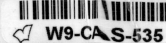

Verbs

25 Forms *196*
26 Tenses *208*
27 Mood *214*
28 Voice *216*
29 Subject-verb agreement *218*

Pronouns

30 Case *224*
31 Pronoun-antecedent agreement *229*
32 Pronoun reference *233*

Modifiers

33 Adjectives and adverbs *236*
34 Misplaced and dangling modifiers *245*

Sentence Faults

35 Fragments *250*
36 Comma splices and fused sentences *253*
37 Mixed sentences *258*

PART 5
Punctuation

38 End punctuation *263*
39 Comma *265*
40 Semicolon *277*
41 Colon *279*
42 Apostrophe *282*
43 Quotation marks *286*
44 Other marks *290*

PART 6
Spelling and Mechanics

45 Spelling and the hyphen *297*
46 Capital letters *303*
47 Italics or underlining *306*
48 Abbreviations *309*
49 Numbers *313*

PART 7
Research Writing

50 Research strategy *317*
51 Finding sources *325*
52 Working with sources *344*
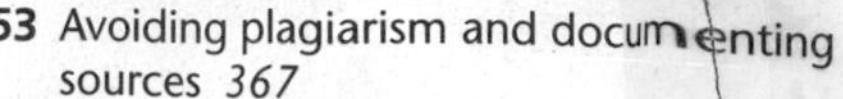
53 Avoiding plagiarism and documenting sources *367*
54 Writing the paper *375*

PART 8
Writing in the Disciplines

55 Goals and requirements of the disciplines *381*
56 Reading and writing about literature *383*
57 Writing in other disciplines *392*
58 MLA documentation and format *406*
59 APA documentation and format *463*
60 Chicago documentation *491*
61 CSE documentation *502*

Glossary / Index / Culture Language Guide

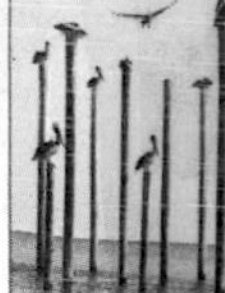

Glossary of Usage *511*
Index *525*

Culture Language Guide *568*

Inside the back cover:
Detailed Contents
Editing Symbols

Writing Process

Why do you need this new edition?

This edition of *The Little, Brown Compact Handbook* differs from the previous edition in countless ways. Here are six that make the book indispensable:

1. More help with college reading and writing ■ A chapter on **academic writing** explains the key academic skill of synthesizing your own and others' views as you write in response to texts and images. ■ A chapter on **academic skills** emphasizes the habits you need to succeed in college.

2. More help with research writing ■ Material on **finding and evaluating sources** covers all kinds of print and electronic resources and shows how to distinguish reliable and unreliable sources. ■ A **research-paper-in-progress** on the environment follows one student's research and writing process, making it easy to see what's expected of you.

3. Up-to-date, more accessible help with citing sources ■ Detailed explanations and highlighted examples present the **most recent revisions of MLA, APA, and CSE documentation styles** and show how to document a wide range of print and electronic sources. A fourth style, **Chicago,** includes models for citing new media. ■ **Annotated sample sources** show you how to find and format bibliographic information in articles, books, and Web sites.

4. New help with the writing process ■ A **student work-in-progress** on globalization and jobs illustrates how the writing process can serve you in college work.

5. Current, more accessible help with grammar and usage ■ Material on **text-message and e-mail shortcuts** gives tips for spotting and editing them in your academic writing. ■ **Checklist and summary boxes** with **color highlighting** offer quick-reference help with crafting clear and correct sentences.

6. Access to *MyCompLab* ■ *The Little, Brown Compact Handbook* is even more useful when you combine it with *MyCompLab,* a Web gateway to resources on grammar, writing, and research developed specifically for writers.

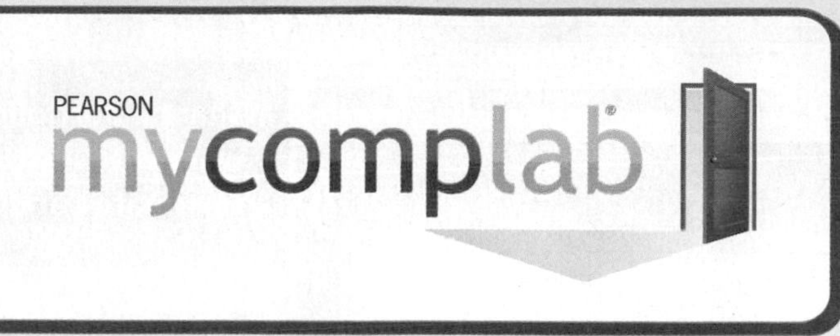

Become a better writer and researcher—and get better grades in all your courses—with *MyCompLab*!

Writing, grammar, and research help are at your fingertips as you draft and revise.

Composing. This dynamic space for composing, revising, and editing is easy to use and built to function like the most popular word-processing programs.

- Use the Writer's Toolkit to search for answers to your writing questions.
- View instructor, peer, and tutor comments on your work in one place.
- Store and manage all your work in one place.
- Access paper review help from experienced tutors through Pearson Tutor Services.

Access instruction, multimedia tutorials, and exercises in the Resources area to help you master skills and get a better grade.

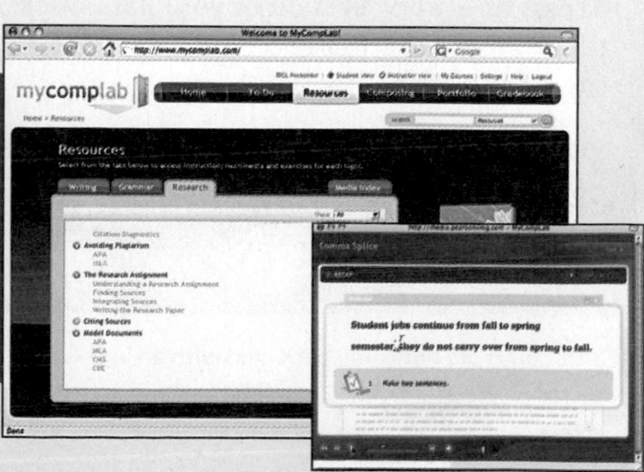

(continued)

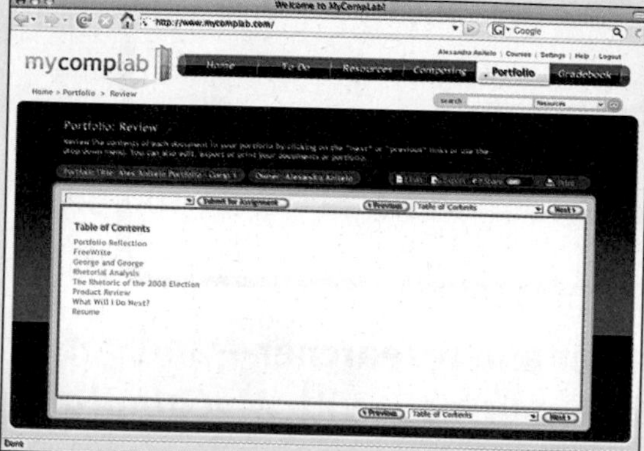

Share e-portfolios of your work with instructors, classmates, and friends.

Portfolio. With this tool, it's easy to create, publish, manage, and share your portfolio. Continue adding material through your college career and beyond!

Manage all your written work and assignments online, in one easy-to-use place.

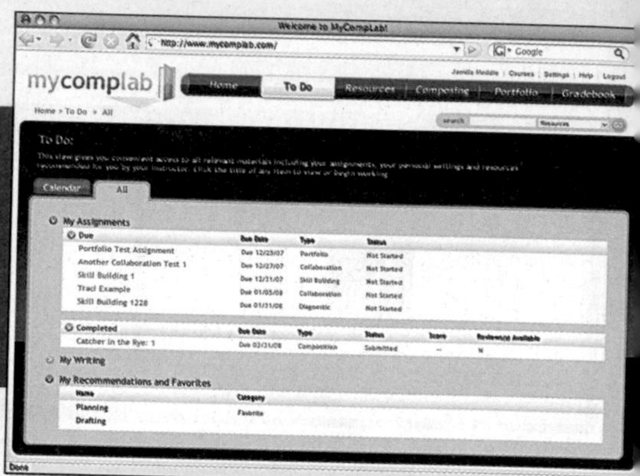

To Do. This area captures assignments and due dates from your instructor along with the personal writing you've done in *MyCompLab*.

Gradebook. This area shows writing and exercise scores. You can see how you are progressing toward a better grade!

Access an e-book version of your handbook

E-book. Access a searchable electronic version of your handbook anywhere you have an Internet connection.

Register for *MyCompLab* today!

Questions? Go to www.mycomplab.com/help.html and click "Student Support."

If this book did not come packaged with an access code to *MyCompLab*, you can purchase access online at **www.mycomplab.com/buy-access.html** or ask your bookstore to order an access card for you.

SEVENTH EDITION

The Little, Brown Compact Handbook

Jane E. Aaron

Longman

New York San Francisco Boston
London Toronto Sydney Tokyo Singapore Madrid
Mexico City Munich Paris Cape Town Hong Kong Montreal

Publisher: Joseph Opiela
Senior Development Editor: Anne Brunell Ehrenworth
Senior Supplements Editor: Donna Campion
Senior Media Producer: Stefanie Liebman
Senior Marketing Manager: Susan Stoudt
Production Manager: Bob Ginsberg
Project Coordination, Text Design, and Electronic Page Makeup: Nesbitt Graphics, Inc.
Cover Design Manager: John Callahan
Cover Designer: Kay Petronio
Cover Photos (*clockwise from top*): Stone/Getty; David Fischer/Digital Vision/Getty Images, Inc.; Image Source/Getty
Photo Researcher: Rebecca Karamehmedovic
Senior Manufacturing Buyer: Roy L. Pickering, Jr.
Printer and Binder: RR Donnelley & Sons Company/Crawfordsville
Cover Printer: Lehigh-Phoenix Color Corporation

For permission to use copyrighted material, grateful acknowledgment is made to the copyright holders on p. 524, which are hereby made part of this copyright page.

Library of Congress Cataloging-in-Publication Data

Aaron, Jane E.
The Little, Brown compact handbook / Jane E. Aaron. -- 7th ed.
p. cm.
Includes bibliographical references and indexes.
ISBN-13: 978-0-205-65163-4
ISBN-10: 0-205-65163-1
1. English language--Grammar--Handbooks, manuals, etc. 2. English language--Rhetoric--Handbooks, manuals, etc. I. Title. II. Title: Compact handbook.
PE1112.A23 2009
808'.042--dc22

2008055656

Longman
is an imprint of

3 4 5 6 7 8 9 10—DOC—12 11 10
ISBN-13: 978-0-205-65163-4
ISBN-10: 0-205-65163-1
www.pearsonhighered.com

Preface for Students

The Little, Brown Compact Handbook contains the basic information you'll need for writing in and out of school. Here you can find how to get ideas, use commas, search the Internet, cite sources, craft an argument, and write a résumé—all in a convenient, accessible package.

This book is mainly a reference for you to dip into as needs arise. You probably won't read the book all the way through, nor will you use everything it contains: you already know much of the content anyway, whether consciously or not. The trick is to figure out what you *don't* know—taking cues from your own writing experiences and the comments of others—and then to find the answers to your questions in these pages.

Using this book will not by itself make you a good writer; for that, you need to care about your work at every level, from finding a subject to spelling words. But learning how to use the handbook and the information in it can give you the means to write *what* you want in the *way* you want.

Reference aids

You have many ways to find what you need in the handbook:

- **Use a directory.** The brief contents inside the front cover displays all the book's parts and chapters. The more detailed contents inside the back cover provides each chapter's subheadings as well.
- **Use a tabbed divider.** At each tab, a detailed outline directs you to the material covered in that part of the book.
- **Use the glossary.** The Glossary of Usage (**Gl** pp. 511–23) clarifies more than 275 words that are commonly confused and misused.
- **Use the index.** On the book's last pages, the extensive index includes every term, concept, and problem word or expression mentioned in the book.
- **Use a list.** Two helpful aids fall at the back of the book. First, the CULTURE LANGUAGE Guide (just before the Contents) pulls together all the material for students using standard American English as a second language or a second dialect. And the list of editing symbols (inside the back cover) explains abbreviations often used to mark papers.
- **Use the elements of the page.** As shown in the following illustrations, each page of the handbook tells you where you are and what you can find there.

The handbook's page elements

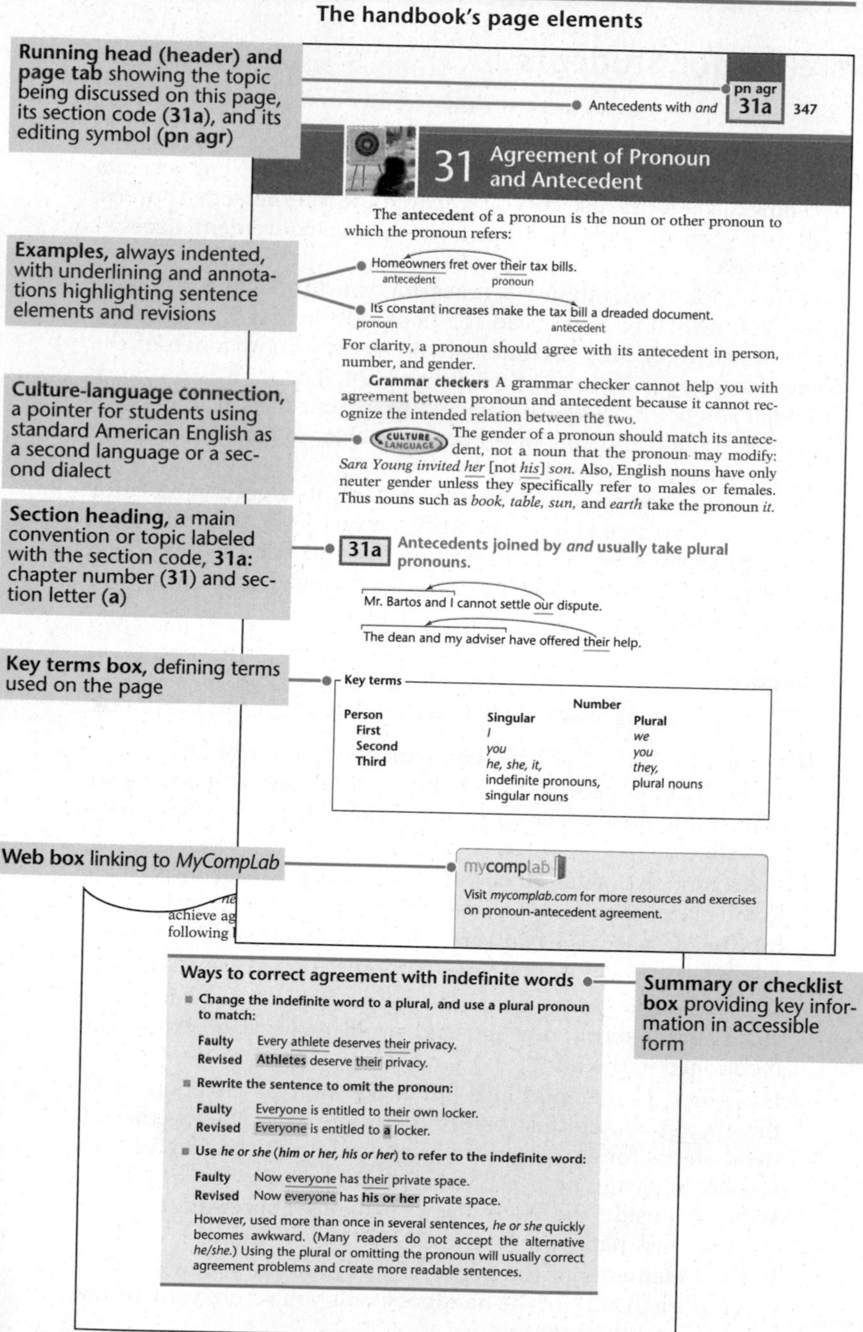

Running head (header) and page tab showing the topic being discussed on this page, its section code (**31a**), and its editing symbol (**pn agr**)
Antecedents with *and*
pn agr
31a
347
31 Agreement of Pronoun and Antecedent
The **antecedent** of a pronoun is the noun or other pronoun to which the pronoun refers:
Examples, always indented, with underlining and annotations highlighting sentence elements and revisions
Homeowners fret over their tax bills.
antecedent
pronoun
Its constant increases make the tax bill a dreaded document.
pronoun
antecedent
For clarity, a pronoun should agree with its antecedent in person, number, and gender.
Grammar checkers A grammar checker cannot help you with agreement between pronoun and antecedent because it cannot recognize the intended relation between the two.
Culture-language connection, a pointer for students using standard American English as a second language or a second dialect
CULTURE LANGUAGE
The gender of a pronoun should match its antecedent, not a noun that the pronoun may modify: *Sara Young invited her* [not *his*] *son.* Also, English nouns have only neuter gender unless they specifically refer to males or females. Thus nouns such as *book, table, sun,* and *earth* take the pronoun *it.*
Section heading, a main convention or topic labeled with the section code, **31a:** chapter number (**31**) and section letter (**a**)
31a
Antecedents joined by *and* usually take plural pronouns.
Mr. Bartos and I cannot settle our dispute.
The dean and my adviser have offered their help.
Key terms box, defining terms used on the page
Key terms
Number
Person
Singular
Plural
First
I
we
Second
you
you
Third
he, she, it,
indefinite pronouns,
singular nouns
they,
plural nouns
Web box linking to *MyCompLab*
mycomplab
Visit *mycomplab.com* for more resources and exercises on pronoun-antecedent agreement.
achieve ag
following
Ways to correct agreement with indefinite words
Summary or checklist box providing key information in accessible form
Change the indefinite word to a plural, and use a plural pronoun to match:
Faulty Every athlete deserves their privacy.
Revised Athletes deserve their privacy.
Rewrite the sentence to omit the pronoun:
Faulty Everyone is entitled to their own locker.
Revised Everyone is entitled to a locker.
Use *he or she* (*him or her, his or her*) to refer to the indefinite word:
Faulty Now everyone has their private space.
Revised Now everyone has his or her private space.
However, used more than once in several sentences, *he or she* quickly becomes awkward. (Many readers do not accept the alternative *he/she.*) Using the plural or omitting the pronoun will usually correct agreement problems and create more readable sentences.

Preface for Instructors

The Little, Brown Compact Handbook provides writers with an accessible reference, one that helps them find what they need and then use what they find. Combining the authority of its parent, *The Little, Brown Handbook*, with a briefer and more convenient format, the *Compact Handbook* addresses writers of varying experience, in varying fields, answering common questions about the writing process, grammar and style, research writing, and more.

This new edition improves on the handbook's strengths as a clear, concise, and accessible reference, while keeping pace with rapid changes in writing and its teaching. In the context of the handbook's many reference functions, the following pages highlight as **New** the most significant additions and changes.

A reference for academic writing

The handbook gives students a solid foundation in the goals and requirements of college writing.

- **New** A reorganized Part 2 ("Writing in and out of College") proceeds through a chapter each on academic skills in general, critical thinking and reading, academic writing, argument, online writing, oral presentations, and public writing.
- **New** The revised chapter on academic skills emphasizes taking notes, reading for comprehension, the basics of academic writing, and preparing for exams.
- **New** The reconceived chapter on academic writing shows students how to write in response to texts.
- **New** Synthesis receives special emphasis wherever students might need help balancing their own and others' views, such as in responding to texts.
- **New** Expanded advice on avoiding plagiarism shows students at every turn how to acknowledge borrowed material.
- **New** A greater stress on opposing views in argument includes discussion of Rogerian approaches.
- Parts 7 and 8 give students a solid foundation in research writing, writing about literature, and writing in other humanities, the social sciences, and the natural and applied sciences. Extensive, specially tabbed sections cover documentation and format in MLA, APA, Chicago, and CSE styles.

A reference for research writing

With detailed advice and a sample MLA paper, the handbook always attends closely to research writing. The discussion stresses using the library as Web gateway, managing information, evaluating and synthesizing sources, integrating source material, and avoiding plagiarism.

- **New** A research-paper-in-progress on green consumerism follows a student through the research process and culminates in an annotated paper documented in MLA style.
- **New** An expanded discussion of evaluating sources illustrates critical criteria with sample articles and Web documents.
- **New** Many kinds of electronic resources—including blogs, wikis, and multimedia as well as Web documents—receive attention as possible sources that require careful evaluation and documentation.
- **New** The advice for generating primary sources now covers conducting observations and surveys.
- **New** Updated source lists in Part 8 provide reliable starting points for research in every discipline.

A reference for documenting sources

The extensive coverage of documentation in four styles—MLA, APA, Chicago, and CSE—reflects each style's latest version and includes many examples of electronic sources.

- **New** MLA style is expanded and completely updated to reflect the 2009 *MLA Handbook for Writers of Research Papers,* Seventh Edition.
- **New** APA style is updated to reflect the 2010 *Publication Manual of the American Psychological Association*, Sixth Edition.
- **New** CSE style is updated to reflect the 2006 *Scientific Style and Format: The CSE Manual for Authors, Editors, and Publishers,* Seventh Edition.
- **New** Annotated samples of key source types accompany MLA and APA documentation, showing students how to find the bibliographical information needed to cite each type.
- **New** For all styles, color highlighting makes authors, titles, dates, and other citation elements easy to grasp.

A reference for the writing process

The handbook takes a practical approach to assessing the writing situation, generating ideas, developing the thesis statement, revising, and other elements of the writing process.

- **New** A student's work-in-progress on globalization and outsourcing illustrates the stages of the writing process.
- **New** Coverage of thesis development now includes discussion and examples of explanatory and argumentative thesis statements.
- An extensive chapter on paragraphs provides twenty-five examples.
- An extensive chapter on document design includes help with using illustrations and a section on designing for readers with vision loss.

A reference on usage, grammar, and punctuation

The handbook's core reference material reliably and concisely explains basic concepts and common errors and provides hundreds of annotated examples from across the curriculum.

- **New** Five added boxes cover coordination, subordination, helping verbs, sentence patterns, and sentence fragments.
- **New** Color highlighting in boxes stresses and distinguishes sentence elements for quick reference.
- **New** Advice on avoiding the informalities common to online communication targets nonstandard grammar, punctuation, abbreviations, and spelling.

A guide for culturally and linguistically diverse writers

At notes and sections labeled CULTURE LANGUAGE, the handbook provides extensive rhetorical and grammatical help for writers whose first language or dialect is not standard American English.

- Fully integrated coverage, instead of a separate section, means that students can find what they need without having to know which problems they do and don't share with native SAE speakers.
- The CULTURE LANGUAGE Guide, just before the back endpapers, orients students with advice on mastering SAE and pulls all the integrated coverage together in one place.

A guide to visual literacy

The handbook helps students process visual information and use it effectively in their writing.

- **New** The discussion of viewing images critically uses fresh and diverse examples to demonstrate identifying and analyzing visual elements.

- **New** A student's work illustrates the process of analyzing an advertisement.
- **New** The discussion of reading and using visual arguments includes a new graph, a new photograph, and new advertisements for analysis.
- Detailed help with preparing or finding illustrations appears in the discussions of document design, research writing, and Web composition.
- Illustrations in several of the handbook's student papers show various ways to support written ideas with visual information.

An accessible reference guide

The handbook is an open book for students, with a convenient lay-flat binding, tabbed dividers, and many internal features that help students navigate and use the content.

- **New** A clean, uncluttered page design uses color and type to distinguish parts of the book and elements of the pages.
- **New** A brief table of contents inside the front cover provides an at-a-glance overview of the book. As before, a detailed table of contents appears inside the back cover.
- **New** Color highlighting in boxes and on documentation models distinguishes important elements.
- A unique approach to terminology facilitates reference and reading. Headings in the text and tables of contents avoid or explain terms. And "Key terms" boxes in the text provide essential definitions, dramatically reducing cross-references and page flipping.
- An unusually accessible organization groups related problems so that students can easily find what they need.
- Cross-references give divider numbers in addition to page numbers, sending students directly to the appropriate tabbed section—for instance, "See **3** pp. 143–45."
- Annotations on both visual and verbal examples connect principles and illustrations.
- Dictionary-style headers in the index make it easy to find entries.
- A preface just for students details reference aids and explains the page layout.

Two versions of the handbook

The handbook is available with a full complement of exercises built into the book. Otherwise identical to the book you're holding, *The Little, Brown Compact Handbook with Exercises* includes more than 140 sets of exercises on usage, grammar, punctuation, and mechanics as well as rhetorical concerns such as thesis statements and paraphrasing. The exercises are in connected discourse, and their subjects come from across the academic curriculum.

Supplements

Pearson offers a variety of support materials to make teaching easier and to help students improve as writers. The following are geared specifically to *The Little, Brown Compact Handbook.* Visit *pearsonhighered.com* or contact your local Pearson sales representative for more information on these and scores of additional supplements.

- **New** mycomplab The Web site *MyCompLab* (*mycomplab.com*) integrates instruction, multimedia tutorials, and exercises for writing, grammar, and research with an online composing space and assessment tools. This seamless, flexible environment comes from extensive research in partnership with composition faculty and students across the country. It provides help for writers in the context of their writing, with functions for instructors' and peers' commentary. Special features include an e-portfolio, a bibliography tool, tutoring services, an assignment builder, and a gradebook and course-management organization created specifically for writing classes. In addition, an e-book version of *The Little, Brown Compact Handbook* integrates the many resources of *MyCompLab* into the text.
- **New** Students can subscribe to *The Little, Brown Compact Handbook* as a *CourseSmart* e-textbook. The site includes all of the handbook's content in a format that enables students to search the text, bookmark passages, integrate their notes, and print reading assignments that incorporate lecture notes. For more information, or to subscribe to the *CourseSmart* e-textbook, visit *coursesmart.com*.
- *Exercises to Accompany The Little, Brown Compact Handbook* offers the same activities found in the exercise version of the handbook, all double-spaced so that students can work directly in the book. An answer key is available.
- *Developmental Exercises to Accompany The Little, Brown Compact Handbook* provides activities in workbook format for developmental writers. An answer key is available.
- vango notes *VangoNotes* are study guides in MP3 format that enable students to download handbook information into their own players and then listen to it whenever and wherever they wish. The notes include "need to know" tips for each handbook chapter, practice tests, audio flash cards for learning key concepts

and terms, and a rapid review for exams. For more information, visit *VangoNotes.com*.

- *Diagnostic and Editing Tests and Exercises* are cross-referenced to *The Little, Brown Compact Handbook* and are available both in print and online.

Acknowledgments

The Little, Brown Compact Handbook stays fresh and useful because instructors talk with the publisher's sales representatives and editors, answer questionnaires, write detailed reviews, and send me personal notes.

For the seventh edition, the following instructors earn special thanks for detailed reviews in which they drew on their rich experience to offer insights into the handbook and suggestions for its improvement: David L. Anderson, Butler County Community College; Martha Bachman, Camden County College; Mike Barrett, Moberly Area Community College; Debbie Bush, Copiah-Lincoln Community College; Lucia Cherciu, Dutchess Community College; Barbara Goldstein, Hillsborough Community College; Andrew Green, University of Miami; Kathleen Green, Pasadena City College; Harold William Halberg, Montgomery County Community College; Kimberly Harrison, Florida International University; Anne Helms, Alamance Community College; Ann Jagoe, North Central Texas College; Tracy Johnson, Butte College; Michael Lueker, Our Lady of the Lakes University; Angie Macri, Pulaski Technical College; Marilee Motto, Owens Community College; Kathryn Scrivener, Clark College; Nanette Tamer, Villa Julie College; and Lori Truman, Kilgore College.

In responding to the ideas of these thoughtful critics, I had the help of several creative people. Caroline Crouse, George Washington University, guided me through the labyrinth of the contemporary library. Sylvan Barnet, Tufts University, continued to lend his expertise in the chapter "Reading and Writing About Literature," which is adapted from his *Short Guide to Writing About Literature* and *Introduction to Literature* (with William Burto and William E. Cain). Ellen Kuhl provided creative, meticulous, and invaluable help with the material on research writing. And Carol Hollar-Zwick, sine qua non, served brilliantly as originator, sounding board, critic, coordinator, researcher, producer, and friend.

A superb publishing team helped to make this book. At Longman, editors Joe Opiela and Anne Brunell Ehrenworth offered perceptive insights into instructors' and students' needs, while production editor Bob Ginsberg helped resolve sometimes competing production goals in favor of quality and accuracy. At Nesbitt Graphics, Jerilyn Bockorick created the striking new design, and Susan McIntyre performed her usual calm (and calming) miracles of scheduling and management to produce the book. I am grateful to all these collaborators.

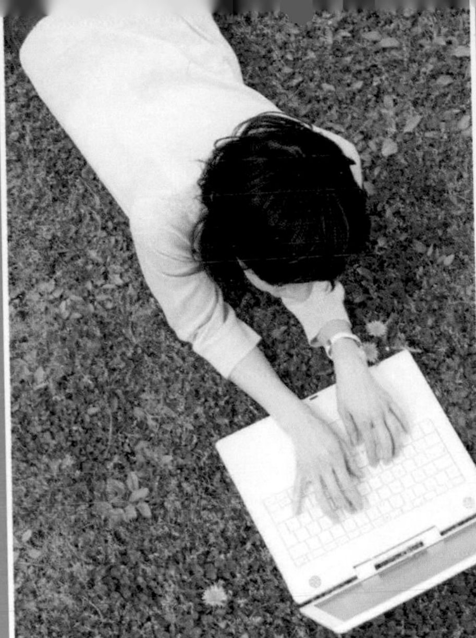

PART 1

The Writing Process

1 The Writing Situation 3

2 Invention 8

3 Thesis and Organization 14

4 Drafting 21

5 Revising and Editing 24

6 Paragraphs 38

7 Document Design 52

PART 1

The Writing Process

1 The Writing Situation *3*

- a Assessment *3*
- b Subject *5*
- c Purpose *6*
- d Audience *7*

2 Invention *8*

- a Keeping a journal *9*
- b Observing *10*
- c Freewriting *10*
- d Brainstorming *11*
- e Clustering *12*
- f Asking questions *13*

3 Thesis and Organization *14*

- a Thesis statement *14*
- b Organization *16*

4 Drafting *21*

- a Starting to draft *21*
- b Maintaining momentum *22*
- c Sample first draft *22*

5 Revising and Editing *24*

- a Revising the whole essay *25*
- b Sample revision *27*
- c Editing the revised draft *28*
- d Formatting and proofreading the final draft *33*
- e Sample final draft *33*
- f Revising collaboratively *35*
- g Preparing a writing portfolio *37*

6 Paragraphs *38*

- a Unity *38*
- b Coherence *39*
- c Development *45*
- d Introductions and conclusions *49*

7 Document Design *52*

- a Academic papers and other documents *53*
- b Principles of design *53*
- c Elements of design *56*
- d Illustrations *60*
- e Readers with vision loss *64*

1 The Writing Situation

Like most writers (even very experienced ones), you may find writing sometimes easy but more often challenging, sometimes smooth but more often halting. Writing involves creation, and creation requires freedom, experimentation, and even missteps. Instead of proceeding in a straight line on a clear path, you might start writing without knowing what you have to say, circle back to explore a new idea, or keep going even though you're sure you'll have to rewrite later.

As uncertain as the writing process may be, you can bring some control to it by assessing your writing situation, particularly your subject, audience, and purpose.

1a Assessing the writing situation

Any writing you do for others occurs in a context that both limits and clarifies your choices. You are communicating something about a particular subject to a particular audience of readers for a specific reason. You may need to conduct research. You'll probably be up against a length requirement and a deadline. And you may be expected to present your work in a certain format.

These are the elements of the **writing situation**, and analyzing them at the very start of a project can tell you much about how to proceed.

Context

- **What is your writing for?** A course in school? Work? Something else? What do you know of the requirements for writing in this context?
- **Will you present your writing on paper, online, or orally?** What does the presentation method require in preparation time, special skills, and use of technology?
- **How much leeway do you have for this writing?** What does the stated or implied assignment tell you?

Subject (pp. 5–6)

- **What does your writing assignment require you to write about?** If you don't have a specific assignment, what subjects might be appropriate for this situation?

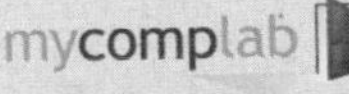

Visit *mycomplab.com* for more resources as well as exercises on the writing situation.

- **What interests you about the subject?** What do you already know about it? What questions do you have about it?
- **What does the assignment require you to do with the subject?**

Purpose (pp. 6–7)

- **What aim does your assignment specify?** For instance, does it ask you to explain something or argue a point?
- **Why are you writing?**
- **What do you want your work to accomplish?** What effect do you intend it to have on readers?
- **How can you best achieve your purpose?**

Audience (pp. 7–8)

- **Who will read your writing?**
- **What do your readers already know and think about your subject?** Do they have any characteristics—such as educational background, experience in your field, or political views—that could influence their reception of your writing?
- **How should you project yourself in your writing?** What role should you play in relation to readers, and what information should you give? How informal or formal should your writing be?
- **What do you want readers to do or think after they read your writing?**

Research (**7** pp. 317–77)

- **What kinds of evidence will best suit your subject, purpose, and audience?** What combination of facts, examples, and expert opinions will support your ideas?
- **Does your assignment require research?** Will you need to consult sources of information or conduct other research, such as interviews, surveys, or experiments?
- **Even if research is not required, what additional information do you need to develop your subject?** How will you obtain it?
- **What style should you use to cite your sources?** (See **7** pp. 374–75 on source documentation in the academic disciplines.)

Deadline and length

- **When is the assignment due?** How will you apportion the work you have to do in the available time?
- **How long should your writing be?** If no length is assigned, what seems appropriate for your subject, purpose, and audience?

Document design

- **What organization and format does the assignment require?** (See p. 53 on format in the academic disciplines and **2** pp. 128–29 on format in public writing.)

- **How might you use margins, headings, and other elements to achieve your purpose?** (See pp. 54–60.)
- **How might you use graphs, photographs, or other illustrations to support ideas and interest readers?** (See pp. 60–64 and **2** pp. 105–11 on using illustrations in writing.)

1b Finding your subject

A subject for writing has several basic requirements:

- **It should be suitable for the assignment.**
- **It should be neither too general nor too limited for the assigned deadline and paper length.**
- **It should be something you are willing to learn more about, even something you care about.**

When you receive an assignment, study its wording and its implications about your writing situation to guide your choice of subject:

- **What's wanted from you?** Many writing assignments contain words such as *discuss, describe, analyze, report, interpret, explain, define, argue,* or *evaluate.* These words specify the way you are to approach your subject, what kind of thinking is expected of you, and what your general purpose is. (See pp. 6–7.)
- **For whom are you writing?** Many assignments will specify or imply your readers, but sometimes you will have to figure out for yourself who your audience is and what it expects of you. (For more on analyzing your audience, see pp. 7–8.)
- **What kind of research is required?** An assignment may specify the kinds of sources you are expected to consult, and you can use such information to choose your subject. (If you are unsure whether research is required, check with your instructor.)
- **Does the subject need to be narrowed?** To do the subject justice in the length and time required, you'll often need to limit it. (See below.)

Answering questions about your assignment will help set some boundaries for your choice of subject. Then you can explore your own interests and experiences to narrow the subject so that you can cover it adequately within the space and time assigned. Federal aid to college students could be the subject of a book; the kinds of aid available or why the government should increase aid would be a more appropriate subject for a four-page paper due in a week. Here are some guidelines for narrowing broad subjects:

- **Break your broad subject into as many specific subjects as you can think of. Make a list.**

- **For each specific subject that interests you and fits the assignment, roughly sketch out the main ideas.** Consider how many paragraphs or pages of specific facts, examples, and other details you would need to pin those ideas down. This thinking should give you at least a vague idea of how much work you'd have to do and how long the resulting paper might be.
- **Break a too-broad subject down further,** repeating the previous steps.

The Internet can also help you limit a general subject. On the Web, browse a directory such as *BUBL LINK* (*bubl.ac.uk/link*). As you pursue increasingly narrow categories, you may find a suitably limited topic.

1c Defining your purpose

Your **purpose** in writing is your chief reason for communicating something about your subject to a particular audience of readers. It is your answer to a potential reader's question, "So what?"

Most writing you do will have one of four main purposes:

- **To entertain readers.**
- **To express your feelings or ideas.**
- **To explain something to readers (exposition).**
- **To persuade readers to accept or act on your opinion (argument).**

These purposes often overlap in a single essay, but usually one predominates. And the dominant purpose will influence your slant on your subject, the details you choose, and even the words you use.

Many writing assignments narrow the purpose by using a signal word, such as the following:

- **Report:** Survey, organize, and objectively present the available evidence on the subject.
- **Summarize:** Concisely state the main points in a text, argument, theory, or other work.
- **Discuss:** Examine the main points, competing views, or implications of the subject.
- **Compare and contrast:** Explain the similarities and differences between two subjects. (See also pp. 47–48.)
- **Define:** Specify the meaning of a term or a concept—distinctive characteristics, boundaries, and so on. (See also pp. 46–47.)
- **Analyze:** Identify the elements of the subject, and discuss how they work together. (See also p. 47 and **2** p. 81.)
- **Interpret:** Infer the subject's meaning or implications.

- **Evaluate:** Judge the quality or significance of the subject, considering pros and cons. (See also **2** p. 83.)
- **Argue:** Take a position on the subject, and support your position with evidence. (See also **2** pp. 97–105.)

You can conceive of your purpose more specifically, too, in a way that incorporates your particular subject and the outcome you intend:

> To explain how Annie Dillard's "Total Eclipse" builds to its climax so that readers appreciate the author's skill
>
> To explain the methods of an engineering study so that readers understand and accept your conclusions
>
> To explain the steps in a new office procedure so that staffers will be able to follow it without difficulty
>
> To argue against additional regulation of health-maintenance organizations so that readers will perceive the disadvantages for themselves

1d Considering your audience

The readers likely to see your work—your **audience**—may influence your choice of subject and your definition of purpose. Your audience certainly will influence what you say about your subject and how you say it—for instance, how much background information you give and whether you adopt a serious or a friendly tone.

For much academic and public writing, readers have specific needs and expectations. You still have many choices to make based on audience, but the options are somewhat defined. (See **2** pp. 90–96 and **8** pp. 381–402 on academic writing and **2** pp. 128–39 on public writing.) In other writing situations, the conventions are vaguer and the choices are more open. The following box contains questions that can help you define and make these choices.

Questions about audience

Identity and expectations

- **Who *are* my readers?**
- **What are my readers' expectations for the kind of writing I'm doing?** Do they expect features such as a particular organization and format, distinctive kinds of evidence, or a certain style of documenting sources?
- **What do I want readers to know or do after reading my work?** How should I make that clear to them?
- **How should I project myself to my readers?** How formal or informal will they expect me to be? What role and tone should I assume?

(continued)

Questions about audience

(continued)

Characteristics, knowledge, and attitudes

- **What characteristics of readers are relevant for my subject and purpose?** For instance:

  Age and sex
  Occupation: students, professional colleagues, etc.
  Social or economic role: subject-matter experts, voters, car buyers, potential employers, etc.
  Economic or educational background
  Ethnic background
  Political, religious, or moral beliefs and values
  Hobbies or activities

- **How will the characteristics of readers influence their attitudes toward my subject?**
- **What do readers already know and *not* know about my subject?** How much do I have to tell them?
- **How should I handle any specialized terms?** Will readers know them? If not, should I define them?
- **What ideas, arguments, or information might surprise, excite, or offend readers?** How should I handle these points?
- **What misconceptions might readers have of my subject and/or my approach to it?** How can I dispel these misconceptions?

Uses and format

- **What will readers do with my writing?** Should I expect them to read every word from the top, to scan for information, or to look for conclusions? Can I help by providing a summary, headings, illustrations, or other aids? (See pp. 52–65 on document design.)

2 Invention

Writers use a host of techniques to help invent or discover ideas and information about their subjects. **Whichever of the following techniques you use, do your work in writing, not just in your head.** Your ideas will then be retrievable, and the very act of writing will lead you to fresh insights.

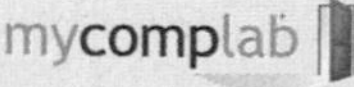

Visit *mycomplab.com* for more resources as well as exercises on invention.

CULTURE LANGUAGE The discovery process encouraged here rewards rapid writing without a lot of thinking beforehand about what you will write or how. If your first language is not standard American English, you may find it helpful initially to do this exploratory writing in your native language or dialect and then to translate the worthwhile material for use in your drafts. This process can be productive, but it is extra work. You may want to try it at first and gradually move to composing in standard American English.

2a Keeping a journal

A **journal** is a diary of ideas kept on paper or on a computer. It gives you a place to record your responses, thoughts, and observations about what you read, see, hear, or experience. It can also provide ideas for writing. Because you write for yourself, you can work out your ideas without the pressure of an audience "out there" who will evaluate logic or organization or correctness. If you write every day, even just for a few minutes, the routine will loosen your writing muscles and improve your confidence.

You can use a journal for varied purposes: perhaps to confide your feelings, explore your responses to movies and other media, practice certain kinds of writing (such as poems or news stories), pursue ideas from your course, or think critically about what you read. One student, Katy Moreno, used her journal for the last purpose. Her composition instructor had distributed "It's a Flat World, After All," an essay by Thomas L. Friedman about globalization and the job market. The instructor then gave the following assignment, calling for a response to reading:

> In "It's a Flat World, After All," Thomas L. Friedman describes today's global job market, focusing not on manufacturing jobs that have been "outsourced" to overseas workers but on jobs that require a college degree and are no longer immune to outsourcing. Friedman argues that keeping jobs in the United States requires that US students, parents, and educators improve math and science education. As a college student, how do you respond to this analysis of the global market for jobs? Does anything Friedman says cause you to rethink how you will spend your college years or what your major will be?

On first reading the essay, Moreno had found it convincing because Friedman's description of the job market matched her family's experience: her mother had lost her job when it was outsourced to India. After rereading the essay, however, Moreno was not persuaded that more math and science would necessarily improve students' opportunities and preserve their future jobs. She compared Friedman's advice with details she recalled from her mother's experience, and she began to develop a response by writing in her journal:

> Friedman is certainly right that more jobs than we realize are going overseas—that's what happened to Mom's job and we were shocked! But he gives only one way for students like me to compete—take more math and science. At first I thought he's totally right. But then I thought that what he said didn't really explain what happened to Mom—she had lots of math + science + tons of experience, but it was her salary, not better training, that caused her job to be outsourced. An overseas worker would do her job for less money. So she lost her job because of money + because she wasn't a manager. Caught in the middle. I want to major in computer science, but I don't think it's smart to try for the kind of job Mom had—at least not as long as it's so much cheaper for companies to hire workers overseas.

(Further examples of Moreno's writing appear in the next three chapters.)

CULTURE LANGUAGE A journal can be especially helpful if your first language is not standard American English. You can practice writing to improve your fluency, try out sentence patterns, and experiment with vocabulary words. Equally important, you can experiment with applying what you know from experience to what you read and observe.

2b Observing your surroundings

Sometimes you can find a good subject or good ideas by looking around you, not in the half-conscious way most of us move from place to place in our daily lives but deliberately, all senses alert. On a bus, for instance, are there certain types of passengers? What seems to be on the driver's mind? To get the most from observation, you should have a notepad and pen or a handheld computer available for taking notes and making sketches. Back at your desk, study your notes and sketches for oddities or patterns that you'd like to explore further.

2c Freewriting

Writing into a subject

Many writers find subjects or discover ideas by **freewriting:** writing without stopping for a certain amount of time (say, ten minutes) or to a certain length (say, one page). The goal of freewriting is to generate ideas and information from *within* yourself by going around the part of your mind that doesn't want to write or can't think of anything to write. You let words themselves suggest other words. *What* you write is not important; that you *keep* writing is. Don't stop, even if that means repeating the same words until new words come. Don't go back to reread, don't censor ideas that seem dumb or repetitious, and above all don't stop to edit: grammar, punctuation, spelling, and the like are irrelevant at this stage.

If you write on a computer, try this technique for moving forward while freewriting: turn off your computer's monitor, or turn its brightness control all the way down so that the screen is dark. The computer will record what you type but keep it from you and thus prevent you from tinkering with your prose. This **invisible writing** may feel uncomfortable at first, but it can free the mind for very creative results.

CULTURE LANGUAGE Invisible writing can be especially helpful if you are uneasy writing in standard American English and you tend to worry about errors while writing. The blank computer screen leaves you no choice but to explore ideas without regard for their expression. If you choose to write with the monitor on, concentrate on *what* you want to say, not *how* you're saying it.

Focused freewriting

Focused freewriting is more concentrated: you start with your subject and write about it without stopping for, say, fifteen minutes or one full page. As in all freewriting, you push to bypass mental blocks and self-consciousness, not debating what to say or editing what you've written. With focused freewriting, though, you let the physical act of writing take you into and around your subject.

An example of focused freewriting can be found in Katy Moreno's journal response to Thomas L. Friedman's "It's a Flat World, After All" on the previous page. Since she already had an idea about Friedman's essay, Moreno was able to start there and expand on the idea.

2d Brainstorming

A method similar to freewriting is **brainstorming**—focusing intently on a subject for a fixed period (say, fifteen minutes), pushing yourself to list every idea and detail that comes to mind. Like freewriting, brainstorming requires turning off your internal editor so that you keep moving ahead. (The technique of invisible writing on a computer, described above, can help you move forward.)

Here is an example of brainstorming by a student, Johanna Abrams, on what a summer job can teach:

summer work teaches—
how to look busy while doing nothing
how to avoid the sun in summer
seriously: discipline, budgeting money, value of money

which job? Burger King cashier? baby sitter? mail-room clerk?
mail room: how to sort mail into boxes: this is learning??
how to survive getting fired—humiliation, outrage
Mrs. King! the mail-room queen as learning experience
the shock of getting fired: what to tell parents, friends?
Mrs. K was so rigid—dumb procedures
initials instead of names on the mail boxes—confusion!
Mrs. K's anger, resentment: the disadvantages of being smarter than your boss
The odd thing about working in an office: a world with its own rules for how to act
what Mr. D said about the pecking order—big chick (Mrs. K) pecks on little chick (me)
a job can beat you down—make you be mean to other people

2e Clustering

Like freewriting and brainstorming, **clustering** also draws on free association and rapid, unedited work. But it emphasizes the relations between ideas by combining writing and nonlinear drawing. When clustering, you radiate outward from a center point—your subject. When an idea occurs, you pursue related ideas in a branching structure until they seem exhausted. Then you do the same with other ideas, continuously branching out or drawing arrows.

The example below shows how a student used clustering for ten minutes to expand on a subject he arrived at through freewriting: writing as a means of disguise.

Clustering

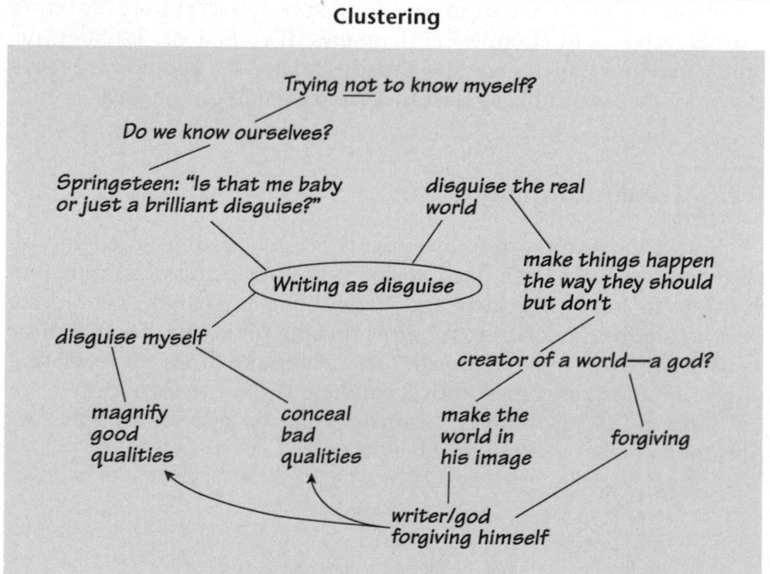

2f Asking questions

Asking yourself a set of questions about your subject—and writing out the answers—can help you look at the subject objectively and see fresh possibilities in it.

1 Journalist's questions

A journalist with a story to report poses a set of questions:

- **Who was involved?**
- **What happened, and what were the results?**
- **When did it happen?**
- **Where did it happen?**
- **Why did it happen?**
- **How did it happen?**

These questions can also be useful in probing an essay subject, especially when you are telling a story or examining causes and effects.

2 Questions about patterns

We think about and understand a vast range of subjects through patterns such as narration, classification, and comparison and contrast. Asking questions based on the patterns can help you view your subject from many angles. Sometimes you may want to develop an entire essay using just one pattern.

- **How did it happen?** (Narration)
- **How does it look, sound, feel, smell, taste?** (Description)
- **What are examples of it or reasons for it?** (Illustration or support)
- **What is it? What does it encompass, and what does it exclude?** (Definition)
- **What are its parts or characteristics?** (Division or analysis)
- **What groups or categories can it be sorted into?** (Classification)
- **How is it like, or different from, other things?** (Comparison and contrast)
- **Why did it happen? What results did or could it have?** (Cause-and-effect analysis)
- **How do you do it, or how does it work?** (Process analysis)

For more on these patterns, including paragraph-length examples, see pp. 45–49.

3 Thesis and Organization

Shaping your raw material helps you clear away unneeded ideas, spot possible gaps, and energize your subject. The two main operations in shaping material are focusing on a thesis (below) and organizing ideas (p. 16).

3a Conceiving a thesis statement

Your readers will expect your essay to be focused on and controlled by a main idea, or **thesis.** In your final draft you may express this idea in a **thesis statement,** often at the end of your introduction.

1 Functions of the thesis statement

As an expression of the thesis, the thesis statement serves three crucial functions and one optional one:

The thesis statement

- The thesis statement **narrows your subject** to a single, central idea that you want readers to gain from your essay.
- It **claims something specific and significant** about your subject, a claim that requires support.
- It **conveys your purpose**—often explanatory or argumentative in college writing.
- It often concisely **previews the arrangement of ideas,** in which case it can also help you organize your essay.

All of the following thesis statements fulfill the first three functions listed in the box (the nature of the claim is highlighted in brackets). Examples 2 and 5 also fulfill the fourth function, previewing organization. Notice the purposes of the statements. Statements 1 and 2 are **explanatory:** the writers mainly want to explain something to readers. Statements 3–5 are **argumentative:** the authors mainly want to convince readers of something.

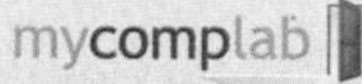

Visit *mycomplab.com* for more resources as well as exercises on thesis and organization.

Subject	Explanatory thesis statement
1. Abraham Lincoln's delay in emancipating the slaves	Lincoln delayed emancipating any slaves until 1863 because his primary goal was to restore and preserve the Union, with or without slavery. [**Topic:** Lincoln's delay. **Claim:** was caused by his goal of preserving the Union.]
2. Preventing juvenile crime	Juveniles can be diverted from crime by active learning programs, full-time sports, and intervention by mentors and role models. [**Topic:** juveniles. **Claim:** can be diverted from crime in three ways.]

Subject	Argumentative thesis statement
3. Drivers' use of cell phones	Drivers' use of cell phones should be outlawed because people who talk and drive at the same time cause accidents. [**Topic:** drivers' use of cell phones. **Claim:** should be outlawed because it causes accidents.]
4. Federal aid to college students	As an investment in its own economy, the federal government should provide a tuition grant to any college student who qualifies academically. [**Topic:** federal government. **Claim:** should provide a tuition grant to any college student who qualifies academically.]
5. The effects of strip-mining	Strip-mining should be tightly controlled in this region to reduce its pollution of water resources, its destruction of the land, and its devastating effects on people's lives. [**Topic:** strip-mining. **Claim:** should be tightly controlled for three reasons.]

CULTURE LANGUAGE In some cultures it is considered rude or unnecessary for a writer to state his or her main idea outright. When writing in standard American English for school or work, you can assume that readers expect a clear and early idea of what you think.

2 Development of the thesis statement

A thesis will not usually leap fully formed into your head: you will have to develop and shape the idea as you develop and shape your essay. Still, trying to draft a thesis statement early can give you a point of reference when changes inevitably occur.

While you are developing your thesis statement, ask the following questions about each attempt:

Checklist for revising the thesis statement

- How well does the **subject** of your statement capture the subject of your paper?
- What **claim** does your statement make about your subject?
- What is the **significance** of the claim? How does it answer "So what?" and convey your purpose?
- How can the claim be **limited** or made more **specific?** Does it state a single idea and clarify the boundaries of the idea?
- How **unified** is the statement? How does each word and phrase contribute to a single idea?

Here are examples of thesis statements revised to meet these requirements:

Original	**Revised**
This new product brought in over $300,000 last year. [A statement of fact, not a claim about the product: what is significant about the product's success?]	This new product succeeded because of its innovative marketing campaign, including widespread press coverage, instore entertainment, and a consumer newsletter.
People should not go on fad diets. [A vague statement that needs limiting with one or more reasons: what's wrong with fad diets?]	Fad diets can be dangerous when they deprive the body of essential nutrients or rely excessively on potentially harmful foods.
Televised sports are different from live sports. [A general statement that needs to be made more specific: how are they different, and why is the difference significant?]	Although television cannot transmit all the excitement of a live game, its close-ups and slow-motion replays reveal much about the players and the strategy of the game.
Seat belts can save lives, but now carmakers are installing air bags. [Not unified: how do the two parts of the sentence relate to each other?]	If drivers had used lifesaving seat belts more often, carmakers might not have needed to install air bags.

3b Organizing your ideas

Most essays share a basic pattern of introduction (states the subject), body (develops the subject), and conclusion (pulls the essay's ideas together). Introductions and conclusions are discussed on pp. 49–52. Within the body, every paragraph develops some aspect of the essay's main idea, or thesis. See pp. 33–35 for Katy Moreno's essay, with annotations highlighting the body's pattern of support for the thesis statement.

CULTURE LANGUAGE If you are not used to reading and writing American academic prose, its pattern of introduction-body-conclusion and the particular schemes discussed below and on the next page may seem unfamiliar. For instance, instead of introductions that focus quickly on the topic and thesis, you may be used to openings that establish personal connections with readers. And instead of body paragraphs that stress general points and support those points with evidence, you may be used to general statements without support (because writers can assume that readers will supply the evidence themselves) or to evidence without explanation (because writers can assume that readers will infer the general points). When writing American academic prose, you need to take into account readers' expectations for directness and for the statement and support of general points.

1 The general and the specific

To organize material for an essay, you need to distinguish general and specific ideas and see the relations between ideas. General and specific refer to the number of instances or objects included in a group signified by a word. The following "ladder" illustrates a general-to-specific hierarchy:

Most general
↑ life form
plant
rose
↓ Uncle Dan's prize-winning American Beauty rose
Most specific

As you arrange your material, pick out the general ideas and then the specific points that support them. Set aside points that seem irrelevant to your key ideas. On a computer you can easily experiment with various arrangements of general ideas and supporting information: save your master list of ideas, duplicate it, and then use the Cut and Paste functions to move material around or (a little quicker) drag selected text to where you want it.

2 Schemes for organizing essays

An essay's body paragraphs may be arranged in many ways that are familiar to readers. The choice depends on your subject, purpose, and audience.

- **Spatial:** In describing a person, place, or thing, move through space systematically from a starting point to other features—for instance, top to bottom, near to far, left to right.
- **Chronological:** In recounting a sequence of events, arrange the events as they actually occurred in time, first to last.

- **General to specific:** Begin with an overall discussion of the subject; then fill in details, facts, examples, and other support.
- **Specific to general:** First provide the support; then draw a conclusion from it.
- **Climactic:** Arrange ideas in order of increasing importance to your thesis or increasing interest to the reader.
- **Problem-solution:** First outline a problem that needs solving; then propose a solution.

3 Outlines

It's not essential to craft a detailed outline before you begin drafting an essay; in fact, too detailed a plan could prevent you from discovering ideas while you draft. Still, even a rough scheme can show you patterns of general and specific, suggest proportions, and highlight gaps or overlaps in coverage.

There are several kinds of outlines, some more flexible than others.

Scratch or informal outline

A scratch or informal outline includes key general points in the order they will be covered. It may also list evidence for the points.

Here is Katy Moreno's scratch outline for her essay on the global job market:

Thesis statement

My mother's experience of having her job outsourced taught a lesson that Thomas L. Friedman overlooks: technical training by itself can be too narrow to produce the communicators and problem solvers needed by contemporary businesses.

Scratch outline

Mom's outsourcing experience
- Excellent tech skills
- Salary too high compared to overseas tech workers
- Lack of planning + communication skills, unlike managers who kept jobs

Well-rounded education to protect vs. outsourcing
- Tech training, as Friedman says
- Also, experience in communication, problem solving, other management skills

Tree diagram

In a tree diagram, ideas and details branch out in increasing specificity. Unlike more linear outlines, this diagram can be supplemented and extended indefinitely, so it is easy to alter. Johanna

Abrams developed the following example from her brainstorming about a summer job (pp. 11–12):

Thesis statement

Two months working in a large agency taught me that an office's pecking order should be respected.

Tree diagram

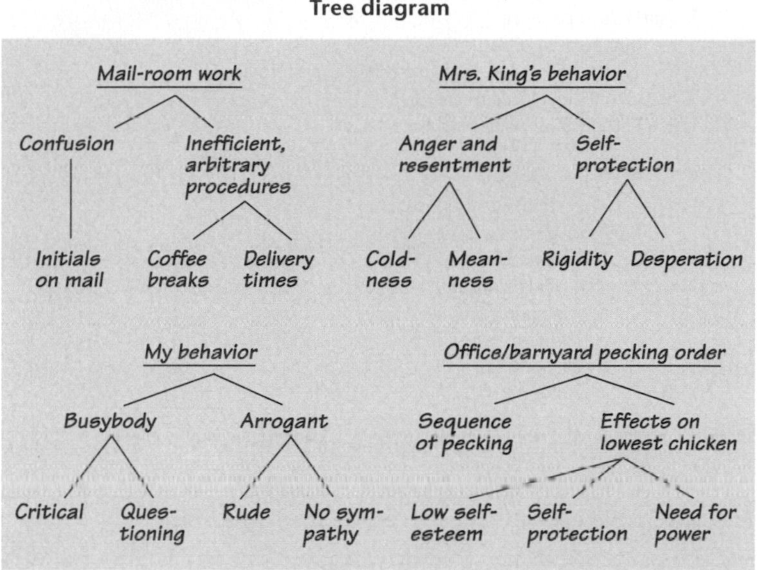

A tree diagram or other visual map can be especially useful for planning a project for the Web. The diagram can help you lay out the organization of your project and its links and then later can serve as a site map for your readers. (For more on writing for the Web, see **2** pp. 119–24.)

Formal outline

A formal outline not only lays out main ideas and their support but also shows the relative importance of all the essay's elements. On the basis of her scratch outline (previous page), Katy Moreno prepared a formal outline for her essay on the global job market:

Thesis statement

My mother's experience of having her job outsourced taught a lesson that Thomas L. Friedman overlooks: technical training by itself can be too narrow to produce the communicators and problem solvers needed by contemporary businesses.

Formal outline

I. Summary of Friedman's article
   A. Reasons for outsourcing
      1. Improved technology and access
      2. Well-educated workers
      3. Productive workers
      4. Lower wages
   B. Need for improved technical training in US
II. Mother's experience
   A. Outsourcing of job
      1. Mother's education, experience, performance
      2. Employer's cost savings
   B. Retention of managers' jobs
      1. Planning skills
      2. Communication skills
III. Conclusions about ideal education
   A. Needs of US businesses
      1. Technical skills
      2. Management skills
         a. Communication
         b. Problem solving
         c. Versatility
   B. Personal goals
      1. Technical training
      2. English and history courses for management skills

This example illustrates several principles of outlining that can ensure completeness, balance, and clear relationships:

- **All parts are systematically indented and labeled:** Roman numerals (I, II) for primary divisions; indented capital letters (A, B) for secondary divisions; further indented Arabic numerals (1, 2) for supporting examples. The next level down is indented further still and labeled with small letters: a, b.
- **The outline divides the material into several groups.** A long list of points at the same level should be broken up into groups.
- **Topics of equal generality appear in parallel headings,** with the same indention and numbering or lettering.
- **All subdivided headings break into at least two parts.** A topic cannot logically be divided into only one part.
- **All headings are expressed in parallel grammatical form**—in the example, as phrases using a noun plus modifiers. This is a topic outline; in a sentence outline all headings are expressed as full sentences (see **8** p. 450).

Note Because of its structure, a formal outline can be an excellent tool for analyzing a draft before revising it. See p. 25.

4 Unity and coherence

Two qualities of effective writing relate to organization; unity and coherence. When you perceive that someone's writing "flows well," you are probably appreciating these qualities.

To check an outline or draft for **unity**, ask these questions:

- **Is each section relevant to the main idea (thesis) of the essay?**
- **Within main sections, does each example or detail support the principal idea of that section?**

To check your outline or draft for **coherence**, ask the following questions:

- **Do the ideas follow a clear sequence?**
- **Are the parts of the essay logically connected?**
- **Are the connections clear and smooth?**

See also pp. 39–44 on unity and coherence in paragraphs.

4 Drafting

Drafting is an occasion for exploration. Don't expect to transcribe solid thoughts into polished prose: solidity and polish will come with revision and editing. Instead, while drafting let the very act of writing help you find and form your meaning.

4a Starting to draft

Beginning a draft sometimes takes courage, even for seasoned professionals. Procrastination may actually help if you let ideas for writing simmer at the same time. At some point, though, you'll have to face the blank paper or computer screen. The following techniques can help you begin:

- **Read over what you've already written**—notes, outlines, and so on—and immediately start your draft with whatever comes to mind.
- **Freewrite** (see p. 10).

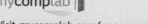

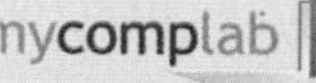

Visit *mycomplab.com* for more resources as well as exercises on drafting.

- **Skip the opening and start in the middle.** Or write the conclusion.
- **Write a paragraph.** Explain what you think your essay will be about when you finish it.
- **Start writing the part that you understand best.** Using your outline, divide your essay into chunks—say, one for the introduction, another for the first point, and so on. One of these chunks may call out to be written.

4b Maintaining momentum

Drafting requires momentum: the forward movement opens you to fresh ideas and connections. To keep moving while drafting, try one or more of these techniques.

- **Set aside enough time for yourself.** For a brief essay, a first draft is likely to take at least an hour or two.
- **Work in a quiet place.**
- **If you must stop working, write down what you expect to do next.** Then you can pick up where you stopped with minimal disruption.
- **Be as fluid as possible.** Spontaneity will allow your attitudes toward your subject to surface naturally in your sentences.
- **Keep going.** Skip over sticky spots; leave a blank if you can't find the right word; put alternative ideas or phrasings in brackets so that you can consider them later. If an idea pops out of nowhere but doesn't seem to fit in, quickly jot it down, or write it into the draft and bracket or boldface it for later attention.
- **Resist self-criticism.** Don't worry about your style, grammar, spelling, punctuation, and the like. Don't worry about what your readers will think. These are very important matters, but save them for revision.
- **Use your thesis statement and outline.** They can remind you of your planned purpose, organization, and content. However, if your writing leads you in a more interesting direction, follow.

If you write on a computer, frequently save the text you're drafting—at least every five or ten minutes and every time you leave the computer.

4c Examining a sample first draft

Katy Moreno's first-draft response to Thomas L. Friedman's "It's a Flat World, After All" appears on the next two pages. As part of her assignment, Moreno showed the draft to four classmates whose suggestions for revision appear in the margin of this draft. They used the Comment function of *Microsoft Word*, which allows users to add comments without inserting words into the document's text. (Notice that the classmates ignore errors in grammar and punctuation, concentrating instead on larger issues such as thesis, clarity of ideas, and unity.)

Title?

In "It's a Flat World, After All," Thomas L. Friedman argues that, most US students are not preparing themselves as well as they should to compete in today's economy. Not like students in India, China, and other countries are. The outsourcing of my mother's job proves that Thomas L. Friedman's advice to improve students' technical training is too narrow.

> **Comment [Jared]:** Your mother's job being outsourced is interesting, but your introduction seems rushed.

> **Comment [Rabia]:** The end of your thesis statement is a little unclear—too narrow for what?

Friedman describes a "flat" world where recent technology like the Internet and wireless communication make it possible for college graduates all over the globe, in particular in India and China, to get jobs that once were gotten by graduates of US colleges and universities. He argues that US students need more math and science in order to compete.

> **Comment [Erin]:** Can you include the reasons Friedman gives for overseas students' success?

I came to college with first-hand knowledge of globalization and outsourcing. My mother, who worked for sixteen years in the field of information technology (IT), was laid off six months ago when the company she worked for decided to outsource much of its IT work to a company based in India. My mother majored in computer science, had sixteen years of experience, and her bosses always gave her good reviews. She never expected to be laid off and was surprised when she was. She wasn't laid off because of her background and performance. In fact, my mother had a very strong background in math and science and years of training and job experience. The reason was because her salary and benefits cost the company more than outsourcing her job did. Which hurt my family financially, as you can imagine.

> **Comment [Nathaniel]:** Tighten this paragraph to avoid repetition? Also, how does your mother's experience relate to Friedman and your thesis?

A number of well-paid people in the IT department where my mother worked, namely IT managers, were not laid off. As my mother explained at the time, they kept their jobs because they were better at planning and they communicated

> **Comment [Erin]:** What were the managers better at planning for?

better, they were better writers and speakers than my mother.

Like my mother, I am more comfortable in front of a computer than I am in front of a group of people. I planned to major in computer science. Since my mother lost her job, though, I have decided to take courses in English and history too, where the classes will require me to do different kinds of work. When I enter the job market, my well-rounded education will make me a more attractive job candidate, and, will help me to be a versatile, productive employee.

Comment [Nathaniel]: Can you be more specific about the kinds of work you'll need to do?

Comment [Rabia]: Can you work this point into your thesis?

We know from our history that Americans have been innovative, hard-working people. We students have educational opportunities to compete in the global economy, but we must use our time in college wisely. As Thomas L. Friedman says, my classmates and I need to be ready for a rapidly changing future. We will have to work hard each day, which means being prepared for class, getting the best grades we can, and making the most of each class. Our futures depend on the decisions we make today.

Comment [Jared]: Conclusion seems to go off in a new direction. Friedman mentions hard work, but it hasn't been your focus before.

Comment [Rabia]: Don't forget your works cited.

5 Revising and Editing

During revision—literally “re-seeing”—you shift your focus outward from yourself and your subject toward your readers, concentrating on what will help them respond as you want. It's wise to revise in at least two stages, one devoted to fundamental meaning and structure (here called **revising**) and one devoted to word choice, grammar, punctuation, and other surface features (here called **editing**). Knowing that you will edit later gives you the freedom at first to look beyond the confines of the page or screen to the whole paper.

mycomplab

Visit *mycomplab.com* for more resources as well as exercises on revising and editing.

5a Revising the whole essay

To revise your writing, you have to read it critically, and that means you have to create some distance between your draft and yourself. One of the following techniques may help you to see your work objectively.

- **Take a break after finishing the draft.** A few hours may be enough; a whole night or day is preferable.
- **Ask someone to read and react to your draft.** If your instructor encourages collaboration among students, by all means take advantage of the opportunity to hear the responses of others. (See pp. 35–37 for more on collaboration.)
- **Type a handwritten draft.** The act of transcription can reveal gaps in content or problems in structure.
- **Outline your draft.** Highlight the main points supporting the thesis, and convert these sentences to outline form. Then examine the outline you've made for logical order, gaps, and digressions. A formal outline can be especially illuminating because of its careful structure (see pp. 19–20).
- **Listen to your draft.** Read the draft out loud to yourself or a friend or classmate, record and listen to it, or have someone read the draft to you.
- **Ease the pressure.** Don't try to re-see everything in your draft at once. Use the checklist on the next page, making a separate pass through the draft for each item.

1 Revising on a word processor

When you revise on a computer, take a few precautions to avoid losing your work and to keep track of your drafts:

- **Save your work every five to ten minutes.**
- **After doing any major work on a project, create a backup version of the file.**
- **Work on a duplicate of your latest draft.** Then the original will remain intact until you're truly finished with it. On the duplicate you can use your word processor's Track Changes function, which shows changes alongside the original text and allows you to accept or reject alterations later.
- **Save each draft under its own file name.** You may need to consult previous drafts for ideas or phrasings.

2 Titling your essay

The revision stage is a good time to consider a title because attempting to sum up your essay in a phrase can focus your attention

Checklist for revision

Purpose

What is the essay's purpose? Does it conform to the assignment? Is it consistent throughout the paper? (See pp. 6–7.)

Thesis

What is the thesis of the essay? Where does it become clear? How well do thesis and paper match: Does the paper stray from the thesis? Does it fulfill the commitment of the thesis? (See pp. 14–16.)

Structure

What are the main points of the paper? (List them.) How well does each support the thesis? How effective is their arrangement for the paper's purpose? (See pp. 16–20.)

Development

How well do details, examples, and other evidence support each main point? Where, if at all, might readers find support skimpy or have trouble understanding the content? (See pp. 6–7, 45–49.)

Tone

What is the tone of the paper? How do particular words and sentence structures create the tone? How appropriate is it for the purpose, topic, and intended readers? Where is it most and least successful?

Unity

What does each sentence and paragraph contribute to the thesis? Where, if at all, do digressions occur? Should these be cut, or can they be rewritten to support the thesis? (See pp. 20–21, 38–39.)

Coherence

How clearly and smoothly does the paper flow? Where does it seem rough or awkward? Can any transitions be improved? (See pp. 20–21, 39–43.)

Title, introduction, conclusion

How accurately and interestingly does the title reflect the essay's content? (See previous page and below.) How well does the introduction engage and focus readers' attention? (See pp. 49–51.) How effective is the conclusion in providing a sense of completion? (See pp. 51–52.)

sharply on your topic, purpose, and audience. The title should tell the reader what your paper is about, but it should not restate the assignment or the thesis statement. Most titles fall into one of these categories:

- **A *descriptive title* announces the subject clearly and accurately.** Such a title is almost always appropriate and is usually expected for academic writing. Katy Moreno's final title—"Can We Compete? College Education for the Global Economy"—is an example.

- A *suggestive title* **hints at the subject to arouse curiosity.** Such a title is common in popular magazines and may be appropriate for writing that is somewhat informal. Moreno might have chosen a suggestive title such as "Training for the New World" or "Education for a Flat World" (echoing Thomas L. Friedman's title).

For more information on essay titles, see **MLA** pp. 448–49 (MLA format), **APA** p. 481 (APA format), and **6** p. 306 (capitalizing words in a title).

5b Examining a sample revision

Katy Moreno was satisfied with her first draft: she had her ideas down, and the arrangement seemed logical. Still, from the revision checklist she knew the draft needed work, and her classmates' comments (pp. 23–24) highlighted what she needed to focus on. Following is the first half of her revised draft with marginal annotations highlighting the changes. Moreno used the Track Changes function on her word processor, so that deletions are crossed out and additions are in blue.

Can We Compete?

College Education for the Global Economy

~~Title?~~

Descriptive title names topic and forecasts approach.

Today's students cannot miss news stories about globalization of the economy and outsourcing of jobs, but are students aware of how these trends are affecting the job market? In "It's a Flat World, After All," Thomas L. Friedman argues that most US students are not preparing themselves as well as ~~they should to compete in today's economy. Not like~~ students in India, China, and other countries ~~are.~~ to compete in today's economy, which requires hard-working, productive scientists and engineers. Friedman's argument speaks to me because my mother recently lost her job when it was outsourced to India. But her experience taught a lesson that Friedman overlooks: technical training by itself can be too narrow to produce the communicators and problem solvers needed by contemporary businesses. ~~The outsourcing of my mother's job proves that Thomas L. Friedman's advice to improve students' technical training is too narrow.~~

Expanded introduction draws readers into Moreno's topic, clarifies her point of agreement with Friedman, and states her revised thesis.

Friedman describes a "flat" world where recent technology like the Internet and wireless communication makes it possible for college graduates

Expanded summary of Friedman's article specifies qualities of overseas workers.

all over the globe~~, in particular~~ to compete for high paying jobs that once belonged to graduates of US colleges and universities. He focuses on workers in India and China~~,~~ who graduate from college with excellent educations in math and science, who are eager for new opportunities, and who are willing to work exceptionally hard, often harder than their American counterparts and, for less money. ~~to get jobs that once were gotten by graduates of US colleges and universities. He~~ Friedman argues that US students must be better prepared academically, especially in ~~need more~~ math and science, so that they can get and keep jobs that will otherwise go overseas. ~~in order to compete.~~

New opening sentences connect to introduction and thesis statement, restating points of agreement and disagreement with Friedman.

Revisions condense long example of mother's experience.

~~I came to college with first hand knowledge of globalization and outsourcing. My mother, who worked for sixteen years in the field of information technology (IT), was laid off six months ago when the company she worked for decided to outsource much of its IT work to a company based in India. My mother~~ At first glance, my mother's experience of losing her job might seem to support the argument of Friedman that better training in math and science is the key to competing in the global job market. Her experience, however, adds dimensions to the globalization story, which Friedman misses. First my mother had the kind of strong background in math and science that Friedman says, today's workers need. She majored in computer science, rose within the information technology (IT) department of a large company, ~~had sixteen years of experience,~~ and her bosses always gave her good performance reviews. Still, when her employer decided to outsource most of its IT work, my mother lost her job. ~~She never expected to be laid off and was surprised when she was. She wasn't laid off because of her background and performance. In fact, my mother had a very strong background in math and science and years of training and job experience.~~ The reason wasn't because her technical skills were inadequate. Instead, her salary and benefits cost the company more than outsourcing her job did. Until wages rise around the globe, jobs like my mother's will be vulnerable. No matter how well you are trained. ~~Which hurt my family financially, as you can imagine.~~

Concluding sentences reinforce the point of the paragraph and connect to thesis statement.

5c Editing the revised draft

After you've revised your essay so that all the content is in place, then turn to the important work of removing any surface problems that could interfere with a reader's understanding or enjoyment of your ideas.

1 Strategies for editing

Try these approaches to discover what needs editing:

- **Take a break.** Even fifteen minutes can clear your head.
- **Read the draft slowly, and read what you actually see.** Otherwise, you're likely to read what you intended to write but didn't. (If you have trouble slowing down, try reading your draft from back to front, sentence by sentence.)
- **Read as if you are encountering the draft for the first time.** Put yourself in the reader's place.
- **Have a classmate, friend, or relative read your work.** Make sure you understand and consider the reader's suggestions, even if eventually you decide not to take them.
- **Read the draft aloud or, even better, record it.** Listen for awkward rhythms, repetitive sentence patterns, and missing or clumsy transitions.
- **Learn from your own experience.** Keep a record of the problems that others have pointed out in your writing. When editing, check your work against this record.

In editing, work first for clear and effective sentences that flow smoothly from one to the next. Then check your sentences for correctness. Use the questions in the checklist on the next page to guide your editing, referring to the page numbers in parentheses as needed.

2 A sample edited paragraph

The third paragraph of Katy Moreno's edited draft appears below. Among other changes, she tightened wording, improved parallelism (with *consistently received*), corrected several comma errors, and repaired the final sentence fragment.

At first glance, my mother's experience of losing her job might seem to support ~~the~~ Friedman's argument ~~of Friedman~~ that better training in math and science is the key to competing in the global job market. However, ~~H~~her experience~~,~~ ~~however,~~ adds dimensions to the globalization story~~, which~~ that Friedman misses. First, my mother had the kind of strong background in math and science that Friedman says~~,~~ today's workers need. She majored in computer science, rose within the information technology (IT) department of a large company, and consistently received ~~her bosses always gave her~~ good performance reviews. Still, when her employer decided to outsource most of its IT work, my mother lost her job. The reason wasn't ~~because~~that her technical skills were inadequate. Instead, her salary and benefits cost the company more than outsourcing her job did. Until wages rise around the globe, jobs like my mother's will be vulnerable,~~. N~~no matter how well ~~you are~~ a person is trained.

Checklist for editing

Are my sentences clear?

Do my words and sentences mean what I Intend them to mean? Is anything confusing? Check especially for these:

Exact language (**3** pp. 165–71)
Parallelism (**3** pp. 151–53)
Clear modifiers (**4** pp. 245–49)
Clear reference of pronouns (**4** pp. 233–35)
Complete sentences (**4** pp. 250–53)
Sentences separated correctly (**4** pp. 253–57)

Are my sentences effective?

How well do words and sentences engage and hold readers' attention? Where does the writing seem wordy, choppy, or dull? Check especially for these:

Emphasis of main ideas (**3** pp. 143–51)
Smooth and informative transitions (pp. 43–44)
Variety in sentence length and structure (**3** pp. 154–57)
Appropriate language (**3** pp. 158–64)
Concise sentences (**3** pp. 172–76)

Do my sentences contain errors?

Where do surface errors interfere with the clarity and effectiveness of my sentences? Check especially for these:

- **Spelling errors** (**6** pp. 297–301)
- **Sentence fragments** (**4** pp. 250–53)
- **Comma splices** (**4** pp. 254–57)
- **Verb errors**
  Verb forms, especially *-s* and *-ed* endings, correct forms of irregular verbs, and appropriate helping verbs (**4** pp. 196–208)
  Verb tenses, especially consistency (**4** pp. 208–14)
  Agreement between subjects and verbs, especially when words come between them or the subject is *each, everyone,* or a similar word (**4** pp. 218–23)
- **Pronoun errors**
  Pronoun forms, especially subjective (*he, she, they, who*) vs. objective (*him, her, them, whom*) (**4** pp. 224–29)
  Agreement between pronouns and antecedents, especially when the antecedent contains *or* or the antecedent is *each, everyone, person,* or a similar word (**4** pp. 229–32)
- **Punctuation errors**
  Commas, especially with comma splices (**4** pp. 254–57) and with *and* or *but,* with introductory elements, with nonessential elements, and with series (**5** pp. 265–76)
  Apostrophes in possessives but not plural nouns (*Dave's/witches*) and in contractions but not possessive personal pronouns (*it's/its*) (**5** pp. 282–85)

3 Editing on a computer

When you write on a word processor, consider these additional approaches to editing:

- **Don't rely on a spelling or grammar/style checker to find what needs editing.** See the discussion of these checkers below.
- **If possible, work on a double-spaced paper copy.** Most people find it much harder to spot errors on a computer screen than on paper.
- **Use the Find command to locate and correct your common problems**—certain misspellings, overuse of *there is,* wordy phrases such as *the fact that,* and so on.
- **Resist overediting.** The ease of editing on a computer can lead to rewriting sentences over and over, stealing the life from your prose. If your grammar/style checker contributes to the temptation, consider turning it off.
- **Take special care with additions and omissions.** Make sure you haven't omitted needed words or left in unneeded words.

4 Working with spelling and grammar/style checkers

A spelling checker and grammar/style checker can be helpful *if* you work within their limitations. The programs miss many problems and may even flag items that are actually correct. Further, they know nothing of your purpose and your audience, so they cannot make important decisions about your writing. Always use these tools critically:

- **Read your work yourself to ensure that it's clear and error-free.**
- **Consider a checker's suggestions carefully, weighing each one against your intentions.** If you aren't sure whether to accept a checker's suggestion, consult a dictionary, writing handbook, or other source. Your version may be fine.

Using a spelling checker

Your word processor's spelling checker can be a great ally: it will flag words that are spelled incorrectly and will usually suggest alternative spellings that resemble what you've typed. However, this ally can also undermine you because of its limitations:

- **The checker may flag a word that you've spelled correctly** just because the word does not appear in its dictionary.
- **The checker may suggest incorrect alternatives.** In providing a list of alternative spellings for your word, the checker may highlight the one it considers most likely to be correct. For

example, if you misspell *definitely* by typing *definately*, your checker may highlight *defiantly* as the correct option. You need to verify that the alternative suggested by the checker is actually what you intend before selecting it. Consult an online or printed dictionary when you aren't sure about the checker's recommendations.

- **Most important, a spelling checker will not flag words that appear in its dictionary but you have misused.** The jingle in the following screen shot has circulated widely as a warning about spelling checkers.

Spelling checker

A spelling checker failed to catch any of the thirteen errors in this jingle. Can you spot them?

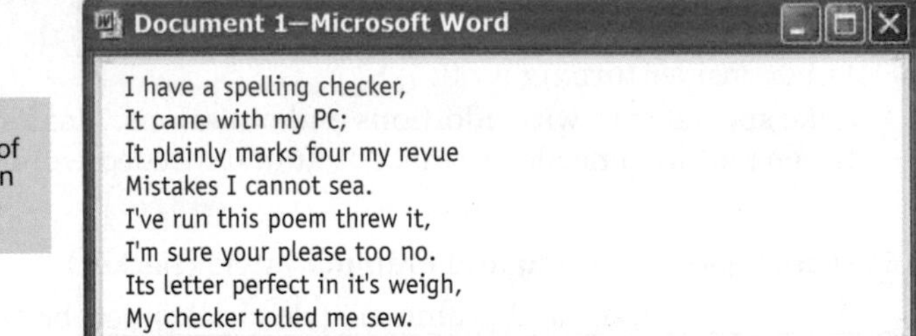

Document 1—Microsoft Word
I have a spelling checker,
It came with my PC;
It plainly marks four my revue
Mistakes I cannot sea.
I've run this poem threw it,
I'm sure your please too no.
Its letter perfect in it's weigh,
My checker tolled me sew.

Using a grammar/style checker

Grammar/style checkers can flag incorrect grammar or punctuation and wordy or awkward sentences. However, these programs can call your attention only to passages that *may* be faulty. They miss many errors because they are not yet capable of analyzing language in all its complexity. (For instance, they can't accurately distinguish a word's part of speech when there are different possibilities, as *light* can be a noun, a verb, or an adjective.) And they often question passages that don't need editing, such as an appropriate passive verb or a deliberate and emphatic use of repetition.

You can customize a grammar/style checker to suit your needs and habits as a writer. (Select Options under the Tools menu.) Most checkers allow you to specify whether to check grammar only or grammar and style. Some style checkers can be set to the level of writing you intend, such as formal, standard, and informal. (For academic writing choose formal.) You can also instruct the checker to flag specific grammar and style problems that tend to occur in your writing, such as mismatched subjects and verbs, apostrophes in plural nouns, overused passive voice, or a confusion between *its* and *it's*.

5d Formatting and proofreading the final draft

After editing your essay, retype or print it one last time. Follow the wishes of your instructor in formatting your document. Two common formats are discussed and illustrated in this book: MLA (**MLA** pp. 447–49) and APA (**APA** pp. 481–84). In addition, pp. 52–65 treat principles and elements of document design.

Be sure to proofread the final essay several times to spot and correct errors. To increase the accuracy of your proofreading, you may need to experiment with ways to keep yourself from relaxing into the rhythm and the content of your prose. Here are a few tricks, including some used by professional proofreaders:

- **Read printed copy,** even if you will eventually submit the paper electronically. Most people proofread more accurately when reading type on paper than when reading it on a computer screen. (At the same time, don't view the printed copy as error-free just because it's clean. Clean-looking copy may still harbor errors.)
- **Read the paper aloud,** very slowly, and distinctly pronounce exactly what you see.
- **Place a ruler under each line as you read it.**
- **Read "against copy,"** comparing your final draft one sentence at a time against the edited draft.
- **Ignore content.** To keep the content of your writing from distracting you, read the essay backward sentence by sentence. Or print each paragraph on a separate page to isolate it. (Of course, reassemble the paragraphs before submitting the paper.)

5e Examining a sample final draft

Katy Moreno's final essay appears on these pages, typed in MLA format except for page numbers. Comments in the margins point out key features of the essay's content.

Katy Moreno

Professor Lacourse

English 110

14 November 2008

Can We Compete?

College Education for the Global Economy

Descriptive title

Introduction

Today's students cannot miss news stories about globalization of the economy and outsourcing of jobs, but are students aware of how these trends are affecting the job market? In "It's a Flat World, After All,"

Thesis statement: basic disagreement with Friedman

Thomas L. Friedman argues that most US students are not preparing themselves as well as students in India, China, and other countries to compete in today's economy, which requires hard-working, productive scientists and engineers. Friedman's argument speaks to me because my mother lost her job when it was outsourced to India. But her experience taught a lesson that Friedman overlooks: technical training by itself can be too narrow to produce the communicators and problem solvers needed by contemporary businesses.

Summary of Friedman's article

No source citation for Friedman because paragraph summarizes entire article and mentions Friedman's name

Friedman describes a "flat" world where recent technology like the Internet and wireless communication makes it possible for college graduates all over the globe to compete for high-paying jobs that once belonged to graduates of US colleges and universities. He focuses on workers in India and China who graduate from college with excellent educations in math and science, who are eager for new opportunities, and who are willing to work exceptionally hard, often harder than their American counterparts, and for less money. Friedman argues that US students must be better prepared academically, especially in math and science, so that they can get and keep jobs that will otherwise go overseas.

Transition to disagreements with Friedman

First disagreement with Friedman

Examples to support first disagreement

Example to qualify first disagreement

Clarification of first disagreement

At first glance, my mother's experience of losing her job might seem to support Friedman's argument that better training in math and science is the key to competing in the global job market. However, her experience adds dimensions to the globalization story that Friedman misses. First, my mother had the kind of strong background in math and science that Friedman says today's workers need. She majored in computer science, rose within the information technology (IT) department of a large company, and consistently received good performance reviews. Still, when her employer decided to outsource most of its IT work, my mother lost her job. The reason wasn't that her technical skills were inadequate; instead, her salary and benefits cost the company more than outsourcing her job did. Until wages rise around the globe, jobs like my mother's will be vulnerable, no matter how well a person is trained.

Second disagreement with Friedman

Explanation of second disagreement

Conclusion summarizing both disagreements with Friedman

The second dimension that Friedman misses is that a number of well-paid people in my mother's IT department, namely IT managers, were not laid off. As my mother explained at the time, they kept their jobs because they were experienced at figuring out the company's IT needs, planning for changes, researching and proposing solutions, and communicating in writing and speech—skills that her more narrow training and experience had missed. Friedman misses these skills by focusing only on technical training. Without the ability to solve problems creatively and to communicate, people with technical expertise alone may not have enough to save their jobs, as my mother learned.

Like my mother, I am more comfortable in front of a computer than I am in front of a group of people, and I had planned to major in computer science. Since my mother lost her job, however, I have decided to take courses in English and history as well. Classes in these subjects will require me to read broadly, think critically, research, and communicate ideas in writing—in short, to develop skills that make managers. When I enter the job market, my well-rounded education will make me a more attractive job candidate and will help me to become the kind of forward-thinking manager that US companies will always need to employ here in the US.

Final point: business needs and author's personal goals

Explanation of final point

Many jobs that require a college degree are indeed going overseas, as Thomas L. Friedman says, and my classmates and I need to be ready for a rapidly changing future. But rather than focus only on math and science, we need to broaden our academic experiences so that the skills we develop make us not only employable but also indispensable.

Conclusion recapping points of agreement and disagreement with Friedman and summarizing essay

Work Cited

Friedman, Thomas L. "It's a Flat World, After All." *New York Times Magazine* 3 Apr. 2005: 32-37. Print.

Work cited in MLA style (see **MLA** p. 415)

5f Revising collaboratively

In many writing courses students work together on writing, most often commenting on each other's work to help with revision. This collaborative writing gives experience in reading written work critically and in reaching others through writing. Collaboration may occur face to face in small groups, via drafts and comments on paper, or on computers.

Whether you collaborate in person, on paper, or on a computer, you will be more comfortable and helpful and will benefit more from others' comments if you follow a few guidelines.

Commenting on others' writing

- **Be sure you know what the writer is saying.** If necessary, summarize the paper to understand its content. (See **2** pp. 72–74.)
- **Address only your most significant concerns with the work.** Use the revision checklist on p. 26 as a guide to what is significant. Unless you have other instructions, ignore mistakes in grammar, punctuation, and the like. (The temptation to focus on such errors may be especially strong if the writer is less experienced than you are with standard American English.) Emphasizing mistakes will contribute little to the writer's revision.

- **Remember that you are the reader, not the writer.** Don't edit sentences, add details, or otherwise assume responsibility for the paper.
- **Phrase your comments carefully.** Avoid misunderstandings by making sure comments are both clear and respectful. If you are responding on paper or online, not face to face with the writer, remember that the writer has nothing but your written words to go on. He or she can't ask you for immediate clarification and can't infer your attitudes from gestures, facial expressions, and tone of voice.
- **Be specific.** If something confuses you, say *why.* If you disagree with a conclusion, say *why.*
- **Be supportive as well as honest.** Tell the writer what you like about the paper. Word comments positively: instead of *This paragraph doesn't interest me,* say *You have an interesting detail here that I almost missed.* Question the writer in a way that emphasizes the effect of the work on you, the reader: *This paragraph confuses me because. . . .* And avoid measuring the work against a set of external standards: *This essay is poorly organized. Your thesis statement is inadequate.*
- **While reading, make your comments in writing.** Even if you will be delivering your comments in person later on, the written record will help you recall what you thought.
- **Link comments to specific parts of a paper.** Especially if you are reading the paper on a computer, be clear about what in the paper each comment relates to. You can embed your comments directly into the paper, distinguishing them with highlighting or color, or you can use a word processor's Comment function.

Benefiting from comments on your writing

- **Think of your readers as counselors or coaches.** They can help you see the virtues and flaws in your work and sharpen your awareness of readers' needs.
- **Read or listen to comments closely.**
- **Know what the critic is saying.** If you need more information, ask for it, or consult the appropriate section of this handbook.
- **Don't become defensive.** Letting comments offend you will only erect a barrier to improvement in your writing. As one writing teacher advises, "Leave your ego at the door."
- **Revise your work in response to appropriate comments,** even if you are not required to do so. You will learn more from actually revising than from just thinking about it.
- **Remember that you are the final authority on your work.** You should be open to suggestions, but you are free to decline advice when you think it is inappropriate.

- **Keep track of both the strengths and weaknesses others identify.** Then in later assignments you can build on your successes and give special attention to problem areas.

CULTURE LANGUAGE In some cultures writers do not expect criticism from readers, or readers do not expect to think and speak critically about what they read. If critical responses are uncommon in your native culture, collaboration may at first be uncomfortable for you. As a writer, think of a draft or even a final paper as more an exploration of ideas than the last word on your subject; then you may be more receptive to readers' suggestions. As a reader, allow yourself to approach a text skeptically, and know that your tactful questions and suggestions will usually be considered appropriate.

5g Preparing a writing portfolio

Your writing instructor may ask you to assemble samples of your writing into a portfolio, or folder, once or more during the course. Such a portfolio gives you a chance to consider all your writing over a period and to showcase your best work.

Although the requirements for portfolios vary, most instructors are looking for a range of writing that demonstrates your progress and strengths as a writer. You, in turn, see how you have advanced from one assignment to the next, as you've had time for new knowledge to sink in and time for practice. Instructors often allow students to revise papers before placing them in the portfolio, even if the papers were submitted earlier. In that case, every paper in the portfolio can benefit from all your learning.

An assignment to assemble a writing portfolio will probably also provide guidelines for what to include, how the portfolio will be evaluated, and how (or whether) it will be weighted for a grade. Be sure you understand the purpose of the portfolio and who will read it. For instance, if your composition instructor will be the only reader and his or her guidelines encourage you to show evidence of progress, you might include a paper that took big risks but never entirely succeeded. In contrast, if a committee of instructors will read your work and the guidelines urge you to demonstrate your competence as a writer, you might include only papers that did succeed.

Unless the guidelines specify otherwise, provide error-free copies of your final drafts, label all your samples with your name, and assemble them all in a folder. Add a cover letter or memo that lists the samples, explains why you've included each one, and evaluates your progress as a writer. The self-evaluation involved should be a learning experience for you and will help your readers assess your development as a writer.

6 Paragraphs

A **paragraph** is a group of related sentences set off by a beginning indention or, sometimes, by extra space. Paragraphs give you and your readers a breather from long stretches of text, and they indicate key steps in the development of your thesis.

This chapter discusses the three qualities of an effective body paragraph: unity (below), coherence (next page), and development (p. 45). In addition, the chapter discusses two special kinds of paragraphs: introductions and conclusions (pp. 49 and 51).

CULTURE LANGUAGE Not all cultures share the paragraphing conventions of American academic writing. In some other languages, writing moves differently from English—not from left to right, but from right to left or down rows from top to bottom. Even in languages that move as English does, writers may not use paragraphs at all. Or they may use paragraphs but not state the central ideas or provide transitional expressions to show readers how sentences relate. If your native language is not English and you have difficulty with paragraphs, don't worry about paragraphing during drafting. Instead, during a separate step of revision, divide your text into parts that develop your main points. Mark those parts with indentions.

6a Maintaining paragraph unity

An effective paragraph develops one central idea—in other words, it is **unified.** Here is an example:

> Some people really like chili, apparently, but nobody can agree how the stuff should be made. C. V. Wood, twice winner at Terlingua, uses flank steak, pork chops, chicken, and green chilis. My friend Hughes Rudd of CBS News, who imported five hundred pounds of chili powder into Russia as a condition of accepting employment as Moscow correspondent, favors coarse-ground beef. Isadore Bleckman, the cameraman I must live with on the road, insists upon one-inch cubes of stew beef and puts garlic in his chili, an Illinois affectation. An Indian of my acquaintance, Mr. Fulton Batisse, who eats chili for breakfast when he can, uses buffalo meat and plays an Indian drum while it's cooking. I ask you.
>
> —Charles Kuralt, *Dateline America*

mycomplab

Visit *mycomplab.com* for more resources as well as exercises on paragraphs.

Checklist for revising paragraphs

- **Is the paragraph unified?** Does it adhere to one general idea that is either stated in a topic sentence or otherwise apparent? (See previous page and below.)
- **Is the paragraph coherent?** Do the sentences follow a clear sequence? Are the sentences linked as needed by parallelism, repetition or restatement, pronouns, consistency, and transitional expressions? (See below.)
- **Is the paragraph developed?** Is the general idea of the paragraph well supported with specific evidence such as details, facts, examples, and reasons? (See p. 45.)

Kuralt's paragraph works because it follows through on its central idea, which is stated in the first sentence, the **topic sentence.** After the topic sentence, each of the next four sentences offers an example of a chili concoction. (In the final sentence Kuralt comments on the examples.)

What if instead Kuralt had written his paragraph as follows? Here the topic of chili preparation is forgotten mid-paragraph, as the sentences digress to describe life in Moscow:

> Some people really like chili, apparently, but nobody can agree how the stuff should be made. C. V. Wood, twice winner at Terlingua, uses flank steak, pork chops, chicken, and green chilis. My friend Hughes Rudd, who imported five hundred pounds of chili powder into Russia as a condition of accepting employment as Moscow correspondent, favors coarse-ground beef. He had some trouble finding the beef in Moscow, though. He sometimes had to scour all the markets and wait in long lines. For any American used to overstocked supermarkets and department stores, Russia can be quite a shock.

Instead of following through on its topic sentence, the paragraph loses its way. It is not unified.

A topic sentence need not always come first in the paragraph. For instance, it may come last, presenting your idea only after you have provided the evidence for it. Or it may not be stated at all, especially in narrative or descriptive writing in which the point becomes clear in the details. But always the idea should govern the paragraph's content as if it were standing guard at the opening.

6b Achieving paragraph coherence

When a paragraph is **coherent,** readers can see how it holds together: the sentences seem to flow logically and smoothly into one another. Exactly the opposite happens with this paragraph:

> The ancient Egyptians were masters of preserving dead people's bodies by making mummies of them. Mummies several thousand years old have been discovered nearly intact. The skin, hair, teeth, finger- and toenails, and facial features of the mummies were evident. One can diagnose the diseases they suffered in life, such as smallpox, arthritis, and nutritional deficiencies. The process was remarkably effective. Sometimes apparent were the fatal afflictions of the dead people: a middle-aged king died from a blow on the head, and polio killed a child king. Mummification consisted of removing the internal organs, applying natural preservatives inside and out, and then wrapping the body in layers of bandages.

The paragraph is hard to read. The sentences lurch instead of gliding from point to point.

The paragraph as it was actually written appears below. It is much clearer because the writer arranged information differently and also built links into his sentences so that they would flow smoothly:

- After stating the central idea in a topic sentence, the writer moves to two more specific explanations and illustrates the second with four sentences of examples.
- Circled words repeat or restate key terms or concepts.
- Boxed words link sentences and clarify relationships.
- Underlined phrases are in parallel grammatical form to reflect their parallel content.

> Central idea
> The ancient Egyptians were masters of preserving dead people's bodies by making mummies of them. Explanation Basically, mummification consisted of removing the internal organs, applying natural preservatives inside and out, and then wrapping the body in layers of bandages. Explanation And the process was remarkably effective. Indeed, mummies several thousand years old have been discovered nearly intact. Specific examples Their skin, hair, teeth, finger- and toenails, and facial features are still evident. Their diseases in life, such as smallpox, arthritis, and nutritional deficiencies, are still diagnosable. Even their fatal afflictions are still apparent: a middle-aged king died from a blow on the head; a child king died from polio.
>
> —Mitchell Rosenbaum (student), "Lost Arts of the Egyptians"

1 Paragraph organization

A coherent paragraph organizes information so that readers can easily follow along. These are common paragraph schemes:

- **General to specific:** Sentences downshift from more general statements to more specific ones. (See the paragraph by Rosenbaum on the previous page.)
- **Climactic:** Sentences increase in drama or interest, ending in a climax. (See the paragraph below about sleep.)
- **Spatial:** Sentences scan a person, place, or object from top to bottom, from side to side, or in some other way that approximates the way people actually look at things. (See the paragraph by Woolf on p. 45.)
- **Chronological:** Sentences present events as they occurred in time, earlier to later. (See the paragraph by LaFrank on p. 43.)

2 Parallelism

Parallelism helps tie sentences together. In the following paragraph the underlined parallel structures of *She* and a verb link all sentences to the first one. Parallelism also appears *within* many of the sentences. Aphra Behn (1640–89) was the first Englishwoman to write professionally.

> In addition to her busy career as a writer, Aphra Behn also found time to briefly marry and spend a little while in debtor's prison. She found time to take up a career as a spy for the English in their war against the Dutch. She made the long and difficult voyage to Suriname [in South America] and became involved in a slave rebellion there. She plunged into political debate at Will's Coffee House and defended her position from the stage of the Drury Lane Theater. She actively argued for women's rights to be educated and to marry whom they pleased, or not at all. She defied the seventeenth-century dictum that ladies must be "modest" and wrote freely about sex.
>
> —Angeline Goreau, "Aphra Behn"

3 Repetition and restatement

Repeating or restating key words helps make a paragraph coherent and also reminds readers what the topic is. In the following paragraph note the underlined repetition of *sleep* and the restatement of *adults*.

> Perhaps the simplest fact about sleep is that individual needs for it vary widely. Most adults sleep between seven and nine hours, but occasionally people turn up who need twelve hours or so, while some rare types can get by on three or four. Rarest of all are those legendary types

Key term

parallelism The use of similar grammatical structures for similar elements of meaning within or among sentences: *The book caused a stir in the media and aroused debate in Congress.* (See also **3** pp. 151–53.)

who require almost no sleep at all; respected researchers have recently studied three such people. One of them—a healthy, happy woman in her seventies—sleeps about an hour every two or three days. The other two are men in early middle age, who get by on a few minutes a night. One of them complains about the daily fifteen minutes or so he's forced to "waste" in sleeping.

—Lawrence A. Mayer, "The Confounding Enemy of Sleep"

4 Pronouns

Because pronouns refer to nouns, they can help relate sentences to each other. In the paragraph on the previous page by Angeline Goreau, *she* works just this way by substituting for *Aphra Behn* in every sentence after the first.

5 Consistency

Consistency (or the lack of it) occurs primarily in the person and number of nouns and pronouns and in the tense of verbs. Any inconsistencies not required by meaning will interfere with a reader's ability to follow the development of ideas.

Note the underlined inconsistencies in the next paragraphs:

Shifts in tense

In the Hopi religion, water is the driving force. Since the Hopi lived in the Arizona desert, they needed water urgently for drinking, cooking, and irrigating crops. Their complex beliefs are focused in part on gaining the assistance of supernatural forces in obtaining water. Many of the Hopi kachinas, or spirit essences, were directly concerned with clouds, rain, and snow.

Shifts in number

Kachinas represent the things and events of the real world, such as clouds, mischief, cornmeal, and even death. A kachina is not worshiped as a god but regarded as an interested friend. They visit the Hopi from December through July in the form of men who dress in kachina costumes and perform dances and other rituals.

Key terms

pronoun A word that refers to and functions as a noun, such as *I, you, he, she, it, we, they: The bush had a beehive in it.* (See **4** p. 181.)

tense The form of a verb that indicates the time of its action, such as present (*I run*), past (*I ran*), or future (*I will run*). (See **4** p. 208.)

number The form of a noun, pronoun, or verb that indicates whether it is singular (one) or plural (more than one): *boy is, boys are.*

person The form of a pronoun that indicates whether the subject is speaking (first person: *I, we*), spoken to (second person: *you*), or spoken about (third person: *he, she, it, they*). All nouns are in the third person.

Shifts in person

Unlike the man, the Hopi woman does not keep contact with kachinas through costumes and dancing. Instead, one receives a small likeness of a kachina, called a *tihu*, from the man impersonating the kachina. You are more likely to receive a tihu as a girl approaching marriage, though a child or older woman may receive one, too.

Grammar checkers A grammar checker cannot help you locate shifts in tense, number, or person among sentences. Shifts are sometimes necessary (as when tenses change to reflect actual differences in time). Furthermore, a passage with needless shifts may still consist of sentences that are grammatically correct, as all the sentences are in the preceding examples.

6 Transitional expressions

Transitional expressions such as *therefore, in contrast,* or *meanwhile* can forge specific connections between sentences, as do the underlined expressions in this paragraph:

> Medical science has thus succeeded in identifying the hundreds of viruses that can cause the common cold. It has also discovered the most effective means of prevention. One person transmits the cold viruses to another most often by hand. For instance, an infected person covers his mouth to cough. He then picks up the telephone. Half an hour later, his daughter picks up the same telephone. Immediately afterward, she rubs her eyes. Within a few days, she, too, has a cold. And thus it spreads. To avoid colds, therefore, people should wash their hands often and keep their hands away from their faces.
>
> —Kathleen LaFrank (student), "Colds: Myth and Science"

Note that you can use transitional expressions to link paragraphs as well as sentences. In the first sentence of LaFrank's paragraph, the word *thus* signals that the sentence refers to an effect discussed in the preceding paragraph.

The following box lists many transitional expressions by the functions they perform.

Transitional expressions

To add or show sequence

again, also, and, and then, besides, equally important, finally, first, further, furthermore, in addition, in the first place, last, moreover, next, second, still, too

To compare

also, in the same way, likewise, similarly

(continued)

Transitional expressions

(continued)

To contrast

although, and yet, but, but at the same time, despite, even so, even though, for all that, however, in contrast, in spite of, nevertheless, notwithstanding, on the contrary, on the other hand, regardless, still, though, yet

To give examples or intensify

after all, an illustration of, even, for example, for instance, indeed, in fact, it is true, of course, specifically, that is, to illustrate, truly

To indicate place

above, adjacent to, below, elsewhere, farther on, here, near, nearby, on the other side, opposite to, there, to the east, to the left

To indicate time

after a while, afterward, as long as, as soon as, at last, at length, at that time, before, earlier, eventually, formerly, immediately, in the meantime, in the past, lately, later, meanwhile, now, presently, shortly, simultaneously, since, so far, soon, subsequently, suddenly, then, thereafter, until, until now, when

To repeat, summarize, or conclude

all in all, altogether, as has been said, in brief, in conclusion, in other words, in particular, in short, in simpler terms, in summary, on the whole, that is, therefore, to put it differently, to summarize

To show cause or effect

accordingly, as a result, because, consequently, for this purpose, hence, otherwise, since, then, therefore, thereupon, thus, to this end, with this object

Note Draw carefully on this list of transitional expressions because the ones in each group are not interchangeable. For instance, *besides, finally,* and *second* may all be used to add information, but each has its own distinct meaning.

CULTURE LANGUAGE If transitional expressions are not common in your native language, you may be tempted to compensate when writing in English by adding them to the beginnings of most sentences. But such explicit transitions aren't needed everywhere, and in fact too many can be intrusive and awkward. When inserting transitional expressions, consider the reader's need for a signal: often the connection from sentence to sentence is already clear from the context or can be made clear by relating the content of sentences more closely (see **3** pp. 145–47). When you do need transitional expressions, try varying their positions in your sentences, as illustrated in the sample paragraph on the previous page.

6c Developing paragraphs

An effective, well-developed paragraph always provides the specific information that readers need and expect in order to understand you and to stay interested in what you say. Paragraph length can be a rough gauge of development: anything much shorter than 100 to 150 words may leave readers with a sense of incompleteness.

To develop or shape an idea in a paragraph, one or more of the following patterns may help. (These patterns may also be used to develop entire essays. See p. 13.)

1 Narration

Narration retells a significant sequence of events, usually in the order of their occurrence (that is, chronologically). A narrator is concerned not just with the sequence of events but also with their consequence, their importance to the whole.

> Jill's story is typical for "recruits" to religious cults. She was very lonely in college and appreciated the attention of the nice young men and women who lived in a house near campus. They persuaded her to share their meals and then to move in with them. Between intense bombardments of "love," they deprived her of sleep and sometimes threatened to throw her out. Jill became increasingly confused and dependent, losing touch with any reality besides the one in the group. She dropped out of school and refused to see or communicate with her family. Before long she, too, was preying on lonely college students.
>
> —Hillary Begas (student), "The Love Bombers"

2 Description

Description details the sensory qualities of a person, scene, thing, or feeling, using concrete and specific words to convey a dominant mood, illustrate an idea, or achieve some other purpose.

> The sun struck straight upon the house, making the white walls glare between the dark windows. Their panes, woven thickly with green branches, held circles of impenetrable darkness. Sharp-edged wedges of light lay upon the window-sill and showed inside the room plates with blue rings, cups with curved handles, the bulge of a great bowl, the criss-cross pattern in the rug, and the formidable corners and lines of cabinets and bookcases. Behind their conglomeration hung a zone of shadow in which might be a further shape to be disencumbered of shadow or still denser depths of darkness. —Virginia Woolf, *The Waves*

3 Illustration or support

An idea may be developed with several specific examples, like those used by Charles Kuralt on p. 38, or with a single extended example, as in the next paragraph:

The language problem that I was attacking loomed larger and larger as I began to learn more. When I would describe in English certain concepts and objects enmeshed in Korean emotion and imagination, I became slowly aware of nuances, of differences between two languages even in simple expression. The remark "Kim entered the house" seems to be simple enough, yet, unless a reader has a clear visual image of a Korean house, his understanding of the sentence is not complete. When a Korean says he is "in the house," he may be in his courtyard, or on his porch, or in his small room! If I wanted to give a specific picture of entering the house in the Western sense, I had to say "room" instead of house—sometimes. I say "sometimes" because many Koreans entertain their guests on their porches and still are considered to be hospitable, and in the Korean sense, going into the "room" may be a more intimate act than it would be in the English sense. Such problems!

—Kim Yong Ik, "A Book-Writing Venture"

Sometimes you can develop a paragraph by providing your reasons for stating a general idea. For instance:

There are three reasons, quite apart from scientific considerations, that mankind needs to travel in space. The first reason is the need for garbage disposal: we need to transfer industrial processes into space, so that the earth may remain a green and pleasant place for our grandchildren to live in. The second reason is the need to escape material impoverishment: the resources of this planet are finite, and we shall not forgo forever the abundant solar energy and minerals and living space that are spread out all around us. The third reason is our spiritual need for an open frontier: the ultimate purpose of space travel is to bring to humanity not only scientific discoveries and an occasional spectacular show on television but a real expansion of our spirit.

—Freeman Dyson, "Disturbing the Universe"

4 Definition

Defining a complicated, abstract, or controversial term often requires extended explanation. The following definition comes from an essay asserting that "quality in product and effort has become a vanishing element of current civilization." Notice how the writer pins down meaning with examples and contrasts.

In the hope of possibly reducing the hail of censure which is certain to greet this essay (I am thinking of going to Alaska or possibly Patagonia in the week it is published), let me say that quality, as I understand it, means investment of the best skill and effort possible to produce the finest and most admirable result possible. Its presence or absence in some degree characterizes every manmade object, service, skilled or unskilled labor—laying bricks, painting a picture, ironing shirts, practicing medicine, shoemaking, scholarship, writing a book. You do it well or you do it half-well. Materials are sound and durable or they are sleazy; method is painstaking or whatever is easiest. Quality is achieving or reaching for the highest standard as against being satisfied with the sloppy or fraudulent. It is honesty of purpose as against catering to cheap or sensational sentiment. It does not allow compromise with the second-rate. —Barbara Tuchman, "The Decline of Quality"

5 Division or analysis

With division or analysis, you separate something into its elements—for instance, you might divide a newspaper into its sections. You may also approach the elements critically, interpreting their meaning and significance (see also **2** pp. 81–83):

> The surface realism of the soap opera conjures up an illusion of "liveness." The domestic settings and easygoing rhythms encourage the viewer to believe that the drama, however ridiculous, is simply an extension of daily life. The conversation is so slow that some have called it "radio with pictures." (Advertisers have always assumed that busy housewives would listen, rather than watch.) Conversation is casual and colloquial, as though one were eavesdropping on neighbors. There is plenty of time to "read" the character's face; close-ups establish intimacy. The sets are comfortably familiar: well-lit interiors of living rooms, restaurants, offices, and hospitals. Daytime soaps have little of the glamour of their prime-time relations. The viewer easily imagines that the conversation is taking place in real time.
>
> —Ruth Rosen, "Search for Yesterday"

6 Classification

When you classify items, you sort them into groups. The classification allows you to see and explain the relations among the items. The following paragraph identifies three groups, or classes, of parents:

> In my experience, the parents who hire daytime sitters for their school-age children tend to fall into one of three groups. The first group includes parents who work and want someone to be at home when the children return from school. These parents are looking for an extension of themselves, someone who will give the care they would give if they were at home. The second group includes parents who may be home all day themselves but are too disorganized or too frazzled by their children's demands to handle child care alone. They are looking for an organizer and helpmate. The third and final group includes parents who do not want to be bothered by their children, whether they are home all day or not. Unlike the parents in the first two groups, who care for their children however they can, these parents seek a permanent substitute for themselves. —Nancy Whittle (student), "Modern Parenting"

7 Comparison and contrast

Comparison and contrast may be used separately or together to develop an idea. The following paragraph illustrates one of two common ways of organizing a comparison and contrast: **subject by subject,** first one subject and then the other.

> Consider the differences also in the behavior of rock and classical music audiences. At a rock concert, the audience members yell, whistle, sing along, and stamp their feet. They may even stand during the entire performance. The better the music, the more active they'll be. At a classical concert, in contrast, the better the performance, the more *still* the audience is. Members of the classical audience are so highly disciplined that they refrain from even clearing their throats or coughing. No matter what effect the powerful music has on their intellects and feelings, they sit on their hands.
>
> —Tony Nahm (student), "Rock and Roll Is Here to Stay"

The next paragraph illustrates the other common organization: **point by point,** with the two subjects discussed side by side and matched feature for feature:

> Arguing is often equated with fighting, but there are key differences between the two. Participants in an argument approach the subject to find common ground, or points on which both sides agree, while people engaged in a fight usually approach the subject with an "us-versus-them" attitude. Participants in an argument are careful to use respectful, polite language, in contrast to the insults and worse that people in a fight use to get the better of their opponents. Finally, participants in an argument commonly have the goal of reaching a new understanding or larger truth about the subject they're debating, while those in a fight have winning as their only goal.
>
> —Erica Ito (student),"Is an Argument Always a Fight?"

8 Cause-and-effect analysis

When you use analysis to explain why something happened or what did or may happen, then you are determining causes or effects. In the following paragraph the author looks at the cause of an effect—Japanese collectivism:

> The *shinkansen* or "bullet train" speeds across the rural areas of Japan giving a quick view of cluster after cluster of farmhouses surrounded by rice paddies. This particular pattern did not develop purely by chance, but as a consequence of the technology peculiar to the growing of rice, the staple of the Japanese diet. The growing of rice requires the construction and maintenance of an irrigation system, something that takes many hands to build. More importantly, the planting and the harvesting of rice can only be done efficiently with the cooperation of twenty or more people. The "bottom line" is that a single family working alone cannot produce enough rice to survive, but a dozen families working together can produce a surplus. Thus the Japanese have had to develop the capacity to work together in harmony, no matter what the forces of disagreement or social disintegration, in order to survive.
>
> —William Ouchi, *Theory Z*

9 Process analysis

When you analyze how to do something or how something works, you explain a process. The following example identifies a process, describes the equipment needed, and details the steps in the process:

> As a car owner, you waste money when you pay a mechanic to change the engine oil. The job is not difficult, even if you know little about cars. All you need is a wrench to remove the drain plug, a large, flat pan to collect the draining oil, plastic bottles to dispose of the used oil, and fresh oil. First, warm up the car's engine so that the oil will flow more easily. When the engine is warm, shut it off and remove its oil-filler cap (the owner's manual shows where this cap is). Then locate the drain plug under the engine (again consulting the owner's manual for its location) and place the flat pan under the plug. Remove the plug with the wrench, letting the oil flow into the pan. When the oil stops flowing, replace the plug and, at the engine's filler hole, add the amount and kind of fresh oil specified by the owner's manual. Pour the used oil into the plastic bottles and take it to a waste-oil collector, which any garage mechanic can recommend.
>
> —Anthony Andreas (student), "Do-It-Yourself Car Care"

6d Writing introductory and concluding paragraphs

1 Introductions

An introduction draws readers from their world into yours.

- **It focuses readers' attention on the topic and arouses their curiosity about what you have to say.**
- **It specifies your subject and implies your attitude.**
- **Often it includes your thesis statement.**
- **It is concise and sincere.**

The box below gives options for focusing readers' attention.

Some strategies for introductions

- Ask a question.
- Relate an incident.
- Use a vivid quotation.
- Create a visual image that represents your subject.
- Offer a surprising statistic or other fact.
- Provide background.
- State an opinion related to your thesis.
- Outline the argument your thesis refutes.
- Make a historical comparison or contrast.
- Outline a problem or dilemma.
- Define a word central to your subject.
- In some business or technical writing, simply state your main idea.

CULTURE LANGUAGE These options for an introduction may not be what you are used to if your native language is not English. In other cultures readers may seek familiarity or reassurance from an author's introduction, or they may prefer an indirect approach to the subject. In academic and business English, however, writers and readers prefer concise, direct expression.

Effective openings

A very common introduction opens with a statement of the essay's general subject, clarifies or limits the subject in one or more sentences, and then asserts the point of the essay in the thesis statement (underlined in the following examples):

> Can your home or office computer make you sterile? Can it strike you blind or dumb? The answer is: probably not. Nevertheless, reports of side effects relating to computer use should be examined, especially in the area of birth defects, eye complaints, and postural difficulties. Although little conclusive evidence exists to establish a causal link between computer use and problems of this sort, the circumstantial evidence can be disturbing.
>
> —Thomas Hartmann, "How Dangerous Is Your Computer?"

> The Declaration of Independence is so widely regarded as a statement of American ideals that its origins in practical politics tend to be forgotten. Thomas Jefferson's draft was intensely debated and then revised in the Continental Congress. Jefferson was disappointed with the result. However, a close reading of both the historical context and the revisions themselves indicates that the Congress improved the document for its intended purpose.
>
> —Ann Weiss (student), "The Editing of the Declaration of Independence"

In much public writing, it's more important to tell readers immediately what your point is than to try to engage them. This introduction to a brief memo quickly outlines a problem and (in the thesis statement) suggests a way to solve it:

> Starting next month, the holiday rush and staff vacations will leave our department short-handed. We need to hire two or perhaps three temporary keyboarders to maintain our schedules for the month.

Additional effective introductions appear in sample papers elsewhere in this book: pp. 33–34, **2** p. 111, **8** p. 390, and **MLA** p. 452.

Openings to avoid

When writing and revising your introduction, avoid approaches that are likely to bore or confuse readers:

- **A vague generality or truth.** Don't extend your reach too wide with a line such as *Throughout human history . . .* or *In today's* *world.* . . . You may have needed a warm-up paragraph to start drafting, but your readers can do without it.

- **A flat announcement.** Don't start with *The purpose of this essay is . . . , In this essay I will . . . ,* or any similar presentation of your intention or topic.
- **A reference to the essay's title.** Don't refer to the title of the essay in the first sentence—for example, *This is a big problem* or *This book is about the history of the guitar.*
- **According to Webster. . . .** Don't start by citing a dictionary definition. A definition can be an effective springboard to an essay, but this kind of lead-in has become dull with overuse.
- **An apology.** Don't fault your opinion or your knowledge with *I'm not sure if I'm right, but I think . . . , I don't know much about this, but . . . ,* or a similar line.

2 Conclusions

Your conclusion finishes off your essay and tells readers where you think you have brought them. It answers the question "So what?"

Effective conclusions

Usually set off in its own paragraph, the conclusion may consist of a single sentence or a group of sentences. It may take one or more of the approaches listed in the box below.

Some strategies for conclusions

- Recommend a course of action.
- Summarize the paper.
- Echo the approach of the introduction.
- Restate your thesis and reflect on its implications.
- Strike a note of hope or despair.
- Give a symbolic or powerful fact or other detail.
- Give an especially compelling example.
- Create an image that represents your subject.
- Use a quotation.

The following paragraph concludes the essay on the Declaration of Independence whose introduction appears on the previous page. The writer both summarizes her essay and echoes her introduction.

> The Declaration of Independence has come to be a statement of this nation's political philosophy, but that was not its purpose in 1776. Jefferson's passionate expression had to bow to the goals of the Congress as a whole to forge unity among the colonies and to win the support of foreign nations.
>
> —Ann Weiss (student), "The Editing of the Declaration of Independence"

In the next paragraph the author concludes an essay on environmental protection with a call for action:

> Until we get the answers, I think we had better keep on building power plants and growing food with the help of fertilizers and such insect-controlling chemicals as we now have. The risks are well known, thanks to the environmentalists. If they had not created a widespread public awareness of the ecological crisis, we wouldn't stand a chance. But such awareness by itself is not enough. Flaming manifestos and prophecies of doom are no longer much help, and a search for scapegoats can only make matters worse. The time for sensations and manifestos is about over. Now we need rigorous analysis, united effort and very hard work.
>
> —Peter F. Drucker, "How Best to Protect the Environment"

Conclusions to avoid

Several kinds of conclusions rarely work well:

- **A repeat of the introduction.** Don't simply replay your introduction. The conclusion should capture what the paragraphs of the body have added to the introduction.
- **A new direction.** Don't introduce a subject different from the one your essay has been about.
- **A sweeping generalization.** Don't conclude more than you reasonably can from the evidence you have presented. If your essay is about your frustrating experience trying to clear a parking ticket, you cannot reasonably conclude that *all* local police forces are too tied up in red tape to be of service to the people.
- **An apology.** Don't cast doubt on your essay. Don't say, *Even though I'm no expert* or *This may not be convincing, but I believe it's true* or anything similar. Rather, to win your readers' confidence, display confidence.

7 Document Design

Imaginehowharditwouldbetoreadandwriteiftextlookedlikethis. To make reading and writing easier, we place spaces between words. This convention and many others—such as page margins, paragraph breaks, and headings—have evolved over time to help writers communicate clearly with readers.

> **mycomplab**
>
> Visit *mycomplab.com* for more resources as well as exercises on document design.

7a Designing academic papers and other documents

The design guidelines offered in this chapter apply to all types of documents, including academic papers, Web sites, business reports, flyers, and newsletters. Each type has specific requirements as well, covered elsewhere in this book.

1 Designing academic papers

Many academic disciplines prefer specific formats for students' papers. This book details two such formats:

- **Modern Language Association,** used in English, foreign languages, and other humanities (**MLA** pp. 447–49).
- **American Psychological Association,** used in the social sciences and some natural and applied sciences (**APA** pp. 481–84).

Other academic formats can be found in the discipline style guides listed in **8** pp. 395, 398, and 402.

The design guidelines in this chapter extend the range of elements and options covered by most academic styles. Your instructors may want you to adhere strictly to a particular style or may allow some latitude in design. Ask them for their preferences.

2 Writing online

In and out of school, you are likely to do a lot of online writing—certainly e-mail and possibly blogs and other Web sites. The purposes and audiences for online writing vary widely, and so do readers' expectations for its design. See **2** pp. 115–24 for the approaches you can take in different online writing situations.

3 Designing business documents and other public writing

When you write outside your college courses, your audience will have certain expectations for how your documents should look and read. Guidelines for such writing appear later in this book:

- **Public writing,** including letters, job applications, reports, proposals, flyers, newsletters, and brochures (**2** pp. 128–39).
- **Oral presentations,** including *PowerPoint* slides and other visual aids (**2** pp. 124–28).

7b Considering principles of design

Most of the principles of design respond to the ways we read. White space, for instance, relieves our eyes and helps to lead us through a document. Groupings or lists help to show relationships.

Type sizes, images, and color add variety and help to emphasize important elements.

The sample documents on these two pages illustrate quite different ways of presenting a report for a marketing course. Even at a glance, the second document is easier to scan and read. It makes better use of white space, groups similar elements, uses bullets and fonts for emphasis, and more successfully integrates the visual data of the chart.

As you design your own documents, think about your purpose, the expectations of your readers, and how readers will move through your document. Also consider the following general principles, noting that they overlap and support one another:

- **Conduct readers through the document.** Establish flow, a pattern for the eye to follow, with headings, lists, and other elements.

Original design

Runs title and subtitle together. Does not distinguish title from text.

Crowds the page with minimal margins.

Downplays paragraph breaks with small indentions.

Buries statistics in a paragraph. Obscures relationships with non-parallel wording.

Does not introduce the figure, leaving readers to infer its meaning and purpose.

Overemphasizes the figure with large size and excessive white space.

Presents the figure undynamically, flat on.

Does not caption the figure to explain what it shows, offering only a figure number and a partial text explanation.

Generation Online: College Students and the Internet

College life once meant classrooms of students listening to teachers or groups of students talking over lunch in the union. But the reality today is more complex: students interact with their peers and professors by computer as much as face to face. As these students graduate and enter the workforce, all of society will be affected by their experience.

According to the Pew Internet Research Center (2008), today's college students are practiced computer and Internet users. The Pew Center reports that 24 percent of students in college today started using computers between ages five and eight. By age eighteen all students were using computers. Almost all college students, 92 percent, rely on the Internet, with 66 percent of students using more than one e-mail address. Computer ownership among this group is also very high: 85 percent have purchased or have been given at least one computer.

Students are eager to tap into the Internet's benefits and convenience.

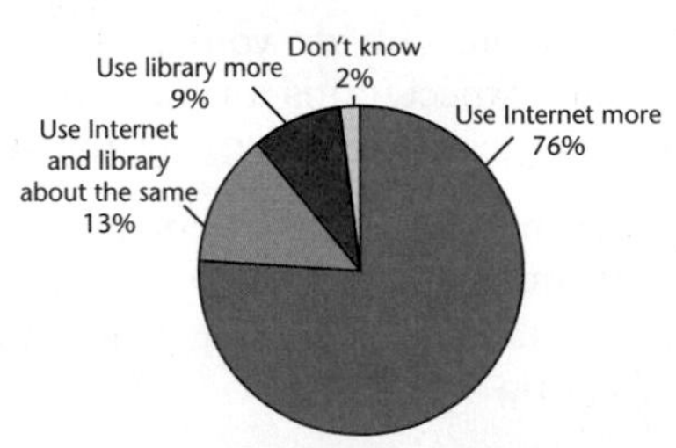

Figure 1

The Internet has eclipsed the library as the site of college students' research, as shown in Figure 1 from the Pew Report. In fact, a mere 9 percent of students

- **Use white space to ease crowding and focus readers' attention.** Provide ample margins, and give breathing room to headings, lists, and other elements. Even the space indicating new paragraphs (indentions or blank lines) gives readers a break and reassures them that ideas are divided into manageable chunks.
- **Group information to show relationships.** Use headings (like those in this chapter) and lists (like the one you're reading) to convey the similarities and differences among parts of a document.
- **Emphasize important elements.** Establish hierarchies of information with type fonts and sizes, headings, indentions, color, boxes, and white space. In this book, for example, the importance of headings is clear from their size and color and from the presence of decorative elements, such as the box around 7c in the heading on the next page.

Revised design

Generation Online:
College Students and the Internet

Distinguishes title from subtitle and both from text.

College life once meant classrooms of students listening to teachers or groups of students talking over lunch in the union. But the reality today is more complex: students interact with their peers and professors by computer as much as face to face. As these students graduate and enter the workforce, all of society will be affected by their experience.

Provides adequate margins.

According to the Pew Internet Research Center (2008), today's college students are practiced computer users and Internet users.

Emphasizes paragraph breaks with white space.

- They started young: 24 percent were using computers between ages five and eight, and all were using them by age eighteen.
- They rely on the Internet: 92 percent have used the network, and 66 percent use more than one e-mail address.
- They own computers: 85 percent have purchased or have been given at least one computer.

Groups statistics in a bulleted list set off with white space. Uses parallel wording for parallel information.

Students are eager to tap into the Internet's benefits and convenience. Figure 1, from the Pew Report, shows that the Internet has eclipsed the library as the site of college students' research. In fact, a mere 9 percent of students reported using the library more than the Internet as a starting point for research.

Introduces the figure to indicate its meaning and purpose.

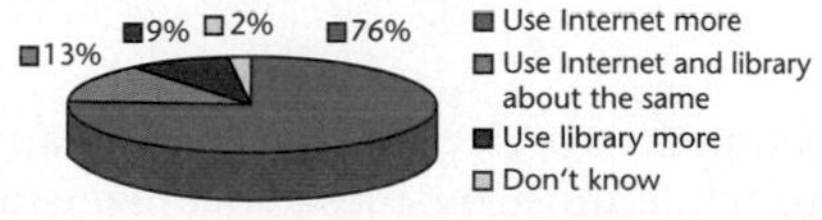

Figure 1. College students' use of the Internet and the library for research

Reduces white space around the figure.

Presents the figure to emphasize the most significant segment.

Captions the figure so that it can be read independently from the text.

- **Standardize to create and fulfill expectations.** Help direct readers through a document by, for instance, using the same size and color for all headings at the same level of importance. Standardizing also reduces clutter, making it easier for readers to determine the significance of the parts.

7c Using the elements of design

Applying the preceding principles involves margins, text, lists, headings, color, and illustrations. You won't use all these elements for every project, and in many writing situations you will be required to follow a prescribed format (see p. 53 on formats in academic writing). If you are addressing readers who have vision loss, consider the additional guidelines discussed on pp. 64–65.

Note Your word processor may provide wizards or templates for many kinds of documents, such as letters, memos, reports, agendas, résumés, and brochures. **Wizards** guide you through setting up and writing complicated documents. **Templates** are preset forms to which you add your own text, headings, and other elements. Wizards and templates can be helpful, but not if they lead you to create cookie-cutter documents no matter what the writing situation. Always keep in mind that a document should be appropriate for your subject, audience, and purpose.

1 Setting margins

Margins at the top, bottom, and sides of a page help to prevent the page from overwhelming readers with unpleasant crowding. Most academic and business documents use a minimum one-inch margin on all sides. Publicity documents, such as flyers and brochures, often use narrower margins, compensating with white space between elements. (See **2** pp. 137–38.)

2 Creating readable text

A document must be readable. You can make text readable by attending to line spacing, type fonts and sizes, highlighting, word spacing, and line breaks.

Line spacing

Most academic documents are double-spaced, with an initial indention for paragraphs, while most business documents are single-spaced, with an extra line of space between paragraphs. Double or triple spacing sets off headings in both types. Web sites and publicity documents, such as flyers and brochures, tend to use more line spacing to separate and group distinct parts of the content.

Type fonts and sizes

The readability of text also derives from the type fonts (or faces) and their sizes. For academic and business documents, generally choose a type size of 10 or 12 points, as in these samples:

10-point Courier	10-point Times New Roman
12-point Courier	12-point Times New Roman

These fonts and the one you're reading have **serifs**—the small lines that finish the letters. Serif fonts are suitable for formal writing and are often easier to read on paper. **Sans serif** fonts (*sans* means "without" in French) include this one found on many word processors:

10-point Arial 12-point Arial

Sans serif fonts can be easier to read on a computer screen and are clearer on paper for readers with some vision loss (see p. 65).

Your word processor probably offers many decorative fonts:

10-point Bodega Sans	10-POINT COMIC
10-POINT STENCIL	*10-point Park Avenue*

Decorative fonts are generally inappropriate for academic and business writing, where letter forms should be conventional and regular. But on some Web sites and in publicity documents, decorative fonts can attract attention, create motion, and reinforce a theme.

Note The point size of a type font is often an unreliable guide to its actual size, as the decorative fonts above illustrate. Before you use a font, print out a sample to be sure it is the size you want.

Highlighting

Within a document's text, underlined, *italic,* **boldface,** or even color type can emphasize key words or sentences. Underlining is rarest these days, having been replaced by italics. Both academic and business writing sometimes use boldface for strong emphasis—as with a term being defined—and publicity documents often rely extensively on boldface to draw the reader's eye. Neither academic nor business writing generally uses color within passages of text. In Web and publicity documents, however, color may be effective if it is dark enough to be readable. (See pp. 59–60 for more on color.)

No matter what your writing situation, use highlighting selectively to complement your meaning, not merely for decoration.

Word spacing

In most writing situations, follow these guidelines for spacing within and between words:

- **Leave one space between words.**

- **Leave one space after all punctuation, with these exceptions:**

Dash (two hyphens or the so-called em dash on a computer)	book--its	book—its
Hyphen	one-half	
Apostrophe within a word	book's	
Two or more adjacent marks	book.")	
Opening quotation mark, parenthesis, or bracket	("book	[book

- **Leave one space before and after an ellipsis mark.** In the examples below, ellipsis marks indicate omissions within a sentence and at the end of a sentence. See **5** pp. 292–94 for additional examples.

  book . . . in   book. . . . The

Line breaks

Your word processor will generally insert appropriate breaks between lines of continuous text: it will not, for instance, automatically begin a line with a comma or period, and it will not end a line with an opening parenthesis or bracket. However, you will have to prevent it from breaking a two-hyphen dash or a three-dot ellipsis mark by spacing to push the beginning of each mark to the next line.

When you instruct it to do so (usually under the Tools menu), your word processor will also automatically hyphenate words to prevent very short lines. If you must decide yourself where to break words, see **6** pp. 301–02.

3 Using lists

Lists give visual reinforcement to the relations between like items—for example, the steps in a process or the elements of a proposal. A list is easier to read than a paragraph and adds white space to the page.

When wording a list, work for parallelism among items—for instance, all complete sentences or all phrases (see also **3** p. 153). Set the list with space above and below and with numbering or bullets (centered dots or other devices, such as the blue squares used in this book). On most word processors you can format a numbered or bulleted list automatically using the Format menu.

4 Using headings

Headings are signposts: they direct the reader's attention by focusing the eye on a document's most significant content. Most Web and publicity documents use headings both decoratively and functionally, to capture and then direct readers' attention. In contrast, most academic and business documents use headings only functionally, to divide text, orient readers, and create emphasis.

When you use headings in academic and business documents, follow these guidelines:

- **Use one, two, or three levels of headings** depending on the needs of your material and the length of your document. Some level of heading every two or so pages will help keep readers on track.
- **Create an outline of your document** to plan where headings should go. Use the first level of heading for the main points (and sections) of your document. Use a second and perhaps a third level of heading to mark subsections of supporting information.
- **Keep headings as short as possible** while making them specific about the material that follows.
- **Word headings consistently**—for instance, all questions (*What Is the Scientific Method?*), all phrases with *-ing* words (*Understanding the Scientific Method*), or all phrases with nouns (*The Scientific Method*).
- **Indicate the relative importance of headings** with type size, positioning, and highlighting, such as capital letters, underlining, or boldface.

  First-Level Heading

  Second-Level Heading

  Third-Level Heading

  Generally, you can use the same type font and size for headings as for the text.
- **Don't break a page immediately after a heading.** Push the heading to the next page.

Note Document format in psychology and some other social sciences requires a particular treatment of headings. See **APA** pp. 481–84.

5 Using color

With a computer and a color printer, most writers can produce documents that use color for bullets, headings, borders, boxes, illustrations, and other elements. Web and publicity documents almost always use color, whereas academic and business documents consisting only of headings and text may not need color at all. (Ask your instructor or supervisor for his or her preferences.) If you do use color in an academic document, follow these guidelines:

- **Print text in black,** not red, blue, or another color.
- **Make sure that color headings are dark enough to be readable.**
- **Stick to the same color for all headings at the same level**—for instance, red for main headings, black for secondary headings.

- **Use color for bullets, lines, and other nontext elements.** But use no more than a few colors to keep pages clean.
- **Use color to distinguish the parts of illustrations**—the segments of charts, the lines of graphs, and the parts of diagrams. Use only as many colors as you need to make your illustration clear.

See also p. 65 on the use of color for readers who have vision loss.

7d Using illustrations

An illustration can often make a point for you more efficiently than words can. Tables present data. Figures (such as graphs and charts) usually recast data in visual form. Diagrams, drawings, and photographs can explain processes, represent what something looks like, or add emphasis.

1 Using illustrations appropriately for the writing situation

Academic and many business documents tend to use illustrations differently from publicity documents. In the latter, illustrations generally attract attention, enliven the piece, or emphasize a point, and they may not be linked directly to the document's text. In academic and business writing, however, illustrations directly reinforce and amplify the text. Follow these guidelines for academic and most business writing:

- **Focus on a purpose for each illustration**—a reason for including it and a point you want it to make. Otherwise, readers may find it irrelevant or confusing.
- **Provide a source note for someone else's independent material**—whether data or an entire illustration (see **7** p. 340). Each discipline has a slightly different style for such source notes: those in the illustrations on the next several pages reflect MLA style for English and some other humanities.
- **Number figures, photographs, and other images together:** Figure 1, Figure 2, and so on.
- **Number and label tables separately:** Table 1, Table 2, and so on.
- **Refer to each illustration in your text**—for instance, "See fig. 2." Place the reference at the point(s) in the text where readers will benefit by consulting the illustration.
- **Determine the placement of illustrations.** The social sciences and some other disciplines require each illustration to fall on a page by itself immediately after the text reference to it (see **APA** p. 484). You may want to follow this rule in other situations as

well if you have a large number of illustrations. Otherwise, you can embed them in your text pages just after you refer to them. When embedding illustrations, consider where they will help but not distract readers.

2 Using tables

Tables usually present raw data, making complex information accessible to readers. The data may show how variables relate to one another, how variables change over time, or how two or more groups contrast. The following table emphasizes the last function.

Table

A self-explanatory title falls above the table.

Self-explanatory headings label horizontal rows and vertical columns.

The layout of rows and columns is clear: headings align with their data, and numbers align vertically down columns.

Table 1

Public- and private-school enrollment of US students age five and older, 2006

	Number of students	Percentage in public school	Percentage in private school
All students	74,220,937	83.2	16.8
Kindergarten	4,012,680	86.0	14.0
Grades 1-4	15,758,734	88.8	11.2
Grades 5-8	16,498,217	89.4	10.6
Grades 9-12	17,500,473	90.5	9.5
College (undergraduate)	17,063,732	77.0	23.0
Graduate and professional school	3,387,101	59.8	40.2

Source: Data from *2006 American Community Survey*; US Census Bureau, n.d.; Web; 10 Oct. 2008; table S1404.

3 Using figures

Figures represent data or show concepts visually. They include charts, graphs, diagrams, and photographs.

Pie charts

Pie charts show the relations among the parts of a whole. The whole totals 100 percent, and each pie slice is proportional in size to its share of the whole. Use a pie chart when shares, not the underlying data, are your focus.

Pie chart

Color distinguishes segments of the chart. Use distinct shades of gray, black, and white if your paper will not be read in color.

Segment percentages total 100.

Every segment is clearly labeled. You can also use a key, as in the chart on p. 57.

Self-explanatory caption falls below the chart.

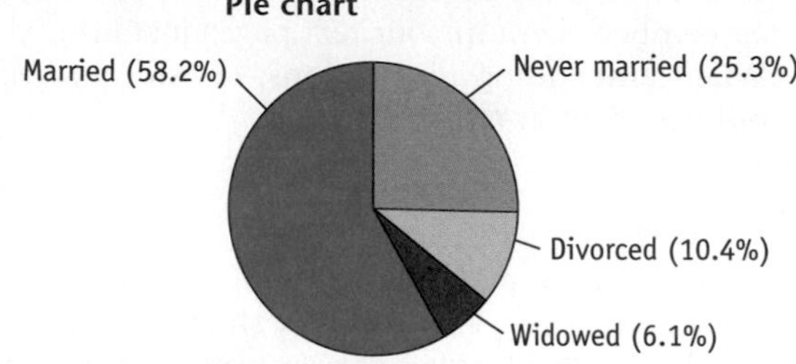

Fig. 1. Marital status in 2006 of adults age eighteen and over. Data from *Statistical Abstract of the United States: 2008*; US Census Bureau, 27 Mar. 2007; Web; 10 Oct. 2008.

Bar charts

Bar charts compare groups or time periods on a measure such as quantity or frequency. Use a bar chart when relative size is your focus. Be sure to start with a zero point in the lower left corner so that the values on the vertical axis are clear.

Bar chart

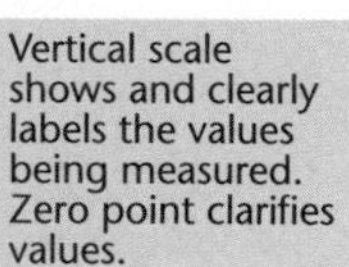

Vertical scale shows and clearly labels the values being measured. Zero point clarifies values.

Horizontal scale shows and clearly labels the groups being compared.

Self-explanatory caption falls below the chart.

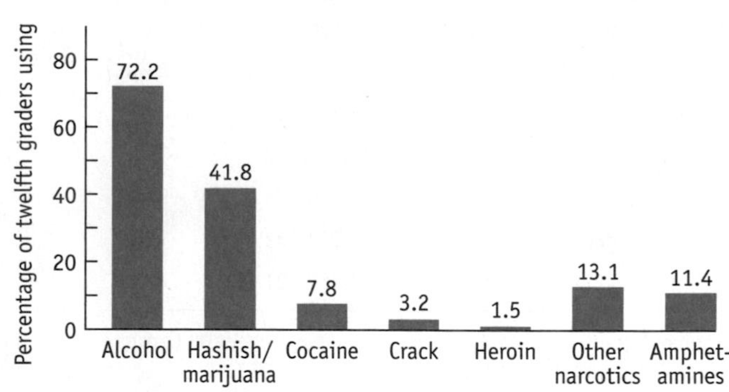

Fig. 2. Lifetime prevalence of use of alcohol and other drugs among twelfth graders in 2007. Data from *Monitoring the Future: A Continuing Study of American Youth*; U of Michigan, 11 Dec. 2007; Web; 10 Aug. 2008.

Line graphs

Line graphs show change over time in one or more subjects. They are an economical and highly visual way to compare many points of data. Be sure to start with a zero point in the lower left corner so that the values on the vertical axis are clear.

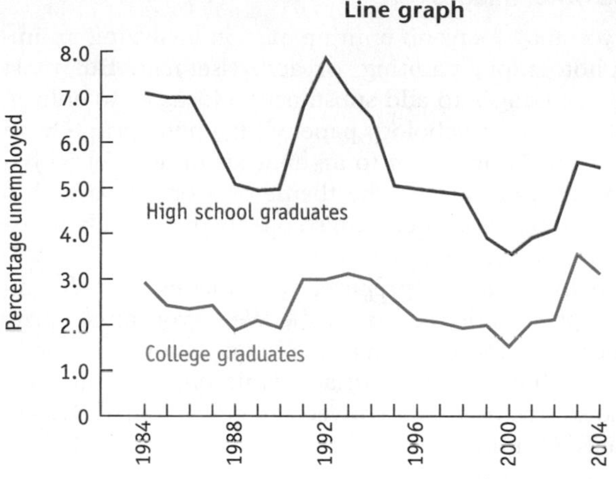

Vertical scale shows and clearly labels the values being measured. Zero point clarifies values.

Color and labels distinguish the subjects being compared. Use dotted and dashed black lines if your paper will not be read in color.

Horizontal scale shows and clearly labels the range of dates.

Fig. 3. Unemployment rates of high school graduates and college graduates, 1984-2004. Data from Antony Davies; *The Economics of College Tuition*; Mercatus Center, George Mason U, 3 Mar. 2005; Web; 26 June 2008.

Self-explanatory caption falls below the graph.

Diagrams

Diagrams show concepts visually, such as the structure of an organization, the way something works or looks, or the relations among subjects. Often, diagrams show what can't be described economically in words.

Diagram

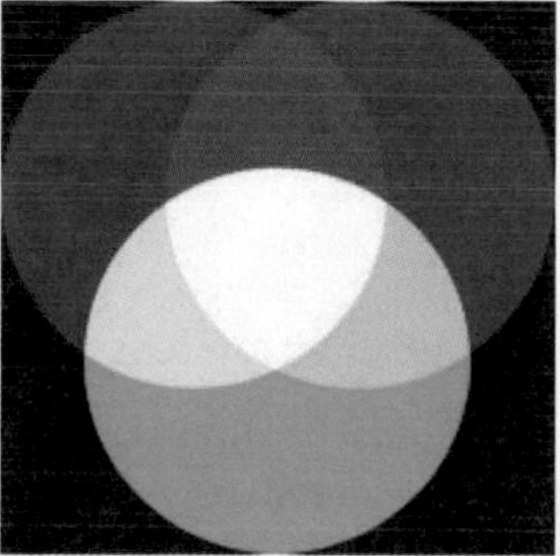

Diagram makes concept comprehensible.

Fig. 4. RGB color theory, applied to televisions and computer monitors, in which all possible colors and white are created from red, green, and blue. From "Color Theory"; *Wikipedia*; Wikimedia, 15 Mar. 2005; Web; 13 May 2008.

Self-explanatory caption falls below the diagram.

Photographs and other images

Sometimes you may focus an entire paper on analyzing an image such as a photograph, painting, or advertisement. But most commonly you'll use images to add substance to ideas or to enliven them. You might clarify a psychology paper with a photograph from a key experiment, add information to an analysis of a novel with a drawing of the author, or capture the theme of a brochure with a cartoon. Images grab readers' attention, so use them carefully to explain, reinforce, or enhance your writing.

Note When using an image prepared by someone else—for instance, a photograph downloaded from the Web—you must verify that the source permits reproduction of the image before you use it. In most documents, but especially in academic papers, you must also fully cite the source of any borrowed image. See **7** pp. 372–73 on copyright issues with Internet sources.

Photograph

Photograph shows subject more economically and dramatically than words could.

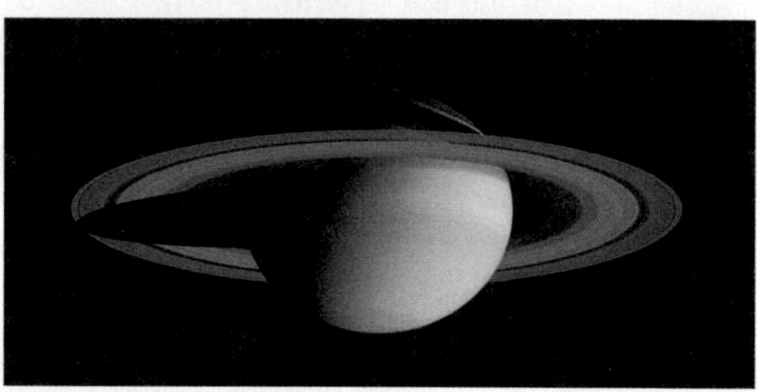

Self-explanatory caption falls below the image.

Fig. 5. View of Saturn from the *Cassini* spacecraft, showing the planet and its rings. From United States, Natl. Atmospheric and Space Administration, Jet Propulsion Laboratory; *Cassini-Huygens: Mission to Saturn and Titan*; NASA, 24 Feb. 2005; Web; 26 Apr. 2008.

7e Considering readers with vision loss

Your audience may include readers who have low vision, problems with color perception, or difficulties processing visual information. If so, consider adapting your design to meet these readers' needs. Here are a few pointers:

- **Use large type fonts.** Most guidelines call for 14 points or larger.
- **Use standard type fonts.** Many people with low vision find it easier to read sans serif fonts such as Arial than serif fonts (see

p. 55). Avoid decorative fonts with unusual flourishes, even in headings.

- **Avoid words in all-capital letters.**
- **Avoid relying on color alone to distinguish elements.** Label elements, and distinguish them by position or size.
- **Use red and green selectively.** To readers who are red-green colorblind, these colors will appear in shades of gray, yellow, or blue.
- **Use contrasting colors.** To make colors distinct, choose them from opposite sides of the color spectrum—violet and yellow, for instance, or orange and blue.
- **Use only light colors for tints behind type.** Make the type itself black or a very dark color.

PART 2

Writing in and out of College

8 Academic Skills *69*

9 Critical Thinking and Reading *77*

10 Academic Writing *90*

11 Argument *97*

12 Online Writing *115*

13 Oral Presentations *124*

14 Public Writing *128*

PART 2

Writing in and out of College

8 Academic Skills *69*

- a Listening and taking notes in class *69*
- b Reading for comprehension *70*
- c Becoming an academic writer *74*
- d Preparing for exams *75*

9 Critical Thinking and Reading *77*

- a Using techniques of critical reading *77*
- b Developing a critical response *81*
- c Viewing images critically *83*

10 Academic Writing *90*

- a Writing in response to texts *90*
- b Purpose *92*
- c Audience *93*
- d Structure and content *93*
- e Language *94*

11 Argument *97*

- a Elements of argument *97*
- b Reasonableness *100*
- c Organization *104*
- d Visual arguments *105*
- e Sample argument *111*

12 Online Writing *115*

- a E-mail *116*
- b Collaboration *118*
- c Web compositions *119*

13 Oral Presentations *124*

- a Organization *124*
- b Delivery *125*

14 Public Writing *128*

- a Business letters and résumés *129*
- b Memos, reports, and proposals *134*
- c Community work: flyers, newsletter, brochures *136*

8 Academic Skills

When you take college courses, you enter an academic discipline—a community of instructors and students whose basic goal is to build knowledge about a subject, whether it is English, history, engineering, or something else. You participate in a discipline community first by studying a subject, acquiring its vocabulary, and learning to express yourself in its ways. As you gain experience and knowledge, you contribute to the community by asking questions and communicating your answers in writing. This active, involved learning is the core of academic work. It may seem beyond you at first, as you try to grasp the content of readings and identify important ideas. But the transition will be easier if you follow this chapter's advice for getting the most from your classes, understanding assigned reading, becoming an academic writer, and preparing for exams.

8a Listening and taking notes in class

When you begin each class meeting, push aside other concerns so that you can focus and listen. Either on paper or on a computer, record what you hear as completely as possible while sorting out the main ideas from the secondary and supporting ones. (See the following box.) Such active note taking will help you understand the instructor's approach to the course and provide you with complete material for later study.

Tips for taking class notes

- **Use your own words.** You will understand and retain the material better if you rephrase it. But use the speaker's words if necessary to catch everything.
- **Leave space in your notes if you miss something.** Ask someone for the missing information as soon as possible after class.
- **Include any reading content mentioned by your instructor.** Use your notes to integrate all the components of the course—your instructor's views, your own thoughts, and the assigned reading.

(continued)

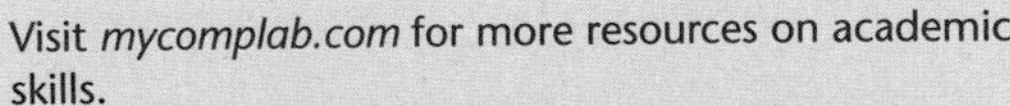

Visit *mycomplab.com* for more resources on academic skills.

Tips for taking class notes

(continued)

- **Review your notes shortly after class.** Reinforce your new knowledge when it is fresh by underlining key words and ideas, adding headings and comments in the margins, converting your notes to questions, or outlining the lecture based on your notes.

8b Reading for comprehension

The assigned reading you do for college courses—such as textbooks, journal articles, essays, and works of literature—requires a greater focus on understanding and retention than does the reading you do for entertainment or for practical information. The process outlined below may seem time consuming, but with practice you'll become efficient at it.

Note The following process stresses ways of understanding what you read. In critical reading, covered in the next chapter, you extend this process to analyze and evaluate what you read and see.

1 Writing while reading

Reading for comprehension is an *active* process. Students often believe they are reading actively when they roll a highlighter over the important ideas in a text, but truly engaged reading requires more than that. If you take notes while reading, you "translate" the work into your own words and reconstruct it for yourself.

The substance of your reading notes will change as you preview, read, and summarize. At first, you may jot quick, short notes in the margins, on separate pages, or on a computer. (Use the last two for material you don't own or are reading online.) As you delve into the work, the notes should become more detailed, restating important points, asking questions, connecting ideas. (See p. 80 for an example of a text annotated in this way by a student.) For some reading, you may want to keep a reading journal that records both what the work says and what you think about it.

2 Previewing

For most course reading, you should skim before reading word for word. Skimming gives you an overview of the material: its length and difficulty, organization, and principal ideas.

- **Gauge length and level.** Is the material brief and straightforward enough to read in one sitting, or do you need more time?
- **Examine the title and introduction.** The title and first couple of paragraphs will give you a sense of the topic, the author's approach, and the main ideas. As you read them, ask yourself what you already know about the subject so that you can integrate new information with old.
- **Move from heading to heading or paragraph to paragraph.** Viewing the headings as headlines or as the levels of an outline will give you a feeling for which ideas the author sees as primary and which subordinate. In a text without headings, reading the first sentence of each paragraph will give you a sense of the author's important ideas.
- **Note highlighted words.** You will likely need to learn the meanings of terms in **bold**, *italic*, or color.
- **Slow down for pictures, diagrams, tables, graphs, and other illustrations.** They often contain concentrated information.
- **Read the summary or conclusion.** These paragraphs often recap the main ideas.
- **Think over what you've skimmed.** Try to recall the central idea, or thesis, and the sequence of ideas.

3 Reading

After previewing a text, you can settle into it to learn what it has to say.

First reading

The first time through new material, read as steadily and smoothly as possible, trying to get the gist of what the author is saying.

- **Read in a place where you can concentrate.** Choose a quiet environment away from distractions such as music or talking.
- **Give yourself time.** Rushing yourself or worrying about something else you have to do will prevent you from grasping what you read.
- **Try to enjoy the work.** Seek connections between it and what you already know. Appreciate new information, interesting relationships, forceful writing, humor, good examples.
- **Make notes sparingly during this first reading.** Mark major stumbling blocks—such as a paragraph you don't understand—so that you can try to resolve them before rereading.

CULTURE LANGUAGE If English is not your first language and you come across unfamiliar words don't stop and look up every one. You will lose more in concentration than you will gain in understanding. Instead, try to guess the meanings of unfamiliar words from their contexts, circle them, and look them up later.

Rereading

After the first reading, plan on at least one other. This time read *slowly.* Your main concern should be to grasp the content and how it is constructed. That means rereading a paragraph if you didn't get the point or using a dictionary to look up words you don't know.

Use your pen, pencil, or keyboard freely to highlight and distill the text:

- **Distinguish main ideas from supporting ideas.** Look for the central idea, or thesis, for the main idea of each paragraph or section, and for the evidence supporting ideas.
- **Learn key terms.** Understand both their meanings and their applications.
- **Discern the connections among ideas.** Be sure you see why the author moves from point A to point B to point C and how those points work together to support the central idea. It often helps to outline the text or summarize it (see below).
- **Add your own comments.** In the margins or separately, note links to other readings or to class discussions, questions to explore further, possible topics for your writing, points you find especially strong or weak. (This last category will occupy much of your time when you are expected to read critically. See pp. 81–83.)

4 Summarizing

A good way to master the content of a text is to summarize it: reduce it to its main points, in your own words.

Writing a summary

- **Understand the meaning.** Look up words or concepts you don't know so that you understand the author's sentences and how they relate to one another.
- **Understand the organization.** Work through the text to identify its sections—single paragraphs or groups of paragraphs focused on a single topic. To understand how parts of a work relate to one another, try drawing a tree diagram or creating an outline (1 pp. 18–20).
- **Distill each section.** Write a one- or two-sentence summary of each section you identify. Focus on the main point of the section, omitting examples, facts, and other supporting evidence.

- **State the main idea.** Write a sentence or two capturing the author's central idea.
- **Support the main idea.** Write a full paragraph (or more, if needed) that begins with the central idea and supports it with the sentences that summarize sections of the work. The paragraph should concisely and accurately state the thrust of the entire work.
- ***Use your own words.*** By writing, you re-create the meaning of the work in a way that makes sense for you.

Summarizing even a passage of text can be tricky. Below is one attempt to summarize the following material from an introductory biology textbook.

Original text

As astronomers study newly discovered planets orbiting distant stars, they hope to find evidence of water on these far-off celestial bodies, for water is the substance that makes possible life as we know it here on Earth. All organisms familiar to us are made mostly of water and live in an environment dominated by water. They require water more than any other substance. Human beings, for example, can survive for quite a few weeks without food, but only a week or so without water. Molecules of water participate in many chemical reactions necessary to sustain life. Most cells are surrounded by water, and cells themselves are about 70–95% water. Three-quarters of Earth's surface is submerged in water. Although most of this water is in liquid form, water is also present on Earth as ice and vapor. Water is the only common substance to exist in the natural environment in all three physical states of matter: solid, liquid, and gas.

—Neil A. Campbell and Jane B. Reece, *Biology*

Draft summary

Astronomers look for water in outer space because life depends on it. It is the most common substance on Earth and in living cells, and it can be a liquid, a solid (ice), or a gas (vapor).

This summary accurately restates ideas in the original, but it does not pare the passage to its essence. The work of astronomers and the three physical states of water add color and texture to the original, but they are asides to the key concept that water sustains life because of its role in life. The following revision narrows the summary to this concept:

Revised summary

Water is the most essential support for life—the dominant substance on Earth and in living cells and a component of life-sustaining chemical processes.

Note Do not count on the AutoSummarize function on your word processor for summarizing texts that you may have copied onto your computer. The summaries are rarely accurate, and you will not gain the experience of interacting with the texts on your own.

8c Becoming an academic writer

As a member of an academic community, you will communicate with other members mainly through writing. Chapter 10 provides a detailed introduction to academic writing, and **8** (Chapters 55–57) treats writing in specific disciplines. The disciplines do differ in their conventions for writing, but in all of them you will be expected to do the following:

- **Know the writing situation posed in each assignment.** Most assignments will at least suggest possible subjects and imply a purpose and an audience. In that context, you refine your subject, your purpose, and your sense of audience as you proceed through the writing process. For a review of assessing the writing situation, see **1** pp. 3–5.
- **Develop and organize your writing.** Most academic papers center on a main point, or thesis, and support the thesis with evidence. For more on developing a thesis and organizing a paper, see **1** pp. 14–20.
- **Synthesize your own and others' ideas.** Academic writing often involves interacting with the works of other writers—responding to them, comparing them, and using them to answer questions. Such interaction requires you to read critically (the subject of the next chapter) and to **synthesize**, or integrate, others' ideas into your own. For more on synthesis, see p. 92.
- **Revise and edit your writing.** Academic writing is careful writing. Allow yourself enough time to revise and edit so that readers can see your main ideas, follow your train of thought, and make sense of your sentences. Consult this book's revision and editing checklists in **1** pp. 26 and 30.
- **Acknowledge your sources.** Academic writers build on the work of others by fully crediting borrowed ideas and information. Always record the publication information of any source you consult so that you can cite it if you decide to use it later in your writing. See **7** pp. 367–73 for a discussion of avoiding plagiarism. For guides to specific documentation styles, see **MLA** pp. 406–07 (English and some other humanities), **APA** pp. 463–81 (social sciences), **Chic** pp. 491–501 (history, philosophy,

and other humanities), and **CSE** pp. 502–08 (natural and applied sciences).

8d Preparing for exams

Studying for an exam involves three main steps, each requiring about a third of the preparation time: reviewing the material, organizing summaries of the material, and testing yourself. Your main goals are to strengthen your understanding of the subject, making both its ideas and its details more memorable, and to increase the flexibility of your new knowledge so that you can apply it in new contexts.

Note Cramming for an exam is about the least effective way of preparing for one. It takes longer to learn under stress, and the learning is shallower, more difficult to apply, and more quickly forgotten. Information learned under stress is even harder to apply in stressful situations such as taking an exam. And the lack of sleep that usually accompanies cramming makes a good performance even more unlikely. If you must cram for a test, face the fact that you can't learn everything. Spend your time reviewing main concepts and facts.

1 Reviewing and memorizing the material

Divide your class notes and reading assignments into manageable units. Reread the material, recite or write out the main ideas and selected supporting ideas and examples, and then skim for an overview. Proceed in this way through all the units of the course, returning to earlier ones as needed to refresh your memory or to relate ideas.

During this stage you should be memorizing what you don't already know by heart. Try these strategies for strengthening your memory:

- **Link new and known information.** For instance, to remember a sequence of four dates in twentieth-century African history, link the dates to simultaneous and more familiar events in the United States.
- **Create groups of ideas or facts that make sense to you.** For instance, memorize French vocabulary words in related groups, such as words for parts of the body or parts of a house. Keep the groups small: research has shown that we can easily memorize about seven items at a time but have trouble with more.
- **Create narratives and visual images.** You may recall a story or a picture more easily than words. For instance, to remember

how the economic laws of supply and demand affect the market for rental housing, you could tie the principles to a narrative about the aftermath of the 1906 San Francisco earthquake, when half the population was suddenly homeless. Or you could visualize a person who has dollar signs for eyes and is converting a spare room into a high-priced rental unit, as many did after the earthquake to meet the new demand for housing.

- **Use *mnemonic devices,* or tricks for remembering.** Say the history dates you want to remember are separated by five years, then four, then nine. By memorizing the first date and recalling 5 + 4 = 9, you'll have command of all four dates.

2 Organizing summaries of the material

Allow time to reorganize the material in your own way, creating categories that will help you apply the information in various contexts. For instance, in studying for a biology exam, work to understand a process, such as how a plant develops or how photosynthesis occurs. Or in studying for an American government test, explain the structures of the local, state, and federal levels of government. Other useful categories include advantages/disadvantages and causes/effects. Such analytical thinking will improve your mastery of the course material and may even prepare you directly for specific essay questions.

3 Testing yourself

Convert each heading in your lecture notes and course reading into a question. Answer in writing, going back to the course material to fill in what you don't yet know. Be sure you can define and explain all key terms. For subjects that require solving problems (such as mathematics, statistics, or physics), work out a difficult problem for every type on which you will be tested. For all subjects, focus on the main themes and questions of the course. In a psychology course, for example, be certain you understand principal theories and their implications. In a literature course, test your knowledge of literary movements and genres or the relations among specific works.

When you are satisfied with your preparation, stop studying. If your exam is the next day, get as much sleep as your schedule allows. You will be able to think more clearly on exam day if you are rested.

9 Critical Thinking and Reading

Throughout college and beyond, you will be expected to think, read, and write critically. **Critical** here does not mean "negative" but "skeptical," "exacting," "creative." You already operate critically every day as you figure out why things happen to you or what your experiences mean. This chapter introduces more formal methods for reading texts critically (below), developing a critical response (p. 81), and viewing images critically (p. 83).

Note Critical thinking plays a large role in research writing. See **7** pp. 345–56 on evaluating print and online sources and **7** pp. 356–57 on synthesizing sources.

9a Using techniques of critical reading

In college and work, much of your critical thinking will focus on written texts (a short story, a journal article, a blog) or on visual objects (a photograph, a chart, a film). Like all subjects worthy of critical consideration, such works operate on at least three levels: (1) what the creator actually says or shows, (2) what the creator does not say or show explicitly but builds into the work (intentionally or not), and (3) what you think. Discovering the first of these levels—reading for comprehension—is discussed in the preceding chapter as part of academic skills (see pp. 70–72). This chapter builds on the earlier material to help you discover the other two levels.

CULTURE LANGUAGE The idea of reading critically may require you to make some adjustments if readers in your native culture tend to seek understanding or agreement more than engagement from what they read. Readers of English use texts for all kinds of reasons, including pleasure, reinforcement, and information. But they also read skeptically, critically, to see the author's motives, test their own ideas, and arrive at new knowledge.

1 Previewing the material

When you're reading a work of literature, such as a short story or a poem, it's often best just to plunge right in. But for critical reading of other works, it's worthwhile to skim before reading word for word, forming expectations and even some preliminary questions. The preview will make your reading more informed and fruitful.

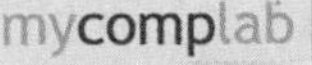

Visit *mycomplab.com* for more resources on critical thinking and reading.

- **What is the work's subject and structure?** Following the steps outlined on p. 71, gauge the length and level, read the title and introduction for clues to the topic and main ideas, read the headings, note highlighted words (defined terms), examine illustrations, and read the summary or conclusion.
- **What are the facts of publication?** Does the date of publication suggest currency or datedness? Does the publisher or publication specialize in a particular kind of material—for instance, scholarly articles or popular books? For a Web document, who or what sponsors the site: an individual? a nonprofit organization? an academic institution? a corporation? a government body?
- **What do you know about the author?** Does a biography tell you about the author's publications, interests, biases, and reputation in the field? For an online source, which may be posted by an unfamiliar or anonymous author, what can you gather about the author from his or her words? If possible, trace unfamiliar authors to learn more about them.
- **What is your preliminary response?** What do you already know about the author's subject? What questions do you have about either the subject or the author's approach to it? What biases of your own might influence your reception of the work—for instance, curiosity, boredom, or an outlook similar or opposed to the author's?

Reprinted on these pages is an essay by Thomas Sowell, an economist, newspaper columnist, and author of many books on economics, politics, and education. The essay was first published in the 1990s, but the debate over student loans has never died down. Preview the essay using the preceding guidelines, and then read it once or twice, until you think you understand what the author is saying. Note your questions and reactions in writing.

Student Loans

The first lesson of economics is scarcity: There is never enough of anything to fully satisfy all those who want it. 1

The first lesson of politics is to disregard the first lesson of economics. When politicians discover some group that is being vocal about not having as much as they want, the "solution" is to give them more. Where do politicians get this "more"? They rob Peter to pay Paul. 2

After a while, of course, they discover that Peter doesn't have enough. Bursting with compassion, politicians rush to the rescue. Needless to say, they do not admit that robbing Peter to pay Paul was a dumb idea in the first place. On the contrary, they now rob Tom, Dick, and Harry to help Peter. 3

The latest chapter in this long-running saga is that politicians have now suddenly discovered that many college students graduate heavily in 4

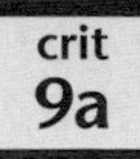

debt. To politicians it follows, as the night follows the day, that the government should come to their rescue with the taxpayers' money.

How big is this crushing burden of college students' debt that we 5
hear so much about from politicians and media deep thinkers? For those students who graduate from public colleges owing money, the debt averages a little under $7000. For those who graduate from private colleges owing money, the average debt is a little under $9000.

Buying a very modestly priced automobile involves more debt than 6
that. And a car loan has to be paid off faster than the ten years that college graduates get to repay their student loans. Moreover, you have to keep buying cars every several years, while one college education lasts a lifetime.

College graduates of course earn higher incomes than other peo- 7
ple. Why, then, should we panic at the thought that they have to repay loans for the education which gave them their opportunities? Even graduates with relatively modest incomes pay less than 10 percent of their annual salary on the first loan the first year—with declining percentages in future years, as their pay increases.

Political hysteria and media hype may focus on the low-income 8
student with a huge debt. That is where you get your heart-rending stories—even if they are not all that typical. In reality, the soaring student loans of the past decade have resulted from allowing high-income people to borrow under government programs.

Before 1978, college loans were available through government pro- 9
grams only to students whose family income was below some cut-off level. That cut-off level was about double the national average income, but at least it kept out the Rockefellers and the Vanderbilts. But, in an era of "compassion," Congress took off even those limits.

That opened the floodgates. No matter how rich you were, it still 10
paid to borrow money through the government at low interest rates. The money you had set aside for your children's education could be invested somewhere else, at higher interest rates. Then, when the student loan became due, parents could pay it off with the money they had set aside—pocketing the difference in interest rates.

To politicians and the media, however, the rapidly growing loans 11
showed what a great "need" there was. The fact that many students welshed when time came to repay their loans showed how "crushing" their burden of debt must be. In reality, those who welsh typically have smaller loans, but have dropped out of college before finishing. People who are irresponsible in one way are often irresponsible in other ways.

No small amount of the deterioration of college standards has been 12
due to the increasingly easy availability of college to people who are not very serious about getting an education. College is not a bad place to hang out for a few years, if you have nothing better to do, and if someone else is paying for it. Its costs are staggering, but the taxpayers carry much of that burden, not only for state universities and city colleges, but also to an increasing extent even for "private" institutions.

Numerous government subsidies and loan programs make it possi- 13
ble for many people to use vast amounts of society's resources at low cost to themselves. Whether in money terms or in real terms, federal aid to higher education has increased several hundred percent since 1970.

That has enabled colleges to raise their tuition by leaps and bounds and enabled professors to be paid more and more for doing less and less teaching.

Naturally all these beneficiaries are going to create hype and hysteria 14
to keep more of the taxpayers' money coming in. But we would be fools to keep on writing blank checks for them.

When you weigh the cost of things, in economics that's called 15
"trade-offs." In politics, it's called "mean-spirited." Apparently, if we just took a different attitude, scarcity would go away.

—Thomas Sowell

2 Reading

Reading is itself more than a one-step process. You want to understand the first level on which the text operates—what the author actually says—and begin to form your impressions.

A procedure for this stage appears in the preceding chapter (pp. 71–72). To recap: Read once through fairly smoothly, trying to appreciate the work and keeping your notes to a minimum. Then read again more carefully, this time making detailed notes, to grasp the ideas and their connections and to pose questions. In the following example, a student, Charlene Robinson, annotates the first four paragraphs of "Student Loans":

The first lesson of economics is scarcity: There is never enough of anything to fully satisfy all those who want it.

The first lesson of politics is to disregard the first lesson of economics. When politicians discover some group that is being vocal about not having as much as they want, the "solution" is to give them more. Where do politicians get this "more"? They rob Peter to pay Paul.

Basic contradiction between economics and politics

biblical reference?

After a while, of course, they discover that Peter doesn't have enough. Bursting with compassion, politicians rush to the rescue. Needless to say, they do not admit that robbing Peter to pay Paul was a dumb idea in the first place. On the contrary, they now rob Tom, Dick, and Harry to help Peter.

ironic and dismissive language

The latest chapter in this long-running saga is that politicians have now suddenly discovered that many college students graduate heavily in debt. To politicians it follows, as the night follows the day, that the government should come to their rescue with the taxpayers' money.

politicians = fools? or irresponsible

3 Summarizing

Summarizing a text—distilling it to its essential ideas, in your own words—is an important step for comprehending it and is discussed in detail in the previous chapter (pp. 72–74). Here, we'll look at how Charlene Robinson summarized paragraphs 1–4 of Thomas Sowell's "Student Loans." She first drafted this sentence:

Draft summary

As much as politicians would like to satisfy voters by giving them everything they ask for, the government cannot afford a student loan program.

Reading the sentence and Sowell's paragraphs, Robinson saw that this draft misread the text by asserting that the government cannot afford student loans. She realized that Sowell's point is more complicated than that and rewrote her summary:

Revised summary

As their support of the government's student loan program illustrates, politicians ignore the economic reality that using resources to benefit one group (students in debt) involves taking the resources from another group (taxpayers).

Note Using your own words when writing a summary not only helps you understand the meaning but also constitutes the first step in avoiding plagiarism. The second step is to cite the source when you use it in something written for others. See **7** pp. 367–75.

9b Developing a critical response

Once you've grasped the content of what you're reading—what the author says—then you can turn to understanding what the author does not say outright but suggests or implies or even lets slip. At this stage you are concerned with the purpose or intention of the author and with how he or she carries it out.

Critical thinking and reading consist of four overlapping operations: analyzing, interpreting, synthesizing, and (often) evaluating.

1 Analyzing

Analysis is the separation of something into its parts or elements, the better to understand it. To see these elements in what you are reading, begin with a question that reflects your purpose in analyzing the text: why you're curious about it or what you're trying to make out of it. This question will serve as a kind of lens that highlights some features and not others.

Analyzing Thomas Sowell's "Student Loans" (pp. 78–80), you might ask one of these questions:

Questions for analysis	Elements
What is Sowell's attitude toward politicians?	References to politicians: content, words, tone
How does Sowell support his assertions about the loan program's costs?	Support: evidence, such as statistics and examples

2 Interpreting

Identifying the elements of something is only a start: you also need to interpret the meaning or significance of the elements and of the whole. Interpretation usually requires you to infer the author's **assumptions**—opinions or beliefs about what is or what could or should be. (*Infer* means to draw a conclusion based on evidence.)

Assumptions are pervasive: we all adhere to certain values, beliefs, and opinions. But assumptions are not always stated outright. Speakers and writers may judge that their audience already understands and accepts their assumptions; they may not even be aware of their assumptions; or they may deliberately refrain from stating their assumptions for fear that the audience will disagree. That is why your job as a critical thinker is to interpret what the assumptions are.

Thomas Sowell's "Student Loans" is based on certain assumptions, some obvious, some not. Analyzing Sowell's attitude toward politicians requires focusing on the statements about them. They "disregard the first lesson of economics" (paragraph 2), which implies that they ignore important principles (knowing that Sowell is an economist himself makes this a reasonable assumption). Politicians also "rob Peter to pay Paul," are "[b]ursting with compassion," "do not admit . . . a dumb idea," are characters in a "long-running saga," and arrive at the solution of spending taxes "as the night follows the day"—that is, inevitably (paragraphs 2–4). From these statements and others, we can infer the following:

> Sowell assumes that politicians become compassionate when a cause is loud and popular, not necessarily just, and they act irresponsibly by trying to solve the problem with other people's (taxpayers') money.

3 Synthesizing

If you stopped at analysis and interpretation, critical thinking and reading might leave you with a pile of elements and possible meanings but no vision of the whole. With **synthesis** you make connections among parts *or* among wholes. You use your perspective—your knowledge and beliefs—to create a new whole by drawing conclusions about relationships and implications.

A key component of academic reading and writing, synthesis receives attention in the next chapter (p. 92) and then in the context of research writing (see **7** pp. 356–57). Sometimes you'll respond directly to a text, as in the following statement about Thomas Sowell's essay "Student Loans," which connects Sowell's assumptions about politicians to a larger idea also implied by the essay:

> Sowell's view that politicians are irresponsible with taxpayers' money reflects his overall opinion that the laws of economics, not politics, should drive government.

Often synthesis will take you outside the text to its surroundings. The following questions can help you investigate the context of a work:

- **How does the work compare with works by others?** For instance, how have other writers responded to Sowell's views on student loans?
- **How does the work fit into the context of other works by the same author or group?** How do Sowell's views on student loans typify, or not, the author's other writing on political and economic issues?
- **What cultural, economic, or political forces influence the work?** What other examples might Sowell have given to illustrate his view that economics, not politics, should determine government spending?
- **What historical forces influence the work?** How has the indebtedness of college students changed over the past four decades?

4 Evaluating

Critical reading and writing often end at synthesis: you form and explain your understanding of what the work says and doesn't say. If you are also expected to **evaluate** the work, however, you will go further to judge its quality and significance. You may be evaluating a source you've discovered in research (see **7** pp. 343–58), or you may be completing an assignment to state and defend a judgment, such as *Thomas Sowell does not summon the evidence to support his case*. You can read Charlene Robinson's critical response to Thomas Sowell's "Student Loans" by following the links in the e-book version of this handbook at *mycomplab.com.*

Evaluation takes a certain amount of confidence. You may think that you lack the expertise to cast judgment on another's work, especially if the work is difficult or the author well known. True, the more informed you are, the better a critical reader you are. But conscientious reading and analysis will give you the internal authority to judge a work *as it stands* and *as it seems to you,* against your own unique bundle of experiences, observations, and attitudes.

9c Viewing images critically

Every day we are bombarded with images—pictures on billboards, commercials on television, graphs and charts in newspapers and textbooks, to name just a few examples. Most images slide by without our noticing them, or so we think. But images, sometimes even more than text, can influence us covertly. Their creators have purposes, some worthy, some not, and understanding those purposes requires critical reading. The method parallels that in the previous section for reading text critically: preview, read for comprehension, analyze, interpret, synthesize, and (often) evaluate.

1 Previewing an image

Your first step in exploring an image is to form initial impressions of the work's origin and purpose and to note distinctive features. This previewing process is like the one for previewing a text (pp. 77–78):

- **What do you see?** What is most striking about the image? What is its subject? What is the gist of any text or symbols? What is the overall effect of the image?
- **What are the facts of publication?** Where did you first see the image? Do you think the image was created especially for that location or for others as well? What can you tell about when the image was created?
- **What do you know about the person or group that created the image?** For instance, was the creator an artist, scholar, news organization, or corporation? What seems to have been the creator's purpose?
- **What is your preliminary response?** What about the image interests, confuses, or disturbs you? Are the form, style, and subject familiar or unfamiliar? How might your knowledge, experiences, and values influence your reception of the image?

If possible, print a copy of the image or scan it into your reading journal, and write comments in the image margins or separately.

2 Reading an image

Reading an image requires the same level of concentration as reading a text. Try to answer the following questions about the image. If some answers aren't clear at this point, skip the question until later.

- **What is the purpose of the image?** Is it mainly explanatory, conveying information, or is it argumentative, trying to convince readers of something or to persuade them to act? What information or point of view does it seem intended to get across?
- **Who is the intended audience for the image?** What does the source of the image, including its publication facts, tell about the image creator's expectations for readers' knowledge, interests, and attitudes? What do the features of the image itself add to your impression?
- **What do any words or symbols add to the image?** Whether located on the image or outside it (such as in a caption), do words

or symbols add information, focus your attention, or alter your impression of the image?

- **What people, places, things, or action does the image show?** Does the image tell a story? Do its characters or other features tap into your knowledge, or are they unfamiliar?
- **What is the form of the image?** Is it a photograph, advertisement, painting, graph, diagram, cartoon, or something else? How do its content and apparent purpose and audience relate to its form?

The illustration below shows the notes that a student, Matthew Greene, made on an advertisement for *BoostUp.org*.

Annotation of an image

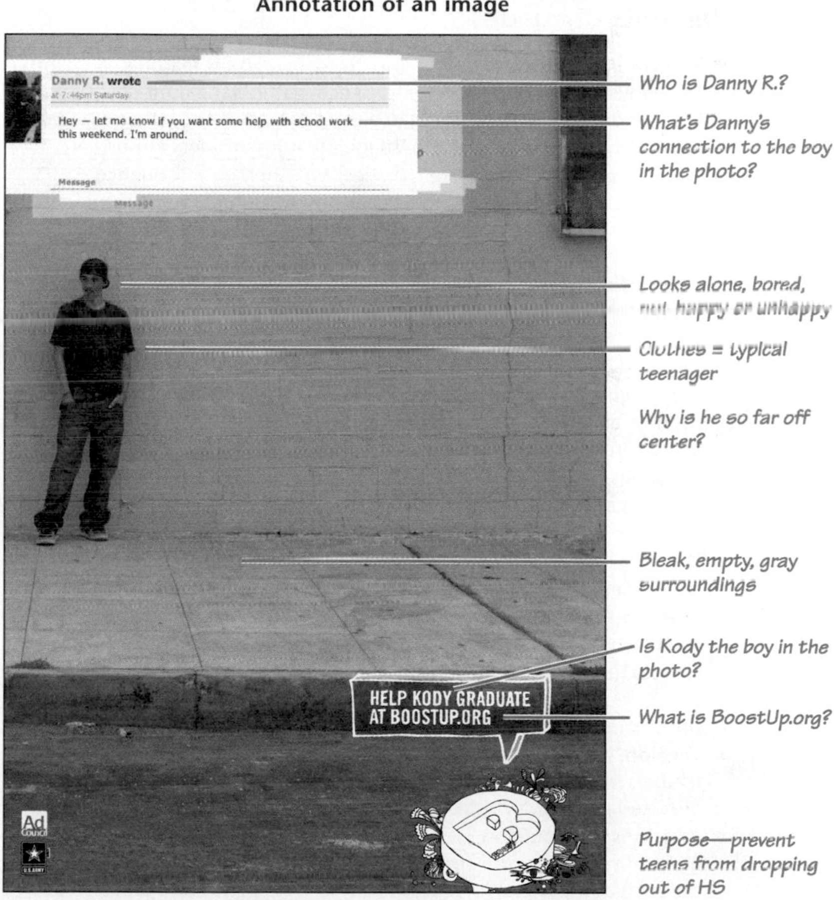

Advertisement for *BoostUp.org*, 2007

3 Analyzing an image

Elements for analysis

As when analyzing a written work, you analyze an image by identifying its elements. The image elements you might consider appear in the box below. Keep in mind that an image is a visual *composition* whose every element likely reflects a deliberate effort to communicate. Still, few images include all the elements, and you can narrow the list further by posing a question about the image you are reading, as illustrated opposite.

Elements of images

- **Emphasis:** Most images pull your eyes to certain features: a graph line moving sharply upward, a provocative figure, bright color, thick lines, and so on. The cropping of a photograph or the date range in a chart will also reflect what the image creator considers important.
- **Narration:** Most images tell stories, whether in a sequence (a TV commercial or a graph showing changes over time) or at a single moment (a photograph, a painting, or a pie chart). Sometimes dialog or a title or caption contributes to the story.
- **Point of view:** The image creator influences responses by taking account of both the viewer's physical relation to the image subject—for instance, whether it is seen head-on or from above—and the viewer's assumed attitude toward the subject.
- **Arrangement:** Patterns among colors or forms, figures in the foreground and background, and elements that are juxtaposed or set apart contribute to the image's meaning and effect.
- **Color:** An image's colors can direct the viewer's attention and convey the creator's attitude toward the subject. Color may also suggest a mood, an era, a cultural connection, or another frame in which to view the image.
- **Characterization:** The figures and objects in an image have certain qualities—sympathetic or not, desirable or not, and so on. Their characteristics reflect the roles they play in the image's story.
- **Context:** The source of an image or the background in an image affects its meaning, whether it is a graph from a scholarly journal or a photo of a car on a sunny beach.
- **Tension:** Images often communicate a problem or seize attention with features that seem wrong, such as misspelled or misaligned words, distorted figures, or controversial relations between characters.
- **Allusions:** An **allusion** is a reference to something the audience is likely to recognize and respond to. Examples include a cultural symbol such as a dollar sign, a mythological figure such as a unicorn, or a familiar movie character such as Darth Vader from *Star Wars*.

Question for analysis

You can focus your analysis of elements by framing your main interest in the image as a question. Matthew Greene posed this question about the *BoostUp.org* ad: *Does the ad move readers to learn more about* BoostUp.org *and how they can help teens to graduate*? The question led Greene to focus on certain elements of the ad:

Image elements	Responses
Emphasis	The ad's grayness and placement of Kody at the far left puts primary emphasis on the boy's isolation. Danny R.'s message, breaking up the gray, receives secondary emphasis.
Narration	The taped-on message suggests a story and connection between Kody and Danny R. Danny R. might be a friend, relative, or mentor. Based on the direct appeal in the word bubble, it appears that Danny R. is trying to help Kody graduate by offering to help him with schoolwork.
Arrangement	The ad places Danny R. and Kody together on the left side of the page, with Danny's message a bright spot on the dull landscape. The appeal to help Kody graduate is subtle and set on its own—the last thing readers look at. It also pulls the elements together so that the ad makes sense.
Color	The lack of color in most of the photo emphasizes Kody's isolation. The whiteness of Danny R.'s message relieves the grayness, like a ray of hope.

Sample Web pages for analysis

The screen shots on the next page are from *AIDS Clock*, an interactive Web site sponsored by the United Nations Population Fund (*www.unfpa.org/aids_clock*). The top image is the home page, displaying a traditional world map. The bottom image appears when viewers click on "Resize the map": now each country's size reflects the number of its people who live with HIV, the virus that causes AIDS. (For example, South Africa grows while the United States shrinks.) The large red number in the upper right changes every fifteen seconds. The "Wake up video" to its left scrolls through photos of people along with text urging viewers to join the World AIDS Campaign. Try to answer the questions in the annotations above the screen shots.

4 Interpreting an image

The strategies for interpreting an image parallel those for interpreting a written text (p. 82). In this process you look more deeply at the elements, considering them in relation to the image creator's

Elements of Web pages

Emphasis and color: What elements on these pages draw your attention? How does color distinguish and emphasize elements?

Narration: What story do the two Web pages tell? What does each map contribute to the story? What does the red number contribute? (Notice that the number changes from the first screen to the second.)

Arrangement: What does the arrangement of elements on the pages contribute to the story being told?

Tension: How do you respond to the distorted map in the second image? What does the distortion contribute to your view of the Web site's effectiveness?

Context: How does knowing the Web site's sponsoring organization, the United Nations Population Fund, affect your response to these images?

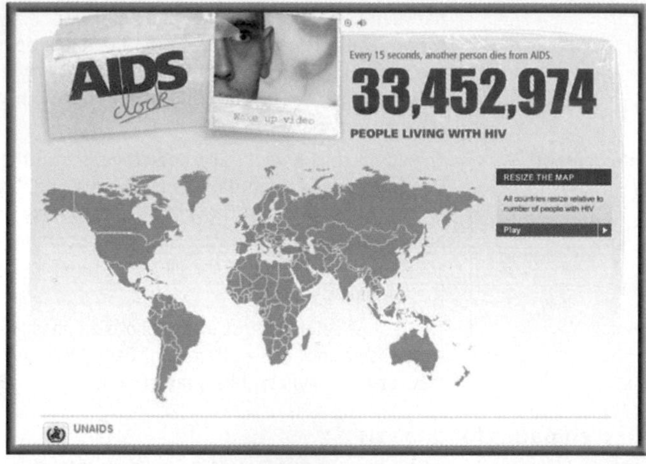

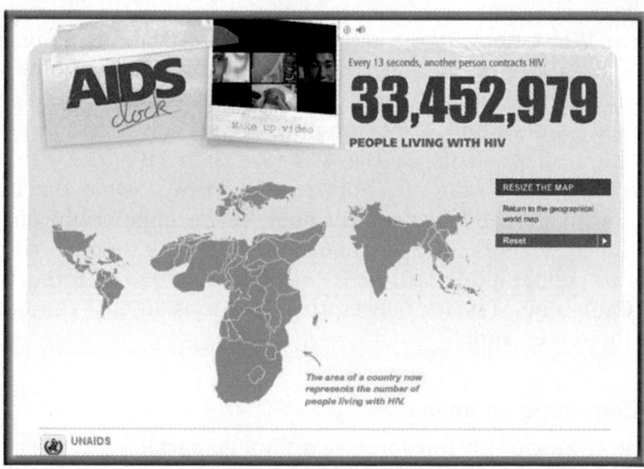

AIDS Clock Web pages, 2008

likely assumptions and intentions. You aim to draw reasonable inferences about *why* the image looks as it does, such as this inference about the *BoostUp.org* advertisement on p. 85:

> The creators of the *BoostUp.org* ad assume that readers want students to graduate from high school.

This statement is supported by the ad's text: the word bubble connecting to the *BoostUp.org* logo specifically says, "Help Kody graduate at BoostUp.org."

5 Synthesizing ideas about an image

As discussed on pp. 82–83, with synthesis you take analysis and interpretation a step further to consider how a work's elements and underlying assumptions relate and what the overall message is. You may also expand your synthesis to view the whole image in a larger context: How does the work fit into the context of other works? What cultural, economic, political, or historical forces influence the work?

Placing an image in its context often requires research. For instance, to learn more about the assumptions underlying the *BoostUp.org* advertisement and the goals of the larger ad campaign, Matthew Greene visited the Web sites of *BoostUp.org* and the Ad Council, one of the ad's sponsors. The following entry from his reading journal synthesizes this research and his own ideas about the ad:

> The *BoostUp.org* magazine ad that features Kody is part of a larger campaign designed to raise public awareness about high school dropouts and encourage pubic support to help teens stay in school. Sponsored by the US Army and the nonprofit Ad Council, *BoostUp.org* profiles high school seniors who are at risk of dropping out and asks individuals to write the students personal messages of support. Ads like "Kody" are the first point of contact between the public and the teens, but they don't by themselves actually help the teens. For that, readers need to visit *BoostUp.org*. Thus the ad's elements work together like pieces of a puzzle, with the solution to be found only on the Web site.

6 Evaluating an image

If your critical reading moves on to evaluation, you'll form judgments about the quality and significance of the image: Is the message of the image accurate and fair, or is it distorted and biased? Can you support, refute, or extend the message? Does the image achieve its apparent purpose, and is the purpose worthwhile? How does the image affect you?

You can read Matthew Greene's critical response to the *BoostUp.org* advertisement in the e-book version of this handbook at *mycomplab.com*.

10 Academic Writing

The academic disciplines differ widely in their subjects and approaches, but they all share the common goal of building knowledge through questioning, research, and communication. The differences among disciplines lie mainly in the kinds of questions asked, the kinds of research done to find the answers, and the **genres,** or types of writing, used to communicate the answers, such as case studies, research reports, literary analyses, and reviews of others' writings.

Both a discipline's concerns and the kind of writing create an academic writing situation, which in turn shapes a writer's choice of subject, conception of audience, definition of purpose, choice of structure and content, and even choice of language. This chapter introduces academic writing situations in general. See **8** (Chapters 55–57) for the particular goals and expectations of writing about literature and in other humanities, the social sciences, and the natural and applied sciences.

10a Writing in response to texts

Academic knowledge building depends on reading, analyzing, and expanding on the work of others. Thus many academic writing assignments require you to respond to one or more texts—not only to written products such as short stories and journal articles but also to visual communications such as images, charts, films, and advertisements. As you form a response to a text, you will synthesize, or integrate, its ideas and information with yours to come to your own conclusions.

Note A common academic assignment, the research paper, expects you to consult and respond to multiple texts in order to support and extend your ideas. See **7** (Chapters 50–54). This section focuses on responding directly to a single text, but the skills involved apply to research writing as well.

1 Deciding how to respond

When an assignment asks you to respond directly to a text, you might take one of the following approaches. (Note that the word

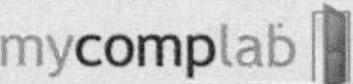

Visit *mycomplab.com* for more resources on academic writing.

author refers to a photographer, painter, or other creator as well as to a writer.)

- **Agree with and extend the author's ideas,** exploring related ideas and providing additional examples.
- **Agree with the author on some points but disagree on others.**
- **Disagree with the author on one or more main points.**
- **Explain how the author achieves a particular effect,** such as evoking a historical period or balancing opposing views.
- **Analyze the overall effectiveness of a text**—for example, how well a writer supports a thesis with convincing evidence or whether an advertisement succeeds in its unstated purpose.

2 Forming a response

You will likely have an immediate response to at least some of the texts you analyze: you may agree or disagree strongly with what the author is saying. But for some other responses, you may need time and thought to determine what the author is saying and what you think about it.

Whatever your assignment, your first task is to examine the text thoroughly so that you're sure you understand what the author says outright and also assumes or implies. You can use the process of critical reading described in the previous chapter to take notes on the text, summarize it, and develop a critical response. Then, as you write, you can use the tips in the following box to convey your response to readers.

Responding to a text

- **Make sure your writing has a point**—a central idea, or thesis, that focuses your response. (For more on developing a thesis, see **1** pp. 14–16.)
- **Include a very brief summary if readers may be unfamiliar with your subject.** But remember that your job is not just to report what the text says or what an image shows; it is to *respond* to the work from your own critical perspective. (For more on summary, see pp. 72–74.)
- **Center each paragraph on an idea of your own that supports your thesis.** Generally, state the idea outright, in your own voice.
- **Support the paragraph idea with evidence from the text**—quotations, paraphrases, details, and examples.
- **Conclude each paragraph with your interpretation of the evidence.** As a general rule, avoid ending paragraphs with source evidence; instead, end with at least a sentence that explains what the evidence shows.

3 Emphasizing synthesis in your response

Following the suggestions in the preceding box will lead you to show readers the synthesis you achieved by thinking critically about the text. That is, you integrate your perspective with that of the author in order to support a conclusion of your own about the work.

A key to synthesis is deciding how to present evidence from your reading and observation in your writing. Especially when you are writing about a relatively unfamiliar subject, you may be tempted to let a text or other source do the talking for you through extensive summary or quotations. However, readers of your academic writing will expect to see you managing ideas and information to make your points. Thus a typical paragraph of text-based writing should open with your own idea, give evidence from the text, and conclude with your interpretation of the evidence. You can see examples of this paragraph pattern in the research paper in **MLA** pp. 452–60.

Note Effective synthesis requires careful handling of evidence from the text (quotations and paraphrases) so that it meshes smoothly into your sentences yet is clearly distinct from your own ideas. See **7** pp. 362–67 on integrating borrowed material.

10b Determining purpose

For most academic writing, your general purpose will be mainly explanatory or mainly argumentative. That is, you will aim to clarify your subject so that readers understand it as you do, or you will aim to gain readers' agreement with a debatable idea about the subject. (See **1** pp. 6–7 for more on general purposes and pp. 97–111 for more on argument.)

Your specific purpose—including your subject and how you hope readers will respond—depends on the kind of writing you're doing. For instance, in a literature review for a biology class, you want readers to understand the research area you're covering, the recent contributions made by researchers, the issues needing further research, and the sources you consulted. Not coincidentally, these topics correspond to the major sections of a literature review. In following the standard format, you both help to define your purpose and begin to meet the discipline's (and thus your instructor's) expectations.

Your specific purpose will be more complex as well. You take a course to learn about a subject and the ways experts think about it. Your writing, in return, contributes to the discipline through the knowledge you uncover and the lens of your perspective. At the same time, as a student you want to demonstrate your competence with research, evidence, format, and other requirements of the discipline.

10c Analyzing audience

Many academic writing assignments will specify or assume an educated audience or an academic audience. Such readers look for writing that is clear, balanced, well organized, and well reasoned, among other qualities discussed in the next section. Other assignments will specify or assume an audience of experts on your subject, readers who look in addition for writing that meets the subject's requirements for claims and evidence, organization, language, format, and other qualities.

Of course, much of your academic writing will have only one reader besides you: the instructor of the course for which you are writing. Instructors fill two main roles as readers:

- **They represent the audience you are addressing.** They may actually be members of the audience, as when you address academic readers or subject experts. Or they may imagine themselves as members of your audience—reading, for instance, as if they sat on the city council. In either case, they're interested in how effectively you write for the audience.
- **They serve as coaches,** guiding you toward achieving the goals of the course and, more broadly, toward the academic aims of building and communicating knowledge.

Like everyone else, instructors have preferences and peeves, but you'll waste time and energy trying to anticipate them. Do attend to written and spoken directions for assignments, of course. But otherwise view your instructors as representatives of the community you are writing for. Their responses will be guided by the community's aims and expectations and by a desire to teach you about them.

10d Choosing structure and content

Many academic writing assignments will at least imply how you should organize your paper and even how you should develop your ideas. Like the literature review mentioned opposite, the type of paper required will break into discrete parts, each with its own requirements for content.

No matter what type of paper an assignment specifies, the broad academic aims of building and exchanging knowledge determine features that are common across disciplines. Follow these general guidelines for your academic writing, supplementing them as indicated with others elsewhere in this book:

- **Develop a thesis**—a central idea or claim to which everything in the paper clearly relates. Usually, state your thesis near the beginning of the paper. For more on theses, see **1** pp. 14–16.
- **Support the thesis with evidence,** drawn usually from research and sometimes from your own experience. The kinds of evidence will depend on the discipline you're writing in and the type of paper you're doing. For more on evidence in the disciplines, see **8** pp. 384–87 (literature), 392 (other humanities), 395–96 (social sciences), and 399 (natural and applied sciences).
- **Synthesize.** Put your sources to work for you by thinking critically about them. Integrate them into your own perspective using your own voice. For more on synthesis, see p. 92 and **7** pp. 356–57 in the discussion of research writing.
- **Acknowledge sources fully, including online sources.** *Not* acknowledging sources undermines the knowledge-sharing foundation of academic writing and opens you to charges of plagiarism, which can be punishable (see **7** pp. 367–73). For lists of disciplines' documentation guides, see **8** pp. 395, 398, and 402. For documentation guidelines and samples, see **MLA** pp. 406–07 (English and some other humanities), **APA** pp. 463–81 (social sciences), **Chic** pp. 491–501 (history, philosophy, and other humanities), and **CSE** pp. 502–08 (natural and applied sciences).
- **Organize clearly within the framework of the type of writing you're doing.** Develop your ideas as simply and directly as your purpose and content allow. Clearly relate sentences, paragraphs, and sections so that readers always know where they are in the paper's development.

CULTURE LANGUAGE These features are far from universal. In other cultures, for instance, academic writers may be indirect or may not have to acknowledge well-known sources. Recognizing such differences between practices in your native culture and in the United States can help you adapt to US academic writing.

10e Using academic language

American academic writing relies on a dialect called standard American English. The dialect is also used in business, the professions, government, the media, and other sites of social and economic power where people of diverse backgrounds must communicate with one another. It is "standard" not because it is better than other forms of English, but because it is accepted as the common language, much as the dollar bill is accepted as the common currency.

Standard American English varies a great deal, from the formal English of a President's State of the Union address through the middle formality of this handbook to the informal chitchat between anchors on morning TV. Even in academic writing, standard American English allows much room for the writer's own tone and voice, as these passages on the same topic show:

More formal

Using the technique of "color engineering," manufacturers and advertisers can heighten the interest of consumers in a product by adding color that does not contribute to the utility of the product but appeals more to emotions. In one example from the 1920s, manufacturers of fountain pens, which had previously been made of hard black rubber, dramatically increased sales simply by producing the pens in bright colors.

Two complicated sentences, one explaining the technique and one giving the example

Drawn-out phrasing, such as *interest of consumers* instead of *consumers' interest*

Formal vocabulary, such as *heighten, contribute,* and *utility*

Less formal

A touch of "color engineering" can sharpen the emotional appeal of a product or its ad. New color can boost sales even when the color serves no use. In the 1920s, for example, fountain-pen makers introduced brightly colored pens along with the familiar ones of hard black rubber. Sales shot up.

Four sentences, two each for explaining the technique and giving the example

More informal phrasing, such as *Sales shot up*

More informal vocabulary, such as *touch, boost,* and *ad*

As different as they are, both examples illustrate several common features of academic language:

- **It follows the conventions of standard American English for grammar and usage.** These conventions are described in guides to the dialect, such as this handbook. Note that standard American English excludes many forms that are encouraged by rapid communication in e-mail and in text or instant messaging, such as incomplete sentences, no capital letters, and shortened spellings (*u* for *you, b4* for *before, thru* for *through,* and so on). (See **3** p. 159 for more on these forms.)
- **It uses a standard vocabulary,** not one that only some groups understand, such as slang, an ethnic or regional dialect, or another language. (See **3** pp. 158–59 and 160–61 for more on specialized vocabularies.)
- **It creates some distance between writer and reader with the third person (*he, she, it, they*).** The first person (*I, we*) is sometimes appropriate to express personal opinions or invite readers to think along, but not with a strongly explanatory purpose (*I*

discovered that "color engineering" can heighten . . .). The second person (*you*) is appropriate only in addressing readers directly (as in this handbook), and even then it may seem condescending or too chummy (*You should know that "color engineering" can heighten . . .*).

- **It is authoritative and neutral.** In the preceding examples, the writers express themselves confidently, not timidly (as in *One possible example of color engineering that might be considered in this case is . . .*). They also refrain from hostility (*Advertisers will stop at nothing to achieve their goals*) and enthusiasm (*Color engineering is genius at work*).

At first, the diverse demands of academic writing may leave you groping for an appropriate voice. In an effort to sound fresh and confident, you may write too casually:

Too casual

"Color engineering" is a great way to get at consumers' feelings. . . . When the guys jazzed up the color, sales shot through the roof.

In an effort to sound "academic," you may produce wordy and awkward sentences:

Wordy and awkward

The emotions of consumers can be made more engaged by the technique known as "color engineering." . . . A very large increase in the sales of fountain pens was achieved by the manufacturers of the pens as a result of this color enhancement technique. [The passive voice in this example, such as *increase . . . was achieved* instead of *the manufacturers achieved,* adds to its wordiness and indirection. See **4** pp. 218–19 for more on verb voice.]

A cure for writing too informally or too stiffly is to read academic writing so that the language and style become familiar and to edit your writing (see **1** pp. 28–30).

CULTURE LANGUAGE If your first language is not English or is an English dialect besides standard American, you know well the power of communicating with others who share your language. Learning to write standard American English in no way requires you to abandon your first language. Like most multilingual people, you are probably already adept at switching between languages as the situation demands—speaking one way with your relatives, say, and another way with an employer. As you practice academic writing, you'll develop the same flexibility with it.

11 Argument

Argument is writing that attempts to solve a problem, open readers' minds to an opinion, change readers' own opinions, or move readers to action. Using a variety of techniques, you engage readers to find common ground and narrow the distance between your views and theirs.

CULTURE LANGUAGE The ways of conceiving and writing arguments described here may be initially uncomfortable to you if your native culture approaches such writing differently. In some cultures, for example, a writer is expected to begin indirectly, to avoid asserting his or her opinion outright, to rely for evidence on appeals to tradition, or to establish a compromise rather than argue a position. In American academic and business settings, writers aim for a well-articulated opinion, evidence gathered from many sources, and a direct and concise argument for the opinion.

11a Understanding and using the elements of argument

An argument has four main elements: subject, claims, evidence, and assumptions. (The last three are adapted from the work of the British philosopher Stephen Toulmin.)

1 The subject

An argument starts with a subject and often with a view of the subject as well—that is, an idea that makes you want to write about the subject. (If you don't have a subject or you aren't sure what you think, see **1** pp. 9–13 for some invention techniques.) Your subject should meet several requirements:

- **It can be disputed:** reasonable people can disagree over it.
- **It *will* be disputed:** it is controversial.
- **It is narrow enough to research and argue in the space and time available.**

On the flip side of these requirements are several kinds of subjects that will not work as the starting place of argument: indisputable facts, such as the functions of the human liver; personal preferences or beliefs, such as a moral commitment to vegetarianism; and ideas that few would disagree with, such as the virtues of a secure home.

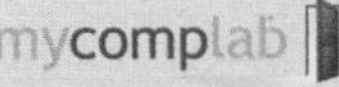

Visit *mycomplab.com* for more resources as well as exercises on argument.

2 Claims

Claims are statements that require support. In an argument you develop your subject into a central claim or **thesis,** asserted outright in a **thesis statement** (see **1** pp. 14–16). This central claim is what the argument is about.

A thesis statement is always an **opinion**—that is, a judgment based on facts and arguable on the basis of facts. It may be one of the following:

- **A claim about past or present reality:**

  In both its space and its equipment, the college's chemistry laboratory is outdated.

  Academic cheating increases with students' economic insecurity.

- **A claim of value:**

  The new room fees are unjustified given the condition of the dormitories.

  Computer music pirates undermine the system that encourages the very creation of music.

- **A recommendation for a course of action,** often a solution to a perceived problem:

  The college's outdated chemistry laboratory should be replaced incrementally over the next five years.

  Schools and businesses can help to resolve the region's traffic congestion by implementing car pools and rewarding participants.

The backbone of an argument consists of specific claims that support the thesis statement. These may also be statements of opinion, or they may fall into one of two other categories:

- **Statements of** ***fact,*** including facts that are generally known or are verifiable (such as the cost of tuition at your school) and those that can be inferred from verifiable facts (such as the monetary value of a college education).
- **Statements of** ***belief,*** or convictions based on personal faith or values, such as *The primary goal of government should be to provide equality of opportunity for all.* Although seemingly arguable, a statement of belief is not based on facts and so cannot be contested on the basis of facts.

3 Evidence

Evidence demonstrates the validity of your claims. The evidence to support the claim that the school needs a new chemistry lab might include the present lab's age, an inventory of facilities and equipment, and the testimony of chemistry professors.

There are several kinds of evidence:

- **Facts,** statements whose truth can be verified or inferred: *Poland is slightly smaller than New Mexico.*
- **Statistics,** facts expressed as numbers: *Of those polled, 22 percent prefer a flat tax.*
- **Examples,** specific instances of the point being made: *Many groups, such as the elderly and people with disabilities, would benefit from this policy.*
- **Expert opinions,** the judgments formed by authorities on the basis of their own examination of the facts: *Affirmative action is necessary to right past injustices, a point argued by Howard Glickstein, a past director of the US Commission on Civil Rights.*
- **Appeals to readers' beliefs or needs,** statements that ask readers to accept a claim in part because it states something they already accept as true without evidence: *The shabby, antiquated chemistry lab shames the school, making it seem a second-rate institution.*

Evidence must be reliable to be convincing. Ask these questions about your evidence:

- **Is it accurate**—trustworthy, exact, and undistorted?
- **Is it relevant**—authoritative, pertinent, and current?
- **Is it representative**—true to its context, neither under- nor overrepresenting any element of the sample it's drawn from?
- **Is it adequate**—plentiful and specific?

4 Assumptions

An **assumption** is an opinion, a principle, or a belief that ties evidence to claims: the assumption explains why a particular piece of evidence is relevant to a particular claim. For instance:

Claim: The college needs a new chemistry laboratory.
Evidence (in part): The testimony of chemistry professors.
Assumption: Chemistry professors are the most capable of evaluating the present lab's quality.

Assumptions are not flaws in arguments but necessities: we all acquire beliefs and opinions that shape our views of the world. Interpreting a work's assumptions is a significant part of critical reading and viewing (see pp. 82 and 87–88), and discovering your own assumptions is a significant part of argument. If your readers do not share your assumptions or if they perceive that you are not forthright about your biases, they will be less receptive to your argument.

11b Writing reasonably

Reasonableness is essential if an argument is to establish common ground between you and your readers. Readers expect logical thinking, appropriate appeals, fairness toward the opposition, and, combining all of these, writing that is free of fallacies.

1 Logical thinking

The thesis of your argument is a conclusion you reach by reasoning about evidence. Two processes of reasoning, induction and deduction, are familiar to you even if you aren't familiar with their names.

Induction

When you're about to buy a used car, you consult friends, relatives, and consumer guides before deciding what kind of car to buy. Using **induction,** or **inductive reasoning,** you make specific observations about cars (your evidence) and you induce, or infer, a **generalization** that Car X is most reliable. The generalization is a claim supported by your observations.

You might also use inductive reasoning in a term paper on print advertising:

Evidence: Advertisements in newspapers and magazines.
Evidence: Comments by advertisers and publishers.
Evidence: Data on the effectiveness of advertising.
Generalization or claim: Print is the most cost-effective medium for advertising.

Reasoning inductively, you connect your evidence to your generalization by assuming that what is true in one set of circumstances (the evidence you examine) is also true in a similar set of circumstances (evidence you do not examine). With induction you create new knowledge out of old.

The more evidence you accumulate, the more probable it is that your generalization is true. Note, however, that absolute certainty is not possible. At some point you must *assume* that your evidence justifies your generalization, for yourself and your readers. Most errors in inductive reasoning involve oversimplifying either the evidence or the generalization. See pp. 103–04 on fallacies.

Deduction

You use **deduction,** or **deductive reasoning,** when you proceed from your generalization that Car X is the most reliable used car to your own specific circumstances (you want to buy a used car) to the conclusion that you should buy Car X. In deduction your assumption is a generalization, principle, or belief that you think is true. It links the evidence (new information) to the claim (the conclusion you draw). With deduction you apply old information to new.

Say that you want the school administration to postpone new room fees for one dormitory. You can base your argument on a deductive **syllogism:**

> **Premise:** The administration should not raise fees on dorm rooms in poor condition. [A generalization or belief that you assume to be true.]
> **Premise:** The rooms in Polk Hall are in poor condition. [New information: a specific case of the first premise.]
> **Conclusion:** The administration should not raise fees on the rooms in Polk Hall. [Your claim.]

As long as the premises of a syllogism are true, the conclusion derives logically and certainly from them. Errors in constructing syllogisms lie behind many of the fallacies discussed on pp. 102–03.

2 Rational, emotional, and ethical appeals

In most arguments you will combine **rational appeals** to readers' capacities for logical reasoning with **emotional appeals** to readers' beliefs and feelings. The following example illustrates both: the second sentence makes a rational appeal (to the logic of financial gain), and the third sentence makes an emotional appeal (to the sense of fairness and open-mindedness).

> Advertising should show more physically challenged people. The millions of Americans with disabilities have considerable buying power, yet so far advertisers have made no attempt to tap that power. Further, by keeping people with disabilities out of the mainstream depicted in ads, advertisers encourage widespread prejudice against disability, prejudice that frightens and demeans those who hold it.

For an emotional appeal to be successful, it must be appropriate for the audience and the argument:

- **It must not misjudge readers' actual feelings.**
- **It must not raise emotional issues that are irrelevant to the claims and the evidence.** See p. 103 on specific inappropriate appeals, such as bandwagon and ad hominem.

A third kind of approach to readers, the **ethical appeal,** is the sense you give of being a competent, fair person who is worth heeding. A rational appeal and an appropriate emotional appeal contribute to your ethical appeal, and so does your acknowledging opposing views (see the next page). An argument that is concisely written and correct in grammar, spelling, and other matters will underscore your competence. In addition, a sincere and even tone will assure readers that you are a balanced person who wants to reason with them.

A sincere and even tone need not exclude language with emotional appeal—words such as *frightens* and *demeans* at the end of the example about advertising. But avoid certain forms of expression that will mark you as unfair:

- **Insulting words,** such as *idiotic* or *fascist.*
- **Biased language,** such as *fags* or *broads* (see **3** pp. 161–64).
- **Sarcasm,** such as the phrase *What a brilliant idea* to indicate contempt for the idea and its originator.
- **Exclamation points!** They'll make you sound shrill!

3 Acknowledgment of opposing views

A good test of your fairness in argument is how you handle possible objections. Assuming your thesis is indeed arguable, then others can marshal their own evidence to support a different view or views. By dealing squarely with these opposing views, you show yourself to be honest and fair. You strengthen your ethical appeal and thus your entire argument.

Before or while you draft your essay, list for yourself all the opposing views you can think of. You'll find them in your research, by talking to friends and classmates, and by critically thinking about your own ideas. You can also look for a range of views in an online discussion that deals with your subject. Two places to start are the *Yahoo!* archive of discussion groups at *groups.yahoo.com* and the *Google* blog directory at *blogsearch.google.com*.

A common way to handle opposing views is to state them, refute those you can, grant the validity of others, and demonstrate why, despite their validity, the opposing views are less compelling than your own. A somewhat different approach, developed by the psychologist Carl Rogers, emphasizes the search for common ground. In a **Rogerian argument** you start by showing that you understand readers' views and by establishing points on which you and readers agree and disagree. Creating a connection in this way can be especially helpful when you expect readers to resist your argument, as it encourages them to hear you out as you develop your claims.

4 Fallacies

Fallacies—errors in argument—either evade the issue of the argument or treat the argument as if it were much simpler than it is.

Evasions

An effective argument squarely faces the central issue or question it addresses. An ineffective argument may dodge the issue in one of the following ways:

- **Begging the question:** treating an opinion that is open to question as if it were already proved or disproved.

  The college library's expenses should be reduced by cutting subscriptions to useless periodicals. [Begged questions: Are some of the library's periodicals useless? Useless to whom?]

- **Non sequitur** (Latin: "It does not follow"): linking two or more ideas that in fact have no logical connection.

  She uses a wheelchair, so she must be unhappy. [The second clause does not follow from the first.]

- **Red herring:** introducing an irrelevant issue intended to distract readers from the relevant issues.

  A campus speech code is essential to protect students, who already have enough problems coping with rising tuition. [Tuition costs and speech codes are different subjects. What protections do students need that a speech code will provide?]

- **Appeal to readers' fear or pity:** substituting emotions for reasoning.

  She should not have to pay taxes because she is an aged widow with no friends or relatives. [Appeals to people's pity. Should age and loneliness, rather than income, determine a person's tax obligation?]

- **Bandwagon:** inviting readers to accept a claim because everyone else does.

  As everyone knows, marijuana use leads to heroin addiction. [What is the evidence?]

- **Ad hominem** (Latin: "to the man"): attacking the qualities of the people holding an opposing view rather than the substance of the view itself.

  One of the scientists has been treated for emotional problems, so his pessimism about nuclear waste merits no attention. [Do the scientist's previous emotional problems invalidate his current views?]

Oversimplifications

In a vain attempt to create something neatly convincing, an ineffective argument may conceal or ignore complexities in one of the following ways:

- **Hasty generalization:** making a claim on the basis of inadequate evidence.

  It is disturbing that several of the youths who shot up schools were users of violent video games. Obviously, these games can breed violence, and they should be banned. [A few cases do not establish the relation between the games and violent behavior. Most youths who play violent video games do not behave violently.]

- **Sweeping generalization:** making an insupportable statement. Many sweeping generalizations are **absolute statements** involving words such as *all, always, never,* and *no one* that allow no exceptions. Others are **stereotypes,** conventional and oversimplified characterizations of a group of people:

  People who live in cities are unfriendly.
  Californians are fad-crazy.
  Women are emotional.
  Men can't express their feelings.

  (See also **3** pp. 161–64 on sexist and other biased language.)
- **Reductive fallacy:** oversimplifying (reducing) the relation between causes and effects.

  Poverty causes crime. [If so, then why do people who are not poor commit crimes? And why aren't all poor people criminals?]
- **Post hoc fallacy** (from Latin, *post hoc, ergo propter hoc:* "after this, therefore because of this"): assuming that because *A* preceded *B,* then *A* must have caused *B.*

  The town council erred in permitting the adult bookstore to open, for shortly afterward two women were assaulted. [It cannot be assumed without evidence that the women's assailants visited or were influenced by the bookstore.]
- **Either/or fallacy:** assuming that a complicated question has only two answers, one good and one bad, both good, or both bad.

  Either we permit mandatory drug testing in the workplace or productivity will continue to decline. [Productivity is not necessarily dependent on drug testing.]

11c Organizing an argument

All arguments include the same parts:

- **The *introduction* establishes the significance of the subject and provides background.** The introduction may run a paragraph or two, and it generally includes the thesis statement. However, the thesis statement may come later in the paper if you think readers may have difficulty accepting it before they see at least some support for it. (See **1** pp. 49–51 for more on introductions.)
- **The *body* states and develops the claims supporting the thesis.** In one or more paragraphs, the body develops each claim with relevant evidence. See the next page on organizing the body.
- **The *response to opposing views*** details and addresses those views, either conceding them or demonstrating your argument's greater strengths. See the next page on organizing this response.

- **The *conclusion* completes the argument,** restating the thesis, summarizing the supporting claims, and making a final appeal to readers. (See **1** pp. 51–52 for more on conclusions.)

The structure of the body and the response to opposing views depends on your subject, purpose, audience, and form of reasoning. Here are several possible arrangements:

A common scheme
Claim 1 and evidence
Claim 2 and evidence
Claim X and evidence
Response to opposing views

A variation
Claim 1 and evidence
Response to opposing views
Claim 2 and evidence
Response to opposing views
Claim X and evidence
Response to opposing views

The Rogerian scheme
Common ground and concession to opposing views
Claim 1 and evidence
Claim 2 and evidence
Claim X and evidence

The problem-solution scheme
The problem: claims and evidence
The solution: claims and evidence
Response to opposing views

11d Using visual arguments

In a **visual argument** you use one or more images to engage and convince readers. Advertisements often provide the most vivid and memorable examples of visual arguments, but writers in almost every academic discipline support their claims with images. The main elements of written arguments discussed on pp. 98–99—claims, evidence, and assumptions—appear also in visual arguments.

1 Claims

The claims in an image may be made by composition as well as by content, with or without accompanying words. For instance:

Image A photograph framing hundreds of chickens crammed into small cages, resembling familiar images of World War II concentration camps.

Claim Commercial poultry-raising practices are cruel and unethical.

Image A chart with dramatically contrasting bars that represent the optimism, stress, and heart disease reported by people before and after they participated in a program of daily walking.

Claim Daily exercise leads to a healthier and happier life.

The following advertisement is one of a series featuring unnamed but well-known people as milk drinkers. The celebrity here is Serena Williams, a tennis champion. The ad makes several claims both in the photograph and in the text.

Claims in an image

Image claim: Strong, shapely women drink milk.

Image claim: Attractive people drink milk.

Image claim: Athletes drink milk.

Text claim: Milk can help dieters reduce to a healthy weight.

got milk?
Lean machine.
When it comes to winning titles, perfect form helps. So I serve up milk. Studies suggest people pursuing a healthy weight could lose more weight and burn more fat by including 24 ounces a day of lowfat or fat free milk in their reduced-calorie diet, instead of 8 ounces or less. That's what I call a nice return.
milk your diet. Lose weight!
24 24

Advertisement by the Milk Processor Education Program

2 Evidence

The kinds of evidence offered by images parallel those found in written arguments:

- **Facts:** You might provide facts in the form of data, as in a graph showing a five-year rise in oil prices. Or you might draw an inference from data, as the ad above does by stating that milk can help dieters "lose weight and burn more fat."
- **Examples:** Most often, you'll use examples to focus on an instance of your argument's claims, as Serena Williams represents milk drinkers in the ad above.

- **Expert opinions:** You might present a chart from an expert showing a trend in unemployment among high school graduates.
- **Appeals to beliefs or needs:** You might depict how things clearly ought to be (an anti-drug brochure featuring a teenager who is confidently refusing peer pressure) or, in contrast, show how things clearly should not be (a Web site for an anti-hunger campaign featuring images of emaciated children).

To make an image work hard as evidence, be sure it relates directly to a point in your argument, adds to that point, and gives readers something to think about. Always include a caption that provides source information and that explicitly ties the image to your text, so that readers don't have to puzzle out your intentions. Number images in sequence (Fig. 1, Fig. 2, and so on), and refer to them by number at the appropriate points in your text. (See **1** pp. 60–64 for more on captioning and numbering illustrations.)

The images below and on the next page supported an argument with this thesis: *Despite proof that the depiction of smoking in movies encourages children and teens to smoke, studios continue to release youth-oriented movies that show stars smoking.*

Image as evidence

Photograph of an actress smoking in a PG-13 movie —a visual example of the claim that youth-oriented movies depict smoking

Fig. 1. The actress Kate Hudson in *Raising Helen,* one of many PG-13 movies released each year in which characters smoke. Photograph by Peggy Storm; *gettyimages.com*; Getty Images, 2003; Web; 21 Apr. 2008.

Caption explaining the image, tying it to the text of the paper and providing source information

Image as evidence

Advertisement by a reputable research and advocacy group, reinforcing the thesis and providing data about depictions of smoking in movies

[One in a Series]
Eighty percent of this year's nominated movies feature smoking. And the winner is
the global tobacco industry. It gains at least $4 billion in lifetime sales revenue, in the U.S. alone, from the new teen smokers recruited to smoke by films each year. In 2007, two-thirds of new U.S. releases featured smoking: 39% of G/PG movies, 66% of PG-13 films, 84% of R-rated films. Together, these movies delivered **6.6 billion tobacco impressions** to North American theater audiences. R-rating smoking is reasonable, responsible—and inevitable. You'll still be able to include smoking in any film, just like this year's R-rated nominees for Best Picture. Yet by keeping smoking out of the G/PG/PG-13 films that kids see most, you'll save 60,000 lives a year. So who's trying to stop the "R"? Must be somebody with a lot to lose.
SMOKE FREE MOVIES
SmokeFreeMovies.ucsf.edu

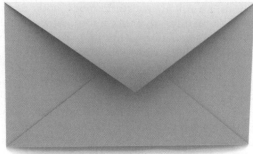

Caption interpreting the ad and providing source information

Fig. 2. Advertisement by the research and advocacy group Smoke Free Movies, providing data on the depiction of smoking in movies and linking the tobacco industry to the practice. From "Our Ads"; *Smoke Free Movies*; U of California, San Francisco, Cardiovascular Research Inst., 2008; Web; 23 Apr. 2008.

3 Assumptions

Like a written argument, a visual argument is based on assumptions—your ideas about the relation between evidence and claims (p. 99). Look again at the milk ad featuring Serena Williams (p. 106). The advertiser seems to have assumed that a celebrity endorsement would strengthen the claims and evidence about the benefits of drinking milk. In addition, the photograph of Williams emphasizes qualities that the advertiser presumably thought would appeal to readers: strength, shapeliness, beauty, even glamour.

As in written arguments, the assumptions in visual arguments must be appropriate for your readers if the argument is to succeed with them. The milk ad originally appeared in sports magazines, so the advertiser could assume that readers knew of and admired Williams. But to readers uninterested in sports or tennis, the photograph might actually undermine the ad's effectiveness.

4 Appeals

Images can help to strengthen the rational, emotional, and ethical appeals of your written argument (pp. 101–02):

- **Images can contribute evidence,** as long as they come from reliable sources, present information accurately and fairly, and relate clearly to the argument's claims.
- **Images can appeal to a host of ideas and emotions,** including patriotism, curiosity, moral values, sympathy, and anger. Any such appeal should correctly gauge readers' beliefs and feelings, and it should be clearly relevant to the argument.
- **Images can show that you are a competent, fair, and trustworthy source of information,** largely through their relevance, reliability, and sensitivity to readers' needs and feelings.

To see how appeals can work in images, look at a photograph used in the sample argument paper on p. 112. This image illustrates the writer's claim that television can ease loneliness.

Appeals in an image

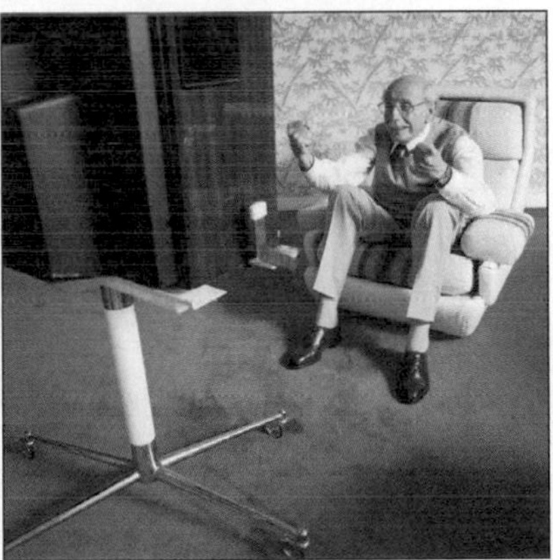

Rational appeal: Backs up the writer's claim that TV can ease loneliness: the man appears to live alone (only one chair is visible) and is interacting enthusiastically with the TV

Emotional appeal: Reinforces the benefits of TV watching: the man's isolation may be disturbing, but his excitement is pleasing

Ethical appeal: Conveys the writer's competence through the appropriateness of the image for the point being made

Fig. 1. Television can be a source of companionship for people whose living situations and limited mobility leave them lonely. Photograph by Jean Michel Foujols; *Corbis*; Corbis, 2005; Web; 13 Oct. 2008.

5 Recognizing fallacies

When making a visual argument, you'll need to guard against all the fallacies discussed on pp. 102–04. Here we'll focus on specific visual examples. The first, the milk ad on p. 106, uses Serena Williams for snob appeal, inviting readers to be like someone they admire. If you drink milk, the ad says subtly, you too may become strong, beautiful, and fearless (notice that Williams looks unguardedly into the camera). The ad does have some substance in its specific and verifiable claim that drinking "24 ounces a day of lowfat or fat free milk" could help people reduce to a healthy weight, but Williams herself, with her milk mustache, makes a stronger claim.

Another example of a visual fallacy is the hasty generalization, a claim that is based on too little evidence or that misrepresents the facts. This fallacy appears in the following graph, which is intended to support this claim: *After a steep decline over the preceding five years, the teen birthrate shot up in 2006.* At first glance, the graph seems to demonstrate the claim, but a close look reveals that it badly misrepresents the data. If the graph were not distorted, the line would be nearly flat.

Fallacy in an image

The vertical axis lacks a zero point and covers a small span, thus misrepresenting and exaggerating both the decline and the increase in the birthrate.

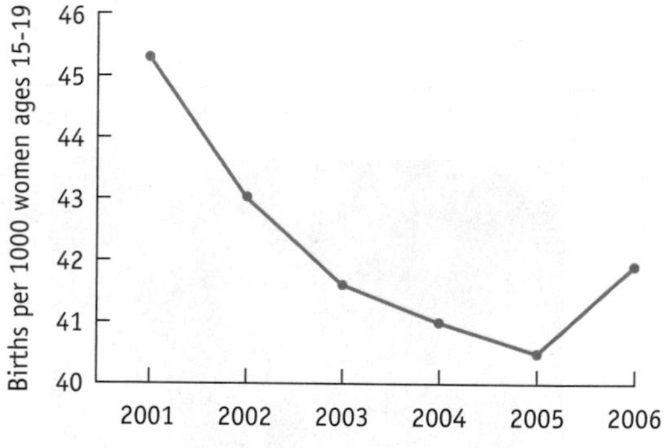

Fig. 2. Steep decline and sharp increase in the birthrate among women ages 15 to 19 in the United States, 2001-06. Data from Brady E. Hamilton et al.; *National Vital Statistics Reports*; US Dept. of Health and Human Services, Centers for Disease Control and Prevention, 1 May 2008; Web; 10 July 2008.

6 Choice of images

You can wait until you've drafted an argument before concentrating on what images to include. This approach keeps your focus on the research and writing needed to craft the best argument from sources. But you can also begin thinking visually at the beginning of a project, as you might if your initial interest in the subject was sparked by a compelling image. Either way, ask yourself some basic questions as you consider visual options:

- **Which parts of your argument require visual evidence or can use visual reinforcement?** Do readers need a visual to understand your argument? Can a claim be explained better visually than verbally? Can a graph or chart present data compactly and interestingly? Can a photograph appeal effectively to readers' beliefs and values?
- **What are the limitations or requirements of your writing situation?** What do the type of writing you're doing and its format allow? Look through examples of similar writing to gauge the kinds of illustrations readers will expect.
- **What kinds of visuals are readily available on your subject?** As you researched your subject, what images seemed especially effective? What sources have you not yet explored? (See **7** pp. 341–42 for tips on locating images.)
- **Should you create original images tailored to your argument?** Instead of searching for existing images, would your time be better spent taking your own photographs or using computer software to compose visual explanations, such as charts and graphs?

Note Any image you include in a paper requires the same detailed citation as a written source. If you plan to publish your argument online, you will also need to seek permission from the author. See **7** pp. 367–75 on citing sources and obtaining permissions.

11e Examining a sample argument

The following essay by Craig Holbrook, a student, illustrates the principles discussed in this chapter. As you read the essay, notice especially the structure, the relation of claims and supporting evidence (including illustrations), the kinds of appeals Holbrook makes, and the ways he addresses opposing views.

TV Can Be Good for You

Television wastes time, pollutes minds, destroys brain cells, and turns some viewers into murderers. Thus runs the prevailing talk about the medium, supported by serious research as well as simple belief. But television has at least one strong virtue, too, which helps to explain its endurance as a cultural force. It provides replacement voices that ease loneliness, spark healthful laughter, and even educate young children.

Introduction

Identification of prevailing view

Disagreement with prevailing view

Thesis statement making three claims for television

Background for claim 1: effects of loneliness

Most people who have lived alone understand the curse of silence, when the only sound is the buzz of unhappiness or anxiety inside one's own head. Although people of all ages who live alone can experience intense loneliness, the elderly are especially vulnerable to solitude. For example, they may suffer increased confusion or depression when left alone for long periods but then rebound when they have steady companionship (Bondevik and Skogstad 329-30).

Evidence for effects of loneliness

Evidence for effects of television on loneliness

A study of elderly men and women in New Zealand found that television can actually serve as a companion by assuming "the role of social contact with the wider world," reducing "feelings of isolation and loneliness because it directs viewers' attention away from themselves" ("Television Programming"). (See fig. 1.) Thus television's replacement voices can provide comfort because they distract from a focus on being alone.

Statement of claim 1

Illustration supporting claim 1

Fig. 1. Television can be a source of companionship for people whose living situations and limited mobility leave them lonely. Photograph by Jean Michel Foujols; *Corbis*; Corbis, 2005; Web; 13 Oct. 2008.

Background for claim 2: effects of laughter

The absence of real voices can be most damaging when it means a lack of laughter. Here, too, research shows that television can have a positive effect on health. Laughter is one of the most powerful calming forces available to human beings, proven in many studies to reduce heart rate, lower blood pressure, and ease other stress-related ailments (Burroughs, Mahoney, and Lippman 172; Griffiths 18). (See fig. 2.) Television offers plenty of laughter: the recent listings for a single Friday night included more than twenty comedy programs running on the networks and on basic cable.

Evidence for effects of laughter

Evidence for comedy on television

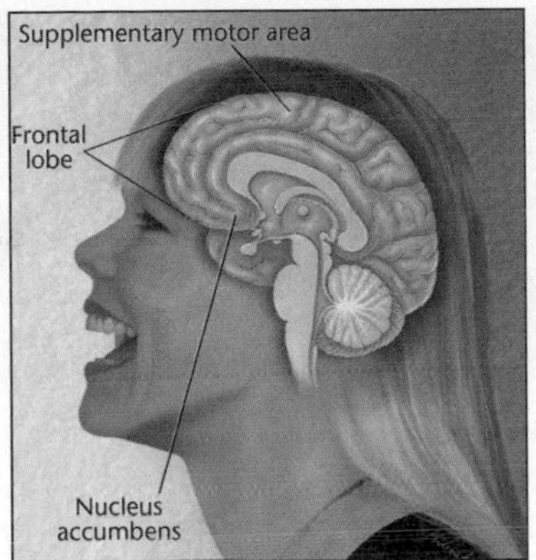

Illustration supporting healthful effects of laughter

Fig. 2. According to the Society for Neuroscience, the process of understanding and being amused by something funny stimulates at least three main areas of the brain. The society makes no recommendation about TV watching, but other studies show the healthful effects of the activity. Illustration by Lydia Kibiuk from *Brain Briefings;* Soc. for Neuroscience, Dec. 2001; Web; 12 Oct. 2008.

Evidence for effects of laughter in response to television

A study reported in a health magazine found that laughter inspired by television and video is as healthful as the laughter generated by live comedy. Volunteers laughing at a video comedy routine "showed significant improvements in several immune functions, such as natural killer-cell activity" (Laliberte 78). Further, the effects of the comedy were so profound that "merely anticipating watching a funny video improved mood, depression, and anger as much as two days beforehand" (Laliberte 79). Even for people with plenty of companionship, television's replacement voices can have healthful effects by causing laughter.

Statement of claim 2

Background for claim 3: educational effects

Television also provides information about the world. This service can be helpful to everyone but especially to children, whose natural curiosity can exhaust the knowledge and patience of their parents and caretakers. While the TV may be baby-sitting children, it can also enrich them. For example, educational programs such as those on the Discovery Channel, the Disney Channel, and PBS offer a steady stream of information at various cognitive levels. (See fig. 3.) Even many cartoons, which are generally dismissed as mindless entertainment or worse, can familiarize children with the material of literature, including strong characters enacting classic narratives.

Evidence for educational programming on television

Illustration supporting claim 3

Fig. 3. Educational television programs such as *Sesame Street* are an important source of learning for children. Characters such as Elmo (shown here) promote reading, learning, and healthy behaviors. Photograph from *The State of the World's Children*; United Nations Children's Fund, 2002; Web; 12 Oct. 2008.

Evidence for educational effects of television on children

Three researchers conducting a review of studies involving children and television found that TV can inspire imaginative play, which psychologists describe as important for children's cognitive development (Thakkar, Garrison, and Christakis 2028). In the studies reviewed, children who watched *Mister Rogers' Neighborhood,* a show that emphasized make-believe, demonstrated significant increases in imaginative play (2029). Thus high-quality educational programming can both inform young viewers and improve their cognitive development.

Statement of claim 3

Anticipation of objection: harm of television

The value of these replacement voices should not be oversold. Almost everyone agrees that too much TV does no one any good and may cause much harm. Many studies show that excessive TV watching increases violent behavior, especially in children, and can cause, rather than ease, other antisocial behaviors (Reeks 114; Walsh 34). In addition, human beings require the give and take of actual interaction. Steven Pinker, an expert in children's language acquisition, warns that children cannot develop language properly by watching television. They need to interact with actual speakers who respond directly to their needs (282). Replacement voices are not real voices and in the end can do only limited good.

Anticipation of objection: need for actual interaction

Qualification of claims in response to objections

Conclusion

But even limited good is something, especially for those who are lonely or neglected. Television is not an entirely positive force, but neither is it an entirely negative one. Its voices can provide company, laughter, and information whenever they're needed.

Works cited in MLA style

No works cited entries for illustrations because captions provide complete source information

Works Cited

Bondevik, Margareth, and Anders Skogstad. "The Oldest Old, ADL, Social Network, and Loneliness." *Western Journal of Nursing Research* 20.3 (1998): 325-43. Print.

Burroughs, W. Jeffrey, Diana L. Mahoney, and Louis G. Lippman. "Attributes of Health-Promoting Laughter: Cross-Generational Comparison." *Journal of Psychology* 136.2 (2004): 171-81. Print.

Griffiths, Joan. "The Mirthful Brain." *Omni* Aug. 1996: 18-19. Print.

Laliberte, Richard W. "The Benefits of Laughter." *Shape* Sept. 2003: 78-79. Print.

Pinker, Steven. *The Language Instinct: How the Mind Creates Language*. New York: Harper, 1994. Print.

Reeks, Anne. "Kids and TV: A Guide." *Parenting* Apr. 2005: 110-15. Print.

"Television Programming for Older People: Summary Research Report." *NZ on Air*. NZ on Air, 25 July 2004. Web. 15 Oct. 2008.

Thakkar, Rupin R., Michelle M. Garrison, and Dimitri A. Christakis. "A Systematic Review for the Effects of Television Viewing by Infants and Preschoolers." *Pediatrics* 18.5 (2006): 2025-31. Web. 12 Oct. 2008.

Walsh, Teri. "Too Much TV Linked to Depression." *Prevention* Feb. 2001: 34-36. Print.

—Craig Holbrook (student)

12 Online Writing

In and out of college, you will write extensively online. Many forms of online writing expand your options as a writer, but they also present distinctive challenges. This chapter discusses some of the options and challenges of e-mail (next page), online collaboration (p. 118), and Web composition (p. 119).

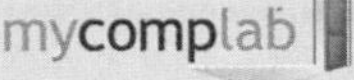

Visit *mycomplab.com* for more resources as well as exercises on online writing.

12a Using e-mail

To use e-mail productively for college work, pause to weigh each element of the message. Consider especially your audience and purpose and how your tone will come across to readers. In the message shown below, the writer knows the recipients well and yet has serious information to convey to them, so he writes informally but states his points and concerns carefully. Writing to the corporation mentioned in the message, the writer would be more formal in both tone and approach. Although e-mail is typically more casual than printed correspondence, in academic settings a crafted message is more likely to achieve the intended purpose. Proofread all but the most informal messages for errors in grammar, punctuation, and spelling.

For more on using e-mail to interact with other students in a course, see p. 118. For more on using e-mail as a research tool, see **7** p. 339.

1 Addressing messages

Send a message only to the people who need to read it. As a general rule, avoid sending messages to many recipients at once—all the students in a course, say, or all the participants in a discussion group—unless what you have to say applies to all of them. Occasionally, you may indeed have a worthwhile idea or important

E-mail message

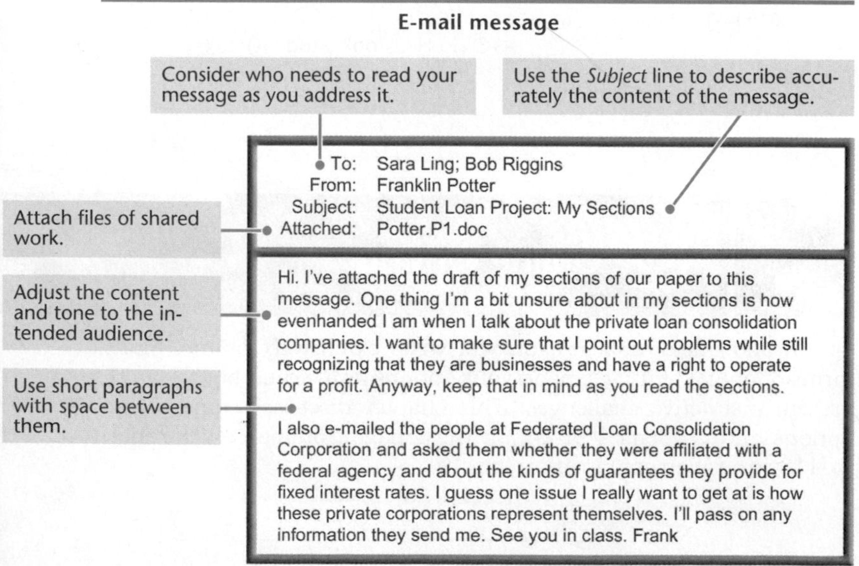
Consider who needs to read your message as you address it.
Use the *Subject* line to describe accurately the content of the message.
Attach files of shared work.
Adjust the content and tone to the intended audience.
Use short paragraphs with space between them.
To: Sara Ling; Bob Riggins
From: Franklin Potter
Subject: Student Loan Project: My Sections
Attached: Potter.P1.doc
Hi. I've attached the draft of my sections of our paper to this message. One thing I'm a bit unsure about in my sections is how evenhanded I am when I talk about the private loan consolidation companies. I want to make sure that I point out problems while still recognizing that they are businesses and have a right to operate for a profit. Anyway, keep that in mind as you read the sections.
I also e-mailed the people at Federated Loan Consolidation Corporation and asked them whether they were affiliated with a federal agency and about the kinds of guarantees they provide for fixed interest rates. I guess one issue I really want to get at is how these private corporations represent themselves. I'll pass on any information they send me. See you in class. Frank

information that everyone on the list will want to know. But spamming—flooding entire lists with irrelevant messages—is rude and irritating.

Similarly, avoid sending frivolous messages to all the members of a group. Instead of dashing off "I agree" and distributing the two-word message widely, put some time into composing a thoughtful response and send it only to those who will be interested.

2 Composing messages

The messages you send are going to people, not just inboxes, so craft your messages with the recipients in mind.

- **Don't say or do anything you wouldn't say or do face to face.**
- **Use names.** In the body of your message, address your reader(s) by name if possible and sign off with your own name and information on how to contact you. Your own name is especially important if your e-mail address does not spell it out.
- **Pay careful attention to tone.** Refrain from flaming, or attacking, correspondents. Don't use all capital letters, which SHOUT. And use irony or sarcasm only cautiously: in the absence of facial expressions, either one can lead to misunderstanding. To indicate irony and emotions, you can use an emoticon such as the smiley :). These sideways faces can easily be overused, though, and should not substitute for thoughtfully worded opinions.
- **Avoid saying anything in e-mail that you would not say in a printed document such as a letter or memo.** E-mail can usually be retrieved from the server, and in business and academic settings it may well be retrieved in disputes over contracts, grades, and other matters.

3 Reading and responding to messages

When you read and respond to messages, again consider the people behind them.

- **Be a forgiving reader.** Avoid nitpicking over spelling or other surface errors. And because attitudes are sometimes difficult to convey, give authors an initial benefit of the doubt: a writer who at first seems hostile may simply have tried too hard to be concise; a writer who at first seems unserious may simply have failed at injecting humor into a worthwhile message.
- **Consider who will read your response.** The Reply function will automatically address the person who wrote you, whereas the

Reply All function will address others who may have been sent copies of the original message. Before you send the message, choose the readers who need to see it.

- **Respect others' privacy.** Forward messages only with permission or only if you know that the author of the message won't mind. If you add more recipients to your response, make sure not to pass on previous private messages by mistake.
- **Avoid participating in flame "wars,"** overheated dialogs that contribute little or no information or understanding. If a war breaks out in a discussion, ignore it: don't rush to defend someone who is being attacked, and don't respond even if you are under attack yourself.

12b Collaborating online

Many instructors integrate online collaboration into their courses, encouraging students to work in groups for discussing ideas and exchanging and commenting on drafts of projects.

1 Participating in discussions

Online conversations in your courses will occur either in real-time chat, which occurs immediately, like a telephone conversation, or in a delayed medium such as e-mail, a blog, or a wiki. Chat discussions can be fast-paced and often work better for brain-storming topics and exchanging impressions than for careful articulation of ideas. Delayed conversations allow detailed, thoughtful messages and responses, so they are good places to develop ideas, explore assignments, and respond to others' work. For either type of conversation, observe the guidelines for composing and responding to messages in the preceding section.

2 Working on drafts

In writing and other courses, you and your fellow students may be invited to exchange and respond to one another's projects by e-mail or over the Web. To guide your reading of others' work, use the revision checklist in **1** p. 26 and the collaboration tips in **1** pp. 35–37. Focus on the deep issues in others' drafts, especially early drafts: thesis, purpose, audience, organization, and support for the thesis. Hold comments on style, grammar, punctuation, and other surface matters until you're reviewing later drafts, if indeed you are expected to comment on them at all.

12c Creating Web compositions

Creating a Web page or site is sometimes as simple as saving a document in a different format, but more often it means thinking in a new way.

The diagrams on the next page show a key difference between traditional printed documents and Web sites. Most traditional documents are meant to be read in sequence from start to finish. In contrast, most Web sites are intended to be examined in whatever order readers choose as they follow links to pages within the site and to other sites. A Web site thus requires careful planning of the links between pages and thoughtful cues to orient readers.

When you create a composition for the Web, it will likely fall into one of two categories: pages such as class papers that resemble printed documents in being linear and text-heavy and that call for familiar ways of writing and reading; or "native" hypertext documents that you build from scratch, which call for screen-oriented writing and reading. These two categories are discussed on pp. 121–24.

Note If you anticipate that some of your readers may have visual, hearing, or reading disabilities, you'll need to consider their needs while designing Web sites. Some of these considerations are covered under document design in **1** pp. 64–65, and others are fundamental to any effective Web design, as discussed in this section. In addition, avoid any content that relies exclusively on images or sound, instead supplementing such elements with text descriptions, and try to provide key concepts both as text and as images and sound. For more on Web design for readers with disabilities, visit the World Wide Web Consortium at *www.w3.org/WAI* or the American Council for the Blind at *acb.org/accessible-formats.html.*

1 Using HTML

Most Web pages are created using hypertext markup language, or HTML, and an HTML editor. The HTML editing program inserts command codes into your document that achieve the effects you want when the material appears on the Web.

From the user's point of view, most HTML editors work much as word processors do, with similar options for sizing, formatting, and highlighting copy and with a display that shows what you will see in the final version. You can compose a Web page without bothering at all about the behind-the-scenes HTML coding. As you gain experience with Web building, however, you may want to create more sophisticated pages by editing the codes themselves.

Traditional print document

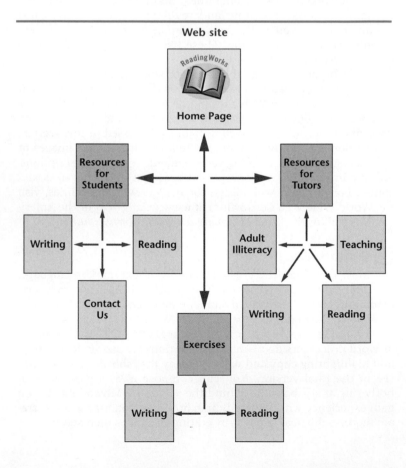

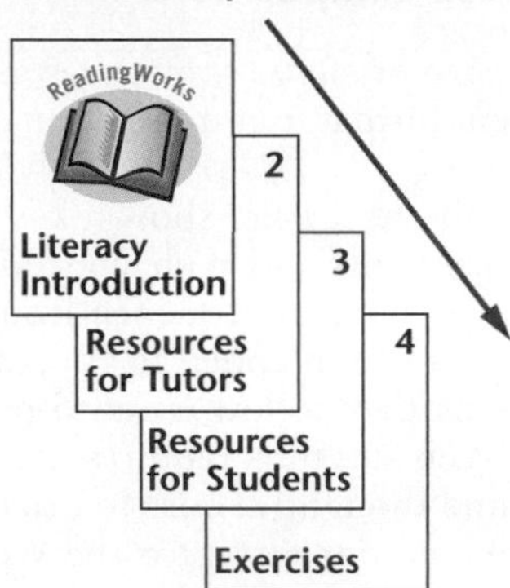

Web site

ReadingWorks
Home Page

Resources for Students

Resources for Tutors

Writing

Reading

Contact Us

Adult Illiteracy

Teaching

Writing

Reading

Exercises

Writing

Reading

2 Creating online papers

If an instructor asks you to post a paper to a Web site or blog, you can compose it on your word processor and then use the Save As HTML function available on most word processors to translate it into a Web page. After translating the paper, your word processor should allow you to modify some of the elements on the page, or you can open the translated document in an HTML editor. The illustration below shows the opening screen of a student's project for a composition course.

Paper submitted on the Web

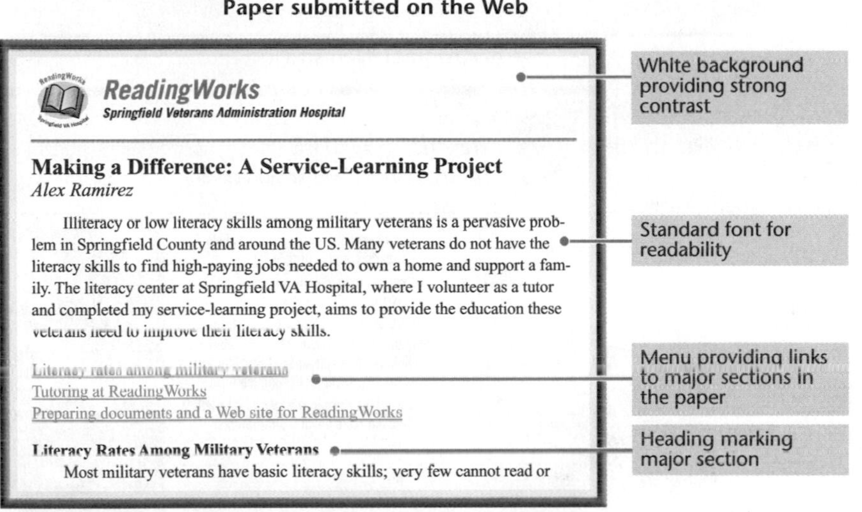

3 Creating original sites

When you create an original Web site, you need to be aware that Web readers generally alternate between skimming pages for highlights and focusing intently on sections of text. To facilitate this kind of reading, you'll want to consider your site's structure and content, flow, ease of navigation, and use of images, video, and sound.

Structure and content

Organize your site so that it efficiently arranges your content and orients readers:

- **Sketch possible site plans before getting started.** (See the previous page for an example.) Your aim is to develop a sense of the major components of your project and to create a logical space for each component.

- **Consider how menus on the site's pages can provide overviews of the organization as well as direct access to the pages.** The Web page below includes a menu on the left.
- **Treat the first few sentences of any page as a get-acquainted space for you and your readers.** On the page below, the text hooks readers with questions and then orients them with general information.
- **Distill your text so that it includes only essential information.** Concise prose is essential in any writing situation, of course. But Web readers expect to scan text quickly and, in any event, have difficulty following long text passages on a computer screen.

Original Web site

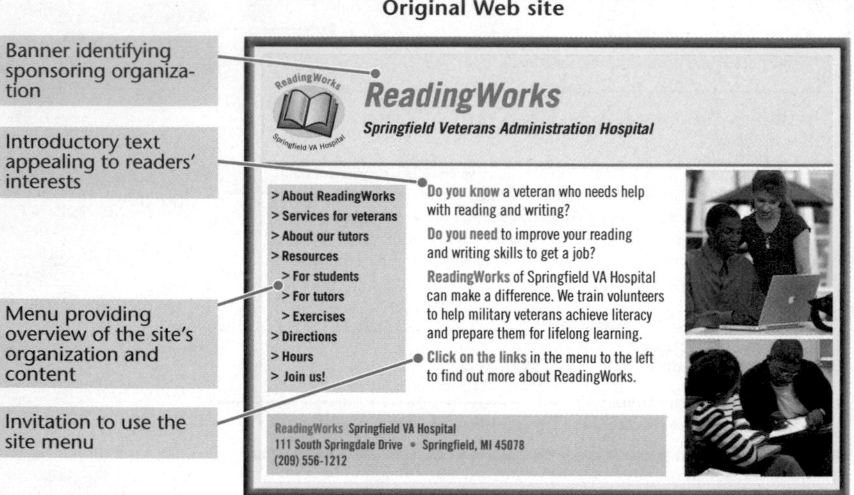

Banner identifying sponsoring organization
Introductory text appealing to readers' interests
Menu providing overview of the site's organization and content
Invitation to use the site menu
ReadingWorks
Springfield Veterans Administration Hospital
> About ReadingWorks
> Services for veterans
> About our tutors
> Resources
> For students
> For tutors
> Exercises
> Directions
> Hours
> Join us!
Do you know a veteran who needs help with reading and writing?
Do you need to improve your reading and writing skills to get a job?
ReadingWorks of Springfield VA Hospital can make a difference. We train volunteers to help military veterans achieve literacy and prepare them for lifelong learning.
Click on the links in the menu to the left to find out more about ReadingWorks.
ReadingWorks Springfield VA Hospital
111 South Springdale Drive • Springfield, MI 45078
(209) 556-1212

Flow

Beginning Web authors sometimes start at the top of the page and then add element upon element until information proceeds down the screen much as it would in a printed document. However, by thinking about how information will flow on a page, you can take better advantage of the Web's visual nature. Follow these guidelines:

- **Standardize elements of your design to create expectations in readers and to fulfill those expectations.** For instance, develop a uniform style for the main headings of pages, for headings within pages, and for menus.
- **Make scanning easy for readers.** Focus readers on crucial text by adding space around it or enlarging it. Add headings to break

up text and to highlight content. Use lists to reinforce the parallel importance of items. (See **1** pp. 58–59 for more on headings and lists.)

Easy navigation

A Web site of more than a few pages requires a menu on every page that lists the features of the site, giving its plan at a glance. By clicking on any item in the menu, readers can go directly to a page that interests them.

You can embed a menu at the top, side, or bottom of a page. Menus at the top or side are best on short pages because they will not scroll off the screen as readers move down the page. On longer pages, menus at the bottom prevent readers from reaching a dead end, a point where they can't easily move forward or backward. You can also use a combination of menus.

Images, video, and sound

Most Web readers expect at least some enhancement of text with multimedia elements—images, video, and sound.

Note See **7** p. 373 on observing copyright restrictions with images, video, and sound.

Images

To use photographs, charts, and other images effectively, follow these guidelines:

- **Use visual elements for a purpose.** They should supplement text, highlight important features, and direct the flow of information. Don't use them as mere decoration.
- **Compose descriptions of images that relate them to your text.** Don't ask the elements to convey your meaning by themselves.
- **Provide alternative descriptions of images** for readers with vision loss or readers whose Web browsers can't display the images.

Video and sound

Video and sound files can provide information that is simply unavailable in printed documents. For instance, as part of a film review you might show and analyze a short clip from the film. Or as part of a project on a controversial issue you might provide links to sound files containing political speeches.

Video and sound files can be difficult to work with and can be slow to download at the reader's end. Make sure they're worth the time: they should provide essential information and should be well integrated with the rest of your composition.

Sources of multimedia elements

You can use your own multimedia elements or obtain them from other sources:

- **Create your own graphs, diagrams, and other illustrations using a graphics program.** Any graphics program requires learning and practice to be used efficiently but can produce professional-looking illustrations.
- **Incorporate your own artwork, photographs, video clips, and sound recordings.** You may be able to find the needed equipment and software at your campus computer lab.
- **Obtain icons, video, and other multimedia elements from other electronic sources.** Be sure to acknowledge your sources and to obtain reprint permission if needed (see **7** pp. 372–73).

13 Oral Presentations

Effective speakers use organization, voice, and other techniques to help their audiences follow and appreciate their presentations.

13a Organizing the presentation

Give your oral presentation a recognizable shape so that listeners can see how ideas and details relate to each other.

The introduction

The beginning of an oral presentation should try to accomplish three goals:

- **Gain the audience's attention and interest.** Begin with a question, an unusual example or statistic, or a short, relevant story.
- **Put yourself in the speech.** Demonstrate your expertise, experience, or concern to gain the interest and trust of your audience.
- **Introduce and preview your topic and purpose.** By the time your introduction is over, listeners should know what your subject is and the direction you'll take to develop your ideas.

mycomplab

Visit *mycomplab.com* for more resources as well as exercises on oral presentations.

Your introduction should prepare your audience for your main points but not give them away. Think of it as a sneak preview of your speech, not the place for an apology such as *I wish I'd had more time to prepare . . .* or a dull statement such as *My speech is about. . . .*

Supporting material

Just as you do when writing, you should use facts, statistics, examples, and expert opinions to support the main points of your oral presentation. In addition, you can make your points more memorable with vivid description, well-chosen quotations, true or fictional stories, and analogies.

The conclusion

You want your conclusion to be clear, of course, but you also want it to be memorable. Remind listeners of how your topic and main idea connect to their needs and interests. If your speech was motivational, tap an emotion that matches your message. If your speech was informational, give some tips on how to remember important details.

13b Delivering the presentation

Methods of delivery

You can deliver an oral presentation in several ways:

- **Impromptu, without preparation:** Make a presentation without planning what you will say. Impromptu speaking requires confidence and excellent general preparation.
- **Extemporaneously:** Prepare notes to glance at but not read from. This method allows you to look and sound natural while ensuring that you don't forget anything.
- **Speaking from a text:** Read aloud from a written presentation. You won't lose your way, but you may lose your audience. Avoid reading for an entire presentation.
- **Speaking from memory:** Deliver a prepared presentation without notes. You can look at your audience every minute, but the stress of retrieving the next words may make you seem tense and unresponsive.

Vocal delivery

The sound of your voice will influence how listeners receive you. Rehearse your presentation several times until you are confident that you are speaking loudly, slowly, and clearly enough for your audience to understand you.

Physical delivery

You are more than your spoken words when you make an oral presentation. If you are able, stand up to deliver your presentation, turning your body toward one side of the room and then the other, stepping out from behind any lectern or desk, and gesturing as appropriate. Above all, make eye contact with your audience as you speak. Looking directly in your listeners' eyes conveys your honesty, your confidence, and your control of the material.

Visual aids

You can supplement an oral presentation with visual aids such as posters, models, slides, or videos.

- **Use visual aids to underscore your points.** Short lists of key ideas, illustrations such as graphs or photographs, or objects such as models can make your presentation more interesting and memorable. But use visual aids judiciously: a battery of illustrations or objects will bury your message rather than amplify it.
- **Coordinate visual aids with your message.** Time each visual to reinforce a point you're making. Tell listeners what they're looking at. Give them enough viewing time so they don't mind turning their attention back to you.
- **Show visual aids only while they're needed.** To regain your audience's attention, remove or turn off any aid as soon as you have finished with it.

Many speakers use *PowerPoint* or other software to present visual aids. Screens of brief points supported by data, images, or video can help listeners follow your main points. (See the next page for examples.) To use *PowerPoint* or other software effectively, follow the guidelines above and also the following:

- **Don't put your whole presentation on screen.** Select your key points, and distill them to as few words as possible. Think of the slides as quick, easy-to-remember summaries.
- **Use a simple design.** Avoid turning your presentation into a show about the software's many capabilities.
- **Use a consistent design.** For optimal flow through the presentation, each slide should be formatted similarly.
- **Add only relevant illustrations.** Avoid loading the presentation with mere decoration.

Practice

Take time to rehearse your presentation out loud, with the notes you will be using. Gauge your performance by making an audio- or videotape of yourself or by practicing in front of a mirror.

PowerPoint slides

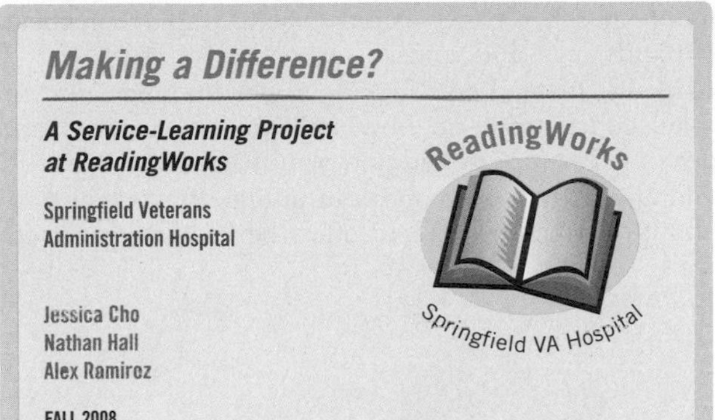

First slide, introducing the project and presentation

Simple, consistent slide design focusing viewers' attention on information, not *PowerPoint* features

Semester goals

- Tutor military veterans
- Research adult litoracy
- Keep a journal
- Collaborate on documents for ReadingWorks
- Report experiences and findings

Later slide, using brief, bulleted points to be explained by the speaker

Photographs reinforcing the project's activities

Practicing out loud will also tell you if your presentation is running too long or too short.

If you plan to use visual aids, you'll need to practice with them, too. Your goal is to eliminate hitches (upside-down slides, missing charts) and to weave the visuals seamlessly into your presentation.

Stage fright

Many people report that speaking in front of an audience is their number-one fear. Even many experienced and polished speakers have some anxiety about delivering an oral presentation, but they use this nervous energy to their advantage, letting it propel them into working hard on each presentation. Several techniques can help you reduce anxiety:

- **Use simple relaxation exercises.** Deep breathing or tensing and relaxing your stomach muscles can ease some of the physical symptoms of speech anxiety—stomachache, rapid heartbeat, and shaky hands, legs, and voice.
- **Think positively.** Instead of worrying about the mistakes you might make, concentrate on how well you've prepared and practiced your presentation and how significant your ideas are.
- **Don't avoid opportunities to speak in public.** Practice and experience build speaking skills and offer the best insurance for success.

14 Public Writing

Writing outside of school, such as for business or for community work, resembles academic writing in many ways. It usually involves the same basic writing process, discussed in **1** pp. 3–33: assessing the writing situation, developing what you want to say, freely working out your meaning in a draft, and revising and editing so that your writing will achieve your purpose with readers. It often involves research, as discussed in **7** pp. 317–75. And it involves the standards of conciseness, appropriate and exact language, and correct grammar and usage discussed in **3** through **6**.

But public writing has its own conventions, too. They vary widely, depending on what you're writing and why, whether it's a proposal for your job or a flyer for a community group. This chapter covers several types of public writing: business letters and résumés (next page); memos, reports, and proposals (p. 134); and flyers, newsletters, and brochures for community work (p. 136).

CULTURE LANGUAGE Public writing in the United States, especially business writing, favors efficiency and may seem abrupt or impolite compared with such writing in your native culture. For instance, a business letter elsewhere may be expected to begin with polite questions about the addressee or with compliments for the addressee's company, whereas US business letters are expected to get right to the point.

mycomplab

Visit *mycomplab.com* for more resources as well as exercises on public writing.

14a Writing business letters and résumés

When you write for business, you are addressing busy people who want to see quickly why you are writing and how they should respond to you. Follow these general guidelines:

- **State your purpose right at the start.**
- **Be straightforward, clear, concise, objective, and courteous.**
- **Observe conventions of grammar and usage,** which make your writing clear and impress your reader with your care.

1 Business letter format

For any business letter, use either unlined white paper measuring 8½″ × 11″ or what is called letterhead stationery with your address printed at the top of the sheet. Type the letter single-spaced (with double spacing between elements) on only one side of a sheet.

A common business-letter form is illustrated on the next page:

- **The *return-address heading* gives your address and the date.** Do not include your name. If you are using stationery with a printed heading, you need only give the date.
- **The *inside address* shows the name, title, and complete address of the person you are writing to.**
- **The *salutation* greets the addressee.** Whenever possible, address your letter to a specific person. (Call the company or department to ask whom to address.) If you can't find a person's name, then use a job title (*Dear Human Resources Manager, Dear Customer Service Manager*) or use a general salutation (*Dear Smythe Shoes*). Use *Ms.* as the title for a woman when she has no other title, when you don't know how she prefers to be addressed, or when you know that she prefers *Ms.*
- **The *body* contains the substance.** Instead of indenting the first line of each paragraph, double-space between paragraphs.
- **The *close* should reflect the level of formality in the salutation:** *Respectfully, Cordially, Yours truly,* and *Sincerely* are more formal closes; *Regards* and *Best wishes* are less formal.
- **The *signature* has two parts:** your name typed four lines below the close, and your handwritten signature in the space between. Give your name as you sign checks and other documents.
- **Include any additional information below the signature,** such as *Enc.* (indicating an enclosure with the letter) or *cc: Margaret Zusky* (indicating that a copy is being sent to the person named).

Use an envelope that will accommodate the letter once it is folded horizontally in thirds. The envelope should show your name and address in the upper left corner and the addressee's name, title,

Business letter (job application)

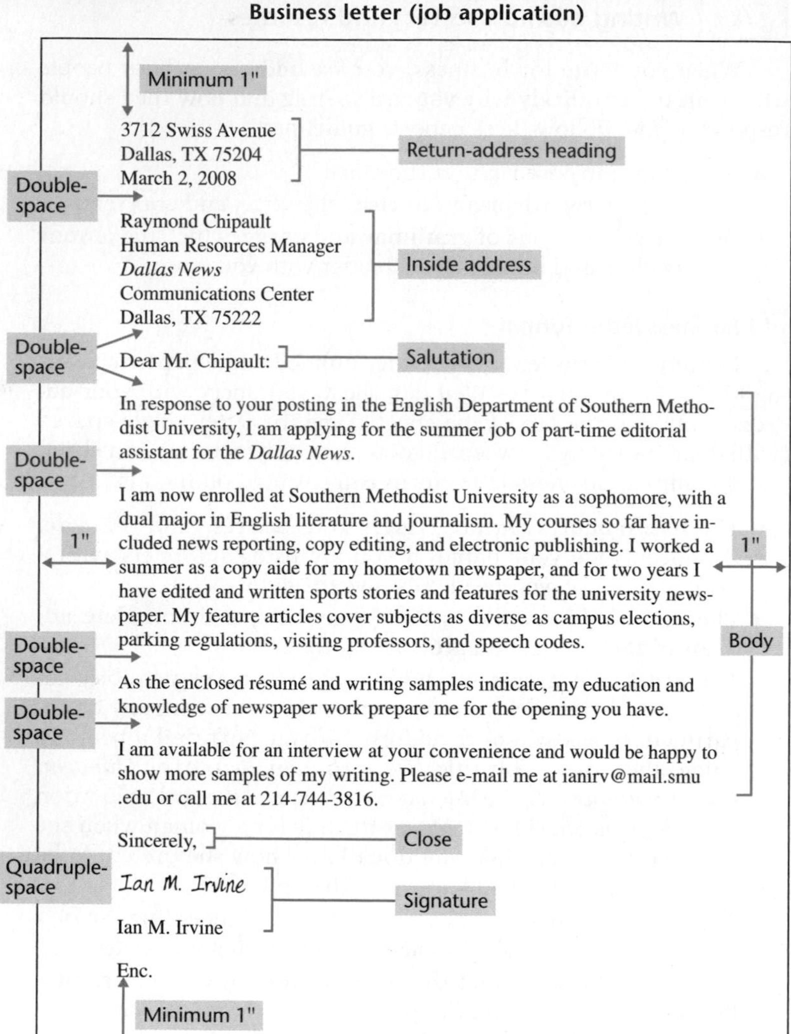
Minimum 1"

3712 Swiss Avenue
Dallas, TX 75204
March 2, 2008

Raymond Chipault
Human Resources Manager
Dallas News
Communications Center
Dallas, TX 75222

Dear Mr. Chipault:

In response to your posting in the English Department of Southern Methodist University, I am applying for the summer job of part-time editorial assistant for the *Dallas News*.

I am now enrolled at Southern Methodist University as a sophomore, with a dual major in English literature and journalism. My courses so far have included news reporting, copy editing, and electronic publishing. I worked a summer as a copy aide for my hometown newspaper, and for two years I have edited and written sports stories and features for the university newspaper. My feature articles cover subjects as diverse as campus elections, parking regulations, visiting professors, and speech codes.

As the enclosed résumé and writing samples indicate, my education and knowledge of newspaper work prepare me for the opening you have.

I am available for an interview at your convenience and would be happy to show more samples of my writing. Please e-mail me at ianirv@mail.smu .edu or call me at 214-744-3816.

Sincerely,

Ian M. Irvine

Ian M. Irvine

Enc.

and address in the center. For easy machine reading, the United States Postal Service recommends all capital letters and no punctuation (spaces separate the elements on a line), as in this address:

RAYMOND CHIPAULT
HUMAN RESOURCES MANAGER
DALLAS NEWS
COMMUNICATIONS CENTER
DALLAS TX 75222-0188

2 Job-application letter

The sample on the preceding page illustrates the key features of a job-application letter:

- **Interpret your résumé for the particular job.** Don't detail your entire résumé, reciting your job history. Instead, highlight and reshape only the relevant parts.
- **Announce at the outset what job you seek and how you heard about it.**
- **Include any special reason you have for applying,** such as a specific career goal.
- **Summarize your qualifications for this particular job,** including relevant facts about education and employment history and emphasizing notable accomplishments. Mention that additional information appears in an accompanying résumé.
- **Describe your availability.** At the end of the letter, mention that you are free for an interview at the convenience of the addressee, or specify when you will be available (for instance, when your current job or classes leave you free, or when you could travel to the employer's city).

3 Résumé

The résumé that accompanies a job application should provide information in table format that allows a potential employer to evaluate your qualifications. The résumé should include your name and address, a career objective, your education and employment history, special skills or awards, and information about how to obtain your references. Fit all the information on one uncrowded page unless your education and experience are extensive. The sample on the next page gives guidelines for a résumé that you submit in print.

Employers may ask for an electronic version of your résumé so that they can add it to a computerized database of applicants. The employers may scan your printed résumé to convert it to an electronic file, which they can then store in an appropriate database, or they may request that you embed your résumé in an e-mail message. To produce a scannable or electronic résumé, follow the guidelines below and consult the sample on p. 133.

- **Keep the design simple for accurate scanning or electronic transmittal.** Avoid images, unusual type, more than one column, vertical or horizontal lines, italics, and underlining.
- **Use concise, specific words to describe your skills and experience.** The employer's computer may use keywords (often nouns) to identify the résumés of suitable job candidates, and you want to ensure that your résumé includes the appropriate

Résumé (print)

Name and contact information	***Ian M. Irvine*** — 3712 Swiss Avenue Dallas, TX 75204 214-744-3816 ianirv@mail.smu.edu
Career objective stated simply and clearly	***Position desired*** — Part-time editorial assistant.
Education before work experience for most college students	***Education*** — *Southern Methodist University*, 2006 to present. Current standing: sophomore. Major: English literature and journalism. Journalism courses: news reporting, copy editing, electronic publishing, communication arts, broadcast journalism. *Abilene (Texas) Senior High School*, 2002-06. Graduated with academic, college-preparatory degree.
Headings marking sections, set off with space and highlighting Conventional use of capital letters: yes for proper nouns and after periods; no for job titles, course names, department names, and so on	***Employment history*** — 2006 to present. Reporter, *Daily Campus*, student newspaper of Southern Methodist University. Write regular coverage of baseball, track, and soccer teams. Write feature stories on campus policies and events. Edit sports news, campus listings, features. Summer 2007. Copy aide, *Abilene Reporter-News*. Assisted reporters with copy routing and research. Summer 2006. Painter, Longhorn Painters, Abilene. Prepared and painted exteriors and interiors of houses.
	Special skills — Fluent in Spanish. Proficient in Internet research and word processing.
Standard, consistent type font	***References*** — Available on request: Placement Office Southern Methodist University Dallas, TX 75275

keywords. Name your specific skills—for example, the computer programs you can operate—and write concretely with words like *manager* (not *person with responsibility for*) and *reporter* (not *staff member who reports*). Look for likely keywords in the employer's description of the job you seek.

4 Electronic communication

Electronic communication—mainly e-mail and faxes—adds a few twists to business writing. E-mail now plays such a prominent

Résumé (scannable or electronic)

Ian M. Irvine
3712 Swiss Avenue
Dallas, TX 75204
214-744-3816
ianirv@mail.smu.edu

KEYWORDS: Editor, editorial assistant, publishing, electronic publishing.

OBJECTIVE
Part-time editorial assistant.

EDUCATION
Southern Methodist University, 2006 to present.
Major: English literature and journalism.
Journalism courses: news reporting, copy editing, electronic publishing, communication arts, broadcast journalism.

Abilene (Texas) Senior High School, 2002-06.
Academic, college preparatory degree.

EMPLOYMENT HISTORY
Reporter, Daily Campus, Southern Methodist University, 2006 to present.
Writer of articles for student newspaper on sports teams, campus policies, and local events. Editor of sports news, campus listings, and features.

Copy aide, Abilene Reporter-News, Abilene, summer 2007.
Assistant to reporters, routing copy and doing research.

Painter, Longhorn Painters, Abilene, summer 2006.
Preparation and painting of exteriors and interiors of houses.

SPECIAL SKILLS
Fluent in Spanish.
Proficient in Internet research and word processing.

REFERENCES
Available on request:
Placement Office
Southern Methodist University
Dallas, TX 75275

Accurate keywords, allowing the employer to place the résumé into an appropriate database

Simple design, avoiding unusual type, italics, multiple columns, decorative lines, and images

Standard font easily read by scanners

Every line aligning at left margin

role in communication of all sorts that it is discussed extensively as part of writing online (see pp. 116–18). Generally, the standards for business e-mail are the same as for other business correspondence.

Faxes follow closely the formats of print documents, but there are unique concerns:

- **Consider legibility.** Small type, photographs, horizontal lines, and other elements that look fine on your copy may not be legible to the addressee.

- **Include a cover sheet.** Most faxes require a cover sheet with the addressee's name, company, and fax number; the date, time, and subject; your own name and fax and telephone numbers; and the total number of pages (including the cover sheet) in the fax.
- **Advise your addressee to expect a fax.** Fax transmissions can go astray. The advice is essential if the fax is confidential, because the machine is often shared.
- **Consider urgency.** Transmission by fax can imply that the correspondence is urgent. If yours isn't, you may want to use the mail instead.

14b Writing memos, reports, and proposals

1 Memos

Business memorandums (memos, for short) address people within the same organization. Most memos deal briefly with a specific topic, such as an answer to a question or an evaluation.

Both the form and the structure of a memo are designed to get to the point and dispose of it quickly (see the sample on the next page). State your reason for writing in the first sentence. Devote the first paragraph to a concise presentation of your answer, conclusion, or evaluation. In the rest of the memo explain your reasoning or evidence. Use headings or lists as appropriate to highlight key information.

2 Reports and proposals

Reports and proposals are text-heavy documents, sometimes lengthy, that convey information such as the results of research, a plan for action, or a recommendation for change. As with other business correspondence, you will prepare a report or proposal for a specific purpose, and you will be addressing interested but busy readers.

Reports and proposals usually divide into sections. The sections vary depending on the purpose of the document, but usually they include an overview or summary, which tells the reader what the document is about; a statement of the problem or need, which justifies the report or proposal; a statement of the plan or solution, which responds to the need or problem; and a recommendation or evaluation. Consider the following guidelines as you prepare a report or proposal:

- **Do your research.** The standard formats of reports and proposals require you to be well informed, so be alert to where you have enough information or where you don't.
- **Focus on the purpose of each section.** Stick to the point of each section, saying only what you need to say, even if you have

Business memo

Bigelow Wax Company

TO: Aileen Rosen, Director of Sales
FROM: Patricia Phillips, Territory 12 *PP*
DATE: March 17, 2008
SUBJECT: 2007 sales of Quick Wax in Territory 12

Heading: company's name, addressee's name, writer's name and initials, date, and subject description

Since it was introduced in January 2007, Quick Wax has been unsuccessful in Territory 12 and has not affected the sales of our Easy Shine. Discussions with customers and my own analysis of Quick Wax suggest three reasons for its failure to compete with our product.

Body: single-spaced with double spacing between paragraphs; paragraphs not indented

1. Quick Wax has not received the promotion necessary for a new product. Advertising—primarily on radio—has been sporadic and has not developed a clear, consistent image for the product. In addition, the Quick Wax sales representative in Territory 12 is new and inexperienced; he is not known to customers, and his sales pitch (which I once overheard) is weak. As far as I can tell, his efforts are not supported by phone calls or mailings from his home office.

2. When Quick Wax does make it to the store shelves, buyers do not choose it over our product. Though priced competitively with our product, Quick Wax is poorly packaged. The container seems smaller than ours, though in fact it holds the same eight ounces. The lettering on the Quick Wax package (red on blue) is difficult to read, in contrast to the white-on-green lettering on the Easy Shine package.

3. Our special purchase offers and my increased efforts to serve existing customers have had the intended effect of keeping customers satisfied with our product and reducing their inclination to stock something new.

Copies: L. Mendes, Director of Marketing
J. MacGregor, Customer Service Manager

People receiving copies

additional information. Each section should accomplish its purpose and contribute to the whole.

- **Follow an appropriate format.** In many businesses, reports and proposals have specific formatting requirements. If you are unsure about the requirements, ask your supervisor.

A sample report appears on the next page. For a sample proposal, follow the links in the e-book version of this handbook at *mycomplab.com*.

Report

Descriptive title conveying report's contents

Standard format: summary, statement of the problem, solutions, and (not shown) recommendations

Major sections delineated by headings

Formal tone, appropriate to a business-writing situation

Single spacing with double spacing between paragraphs and around the list

Bulleted list emphasizing alternative solutions

Canada Geese at ABC Institute: An Environmental Problem

Summary

The flock of Canada geese on and around ABC Institute's grounds has grown dramatically in recent years to become a nuisance and an environmental problem. This report reviews the problem, considers possible solutions, and proposes that ABC Institute and the US Fish and Wildlife Service cooperate to reduce the flock by humane means.

The Problem

Canada geese began living at Taylor Lake next to ABC Institute when they were relocated there in 1985 by the state game department. As a nonmigratory flock, the geese are present year-round, with the highest population each year occurring in early spring. In recent years the flock has grown dramatically. The Audubon Society's annual Christmas bird census shows a thirty-fold increase from the 37 geese counted in 1986 to the 1125 counted in 2008.

The principal environmental problem caused by the geese is pollution of grass and water by defecation. Geese droppings cover the ABC Institute's grounds as well as the park's picnicking areas. The runoff from these droppings into Taylor Lake has substantially affected the quality of the lake's water, so that local authorities have twice (2007 and 2008) issued warnings against swimming.

Possible Solutions

The goose overpopulation and resulting environmental problems have several possible solutions:

- Harass the geese with dogs and audiovisual effects (light and noise) so that the geese choose to leave. This solution is inhumane to the geese and unpleasant for human neighbors.
- Feed the geese a chemical that will weaken the shells of their eggs and thus reduce growth of the flock. This solution is inhumane to the geese and also impractical, because geese are long-lived.
- Kill adult geese. This solution is, obviously, inhumane to the geese.
- Thin the goose population by trapping and removing many geese (perhaps 600) to areas less populated by humans, such as wildlife preserves.

Though costly (see figures below), the last solution is the most humane. It would be harmless to the geese, provided that sizable netted enclosures are used for traps. [Discussion of solution and "Recommendations" section follow.]

14c Writing for community work

At some point in your life, you're likely to volunteer for a community organization such as a soup kitchen, a daycare center, or a literacy program. Many college courses involve service learning, in which you do such volunteer work, write about the experience for your course, and write *for* the organization you're helping.

The writing you do for a community group may range from flyers to grant proposals. Two guidelines will help you prepare effective projects like the ones here, for a literacy program.

- **Craft each document for its purpose and audience.** You are trying to achieve a specific aim with your readers, and the approach and tone you use will influence their responses. If, for example, you are writing letters to local businesses to raise funds for a homeless shelter, bring to mind the people who will

Flyer

FIRST ANNUAL AWARDS DINNER

WHEN

Friday night
May 23
7:30 to 10:30

WHERE

Suite 42
Springfield VA Hospital

WHO

Students, tutors, and their families are invited to join us for an evening of food and music as we celebrate their efforts and accomplishments.

For information contact ReadingWorks 209-556-1212

ReadingWorks of Springfield Veterans Administration Hospital
111 South Springdale Drive
Springfield, MI 45078

Large type and color focusing a distant reader's attention on important information: what's happening, when, where, and who is invited

White space drawing viewers' eyes to main message and creating flow among elements

Color highlighting only key information

Less important information set in smaller type

read your letter. How can you best persuade those readers to donate money?

- **Expect to work with others.** Much public writing is the work of more than one person. Even if you draft the document on your own, others will review the content, tone, and design. Such collaboration is rewarding, but it sometimes requires patience and goodwill. See **1** pp. 35–37 for advice on collaborating.

Newsletter

Multicolumn format allowing room for headings, articles, and other elements on a single page

Two-column heading emphasizing the main article

Elements helping readers skim for highlights: spacing, varied font sizes, lines, and a bulleted list

Color focusing readers' attention on banner, headlines, and table of contents

Lively but uncluttered overall appearance

Box in the first column highlighting table of contents

ReadingWorks

Springfield Veterans Administration Hospital SUMMER 2008

From the director

Can you help? With more and more learners in the ReadingWorks program, we need more and more tutors. You may know people who would be interested in participating in the program, if only they knew about it.

Those of you who have been tutoring VA patients in reading and writing know both the great need you fulfill and the great benefits you bring to the students. New tutors need no special skills—we'll provide the training—only patience and an interest in helping others.

We've scheduled an orientation meeting for Friday, September 12, at 6:30 PM. Please come and bring a friend who is willing to contribute a couple of hours a week to our work.

Thanks,
Kate Goodman

IN THIS ISSUE

First Annual Awards Dinner	1
New Guidelines on PTSD	1
Textbooks	2
Lesson Planning	2
Dyslexia Workshop	2
Support for Tutors	3
Writing by Students	3
Calendar of Events	4

FIRST ANNUAL AWARDS DINNER

A festive night for students and tutors

The first annual ReadingWorks Awards Dinner on May 23rd was a great success. Springfield's own Golden Fork provided tasty food and Amber Allen supplied lively music. The students decorated Suite 42 on the theme of books and reading. In all, 127 people attended.

The highlight of the night was the awards ceremony. Nine students, recommended by their tutors, received certificates recognizing their efforts and special accomplishments in learning to read and write:

Ramon Berva
Edward Byar
David Dunbar
Tony Garnier
Chris Guigni
Akili Haynes
Josh Livingston
Alex Obeld
B. J. Resnansky

In addition, nine tutors received certificates commemorating five years of service to ReadingWorks:

Anita Crumpton
Felix Cruz-Rivera
Bette Elgen
Kayleah Bortoluzzi
Harriotte Henderson
Ben Obiso
Meggie Puente
Max Smith
Sara Villante

Congratulations to all!

PTSD: New Guidelines

Most of us are working with veterans who have been diagnosed with post-traumatic stress disorder. Because this disorder is often complicated by alcoholism, depression, anxiety, and other problems, the National Center for PTSD has issued some guidelines for helping PTSD patients in ways that reduce their stress.

- The hospital must know your tutoring schedule, and you need to sign in and out before and after each tutoring session.
- To protect patients' privacy, meet them only in designated visiting and tutoring areas, never in their rooms.
- Treat patients with dignity and respect, even when (as sometimes happens) they grow frustrated and angry. Seek help from a nurse or orderly if you need it.

Brochure

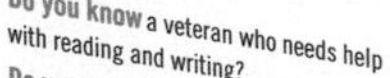

Do you know a veteran who needs help with reading and writing?

Do you need to improve your reading and writing skills to get a job?

ReadingWorks can make a difference. We organize volunteers to help military veterans achieve literacy and to prepare them for life-long learning.

For more information about our services, call Kate Goodman at 209-556-1212 or visit www.readingworks.org.

ReadingWorks
Springfield VA Hospital
111 South Springdale Drive
Springfield, MI 45078

ReadingWorks
Springfield VA Hospital

Helping military veterans achieve literacy

Panel 2: The right page when the cover is opened, the first one readers see, containing key information

Panel 6: The back, usually including the return address and space for a mailing label and postage

Panel 1: The cover, drawing readers' attention to the group's name, purpose, and affiliation

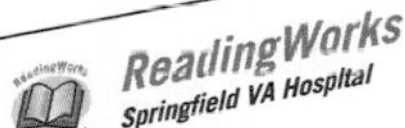

ReadingWorks
Springfield VA Hospital

OUR MISSION

- We provide workshops and formal lessons for veterans wishing to develop their reading and writing skills
- We train volunteers to tutor veterans one on one.
- We maintain outreach programs to provide access to literacy training for all veterans.
- We create literacy resources and share them with others who promote literacy for veterans.

OUR SERVICES

One-on-one tutoring
One to three hours a week with a trained volunteer tutor.

Workshops and classes
Small-group meetings centered on reading and writing, computer skills, and English as a second language.

Library
Books and other resources for students at various literacy levels.

Computer lab
Five computers with high-speed Internet access and a full range of software.

OUR TUTORS

The goodwill and generosity of our volunteer tutors allows us to reach out to those who have served our country.

If you or someone you know can join our team, contact Kate Goodman at 209-556-1212.

Hours
12:00 to 8:00, Mon., Wed.
9:00 to 5:00, Tues., Thurs., Fri.

Eligibility
Any veteran of the US military is eligible for our services.

How to reach us
Springfield VA Hospital
Room 172, first floor
111 South Springdale Drive
Springfield, MI 45078
209-556-1212
www.readingworks.org

Panel 3: The left page when the cover is opened, reinforcing the message of panel 2

Varied type, color, and photographs, adding visual interest and focusing readers' attention

Panels 4 and 5: The inside panels, containing contact information and other details

PART 3

Clarity and Style

15 Emphasis *143*

16 Parallelism *151*

17 Variety and Details *154*

18 Appropriate and Exact Language *158*

19 Completeness *171*

20 Conciseness *172*

PART 3

Clarity and Style

15 Emphasis *143*

- **a** Effective subjects and verbs *143*
- **b** Sentence beginnings and endings *145*
- **c** Coordination *147*
- **d** Subordination *149*

16 Parallelism *151*

- **a** With *and, but, or, nor, yet* *151*
- **b** With *both . . . and, not . . . but,* etc. *152*
- **c** In comparisons *153*
- **d** With lists, headings, and outlines *153*

17 Variety and Details *154*

- **a** Sentence length *154*
- **b** Sentence structure *154*
- **c** Details *157*

18 Appropriate and Exact Language *158*

- **a** Appropriate language *158*
- **b** Exact language *165*

19 Completeness *171*

- **a** Compounds *171*
- **b** Needed words *172*

20 Conciseness *172*

- **a** Focusing on subject and verb *173*
- **b** Cutting empty words *174*
- **c** Cutting repetition *175*
- **d** Reducing clauses and phrases *175*
- **e** Revising *there is, here is,* or *it is* *176*
- **f** Combining sentences *176*
- **g** Rewriting jargon *176*

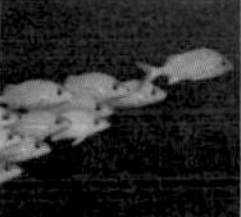

15 Emphasis

Emphatic writing leads readers to see your main ideas both within and among sentences. You can achieve emphasis by attending to your subjects and verbs (below), using sentence beginnings and endings (p. 145), coordinating equally important ideas (p. 147), and subordinating less important ideas (p. 149). In addition, emphatic writing is concise writing, the subject of Chapter 20.

Grammar checkers A grammar checker may spot some problems with emphasis, such as nouns made from verbs, passive voice, wordy phrases, and long sentences that may also be flabby and unemphatic. However, no checker can help you identify the important ideas in your sentences or determine whether those ideas receive appropriate emphasis.

15a Using subjects and verbs effectively

The heart of every sentence is its subject, which usually names the actor, and its predicate verb, which usually specifies the subject's action: *Children* [subject] *grow* [verb]. When these elements do not identify the key actor and action in the sentence, readers must find that information elsewhere and the sentence may be wordy and unemphatic.

In the following sentences, the subjects and verbs are underlined.

Unemphatic The intention of the company was to expand its workforce. A proposal was also made to diversify the backgrounds and abilities of employees.

These sentences are unemphatic because their key ideas do not appear in their subjects and verbs. In the revision on the next page the sentences are not only clearer but more concise.

Key terms

subject Who or what a sentence is about: *Biologists often study animals.* (See **4** pp. 186–87.)

predicate The part of a sentence containing a verb that asserts something about the subject: *Biologists often study animals.* (See **4** pp. 186–87.)

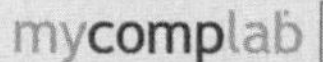

Visit *mycomplab.com* for more resources as well as exercises on emphasis.

Revised The company intended to expand its workforce. It also proposed to diversify the backgrounds and abilities of employees.

The constructions discussed below and opposite usually drain meaning from a sentence's subject and verb.

Nouns made from verbs

Nouns made from verbs can obscure the key actions of sentences and add words. These nouns include *intention* (from *intend*), *proposal* (from *propose*), *decision* (from *decide*), *expectation* (from *expect*), and *inclusion* (from *include*).

Unemphatic After the company made a decision to hire more workers with disabilities, its next step was the construction of wheelchair ramps and other facilities.

Revised After the company decided to hire more workers with disabilities, it next constructed wheelchair ramps and other facilities.

Weak verbs

Weak verbs, such as *made* and *was* in the unemphatic sentence above, tend to stall sentences just where they should be moving and often bury key actions:

Unemphatic The company is now the leader among businesses in complying with the 1990 disabilities act. Its officers make frequent speeches on the act to business groups.

Revised The company now leads other businesses in complying with the 1990 disabilities act. Its officers frequently speak on the act to business groups.

Forms of *be, have,* and *make* are often weak, but don't try to eliminate every use of them: *be* and *have* are essential as helping verbs (*is going, has written*); *be* links subjects and words describing them (*Planes are noisy*); and *have* and *make* have independent meanings (among them "possess" and "force," respectively). But do consider replacing forms of *be, have,* and *make* when one of the words following the verb could be made into a strong verb itself, as in the following examples.

Key terms

noun A word that names a person, thing, quality, place, or idea: *student, desk, happiness, city, democracy.* (See **4** pp. 180–81.)

helping verb A verb used with another verb to convey time, obligation, and other meanings: *was drilling, would have been drilling.* (See **4** p. 183.)

Unemphatic	**Emphatic**
was influential	influenced
is a glorification	glorifies
have a preference	prefer
had the appearance	appeared, seemed
made a claim	claimed

Passive voice

Verbs in the passive voice state actions received by, not performed by, their subjects. Thus the passive de-emphasizes the true actor of the sentence, sometimes omitting it entirely. Generally, prefer the active voice, in which the subject performs the action. (See also **4** pp. 216–17 for help with editing the passive voice.)

Unemphatic The 1990 law is seen by most businesses as fair, but the costs of complying have sometimes been objected to.

Revised Most businesses see the 1990 law as fair, but some have objected to the costs of complying.

15b Using sentence beginnings and endings

Readers automatically seek a writer's principal meaning in the main clause of a sentence—essentially, in the subject that names the actor and in the verb that usually specifies the action (see p. 143). Thus you can help readers understand the meaning you intend by controlling the information in your subjects and the relation of the main clause to any modifiers attached to it.

Old and new information

Generally, readers expect the beginning of a sentence to contain information that they already know or that you have already introduced. They then look to the ending for new information. In the

Key terms

passive voice The verb form when the subject names the *receiver* of the verb's action: *The house was destroyed by the tornado.*

active voice The verb form when the subject names the *performer* of the verb's action: *The tornado destroyed the house.*

main clause A word group that can stand alone as a sentence, containing a subject and a predicate and not beginning with a subordinating word: *The books were expensive.* (See **4** p. 193.)

modifier A word or word group that describes another word or word group: *sweet candy, running in the park.* (See **4** pp. 183–84 and 190–92.)

unemphatic passage below, the second and third sentences both begin with new topics, while the old topics appear at the ends of the sentences. The pattern of the passage is A→B. C→B. D→A.

Unemphatic Education (A) often means controversy (B) these days, with rising costs and constant complaints about its inadequacies. But the value (C) of schooling should not be obscured by the controversy (B). The single best means (D) of economic advancement, despite its shortcomings, remains education (A).

In the more emphatic revision, the old information begins each sentence and new information ends the sentence. The passage follows the pattern A→B. B→C. A→D.

Revised Education (A) often means controversy (B) these days, with rising costs and constant complaints about its inadequacies. But the controversy (B) should not obscure the value (C) of schooling. Education (A) remains, despite its shortcomings, the single best means of economic advancement (D).

Cumulative and periodic sentences

You can call attention to information by placing it first or last in a sentence, reserving the middle for incidentals:

Unemphatic Education remains the single best means of economic advancement, despite its shortcomings. [Emphasizes shortcomings.]

Revised Despite its shortcomings, education remains the single best means of economic advancement. [Emphasizes advancement more than shortcomings.]

Revised Education remains, despite its shortcomings, the single best means of economic advancement. [De-emphasizes shortcomings.]

A sentence that adds modifiers to the main clause is called **cumulative** because it accumulates information as it proceeds:

Cumulative Education has no equal in opening minds, instilling values, and creating opportunities.

Cumulative Most of the Great American Desert is made up of bare rock, rugged cliffs, mesas, canyons, mountains, separated from one another by broad flat basins covered with sunbaked mud and alkali, supporting a sparse and measured growth of sagebrush or creosote or saltbush, depending on location and elevation. —Edward Abbey

The opposite kind of sentence, called **periodic,** saves the main clause until just before the end (the period) of the sentence. Everything before the main clause points toward it:

Periodic In opening minds, instilling values, and creating opportunities, education has no equal.

Periodic With people from all over the world—Korean doctors, Jamaican cricket players, Vietnamese engineers, Haitian cabdrivers, Chinese grocers, Indian restaurant owners—the American mosaic is continually changing.

The periodic sentence creates suspense by reserving important information for the end. But readers should already have an idea of the sentence's subject—because it was mentioned in the preceding sentence—so that they know what the opening modifiers describe.

15c Using coordination

Use **coordination** to show that two or more elements in a sentence are equally important in meaning and thus to clarify the relationship between them:

Ways to coordinate information in sentences

- **Link main clauses with a comma and a coordinating conjunction:** *and, but, or, nor, for, so, yet.*

  Independence Hall in Philadelphia is faithfully restored, but many years ago it was in bad shape.

- **Relate main clauses with a semicolon alone or a semicolon and a conjunctive adverb:** *however, indeed, thus,* etc.

  The building was standing; however, it suffered from neglect.

- **Within clauses, link words and phrases with a coordinating conjunction:** *and, but, or, nor.*

  The people and officials of the nation were indifferent to independence Hall or took it for granted.

- **Link main clauses, words, or phrases with a correlative conjunction:** *both . . . and, not only . . . but also,* etc.

  People not only took the building for granted but also neglected it.

Grammar checkers A grammar checker may spot some errors in punctuating coordinated elements, and it can usually flag long sentences that may contain excessive coordination. But otherwise a checker can provide little help with coordination because it cannot recognize the relations among ideas in sentences.

1 Coordinating to relate equal ideas

Coordination shows the equality between elements, as illustrated by the examples in the preceding box. At the same time that it clarifies meaning, it can also help smooth choppy sentences:

Choppy sentences We should not rely so heavily on oil. Coal and uranium are also overused. We have a substantial energy resource in the moving waters of our rivers. Smaller streams add to the total volume of water. The resource renews itself. Oil and coal are irreplaceable. Uranium is also irreplaceable. The cost of water does not increase much over time. The costs of coal, oil, and uranium rise dramatically.

The revision groups coal, oil, and uranium and clearly opposes them to water (the connecting words are underlined):

Ideas coordinated We should not rely so heavily on oil, coal, <u>and</u> uranium, <u>for</u> we have a substantial energy resource in the moving waters of our rivers <u>and</u> streams. Oil, coal, <u>and</u> uranium are irreplaceable <u>and</u> thus subject to dramatic cost increases; water, <u>however,</u> is self-renewing <u>and</u> more stable in cost.

2 Coordinating effectively

Use coordination only to express the *equality* of ideas or details. A string of coordinated elements—especially main clauses—implies that all points are equally important:

Excessive coordination The weeks leading up to the resignation of President Nixon were eventful, and the Supreme Court and the Congress closed in on him, and the Senate Judiciary Committee voted to begin impeachment proceedings, and finally the President resigned on August 9, 1974.

Key terms

coordinating conjunctions *And, but, or, nor,* and sometimes *for, so, yet.* (See **4** p. 185.)

conjunctive adverbs Modifiers that describe the relation of the ideas in two clauses, such as *hence, however, indeed,* and *thus.* (See **4** p. 257.)

correlative conjunctions Pairs of connecting words, such as *both . . . and, either . . . or, not only . . . but also.* (See **4** p. 186.)

Such a passage needs editing to stress the important points (underlined below) and to de-emphasize the less important information:

Revised The weeks leading up to the resignation of President Nixon were eventful, as the Supreme Court and the Congress closed in on him and the Senate Judiciary Committee voted to begin impeachment proceedings. Finally, the President resigned on August 9, 1974.

Even within a single sentence, coordination should express a logical equality between ideas:

Faulty John Stuart Mill was a nineteenth-century utilitarian, and he believed that actions should be judged by their usefulness or by the happiness they cause. [The two clauses are not separate and equal: the second expands on the first by explaining what a utilitarian such as Mill believed.]

Revised John Stuart Mill, a nineteenth-century utilitarian, believed that actions should be judged by their usefulness or by the happiness they cause.

15d Using subordination

Use **subordination** to indicate that some elements in a sentence are less important than others for your meaning. Usually, the main idea appears in the main clause, and supporting details appear in subordinate structures:

Ways to subordinate information in sentences

- **Use a subordinate clause beginning with a subordinating word:** *who (whom), that, which, although, because, if,* etc.

  Although some citizens had tried to rescue Independence Hall, they had not gained substantial public support.

  The first strong step was taken by the federal government, which made the building a national monument.

- **Use a phrase.**

  Like most national monuments, Independence Hall is protected by the National Park Service.

  Protecting many popular tourist sites, the service is a highly visible government agency.

- **Use a short modifier.**

  At the red brick Independence Hall, park rangers give guided tours and protect the irreplaceable building from vandalism.

Grammar checkers A grammar checker may spot some errors in punctuating subordinated elements, and it can usually flag long sentences that may contain excessive subordination. But otherwise a checker can provide little help with subordination because it cannot recognize the relations among ideas in sentences.

1 Subordinating to emphasize main ideas

A string of main clauses can make everything in a passage seem equally important:

String of main clauses Computer prices have dropped, and production costs have dropped more slowly, and computer manufacturers have had to struggle, for their profits have been shrinking.

Emphasis comes from keeping the truly important information in the main clause (underlined) and subordinating the less important details:

Revised Because production costs have dropped more slowly than prices, computer manufacturers have had to struggle with shrinking profits.

2 Subordinating effectively

Use subordination only for the less important information in a sentence.

Faulty Ms. Angelo was in her first year of teaching, although she was a better instructor than others with many years of experience.

The preceding sentence suggests that Angelo's inexperience is the main idea, whereas the writer intended to stress her skill *despite* her inexperience. Reducing the inexperience to a subordinate clause and elevating the skill to the main clause (underlined) gives appropriate emphasis:

Revised Although Ms. Angelo was in her first year of teaching, she was a better instructor than others with many years of experience.

Key terms

subordinate clause A word group that contains a subject and verb, begins with a subordinating word such as *because* or *who,* and is not a question: *Words can do damage when they hurt feelings*. (See **4** p. 193.)

phrase A word group that lacks a subject or predicate or both: *Words can do damage by hurting feelings*. (See **4** p. 190.)

Subordination loses its power to organize and emphasize when too much loosely related detail crowds into one long, meandering sentence:

Overloaded The boats that were moored at the dock when the hurricane, which was one of the worst in three decades, struck were ripped from their moorings, because the owners had not been adequately prepared, since the weather service had predicted that the storm would blow out to sea, which they do at this time of year.

The revision stresses important information in the main clauses (underlined):

Revised Struck by one of the worst hurricanes in three decades, the boats at the dock were ripped from their moorings. The owners were unprepared because the weather service had said that hurricanes at this time of year blow out to sea.

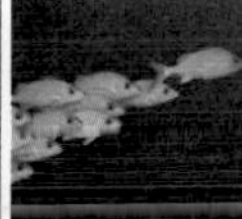

16 Parallelism

Parallelism gives similar grammatical form to sentence elements that have similar function and importance.

The air is dirtied by factories belching smoke
and
cars spewing exhaust.

In this example the two underlined phrases have the same function and importance (both specify sources of air pollution), so they also have the same grammatical construction. Parallelism makes form follow meaning.

Grammar checkers A grammar checker cannot recognize faulty parallelism because it cannot recognize the relations among ideas.

16a Using parallelism with *and, but, or, nor, yet*

The coordinating conjunctions *and, or, nor,* and *yet* always signal a need for parallelism.

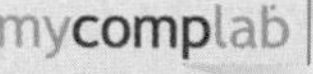

Visit *mycomplab.com* for more resources as well as exercises on parallelism.

The industrial base was shifting and shrinking. [Parallel words.]

Politicians rarely acknowledged the problem or proposed alternatives. [Parallel phrases.]

Industrial workers were understandably disturbed that they were losing their jobs and that no one seemed to care. [Parallel clauses.]

When sentence elements linked by coordinating conjunctions are not parallel in structure, the sentence is awkward and distracting:

Nonparallel	The reasons steel companies kept losing money were that their plants were inefficient, high labor costs, and foreign competition was increasing.
Revised	The reasons steel companies kept losing money were inefficient plants, high labor costs, and increasing foreign competition.
Nonparallel	Success was difficult even for efficient companies because of the shift away from all manufacturing in the United States and the fact that steel production was shifting toward emerging nations.
Revised	Success was difficult even for efficient companies because of the shift away from all manufacturing in the United States and toward steel production in emerging nations.

All the words required by idiom or grammar must be stated in compound constructions (see also p. 171):

Faulty	Given training, workers can acquire the skills and interest in other jobs. [Idiom dictates different prepositions with *skills* and *interest*.]
Revised	Given training, workers can acquire the skills for and interest in other jobs.

16b Using parallelism with *both . . . and, not . . . but,* or another correlative conjunction

Correlative conjunctions stress equality and balance between elements. Parallelism confirms the equality.

Key terms

coordinating conjunctions Words that connect elements of the same kind and importance: *and, but, or, nor,* and sometimes *for, so, yet.* (See **4** p. 185.)

correlative conjunctions Pairs of words that connect elements of the same kind and importance, such as *but . . . and, either . . . or, neither . . . nor, not . . . but, not only . . . but also.* (See **4** p. 186.)

It is not a tax bill but a tax relief bill, providing relief not for the needy but for the greedy.

—Franklin Delano Roosevelt

With correlative conjunctions, the element after the second connector must match the element after the first connector:

Nonparallel Huck Finn learns not only that human beings have an enormous capacity for folly but also enormous dignity. [The first element includes *that human beings have;* the second element does not.]

Revised Huck Finn learns that human beings have not only an enormous capacity for folly but also enormous dignity. [Repositioning *that human beings have* makes the two elements parallel.]

16c Using parallelism in comparisons

Parallelism confirms the likeness or difference between two elements being compared using *than* or *as:*

Nonparallel Huck Finn proves less a bad boy than to be an independent spirit. In the end he is every bit as determined in rejecting help as he is to leave for "the territory."

Revised Huck Finn proves less a bad boy than an independent spirit. In the end he is every bit as determined to reject help as he is to leave for "the territory."

(See also **4** pp. 240–41 on making comparisons logical.)

16d Using parallelism with lists, headings, and outlines

The items in a list or outline are coordinate and should be parallel. Parallelism is essential in a formal topic outline and in the headings that divide a paper into sections. (See **1** pp. 19–20 and 58–59 for more on outlines and headings.)

Nonparallel	**Revised**
Changes in Renaissance England	Changes in Renaissance England
1. Extension of trade routes	1. Extension of trade routes
2. Merchant class became more powerful	2. Increased power of the merchant class
3. The death of feudalism	3. Death of feudalism
4. Upsurging of the arts	4. Upsurge of the arts
5. Religious quarrels began	5. Rise of religious quarrels

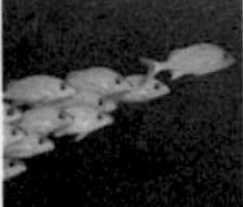

17 Variety and Details

Writing that's interesting as well as clear has at least two features: the sentences vary in length and structure, and they are well textured with details.

Grammar checkers Some grammar checkers will flag long sentences, and you can check for appropriate variety in a series of such sentences. But generally these programs cannot help you see where variety may be needed because they cannot recognize the relative importance and complexity of your ideas.

17a Varying sentence length

In most contemporary writing, sentences tend to vary from about ten to about forty words. When sentences are all at one extreme or the other, readers may have difficulty focusing on main ideas and seeing the relations among them.

- **Long sentences.** If most of your sentences contain thirty-five words or more, your main ideas may not stand out from the details that support them. Break some of the long sentences into shorter, simpler ones.
- **Short sentences.** If most of your sentences contain fewer than ten or fifteen words, all your ideas may seem equally important and the links between them may not be clear. Try combining sentences with coordination (p. 147) and subordination (p. 149) to show relationships and stress main ideas over supporting information.

17b Varying sentence structure

A passage will be monotonous if all its sentences follow the same pattern, like soldiers marching in a parade. Try the following techniques for varying structure.

1 Subordination

A string of main clauses in simple or compound sentences can be especially plodding.

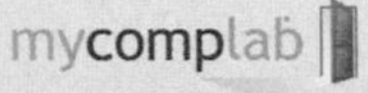

Visit *mycomplab.com* for more resources on variety and details.

Monotonous The moon is now drifting away from the earth. It moves away at the rate of about one inch a year. This movement is lengthening our days. They increase a thousandth of a second every century. Forty-seven of our present days will someday make up a month. We might eventually lose the moon altogether. Such great planetary movement rightly concerns astronomers, but it need not worry us. It will take 50 million years.

Enliven such writing—and make the main ideas stand out—by expressing the less important information in subordinate clauses and phrases. In the revision below, underlining indicates subordinate structures that used to be main clauses:

Revised The moon is now drifting away from the earth about one inch a year. At a thousandth of a second every century, this movement is lengthening our days. Forty-seven of our present days will someday make up a month, if we don't eventually lose the moon altogether. Such great planetary movement rightly concerns astronomers, but it need not worry us. It will take 50 million years.

2 Sentence combining

As the preceding example shows, subordinating to achieve variety often involves combining short, choppy sentences into longer units that link related information and stress main ideas. Here is another unvaried passage:

Monotonous Astronomy may seem a remote science. It may seem to have little to do with people's daily lives. Many astronomers find otherwise. They see their science as soothing. It gives perspective to everyday routines and problems.

Key terms

main clause A word group that can stand alone as a sentence because it contains a subject and a predicate and does not begin with a subordinating word: *Tourism is an industry. It brings in over $2 billion a year.* (See **4** p. 193.)

subordinate clause A word group that contains a subject and predicate, begins with a subordinating word such as *because* or *who,* and is not a question: *Tourism is an industry that brings in over $2 billion a year.* (See **4** p. 193.)

phrase A word group that lacks a subject or predicate or both: *Tourism is an Industry valued at over $2 billion a year.* (See **4** p. 190.)

Combining five sentences into one, the following revision is both clearer and easier to read. Underlining highlights the changes.

Revised Astronomy may seem a remote science having little to do with people's daily lives, but many astronomers find their science soothing because it gives perspective to everyday routines and problems.

3 Varied sentence beginnings

An English sentence often begins with its subject, which generally captures old information from a preceding sentence (see p. 145):

The defendant's lawyer was determined to break the prosecution's witness. He relentlessly cross-examined the stubborn witness for a week.

However, an unbroken sequence of sentences beginning with the subject quickly becomes monotonous:

Monotonous The defendant's lawyer was determined to break the prosecution's witness. He relentlessly cross-examined the witness for a week. The witness had expected to be dismissed within an hour and was visibly irritated. She did not cooperate. She was reprimanded by the judge.

Beginning some of these sentences with other expressions improves readability and clarity:

Revised The defendant's lawyer was determined to break the prosecution's witness. For a week he relentlessly cross-examined the witness. Expecting to be dismissed within an hour, the witness was visibly irritated. She did not cooperate. Indeed, she was reprimanded by the judge.

The underlined expressions represent the most common choices for varying sentence beginnings:

- **Adverb modifiers,** such as *For a week* (modifies the verb *cross-examined*).
- **Adjective modifiers,** such as *Expecting to be dismissed within an hour* (modifies *witness*).
- **Transitional expressions,** such as *Indeed.* (See **1** pp. 43–44 for a list.)

Key terms

adverb A word or word group that describes a verb, an adjective, another adverb, or a whole sentence: *dressed sharply, clearly unhappy, soaring from the mountain.* (See **4** pp. 183–84.)

adjective A word or word group that describes a noun or pronoun: *sweet smile, certain someone.* (See **4** p. 183.)

CULTURE LANGUAGE In standard American English, placing certain adverb modifiers at the beginning of a sentence requires you to alter the normal subject-verb order as well. The most common of these modifiers are negatives, including *seldom, rarely, in no case, not since,* and *not until.*

	adverb subject verb phrase
Faulty	Seldom a witness has held the stand so long.
	adverb helping verb subject main verb
Revised	Seldom has a witness held the stand so long.

4 Varied word order

Occasionally you can vary a sentence and emphasize it at the same time by inverting the usual order of parts:

> A dozen witnesses testified for the prosecution, and the defense attorney barely questioned eleven of them. The twelfth, however, he grilled. [Normal word order: *He grilled the twelfth, however.*]

Inverted sentences used without need are artificial. Use them only when emphasis demands.

17c Adding details

Relevant details such as facts and examples create the texture and life that keep readers awake and help them grasp your meaning. For instance:

Flat Constructed after World War II, Levittown, New York, consisted of thousands of houses in two basic styles. Over the decades, residents have altered the houses so dramatically that the original styles are often unrecognizable.

Detailed Constructed on potato fields after World War II, Levittown, New York, consisted of more than seventeen thousand houses in Cape Cod and ranch styles. Over the decades, residents have added expansive front porches, punched dormer windows through roofs, converted garages to sun porches, and otherwise altered the houses so dramatically that the original styles are often unrecognizable.

18 Appropriate and Exact Language

The clarity and effectiveness of your writing will depend greatly on the use of language that is appropriate for your writing situation (below) and that expresses your meaning exactly (p. 165).

18a Choosing appropriate language

Appropriate language suits your writing situation—your subject, purpose, and audience. In most college and career writing you should rely on what's called **standard American English,** the dialect of English normally expected and used in school, business, the professions, government, and the communications media. (For more on its role in academic writing, see **2** pp. 94–96.)

The vocabulary of standard American English is huge, allowing expression of an infinite range of ideas and feelings; but it does exclude words that only some groups of people use, understand, or find inoffensive. Some of these more limited vocabularies should be avoided altogether; others should be used cautiously and in relevant situations, as when aiming for a special effect with an audience you know will appreciate it. Whenever you doubt a word's status, consult a dictionary (see p. 165).

Grammar checkers A grammar checker can often be set to flag potentially inappropriate words, such as nonstandard dialect, slang, colloquialisms, and gender-specific terms (*manmade, mailman*). However, the checker can flag only words listed in its dictionary of questionable words. For example, a checker flagged *businessman* as potentially sexist in *A successful businessman puts clients first,* but the checker did not flag *his* in *A successful businessperson listens to his clients.* If you use a checker to review your language, you'll need to determine whether a flagged word is or is not appropriate for your writing situation.

1 Nonstandard dialect 

Like many countries, the United States includes scores of regional, social, and ethnic groups with their own distinct **dialects,** or versions of English. Standard American English is one of those dialects, and so are Black English, Appalachian English, Creole, and

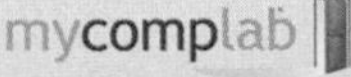

Visit *mycomplab.com* for more resources as well as exercises on appropriate and exact language.

the English of coastal Maine. All the dialects of English share many features, but each also has its own vocabulary, pronunciation, and grammar.

If you speak a dialect of English besides standard American English, be careful about using your dialect in situations where standard English is the norm, such as in academic or business writing. Dialects are not wrong in themselves, but forms imported from one dialect into another may still be perceived as unclear or incorrect. When you know standard English is expected in your writing, edit to eliminate expressions in your dialect that you know (or have been told) differ from standard English. These expressions may include *theirselves, hisn, them books,* and others labeled "nonstandard" by a dictionary. They may also include certain verb forms, as discussed in **4** pp. 199–208. For help identifying and editing nonstandard language, see the CULTURE LANGUAGE Guide just before the back endpapers of this book.

Your participation in the community of standard English does not require you to abandon your own dialect. You may want to use it in writing you do for yourself, such as journals, notes, and drafts, which should be composed as freely as possible. You may want to quote it in an academic paper, as when analyzing or reporting conversation in dialect. And, of course, you will want to use it with others who speak it.

2 Shortcuts of online communication

Rapid communication by e-mail and text or instant messaging encourages some informalities that are inappropriate for academic writing. If you use these media frequently, you may need to proofread your academic papers especially to identify and revise errors such as the following:

- **Sentence fragments.** Make sure every sentence has a subject and a predicate. Avoid fragments such as *Observing the results* or *After the meeting.* For more on fragments, see **4** pp. 250–53.
- **Missing punctuation.** Between and within sentences, use standard punctuation marks. Check especially for missing commas within sentences and missing apostrophes in possessives and contractions. See **5** pp. 265–76 and 282–85.
- **Missing capital letters.** Use capital letters at the beginnings of sentences, for proper nouns and adjectives, and in titles. See **6** pp. 303–06.
- **Nonstandard abbreviations and spellings.** Avoid forms such as 2 for *to* or *too, b4* for *before, bc* for *because, ur* for *you are* or *you're,* and + or & for *and.* See **6** pp. 297–301 and 309–11.

3 Slang

Slang is the language used by a group, such as musicians or computer programmers, to reflect common experiences and to make technical references efficient. The following example is from an essay on the slang of "skaters" (skateboarders):

> Curtis slashed ultra-punk crunchers on his longboard, while the Rube-man flailed his usual Gumbyness on tweaked frontsides and lofty fakie ollies.
>
> —Miles Orkin, "Mucho Slingage by the Pool"

Among those who understand it, slang may be vivid and forceful. It often occurs in dialog, and an occasional slang expression can enliven an informal essay. But most slang is too flippant and imprecise for effective communication, and it is generally inappropriate for college or business writing. Notice the gain in seriousness and precision achieved in the following revision:

Slang Many students start out pretty together but then get weird.

Revised Many students start out with clear goals but then lose their direction.

4 Colloquial language

Colloquial language is the everyday spoken language, including expressions such as *get together, go crazy, do the dirty work,* and *get along.*

When you write informally, colloquial language may be appropriate to achieve the casual, relaxed effect of conversation. An occasional colloquial word dropped into otherwise more formal writing can also help you achieve a desired emphasis. But most colloquial language is not precise enough for college or career writing. In such writing you should generally avoid any words and expressions labeled "informal" or "colloquial" in your dictionary.

Colloquial According to a Native American myth, the Great Creator had a dog hanging around with him when he created the earth.

Revised According to a Native American myth, the Great Creator was accompanied by a dog when he created the earth.

5 Technical words

All disciplines and professions rely on specialized language that allows the members to communicate precisely and efficiently with each other. Chemists, for instance, have their *phosphatides,* and literary critics have their *motifs* and *subtexts.* Without explanation, technical words are meaningless to nonspecialists. When you are writing for nonspecialists, avoid unnecessary technical terms and carefully define terms you must use.

6 Indirect and pretentious writing

Small, plain, and direct words are almost always preferable to big, showy, or evasive words. Take special care to avoid euphemisms, double talk, and pretentious writing.

A **euphemism** is a presumably inoffensive word that a writer or speaker substitutes for a word deemed potentially offensive or too blunt, such as *passed away* for *died* or *misspeak* for *lie.* Use euphemisms only when you know that blunt, truthful words would needlessly hurt or offend members of your audience.

A kind of euphemism that deliberately evades the truth is **double talk** (also called **doublespeak** or **weasel words**): language intended to confuse or to be misunderstood. Today double talk is unfortunately common in politics and advertising—the *revenue enhancement* that is really a tax, the *peace-keeping function* that is really war making, the *biodegradable* bags that last decades. Double talk has no place in honest writing.

Euphemism and sometimes double talk seem to keep company with **pretentious writing**, fancy language that is more elaborate than its subject requires. Choose your words for their exactness and economy. The big, ornate word may be tempting, but pass it up. Your readers will be grateful.

Pretentious To perpetuate our endeavor of providing funds for our elderly citizens as we do at the present moment, we will face the exigency of enhanced contributions from all our citizens.

Revised We cannot continue to fund Social Security and Medicare for the elderly unless we raise taxes.

7 Sexist and other biased language

Even when we do not mean it to, our language can reflect and perpetuate hurtful prejudices toward groups of people. Such biased language can be obvious—words such as *nigger, honky, mick, kike, fag, dyke,* and *broad.* But it can also be subtle, generalizing about groups in ways that may be familiar but that are also inaccurate or unfair.

Biased language reflects poorly on the user, not on the person or persons whom it mischaracterizes or insults. Unbiased language does not submit to false generalizations. It treats people respectfully as individuals and labels groups as they wish to be labeled.

Stereotypes of race, ethnicity, religion, age, and other characteristics

A **stereotype** is a generalization based on poor evidence, a kind of formula for understanding and judging people simply because of their membership in a group:

Men are uncommunicative.
Women are emotional.
Liberals want to raise taxes.
Conservatives are affluent.

At best, stereotypes betray a noncritical writer, one who is not thinking beyond notions received from others. In your writing, be alert for statements that characterize whole groups of people:

Stereotype Elderly drivers should have their licenses limited to daytime driving only. [Asserts that all elderly people are poor night drivers.]

Revised Drivers with impaired night vision should have their licenses limited to daytime driving only.

Some stereotypes have become part of the language, but they are still potentially offensive:

Stereotype The administrators are too blind to see the need for a new gymnasium. [Equates vision loss and lack of understanding.]

Revised The administrators do not understand the need for a new gymnasium.

Sexist language

Among the most subtle and persistent biased language is that expressing narrow ideas about men's and women's roles, position, and value in society. Like other stereotypes, this **sexist language** can wound or irritate readers, and it indicates the writer's thoughtlessness or unfairness. The box on the next two pages suggests some ways of eliminating sexist language.

CULTURE LANGUAGE Forms of address vary widely from culture to culture. In some cultures, for instance, one shows respect by referring to all older women as if they were married, using the equivalent of *Mrs.* Usage in the United States is changing toward making no assumptions about marital status, rank, or other characteristics—for instance, addressing a woman as *Ms.* unless she is known to prefer *Mrs.* or *Miss.*

Eliminating sexist language

- **Avoid demeaning and patronizing language:**

Sexist Dr. Keith Kim and Lydia Hawkins coauthored the article.
Revised Dr. Keith Kim and Dr. Lydia Hawkins coauthored the article.
Revised Keith Kim and Lydia Hawkins coauthored the article.

Sexist Ladies are entering almost every occupation formerly filled by men.
Revised Women are entering almost every occupation formerly filled by men.

- **Avoid occupational or social stereotypes:**

Sexist The considerate doctor commends a nurse when she provides his patients with good care.
Revised The considerate doctor commends a nurse who provides good care for patients.

Sexist The grocery shopper should save her coupons.
Revised Grocery shoppers should save their coupons.

- **Avoid referring needlessly to gender:**

Sexist Marie Curie, a woman chemist, discovered radium.
Revised Marie Curie, a chemist, discovered radium.

Sexist The patients were tended by a male nurse.
Revised The patients were tended by a nurse.

- **Avoid using *man* or words containing *man* to refer to all human beings.** Here are a few alternatives:

businessman	businessperson
chairman	chair, chairperson
congressman	representative in Congress, legislator
craftsman	craftsperson, artisan
layman	layperson
mankind	humankind, humanity, human beings, humans
manmade	handmade, manufactured, synthetic, artificial
manpower	personnel, human resources
policeman	police officer
salesman	salesperson

Sexist Man has not reached the limits of social justice.
Revised Humankind [or Humanity] has not reached the limits of social justice.

Sexist The furniture consists of manmade materials.
Revised The furniture consists of synthetic materials.

(continued)

Eliminating sexist language

(continued)

- **Avoid the generic *he*,** the male pronoun used to refer to both genders. (See also **4** pp. 231–32.)

Sexist The newborn child explores his world.

Revised Newborn children explore their world. [Use the plural for the pronoun and the word it refers to.]

Revised The newborn child explores the world. [Avoid the pronoun altogether.]

Revised The newborn child explores his or her world. [Substitute male and female pronouns.]

Use the last option sparingly—only once in a group of sentences and only to stress the singular individual.

Appropriate labels

We often need to label groups: *swimmers, politicians, mothers, Christians, Westerners, students*. But labels can be shorthand stereotypes, slighting the person labeled and ignoring the preferences of the group members themselves. Although sometimes dismissed as "political correctness," showing sensitivity about labels hurts no one and helps gain your readers' trust and respect.

- **Avoid labels that (intentionally or not) disparage the person or group you refer to.** A person with emotional problems is not a *mental patient*. A person with cancer is not a *cancer victim*. A person using a wheelchair is not *wheelchair-bound*.
- **Use names for racial, ethnic, and other groups that reflect the preferences of each group's members,** or at least many of them. Examples of current preferences include *African American* or *black, latino/latina* (for Americans and American immigrants of Spanish-speaking descent), and *people with disabilities* (rather than *the disabled* or *the handicapped*). But labels change often. To learn how a group's members wish to be labeled, ask them directly, attend to usage in reputable periodicals, or check a recent dictionary.
- **Identify a person's group only when it is relevant to the point you're making.** Consider the context of the label: Is it a necessary piece of information? If not, don't use it.

A helpful reference for appropriate labels is *Guidelines for Bias-Free Writing*, by Marilyn Schwartz and the Task Force on Bias-Free Language of the Association of American University Presses.

18b Choosing exact language

To write clearly and effectively, you will want to find the words that fit your meaning exactly and convey your attitude precisely.

Grammar checkers A grammar checker can provide some help with inexact language. For instance, you can set it to flag commonly confused words (such as *continuous/continual*), misused prepositions in idioms (such as *accuse for* instead of *accuse of*), and clichés. But a checker can't help you at all with inappropriate connotation, excessive abstraction, or other problems discussed in this section.

1 Word meanings and synonyms

For writing exactly, a dictionary is essential and a thesaurus can bc helpful.

Desk dictionaries

A desk dictionary defines about 150,000 to 200,000 words and provides pronunciation, grammatical functions, etymology (word history), and other information. The sample below is from *Merriam-Webster's Collegiate Dictionary.*

Dictionary entry for *reckon*

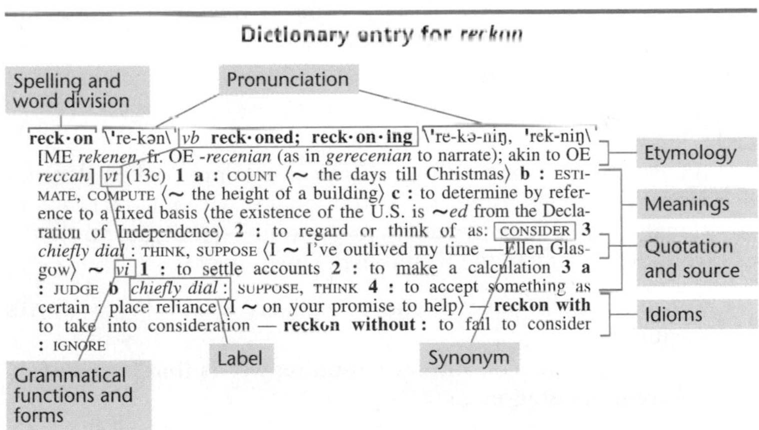

Spelling and word division
Pronunciation
Etymology
Meanings
Quotation and source
Idioms
Grammatical functions and forms
Label
Synonym
reck·on \'re-kən\ *vb* **reck·oned; reck·on·ing** \'re-kə-niŋ, 'rek-niŋ\ [ME *rekenen*, fr. OE *-recenian* (as in *gerecenian* to narrate); akin to OE *reccan*] *vt* (13c) **1 a :** COUNT ⟨~ the days till Christmas⟩ **b :** ESTIMATE, COMPUTE ⟨~ the height of a building⟩ **c :** to determine by reference to a fixed basis ⟨the existence of the U.S. is ~*ed* from the Declaration of Independence⟩ **2 :** to regard or think of as: CONSIDER **3** *chiefly dial* : THINK, SUPPOSE ⟨I ~ I've outlived my time —Ellen Glasgow⟩ ~ *vi* **1 :** to settle accounts **2 :** to make a calculation **3 a :** JUDGE **b** *chiefly dial* : SUPPOSE, THINK **4 :** to accept something as certain : place reliance ⟨I ~ on your promise to help⟩ — **reckon with :** to take into consideration — **reckon without :** to fail to consider : IGNORE

Good desk dictionaries, in addition to *Merriam-Webster's,* include the *American Heritage College Dictionary,* the *Random House Webster's College Dictionary,* and *Webster's New World Dictionary.* Most of these are available in both print and electronic form (CD-ROM or online). In addition, several Web sites provide online dictionaries or links to online dictionaries.

CULTURE LANGUAGE If English is not your native language, you may want a dictionary prepared especially for students using English as a second language (ESL). Such a dictionary contains special information on prepositions, count versus noncount nouns, and many other matters. Reliable ESL dictionaries include *COBUILD English Language Dictionary, Longman Dictionary of Contemporary English,* and *Oxford Advanced Learner's Dictionary.*

Thesauruses

To find a word with the exact shade of meaning you intend, you may want to consult a thesaurus, or book of **synonyms**—words with approximately the same meaning. A thesaurus such as *Roget's International Thesaurus* lists most imaginable synonyms for thousands of words. The word *news,* for instance, has half a page of synonyms in *Roget's International,* including *tidings, gossip,* and *journalism.*

Since a thesaurus aims to open up possibilities, its lists of synonyms include approximate as well as precise matches. The thesaurus does not define synonyms or distinguish among them, however, so you need a dictionary to discover exact meanings. In general, don't use a word from a thesaurus—even one you like the sound of—until you know it is appropriate for your meaning.

Note Your word processor may also include a thesaurus, making it easy to look up synonyms and insert the chosen word into your text. But still you should consult a dictionary unless you are certain of the word's meaning.

2 The right word for your meaning

All words have one or more basic meanings, called **denotations**—the meanings listed in the dictionary, without reference to emotional associations. If readers are to understand you, you must use words according to their established meanings.

- **Consult a dictionary whenever you are unsure of a word's meaning.**
- **Distinguish between similar-sounding words that have widely different denotations:**

  Inexact Older people often suffer infirmaries [places for the sick].
  Exact Older people often suffer infirmities [disabilities].

  Some words, called **homonyms,** sound exactly alike but differ in meaning: for example, *principal/principle* and *rain/reign/rein.* (See **6** pp. 297–98 for a list of commonly confused homonyms.)
- **Distinguish between words with related but distinct meanings:**

  Inexact Television commercials continuously [unceasingly] interrupt programming.

Exact Television commercials continually [regularly] interrupt programming.

In addition to their emotion-free meanings, many words carry related meanings that evoke specific feelings. These **connotations** can shape readers' responses and are thus a powerful tool for writers. The following word pairs have related denotations but very different connotations:

pride: sense of self-worth
vanity: excessive regard for oneself

firm: steady, unchanging, unyielding
stubborn: unreasonable, bullheaded

enthusiasm: excitement
mania: excessive interest or desire

A dictionary can help you track down words with the exact connotations you want. Besides providing meanings, your dictionary may also list and distinguish synonyms to guide your choices. A thesaurus can also help if you use it carefully, as discussed on the previous page.

3 Concrete and specific words

Clear, exact writing balances abstract and general words, which outline ideas and objects, with concrete and specific words, which sharpen and solidify.

- **Abstract words** name ideas: *beauty, inflation, management, culture, liberal.* **Concrete words** name qualities and things we can know by our five senses of sight, hearing, touch, taste, and smell: *sleek, humming, rough, salty, musty.*
- **General words** name classes or groups of things, such as *birds, weather,* and *buildings,* and include all the varieties of the class. **Specific words** limit a general class, such as *buildings,* by naming a variety, such as *skyscraper, Victorian courthouse,* or *hut.*

Abstract and general words are useful in the broad statements that set the course for your writing.

The wild horse in America has a romantic history.

Relations between the sexes today are more relaxed than they were in the past.

But such statements need development with concrete and specific detail. Detail can turn a vague sentence into an exact one:

Vague The size of his hands made his smallness real. [How big were his hands? How small was he?]

Exact Not until I saw his delicate, doll-like hands did I realize that he stood a full head shorter than most other men.

Note You can use your computer's Find function to help you find and revise abstract and general words that you tend to overuse. Examples of such words include *nice, interesting, things, very, good, a lot, a little,* and *some.*

4 Idioms

Idioms are expressions in any language that do not fit the rules for meaning or grammar—for instance, *put up with, plug away at, make off with.*

Idioms that involve prepositions can be especially confusing for both native and nonnative speakers of English. Some idioms with prepositions are listed in the following box. (More appear in **4** pp. 207–08.)

Idioms with prepositions

- abide by a rule
  - in a place or state
- according to
- accords with
- accuse of a crime
- accustomed to
- adapt from a source
  - to a situation
- afraid of
- agree on a plan as a group
  - to someone else's plan
  - with a person
- angry with
- aware of
- based on
- belong in or on a place
  - to a group
- capable of
- certain of
- charge for a purchase
  - with a crime
- concur in an opinion
  - with a person
- contend for a principle
  - with a person
- dependent on
- differ about or over a question
  - from in some quality
  - with a person
- disappointed by or in a person
  - in or with a thing
- familiar with
- identical with or to
- impatient for a raise
  - with a person
- independent of
- infer from
- inferior to
- involved in a task
  - with a person
- oblivious of or to one's surroundings
  - of something forgotten
- occupied by a person
  - in study
  - with a thing
- opposed to
- part from a person
  - with a possession
- prior to
- proud of

related to	superior to
rewarded by the judge	wait at a place
for something done	for a train, a person
with a gift	in a room
similar to	on a customer
sorry about an error	
for a person	

CULTURE LANGUAGE If you are learning standard American English, you are justified in stumbling over its prepositions: their meanings can shift depending on context, and they have many idiomatic uses. In mastering the prepositions of standard English, you probably can't avoid memorization. But you can help yourself by memorizing related groups, such as *at/in/on* and *for/since*.

***At, in,* or *on* in expressions of time**

- Use *at* before actual clock time: *at 8:30.*
- Use *in* before a month, year, century, or period: *in April, in 2007, in the twenty-first century, in the next month.*
- Use *on* before a day or date: *on Tuesday, on May 3, on Labor Day.*

***At, in,* or *on* in expressions of place**

- Use *at* before a specific place or address: *at the school, at 511 Iris Street.*
- Use *in* before a place with limits or before a city, state, country, or continent: *in the house, in a box, in Oklahoma City, in China, in Asia.*
- Use *on* to mean "supported by" or "touching the surface of": *on the table, on Iris Street, on page 150.*

***For* or *since* in expressions of time**

- Use *for* before a period of time: *for an hour, for two years.*
- Use *since* before a specific point in time: *since 1999, since Friday.*

A dictionary of English as a second language is the best source for the meanings of prepositions; see the suggestions on p. 166.

5 Figurative language

Figurative language (or a **figure of speech**) departs from the literal meanings of words, usually by comparing very different ideas or objects:

Literal As I try to write, I can think of nothing to say.
Figurative As I try to write, my mind is a slab of black slate.

Imaginatively and carefully used, figurative language can capture meaning more precisely and emotionally than literal language. Here is a figure of speech at work in technical writing (paraphrasing the physicist Edward Andrade):

> The molecules in a liquid move continuously like couples on an over-crowded dance floor, jostling each other.

The two most common figures of speech are the simile and the metaphor. Both compare two things of different classes, often one abstract and the other concrete. A **simile** makes the comparison explicit and usually begins with *like* or *as:*

> Whenever we grow, we tend to feel it, as a young seed must feel the weight and inertia of the earth when it seeks to break out of its shell on its way to becoming a plant.
> —Alice Walker

A **metaphor** claims that the two things are identical, omitting such words as *like* and *as:*

> A school is a hopper into which children are heaved while they are young and tender; therein they are pressed into certain standard shapes and covered from head to heels with official rubber stamps.
> —H. L. Mencken

To be successful, figurative language must be fresh and unstrained, calling attention not to itself but to the writer's meaning. Be especially wary of mixed metaphors, which combine two or more incompatible figures:

Mixed Various thorny problems that we try to sweep under the rug continue to bob up all the same.

Improved Various thorny problems that we try to weed out continue to thrive all the same.

6 Trite expressions

Trite expressions, or **clichés,** are phrases so old and so often repeated that they have become stale. They include the following:

add insult to injury
better late than never
crushing blow
green with envy
hard as a rock
heavy as lead
hit the nail on the head
hour of need
ladder of success
moving experience
a needle in a haystack
point with pride
pride and joy
easier said than done
face the music
few and far between
ripe old age
rude awakening
shoulder the burden
shoulder to cry on
sneaking suspicion
stand in awe
strong as an ox
thin as a rail
tried and true
wise as an owl

To edit clichés, listen to your writing for any expressions that you have heard or used before. You can also supplement your efforts with a style checker, which may include a cliché detector. When you find a cliché, substitute fresh words of your own or restate the idea in plain language.

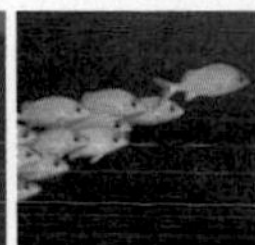

19 Completeness

The most serious kind of incomplete sentence is the grammatical fragment (see **4** pp. 250–53). But sentences are also incomplete when they omit one or more words needed for clarity.

Grammar checkers A grammar checker will not flag most kinds of incomplete sentences discussed in this chapter.

19a Writing complete compounds

You may omit words from a compound construction when the omission will not confuse readers.

> Environmentalists have hopes for alternative fuels and [for] public transportation.
>
> Some cars will run on electricity, some [will run] on ethanol, and some [will run] on hydrogen.

Such omissions are possible only when the words omitted are common to all the parts of a compound construction. When the parts differ in any way, all words must be included in all parts.

> One new car gets eighty miles per gallon; some old cars get as little as five miles per gallon. [One verb is singular, the other plural.]
>
> Environmentalists believe in and work for fuel conservation. [Idiom requires different prepositions with *believe* and *work*.]

Key term

compound construction Two or more elements (words, phrases, clauses) that are equal in importance and that function as a unit: *Rain fell, and streams overflowed* (clauses); *dogs and cats* (words).

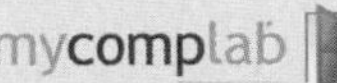

Visit *mycomplab.com* for more resources on complete sentences.

19b Adding needed words

In haste or carelessness, do not omit small words that are needed for clarity:

Incomplete Regular payroll deductions are a type painless savings. You hardly notice missing amounts, and after period of years the contributions can add a large total.

Revised Regular payroll deductions are a type of painless savings. You hardly notice the missing amounts, and after a period of years the contributions can add up to a large total.

Attentive proofreading is the only insurance against this kind of omission. *Proofread all your papers carefully.* See **1** p. 33 for tips.

CULTURE LANGUAGE If your native language or dialect is not standard American English, you may have difficulty knowing when to use the English articles *a, an,* and *the.* For guidelines see **4** pp. 240–42.

20 Conciseness

Concise writing makes every word count. Conciseness is not the same as mere brevity: detail and originality should not be cut with needless words. Rather, the length of an expression should be appropriate to the thought.

You may find yourself writing wordily when you are unsure of your subject or when your thoughts are tangled. It's fine, even necessary, to grope while drafting. But you should straighten out your ideas and eliminate wordiness during revision and editing.

Grammar checkers A grammar checker will identify at least some wordy structures, such as repeated words, weak verbs, passive voice, and *there is* and *it is* constructions. But a checker can't identify all potentially wordy structures, nor can it tell you whether a structure is appropriate for your ideas.

CULTURE LANGUAGE As you'll see in the examples that follow, wordiness is not a problem of incorrect grammar. A sentence may be perfectly grammatical but still contain unneeded words that interfere with the clarity and force of your idea.

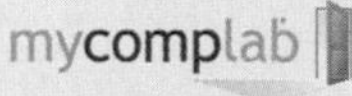

Visit *mycomplab.com* for more resources as well as exercises on writing concisely.

Ways to achieve conciseness

Wordy (87 words)

The highly pressured nature of critical-care nursing is due to the fact that the patients have life-threatening illnesses. Critical-care nurses must have possession of steady nerves to care for patients who are critically ill and very sick. The nurses must also have possession of interpersonal skills. They must also have medical skills. It is considered by most health-care professionals that these nurses are essential if there is to be improvement of patients who are now in critical care from that status to the status of intermediate care.

- Focus on subject and verb, and cut or shorten empty words and phrases.
- Avoid nouns made from verbs.
- Cut unneeded repetition.
- Combine sentences.
- Change passive voice to active voice.
- Revise *there is* constructions.
- Cut unneeded repetition, and reduce clauses and phrases.

Concise (37 words)

Critical-care nursing is highly pressured because the patients have life-threatening illnesses. Critical-care nurses must possess steady nerves and interpersonal and medical skills. Most health-care professionals consider these nurses essential if patients are to improve to intermediate care.

20a Focusing on the subject and verb

Using the subjects and verbs of your sentences for the key actors and actions will reduce words and emphasize important ideas. (See pp. 143–45 for more on this topic.)

Wordy The reason why most of the country shifts to daylight time is that winter days are much shorter than summer days.

Concise Most of the country shifts to daylight time because winter days are much shorter than summer days.

Focusing on subjects and verbs will also help you avoid several other causes of wordiness discussed further on pp. 144–45:

Nouns made from verbs

Wordy The occurrence of the winter solstice, the shortest day of the year, is an event occurring about December 22.

Concise The winter solstice, the shortest day of the year, occurs about December 22.

Weak verbs

Wordy The earth's axis has a tilt as the planet is in orbit around the sun so that the northern and southern hemispheres are alternately in alignment toward the sun.

Concise The earth's axis tilts as the planet orbits the sun so that the northern and southern hemispheres alternately align toward the sun.

Passive voice

Wordy During its winter the northern hemisphere is tilted farthest away from the sun, so the nights are made longer and the days are made shorter.

Concise During its winter the northern hemisphere tilts away from the sun, making the nights longer and the days shorter.

See also **4** pp. 216–17 on changing the passive voice to the active voice, as in the example above.

20b Cutting empty words

Empty words walk in place, gaining little or nothing in meaning. Many can be cut entirely. The following are just a few examples:

all things considered
as far as I'm concerned
for all intents and purposes
for the most part
in a manner of speaking
in my opinion
last but not least
more or less

Other empty words can also be cut, usually along with some of the words around them.

area	case	factor	kind	nature	thing
aspect	element	field	manner	situation	type

Still others can be reduced from several words to a single word:

For	Substitute
at the present time	now, yet
because of the fact that	because
due to the fact that	because
for the purpose of	for
in order to	to
in the event that	if
in the final analysis	finally

Key terms

passive voice The verb form when the subject names the *receiver* of the verb's action: *The house was destroyed by the tornado.* (See **4** p. 216.)

active voice The verb form when the subject names the *performer* of the verb's action: *The tornado destroyed the house.* (See **4** p. 216.)

Cutting or reducing such words and phrases will make your writing move faster and work harder:

Wordy In my opinion, the council's proposal to improve the city center is inadequate, all things considered.

Revised The council's proposal to improve the city center is inadequate.

20c Cutting unneeded repetition

Unnecessary repetition weakens sentences:

Wordy Many unskilled workers without training in a particular job are unemployed and do not have any work.

Concise Many unskilled workers are unemployed.

Be especially alert to phrases that say the same thing twice. In the examples below, the unneeded words are underlined:

circle around
consensus of opinion
cooperate together
final completion
frank and honest exchange
the future to come
important [basic] essentials
puzzling in nature
repeat again
return again
square [round] in shape
surrounding circumstances

CULTURE LANGUAGE The preceding phrases are redundant because the main word already implies the underlined word or words. A dictionary will tell you what meanings a word implies. *Assassinate,* for instance, means "murder someone well known," so the following sentence is redundant: *Julius Caesar was assassinated and killed.*

20d Reducing clauses and phrases

Modifiers can be expanded or contracted depending on the emphasis you want to achieve. (Generally, the longer a construction, the more emphatic it is.) When editing sentences, consider whether any modifiers can be reduced without loss of emphasis or clarity.

Wordy The Channel Tunnel, which runs between Britain and France, bores through a bed of solid chalk that is twenty-three miles across.

Concise The Channel Tunnel between Britain and France bores through twenty-three miles of solid chalk.

Key term

modifier A word or word group that limits or qualifies another word: *slippery road, cars with tire chains.*

20e Revising *there is, here is,* or *it is*

You can postpone the sentence subject with the words *there, here,* and *it: There are three tests. Here is the main problem. It was not fair that only seniors could vote.* These **expletive constructions** can be useful to emphasize the subject (as when introducing it for the first time) or to indicate a change in direction. But often they just add words and create limp substitutes for more vigorous sentences:

Wordy There were delays and cost overruns that plagued construction of the Channel Tunnel. It had been the hope of investors that they would see earnings soon after there were trains passing through the tunnel, but profits took years to come.

Concise Delays and cost overruns plagued construction of the Channel Tunnel. Investors had hoped to see earnings soon after trains began passing through the tunnel, but profits took years to come.

CULTURE LANGUAGE When you must use an expletive construction, be careful to include *there, here,* or *it.* Only commands and some questions can begin with verbs.

20f Combining sentences

Often the information in two or more sentences can be combined into one tight sentence:

Wordy An unexpected problem with the Channel Tunnel is stowaways. The stowaways are mostly illegal immigrants. They are trying to smuggle themselves into England.

Concise An unexpected problem with the Channel Tunnel is stowaways, mostly illegal immigrants who are trying to smuggle themselves into England.

20g Rewriting jargon

Jargon can refer to the special vocabulary of any discipline or profession. But it has also come to describe vague, inflated language that is overcomplicated, even incomprehensible. When it comes from government or business, we call it **bureaucratese.**

Jargon The necessity for individuals to become separate entities in their own right may impel children to engage in open rebelliousness against parental authority or against sibling influence, with resultant bewilderment of those being rebelled against.

Translation Children's natural desire to become themselves may make them rebel against bewildered parents or siblings.

PART 4

Sentence Parts and Patterns

Basic Grammar *180*

Verbs *196*

Pronouns *224*

Modifiers *236*

Sentence Faults *250*

PART 4

Sentence Parts and Patterns

Basic Grammar

21 Parts of Speech *180*

- a Nouns *180*
- b Pronouns *181*
- c Verbs *182*
- d Adjectives and adverbs *183*
- e Connecting words: prepositions and conjunctions *184*
- f Interjections *186*

22 The Sentence *186*

- a Subject and predicate *186*
- b Predicate patterns *188*

23 Phrases and Subordinate Clauses *191*

- a Phrases *191*
- b Subordinate clauses *193*

24 Sentence Types *194*

- a Simple sentences *195*
- b Compound sentences *195*
- c Complex sentences *195*
- d Compound-complex sentences *195*

Verbs

25 Forms *196*

- a *Sing/sang/sung* and other irregular verbs *196*
- b *Sit/set; lie/lay; rise/raise* *198*
- c *-s* and *-ed* forms *199*
- d *Be, have,* and other helping verbs *200*
- e Verbs + gerund or infinitive: *stop eating* vs. *stop to eat* *205*
- f Verb + particle: *look up, look over,* etc. *207*

26 Tenses *208*

- a Present tense: *sing* *210*
- b Perfect tenses: *have/had/will have sung* *210*
- c Progressive tenses: *is/was/will be singing* *211*
- d Consistency *211*
- e Sequence *212*

27 Mood *214*

- a Subjunctive: *I wish I were* *214*
- b Consistency *215*

28 Voice *216*

- a *She wrote it* (active) vs. *It was written* (passive) *216*
- b Consistency *217*

29 Subject-Verb Agreement *218*

- a *-s* and *-es* endings *218*
- b Intervening words *219*
- c Subjects with *and* *220*
- d Subjects with *or* or *nor* *220*

e *Everyone* and other indefinite pronouns *220*
f *Team* and other collective nouns *221*
g *Who, which, that* as subjects *222*
h *News* and other singular nouns ending in *-s* *222*
i Verb preceding subject *223*
j *Is, are,* and other linking verbs *223*
k Titles and words being defined *223*

Pronouns

30 Case *224*

a *She and I* vs. *her and me* *225*
b *It was she* vs. *It was her* *226*
c *Who* vs. *whom* *226*
d Other constructions *228*

31 Pronoun-Antecedent Agreement *229*

a Antecedents with *and* *230*
b Antecedents with *or* or *nor* *230*
c *Everyone, person,* and other indefinite words *231*
d *Team* and other collective nouns *232*

32 Pronoun Reference *233*

a Clear reference *233*
b Close reference *233*
c Specific reference *234*
d Appropriate *you* *235*
e Consistency *235*

Modifiers

33 Adjectives and Adverbs *236*

a Adjective vs. adverb *236*
b Adjective with linking verb: *felt bad* *237*
c *Bigger, most talented,* and other comparisons *237*
d Double negatives *239*
e Present and past participles: *boring* vs. *bored* *240*
f *A, an, the,* and other determiners *240*

34 Misplaced and Dangling Modifiers *245*

a Misplaced modifiers *245*
b Dangling modifiers *248*

Sentence Faults

35 Fragments *250*

a Tests *250*
b Revision *252*
c Acceptable fragments *252*

36 Comma Splices and Fused Sentences *253*

a Main clauses without *and, but,* etc. *255*
b Main clauses with *however, for example,* etc. *256*

37 Mixed Sentences *258*

a *Reason is because* and other mixed meanings *258*
b Tangled grammar *259*
c Repeated subjects and other parts *260*

Basic Grammar

Grammar describes how language works, and understanding it can help you create clear and accurate sentences. This section explains the kinds of words in sentences (Chapter 21) and how to build basic sentences (22), expand them (23), and classify them (24).

Grammar checkers A grammar checker can both offer assistance and cause problems as you compose sentences. Look for the cautions and tips for using a checker in this and the next part of this book. For more information about grammar checkers, see **1** p. 31.

21 Parts of Speech

All English words fall into eight groups, called **parts of speech:** nouns, pronouns, verbs, adjectives, adverbs, prepositions, conjunctions, and interjections.

Note In different sentences a word may serve as different parts of speech. For example:

> The government sent aid to the city. [*Aid* is a noun.]
> Governments aid citizens. [*Aid* is a verb.]

The *function* of a word in a sentence always determines its part of speech in that sentence.

21a Recognizing nouns

Nouns name. They may name a person (*Helen Mirren, Jesse Jackson, astronaut*), a thing (*chair, book, Mt. Rainier*), a quality (*pain, mystery, simplicity*), a place (*city, Washington, ocean, Red Sea*), or an idea (*reality, peace, success*).

The forms of nouns depend partly on where they fit in certain groups. As the following examples indicate, the same noun may appear in more than one group.

- **A *common noun* names a general class of things and does not begin with a capital letter:** *earthquake, citizen, earth, fortitude, army.*

- A *proper noun* names a specific person, place, or thing and begins with a capital letter: *Angelina Jolie, Washington Monument, El Paso, US Congress.*
- A *count noun* names a thing considered countable in English. Most count nouns add *-s* or *-es* to distinguish between singular (one) and plural (more than one): *citizen, citizens; city, cities.* Some count nouns form irregular plurals: *woman, women; child, children.*
- A *noncount noun* names things or qualities that aren't considered countable in English: *earth, sugar, chaos, fortitude.* Noncount nouns do not form plurals.
- A *collective noun* is singular in form but names a group: *army, family, herd, US Congress.*

In addition, most nouns form the **possessive** by adding *-'s* to show ownership (*Nadia's books, citizen's rights*), source (*Auden's poems*), and some other relationships.

21b Recognizing pronouns

Most **pronouns** substitute for nouns and function in sentences as nouns do: *Susanne Ling enlisted in the Air Force when she graduated.*

Pronouns fall into groups depending on their form or function:

- A *personal pronoun* refers to a specific individual or to individuals: *I, you, he, she, it, we,* and *they.*
- An *indefinite pronoun* does not refer to a specific noun: *anyone, everything, no one, somebody,* and so on. *No one came. Nothing moves. Everybody speaks.*
- A *relative pronoun* relates a group of words to a noun or another pronoun: *who, whoever, which, that. Everyone who attended received a prize. The book that won is a novel.*
- An *interrogative pronoun* introduces a question: *who, whom, whose, which, what. What song is that? Who will contribute?*
- A *demonstrative pronoun* identifies or points to a noun: *this, these, that, those,* and so on. *Those berries are ripe. This is the site.*
- An *intensive pronoun* emphasizes a noun or another pronoun: *myself, himself, itself, themselves,* and so on. *I myself asked that question. The price itself is in doubt.*
- A *reflexive pronoun* indicates that the sentence subject also receives the action of the verb: *myself, himself, itself, themselves,* and so on. *He perjured himself. They injured themselves.*

The personal pronouns *I, he, she, we,* and *they* and the relative pronouns *who* and *whoever* change form depending on their function in the sentence. (See Chapter 30.)

21c Recognizing verbs

Verbs express an action (*bring, change, grow, consider*), an occurrence (*become, happen, occur*), or a state of being (*be, seem, remain*).

1 Forms of verbs

Verbs have five distinctive forms. If the form can change as described here, the word is a verb:

- **The *plain form* is the dictionary form of the verb.** When the subject is a plural noun or the pronoun *I, we, you,* or *they,* the plain form indicates action that occurs in the present, occurs habitually, or is generally true.

  A few artists live in town today.
  They hold classes downtown.

- **The *-s form* ends in *-s* or *-es*.** When the subject is a singular noun, a pronoun such as *everyone,* or the personal pronoun *he, she,* or *it,* the *-s* form indicates action that occurs in the present, occurs habitually, or is generally true.

  The artist lives in town today.
  She holds classes downtown.

- **The *past-tense form* indicates that the action of the verb occurred before now.** It usually adds *-d* or *-ed* to the plain form, although most irregular verbs create it in different ways (see pp. 196–98).

  Many artists lived in town before this year.
  They held classes downtown. [Irregular verb.]

- **The *past participle* is usually the same as the past-tense form, except in most irregular verbs.** It combines with forms of *have* or *be* (*has climbed, was created*), or by itself it modifies nouns and pronouns (*the sliced apples*).

  Artists have lived in town for decades.
  They have held classes downtown. [Irregular verb.]

- **The *present participle* adds *-ing* to the verb's plain form.** It combines with forms of *be* (*is buying*), modifies nouns and pronouns (*the boiling water*), or functions as a noun (*Running exhausts me*).

  A few artists are living in town today.
  They are holding classes downtown.

The verb *be* has eight forms rather than the five forms of most other verbs:

Plain form	be		
Present participle	being		
Past participle	been		
	I	***he, she, it***	***we, you, they***
Present tense	am	is	are
Past tense	was	was	were

2 Helping verbs

Some verb forms combine with **helping verbs** to indicate time, possibility, obligation, necessity, and other kinds of meaning: *can run, was sleeping, had been working.* In these **verb phrases** *run, sleeping,* and *working* are **main verbs**—they carry the principal meaning.

Verb phrase	
Helping	***Main***
Artists can	train others to draw.
The techniques have	changed little.

The most common helping verbs are listed in the box below. See pp. 200–05 for more on helping verbs.

Common helping verbs

Forms of *be:* be, am, is, are, was, were, been, being
Forms of *have:* have, has, had, having
Forms of *do:* do, does, did

be able to	could	may	ought to	used to
be supposed to	had better	might	shall	will
can	have to	must	should	would

21d Recognizing adjectives and adverbs

Adjectives describe or modify nouns and pronouns. They specify which one, what quality, or how many.

old	city	generous	one	two	pears
adjective	noun	adjective	pronoun	adjective	noun

Adverbs describe or modify verbs, adjectives, other adverbs, and whole groups of words. They specify when, where, how, and to what extent.

nearly	destroyed	too	quickly
adverb	verb	adverb	adverb

very generous — adverb, adjective

Unfortunately, taxes will rise. — adverb, word group

An *-ly* ending often signals an adverb, but not always: *friendly* is an adjective; *never* and *not* are adverbs. The only way to tell whether a word is an adjective or an adverb is to determine what part of speech it modifies.

Adjectives and adverbs appear in three forms: **positive** (*green, angrily*), **comparative** (*greener, more angrily*), and **superlative** (*greenest, most angrily*).

See Chapter 33 for more on adjectives and adverbs.

21e Recognizing connecting words: Prepositions and conjunctions

Connecting words are mostly small words that link parts of sentences. They never change form.

1 Prepositions

Prepositions form nouns or pronouns (plus any modifiers) into word groups called **prepositional phrases:** *about love, down the stairs*. These phrases usually serve as modifiers in sentences, as in *The plants trailed down the stairs*. (See p. 191.)

Common prepositions

about	before	except for	of	throughout
above	behind	excepting	off	till
according to	below	for	on	to
across	beneath	from	onto	toward
after	beside	in	on top of	under
against	between	in addition to	out	underneath
along	beyond	inside	out of	unlike
along with	by	inside of	outside	until
among	concerning	in spite of	over	up
around	despite	instead of	past	upon
as	down	into	regarding	up to
aside from	due to	like	round	with
at	during	near	since	within
because of	except	next to	through	without

The meanings and uses of English prepositions can be difficult to master. See **3** pp. 168–69 for a discussion of prepositions in idioms. See pp. 207–08 for uses of prepositions in two-word verbs such as *look after* or *look up.*

2 Subordinating conjunctions

Subordinating conjunctions form sentences into word groups called **subordinate clauses,** such as *when the meeting ended* or *that she knew.* These clauses serve as parts of sentences: *Everyone was relieved when the meeting ended. She said that she knew.* (See pp. 193–94.)

Common subordinating conjunctions

after	even if	rather than	until
although	even though	since	when
as	if	so that	whenever
as if	if only	than	where
as long as	in order that	that	whereas
as though	now that	though	wherever
because	once	till	whether
before	provided	unless	while

CULTURE LANGUAGE Subordinating conjunctions convey meaning without help from other function words, such as the coordinating conjunctions *and, but, for,* or *so:*

Faulty Even though the parents are illiterate, but their children may read well. [*Even though* and *but* have the same meaning, so both are not needed.]

Revised Even though the parents are illiterate, their children may read well.

3 Coordinating and correlative conjunctions

Coordinating and correlative conjunctions connect words or word groups of the same kind, such as nouns or sentences.

Coordinating conjunctions consist of a single word:

Coordinating conjunctions

and	nor	for	yet
but	or	so	

Biofeedback or simple relaxation can relieve headaches.
Relaxation works well, and it is inexpensive.

Correlative conjunctions are combinations of coordinating conjunctions and other words:

Common correlative conjunctions

both . . . and
not only . . . but also
not . . . but
either . . . or
neither . . . nor
whether . . . or
as . . . as

Both biofeedback and relaxation can relieve headaches.

The headache sufferer learns not only to recognize the causes of headaches but also to control those causes.

21f Recognizing interjections

Interjections express feeling or command attention. They are rarely used in academic or business writing.

Oh, the meeting went fine.
They won seven thousand dollars! Wow!

22 The Sentence

The **sentence** is the basic unit of expression. It is grammatically complete and independent: it does not serve as an adjective, adverb, or other single part of speech.

22a Recognizing subjects and predicates

Most sentences make statements. First the **subject** names something; then the **predicate** makes an assertion about the subject or describes an action by the subject.

Subject	**Predicate**
Art	thrives.

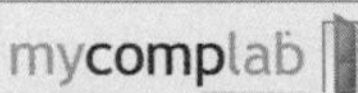

Visit *mycomplab.com* for more resources as well as exercises on the sentence.

The **simple subject** consists of one or more nouns or pronouns, whereas the **complete subject** also includes any modifiers. The **simple predicate** consists of one or more verbs, whereas the **complete predicate** adds any words needed to complete the meaning of the verb plus any modifiers.

Sometimes, as in *Art thrives,* the simple and complete subject and predicate are the same. More often, they are different:

Subject	Predicate
complete / simple	complete / simple
Some contemporary art	stirs controversy.
complete / simple	complete / simple
Congress and the media	discuss and dispute its value.

In the second example, the simple subject and simple predicate are both **compound:** in each, two words joined by a coordinating conjunction (*and*) serve the same function.

Tests to find subjects and predicates

The tests below use the following example:

Art that makes it into museums has often survived controversy.

Identify the subject.

- **Ask *who* or *what* is acting or being described in the sentence.**

  Complete subject art that makes it into museums

- **Isolate the simple subject by deleting modifiers**—words or word groups that don't name the actor of the sentence but give information about it. In the example, the word group *that makes it into museums* does not name the actor but modifies it.

  Simple subject art

Identify the predicate.

- **Ask what the sentence asserts about the subject:** what is its action, or what state is it in? In the example, the assertion about *art* is that it *has often survived controversy.*

  Complete predicate has often survived controversy

- **Isolate the verb, the simple predicate, by changing the time of the subject's action.** The simple predicate is the word or words that change as a result.

Example	Art . . . has often survived controversy.
Present	Art . . . often survives controversy.
Future	Art . . . will often survive controversy.
Simple predicate	has survived

Note If a sentence contains a word group such as *that makes it into museums* or *because viewers agree about its quality,* you may be tempted to mark the subject and verb in the word group as the subject and verb of the sentence. But these word groups are subordinate clauses, made into modifiers by the words they begin with: *that* and *because.* See pp. 193–94 for more on subordinate clauses.

CULTURE LANGUAGE The subject of a sentence in standard American English may be a noun (*art*) or a pronoun that refers to the noun (*it*), but not both. (See p. 260.)

Faulty Some art it stirs controversy.
Revised Some art stirs controversy.

22b Recognizing predicate patterns

All English sentences are based on five patterns, each differing in the complete predicate (the verb and any words following it).

CULTURE LANGUAGE Word order in English sentences may not correspond to word order in the sentences of your native language or dialect. English, for instance, strongly prefers subject first, then verb, whereas some other languages prefer the verb first.

Pattern 1: The earth trembled.

In the simplest pattern the predicate consists only of an **intransitive verb,** a verb that does not require a following word to complete its meaning.

Subject	Predicate
	Intransitive verb
The earth	trembled.
The hospital	may close.

Pattern 2: The earthquake destroyed the city.

In pattern 2 the verb is followed by a **direct object**, a noun or pronoun that identifies who or what receives the action of the verb. A verb that requires a direct object to complete its meaning is called **transitive.**

Subject	Predicate	
	Transitive verb	*Direct object*
The earthquake	destroyed	the city.
Education	opens	doors.

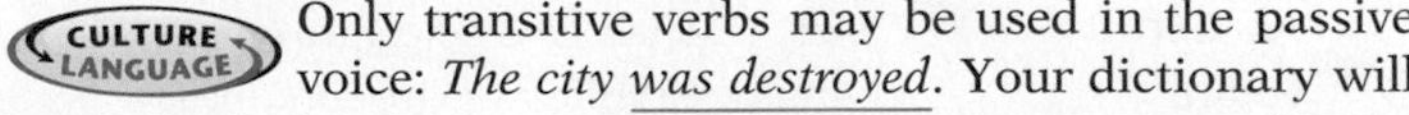
CULTURE LANGUAGE Only transitive verbs may be used in the passive voice: *The city was destroyed*. Your dictionary will

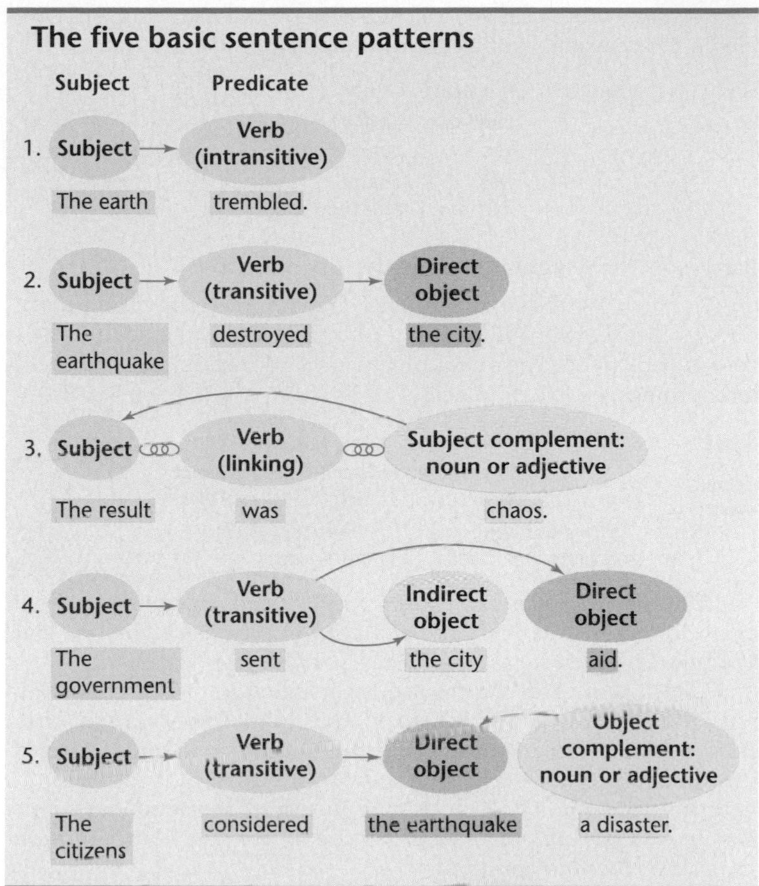

indicate whether a verb is transitive or intransitive. For some verbs (*begin, learn, read, write,* and others), it will indicate both uses.

Pattern 3: The result was chaos.

In pattern 3 the verb is followed by a **subject complement,** a word that renames or describes the subject. A verb in this pattern is called a **linking verb** because it links its subject to the description following. The linking verbs include *be, seem, appear, become, grow,*

Key term

passive voice The verb form when the subject names the receiver of the verb's action: *Bad weather was predicted.* (See p. 216.)

remain, stay, prove, feel, look, smell, sound, and *taste.* Subject complements are usually nouns or adjectives.

Subject	Predicate	
	Linking verb	*Subject complement*
The result	was	chaos.
The man	became	an accountant.

Pattern 4: The government sent the city aid.

In pattern 4 the verb is followed by a direct object and an **indirect object,** a word identifying to or for whom the action of the verb is performed. The direct object and indirect object refer to different things, people, or places.

Subject	Predicate		
	Transitive verb	*Indirect object*	*Direct object*
The government	sent	the city	aid.
One company	offered	its employees	bonuses.

A number of verbs can take indirect objects, including *send* and *offer* (preceding examples) and *allow, bring, buy, deny, find, get, give, leave, make, pay, read, sell, show, teach,* and *write.*

CULTURE LANGUAGE Some verbs are never followed by an indirect object—*admit, announce, demonstrate, explain, introduce, mention, prove, recommend, say,* and some others. However, the direct objects of these verbs may be followed by *to* or *for* and a noun or pronoun that specifies to or for whom the action was done: *The manual explains the new procedure to workers. A video demonstrates the procedure for us.*

Pattern 5: The citizens considered the earthquake a disaster.

In pattern 5 the verb is followed by a direct object and an **object complement,** a word that renames or describes the direct object. Object complements may be nouns or adjectives.

Subject	Predicate		
	Transitive verb	*Direct object*	*Object complement*
The citizens	considered	the earthquake	a disaster.
Success	makes	some people	nervous.

23 Phrases and Subordinate Clauses

Most sentences contain word groups that serve as adjectives, adverbs, or nouns and thus cannot stand alone as sentences.

- A *phrase* lacks either a subject or a predicate or both: *fearing an accident; in a panic.*
- A *subordinate clause* contains a subject and a predicate but begins with a subordinating word: *when prices rise; whoever laughs.*

23a Recognizing phrases

1 Prepositional phrases

A **prepositional phrase** consists of a preposition plus a noun, a pronoun, or a word group serving as a noun, called the **object of the preposition.** A list of prepositions appears on p. 184.

Preposition	Object
of	spaghetti
on	the surface
with	great satisfaction
upon	entering the room
from	where you are standing

Prepositional phrases usually function as adjectives or adverbs.

Life on a raft was an opportunity for adventure.
adjective phrase — adjective phrase

Huck Finn rode the raft by choice.
adverb phrase

With his companion, Jim, Huck met many types of people.
adverb phrase — adjective phrase

2 Verbal phrases

Certain forms of verbs, called **verbals,** can serve as modifiers or nouns. Often these verbals appear with their own modifiers and objects in **verbal phrases.**

Note Verbals cannot serve as verbs in sentences. *The sun rises over the dump* is a sentence; *The sun rising over the dump* is a sentence fragment. (See p. 251.)

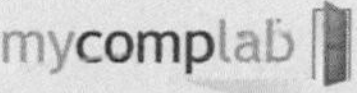

Visit *mycomplab.com* for more resources as well as exercises on phrases and subordinate clauses.

Participial phrases

A **participle** is a verb form ending in *-ing* (*walking*) or, often, *-d* or *-ed* (*walked*). Participles and participial phrases serve as adjectives.

Strolling shoppers fill the malls.
adjective

They make selections determined by personal taste.
adjective phrase

Note With irregular verbs, the past participle may have a different ending—for instance, *hidden funds.* (See pp. 196–98.)

CULTURE LANGUAGE For verbs expressing feeling, the present and past participles have different meanings: *It was a boring lecture. The bored students slept.* (See p. 240.)

Gerund phrases

A **gerund** is the *-ing* form of a verb when it serves as a noun. Gerunds and gerund phrases can do whatever nouns can do.

sentence subject
Shopping satisfies personal needs.
noun

object of preposition
Malls are good at creating such needs.
noun phrase

Infinitive phrases

An **infinitive** is the plain form of a verb plus *to: to hide.* Infinitives and infinitive phrases serve as adjectives, adverbs, or nouns.

sentence subject — subject complement
To design a mall is to create an artificial environment.
noun phrase — noun phrase

Malls are designed to make shoppers feel safe.
adverb phrase

The environment supports the impulse to shop.
adjective

CULTURE LANGUAGE Infinitives and gerunds may follow some verbs and not others and may differ in meaning after a verb: *The cowboy stopped to sing. The cowboy stopped singing.* (See pp. 205–07.)

3 Absolute phrases

An **absolute phrase** consists of a noun or pronoun and a participle, plus any modifiers. It modifies the entire rest of the sentence it appears in.

absolute phrase

Their own place established, many ethnic groups are making way for new arrivals.

Unlike a participial phrase (opposite), an absolute phrase always contains a noun that serves as a subject.

participial phrase

Learning English, many immigrants discover American culture.

absolute phrase

Immigrants having learned English, their opportunities widen.

4 Appositive phrases

An **appositive** is usually a noun that renames another noun. An appositive phrase includes modifiers as well.

appositive phrase

Bizen ware, a dark stoneware, is produced in Japan.

Appositives and appositive phrases sometimes begin with *that is, such as, for example,* or *in other words.*

appositive phrase

Bizen ware is used in the Japanese tea ceremony, that is, the Zen Buddhist observance that links meditation and art.

23b Recognizing subordinate clauses

A **clause** is any group of words that contains both a subject and a predicate. There are two kinds of clauses, and the distinction between them is important.

- **A** ***main clause*** **makes a complete statement and can stand alone as a sentence:** *The sky darkened.*
- **A** ***subordinate clause*** **is just like a main clause** ***except*** **that it begins with a subordinating word:** *when the sky darkened; whoever calls.* The subordinating word reduces the clause from a complete statement to a single part of speech: an adjective, adverb, or noun. Use subordinate clauses to support the ideas in main clauses, as described in **3** pp. 149–50.

Note A subordinate clause punctuated as a sentence is a sentence fragment. (See p. 252.)

Adjective clauses

An **adjective clause** modifies a noun or pronoun. It usually begins with the relative pronoun *who, whom, whose, which,* or *that.*

The relative pronoun is the subject or object of the clause it begins. The clause ordinarily falls immediately after the word it modifies.

adjective clause

Parents who cannot read may have bad memories of school.

adjective clause

One school, which is open year-round, helps parents learn to read.

Adverb clauses

An **adverb clause** modifies a verb, an adjective, another adverb, or a whole word group. It always begins with a subordinating conjunction, such as *although, because, if,* or *when* (see p. 185 for a list).

adverb clause

The school began teaching parents when adult illiteracy gained national attention.

adverb clause — main clause

Because it was directed at people who could not read, advertising had to be inventive.

Noun clauses

A **noun clause** replaces a noun in a sentence and serves as a subject, object, or complement. It begins with *that, what, whatever, who, whom, whoever, whomever, when, where, whether, why,* or *how*.

sentence subject

Whether the program would succeed depended on door-to-door advertising.

noun clause

object of verb

Teachers explained in person how the program would work.

noun clause

24 Sentence Types

The four basic sentence structures vary in the number of main and subordinate clauses. Each structure gives different emphasis to the main and supporting information in a sentence.

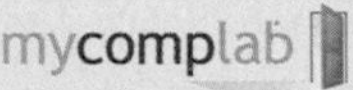

Visit *mycomplab.com* for more resources as well as exercises on sentence types.

24a Recognizing simple sentences

A **simple sentence** consists of a single main clause and no subordinate clause.

main clause
Last summer was unusually hot.

main clause
The summer made many farmers leave the area for good or reduced them to bare existence.

24b Recognizing compound sentences

A **compound sentence** consists of two or more main clauses and no subordinate clause.

main clause / main clause
Last July was hot, but August was even hotter.

main clause / main clause
The hot sun scorched the earth, and the lack of rain killed many crops.

24c Recognizing complex sentences

A **complex sentence** consists of one main clause and one or more subordinate clauses.

main clause / subordinate clause
Rain finally came, although many had left the area by then.

main clause / subordinate clause
Those who remained were able to start anew because the government came to their aid.
subordinate clause

24d Recognizing compound-complex sentences

A **compound-complex sentence** has the characteristics of both the compound sentence (two or more main clauses) and the complex sentence (at least one subordinate clause).

subordinate clause / main clause
When government aid finally came, many people had already been reduced to poverty and others had been forced to move.
main clause

Verbs

Verbs express actions, conditions, and states of being. The basic uses and forms of verbs are described on pp. 182–83. This section explains and solves the most common problems with verbs' forms (Chapter 25), tenses (26), mood (27), and voice (28) and shows how to make verbs match their subjects (29).

25 Verb Forms

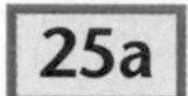

25a Use the correct forms of *sing/sang/sung* and other irregular verbs.

Most verbs are **regular:** they form their past tense and past participle by adding *-d* or *-ed* to the plain form.

Plain form	Past tense	Past participle
live	lived	lived
act	acted	acted

About two hundred English verbs are **irregular:** they form their past tense and past participle in some irregular way. Check a dictionary under the verb's plain form if you have any doubt about its other forms. If the verb is irregular, the dictionary will list the plain form, the past tense, and the past participle in that order (*go, went, gone*). If the dictionary gives only two forms (as in *think, thought*), then the past tense and the past participle are the same.

Grammar checkers A grammar checker may not flag incorrect forms of irregular verbs. For example, a checker flagged *The runner*

Key terms

plain form The dictionary form of the verb: *I walk. You forget.* (See p. 184.)

past-tense form The verb form indicating action that occurred in the past: *I walked. You forgot.* (See p. 184.)

past participle The verb form used with *have, has,* or *had: I have walked.* It may serve as a modifier: *It is a forgotten book.* (See p. 184.)

mycomplab

Visit *mycomplab.com* for more resources as well as exercises on verb forms.

Common irregular verbs

Plain form	Past tense	Past participle
be	was, were	been
become	became	become
begin	began	begun
bid	bid	bid
bite	bit	bitten, bit
blow	blew	blown
break	broke	broken
bring	brought	brought
burst	burst	burst
buy	bought	bought
catch	caught	caught
choose	chose	chosen
come	came	come
cut	cut	cut
dive	dived, dove	dived
do	did	done
dream	dreamed, dreamt	dreamed, dreamt
drink	drank	drunk
drive	drove	driven
eat	ate	eaten
fall	fell	fallen
find	found	found
flee	fled	fled
fly	flew	flown
forget	forgot	forgotten, forgot
freeze	froze	frozen
get	got	got, gotten
give	gave	given
go	went	gone
grow	grew	grown
hang (suspend)	hung	hung
have	had	had
hear	heard	heard
hide	hid	hidden
hold	held	held
keep	kept	kept
know	knew	known
lead	led	led
leave	left	left
lend	lent	lent
let	let	let
lose	lost	lost
pay	paid	paid
ride	rode	ridden
ring	rang	rung

(continued)

Common irregular verbs
(continued)

Plain form	Past tense	Past participle
run	ran	run
say	said	said
see	saw	seen
shake	shook	shaken
shrink	shrank, shrunk	shrunk, shrunken
sing	sang, sung	sung
sink	sank, sunk	sunk
sleep	slept	slept
slide	slid	slid
speak	spoke	spoken
spring	sprang, sprung	sprung
stand	stood	stood
steal	stole	stolen
swim	swam	swum
swing	swung	swung
take	took	taken
tear	tore	torn
throw	threw	thrown
wear	wore	worn
write	wrote	written

stealed second base (*stole* is correct) but not *The runner had steal second base* (*stolen* is correct). When in doubt about the forms of irregular verbs, refer to the preceding list or consult a dictionary.

CULTURE LANGUAGE Some English dialects use distinctive verb forms that differ from those of standard American English: for instance, *drug* for *dragged, growed* for *grew, come* for *came,* or *went* for *gone.* In situations requiring standard American English, use the forms in the list here or in a dictionary.

25b Distinguish between *sit* and *set, lie* and *lay,* and *rise* and *raise.*

The forms of *sit* and *set, lie* and *lay,* and *rise* and *raise* are easy to confuse.

Plain form	Past tense	Past participle
sit	sat	sat
set	set	set
lie	lay	lain
lay	laid	laid
rise	rose	risen
raise	raised	raised

In each of these confusing pairs, one verb is intransitive (it does not take an object) and one is transitive (it does take an object). (See pp. 188–89 for more on this distinction.)

Intransitive

The patients lie in their beds. [*Lie* means "recline" and takes no object.]

Visitors sit with them. [*Sit* means "be seated" or "be located" and takes no object.]

Patients' temperatures rise. [*Rise* means "increase" or "get up" and takes no object.]

Transitive

Orderlies lay the dinner trays on tables. [*Lay* means "place" and takes an object, here *trays.*]

Orderlies set the trays down. [*Set* means "place" and takes an object, here *trays.*]

Nursing aides raise the shades. [*Raise* means "lift" or "bring up" and takes an object, here *shades.*]

25c Use the *-s* and *-ed* forms of the verb when they are required.

Speakers of some English dialects and nonnative speakers of English sometimes omit the *-s* and *-ed* verb endings when they are required in standard American English.

Grammar checkers A grammar checker will flag many omitted *-s* and *-ed* endings from verbs, as in *he ask* and *was ask.* But it will miss many omissions, too.

1 Required *-s* ending

Use the *-s* form of a verb when *both* of these situations hold:

- **The subject is a singular noun (*boy*), an indefinite pronoun (*everyone*), or *he, she,* or *it*.** These subjects are **third person,** used when someone or something is being spoken about.
- **The verb's action occurs in the present.**

The letter asks [not ask] for a quick response.
Delay costs [not cost] money.

Be especially careful with the *-s* forms of *be* (*is*), *have* (*has*), and *do* (*does, doesn't*). These forms should always be used to indicate present time with third-person singular subjects.

The company is [not be] late in responding.
It has [not have] problems.
It doesn't [not don't] have the needed data.
The contract does [not do] depend on the response.

In addition, *be* has an *-s* form in the past tense with *I* and third-person singular subjects:

The company was [not were] in trouble before.

I, you, and plural subjects do *not* take the *-s* form of verbs:

I am [not is] a student.
You are [not is] also a student.
They are [not is] students, too.

2 Required *-ed* or *-d* ending

The *-ed* or *-d* verb form is required in *any* of these situations:

- **The verb's action occurred in the past:**

  The company asked [not ask] for more time.

- **The verb form functions as a modifier:**

  The data concerned [not concern] should be retrievable.

- **The verb form combines with a form of *be* or *have*:**

  The company is supposed [not suppose] to be the best.
  It has developed [not develop] an excellent reputation.

Watch especially for a needed *-ed* or *-d* ending when it isn't pronounced clearly in speech, as in *asked, discussed, mixed, supposed, walked,* and *used.*

25d Use helping verbs with main verbs appropriately.

Helping verbs combine with main verbs in verb phrases: *The line should have been cut. Who was calling?*

Grammar checkers A grammar checker often spots omitted helping verbs and incorrect main verbs with helping verbs, but sometimes it does not. A checker flagged *Many been fortunate* and *She working* but overlooked other errors, such as *The conference will be occurred.*

Key terms

helping verb A word such as *can, may, be, have,* or *do* that forms a verb phrase with another verb to show time, permission, and other meanings. (See p. 183.)

main verb The verb that carries the principal meaning in a verb phrase: *has walked, could be happening.* (See p. 183.)

verb phrase A helping verb plus a main verb: *will be singing, would speak.* (See p. 183.)

1 Required helping verbs

Standard American English requires helping verbs in certain situations:

- **The main verb ends in *-ing:***

  Researchers are conducting fieldwork all over the world. [Not Researchers conducting. . . .]

- **The main verb is *been* or *be:***

  Many have been fortunate in their discoveries. [Not Many been. . . .]
  Some could be real-life Indiana Joneses. [Not Some be. . . .]

- **The main verb is a past participle**, such as *talked, begun,* or *thrown.*

  Their discoveries were covered in newspapers and magazines. [Not Their discoveries covered. . . .]

  The researchers have given interviews on TV. [Not The researchers given. . . .]

The omission of a helping verb may create an incomplete sentence, or **sentence fragment**, because a present participle (*conducting*), an irregular past participle (*been*), or the infinitive *be* cannot stand alone as the only verb in a sentence (see p. 250). To work as sentence verbs, these verb forms need helping verbs.

2 Combination of helping verb + main verb

Helping verbs and main verbs combine into verb phrases in specific ways.

Note The main verb in a verb phrase (the one carrying the main meaning) does not change to show a change in subject or time: *she has sung, you had sung*. Only the helping verb may change.

Form of *be* + present participle

The **progressive tenses** indicate action in progress. Create them with *be, am, is, are, was, were,* or *been* followed by the main verb's present participle:

She is working on a new book.

Key terms

present participle The *-ing* form of a verb: *flying, playing.* (See p. 182.)

progressive tenses Verb tenses expressing action in progress—for instance, *I am flying. I was flying. I will be flying.* (See p. 211.)

Be and *been* always require additional helping verbs to form progressive tenses:

can	might	should	be working	have	been working
could	must	will		has	
may	shall	would		had	

When forming the progressive tenses, be sure to use the *-ing* form of the main verb.

Faulty Her ideas are grow more complex. She is developed a new approach to ethics.

Revised Her ideas are growing more complex. She is developing a new approach to ethics.

Form of *be* + past participle

The **passive voice** of the verb indicates that the subject *receives* the action of the verb. Create the passive voice with a form of *be* (*be, am, is, are, was, were, being,* or *been*) followed by the main verb's past participle:

Her latest book was completed in four months.

Be, being, and *been* always require additional helping verbs to form the passive voice:

have	been completed	am	was	being completed
has		is	were	
had		are		

will be completed

Be sure to use the main verb's past participle for the passive voice:

Faulty Her next book will be publish soon.

Revised Her next book will be published soon.

Note Only transitive verbs may form the passive voice:

Faulty A philosophy conference will be occurred in the same week. [*Occur* is not a transitive verb.]

Revised A philosophy conference will occur in the same week.

Key terms

past participle The *-d* or *-ed* form of a regular verb: *hedged, walked.* Most irregular verbs have distinctive past participles: *eaten, swum.* (See p. 184.)

passive voice The verb form when the subject names the receiver of the verb's action: *An essay was written by every student.* (See p. 218.)

See pp. 216–17 for advice on when to use and when to avoid the passive voice.

Forms of *have*

Four forms of *have* serve as helping verbs: *have, has, had, having.* One of these forms plus the main verb's past participle creates one of the **perfect tenses,** those expressing action completed before another specific time or action:

Some students have complained about the laboratory.
Others had complained before.

Will and other helping verbs sometimes accompany forms of *have* in the perfect tenses:

Several more students will have complained by the end of the week.

Forms of *do*

Do, does, and *did* have three uses as helping verbs, always with the plain form of the main verb:

- **To pose a question:** *How did the trial end?*
- **To emphasize the main verb:** *It did end eventually.*
- **To negate the main verb, along with *not* or *never*:** *The judge did not withdraw.*

Be sure to use the main verb's plain form with any form of *do.*

Faulty The judge did remained in court.
Revised The judge did remain in court.

Modals

The modal helping verbs include *can, could, may,* and *might,* along with several two- and three-word combinations, such as *have to* and *be able to.* (See p. 183 for a list of helping verbs.) Use the plain form of the main verb with a modal unless the modal combines with another helping verb (usually *have*):

Faulty The equipment can detects small vibrations. It should have detect the change.

Revised The equipment can detect small vibrations. It should have detected the change.

Key terms

transitive verb A verb that requires an object to complete its meaning: *Every student completed an essay* (*essay* is the object of *completed*). (See p. 188.)

perfect tenses Verb tenses expressing an action completed before another specific time or action: *We have eaten. We had eaten. We will have eaten.* (See p. 212.)

Modals convey various meanings, with these being most common:

- **Ability:** *can, could, be able to*

  The equipment can detect small vibrations. [Present.]

  The equipment could detect small vibrations. [Past.]

  The equipment is able to detect small vibrations. [Present. Past: *was able to.* Future: *will be able to.*]

- **Possibility:** *could, may, might; could/may/might have* + past participle

  The equipment could fail. [Present.]
  The equipment may fail. [Present or future.]
  The equipment might fail. [Present or future.]
  The equipment may have failed. [Past.]

- **Necessity or obligation:** *must, have to, be supposed to*

  The lab must purchase a backup. [Present or future.]
  The lab has to purchase a backup. [Present or future. Past: *had to.*]
  The lab will have to purchase a backup. [Future.]
  The lab is supposed to purchase a backup. [Present. Past: *was supposed to.*]

- **Permission:** *may, can, could*

  The lab may spend the money. [Present or future.]
  The lab can spend the money. [Present or future.]
  The lab could spend the money. [Present or future, more tentative.]
  The lab could have spent the money. [Past.]

- **Intention:** *will, shall, would*

  The lab will spend the money. [Future.]

  Shall we offer advice? [Future. Use *shall* for questions requesting opinion or consent.]

  We would have offered advice. [Past.]

- **Request:** *could, can, would*

  Could [or Can or Would] you please obtain a bid? [Present or future.]

- **Advisability:** *should, had better, ought to; should have* + past participle

  You should obtain three bids. [Present or future.]
  You had better obtain three bids. [Present or future.]
  You ought to obtain three bids. [Present or future.]
  You should have obtained three bids. [Past.]

- **Past habit:** *would, used to*

In years past we would obtain five bids.
We used to obtain five bids.

25e Use a gerund or an infinitive after a verb as appropriate.

Nonnative speakers of English sometimes stumble over whether to use a gerund or an infinitive after a verb. Gerunds and infinitives may follow certain verbs but not others. And sometimes the use of a gerund or infinitive with the same verb changes the meaning.

Grammar checkers A grammar checker will spot some but not all errors in matching gerunds or infinitives with verbs. For example, a checker failed to flag *I practice to swim* and *I promise helping out.* Use the lists given here and a dictionary of English as a second language to determine whether an infinitive or a gerund is appropriate. (See **3** p. 166 for a list of ESL dictionaries.)

1 Either gerund or infinitive

A gerund or an infinitive may come after the following verbs with no significant difference in meaning.

begin	continue	intend	prefer
can't bear	hate	like	start
can't stand	hesitate	love	

The pump began working.
The pump began to work.

2 Meaning change with gerund or infinitive

With four verbs, a gerund has quite a different meaning from an infinitive:

forget	stop
remember	try

The engineer stopped eating. [He no longer ate.]
The engineer stopped to eat. [He stopped in order to eat.]

Key terms

gerund The *-ing* form of the verb used as a noun: *Smoking is unhealthful.* (See p. 192.)

infinitive The plain form of the verb usually preceded by *to: to smoke.* An infinitive may serve as an adjective, adverb, or noun. (See p. 192.)

3 Gerund, not infinitive

Do not use an infinitive after these verbs:

admit	discuss	mind	recollect
adore	dislike	miss	resent
appreciate	enjoy	postpone	resist
avoid	escape	practice	risk
consider	finish	put off	suggest
deny	imagine	quit	tolerate
detest	keep	recall	understand

Faulty He finished to eat lunch.
Revised He finished eating lunch.

4 Infinitive, not gerund

Do not use a gerund after these verbs:

agree	claim	manage	promise
appear	consent	mean	refuse
arrange	decide	offer	say
ask	expect	plan	wait
assent	have	prepare	want
beg	hope	pretend	wish

Faulty He decided checking the pump.
Revised He decided to check the pump.

5 Noun or pronoun + infinitive

Some verbs may be followed by an infinitive alone or by a noun or pronoun and an infinitive. The presence of a noun or pronoun changes the meaning.

ask	dare	need	wish
beg	expect	promise	would like
choose	help	want	

He expected to watch.
He expected his workers to watch.

Some verbs *must* be followed by a noun or pronoun before an infinitive:

advise	encourage	oblige	require
allow	forbid	order	teach
cause	force	permit	tell
challenge	hire	persuade	train
command	instruct	remind	urge
convince	invite	request	warn

He instructed his workers to watch.

Do not use *to* before the infinitive when it follows one of these verbs and a noun or pronoun:

feel	hear	make ("force")	watch
have	let	see	

He let his workers learn by observation.

25f Use the appropriate particles with two-word verbs.

Standard American English includes some verbs that consist of two words: the verb itself and a **particle**, a preposition or adverb that affects the meaning of the verb.

Look up the answer. [Research the answer.]
Look over the answer. [Examine the answer.]

The meanings of these two-word verbs are often quite different from the meanings of the individual words that make them up. (There are some three-word verbs, too, such as *put up with* and *run out of*.) A dictionary of English as a second language will define two-word verbs and say whether the verbs may be separated in a sentence, as explained below and on the next page. (See **3** p. 166 for a list of ESL dictionaries.) A grammar checker will recognize few if any misuses of two-word verbs.

Note Many two-word verbs are more common in speech than in more formal academic or business writing. For formal writing, consider using *research* instead of *look up*, *examine* or *inspect* instead of *look over*.

1 Inseparable two-word verbs

Verbs and particles that may not be separated by any other words include the following:

catch on	go over	play around	stay away
come across	grow up	run into	stay up
get along	keep on	run out of	take care of
give in	look into	speak up	turn up at

Faulty Children grow quickly up.
Revised Children grow up quickly.

Key terms

preposition A word such as *about*, *for*, or *to* that takes a noun or pronoun as its object: *at the house*, *in the woods*. (See p. 184 for a list of prepositions.)

adverb A word that modifies a verb, adjective, other adverb, or whole word group. (See pp. 183–84.)

2 Separable two-word verbs

Most two-word verbs that take direct objects may be separated by the object.

> Parents help out their children.
> Parents help their children out.

If the direct object is a pronoun, the pronoun *must* separate the verb from the particle.

> **Faulty** Parents help out them.
> **Revised** Parents help them out.

The separable two-word verbs include the following:

bring up	give back	make up	throw out
call off	hand in	point out	try on
call up	hand out	put away	try out
drop off	help out	put back	turn down
fill out	leave out	put off	turn on
fill up	look over	take out	turn up
give away	look up	take over	wrap up

26 Verb Tenses

Tense shows the time of a verb's action. The box on the next page illustrates the tense forms for a regular verb. (Irregular verbs have different past-tense and past-participle forms. See pp. 196–98.)

Grammar checkers A grammar checker can provide little help with incorrect verb tenses and tense sequences because correctness usually depends on meaning.

CULTURE LANGUAGE In standard American English, a verb conveys time and sequence through its form. In some other languages and English dialects, various markers besides verb form may indicate the time of a verb. For instance, in African American dialect *I be attending class on Friday* means that the speaker attends class every Friday. To a speaker of standard American English,

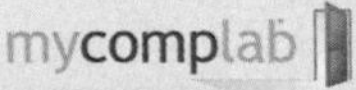

Visit *mycomplab.com* for more resources as well as exercises on verb tenses.

Tenses of a regular verb (active voice)

Present Action that is occurring now, occurs habitually, or is generally true

Simple present Plain form or *-s* form

I walk.
You/we/they walk.
He/she/it walks.

Present progressive *Am, is,* or *are* plus *-ing* form

I am walking.
You/we/they are walking.
He/she/it is walking.

Past Action that occurred before now

Simple past Past-tense form (*-d* or *-ed*)

I/he/she/it walked.
You/we/they walked.

Past progressive *Was* or *were* plus *-ing* form

I/he/she/it was walking.
You/we/they were walking.

Future Action that will occur in the future

Simple future Plain form plus *will*

I/you/he/she/it/we/they will walk.

Future progressive *Will be* plus *-ing* form

I/you/he/she/it/we/they will be walking.

Present perfect Action that began in the past and is linked to the present

Present perfect *Have* or *has* plus past participle (*-d* or *-ed*)

I/you/we/they have walked.
He/she/it has walked.

Present perfect progressive *Have been* or *has been* plus *-ing* form

I/you/we/they have been walking.
He/she/it has been walking.

Past perfect Action that was completed before another past action

Past perfect *Had* plus past participle (*-d* or *-ed*)

I/you/he/she/it/we/they had walked.

Past perfect progressive *Had been* plus *-ing* form

I/you/he/she/it/we/they had been walking.

Future perfect Action that will be completed before another future action

Future perfect *Will have* plus past participle (*-d* or *-ed*)

I/you/he/she/it/we/they will have walked.

Future perfect progressive *Will have been* plus *-ing* form

I/you/he/she/it/we/they will have been walking.

however, the sentence may be unclear: last Friday? this Friday? every Friday? The intended meaning must be indicated by verb tense. *I attended class on Friday. I will attend class on Friday. I attend class on Friday.*

26a Observe the special uses of the present tense (*sing*).

The present tense has several distinctive uses.

Action occurring now

She understands the problem.
We define the problem differently.

Habitual or recurring action

Banks regularly undergo audits.
The audits monitor the banks' activities.

A general truth

The mills of the gods grind slowly.
The earth is round.

Discussion of literature, film, and so on

Huckleberry Finn has adventures we all envy.
In that article the author examines several causes of crime.

Future time

Next week we draft a new budget.
Funding ends in less than a year.

(The present tense shows future time with expressions like those in the examples above: *next week, in less than a year.*)

26b Observe the uses of the perfect tenses (*have/had/will have sung*).

The **perfect tenses** consist of a form of *have* plus the verb's past participle (*closed, hidden*). They indicate an action completed before another specific time or action. The present perfect tense also indicates action begun in the past and continued into the present.

present perfect
The dancer has performed here only once. [The action is completed at the time of the statement.]

present perfect
Critics have written about the performance ever since. [The action began in the past and continues now.]

past perfect
The dancer had trained in Asia before his performance. [The action was completed before another past action.]

future perfect
He will have danced here again by the end of the year. [The action begins now or in the future and will be completed by a specific time in the future.]

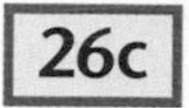 With the present perfect tense, the words *since* and *for* are followed by different information. After *since,* give a specific point in time: *The play has run since 1989.* After *for,* give a span of time: *It has run for decades.*

26c Observe the uses of the progressive tenses (*is/was/will be singing*).

The **progressive tenses** indicate continuing (therefore progressive) action. In standard American English the progressive tenses consist of a form of *be* plus the verb's *-ing* form (present participle). (The words *be* and *been* must be combined with other helping verbs. See pp. 201–02.)

The economy is improving. (present progressive)

Last year the economy was stagnating. (past progressive)

Economists will be watching for signs of growth. (future progressive)

The government has been expecting an upturn. (present perfect progressive)

Various indicators had been suggesting improvement. (past perfect progressive)

By the end of this year, investors will have been watching interest rates nervously for nearly a decade. (future perfect progressive)

Note Verbs that express unchanging states (especially mental states) rather than physical actions do not usually appear in the progressive tenses. These verbs include *adore, appear, believe, belong, care, hate, have, hear, know, like, love, mean, need, own, prefer, remember, see, sound, taste, think, understand,* and *want.*

Faulty She is wanting to study ethics.
Revised She wants to study ethics.

26d Keep tenses consistent.

Within a sentence, the tenses of verbs and verb forms need not be identical as long as they reflect actual changes in time: *Ramon will graduate from college thirty years after his father arrived in America.* But needless shifts in tense will confuse or distract readers:

Inconsistent Immediately after Booth shot Lincoln, Major Rathbone threw himself upon the assassin. But Booth pulls a knife and plunges it into the major's arm.

Revised Immediately after Booth shot Lincoln, Major Rathbone threw himself upon the assassin. But Booth pulled a knife and plunged it into the major's arm.

Inconsistent The main character in the novel suffers psychologically because he has a clubfoot, but he eventually triumphed over his disability.

Revised The main character in the novel suffers psychologically because he has a clubfoot, but he eventually triumphs over his disability. [Use the present tense to discuss the content of literature, film, and so on.]

26e Use the appropriate sequence of verb tenses.

The **sequence of tenses** is the relation between the verb tense in a main clause and the verb tense in a subordinate clause. The tenses should change when necessary to reflect changes in actual or relative time. The main difficulties with tense sequence are discussed on these pages.

1 Past or past perfect tense in main clause

When the verb in the main clause is in the past or past perfect tense, the verb in the subordinate clause must also be past or past perfect:

main clause: past — subordinate clause: past

The researchers discovered that people varied widely in their knowledge of public events.

main clause: past — subordinate clause: past perfect

The variation occurred because respondents had been born in different decades.

main clause: past perfect — subordinate clause: past

None of them had been born when Dwight Eisenhower was President.

Key terms

main clause A word group that can stand alone as a sentence because it contains a subject and a predicate and does not begin with a subordinating word. *Books are valuable.* (See p. 193.)

subordinate clause A word group that contains a subject and a predicate, begins with a subordinating word such as *because* or *who,* and is not a question: *Books are valuable when they enlighten.* (See p. 193.)

Exception Always use the present tense for a general truth, such as *The earth is round:*

main clause: past — subordinate clause: present

Most understood that popular Presidents are not necessarily good Presidents.

2 Conditional sentences

A **conditional sentence** states a factual relation between cause and effect, makes a prediction, or speculates about what might happen. Such a sentence usually contains a subordinate clause beginning with *if, when,* or *unless* and a main clause stating the result. The three kinds of conditional sentences use distinctive verbs.

Factual relation

Statements linking factual causes and effects use matched tenses in the subordinate and main clauses:

subordinate clause: present — main clause: present

When a voter casts a ballot, he or she has complete privacy.

subordinate clause: past — main clause: past

When voters registered in some states, they had to pay a poll tax.

Prediction

Predictions generally use the present tense in the subordinate clause and the future tense in the main clause:

subordinate clause: present — main clause: future

Unless citizens regain faith in politics, they will not vote.

Sometimes the verb in the main clause consists of *may, can, should,* or *might* plus the verb's plain form: *If citizens regain faith, they may vote.*

Speculation

The verbs in speculations depend on whether the linked events are possible or impossible. For possible events in the present, use the past tense in the subordinate clause and *would, could,* or *might* plus the verb's plain form in the main clause:

subordinate clause: past — main clause: *would* + verb

If voters had more confidence, they would vote more often.

Use *were* instead of *was* in the subordinate clause, even when the subject is *I, he, she, it,* or a singular noun. (See pp. 214–15 for more on this distinctive verb form.)

subordinate clause: past — main clause: *would* + verb

If the voter were more confident, he or she would vote more often.

For impossible events in the present—events that are contrary to fact—use the same forms as above (including the distinctive *were* when applicable):

subordinate clause: past — main clause: *might* + verb

If Lincoln were alive, he might inspire confidence.

For impossible events in the past, use the past perfect tense in the subordinate clause and *would, could,* or *might* plus the present perfect tense in the main clause:

subordinate clause: past perfect — main clause: *might* + present perfect

If Lincoln had lived past the Civil War, he might have helped stabilize the country.

27 Verb Mood

Mood in grammar is a verb form that indicates the writer's or speaker's attitude toward what he or she is saying. The **indicative mood** states a fact or opinion or asks a question: *The theater needs help.* The **imperative mood** expresses a command or gives a direction. It omits the subject of the sentence, *you: Help the theater.*

The **subjunctive mood** is trickier and requires distinctive verb forms described below and opposite.

Grammar checkers A grammar checker may spot some errors in the subjunctive mood, but it may miss others. For example, a checker flagged *I wish I was home* (should be *were home*) but not *If I were home, I will not leave* (should be *would not leave*).

27a Use the subjunctive verb forms appropriately, as in *I wish I were.*

The subjunctive mood expresses a suggestion, requirement, or desire, or it states a condition that is contrary to fact (that is, imaginary or hypothetical).

mycomplab

Visit *mycomplab.com* for more resources as well as exercises on verb mood.

- **Verbs such as *ask, insist, urge, require, recommend,* and *suggest* indicate request or requirement.** They often precede a subordinate clause beginning with *that* and containing the substance of the request or requirement. For all subjects, the verb in the *that* clause is the plain form:

  Rules require that every donation be mailed. [plain form: be]

- **Contrary-to-fact clauses state imaginary or hypothetical conditions and usually begin with *if* or *unless* or follow *wish*.** For present contrary-to-fact clauses, use the verb's past-tense form (for *be,* use the past-tense form *were*):

  If the theater were in better shape and had more money, its future would be assured. [past: were; past: had]

  I wish I were able to donate money. [past: were]

  For past contrary-to-fact clauses, use the verb's past perfect form (*had* + past participle):

  The theater would be better funded if it had been better managed. [past perfect: had been]

  Note Do not use the helping verb *would* or *could* in a contrary-to fact clause beginning with *if:*

Not	Many people would have helped if they would have known.
But	Many people would have helped if they had known.

See also pp. 213–14 on verb tenses in sentences like these.

27b Keep mood consistent.

Shifts in mood within a sentence or among related sentences can be confusing. Such shifts occur most frequently in directions.

Inconsistent	Cook the mixture slowly, and you should stir it until the sugar is dissolved. [Mood shifts from imperative to indicative.]
Revised	Cook the mixture slowly, and stir it until the sugar is dissolved. [Consistently imperative.]

28 Verb Voice

The **voice** of a verb tells whether the subject of the sentence performs the action (**active**) or is acted upon (**passive**). The actor in a passive sentence may be named in a prepositional phrase (as in *Rents are controlled by the city*), or the actor may be omitted (as in *Rents are controlled*).

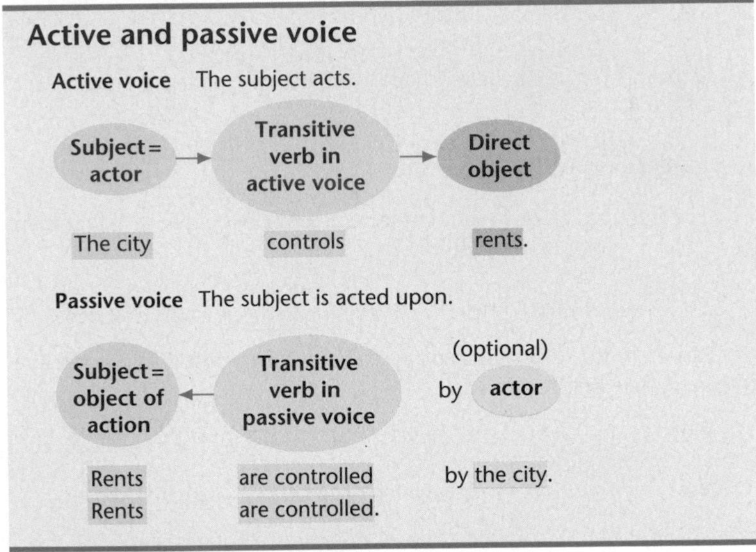

Active and passive voice
Active voice The subject acts.
Subject = actor
Transitive verb in active voice
Direct object
The city
controls
rents.
Passive voice The subject is acted upon.
Subject = object of action
Transitive verb in passive voice
(optional)
by actor
Rents
are controlled
by the city.
Rents
are controlled.

CULTURE LANGUAGE A passive verb always consists of a form of *be* plus the past participle of the main verb: *rents are controlled, people were inspired*. Other helping verbs must also be used with the words *be, being,* and *been: rents have been controlled, people would have been inspired*. Only a transitive verb (one that takes an object) may be used in the passive voice. (See p. 188.)

28a Generally, prefer the active voice. Use the passive voice when the actor is unknown or unimportant.

The active voice is usually clearer, more concise, and more forthright than the passive voice.

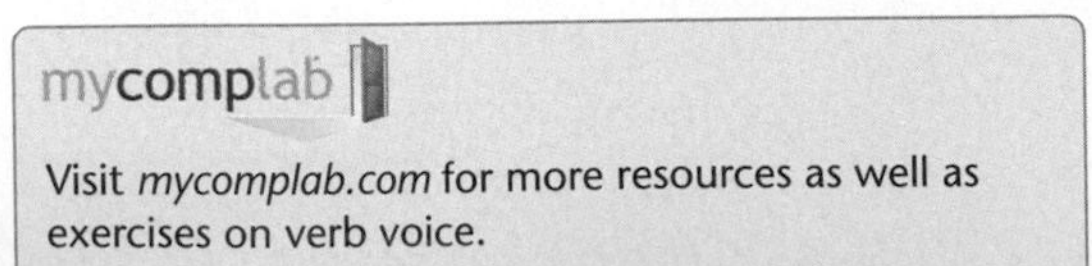

mycomplab
Visit mycomplab.com for more resources as well as exercises on verb voice.

Weak passive The library is used by both students and teachers for studying and research, and the plan to expand it has been praised by many.

Strong active Both students and teachers use the library for studying and research, and many have praised the plan to expand it.

The passive voice is useful in two situations: when the actor is unknown and when the actor is unimportant or less important than the object of the action.

> The Internet was established in 1969 by the US Department of Defense. The network has been extended internationally to governments, universities, foundations, corporations, and private individuals. [In the first sentence the writer wishes to stress the Internet rather than the Department of Defense. In the second sentence the actor is unknown or too complicated to name.]
>
> After the solution had been cooled to 10°C, the acid was added. [The person who cooled and added, perhaps the writer, is less important than the facts that the solution was cooled and acid was added. Passive sentences are common in scientific writing.]

Grammar checkers Most grammar checkers can be set to spot the passive voice. But they will also flag appropriate uses of the passive voice (such as when the actor is unknown).

28b Keep voice consistent.

Shifts in voice that involve shifts in subject are usually unnecessary and confusing.

Inconsistent Internet blogs cover an enormous range of topics. Opportunities for people to discuss pet issues are provided on these sites.

Revised Internet blogs cover an enormous range of topics and provide opportunities for people to discuss pet issues.

A shift in voice is appropriate when it helps focus the reader's attention on a single subject, as in *The candidate campaigned vigorously and was nominated on the first ballot.*

29 Agreement of Subject and Verb

A subject and its verb should agree in number and person.

More Japanese Americans live in Hawaii and California than elsewhere.
subject verb

Daniel Inouye was the first Japanese American in Congress.
subject verb

Most problems of subject-verb agreement arise when endings are omitted from subjects or verbs or when the relation between sentence parts is uncertain.

Grammar checkers A grammar checker will catch many simple errors in subject-verb agreement, such as *Addie and John is late,* and some more complicated errors, such as *Is Margaret and Tom going with us?* (should be *are* in both cases). But a checker failed to flag *The old group has gone their separate ways* (should be *have*) and offered a wrong correction for *The old group have gone their separate ways,* which is already correct.

29a The *-s* and *-es* endings work differently for nouns and verbs.

An *-s* or *-es* ending does opposite things to nouns and verbs: it usually makes a noun *plural,* but it always makes a present-tense verb *singular.* Thus a singular-noun subject will not end in *-s,* but its verb will. A plural-noun subject will end in *-s,* but its verb will not. Between them, subject and verb use only one *-s* ending.

Singular subject	**Plural subject**
The boy plays.	The boys play.
The bird soars.	The birds soar.

Key terms

	Number	
Person	**Singular**	**Plural**
First	I eat.	We eat.
Second	You eat.	You eat.
Third	He/she/it eats.	They eat.
	The bird eats.	Birds eat.

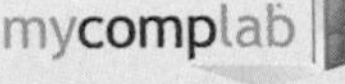

Visit *mycomplab.com* for more resources as well as exercises on subject-verb agreement.

The only exceptions to these rules involve the nouns that form irregular plurals, such as *child/children, woman/women.* The irregular plural still requires a plural verb: *The children play. The women read.*

CULTURE LANGUAGE If your first language or dialect is not standard American English, subject-verb agreement may be problematic, especially for the following reasons:

- **Some English dialects follow different rules for subject-verb agreement,** such as omitting the *-s* ending for singular verbs or using the *-s* ending for plural verbs.

  Nonstandard The voter resist change.
  Standard The voter resists change.
  Standard The voters resist change.

  The verb *be* changes spelling for singular and plural in both present and past tense. (See also pp. 182–83.)

  Nonstandard Taxes is high. They was raised just last year.
  Standard Taxes are high. They were raised just last year.

  Have also has a distinctive *-s* form, *has:*

  Nonstandard The new tax have little chance of passing.
  Standard The new tax has little chance of passing.

- **Some other languages change all parts of verb phrases to match their subjects.** In English verb phrases, however, only the helping verbs *be, have,* and *do* change for different subjects. The modal helping verbs—*can, may, should, will,* and others—do not change:

  Nonstandard The tax mays pass next year.
  Standard The tax may pass next year.

  The main verb in a verb phrase also does not change for different subjects:

  Nonstandard The tax may passes next year.
  Standard The tax may pass next year.

29b Subject and verb should agree even when other words come between them.

The catalog of course requirements often baffles [not baffle] students.

The requirements stated in the catalog are [not is] unclear.

Note Phrases beginning with *as well as, together with, along with,* and *in addition to* do not change a singular subject to plural:

The president, as well as the deans, has [not have] agreed.

29c Subjects joined by *and* usually take plural verbs.

Frost and Roethke were contemporaries.

Exceptions When the parts of the subject form a single idea or refer to a single person or thing, they take a singular verb:

Avocado and bean sprouts is a California sandwich.

When a compound subject is preceded by the adjective *each* or *every,* the verb is usually singular:

Each man, woman, and child has a right to be heard.

29d When parts of a subject are joined by *or* or *nor,* the verb agrees with the nearer part.

Either the painter or the carpenter knows the cost.

The cabinets or the bookcases are too costly.

When one part of the subject is singular and the other plural, avoid awkwardness by placing the plural part closer to the verb so that the verb is plural:

Awkward Neither the owners nor the contractor agrees.

Revised Neither the contractor nor the owners agree.

29e With *everyone* and other indefinite pronouns, use a singular or plural verb as appropriate.

Most indefinite pronouns are singular in meaning (they refer to a single unspecified person or thing), and they take a singular verb:

Something smells. Neither is right.

The plural indefinite pronouns refer to more than one unspecified thing, and they take a plural verb:

Both are correct. Several were invited.

The other indefinite pronouns take a singular or a plural verb depending on whether the word they refer to is singular or plural:

All of the money is reserved for emergencies.

All of the funds are reserved for emergencies.

CULTURE LANGUAGE See p. 244 for the distinction between *few* ("not many") and *a few* ("some").

29f Collective nouns such as *team* take singular or plural verbs depending on meaning.

Use a singular verb with a collective noun when the group acts as a unit:

The team has won five of the last six meets.

But when the group's members act separately, not together, use a plural verb:

The old team have gone their separate ways.

The collective noun *number* may be singular or plural. Preceded by *a*, it is plural; preceded by *the*, it is singular:

A number of people are in debt.

The number of people in debt is very large.

CULTURE LANGUAGE Some noncount nouns (nouns that don't form plurals) are collective nouns because they name groups: for instance, *furniture, clothing, mail, machinery, equipment, military, police.* These noncount nouns usually take singular verbs: *Mail arrives daily.* But some of these nouns take plural verbs,

Key terms

indefinite pronoun A pronoun that does not refer to a specific person or thing:

Singular			*Singular or plural*	*Plural*
anybody	everyone	nothing	all	both
anyone	everything	one	any	few
anything	much	somebody	more	many
each	neither	someone	most	several
either	nobody	something	none	
everybody	no one		some	

collective noun A noun with singular form that names a group of individuals or things—for instance, *army, audience, committee, crowd, family.*

including *clergy, military, people, police,* and any collective noun that comes from an adjective, such as *the poor, the rich, the young, the elderly.* If you mean one representative of the group, use a singular noun such as *police officer* or *poor person.*

29g *Who, which,* and *that* take verbs that agree with their antecedents.

When used as subjects, *who, which,* and *that* refer to another word in the sentence, called the **antecedent.** The verb agrees with the antecedent:

> Mayor Garber ought to listen to the people who work for her.
>
> Bardini is the only aide who has her ear.

Agreement problems often occur with *who* and *that* when the sentence includes *one of the* or *the only one of the:*

> Bardini is one of the aides who work unpaid. [Of the aides who work unpaid, Bardini is one.]
>
> Bardini is the only one of the aides who knows the community. [Of the aides, only one, Bardini, knows the community.]

CULTURE LANGUAGE In phrases beginning with *one of the,* be sure the noun is plural: *Bardini is one of the aides* [not *aide*] *who work unpaid.*

29h *News* and other singular nouns ending in *-s* take singular verbs.

Singular nouns ending in *-s* include *athletics, economics, mathematics, measles, mumps, news, physics, politics,* and *statistics,* as well as place names such as *Athens, Wales,* and *United States.*

> After so long a wait, the news has to be good.
>
> Statistics is required of psychology majors.

A few of these words also take plural verbs, but only when they describe individual items rather than whole bodies of activity or knowledge: *The statistics prove him wrong.*

Measurements and figures ending in *-s* may also be singular when the quantity they refer to is a unit:

> Three years is a long time to wait.

Three-fourths of the library consists of reference books.

29i The verb agrees with the subject even when it precedes the subject.

The verb precedes the subject mainly in questions and in constructions beginning with *there* or *here* and a form of *be:*

Is voting a right or a privilege?

Are a right and a privilege the same thing?

There are differences between them.

29j *Is, are,* and other linking verbs agree with their subjects, not subject complements.

Make a linking verb agree with its subject, usually the first element in the sentence, not with the noun or pronoun serving as a subject complement.

The child's sole support is her court-appointed guardians.

Her court-appointed guardians are the child's sole support.

29k Use singular verbs with titles and with words being defined.

Hakada Associates is a new firm.

Dream Days remains a favorite book.

Folks is a down-home word for *people*.

Key terms

linking verb A verb that connects or equates the subject and subject complement: for example, *seem, become, appear,* and forms of *be.* (See p. 189.)

subject complement A word that describes or renames the subject: *They became chemists*. (See p. 189.)

Pronouns

Pronouns—words such as *she* and *who* that refer to nouns—merit special care because all their meaning comes from the other words they refer to. This section discusses pronoun case (Chapter 30), matching pronouns and the words they refer to (31), and making sure pronouns refer to the right nouns (32).

30 Pronoun Case

Case is the form of a noun or pronoun that shows the reader how it functions in a sentence.

- **The subjective case** indicates that the word is a subject or subject complement.
- **The objective case** indicates that the word is an object of a verb or preposition.
- **The possessive case** indicates that the word owns or is the source of a noun in the sentence.

Nouns change form only to show possession: *teacher's* (see **5** pp. 282–85). Most of the pronouns listed on the next page change more frequently.

Key terms

subject Who or what a sentence is about: *Biologists often study animals. They often work in laboratories.* (See pp. 186–87.)

subject complement A word or words that rename or describe the sentence subject: *Biologists are scientists. The best biologists are she and Scoggins.* (See p. 189.)

object of verb The receiver of the verb's action (**direct object**): *Many biologists study animals. The animals teach them.* Or the person or thing the action is performed for (**indirect object**): *Some biologists give animals homes. The animals give them pleasure.* (See pp. 188–90.)

object of preposition The word linked by *with, for,* or another preposition to the rest of the sentence: *Many biologists work in a laboratory. For them the lab often provides a second home.* (See p. 191.)

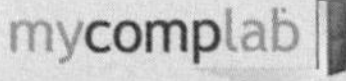

Visit *mycomplab.com* for more resources as well as exercises on pronoun case.

Subjective	Objective	Possessive
I	me	my, mine
you	you	your, yours
he	him	his
she	her	her, hers
it	it	its
we	us	our, ours
you	you	your, yours
they	them	their, theirs
who	whom	whose
whoever	whomever	—

Grammar checkers A grammar checker may flag some problems with pronoun case, but it will also miss a lot. For instance, one checker spotted the error in *We asked whom would come* (should be *who would come*), but it overlooked *We dreaded them coming* (should be *their coming*).

CULTURE LANGUAGE In standard American English, *-self* pronouns do not change form to show function. Their only forms are *myself, yourself, himself, herself, itself, ourselves, yourselves, themselves.* Avoid nonstandard forms such as *hisself, ourself,* and *theirselves.*

30a Distinguish between compound subjects and compound objects: *she and I* vs. *her and me.*

Compound subjects or objects—those consisting of two or more nouns or pronouns—have the same case forms as they would if one noun or pronoun stood alone:

compound subject
She and Novick discussed the proposal.

compound object
The proposal disappointed her and him.

If you are in doubt about the correct form, try the test in the following box:

A test for case forms in compound constructions

1. **Identify a compound construction** (one connected by *and, but, or, nor*).

   [He, Him] and [I, me] won the prize.
   The prize went to [he, him] and [I, me].

(continued)

A test for case forms in compound constructions
(continued)

2. **Write a separate sentence for each part of the compound:**

   [He, Him] won the prize. [I, Me] won the prize.
   The prize went to [he, him]. The prize went to [I, me].

3. **Choose the pronouns that sound correct.**

   He won the prize. I won the prize. [Subjective.]
   The prize went to him. The prize went to me. [Objective.]

4. **Put the separate sentences back together.**

   He and I won the prize.
   The prize went to him and me.

30b Use the subjective case for subject complements: *It was she.*

After a linking verb, a pronoun renaming the subject (a subject complement) should be in the subjective case:

subject complement
The ones who care most are she and Novick.

subject complement
It was they whom the mayor appointed.

If this construction sounds stilted to you, use the more natural order: *She and Novick are the ones who care most. The mayor appointed them.*

30c The use of *who* vs. *whom* depends on the pronoun's function in its clause.

Use *who* where you would use *he* or *she*—all ending in vowels. Use *whom* where you would use *him* or *her*—all ending in consonants.

1 Questions

At the beginning of a question, use *who* for a subject and *whom* for an object:

subject → Who wrote the policy? object ← Whom does it affect?

Key term

linking verb A verb, such as a form of *be,* that connects a subject and a word that renames or describes the subject (subject complement): *They are biologists.* (See p. 189.)

To find the correct case of *who* in a question, use the following test:

1. **Pose the question:**

   [Who, Whom] makes that decision?
   [Who, Whom] does one ask?

2. **Answer the question, using a personal pronoun.** Choose the pronoun that sounds correct, and note its case:

   [She, Her] makes that decision. She makes that decision. [Subjective.]
   One asks [she, her]. One asks her. [Objective.]

3. **Use the same case (*who* or *whom*) in the question:**

   Who makes that decision? [Subjective.]
   Whom does one ask? [Objective.]

2 Subordinate clauses

In a subordinate clause, use *who* or *whoever* for a subject, *whom* or *whomever* for an object.

subject →
Give old clothes to whoever needs them.

object ←
I don't know whom the mayor appointed.

To determine which form to use, try the following test:

1. **Locate the subordinate clause:**

   Few people know [who, whom] they should ask.
   They are unsure [who, whom] makes the decision.

2. **Rewrite the subordinate clause as a separate sentence, substituting a personal pronoun for *who, whom*.** Choose the pronoun that sounds correct, and note its case:

   They should ask [she, her]. They should ask her. [Objective.]
   [She, Her] makes the decision. She makes the decision. [Subjective.]

3. **Use the same case (*who* or *whom*) in the subordinate clause:**

   Few people know whom they should ask. [Objective.]
   They are unsure who makes the decision. [Subjective.]

Key term

subordinate clause A word group that contains a subject and a predicate and also begins with a subordinating word, such as *who, whom,* or *because.* (See p. 193.)

Note Don't let expressions such as *I think* and *she says* mislead you into using *whom* rather than *who* for the subject of a clause.

subject

He is the one who I think is best qualified.

To choose between *who* and *whom* in such constructions, delete the interrupting phrase so that you can see the true relation between parts: *He is the one who is best qualified.*

30d Use the appropriate case in other constructions.

1 *We* or *us* with a noun

The choice of *we* or *us* before a noun depends on the use of the noun:

object of preposition

Freezing weather is welcomed by us skaters.

subject

We skaters welcome freezing weather.

2 Pronoun in an appositive

In an appositive the case of a pronoun depends on the function of the word the appositive describes or identifies:

appositive identifies object

The class elected two representatives, DeShawn and me.

appositive identifies subject

Two representatives, DeShawn and I, were elected.

3 Pronoun after *than* or *as*

When a pronoun follows *than* or *as* in a comparison, the case of the pronoun indicates what words may have been omitted. A subjective pronoun must be the subject of the omitted verb:

subject

Some critics like Glass more than he [does].

An objective pronoun must be the object of the omitted verb:

object

Some critics like Glass more than [they like] him.

Key term

appositive A noun or noun substitute that renames another noun immediately before it. (See p. 193.)

4 Subject and object of infinitive

Both the object *and* the subject of an infinitive are in the objective case:

subject of infinitive
The school asked him to speak.

object of infinitive
Students chose to invite him.

5 Case before a gerund

Ordinarily, use the possessive form of a pronoun or noun immediately before a gerund:

The coach disapproved of their lifting weights.

The coach's disapproving was a surprise.

31 Agreement of Pronoun and Antecedent

The antecedent of a pronoun is the noun or other pronoun to which the pronoun refers:

Homeowners fret over their tax bills.
antecedent pronoun

Its constant increases make the tax bill a dreaded document.
pronoun antecedent

For clarity, a pronoun should agree with its antecedent in person, number, and gender.

Grammar checkers A grammar checker cannot help you with agreement between pronoun and antecedent because it cannot recognize the intended relation between the two.

Key terms

infinitive The plain form of the verb plus *to: to run.* (See p. 192.)

gerund The *-ing* form of a verb used as a noun: *Running is fun.* (See p. 192.)

CULTURE LANGUAGE The gender of a pronoun should match its antecedent, not a noun that the pronoun may modify: *Sara Young invited her* [not *his*] *son.* Also, English nouns have only neuter gender unless they specifically refer to males or females. Thus nouns such as *book, table, sun,* and *earth* take the pronoun *it.*

31a Antecedents joined by *and* usually take plural pronouns.

Mr. Bartos and I cannot settle our dispute.

The dean and my adviser have offered their help.

Exceptions When the compound antecedent refers to a single idea, person, or thing, then the pronoun is singular:

My friend and adviser offered her help.

When the compound antecedent follows *each* or *every,* the pronoun is singular:

Every girl and woman took her seat.

31b When parts of an antecedent are joined by *or* or *nor,* the pronoun agrees with the nearer part.

Tenants or owners must present their grievances.

Either the tenant or the owner will have her way.

When one subject is plural and the other singular, the sentence will be awkward unless you put the plural subject second:

Awkward Neither the tenants nor the owner has yet made her case.

Revised Neither the owner nor the tenants have yet made their case.

Key terms

	Number	
Person	**Singular**	**Plural**
First	*I*	*we*
Second	*you*	*you*
Third	*he, she, it,* indefinite pronouns, singular nouns	*they,* plural nouns
Gender		
Masculine	*he,* nouns naming males	
Feminine	*she,* nouns naming females	
Neuter	*it,* all other nouns	

31c With *everyone, person,* and other indefinite words, use a singular or plural pronoun as appropriate.

Indefinite words—indefinite pronouns and generic nouns—do not refer to any specific person or thing. Most indefinite pronouns and all generic nouns are singular in meaning. When they serve as antecedents of pronouns, the pronouns should be singular:

> Everyone on the women's team now has her own locker.
> indefinite pronoun
>
> Every person on the women's team now has her own locker.
> generic noun

Six indefinite pronouns—*all, any, more, most, none, some*—may be singular or plural in meaning depending on what they refer to:

> Few women athletes had changing spaces, so most had to change in their rooms.
>
> Most of the changing space was dismal, its color a drab olive green.

Four indefinite pronouns—*both, few, many, several*—are always plural in meaning:

> Few realize how their athletic facilities have changed.

Most agreement problems arise with the singular indefinite words. We often use these words to mean "many" or "all" rather than "one" and then refer to them with plural pronouns, as in *Everyone has their own locker.* Often, too, we mean indefinite words to include both masculine and feminine genders and thus resort to *they* instead of the **generic *he***—the masculine pronoun referring to both genders, as in *Everyone deserves his privacy.* (For more on the

Key terms

indefinite pronoun A pronoun that does not refer to a specific person or thing:

Singular			*Singular or plural*	*Plural*
anybody	everyone	nothing	all	both
anyone	everything	one	any	few
anything	much	somebody	more	many
each	neither	someone	most	several
either	nobody	something	none	
everybody	no one		some	

generic noun A singular noun such as *person* and *student* when it refers to a typical member of a group, not to a particular individual.

generic *he,* which many readers view as sexist, see **3** p. 164.) To achieve agreement in such cases, you have the following options.

Ways to correct agreement with indefinite words

- **Change the indefinite word to a plural, and use a plural pronoun to match:**

  Faulty Every athlete deserves their privacy.
  Revised **Athletes** deserve their privacy.

- **Rewrite the sentence to omit the pronoun:**

  Faulty Everyone is entitled to their own locker.
  Revised Everyone is entitled to **a** locker.

- **Use *he or she* (*him or her, his or her*) to refer to the indefinite word:**

  Faulty Now everyone has their private space.
  Revised Now everyone has **his or her** private space.

  However, used more than once in several sentences, *he or she* quickly becomes awkward. (Many readers do not accept the alternative *he/she.*) Using the plural or omitting the pronoun will usually correct agreement problems and create more readable sentences.

31d Collective nouns such as *team* take singular or plural pronouns depending on meaning.

Use a singular pronoun with a collective noun when referring to the group as a unit:

The committee voted to disband itself.

When referring to the individual members of the group, use a plural pronoun:

The old team have gone their separate ways.

CULTURE LANGUAGE In standard American English, collective nouns that are noncount nouns (they don't form plurals) usually take singular pronouns: *The mail sits in its own basket.* A few noncount nouns take plural pronouns, including *clergy, military, police, the rich,* and *the poor: The police support their unions.*

Key term

collective noun A noun with singular form that names a group of individuals or things—for instance, *army, audience, committee, crowd, family, group, team.*

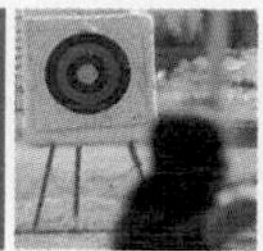

32 Reference of Pronoun to Antecedent

A **pronoun** should refer clearly to its **antecedent,** the noun it substitutes for. Otherwise, readers will have difficulty grasping the pronoun's meaning.

Grammar checkers A grammar checker cannot recognize unclear pronoun reference. For instance, a checker did not flag any of the confusing examples in this chapter.

CULTURE LANGUAGE In standard American English, a pronoun needs a clear antecedent nearby, but don't use both a pronoun and its antecedent as the subject of the same clause: *Jim* [not *Jim he*] *told Mark to go alone.* (See also p. 260.)

32a Make a pronoun refer clearly to one antecedent.

When either of two nouns can be a pronoun's antecedent, the reference will not be clear.

Confusing Emily Dickinson is sometimes compared with Jane Austen, but she was quite different.

Revise such a sentence in one of two ways:

- **Replace the pronoun with the appropriate noun.**

Clear Emily Dickinson is sometimes compared with Jane Austen, but Dickinson [or Austen] was quite different.

- **Avoid repetition by rewriting the sentence.** If you use the pronoun, make sure it has only one possible antecedent.

Clear Despite occasional comparison, Emily Dickinson and Jane Austen were quite different.

Clear Though sometimes compared with her, Emily Dickinson was quite different from Jane Austen.

32b Place a pronoun close enough to its antecedent to ensure clarity.

A clause beginning with *who, which,* or *that* should generally fall immediately after the word to which it refers.

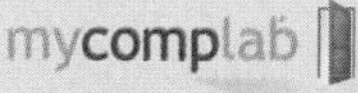

Visit *mycomplab.com* for more resources as well as exercises on pronoun reference.

Confusing Jody found a lamp in the attic that her aunt had used.

Clear In the attic Jody found a lamp that her aunt had used.

32c Make a pronoun refer to a specific antecedent, not an implied one.

A pronoun should refer to a specific noun or other pronoun. A reader can only guess at the meaning of a pronoun when its antecedent is implied by the context, not stated outright.

1 Vague *this, that, which,* or *it*

This, that, which, or *it* should refer to a specific noun, not to a whole word group expressing an idea or situation.

Confusing The British knew little of the American countryside, and they had no experience with the colonists' guerrilla tactics. This gave the colonists an advantage.

Clear The British knew little of the American countryside, and they had no experience with the colonists' guerrilla tactics. This ignorance and inexperience gave the colonists an advantage.

2 Indefinite antecedents with *it* and *they*

It and *they* should have definite noun antecedents. Rewrite the sentence if the antecedent is missing.

Confusing In Chapter 4 of this book it describes the early flights of the Wright brothers.

Clear Chapter 4 of this book describes the early flights of the Wright brothers.

Confusing Even in reality TV shows, they present a false picture of life.

Clear Even reality TV shows present a false picture of life.

3 Implied nouns

A noun may be implied in some other word or phrase, as *happiness* is implied in *happy*, *driver* is implied in *drive*, and *mother* is implied in *mother's*. But a pronoun cannot refer clearly to an implied noun, only to a specific, stated one.

Confusing Cohen's report brought her a lawsuit.

Clear Cohen was sued over her report.

Confusing	Her reports on psychological development generally go unnoticed outside it. ?
Clear	Her reports on psychological development generally go unnoticed outside the field.

32d Use *you* only to mean "you, the reader."

You should clearly mean "you, the reader." The context must be appropriate for such a meaning:

Inappropriate	In the fourteenth century you had to struggle simply to survive.
Revised	In the fourteenth century one [or a person] had to struggle simply to survive.

Writers sometimes drift into *you* because *one, a person,* or a similar indefinite word can be difficult to sustain. Sentence after sentence, the indefinite word may sound stuffy, and it requires *he* or *he or she* for pronoun-antecedent agreement (see pp. 231–32). To avoid these problems, try using plural nouns and pronouns:

Original	In the fourteenth century one had to struggle simply to survive.
Revised	In the fourteenth century people had to struggle simply to survive.

32e Keep pronouns consistent.

Within a sentence or a group of related sentences, pronouns should be consistent. Partly, consistency comes from making pronouns and their antecedents agree (see Chapter 31). In addition, the pronouns within a passage should match each other.

Inconsistent	One finds when reading that your concentration improves with practice, so that I now comprehend more in less time.
Revised	I find when reading that my concentration improves with practice, so that I now comprehend more in less time.

Modifiers

Modifiers describe or limit other words in a sentence. They are adjectives, adverbs, or word groups serving as adjectives or adverbs. This section shows how to solve problems in the forms of modifiers (Chapter 33) and in their relation to the rest of the sentence (34).

33 Adjectives and Adverbs

Adjectives modify nouns (*happy child*) and pronouns (*special someone*). **Adverbs** modify verbs (*almost see*), adjectives (*very happy*), other adverbs (*not very*), and whole word groups (*Otherwise, I'll go*). The only way to tell whether a modifier should be an adjective or an adverb is to determine its function in the sentence.

Grammar checkers A grammar checker will spot some but not all problems with misused adjectives and adverbs. For instance, a checker flagged *Some children suffer bad* and *Jenny did not feel nothing*. But it did not flag *Educating children good should be everyone's focus*.

CULTURE LANGUAGE In standard American English, an adjective does not change along with the noun it modifies to show plural number: *square* [not *squares*] *spaces*. Only nouns form plurals.

33a Use adjectives only to modify nouns and pronouns.

Do not use adjectives instead of adverbs to modify verbs, adverbs, or other adjectives:

Faulty Educating children good should be everyone's focus.

Revised Educating children well should be everyone's focus.

Faulty Some children suffer bad.

Revised Some children suffer badly.

CULTURE LANGUAGE To negate a verb or an adjective, use the adverb *not*.

They are not learning. They are not stupid.

mycomplab

Visit *mycomplab.com* for more resources as well as exercises on adjectives and adverbs.

To negate a noun, use the adjective *no*.

> No child should fail to read.

33b Use an adjective after a linking verb to modify the subject. Use an adverb to modify a verb.

Some verbs may or may not be linking verbs, depending on their meaning in the sentence. When the word after the verb modifies the subject, the verb is linking and the word should be an adjective: *He looked happy*. When the word modifies the verb, however, it should be an adverb: *He looked carefully*.

Two word pairs are especially tricky. One is *bad* and *badly:*

> The weather grew bad. (grew: linking verb; bad: adjective)
>
> She felt bad. (felt: linking verb; bad: adjective)
>
> Flowers grow badly in such soil. (grow: verb; badly: adverb)

The other pair is *good* and *well. Good* serves only as an adjective. *Well* may serve as an adverb with a host of meanings or as an adjective meaning only "fit" or "healthy."

> Decker trained well. (trained: verb; well: adverb)
>
> She felt well. (felt: linking verb; well: adjective)
>
> Her health was good. (was: linking verb; good: adjective)

33c Use the comparative and superlative forms of adjectives and adverbs appropriately.

Adjectives and adverbs can show degrees of quality or amount with the endings *-er* and *-est* or with the words *more* and *most* or *less* and *least.* Most modifiers have three forms:

Positive The basic form listed in the dictionary	**Comparative** A greater or lesser degree of the quality	**Superlative** The greatest or least degree of the quality
Adjectives		
red	redder	reddest
awful	more/less awful	most/least awful
Adverbs		
soon	sooner	soonest
quickly	more/less quickly	most/least quickly

Key term

linking verb A verb that connects a subject and a word that describes the subject: *They are golfers.* Linking verbs include *look, sound, feel, appear, seem, become,* and forms of *be.* (See p. 189.)

If sound alone does not tell you whether to use *-er/-est* or *more/most,* consult a dictionary. If the endings can be used, the dictionary will list them. Otherwise, use *more* or *most.*

1 Irregular adjectives and adverbs

Irregular modifiers change the spelling of their positive form to show comparative and superlative degrees.

Positive	Comparative	Superlative
Adjectives		
good	better	best
bad	worse	worst
little	littler, less	littlest, least
many, some, much	more	most
Adverbs		
well	better	best
badly	worse	worst

2 Double comparisons

A double comparative or double superlative combines the *-er* or *-est* ending with the word *more* or *most.* It is redundant.

Chang was the wisest [not most wisest] person in town.
He was smarter [not more smarter] than anyone else.

3 Logical comparisons

Absolute modifiers

Some adjectives and adverbs cannot logically be compared—for instance, *perfect, unique, dead, impossible, infinite.* These absolute words can be preceded by adverbs like *nearly* or *almost* that mean "approaching," but they cannot logically be modified by *more* or *most* (as in *most perfect*).

Not He was the most unique teacher we had.
But He was a unique teacher.

Completeness

To be logical, a comparison must also be complete in the following ways:

- **The comparison must state a relation fully enough for clarity.**

Unclear Carmakers worry about their industry more than environmentalists.

Clear Carmakers worry about their industry more than environmentalists do.

Clear Carmakers worry about their industry more than they worry about environmentalists.

- **The items being compared should in fact be comparable.**

Illogical The cost of a hybrid car can be greater than a gasoline-powered car. [Illogically compares a cost and a car.]

Revised The cost of a hybrid car can be greater than the cost of [or that of] a gasoline-powered car.

See also **3** p. 153 on parallelism with comparisons.

Any versus *any other*

Use *any other* when comparing something with others in the same group. Use *any* when comparing something with others in a different group.

Illogical Los Angeles is larger than any city in California. [Since Los Angeles is itself a city in California, the sentence seems to say that Los Angeles is larger than itself.]

Revised Los Angeles is larger than any other city in California.

Illogical Los Angeles is larger than any other city in Canada. [The cities in Canada constitute a group to which Los Angeles does not belong.]

Revised Los Angeles is larger than any city in Canada.

33d Watch for double negatives.

In a **double negative** two negative words such as *no, not, none, neither, barely, hardly,* or *scarcely* cancel each other out. Some double negatives are intentional: for instance, *She was not unhappy* indicates with understatement that she was indeed happy. But most double negatives say the opposite of what is intended: *Jenny did not feel nothing* asserts that Jenny felt other than nothing, or something. For the opposite meaning, one of the negatives must be eliminated (*She felt nothing*) or one of them must be changed to a positive (*She did not feel anything*).

Faulty The IRS cannot hardly audit all tax returns. None of its audits never touch many cheaters.

Revised The IRS cannot audit all tax returns. Its audits never touch many cheaters.

33e Distinguish between present and past participles as adjectives.

Both present participles and past participles may serve as adjectives: *a burning building, a burned building.* As in the examples, the two participles usually differ in the time they indicate.

But some present and past participles—those derived from verbs expressing feeling—can have altogether different meanings. The present participle modifies something that causes the feeling: *That was a frightening storm* (the storm frightens). The past participle modifies something that experiences the feeling: *They quieted the frightened horses* (the horses feel fright).

The following participles are among those likely to be confused:

amazing/amazed
amusing/amused
annoying/annoyed
astonishing/astonished
boring/bored
confusing/confused
depressing/depressed
embarrassing/embarrassed
exciting/excited
exhausting/exhausted
fascinating/fascinated
frightening/frightened
frustrating/frustrated
interesting/interested
pleasing/pleased
satisfying/satisfied
shocking/shocked
surprising/surprised
tiring/tired
worrying/worried

33f Use *a, an, the,* and other determiners appropriately.

Determiners are special kinds of adjectives that mark nouns because they always precede nouns. Some common determiners are *a, an,* and *the* (called **articles**) and *my, their, whose, this, these, those, one, some,* and *any.*

Native speakers of standard American English can rely on their intuition when using determiners, but speakers of other languages

Key terms

present participle The *-ing* form of a verb: *flying, writing.* (See p. 182.)

past participle The *-d* or *-ed* form of a regular verb: *slipped, walked.* Most irregular verbs have distinctive past participles, such as *eaten* or *swum.* (See p. 182.)

and dialects often have difficulty with them. In standard American English, the use of determiners depends on the context they appear in and the kind of noun they precede:

- **A *proper noun* names a particular person, place, or thing and begins with a capital letter:** *February, Joe Allen, Red River.* Most proper nouns are not preceded by determiners.
- **A *count noun* names something that is countable in English and can form a plural:** *girl/girls, apple/apples, child/children.* A singular count noun is always preceded by a determiner; a plural count noun sometimes is.
- **A *noncount noun* names something not usually considered countable in English, and so it does not form a plural.** A noncount noun is sometimes preceded by a determiner. Here is a sample of noncount nouns, sorted into groups by meaning:

  Abstractions: confidence, democracy, education, equality, evidence, health, information, intelligence, knowledge, luxury, peace, pollution, research, success, supervision, truth, wealth, work

  Food and drink: bread, candy, cereal, flour, meat, milk, salt, water, wine

  Emotions: anger, courage, happiness, hate, joy, love, respect, satisfaction

  Natural events and substances: air, blood, dirt, gasoline, gold, hair, heat, ice, oil, oxygen, rain, silver, smoke, weather, wood

  Groups: clergy, clothing, equipment, furniture, garbage, jewelry, junk, legislation, machinery, mail, military, money, police, vocabulary

  Fields of study: architecture, accounting, biology, business, chemistry, engineering, literature, psychology, science

A dictionary of English as a second language will tell you whether a noun is a count noun, a noncount noun, or both. (See **3** p. 166 for recommended dictionaries.)

Note Many nouns are sometimes count nouns and sometimes noncount nouns:

> The library has a room for readers. [*Room* is a count noun meaning "walled area."]
>
> The library has room for reading. [*Room* is a noncount noun meaning "space."]

Grammar checkers Partly because the same noun may fall into different groups, a grammar checker is an unreliable guide to missing or misused articles and other determiners. For instance, a checker flagged the omitted *a* before *Scientist* in *Scientist developed new processes;* it did not flag the omitted *a* before *new* in *A scientist developed new process;* and it mistakenly flagged the correctly omitted article *the* before *Vegetation* in *Vegetation suffers from drought.*

1 *A, an,* and *the*

With singular count nouns

A or *an* precedes a singular count noun when the reader does not already know its identity, usually because you have not mentioned it before:

> A scientist in our chemistry department developed a process to strengthen metals. [*Scientist* and *process* are being introduced for the first time.]

The precedes a singular count noun that has a specific identity for the reader, for one of the following reasons:

- **You have mentioned the noun before:**

  A scientist in our chemistry department developed a process to strengthen metals. The scientist patented the process. [*Scientist* and *process* were identified in the preceding sentence.]

- **You identify the noun immediately before or after you state it:**

  The most productive laboratory is the research center in the chemistry department. [*Most productive* identifies *laboratory. In the chemistry department* identifies *research center.* And *chemistry department* is a shared facility—see below.]

- **The noun names something unique—the only one in existence:**

  The sun rises in the east. [*Sun* and *east* are unique.]

- **The noun names an institution or facility that is shared by the community of readers:**

  Many men and women aspire to the presidency. [*Presidency* is a shared institution.]

  The cell phone has changed business communication. [*Cell phone* is a shared facility.]

The is not used before a singular noun that names a general category:

> Wordsworth's poetry shows his love of nature [not the nature].
> General Sherman said that war is hell. [*War* names a general category.]
> The war in Iraq left many wounded. [*War* names a specific war.]

With plural count nouns

A or *an* never precedes a plural noun. *The* does not precede a plural noun that names a general category. *The* does precede a plural noun that names specific representatives of a category.

Men and women are different. [*Men* and *women* name general categories.]

The women formed a team. [*Women* refers to specific people.]

With noncount nouns

A or *an* never precedes a noncount noun. *The* does precede a noncount noun that names specific representatives of a general category.

Vegetation suffers from drought. [*Vegetation* names a general category.]

The vegetation in the park withered or died. [*Vegetation* refers to specific plants.]

With proper nouns

A or *an* never precedes a proper noun. *The* generally does not precede proper nouns.

Garcia lives in Boulder.

There are exceptions, however. For instance, we generally use *the* before plural proper nouns (*the Murphys, the Boston Celtics*) and before the names of groups and organizations (*the Department of Justice, the Sierra Club*), ships (*the Lusitania*), oceans (*the Pacific*), mountain ranges (*the Alps*), regions (*the Middle East*), rivers (*the Mississippi*), and some countries (*the United States, the Netherlands*).

2 Other determiners

The uses of English determiners besides articles also depend on context and kind of noun. The following determiners may be used as indicated with singular count nouns, plural count nouns, or noncount nouns.

With any kind of noun (singular count, plural count, noncount)

my, our, your, his, her, its, their, possessive nouns (*boy's, boys'*)
whose, which(ever), what(ever)
some, any, the other
no

Their account is overdrawn. [Singular count.]
Their funds are low. [Plural count.]
Their money is running out. [Noncount.]

Only with singular nouns (count and noncount)

this, that

This account has some money. [Count.]
That information may help. [Noncount.]

Only with noncount nouns and plural count nouns

most, enough, other, such, all, all of the, a lot of

Most funds are committed. [Plural count.]
Most money is needed elsewhere. [Noncount.]

Only with singular count nouns

one, every, each, either, neither, another

One car must be sold. [Singular count.]

Only with plural count nouns

these, those
both, many, few, a few, fewer, fewest, several
two, three, and so forth

Two cars are unnecessary. [Plural count.]

Note *Few* means "not many" or "not enough." *A few* means "some" or "a small but sufficient quantity."

Few committee members came to the meeting.
A few members can keep the committee going.

Do not use *much* with a plural count noun.

Many [not Much] members want to help.

Only with noncount nouns

much, more, little, a little, less, least, a large amount of

Less luxury is in order. [Noncount.]

Note *Little* means "not many" or "not enough." *A little* means "some" or "a small but sufficient quantity."

Little time remains before the conference.
The members need a little help from their colleagues.

Do not use *many* with a noncount noun.

Much [not Many] work remains.

34 Misplaced and Dangling Modifiers

The arrangement of words in a sentence is an important clue to their relationships. Modifiers will be unclear if readers can't connect them to the words they modify.

Grammar checkers A grammar checker cannot recognize most problems with modifiers. For instance, a checker failed to flag the misplaced modifiers in *Gasoline high prices affect usually car sales* or the dangling modifier in *The vandalism was visible passing the building.*

34a Reposition misplaced modifiers.

A **misplaced modifier** falls in the wrong place in a sentence. It is usually awkward or confusing. It may even be unintentionally funny.

1 Clear placement

Readers tend to link a modifier to the nearest word it could modify. Any other placement can link the modifier to the wrong word.

Confusing He served steak to the men on paper plates.

Clear He served the men steak on paper plates.

Confusing According to the police, many dogs are killed by automobiles and trucks roaming unleashed.

Clear According to the police, many dogs roaming unleashed are killed by automobiles and trucks.

2 *Only* and other limiting modifiers

Limiting modifiers include *almost, even, exactly, hardly, just, merely, nearly, only, scarcely,* and *simply*. For clarity place such a modifier immediately before the word or word group you intend it to limit.

Unclear The archaeologist only found the skull on her last dig.

Clear The archaeologist found only the skull on her last dig.

Clear The archaeologist found the skull only on her last dig.

mycomplab

Visit *mycomplab.com* for more resources as well as exercises on misplaced and dangling modifiers.

3 Adverbs with grammatical units

Adverbs can often move around in sentences, but some will be awkward if they interrupt certain grammatical units:

- **A long adverb stops the flow from subject to verb.**

subject — adverb — verb
Awkward The city, after the hurricane, began massive rebuilding.

adverb — subject verb
Revised After the hurricane, the city began massive rebuilding.

- **Any adverb is awkward between a verb and its direct object.**

verb — adverb — object
Awkward The hurricane had damaged badly many homes in the city.

verb — object
Revised The hurricane had badly damaged many homes in the city.
adverb

- **A *split infinitive*—an adverb placed between *to* and the verb—annoys many readers.**

infinitive
Awkward The weather service expected temperatures to not rise.

infinitive
Revised The weather service expected temperatures not to rise.

A split infinitive may sometimes be natural and preferable, though it may still bother some readers.

infinitive
Several US industries expect to more than triple their use of robots.

Here the split infinitive is more economical than the alternatives, such as *Several US industries expect to increase their use of robots by more than three times.*

- **A long adverb is usually awkward inside a verb phrase.**

helping verb — adverb
Awkward People who have osteoporosis can, by increasing their daily intake of calcium and vitamin D, improve their bone density.
main verb

Key terms

adverb A word or word group that describes a verb, adjective, other adverb, or whole word group, specifying how, when, where, or to what extent: *quickly see, solid like a boulder*.

direct object The receiver of the verb's action: *The car hit a tree.* (See p. 188.)

infinitive A verb form consisting of *to* plus the verb's plain (or dictionary) form: *to produce, to enjoy.* (See p. 192.)

adverb

Revised By increasing their daily intake of calcium and vitamin D,

verb phrase

people who have osteoporosis can improve their bone density.

CULTURE LANGUAGE In a question, place a one-word adverb after the first helping verb and subject:

helping verb | subject | adverb | rest of verb phrase

Will spacecraft ever be able to leave the solar system?

4 Other adverb positions

Placements of a few adverbs can be difficult for nonnative speakers of English:

- **Adverbs of frequency** include *always, never, often, rarely, seldom, sometimes,* and *usually.* They generally appear at the beginning of a sentence, before a one-word verb, or after the helping verb in a verb phrase.

  helping verb | adverb | main verb

  Robots have sometimes put humans out of work.

  adverb | verb phrase

  Sometimes robots have put humans out of work.

  Adverbs of frequency always follow the verb *be.*

  verb | adverb

  Robots are often helpful to workers.

  verb | adverb

  Robots are seldom useful around the house.

- **Adverbs of degree** include *absolutely, almost, certainly, completely, definitely, especially, extremely, hardly,* and *only.* They fall just before the word modified (an adjective, another adverb, sometimes a verb).

  adverb | adjective

  Robots have been especially useful in making cars.

- **Adverbs of manner** include *badly, beautifully, openly, sweetly, tightly, well,* and others that describe how something is done. They usually fall after the verb.

  verb | adverb

  Robots work smoothly on assembly lines.

Key term

verb phrase A verb consisting of a helping verb and a main verb that carries the principal meaning: *will have begun, can see.* (See p. 183.)

- **The adverb *not*** changes position depending on what it modifies. When it modifies a verb, place it after the helping verb (or the first helping verb if more than one).

  helping verb — main verb
  Robots do not think.

  When *not* modifies another adverb or an adjective, place it before the other modifier.

  adjective
  Robots are not sleek machines.

5 Order of adjectives

English follows distinctive rules for arranging two or three adjectives before a noun. (A string of more than three adjectives before a noun is rare.) The order is shown in the chart below.

Determiner	Opinion	Size or shape	Color	Origin	Material	Noun used as adjective	Noun
many						state	**laws**
	lovely		green	Thai			**birds**
a	fine			German			**camera**
this		square			wooden		**table**
all						business	**reports**
the			blue		litmus		**paper**

See **5** pp. 276–77 on punctuating adjectives before a noun.

34b Connect dangling modifiers to their sentences.

A **dangling modifier** does not sensibly modify anything in its sentence.

Dangling Passing the building, the vandalism became visible.

Dangling modifiers usually introduce sentences, contain a verb form, and imply but do not name a subject. In the example above, the implied subject is the someone or something passing the build-

> **Key term**
> **adjective** A word that describes a noun or pronoun, specifying which one, what quality, or how many: *good one, three cars*. (See p. 183.)

Identifying and revising dangling modifiers

- **Find a subject.** If the modifier lacks a subject of its own (e.g., *when in diapers*), identify what it describes.
- **Connect the subject and modifier.** Verify that what the modifier describes is in fact the subject of the main clause. If it is not, the modifier is probably dangling:

  modifier — subject

  Dangling When in diapers, my mother remarried.
- **Revise as needed.** Revise a dangling modifier (*a*) by recasting it with a subject of its own or (*b*) by changing the subject of the main clause:

  Revision *a* When I was in diapers, my mother remarried.

  Revision *b* When in diapers, I attended my mother's second wedding.

ing. Readers assume that this implied subject is the same as the subject of the sentence (*vandalism* in the example), but vandalism does not pass buildings. The modifier "dangles" because it does not connect sensibly to the rest of the sentence. Here is another example:

Dangling Although intact, graffiti covered every inch of the walls and windows. [The walls and windows, not the graffiti, were intact.]

To revise a dangling modifier, you have to recast the sentence it appears in. (Revising just by moving the modifier will leave it dangling: *The vandalism became visible passing the building.*) Choose a revision method depending on what you want to emphasize in the sentence.

- **Rewrite the dangling modifier as a complete clause with its own stated subject and verb.** Readers can accept that the new subject and the sentence subject are different.

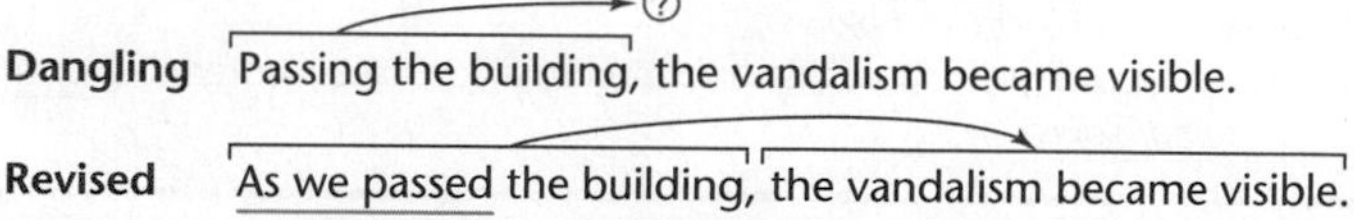

Dangling Passing the building, the vandalism became visible.

Revised As we passed the building, the vandalism became visible.

- **Change the subject of the sentence to a word the modifier properly describes.**

Dangling Trying to understand the causes, vandalism has been extensively studied.

Revised Trying to understand the causes, researchers have extensively studied vandalism.

Sentence Faults

A word group punctuated as a sentence will confuse or annoy readers if it lacks needed parts, has too many parts, or has parts that don't fit together.

35 Sentence Fragments

A **sentence fragment** is part of a sentence that is set off as if it were a whole sentence by an initial capital letter and a final period or other end punctuation. Although writers occasionally use fragments deliberately and effectively (see pp. 252–53), readers perceive most fragments as serious errors.

Grammar checkers A grammar checker can spot many but not all sentence fragments, and it may flag sentences that are actually commands, such as *Continue reading.*

35a Test your sentences for completeness.

A word group punctuated as a sentence should pass *all three* of the following tests. If it does not, it is a fragment and needs revision.

Complete sentence versus sentence fragment

A complete sentence or main clause

1. contains a subject and a predicate verb (The wind blows)
2. and is not a subordinate clause (beginning with a word such as *because* or *who*).

A sentence fragment

1. lacks a predicate verb (*The wind blowing*),
2. or lacks a subject (*And blows*),
3. or is a subordinate clause not attached to a complete sentence (*Because the wind blows*).

Test 1: Find the predicate verb.

Look for a verb that can serve as the predicate of a sentence. Some fragments lack any verb at all.

mycomplab

Visit *mycomplab.com* for more resources as well as exercises on sentence fragments.

Fragment	Uncountable numbers of sites on the Web.
Revised	Uncountable numbers of sites make up the Web.

Other fragments may include a verb form but not a **finite verb**, one that changes form as indicated below. A verbal does not change; it cannot serve as a predicate verb without the aid of a helping verb.

	Finite verbs in complete sentences	**Verbals in sentence fragments**
Singular	The network grows.	The network growing.
Plural	Networks grow.	Networks growing.
Present	The network grows.	
Past	The network grew.	The network growing.
Future	The network will grow.	

CULTURE LANGUAGE Some languages allow forms of *be* to be omitted as helping verbs or linking verbs. But English requires stating forms of *be*, as shown in the following revised example.

Fragments	The network growing. It much larger than its developers anticipated.
Revised	The network is growing. It is much larger than its developers anticipated.

Test 2: Find the subject.

The subject of the sentence will usually come before the verb. If there is no subject, the word group is probably a fragment:

Fragment	And has enormous popular appeal.
Revised	And the Web has enormous popular appeal.

In one kind of complete sentence, a command, the subject *you* is understood: [*You*] *Experiment with the Web.*

CULTURE LANGUAGE Some languages allow the omission of the sentence subject, especially when it is a pronoun. But in English, except in commands, the subject is always stated.

Key terms

predicate The part of a sentence containing a verb that asserts something about the subject: *Ducks swim.* (See pp. 186–87.)

verbal A verb form that can serve as a noun, a modifier, or a part of a sentence verb, but not alone as the only verb of a sentence: *drawing, to draw, drawn.* (See p. 191.)

helping verb A verb such as *is, were, have, might,* and *could* that combines with various verb forms to indicate time and other kinds of meaning: for instance, *were drawing, might draw.* (See p. 183.)

subject The part of a sentence that names who or what performs the action or makes the assertion of the predicate: *Ducks swim.* (See pp. 186–87.)

Fragment	Web commerce has expanded. Has hurt traditional stores.
Revised	Web commerce has expanded. It has hurt traditional stores.

Test 3: Make sure the clause is not subordinate.

A subordinate clause usually begins with a subordinating word, such as one of the following:

Subordinating conjunctions			**Relative pronouns**	
after	once	until	that	who/whom
although	since	when	which	whoever/whomever
as	than	where		whose
because	that	whereas		
if	unless	while		

Subordinate clauses serve as parts of sentences (as nouns or modifiers), not as whole sentences:

Fragment	When the government devised the Internet.
Revised	The government devised the Internet.
Revised	When the government devised the Internet, no expansive computer network existed.
Fragment	The reason that the government devised the Internet.
Revised	The reason that the government devised the Internet was to link departments and defense contractors.

Note Questions beginning with *how, what, when, where, which, who, whom, whose,* and *why* are not sentence fragments: *Who was responsible? When did it happen?*

35b Revise sentence fragments.

Almost all sentence fragments can be corrected in one of the two ways shown in the box on the facing page. The choice depends on the importance of the information in the fragment and thus how much you want to stress it.

35c Be aware of the acceptable uses of incomplete sentences.

A few word groups lacking the usual subject-predicate combination are incomplete sentences, but they are not fragments because they conform to the expectations of most readers. They include commands (*Move along. Shut the window.*); exclamations (*Oh*

Key term

subordinate clause A word group that contains a subject and a predicate, begins with a subordinating word such as *because* or *who,* and is not a question: *Ducks can swim when they are young.* A subordinate clause may serve as a modifier or as a noun. (See p. 193.)

Revision of sentence fragments

Option 1

Rewrite the fragment as a complete sentence. This revision gives the information in the fragment the same importance as that in other complete sentences.

Fragment A major improvement in public health occurred with the widespread use of vaccines. Which protected children against life-threatening diseases.

Revised A major improvement in public health occurred with the widespread use of vaccines. They protected children against life-threatening diseases.

Two main clauses may be separated by a semicolon instead of a period (see **5** p. 277).

Option 2

Combine the fragment with a main clause. This revision subordinates the information in the fragment to the information in the main clause.

Fragment The polio vaccine eradicated the disease from most of the globe. The first vaccine to be used widely.

Revised The polio vaccine, the first to be used widely, eradicated the disease from most of the globe.

no!); questions and answers (*Where next? To Kansas.*); and descriptions in employment résumés (*Weekly volunteer in soup kitchen.*)

Experienced writers sometimes use sentence fragments when they want to achieve a special effect. Such fragments appear more in informal than in formal writing. Unless you are experienced and thoroughly secure in your own writing, you should avoid all fragments and concentrate on writing clear, well-formed sentences.

36 Comma Splices and Fused Sentences

When two main clauses fall in a row, readers need a signal that one main clause is ending and another is beginning. The four ways to provide this signal appear in the box on the next page.

Visit *mycomplab.com* for more resources as well as exercises on comma splices and fused sentences.

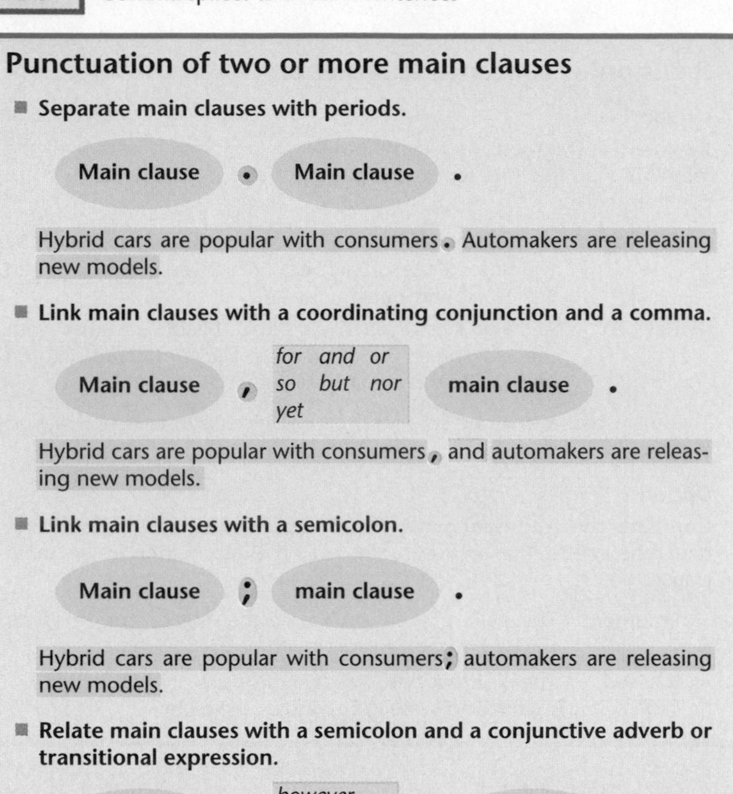

Punctuation of two or more main clauses

- **Separate main clauses with periods.**

  Main clause **.** **Main clause** **.**

  Hybrid cars are popular with consumers. Automakers are releasing new models.

- **Link main clauses with a coordinating conjunction and a comma.**

  Main clause **,** *for and or so but nor yet* **main clause** **.**

  Hybrid cars are popular with consumers, and automakers are releasing new models.

- **Link main clauses with a semicolon.**

  Main clause **;** **main clause** **.**

  Hybrid cars are popular with consumers; automakers are releasing new models.

- **Relate main clauses with a semicolon and a conjunctive adverb or transitional expression.**

  Main clause **;** *however, for example,* etc. **,** **main clause** **.**

  Hybrid cars are popular with consumers; as a result, automakers are releasing new models.

Two problems in punctuating main clauses fail to signal the break between main clauses. One is the **comma splice**, in which the clauses are joined (or spliced) *only* with a comma.

Key terms

main clause A word group that can stand alone as a sentence because it contains a subject and a predicate and does not begin with a subordinating word: *A dictionary is essential.*

coordinating conjunction *And, but, or, nor, for, so, yet.* (See p. 185.)

conjunctive adverb A modifier that describes the relation of the ideas in two clauses, such as *consequently, however, indeed,* and *therefore.* (See p. 257.)

Comma splice The ship was huge, its mast stood eighty feet high.

The other is the **fused sentence** (or **run-on sentence**), in which no punctuation or conjunction appears between the clauses.

Fused sentence The ship was huge its mast stood eighty feet high.

Grammar checkers A grammar checker can detect many comma splices, but it will miss most fused sentences. For example, a checker flagged *Money is tight, we need to spend carefully* but not *Money is tight we need to spend carefully*. A checker may also question sentences that are actually correct, such as *Money being tighter now than before, we need to spend carefully*.

CULTURE LANGUAGE In standard American English, a sentence may not include more than one main clause unless the clauses are separated by a comma and a coordinating conjunction or by a semicolon. If your native language does not have such a rule or has accustomed you to writing long sentences, you may need to edit your English writing especially for comma splices and fused sentences.

36a Separate main clauses not joined by *and, but,* or another coordinating conjunction.

If your readers point out comma splices or fused sentences in your writing, you're not creating enough separation between main clauses in your sentences. Punctuate consecutive main clauses in the following ways.

Separate sentences

Make the clauses into separate sentences when the ideas expressed are only loosely related:

Comma splice Chemistry has contributed much to our understanding of foods, many foods such as wheat and beans can be produced in the laboratory.

Revised Chemistry has contributed much to our understanding of foods. Many foods such as wheat and beans can be produced in the laboratory.

Coordinating conjunction

Insert a coordinating conjunction in a comma splice when the ideas in the main clauses are closely related and equally important:

Comma splice Some laboratory-grown foods taste good, they are nutritious.

Revised	Some laboratory-grown foods taste good, and they are nutritious.

In a fused sentence insert a comma and a coordinating conjunction:

Fused sentence	Chemists have made much progress they still have a way to go.
Revised	Chemists have made much progress, but they still have a way to go.

Semicolon

Insert a semicolon between clauses if the relation between the ideas is very close and obvious without a conjunction:

Comma splice	Good taste is rare in laboratory-grown vegetables, they are usually bland.
Revised	Good taste is rare in laboratory-grown vegetables; they are usually bland.

Subordination

When one idea is less important than the other, express the less important idea in a subordinate clause:

Comma splice	The vitamins are adequate, the flavor is deficient.
Revised	Even though the vitamins are adequate, the flavor is deficient.

36b Separate main clauses related by *however, for example,* and so on.

Two groups of words, shown in the box opposite, describe how one main clause relates to another: **conjunctive adverbs** and other **transitional expressions.** (See **1** pp. 43–44 for a longer list of transitional expressions.)

When two main clauses are related by a conjunctive adverb or another transitional expression, they must be separated by a period or by a semicolon. The adverb or expression is also generally set off by a comma or commas.

Key term

subordinate clause A word group that contains a subject and a predicate, begins with a subordinating word such as *because* or *who,* and is not a question: *Ducks can swim when they are young.* A subordinate clause may serve as a modifier or as a noun. (See p. 193.)

Common conjunctive adverbs and transitional expressions

accordingly	for instance	instead	on the contrary
anyway	further	in the meantime	otherwise
as a result	furthermore	in the past	similarly
at last	hence	likewise	still
besides	however	meanwhile	that is
certainly	incidentally	moreover	then
consequently	in contrast	namely	thereafter
even so	indeed	nevertheless	therefore
finally	in fact	nonetheless	thus
for all that	in other words	now	undoubtedly
for example	in short	of course	until now

Comma splice Healthcare costs are higher in the United States than in many other countries, consequently health insurance is also more costly.

Revised Healthcare costs are higher in the United States than in many other countries. Consequently, health insurance is also more costly.

Revised Healthcare costs are higher in the United States than in many other countries; consequently, health insurance is also more costly.

Conjunctive adverbs and transitional expressions are different from coordinating conjunctions (*and, but,* and so on) and subordinating conjunctions (*although, because,* and so on):

- **Unlike conjunctions, conjunctive adverbs and transitional expressions do not join two clauses into a grammatical unit.** They merely describe the way two clauses relate in meaning.
- **Unlike conjunctions, conjunctive adverbs and transitional expressions can be moved within a clause.** No matter where in the clause an adverb or expression falls, though, the clause must be separated from another main clause by a period or semicolon:

  Most Americans refuse to give up unhealthful habits; our medical costs, consequently, are higher than those of many other countries.

37 Mixed Sentences

A **mixed sentence** contains parts that do not fit together. The misfit may be in meaning or in grammar.

Grammar checkers A grammar checker may recognize a simple mixed construction such as *reason is because,* but it will fail to flag most mixed sentences.

37a Match subjects and predicates in meaning.

In a sentence with mixed meaning, the subject is said to do or be something illogical. Such a mixture is sometimes called **faulty predication** because the predicate conflicts with the subject.

1 Illogical equation with *be*

When a form of *be* connects a subject and a word that describes the subject (a complement), the subject and complement must be logically related:

Mixed A compromise between the city and the country would be the ideal place to live.

Revised A community that offered the best qualities of both city and country would be the ideal place to live.

2 *Is when, is where*

Definitions require nouns on both sides of *be.* Clauses that define and begin with *when* or *where* are common in speech but should be avoided in writing:

Mixed An examination is when you are tested on what you know.

Revised An examination is a test of what you know.

Key terms

subject The part of a sentence that names who or what performs the action or makes the assertion of the predicate: *Geese fly.* (See pp. 186–87.)

predicate The part of a sentence containing a verb that asserts something about the subject: *Geese fly.* (See pp. 186–87.)

mycomplab

Visit *mycomplab.com* for more resources on mixed sentences.

3 *Reason is because*

The commonly heard construction *reason is because* is redundant since *because* means "for the reason that":

Mixed The reason the temple requests donations is because the school needs expansion.

Revised The reason the temple requests donations is that the school needs expansion.

Revised The temple requests donations because the school needs expansion.

4 Other mixed meanings

Faulty predications are not confined to sentences with *be:*

Mixed The use of emission controls was created to reduce air pollution.

Revised Emission controls were created to reduce air pollution.

37b Untangle sentences that are mixed in grammar.

Many mixed sentences start with one grammatical plan or construction but end with a different one:

Mixed By paying more attention to impressions than facts leads us to misjudge others. [modifier (prepositional phrase): By paying more attention to impressions than facts; verb: leads]

Revised By paying more attention to impressions than facts, we misjudge others. [modifier (prepositional phrase): By paying more attention to impressions than facts; subject: we; verb: misjudge]

Constructions that use *Just because* clauses as subjects are common in speech but should be avoided in writing:

Mixed Just because no one is watching doesn't mean we have license to break the law. [modifier (subordinate clause): Just because no one is watching; verb: doesn't mean]

Revised Even when no one is watching, we don't have license to break the law. [modifier (subordinate clause): Even when no one is watching; subject + verb: we don't have]

A mixed sentence is especially likely when you are working on a computer and connect parts of two sentences or rewrite half a sentence but not the other half. A mixed sentence may also occur when you don't make the subject and predicate verb carry the principal meaning. (See **3** p. 143.)

37c State parts of sentences, such as subjects, only once.

In some languages other than English, certain parts of sentences may be repeated. These include the subject in any kind of clause or an object or adverb in an adjective clause. In English, however, these parts are stated only once in a clause.

1 Repetition of subject

You may be tempted to restate a subject as a pronoun before the verb. But the subject needs stating only once in its clause:

Faulty The liquid it reached a temperature of 180°F.
Revised The liquid reached a temperature of 180°F.

Faulty Gases in the liquid they escaped.
Revised Gases in the liquid escaped.

2 Repetition in an adjective clause

Adjective clauses begin with *who, whom, whose, which, that, where,* and *when* (see also pp. 193–94). The beginning word replaces another word: the subject (*He is the person who called*), an object of a verb or preposition (*He is the person whom I mentioned*), or a preposition and pronoun (*He knows the office where* [*in which*] *the conference will occur*).

Do not state the word being replaced in an adjective clause:

Faulty The technician whom the test depended on her was burned. [*Whom* should replace *her.*]
Revised The technician whom the test depended on was burned.

Adjective clauses beginning with *where* or *when* do not need an adverb such as *there* or *then:*

Faulty Gases escaped at a moment when the technician was unprepared then.
Revised Gases escaped at a moment when the technician was unprepared.

Note *Whom, which,* and similar words are sometimes omitted but are still understood by the reader. Thus the word being replaced should not be stated.

Faulty Accidents rarely happen to technicians the lab has trained *them*. [*Whom* is understood: . . . *technicians whom the lab has trained.*]
Revised Accidents rarely happen to technicians the lab has trained.

PART 5

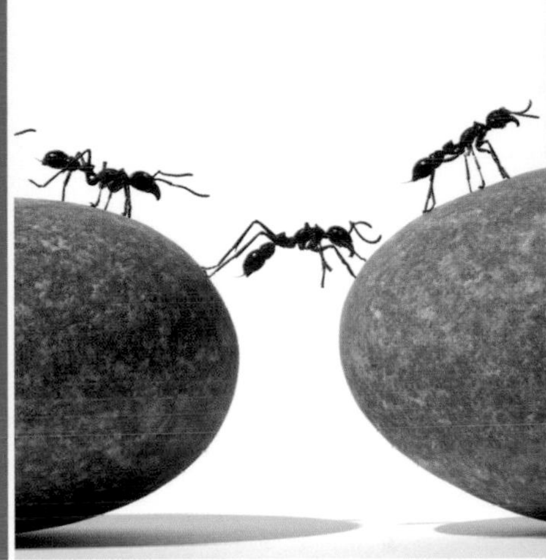

Punctuation

38 End Punctuation *263*

39 The Comma *265*

40 The Semicolon *277*

41 The Colon *279*

42 The Apostrophe *282*

43 Quotation Marks *286*

44 Other Marks *290*

PART 5

Punctuation

38 End Punctuation *263*

- **a** Period *263*
- **b** Question mark *264*
- **c** Exclamation point *264*

39 The Comma *265*

- **a** Main clauses with *and, but,* etc. *265*
- **b** Introductory elements *267*
- **c** Nonessential elements *268*
- **d** Items in series *272*
- **e** Two or more adjectives *272*
- **f** Dates, addresses, place names, long numbers *273*
- **g** *She said,* etc., with quotations *273*
- **h** Misuses *274*
  - **1** Between subject-verb, verb-object, preposition-object *275*
  - **2** In compound subject, predicate, etc. *275*
  - **3** After conjunction *275*
  - **4** Around essential elements *276*
  - **5** Around series *276*
  - **6** Before indirect quotation *276*

40 The Semicolon *277*

- **a** Main clauses without *and, but,* etc. *277*
- **b** Main clauses with *however, for example,* etc. *277*
- **c** Main clauses or series items with commas *278*
- **d** Misuses *278*

41 The Colon *279*

- **a** Concluding explanation, series, etc. *280*
- **b** Salutation of business letter, title and subtitle, divisions of time *281*
- **c** Misuses *281*

42 The Apostrophe *282*

- **a** Possession *282*
- **b** Misuses *284*
  - **1** Plural nouns: *Joneses,* not *Jones' 284*
  - **2** Singular verbs: *makes,* not *make's 284*
  - **3** Possessive personal pronouns: *its,* not *it's 285*
- **c** Contractions *285*
- **d** Plural abbreviations, etc. *285*

43 Quotation Marks *286*

- **a** Direct quotations *286*
- **b** Quotation within quotation *287*
- **c** Dialog *287*
- **d** Titles of works *287*
- **e** Words used in a special sense *288*
- **f** Misuses *288*
- **g** With other punctuation *289*

44 Other Marks *290*

- **a** Dash or dashes *290*
- **b** Parentheses *291*
- **c** Ellipsis mark *292*
- **d** Brackets *294*
- **e** Slash *294*

38 End Punctuation

End a sentence with one of three punctuation marks: a period (.), a question mark (?), or an exclamation point (!).

Grammar checkers A grammar checker may flag missing question marks after direct questions or incorrect combinations of marks (such as a question mark and a period at the end of a sentence), but it cannot do much else.

38a Use a period after most sentences and with some abbreviations.

1 Statements, mild commands, and indirect questions

Statement

The airline went bankrupt. It no longer flies.

Mild command

Think of the possibilities. Please consider others.

Indirect question

An **indirect question** reports what someone asked but not in the exact form or words of the original question:

The judge asked why I had been driving with my lights off.
No one asked how we got home.

CULTURE LANGUAGE In standard American English, an indirect question uses the wording and subject-verb order of a statement: *The reporter asked why the negotiations failed* [not *why did the negotiations fail*].

2 Abbreviations

Use periods with abbreviations that consist of or end in small letters. Otherwise, omit periods from abbreviations.

Dr.	Mr., Mrs.	e.g.	Feb.	ft.
St.	Ms.	i.e.	p.	a.m., p.m.
PhD	BC, BCE	USA	IBM	AM, PM
BA	AD, CE	US	USMC	AIDS

Note When a sentence ends in an abbreviation with a period, don't add a second period: *My first class is at 8 a.m.*

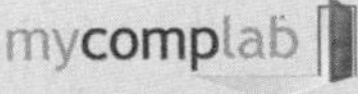

Visit *mycomplab.com* for more resources as well as exercises on end punctuation.

38b Use a question mark after a direct question and sometimes to indicate doubt.

1 Direct questions

Who will follow her?
What is the difference between these two people?

After indirect questions, use a period: *We wondered who would follow her.* (See the preceding page.)

Questions in a series are each followed by a question mark:

The officer asked how many times the suspect had been arrested. Three times? Four times? More than that?

Note Do not combine question marks with other question marks, periods, commas, or other punctuation.

2 Doubt

A question mark within parentheses can indicate doubt about a number or date.

The Greek philosopher Socrates was born in 470 (?) BC and died in 399 BC from drinking poison. [Socrates's birthdate is not known for sure.]

Use sentence structure and words, not a question mark, to express sarcasm or irony.

Not Stern's friendliness (?) bothered Crane.
But Stern's insincerity bothered Crane.

38c Use an exclamation point after an emphatic statement, interjection, or command.

No! We must not lose this election!
Come here immediately!

Follow mild interjections and commands with commas or periods, as appropriate: *Oh, call whenever you can.*

Note Do not combine exclamation points with periods, commas, or other punctuation marks. And use exclamation points sparingly, even in informal writing. Overused, they'll fail to impress readers, and they may make you sound overemotional.

Key term

interjection A word that expresses feeling or commands attention, either alone or within a sentence: *Oh! Hey! Wow!*

39 The Comma

The comma (,) is the most common punctuation mark inside sentences. Its main uses are shown in the box on the next page.

Grammar checkers A grammar checker will ignore many comma errors. For example, a checker failed to catch the missing commas in *We cooked lasagna spinach and apple pie* and the misused commas in *The trip was short but, the weather was perfect* and *The travelers were tempted by, the many shops.*

39a Use a comma before *and, but,* or another coordinating conjunction linking main clauses.

When a coordinating conjunction links words or phrases, do not use a comma: *Dugain plays and sings Irish and English folk songs.* However, *do* use a comma when a coordinating conjunction joins main clauses, as in the next examples.

> Caffeine can keep coffee drinkers alert, and it may elevate their mood.
>
> Caffeine was once thought to be safe, but now researchers warn of harmful effects.
>
> Coffee drinkers may suffer sleeplessness, for the drug acts as a stimulant to the nervous system.

Note The comma goes *before,* not after, a coordinating conjunction that links main clauses: *Caffeine increases heart rate, and it* [not *and, it*] *constricts blood vessels.*

Exception Some writers omit the comma between main clauses that are very short and closely related in meaning: *Caffeine helps but it also hurts.* If you are in doubt about whether to use the comma in such a sentence, use it. It will always be correct.

Key terms

coordinating conjunctions *And, but, or, nor,* and sometimes *for, so, yet.* (See **4** p. 185.)

main clause A word group that can stand alone as a sentence because it contains a subject and a predicate and does not begin with a subordinating word: *Water freezes at temperatures below 32°F.* (See **4** p. 193.)

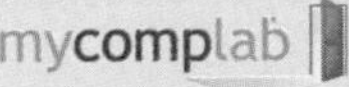

Visit *mycomplab.com* for more resources as well as exercises on the comma.

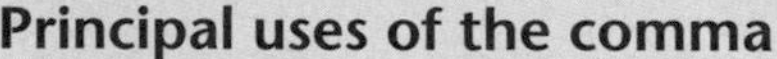

Principal uses of the comma

- **Separate main clauses linked by a coordinating conjunction** (previous page):

Main clause , *for and or so but nor yet* main clause .

The building is finished, but it has no tenants.

- **Set off most introductory elements** (opposite):

Introductory element , main clause .

Unfortunately, the only tenant pulled out.

- **Set off nonessential elements** (p. 268):

Main clause , nonessential element .

The empty building symbolizes a weak local economy, which affects everyone.

Beginning of main clause , nonessential element , end of main clause .

The primary cause, the decline of local industry, is not news.

- **Separate items in a series** (p. 272):

. . . item 1 , item 2 , *and or* item 3 . . .

The city needs healthier businesses, new schools, and improved housing.

- **Separate coordinate adjectives** (p. 272):

. . . first adjective , second adjective word modified . . .

A tall, sleek skyscraper is not needed.

Other uses of the comma:

Separate parts of dates, addresses, long numbers (p. 273).
Separate quotations and signal phrases (p. 273).

See also p. 274 for when *not* to use the comma.

Use a comma to set off most introductory elements.

An **introductory element** begins a sentence and modifies a word or words in the main clause. It is usually followed by a comma.

Subordinate clause

Even when identical twins are raised apart, they grow up very like each other.

Verbal or verbal phrase

Explaining the similarity, some researchers claim that one's genes are one's destiny.

Concerned, other researchers deny the claim.

Prepositional phrase

In a debate that has lasted centuries, scientists use identical twins to argue for or against genetic destiny.

Transitional expression

Of course, scientists can now look directly at the genes themselves to answer questions.

You may omit the comma after a short subordinate clause or prepositional phrase if its omission does not create confusion: *When snow falls the city collapses. By the year 2000 the world population had topped 6 billion.* You may also omit the comma after some transitional expressions when they start sentences: *Thus the debate continues* (see p. 271). However, in both situations the comma is never wrong.

Note Take care to distinguish *-ing* words used as modifiers from *-ing* words used as subjects. The former almost always take a comma; the latter never do.

Key terms

subordinate clause A word group that contains a subject and a predicate, begins with a subordinating word such as *because* or *who,* and is not a question: *When water freezes, crystals form.* (See **4** p. 193.)

verbal A verb form used as an adjective, adverb, or noun. A verbal plus any object or modifier is a **verbal phrase:** *frozen water, ready to freeze, rapid freezing.* (See **4** p. 191.)

prepositional phrase A word group consisting of a preposition, such as *for* or *in,* followed by a noun or pronoun plus any modifiers: *in a jar, with a spoon.* (See **4** p. 191.)

transitional expression A word or phrase that shows the relationship between sentences: *for example, however, in fact, of course.* (See **1** pp. 43–44.)

modifier — subject — verb
Studying identical twins, geneticists learn about inheritance.

subject — verb
Studying identical twins helps geneticists learn about inheritance.

39c Use a comma or commas to set off nonessential elements.

Commas around part of a sentence often signal that the element is not necessary to the meaning. This **nonessential element** may modify or rename the word it refers to, but it does not limit the word to a particular individual or group. The meaning of the word would still be clear if the element were deleted:

Nonessential element
The company, which is located in Oklahoma, has a good reputation.

(Because it does not restrict meaning, a nonessential element is also called a **nonrestrictive element**.)

In contrast, an **essential** (or **restrictive**) **element** *does* limit the word it refers to: the element cannot be omitted without leaving the meaning too general. Because it is essential, such an element is *not* set off with a comma or commas.

Essential element
The company rewards employees who work hard.

Omitting the underlined words would distort the meaning: the company doesn't necessarily reward *all* employees, only the hardworking ones.

The same element in the same sentence may be essential or nonessential depending on your meaning and the context:

Essential
Not all the bands were equally well received, however. The band playing old music held the audience's attention. The other groups created much less excitement. [*Playing old music* identifies a particular band.]

Nonessential
A new band called Fats made its debut on Saturday night. The band, playing old music, held the audience's attention. If this performance is typical, the group has a bright future. [*Playing old music* adds information about a band already named.]

Note When a nonessential element falls in the middle of a sentence, be sure to set it off with a pair of commas, one *before* and one *after* the element.

A test for nonessential and essential elements

1. **Identify the element:**

   Hai Nguyen who emigrated from Vietnam lives in Dallas.
   Those who emigrated with him live elsewhere.

2. **Remove the element.** Does the fundamental meaning of the sentence change?

   Hai Nguyen lives in Dallas. ***No.***
   Those live elsewhere. ***Yes.*** [Who are *Those?*]

3. **If *no,* the element is *nonessential* and *should* be set off with punctuation:**

   Hai Nguyen, who emigrated from Vietnam, lives in Dallas.

   If *yes,* the element is *essential* and should *not* be set off with punctuation:

   Those who emigrated with him live elsewhere.

1 Nonessential phrases and clauses

Most nonessential phrases and subordinate clauses function as adjectives or, less commonly, as adverbs. In each of the following examples, the underlined words could be omitted with no loss of clarity.

> Elizabeth Blackwell was the first woman to graduate from an American medical school, in 1849. [Phrase.]
>
> She was a medical pioneer, helping to found the first medical college for women. [Phrase.]
>
> She taught at the school, which was affiliated with the New York Infirmary. [Clause.]
>
> Blackwell, who published books and papers on medicine, practiced pediatrics and gynecology. [Clause.]

Note Use *that* only in an essential clause, never in a nonessential clause: . . . *school, which* [not *that*] *was affiliated*. . . . Many writers reserve *which* for nonessential clauses.

Key terms

phrase A word group lacking a subject or a verb or both: *in Duluth, carrying water.* (See **4** p. 191.)

subordinate clause A word group that contains a subject and a predicate, begins with a subordinating word such as *who* or *although,* and is not a question: *Samson, who won a gold medal, coaches in Utah.* (See **4** p. 193.)

2 Nonessential appositives

A nonessential appositive merely adds information about the word it refers to.

> Toni Morrison's fifth novel, *Beloved*, won the Pulitzer Prize in 1988. [The word *fifth* identifies the novel, while the title adds a detail.]

In contrast, an essential appositive limits or defines the word it refers to:

> Morrison's novel *The Bluest Eye* is about an African American girl who longs for blue eyes. [Morrison has written more than one novel, so the title is essential to identify the intended one.]

3 Other nonessential elements

Like nonessential modifiers or appositives, many other elements contribute to texture, tone, or overall clarity but are not essential to the meaning. Unlike nonessential modifiers or appositives, these other nonessential elements generally do not refer to any specific word in the sentence.

Note Use a pair of commas—one before, one after—when any of these elements falls in the middle of a sentence.

Absolute phrases

> Household recycling having succeeded, the city now wants to extend the program to businesses.
>
> Many businesses, their profits already squeezed, resist recycling.

Parenthetical and transitional expressions

Generally, set off parenthetical and transitional expressions with commas:

> The world's most celebrated holiday is, perhaps surprisingly, New Year's Day. [Parenthetical expression.]
>
> Interestingly, Americans have relatively few holidays. [Parenthetical expression.]

Key terms

appositive A noun that renames another noun immediately before it: *His wife, Kyra Sedgwick, is also an actor.* (See **4** p. 193.)

absolute phrase A phrase modifying a whole main clause and consisting of a participle and its subject: *Their homework completed, the children watched TV.* (See **4** p. 192.)

parenthetical expression An explanatory or supplemental word or phrase, such as *all things considered, to be frank,* or a brief example. (See p. 291.)

transitional expression A word or phrase that shows the relationship between sentences: *for example, however, in fact, of course.* (See **1** pp. 43–44.)

US workers, for example, receive fewer holidays than European workers do. [Transitional expression.]

(Dashes and parentheses may also set off parenthetical expressions. See pp. 290–91.)

When a transitional expression links main clauses, precede it with a semicolon and follow it with a comma (see pp. 277–78):

European workers often have long paid vacations; indeed, they may receive a full month after just a few years with a company.

Exception The conjunctions *and* and *but,* sometimes used as transitional expressions, are never followed by commas (see p. 267). Usage varies with some other transitional expressions, depending on the expression and the writer's judgment. Many writers omit commas with expressions that we read without pauses, such as *also, hence, next, now, then,* and *thus.* The same applies to *therefore* and *instead* when they fall inside or at the ends of clauses.

US workers therefore put in more work days. But the days themselves may be shorter.

Then the total hours worked would come out roughly the same.

Phrases of contrast

The substance, not the style, is important.

Substance, unlike style, cannot be faked.

Tag questions

They don't stop to consider others, do they?

Jones should be allowed to vote, shouldn't he?

Yes* and *no

Yes, the editorial did have a point.

No, that can never be.

Words of direct address

Cody, please bring me the newspaper.

With all due respect, sir, I will not.

Mild interjections

Well, you will never know who did it.

Oh, they forgot all about the baby.

Key terms

tag question A question at the end of a statement, consisting of a pronoun, a helping verb, and sometimes *not: It isn't wet, is it?*

interjection A word that expresses feeling or commands attention: *Oh, must we?*

39d Use commas between items in a series.

A **series** consists of three or more items of equal importance. The items may be words, phrases, or clauses.

Anna Spingle married at the age of seventeen, had three children by twenty-one, and divorced at twenty-two.

She worked as a cook, a baby-sitter, and a crossing guard.

Some writers omit the comma before the coordinating conjunction in a series (*Breakfast consisted of coffee, eggs and kippers*). But the final comma is never wrong, and it always helps the reader see the last two items as separate.

39e Use commas between two or more adjectives that equally modify the same word.

Adjectives that equally modify the same word—**coordinate adjectives**—may be separated either by *and* or by a comma.

Spingle's scratched and dented car is old, but it gets her to work.

She has dreams of a sleek, shiny car.

Adjectives are not coordinate—and should not be separated by commas—when the one nearer the noun is more closely related to the noun in meaning.

Spingle's children work at various part-time jobs.

They all expect to go to a nearby community college.

Tests for commas with adjectives

1. **Identify the adjectives.**

   She was a faithful sincere friend.
   They are dedicated medical students.

2. **Can the adjectives be reversed without changing meaning?**

   She was a sincere faithful friend. ***Yes.***
   They are medical dedicated students. ***No.***

3. **Can the word *and* be sensibly inserted between the adjectives?**

   She was a faithful and sincere friend. ***Yes.***
   They are dedicated and medical students. ***No.***

4. **If *yes* to both questions, the adjectives *are* coordinate and *should* be separated by a comma.**

   She was a faithful, sincere friend.

   If *no* to both questions, the adjectives are *not* coordinate and should *not* be separated by a comma.

   They are dedicated medical students.

39f Use commas in dates, addresses, place names, and long numbers.

Within a sentence, any date, address, or place name that contains a comma should also end with a comma.

Dates

July 4, 1776, is the date the Declaration was signed.

The bombing of Pearl Harbor on Sunday, December 7, 1941, prompted American entry into World War II.

Do not use commas between the parts of a date in inverted order (*15 December 1992*) or in dates consisting of a month or season and a year (*December 1941*).

Addresses and place names

Use the address 220 Cornell Road, Woodside, California 94062, for all letters. [Do not use a comma between a state name and a zip code.]

Columbus, Ohio, is the location of Ohio State University.

Long numbers

Use the comma to separate the figures in long numbers into groups of three, counting from the right. With numbers of four digits, the comma is optional.

The new assembly plant cost $7,525,000.

A kilometer is 3,281 feet [*or* 3281 feet].

CULTURE LANGUAGE Usage in standard American English differs from that in some other languages and dialects, which use a period, not a comma, to separate the figures in long numbers.

39g Use commas with quotations according to standard practice.

The words *she said, he writes,* and so on identify the source of a quotation. These **signal phrases** should be separated from the quotation by punctuation, usually a comma or commas.

"Knowledge is power," writes Francis Bacon.

"The shore has a dual nature," observes Rachel Carson, "changing with the swing of the tides." [The signal phrase interrupts the quotation at a comma and thus ends with a comma.]

Exceptions When a signal phrase interrupts a quotation between main clauses, follow the signal phrase with a semicolon or a period. The choice depends on the punctuation of the original.

Not "That part of my life was over," she wrote, "his words had sealed it shut."

But "That part of my life was over," she wrote. "His words had sealed it shut." [*She wrote* interrupts the quotation at a period.]

Or "That part of my life was over," she wrote; "his words had sealed it shut." [*She wrote* interrupts the quotation at a semicolon.]

Do not use a comma when a signal phrase follows a quotation ending in an exclamation point or a question mark:

"Claude!" Mrs. Harrison called.

"Why must I come home?" he asked.

Do not use a comma with a quotation that is integrated into your sentence structure, including one introduced by *that:*

James Baldwin insists that "one must never, in one's life, accept . . . injustices as commonplace."

Baldwin thought that the violence of a riot "had been devised as a corrective" to his own violence.

Do not use a comma with a quoted title unless it is a nonessential appositive:

The Beatles recorded "She Loves You" in 1963.

The Beatles' first huge US hit, "She Loves You," appeared in 1963.

39h Delete commas where they are not required.

Commas can make sentences choppy and even confusing if they are used more often than needed.

Key term

nonessential appositive A word or words that rename an immediately preceding noun but do not limit or define the noun: *The author's first story, "Biloxi," won a prize.* (See p. 270.)

1 No comma between subject and verb, verb and object, or preposition and object

Not The returning soldiers, received a warm welcome. [Separated subject and verb.]

But The returning soldiers received a warm welcome.

Not They had chosen, to fight for their country despite, the risks. [Separated verb *chosen* and its object; separated preposition *despite* and its object.]

But They had chosen to fight for their country despite the risks.

2 No comma in most compound constructions

Compound constructions consisting of two elements almost never require a comma. The only exception is the sentence consisting of two main clauses linked by a coordinating conjunction: *The computer failed, but employees kept working* (see p. 265).

Not Banks, and other financial institutions [compound subject] have helped older people with money management, and investment [compound object of preposition].

But Banks and other financial institutions have helped older people with money management and investment.

Not One bank created special accounts for older people, and held [compound predicate] classes, and workshops [compound object of verb].

But One bank created special accounts for older people and held classes and workshops.

3 No comma after a conjunction

Not Parents of adolescents notice increased conflict at puberty, and, they complain of bickering.

But Parents of adolescents notice increased conflict at puberty, and they complain of bickering.

Key terms

compound construction Two or more words, phrases, or clauses connected by a coordinating conjunction, usually *and, but, or, nor: man and woman, old or young, leaking oil and spewing steam.*

conjunction A connecting word such as a **coordinating conjunction** (*and, but, or,* and so on) or a **subordinating conjunction** (*although, because, when,* and so on). (See **4** p. 185.)

Not Although, other primates leave the family at adolescence, humans do not.

But Although other primates leave the family at adolescence, humans do not.

4 No commas around essential elements

Not Hawthorne's work, *The Scarlet Letter*, was the first major American novel. [The title is essential to distinguish the novel from the rest of Hawthorne's work.]

But Hawthorne's work *The Scarlet Letter* was the first major American novel.

Not The symbols, that Hawthorne uses, have influenced other novelists. [The clause identifies which symbols have been influential.]

But The symbols that Hawthorne uses have influenced other novelists.

5 No commas around a series

Commas separate the items *within* a series (p. 272) but do not separate the series from the rest of the sentence.

Not The skills of, hunting, herding, and agriculture, sustained the Native Americans.

But The skills of hunting herding, and agriculture sustained the Native Americans.

6 No comma before an indirect quotation

Not The report concluded, that dieting could be more dangerous than overeating.

But The report concluded that dieting could be more dangerous than overeating.

Key term

essential element Limits the word it refers to and thus can't be omitted without leaving the meaning too general. (See pp. 268–69.)

40 The Semicolon

The semicolon (;) separates equal and balanced sentence elements—usually main clauses (below) and occasionally items in series (p. 278).

Grammar checkers A grammar checker can spot a few errors in the use of semicolons. For example, a checker suggested using a semicolon after *perfect* in *The set was perfect, the director had planned every detail,* thus correcting a comma splice. But it missed the incorrect semicolon in *The set was perfect; deserted streets, dark houses, and gloomy mist* (a colon would be correct).

40a Use a semicolon between main clauses not joined by *and, but,* or another coordinating conjunction.

When no coordinating conjunction links two main clauses, the clauses should be separated by a semicolon.

> A new ulcer drug arrived on the market with a mixed reputation**;** doctors find that the drug works but worry about its side effects.
>
> The side effects are not minor**;** some leave the patient quite uncomfortable or even ill.

Note This rule prevents the errors known as comma splices and fused sentences. (See **4** pp. 255–56.)

40b Use a semicolon between main clauses related by *however, for example,* and so on.

When a conjunctive adverb or another transitional expression relates two main clauses in a single sentence, the clauses should be separated with a semicolon:

> An American immigrant, Levi Strauss, invented blue jeans in the 1860s**;** eventually, his product clothed working men throughout the West.

Key terms

main clause A word group that can stand alone as a sentence because it contains a subject and a predicate and does not begin with a subordinating word: *Parks help cities breathe.* (See **4** p. 193.)

coordinating conjunctions *And, but, or, nor,* and sometimes *for, so, yet.*

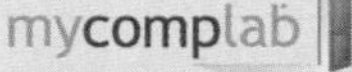

Visit *mycomplab.com* for more resources as well as exercises on the semicolon.

The position of the semicolon between main clauses never changes, but the conjunctive adverb or transitional expression may move around within the second clause. Wherever the adverb or expression falls, it is usually set off with a comma or commas. (See pp. 270–71.)

> Blue jeans have become fashionable all over the world; however, the American originators still wear more jeans than anyone else.
>
> Blue jeans have become fashionable all over the world; the American originators, however, still wear more jeans than anyone else.
>
> Blue jeans have become fashionable all over the world; the American originators still wear more jeans than anyone else, however.

Note This rule prevents the errors known as comma splices and fused sentences. (See **4** pp. 256–57.)

40c Use semicolons between main clauses or series items containing commas.

Normally, commas separate main clauses linked by coordinating conjunctions (*and, but, or, nor*) and separate items in a series. But when the clauses or series items contain commas, a semicolon between them makes the sentence easier to read.

> Lewis and Clark led the men of their party with consummate skill, inspiring and encouraging them, doctoring and caring for them; and they kept voluminous journals. —Page Smith
>
> The custody case involved Amy Dalton, the child; Ellen and Mark Dalton, the parents; and Ruth and Hal Blum, the grandparents.

40d Delete or replace unneeded semicolons.

Too many semicolons can make writing choppy. And semicolons are often misused in certain constructions that call for other punctuation or no punctuation.

Key terms

conjunctive adverb A modifier that describes the relation of the ideas in two clauses, such as *consequently, hence, however, indeed, instead, nonetheless, otherwise, still, then, therefore, thus.* (See **4** p. 257.)

transitional expression A word or phrase that shows the relationship between ideas. Transitional expressions include conjunctive adverbs as well as *for example, in fact, of course,* and many other words and phrases. (See **1** pp. 43–44.)

1 No semicolon between a main clause and a subordinate clause or phrase

The semicolon does not separate unequal parts, such as main clauses and subordinate clauses or phrases.

Not Pygmies are in danger of extinction; because of encroaching development.

But Pygmies are in danger of extinction because of encroaching development.

Not According to African authorities; only about 35,000 Pygmies exist today.

But According to African authorities, only about 35,000 Pygmies exist today.

2 No semicolon before a series or explanation

Colons and dashes, not semicolons, introduce series, explanations, and so forth. (See the next page and p. 290.)

Not Teachers have heard all sorts of reasons why students do poorly; psychological problems, family illness, too much work, too little time.

But Teachers have heard all sorts of reasons why students do poorly: psychological problems, family illness, too much work, too little time.

41 The Colon

The colon (:) is mainly a mark of introduction: it signals that the words following will explain or amplify (next page). The colon also has several conventional uses, such as in expressions of time (p. 281).

Grammar checkers Many grammar checkers cannot recognize missing or misused colons and instead simply ignore them.

mycomplab

Visit *mycomplab.com* for more resources as well as exercises on the colon.

41a Use a colon to introduce a concluding explanation, a series, an appositive, and some quotations.

As an introducer, a colon is always preceded by a complete main clause. It may or may not be followed by a main clause. This is one way the colon differs from the semicolon, which generally separates main clauses only. (See pp. 277–78.)

Explanation

Soul food has a deceptively simple definition: the ethnic cooking of African Americans.

Sometimes a concluding explanation is preceded by *the following* or *as follows* and a colon:

A more precise definition might be the following: soul food draws on ingredients, cooking methods, and dishes that originated in Africa, were brought to the New World by slaves, and were modified or supplemented in the Caribbean and the American South.

Note A complete sentence *after* a colon may begin with a capital letter or a small letter (as in the preceding example). Just be consistent throughout an essay.

Series

At least three soul food dishes are familiar to most Americans: fried chicken, barbecued spareribs, and sweet potatoes.

Appositive

Soul food has only one disadvantage: fat.

Namely, that is, and other expressions that introduce appositives *follow* the colon: *Soul food has only one disadvantage: namely, fat.*

Quotation

One soul food chef has a solution: "Soul food doesn't have to be greasy to taste good. Instead of using ham hocks to flavor beans, I use smoked turkey wings. The soulful, smoky taste remains, but without all the fat of pork."

Use a colon before a quotation when the introduction is a complete sentence.

Key terms

main clause A word group that can stand alone as a sentence because it contains a subject and a predicate and does not begin with a subordinating word: *Soul food is a varied cuisine.* (See **4** p. 193.)

appositive A noun or noun substitute that renames another noun immediately before it: *my brother, Jack.* (See **4** p. 193.)

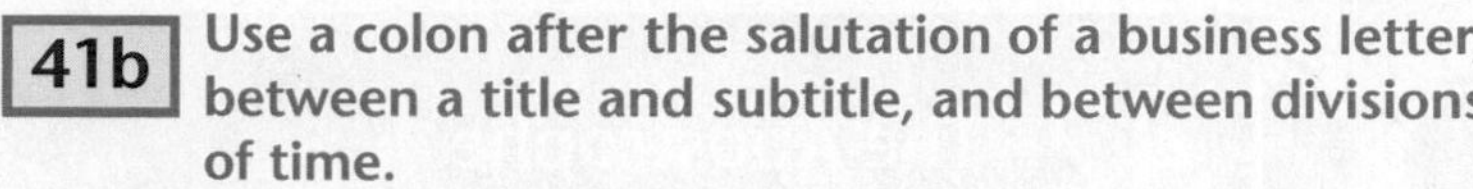

41b Use a colon after the salutation of a business letter, between a title and subtitle, and between divisions of time.

Salutation of business letter

Dear Ms. Burak:

Title and subtitle

Charles Dickens: An Introduction to His Novels

Time

12:26 AM 6:00 PM

41c Delete or replace unneeded colons.

Use the colon only at the end of a main clause, not in the following situations:

- **Delete a colon after a verb.**

Not The best-known soul food dish is: fried chicken.

But The best-known soul food dish is fried chicken.

- **Delete a colon after a preposition.**

Not Soul food recipes can be found in: mainstream cookbooks as well as specialized references.

But Soul food recipes can be found in mainstream cookbooks as well as specialized references.

- **Delete a colon after *such as* or *including*.**

Not Many Americans have not tasted delicacies such as: chitlins and black-eyed peas.

But Many Americans have not tasted delicacies such as chitlins and black-eyed peas.

Key term

preposition *In, on, outside,* or another word that takes a noun or pronoun as its object: *in the house.* (See **4** p. 184.)

42 The Apostrophe

The apostrophe (') appears as part of a word to indicate possession (below), the omission of one or more letters (p. 285), or sometimes plural number (p. 285).

Grammar checkers A grammar checker usually has mixed results in recognizing apostrophe errors. For instance, it may flag missing apostrophes in contractions (as in *isnt*) but may not distinguish between *its* and *it's, their* and *they're, your* and *you're, whose* and *who's*. A checker may identify some apostrophe errors in possessives but overlook others, and it may flag correct plurals. Instead of relying on your checker, try using your computer's Search or Find function to hunt for all words you have ended in *-s*. Then check them to ensure that apostrophes are used correctly.

42a Use the apostrophe to show possession.

A noun or indefinite pronoun shows possession with an apostrophe and, usually, an *-s: the dog's hair, everyone's hope*. Only personal pronouns such as *hers* and *its* do not use apostrophes for possession.

Note Apostrophes are easy to misuse. Always check your drafts to be sure that all words ending in *-s* neither omit needed apostrophes nor add unneeded ones. Also, remember that the apostrophe or apostrophe-plus-*s* is an *addition*. Before this addition, always spell the name of the owner or owners without dropping or adding letters.

1 Singular words: Add -'*s*.

Bill Boughton**'s** skillful card tricks amaze children.
Anyone**'s** eyes would widen.
Most tricks will pique an adult**'s** curiosity, too.

The -'*s* ending for singular words pertains also to singular words ending in *-s*, as the next examples show.

Henry James**'s** novels reward the patient reader.
The business**'s** customers filed suit.

Key term

indefinite pronoun A pronoun that does not refer to a specific person or thing, such as *anyone, each, everybody, no one,* or *something.* (See **4** p. 231.)

mycomplab

Visit *mycomplab.com* for more resources as well as exercises on the apostrophe.

Uses and misuses of the apostrophe

Uses of the apostrophe

- **Use an apostrophe to form the possessives of nouns and indefinite pronouns** (previous page).

Singular	**Plural**
Ms. Park's	the Parks'
lawyer's	lawyers'
everyone's	two weeks'

- **Use an apostrophe to form contractions** (p. 285).

it's a girl	shouldn't
you're	won't

- **The apostrophe is optional for plurals of abbreviations, dates, and words or characters named as words** (p. 285).

MAs or MA's	*C*s or *C*'s
1960s or 1960's	*if*s or *if*'s

Misuses of the apostrophe

- **Do not use an apostrophe plus *-s* to form the possessives of plural nouns ending in *-s*** (next page). Instead, use an apostrophe alone after the *-s* that forms the plural.

Not	**But**
the Kim's car	the Kims' car
boy's fathers	boys' fathers

- **Do not use an apostrophe to form plurals of nouns** (p. 284).

Not	**But**
book's are	books are
the Freed's	the Freeds

- **Do not use an apostrophe with verbs ending in *-s*** (p. 284).

Not	**But**
swim's	swims

- **Do not use an apostrophe to form the possessives of personal pronouns** (p. 285).

Not	**But**
it's toes	its toes
your's	yours

Exception An apostrophe alone may be added to a singular word ending in *-s* when another *s* would make the word difficult to say: *Moses' mother, Joan Rivers' jokes*. But the added *-s* is never wrong (*Moses's*, *Rivers's*).

2 Plural words ending in *-s:* Add -' only.

Workers' incomes have fallen slightly over the past year.
Many students benefit from several years' work after high school.
The Jameses' talents are extraordinary.

Note the difference in the possessives of singular and plural words ending in *-s.* The singular form usually takes the apostrophe plus *-s: James's.* The plural takes only the apostrophe: *Jameses'.*

3 Plural words not ending in -*s:* Add -'*s.*

Children's educations are at stake.
We need to attract the media's attention.

4 Compound words: Add -'*s* only to the last word.

The brother-in-law's business failed.
Taxes are always somebody else's fault.

5 Two or more owners: Add -'*s* depending on possession.

Individual possession
Zimbale's and Mason's comedy techniques are similar. [Each comedian has his own technique.]

Joint possession
The child recovered despite her mother and father's neglect. [The mother and father were jointly neglectful.]

42b Delete or replace any apostrophe in a plural noun, a singular verb, or a possessive personal pronoun.

1 Plural nouns

The plurals of nouns are generally formed by adding *-s* or *-es,* never with an apostrophe: *boys, families, Joneses, Murphys.*

Not The Jones' controlled the firm's until 2001.
But The Joneses controlled the firms until 2001.

2 Singular verbs

Verbs ending in *-s* never take an apostrophe:

Not The subway break's down less often now.
But The subway breaks down less often now.

3 Possessives of personal pronouns

His, hers, its, ours, yours, theirs, and *whose* are possessive forms of *he, she, it, we, you, they,* and *who.* They do not take apostrophes:

Not The house is her's. It's roof leaks.
But The house is hers. Its roof leaks.

Don't confuse possessive pronouns with contractions. See below.

42c Use the apostrophe to form contractions.

A **contraction** replaces one or more letters, numbers, or words with an apostrophe, as in the following examples:

it is, it has	it's	cannot	can't
they are	they're	does not	doesn't
you are	you're	were not	weren't
who is, who has	who's	class of 2012	class of '12

Note Don't confuse contractions with personal pronouns:

Contractions	Personal pronouns
It's a book.	Its cover is green.
They're coming.	Their car broke down.
You're right.	Your idea is good.
Who's coming?	Whose party is it?

42d The apostrophe is optional to mark plural abbreviations, dates, and words or characters named as words.

You'll sometimes see apostrophes used to form the plurals of abbreviations (BA's), dates (1900's), and words or characters named as words (*but*'s). However, most current style guides recommend against the apostrophe in these cases.

BAs PhDs
1990s 2000s

The sentence has too many *but*s.
Two *3*s end the zip code.

Note Italicize or underline a word or character named as a word (see **6** p. 308), but not the added *-s*.

43 Quotation Marks

Quotation marks—either double (" ") or single (' ')—mainly enclose direct quotations from speech or writing, enclose certain titles, and highlight words used in a special sense. These are the uses covered in this chapter, along with placing quotation marks outside or inside other punctuation marks. Additional information on using quotations appears elsewhere in this book:

- **Using commas with signal phrases introducing quotations.** See pp. 273–74.
- **Using the ellipsis mark and brackets to indicate changes in quotations.** See pp. 292–94.
- **Quoting sources versus paraphrasing or summarizing them.** See **7** pp. 359–62.
- **Integrating quotations into your text.** See **7** pp. 362–67.
- **Acknowledging the sources of quotations to avoid plagiarism.** See **7** pp. 370–72.
- **Formatting long prose quotations and poetry quotations.** See **MLA** p. 449 and **APA** p. 483.

Note Always use quotation marks in pairs, one at the beginning of a quotation and one at the end.

Grammar checkers A grammar checker will help you use quotation marks in pairs by flagging a lone mark. It may also look for punctuation inside or outside quotation marks, but it may not detect errors when punctuation should actually fall outside quotation marks.

43a Use double quotation marks to enclose direct quotations.

A **direct quotation** reports what someone said or wrote, in the exact words of the original:

> "Life," said the psychoanalyst Karen Horney, "remains a very efficient therapist."

Note Do not use quotation marks with a direct quotation that is set off from your text. See **MLA** p. 449 and **APA** p. 483. Also do

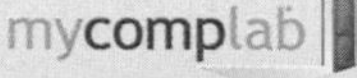

Visit *mycomplab.com* for more resources as well as exercises on quotation marks.

not use quotation marks with an **indirect quotation,** which reports what someone said or wrote but not in the exact words.

> The psychoanalyst Karen Horney claimed that life is a good therapist.

43b Use single quotation marks to enclose a quotation within a quotation.

> "In formulating any philosophy," Woody Allen writes, "the first consideration must always be: What can we know? Descartes hinted at the problem when he wrote, 'My mind can never know my body, although it has become quite friendly with my leg.'"

Notice that two different quotation marks appear at the end of the sentence—one single (to finish the interior quotation) and one double (to finish the main quotation).

43c Set off quotations of dialog according to standard practice.

When quoting conversations, begin a new paragraph for each speaker.

> "What shall I call you? Your name?" Andrews whispered rapidly, as with a high squeak the latch of the door rose.
>
> "Elizabeth," she said. "Elizabeth."
>
> —Graham Greene, *The Man Within*

When you quote a single speaker for more than one paragraph, put quotation marks at the beginning of each paragraph but at the end of only the last paragraph.

Note Quotation marks are optional for quoting unspoken thoughts or imagined dialog:

> I asked myself, "How can we solve this?"
> I asked myself, How can we solve this?

43d Put quotation marks around the titles of works that are parts of other works.

Use quotation marks to enclose the titles of works that are published or released within larger works. (See the following box.) Use single quotation marks for a quotation within a quoted title, as in the article title and essay title in the box. And enclose all punctuation in the title within the quotation marks, as in the article title.

Titles to be enclosed in quotation marks

Other titles should be italicized or underlined. (See **6** p. 307.)

Song
"The Star-Spangled Banner"

Short poem
"Mending Wall"

Short story
"The Gift of the Magi"

Article in periodical
"Does 'Scaring' Work?"

Essay
"Joey: A 'Mechanical Boy'"

Page or document on a Web site
"Readers' Page" (on the site *Friends of Prufrock*)

Episode of a television or radio program
"The Mexican Connection" (on *60 Minutes*)

Subdivision of a book
"The Mast Head" (Chapter 35 of *Moby-Dick*)

Note Some academic disciplines do not require quotation marks for titles within source citations. See **APA** p. 468 and **CSE** p. 504.

43e Quotation marks may enclose words being used in a special sense.

On movie sets movable "wild walls" make a one-walled room seem four-walled on film.

Note Use italics or underlining for defined words. (See **6** p. 308.)

43f Delete quotation marks where they are not required.

Title of your paper

Not "The Death Wish in One Poem by Robert Frost"

But The Death Wish in One Poem by Robert Frost

Or The Death Wish in "Stopping by Woods on a Snowy Evening"

Common nickname

Not As President, "Jimmy" Carter preferred to use his nickname.

But As President, Jimmy Carter preferred to use his nickname.

Slang or trite expression

Quotation marks will not excuse slang or a trite expression that is inappropriate to your writing. If slang is appropriate, use it without quotation marks.

Not We should support the President in his "hour of need" rather than "wimp out on him."

But We should give the President the support he needs rather than turn away like cowards.

43g Place other punctuation marks inside or outside quotation marks according to standard practice.

1 Commas and periods: Inside quotation marks

Swift uses irony in his essay "A Modest Proposal."

Many first-time readers are shocked to see infants described as "delicious."

"'A Modest Proposal,'" writes one critic, "is so outrageous that it cannot be believed."

Exception When a parenthetical source citation immediately follows a quotation, place any period or comma *after* the citation:

One critic calls the essay "outrageous" (Olms 26).

Partly because of "the cool calculation of its delivery" (Olms 27), Swift's satire still chills a modern reader.

2 Colons and semicolons: Outside quotation marks

A few years ago the slogan in elementary education was "learning by playing"; now educators are concerned with basic skills.

We all know what is meant by "inflation": more money buys less.

3 Dashes, question marks, and exclamation points: Inside quotation marks only if part of the quotation

When a dash, question mark, or exclamation point is part of the quotation, place it *inside* quotation marks. Don't use any other punctuation, such as a period or comma:

"But must you—" Marcia hesitated, afraid of the answer.

"Go away!" I yelled.

Did you say, "Who is she?" [When both your sentence and the quotation would end in a question mark or exclamation point, use only the mark in the quotation.]

When a dash, question mark, or exclamation point applies only to the larger sentence, not to the quotation, place it *outside* quotation marks—again, with no other punctuation:

One evocative line in English poetry—"After many a summer dies the swan"—comes from Alfred, Lord Tennyson.

Who said, "Now cracks a noble heart"?

The woman called me "stupid"!

44 Other Marks

The other marks of punctuation are the dash (below), parentheses (p. 291), the ellipsis mark (p. 292), brackets (p. 294), and the slash (p. 295).

Grammar checkers A grammar checker may flag a lone parenthesis or bracket so that you can match it with another parenthesis or bracket. But most checkers cannot recognize other misuses of the marks covered here and instead simply ignore the marks.

44a Use the dash or dashes to indicate shifts and to set off some sentence elements.

The dash (—) is mainly a mark of interruption: it signals a shift, insertion, or break. In your papers, form a dash with two hyphens (--) or use the character called an em dash on your word processor. Do not add extra space around or between the hyphens or around the em dash.

Note When an interrupting element starting with a dash falls in the middle of a sentence, be sure to add the closing dash to signal the end of the interruption. See the first example below.

1 Shifts in tone or thought

The novel—if one can call it that—appeared in 2005.
If the book had a plot—but a plot would be conventional.

2 Nonessential elements

Dashes may be used instead of commas to set off and emphasize modifiers, parenthetical expressions, and other nonessential elements, especially when these elements are internally punctuated:

The qualities Monet painted—sunlight, rich shadows, deep colors—abounded near the rivers and gardens he used as subjects.

Though they are close together—separated by only a few blocks—the two neighborhoods could be in different countries.

Key term

nonessential element Gives added information but does not limit the word it refers to. (See pp. 268–69.)

mycomplab

Visit *mycomplab.com* for more resources as well as exercises on the dash, parentheses, the ellipsis mark, brackets, and the slash.

3 Introductory series and concluding series and explanations

Shortness of breath, skin discoloration or the sudden appearance of moles, persistent indigestion, the presence of small lumps—all these may signify cancer. [Introductory series.]

The patient undergoes a battery of tests—MRI, bronchoscopy, perhaps even biopsy. [Concluding series.]

Many patients are disturbed by the MRI—by the need to keep still for long periods in an exceedingly small space. [Concluding explanation.]

A colon could be used instead of a dash in the last two examples. The dash is more informal.

4 Overuse

Too many dashes can make writing jumpy or breathy.

Not In all his life—eighty-seven years—my great-grandfather never allowed his picture to be taken—not even once. He claimed the "black box"—the camera—would steal his soul.

But In all his eighty-seven years, my great-grandfather did not allow his picture to be taken even once. He claimed the "black box"—the camera—would steal his soul.

44b Use parentheses to enclose parenthetical expressions and labels for lists within sentences.

Note Parentheses *always* come in pairs, one before and one after the punctuated material.

1 Parenthetical expressions

Parenthetical expressions include explanations, facts, digressions, and examples that may be helpful or interesting but are not essential to meaning. Parentheses de-emphasize parenthetical expressions. (Commas emphasize them more than parentheses do, and dashes emphasize them still more.)

The population of Philadelphia (now about 1.5 million) has declined since 1950.

Note Don't put a comma before a parenthetical expression enclosed in parentheses. Punctuation after the parenthetical expression should be placed outside the closing parenthesis.

Not The population of Philadelphia compares with that of Phoenix, (just over 1.6 million.)

But The population of Philadelphia compares with that of Phoenix (just over 1.6 million).

If you enclose a complete sentence in parentheses, capitalize the sentence and place the closing period *inside* the closing parenthesis:

In general, coaches will tell you that scouts are just guys who can't coach. (But then, so are brain surgeons.) —Roy Blount

2 Labels for lists within sentences

Outside the Middle East, the countries with the largest oil reserves are (1) Venezuela (63 billion barrels), (2) Russia (57 billion barrels), and (3) Mexico (51 billion barrels).

When you set a list off from your text, do not enclose such labels in parentheses.

44c Use the ellipsis mark to indicate omissions from quotations.

The ellipsis mark, consisting of three periods separated by space (. . .), generally indicates an omission from a quotation. All the following examples quote from this passage about environmentalism:

Original quotation

"At the heart of the environmentalist world view is the conviction that human physical and spiritual health depends on sustaining the planet in a relatively unaltered state. Earth is our home in the full, genetic sense, where humanity and its ancestors existed for all the millions of years of their evolution. Natural ecosystems—forests, coral reefs, marine blue waters—maintain the world exactly as we would wish it to be maintained. When we debase the global environment and extinguish the variety of life, we are dismantling a support system that is too complex to understand, let alone replace, in the foreseeable future."

—Edward O. Wilson, "Is Humanity Suicidal?"

1. Omission of the middle of a sentence

"Natural ecosystems . . . maintain the world exactly as we would wish it to be maintained."

2. Omission of the end of a sentence, without source citation

"Earth is our home. . . ." [The sentence period, closed up to the last word, precedes the ellipsis mark.]

3. Omission of the end of a sentence, with source citation

"Earth is our home . . ." (Wilson 27). [The sentence period follows the source citation.]

4. Omission of parts of two or more sentences

Wilson writes, "At the heart of the environmentalist world view is the conviction that human physical and spiritual health depends on sustaining the planet . . . where humanity and its ancestors existed for all the millions of years of their evolution."

5. Omission of one or more sentences

As Wilson puts it, "At the heart of the environmentalist world view is the conviction that human physical and spiritual health depends on sustaining the planet in a relatively unaltered state. . . . When we debase the global environment and extinguish the variety of life, we are dismantling a support system that is too complex to understand, let alone replace, in the foreseeable future."

6. Omission from the middle of a sentence through the end of another sentence

"Earth is our home. . . . When we debase the global environment and extinguish the variety of life, we are dismantling a support system that is too complex to understand, let alone replace, in the foreseeable future."

7. Omission of the beginning of a sentence, leaving a complete sentence

a. Bracketed capital letter

"[H]uman physical and spiritual health," Wilson writes, "depends on sustaining the planet in a relatively unaltered state." [No ellipsis mark is needed because the brackets around the *H* indicate that the letter was not capitalized originally and thus that the beginning of the sentence has been omitted.]

b. Small letter

According to Wilson, "human physical and spiritual health depends on sustaining the planet in a relatively unaltered state." [No ellipsis mark is needed because the small *h* indicates that the beginning of the sentence has been omitted.]

c. Capital letter from the original

Hami comments, ". . . Wilson argues eloquently for the environmentalist world view." [An ellipsis mark *is* needed because the quoted part of the sentence begins with a capital letter and it is otherwise not clear that the beginning of the original sentence has been omitted.]

8. Use of a word or phrase

Wilson describes the earth as "our home." [No ellipsis mark needed.]

Note these features of the examples:

- **Use an ellipsis mark when it is not otherwise clear that you have left out material from the source,** as when you omit one or more sentences (examples 5 and 6) or when the words you quote form a complete sentence that is different in the original (examples 1–4 and 7c).
- **You don't need an ellipsis mark when it is obvious that you have omitted something,** such as when a bracketed letter or a small letter indicates omission (examples 7a and 7b) or when a phrase clearly comes from a larger sentence (example 8).

- **Place an ellipsis mark after a sentence period *except* when a parenthetical source citation follows the quotation,** as in example 3. Then the sentence period falls after the citation.

If you omit one or more lines of poetry or paragraphs of prose from a quotation, use a separate line of ellipsis marks across the full width of the quotation to show the omission.

> In "Song: Love Armed" from 1676, Aphra Behn contrasts two lovers' experiences of a romance:
>
> Love in fantastic triumph sate,
> Whilst bleeding hearts around him flowed,
> . . . .
> But my poor heart alone is harmed,
> Whilst thine the victor is, and free. (lines 1-2, 15-16)

(See **MLA** p. 449 for the format of such displayed quotations.)

44d Use brackets to indicate changes in quotations.

Brackets have specialized uses in mathematical equations, but their main use for all kinds of writing is to indicate that you have altered a quotation to explain, clarify, or correct it.

> "That Texaco station [just outside Chicago] is one of the busiest in the nation," said a company spokesperson.

The word *sic* (Latin for "in this manner") in brackets indicates that an error in the quotation appeared in the original and was not made by you. Do not use *sic* to make fun of a writer or to note errors in a passage that is clearly nonstandard.

> According to the newspaper report, "The car slammed thru [sic] the railing and into oncoming traffic."

44e Use the slash between options and between lines of poetry run into the text.

Option

Some teachers oppose pass/fail courses.

Poetry

Many readers have sensed a reluctant turn away from death in Frost's lines "The woods are lovely, dark and deep, / But I have promises to keep" (13-14).

When separating lines of poetry in this way, leave a space before and after the slash. (See **MLA** p. 449 for more on quoting poetry.)

PART 6

Spelling and Mechanics

45 Spelling and the Hyphen *297*

46 Capital Letters *303*

47 Italics or Underlining *306*

48 Abbreviations *309*

49 Numbers *312*

PART 6

Spelling and Mechanics

45 Spelling and the Hyphen *297*

- **a** Typical spelling problems *297*
- **b** Spelling rules *299*
- **c** The hyphen *301*

46 Capital Letters *303*

- **a** First word of sentence *303*
- **b** Proper nouns and adjectives *304*
- **c** Titles and subtitles of works *306*
- **d** Online communication *306*

47 Italics or Underlining *306*

- **a** Titles of works *307*
- **b** Ships, aircraft, spacecraft, trains *308*
- **c** Foreign words *308*
- **d** Words or characters named as words *308*
- **e** Emphasis *308*
- **f** Online communication *309*

48 Abbreviations *309*

- **a** Titles before and after proper names *310*
- **b** Familiar abbreviations and acronyms *310*
- **c** *BC, BCE, AD, CE, AM, PM, no., $* *310*
- **d** Latin abbreviations *310*
- **e** *Inc., Bros., Co., &* *311*
- **f** Units of measurement, names, etc. *311*

49 Numbers *312*

- **a** Numerals vs. words *312*
- **b** Dates, addresses, etc. *313*
- **c** Beginning sentences *313*

45 Spelling and the Hyphen

You can train yourself to spell better, and this chapter will tell you how. But you can improve instantly by acquiring three habits:

- **Carefully proofread your writing.**
- **Cultivate a healthy suspicion of your spellings.**
- **Check a dictionary *every time* you doubt a spelling.**

Spelling checkers A spelling checker can help you find and track spelling errors in your papers. But its usefulness is limited, mainly because it can't spot the confusion of words with similar spellings, such as *now/not, to/too*, and *their/they're/there*. See **1** pp. 31–32 for more on spelling checkers.

45a Anticipate typical spelling problems.

Certain situations, such as misleading pronunciation, commonly lead to misspelling.

1 Pronunciation

In English, pronunciation of words is an unreliable guide to how they are spelled. Pronunciation is especially misleading with **homonyms**, words pronounced the same but spelled differently. Some homonyms and near-homonyms appear in the following box.

Words commonly confused

accept (to receive)
except (other than)

affect (to have an influence on)
effect (a result)

all ready (prepared)
already (by this time)

allusion (an indirect reference)
illusion (an erroneous belief or perception)

ascent (a movement up)
assent (to agree, or an agreement)

bare (unclothed)
bear (to carry, or an animal)

board (a plane of wood)
bored (uninterested)

brake (to stop)
break (to smash)

(continued)

mycomplab

Visit *mycomplab.com* for more resources as well as exercises on spelling and the hyphen.

Words commonly confused

(continued)

buy (to purchase)
by (next to)

cite (to quote an authority)
sight (the ability to see)
site (a place)

desert (to abandon)
dessert (after-dinner course)

discreet (reserved, respectful)
discrete (individual, distinct)

fair (average, or lovely)
fare (a fee for transportation)

forth (forward)
fourth (after *third*)

hear (to perceive by ear)
here (in this place)

heard (past tense of *hear*)
herd (a group of animals)

hole (an opening)
whole (complete)

its (possessive of *it*)
it's (contraction of *it is* or *it has*)

know (to be certain)
no (the opposite of *yes*)

loose (not attached)
lose (to misplace)

meat (flesh)
meet (to encounter, or a competition)

passed (past tense of *pass*)
past (after, or a time gone by)

patience (forbearance)
patients (persons under medical care)

peace (the absence of war)
piece (a portion of something)

plain (clear)
plane (a carpenter's tool, or an airborne vehicle)

presence (the state of being at hand)
presents (gifts)

principal (most important, or the head of a school)
principle (a basic truth or law)

rain (precipitation)
reign (to rule)
rein (a strap for an animal)

right (correct)
rite (a religious ceremony)
write (to make letters)

road (a surface for driving)
rode (past tense of *ride*)

scene (where an action occurs)
seen (past participle of *see*)

stationary (unmoving)
stationery (writing paper)

their (possessive of *they*)
there (opposite of *here*)
they're (contraction of *they are*)

to (toward)
too (also)
two (following *one*)

waist (the middle of the body)
waste (discarded material)

weak (not strong)
week (Sunday through Saturday)

weather (climate)
whether (*if,* or introducing a choice)

which (one of a group)
witch (a sorcerer)

who's (contraction of *who is* or *who has*)
whose (possessive of *who*)

your (possessive of *you*)
you're (contraction of *you are*)

2 Different forms of the same word

Often, the noun form and the verb form of the same word are spelled differently: for example, *advice* (noun) and *advise* (verb). Sometimes the noun and the adjective forms of the same word differ: *height* and *high*. Similar changes occur in the parts of some irregular verbs (*know, knew, known*) and the plurals of irregular nouns (*man, men*).

3 American vs. British spellings 

If you learned English outside the United States, you may be accustomed to British rather than American spellings. Here are the chief differences:

American	British
color, humor	colour, humour
theater, center	theatre, centre
canceled, traveled	cancelled, travelled
judgment	judgement
realize, civilize	realise, civilise
connection	connexion

Your dictionary may list both spellings, but it will specially mark the British one with *chiefly Brit* or a similar label.

45b Follow spelling rules.

1 *ie* vs. *ei*

To distinguish between *ie* and *ei*, use the familiar jingle:

I before *e*, except after *c*, or when pronounced "ay" as in *neighbor* and *weigh*.

I* before *e	believe	thief	hygiene
ei* after *c	ceiling	conceive	perceive
***ei* sounded as "ay"**	sleigh	eight	beige

Exceptions For some exceptions, remember this sentence:

The weird foreigner neither seizes leisure nor forfeits height.

2 Final *e*

When adding an ending to a word with a final *e*, drop the *e* if the ending begins with a vowel:

advise + able = advisable   surprise + ing = surprising

Keep the *e* if the ending begins with a consonant:

care + ful = careful   like + ly = likely

Exceptions Retain the *e* after a soft *c* or *g*, to keep the sound of the consonant soft rather than hard: *courageous, changeable.* And drop the *e* before a consonant when the *e* is preceded by another vowel: *argue + ment = argument, true + ly = truly.*

3 Final *y*

When adding an ending to a word with a final *y*, change the *y* to *i* if it follows a consonant:

beauty, beauties   worry, worried   supply, supplies

But keep the *y* if it follows a vowel, if it ends a proper name, or if the ending is *-ing:*

day, days   Minsky, Minskys   cry, crying

4 Final consonants

When adding an ending to a one-syllable word ending in a consonant, double the final consonant when it follows a single vowel. Otherwise, don't double the consonant.

slap, slapping   park, parking   pair, paired

In words of more than one syllable, double the final consonant when it follows a single vowel *and* when it ends a stressed syllable once the new ending is added. Otherwise, don't double the consonant.

refer, referring   refer, reference   relent, relented

5 Prefixes

When adding a prefix, do not drop a letter from or add a letter to the original word:

unnecessary   disappoint   misspell

6 Plurals

Most nouns form plurals by adding *s* to the singular form. Add *es* for the plural of nouns ending in *s, sh, ch,* or *x.*

boy, boys   kiss, kisses   church, churches

Nouns ending in *o* preceded by a vowel usually form the plural with *s.* Those ending in *o* preceded by a consonant usually form the plural with *es.*

ratio, ratios   hero, heroes

Some very common nouns form irregular plurals.

child, children woman, women mouse, mice

Some English nouns that were originally Italian, Greek, Latin, or French form the plural according to their original language:

analysis, analyses criterion, criteria piano, pianos
basis, bases datum, data thesis, theses
crisis, crises medium, media

A few such nouns may form irregular *or* regular plurals: for instance, *index, indices, indexes; curriculum, curricula, curriculums*. The regular plural is more contemporary.

With compound nouns, add *s* to the main word of the compound. Sometimes this main word is not the last word.

city-states fathers-in-law passersby

CULTURE LANGUAGE Noncount nouns do not form plurals, either regularly (with an added *s*) or irregularly. Examples of noncount nouns include *equipment, intelligence,* and *wealth.* See **4** p. 241.

45c Use the hyphen to form or divide words.

The hyphen is used either to form compound words or to divide words at the ends of lines.

1 Compound adjectives

When two or more words serve together as a single modifier before a noun, a hyphen forms the modifying words clearly into a unit.

She is a well-known actor.
Some Spanish-speaking students work as translators.

When such a compound adjective follows the noun, the hyphen is unnecessary.

The actor is well known.
Many students are Spanish speaking.

The hyphen is also unnecessary in a compound modifier containing an *-ly* adverb, even before the noun: *clearly defined terms*.

When part of a compound adjective appears only once in two or more parallel compound adjectives, hyphens indicate which words the reader should mentally join with the missing part.

School-age children should have eight- or nine-o'clock bedtimes.

2 Fractions and compound numbers

Hyphens join the numerator and denominator of fractions: *one-half, three-fourths*. Hyphens also join the parts of the whole numbers *twenty-one* to *ninety-nine*.

When a hyphenated number is part of a compound adjective before a noun, join all parts of the modifier with hyphens: *sixty-three-foot wall*.

3 Prefixes and suffixes

Do not use hyphens with prefixes except as follows:

- **With the prefixes *self-*, *all-*, and *ex-*:** *self-control, all-inclusive, ex-student.*
- **With a prefix before a capitalized word:** *un-American.*
- **With a capital letter before a word:** *T-shirt.*
- **To prevent misreading:** *de-emphasize, re-create a story.*

The only suffix that regularly requires a hyphen is *-elect,* as in *president-elect*.

4 Words at the ends of lines

You can avoid occasional short lines in your documents by setting your word processor to divide words automatically at appropriate breaks. (In the Tools menu, select Language and then Hyphenation.) To divide words manually, follow these guidelines:

- **Divide words only between syllables**—for instance, *win-dows,* not *wi-ndows.* Check a dictionary for correct syllable breaks.
- **Never divide a one-syllable word.**
- **Leave at least two letters on the first line and three on the second line.** If a word cannot be divided to follow this rule (for instance, *a-bus-er*), don't divide it.

If you must break an electronic address—for instance, in a source citation—do so only after a slash. Do not hyphenate, because readers may perceive any added hyphen as part of the address.

Not http://www.library.miami.edu/staff/lmc/soc-
race.html

But http://www.library.miami.edu/staff/lmc/
socrace.html

46 Capital Letters

Generally, capitalize a word only when a dictionary or conventional use says you must. Consult one of the style guides listed in **8** pp. 398 and 402 for special uses of capitals in the social, natural, and applied sciences.

Grammar checkers A grammar checker will flag overused capital letters and missing capitals at the beginnings of sentences. It will also spot missing capitals at the beginnings of proper nouns and adjectives—*if* the nouns and adjectives are in the checker's dictionary. For example, a checker caught *christianity* and *europe* but not *china* (for the country) or *Stephen king*.

CULTURE LANGUAGE Conventions of capitalization vary from language to language. English, for instance, is the only language to capitalize the first-person singular pronoun (*I*), and its practice of capitalizing proper nouns but not most common nouns also distinguishes it from some other languages.

46a Capitalize the first word of every sentence.

No one expected the outcome.

When quoting other writers, you should reproduce the capital letters beginning their sentences or indicate that you have altered the source's capitalization. Whenever possible, integrate the quotation into your own sentence so that its capitalization coincides with yours:

> "Psychotherapists often overlook the benefits of self-deception," the author argues.
>
> The author argues that "the benefits of self-deception" are not always recognized by psychotherapists.

If you need to alter the capitalization in the source, indicate the change with brackets:

> "[T]he benefits of self-deception" are not always recognized by psychotherapists, the author argues.
>
> The author argues that "[p]sychotherapists often overlook the benefits of self-deception."

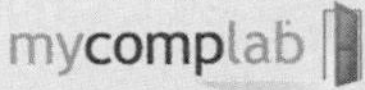

Visit *mycomplab.com* for more resources as well as exercises on capital letters.

Note Capitalization of questions in a series is optional. Both of the following examples are correct:

Is the population a hundred? Two hundred? More?
Is the population a hundred? two hundred? more?

Also optional is capitalization of the first word in a complete sentence after a colon.

46b Capitalize proper nouns, proper adjectives, and words used as essential parts of proper nouns.

1 Proper nouns and proper adjectives

Proper nouns name specific persons, places, and things: *Shakespeare, California, World War I.* **Proper adjectives** are formed from some proper nouns: *Shakespearean, Californian.* Capitalize all proper nouns and proper adjectives but not the articles (*a, an, the*) that precede them:

Proper nouns and adjectives to be capitalized

Specific persons and things

Stephen King	Boulder Dam
Napoleon Bonaparte	the Empire State Building

Specific places and geographical regions

New York City	the Mediterranean Sea
China	the Northeast, the South

But: northeast of the city, going south

Days of the week, months, holidays

Monday	Yom Kippur
May	Christmas

Historical events, documents, periods, movements

the Vietnam War	the Renaissance
the Constitution	the Romantic Movement

Government offices or departments and institutions

House of Representatives	Polk Municipal Court
Department of Defense	Northeast High School

Political, social, athletic, and other organizations and associations and their members

Democratic Party, Democrats	League of Women Voters
Sierra Club	Boston Celtics
B'nai B'rith	Chicago Symphony Orchestra

Races, nationalities, and their languages

Native American	Germans
African American	Swahili
Caucasian	Italian

But: blacks, whites

Religions, their followers, and terms for the sacred

Christianity, Christians	God
Catholicism, Catholics	Allah
Judaism, Orthodox Jews	the Bible [**but** biblical]
Islam, Muslims	the Koran, the Qur'an

2 Common nouns used as essential parts of proper nouns

Capitalize the common nouns *street, avenue, park, river, ocean, lake, company, college, county,* and *memorial* when they are part of proper nouns naming specific places or institutions:

Main Street	Lake Superior
Central Park	Ford Motor Company
Mississippi River	Madison College
Pacific Ocean	George Washington Memorial

3 Compass directions

Capitalize compass directions only when they name a specific region instead of a general direction:

Students from the West often melt in eastern humidity.

4 Relationships

Capitalize the names of relationships only when they precede or replace proper names:

Our aunt scolded us for disrespecting Father and Uncle Jake.

5 Titles with persons' names

Before a person's name, capitalize his or her title. After or apart from the name, do not capitalize the title.

Professor Otto Osborne	Otto Osborne, a professor
Doctor Jane Covington	Jane Covington, a doctor
Governor Ella Moore	Ella Moore, the governor

Note Many writers capitalize a title denoting very high rank even when it follows a name or is used alone: *Ronald Reagan, past President of the United States.*

46c Capitalize most words in titles and subtitles of works.

Within your text, capitalize all the words in a title *except* the following: articles (*a, an, the*); *to* in infinitives; and connecting words (prepositions and conjunctions) of fewer than five letters. Capitalize even these short words when they are the first or last word in a title or when they fall after a colon or semicolon.

"Courtship Through the Ages"	*Management: A New Theory*
A Diamond Is Forever	"Once More to the Lake"
"Knowing Whom to Ask"	*An End to Live For*
Learning from Las Vegas	*File Under Architecture*

Note The style guides of the academic disciplines have their own rules for capitals in titles. For instance, MLA style for English and some other humanities capitalizes all subordinating conjunctions but no prepositions. In addition, APA style for the social sciences and CSE style for the sciences capitalize only the first word and proper names in book and article titles within source citations (see **APA** p. 468 and **CSE** p. 504).

46d Use capitals according to convention in online communication.

Online messages written in all-capital letters or with no capital letters are difficult to read. Further, messages in all-capital letters may be taken as rude (see also **2** p. 117). Use capital letters according to rules 46a–46c in all your online communication.

47 Italics or Underlining

Italic type and underlining indicate the same thing: the word or words are being distinguished or emphasized. Italic type is now used almost universally in academic and business writing, and it has recently become the preferred style of the Modern Language Association (see **MLA** p. 406). Some instructors recommend underlining, so ask your instructor for his or her preference.

> **mycomplab**
>
> Visit *mycomplab.com* for more resources as well as exercises on italics or underlining.

Always use either italics or underlining consistently throughout a document in both text and source citations. If you are using italics, make sure that the italic characters are clearly distinct from the regular type. If you are using underlining and you underline two or more words in a row, underline the space between the words, too: Criminal Statistics: Misuses of Numbers.

Grammar checkers A grammar checker cannot recognize problems with italics or underlining. Check your work to ensure that you have used highlighting appropriately.

47a Italicize or underline the titles of works that appear independently.

Within your text, underline or italicize the titles of works that are published, released, or produced separately from other works. (See the box below.) Use quotation marks for all other titles. (See **5** p. 288.)

Titles to be italicized or underlined

Other titles should be placed in quotation marks. (See **5** p. 288.)

Books
War and Peace
And the Band Played On

Plays
Hamlet
The Phantom of the Opera

Computer software
Microsoft Internet Explorer
Acrobat Reader

Web sites
Google
Friends of Prufrock

Pamphlets
The Truth About Alcoholism

Long musical works
Tchaikovsky's *Swan Lake*
But: Symphony in C

Television and radio programs
The Shadow
NBC Sports Hour

Long poems
Beowulf
Paradise Lost

Periodicals
Time
Philadelphia Inquirer

Published speeches
Lincoln's *Gettysburg Address*

Movies, DVDs, and videos
Schindler's List
How to Relax

Works of visual art
Michelangelo's *David*
Picasso's *Guernica*

Exceptions Legal documents, the Bible, the Koran, and their parts are generally not italicized or underlined:

Not We studied the *Book of Revelation* in the *Bible*.
But We studied the Book of Revelation in the Bible.

47b Italicize or underline the names of ships, aircraft, spacecraft, and trains.

Challenger *Orient Express* *Queen Mary 2*
Apollo XI *Montrealer* *Spirit of St. Louis*

47c Italicize or underline foreign words that are not part of the English language.

Italicize or underline a foreign expression that has not been absorbed into English. A dictionary will say whether a word is still considered foreign to English.

The scientific name for the brown trout is *Salmo trutta*. [The Latin scientific names for plants and animals are always italicized or underlined.]

The Latin *De gustibus non est disputandum* translates roughly as "There's no accounting for taste."

47d Italicize or underline words or characters named as words.

Use italics or underlining to indicate that you are citing a character or word as a word rather than using it for its meaning. Words you are defining fall under this convention.

The word *syzygy* refers to a straight line formed by three celestial bodies, as in the alignment of the earth, sun, and moon.

Some people say *th*, as in *thought*, with a faint *s* or *f* sound.

47e Occasionally, italics or underlining may be used for emphasis.

Italics or underlining can stress an important word or phrase, especially in reporting how someone said something. But use such emphasis very rarely, or your writing may sound immature or hysterical.

47f In online communication, use alternatives for italics or underlining.

Some forms of online communication do not allow conventional highlighting such as italics or underlining for the purposes described in this chapter. (On Web sites, for instance, underlining often indicates a link to another site.)

To distinguish book titles and other elements that usually require italics or underlining, type an underscore before and after the element: *Measurements coincide with those in _Joule's Handbook_.* You can also emphasize words with asterisks before and after: *I *will not* be able to attend.*

Don't use all-capital letters for emphasis; they yell too loudly. (See also p. 306.)

48 Abbreviations

The following guidelines on abbreviations pertain to the text of a nontechnical document. All academic disciplines use abbreviations in source citations, and much technical writing, such as in the sciences and engineering, uses many abbreviations in the document text. For the in-text requirements of the discipline you are writing in, consult one of the style guides listed in **8** pp. 395 (humanities), 398 (social sciences), and 402 (natural and applied sciences).

Usage varies, but writers increasingly omit periods from abbreviations that consist of or end in capital letters: *US, BA, USMC, PhD.* See **5** p. 263 on punctuating abbreviations.

Grammar and spelling checkers A grammar checker may flag some abbreviations, such as *ft.* (for *foot*) and *st.* (for *street*). A spelling checker will flag abbreviations it does not recognize. But neither checker can tell you whether an abbreviation is appropriate for your writing situation or will be clear to your readers.

mycomplab

Visit *mycomplab.com* for more resources as well as exercises on abbreviations.

48a Use standard abbreviations for titles immediately before and after proper names.

Before the name	**After the name**
Dr. James Hsu	James Hsu, MD
Mr., Mrs., Ms., Hon.,	DDS, DVM, PhD,
St., Rev., Msgr., Gen.	EdD, OSB, SJ, Sr., Jr.

Do not use abbreviations such as *Rev., Hon., Prof., Rep., Sen., Dr.,* and *St.* (for *Saint*) unless they appear before a proper name.

48b Familiar abbreviations and acronyms are acceptable in most writing.

An **acronym** is an abbreviation that spells a pronounceable word, such as WHO, NATO, and AIDS. These and other abbreviations using initials are acceptable in most writing as long as they are familiar to readers.

Institutions	LSU, UCLA, TCU
Organizations	CIA, FBI, YMCA, AFL-CIO
Corporations	IBM, CBS, ITT
People	JFK, LBJ, FDR
Countries	US, USA

Note If a name or term (such as *operating room*) appears often in a piece of writing, then its abbreviation (*OR*) can cut down on extra words. Spell out the full term at its first appearance, indicate its abbreviation in parentheses, and then use the abbreviation.

48c Use *BC, BCE, AD, CE, AM, PM, no.,* and *$* only with specific dates and numbers.

44 BC	AD 1492	11:26 AM (*or* a.m.)	no. 36 (*or* No. 36)
44 BCE	1492 CE	8:05 PM (*or* p.m.)	$7.41

The abbreviations BC ("before Christ"), BCE ("before the common era"), and CE ("common era") always follow a date. In contrast, AD (*anno Domini,* Latin for "in the year of the Lord") precedes a date.

48d Generally reserve Latin abbreviations for source citations and comments in parentheses.

Latin abbreviations are generally not italicized or underlined.

i.e.	*id est:* that is
cf.	*confer:* compare

e.g.	*exempli gratia:* for example
et al.	*et alii:* and others
etc.	*et cetera:* and so forth
NB	*nota bene:* note well

He said he would be gone a fortnight (i.e., two weeks).
Bloom et al., editors, *Anthology of Light Verse*
Trees, too, are susceptible to disease (e.g., Dutch elm disease).

Some writers avoid these abbreviations in formal writing, even within parentheses.

48e Use *Inc., Bros., Co.,* or & (for *and*) only in official names of business firms.

Not The Santini bros. operate a large moving firm in New York City & environs.

But The Santini brothers operate a large moving firm in New York City and environs.

Or Santini Bros. is a large moving firm in New York City and environs.

48f Generally spell out units of measurement and names of places, calendar designations, people, and courses.

In most academic, general, and business writing, the types of words listed below should always be spelled out. (In source citations and technical writing, however, these words are more often abbreviated.)

Units of measurement
The dog is thirty inches [not in.] high.

Geographical names
The publisher is in Massachusetts [not Mass. or MA].

Names of days, months, and holidays
The truce was signed on Tuesday [not Tues.], April [not Apr.] 16.

Names of people
Robert [not Robt.] Frost wrote accessible poems.

Courses of instruction
I'm majoring in political science [not poli. sci.].

49 Numbers

This chapter addresses the use of numbers (numerals versus words) in the text of a document. All disciplines use many more numerals in source citations.

Grammar checkers A grammar checker will flag numerals beginning sentences and can be customized to ignore or to look for numerals. But it can't tell you whether numerals or spelled-out numbers are appropriate for your writing situation.

49a Use numerals according to standard practice in the field you are writing in.

Always use numerals for numbers that require more than two words to spell out:

> The leap year has 366 days.
> The population of Minot, North Dakota, is about 32,800.

In nontechnical academic writing, spell out numbers of one or two words:

> Twelve nations signed the treaty.
>
> The ball game drew forty-two thousand people. [A hyphenated number may be considered one word.]

In much business writing, use numerals for all numbers over ten: *five reasons, 11 participants*. In technical academic and business writing, such as in science and engineering, use numerals for all numbers over ten, and use numerals for zero through nine when they refer to exact measurements: *2 liters, 1 hour*. (Consult one of the style guides listed in **8** pp. 398 and 402 for more details.)

Note Use a combination of numerals and words for round numbers over a million: *26 million, 2.45 billion*. And use either all numerals or all words when several numbers appear together in a passage, even if convention would require a mixture.

CULTURE LANGUAGE In standard American English, a comma separates the numerals in long numbers (*26,000*), and a period functions as a decimal point (*2.06*).

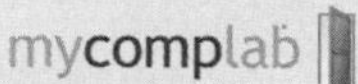

Visit *mycomplab.com* for more resources as well as exercises on numbers.

49b Use numerals according to convention for dates, addresses, and other information.

Days and years
June 18, 1985 AD 12
456 BCE 2010

The time of day
9:00 AM 3:45 PM

Addresses
355 Clinton Avenue
Washington, DC 20036

Exact amounts of money
$3.5 million $4.50

Decimals, percentages, and fractions
22.5 3½
48% (*or* 48 percent)

Scores and statistics
21 to 7 a ratio of 8 to 1
a mean of 26

Pages, chapters, volumes, acts, scenes, lines
Chapter 9, page 123
Hamlet, act 5, scene 3

Exceptions Round dollar or cent amounts of only a few words may be expressed in words: *seventeen dollars; sixty cents*. When the word *o'clock* is used for the time of day, also express the number in words: *two o'clock* (not *2 o'clock*).

49c Spell out numbers that begin sentences.

For clarity, spell out any number that begins a sentence. If the number requires more than two words, reword the sentence so that the number falls later and can be expressed as a numeral.

Not 3.9 billion people live in Asia.
But The population of Asia is 3.9 billion.

Research Writing

50 Research Strategy *317*

51 Finding Sources *325*

52 Working with Sources *344*

53 Avoiding Plagiarism and Documenting Sources *367*

54 Writing the Paper *375*

PART 7

Research Writing

50 Research Strategy *317*

- a Planning *317*
- b Research journal *318*
- c Researchable subject and question *319*
- d Goals for sources *320*
- e Working, annotated bibliography *323*

51 Finding Sources *325*

- a Your library's Web site *326*
- b Searching electronically *326*
- c Reference works *329*
- d Books *330*
- e Periodicals *331*
- f The Web *335*
- g Other online sources *338*
- h Government publications *340*
- i Images, audio, and video *340*
- j Your own sources *342*

52 Working with Sources *344*

- a Evaluating sources *345*
- b Synthesizing sources *356*
- c Gathering information *358*
- d Using summary, paraphrase, and quotation *359*
- e Integrating sources *362*

53 Avoiding Plagiarism and Documenting Sources *367*

- a Plagiarism and the Internet *368*
- b What not to acknowledge *370*
- c What *must* be acknowledged *370*
- d Online sources *372*
- e Documenting sources *374*

54 Writing the Paper *375*

- a Focusing and organizing *375*
- b Drafting, revising, and formatting *376*

50 Research Strategy

Research writing gives you a chance to work like a detective solving a case. The mystery is the answer to a question you care about. The search for the answer leads you to consider what others think about your subject, but you do more than simply report their views. You build on them to develop and support your own opinion, and ultimately you become an expert in your own right.

Your investigation will be more productive and enjoyable if you take some steps described in this chapter: plan your work (below), keep a research journal (next page), find an appropriate subject and research question (p. 319), set goals for your sources (p. 320), and keep a working, annotated bibliography (p. 323).

50a Planning your work

Research writing is a *writing* process:

- **You work within a particular situation of subject, purpose, audience, and other factors** (see **1** pp. 3–8).
- **You gather ideas and information about your subject** (**1** pp. 8–13).
- **You focus and arrange your ideas** (**1** pp. 14–21).
- **You draft to explore your meaning** (**1** pp. 21–22).
- **You revise and edit to develop, shape, and polish** (**1** pp. 24–33).

Although the process seems neatly sequential in this list, you know from experience that the stages overlap—that, for instance, you may begin drafting before you've gathered all the information you expect to find, and then while drafting you may discover a source that causes you to rethink your approach. Anticipating the process of research writing can free you to be flexible in your search and open to discoveries.

A thoughtful plan and systematic procedures can help you follow through on the diverse activities of research writing. One step is to make a schedule like the one on the next page that apportions the available time to the necessary work. You can estimate that each segment marked off by a horizontal line will occupy *roughly* one-quarter of the total time—for example, a week in a four-week assignment or two weeks in an eight-week assignment. The most

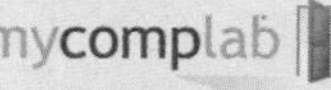

Visit *mycomplab.com* for more resources as well as exercises on research strategy.

unpredictable segments are the first two, so get started early enough to accommodate the unexpected.

Complete by:

_______ 1. Setting a schedule and beginning a research journal (here and below)
_______ 2. Finding a researchable subject and question (facing page)
_______ 3. Setting goals for sources (p. 320)
_______ 4. Finding print and electronic sources (p. 325), and making a working, annotated bibliography (p. 323)

_______ 5. Evaluating and synthesizing sources (pp. 345, 356)
_______ 6. Gathering information from sources (p. 358), often using summary, paraphrase, and direct quotation (p. 359)
_______ 7. Taking steps to avoid plagiarism (p. 367)

_______ 8. Developing a thesis statement and creating a structure (p. 375)
_______ 9. Drafting the paper (p. 376), integrating summaries, paraphrases, and direct quotations into your ideas (p. 362)

_______ 10. Revising and editing the paper (p. 376)
_______ 11. Citing sources in your text (p. 374)
_______ 12. Preparing the list of works cited or references (p. 374)
_______ 13. Preparing the final manuscript (p. 377)
_______ Final paper due

50b Keeping a research journal

While working on a research project, carry a notebook or a computer with you at all times to use as a **research journal,** a place to record your activities and ideas. (See **1** p. 9 on journal keeping.) In the journal's dated entries, you can write about the sources you consult, the leads you want to pursue, and any difficulties you encounter. Most important, you can record your thoughts about sources, leads, dead ends, new directions, relationships, and anything else that strikes you. The very act of writing in the journal can expand and clarify your thinking.

Note The research journal is the place to track and develop your own ideas. To avoid mixing up your thoughts and those of others, keep separate notes on what your sources actually say, using one of the methods discussed on pp. 358–59.

50c Finding a researchable subject and question

Before reading this section, review the suggestions given in Chapter 1 for finding and narrowing a writing subject (**1** pp. 5–6). Generally, the same procedure applies to writing any kind of research paper. However, selecting and limiting a subject for a research paper can present special opportunities and problems. And before you proceed with your subject, you'll want to transform it into a question that can guide your search for sources.

1 Appropriate subject

Seek a research subject that interests you and that you care about. (It may be a subject you've already written about without the benefit of research.) Starting with your own views will motivate you, and you will be a participant in a dialog when you begin examining sources.

When you settle on a subject, ask the following questions about it. For each requirement, there are corresponding pitfalls.

- **Are ample sources of information available on the subject?**

  Avoid very recent subjects, such as a newly announced medical discovery or a breaking story in today's newspaper.

- **Does the subject encourage research in the kinds and number of sources required by the assignment?**

  Avoid (*a*) subjects that depend entirely on personal opinion and experience, such as the virtues of your hobby, and (*b*) subjects that require research in only one source, such as a straight factual biography.

- **Will the subject lead you to an objective assessment of sources and to defensible conclusions?**

  Avoid subjects that rest entirely on belief or prejudice, such as when human life begins or why women (or men) are superior. Your readers are unlikely to be swayed from their own beliefs.

- **Does the subject suit the length of paper assigned and the time given for research and writing?**

  Avoid broad subjects that have too many sources to survey adequately, such as a major event in history.

2 Research question

Asking a question about your subject can give direction to your research by focusing your thinking on a particular approach. To discover your question, consider what about your subject intrigues or perplexes you, what you'd like to know more about. (See below for suggestions on using your own knowledge.)

Try to narrow your research question so that you can answer it in the time and space you have available. The question *How does human activity affect the environment?* is very broad, encompassing issues as diverse as pollution, distribution of resources, climate change, population growth, land use, biodiversity, and the ozone layer. In contrast, the question *How can buying environmentally friendly products help the environment?* or *How, if at all, should carbon emissions be taxed?* is much narrower. Each question also requires more than a simple *yes* or *no* answer, so that answering, even tentatively, demands thought about pros and cons, causes and effects.

As you read and write, your question will probably evolve to reflect your increasing knowledge of the subject, and eventually its answer will become your main idea, or thesis statement (see p. 375).

50d Setting goals for sources

Before you start looking for sources, consider what you already know about your subject and where you are likely to find information on it.

1 Your own knowledge

Discovering what you already know about your topic will guide you in discovering what you don't know. Take some time to spell out facts you have learned, opinions you have heard or read elsewhere, and of course your own opinions. Use one of the discovery techniques discussed in **1** pp. 9–13 to explore and develop your ideas: keeping a journal, observing your surroundings, freewriting, brainstorming, clustering, and asking questions.

When you've explored your thoughts, make a list of questions for which you don't have answers, whether factual (*How much do Americans spend on green products?*) or more open-ended (*Are green products worth the higher prices?*). These questions will give you clues about the sources you need to look for first.

2 Kinds of sources

For many research projects, you'll want to consult a mix of sources, as described on the next two pages. You may start by seeking the outlines of your topic—the range and depth of opinions about it—in reference works and articles in popular periodicals or through a Web search. Then, as you refine your views and your research question, you'll move on to more specialized sources, such as scholarly books and periodicals and your own interviews or surveys. (See pp. 329–44 for more on each kind of source.)

The mix of sources you choose depends heavily on your subject. For example, a paper on green consumerism would require the use of very recent sources because environmentally friendly products are fairly new to the marketplace. Your mix of sources may also be specified by your instructor or limited by the requirements of your assignment.

Library and Internet sources

The print and electronic sources available through your library—mainly reference works, periodicals, and books—have two big advantages over most of what you'll find on the open Web: they are cataloged and indexed for easy retrieval; and they are generally reliable, having been screened first by their publishers and then by the library's staff. In contrast, the Internet's retrieval systems are more difficult to use effectively, and Internet sources tend to be less reliable because most do not pass through any screening before being posted. (There are many exceptions, such as online scholarly journals and reference works. But these sources are generally available through your library's Web site as well.)

Most instructors expect research writers to consult library sources. But they'll accept Internet sources, too, if you have used them judiciously. Even with its disadvantages, the Internet can be a valuable resource for primary sources, current information, and a diversity of views. For guidelines on evaluating both library and Internet sources, see pp. 345–56.

Primary and secondary sources

Use **primary sources** when they are available or are required by your assignment. These sources are firsthand accounts, such as works of literature, historical documents (letters, speeches, and so on), eyewitness reports (including articles by journalists who are on location), reports on experiments or surveys conducted by the writer, and your own interviews, experiments, observations, or correspondence.

Many assignments will allow you to use **secondary sources,** which report and analyze information drawn from other sources, often primary ones. Examples include a reporter's summary of a controversial issue, a historian's account of a battle, a critic's reading of a poem, and a psychologist's evaluation of several studies. Secondary sources may contain helpful summaries and interpretations that direct, support, and extend your own thinking. However, most research-writing assignments expect your own ideas to go beyond those in such sources.

Scholarly and popular sources

The scholarship of acknowledged experts is essential for depth, authority, and specificity. Most instructors expect students to emphasize scholarly sources in their research. But the general-interest views and information of popular sources can help you apply more scholarly approaches to daily life.

- **Check the title.** Is it technical, or does it use a general vocabulary?
- **Check the publisher.** Is it a scholarly journal (such as *Cultural Geographies*) or a publisher of scholarly books (such as Harvard University Press), or is it a popular magazine (such as *Consumer Reports* or *Newsweek*) or a publisher of popular books (such as Little, Brown)?
- **Check the length of periodical articles.** Scholarly articles are generally much longer than magazine and newspaper articles.
- **Check the author.** Have you seen the name elsewhere, which might suggest that the author is an expert?
- **Check the electronic address.** Addresses, or URLs, for Internet sources include an abbreviation that tells you something about the origin of the source: scholarly sources end in *edu, org,* or *gov,* while popular sources usually end in *com.* (See pp. 335–42 and 350–51 for more on types of online sources.)

Older and newer sources

Check the publication date. For most subjects a combination of older, established sources (such as books) and current sources (such as newspaper articles, interviews, or Web sites) will provide both background and up-to-date information. Only historical subjects or very current subjects require an emphasis on one extreme or another.

Impartial and biased sources

Seek a range of viewpoints. Sources that attempt to be impartial can offer an overview of your subject and trustworthy facts. Sources with clear biases can offer a diversity of opinion. Of course, to discover bias, you may have to read the source carefully (see pp. 345–56); but you can infer quite a bit just from a bibliographical listing.

- **Check the author.** You may have heard of the author as a respected researcher (thus more likely to be objective) or as a leading proponent of a certain view (less likely to be objective).
- **Check the title.** It may reveal something about point of view. (Consider these contrasting titles: "Go for the Green" versus "Green Consumerism and the Struggle for Northern Maine.")

Note Sources you find on the Internet must be approached with particular care. See pp. 347–56.

Sources with helpful features

Depending on your topic and how far along your research is, you may want to look for sources with features such as illustrations (which can clarify important concepts), bibliographies (which can direct you to other sources), and indexes (which can help you develop keywords for electronic searches; see pp. 327–29).

50e Keeping a working, annotated bibliography

To track where sources are, compile a **working bibliography** as you uncover possibilities. When you have a substantial file—say, ten to thirty sources—you can decide which ones seem most promising and look them up first.

1 Source information

When you turn in your paper, you will be expected to attach a list of the sources you have used. So that readers can check or follow up on your sources, your list must include all the information needed to find the sources, in a format readers can understand. (See pp. 374–75.) The box on the next page shows the information you should record for each type of source so that you will not have to retrace your steps later.

Note Whenever possible, record source information in the correct format for the documentation style you will be using. Then you will be less likely to omit needed information or to confuse numbers, dates, and other data when it's time to write your citations. This book describes four styles: MLA (see **MLA** p. 406), APA (see **APA** p. 463), Chicago (see **Chic** p. 491), and CSE (see **CSE** p. 502). For others, consult one of the guides listed in **8** pp. 398 and 402.

2 Annotations

Creating annotations for a working bibliography converts it from a simple list into a tool for assessing sources. When you discover a possible source, record not only its publication information but also the following:

- **What you know about the content of the source.** Periodical databases and book catalogs generally include abstracts, or summaries, of sources that can help with this part of the annotation.
- **How you think the source may be helpful in your research.** Does it offer expert opinion, statistics, an important example, or a range of views? Does it place your subject in a historical, social, or economic context?

Information for a working bibliography

For books

Library call number
Name(s) of author(s), editor(s), translator(s), or others listed
Title and subtitle
Publication data:
  Place of publication
  Publisher's name
  Date of publication
Other important data, such as edition or volume number
Medium (print, Web, etc.)

For periodical articles

Name(s) of author(s)
Title and subtitle of article
Title of periodical
Publication data:
  Volume number and issue number (if any) in which article appears
  Date of issue
  Page numbers on which article appears
Medium (print, Web, etc.)

For electronic sources

Name(s) of author(s)
Title and subtitle of source
Title of Web site, periodical, or other larger work
Publication data, such as data listed above for a book or article; the publisher or sponsor of a Web site; and the date of release, revision, or online posting
Any publication data for the source in another medium (print, film, etc.)
Format of online source (Web site or page, podcast, e-mail, etc.)
Date you consulted the source
Title of any database used to reach the source
Complete URL (but see the note below)
Digital Object Identifier, if any (for APA style)
Medium (Web, CD-ROM, etc.)

For other sources

Name(s) of author(s), creator(s), or others listed, such as a government department, recording artist, or photographer
Title of work
Format, such as unpublished letter, live performance, or photograph
Publication or production data:
  Publication title
  Publisher's or producer's name
  Date of publication, release, or production
Identifying numbers (if any)
Medium (print, typescript, etc.)

Note MLA documentation style does not require URLs for citations of most electronic sources; other styles do require them. Recording URLs will ensure that you have them if you need them and will make it easy to track down sources if you want to consult them again. For sources you reach through databases, record URLs only if they are usable by others outside your school. Most database URLs are unique to the search or the subscriber.

Taking the time with your annotations can help you discover gaps that may remain in your sources and will later help you decide which sources to pursue in depth. One student annotated a bibliography entry on his computer with a summary and a note on the source features he thought would be most helpful to him:

Entry for an annotated working bibliography

> Gore, Al. *An Inconvenient Truth: The Planetary Emergency of Global Warming and What We Can Do about It*. Emmaus: Rodale, 2006. Print.
>
> Book version of the documentary movie supporting Gore's argument that global warming is a serious threat to the planet. Includes summaries of scientific studies, short essays on various subjects, and dozens of images, tables, charts, and graphs. Last chapter offers several suggestions for ways to solve the problem, with an emphasis on changing individual buying habits.

Publication information for source

Summary of source

Ideas on use of source

As you become more familiar with your sources, you can use your initial annotated bibliography to record your evaluations of them as well as more detailed thoughts on how they fit into your research.

51 Finding Sources

This chapter discusses conducting electronic searches (next page) and taking advantage of the range of sources, both print and electronic, that you have access to: reference works (p. 329); books (p. 330); periodicals (p. 331); the Web (p. 335); other online sources (p. 338); government publications (p. 340); images, audio, and video (p. 340); and your own interviews, surveys, and other primary sources (p. 342).

Note As you look for sources, avoid the temptation to seek a "silver bullet"—that is, to locate two or three perfect sources that already say everything you want to say about your subject. Instead of merely repeating others' ideas, read and synthesize many sources so that you develop your own ideas. For more on synthesis, see pp. 356–57.

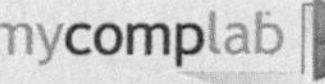

Visit *mycomplab.com* for more resources as well as exercises on finding sources.

51a Starting with your library's Web site

As you conduct research, the Web will be your gateway to ideas and information. Always start with your library's Web site, not with a public search engine such as *Google*. The library site will lead you to vast resources, including books, periodical articles, and reference works that aren't available on the open Web. More important, unlike many sources on the open Web, every source you find on the library site will have passed through filters to ensure its value. A scholarly journal article, for instance, undergoes at least three successive reviews: subject-matter experts first deem it worth publishing in the journal; then a database vendor deems the journal worth including in the database; and finally your school's librarians deem the database worth subscribing to.

Google and other search engines may seem more user-friendly than the library's Web site and may seem to return plenty of sources for you to work with. Many of the sources may indeed be reliable and relevant to your research, but many more will not be. In the end, a library Web search will be more efficient and more effective than a direct Web search. (For help with evaluating sources from any resource, see pp. 345–56.)

Note Start with the library's Web site, but don't stop there. Many books, periodicals, and other excellent sources are available only on library shelves, not online, and most instructors expect research papers to be built to some extent on these resources. When you spot promising print sources while browsing the library's online databases, make records of them and then look them up at the library.

51b Searching electronically

Searching electronically requires careful planning. Become familiar with the kinds of electronic resources available to you, understand the different search strategies they demand, and take the time to develop **keywords** that name your subject for databases and Web search engines.

1 Kinds of electronic sources

Your school's library, its Web site, and the open Web offer several kinds of electronic resources that are suitable for academic research:

- **The library's catalog of holdings** is a database that lists all the resources that the library owns or subscribes to: books, journals, magazines, newspapers, reference works, and more. The

A tip for researchers

Take advantage of two valuable resources offered by your library:

- **An orientation,** which introduces the library's resources and explains how to reach and use the Web site and the print holdings.
- **Reference librarians,** whose job it is to help you and others navigate the library's resources. Even very experienced researchers often consult reference librarians.

catalog may also include the holdings of other school libraries nearby or in your state.

- **Online databases** include indexes, bibliographies, and other reference works. They are your main route to articles in periodicals, providing publication information, summaries, and often full text. Your library subscribes to the databases and makes them available through its Web site. (You may also discover databases directly on the Web, but, again, the library is a more productive starting place.)
- **Databases on CD-ROM** include the same information as online databases, but they must be read at a library computer terminal. Increasingly, libraries are moving away from CD-ROMs in favor of online databases.
- **Full-text resources** contain the entire contents of articles, book chapters, and even whole books. The library's databases provide access to the full text of many listed sources. In addition, the Web sites of many periodicals and organizations, such as government agencies, offer the full text of articles, reports, and other publications.

2 Databases vs. the open Web

To develop keywords it helps to understand an important difference in how library databases and the open Web work:

- **A database indexes sources by authors, titles, publication years, and its own subject headings.** The subject headings reflect the database's directory of terms and are assigned by people who have read the sources. You can find these subject headings by using your own keywords until you locate a promising source. The information for the source will list the headings under which the database indexes it and other sources like it. (See p. 334 for an illustration.) You can then use those headings for further searches.
- **A Web search engine seeks your keywords in the titles and texts of sites.** The process is entirely electronic, so the results from a search engine will depend on how well your keywords

describe your subject and anticipate the words used in sources. If you describe your subject too broadly or describe it specifically but don't match the vocabulary in relevant sources, your search will turn up few relevant sources and probably many that aren't relevant.

3 Keyword refinement

Every database and search engine provides a system that you can use to refine your keywords for a productive search. The basic operations appear in the following box, but resources do differ. For instance, some assume that *AND* should link keywords, while others provide options specifying "Must contain all the words" and other equivalents for the operations in the box. You can learn a search engine's system by consulting its Advanced Search page.

Ways to refine keywords

Most databases and many search engines work with **Boolean operators,** terms or symbols that allow you to expand or limit your keywords and thus your search.

- **Use *AND* or + to narrow the search** by including only sources that use all the given words. The keywords *green AND products* request only the sources in the shaded area.

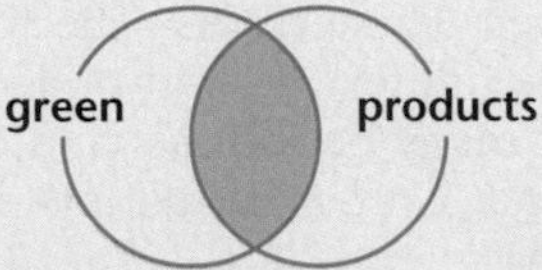

- **Use *NOT* or – ("minus") to narrow the search** by excluding irrelevant words. The keywords *green AND products NOT guide* exclude sources that use the word *guide:*

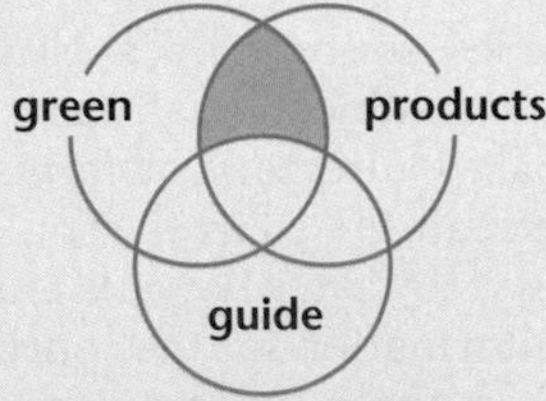

- **Use *OR* to broaden the search** by giving alternate keywords. The keywords *green AND products OR goods* allow for sources that use a synonym for *products:*

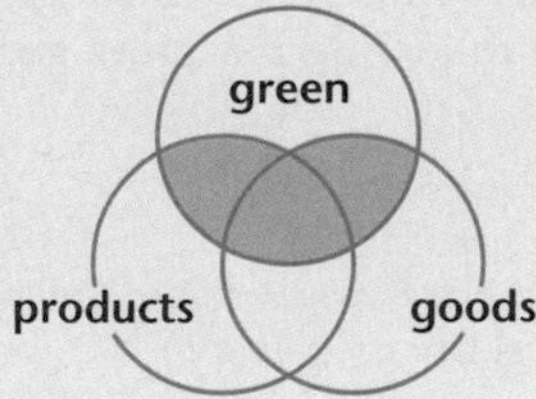

- **Use parentheses or quotation marks to form search phrases.** For instance, *(green products)* requests the exact phrase, not the separate words. Only sources using *green products* would turn up.
- **Use wild cards to permit different versions of the same word.** In *consum**, for instance, the wild card * indicates that sources may include *consume, consumer, consumerism,* and *consumption* as well as *consumptive, consumedly,* and *consummate.* The example suggests that you have to consider all the variations allowed by a wild card and whether it opens up your search too much. If you seek only two or three from many variations, you may be better off using *OR: consumption OR consumerism.* (Note that some systems use ?, :, or + for a wild card instead of *.)
- **Be sure to spell your keywords correctly.** Some search tools will look for close matches or approximations, but correct spelling gives you the best chance of finding relevant sources.

Note You will probably have to use trial and error in developing your keywords, sometimes running dry (turning up few or no sources) and sometimes hitting uncontrollable gushers (turning up thousands or millions of mostly irrelevant sources). But the process is not busywork—far from it. Besides leading you eventually to worthwhile sources, it can also teach you a great deal about your subject: how you can or should narrow it, how it is and is not described by others, what others consider interesting or debatable about it, and what the major arguments are. See pp. 337–38 for an example of a student's keyword search of the Web.

51c Finding reference works

Reference works, often available online, include encyclopedias, dictionaries, digests, bibliographies, indexes, atlases, almanacs, and handbooks. Your research *must* go beyond these sources, but they can help you decide whether your topic really interests you and whether it meets the requirements for a research paper (p. 319). Preliminary research in reference works can also help you develop keywords for electronic searches and can direct you to more detailed sources on your topic.

You'll find many reference works through your library and directly on the Web. The following list gives general Web references for all disciplines:

Internet Public Library (*www.ipl.org*)
Library of Congress (*lcweb.loc.gov*)
LSU Libraries Webliography (*www.lib.lsu.edu/weblio.html*)
World Wide Web Virtual Library (*vlib.org*)

For Web sites in specific academic disciplines, see **8** pp. 388–89 (literature), 394 (other humanities), 398 (social sciences), and 401–02 (natural and applied sciences).

Note The Web-based encyclopedia *Wikipedia* (found at *wikipedia.org*) is one of the largest reference sites on the Internet. Like any encyclopedia, *Wikipedia* can provide background information for research on a topic; but unlike other encyclopedias, *Wikipedia* is a **wiki**, a kind of Web site that can be contributed to or edited by anyone. Ask your instructor whether *Wikipedia* is an acceptable source before you use it. If you do use it, you must carefully evaluate any information you find, using the guidelines on pp. 347–54.

51d Finding books

Your library's catalog is searchable at a terminal in the library and via the library's Web site. You can search the catalog by author or title, of course, and by your own keywords or the headings found in *Library of Congress Subject Headings* (*LCSH*). The screen shot below shows the complete record for a book, including the *LCSH* headings that can be used to find similar sources.

Book catalog full record

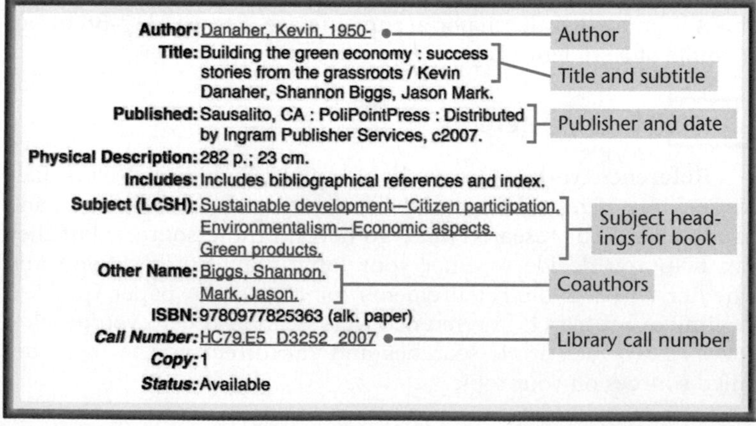

51e Finding periodicals

Periodicals include newspapers, journals, and magazines. Newspapers, the easiest to recognize, are useful for detailed accounts of past and current events. Journals and magazines can be harder to distinguish, but their differences are important. Most college instructors expect students' research to rely more on journals than on magazines.

	Journals	Magazines
Examples	*American Anthropologist, Journal of Black Studies, Journal of Chemical Education*	*The New Yorker, Time, Rolling Stone, People*
Availability	Mainly through college and university libraries	Public libraries, newsstands, and bookstores
Purpose	Advance knowledge in a particular field	Express opinion, inform, or entertain
Authors	Specialists in the field	May or may not be specialists in their subjects
Readers	Often specialists in the field	Members of the general public or a subgroup with a particular interest
Source citations	Source citations always included	Source citations rarely included
Length of articles	Usually long, ten pages or more	Usually short, fewer than ten pages
Appearance	Bland, with black-only type, little or no decoration, and only illustrations that directly amplify the text, such as graphs	Generally lively, with color, decoration (headings, sidebars, and other elements), and illustrations (drawings, photographs)
Frequency of publication	Quarterly or less often	Weekly, biweekly, or monthly
Pagination of issues	May be paged separately (like a magazine) or may be paged sequentially throughout an annual volume, so that issue number 3 (the third issue of the year) could open on page 373	Paged separately, each beginning on page 1

1 Indexes to periodicals

How indexes work

Periodical databases index the articles in journals, magazines, and newspapers. Often these databases include abstracts, or summaries, of the articles, and they may offer the full text of the articles as well. Your library subscribes to many periodical databases and to services that offer multiple databases. (See p. 335 for a list.) Most databases and services will be searchable through the library's Web site.

Note The search engine *Google* is developing *Google Scholar,* a search engine at *scholar.google.com* that seeks out scholarly articles. It is particularly useful for subjects that range across disciplines, for which discipline-specific databases can be too limited. *Google Scholar* can connect to your library's holdings if you tell it to do so under Scholar Preferences. Keep in mind, however, that *Google Scholar*'s searches are not as yet exhaustive. Your library probably subscribes to most of the periodicals searched by *Google Scholar,* so begin there.

Selection of databases

To decide which databases to consult, you'll need to consider what you're looking for:

- **How broadly and deeply should you search?** Periodical databases vary widely in what they index. Some, such as *ProQuest Research Library,* cover many subjects but don't index the full range of periodicals in each subject. Others, such as *Historical Abstracts,* cover a single subject but then include most of the available periodicals. If your subject ranges across disciplines, then start with a broad database. If your subject focuses on a particular discipline, then start with a narrower database.
- **Which databases most likely include the kinds of resources you need?** The Web sites of most libraries allow you to narrow a database search to a particular kind of periodical (such as newspapers or journals) or to a particular discipline. You can then discover each database's focus by checking the description of the database (sometimes labeled "Help" or "Guide") or the list of indexed resources (sometimes labeled "Publications" or "Index"). The description will also tell you the time period the database covers, so you'll know whether you also need to consult older print indexes at the library.

Database searches

When you first search a database, use your own keywords to locate sources. The procedure is illustrated in the three screen shots shown below and on the next page. Your goal is to find at least one source that seems just right for your subject, so that you can see what subject headings the database itself uses for such sources. Using one or more of those headings will focus and speed your search.

1. Initial keyword search of a periodical database

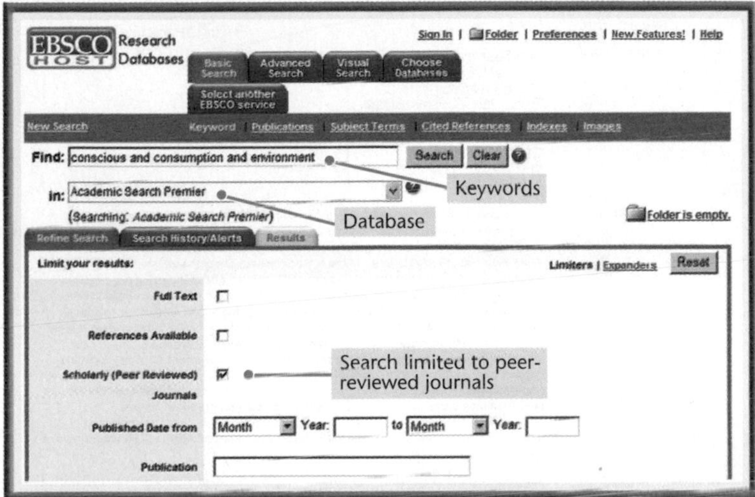

2. Partial keyword search results

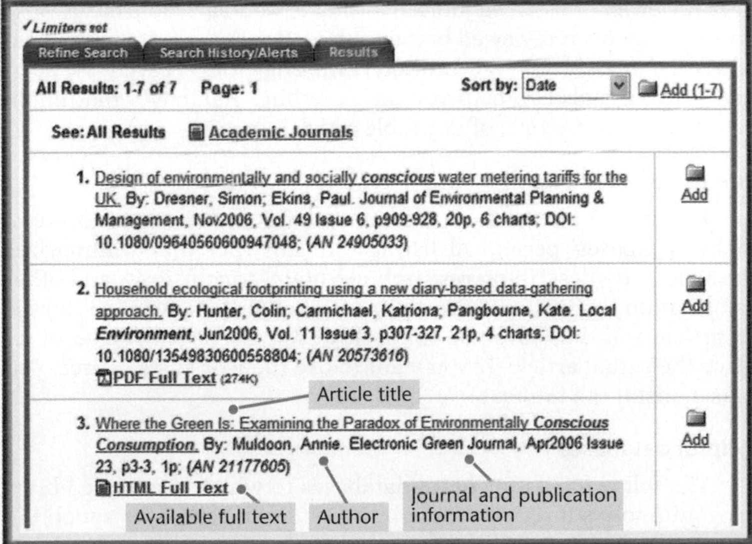

3. Full article record with abstract

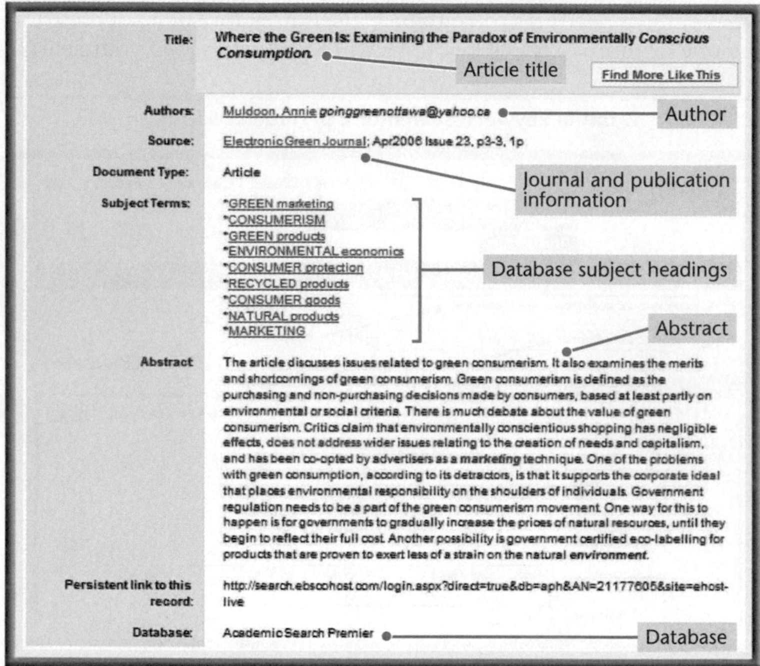
Title: Where the Green Is: Examining the Paradox of Environmentally *Conscious* *Consumption.*
Article title
Find More Like This
Authors: Muldoon, Annie goinggreenottawa@yahoo.ca
Author
Source: Electronic Green Journal; Apr2006 Issue 23, p3-3, 1p
Document Type: Article
Journal and publication information
Subject Terms: *GREEN marketing
*CONSUMERISM
*GREEN products
*ENVIRONMENTAL economics
*CONSUMER protection
*RECYCLED products
*CONSUMER goods
*NATURAL products
*MARKETING
Database subject headings
Abstract
Abstract: The article discusses issues related to green consumerism. It also examines the merits and shortcomings of green consumerism. Green consumerism is defined as the purchasing and non-purchasing decisions made by consumers, based at least partly on environmental or social criteria. There is much debate about the value of green consumerism. Critics claim that environmentally conscientious shopping has negligible effects, does not address wider issues relating to the creation of needs and capitalism, and has been co-opted by advertisers as a *marketing* technique. One of the problems with green consumption, according to its detractors, is that it supports the corporate ideal that places environmental responsibility on the shoulders of individuals. Government regulation needs to be a part of the green consumerism movement. One way for this to happen is for governments to gradually increase the prices of natural resources, until they begin to reflect their full cost. Another possibility is government certified eco-labelling for products that are proven to exert less of a strain on the natural *environment.*
Persistent link to this record: http://search.ebscohost.com/login.aspx?direct=true&db=aph&AN=21177605&site=ehost-live
Database: Academic Search Premier
Database

Note Many databases allow you to limit your search to so-called peer-reviewed or refereed journals—that is, scholarly journals whose articles have been reviewed before publication by experts in the field and then revised by the author. Limiting your search to peer-reviewed journals can help you navigate huge databases that might otherwise return scores of unusable articles.

The use of abstracts

In screen 3 above, the full article record shows a key feature of many databases' periodical listings: an **abstract** that summarizes the article. By describing research methods, conclusions, and other information, an abstract can tell you whether you want to pursue an article and thus save you time. However, the abstract cannot replace the actual article. If you want to use the work as a source, you must consult the full text.

Helpful databases

The following list includes databases to which academic libraries commonly subscribe. Some of these databases cover much the same material, so your library may not subscribe to all of them.

EBSCOhost Academic Search. A periodical index covering magazines and journals in the social sciences, sciences, arts, and humanities. Many articles are available full-text.

InfoTrac Expanded Academic. The Gale Group's general periodical index covering the social sciences, sciences, arts, and humanities as well as national news periodicals. It includes full-text articles.

LexisNexis Academic. An index of news and business, legal, and reference information, with full-text articles. *LexisNexis* includes international, national, and regional newspapers, news magazines, legal and business publications, and court cases.

ProQuest Research Library. A periodical index covering the sciences, social sciences, arts, and humanities, including many full-text articles.

2 Locations of periodicals

If an index listing does not include or link directly to the full text of an article, you'll need to consult the periodical itself. Recent issues of periodicals are probably held in the library's periodical room. Back issues are usually stored elsewhere, either in bound volumes or on film that requires a special machine to read. A librarian will show you how to operate the machine.

51f Finding sources on the Web

As an academic researcher, you enter the Web in two ways: through your library's Web site, and through public search engines such as *Yahoo!* and *Google*. The library entrance, covered in the preceding sections, is your main path to the books and periodicals that, for most subjects, should make up most of your sources. The public entrance, discussed here, can lead to a wealth of information and ideas, but it also has a number of disadvantages:

- **The Web is a wide-open network.** Anyone with the right hardware and software can place information on the Internet, and even a carefully conceived search can turn up sources with widely varying reliability: journal articles, government documents, scholarly data, term papers written by high school students, sales pitches masked as objective reports, wild theories. You must be especially diligent about evaluating Internet sources (see pp. 347–56).
- **The Web changes constantly.** No search engine can keep up with the Web's daily additions and deletions, and a source you find today may be different or gone tomorrow. You should not put off consulting an online source that you think you may want to use.
- **The Web provides limited information on the past.** Sources dating from before the 1980s or even more recently probably will not appear on the Web.

- **The Web is not all-inclusive.** Most books and many periodicals are available only via the library, not directly via the Web.

Clearly, the Web warrants cautious use. It should not be the only resource you work with.

Note Open-source wikis, such as *Wikipedia* and *SourceWatch*, are Web sites that can be contributed to and edited by anyone. Ask your instructor whether wikis are acceptable sources before using one, and evaluate any information you find on a wiki using the guidelines on pp. 347–54.

1 Search engines

To find sources on the Web, you use a **search engine** that catalogs Web sites in a series of directories and conducts keyword searches. Generally, use a directory when you haven't yet refined your topic or you want a general overview. Use keywords when you have refined your topic and you seek specific information.

Current search engines

The box below lists popular search engines. To reach any one of them, enter its address in the Address or Location field of your Web browser.

Web search engines

The features of search engines change often, and new ones appear constantly. For the latest on search engines, see the links collected by *Easy Searcher* at *easysearcher.com.*

Directories that review sites

BUBL Link (bubl.ac.uk)
Internet Public Library (ipl.org/div/subject)
Internet Scout Project (scout.wisc.edu/archives)
Librarians' Internet Index (lii.org)

Search engines

AlltheWeb (alltheweb.com)
AltaVista (altavista.com)
Ask.com (ask.com)
Dogpile (dogpile.com)
Google (google.com)
Livesearch.com (livesearch.com)
MetaCrawler (metacrawler.com)
Yahoo! (yahoo.com)

Note For a good range of reliable sources, try out more than a single search engine, perhaps as many as four or five. No search engine can catalog the entire Web—indeed, even the most powerful engine may not include half the sites available at any given time, and most engines include only a fifth or less. In addition, most search engines accept paid placements, giving higher billing to sites that pay a fee. These so-called sponsored links are usually marked as such, but they can compromise a search engine's method for arranging sites in response to your keywords.

Customized searches

The home page of a search engine includes a field for you to type your keywords into. Generally, it will also include an Advanced Search link that you can use to customize your search. For instance, you may be able to select a range of dates, a language, or a number of results to see. Advanced Search will also explain how to use operators such as *AND* and *NOT* to limit or expand your search.

Search records

Your Web browser includes functions that allow you to keep track of Web sources and your search:

- **Use *Favorites* or *Bookmarks* to save site addresses as links.** Click one of these terms near the top of the browser screen to add a site you want to return to. A favorite or bookmark remains on file until you delete it.
- **Use *History* to locate sites you have visited before.** The browser records visited sites for a certain period, such as a single online session or a week's sessions. (After that period, the history is deleted.) If you forgot to bookmark a site, you can click History or Go to locate your search history and recover the site.

2 A sample search

The following sample Web search illustrates how the refinement of keywords can narrow a search to maximize the relevant hits and minimize the irrelevant ones. Justin Malik, a student researching the environmental effects of green consumer products, first used the keywords *green consumption* on *Google*. But, as shown on screen 1 on the next page, the search produced more than 3.4 *million* hits, an unusably large number and a sure sign that Malik's keywords needed revision.

After several tries, Malik arrived at *"green consumption" "environmental issues"* to describe his subject more precisely. He then added *site:.org* to limit the results to nonprofit organizations. Narrowed in this way, Malik's search still produced 387 hits, but this large number included many potential sources on the first few screens, as shown on screen 2 on the next page.

1. First *Google* search results

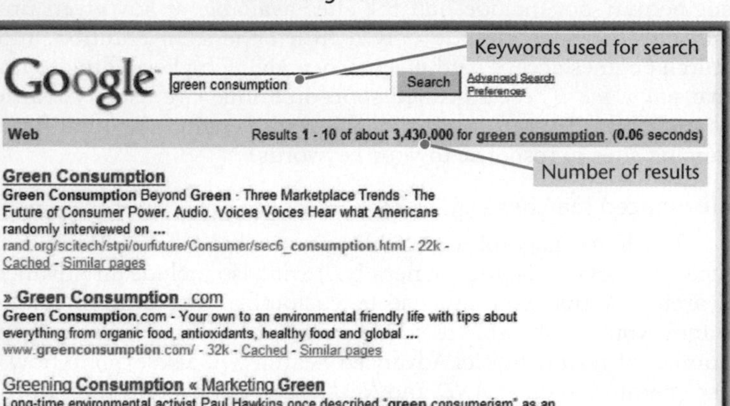

2. *Google* results with refined keywords

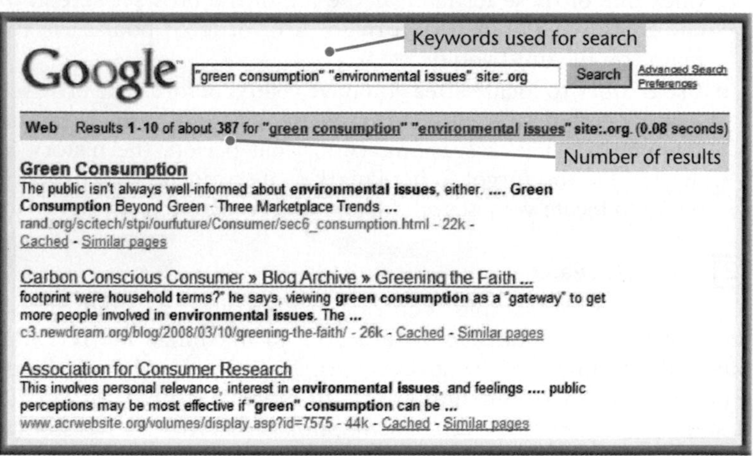

51g Finding other online sources

Several online sources can put you directly in touch with experts and others whose ideas and information may inform your research. Because these sources, like Web sites, are unfiltered, you must always evaluate them carefully. (See pp. 354–56.)

1 E-mail

As a research tool, e-mail allows you to communicate with others who are interested in your topic. You might, for instance, carry on an e-mail conversation with a teacher at your school or interview an expert in another state to follow up on a scholarly article he or she published. (See **2** pp. 116–18 for more on using e-mail.)

2 Blogs

Blogs (Web logs) are personal sites on which an author posts time-stamped comments, generally centering on a common theme, in a format that allows readers to respond to the author or to each other. You can find a directory of blogs at *blogcatalog.com*.

Like all other online media discussed in this section, blogs consulted as potential sources must be evaluated carefully. Some are reliable sources of opinion, news, or evolving scholarship, and many refer to worthy books, articles, Web sites, and other resources. But lots of blogs are little more than outlets for their authors' gripes and prejudices. See pp. 354–56 for tips on telling the good from the bad.

3 Discussion lists

A **discussion list** (sometimes called a **listserv** or just a **list**) uses e-mail to connect individuals who are interested in a common subject, often with a scholarly or technical focus. By sending a question to an appropriate list, you may be able to reach scores of people who know something about your topic. For an index of discussion lists, see *tile.net/lists*.

When conducting research on a discussion list, follow the guidelines for writing e-mail (**2** pp. 116–18) as well as these:

- ***Lurk* for a while**—read without posting messages. Make sure the discussion is relevant to your topic, and get a sense of how the group interacts.
- **Consult the list's archive.** Your question may already have been answered.
- **Don't ask for information you can find elsewhere.** Most list members are glad to help with legitimate questions but resent messages that rehash familiar debates or that ask them to do someone else's work.
- **Evaluate messages carefully.** Many list subscribers are passionate experts with fair-minded approaches to their topics, but almost anyone with an Internet connection can post a message to a list. See pp. 354–56 on evaluating online sources.

4 Web forums and newsgroups

Web forums and newsgroups are more open and less scholarly than discussion lists, so their messages require even more diligent evaluation. **Web forums** allow participants to join a conversation simply by selecting a link on a Web page. For a directory of forums, see *delphiforums.com.* **Newsgroups** are organized under subject headings such as *soc* for social issues and *biz* for business. For a directory of newsgroups, see *groups.google.com.*

51h Using government publications

Government publications provide a vast array of data, reports, policy statements, public records, and other historical and contemporary information. For US government publications, consult the Government Printing Office's *GPO Access* at *www.gpoaccess.gov.* Also helpful is *Google US Government Search* (*google.com/unclesam*) because it returns *.gov* (government) and *.mil* (military) documents and its ranking system emphasizes the most useful documents. Many federal, state, and local government agencies post important publications—legislation, reports, press releases—on their own Web sites. You can find lists of sites for various federal agencies by using the keywords *United States federal government* with a search engine. Use the name of a state, city, or town with *government* for state and local information.

51i Finding images, audio, and video

Images, audio, and video can be used as both primary and secondary sources in a research project. A painting, an advertisement, or a video of a speech might be the subject of a paper and thus a primary source. A podcast of a radio interview with an expert on your subject or a college lecture might serve as a secondary source. Because many of these sources are unfiltered—they can be posted by anyone—you must always evaluate them as carefully as you would any source you find on the open Web.

Note You must also cite every image, audio, and video source fully in your paper, just as you cite text sources, with author, title, and publication information. In addition, some sources will require that you seek permission from the copyright holder, either the source itself or a third party such as a photographer or the creator of video. Permission is especially likely to be required if you are submitting your paper on the public Web. See p. 373 for more about online publication.

1 Images

The use of images to support an argument is discussed in **2** pp. 105–11. To find images, you have a number of options.

- **Scout for images while reading sources.** Your sources may include charts, graphs, photographs, and other images that can support your ideas. When you find an image you may want to use, photocopy or download it so you'll have it available later.
- **Create your own images,** such as photographs or charts. See **1** pp. 61–64 for examples.
- **Use an image search engine.** *Google, Yahoo!, AlltheWeb,* and some other search engines conduct specialized image searches. They can find scores of images, but the results may be inaccurate or incomplete because the sources surveyed often do not include descriptions of the images. (The engines will search file names and any text accompanying the images.)
- **Use a public image database.** The following sites generally conduct accurate searches because their images are filed with information such as a description of the image, the artist's name, and the image's date:

  Adflip (*adflip.com*): Historical and contemporary print advertisements

  Duke University, *Ad*Access* (*library.duke.edu/digitalcollections/adaccess*): Print advertisements spanning 1911–55

  Library of Congress, *American Memory* (*memory.loc.gov/ammem*): Maps, photographs, and prints documenting the American experience

  Library of Congress, *Prints and Photographs Online Catalog* (*loc.gov/rr/print/catalog.html*): Images from the library's collection, including those available through *American Memory*

  New York Public Library Digital Gallery (*digitalgallery.nypl.org/nypldigital*): Maps, drawings, photographs, and paintings from the library's collection

  Political Cartoons (*politicalcartoons.com*): Cartoons on contemporary issues and events

- **Use a public image directory.** The following sites collect links to image sources:

  Art Source (*ilpi.com/artsource/general.html*): Sources on art and architecture

  Museum Computer Network (*mcn.edu/resources/sitesonline.htm*): Museum collections

  MuseumLink's Museum of Museums (*museumlink.com*): Links to museums all over the world

  Washington State University, *Popular Culture: Resources for Critical Analysis* (*wsu.edu/~amerstu/pop*): Sources on advertising, fashion, magazines, toys, and other artifacts of popular culture

  Yale University Arts Library, *Image Resources* (*library.yale.edu/art*): Sources on the visual and performing arts

- **Use a subscription database.** Your library may subscribe to the following resources:

  ARTstor: Museum collections and a database of images typically used in art history courses
  Associated Press, *AccuNet/AP Multimedia Archives*: Historical and contemporary news images
  Grove Art Online: Art images and links to museum sites

Many images you find will be available for free, but some sources do charge a fee for use. Before paying for an image, check with a librarian to see if it is available elsewhere for free.

2 Audio and video

Audio and video, widely available on the Web and on CD-ROM, can provide your readers with the experience of "being there." For example, if you are researching the media response to Martin Luther King's famous "I Have a Dream" speech and you are publishing your paper electronically, you might insert links to the speech and to TV and radio coverage of it.

- **Audio files** such as podcasts, Webcasts, and CDs record radio programs, interviews, speeches, lectures, and music. They are available on the Web and through your library. Online sources of audio include Congress's *American Memory* (see the previous page) and podcasts at *www.podcastdirectory.com.*
- **Video files** capture performances, public presentations and speeches, news events, and other activities. They are available on the Web and through your library on DVD. Online sources of video include the Library of Congress's *American Memory* (see the previous page); *YouTube*, which includes commercials, historical footage, current events, and much more (*youtube.com*); and search engines such as *Google* (*video.google.com*).

51j Generating your own sources

Academic writing will often require you to conduct primary research for information of your own. For instance, you may need to analyze a poem, conduct an experiment, or interview an expert. Three common forms of primary research are observation, personal interviews, and surveys.

1 Observation

Observation can be an effective way to gather fresh information on your subject. You may observe in a controlled setting—for instance, watching the behavior of children playing in a child-development lab. Or you may observe in a more open setting—for instance, watching the interactions among students at a cafeteria on your campus. Be sure your observation has a well-defined purpose that relates to your research project. Throughout the observation, take careful notes, either on paper or on a handheld computer, and always record the date, time, and location for each session.

2 Personal interviews

An interview can be especially helpful for a research project because it allows you to ask questions precisely geared to your topic. You can conduct an interview in person, over the telephone, or online. A personal interview is preferable if you can arrange it, because you can see the person's expressions and gestures as well as hear his or her tone.

Here are a few guidelines for interviews:

- **Call or write for an appointment.** Tell the person exactly why you are calling, what you want to discuss, and how long you expect the interview to take. Be true to your word on all points.
- **Prepare a list of open-ended questions to ask**—perhaps ten or twelve for a one-hour interview. Plan on doing some research for these questions to discover background on the issues and your subject's published views on the issues.
- **Pay attention to your subject's answers** so that you can ask appropriate follow-up questions. Take care in interpreting answers, especially if you are online and thus can't depend on facial expressions, gestures, and tone of voice to convey the subject's attitudes.
- **Keep thorough notes.** Take notes during an in-person or telephone interview, or record the interview if you have the equipment and your subject agrees. For online interviews, save the discussion in a file of its own.
- **Verify quotations.** Before you quote your subject in your paper, check with him or her to ensure that the quotations are accurate.
- **Send a thank-you note immediately after the interview.** Promise your subject a copy of your finished paper, and send the paper promptly.

3 Surveys

Asking questions of a defined group of people can provide information about respondents' attitudes, behavior, backgrounds, and expectations. Use the following tips to plan and conduct a survey:

- **Decide what you want to find out.** The questions you ask should be dictated by your purpose. Formulating a **hypothesis** about your subject—a generalization that can be tested—will help you refine your purpose.

- **Define your population.** Think about the kinds of people your hypothesis is about—for instance, college men or preschool children. Plan to sample this population so that your findings will be representative.
- **Write your questions.** Surveys may contain closed questions that direct the respondent's answers (checklists and multiple-choice, true/false, or yes/no questions) or open-ended questions that allow brief, descriptive answers. Avoid loaded questions that reveal your own biases or make assumptions about subjects' answers.
- **Test your questions.** Use a few respondents with whom you can discuss the answers. Eliminate or recast questions that respondents find unclear, discomforting, or unanswerable.
- **Tally the results.** Count the actual numbers of answers, including any nonanswers.
- **Seek patterns in the raw data.** Such patterns may confirm or contradict your hypothesis. Revise the hypothesis or conduct additional research if necessary.

52 Working with Sources

Research writing is much more than finding sources and reporting their contents. The challenge and interest come from interacting with and synthesizing sources: reading them critically to discover their meanings, judge their relevance and reliability, and create relationships among them; and using them to extend and support your own ideas so that you make your subject your own.

CULTURE LANGUAGE Making a subject your own requires thinking critically about sources and developing independent ideas. These goals may at first be uncomfortable if your native culture emphasizes understanding and respecting established authority more than questioning and enlarging it. The information here will help you work with sources so that you can become an expert in your own right and convincingly convey your expertise to others.

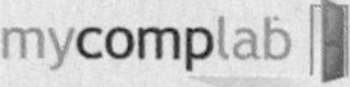

Visit *mycomplab.com* for more resources as well as exercises on working with sources.

52a Evaluating sources

Before you gather information and ideas from sources, scan them to evaluate what they have to offer and how you might use them.

Note In evaluating sources, you need to consider how they come to you. The sources you find through the library, both in print and on the Web, have been previewed for you by their publishers and by the library's staff. They still require your critical reading, but you can have some confidence in the information they contain. With online sources you reach directly, however, you can't assume similar previewing, so your critical reading must be especially rigorous. Special tips for evaluating Web sites and other online sources begin on p. 347.

1 Relevance and reliability

Not all the sources you find will prove worthwhile: some may be irrelevant to your subject, and others may be unreliable. Gauging the relevance and reliability of sources is the essential task of evaluating them. If you haven't already done so, read this book's chapter on critical thinking and reading (**2** pp. 77–89). It provides a foundation for answering the questions in the following box.

Questions for evaluating sources

For online sources, supplement these questions with those on pp. 347 and 354–55.

Relevance

- **Does the source devote some attention to your subject?** Does it focus on your subject or cover it marginally? How does it compare to other sources you've found?
- **Is the source appropriately specialized for your needs?** Check the source's treatment of a topic you know something about, to ensure that it is neither too superficial nor too technical.
- **Is the source up to date enough for your subject?** When was it published? If your subject is current, your sources should be, too.

Reliability

- **Where does the source come from?** Did you find it through your library or directly through the Internet? (If the latter, see pp. 347 and 350–56.) Is the source popular or scholarly?
- **Is the author an expert in the field?** Check the author's credentials in a biography (if the source includes one), in a biographical reference, or by a keyword search of the Web.

(continued)

Questions for evaluating sources

(continued)

- **What is the author's bias?** How do the author's ideas relate to those in other sources? What areas does the author emphasize, ignore, or dismiss?
- **Is the source fair, reasonable, and well-written?** Does it provide sound reasoning and a fair picture of opposing views? Is the tone calm and objective? Is the source logically organized and error-free?
- **Are the author's claims well supported?** Does the author provide accurate, relevant, representative, and adequate evidence to back up his or her claims? Does the author cite sources, and if so are they reliable?

2 Evaluating library sources

To evaluate sources you find through your library, either in print or on the library's Web site, look at dates, titles, summaries, introductions, headings, author biographies, and any source notes. The following criteria expand on the most important tips in the preceding box. On pp. 348–49 you can see how Justin Malik applied these criteria to two print sources, a magazine article and a journal article, that he consulted while researching green consumerism.

Identify the origin of the source.

Check whether a library source is popular or scholarly. Scholarly sources, such as refereed journals and university press books, are generally deeper and more reliable, though some popular sources, such as first-hand newspaper accounts and books for a general audience, are often appropriate for research projects.

Check the author's expertise.

The authors of scholarly publications tend to be experts whose authority can be verified. Check the source to see whether it contains a biographical note about the author, check a biographical reference, or check the author's name in a keyword search of the Web. Look for other publications by the author and for his or her job and any affiliation, such as teacher at a university, researcher with a nonprofit organization, author of general-interest books, or writer for popular magazines.

Identify the author's bias.

Every author has a point of view that influences the selection and interpretation of evidence. You may be able to learn about an author's bias from biographies, citation indexes, and review indexes. But also look at the source itself. How do the author's ideas relate to those in other sources? What areas does the author emphasize, ignore, or dismiss? When you're aware of sources' biases, you can attempt to balance them.

Determine whether the source is fair, reasonable, and well written.

Even a strongly biased work should present solid reasoning and give balanced coverage to opposing views—all in an objective tone. Any source should be organized logically and should be written in clear, error-free sentences. The absence of any of these qualities should raise a warning flag.

Analyze support for the author's claims.

Evidence should be accurate, relevant to the argument, representative of its context, and adequate for the point being made (see **2** pp. 98–99). The author's sources should themselves be reliable.

3 Evaluating Web sites

To a great extent, the same critical reading that helps you evaluate library sources will help you evaluate Web sites that you reach directly. But most Web sites have not undergone prior screening by editors and librarians. On your own, you must distinguish scholarship from corporate promotion, valid data from invented statistics, well-founded opinion from clever propaganda.

The strategy summarized in the box below can help you make such distinctions. On pp. 352–53 you can see how Justin Malik applied this strategy to two Web sites that he consulted while researching green consumerism.

Questions for evaluating Web sites

Supplement these questions with those on pp. 345–46.

- **What type of site are you viewing?** What does the type lead you to expect about the site's purpose and content?
- **Who is the author or sponsor?** How credible is the person or group responsible for the site?
- **What is the purpose of the site?** What does the site's author or sponsor intend to achieve?
- **What does context tell you?** What do you already know about the site's subject that can inform your evaluation? What kinds of support or other information do the site's links provide?
- **What does presentation tell you?** Is the site's design well thought out and effective? Is the writing clear and error-free?
- **How worthwhile is the content?** Are the site's claims well supported by evidence? Is the evidence from reliable sources? When was the site last updated?

(continued on p. 350)

Evaluating library sources

Opposite are sample pages from two library sources that Justin Malik considered for his paper on green consumerism. Malik evaluated the sources using the questions and guidelines on pp. 345–47.

Makower	Jackson
Origin	
Interview with Joel Makower published in *Vegetarian Times*, a popular magazine.	Article by Tim Jackson published in *Journal of Industrial Ecology*, a scholarly journal sponsored by two reputable universities: MIT and Yale.
Author	
Gives Makower's credentials at the beginning of the interview: the author of a book on green products and of a monthly newsletter on green businesses. Quotes another source that calls Makower the "guru of green business practice."	Includes a biography at the end of the article that describes Jackson as a professor at the University of Surrey (UK) and lists his professional activities related to the environment.
Bias	
Describes and promotes green products. Concludes with an endorsement of a for-profit Web site that tracks and sells green products.	Presents multiple views of green consumerism. Argues that a solution to environmental problems will involve green products and less consumption but in different ways than currently proposed.
Reasonableness and writing	
Presents Makower's data and perspective on distinguishing good from bad green products, using conversational writing in an informal presentation.	Presents and cites opposing views objectively, using formal academic writing.
Source citations	
Lacks source citations for claims and data.	Includes more than three pages of source citations, many of scholarly and government sources and all cited within the article.
Assessment	
Probably unreliable: Despite Makower's reputation, the article comes from a nonscholarly source, takes a one-sided approach to consumption, and depends on statistics credited only to Makower.	**Probably reliable:** The article comes from a scholarly journal, the author is an expert in the field, he discusses many views and concedes some, and his source citations confirm evidence from reliable sources.

First and last pages of an interview with Joel Makower, published in *Vegetarian Times*

Largest manufacturer of renewable energy equipment in the United States?
General Electric

Largest buyer of green energy in the United States?
Johnson & Johnson

Largest buyer of fair-trade coffee in the world?
Starbucks

a greater capacity than they did 10 years ago because landfill operators are more sophisticated about compacting.

The problem with landfills is the energy and resources used to make the stuff that goes into them. Over 95 percent of the things we buy—disposable razors, single-use water bottles—have a useful life of less than six weeks, and sometimes less than a day. Almost every environmental problem we face is a result of our own wastefulness. We pay a high price for being a consumer society, and not just at the checkout counter. The promise of green consumerism is that we won't have to do without things we want or need. But that means demanding that manufacturers find better ways to make these things and rewarding the companies that do by buying their products.

q:
Who are they?

q:
Can we really do much in our own homes?

a:
Sure. I live in the house where I grew up. We've made a series of eco-friendly renovations, using wood that is harvested in a sustainable way, paints that don't emit harmful chemicals, energy-efficient appliances and windows. We also asked that the contractors recycle all of the waste from the work they did. Because we live in California, which is a pretty eco-conscious state, contractors get asked to do that quite a lot. But you have to ask. That's what creates a demand for the service.

Being a green consumer isn't just passively selecting the right item at your supermarket. It involves complaining when complaining is warranted, demanding new products and services when they don't exist and buying them when they appear. It means taking action. ■

go for the green

interview by alan pell crawford

buying beer? sneakers? a car? the most eco-conscious companies aren't always the most obvious

If anybody knows how corporations have responded to this demand for environmentally responsible products, it's Makower. General Electric, General Motors, Hewlett-Packard, Levi Strauss & Co., Nike and Procter & Gamble have all had the benefit of his counsel. Now it's your turn.

green-rated products

…nova.com—from the Latin *ab novo* for "nurturing change"—is an online eco-shopping service that's associated with Amazon.com. Find a product on Alonovo, and in addition to the description, reviews and price, you'll also see a five-dot rating for the company that produced it. Better still, Alonovo allows you to influence the ratings that products and companies receive by weighting the values most important to you—Healthy Environment, Business Ethics and so forth. Best of all, you can buy products through Alonovo at Amazon prices but 20 percent of revenues are sent to a nonprofit that you specify. Amazon processes the transaction and ships the goods.

Launched in August 2005, Alonovo (a for-profit company) is one of a number of new services designed to help consumers make smart choices. Similar in concept is Idealswork (idealswork.com), which allows you to put more emphasis on a company's animal-welfare policies, for example, than on its concern for workplace equity—or vice versa.

How good will Alonovo be? "If it catches on," says Joel Makower, "it could be one of the most powerful social change tools ever put into consumers' hands."

www.vegetariantimes.com 87

STATE OF THE DEBATE

Live Better by Consuming Less?

Is There a "Double Dividend" in Sustainable Consumption?

Tim Jackson

Keywords
consumer behavior
consumer choice
consumer culture
evolutionary psychology
industrial ecology
symbolic interactionism

Summ…

Industri… the effic… tion is al… ment. Th… this. But… really be… debates… self. This article explores some of these wider debates. In particular, it draws attention to a fundamental disagreement that runs through the literature on consumption and haunts the debate on sustainable consumption: the question of whether, or to what extent, consumption can be taken as "good for us." Some approaches assume that increasing consumption is more or less synonymous with improved well-being: the more we consume the better off we are. Others argue, just as vehemently, that the scale of consumption in modern society is both environmentally and psychologically damaging, and that we could reduce consumption significantly without threatening the quality of our lives. This second viewpoint suggests that a kind of "double dividend" is inherent in sustainable consumption: the ability to live better by consuming less and reduce our impact on the environment in the process. In the final analysis, this article argues, such "win-win" solutions may exist but will require a concerted societal effort to realize.

…for fundamental change. …penter Publishing.

UNDP (United Nations Development Programme) 1998. *Human development report 1998*. Oxford, UK: Oxford University Press.

UNEP (United Nations Environment Programme) 2001. Consumption opportunities: Strategies for change. Paris: UNEP.

Van den Bergh, J. C. J. M., A. Ferrer-i-Carbonell, and G. Munda. 2000. Alternative models of individual behaviour and implications for environmental policy. *Ecological Economics* 32(1): 43–61.

About the Author

Tim Jackson is Professor of Sustainable Development at the Centre for Environmental Strategy (CES) in the University of Surrey, Guildford, United Kingdom. He currently holds a research fellowship in sustainable consumption funded by the Economic and Social Research Council and leads the Ecological Economics Research Group at CES. He is also chair of the Economics Steering Group of the U.K. Sustainable Development Commission and sits on the U.K. Round Table on Sustainable Consumption.

http://mitpress.mit.edu/jie *Journal of Industrial Ecology* 19

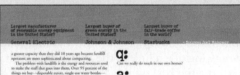

First and last pages of an article by Tim Jackson, published in the *Journal of Industrial Ecology*

(continued from p. 347)

Note To evaluate a Web document, you'll often need to travel to the site's home page to discover the author or sponsor, date of publication, and other relevant information. The page you're reading may include a link to the home page. If it doesn't, you can find it by editing the URL in the Address or Location field of your browser. Working backward, delete the end of the URL up to the last slash and hit Enter. Repeat this step until you reach the home page. There you may also find a menu option, often labeled "About," that will lead you to a description of the site's author or sponsor.

Determine the type of site.

When you search the Web, you're likely to encounter various types of sites. Although they overlap—a primarily informational site may include scholarship as well—the types can usually be identified by their content and purposes. Here are the main types:

- **Scholarly sites:** These sites have a knowledge-building interest and include research reports with supporting data and extensive documentation of scholarly sources. The URLs of the sites generally end in *edu* (originating from an educational institution), *org* (a nonprofit organization), or *gov* (a government department or agency). Such sites are more likely to be reliable than the others described below.
- **Informational sites:** Individuals, nonprofit organizations, corporations, schools, and government bodies all produce sites intended to centralize information on particular subjects. The sites' URLs may end in *edu, org, gov,* or *com* (originating from a commercial organization). Such sites generally do not have the knowledge-building focus of scholarly sites and may omit supporting data and documentation, but they can provide useful information and often include links to scholarly sources.
- **Advocacy sites:** Many sites present the views of individuals or organizations that promote certain policies or actions. Their URLs usually end in *org*, but they may end in *edu* or *com*. Some advocacy sites include serious, well-documented research to support their positions, but others select or distort evidence.
- **Commercial sites:** Corporations and other businesses maintain Web sites to explain or promote themselves or to sell goods and services. The URLs of commercial sites end in *com*. The information on such a site furthers the sponsor's profit-making purpose, but it can include reliable data.
- **Personal sites:** The sites maintained by individuals range from diaries of a family's travels to opinions on political issues to reports on evolving scholarship. The sites' URLs usually end in

com or *edu*. Personal sites are only as reliable as their authors, but some do provide valuable eyewitness accounts, links to worthy sources, and other usable information. A particular kind of personal site, the blog, is discussed on pp. 339 and 354–56.

Note Informational sites called wikis allow anyone to contribute and edit information on the site. Older entries on reputable wikis, such as *Wikipedia,* tend to be reliable because they have been reviewed and edited by experts, but recent entries may contain errors and even misinformation. Ask your instructor whether wikis are acceptable sources. If so, evaluate them carefully against other, more reliable sources using the following guidelines.

Identify the author and sponsor.

A reputable site will list its authors, will name the group responsible for the site, and will provide information or a link for contacting the author and the sponsor. If none of this information is provided, you should not use the source. If you have only the author's or the sponsor's name, you may be able to discover more in a biographical dictionary, through a keyword search, or in your other sources. Make sure the author and the sponsor have expertise on the subject they're presenting: if an author is a doctor, for instance, what is he or she a doctor of?

Gauge purpose and bias.

A Web site's purpose determines what ideas and information it offers. Inferring that purpose tells you how to interpret what you see on the site. If a site is intended to sell a product or an opinion, it will likely emphasize favorable ideas and information while ignoring or even distorting what is unfavorable. In contrast, if a site is intended to build knowledge—for instance, a scholarly project or journal—it will likely acknowledge diverse views and evidence.

Determining the purpose of a site often requires looking beyond the first page and beneath the surface of words and images. To start, read what the site says about itself, usually found on a page labeled "About." Be suspicious of any site that doesn't provide information about itself and its goals.

Consider context.

Your evaluation of a Web site should be informed by considerations outside the site itself. Chief among these is your own knowledge. What do you already know about the site's subject and the prevailing views of it? Where does this site seem to fit into that picture? What can you learn from this site that you don't already know?

(continued on p. 354)

Evaluating Web sites

Opposite are screen shots from two Web sites that Justin Malik considered for his paper on green consumerism. Malik evaluated the sources using the questions in the boxes on pp. 345–46 and 347.

	Allianz Knowledge Partnersite	*Nature Reports: Climate Change*
Author and sponsor	Site sponsor is the Allianz Group, a global insurance company partnering with well-known organizations to provide information on a variety of issues. Author of article is identified as an editor, not a scientist.	Listed authors are scientists, experts on climate change. (Biographies appear at the end of the article.) Site sponsor is the Nature Publishing Group, which also publishes the reputable science journal *Nature*.
Purpose and bias	Educational page on a corporate-sponsored Web site with the self-stated purpose of gathering information about global issues and making it available to an international audience.	Informational site with the self-stated purpose of providing "authoritative, in-depth reporting on climate change and its wider implications for policy, society and the economy." Article expresses bias toward reducing pollution to stop climate change.
Context	One of many sites publishing current information on climate issues.	One of many sites publishing current research on climate issues.
Presentation	Clean, professionally designed site with mostly error-free writing.	Clean, professionally designed site with error-free writing.
Content	Article gives basic information about climate change and provides links to other pages that expand on its claims. Probably because of the intended general (nonscientist) audience, the pages do not include citations of scholarly research.	Article is current (date above the title) and clearly explains the science of climate change with references and links to scholarly sources. Other links connect to hundreds of articles elsewhere on the site about climate-related topics.
Assessment	**Probably unreliable:** Despite the wealth of information in the article and its links, the material lacks the scholarly source citations necessary for its use as evidence in an academic paper.	**Probably reliable:** The article has an explicit bias toward stopping climate change, but the site sponsor has a scholarly reputation, the authors are climate-change experts, and the references cite many scholarly and government sources.

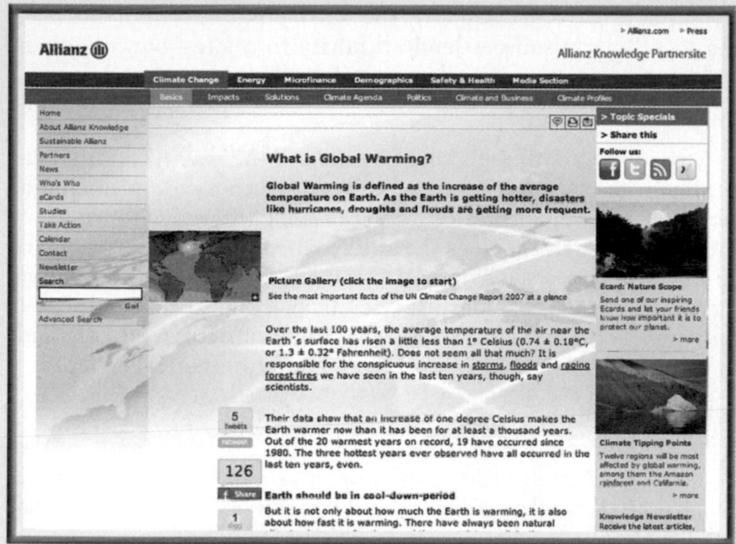

Article published on the Web site *Allianz Knowledge Partnersite*

Article published on the Web site *Nature Reports: Climate Change*

(continued from p. 351)

In addition, you can follow some of the site's links to see how they support, or don't support, the site's credibility. For instance, links to scholarly sources lend authority to a site—but *only* if the scholarly sources actually relate to and back up the site's claims.

Look at presentation.

Considering both the look of a site and the way it's written can illuminate its intentions and reliability. Are the site's elements all functional and well integrated, or is the site cluttered with irrelevant material and graphics? Does the site seem carefully constructed and well maintained, or is it sloppy? Does the design reflect the apparent purpose of the site, or does it undercut or conceal that purpose in some way? Is the text clearly written, or is it difficult to understand? Is it error-free, or does it contain typos and grammatical errors?

Analyze content.

With information about a site's author, purpose, and context, you're in a position to evaluate its content. Are the ideas and information current, or are they dated? (Check the publication date.) Are they slanted and, if so, in what direction? Are the views and data authoritative, or do you need to balance them—or even reject them? Are claims made on the site supported by evidence drawn from reliable sources? These questions require close reading of both the text and its sources.

4 Evaluating other online sources

Blogs, online discussions, and online images, video, and audio require the same critical scrutiny as Web sites do. Blogs and discussion groups can be sources of reliable data and opinions, but you will also encounter wrong or misleading data and skewed opinions. One podcast may provide an interview with a recognized expert while another claims authority that it doesn't deserve. A *YouTube* search using "I have a dream" brings up videos of Martin Luther King, Jr., delivering his famous speech as well as videos of people speaking hatefully about King and the speech.

Use the following strategy for evaluating blogs, discussion groups, and multimedia sources:

Questions for evaluating blogs, online discussions, images, video, and audio

Supplement these questions with those on pp. 345–46.

- **Who is the author or creator?** How credible is he or she?
- **What is the author's or creator's purpose?** What can you tell about why the author or creator is publishing the work?

- **What does the context reveal?** What do other responses to the work, including responses to a blog posting or the other messages in a discussion thread, indicate about the source's balance and reliability?
- **How worthwhile is the content?** Are the claims made by the author or creator supported by evidence? Is the evidence from reliable sources?
- **How does the source compare with other sources?** Do the claims made by the author or creator seem accurate and fair given what you've seen in sources you know to be reliable?

Identify the author or creator.

Checking out the author or creator of a blog, online posting, video file, or podcast can help you judge its reliability. If the author or creator uses a screen name, write directly to him or her requesting full name and credentials. Do not use the source if you don't get a response. Once you know the person's name, you may be able to obtain background information from a keyword search of the Web or a biographical dictionary.

You can also get a sense of the interests and biases of an author or creator by tracking down his or her other publications. For a blog, check whether the author cites or links to other publications. For a discussion-group posting, look for an archive or other feature that allows you to find additional messages by the same author. For multimedia sources, try to gain an overview of the creator's work.

Analyze the author's or creator's purpose.

What can you tell about *why* the author or creator is publishing the work? Look for claims, the use (or lack) of evidence, and the treatment of opposing views. All these convey the person's stand on the subject and general fairness, and they will help you position the source among your other sources.

Consider the context.

Blogs, discussion-group postings, and multimedia sources are often difficult to evaluate in isolation. Looking beyond a particular contribution to the responses of others will give you a sense of how the author or creator is regarded. On a blog, look at the comments others have posted. Do the same with postings, going back to the initial posting in the discussion thread and reading forward.

Analyze content.

A reliable source will offer evidence for claims and sources for evidence. If you don't see such supporting information, ask the author or creator for it. (If he or she fails to respond, don't use the source.) Then verify the sources with your own research: are they reputable?

The tone of writing can also be a clue to its purpose and reliability. Blogs, online discussions, and some podcasts tend to be more informal and often more heated than other kinds of dialog, but look askance at writing that's contemptuous, dismissive, or shrill.

Compare with other sources.

Always consider blogs, postings, and multimedia sources in comparison to other sources so that you can distinguish singular, untested views from more mainstream views that have been subject to verification. Don't assume that a blog author's information and opinions are mainstream just because you see them on other blogs. The technology allows content to be picked up instantly by other blogs, so widespread distribution indicates only popularity, not reliability.

Be wary of blogs or postings that reproduce periodical articles, reports, or other publications. Try to locate the original version of the publication to be sure it has been reproduced fully and accurately, not quoted selectively or distorted. If you can't locate the original version, don't use the publication as a source.

52b Synthesizing sources

When you begin to locate the differences and similarities among sources, you move into the most significant part of research writing: forging relationships for your own purpose. This **synthesis** is an essential step in reading sources critically, and it continues through the drafting and revision of a research paper. As you infer connections—say, between one writer's opinions and another's or between two works by the same author—you create new knowledge.

Your synthesis of sources will grow more detailed and sophisticated as you proceed through the process of working with sources described in the balance of this chapter: gathering information from sources (pp. 358–59); deciding whether to summarize, paraphrase, or quote directly from sources (pp. 359–62); and integrating sources into your sentences (pp. 362–67). Unless you are analyzing primary sources such as the works of a poet, at first read your sources quickly and selectively to obtain an overview of your subject and a sense of how the sources approach it. Don't get bogged down in gathering detailed information, but *do* record your ideas about sources in your research journal (p. 318) or your annotated bibliography (p. 323).

Respond to sources.

Write down what your sources make you think. Do you agree or disagree with the author? Do you find his or her views narrow, or do they open up new approaches for you? Is there anything in the source that you need to research further before you can understand it? Does the source prompt questions that you should keep in mind while reading other sources?

Connect sources.

When you notice a link between sources, jot it down. Do two sources differ in their theories or their interpretations of facts? Does one source illuminate another—perhaps commenting or clarifying or supplying additional data? Do two or more sources report studies that support a theory you've read about or an idea of your own?

Heed your insights.

Apart from ideas prompted by your sources, you are sure to come up with independent thoughts: a conviction, a point of confusion that suddenly becomes clear, a question you haven't seen anyone else ask. These insights may occur at unexpected times, so it's good practice to keep a notebook or computer handy to record them.

Draw your own conclusions.

As your research proceeds, the responses, connections, and insights you form through synthesis will lead you to answer your starting research question with a statement of your thesis (see p. 375). They will also lead you to the main ideas supporting your thesis—conclusions you have drawn from your synthesis of sources, forming the main divisions of your paper.

Use sources to support your conclusions.

Effective synthesis requires careful handling of evidence from sources so that it meshes smoothly into your sentences and yet is clearly distinct from your own ideas. When drafting your paper, make sure that each paragraph focuses on an idea of your own, with the support for the idea coming from your sources. Generally, open each paragraph with your idea, provide evidence from a source or sources with appropriate citations, and close with an interpretation of the evidence. (Avoid ending a paragraph with a source citation; instead, end with your own idea.) In this way, your paper will synthesize others' work into something wholly your own. For more on structuring paragraphs in academic writing, see **2** p. 91.

52c Gathering information from sources

You can accomplish a great deal of synthesis while gathering information from your sources. This information gathering is not a mechanical process. Rather, as you read you assess and organize the information in your sources.

Researchers vary in their methods for working with sources, but all methods share the same goals:

- **Keep accurate records of what sources say.** Accuracy helps prevent misrepresentation and plagiarism.
- **Keep accurate records of how to find sources.** These records are essential for retracing steps and for citing sources in the final paper. (See pp. 323–25 on keeping a working bibliography.)
- **Synthesize sources.** Information gathering is a critical process, leading to an understanding of sources, the relationships among them and your own ideas, and their support for your ideas.

To achieve these goals, you can take handwritten notes, type notes into your computer, annotate photocopies or printouts of sources, or annotate downloaded documents. On any given project, you may use all the methods. Each has advantages and disadvantages.

- **Handwritten notes:** Taking notes by hand is especially useful if you come across a source with no computer or photocopier handy. But handwritten notes can be risky. It's easy to introduce errors as you work from source to paper. And it's possible to copy source language and then later mistake and use it as your own, thus plagiarizing the source. Always take care to make accurate notes and to place big quotation marks around any passage you quote.
- **Notes on computer:** Taking notes on a computer can streamline the path of source to note to paper, because you can import the notes into your draft as you write. However, computer notes have the same disadvantages as handwritten notes: the risk of introducing errors and the risk of plagiarizing. As with handwritten notes, be a stickler for accuracy and use quotation marks for quotations.
- **Photocopies and printouts:** Photocopying from print sources or printing out online sources each has the distinct advantages of convenience and reduction in the risks of error and plagiarism during information gathering. But each method has disadvantages, too. The busywork of copying or printing can distract you from the crucial work of synthesizing sources. And you have to make a special effort to annotate copies and

printouts with the publication information for sources. If you don't have this information for your final paper, you can't use the source.

- **Downloads:** Researching online, you can usually download full-text articles, Web pages, discussion-group messages, and other materials onto your computer. While drafting, you can import source information from one file into another. Like photocopies and printouts, though, downloads can distract you from interacting with sources and can easily become separated from the publication information you must have in order to use the sources. Even more important, directly importing source material creates a high risk of plagiarism. You must keep clear boundaries between your own ideas and words and those of others.

52d Using summary, paraphrase, and quotation

Deciding whether to summarize, paraphrase, or quote directly from sources is an important step in synthesizing the sources' ideas and your own. You engage in synthesis when you use your own words to summarize an author's argument or paraphrase a significant example or when you select a significant passage to quote. Choosing summary, paraphrase, or quotation should depend on why you are using a source.

Note Summaries, paraphrases, and quotations all require source citations. A summary or paraphrase without a source citation or a quotation without quotation marks and a source citation is plagiarism. (See pp. 367–73 for more on plagiarism.)

1 Summary

When you **summarize**, you condense an extended idea or argument into a sentence or more in your own words. (See **2** pp. 80–81 for tips.) **Summary** is most useful when you want to record the gist of an author's idea without the background or supporting evidence. Following is a passage from a scholarly essay about consumption and its impact on the environment. Then a sample computer note shows a summary of the passage.

Original quotation

Such intuition is even making its way, albeit slowly, into scholarly circles, where recognition is mounting that ever-increasing pressures on ecosystems, life-supporting environmental services, and critical natural cycles are driven not only by the sheer number of resource users and the inefficiencies of their resource use, but also by the patterns of resource use themselves. In global environmental policymaking arenas, it is becoming more and more difficult to ignore the fact that the overdeveloped North must restrain its consumption if it expects the underdeveloped South to embrace a more sustainable trajectory.

—Thomas Princen, Michael Maniates, and Ken Conca, "Confronting Consumption," p. 4

Summary of source

Environmental consequences of consumption

Princen, Maniates, and Conca 4

Overconsumption may be a more significant cause of environmental problems than increasing population is.

2 Paraphrase

When you **paraphrase,** you follow much more closely the author's original presentation, but you restate it using your own words and sentence structures. Paraphrase is most useful when you want to present or examine an author's line of reasoning but you don't feel the original words merit direct quotation. Here is a paraphrase of the quotation from the essay "Confronting Consumption."

Paraphrase of source

Environmental consequences of consumption

Princen, Maniates, and Conca 4

Scholars are coming to believe that consumption is partly to blame for changes in ecosystems, reduction of essential natural resources, and changes in natural cycles. Policy makers increasingly see that wealthy nations have to start consuming less if they want developing nations to adopt practices that reduce pollution and waste. Rising population around the world does cause significant stress on the environment, but consumption is increasing even more rapidly than population.

Notice that the paraphrase follows the original but uses different words and different sentence structures. In contrast, an unsuccessful paraphrase—one that plagiarizes—copies the author's words or sentence structures or both *without quotation marks.* (See pp. 371–72 for examples.)

Paraphrasing a source

- **Read the relevant material several times to be sure you understand it.**
- **Restate the source's ideas in your own words and sentence structures.** You need not put down in new words the whole passage or all the details. Select what is relevant to your topic, and restate only that. If complete sentences seem too detailed or cumbersome, use phrases.
- **Be careful not to distort meaning.** Don't change the source's emphasis or omit connecting words, qualifiers, and other material whose absence will confuse you later or cause you to misrepresent the source.

CULTURE LANGUAGE If English is not your native language and you have difficulty paraphrasing the ideas in sources, try this. Before attempting a paraphrase, read the original passage several times. Then, instead of "translating" line by line, try to state the gist of the passage without looking at it. Check your effort against the original to be sure you have captured the source author's meaning and emphasis without using his or her words and sentence structures. If you need a synonym for a word, look it up in a dictionary.

3 Direct quotation

Your notes from sources may include many quotations, especially if you rely on photocopies, printouts, or downloads. Whether to use a quotation in your draft, instead of a summary or paraphrase, depends on how important the exact words are and on whether the source is primary or secondary (p. 321):

- **Quote extensively when you are analyzing primary sources,** such as literary works and historical documents. The quotations will often be both the target of your analysis and the chief support for your ideas.
- **Quote selectively when you are drawing on secondary sources.** Favor summaries and paraphrases over quotations, and put every quotation to both tests in the box on the next page. Most papers of ten or so pages should not need more than two or three quotations that are longer than a few lines each.

When you quote a source, either in your notes or in your draft, take precautions to avoid plagiarism or misrepresentation of the source:

- **Copy the material carefully.** Take down the author's exact wording, spelling, capitalization, and punctuation.
- **Proofread every direct quotation at least twice.**

Tests for direct quotations from secondary sources

The author's original satisfies one of these requirements:

- The language is unusually vivid, bold, or inventive.
- The quotation cannot be paraphrased without distortion or loss of meaning.
- The words themselves are at issue in your interpretation.
- The quotation represents and emphasizes a body of opinion or the view of an important expert.
- The quotation emphatically reinforces your own idea.
- The quotation is an illustration, such as a graph, diagram, or table.

The quotation is as short as possible:

- It includes only material relevant to your point.
- It is edited to eliminate examples and other unneeded material, using ellipsis marks and brackets (**5** pp. 292–94).

- **Use quotation marks around the quotation** so that later you won't confuse it with a paraphrase or summary. Be sure to transfer the quotation marks into your draft as well, unless the quotation is long and is set off from your text. For advice on handling long quotations, see **MLA** p. 449 and **APA** p. 483.
- **Use brackets** to add words for clarity or to change the capitalization of letters (see **5** p. 294 and **6** p. 303).
- **Use ellipsis marks** to omit irrelevant material (see **5** pp. 292–94).
- **Cite the source of the quotation in your draft.** See pp. 374–75 on documentation.

52e Integrating sources into your text

Integrating sources into your sentences is key to synthesizing others' ideas and information with your own. Evidence drawn from sources should *back up* your conclusions, not *be* your conclusions: you don't want to let your evidence overwhelm your own point of view. The point of research is to investigate and go beyond sources, to interpret them and use them to support your own independent ideas.

Note The examples in this section use the MLA style of source documentation and also present-tense verbs (such as *disagrees* and *claims*). See pp. 366–67 for specific variations in documentation style and verb tense within the academic disciplines. Several other conventions governing quotations are discussed elsewhere in this book:

- **Using commas to punctuate signal phrases** (**5** pp. 273–74).

- **Placing other punctuation marks with quotation marks (5 p. 289).**
- **Using brackets and the ellipsis mark to indicate changes in quotations (5 pp. 292–94).**
- **Punctuating and placing parenthetical citations (MLA pp. 412–14).**
- **Formatting long prose quotations and poetry quotations (MLA p. 449 and APA p. 483).**

1 Introduction of borrowed material

Readers will be distracted from your point if borrowed material does not fit into your sentence. In the passage below, the writer has not meshed the structures of her own and her source's sentences:

Awkward One editor disagrees with this view and "a good reporter does not fail to separate opinions from facts" (Lyman 52).

In the following revision the writer adds words to integrate the quotation into her sentence:

Revised One editor disagrees with this view, maintaining that "a good reporter does not fail to separate opinions from facts" (Lyman 52).

To mesh your own and your source's words, you may sometimes need to make a substitution or addition to the quotation, signaling your change with brackets:

Words added "The tabloids [of England] are a journalistic case study in bad reporting," claims Lyman (52).

Verb form changed A bad reporter, Lyman implies, is one who "[fails] to separate opinions from facts" (52). [The bracketed verb replaces *fail* in the original.]

Capitalization changed "[T]o separate opinions from facts" is the work of a good reporter (Lyman 52). [In the original, *to* is not capitalized.]

Noun supplied for pronoun The reliability of a news organization "depends on [reporters'] trustworthiness," says Lyman (52). [The bracketed noun replaces *their* in the original.]

2 Interpretation of borrowed material

You need to work borrowed material into your sentences so that readers see without effort how it contributes to the points you are making. If you merely dump source material into your paper without explaining how you intend it to be interpreted, readers will have to struggle to understand your sentences and the relationships you are trying to establish. For example, the following passage forces us to figure out for ourselves that the writer's sentence and the quotation state opposite points of view:

Dumped Many news editors and reporters maintain that it is impossible to keep personal opinions from influencing the selection and presentation of facts. "True, news reporters, like everyone else, form impressions of what they see and hear. However, a good reporter does not fail to separate opinions from facts" (Lyman 52).

In the revision, the underlined additions tell us how to interpret the quotation:

Revised Many news editors and reporters maintain that it is impossible to keep personal opinions from influencing the selection and presentation of facts. Yet not all authorities agree with this view. One editor grants that "news reporters, like everyone else, form impressions of what they see and hear." But, he insists, "a good reporter does not fail to separate opinions from facts" (Lyman 52).

Signal phrases

The words *One editor grants* and *he insists* in the revised passage above are **signal phrases:** they tell readers who the source is and what to expect in the quotations that follow. Signal phrases usually contain (1) the source author's name (or a substitute for it, such as *One editor* and *he*) and (2) a verb that indicates the source author's attitude or approach to what he or she says.

Some verbs for signal phrases appear in the following list. These verbs are in the present tense, which is typical of writing in the humanities. In the social and natural sciences, the past tense (*noted*) or present perfect tense (*has noted*) is more common. See pp. 366–67.

Author is neutral	**Author infers or suggests**	**Author argues**	**Author is uneasy or disparaging**
comments	analyzes	claims	belittles
describes	asks	contends	bemoans
explains	assesses	defends	complains
illustrates	concludes	holds	condemns
notes	considers	insists	deplores
observes	finds	maintains	deprecates
points out	predicts		derides
records	proposes	**Author agrees**	disagrees
relates	reveals	admits	laments
reports	shows	agrees	warns
says	speculates	concedes	
sees	suggests	concurs	
thinks	supposes	grants	
writes			

Vary your signal phrases to suit your interpretation of borrowed material and also to keep readers' interest. A signal phrase may precede, interrupt, or follow the borrowed material:

Precedes	Lyman insists that "a good reporter does not fail to separate opinions from facts" (52).
Interrupts	"However," Lyman insists, "a good reporter does not fail to separate opinions from facts" (52).
Follows	"[A] good reporter does not fail to separate opinions from facts," Lyman insists (52).

Background information

You can add information to a quotation to integrate it into your text and to inform readers why you are using it. In most cases, provide the author's name in the text, especially if the author is an expert or if readers will recognize the name:

Author named	Harold Lyman grants that "news reporters, like everyone else, form impressions of what they see and hear." But, Lyman insists, "a good reporter does not fail to separate opinions from facts" (52).

If the source title contributes information about the author or the context of the quotation, you can provide it in the text:

Title given	Harold Lyman, in his book *The Conscience of the Journalist*, grants that "news reporters, like everyone else, form impressions of what they see and hear." But, Lyman insists, "a good reporter does not fail to separate opinions from facts" (52).

If the quoted author's background and experience reinforce or clarify the quotation, you can provide these credentials in the text:

Credentials given	Harold Lyman, a newspaper editor for more than forty years, grants that "news reporters, like everyone else, form impressions of what they see and hear." But, Lyman insists, "a good reporter does not fail to separate opinions from facts" (52).

You need not name the author, source, or credentials in your text when you are simply establishing facts or weaving together facts and opinions from varied sources. In the following passage, the information is more important than the source, so the name of the source is confined to a parenthetical acknowledgment:

> To end the abuses of the British, many colonists were urging three actions: forming a united front, seceding from Britain, and taking control of their own international relations (Wills 325–36).

3 Discipline styles for integrating sources

The preceding guidelines for introducing and interpreting borrowed material apply generally across academic disciplines, but there are differences in verb tenses and documentation style.

English and some other humanities

Writers in English, foreign languages, and related disciplines use MLA style for documenting sources and generally use the present tense of verbs in signal phrases. In discussing sources other than works of literature, the present perfect tense is also sometimes appropriate:

Lyman insists . . . [present]
Lyman has insisted . . . [present perfect]

In discussing works of literature, use only the present tense to describe both the work of the author and the action in the work:

> Kate Chopin builds irony into every turn of "The Story of an Hour." For example, Mrs. Mallard, the central character, finds joy in the death of her husband, whom she loves, because she anticipates "the long procession of years that would belong to her absolutely" (23).

Avoid shifting tenses in writing about literature. You can, for instance, shorten quotations to avoid their past-tense verbs.

Shift Her freedom elevates her, so that "she carried herself unwittingly like a goddess of victory" (24).

No shift Her freedom elevates her, so that she walks "unwittingly like a goddess of victory" (24).

History and other humanities

Writers in history, art history, philosophy, and related disciplines generally use the present perfect tense or present tense of verbs in signal phrases.

> Lincoln persisted, as Haworth has noted, in "feeling that events controlled him."[3]
>
> What Miller calls Lincoln's "severe self-doubt"[6] undermined his effectiveness on at least two occasions.

The raised numbers after the quotations are part of the Chicago documentation style, used in history and other disciplines.

Social and natural sciences

Writers in the sciences generally use a verb's present tense just for reporting the results of a study (*The data suggest* . . .). Otherwise, they use a verb's past tense or present perfect tense in a signal phrase, as when introducing an explanation, interpretation, or other commentary. (Thus when you are writing for the sciences, generally convert the list of signal-phrase verbs on p. 364 from the present to the present perfect tense or past tense.)

> Lin (1999) has suggested that preschooling may significantly affect children's academic performance through high school (pp. 22–23).
>
> In an exhaustive survey of the literature published between 1990 and 2000, Walker (2001) found "no proof, merely a weak correlation, linking place of residence and rate of illness" (p. 121).

These passages conform to APA documentation style. APA style, or one quite similar to it, is also used in sociology, education, nursing, biology, and many other sciences.

53 Avoiding Plagiarism and Documenting Sources

The knowledge building that is the focus of academic writing rests on the integrity of everyone who participates in using and crediting sources, including students. The work of a writer or creator is his or her intellectual property. You and others may borrow the work's ideas and even its words or an image, but you *must* acknowledge that what you borrowed came from someone else.

When you acknowledge sources in your writing, you are doing more than giving credit to the writer or creator of the work you consulted. You are also showing what your own writing is based on, which in turn gives you credibility as a researcher and writer. Acknowledging sources creates the trust among scholars, students, writers, and readers that knowledge building requires.

Plagiarism (from a Latin word for "kidnapper") is the presentation of someone else's work as your own. Whether deliberate or accidental, plagiarism is a serious offense. It breaks trust, and it undermines or even destroys your credibility as a researcher and writer. In most colleges, a code of academic honesty calls for severe consequences for plagiarism: a reduced or failing grade, suspension from school, or expulsion.

Visit *mycomplab.com* for more resources as well as exercises on avoiding plagiarism and documenting sources.

- *Deliberate* **plagiarism:**

  Copying or downloading a phrase, a sentence, or a longer passage from a source and passing it off as your own by omitting quotation marks and a source citation.

  Summarizing or paraphrasing someone else's ideas without acknowledging your debt in a source citation.

  Handing in as your own work a paper you have bought, copied off the Web, had a friend write, or accepted from another student.

- *Accidental* **plagiarism:**

  Reading a wide variety of sources on a subject without taking notes on them, and then not remembering the difference between what you recently learned and what you already knew.

  Forgetting to place quotation marks around another writer's words.

  Carelessly omitting a source citation for a paraphrase.

  Omitting a source citation for another's idea because you are unaware of the need to acknowledge the idea.

The way to avoid plagiarism is to acknowledge your sources by documenting them. This chapter discusses plagiarism and the Internet, shows how to distinguish what doesn't require acknowledgment from what does, and provides an overview of source documentation.

CULTURE LANGUAGE The concept of intellectual property and thus the rules governing plagiarism are not universal. In some other cultures, for instance, students may be encouraged to copy the words of scholars without acknowledgment in order to demonstrate their mastery of or respect for the scholars' work. In the United States, however, using an author's work without a source citation is considered theft. When in doubt about the guidelines in this chapter, ask your instructor for advice.

53a Committing and detecting plagiarism on the Internet

The Internet has made it easier to plagiarize than ever before, but it has also made plagiarism easier to catch.

Even honest students risk accidental plagiarism by downloading sources and importing portions into their drafts. Dishonest students may take advantage of downloading to steal others' work. They may also use the term-paper businesses on the Web, which offer both ready-made research and complete papers, usually for a fee. **Paying for research or a paper does not make it the buyer's work.** Anyone who submits someone else's work as his or her own is a plagiarist.

Checklist for avoiding plagiarism

Type of source

Are you using

- your own independent material,
- common knowledge, or
- someone else's independent material?

You must acknowledge someone else's material.

Quotations

- Do all quotations exactly match their sources? Check them.
- Have you inserted quotation marks around quotations that are run into your text?
- Have you shown omissions with ellipsis marks and additions with brackets?
- Does every quotation have a source citation?

Paraphrases and summaries

- Have you used your own words and sentence structures for every paraphrase and summary? If not, use quotation marks around the original author's words.
- Does every paraphrase and summary have a source citation?

The Web

- Have you obtained any necessary permission to use someone else's material on the Web?

Source citations

- Have you acknowledged every use of someone else's material in each place you used it?
- Does your list of works cited include entries for all the sources you have used?

Students who plagiarize from the Internet both deprive themselves of an education in honest research and expose themselves to detection. Teachers can use search engines to locate specific phrases or sentences anywhere on the Web, including among scholarly publications, all kinds of Web sites, and term-paper collections. They can search the term-paper sites as easily as students can, looking for similarities with papers they've received. They can also use detection programs such as *Turnitin* that compare students' work with other work anywhere on the Internet, seeking matches as short as a few words.

Some instructors suggest that their students use plagiarism-detection programs to verify that their own work does not include accidental plagiarism from the Internet.

53b Knowing what you need not acknowledge

1 Your independent material

Your own observations, thoughts, compilations of facts, or experimental results—expressed in your words and format—do not require acknowledgment. You should describe the basis for your conclusions so that readers can evaluate your thinking, but you need not cite sources for them.

2 Common knowledge

Common knowledge consists of the standard information on a subject as well as folk literature and commonsense observations.

- **Standard information** includes the major facts of history, such as the dates during which Charlemagne ruled as emperor of Rome (800–14). It does *not* include interpretations of facts, such as a historian's opinion that Charlemagne was sometimes needlessly cruel in extending his power.
- **Folk literature,** such as the fairy tale "Snow White," is popularly known and cannot be traced to a particular writer. Literature traceable to a writer is *not* folk literature, even if it is very familiar.
- **Commonsense observations** are things most people know, such as that inflation is most troublesome for people with low and fixed incomes. However, a particular economist's argument about the effects of inflation on Chinese immigrants is *not* a commonsense observation.

If you do not know a subject well enough to determine whether a piece of information is common knowledge, make a record of the source as you would for any other quotation, paraphrase, or summary. As you read more about the subject, the information may come up repeatedly without acknowledgment, in which case it is probably common knowledge. But if you are still in doubt when you finish your research, always acknowledge the source.

53c Knowing what you *must* acknowledge

You must always acknowledge other people's independent material—that is, any facts or ideas that are not common knowledge or your own. The source may be anything, including a book, an article, a movie, an interview, a microfilmed document, a Web page, a newsgroup posting, or an opinion expressed on the radio. You must acknowledge summaries or paraphrases of ideas or facts as well as quotations of the language and format in which ideas or facts appear: wording, sentence structures, arrangement, and special graphics (such as a diagram). You must acknowledge another's material no matter how you use it, how much of it you use, or how often you use it.

1 Copied language: Quotation marks and a source citation

The following example baldly plagiarizes the original quotation from Jessica Mitford's *Kind and Usual Punishment,* p. 9. Without quotation marks or a source citation, the example matches Mitford's wording (underlined) and closely parallels her sentence structure:

Original quotation "The character and mentality of the keepers may be of more importance in understanding prisons than the character and mentality of the kept."

Plagiarism But the character of prison officials (the keepers) is of more importance in understanding prisons than the character of prisoners (the kept).

To avoid plagiarism, the writer can paraphrase and cite the source (see the examples on the next page) or use Mitford's actual words *in quotation marks* and *with a source citation* (here, in MLA style):

Revision (quotation) According to one critic of the penal system, "The character and mentality of the keepers may be of more importance in understanding prisons than the character and mentality of the kept" (Mitford 9).

Even with a source citation and with a different sentence structure, the next example is still plagiarism because it uses some of Mitford's words (underlined) without quotation marks:

Plagiarism According to one critic of the penal system, the psychology of the kept may say less about prisons than the psychology of the keepers (Mitford 9).

Revision (quotation) According to one critic of the penal system, the psychology of "the kept" may say less about prisons than the psychology of "the keepers" (Mitford 9).

2 Paraphrase or summary: Your own words and sentence structure and a source citation

The following example changes the sentence structure of the original Mitford quotation above, but it still uses Mitford's words (underlined) without quotation marks and without a source citation:

Plagiarism In understanding prisons, we should know more about the character and mentality of the keepers than of the kept.

To avoid plagiarism, the writer can use quotation marks and cite the source (see the previous page) or *use his or her own words* and still *cite the source* (because the idea is Mitford's, not the writer's):

Revision (paraphrase) Mitford holds that we may be able to learn more about prisons from the psychology of the prison officials than from that of the prisoners (9).

Revision (paraphrase) We may understand prisons better if we focus on the personalities and attitudes of the prison workers rather than those of the inmates (Mitford 9).

In the next example, the writer cites Mitford and does not use her words but still plagiarizes her sentence structure:

Plagiarism One critic of the penal system maintains that the psychology of prison officials may be more informative about prisons than the psychology of prisoners (Mitford 9).

Revision (paraphrase) One critic of the penal system maintains that we may be able to learn less from the psychology of prisoners than from the psychology of prison officials (Mitford 9).

53d Using and acknowledging online sources

Online sources are so accessible and so easy to download into your own documents that it may seem they are freely available, exempting you from the obligation to acknowledge them. They are not. Acknowledging online sources is somewhat trickier than acknowledging print sources, but no less essential. Further, if you are publishing your work on the Web, you need to take account of sources' copyright restrictions as well.

1 Online sources in an unpublished project

When you use material from an online source in a print or online document to be distributed just to your class, your obligation to cite sources does not change: you must acknowledge someone else's independent material in whatever form you find it. With online sources, that obligation can present additional challenges:

- **Record complete publication information each time you consult an online source.** Online sources may change or even disappear entirely. See p. 324 for the information to record, such as the electronic address and the publication date. Without the proper information, you *may not* use the source.
- **Acknowledge linked sites.** If you use a Web site and one or more of its linked sites, you must acknowledge the linked sites

as well. One person's use of a second person's work does not release you from the responsibility to cite the second work.

- **Seek the author's permission before using an e-mail message, discussion-group posting, or blog contribution.** Obtaining permission advises the author that his or her ideas are about to be distributed more widely and lets the author verify that you have not misrepresented the ideas.

2 Print and online sources in a Web composition

When you use material from print or online sources in a composition for the Web, you must not only acknowledge your sources but also take the additional precaution of observing copyright restrictions.

A Web site is a medium of publication just as a book or magazine is and so involves the same responsibility to obtain reprint permission from copyright holders. The exception is a password-protected site (such as a course site), which many copyright holders regard as private. You can find information about copyright holders and permissions on the copyright page of a print publication (following the title page) and on a page labeled something like "Terms of Use" on a Web site. If you don't see an explicit release for student use or publication on private Web sites, assume you must seek permission.

The legal convention of fair use allows an author to reprint a small portion of copyrighted material without obtaining the copyright holder's permission, as long as the author acknowledges the source. The online standards of fair use differ for print and online sources and are not fixed in either case. The guidelines below are conservative:

- **Print sources:** Quote without permission fewer than fifty words from an article or fewer than three hundred words from a book. You'll need permission to use any longer quotation from an article or book; any quotation at all from a play, poem, or song; and any use of an entire work, such as a photograph, chart, or other illustration.
- **Online sources:** Quote without permission text that represents just a small portion of the whole—say, up to forty words out of three hundred. Follow the print guidelines above for plays, poems, songs, and illustrations, adding multimedia elements (audio or video clips) to the list of works that require reprint permission for any use.
- **Links:** You may need to seek permission to link your site to another one—for instance, if you rely on the linked site to substantiate your claims or to provide a multimedia element.

53e Documenting sources

Every time you borrow the words, facts, or ideas of others, you must **document** the source—that is, supply a reference (or document) telling readers that you borrowed the material and where you borrowed it from.

Editors and teachers in most academic disciplines require special documentation formats (or styles) in their scholarly journals and in students' papers. All the styles use a citation in the text that serves two purposes: it signals that material is borrowed, and it refers readers to detailed information about the source so that they can locate both the source and the place in the source where the borrowed material appears. The detailed source information appears either in footnotes or at the end of the paper.

Aside from these essential similarities, the disciplines' documentation styles differ markedly in citation form, arrangement of source information, and other particulars. Each discipline's style reflects the needs of its practitioners for certain kinds of information presented in certain ways. For instance, the currency of a source is important in the social sciences, where studies build on and correct each other; thus in-text citations in the social sciences include a source's date of publication. In the humanities, however, currency is less important, so in-text citations do not include date of publication.

The disciplines' documentation formats are described in style guides listed in **8** pp. 395 (literature and other humanities), 398 (social sciences), and 402 (natural and applied sciences). This book also discusses and illustrates four common documentation styles:

- MLA style, used in English, foreign languages, and some other humanities **(MLA** p. 406).
- APA style, used in psychology and some other social sciences (**APA** p. 463).
- Chicago style, used in history, art history, philosophy, religion, and some other humanities (**Chic** p. 491).
- CSE style, used in the biological and some other sciences (**CSE** p. 502).

Always ask your instructor which documentation style you should use. If your instructor does not require a particular style, use the one in this book that's most appropriate for the discipline in which you're writing. Do follow a single system for citing sources so that you provide all the necessary information in a consistent format.

Note Bibliography software—*Zotero, Refworks, Endnote,* and others—can help you format your source citations in the style of your choice. Always ask your instructors if you may use such software for your papers. The programs prompt you for needed information (author's name, book title, and so on) and then arrange, capitalize, underline, and punctuate the information as required by the style. But no program can anticipate all the varieties of source information, nor can it substitute for your own care and attention in giving your sources complete acknowledgment using the required form.

54 Writing the Paper

This chapter complements and extends the detailed discussion of the writing situation and the writing process in Chapters 1–5 (**1** pp. 3–37), which also include many tips for using a word processor. If you haven't already done so, you may want to read those chapters before this one.

54a Focusing and organizing the paper

Before you begin using your source notes in a draft, give some thought to your main idea and your organization.

1 Thesis statement

You began research with a question about your subject (see p. 319). Though that question may have evolved during research, you should be able to answer it once you've consulted most of your sources. Try to state that answer in a **thesis statement,** a claim that narrows your subject to a single idea. Here, for example, are the research question and thesis statement of Justin Malik, whose final paper appears later in this book (**MLA** pp. 452–60):

Research question

How can green consumerism help the environment?

Thesis statement

Although green consumerism can help the environment, consumerism itself is the root of some of the most pressing ecological problems we face. To make a real difference, we must consume less.

A precise thesis statement will give you a focus as you organize and draft your paper. For more on thesis statements, see **1** pp. 14–16.

mycomplab

Visit *mycomplab.com* for more resources as well as exercises on writing and revising a research paper.

2 Organization

To structure your paper, you'll need to synthesize, or forge relationships among ideas (see pp. 356–57). Here is one approach:

- **Arrange source information in categories.** Each group should correspond to a main section of your paper: a key idea of your own that supports the thesis.
- **Review your research journal** for connections between sources and other thoughts that can help you organize your paper.
- **Look objectively at your categories.** If some are skimpy, with little information, consider whether you should drop the categories or conduct more research to fill them out. If most of your information falls into one or two categories, consider whether they are too broad and should be divided. (If any of this rethinking affects your thesis statement, revise it accordingly.)
- **Within each group, distinguish between the main idea and the supporting ideas and evidence.** Only the support should come from your sources. The main idea should be your own.

See **1** pp. 16–20 for more on organizing a paper, including samples of both informal and formal outlines.

54b Drafting, revising, and formatting the paper

1 First draft

In drafting your paper, you do not have to proceed methodically from introduction to conclusion. Instead, draft in sections, beginning with the one you feel most confident about. Each section should center on a principal idea contributing to your thesis, a conclusion you have drawn from reading and responding to sources. Start the section by stating the idea; then support it with information, summaries, paraphrases, and quotations from your notes. Remember to insert source information from your notes as well.

2 Revision and editing

For a complex project like a research paper, you'll certainly want to revise in at least two stages—first for thesis, structure, and other whole-paper issues, and then for clarity, grammar, and other sentence-level issues. Chapter 5 supports this two-stage approach with checklists for revision (**1** p. 26) and editing (**1** p. 30). The following box provides additional steps to take when revising a research paper.

Checklist for revising a research paper

Assignment

How does the draft satisfy all of the criteria stated in your instructor's assignment?

Thesis statement

How well does your thesis statement describe your subject and your perspective as they emerged during drafting?

Structure

(Outlining your draft can help you see structure at a glance. See **1** p. 25.)

How consistently does borrowed material illuminate and support—not lead and dominate—your own ideas? How well is the importance of ideas reflected in the emphasis they receive? Will the arrangement of ideas be clear to readers?

Evidence

Where might evidence seem weak or irrelevant to readers?

Reasonableness and clarity

How reasonable will readers find your argument? (See **2** pp. 100–04.) Where do you need to define terms or concepts that readers may not know or may dispute?

3 Format

The final draft of your paper should conform to the document format recommended by your instructor or by the style guide of the discipline in which you are writing. This book details two common formats: Modern Language Association (**MLA** pp. 447–49) and American Psychological Association (**APA** pp. 481–84).

In any discipline you can use a word processor to present your ideas effectively and attractively with readable typefonts, headings, illustrations, and other elements. See **1** pp. 54–64 for ideas.

PART 8

Writing in the Disciplines

55 Working with the Goals and Requirements of the Disciplines 381

56 Reading and Writing About Literature 383

57 Writing in Other Disciplines 392

58 MLA Documentation and Format 403

59 APA Documentation and Format 461

60 Chicago Documentation 489

61 CSE Documentation 502

PART 8

Writing in the Disciplines

55 Goals and Requirements of the Disciplines *381*

- **a** Methods and evidence *381*
- **b** Writing assignments *382*
- **c** Tools and language *382*
- **d** Documentation and format *383*

56 Reading and Writing About Literature *383*

- **a** Methods and evidence *384*
- **b** Writing assignments *387*
- **c** Tools and language *388*
- **d** Documentation and format *389*
- **e** Sample literary analysis *389*

57 Writing in Other Disciplines *392*

- **a** Humanities *392*
- **b** Social sciences *395*
- **c** Natural and applied sciences *399*

58 MLA Documentation and Format *403*

Indexes to models *404–06*

- **a** Parenthetical text citations *407*
- **b** List of works cited *415*
- **c** Format of paper *447*
- **d** Sample paper *450*

59 APA Documentation and Format *461*

Indexes to models *462–63*

- **a** Parenthetical text citations *464*
- **b** List of references *467*
- **c** Format of paper *481*
- **d** Sample paper *484*

60 Chicago Documentation *489*

Index to models *490*

- **a** Notes and works-cited entries *491*
- **b** Models *494*

61 CSE Documentation *502*

Index to models *491*

- **a** Name-year text citations *502*
- **b** Numbered text citations *502*
- **c** List of references *503*

55 Working with the Goals and Requirements of the Disciplines

Chapter 10 (**2** p. 90) outlines the general concerns of subject, purpose, and audience that figure in most academic writing situations. The disciplines have more in common as well: methods of gathering evidence, kinds of assignments, scholarly tools, language conventions, and styles for source citations and document format. This chapter introduces these common goals and requirements. The following chapters then distinguish the disciplines along the same lines, focusing on literature (Chapter 56) and on other humanities, the social sciences, and the natural and applied sciences (Chapter 57).

55a Using methods and evidence

The **methodology** of a discipline is the way its practitioners study their subjects—that is, how they proceed when investigating the answers to questions. Methodology relates to the way practitioners analyze evidence and ideas. For instance, a literary critic and a social historian would probably approach Shakespeare's *Hamlet* quite differently: the literary critic might study the play for a theme among its poetic images; the historian might examine the play's relation to Shakespeare's context—England at the turn of the seventeenth century.

Whatever their approach, academic writers do not compose entirely out of their personal experience. Rather, they combine the evidence of their experience with that appropriate to the discipline, drawing well-supported conclusions about their subjects. The evidence of the discipline comes from research using primary or secondary sources.

- **Primary sources** are firsthand or original accounts, such as historical documents, works of art, and reports on experiments that the writer has conducted. When you use primary sources, you conduct original research and generate your own evidence. You might use your analysis of a painting as evidence for an interpretation of the painting. Or you might use data from your own survey of students to support your conclusions about students' attitudes.
- **Secondary sources** are books and articles written *about* primary sources. Much academic writing requires that you use

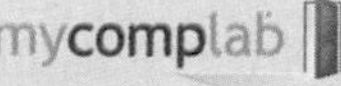

Visit *mycomplab.com* for more resources on writing in the disciplines.

Guidelines for academic writers

- **Become familiar with the methodology and the kinds of evidence appropriate for the discipline in which you are writing.**
- **Analyze the special demands of each assignment.** The questions you set out to answer, the assertions you wish to support, will govern how you choose your sources and evidence.
- **Become familiar with the discipline's specialized tools and language.**
- **Use the discipline's style for source citations and document format.**

such sources to spark, extend, or support your own ideas, as when you review the published opinions on your subject before contributing conclusions from your original research.

55b Understanding writing assignments

For most academic writing, your primary purpose will be either to explain something to your readers or to persuade them to accept your conclusions. To achieve your purpose, you will adapt your writing process to the writing situation, particularly to your reader's likely expectations for evidence and how you use it. Most assignments will contain keywords that imply some of these expectations—words such as *compare, define, analyze,* and *illustrate* that express customary ways of thinking about and organizing a vast range of subjects. (See **1** p. 13 for more on these so-called patterns of development.) You should be aware of such keywords and alert to them in the wording of assignments.

55c Using tools and language

When you write in an academic discipline, you use the scholarly tools of that discipline, particularly its periodical indexes. In addition, you may use the aids developed by practitioners of the discipline for efficiently and effectively approaching research, conducting it, and recording the findings. Many of these aids, such as a system for recording evidence from sources, are discussed in **7** pp. 317–75 and can be adapted to any discipline. Other aids are discussed in the next two chapters.

Pay close attention to the texts assigned in a course and any materials given out in class, for these items may introduce you to valuable references and other research aids, and they will use the specialized language of the discipline. This specialized language allows practitioners to write to each other both efficiently and precisely. It also furthers certain concerns of the discipline, such as accuracy and objectivity. Scientists, for example, try to interpret their data objectively, so they avoid *undoubtedly, obviously,* and other words that slant conclusions. Some of the language conventions like this one are discussed in the following chapters. As you gain experience in a particular discipline, keep alert for such conventions and train yourself to follow them.

55d Following styles for source citations and document format

Most disciplines publish journals that require authors to use a certain style for source citations and a certain format for documents. In turn, most instructors in a discipline require the same of students writing papers for their courses.

When you cite your sources, you tell readers which ideas and information you borrowed and where they can find your sources. Thus source citations indicate how much knowledge you have and how broad and deep your research was. They also help you avoid **plagiarism,** the serious offense of presenting the words, ideas, and data of others as if they were your own. (See **7** pp. 367–73 on avoiding plagiarism.)

Document format specifies such features as margins and the placement of the title. But it also extends to special elements of the manuscript, such as tables or an abstract, that may be required by the discipline.

The style guides for various disciplines are listed on pp. 395 (humanities), 398 (social sciences), and 402 (natural and applied sciences). If your instructor does not require a particular style, use that of the Modern Language Association, which is described and illustrated at length in **MLA** pp. 406–60.

56 Reading and Writing About Literature

By Sylvan Barnet

Writers of literature—stories, novels, poems, and plays—are concerned with presenting human experience concretely, with *showing* rather than *telling,* with giving a sense of the feel of life. Reading and writing about literature thus require extremely close attention

mycomplab

Visit *mycomplab.com* for more resources as well as exercises on reading and writing about literature.

to the feel of the words. For instance, the word *woods* in Robert Frost's "Stopping by Woods on a Snowy Evening" has a rural, folksy quality that *forest* doesn't have, and many such small distinctions contribute to the poem's effect.

When you read literature, you interpret distinctions like these, forming an idea of the work. When you write about literature, you state your idea as your thesis, and you support the thesis with evidence from the work. (See **1** pp. 14–16 for more on thesis statements.)

Note Writing about literature is not merely summarizing literature. Your thesis is a claim about the meaning or effect of the literary work, not a statement of its plot. And your paper is a demonstration of your thesis, not a retelling of the work's changes or events.

56a Using the methods and evidence of literary analysis

1 Reading literature

Reading literature critically involves interacting with a text, not in order to make negative judgments but in order to understand the work and evaluate its significance or quality. Such interaction is not passive, like scanning a newspaper or watching television. Instead, it is a process of engagement, of diving into the words themselves.

You will become more engaged if you write while you read. If you own the book you're reading, don't hesitate to underline or highlight passages that especially interest you. Don't hesitate to annotate the margins, indicating your pleasures, displeasures, and uncertainties with remarks such as *Nice detail* or *Do we need this long description?* or *Not believable.* If you don't own the book, make these notes on separate sheets or on your computer.

An effective way to interact with a text is to keep a **reading journal.** A journal is not a diary in which you record your doings; instead, it is a place to develop and store your reflections on what you read, such as an answer to a question you may have posed in the margin of the text or a response to something said in class. You may, for instance, want to reflect on why your opinion is so different from that of another student. You may even make an entry in the form of a letter to the author or from one character to another. (See **1** pp. 9–10 for more on journal keeping.)

2 Meaning in literature

In analyzing literature, you face right off the question of *meaning.* Readers disagree all the time over the meanings of works of literature, partly because (as noted earlier) literature *shows* rather than *tells:* it gives concrete images of imagined human experiences, but it usually does not say how we ought to understand these images. Further, readers bring different experiences to their reading and thus understand images differently. In writing about literature, then, we can offer only our *interpretation* of the meaning rather than *the* meaning. Still, most people agree that there are limits to interpretation: it must be supported by evidence that a reasonable person finds at least plausible if not totally convincing.

3 Questions for a literary analysis

One reason interpretations of meaning differ is that readers approach literary works differently, focusing on certain elements and interpreting those elements distinctively. For instance, some critics look at a literary work mainly as an artifact of the particular time and culture in which it was created, while other critics stress the work's effect on its readers.

This chapter emphasizes so-called formalist criticism, which sees a literary work primarily as something to be understood in itself. This critical framework engages the reader immediately in the work of literature, without requiring extensive historical or cultural background, and it introduces the conventional elements of literature that all critical approaches discuss, even though they view the elements differently. The following list poses questions for each element that can help you think constructively and imaginatively about what you read.

- ***Plot:*** **the relationships and patterns of events.** Even a poem has a plot—for instance, a change in mood from grief to resignation.

  What actions happen?
  What conflicts occur?
  How do the events connect to each other and to the whole?

- ***Characters:*** **the people the author creates,** including the narrator of a story or the speaker of a poem.

  Who are the principal people in the work?
  How do they interact?
  What do their actions, words, and thoughts reveal about their personalities and the personalities of others?
  Do the characters stay the same, or do they change? Why?

- ***Point of view:*** **the perspective or attitude of the speaker in a poem or the voice who tells a story.** The point of view may be **first person** (a participant, using *I*) or **third person** (an outsider, using *he, she, it, they*). A first-person narrator may be a major or a minor character in the narrative and may be **reliable** or **unreliable** (unable to report events wholly or accurately). A third-person narrator may be **omniscient** (knows what goes on in all characters' minds), **limited** (knows what goes on in the mind of only one or two characters), or **objective** (knows only what is external to the characters).

Who is the narrator (or the speaker of a poem)?
How does the narrator's point of view affect the narrative?

- *Tone:* **the narrator's or speaker's attitude,** perceived through the words (for instance, joyful, bitter, or confident).

  What tone (or tones) do you hear? If there is a change, how do you account for it?
  Is there an ironic contrast between the narrator's tone (for instance, confidence) and what you take to be the author's attitude (for instance, pity for human overconfidence)?

- *Imagery:* **word pictures or details involving the senses of sight, sound, touch, smell, and taste.**

  What images does the writer use? What senses do they draw on?
  What patterns are evident in the images (for instance, religious or commercial images)?
  What is the significance of the imagery?

- *Symbolism:* **concrete things standing for larger and more abstract ideas.** For instance, the American flag may symbolize freedom, or a dead flower may symbolize mortality.

  What symbols does the author use? What do they seem to signify?
  How does the symbolism relate to the theme of the work?

- *Setting:* **the place where the action happens.**

  What does the locale contribute to the work?
  Are scene shifts significant?

- *Form:* **the shape or structure of the work.**

  What *is* the form? (For example, a story might divide sharply in the middle, moving from happiness to sorrow.)
  What parts of the work does the form emphasize, and why?

- *Themes:* **the main ideas about human experience suggested by the work as a whole.** A theme is neither a plot (what happens) nor a subject (such as mourning or marriage). Rather it is what the author says with that plot about that subject.

  Can you state each theme in a sentence? Avoid mentioning specific characters or actions; instead, write an observation applicable to humanity in general. For instance, you might state the following about Gwendolyn Brooks's poem "The Bean Eaters" (p. 390): *People can live contentedly despite old age and poverty.*
  Do certain words, passages of dialog or description, or situations seem to represent a theme most clearly?
  How do the work's elements combine to develop a theme?

- *Appeal:* **the degree to which the work pleases you.**

  What do you especially like or dislike about the work? Why?

Do you think your responses are unique, or would they be common to most readers? Why?

4 Using evidence in writing about literature

The evidence for a literary analysis always comes from at least one primary source (the work or works being discussed) and may come from secondary sources (critical and historical works). For example, in the paper on pp. 390–91 about Gwendolyn Brooks's "The Bean Eaters," the primary material is the poem itself, and the secondary material is the three critical studies of the poem. The bulk of the evidence is usually quotations from the work, although summaries and paraphrases can be useful as well.

Your instructor will probably tell you if you are expected to consult secondary sources for an assignment. They can help you understand a writer's work, but your primary concern should always be the work itself, not what critics A, B, and C say about it. In general, then, quote or summarize secondary material sparingly. And always cite your sources.

56b Understanding writing assignments in literature

A literature instructor may ask you to write one or more of the following types of papers. The first two are the most common.

- **A literary analysis paper:** your ideas about a work of literature—your interpretation of its meaning, context, or representations based on specific words, passages, characters, and events.
- **A literary research paper:** analysis of a literary work combined with research about the work and perhaps its author. A literary research paper draws on both primary and secondary sources.
- **A personal response or reaction paper:** your thoughts and feelings about a work of literature.

Key terms

primary source A firsthand account: for instance, a historical document, a work of literature, or your own observations. (See also p. 381.)
secondary source A report on or analysis of other sources, often primary ones: for instance, a historian's account of a battle or a critic's view of a poem. (See also pp. 381–82.)
quotation An exact repetition of an author's words, placed in quotation marks. (See also **7** pp. 461–62.)
paraphrase A restatement of an author's words, closely following the author's line of thought but using different words and sentence structures. (See also **7** pp. 460–61.)
summary A condensation of an extended passage into a sentence or more. (See also **7** pp. 359–60.)

- **A book review:** a summary of a book and a judgment about the book's value.
- **A theater review:** your reactions to and opinions about a theatrical performance.

56c Using the tools and language of literary analysis

1 Writing tools

The fundamental tool for writing about literature is reading critically. Asking analytical questions such as those on pp. 385–87 can help you focus your ideas. In addition, keeping a reading journal can help you develop your thoughts. Make careful, well-organized notes on any research materials. Finally, discuss the work with others who have read it. They may offer reactions and insights that will help you shape your own ideas.

2 Language considerations

Use the present tense of verbs to describe both the action in a literary work and the writing of an author: *The old people live a meager existence. Brooks emphasizes how isolated the couple is. The critic Harry Shaw reads the lines as perhaps despairing.* Use the past tense to describe events that actually occurred in the past: *Brooks was born in 1917.*

Some instructors discourage students from using the first-person *I* (as in *I felt sorry for the character*) in writing about literature. At least use *I* sparingly to avoid sounding egotistical. Rephrase sentences to avoid using *I* unnecessarily—for instance, *The character evokes the reader's sympathy.*

3 Research sources

In addition to the following resources on literature, you may also want to consult some on other humanities (p. 394).

Specialized encyclopedias, dictionaries, and bibliographies

Cambridge Bibliography of English Literature
Cambridge Encyclopedia of Language
Cambridge Guide to Literature in English
Dictionary of Literary Biography
Handbook to Literature
Literary Criticism Index
McGraw-Hill Encyclopedia of World Drama
New Princeton Encyclopedia of Poetry and Poetics
Oxford Companion to American Literature
Oxford Companion to the Theatre
Schomburg Center Guide to Black Literature from the Eighteenth Century to the Present

Library databases and indexes

Abstracts of Folklore Studies
Dissertation Abstracts International (doctoral dissertations)
Early English Books Online
Gale Literary Resource Center
Humanities Index
Literary Criticism Index
Literary Index
Literature Online
MLA International Bibliography of Books and Articles on the Modern Languages and Literatures
World Shakespeare Bibliography

Book reviews

Book Review Digest
Book Review Index

Sources on the open Web

Alex Catalog of Electronic Texts (*infomotions.com/alex*)
EServer (*eserver.org*)
Internet Public Library: Online Literary Criticism (*ipl.org/div/litcrit*)
Literary Resources on the Net (*andromeda.rutgers.edu/~jlynch/Lit*)
Mr. William Shakespeare and the Internet (*Shakespeare.palomar.edu*)
Online Books Page (*onlinebooks.library.upenn.edu/books*)
Voice of the Shuttle (*vos.ucsb.edu*)

56d Documenting sources and formatting papers in literary analysis

Unless your instructor specifies otherwise, use the documentation style of the Modern Language Association, detailed in **MLA** pp. 406–47. In MLA style, parenthetical citations in the text of the paper refer to a list of works cited at the end. Sample papers illustrating this style appear on the following pages, in **2** pp. 111–15, and in **MLA** pp. 452–60.

Use MLA format for headings, margins, long quotations, and other elements, as detailed in **MLA** pp. 447–49.

56e Examining a sample literary analysis

The following pages reprint a poem and a student paper on the work. The author develops a thesis about the poem, supporting this main idea with quotations, paraphrases, and summaries from the work being discussed, a primary source. The author also draws sparingly on secondary sources (other critics' views), which further support his own views.

Note the following features of the student's paper:

- **The writer does not merely summarize the literary work.** He summarizes briefly to make his meaning clear, but his essay consists mostly of his own analysis.
- **The writer uses many quotations from the literary work.** The quotations provide evidence for his ideas and let readers hear the voice of the work.
- **The writer integrates quotations smoothly into his own sentences.** See **7** pp. 362–67.
- **The writer uses the present tense of verbs** to describe both the author's work and the action in the work.

Poem

Gwendolyn Brooks

The Bean Eaters

They eat beans mostly, this old yellow pair.
Dinner is a casual affair.
Plain chipware on a plain and creaking wood,
Tin flatware.

Two who are Mostly Good.
Two who have lived their day,
But keep on putting on their clothes
And putting things away.

And remembering . . .
Remembering, with twinklings and twinges,
As they lean over the beans in their rented back room that
is full of beads and receipts and dolls and cloths,
tobacco crumbs, vases and fringes.

An essay on poetry with secondary sources

Marking Time Versus Enduring in
Gwendolyn Brooks's "The Bean Eaters"

Gwendolyn Brooks's poem "The Bean Eaters" runs only eleven lines. It is written in plain language about very plain people. Yet its meaning is ambiguous. One critic, George E. Kent, says the old couple who eat beans "have had their day and exist now as time-markers" (141). However, another critic, D. H. Melhem, perceives not time marking but "endurance" in the old couple (123). The reader must decide if this poem is a despairing picture of old age or a more positive portrait.

"The Bean Eaters" describes an "old yellow pair" who "eat beans mostly" (line 1) off "Plain chipware" (3) with "Tin flatware" (4) "in their rented back room" (11). Clearly, they are poor. They live alone, not with friends or relatives—children or grandchildren are not mentioned—but with memories and a few possessions (9-11).

They are "Mostly Good" (5), words Brooks capitalizes at the end of a line, perhaps to stress the old people's adherence to traditional values as well as their lack of saintliness. They are unexceptional, whatever message they have for readers.

The isolated routine of the couple's life is something Brooks draws attention to with a separate stanza:

> Two who are Mostly Good.
> Two who have lived their day,
> But keep on putting on their clothes
> And putting things away. (5-8)

Brooks emphasizes how isolated the couple is by repeating "Two who." Then she emphasizes how routine their life is by repeating "putting."

A pessimistic reading of this poem seems justified. The critic Harry B. Shaw reads the lines just quoted as perhaps despairing: "they are putting things away as if winding down an operation and readying for withdrawal from activity" (80). However, Shaw observes, the word "But" also indicates that the couple resist slipping away, that they intend to hold on (80). This dual meaning is at the heart of Brooks's poem: the old people live a meager existence, yes, but their will, their self-control, and their connection with another person—their essential humanity—are unharmed.

The truly positive nature of the poem is revealed in the last stanza. In Brooks's words, the old people remember with some "twinges" perhaps, but also with "twinklings" (10), a cheerful image. As Melhem says, these people are "strong in mutual affection and shared memories" (123). And the final line, which is much longer than all the rest and which catalogs the evidence of the couple's long life together, is almost musically affirmative: "As they lean over the beans in their rented back room that is full of beads and receipts and dolls and cloths, tobacco crumbs, vases and fringes" (11).

What these people have is not much, but it is something.

Works Cited

Brooks, Gwendolyn. "The Bean Eaters." *Literature: Fiction, Poetry, and Drama*. Ed. Sylvan Barnet, William Burto, and William E. Cain. 15th ed. New York: Longman, 2008. 922. Print.

Kent, George E. *A Life of Gwendolyn Brooks*. Lexington: UP of Kentucky, 1990. Print.

Melhem, D. H. *Gwendolyn Brooks: Poetry and the Heroic Voice*. Lexington: UP of Kentucky, 1987. Print.

Shaw, Harry B. *Gwendolyn Brooks*. Boston: Twayne, 1980. Print. Twayne's United States Authors Ser. 395.

—Kenneth Scheff (student)

57 Writing in Other Disciplines

57a Writing in the humanities

The humanities include literature, the visual arts, music, film, dance, history, philosophy, and religion. The preceding chapter discusses the particular requirements of reading and writing about literature. This section concentrates on history. Although the arts, religion, and other humanities have their own concerns, they share many important goals and methods with literature and history.

1 Methods and evidence in the humanities

Writers in the humanities record and speculate about the growth, ideas, and emotions of human beings. Based on the evidence of written words, artworks, and other human traces and creations, humanities writers explain, interpret, analyze, and reconstruct the human experience.

The discipline of history focuses on reconstructing the past. In Greek the word for history means "to inquire": historians inquire into the past to understand the events of the past. Then they report, explain, analyze, and evaluate those events in their context, asking such questions as what happened before or after the events or how the events were related to then existing political and social structures.

Historians' reconstructions of the past—their conclusions about what happened and why—are always supported with reference to the written record. The evidence of history is mainly primary sources, such as eyewitness accounts and contemporary documents, letters, commercial records, and the like. For history papers, you might also be asked to support your conclusions with those in secondary sources.

In reading historical sources, you need to weigh and evaluate their evidence. If, for example, you find conflicting accounts of the same event, you need to consider the possible biases of the authors. In general, the more a historian's conclusions are supported by public records such as deeds, marriage licenses, and newspaper accounts, the more reliable the conclusions are likely to be.

2 Writing assignments in the humanities

Papers in the humanities generally perform one or more of the following operations.

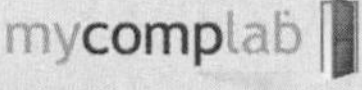

Visit *mycomplab.com* for more resources as well as exercises on writing in the disciplines.

- **Explanation:** for instance, showing how a painter developed a particular technique or clarifying a general's role in a historical battle.
- **Analysis:** examining the elements of a philosophical argument or breaking down the causes of a historical event.
- **Interpretation:** inferring the meaning of a film from its images or the significance of a historical event from contemporary accounts of it.
- **Synthesis:** finding a pattern in a historical period or in a composer's works.
- **Evaluation:** judging the quality of an architect's design or a historian's conclusions.

Most likely, you will use these operations in combination—say, interpreting and explaining the meaning of a painting and then evaluating it. (These operations are discussed in more detail in **2** pp. 81–83.)

3 Tools and language in the humanities

The tools and language of the humanities vary according to the discipline. Major reference works in each field, such as those listed on the next page, can clarify specific tools you need and language you should use.

Writing tools

A useful tool for the arts is to ask a series of questions to analyze and evaluate a work. (A list of such questions for reading literature appears on pp. 385–87.) In any humanities discipline, a journal—a log of questions, reactions, and insights—can help you discover and record your thoughts.

In history the tools are those of any thorough and efficient researcher: a system for finding and tracking sources; a methodical examination of sources, including evaluating and synthesizing them; a system for gathering source information; and a separate system, such as a research journal, for tracking one's own evolving thoughts.

Language considerations

Historians strive for precision and logic. They do not guess about what happened or speculate about "what if." They avoid trying to influence readers' opinions with words having strongly negative or positive connotations, such as *stupid* or *brilliant*. Instead, historians show the evidence and draw conclusions from that. Generally, they avoid using *I* because it tends to draw attention away from the evidence and toward the writer.

Writing about history demands some attention to the tenses of verbs to maintain consistency. Generally, historians use the past tense to refer to events that occurred in the past. They reserve the present tense only for statements about the present or statements of general truths. For example:

> Franklin Delano Roosevelt died in 1945. Many of Roosevelt's economic reforms persist in programs such as Social Security, unemployment compensation, and farm subsidies.

Research sources on the open Web

The following lists give resources in the humanities. (Resources for literature appear on pp. 388–89.)

General

BUBL LINK (bubl.ac.uk/link)
EDSITEment (edsitement.neh.gov)
Voice of the Shuttle (vos.ucsb.edu)

Art

Artnet (artnet.com)
World Wide Arts Resources (wwar.com/browse.html)

Dance

Artslynx International Dance Resources (www.artslynx.org/dance)
BUBL LINK: Dance (bubl.ac.uk/link/d/dance.htm)

Film

Film Studies on the Internet (www.library.ualberta.ca/subject/film/websites/index.cfm)
Internet Movie Database (imdb.com)

History

Best of History Web Sites (besthistorysites.net)
Librarians' Internet Index: History (lii.org/search/file/history)
National Women's History Project (nwhp.org)

Music

American Music Resource (amrhome.net)
Web Resources Research in Music (music.ucc.ie/wrrm)

Philosophy

Social Science Information Gateway: Philosophy (www.intute.ac.uk/artsandhumanities/philosophy)
Stanford Encyclopedia of Philosophy (plato.stanford.edu)

Religion

Academic Info: Religion Gateway (academicinfo.net/religindex.html)
Virtual Religion Index (virtualreligion.net/vri)

Theater

McCoy's Brief Guide to Internet Resources in Theatre and Performance Studies (www2.stetson.edu/csata/thr_guid.html)
Theater Connections (uncc.edu/jvanoate/theater)

4 Documentation and format in the humanities

Writers in the humanities generally rely on one of the following guides for source-citation style:

The Chicago Manual of Style, 15th ed., 2003
A Manual for Writers of Research Papers, Theses, and Dissertations, by Kate L. Turabian, 7th ed., rev. Wayne C. Booth, Gregory G. Colomb, and Joseph M. Williams, 2007
MLA Handbook for Writers of Research Papers, 7th ed., 2009

See **MLA** pp. 406–49 for the recommendations of the *MLA Handbook.* Unless your instructor specifies otherwise, use these recommendations for papers in English and foreign languages. In history, art history, and many other disciplines, however, writers rely on *The Chicago Manual of Style* or the student reference adapted from it, *A Manual for Writers.* Both books detail two documentation styles. One, used mainly by scientists and social scientists, closely resembles the style of the American Psychological Association (see **APA** pp. 463–84). The other style, used more in the humanities, calls for footnotes or endnotes and an optional bibliography. This style is described in **Chic** pp. 491–501.

57b Writing in the social sciences

The social sciences—including anthropology, economics, education, management, political science, psychology, and sociology—focus on the study of human behavior. As the name implies, the social sciences examine the way human beings relate to themselves, to their environment, and to one another.

1 Methods and evidence in the social sciences

Researchers in the social sciences systematically pose a question, formulate a **hypothesis** (a generalization that can be tested), collect data, analyze those data, and draw conclusions to support, refine, or disprove their hypothesis. This is the scientific method developed in the natural sciences (see p. 399).

Social scientists gather data in several ways:

- **They make firsthand observations of human behavior,** recording the observations in writing or electronically.
- **They interview subjects about their attitudes and behavior,** recording responses in writing or electronically. (See **7** p. 343 for guidelines on conducting an interview.)
- **They conduct broader surveys using questionnaires,** asking people about their attitudes and behavior. (See **7** pp. 343–44 for guidelines on conducting a survey.)

- **They conduct controlled experiments,** structuring an environment in which to encourage and measure a specific behavior.

In their writing, social scientists explain their own research or analyze and evaluate others' research.

The research methods of social science generate two kinds of data:

- ***Quantitative data* are numerical,** such as statistical evidence based on surveys, polls, tests, and experiments. When public-opinion pollsters announce that 47 percent of US citizens polled approve of the President's leadership, they are offering quantitative data gained from a survey. Social science writers present quantitative data in graphs, charts, and other illustrations that accompany their text.
- ***Qualitative data* are not numerical but more subjective:** they are based on interviews, firsthand observations, and inferences, taking into account the subjective nature of human experience. Examples of qualitative data include an anthropologist's description of the initiation ceremonies in a culture she is studying or a psychologist's interpretation of interviews he conducted with a group of adolescents.

2 Writing assignments in the social sciences

Depending on what social science courses you take, you may be asked to complete a variety of assignments:

- **A summary or review of research** reports on the available research literature on a subject, such as infants' perception of color.
- **A case analysis** explains the components of a phenomenon, such as a factory closing.
- **A problem-solving analysis** explains the elements of a problem, such as unreported child abuse, and suggests ways to solve it.
- **A research paper** interprets and sometimes analyzes and evaluates the writings of other social scientists about a subject, such as the effect of national appeals in advertising.
- **A research report** explains the author's own original research or the author's attempt to replicate someone else's research. (See **APA** pp. 484–87 for an example of a research report.)

Many social science disciplines have special requirements for the content and organization of each kind of paper. The requirements appear in the style guides of the disciplines, listed on p. 395. For instance, the American Psychological Association specifies the outline for research reports that is illustrated in **APA** pp. 481–84. Because of the differences among disciplines and even among different kinds of papers in the same discipline, you should always ask your instructor what he or she requires for an assignment.

3 Tools and language in the social sciences

The following guidelines for tools and language apply to most social sciences. However, the particular discipline you are writing in, or an instructor in a particular course, may have additional requirements.

Writing tools

Many social scientists rely on a **research journal** or **log**, in which they record their ideas throughout the research-writing process. Even if a research journal is not required in your courses, you may want to use one. As you begin formulating a hypothesis, you can record preliminary questions. Then when you are in the field conducting research, you can use the journal to react to the evidence you are collecting, to record changes in your perceptions and ideas, and to assess your progress.

To avoid confusing your reflections on the evidence with the evidence itself, keep records of actual data—notes from interviews, observations, surveys, and experiments—separately from the journal.

Language considerations

Each social science discipline has specialized terminology for concepts basic to the discipline. In sociology, for example, the words *mechanism, identity,* and *deviance* have specific meanings different from those of everyday usage. And *identity* means something different in sociology, where it applies to groups of people, than in psychology, where it applies to the individual. Social scientists also use precise terms to describe or interpret research. For instance, they say *The subject expressed a feeling of* rather than *The subject felt* because human feelings are not knowable for certain; or they say *These studies indicate* rather than *These studies prove* because conclusions are only tentative.

Just as social scientists strive for objectivity in their research, they also strive to demonstrate their objectivity through language in their writing. They avoid expressions such as *I think* in order to focus attention on what the evidence shows rather than on the researcher's opinions. (However, many social scientists prefer *I* to the artificial *the researcher* when they refer to their own actions, as in *I then interviewed the subjects.* Ask your instructor for his or her preferences.) Social scientists also avoid direct or indirect expression of their personal biases or emotions, either in discussions of other researchers' work or in descriptions of research subjects. Thus one social scientist does not call another's work *sloppy* or *immaculate* and does not refer to his or her own subjects as *drunks* or *innocent victims*. Instead, the writer uses neutral language and ties conclusions strictly to the data.

Research sources on the open Web

General

Data on the Net (*3stages.org/idata*)
Social Science Information Gateway (*sosig.ac.uk*)
WWW Virtual Library: Social and Behavorial Sciences (*vlib.org/SocialSciences*)

Anthropology

Anthro.Net (*home1.gte.net/ericjw1/index.html*)
National Anthropological Archives (*www.nmnh.si.edu/naa/index.htm*)

Business and economics

Resources for Economics on the Internet (*rfe.org*)
Virtual International Business and Economic Sources (*library.uncc.edu/display/?dept=reference&format=open&page=68*)

Education

Educator's Reference Desk (*eduref.org*)
US Department of Education (*ed.gov*)

Ethnic and gender studies

Diversity and Ethnic Studies (*public.iastate.edu/~savega/divweb2.htm*)
Voice of the Shuttle: Gender Studies (*vos.ucsb.edu/browse.asp?id=2711*)

Political science and law

Librarians' Internet Index: Law (*search.lii.org/index.jsp?more=SubTopic3*)
Political Science Resources (*psr.keele.ac.uk*)

Psychology

Psychology: Online Resource Central (*psych-central.com*)
PsychWeb (*psywww.com*)

Sociology

SocioWeb (*socioweb.com*)
WWW Virtual Library: Sociology (*socserv2.mcmaster.ca/w3virtsoclib*)

4 Documentation and format in the social sciences

Some of the social sciences publish style guides that advise practitioners how to organize, document, and type papers. The following is a partial list:

American Anthropological Association, *AAA Style Guide,* 2003 (*www.aaanet.org/publications/guidelines.cfm*)
American Political Science Association, *Style Manual for Political Science,* 2006
American Psychological Association, *Publication Manual of the American Psychological Association,* 6th ed., 2010
American Sociological Association, *ASA Style Guide,* 3rd ed., 2007
Linguistic Society of America, "LSA Style Sheet," published every December in *LSA Bulletin*
A Uniform System of Citation (law), 18th ed., 2005

By far the most widely used style is that of the American Psychological Association, detailed in **APA** pp. 463–84. Always ask your instructor in any discipline what style you should use.

57c Writing in the natural and applied sciences

The natural and applied sciences include biology, chemistry, physics, mathematics, engineering, computer science, and their branches. Their purpose is to understand natural and technological phenomena. (A *phenomenon* is a fact or event that can be known by the senses.) Scientists conduct experiments and write to explain the step-by-step processes in their methods of inquiry and discovery.

1 Methods and evidence in the sciences

Scientists investigate phenomena by the **scientific method**, a process of continual testing and refinement:

The scientific method

- **Observe carefully**. Accurately note all details of the phenomenon being researched.
- **Ask questions about the observations.**
- **Formulate a *hypothesis*, or preliminary generalization, that explains** the observed facts.
- **Test the hypothesis** with additional observations or controlled experiments.
- **If the hypothesis proves accurate, formulate a *theory*,** or unified model, that explains *why*.
- **If the hypothesis is disproved, revise it or start anew.**

Scientific evidence is almost always quantitative—that is, it consists of numerical data obtained from the measurement of phenomena. These data are called **empirical** (from a Greek word for "experience"): they result from observation and experience, generally in a controlled laboratory setting but also (as sometimes in astronomy or biology) in the natural world. Often the empirical evidence for scientific writing comes from library research into other people's reports of their investigations. Surveys of known data or existing literature are common in scientific writing.

2 Writing assignments in the sciences

No matter what your assignment, you will be expected to document and explain your evidence carefully so that anyone reading can check your sources and replicate your research. It is important for your reader to know the context of your research—both the previous experimentation and research on your particular subject (acknowledged in the survey of the literature) and the physical conditions and other variables surrounding your own work.

Assignments in the natural and applied sciences include the following:

- **A summary** distills a research article to its essence in brief, concise form. (Summary is discussed in detail in **2** pp. 72–74.)
- **A critique** summarizes and critically evaluates a scientific report.
- **A laboratory report** explains the procedure and results of an experiment conducted by the writer.
- **A research report** explains the experimental research of other scientists and the writer's own methods, findings, and conclusions.
- **A research proposal** reviews the relevant literature and explains a plan for further research.

A laboratory report has four or five major sections:

1. **"Abstract":** a summary of the report.
2. **"Introduction"** or **"Objective":** a review of why the study was undertaken, a summary of the background of the study, and a statement of the problem being studied.
3. **"Method"** or **"Procedure":** a detailed explanation of how the study was conducted, including any statistical analysis.
4. **"Results":** an explanation of the major findings (including unexpected results) and a summary of the data presented in graphs and tables.
5. **"Discussion":** an interpretation of the results and an explanation of how they relate to the goals of the experiment. This section also describes new hypotheses that might be tested as a result of the experiment. If the discussion is brief, it may be combined with the results in a single section labeled "Conclusions."

In addition, laboratory or research reports may include a list of references (if other sources were consulted). They almost always include tables and figures (graphs and charts) containing the data from the research.

3 Tools and language in the sciences

Tools and language concerns vary from discipline to discipline in the sciences. Consult your instructor for specifics about the field in which you are writing.

Writing tools

In the sciences a **lab notebook** or **scientific journal** is almost indispensable for accurately recording the empirical data from observations and experiments. Use such a notebook or journal for these purposes:

- **Record observations** from reading, from class, or from the lab.
- **Ask questions and refine hypotheses.**
- **Record procedures.**
- **Record results.**
- **Keep an ongoing record of ideas and findings** and how they change as data accumulate.
- **Sequence and organize your material** as you compile your findings and write your report.

Make sure that your records of data are clearly separate from your reflections on the data so that you don't mistakenly confuse the two in drawing your conclusions.

Language considerations

Science writers use objective language that removes the writer as a character in the situation and events being explained, except as the impersonal agent of change, the experimenter. Although usage is changing, scientists still rarely use *I* in their reports and evaluations, and they often resort to the passive voice of verbs, as in *The mixture was then subjected to centrifugal force.* This conscious objectivity focuses attention (including the writer's) on the empirical data and what they show. It discourages the writer from, say, ascribing motives and will to animals and plants. For instance, instead of asserting that the sea tortoise *evolved* its hard shell *to protect* its body, a scientist would write only what could be observed: that the hard shell *covers and thus protects* the tortoise's body.

Science writers typically change verb tenses to distinguish between established information and their own research. For established information, such as that found in journals and other reliable sources, use the present tense: *Baroreceptors monitor blood pressure*. For your own and others' research, use the past tense: *The bacteria died within three hours. Marti reported some success*.

Each discipline in the natural and applied sciences has a specialized vocabulary that permits precise, accurate, and efficient communication. Some of these terms, such as *pressure* in physics, have different meanings in the common language and must be handled carefully in science writing. Others, such as *enthalpy* in chemistry, have no meanings in the common language and must simply be learned and used correctly.

Research sources on the open Web

General

Google Directory: Science Links (directory.google.com/Top/Science)
Librarians' Internet Index: Science (search.lii.org/index.jsp?more=SubTopic13)

WWW Virtual Library: Natural Sciences and Mathematics (*vlib.org/Science.html*)

Biology
Biology.Arizona.Edu (*biology.arizona.edu*)
National Biological Information Infrastructure (*www.nbii.gov*)

Chemistry
Chemistry.org (*chemistry.org/portal/a/c/s/1/home.html*)
WWW Virtual Library: Links for Chemists (*liv.ac.uk/Chemistry/Links/links.html*)

Computer science
IEEE Computer Society (*computer.org*)
University of Texas Virtual Computer Library (*utexas.edu/computer/vcl*)

Engineering
National Academy of Engineering (*nae.edu*)
TechXtra: Engineering, Mathematics, and Computing (*www.techxtra.ac.uk*)

Environmental science
EE-link: Environmental Education on the Internet (*eelink.net*)
EnviroLink (*envirolink.org*)

Geology
American Geological Institute (*www.agiweb.org*)
US Geological Survey Library (*library.usgs.gov*)

Health sciences
Hardin MD (*www.lib.uiowa.edu/hardin/md*)
World Health Organization (*who.int/en*)

Mathematics
Internet Mathematics Library (*mathforum.org/library*)
Mathematical Atlas (*math-atlas.org*)

Physics and astronomy
American Institute of Physics (*aip.org*)
PhysicsWeb (*physicsweb.org*)

4 Documentation and format in the sciences

Within the natural and applied sciences, practitioners use one of two styles of documentation, varying slightly from discipline to discipline. Following are some of the style guides most often consulted:

American Chemical Society, *ACS Style Guide: A Manual for Authors and Editors,* 3rd ed., 2006
American Institute of Physics, *Style Manual for Guidance in the Preparation of Papers,* 4th ed., 1997
American Medical Association Manual of Style, 10th ed., 2007
Council of Science Editors, *Scientific Style and Format: The CSE Manual for Authors, Editors, and Publishers,* 7th ed., 2006

The most thorough and widely used of these guides is the last one, *Scientific Style and Format*. See **CSE** pp. 502–08 for a description of the style.

MLA Documentation and Format

MLA Documentation and Format

58 MLA Documentation and Format *406*

a Parenthetical text citations *407*
b List of works cited *415*
c Format of paper *447*
d Sample paper *450*

MLA parenthetical text citations

1. Author not named in your text *407*
2. Author named in your text *408*
3. A work with two or three authors *408*
4. A work with more than three authors *408*
5. A work by an author of two or more cited works *408*
6. An anonymous work *409*
7. A work with a corporate author *409*
8. A nonprint source *409*
9. A multivolume work *410*
10. An entire work or a work with no page or other reference numbers *410*
11. A work with numbered paragraphs or sections instead of pages *411*
12. An indirect source *411*
13. A literary work *411*
14. The Bible *412*
15. Two or more works in the same citation *412*

MLA works-cited models

1. Authors

1. One author *416*
2. Two or three authors *416*
3. More than three authors *416*
4. The same author(s) for two or more works *417*
5. A corporate author *417*
6. Author not named (anonymous) *417*

2. Periodical print sources

Articles in scholarly journals

7. An article in a journal with volume and issue numbers *418, 419*
8. An article in a journal with only issue numbers *418*
9. An abstract of a journal article or a dissertation *418*

Articles in newspapers

10. An article in a national newspaper *420, 421*
11. An article in a local newspaper *420*

Articles in magazines

12. An article in a weekly or biweekly magazine *420*
13. An article in a monthly or bimonthly magazine *420*

Reviews, editorials, letters to the editor, interviews

14. A review *420*
15. An editorial *422*
16. A letter to the editor *422*
17. An interview *422*

Articles in series or in special issues

18. An article in a series *422*
19. An article in a special issue *422*

3. Nonperiodical print sources

Books

20. Basic format for a book *423, 424*
21. A second or subsequent edition *423*
22. A book with an editor *423*
23. A book with an author and an editor *423*
24. A book with a translator *425*
25. An anthology *425*
26. A selection from an anthology *425*
27. Two or more selections from the same anthology *426*
28. An article in a reference work *426*
29. An illustrated book or graphic narrative *426*
30. A multivolume work *427*
31. A series *427*
32. A republished book *427*
33. The Bible *428*
34. A book with a title in its title *428*
35. Published proceedings of a conference *428*
36. An introduction, preface, foreword, or afterword *428*
37. A book lacking publication information or pagination *429*

Other nonperiodical print sources

38. A government publication *429*
39. A pamphlet or brochure *430*
40. A dissertation *430*
41. A letter *430*

4. Nonperiodical Web sources

Nonperiodical sources available only on the Web

42. A short work with a title *432, 433*
43. A short work without a title *432*
44. An entire site *434*
45. An article in a newspaper *434*
46. An article in a magazine *434*
47. A government publication *435*
48. An article in a reference work *435*
49. An image *435*
50. A television or radio program *436*
51. A video recording *436*
52. A sound recording *436*
53. A podcast *437*
54. A blog entry *437*
55. A wiki *437*

Nonperiodical Web sources also available in print

56. A short work with print publication information *438*
57. A book with print publication information *438*

Nonperiodical Web sources also available in other media

58. A sound recording with other publication information *438*
59. A film or video recording with other publication information *438*
60. An image with other publication information *439*

Citation of a URL

61. A source requiring citation of the URL *439*

5. Journals on the Web and periodicals in online databases

Web journals consulted directly

62. An article in a scholarly journal *440*
63. An abstract of a journal article *441*

Web periodicals consulted in online databases

64. An article in a scholarly journal *441, 442*
65. An abstract of a journal article *441*
66. An article in a newspaper *441*
67. An article in a magazine *442*

6. Other electronic sources

Publications on CD-ROM or DVD-ROM

68. A nonperiodical CD-ROM or DVD-ROM *443*
69. A periodical CD-ROM or DVD-ROM *443*

(continued)

MLA works-cited models

(continued)

E-mail and discussion-group postings

70. An e-mail message *443*
71. A posting to a discussion group *443*

Digital files

72. A text file *444*
73. A media file *444*

7. Other sources

74. A television or radio program *444*
75. A personal or broadcast interview *445*
76. A sound recording *445*
77. A film, DVD, or video recording *445*
78. A painting, photograph, or other work of visual art *446*
79. A personal photograph *446*
80. A map, chart, graph, or diagram *446*
81. A cartoon or comic strip *446*
82. An advertisement *447*
83. A performance *447*
84. A lecture, speech, address, or reading *447*

58 MLA Documentation and Format

English, foreign languages, and some other humanities use the documentation style of the Modern Language Association, recently updated in the *MLA Handbook for Writers of Research Papers* (7th ed., 2009).

- **In your text, a brief parenthetical citation adjacent to the borrowed material directs readers to a complete list of all the works you cite.**
- **At the end of your paper, the list of works cited includes complete bibliographical information for every source.**

Every entry in the list of works cited has at least one corresponding citation in the text, and every in-text citation has a corresponding entry in the list of works cited.

mycomplab

Visit *mycomplab.com* for more resources as well as exercises on MLA documentation and format.

This chapter describes MLA documentation: writing text citations (below), placing citations (p. 412), using supplementary notes (p. 414), and preparing the list of works cited (p. 417). A detailed discussion of MLA document format (p. 447) and a sample MLA paper (p. 452) conclude the chapter.

58a Writing parenthetical text citations

1 Citation formats

In-text citations of sources must include just enough information for the reader to locate the following:

- **The *source* in your list of works cited.**
- **The *place* in the source where the borrowed material appears.**

For any kind of source, you can usually meet both these requirements by providing the author's last name and (if the source uses them) the page numbers where the material appears. The reader can find the source in your list of works cited and find the borrowed material in the source itself.

The following models illustrate the basic text-citation forms and also forms for more unusual sources, such as those with no named author or no page numbers. See the **MLA divider** for an index to all the models.

Note Models 1 and 2 show the direct relationship between what you include in your text and what you include in a parenthetical citation. If you do *not* name the author in your text, you include the name in parentheses before the page reference (model 1). If you *do* name the author in your text, you do not include the name in parentheses (model 2).

1. Author not named in your text

When you have not already named the author in your sentence, provide the author's last name and the page number(s), with no punctuation between them, in parentheses.

> One researcher concludes that "women impose a distinctive construction on moral problems, seeing moral dilemmas in terms of conflicting responsibilities" (Gilligan 105-06).

See model 6 for the form to use when the source does not have an author. And see models 10 and 11 for the forms to use when the source does not provide page numbers.

2. Author named in your text

When you have already given the author's name with the material you're citing, do not repeat it in the parenthetical citation. Give just the page number(s).

> Carol Gilligan concludes that "women impose a distinctive construction on moral problems, seeing moral dilemmas in terms of conflicting responsibilities" (105-06).

See model 6 for the form to use when the source does not list an author. And see models 10 and 11 for the forms to use when the source does not provide page numbers.

3. A work with two or three authors

If the source has two or three authors, give all their last names in the text or in the citation. Separate two authors' names with and.

> As Frieden and Sagalyn observe, "The poor and the minorities were the leading victims of highway and renewal programs" (29).

> According to one study, "The poor and the minorities were the leading victims of highway and renewal programs" (Frieden and Sagalyn 29).

With three authors, add commas and also and before the final name.

> The textbook by Wilcox, Ault, and Agee discusses the "ethical dilemmas in public relations practice" (125).

> One textbook discusses the "ethical dilemmas in public relations practice" (Wilcox, Ault, and Agee 125).

4. A work with more than three authors

If the source has more than three authors, you may list all their last names or use only the first author's name followed by et al. (the abbreviation for the Latin *et alii,* "and others"). The choice depends on what you do in your list of works cited (see pp. 416–17).

> Increased competition means that employees of public relations firms may find their loyalty stretched in more than one direction (Cameron et al. 417).

> Increased competition means that employees of public relations firms may find their loyalty stretched in more than one direction (Cameron, Wilcox, Reber, and Shin 417).

5. A work by an author of two or more cited works

If your list of works cited includes two or more works by the same author, then your citation must tell the reader which of the author's works you are referring to. Give the title either in the text or in a parenthetical citation. In a parenthetical citation, give the full title only if it is brief; otherwise, shorten the title to the first one, two, or three main words (excluding *A, An,* or *The*).

> At about age seven, children begin to use appropriate gestures with their stories (Gardner, *Arts* 144-45).

The full title of Gardner's book is *The Arts and Human Development* (see the works-cited entry on p. 417). This shortened title is italicized because the source is a book.

6. An anonymous work

For a work with no named author or editor (whether an individual or an organization), use a full or shortened version of the title, as explained above. In your list of works cited, you alphabetize an anonymous work by the first main word of the title (see p. 417), so the first word of a shortened title should be the same. The following citations refer to an unsigned source titled "The Right to Die." The title appears in quotation marks because the source is a periodical article.

> One article notes that a death-row inmate may demand his own execution to achieve a fleeting notoriety ("Right" 16).

> "The Right to Die" notes that a death-row inmate may demand execution to achieve a fleeting notoriety (16).

If two or more anonymous works have the same title, distinguish them with additional information in the text citation, such as the publication date.

7. A work with a corporate author

Some works list as author a government body, association, committee, company, or other group. Cite such a work by the organization's name. If the name is long, work it into the text to avoid an intrusive parenthetical citation.

> A 2008 report by the Hawaii Department of Education provides evidence of an increase in graduation rates (12).

8. A nonprint source

Cite a nonprint source such as a Web page or a DVD just as you would any other source. If your works-cited entry lists the source under the name of an author or other contributor, use that name in the text citation. The following example cites an authored source that has page numbers.

> Business forecasts for the fourth quarter tended to be optimistic (White 4).

If your works-cited entry lists the work under its title, cite the work by title in your text, as explained in model 6. The next example cites an entire work (a film on DVD) and gives the title in the text, so it omits a parenthetical citation (see model 10).

> Seven decades after its release, *Citizen Kane* is still remarkable for its rich black-and-white photography.

9. A multivolume work

If you consulted only one volume of a multivolume work, your list of works cited will say so (see model 30 on p. 427), and you can treat the volume as you would any book.

If you consulted more than one volume of a multivolume work, give the appropriate volume in your text citation.

> After issuing the Emancipation Proclamation, Lincoln said, "What I did, I did after very full deliberations, and under a very heavy and solemn sense of responsibility" (5: 438).

The number 5 indicates the volume from which the quotation was taken; the number 438 indicates the page number in that volume. When the author's name appears in such a citation, place it before the volume number with no punctuation: (Lincoln 5: 438).

If you are referring generally to an entire volume of a multivolume work and are not citing specific page numbers, add the abbreviation vol. before the volume number as in (vol. 5) or (Lincoln, vol. 5) (note the comma after the author's name). Then readers will not misinterpret the volume number as a page number.

10. An entire work or a work with no page or other reference numbers

When you cite an entire work rather than a part of it, you may omit any page or other reference number. If the work you cite has an author, try to work the author's name into your text. You will not need a parenthetical citation then, but the source still must appear in your list of works cited.

> Boyd deals with the need to acknowledge and come to terms with our fear of nuclear technology.

Use the same format when you cite a specific passage from a work with no page, paragraph, or other reference numbers, such as a Web source.

If the author's name does not appear in your text, put it in a parenthetical citation.

> Almost 20 percent of commercial banks have been audited for the practice (Friis).

11. A work with numbered paragraphs or sections instead of pages

Some electronic sources number each paragraph or section instead of each page. In citing passages in these sources, give the paragraph or section number(s) and distinguish them from page numbers: after the author's name, put a comma, a space, and par. (one paragraph), pars. (more than one paragraph), sec., or secs.

> Twins reared apart report similar feelings (Palfrey, pars. 6-7).

12. An indirect source

When you want to use a quotation that is already in quotation marks—indicating that the author you are reading is quoting someone else—try to find the original source and quote directly from it. If you can't find the original source, then your citation must indicate that your quotation of it is indirect. In the following citation, qtd. in ("quoted in") says that Davino was quoted by Boyd.

> George Davino maintains that "even small children have vivid ideas about nuclear energy" (qtd. in Boyd 22).

The list of works cited then includes only Boyd (the work consulted), not Davino.

13. A literary work

Novels, plays, and poems are often available in many editions, so your instructor may ask you to provide information that will help readers find the passage you cite no matter what edition they consult.

- **Novels:** The page number comes first, followed by a semicolon and then information on the appropriate part or chapter of the work.

  > Toward the end of James's novel, Maggie suddenly feels "the thick breath of the definite—which was the intimate, the immediate, the familiar, as she hadn't had them for so long" (535; pt. 6, ch. 41).

- **Poems that are not divided into parts:** You may omit the page number and supply the line number(s) for the quotation. To prevent confusion with page numbers, precede the numbers with line or lines in the first citation; then use just the numbers.

  > In Shakespeare's Sonnet 73 the speaker identifies with the trees of late autumn, "Bare ruined choirs, where late the sweet birds sang" (line 4). "In me," Shakespeare writes, "thou seest the glowing of such fire / That on the ashes of his youth doth lie . . ." (9-10).

  (See pp. 390–91 for a sample paper on a poem.)

- **Verse plays and poems that are divided into parts:** Omit a page number and cite the appropriate part—act (and scene, if any), canto, book, and so on—plus the line number(s). Use Arabic numerals for parts, including acts and scenes (3.4), unless your instructor specifies Roman numerals (III.iv).

  Later in Shakespeare's *King Lear* the disguised Edgar says, "The prince of darkness is a gentleman" (3.4.147).

- **Prose plays:** Provide the page number followed by the act and scene, if any. For an example, see the reference to *Death of a Salesman* on p. 414.

14. The Bible

When you cite passages of the Bible in parentheses, abbreviate the title of any book longer than four letters—for instance, Gen. (Genesis), 1 Sam. (1 Samuel), Ps. (Psalms), Prov. (Proverbs), Matt. (Matthew), Rom. (Romans). Then give the chapter and verse(s) in Arabic numerals.

According to the Bible, at Babel God "did . . . confound the language of all the earth" (Gen. 11.9).

15. Two or more works in the same citation

When you refer to more than one work in a single parenthetical citation, separate the references with a semicolon.

Two recent articles point out that a computer badly used can be less efficient than no computer at all (Gough and Hall 201; Richards 162).

Since long citations in the text can distract the reader, you may choose to cite several or more works in an endnote or footnote rather than in the text. See pp. 414–15.

2 Placement and punctuation of parenthetical citations

The following guidelines will help you place and punctuate text citations to distinguish between your own and your sources' ideas and to make your own text readable. See also **7** pp. 362–67 on editing quotations and using signal phrases to integrate source material into your sentences.

Where to place citations

Position text citations to accomplish two goals:

- **Make it clear exactly where your borrowing begins and ends.**
- **Keep the citation as unobtrusive as possible.**

You can accomplish both goals by placing the parenthetical citation at the end of the sentence element containing the borrowed material. This sentence element may be a phrase or a clause, and it may begin, interrupt, or conclude the sentence. Usually, as in the following examples, the element ends with a punctuation mark.

> The inflation rate might climb as high as 30 percent (Kim 164), an increase that could threaten the small nation's stability.
>
> The inflation rate, which might climb as high as 30 percent (Kim 164), could threaten the small nation's stability.
>
> The small nation's stability could be threatened by its inflation rate, which, one source predicts, might climb as high as 30 percent (Kim 164).

In the last example the addition of one source predicts clarifies that Kim is responsible only for the inflation-rate prediction, not for the statement about stability.

When your paraphrase or summary of a source runs longer than a sentence, clarify the boundaries by using the author's name in the first sentence and placing the parenthetical citation at the end of the last sentence.

> Juliette Kim studied the effects of acutely high inflation in several South American and African countries since World War II. She discovered that a major change in government accompanied or followed the inflationary period in 56 percent of cases ([illegible])

When you cite two or more sources in the same paragraph, position authors' names and parenthetical citations so that readers can see who said what. In the following example, the beginnings and ends of sentences clearly mark the different sources.

> Schools use computers extensively for drill-and-practice exercises, in which students repeat specific skills such as spelling words, using the multiplication facts, or, at a higher level, doing chemistry problems. But many education experts criticize such exercises for boring students and failing to engage their critical thinking and creativity. Jane M. Healy, a noted educational psychologist and teacher, takes issue with "interactive" software for children as well as drill-and-practice software, arguing that "some of the most popular 'educational' software . . . may be damaging to independent thinking, attention, and motivation" (20). Another education expert, Harold Wenglinsky of the Educational Testing Service, found in a well-regarded 1998 study that fourth and eighth graders who used computers frequently, including for drill and practice, actually did worse on tests than their peers who used computers less often (*Does It Compute?* 21). In a later article, Wenglinsky concludes that "the quantity

of use matters far less than the quality of use." In schools, he says, high-quality computer work, involving critical thinking, is still rare ("In Search" 17).

How to punctuate citations

Generally place a parenthetical citation *before* any punctuation required by your sentence. If the borrowed material is a quotation, place the citation *between* the closing quotation mark and the punctuation:

> Spelling argues that during the 1970s American automobile manufacturers met consumer needs "as well as could be expected" (26), but not everyone agrees with him.

The exception is a quotation ending in a question mark or exclamation point. Then use the appropriate punctuation inside the closing quotation mark, and follow the quotation with the text citation and a period.

> "Of what use is genius," Emerson asks, "if the organ . . . cannot find a focal distance within the actual horizon of human life?" ("Experience" 60). Mad genius is no genius.

When a citation appears at the end of a quotation set off from the text, place it one space *after* the punctuation ending the quotation. Do not use additional punctuation with the citation or quotation marks around the quotation.

> In Arthur Miller's *Death of a Salesman,* the most poignant defense of Willie Loman comes from his wife, Linda:
>
> > He's not the finest character that ever lived. But he's a human being, and a terrible thing is happening to him. So attention must be paid. He's not to be allowed to fall into his grave like an old dog. Attention, attention must finally be paid to such a person. (56; act 1)

(This citation of a play includes the act number as well as the page number. See p. 412.)

3 Footnotes or endnotes in special circumstances

Footnotes or endnotes may replace parenthetical citations when you cite several sources at once, when you comment on a source, or when you provide information that does not fit easily in the text. Signal a footnote or endnote in your text with a numeral raised above the appropriate line. Then write a note with the same numeral.

Text At least five studies have confirmed these results.[1]

Note 1. Abbott and Winger 266-68; Casner 27; Hoyenga 78-79; Marino 36; Tripp, Tripp, and Walk 179-83.

In a note, the numeral is not raised, is indented one-half inch, and is followed by a period and a space. If the note appears as a footnote, place it at the bottom of the page on which the citation appears, set it off from the text with quadruple spacing, and single-space the note itself. If the note appears as an endnote, place it in numerical order with the other endnotes on a page between the text and the list of works cited. Double-space all the endnotes.

58b Preparing the MLA list of works cited

At the end of your paper, a list titled Works Cited includes all the sources you quoted, paraphrased, or summarized in your paper. (If your instructor asks you to include sources you examined but did not cite, title the list Works Consulted.)

Follow this format for the list of works cited:

- **Arrange your sources in alphabetical order** by the last name of the author. If an author is not given in the source, alphabetize the source by the first main word of the title (excluding *A, An,* or *The*).
- **Type the entire list double-spaced**, both within and between entries.
- **Indent the second and subsequent lines of each entry one-half inch from the left.** Your word processor can format this so-called hanging indent automatically.

For a complete list of works cited, see the paper by Justin Malik (p. 459).

MLA works-cited page

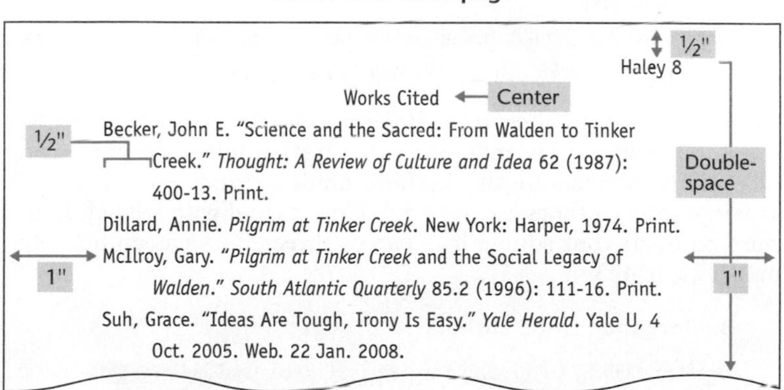

An index to all the following models appears at the **MLA** divider. Use your best judgment in adapting the models to your particular sources. If you can't find a model that exactly matches a source you used, locate and follow the closest possible match. You will certainly need to combine formats—for instance, drawing on model 2 ("Two or three authors") and model 10 ("An article in a national newspaper") for a national newspaper article with two authors.

Note MLA style now requires that you give the medium for every source you cite, such as print, Web, DVD, or television. For example, if you consulted an article in a print magazine, your works-cited entry should list the medium as Print. If you consulted a book on the Web, your works-cited entry should list the medium as Web. The models here all conform to this standard.

1 Listing authors

The following models show how to handle authors' names in citing any kind of source.

1. One author

Ehrenreich, Barbara. *Dancing in the Streets: A History of Collective Joy*. New York: Metropolitan-Holt, 2006. Print.

Give the author's full name—last name first, a comma, first name, and any middle name or initial. Omit any title, such as *Dr.* or *PhD.* End the name with a period. If your source lists an editor as author, see model 22, p. 423.

2. Two or three authors

Lifton, Robert Jay, and Greg Mitchell. *Who Owns Death: Capital Punishment, the American Conscience, and the End of Executions*. New York: Morrow, 2000. Print.

Wilcox, Dennis L., Phillip H. Ault, and Warren K. Agee. *Public Relations: Strategies and Tactics*. 8th ed. New York: Irwin, 2006. Print.

Give the authors' names in the order provided on the title page. Reverse the first and last names of the first author *only,* not of any other authors. Separate two authors' names with a comma and and; separate three authors' names with commas and with and before the third name. If your source lists two or three editors as authors, see model 22, p. 423.

3. More than three authors

Cameron, Glen T., Dennis L. Wilcox, Bryan H. Reber, and Jae-Hwa Shin. *Public Relations Today: Managing Competition and Conflict*. New York: Pearson, 2007. Print.

Cameron, Glen T., et al. *Public Relations Today: Managing Competition and Conflict*. New York: Pearson, 2007. Print.

You may, but need not, give all authors' names if the work has more than three authors. If you choose not to give all names, provide the name of the first author only, and follow the name with a comma and the abbreviation et al. (for the Latin *et alii,* meaning "and others"). If your source lists more than three editors as authors, see model 22, p. 423.

4. The same author(s) for two or more works

Gardner, Howard. *The Arts and Human Development*. New York: Wiley, 1973. Print.

---. *Five Minds for the Future*. Boston: Harvard Business School P, 2007. Print.

Give the author's name only in the first entry. For the second and any subsequent works by the same author, substitute three hyphens for the author's name, followed by a period. Note that the three hyphens stand for *exactly* the same name or names. If the second Gardner source were by Gardner and somebody else, both names would have to be given in full.

Place an entry or entries using three hyphens immediately after the entry that names the author. Within the set of entries by the same author, arrange the sources alphabetically by the first main word of the title, as in the Gardner examples (*Arts*, then *Five*).

If you cite two or more sources that list as author(s) exactly the same editor(s), follow the hyphens with a comma and ed. or eds. as appropriate. (See model 22, p. 423.)

5. A corporate author

Vault Technologies. *Turnkey Parking Solutions*. Salt Lake City: Mills, 2008. Print.

Corporate authors include associations, committees, institutions, government bodies, companies, and other groups. List the name of the group as author when a source gives only that name and not an individual's name.

6. Author not named (anonymous)

The Dorling Kindersley World Reference Atlas. London: Dorling, 2007. Print.

List a work that names no author—neither an individual nor a group—by its full title. If the work is a book, italicize the title. If the work is a periodical article or other short work, enclose the title in quotation marks:

"Let the Horse Race Begin." *Time* 31 Mar. 2008: 22. Print.

Alphabetize the work by the title's first main word, excluding *A, An,* or *The* (*Dorling* in the first example and Let in the second).

2 Listing periodical print sources

Print periodicals include scholarly journals, newspapers, and magazines that are published at regular intervals (quarterly, monthly, weekly, or daily). To cite more than one author, two or more articles by the same author, a corporate author, or an article with no named author, see models 1–6.

Note The treatment of volume and issue numbers and publication dates varies depending on the kind of periodical being cited, as the models indicate. For the distinction between journals and magazines, see **7** p. 331.

Articles in scholarly journals

7. An article in a journal with volume and issue numbers (print)

Bee, Robert. "The Importance of Preserving Paper-Based Artifacts in a Digital Age." *Library Quarterly* 78.2 (2008): 174-94. Print.

The facing page shows the basic format for an article in a print journal and the location of the required information in the journal. See p. 421 for parallel information on a newspaper article.

8. An article in a journal with only issue numbers (print)

Rymhs, Deena. "David Collier's *Surviving Saskatoon* and New Comics." *Canadian Literature* 194 (2007): 75-92. Print.

If a scholarly journal numbers only issues, not volumes, give the issue number alone after the journal title.

9. An abstract of a journal article or a dissertation (print)

Lever, Janet. "Sex Differences in the Games Children Play." *Social Problems* 23.2 (1996): 478-87. *Psychological Abstracts* 63.5 (1996): item 1431. Print.

For an abstract of an article, first provide the publication information for the article, following model 7. Then give the information for the abstract. If the abstract publisher lists abstracts by item rather than page number, add item before the number.

For an abstract appearing in *Dissertation Abstracts* (*DA*) or *Dissertation Abstracts International* (*DAI*), give the author's name and the title, Diss. (for "Dissertation"), the institution granting the author's degree, the date of the dissertation, and the publication information.

Steciw, Steven K. "Alterations to the Pessac Project of Le Corbusier." Diss. U of Cambridge, England, 1986. *DAI* 46.10 (1986): 565C. Print.

Format for a print journal article

① ②
Bee, Robert. "The Importance of Preserving Paper-Based Artifacts in a Digital Age."
③ ④ ⑤ ⑥ ⑦
Library Quarterly 78.2 (2008): 179-94. Print.

Journal cover

THE LIBRARY QVARTERLY

VOLUME 78 · APRIL 2008 · NUMBER 2

⑦ **Medium.** Give the medium of the article, Print, followed by a period.

③ **Title of periodical,** in italics. Omit any *A, An,* or *The* from the beginning of the title. Do not end with a period.

④ **Volume and issue numbers,** in Arabic numerals, separated by a period. Do not add a period after the issue number.

⑤ **Year of publication,** in parentheses and followed by a colon.

② **Title of article,** in quotation marks. Give the full title and any subtitle, separating them with a colon. End the title with a period inside the final quotation mark.

First page of article

THE IMPORTANCE OF PRESERVING PAPER-BASED ARTIFACTS IN A DIGITAL AGE

Robert Bee[1]

The preservation of paper-based artifacts is an essential issue for col
agement in academic libraries. In recent years, the library science pr

[*Library Quarterly*, vol. 78, no. 2, pp. 179–194]
© 2008 by The University of Chicago. All rights reserved.
0024-2519/2008/7802-0002$10.00

179

① **Author.** Give the full name—last name first, a comma, first name, and any middle name or initial. Omit *Dr., PhD,* or any other title. End the name with a period.

⑥ **Inclusive page numbers of article,** without "pp." Provide only as many digits in the last number as needed for clarity, usually two.

See also model 40 on p. 430 (entire dissertation), model 63 on p. 441 (abstract on the Web), and model 65 on p. 441 (abstract in an online database).

Note Most instructors expect you to consult and cite full articles, not abstracts. See **7** p. 334.

Articles in newspapers

10. An article in a national newspaper (print)

Stout, David. "Blind Win Court Ruling on US Currency." *New York Times* 21 May 2008, natl. ed.: A23. Print.

See the facing page for an analysis of this entry and the location of the required information in the newspaper.

11. An article in a local newspaper (print)

Arntaenius, Linda. "Merwick Rezoning Pushes Senior Housing Debate." *Town Topics* [Princeton] 21 May 2008: 1+. Print.

If the city of publication does not appear in the title of a local newspaper, follow the title with the city name, not italicized, in brackets.

Articles in magazines

12. An article in a weekly or biweekly magazine (print)

Fortini, Amanda. "Pomegranate Princess." *New Yorker* 31 Mar. 2008: 92-99. Print.

Give the author, title of the article, and title of the magazine. Follow the magazine title with the day, the month, and the year of publication. (Abbreviate all months except May, June, and July.) Don't place the date in parentheses, and don't provide a volume or issue number. Give the page numbers of the article and the medium, Print.

13. An article in a monthly or bimonthly magazine (print)

Douthat, Ross. "The Return of the Paranoid Style." *Atlantic Monthly* Apr. 2008: 52-59. Print.

Follow the magazine title with the month and the year of publication. (Abbreviate all months except May, June, and July.) Don't place the date in parentheses, and don't provide a volume or issue number. Give the page numbers of the article and the medium, Print.

Reviews, editorials, letters to the editor, interviews

14. A review (print)

Glasswell, Kathryn, and George Kamberelis. "Drawing and Redrawing the Map of Writing Studies." Rev. of *Handbook of Writing Research*, by Charles A.

Format for a print newspaper article

① Stout, David. ② "Blind Win Court Ruling on US Currency." ③ *New York Times* ④ 21 May 2008, ⑤ natl. ed.: ⑥ A23. ⑦ Print.

① **Author.** Give the full name—last name first, a comma, first name, and any middle name or initial. Omit *Dr., PhD,* or any other title. End with a period.

⑥ **Page number of article,** without "pp." Include a section designation before the number when the newspaper does the same, as here. Otherwise, give the section between the edition and the colon. Add a plus sign to the page number when the article continues on a later page.

First page of article

THE NEW YORK TIMES **NATIONAL** WEDNESDAY, MAY 21, 2008 A23

Blind Win Court Ruling on U.S. Currency

By DAVID STOUT

WASHINGTON — In a decision that could radically change the size, the color and even the feel of American money, a federal appeals court ruled on Tuesday that the United States discriminates against the blind and those with limited vision because its paper currency is all the same size regardless of a bill's value.

blind or visually impaired," said Brookly McLaughlin, deputy assistant secretary for public affairs.

Ms. McLaughlin said the Bureau of Engraving and Printing, the Treasury agency that makes paper money, had already contracted with a research firm to study ways to help those who are blind or have poor vision. The re-

in the country could cost $3.5 bil- lion ... introduce ... Other ... fected inc ... money-di ... er machi ... makers ... Judge Randolph said.

The suit was brought under the Rehabilitation Act of 1973, which addresses discrimination in fed-

② **Title of article,** in quotation marks. Give the full title and any subtitle, separating them with a colon. End with a period inside the final quotation mark.

③ **Name of newspaper,** in italics. Give the title as it appears on the first page, omitting any *A, An,* or *The* from the beginning.

First page of newspaper

"All the News That's Fit to Print"

The New York Times

National Edition

VOL. CLVII . . . No. 54,317 WEDNESDAY, MAY 21, 2008 $1.25

⑦ **Medium.** Give the medium of the article, Print, followed by a period.

④ **Date of publication.** Give the day of the month first, then month, then year. Abbreviate all months except May, June, and July. End the date with a comma if listing the newspaper edition and/or the section designation. Otherwise, end with a colon.

⑤ **Edition.** If the newspaper lists an edition at the top of the first page, include it after the date. End with a comma if listing the section designation. Otherwise, end with a colon.

MacArthur, Steve Graham, and Jill Fitzgerald. *Reading Research Quarterly* 42.2 (2007): 304-23. Print.

Rev. is an abbreviation for "Review." The names of the authors of the work being reviewed follow the title of the work, a comma, and by. If the review has no title of its own, then Rev. of and the title of the reviewed work immediately follow the name of the reviewer.

15. An editorial (print)

"A Global AIDS Campaign Stalled." Editorial. *New York Times* 21 June 2008, natl. ed.: A18. Print.

For an editorial with no named author, begin with the title and add the word Editorial after the title, as in the example. For an editorial with a named author, start with his or her name and then proceed as in the example.

16. A letter to the editor (print)

McBride, Thad. "Swapping the Suit and Tie." Letter. *Economist* 29 Mar. 2008: 30. Print.

Add the word Letter after the title, if there is one, or after the author's name.

17. An interview (print)

Aloni, Shulamit. Interview. *Palestine-Israel Journal of Politics, Economics, and Culture* 14.4 (2007): 63-68. Print.

Begin with the name of the person interviewed. If the interview does not have a title (as in the example), add Interview after the name. (Replace this description with the title if there is one.) You may also add the name of the interviewer if you know it—for example, Interview by Benson Wright. See model 75 (p. 445) to cite a broadcast interview or an interview you conduct yourself.

Articles in series or in special issues

18. An article in a series (print)

Kleinfeld, N. R. "Living at an Epicenter of Diabetes, Defiance, and Despair." *New York Times* 10 Jan. 2006, natl. ed.: A1+. Print. Pt. 2 of a series, Bad Blood, begun 9 Jan. 2006.

Cite an article in a series following a model on pp. 418–20 (scholarly journal, newspaper, or magazine). If you wish, end the entry with a description to indicate that the article is part of a series.

19. An article in a special issue (print)

Rubini, Monica, and Michela Menegatti. "Linguistic Bias in Personnel Selection." *Celebrating Two Decades of Linguistic Bias Research.* Ed. Robbie M. Sutton and Karen M. Douglas. Spec. issue of *Journal of Language and Social Psychology* 27.2 (2008): 168-81. Print.

Cite an article in a special issue of a periodical by starting with the author and title of the article. Follow with the title of the special issue, Ed., and the names of the issue's editor(s). Add Spec. issue of before the periodical title. Conclude with publication information, using the appropriate model on pp. 418–20 for a journal or magazine.

3 Listing nonperiodical print sources

Nonperiodical print sources are works that are not published at regular intervals, such as books, government publications, and pamphlets. To cite more than one author, two or more articles by the same author, a corporate author, or a source with no named author, see models 1–6.

Books

20. Basic format for a book (print)

Lahiri, Jhumpa. *Unaccustomed Earth*. New York: Knopf, 2008. Print.

The next page shows the basic format for a book and the location of the required information in the book. When other information is required, put it between the author's name and the title or between the title and the publication information, as in the following models.

21. A second or subsequent edition (print)

Bolinger, Dwight L. *Aspects of Language*. 3rd ed. New York: Harcourt, 1981. Print.

For any edition after the first, place the edition number after the title. (If an editor's name follows the title, place the edition number after the name. See model 26.) Use the appropriate designation for editions that are named or dated rather than numbered—for instance, Rev. ed. for "Revised edition."

22. A book with an editor (print)

Holland, Merlin, and Rupert Hart-Davis, eds. *The Complete Letters of Oscar Wilde*. New York: Holt, 2000. Print.

Handle editors' names like authors' names (models 1–4), but add a comma and the abbreviation ed. (one editor) or eds. (two or more editors) after the last editor's name.

23. A book with an author and an editor (print)

Mumford, Lewis. *The City in History*. Ed. Donald L. Miller. New York: Pantheon, 1986. Print.

When citing the work of the author, give his or her name first, and give the editor's name after the title, preceded by Ed. (singular only, meaning "Edited by"). When citing the work of the editor, use

Format for a print book

① ② ③ ④ ⑤ ⑥

Lahiri, Jhumpa. *Unaccustomed Earth*. New York: Knopf, 2008. Print.

Title page

Unaccustomed Earth

Jhumpa Lahiri

Alfred A. Knopf New York • Toronto 2008

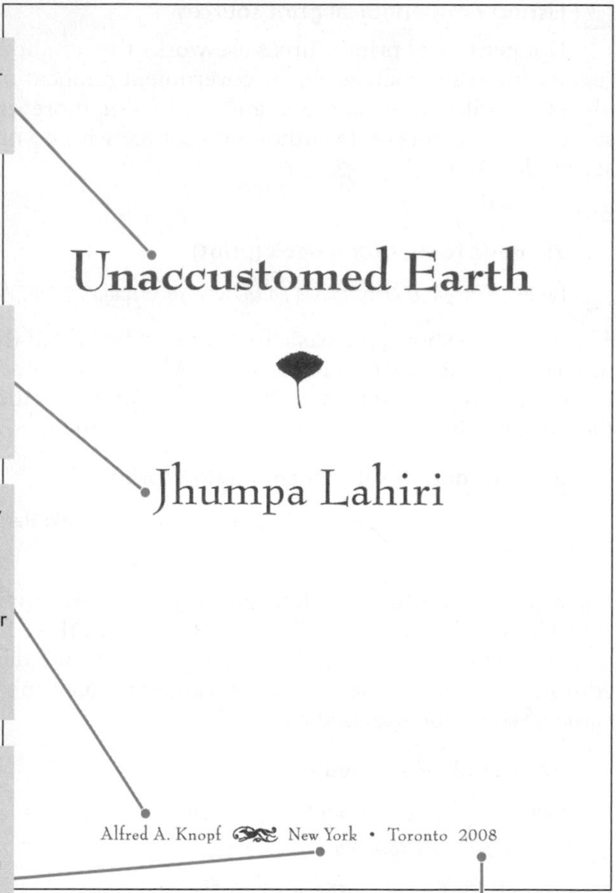

② **Title**, in italics. Give the full title and any subtitle, separating them with a colon. End the title with a period.

① **Author.** Give the full name—last name first, a comma, first name, and any middle name or initial. Omit *Dr., PhD,* or any other title. End the name with a period.

④ **Publisher's name.** Shorten most publishers' names ("UP" for University Press, "Little" for Little, Brown). Give both imprint and publisher's names when they appear on the title page: e.g., "Vintage-Random" for Vintage Books and Random House.

③ **City of publication.** Precede the publisher's name with its city, followed by a colon. Use only the first city if the title page lists more than one.

⑤ **Date of publication.** If the date doesn't appear on the title page, look for it on the next page. End the date with a period.

⑥ **Medium.** Give the medium of the book, Print, followed by a period.

model 22 for a book with an editor, adding By and the author's name after the title:

Miller, Donald L., ed. *The City in History*. By Lewis Mumford. New York: Pantheon, 1986. Print.

24. A book with a translator (print)

Alighieri, Dante. *The Inferno*. Trans. John Ciardi. New York: NAL, 1971. Print.

When citing the work of the author, as in the preceding example, give his or her name first, and give the translator's name after the title, preceded by Trans. ("Translated by").

When citing the work of the translator, give his or her name first, followed by a comma and trans. Follow the title with By and the author's name:

Ciardi, John, trans. *The Inferno*. By Dante Alighieri. New York: NAL, 1971. Print.

When a book you cite by author has a translator *and* an editor, give their names in the order used on the book's title page.

25. An anthology (print)

Kennedy, X. J., and Dana Gioia, eds. *Literature: An Introduction to Fiction, Poetry, and Drama*. 10th ed. New York: Longman, 2007. Print.

Cite an entire anthology only when citing the work of the editor or editors or when your instructor permits cross-referencing like that shown in model 27. Give the name of the editor or editors (followed by ed. or eds.) and then the title of the anthology.

26. A selection from an anthology (print)

Mason, Bobbie Ann. "Shiloh." *Literature: An Introduction to Fiction, Poetry, and Drama*. Ed. X. J. Kennedy and Dana Gioia. 10th ed. New York: Longman, 2007. 604-13. Print.

This listing adds the following to the anthology entry in model 25: author of selection, title of selection (in quotation marks), and inclusive page numbers for the selection (without the abbreviation "pp."). If you wish, you may also supply the original date of publication for the work you are citing, after its title. See model 32 on p. 427.

If the work you cite comes from a collection of works by one author that has no editor, use the following form:

Auden, W. H. "Family Ghosts." *The Collected Poetry of W. H. Auden*. New York: Random, 1945. 132-33. Print.

If the work you cite is a scholarly article that was previously printed elsewhere, provide the complete information for the earlier publication of the piece, followed by Rpt. in ("Reprinted in") and the information for the source in which you found the piece:

Molloy, Francis C. "The Suburban Vision in John O'Hara's Short Stories." *Critique: Studies in Modern Fiction* 25.2 (1984): 101-13. Rpt. in *Short Story Criticism: Excerpts from Criticism of the Works of Short Fiction Writers*. Ed. David Segal. Vol. 15. Detroit: Gale, 1989. 287-92. Print.

27. Two or more selections from the same anthology (print)

Erdrich, Louise. "Indian Boarding School: The Runaways." Kennedy and Gioia 1106.

Kennedy, X. J., and Dana Gioia, eds. *Literature: An Introduction to Fiction, Poetry, and Drama*. 10th ed. New York: Longman, 2007. Print.

Merwin, W. S. "For the Anniversary of My Death." Kennedy and Gioia 877-78.

Stevens, Wallace. "Thirteen Ways of Looking at a Blackbird." Kennedy and Gioia 880-82.

When you are citing more than one selection from the same source, your instructor may allow you to avoid repetition by giving the source in full (the Kennedy and Gioia entry) and then simply cross-referencing it in entries for the works you used. Thus the Erdrich, Merwin, and Stevens examples replace full publication information with Kennedy and Gioia and the appropriate pages in that book. Note that each entry appears in its proper alphabetical place among other works cited. Because each entry cross-references the Kennedy anthology, the medium is not required.

28. An article in a reference work (print)

"Reckon." *Merriam-Webster's Collegiate Dictionary*. 11th ed. 2008. Print.

Wenner, Manfred W. "Arabia." *The New Encyclopaedia Britannica: Macropaedia*. 15th ed. 2007. Print.

List an article in a reference work by its title (first example) unless the article is signed (second example). For works with entries arranged alphabetically, you need not include volume or page numbers. For works that are widely used and often revised, like those above, you may omit the editors' names and all publication information except any edition number, the publication year, and the medium. For works that are specialized—with narrow subjects and audiences—give full publication information:

"Hungarians in America." *The Ethnic Almanac*. Ed. Stephanie Bernardo Johns. 6th ed. New York: Doubleday, 2002. 121-23. Print.

See also models 48 (p. 435) and 68 (p. 443), respectively, to cite reference works appearing on the Web or on a CD-ROM or DVD-ROM.

29. An illustrated book or graphic narrative (print)

Wilson, G. Willow. *Cairo*. Illus. M. K. Perker. New York: Vertigo-DC Comics, 2005. Print.

When citing the work of the writer of a graphic narrative or illustrated book, follow the example above: author's name, title, Illus. ("Illustrated by"), and the illustrator's name. When citing the work of an illustrator, list his or her name first, followed by a comma and illus. ("illustrator"). After the title and By, list the author's name.

Williams, Garth, illus. *Charlotte's Web.* By E. B. White. 1952. New York: Harper, 1999. Print.

30. A multivolume work (print)

Lincoln, Abraham. *The Collected Works of Abraham Lincoln*. Ed. Roy P. Basler. Vol. 5. New Brunswick: Rutgers UP, 1953. Print. 8 vols.

If you use only one volume of a multivolume work, give that volume number before the publication information (Vol. 5 in the preceding example). You may add the total number of volumes at the end of the entry (8 vols. in the example).

If you use two or more volumes of a multivolume work, give the work's total number of volumes before the publication information (8 vols. in the following example). Your text citation will indicate which volume you are citing (see p. 410).

Lincoln, Abraham. *The Collected Works of Abraham Lincoln*. Ed. Roy P. Basler. 8 vols. New Brunswick: Rutgers UP, 1953. Print.

If you cite a multivolume work published over a period of years, give the inclusive years as the publication date: for instance, Cambridge: Harvard UP, 1978-90.

31. A series (print)

Bergman, Ingmar. *The Seventh Seal*. New York: Simon, 1995. Print. Mod. Film Scripts Ser. 12.

Place the name of the series (not quoted or italicized) at the end of the entry, followed by a period, a series number (if any), and another period. Abbreviate common words such as *modern* and *series*.

32. A republished book (print)

James, Henry. *The Bostonians*. 1886. New York: Penguin, 2001. Print.

Republished books include books reissued under new titles and paperbound editions of books originally released in hard covers. Place the original publication date (but not the place of publication or the publisher's name) after the title, and then provide the full publication information for the source you are using. If the book was originally published under a different title, add this title after Rpt. of ("Reprint of") at the end of the entry (after Print) and move the original publication date after the title—for example, Rpt. of *Thomas Hardy: A Life*. 1941.

33. The Bible (print)

The Bible. Print. King James Vers.

The Holy Bible. Trans. Ronald Youngblood et al. Grand Rapids: Zondervan, 1984. Print. New Intl. Vers.

When citing a standard version of the Bible (first example), do not italicize the title or the name of the version at the end. You need not provide publication information. For an edition of the Bible (second example), italicize the title, provide editors' and/or translators' names, give full publication information, and add the version name at the end.

34. A book with a title in its title (print)

Eco, Umberto. *Postscript to* The Name of the Rose. Trans. William Weaver. New York: Harcourt, 1983. Print.

When a book's title contains another book title (here *The Name of the Rose*), do not italicize the second title. When a book's title contains a quotation or the title of a work normally placed in quotation marks, keep the quotation marks and italicize both titles: *Critical Response to Henry James's "The Beast in the Jungle."*

35. Published proceedings of a conference (print)

Stimpson, Bill, ed. *2007 Annual Conference and Exhibition*. Proc. of Amer. Wind Energy Assn. Conf., 3-6 June 2007, New York. Red Hook: Curran, 2008. Print.

To cite the published proceedings of a conference, use a book model—here, an edited book (model 22). Between the title and the publication data, add information about the conference, such as its name, date, and location. You may omit any of this information that already appears in the source title. Treat a particular presentation at the conference like a selection from an anthology (model 26).

36. An introduction, preface, foreword, or afterword (print)

Donaldson, Norman. Introduction. *The Claverings*. By Anthony Trollope. New York: Dover, 1977. vii-xv. Print.

An introduction, foreword, or afterword is often written by someone other than the book's author. When citing such a piece, give its name without quotation marks or italics, as with Introduction above. (If the piece has a title of its own, provide it, in quotation marks, between the name of the author and the name of the book.) Follow the title of the book with By and the book author's name. Give the inclusive page numbers of the part you cite. (In the example above, the small Roman numerals refer to the front matter of the book, before page 1.)

When the author of a preface or introduction is the same as the author of the book, give only the last name after the title:

Gould, Stephen Jay. Prologue. *The Flamingo's Smile: Reflections in Natural History*. By Gould. New York: Norton, 1985. 13-20. Print.

37. A book lacking publication information or pagination (print)

Carle, Eric. *The Very Busy Spider.* New York: Philomel, 1984. N. pag. Print.

Some books are not paginated or do not list a publisher or a place of publication. To cite such a book, provide as much information as you can and indicate the missing information with an abbreviation: N.p. if no city of publication, n.p. if no publisher, n.d. if no publication date, and N. pag. if no page numbers.

Other nonperiodical print sources

38. A government publication (print)

United Nations. Dept. of Economic and Social Affairs. *World Youth Report 2007: Young People's Transition to Adulthood—Progress and Challenges.* New York: United Nations, 2008. Print.

United States. Cong. House. Committee on Agriculture, Nutrition, and Forestry. *Food and Energy Act of 2007*. 110th Cong., 1st sess. Washington: GPO, 2007. Print.

Wisconsin. Dept. of Public Instruction. *Bullying Prevention Program: Grades 6-8.* Madison: Wisconsin Dept. of Public Instruction, 2007. Print.

If a government publication does not list a person as author or editor, give the appropriate agency as author, as in the above examples. Provide information in the order illustrated, separating elements with periods: the name of the government, the name of the agency (which may be abbreviated), and the title and publication information. For a congressional publication (second example), give the house and committee involved before the title, and give the number and session of Congress after the title. In this example, GPO stands for the US Government Printing Office.

If a government publication lists a person as author or editor, treat the source as an authored or edited book:

Putko, Michelle. *Women in Combat Compendium*. Carlisle: US Army War Coll., Strategic Studies Inst., 2008. Print.

See model 47 (p. 435) to cite a government publication you find on the Web.

39. A pamphlet or brochure (print)

Understanding Childhood Obesity. Tampa: Obesity Action Coalition, 2008. Print.

Most pamphlets and brochures can be treated as books. In this example, the pamphlet has no listed author, so the title comes first. If your source has an author, give his or her name first, followed by the title and publication information.

40. A dissertation (print)

McFaddin, Marie Oliver. *Adaptive Reuse: An Architectural Solution for Poverty and Homelessness*. Diss. U of Maryland, 2007. Ann Arbor: UMI, 2007. Print.

Treat a published dissertation like a book, but after the title insert Diss. ("Dissertation"), the institution granting the degree, and the year.

For an unpublished dissertation, use quotation marks rather than italics for the title and omit publication information.

Wilson, Stuart M. "John Stuart Mill as a Literary Critic." Diss. U of Michigan, 1990. Print.

41. A letter (print)

Buttolph, Mrs. Laura E. Letter to Rev. and Mrs. C. C. Jones. 20 June 1857. *The Children of Pride: A True Story of Georgia and the Civil War*. Ed. Robert Manson Myers. New Haven: Yale UP, 1972. 334-35. Print.

List a published letter under the writer's name. Specify that the source is a letter and to whom it was addressed, and give the date on which it was written. Treat the remaining information like that for a selection from an anthology (model 26, p. 425). (See also model 16, p. 422, for the format of a letter to the editor of a periodical.)

For an unpublished letter in the collection of a library or archive, specify the writer, recipient, and date, as for a published letter. Then provide the medium, either MS ("manuscript") or TS ("typescript"). End with the name and location of the archive.

James, Jonathan E. Letter to his sister. 16 Apr. 1970. MS. Jonathan E. James Papers. South Dakota State Archive, Pierre.

For a letter you received, give the name of the writer, note the fact that the letter was sent to you, provide the date of the letter, and add the medium, MS or TS.

Wynne, Ava. Letter to the author. 6 Apr. 2008. MS.

To cite an e-mail message or a discussion-group posting, see models 70–71 (p. 443).

4 Listing nonperiodical Web sources

This section shows how to cite nonperiodical sources that you find on the Web. These sources may be published only once or occasionally, or they may be updated frequently but not regularly. (Most online magazines and newspapers fall into the latter category, even if they relate to printed periodicals, because their content changes often and unpredictably. See models 45 and 46.) Some nonperiodical Web sources are available only on the Web (below); others are available in other media as well, such as print or film (pp. 438–39). See models 62–67 (pp. 440–42) to cite a scholarly journal that you find on the Web and any periodical that you find in an online database.

The MLA no longer recommends providing a URL (electronic address) in Web source citations because URLs change frequently and because users can search for documents using search engines. However, do include a URL if your source is hard to find without it, if your source could be confused with another one, or if your instructor requires you to include URLs. See model 61 (p. 439) for the form to use when citing a URL.

Note The *MLA Handbook* does not label its examples of nonperiodical Web sources as particular types. For ease of reference, the following models identify and illustrate the kinds of Web sources you are likely to encounter. If you don't see just what you need, consult the index of models on the MLA tabbed divider for a similar source type whose format you can adapt. If your source does not include all of the information needed for a complete citation, find and list what you can.

Nonperiodical sources available only on the Web

Many nonperiodical Web sources are available only online. The following list, adapted from the *MLA Handbook,* itemizes the possible elements in a nonperiodical Web publication, in order of their appearance in a works-cited entry:

1. **Name of the author or other person responsible for the source,** such as an editor, translator, director, or performer. See models 1–6 (pp. 416–17) for the handling of authors' names. For other kinds of contributors, see models 22–24 (editors and translators) and models 74, 76–77, and 83 (directors, performers, and so on).
2. **Title of the cited work.** Use quotation marks for titles of articles, blog entries, and other sources that are parts of larger works. Use italics for books, plays, and other sources that are published independently.
3. **Title of the Web site,** in italics.

4. **Version or edition cited,** if any, following model 21 (p. 423)—for example, *Index of History Periodicals*. 2nd ed.
5. **Publisher or sponsor of the site,** followed by a comma. If you cannot find a publisher or sponsor, use N.p. ("No publisher") instead.
6. **Date of electronic publication, latest revision, or posting.** If no date is available, use n.d. ("no date") instead.
7. **Medium of publication:** Web.
8. **Date of your access:** day, month, year.

For some Web sources, you may want to include information that is not on this list, such as the names of both the writer and the performers on a television show.

42. A short work with a title (Web)

Molella, Arthur. "Cultures of Innovation." *The Lemelson Center for the Study of Invention and Innovation*. Smithsonian Inst., Natl. Museum of Amer. Hist., Spring 2005. Web. 3 Aug. 2008.

See the facing page for an analysis of this entry and the location of the required information on the Web site. If the short work you are citing lacks an author, follow model 6 (p. 417) for an anonymous source, starting the entry with the title of the work:

"Clean Energy." *Union of Concerned Scientists: Citizens and Scientists for Environmental Solutions*. Union of Concerned Scientists, 5 Feb. 2008. Web. 11 Mar. 2008.

To cite a short Web source that also appears in another medium (such as print), see models 56–60 (pp. 438–39). To cite an article from a Web journal or from an online database, see models 62–67 (pp. 440–42).

43. A short work without a title (Web)

Crane, Gregory, ed. Home page. *The Perseus Digital Library*. Dept. of Classics, Tufts U, n.d. Web. 21 July 2008.

If you are citing an untitled short work from a Web site, such as the home page of a site or a posting to a blog, insert Home page, Online posting, or another descriptive label in place of the title. Do not use quotation marks or italics for this label.

Note that this source lacks a publication date, indicated by n.d. after the sponsor's name.

Format for a short work on the Web

① Molella, Arthur. ② "Cultures of Innovation." ③ *The Lemelson Center for the Study of Invention and Innovation.* ④ Smithsonian Inst., Natl. Museum of Amer. Hist., ⑤ Spring 2005. ⑥ Web. ⑦ 3 Aug. 2008.

Top of page

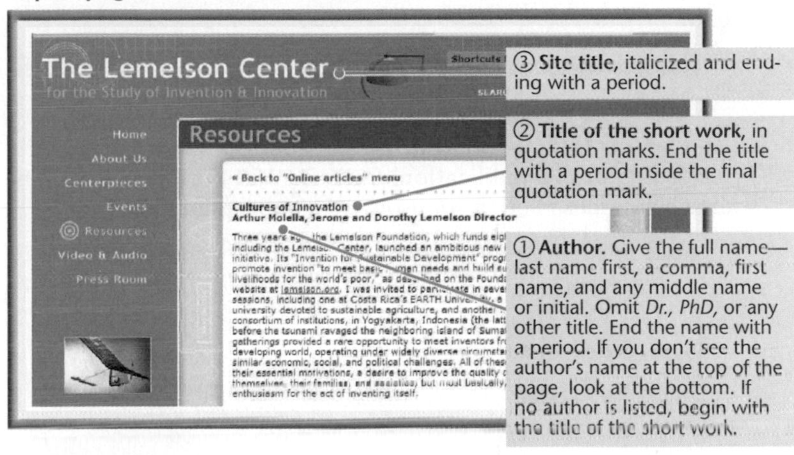

The Lemelson Center
for the Study of Invention & Innovation
Home
About Us
Centerpieces
Events
Resources
Video & Audio
Press Room
Resources
« Back to "Online articles" menu
Cultures of Innovation
Arthur Molella, Jerome and Dorothy Lemelson Director
③ **Site title,** italicized and ending with a period.
② **Title of the short work,** in quotation marks. End the title with a period inside the final quotation mark.
① **Author.** Give the full name—last name first, a comma, first name, and any middle name or initial. Omit *Dr., PhD,* or any other title. End the name with a period. If you don't see the author's name at the top of the page, look at the bottom. If no author is listed, begin with the title of the short work.

Bottom of page

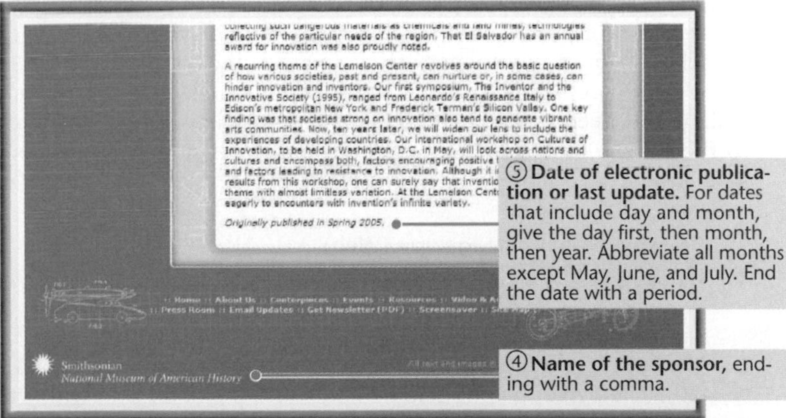

Originally published in Spring 2005.
Smithsonian
National Museum of American History
⑤ **Date of electronic publication or last update.** For dates that include day and month, give the day first, then month, then year. Abbreviate all months except May, June, and July. End the date with a period.
④ **Name of the sponsor,** ending with a comma.

⑥ **Medium.** Give the medium of the article, Web, followed by a period.

⑦ **Date of your access.** Give the day first, then month, then year. Abbreviate all months except May, June, and July. End the date with a period. (Since this date does not appear on the site, you'll need to record it separately.)

44. An entire site (Web)

Cheit, Ross E., ed. *The Recovered Memory Project.* Taubman Center for Public and Amer. Insts., Brown U, July 2007. Web. 8 Oct. 2008.

When citing an entire Web site—for instance, a scholarly project or a foundation site—include the name of the editor, author, or compiler (if available); the title of the site; the sponsor; the date of publication or most recent update; the medium (Web); and your date of access.

If your source lacks a named author or editor, begin with the site title:

Union of Concerned Scientists: Citizens and Scientists for Environmental Solutions. Union of Concerned Scientists, 5 Feb. 2008. Web. 11 Mar. 2008.

If your source lacks a sponsor, use the abbreviation N.p. ("No publisher"). If it lacks a publication date, use the abbreviation n.d. The source below lacks both a sponsor and a publication date:

Corbett, John. *STARN: Scots Teaching and Resource Network.* N.p., n.d. Web. 26 Nov. 2008.

45. An article in a newspaper (Web)

Carvajal, Doreen. "High-Tech Crime Is an Online Bubble That Hasn't Burst." *New York Times.* New York Times, 7 Apr. 2008. Web. 8 Apr. 2008.

List the author, article title, and newspaper title as in model 10 or 11 (p. 420). Then give the publishers's name and the date. End with the medium of publication (Web) and the date of your access. (See model 66 to cite a newspaper article in an online database.)

Use the preceding format to adapt the models for print periodicals if you need to cite a Web newspaper review, editorial, letter to the editor, interview, or article in a series (models 14–18, pp. 420–22).

46. An article in a magazine (Web)

Yabroff, Jennie. "Art Aimed to Shock." *Newsweek.* Newsweek, 26 Apr. 2008. Web. 15 May 2008.

List the author, article title, and magazine title as in model 12 or 13 (p. 420). Then give the publisher's name and the date. End with the medium (Web) and the date of your access. (See model 67 to cite a magazine article in an online database.)

Use the preceding format to adapt the models for print periodicals if you need to cite a Web magazine review, editorial, letter to the editor, interview, article in a series, or special issue (models 14–19, pp. 420–22).

47. A government publication (Web)

United States. Dept. of Agriculture. "Inside the Pyramid." *MyPyramid.gov.* US Dept. of Agriculture, n.d. Web. 1 Mar. 2008.

See model 38 for examples of government publications in print. Provide the same information for online publications along with the facts of Web publication. The example above includes the names of the government and department; the title of the source, in quotation marks; the title of the Web site, in italics; the sponsor; n.d. (because there is no publication date); the medium (Web); and the date of access.

48. An article in a reference work (Web)

"Yi Dynasty." *Encyclopaedia Britannica Online*. Encyclopaedia Britannica, 2008. Web. 7 Apr. 2008.

This source does not list an author, so the entry begins with the title of the article and then proceeds as for other Web sources. If a reference article has an author, place the name before the article title, as in model 42.

For reference works that you find in print or on CD-ROM or DVD-ROM, see models 28 (p. 426) and 68 (p. 443), respectively.

49. An image (Web)

To cite images that are available only on the Web, give the name of the artist or creator, the title of the work, the date of the work (if any), a word describing the type of image (if not otherwise clear from the image or site title), the title of the Web site, the sponsor, the date of the site, the medium (Web), and your date of access. The following examples show a range of possibilities.

A work of visual art:

Simpson, Rick. *Overload. Museum of Computer Art.* Museum of Computer Art, 2008. Web. 1 Apr. 2008.

A photograph:

Touboul, Jean. *Desert 1.* 2002. Photograph. *Artmuse.net.* Jean Touboul, 2007. Web. 14 Nov. 2008.

An advertisement:

United States. Dept. of Educ. Federal Student Aid. Advertisement. *Facebook.* Facebook, 2008. Web. 6 May 2008.

A map, chart, graph, or diagram:

"Greenhouse Effect." Diagram. *Earthguide.* Scripps Inst. of Oceanography, 2008. Web. 17 July 2008.

See also model 60 (p. 439) to cite an image that appears both on the Web and in another medium. And see models 78–82 (pp. 446–47) to cite images that aren't on the Web.

50. A television or radio program (Web)

Seabrook, Andrea, host. *All Things Considered*. Natl. Public Radio, 6 Apr. 2008. Web. 21 Apr. 2008.

The Web sites of television and radio networks and programs often include both content that was broadcast as part of a show and content that is unique to the site. Cite such material by its title or by the name of the person whose work you cite. Identify the role of anyone but an author (host in the example). Give the site title, the sponsor, the date, the medium (Web), and the date of your access. You may also cite other contributors (and their roles) after the title, as in model 52.

See also model 74 (p. 444) to cite a television or radio program that isn't on the Web.

51. A video recording (Web)

Green Children Foundation, prod. *The Green Children Visit China*. *YouTube*. YouTube, 7 Jan. 2008. Web. 28 June 2008.

Cite a video on the Web either by its title or by the name of the person whose work you are citing—in this example, the foundation that produced the video. Identify the role of anyone but an author (prod. in the example). Give the video title, the site title, the sponsor, the date, the medium (Web), and the date of your access. You may also cite other contributors (and their roles) after the title, as in model 52.

See also model 53 to cite a podcast of a video recording; model 59 (p. 438) to cite a video recording or film that appears both on the Web and in another medium (such as DVD); and model 77 (p. 445) to cite a film, DVD, or video recording that isn't on the Web.

52. A sound recording (Web)

Beglarian, Eve. *Five Things*. Perf. Beglarian et al. *Kalvos and Damian*. N.p., 23 Oct. 2001. Web. 8 Mar. 2008.

Cite a musical sound recording by its title or by the name of the person whose work you are citing—in this example, the composer. (If the composer's name comes after the title, precede it with By. See the next example.) This example also gives the work title, the performers of the work, the site title, the sponsor (here unknown, so replaced with N.p.), the date, the medium (Web), and the date of access.

The same format may be used for a spoken-word recording that you find on the Web:

Wasserstein, Wendy, narr. "Afternoon of a Faun." By Wasserstein. *The Borzoi Reader Online*. Knopf, 2001. Web. 14 Feb. 2008.

See also the next model to cite a sound podcast; model 58 to cite a sound recording that appears both on the Web and in another medium (such as CD); and model 76 (p. 445) to cite a sound recording that isn't on the Web.

53. A podcast (Web)

Simon, Bob. "Exonerated." *60 Minutes*. *CBS News*. CBS News, 25 May 2008. Web. 6 June 2008.

This podcast from a news program lists the author of a story on the show, the title of the story (in quotation marks), and the program (italicized) as well as the site title, sponsor, date, medium (Web), and access date. If a podcast does not list an author or other creator, begin with the title.

54. A blog entry (Web)

Marshall, Joshua Micah. "Asking the Tough Questions." *Talking Points Memo*. TPM Media, 15 May 2008. Web. 21 May 2008.

For a blog entry, give the author, the title of the entry, the title of the blog or site, the name of the sponsor (or N.p. if no sponsor is named), the publication date, the medium (Web), and the date of access. See model 43 (p. 432) to cite a blog entry without a title.

55. A wiki (Web)

"Podcast." *Wikipedia*. Wikimedia, n.d. Web. 20 Nov. 2008.

To cite an entry from a wiki, follow the above example: entry title, site title, sponsor, publication date (here n.d. because the wiki entry is undated), medium (Web), and date of access. Begin with the site title if you are citing the entire wiki.

Nonperiodical Web sources also available in print

Some sources you find on the Web may be books, short stories, and other works that have been scanned from print versions. To cite such a source, generally provide the information for both original print publication and Web publication. Begin your entry as if you were citing the print work, consulting models 20–41 for an appropriate format. Then, instead of giving "Print" as the medium, provide the title of the Web site you used, any version or edition number, the medium you used (Web), and the date of your access.

56. A short work with print publication information (Web)

Wheatley, Phillis. "On Virtue." *Poems on Various Subjects, Religious and Moral.* London, 1773. N. pag. *American Verse Project*. Web. 21 July 2008.

The print information for this poem follows model 26 (p. 425) for a selection from an anthology, but it omits the publisher's name because the anthology was published before 1900. The print information ends with N. pag. because the original source has no page numbers.

57. A book with print publication information (Web)

James, Henry. *The Ambassadors*. 1903. New York: Scribner's, 1909. *Oxford Text Archive*. Web. 5 May 2008.

The print information for this novel follows model 32 (p. 427) for a republished book, so it includes both the original date of publication (1903) and the publication information for the scanned book.

Nonperiodical Web sources also available in other media

Some images, films, and sound recordings that you find on the Web may have been published before in other media and then scanned or digitized for the Web. To cite such a source, generally provide the information for original publication as well as that for Web publication. Begin your entry as if you were citing the original, consulting models 74–84 (pp. 444–47) for an appropriate format. Then, instead of giving the original medium of publication, provide the title of the Web site you used, the medium you used (Web), and your date of access.

58. A sound recording with other publication information (Web)

"Rioting in Pittsburgh." CBS Radio, 1968. *Vincent Voice Library*. Web. 7 Dec. 2008.

For Web sound recordings with original publication information, base citations on model 76 (p. 445), adding the information for Web publication.

59. A film or video recording with other publication information (Web)

Coca Cola. Advertisement. Dir. Haskell Wexler. 1971. *American Memory*. Lib. of Cong. Web. 8 Apr. 2008.

For Web films or videos with original publication information, base citations on model 77 (p. 445), adding the information for Web publication.

60. An image with other publication information (Web)

Pollock, Jackson. *Lavender Mist: Number 1.* 1950. Natl. Gallery of Art, Washington. *WebMuseum*. Web. 7 Apr. 2008.

Keefe, Mike. "FAA Inspector in a Quandary." Cartoon. *Denver Post* 5 Apr. 2008. *PoliticalCartoons.com*. Web. 7 Apr. 2008.

For Web images with original publication information, base citations on models 78–82 (pp. 446–47), adding the information for Web publication.

Citation of a URL

61. A source requiring citation of the URL

Joss, Rich. "Dispatches from the Ice: The Second Season Begins." *Antarctic Expeditions*. Smithsonian Natl. Zoo and Friends of the Natl. Zoo, 26 Oct. 2007. Web. 26 Sept. 2008. <http://nationalzoo.si.edu/ConservationAndScience/AquaticEcosystems/Antarctica/Expedition/FieldNew/2-FieldNews.cfm>.

Because a URL does not always provide a convenient or usable route to a source, the MLA no longer recommends including URLs in works-cited entries. However, you should include URLs when your instructor requires them. You should also give a URL when readers may not be able to locate a source without one. For example, using a search engine to find "Dispatches from the Ice" (the title in the example) yields more than ten hits, one of which links to the correct site but the wrong document.

If you need to include a URL, ensure accuracy by using Copy and Paste to duplicate it in a file or an e-mail to yourself. In your list of works cited, give the URL after your date of access and a period. Put angle brackets on both ends of the URL, and end with a period. Break URLs *only* after slashes—do not hyphenate.

5 Listing journals on the Web and periodicals in online databases

This section covers two kinds of periodicals: scholarly journals that you reach directly on the Web (next page) and journals, newspapers, and magazines that you reach in online databases (p. 441). Newspapers and magazines that you reach directly on the Web are typically not periodicals (because their content often changes), so they are covered in models 45 and 46 (p. 434).

Citations for Web journals and for periodicals in online databases resemble those for print periodicals, with some changes for the different medium.

Web journals consulted directly

The journals you find directly on the Web may be published only online or may be published in print versions as well. The citation format is the same in either case: begin with an appropriate print model (pp. 418–20), but replace "Print" with Web and add your access date. Because many Web journals are unpaged, you may have to substitute n. pag. for page numbers.

62. An article in a scholarly journal (Web)

Polletta, Francesca. "Just Talk: Public Deliberation after 9/11." *Journal of Public Deliberation* 4.1 (2008): n. pag. Web. 7 Apr. 2008.

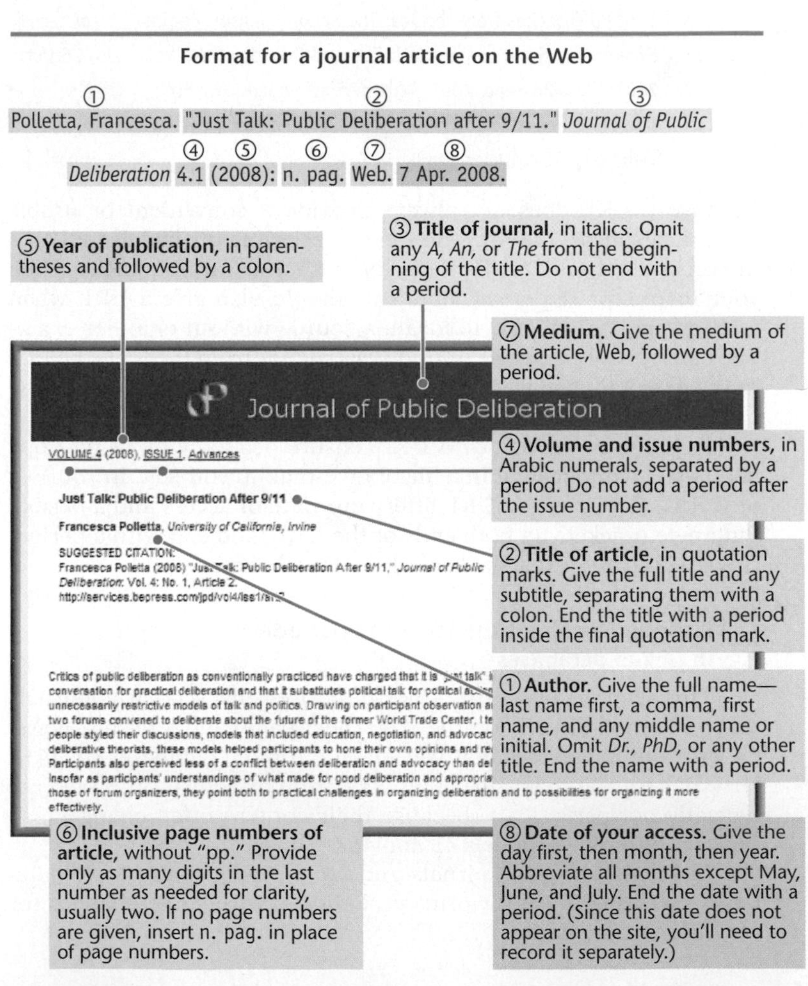

Format for a journal article on the Web
① Polletta, Francesca. ② "Just Talk: Public Deliberation after 9/11." ③ Journal of Public Deliberation ④ 4.1 ⑤ (2008): ⑥ n. pag. ⑦ Web. ⑧ 7 Apr. 2008.
⑤ Year of publication, in parentheses and followed by a colon.
③ Title of journal, in italics. Omit any A, An, or The from the beginning of the title. Do not end with a period.
⑦ Medium. Give the medium of the article, Web, followed by a period.
Journal of Public Deliberation
VOLUME 4 (2008), ISSUE 1, Advances
Just Talk: Public Deliberation After 9/11
Francesca Polletta, University of California, Irvine
SUGGESTED CITATION:
④ Volume and issue numbers, in Arabic numerals, separated by a period. Do not add a period after the issue number.
② Title of article, in quotation marks. Give the full title and any subtitle, separating them with a colon. End the title with a period inside the final quotation mark.
① Author. Give the full name—last name first, a comma, first name, and any middle name or initial. Omit Dr., PhD, or any other title. End the name with a period.
⑥ Inclusive page numbers of article, without "pp." Provide only as many digits in the last number as needed for clarity, usually two. If no page numbers are given, insert n. pag. in place of page numbers.
⑧ Date of your access. Give the day first, then month, then year. Abbreviate all months except May, June, and July. End the date with a period. (Since this date does not appear on the site, you'll need to record it separately.)

See the facing page for an analysis of the preceding example and the location of the required information in the Web journal. (For a journal article reached in an online database, see model 64.)

Use the same format to adapt the models for print periodicals if you need to cite a Web journal review, editorial, letter to the editor, interview, article in a series, or special issue (models 14–19, pp. 420–22).

63. An abstract of a journal article (Web)

Polletta, Francesca. "Just Talk: Public Deliberation after 9/11." *Journal of Public Deliberation* 4.1 (2008): n. pag. Abstract. Web. 7 Apr. 2008.

Treat a Web abstract like a Web journal article, but add Abstract between the publication information and the medium. (You may omit this label if the journal title clearly indicates that the cited work is an abstract.) See model 65 to cite an abstract in an online database.

Web periodicals consulted in online databases

Many articles in journals, newspapers, and magazines are available in online databases that you reach through your library's Web site, such as *Academic Search Premier, ProQuest,* and *Project Muse.* Follow models 7–19 (pp. 418–22) for print periodicals, but replace "Print" with the title of the database you consulted, the medium (Web), and the date of your access.

64. An article in a scholarly journal (online database)

Gorski, Paul C. "Privilege and Repression in the Digital Era: Rethinking the Sociopolitics of the Digital Divide." *Race, Gender and Class* 10.4 (2003): 145-76. *Ethnic NewsWatch.* Web. 23 Apr. 2008.

See the next page for an analysis of this entry and the location of the required information in the database.

65. An abstract of a journal article (online database)

Gorski, Paul C. "Privilege and Repression in the Digital Era: Rethinking the Sociopolitics of the Digital Divide." *Race, Gender and Class* 10.4 (2003): 145-76. Abstract. *Ethnic NewsWatch.* Web. 23 Apr. 2008.

Treat an abstract in an online database like a journal article in a database, but add Abstract between the publication information and the database title. (You may omit this label if the journal title clearly indicates that the cited work is an abstract.)

66. An article in a newspaper (online database)

Buckman, Rebecca. "Driver Cell Phone Bans Questioned." *Wall Street Journal* 13 May 2008, eastern ed.: D2+. *ProQuest.* Web. 12 Oct. 2008.

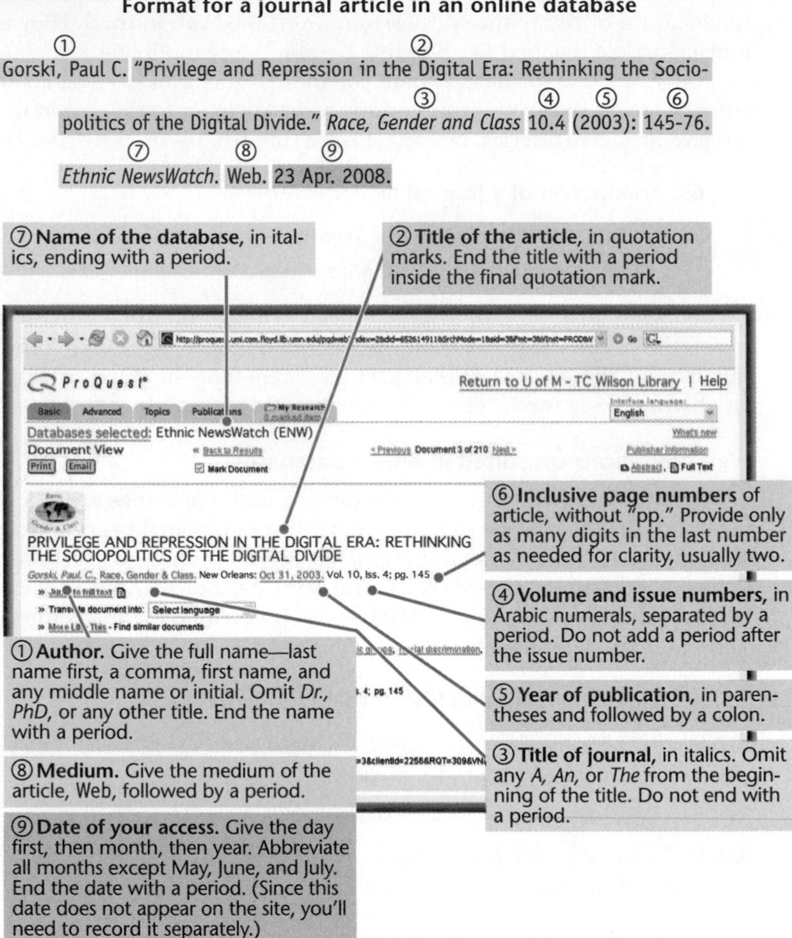

Format for a journal article in an online database
① ②
Gorski, Paul C. "Privilege and Repression in the Digital Era: Rethinking the Socio-
③ ④ ⑤ ⑥
politics of the Digital Divide." Race, Gender and Class 10.4 (2003): 145-76.
⑦ ⑧ ⑨
Ethnic NewsWatch. Web. 23 Apr. 2008.
⑦ Name of the database, in italics, ending with a period.
② Title of the article, in quotation marks. End the title with a period inside the final quotation mark.
ProQuest
Return to U of M - TC Wilson Library | Help
Basic
Advanced
Topics
Publications
My Research
Interface language:
English
Databases selected: Ethnic NewsWatch (ENW)
What's new
Document View
« Back to Results
< Previous Document 3 of 210 Next >
Publisher information
Print
Email
Mark Document
Abstract, Full Text
PRIVILEGE AND REPRESSION IN THE DIGITAL ERA: RETHINKING THE SOCIOPOLITICS OF THE DIGITAL DIVIDE
Gorski, Paul C., Race, Gender & Class. New Orleans: Oct 31, 2003. Vol. 10, Iss. 4; pg. 145
» Jump to full text
» Translate document into: Select language
» More Like This - Find similar documents
⑥ Inclusive page numbers of article, without "pp." Provide only as many digits in the last number as needed for clarity, usually two.
④ Volume and issue numbers, in Arabic numerals, separated by a period. Do not add a period after the issue number.
⑤ Year of publication, in parentheses and followed by a colon.
③ Title of journal, in italics. Omit any A, An, or The from the beginning of the title. Do not end with a period.
① Author. Give the full name—last name first, a comma, first name, and any middle name or initial. Omit Dr., PhD, or any other title. End the name with a period.
⑧ Medium. Give the medium of the article, Web, followed by a period.
⑨ Date of your access. Give the day first, then month, then year. Abbreviate all months except May, June, and July. End the date with a period. (Since this date does not appear on the site, you'll need to record it separately.)

Follow model 10 or 11 (p. 420) for citing author, title of article, title of newspaper, publication date, edition (if any), and page numbers. Add the database title, the medium (Web), and your date of access.

67. An article in a magazine (online database)

Brown, Kathryn. "The Skinny on the Environment." *Scientific American* Jan. 2008: 30-37. *Academic Search Premier*. Web. 3 Aug. 2008.

Follow model 12 or 13 (p. 420) for citing author, title of article, title of magazine, publication date, and page numbers. Add the title of the database, the medium (Web), and the date of your access.

6 Listing other electronic sources

Publications on CD-ROM or DVD-ROM

68. A nonperiodical CD-ROM or DVD-ROM

Nunberg, Geoffrey. "Usage in the Dictionary." *The American Heritage Dictionary of the English Language.* 4th ed. Boston: Houghton, 2000. CD-ROM.

Single-issue CD-ROMs may be encyclopedias, dictionaries, books, and other resources that are published just once, like print books. Follow models 20–37 for print books (pp. 423–29), but replace "Print" with CD-ROM or DVD-ROM. If the disc has a vendor that differs from the publisher of the work, add the vendor's place of publication, name, and publication date after the medium—for instance, Philadelphia: Soquest, 2006.

See also models 28 (p. 426) and 48 (p. 435) to cite reference works in print and on the Web.

69. A periodical CD-ROM or DVD-ROM

Kolata, Gina. "Gauging Body Mass Index in a Changing Body." *New York Times* 28 June 2005, natl. ed.: D1+. CD-ROM. *New York Times Ondisc.* UMI-ProQuest. Sept. 2005.

Databases on CD-ROM or DVD-ROM are issued periodically—for instance, every six months or every year. The journals, newspapers, and other publications included in such a database are generally available in print as well, so your works-cited entry should give the information for both formats. Start with information for the print version, following models 7–19 (pp. 418–22). Then replace "Print" with the medium (CD-ROM or DVD-ROM), the database title, the vendor's name (UMI-ProQuest in the example), and the database publication date.

E-mail and discussion-group postings

70. An e-mail message

Bailey, Elizabeth. "Re: London." Message to the author. 27 Mar. 2008. E-mail.

For e-mail, give the writer's name; the title, if any, from the e-mail's subject heading, in quotation marks; Message to the author (or the name of a recipient besides you); the date of the message; and the medium, E-mail. You do not need to include the date of your access.

71. A posting to a discussion group

Williams, Frederick. "Circles as Primitive." *The Math Forum @ Drexel.* Drexel U, 28 Feb. 2008. E-mail.

Cite a posting to a discussion group like a blog entry (model 54, p. 437). This example for a discussion-list posting includes author's name, title of the posting, title of the list, name of the sponsor, date of the posting, and medium (E-mail). If the posting is untitled, give Online posting instead. You need not add the date of your access.

Digital files

You may want to cite a digital file that is not on the Web or on a disc, such as a PDF document, a JPEG image, or an MP3 sound recording that you downloaded onto your computer. Use the appropriate model for your kind of source (for instance, model 79 for a personal photograph), but replace the medium with the file format you're using. If you don't know the file format, use Digital file.

72. A text file (digital)

Berg, John K. "Estimates of Persons Driving While Intoxicated." *Law Enforcement Today* 17 Apr. 2008. PDF file.

Fernandez, Carlos. "Summers in Spain." 2008. *Microsoft Word* file.

73. A media file (digital)

Springsteen, Bruce. "Empty Sky." *The Rising*. Columbia, 2002. MP3 file.

Boys playing basketball. Personal photograph by Granger Goetz. 2008. JPEG file.

7 Listing other sources

The source types covered in this section are not on a computer or, generally, in printed sources. Most of them have parallel citation formats elsewhere in this chapter when you reach them through electronic and print media. See model 17 (p. 422) to cite an interview in print. See models 49–52 (pp. 435–36) to cite images, television and radio programs, video recordings, and sound recordings that are available only on the Web. See models 58–60 (pp. 438–39) to cite such sources when they are available on the Web and in other media. And see model 73 to cite such sources in digital files.

74. A television or radio program

"Piece of My Heart." By Stacy McKee. Dir. Mark Tinker. *Grey's Anatomy*. ABC. KGO, San Francisco, 1 May 2008. Television.

Start with the title unless you are citing the work of a person or persons. The example here cites an episode title (in quotation marks) and the names of the episode's writer and director. By and Dir. identify their roles. Then the entry gives the program title (in italics), the name of the network, the call letters and city of the local station, the date, and the medium (Television). If you list individuals who worked on the entire program, put their names after the program title.

75. A personal or broadcast interview

Paul, William. Personal interview. 6 June 2008.

Diaz, Junot. Interview by Terry Gross. *Fresh Air*. Natl. Public Radio. WGBH, Boston, 18 Oct. 2007. Radio.

Begin with the name of the person interviewed. For an interview you conducted, specify Personal interview or the medium (such as Telephone interview or E-mail interview), and then give the date. For an interview you heard or saw, provide the title if any or Interview if there is no title. Add the name of the interviewer if he or she is identified. Then follow an appropriate model for the kind of source (here, a radio program), and end with the medium (here, Radio).

76. A sound recording

Rubenstein, Artur, perf. Piano Concerto no. 2 in B-flat. By Johannes Brahms. Cond. Eugene Ormandy. Philadelphia Orch. RCA, 1972. LP.

Springsteen, Bruce. "Empty Sky." *The Rising*. Columbia, 2002. CD.

Begin with the name of the individual whose work you are citing. Unless this person is the composer, identify his or her role, as with perf. ("performer") in the first example. If you're citing a work identified by form, number, and key (first example), do not use quotation marks or italics for the title. If you're citing a song or song lyrics (second example), give the title in quotation marks; then provide the title of the recording in italics. Following the title, identify the composer or author if you haven't already, after By, and name and identify other participants you want to mention. Then provide the manufacturer of the recording, the date of release, and the medium: LP in the first example, CD in the second.

77. A film, DVD, or video recording

A Beautiful Mind. Dir. Ron Howard. Universal, 2001. Film.

Start with the title of the work unless you are citing the work of a person (see the next example). Generally, identify and name the director. You may list other participants (writer, lead performers, and so on) as you judge appropriate. For a film, end with the distributor, date, and medium (Film).

For a DVD or videocassette, include the original release date (if any), the distributor's name, and the medium (DVD or Videocassette).

Balanchine, George, chor. *Serenade*. Perf. San Francisco Ballet. Dir. Hilary Bean. 1991. PBS Video, 2006. DVD.

78. A painting, photograph, or other work of visual art

Arnold, Leslie. *Seated Woman.* N.d. Oil on canvas. DeYoung Museum, San Francisco.

Sugimoto, Hiroshi. *Pacific Ocean, Mount Tamalpais.* 1994. Photograph. Private collection.

To cite an actual work of art, name the artist and give the title (in italics) and the date of creation (or N.d. if the date is unknown). Then provide the medium of the work (such as Oil on canvas or Photograph) and the name and location of the owner, if known. (Use Private collection if not.)

For a work you see only in a reproduction, provide the complete publication information for the source you used. Omit the medium of the work itself, and replace it with the medium of the reproduction (Print in the following example). Omit such information only if you examined the actual work.

Hockney, David. *Place Furstenberg, Paris.* 1985. Coll. Art Gallery, New Paltz. *David Hockney: A Retrospective.* Ed. Maurice Tuchman and Stephanie Barron. Los Angeles: Los Angeles County Museum of Art, 1988. 247. Print.

79. A personal photograph

Common milkweed on Lake Michigan shoreline. Personal photograph by the author. 22 Aug. 2008.

For a personal photograph by you or by someone else, describe the subject (without quotation marks or italics), name the photographer, and add the date. The current edition of the *MLA Handbook* does not cover personal photographs. This format comes from the previous edition.

80. A map, chart, graph, or diagram

"The Sonoran Desert." Map. *Sonoran Desert: An American Deserts Handbook.* By Rose Houk. Tucson: Western Natl. Parks Assn., 2000. 12. Print.

Unless the creator of an illustration is given on the source, list the illustration by its title. Put the title in quotation marks if it comes from another publication or in italics if it is published independently. Then add a description (Map, Chart, and so on), the publication information, and the medium (here, Print).

81. A cartoon or comic strip

Trudeau, Garry. "Doonesbury." Comic strip. *San Francisco Chronicle* 28 Aug. 2008: E6. Print.

Cite a cartoon or comic strip with the artist's name, the title (in quotation marks), the description Cartoon or Comic strip, the publication information, and the medium (here, Print).

82. An advertisement

Escape Hybrid by Ford. Advertisement. *New Yorker* 10 Dec. 2007: 11. Print.

Cite an advertisement with the name of the product or company advertised, the description Advertisement, the publication information, and the medium (Print, Television, Radio, and so on).

83. A performance

Levine, James, cond. Boston Symphony Orch. Symphony Hall, Boston. 2 May 2008. Performance.

The New Century. By Paul Rudnick. Dir. Nicholas Martin. Mitzi E. Newhouse Theater, New York. 6 May 2008. Performance.

For a live performance, generally base your citation on film citations (model 77). Place the title first (second example) unless you are citing the work of an individual (first example). After the title, provide relevant information about participants as well as the theater, city, and performance date. Conclude with the medium (Performance).

84. A lecture, speech, address, or reading

Katrib, Ruba. "New Art: South Florida Exhibit." Museum of Contemporary Art. MOCA at Goldman Warehouse, Miami. 4 Sept. 2007. Address.

Give the speaker's name, the title if any (in quotation marks), the title of the meeting if any, the name of the sponsoring organization, the location of the presentation, and the date. End with a description of the type of presentation (Lecture, Speech, Address, Reading).

Although the MLA does not provide a specific style for citing classroom lectures in your courses, you can adapt the preceding format for this purpose.

Cavanaugh, Carol. Class lecture on teaching mentors. Lesley U. 4 Apr. 2008. Lecture.

58c Formatting a paper in MLA style

The *MLA Handbook* provides guidelines for a fairly simple document format, with just a few elements. For guidelines on type fonts, headings, lists, illustrations, and other features that MLA style does not specify, see **1** pp. 54–60.

The samples on the next page show the formats for the first page and a later page of a paper. For the format of the list of works cited, see p. 415.

First page of MLA paper

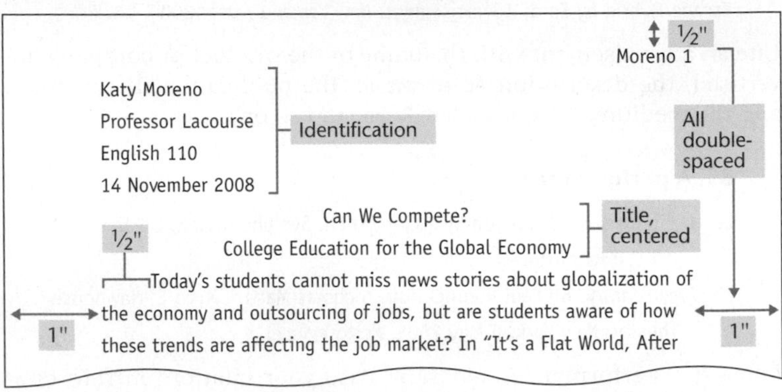

Later page of MLA paper

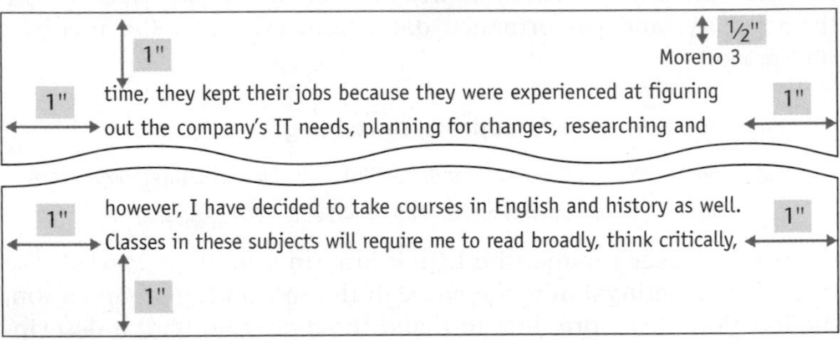

Margins Use minimum one-inch margins on all sides of every page.

Spacing and indentions Double-space throughout. Indent paragraphs one-half inch. (See opposite for indention of poetry and long prose quotations.)

Paging Begin numbering on the first page, and number consecutively through the end (including the list of works cited). Use Arabic numerals (1, 2, 3) positioned in the upper right, about one-half inch from the top. Place your last name before the page number in case the pages later become separated.

Identification and title MLA style does not require a title page for a paper. Instead, give your name, your instructor's name, the course title, and the date on separate lines in the upper left of the first page—one inch from the top of the paper. (See the sample above.) Double-space between all lines of this identification.

Double-space again, and center the title. Do not highlight the title with italics, underlining, boldface, larger type, or quotation marks. Capitalize the words in the title according to the guidelines in **6** p. 306. Double-space the lines of the title and between the title and the text.

Poetry and long prose quotations Treat a single line of poetry like any other quotation, running it into your text and enclosing it in quotation marks. You may run in two or three lines of poetry as well, separating the lines with a slash surrounded by space.

> An example of Robert Frost's incisiveness is in two lines from "Death of the Hired Man": "Home is the place where, when you have to go there / They have to take you in" (119-20).

Always set off from your text a poetry quotation of more than three lines. Use double spacing above and below the quotation and for the quotation itself. Indent the quotation one inch from the left margin. *Do not add quotation marks.*

> Emily Dickinson stripped ideas to their essence, as in this description of "A narrow Fellow in the Grass," a snake:
>
> I more than once at Noon
> Have passed, I thought, a Whip lash
> Unbraiding in the Sun
> When stopping to secure it
> It wrinkled, and was gone – (12-16)

Also set off a prose quotation of more than four typed lines. (See **7** pp. 361–62 on when to use such long quotations.) Double-space and indent as with the preceding poetry example. *Do not add quotation marks.*

> In the influential *Talley's Corner* from 1967, Elliot Liebow observes that "unskilled" construction work requires more skill than is generally assumed:
>
> A healthy, sturdy, active man of good intelligence requires from two to four weeks to break in on a construction job. . . . It frequently happens that his foreman or the craftsman he services is not willing to wait that long for him to get into condition or to learn at a glance the difference in size between a rough 2 x 8 and a finished 2 x 10. (62)

Do not use a paragraph indention for a quotation of a single complete paragraph or a part of a paragraph. Use paragraph indentions of one-quarter inch only for a quotation of two or more complete paragraphs.

58d Examining a sample paper in MLA style

The sample paper beginning on p. 452 follows MLA guidelines for overall format, parenthetical citations, and the list of works cited. Marginal annotations highlight features of the paper.

Note Because the sample paper addresses a current topic, many of its sources come from the Internet and do not use page or other reference numbers. Thus the in-text citations of these sources do not give reference numbers. In a paper relying solely on printed journals, books, and other traditional sources, most if not all in-text citations would include page numbers.

A note on outlines

Some instructors ask students to submit an outline of the final paper. For advice on constructing a formal or topic outline, see **1** pp. 19–20. Below is an outline of the sample paper following, written in complete sentences. Note that the thesis statement precedes either a topic or a sentence outline.

Thesis statement: Although green consumerism can help the environment, consumerism itself is the root of some of the most pressing ecological problems we face. To make a real difference, we must consume less.

I. Green products claiming to help the environment both appeal to and confuse consumers.
   A. The market for ecologically sound products is enormous.
   B. Determining whether or not a product is as green as advertised can be a challenge.
II. Green products don't solve the high rate of consumption that truly threatens the environment.
   A. Overconsumption is a significant cause of three of the most serious environmental problems.
      1. It depletes natural resources.
      2. It contributes to pollution, particularly from the greenhouse gases responsible for global warming.
      3. It produces a huge amount of solid waste.
   B. The availability of greener products has not reduced the environmental effects of consumption.
III. Since buying green products does not reduce consumption, other solutions must be found for environmental problems.
   A. Experts have proposed many far-reaching solutions, but they require concerted government action and could take decades to implement.

B. For shorter-term solutions, individuals can change their own behavior as consumers.
   1. Precycling may be the greenest behavior that individuals can adopt.
      a. Precycling means avoiding purchase of products that use raw materials and excessive packaging.
      b. More important, precycling means avoiding purchases of new products whenever possible.
   2. For unavoidable purchases, individuals can buy green products and influence businesses to embrace ecological goals.

Malik 1

Identification: writer's name, instructor's name, course title, date.

Justin Malik
Ms. Rossi
English 112-02
18 March 2008

Title centered.

Double-space throughout.

The False Promise of Green Consumerism

Introduction: establishes the issue with examples (first paragraph) and background (second paragraph).

They line the aisles of just about any store. They seem to dominate television and print advertising. Chances are that at least a few of them belong to you. From organic jeans to household cleaners to hybrid cars, products advertised as environmentally friendly are readily available and are so popular they're trendy. It's easy to see why Americans are buying these things in record numbers. The new wave of "green" consumer goods makes an almost irresistible promise: we can save the planet by shopping.

Citation form: no parenthetical citation because author and titles are named in the text and discussion cites entire works.

Citation form: shortened title for one of two works by the same author.

Thesis statement.

Saving the planet does seem to be urgent. Thanks partly to former Vice President Al Gore, who sounded the alarm in 1992 with *Earth in the Balance* and again in 2006 with *An Inconvenient Truth,* the threat of global warming has become a regular feature in the news media and a recurring theme in popular culture. Unfortunately, as Gore himself points out, climate change is just one of many environmental problems competing for our attention: the rainforests are vanishing, our air and our water are dangerously polluted, alarming numbers of species are facing extinction, and landfills are overflowing (*Earth* 23-28). All the bad news can be overwhelming, and most people feel powerless to halt the damage. Thus it is reassuring that we may be able to help by making small changes in what we buy—but it is not entirely true. Although green consumerism can help the environment, consumerism itself is the root of some of the most pressing ecological problems we face. To make a real difference, we must consume less.

Background on green products (next two paragraphs).

Citation form: source with more than three authors; no page number because source from an online database is unnumbered.

The market for items perceived as ecologically sound is enormous. Experts estimate that spending on green products already approaches $200 billion a year (Adler et al.). Shoppers respond well to new options, whether the purchase is as minor as a bottle of chemical-free dish soap or as major as a front-loading washing machine. Not surprisingly, businesses are

Malik 2

responding by offering as many new eco-products as they can. Sandra Jones of the *Chicago Tribune* reports that "green product introductions [have] skyrocketed" lately. She cites a market research report by the Mintel International Group: in the first five years of this century, new household products labeled as green rose from zero to 153, eco-conscious health and beauty aids increased by more than a thousand percent, and organic food and beverage options nearly tripled (B1). These new products are offered for sale at stores like Wal-Mart, Target, Home Depot, Starbucks, and Pottery Barn. It seems clear that green consumerism has grown into a mainstream interest.

Brackets signal word added to clarify the quotation.

Source author named in text, so not named in parenthetical citation.

Common-knowledge examples of stores and products do not require source citations.

Determining whether or not a product is as green as advertised can be a challenge. Claims vary: a product might be labeled as organic, biodegradable, energy efficient, recycled, carbon neutral, renewable, or just about anything that sounds environmentally positive. However, none of these terms carries a universally accepted meaning, and no enforceable labeling regulations exist ("It's Not Easy"). Some of the new product options offer clear environmental benefits: for instance, compact fluorescent light bulbs last ten times as long as regular bulbs and draw about a third of the electricity (Gore, *Inconvenient* 306), and paper made from recycled fibers saves many trees. But other "green" products just as clearly do little or nothing to help the environment: a disposable razor made with less plastic is still a disposable razor, destined for a landfill after only a few uses.

Citation form: shortened title for anonymous source; page number for a one-page source not required.

Citation form: author not named in the text; shortened title for one of two works by the same author. Position of citation clarifies which example comes from the source.

Distinguishing truly green products from those that are not so green merely scratches the surface of a much larger issue. The products aren't the problem; it's our high rate of consumption that poses the real threat to the environment. We seek what's newer and better—whether cars, clothes, phones, computers, televisions, shoes, or gadgets—and they all require resources to make, ship, and use them. Political scientists Thomas Princen, Michael Maniates, and Ken Conca maintain that overconsumption is a leading force behind several ecological crises, warning that

Environmental effects of consumption (next four paragraphs). Writer synthesizes information from half a dozen sources to develop his own ideas.

> ever-increasing pressures on ecosystems, life-supporting environmental services, and critical

Quotation over four lines set off without quotation marks. See p. 449.

Ellipsis mark signals omission from quotation.

Citation form with displayed quotation: follows sentence period. Authors named in text, so not named in parenthetical citation.

> natural cycles are driven not only by the sheer number of resource users . . . but also by the patterns of resource use themselves. (4)

Those patterns of resource use are disturbing. In just the second half of the twentieth century, gross world product (the global output of consumer goods) grew at five times the rate of population growth—a difference explained by a huge rise in consumption per person. (See fig. 1.) Such growth might be good for the economy, but it is bad for the environment. As fig. 1 shows, it is accompanied by the depletion of natural resources, increases in the carbon emissions that cause global warming, and increases in the amount of solid waste disposal.

Text refers to figure.

Figure presents numerical data visually.

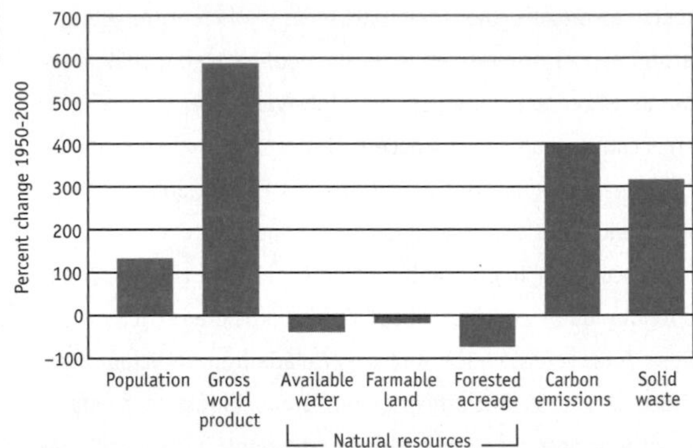

Figure caption explains the chart and gives complete source information.

Fig. 1. Global population, consumption, and environmental impacts, 1950-2000. Data from United Nations Development Programme; *Human Development Report: Changing Today's Consumption Patterns—For Tomorrow's Human Development*; New York: Oxford UP, 1998, 4; print; and from Earth Policy Inst.; "Eco-Economy Indicators"; *Earth Policy Institute*; EPI, Feb. 2008; Web; 6 Mar. 2008.

The first negative effect of overconsumption, the depletion of resources, occurs because the manufacture and distribution of any consumer product depends on the use of water, land, and raw materials such as wood, metal, and oil. Paul Hawken, a respected environmentalist, explains that just in the United States "[i]ndustry moves, mines, extracts, shovels, burns, wastes, pumps, and disposes of *4 million pounds of*

Brackets signal capitalization changed to integrate quotation with writer's sentence.

Malik 4

material in order to provide one average . . . family's needs for a year" (qtd. in DeGraaf, Wann, and Naylor 85; emphasis added). The United Nations Development Programme's 1998 *Human Development Report* (still the most comprehensive study of the environmental impacts of consumerism) warns that many regions in the world don't have enough water, productive soil, or forests to meet the basic needs of their populations (4). More recent data from the Earth Policy Institute show that as manufacturing and per-person consumption continue to rise, the supply of resources needed for survival continues to decline. Thus heavy consumption poses a threat not only to the environment but also to the well-being of the human race.

Citation form: source with three authors; "qtd. in" indicates indirect source (Hawken quoted by DeGraaf, Wann, and Naylor); "emphasis added" indicates italics was not in original quotation.

Citation form: corporate author is named in the text, so page number only.

Citation form: no parenthetical citation because author is named in the text and online source has no page or other reference numbers.

In addition to using up scarce natural resources, manufacturing and distributing products harms the earth by spewing pollution into the water, soil, and air. The most worrisome aspect of that pollution may be its link to global warming. As Al Gore explains, the energy needed to power manufacturing and distribution comes primarily from burning fossil fuels, a process that releases carbon dioxide and other greenhouse gases into the air. Those gases build up and trap heat in the earth's atmosphere. The result, most scientists now believe, is increasing global temperatures that will raise sea levels, expand deserts, and cause more frequent floods and hurricanes (*Inconvenient* 26-27, 81, 118-19, 184). As the preceding bar chart shows, carbon emissions, like production of consumer goods in general, are rising at rates out of proportion with population growth. The more we consume, the more we contribute to global warming.

Summary reduces six pages in the source to three sentences. Signal phrase and parenthetical citation mark boundaries of the summary.

Citation form: shortened title for one of two works by the same author; page numbers indicate exact locations of information in source.

Writer's own conclusion from preceding data.

As harmful as they are, gradual global warming and the depletion of resources half a world away can be difficult to comprehend or appreciate. A more immediate environmental effect of our buying habits can be seen in the volumes of trash those habits create. The US Environmental Protection Agency found that in a single year (2006), US residents, corporations, and institutions produced 251 million tons of municipal solid waste, amounting to "4.6 pounds per person per day" (1-2). Nearly a third of that trash came just from the

Citation form: author (a US government body) named in text.

Malik 5

wrappers, cans, bottles, and boxes used for shipping consumer goods. Yet the mountains of trash left over from consumption are only a part of the problem. In industrial countries overall, 90 percent of waste comes not from what gets thrown out, but from the manufacturing processes of converting natural resources into consumer products (DeGraaf, Wann, and Naylor 192). Nearly everything we buy creates waste in production, comes in packaging that gets discarded immediately, and ultimately ends up in landfills that are already overflowing.

Citation form: source with three authors; authors not named in text.

Unfortunately, the growing popularity of green products has not reduced the environmental effects of consumption. A study conducted by economists Jeff Rubin and Benjamin Tal for the research firm CIBC World Markets found that while eco-friendly and energy-efficient products have become more available, "consumption is growing by ever-increasing amounts." The authors give the example of automobiles: in the last generation, cars have become much more energy efficient, but the average American now drives 2500 more miles a year, for a net gain in energy use (4-5). At the same time, per-person waste production in the United States has risen by more than 20 percent (United States 1). Greener products may reduce our cost of consumption and even reduce our guilt about consumption, but they do not reduce consumption and its effects.

Environmental effects of green consumption.

Citation form: authors are named in the text, so page numbers only.

Citation form: US government source not named in text.

Writer's own conclusion from preceding data.

If buying green won't solve the problems caused by overconsumption, what will? Politicians, environmentalists, and economists have proposed an array of far-reaching ideas, including creating a financial market for carbon credits and offsets, aggressively taxing consumption and pollution, offering financial incentives for environmentally positive behaviors, and even abandoning market capitalism altogether (Muldoon). However, all of these are "top-down" solutions that require concerted government action. Gaining support for any one of them, putting it into practice, and getting results could take decades. In the meantime, the environment would continue to deteriorate. Clearly, short-term solutions are also essential.

Solutions to problem of consumption (next three paragraphs).

Citation form: author's name only, because scholarly article on the Web has no page or other reference numbers.

Malik 6

The most promising short-term solution is for individuals to change their own behavior as consumers. The greenest behavior that individuals can adopt may be precycling, the term widely used for avoiding purchases of products that involve the use of raw materials. Precycling includes choosing eco-friendly products made of recycled or nontoxic materials (such as aluminum-free deodorants and fleece made from soda bottles) and avoiding items wrapped in excessive packaging (such as kitchen tools strapped to cardboard and printer cartridges sealed in plastic clamshells). More important, though, precycling means not buying new things in the first place. Renting and borrowing, when possible, save money and resources; so do keeping possessions in good repair and not replacing them until absolutely necessary. Good-quality used items, from clothing to furniture to electronics, can be obtained for free, or very cheaply, through online communities like *Craigslist* and *Freecycle,* from thrift stores and yard sales, or by trading with friends and relatives. When consumers choose used goods over new, they can help to reduce demand for manufactured products that waste energy and resources, and they can help to keep unwanted items out of the waste stream.

Common-knowledge definition and writer's own examples do not require source citations.

Avoiding unnecessary purchases brings personal benefits as well. Brenda Lin, an environmental activist, explained in an e-mail interview that frugal living not only saves money but also provides pleasure:

Primary source: personal interview by e-mail.

> You'd be amazed at what people throw out or give away: perfectly good computers, oriental rugs, barely used sports equipment, designer clothes, you name it. . . . It's a game for me to find what I need in other people's trash or at Goodwill. You should see the shock on people's faces when I tell them where I got my stuff. I get almost as much enjoyment from that as from saving money and helping the environment at the same time.

Quotation of over four lines set off without quotation marks. See p. 449.

Ellipsis mark signals omission from quotation.

Lin's experience relates to a study of the personal and social consequences of consumerism by the sociologist Juliet B. Schor. Schor found that the more people buy, the less happy they tend to feel because of the stress of working longer

Citation form: no parenthetical citation because author is named in the text and interview has no page or other reference numbers.

hours to afford their purchases (11-12). Researching the opposite effect, Schor conducted interviews with hundreds of Americans who had drastically reduced their spending so that they would be less dependent on paid work. For these people, she discovered, a deliberately lower standard of living improved quality of life by leaving more time to spend with family and pursue personal interests (136-42). Reducing consumption, it turns out, does not have to translate into sacrifice.

Writer's own conclusion from two sources.

Benefits of green consumerism.

For unavoidable purchases like food and light bulbs, buying green can make a difference by influencing corporate decisions. Some ecologists and economists believe that as more shoppers choose earth-friendly products over their traditional counterparts—or boycott products that are clearly harmful to the environment—more manufacturers and retailers will look for ways to limit the environmental effects of their industrial practices and the goods they sell (Gore, *Earth* 193; Muldoon). Indeed, as environmental business consultant Gregory C. Unruh points out in an article for *Harvard Business Review*, several major companies, among them Wal-Mart, Coca-Cola, General Electric, and Nike, have already taken up sustainability initiatives in response to market pressure. In the process, the companies have discovered that environmentally minded practices tend to raise profits and strengthen customer loyalty (111-12). By giving industry solid, bottom-line reasons to embrace ecological goals, consumer demand for earth-friendly products can magnify the effects of individual action.

Citation form: two works in the same citation.

Citation form: author is named in the text, so page numbers only.

Conclusion: summary and a call for action.

Careful shopping can help the environment, but green doesn't necessarily mean "Go." All consumption depletes resources, increases the likelihood of global warming, and creates waste, so even eco-friendly products must be used in moderation. As individuals, we can each play a small role in helping the environment—and help ourselves at the same time—by not buying anything we don't really need, even if it seems environmentally sound. Reducing our personal impact on the earth is a small price to pay for preserving a livable planet for future generations.

Malik 8

New page, double-spaced. Sources alphabetized by authors' last names.

Works Cited

Adler, Jerry, et al. "The Greening of America." *Newsweek* 14 Aug. 2006: 46-50. *Master File Premier*. Web. 20 Feb. 2008.

An article with more than three authors, from a weekly magazine in an online database.

DeGraaf, John, David Wann, and Thomas H. Naylor. *Affluenza: The All-Consuming Epidemic.* San Francisco: Berrett-Koehler, 2001. Print.

A print book with three authors.

Earth Policy Inst. "Eco-Economy Indicators." *Earth Policy Institute.* EPI, Feb. 2008. Web. 6 Mar. 2008.

A short, titled work on a Web site, with a corporate author.

Gore, Al. *Earth in the Balance: Ecology and the Human Spirit.* Boston: Houghton, 1992. Print.

A print book with one author.

---. *An Inconvenient Truth: The Planetary Emergency of Global Warming and What We Can Do about It*. Emmaus: Rodale, 2006. Print.

Second source by author of two or more cited works: three hyphens replace author's name.

"It's Not Easy Buying Green." *Consumer Reports* Sept. 2007: 9. Print.

An anonymous article in a print monthly magazine, listed and alphabetized by title.

Jones, Sandra. "Green! It's Easy Being Green When It's in Vogue." *Chicago Tribune* 27 May 2007, final ed.: B1+. Print.

A print newspaper article.

Lin, Brenda. Message to the author. 7 Mar. 2008. E-mail.

A personal interview by e-mail.

Muldoon, Annie. "Where the Green Is: Examining the Paradox of Environmentally Conscious Consumption." *Electronic Green Journal* 23 (2006): n. pag. Web. 28 Feb. 2008.

An article in a Web scholarly journal that numbers only issues and does not use page numbers.

Princen, Thomas, Michael Maniates, and Ken Conca. Introduction. *Confronting Consumption.* Ed. Princen, Maniates, and Conca. Cambridge: MIT P, 2002. 1-20. Print.

An introduction to a print anthology.

Rubin, Jeff, and Benjamin Tal. "Does Energy Efficiency Save Energy?" *StrategEcon.* CIBC World Markets, 27 Nov. 2007. Web. 13 Mar. 2008.

A short, titled work on a Web site, by two authors.

Schor, Juliet B. *The Overspent American: Upscaling, Downshifting, and the New Consumer.* New York: Basic, 1998. Print.

A print book with one author.

United Nations Development Programme. *Human Development Report 1998: Changing Today's Consumption Patterns—For Tomorrow's Human Development.* New York: Oxford UP, 1998. Print.

A print book with a corporate author.

United States. Environmental Protection Agency. Solid Waste and Emergency Response. *Municipal Solid Waste*

A US government source with no named author, so government body given as author.

Malik 9

Generation, Recycling, and Disposal in the United States: Facts and Figures for 2006. US Environmental Protection Agency, Nov. 2007. Web. 4 Feb. 2008.

Unruh, Gregory C. "The Biosphere Rules." *Harvard Business Review* 86.2 (2008): 111-17. *Business Source Premier.* Web. 14 Mar. 2008.

An article in a scholarly journal that numbers volumes and issues, consulted in an online database.

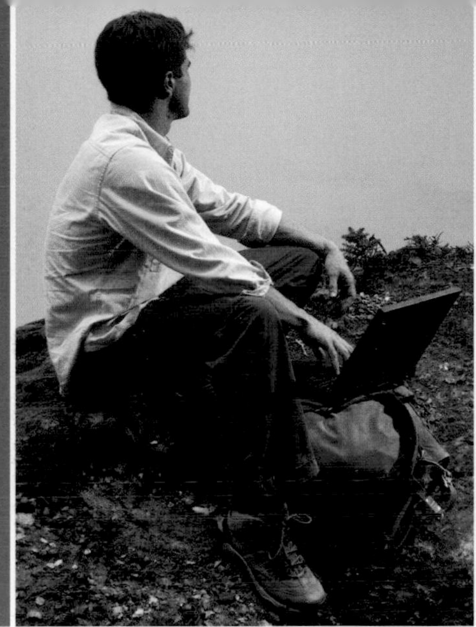

APA Documentation and Format

APA Documentation and Format

59 APA Documentation and Format *463*

a Parenthetical text citations *464*
b List of references *467*
c Format of paper *481*
d Sample paper *484*

APA parenthetical text citations

1. Author not named in your text *464*
2. Author named in your text *464*
3. A work with two authors *464*
4. A work with three to five authors *465*
5. A work with six or more authors *465*
6. A work with a group author *465*
7. A work with no author or an anonymous work *465*
8. One of two or more works by the same author(s) *466*
9. Two or more works by different authors *466*
10. An indirect source *466*
11. An electronic source *466*

APA references

Authors

1. One author *469*
2. Two to seven authors *469*
3. Eight or more authors *469*
4. A group author *469*
5. Author not named (anonymous) *469*
6. Two or more works by the same author(s) published in the same year *470*

Print periodicals

7. An article in a journal *470, 471*
8. An abstract of a journal article *470*
9. An article in a newspaper *472*
10. An article in a magazine *472*
11. A review *472*

Print books

12. Basic format for a book *472*
13. A book with an editor *472*
14. A book with a translator *473*
15. A later edition *473*
16. A work in more than one volume *473*
17. An article or a chapter in an edited book *473*

Web and other electronic sources

18. A journal article with a Digital Object Identifier (DOI) *474, 475*
19. A journal article without a DOI *474*
20. A periodical article in an online database *474*
21. An abstract of a journal article *476*
22. An article in a newspaper *476*
23. An article in a magazine *476*
24. Supplemental periodical content that appears only online *476*
25. A review *476*
26. A report or other material from the Web site of an organization or government *476*

27. A book *477*
28. An article in a reference work *477*
29. An article in a wiki *477*
30. A dissertation *477*
31. A podcast *478*
32. A film or video recording *478*
33. An image *478*
34. A message posted to a blog or discussion group *478*
35. A personal communication *478*

Other sources

36. A report *479*
37. A government publication *479*
38. A dissertation *479*
39. An interview *480*
40. A motion picture *480*
41. A musical recording *480*
42. A television series or episode *481*

59 APA Documentation and Format

The style guide for psychology and some other social sciences is the *Publication Manual of the American Psychological Association* (6th ed., 2010). The guidelines here reflect the second printing of the *Publication Manual,* which corrected some errors in the first printing. (The corrections are posted on the APA's Web site: *apastyle.org*.)

In APA documentation style, you acknowledge each of your sources twice:

- **In your text, a brief parenthetical citation adjacent to the borrowed material directs readers to a complete list of all the works you refer to.**
- **At the end of your paper, the list of references includes complete bibliographical information for every source.**

Every entry in the list of references has at least one corresponding citation in the text, and every in-text citation has a corresponding entry in the list of references.

This chapter describes APA text citations (next page) and references (p. 467), details APA document format (p. 481), and concludes with a sample APA paper (p. 484).

mycomplab

Visit *mycomplab.com* for more resources as well as exercises on APA documentation and format.

59a Writing APA parenthetical text citations

In APA documentation style, parenthetical citations within the text refer the reader to a list of sources at the end of the text. See the **APA** divider for an index to the models for various kinds of sources.

1. Author not named in your text

One critic of Milgram's experiments insisted that the subjects "should have been fully informed of the possible effects on them" (Baumrind, 1988, p. 34).

When you do not name the author in your text, place in parentheses the author's last name, the date of the source, and sometimes the page number as explained below. Separate the elements with commas. Position the reference so that it is clear what material is being documented *and* so that the reference fits as smoothly as possible into your sentence structure. (See **MLA** pp. 412–14 for guidelines.) The following would also be correct:

In the view of one critic of Milgram's experiments (Baumrind, 1988), the subjects "should have been fully informed of the possible effects on them" (p. 34).

Unless none is available, the APA requires a page or other identifying number for a direct quotation (as in the examples above) and recommends an identifying number for a paraphrase. Use an appropriate abbreviation before the number—for instance, p. for *page* and para. for *paragraph*. The identifying number may fall with the author and date (first example) or by itself in a separate pair of parentheses (second example). See also model 11, p. 466.

2. Author named in your text

Baumrind (1988) insisted that the subjects in Milgram's study "should have been fully informed of the possible effects on them" (p. 34).

When you use the author's name in the text, do not repeat it in the reference. Place the source date in parentheses after the author's name. Place any page or paragraph reference either after the borrowed material (as in the example) or with the date: (1988, p. 34). If you cite the same source again in the paragraph, you need not repeat the reference as long as it is clear that you are using the same source and the page number (if any) is the same.

3. A work with two authors

Pepinsky and DeStefano (1997) demonstrated that a teacher's language often reveals hidden biases.

One study (Pepinsky & DeStefano, 1997) demonstrated the hidden biases often revealed in a teacher's language.

When given in the text, two authors' names are connected by and. In a parenthetical citation, they are connected by an ampersand, &.

4. A work with three to five authors

Pepinsky, Dunn, Rentl, and Corson (1999) further demonstrated the biases evident in gestures.

In the first citation of a work with three to five authors, name all the authors. In the second and subsequent references to a work with three to five authors, generally give only the first author's name, followed by et al. (Latin abbreviation for "and others"):

In the work of Pepinsky et al. (1999), the loaded gestures included head shakes and eye contact.

However, two or more sources published in the same year could shorten to the same form—for instance, two references shortening to Pepinsky et al., 1999. In that case, cite the last names of as many authors as you need to distinguish the sources, and then give et al.: for instance, (Pepinsky, Dunn, et al., 1999) and (Pepinsky, Bradley, et al., 1999).

5. A work with six or more authors

One study (Rutter et al., 2003) attempted to explain these geographical differences in adolescent experience.

For six or more authors, even in the first citation of the work, give only the first author's name, followed by et al. If two or more sources published in the same year shorten to the same form, give additional names as explained with model 4.

6. A work with a group author

The students' later work improved significantly (Lenschow Research, 2009).

For a work that lists an institution, agency, corporation, or other group as author, treat the name of the group as if it were one person's name. If the name is long and has a familiar abbreviation, you may use the abbreviation in the second and subsequent citations. For example, you might abbreviate American Psychological Association as APA.

7. A work with no author or an anonymous work

One article ("Right to Die," 1996) noted that a death-row inmate may crave notoriety.

For a work with no named author, use the first two or three words of the title in place of an author's name, excluding an initial *The, A,* or *An.* Italicize book and journal titles, place quotation marks around article titles, and capitalize the significant words in all titles cited in the text. (In the reference list, however, do not use quotation marks for article titles, and capitalize only the first word in all but periodical titles. See p. 468.)

For a work that lists "Anonymous" as the author, use that word in the citation: (Anonymous, 2007).

8. One of two or more works by the same author(s)

At about age seven, most children begin to use appropriate gestures to reinforce their stories (Gardner, 1973a).

When you cite one of two or more works by the same author(s), the date will tell readers which source you mean—as long as your reference list includes only one source published by the author(s) in that year. If your reference list includes two or more works published by the same author(s) *in the same year,* the works should be lettered in the reference list (see p. 470). Then your parenthetical citation should include the appropriate letter with the date: 1973a in the example.

9. Two or more works by different authors

Two studies (Marconi & Hamblen, 1999; Torrence, 2007) found that monthly safety meetings can dramatically reduce workplace injuries.

List the sources in alphabetical order by their authors' names. Insert a semicolon between sources.

10. An indirect source

Supporting data appeared in a study by Chang (as cited in Torrence, 2007).

The phrase as cited in indicates that the reference to Chang's study was found in Torrence. Only Torrence then appears in the list of references.

11. An electronic source

Ferguson and Hawkins (2006) did not anticipate the "evident hostility" of participants (para. 6).

Electronic sources can be cited like printed sources, usually with the author's last name and the publication date. When quoting or paraphrasing electronic sources that number paragraphs instead of pages, provide the paragraph number preceded by para. If the source does not number pages or paragraphs but does include headings, list the heading under which the quotation appears and then (counting paragraphs yourself) the number of the paragraph in which the quotation appears—for example, (Endter & Decker, 2008, Method section, para. 3). When the source does not number pages or paragraphs or provide frequent headings, omit any reference number.

59b Preparing the APA reference list

In APA style, the in-text parenthetical citations refer to the list of sources at the end of the text. This list, titled References, includes full publication information on every source cited in the paper. The list falls at the end of the paper, numbered in sequence with the preceding pages. The sample below shows the elements and their spacing.

APA reference list

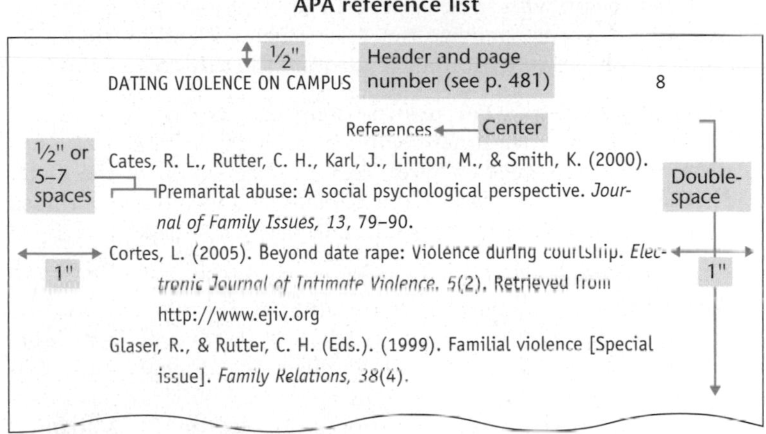

Arrangement Arrange sources alphabetically by the author's last name. If there is no author, alphabetize by the first main word of the title. Do *not* group sources by type (books, journals, and so on).

Spacing Double-space everything in the references, as shown in the sample, unless your instructor requests single spacing. (If you do single-space the entries themselves, always double-space *between* them.)

Indention As illustrated in the sample above, begin each entry at the left margin, and indent the second and subsequent lines five to seven spaces or one-half inch.

Punctuation Separate the parts of the reference (author, date, title, and publication information) with a period and one space. Do not use a final period in references that conclude with a DOI or a URL (see p. 474).

Authors For works with up to seven authors, list all authors with last name first, separating names and parts of names with commas. Use initials for first and middle names. Use an ampersand (&) before the last author's name. See model 3 (opposite) for the treatment of eight or more authors.

Publication date Place the publication date in parentheses after the author's or authors' names, followed by a period. Generally this date is the year only, though for some sources (such as magazine and newspaper articles) it includes the month and sometimes the day as well.

Titles In titles of books and articles, capitalize only the first word of the title, the first word of the subtitle, and proper nouns; all other words begin with small letters. In titles of journals, capitalize all significant words. Italicize the titles of books and journals. Do not italicize or use quotation marks around the titles of articles.

City of publication For print sources that are not periodicals (such as books or government publications), give the city of publication, a comma, the two-letter postal abbreviation of the state, and a colon. Omit the state if the publisher is a university whose name includes the state name, such as University of Arizona.

Publisher's name For nonperiodical print sources, give the publisher's name after the place of publication and a colon. Use shortened names for many publishers (such as Morrow for William Morrow), and omit "Co.," "Inc.," and "Publishers." However, give full names for associations, corporations, and university presses (such as Harvard University Press), and do not omit "Books" or "Press" from a publisher's name.

Page numbers Use the abbreviation p. or pp. before page numbers in books and in newspapers. Do *not* use the abbreviation for journals and magazines. For inclusive page numbers, include all figures: 667-668.

An index to the following models appears at the **APA** divider. If you don't see a model listed for the kind of source you used, try to find one that comes close, and provide ample information so that readers can trace the source. Often you will have to combine models to provide the necessary information on a source—for instance, combining "Two to seven authors" (model 2) and "An article in a journal" (model 7) for a journal article with two or more authors.

1 Listing authors

1. One author

Rodriguez, R. (1982). *A hunger of memory: The education of Richard Rodriguez.* Boston, MA: Godine.

The initial R. appears instead of the author's first name, even though the author's full first name appears on the source. In this book title, only the first words of the title and subtitle and the proper name are capitalized.

2. Two to seven authors

Nesselroade, J. R., & Baltes, P. B. (1999). *Longitudinal research in behavioral studies.* New York, NY: Academic Press.

Separate author's names with commas, and use an ampersand (&) before the last author's name.

3. Eight or more authors

Wimple, P. B., Van Eijk, M., Potts, C. A., Hayes, J., Obergau, W. R., Smith, H., . . . Zimmer, S. (2001). *Case studies in moral decision making among adolescents.* San Francisco, CA: Jossey-Bass.

For a work by eight or more authors, give the first six authors' names, an ellipsis mark (three spaced periods), and then the last author's name.

4. A group author

Lenschow Research. (2008). *Trends in secondary curriculum.* Baltimore, MD: Arrow Books.

For a work with a group author—such as a research group, a government agency, or a corporation—begin the entry with the group name. In the reference list, alphabetize the work as if the first main word (excluding *The, A,* and *An*) were an author's last name.

5. Author not named (anonymous)

Merriam-Webster's collegiate dictionary (11th ed.). (2008). Springfield, MA: Merriam-Webster.

Heros of the environment. (2009, October 5). *Time, 174*(13), 45-54.

When no author is named, list the work under its title and alphabetize it by the first main word (excluding any *The, A, An*).

For a work whose author is actually given as "Anonymous," use that word in place of the author's name and alphabetize it as if it were a name:

Anonymous. (2006). *Teaching research, researching teaching.* New York, NY: Alpine Press.

6. Two or more works by the same author(s) published in the same year

Gardner, H. (1973a). *The arts and human development.* New York, NY: Wiley.

Gardner, H. (1973b). *The quest for mind: Piaget, Lévi-Strauss, and the structuralist movement.* New York, NY: Knopf.

When citing two or more works by exactly the same author(s), published in the same year, arrange them alphabetically by the first main word of the title and distinguish the sources by adding a letter to the date. Both the date and the letter are used in citing the source in your text (see p. 466).

When citing two or more works by exactly the same author(s) but *not* published in the same year, arrange the sources in order of their publication dates, earliest first.

2 Listing print periodicals: Journals, newspapers, magazines

7. An article in a journal (print)

Selwyn, N. (2005). The social processes of learning to use computers. *Social Science Computer Review, 23,* 122-135.

The facing page shows the basic format for a print journal article and the location of the required information in the journal. If the print article has a Digital Object Identifier, add it at the end of the entry. See model 18, page 474.

Note Some journals number the pages of issues consecutively throughout a year, so that each issue after the first begins numbering where the previous issue left off—say, at page 132 or 416. For this kind of journal, give the volume number after the title, as in the preceding example. The page numbers are enough to guide readers to the issue you used. Other journals and most magazines start each issue with page 1. For these journals and magazines, place the issue number (not italicized) in parentheses immediately after the volume number. See model 10 for an example of a volume and issue number.

8. An abstract of a journal article (print)

Emery, R. E. (2006). Marital turmoil: Interpersonal conflict and the children of discord and divorce. *Psychological Bulletin, 92,* 310-330. Abstract obtained from *Psychological Abstracts*, 2007, *69,* Item 1320.

Format for a print journal article

① Selwyn, N. ② (2005). ③ The social processes of learning to use computers. ④ *Social Science Computer Review,* ⑤ *23*, ⑥ 122-135.

Journal cover

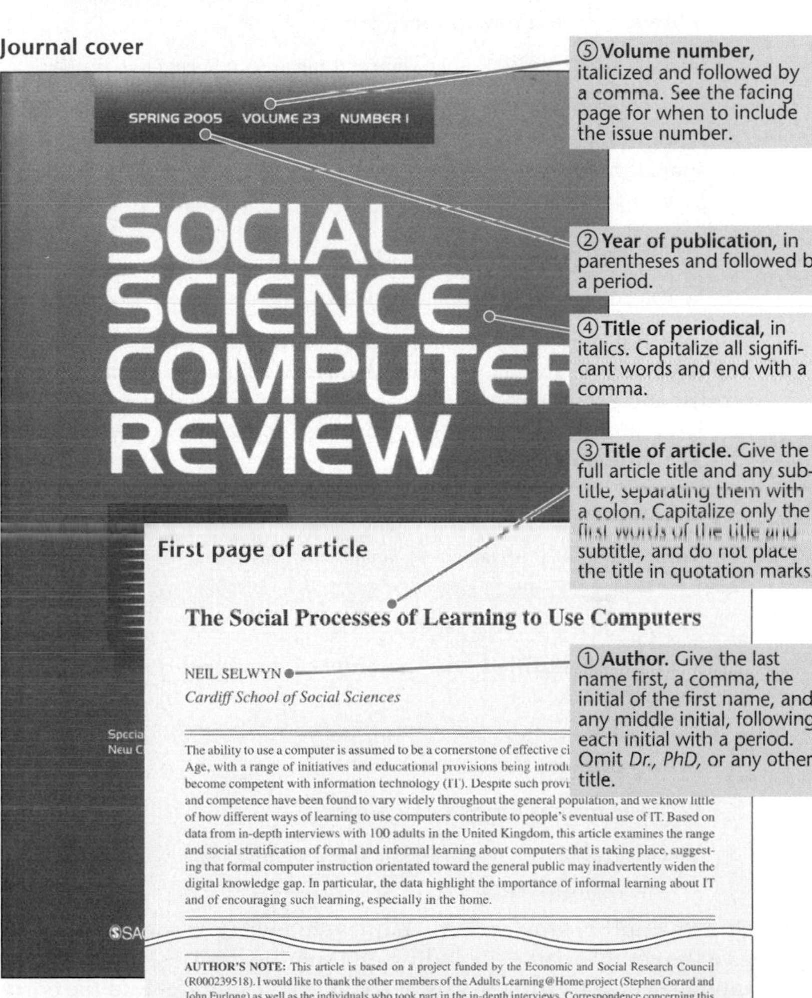

SPRING 2005 VOLUME 23 NUMBER I
SOCIAL SCIENCE COMPUTER REVIEW
First page of article
The Social Processes of Learning to Use Computers
NEIL SELWYN
Cardiff School of Social Sciences
The ability to use a computer is assumed to be a cornerstone of effective ci... Age, with a range of initiatives and educational provisions being introd... become competent with information technology (IT). Despite such provi... and competence have been found to vary widely throughout the general population, and we know little of how different ways of learning to use computers contribute to people's eventual use of IT. Based on data from in-depth interviews with 100 adults in the United Kingdom, this article examines the range and social stratification of formal and informal learning about computers that is taking place, suggesting that formal computer instruction orientated toward the general public may inadvertently widen the digital knowledge gap. In particular, the data highlight the importance of informal learning about IT and of encouraging such learning, especially in the home.
AUTHOR'S NOTE: This article is based on a project funded by the Economic and Social Research Council (R000239518). I would like to thank the other members of the Adults Learning@Home project (Stephen Gorard and John Furlong) as well as the individuals who took part in the in-depth interviews. Correspondence concerning this article may be addressed to Neil Selwyn, School of Social Sciences, Cardiff University, Glamorgan Building, King Edward VII Avenue, Cardiff CF10 3WT, UK; e-mail: selwynnc@cardiff.ac.uk.
122
⑤ **Volume number,** italicized and followed by a comma. See the facing page for when to include the issue number.
② **Year of publication,** in parentheses and followed by a period.
④ **Title of periodical,** in italics. Capitalize all significant words and end with a comma.
③ **Title of article.** Give the full article title and any subtitle, separating them with a colon. Capitalize only the first words of the title and subtitle, and do not place the title in quotation marks.
① **Author.** Give the last name first, a comma, the initial of the first name, and any middle initial, following each initial with a period. Omit *Dr., PhD,* or any other title.
⑥ **Inclusive page numbers of article,** without "pp." Do not omit any numerals.

When you cite the abstract of an article rather than the article itself, give full publication information for the article, followed by Abstract obtained from and the information for the collection of abstracts, including title, date, volume and issue numbers, and either page number or other reference number (Item 1320 in the example).

9. An article in a newspaper (print)

Stout, D. (2008, May 28). Blind win court ruling on U.S. currency. *The New York Times*, p. A23.

Give month *and* day along with year of publication. Use *The* in the newspaper name if the paper itself does. Precede the page number(s) with p. or pp.

10. An article in a magazine (print)

Newton-Small, J. (2009, October 5). Divided loyalties. *Time, 174*(13), 38.

Give the full date of the issue: year, followed by a comma, month, and day (if any). Give all page numbers even when the article appears on discontinuous pages, without "pp." If a magazine has volume and issue numbers, provide both because magazine issues are paginated separately. (See p. 470.)

11. A review (print)

Dinnage, R. (1987, November 29). Against the master and his men [Review of the book *A mind of her own: The life of Karen Horney,* by S. Quinn]. *The New York Times Book Review*, 10-11.

If the review is not titled, use the bracketed information as the title, keeping the brackets.

3 Listing print books

12. Basic format for a book (print)

Ehrenreich, B. (2007). *Dancing in the streets: A history of collective joy.* New York, NY: Holt.

Give the author's or authors' names, following models 1–4. Then give the complete title, including any subtitle. Italicize the title, and capitalize only the first words of the title and subtitle. End the entry with the city and state of publication and the publisher's name. (See p. 468 for how to treat these elements.)

13. A book with an editor (print)

Dohrenwend, B. S., & Dohrenwend, B. P. (Eds.). (1999). *Stressful life events: Their nature and effects*. New York, NY: Wiley.

List the editors' names as if they were authors, but follow the last name with (Eds.).—or (Ed.). with only one editor. Note the periods inside and outside the final parenthesis.

14. A book with a translator (print)

Trajan, P. D. (1927). *Psychology of animals* (H. Simone, Trans.). Washington, DC: Halperin.

The name of the translator appears in parentheses after the title, followed by a comma, Trans. and a closing parenthesis, and a final period.

15. A later edition (print)

Bolinger, D. L. (1981). *Aspects of language* (3rd ed.). New York, NY: Harcourt Brace Jovanovich.

The edition number in parentheses follows the title and is followed by a period.

16. A work in more than one volume (print)

Lincoln, A. (1953). *The collected works of Abraham Lincoln* (R. P. Basler, Ed.). (Vol. 5). New Brunswick, NJ: Rutgers University Press.

Lincoln, A. (1953). *The collected works of Abraham Lincoln* (R. P. Basler, Ed.). (Vols. 1-8). New Brunswick, NJ: Rutgers University Press.

The first entry cites a single volume (5) in the eight-volume set. The second cites all eight volumes. Use the abbreviation Vol. or Vols. in parentheses and follow the closing parenthesis with a period. In the absence of an editor's name, the description of volumes would follow the title directly: *The collected works of Abraham Lincoln* (Vol. 5).

17. An article or a chapter in an edited book (print)

Paykel, E. S. (1999). Life stress and psychiatric disorder: Applications of the clinical approach. In B. S. Dohrenwend & B. P. Dohrenwend (Eds.), *Stressful life events: Their nature and effects* (pp. 239-264). New York, NY: Wiley.

Give the publication date of the collection (1999 here) as the publication date of the article or chapter. After the article or chapter title and a period, say In and then provide the editors' names (in normal order), (Eds.) and a comma, the title of the collection, and the page numbers of the article in parentheses.

4 Listing Web and other electronic sources

In APA style, most electronic references begin as those for print references do: author, date, title. Then you add information on how to retrieve the source, generally giving either a DOI (see model 18) or a URL (see model 19). In addition, note the following:

- APA does not require your access date if the source is unlikely to change or if it has a publication date or edition or version number. See model 29 for use of an access date.
- APA does not require a full URL if the source can be located by searching the home page of a Web site. See model 32 for an example of a complete URL.
- When you need to divide a URL or DOI from one line to the next, APA calls for breaking before punctuation such as a period or slash. (But break after the two slashes in http://.) Do not hyphenate a URL or a DOI.

If you don't see a model for your particular electronic source, consult the index of models at the **APA** divider for a similar source type whose format you can adapt. If your source does not include all of the information needed for a complete citation, find and list what you can.

18. A journal article with a Digital Object Identifier (DOI) (Web)

Cunningham, J. A., & Selby, P. (2007). Relighting cigarettes: How common is it? *Nicotine and Tobacco Research, 9*, 621-623. doi:10.1080/14622200701239688

The facing page shows the basic format for a periodical article that you access either directly online or through an online database as well as the location of the required information on the source.

Many publishers now assign a Digital Object Identifier (DOI) to journal articles and other documents. A DOI functions as a unique identifier and a link to the text. When a DOI is available, include it instead of a URL or a database name. (The DOI may be evident on the source, or it may be found by clicking on "Article" or "CrossRef.") Do not add a period at the end of the DOI.

19. A journal article without a DOI (Web)

Polletta, F. (2008). Just talk: Public deliberation after 9/11. *Journal of Public Deliberation, 4*(1). Retrieved from http://services.bepress.com/jpd

When a journal article does not have a DOI, give the URL of the journal's home page in a statement beginning Retrieved from. Do not add a period at the end of the URL.

20. A journal article in an online database (Web)

Rosen, I. M., Maurer, D. M., & Darnall, C. R. (2008). Reducing tobacco use in adolescents. *American Family Physician, 77*, 483–490. Retrieved from http://www.aafp.org/online/en/home/publications/journals/afp.html

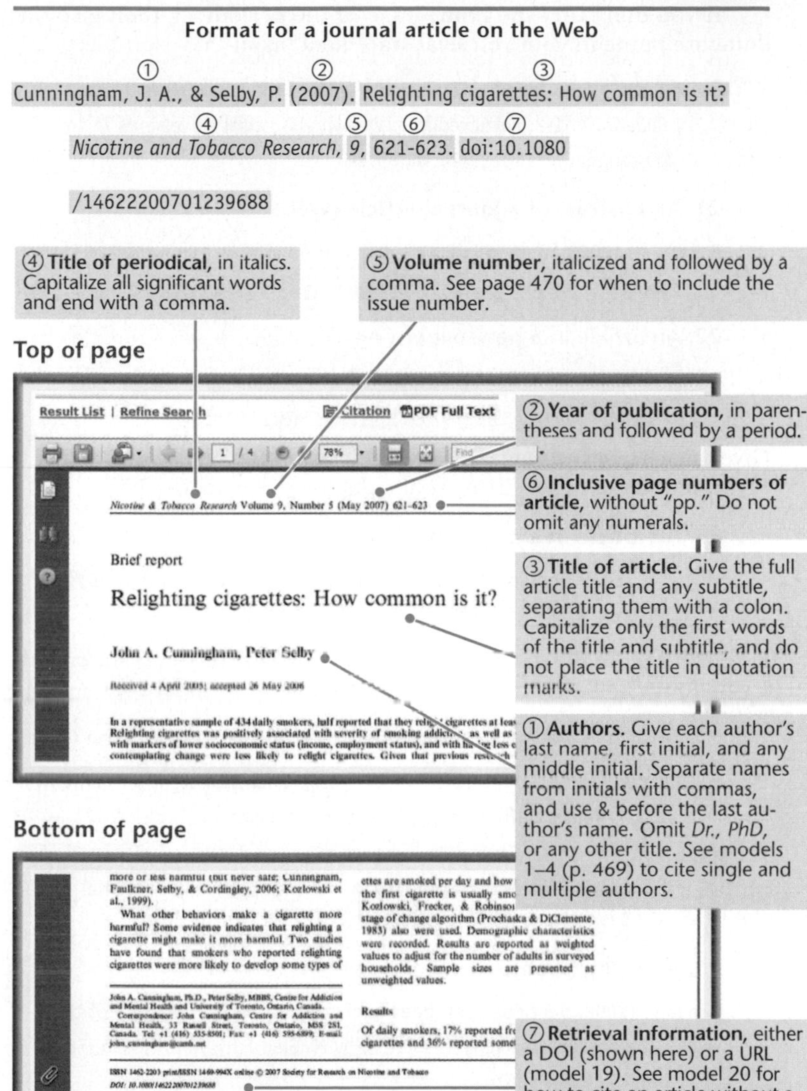
Format for a journal article on the Web
Cunningham, J. A., & Selby, P. (2007). Relighting cigarettes: How common is it?
Nicotine and Tobacco Research, 9, 621-623. doi:10.1080
/14622200701239688
④ Title of periodical, in italics. Capitalize all significant words and end with a comma.
⑤ Volume number, italicized and followed by a comma. See page 470 for when to include the issue number.
Top of page
Result List | Refine Search
Citation
PDF Full Text
Nicotine & Tobacco Research Volume 9, Number 5 (May 2007) 621–623
Brief report
Relighting cigarettes: How common is it?
John A. Cunningham, Peter Selby
② Year of publication, in parentheses and followed by a period.
⑥ Inclusive page numbers of article, without "pp." Do not omit any numerals.
③ Title of article. Give the full article title and any subtitle, separating them with a colon. Capitalize only the first words of the title and subtitle, and do not place the title in quotation marks.
① Authors. Give each author's last name, first initial, and any middle initial. Separate names from initials with commas, and use & before the last author's name. Omit Dr., PhD, or any other title. See models 1–4 (p. 469) to cite single and multiple authors.
Bottom of page
⑦ Retrieval information, either a DOI (shown here) or a URL (model 19). See model 20 for how to cite an article without a DOI that you retrieve from a database.

Generally, do not give the name of the database in which you found your source, because readers may not be able to find the source the same way you did. Instead, use a search engine to find the home page of the periodical and give the home page URL in your retrieval statement (preceding example).

If you don't find the home page of the periodical, then give the database name in your retrieval statement, as in this example:

Smith, E. M. (1926, March). Equal rights—internationally! *Life and Labor Bulletin, 4*, 1-2. Retrieved from Women and Social Movements in the United States, 1600-2000, database.

21. An abstract of a journal article (Web)

Polletta, F. (2008). Just talk: Public deliberation after 9/11. *Journal of Public Deliberation, 4*(1). Abstract retrieved from http://services.bepress.com/jpd

22. An article in a newspaper (Web)

Gootman, E. (2008, June 19). Gifted programs in the city are less diverse. *The New York Times*. Retrieved from http://www.nytimes.com

Give the URL of the magazine's home page in the retrieval statement. If you found the article in an online database, see model 20.

23. An article in a magazine (Web)

Young, E. (2009, February 21). Sleep well, keep sane. *New Scientist, 201*(26), 34-37. Retrieved from http://www.newscientist.com

Give the URL of the magazine's home page in the retrieval statement. If you found the article in an online database, see model 20.

24. Supplemental periodical content that appears only online (Web)

Gawande, A. (2009, June 1). More is less [Supplemental material]. *The New Yorker.* Retrieved from http://www.newyorker.com

If you cite material from a periodical's Web site that is not included in the print version of the publication, add [Supplemental material] after the title and give the URL of the publication's home page.

25. A review (Web)

Bond, M. (2008, December 18). Does genius breed success? [Review of the book *Outliers: The story of success*, by M. Gladwell]. *Nature, 456*, 785. doi:10.1038/456874a

Cite an online review like a print review (model 11, p. 472), concluding with retrieval information (here, a DOI).

26. A report or other material from the Web site of an organization or government (Web)

Ellerman, D., & Joskow, P. L. (2008, May). *The European Union's emissions trading system in perspective*. Retrieved from the Pew Center on Global Climate Change website: http://www.pewclimate.org

Treat the title of an independent Web document like the title of a book. Provide the name of the publishing organization as part of the retrieval statement when the publisher is not listed as the author, as in the preceding example.

If the document you cite is difficult to locate from the organization's home page, give the complete URL in the retrieval statement:

Union of Concerned Scientists. *Clean vehicles*. (2009, April 24). Retrieved from http://www.ucsusa.org/clean_vehicles

If the document you cite is undated, use the abbreviation n.d. in place of the publication date and give the date of your access in the retrieval statement:

U.S. Department of Agriculture. (n.d.). *Inside the Pyramid*. Retrieved April 23, 2008, from http://www.mypyramid.gov/pyramid/index.html

27. A book (Web)

Hernandez, L. M., & Munthali, A. W. (Eds.). (2007). *Training physicians for public health careers*. Retrieved from http://books.nap.edu/catalog.php?record_id=11915

For online books, replace the publisher's city and name with a retrieval statement. See models 14–17 (pp. 472–73) to cite variations in book entries: a translator, a later edition, a book in more than one volume, and an article or a chapter in a book.

28. An article in a reference work (Web)

Perception. (2008). In *Encyclopaedia Britannica Online*. Retrieved from http://www.britannica.com

29. An article in a wiki (Web)

Clinical neuropsychology. (2008, January 27). Retrieved August 3, 2009, from Wikipedia: http://en.wikipedia.org/wiki/Clinical_neuropsychology

Give your date of retrieval for sources that are likely to change, such as this wiki.

30. A dissertation (Web)

A dissertation in a commercial database:

McFaddin, M. O. (2007). *Adaptive reuse: An architectural solution for poverty and homelessness* (Doctoral dissertation). Available from ProQuest Dissertations and Theses database. (ATT 1378764)

If a dissertation is from a commercial database, give the name of the database in the retrieval statement, followed by the accession or order number in parentheses.

A dissertation in an institutional database:

Chang, J. K. (2003). *Therapeutic intervention in treatment of injuries to the hand and wrist* (Doctoral dissertation). Retrieved from http://medsci.archive.liasu.edu/61724

If a dissertation is from an institution's database, give the URL in the retrieval statement.

See also model 38 (p. 479) for examples of print dissertations.

31. A podcast (Web)

Ferracca, J. (Producer). (2008, June 11). Who owns antiquities? [Audio podcast]. *Here on earth: Radio without borders.* Retrieved from http://www.wpr.org/hereonearth

32. A film or video recording (Web)

Green Children Foundation (Producer). (2008, January 7). *The green children visit China* [Video file]. Retrieved from http://youtube.com/watch?v=uD4xfLTxCsY

If the film or video you cite is difficult to locate from the home page of the Web site, give the complete URL in the retrieval statement, as in the example.

33. An image (Web)

United Nations Population Fund (Cartographer). (2005). *Percent of population living on less than $1/day* [Demographic map]. Retrieved from http://www.unfpa.org

34. A message posted to a blog or discussion group (Web)

Munger, D. (2009, May 9). Does recess really improve classroom behavior? [Web log post]. Retrieved from http://scienceblogs.com/cognitivedaily

Include postings to blogs and discussion groups in your list of references *only* if they are retrievable by others. (The source above is retrievable by a search of the home page URL.) Follow the message title with [Web log post], [Electronic mailing list message], or [Online forum comment]. Include the name of the blog or discussion group in the retrieval statement if it isn't part of the URL.

35. A personal communication (text citation)

At least one member of the research team has expressed reservations about the design of the study (L. Kogod, personal communication, February 6, 2006).

Personal e-mail and other online postings that are not retrievable by others should be cited only in your text, as here, not in your list of references.

5 Listing other sources

36. A report (print)

Gerald, K. (2003). *Medico-moral problems in obstetric care* (Report No. NP-71). St. Louis, MO: Catholic Hospital Association.

Treat a printed report like a book, but provide any report number in parentheses immediately after the title, with no punctuation between them.

For a report from the Educational Resources Information Center (ERIC), provide the ERIC document number in parentheses at the end of the entry:

Jolson, M. K. (2001). *Music education for preschoolers* (Report No. TC-622). New York, NY: Teachers College, Columbia University. (ERIC Document Reproduction Service No. ED264488)

37. A government publication (print)

Hawaii. Department of Education. (2008). *Kauai district schools, profile 2007-08.* Honolulu, HI: Author.

Stiller, A. (2002). *Historic preservation and tax incentives*. Washington, DC: U.S. Department of the Interior.

If no person is named as the author, list the publication under the name of the sponsoring agency. When the agency is both the author and the publisher, use Author in place of the publisher's name, as in the first example.

For legal materials such as court decisions, laws, and testimony at hearings, the APA recommends formats that correspond to conventional legal citations. The following example of a congressional hearing includes the full title, the number of the Congress, the page number where the hearing transcript starts in the official publication, and the date of the hearing.

Medicare payment for outpatient physical and occupational therapy services: Hearing before the Committee on Ways and Means, House of Representatives, 110th Cong. 3 (2007).

38. A dissertation (print)

A dissertation abstracted in DAI:

Steciw, S. K. (1986). Alterations to the Pessac project of Le Corbusier. *Dissertation Abstracts International, 46*(6), 565C.

An unpublished dissertation:

Hernandez, A. J. (2005). *Persistent poverty: Transient work and workers in today's labor market* (Unpublished doctoral dissertation). University of Illinois, Urbana-Champaign.

39. An interview (print)

Schenker, H. (2007). No peace without third-party intervention [Interview with Shulamit Aloni]. *Palestine-Israel Journal of Politics, Economics, and Culture, 14*(4), 63-68.

List a published interview under the interviewer's name, and provide the title, if any, without italics or quotation marks. If there is no title, or if the title does not indicate the interview format or the interviewee (as in the example), add a bracketed explanation. End with the publication information for the kind of source the interview appears in (here, a journal).

An interview you conduct yourself should not be included in the list of references. Instead, use an in-text parenthetical citation, as shown in model 35 (p. 478) for a nonretrievable online posting.

40. A motion picture

American Psychological Association (Producer). (2001). *Ethnocultural psychotherapy* [DVD]. Available from http://www.apa.org/videos

Howard, R. (Director). (2001). *A beautiful mind* [Motion picture]. United States: Universal.

Depending on whose work you are citing, begin with the name or names of the creator, director, producer, or primary contributor, followed by the function in parentheses. (The second example would begin with the producer's name if you were citing the motion picture as a whole, not specifically the work of the director.) Add the medium in brackets after the title: [Motion picture] (for film), [DVD], or [Videocassette]. For a work in wide circulation (second example), give the country of origin and the studio that released the picture. For a work that is not widely circulated (first example), give the distributior's address or URL.

41. A musical recording

Springsteen, B. (2002). Empty sky. On *The rising* [CD]. New York, NY: Columbia.

Begin with the name of the writer or composer. (If you cite another artist's recording of the work, provide this information after the title of the work—for example, [Recorded by E. Davila].) Give the medium in brackets ([CD], [LP], and so on). Finish with the city, state, and name of the recording label.

42. A television series or episode

Rhimes, S. (Executive Producer). (2008). *Grey's anatomy* [Television series]. New York, NY: CBS.

McKee S. (Writer), & Tinker, M. (Director). (2008). Piece of my heart [Television series episode]. In S. Rhimes (Executive Producer), *Grey's anatomy*. New York, NY: CBS.

For a television series, begin with the producers' names and identify their function in parentheses. Add [Television series] after the series title, and give the city and name of the network. For an episode, begin with the writer and then the director, identifying the function of each in parentheses, and add [Television series episode] after the episode title. Then provide the series information, beginning with In and the producers' names and function, giving the series title, and ending with the city and name of the network.

59c Formatting a paper in APA style

The following guidelines for document format reflect the second printing of the APA *Publication Manual*, 6th edition, which corrected some errors in the first printing. (The corrections are posted on the APA's Web site: *apastyle.org*.) Check with your instructor for any modifications to this format.

Note See p. 467 for the APA format of a reference list. And see 1 pp. 54–64 for guidelines on type fonts, lists, tables and figures, and other elements of document design.

Margins Use one-inch margins on the top, bottom, and both sides.

Spacing and indentions Double-space everywhere. (The only exception is tables and figures, where related data, labels, and other elements may be single-spaced.) Indent paragraphs and displayed quotations one-half inch or five to seven spaces.

Paging Begin numbering on the title page, and number consecutively through the end (including the reference list). Provide a header about one-half inch from the top of every page, as shown in the samples on the next page. The header consists of the page number on the far right and your full or shortened title on the far left. Type the title in all-capital letters. On the title page only, precede the title with the label Running head and a colon. Omit this label on all other pages.

Title page Include the full title, your name, the course title, the instructor's name, and the date. (See the next page.) Type the title on the top half of the page, followed by the identifying information, all centered horizontally and double-spaced.

APA title page

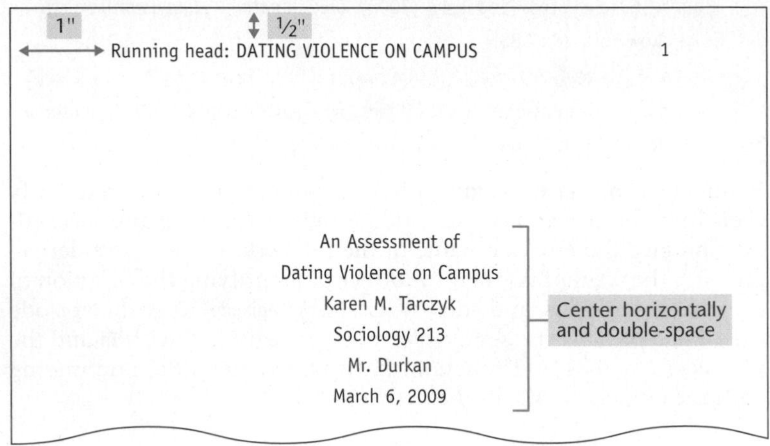

1"
½"
Running head: DATING VIOLENCE ON CAMPUS
1
An Assessment of
Dating Violence on Campus
Karen M. Tarczyk
Sociology 213
Mr. Durkan
March 6, 2009
Center horizontally and double-space

APA abstract

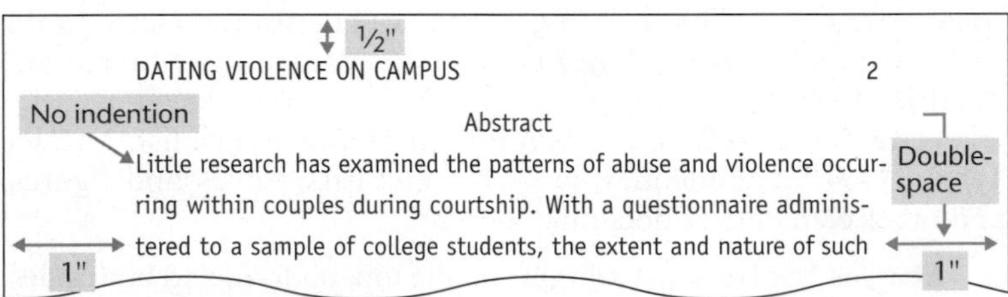

First page of APA body

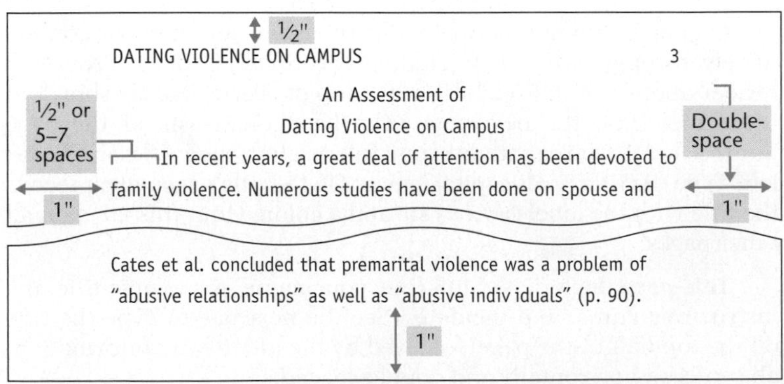

½"
DATING VIOLENCE ON CAMPUS
3
An Assessment of
Dating Violence on Campus
½" or 5–7 spaces
In recent years, a great deal of attention has been devoted to
family violence. Numerous studies have been done on spouse and
Double-space
1"
1"
Cates et al. concluded that premarital violence was a problem of
"abusive relationships" as well as "abusive indiv iduals" (p. 90).
1"

Later page of APA body

DATING VIOLENCE ON CAMPUS 4

All the studies indicate a problem that is being neglected. My objective was to gather data on the extent and nature of premarital violence and to discuss possible interpretations.

Method

Sample

Double-space

I conducted a survey of 200 students (134 females, 66 males) at a large state university in the northeastern United States. The sample consisted of students enrolled in an introductory sociology course.

Abstract Summarize (in a maximum of 120 words) your subject, research method, findings, and conclusions. (See the next page.) Put the abstract on a page by itself.

Body Begin with a restatement of the paper's title and then an introduction (not labeled). The introduction concisely presents the problem you researched, your research method, the relevant background (such as related studies), and the purpose of your research.

The next section, labeled **Method**, provides a detailed discussion of how you conducted your research, including a description of the research subjects, any materials or tools you used (such as questionnaires or surveys), and the procedure you followed. In the illustration on p. 483, the labels **Method** and **Sample** are first-level and second-level headings, respectively. When you need one, two, or three levels of headings, use the following formats, always double-spacing above and below:

First-Level Heading

Second-Level Heading

Third-level heading. Run this heading into the text paragraph.

The **Results** section (labeled with a first-level heading) summarizes the data you collected, explains how you analyzed them, and presents them in detail, often in tables, graphs, or charts.

The **Discussion** section (labeled with a first-level heading) interprets the data and presents your conclusions. (When the discussion is brief, you may combine it with the previous section under the heading **Results and Discussion**.)

The References section, beginning a new page, includes all your sources. See pp. 467–68 for an explanation and sample.

Long quotations Run into your text all quotations of forty words or less, enclosed in quotation marks. For quotations of more than forty words, set them off from your text by indenting all lines one-half inch or five to seven spaces, double-spacing throughout.

> Echoing the opinions of other Europeans at the time, Freud (1961) had a poor view of Americans:
>
> > The Americans are really too bad. . . . Competition is much more pungent with them, not succeeding means civil death to every one, and they have no private resources apart from their profession, no hobby, games, love or other interests of a cultured person. And success means money. (p. 86)

Do not use quotation marks around a quotation displayed in this way.

Illustrations Present data in tables and figures (graphs or charts), as appropriate. (See p. 486 and **1** pp. 61–64 for examples.) Begin each illustration on a separate page. Number each kind of illustration consecutively and separately from the other (Table 1, Table 2, etc., and Figure 1, Figure 2, etc.). Refer to all illustrations in your text—for instance, (see Figure 3). Generally, place illustrations immediately after the text references to them.

59d Examining a sample paper in APA style

The following excerpts from a sociology paper illustrate elements of a research paper using the APA style of documentation and format.

[Title page.]

Shortened title and page number.

Running head: DATING VIOLENCE ON CAMPUS 1

Double-space all information: title, name, course title, instructor, date.

An Assessment of
Dating Violence on Campus
Karen M. Tarczyk
Sociology 213
Mr. Durkan
March 6, 2008

[New page.]

DATING VIOLENCE ON CAMPUS 2

Abstract: summary of subject, research method, conclusions.

Double-space throughout.

Abstract

Little research has examined the patterns of abuse and violence occurring within couples during courtship. With a questionnaire administered to a sample of college students, the extent and nature of such abuse and violence were investigated. The results, interpretations, and implications for further research are discussed.

An Assessment of
Dating Violence on Campus

Title repeated on first text page.

In recent years, a great deal of attention has been devoted to family violence. Numerous studies have been done on spouse and child abuse. However, violent behavior occurs in dating relationships as well, yet the problem of dating violence has been relatively ignored by sociological research. It should be examined further since the premarital relationship is one context in which individuals learn and adopt behaviors that surface in marriage.

Introduction: presentation of the problem researched by the writer.

The sociologist James Makepeace (1989) contended that courtship violence is a "potential mediating link" between violence in one's family of orientation and violence in one's later family of procreation (p. 103). Studying dating behaviors at Bemidji State University in Minnesota, Makepeace reported that one-fifth of the respondents had had at least one encounter with dating violence. He then extended these percentages to students nationwide, suggesting the existence of a major hidden social problem.

Citation form: author named in the text.

Citation form: page number given for quotation.

More recent research supports Makepeace's. Cates, Rutter, Karl, Linton, and Smith (2000) found that 22.3% of respondents at Oregon State University had been either the victim or the perpetrator of premarital violence. Another study (Cortes, 2005) found that so-called date rape, while much more publicized and discussed, was reported by many fewer woman respondents (2%) than was other violence during courtship (21%).

Citation form: source with three to five authors, named in the text.

Citation form: author not named in the text.

[The introduction continues.]

All these studies indicate a problem that is being neglected. My objective was to gather data on the extent and nature of premarital violence and to discuss possible interpretations.

Method

Sample

First- and second-level headings.

I conducted a survey of 200 students (134 females, 66 males) at a large state university in the northeastern United States. The sample consisted of students enrolled in an introductory sociology course.

"Method" section: discussion of how research was conducted.

[The explanation of method continues.]

The Questionnaire

A questionnaire exploring the personal dynamics of relationships was distributed during regularly scheduled class. Questions were answered anonymously in a 30-minute period. The survey consisted of three sections.

DATING VIOLENCE ON CAMPUS 4

[The explanation of method continues.]

Section 3 required participants to provide information about their current dating relationships. Levels of stress and frustration, communication between partners, and patterns of decision making were examined. These variables were expected to influence the amount of violence in a relationship. The next part of the survey was adopted from Murray Strauss's Conflict Tactics Scales (1992). These scales contain 19 items designed to measure conflict and the means of conflict resolution, including reasoning, verbal aggression, and actual violence. The final page of the questionnaire contained general questions on the couple's use of alcohol, sexual activity, and overall satisfaction with the relationship.

"Results" section: summary and presentation of data.

Results

The questionnaire revealed significant levels of verbal aggression and threatened and actual violence among dating couples. A high number of students, 50% (62 of 123 subjects), reported that they had been the victim of verbal abuse, either being insulted or sworn at. In addition, almost 14% (17 of 123) of respondents admitted being threatened with some type of violence, and more than 14% (18 of 123) reported being pushed, grabbed, or shoved. (See Table 1.)

Reference to table.

[The explanation of results continues.]

[Table on a page by itself.]

DATING VIOLENCE ON CAMPUS 5

Table presents data in clear format.

Table 1

Incidence of Courtship Violence

Type of violence	Number of students reporting	Percentage of sample
Insulted or swore	62	50.4
Threatened to hit or throw something	17	13.8
Threw something	8	6.5
Pushed, grabbed, or shoved	18	14.6
Slapped	8	6.5
Kicked, bit, or hit with fist	7	5.7
Hit or tried to hit with something	2	1.6
Threatened with a knife or gun	1	0.8
Used a knife or gun	1	0.8

DATING VIOLENCE ON CAMPUS 6

Discussion

"Discussion" section: interpretation of data and presentation of conclusions.

Violence within premarital relationships has been relatively ignored. The results of the present study indicate that abuse and force do occur in dating relationships. Although the percentages are small, so was the sample. Extending them to the entire campus population of 5,000 would mean significant numbers. For example, if the nearly 6% incidence of being kicked, bitten, or hit with a fist is typical, then 300 students might have experienced this type of violence.

[The discussion continues.]

If the courtship period is characterized by abuse and violence, what accounts for it? The other sections of the survey examined some variables that appear to influence the relationship. Level of stress and frustration, both within the relationship and in the respondent's life, was one such variable. The communication level between partners, both the frequency of discussion and the frequency of agreement, was another.

[The discussion continues.]

The method of analyzing the data in this study, utilizing frequency distributions, provided a clear overview. However, more tests of significance and correlation and a closer look at the social and individual variables affecting the relationship are warranted. The courtship period may set the stage for patterns of married life. It merits more attention.

[New page.]

DATING VIOLENCE ON CAMPUS 7

New page for reference list.

References

Cates, R. L., Rutter, C. H., Karl, J., Linton, M., & Smith, K. (2000). Premarital abuse: A social psychological perspective. *Journal of Family Issues, 13*, 79-90.

Cortes, L. (2005). Beyond date rape: Violence during courtship. *Electronic Journal of Intimate Violence, 5*(2). Retrieved from http://www.ejiv.org

Glaser, R., & Rutter, C. H. (Eds.). (1999). Familial violence [Special issue]. *Family Relations, 38*(4).

Makepeace, J. M. (1989). Courtship violence among college students. *Family Relations, 28*(6), 97-103.

Strauss, M. L. (1992). *Conflict Tactics Scales*. New York, NY: Sociological Tests.

An article in a print journal.

An article in an online journal without a Digital Object Identifier.

A book. ("Tactics Scales" is part of a proper name and so is capitalized.)

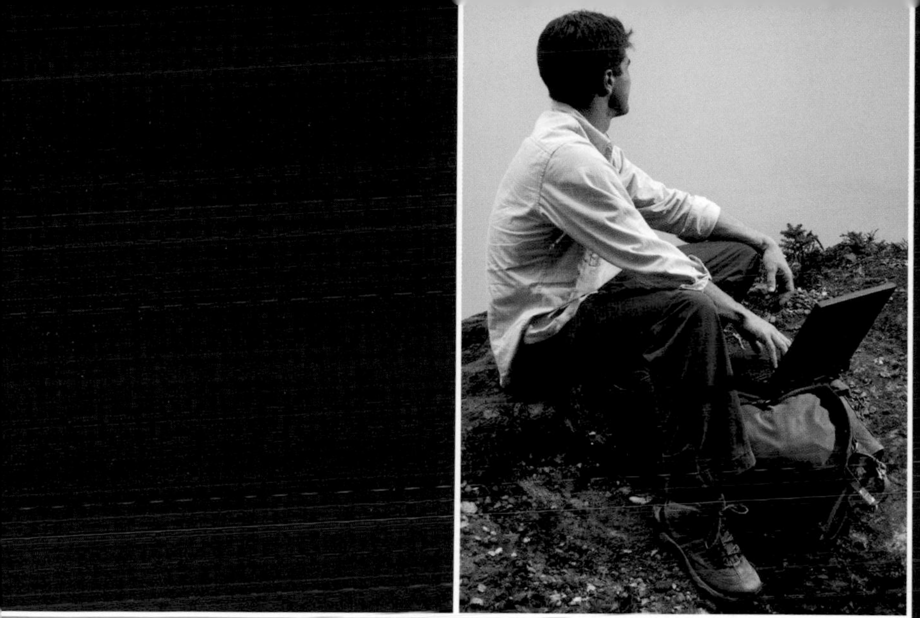

Chicago and CSE Documentation

Chicago and CSE Documentation

60 Chicago Documentation *491*

- a Notes and works-cited entries *491*
- b Models *494*

61 CSE Documentation *502*

- a Name-year text citations *502*
- b Numbered text citations *502*
- c List of references *503*

Chicago note and works-cited models

Authors

1. One, two, or three authors *494*
2. More than three authors *494*
3. Author not named (anonymous) *494*

Print periodicals

4. An article in a journal *495*
5. An article in a newspaper *495*
6. An article in magazine *495*
7. A review *495*

Books

8. Basic format for a book *495*
9. A book with an editor *496*
10. A book with an author and an editor *496*
11. A translation *496*
12. A later edition *496*
13. A work in more than one volume *496*
14. A selection from an anthology *496*
15. A work in a series *497*
16. An article in a reference work *497*

Web and other electronic sources

17. An article in a journal *497*
18. An article in a magazine *497*
19. An article in a newspaper *498*
20. An article in an online database *498*
21. A book *498*
22. An article in a reference work *498*
23. An audio or visual source *498*
24. A message posted to a blog or discussion group *499*
25. Electronic mail *499*
26. A work on CD-ROM or DVD-ROM *499*

Other sources

27. A government publication *499*
28. A published letter *500*
29. A published or broadcast interview *500*
30. A personal letter or interview *500*
31. A work of art *500*
32. A film, DVD, or video recording *500*
33. A sound recording *500*

Shortened notes *501*

CSE references

Authors

1. One author *504*
2. Two to ten authors *504*
3. More than ten authors *504*
4. Author not named *505*
5. Two or more cited works by the same author(s) published in the same year *505*

Print periodicals

6. An article in a journal *505*
7. An article in a newspaper *505*
8. An article in a magazine *505*

Print books

9. Basic format for a book *505*
10. A book with an editor *505*
11. A selection from a book *506*

Web and other electronic sources

12. An article in a journal *506*
13. An article in a database *506*
14. A book *507*
15. A Web site *507*
16. A message posted to a discussion list *507*
17. A personal online communication *507*
18. A document on CD-ROM or DVD-ROM *507*

Other sources

19. A report written and published by the same organization *508*
20. A report written and published by different organizations *508*
21. An audio or visual recording *508*

60 Chicago Documentation

History, art history, philosophy, and some other humanities use endnotes or footnotes to document sources, following one style recommended by *The Chicago Manual of Style* (15th ed., 2003) and the student guide adapted from it, Kate L. Turabian's *A Manual for Writers of Research Papers, Theses, and Dissertations* (7th ed., revised by Wayne C. Booth, Gregory G. Colomb, and Joseph M. Williams, 2007).

60a Using Chicago notes and works-cited entries

In the Chicago note style, raised numerals in the text refer to footnotes (bottoms of pages) or endnotes (end of paper). These

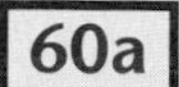

Visit *mycomplab.com* for more resources on Chicago documentation.

notes contain complete source information. A separate list of works cited is optional: ask your instructor for his or her preference.

Whether providing footnotes or endnotes, single-space each note and double-space between notes, as shown in the samples below. Separate footnotes from the text with a short line. Place endnotes directly after the text, beginning on a new page. For the list of sources at the end of the paper, use the format on the facing page. Arrange the sources alphabetically by the authors' last names.

Chicago footnotes

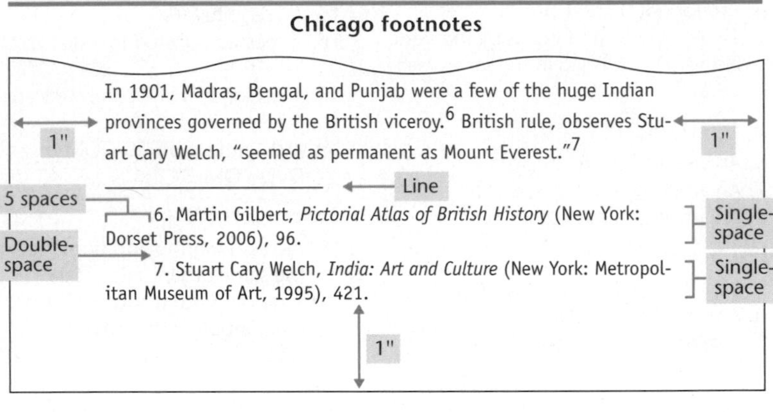

Chicago endnotes

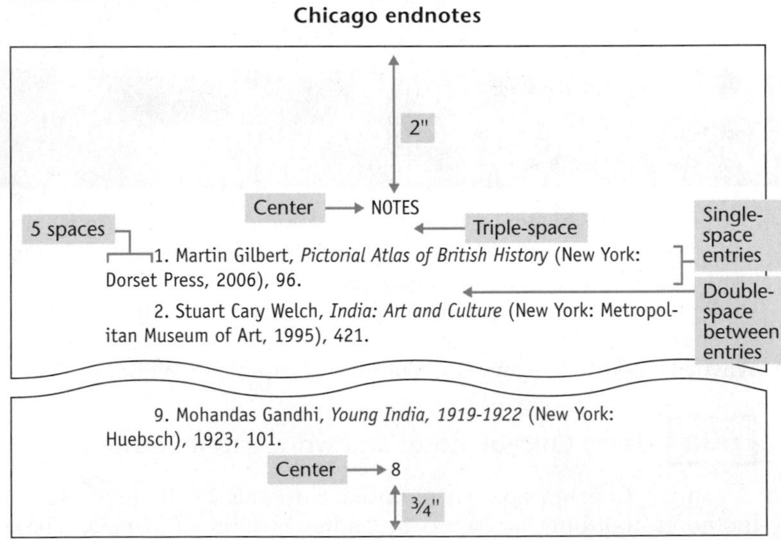

The note and works-cited entry on the facing page illustrate the essentials of each type of reference.

Chicago list of works cited

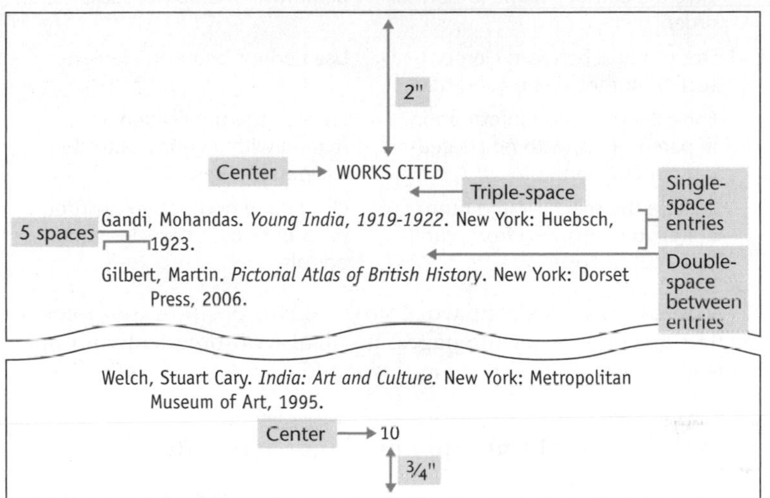

2"
Center → WORKS CITED
Triple-space
Single-space entries
5 spaces
Gandi, Mohandas. *Young India, 1919-1922*. New York: Huebsch, 1923.
Double-space between entries
Gilbert, Martin. *Pictorial Atlas of British History*. New York: Dorset Press, 2006.
Welch, Stuart Cary. *India: Art and Culture*. New York: Metropolitan Museum of Art, 1995.
Center → 10
¾"

Note

6. Martin Gilbert, *Pictorial Atlas of British History* (New York: Dorset Press, 2006), 96.

Works-cited entry

Gilbert, Martin. *Pictorial Atlas of British History*. New York: Dorset Press, 2006.

Treat some features of notes and works-cited entries the same:

- Single-space each note or entry, and double-space between the notes.
- Italicize or underline the titles of books and periodicals. Ask your instructor for his or her preference.
- Enclose in quotation marks the titles of parts of books or articles in periodicals.
- Do not abbreviate publishers' names, but omit "Inc.," "Co.," and similar abbreviations.
- Do not use "p." or "pp." before page numbers.

Treat other features of notes and works-cited entries differently:

Note	**Works-cited entry**
Start with a number that corresponds to the note number in the text.	Do not begin with a number.
Indent the first line five spaces.	Indent the second and subsequent lines five spaces.

Note	Works-cited entry
Give the author's name in normal order.	Begin with the author's last name.
Use commas between elements such as author's name and title.	Use periods between elements.
Enclose publication information in parentheses, with no preceding punctuation.	Precede the publication information with a period, and don't use parentheses.
Include the specific page number(s) you borrowed from, omitting "p." or "pp."	Omit page numbers except for parts of books or articles in periodicals.

You can instruct your word processor to position footnotes at the bottoms of appropriate pages. It will also automatically number notes and even renumber them if you add or delete one or more.

60b Models of Chicago notes and works-cited entries

The models below show notes and works-cited entries together for easy reference. An index to the models appears at the **Chicago** divider. Be sure to use the numbered note form for notes and the unnumbered works-cited form for works-cited entries.

1 Listing authors

1. One, two, or three authors

1. Carol Gilligan, *In a Different Voice: Psychological Theory and Women's Development* (Cambridge: Harvard University Press, 1982), 27.

Gilligan, Carol. *In a Different Voice: Psychological Theory and Women's Development*. Cambridge: Harvard University Press, 1982.

1. Dennis L. Wilcox, Phillip H. Ault, and Warren K. Agee, *Public Relations: Strategies and Tactics,* 6th ed. (New York: Irwin, 2005), 182.

Wilcox, Dennis L., Phillip H. Ault, and Warren K. Agee. *Public Relations: Strategies and Tactics*. 6th ed. New York: Irwin, 2005.

2. More than three authors

2. Geraldo Lopez and others, *China and the West* (Boston: Little, Brown, 2004), 461.

Lopez, Geraldo, Judith P. Salt, Anne Ming, and Henry Reisen. *China and the West*. Boston: Little, Brown, 2004.

3. Author not named (anonymous)

3. *The Dorling Kindersley World Reference Atlas* (London: Dorling Kindersley 2005), 150-51.

The Dorling Kindersley World Reference Atlas. London: Dorling Kindersley, 2005.

2 Listing print periodicals: Journals, newspapers, magazines

4. An article in a journal (print)

4. Janet Lever, "Sex Differences in the Games Children Play," *Social Problems* 23 (1996): 482.

Lever, Janet. "Sex Differences in the Games Children Play." *Social Problems* 23 (1996): 478-87.

Provide the issue number if the journal numbers issues, as shown below. Note that the issue number is required for any journal that pages each issue separately or that numbers only issues, not volumes.

4. Robert Bee, "The Importance of Preserving Paper-Based Artifacts in a Digital Age," *The Library Quarterly* 78, no. 2 (2008): 176.

Bee, Robert. "The Importance of Preserving Paper-Based Artifacts in a Digital Age." *The Library Quarterly* 78, no. 2 (2008): 174-94.

5. An article in a newspaper (print)

5. David Stout, "Blind Win Court Ruling on US Currency," *New York Times*, May 21, 2008, national edition, A23.

Stout, David. "Blind Win Court Ruling on US Currency." *New York Times*, May 21, 2008, national edition, A23.

Chicago style does not require page numbers for newspaper articles, whether in notes or in works-cited entries. Thus A23 could be omitted from the preceding examples.

6. An article in a magazine (print)

6. Amanda Fortini, "Pomegranate Princess," *New Yorker*, March 31, 2008, 94.

Fortini, Amanda. "Pomegranate Princess." *New Yorker*, March 31, 2008, 92-99.

Chicago works-cited style does not require inclusive page numbers for magazine articles, so 92-99 could be omitted from the preceding example.

7. A review (print)

7. John Gregory Dunne, "The Secret of Danny Santiago," review of *Famous All over Town,* by Danny Santiago, *New York Review of Books,* August 16, 1994, 25.

Dunne, John Gregory. "The Secret of Danny Santiago." Review of *Famous All over Town,* by Danny Santiago. *New York Review of Books,* August 16, 1994, 17-27.

3 Listing print books

8. Basic format for a book (print)

8. Barbara Ehrenreich, *Dancing in the Streets: A History of Collective Joy* (New York: Henry Holt, 2006), 97-117.

Ehrenreich, Barbara. *Dancing in the Streets: A History of Collective Joy.* New York: Henry Holt, 2006.

9. A book with an editor (print)

9. Hendrick Ruitenbeek, ed., *Freud as We Knew Him* (Detroit: Wayne State University Press, 1973), 64.

Ruitenbeek, Hendrick, ed. *Freud as We Knew Him.* Detroit: Wayne State University Press, 1973.

10. A book with an author and an editor (print)

10. Lewis Mumford, *The City in History,* ed. Donald L. Miller (New York: Pantheon, 1986), 216-17.

Mumford, Lewis. *The City in History*. Edited by Donald L. Miller. New York: Pantheon, 1986.

11. A translation (print)

11. Dante Alighieri, *The Inferno,* trans. John Ciardi (New York: New American Library, 1971), 51.

Alighieri, Dante. *The Inferno*. Translated by John Ciardi. New York: New American Library, 1971.

12. A later edition (print)

12. Dwight L. Bolinger, *Aspects of Language,* 3rd ed. (New York: Harcourt Brace Jovanovich, 1981), 20.

Bolinger, Dwight L. *Aspects of Language*. 3rd ed. New York: Harcourt Brace Jovanovich, 1981.

13. A work in more than one volume (print)

Citation of one volume without a title:

13. Abraham Lincoln, *The Collected Works of Abraham Lincoln,* ed. Roy P. Basler (New Brunswick: Rutgers University Press, 1953), 5:426-28.

Lincoln, Abraham. *The Collected Works of Abraham Lincoln*. Edited by Roy P. Basler. Vol. 5. New Brunswick: Rutgers University Press, 1953.

Citation of one volume with a title:

13. Linda B. Welkin, *The Age of Balanchine,* vol. 3 of *The History of Ballet* (New York: Columbia University Press, 1999), 56.

Welkin, Linda B. *The Age of Balanchine*. Vol. 3 of *The History of Ballet.* New York: Columbia University Press, 1999.

14. A selection from an anthology (print)

14. Rosetta Brooks, "Streetwise," in *The New Urban Landscape,* ed. Richard Martin (New York: Rizzoli, 2005), 38-39.

Brooks, Rosetta. "Streetwise." In *The New Urban Landscape,* ed. Richard Martin, 37-60. New York: Rizzoli, 2005.

15. A work in a series (print)

15. Ingmar Bergman, *The Seventh Seal,* Modern Film Scripts 12 (New York: Simon and Schuster, 1995), 27.

Bergman, Ingmar. *The Seventh Seal.* Modern Film Scripts 12. New York: Simon and Schuster, 1995.

16. An article in a reference work (print)

16. *Merriam-Webster's Collegiate Dictionary,* 11th ed., s.v. "reckon."

Merriam-Webster's Collegiate Dictionary. 11th ed. S.v. "reckon."

As in the example, use the abbreviation s.v. (Latin *sub verbo,* "under the word") for reference works that are alphabetically arranged. Well-known works like the one listed here do not need publication information except for edition number. Chicago style generally recommends notes only, not works-cited entries, for reference works; however, your instructor may require works-cited entries.

4 Web and other electronic sources

The Chicago Manual's models for documenting electronic sources derive mainly from those for print sources, with the addition of an electronic address (URL) or other indication of the medium along with any other information that may help readers locate the source. Chicago requires the date of your access to an online source only if the source could change significantly (for instance, a blog). However, your instructor may require access dates for a broader range of online sources, so they are included in the following models (in parentheses at the end).

Note Chicago style allows many ways to break URLs between the end of one line and the beginning of the next: after slashes, before most punctuation marks (periods, commas, question marks, and so on), and before or after equal signs and ampersands (&). *Do not* break after a hyphen or add any hyphens.

17. An article in a journal (Web)

17. Andrew Palfrey, "Choice of Mates in Identical Twins," *Modern Psychology* 4, no. 1 (2003): 28, http://www.liasu/edu/modpsy/palfrey4(1).htm (accessed February 25, 2008).

Palfrey, Andrew. "Choice of Mates in Identical Twins." *Modern Psychology* 4, no. 1 (2003): 26-40. http://www.liasu/edu/modpsy/palfrey4(1).htm (accessed February 25, 2008).

18. An article in a magazine (Web)

18. Nina Shen Rastogi, "Peacekeepers on Trial," *Slate,* May 28, 2008, http://www.slate.com/id/2192272 (accessed June 20, 2008).

Rastogi, Nina Shen. "Peacekeepers on Trial." *Slate,* May 28, 2008. http://www.slate.com/id/2192272 (accessed June 20, 2008).

19. An article in a newspaper (Web)

19. Elissa Gootman, "Gifted Programs in the City Are Less Diverse," *New York Times,* June 19, 2008, http://www.nytimes.com/2008/06/19/nyregion/19gifted.html (accessed August 17, 2008).

Gootman, Elissa. "Gifted Programs in the City Are Less Diverse." *New York Times,* June 19, 2008. http://www.nytimes.com/2008/06/19/nyregion/19gifted.html (accessed August 17, 2008).

20. An article in an online database (Web)

20. Irina Netchaeva, "E-Government and E-Democracy," *International Journal for Communication Studies* 64 (2002): 470-71, http://www.epnet.com (accessed June 20, 2008).

Netchaeva, Irina. "E-Government and E-Democracy." *International Journal for Communication Studies* 64 (2002): 467-78. http://www.epnet.com (accessed June 20, 2008).

For news and journal databases, including those to which your library subscribes, you may omit the name of the database. Give its main URL (as in the examples) unless the work has a usable URL of its own.

21. A book (Web)

21. Jane Austen, *Emma,* ed. R. W. Chapman (1816; Oxford: Clarendon, 1926; Oxford Text Archive, 2004), chap. 1, http://ota.ahds.ac.uk/Austen/Emma.1519 (accessed July 15, 2008).

Austen, Jane. *Emma.* Edited by R. W. Chapman. 1816. Oxford: Clarendon, 1926. Oxford Text Archive, 2004. http://ota.ahds.ac.uk/Austen/Emma.1519 (accessed July 15, 2008).

Provide print publication information, if any.

22. An article in a reference work (Web)

22. *Encyclopaedia Britannica Online,* s.v. "Wu-ti," http://www.eb.com:80 (accessed September 23, 2008).

Encyclopaedia Britannica Online. S.v. "Wu-ti." http://www.eb.com:80 (accessed September 23, 2008).

23. An audio or visual source (Web)

A work of art:

23. Jackson Pollock, *Shimmering Substance,* 1946, Museum of Modern Art, New York, http://moma.org/collection/conservation/pollock/shimmering_substance.html (accessed March 12, 2008).

Pollock, Jackson. *Shimmering Substance.* 1946. Museum of Modern Art, New York. http://moma.org/collection/conservation/pollock/shimmering_substance.html (accessed March 12, 2008).

See also model 30 to cite a work of art that you view in person.

A sound recording:

23. Ronald W. Reagan, State of the Union Address, January 26, 1982, Vincent Voice Library, Digital and Multimedia Center, University of Michigan, http://www.lib.msu.edu/vincent/presidents/reagan.html (accessed May 6, 2008).

Reagan, Ronald W. State of the Union Address. January 26, 1982. Vincent Voice Library. Digital and Multimedia Center, University of Michigan. http://www.lib.msu.edu/vincent/presidents/reagan.html (accessed May 6, 2008).

A film or film clip:

23. Leslie J. Stewart, *96 Ranch Rodeo and Barbecue* (1951); 16mm; from Library of Congress, *Buckaroos in Paradise: Ranching Culture in Northern Nevada, 1945-1982,* MPEG, http://memory.loc.gov/cgi-bin/query (accessed January 7, 2008).

Stewart, Leslie J. 96 *Ranch Rodeo and Barbecue*. 1951; 16 mm. From Library of Congress, *Buckaroos in Paradise: Ranching Culture in Northern Nevada, 1945-1982*. MPEG, http://memory.loc.gov/cgi-bin/query (accessed January 7, 2008).

24. A message posted to a blog or discussion group (Web)

24. Chris Horner, "EU Emissions," Cooler Heads Blog, June 18, 2008, http://www.globalwarming.org/node/2362 (accessed July 2, 2008).

Horner, Chris. "EU Emissions." Cooler Heads Blog. June 18, 2008. http://www.globalwarming.org/node/2362 (accessed July 2, 2008).

24. Michael Tourville, "European Currency Reform," e-mail to International Finance discussion list, January 6, 2008, http://www.weg.isu.edu/finance-dl/archive/46732 (accessed January 12, 2008).

Tourville, Michael. "European Currency Reform." E-mail to International Finance discussion list. January 6, 2008. http://www.weg.isu.edu/finance-dl/archive/46732 (accessed January 12, 2008).

25. Electronic mail

25. Elizabeth Bailey, "Re: London," e-mail message to author, May 4, 2008.

Bailey, Elizabeth. "Re: London." E-mail message to author. May 4, 2008.

26. A work on CD-ROM or DVD-ROM

26. *The American Heritage Dictionary of the English Language,* 4th ed. (Boston: Houghton Mifflin, 2000), CD-ROM.

The American Heritage Dictionary of the English Language. 4th ed. Boston: Houghton Mifflin, 2000. CD-ROM.

5 Listing other sources

27. A government publication (print)

27. House Committee on Ways and Means, *Medicare Payment for Outpatient Physical and Occupational Therapy Services,* 110th Cong., 1st sess., 2007, H. Doc. 772, 18-19.

U.S. Congress. House. Committee on Ways and Means. *Medicare Payment for Outpatient Physical and Occupational Therapy Services*. 110th Cong., 1st sess., 2007. H. Doc. 772.

27. Hawaii Department of Education, *Kauai District Schools, Profile 2007-08* (Honolulu, 2008), 38.

Hawaii. Department of Education. *Kauai District Schools, Profile 2007-08*. Honolulu, 2008.

28. A published letter (print)

28. Mrs. Laura E. Buttolph to Rev. and Mrs. C. C. Jones, June 20, 1857, in *The Children of Pride: A True Story of Georgia and the Civil War,* ed. Robert Manson Myers (New Haven, CT: Yale University Press, 1972), 334.

Buttolph, Laura E. Mrs. Laura E. Buttolph to Rev. and Mrs. C. C. Jones, June 20, 1857. In *The Children of Pride: A True Story of Georgia and the Civil War,* edited by Robert Manson Myers. New Haven, CT: Yale University Press, 1972.

29. A published or broadcast interview

29. Junot Diaz, interview by Terry Gross, *Fresh Air,* NPR, October 18, 2007.

Diaz, Junot. Interview by Terry Gross. *Fresh Air.* NPR. October 18, 2007.

30. A personal letter or interview

30. Ann E. Packer, letter to author, June 15, 2008.

Packer, Ann E. Letter to author. June 15, 2008.

30. William Paul, interview by author, December 19, 2005.

Paul, William. Interview by author. December 19, 2005.

31. A work of art

31. John Singer Sargent, *In Switzerland,* 1908, Metropolitan Museum of Art, New York.

Sargent, John Singer. *In Switzerland*. 1908. Metropolitan Museum of Art, New York.

32. A film, DVD, or video recording

32. George Balanchine, *Serenade,* DVD, San Francisco Ballet (New York: PBS Video, 2006).

Balanchine, George. *Serenade*. DVD. San Francisco Ballet. New York: PBS Video, 2006.

33. A sound recording

33. Johannes Brahms, *Piano Concerto no. 2 in B-flat,* Artur Rubinstein, Philadelphia Orchestra, Eugene Ormandy, compact disc, RCA BRC4-6731.

Brahms, Johannes. *Piano Concerto no. 2 in B-flat*. Artur Rubinstein. Philadelphia Orchestra. Eugene Ormandy. Compact disc. RCA BRC4-6731.

6 Using shortened notes

To streamline documentation, Chicago style recommends shortened notes for sources that are fully cited elsewhere, either in a complete list of works cited or in previous notes. Ask your instructor whether your paper should include a list of works cited and, if so, whether you may use shortened notes for first references to sources as well as for subsequent references.

A shortened note contains the author's last name, the work's title (minus any initial *A*, *An*, or *The*), and the page number. Reduce long titles to four or fewer key words.

Complete note

4. Janet Lever, "Sex Differences in the Games Children Play," *Social Problems* 23 (1996): 482.

Complete works-cited entry

Lever, Janet. "Sex Differences in the Games Children Play." *Social Problems* 23 (1996): 478-87.

Shortened note

12. Lever, "Sex Differences," 483.

You may use the Latin abbreviation ibid. (meaning "in the same place") to refer to the same source cited in the preceding note. Give a page number if it differs from that in the preceding note.

12. Lever, "Sex Differences," 483.
13. Gilligan, *In a Different Voice,* 92.
14. Ibid., 93.
15. Lever, "Sex Differences," 483.

Chicago style allows for in-text parenthetical citations when you cite one or more works repeatedly. In the following example, the raised number 2 refers to the source information in a note; the number in parentheses is a page number in the same source.

British rule, observes Stuart Cary Welch, "seemed as permanent as Mount Everest."[2] Most Indians submitted, willingly or not, to British influence in every facet of life (42).

61 CSE Documentation

Writers in the life sciences, physical sciences, and mathematics rely for documentation style on *Scientific Style and Format: The CSE Manual for Authors, Editors, and Publishers* (7th ed., 2006), published by the Council of Science Editors.

Scientific Style and Format details both styles of scientific documentation: one using author and date and one using numbers. Both types of text citation refer to a list of references at the end of the paper. Ask your instructor which style you should use.

61a Writing CSE name-year text citations

In the CSE name-year style, parenthetical text citations provide the last name of the author being cited and the source's year of publication. At the end of the paper, a list of references, arranged alphabetically by authors' last names, provides complete information on each source. (See opposite.)

The CSE name-year style closely resembles the APA name-year style detailed in **APA** pp. 464–67. You can follow the APA examples for in-text citations, making several notable changes for CSE:

- **Do not use a comma to separate the author's name and the date:** (Baumrind 1968, p. 34).
- **Separate two authors' names with and (not "&"):** (Pepinsky and DeStefano 1997).
- **For sources with three or more authors, use et al. (Latin abbreviation for "and others") after the first author's name:** (Rutter et al. 1996).

61b Writing CSE numbered text citations

In the CSE number style, raised numbers in the text refer to a numbered list of references at the end of the paper.

Two standard references[1,2] use this term.

These forms of immunity have been extensively researched.[3]

Hepburn and Tatin[2] do not discuss this project.

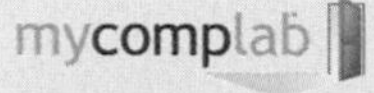

Visit *mycomplab.com* for more resources on CSE documentation.

Assignment of numbers The number for each source is based on the order in which you cite the source in the text: the first cited source is 1, the second is 2, and so on.

Reuse of numbers When you cite a source you have already cited and numbered, use the original number again (see the last example on the previous page, which reuses the number 2 from the first example).

This reuse is the key difference between the CSE numbered citations and numbered references to footnotes or endnotes. In the CSE style, each source has only one number, determined by the order in which the source is cited. With notes, in contrast, the numbering proceeds in sequence, so that each source has as many numbers as it has citations in the text.

Citation of two or more sources When you cite two or more sources at once, arrange their numbers in sequence and separate them with a comma and no space, as in the first example on the previous page.

61c Preparing the CSE reference list

For both the name-year and the number styles of in-text citation, provide a list, titled References, of all sources you have cited. Format the page as shown for APA references in APA p. 467, except that CSE entries are single-spaced.

The following examples show the differences and similarities between the name-year and number styles:

Name-year style

Hepburn PX, Tatin JM. 2005. Human physiology. New York (NY): Columbia University Press.

Number style

2. Hepburn PX, Tatin JM. Human physiology. New York (NY): Columbia University Press; 2005.

Spacing In both styles, single-space each entry and double-space between entries.

Arrangement In the name-year style, arrange entries alphabetically by authors' last names. In the number style, arrange entries in numerical order—that is, in order of their citation in the text.

Format In both styles, begin the first line of each entry at the left margin and indent subsequent lines.

Authors In both styles, list each author's name with the last name first, followed by initials for first and middle names. Do not use a comma between an author's last name and initials, and do not use periods or space with the initials. Do use a comma to separate authors' names.

Placement of dates In the name-year style, the date follows the author's or authors' names. In the number style, the date follows the publication information (for a book) or the periodical title (for a journal, magazine, or newspaper).

Journal titles In both styles, do not italicize or underline journal titles. For titles of two or more words, abbreviate words of six or more letters (without periods) and omit most prepositions, articles, and conjunctions. Capitalize each word. For example, *Journal of Chemical and Biochemical Studies* becomes J Chem Biochem Stud.

Book and article titles In both styles, do not italicize, underline, or use quotation marks around a book or an article title. Capitalize only the first word and any proper nouns.

Publication information for journal articles The name-year and number styles differ in the placement of the publication date (see the previous page). However, both styles end with the journal's volume number, any issue number in parentheses, a colon, and the article's page numbers, run together without space: 28:329-30 or 62(2):26-40.

The following examples show both a name-year reference and a number reference for each type of source. An index to all the models appears opposite the **CSE** divider (p. 491).

1 Listing authors

1. One author

Gould SJ. 1987. Time's arrow, time's cycle. Cambridge (MA): Harvard University Press.

1. Gould SJ. Time's arrow, time's cycle. Cambridge (MA): Harvard University Press; 1987.

2. Two to ten authors

Hepburn PX, Tatin JM, Tatin JP. 2008. Human physiology. New York (NY): Columbia University Press.

2. Hepburn PX, Tatin JM, Tatin JP. Human physiology. New York (NY): Columbia University Press; 2008.

3. More than ten authors

Evans RW, Bowditch L, Dana KL, Drumond A, Wildovitch WP, Young SL, Mills P, Mills RR, Livak SR, Lisi OL, et al. 2004. Organ transplants: ethical issues. Ann Arbor (MI): University of Michigan Press.

3. Evans RW, Bowditch L, Dana KL, Drummond A, Wildovitch WP, Young SL, Mills P, Mills RR, Livak SR, Lisi OL, et al. Organ transplants: ethical issues. Ann Arbor (MI): University of Michigan Press; 2004.

4. Author not named

Health care for children with diabetes. 2008. New York (NY): US Health Care.

4. Health care for children with diabetes. New York (NY): US Health Care; 2008.

5. Two or more cited works by the same author(s) published in the same year

Gardner H. 1973a. The arts and human development. New York (NY): Wiley.

Gardner H. 1973b. The quest for mind: Piaget, Lévi-Strauss, and the structuralist movement. New York (NY): Knopf.

(The number style does not require such forms.)

2 Listing print periodicals: Journals, newspapers, magazines

6. An article in a journal (print)

Kim P. 2006. Medical decision making for the dying. Milbank Quar. 64(2):26-40.

6. Kim P. Medical decision making for the dying. Milbank Quar. 2006;64(2):26-40.

If a journal article has a Digital Object Identifier (DOI), you may include the number at the end of the entry for readers' convenience. (See APA p. 471 for more on DOIs.)

7. An article in a newspaper (print)

Stout D. 2008 May 28. Blind win court ruling on US currency. New York Times (National Ed.). Sect. A:23 (col. 3).

7. Stout D. Blind win court ruling on US currency. New York Times (National Ed.). 2008 May 28;Sect. A:23 (col. 3).

8. An article in a magazine (print)

Wilkinson A. 2008 June 2. Crime fighting of the future. New Yorker. 26-33.

8. Wilkinson A. Crime fighting of the future. New Yorker. 2008 June 2:26-33.

3 Listing print books

9. Basic format for a book (print)

Wilson EO. 2004. On human nature. Cambridge (MA): Harvard University Press.

9. Wilson EO. On human nature. Cambridge (MA): Harvard University Press; 2004.

10. A book with an editor (print)

Jonson P, editor. 2008. Anatomy yearbook 2008. Los Angeles (CA): Anatco.

10. Jonson P, editor. Anatomy yearbook 2008. Los Angeles (CA): Anatco; 2008.

11. A selection from a book (print)

Krigel R, Laubenstein L, Muggia F. 2005. Kaposi's sarcoma. In: Ebbeson P, Biggar RS, Melbye M, editors. AIDS: a basic guide for clinicians. 2nd ed. Philadelphia (PA): Saunders. p. 100-26.

11. Kriegel R, Laubenstein L, Muggia F. Kaposi's sarcoma. In: Ebbeson P, Biggar RS, Melbye M, editors. AIDS: a basic guide for clinicians. 2nd ed. Philadelphia (PA): Saunders; 2005. p. 100-26.

4 Listing Web and other electronic sources

Do not add a period after a URL at the end of an entry. If you must break a URL from one line to the next, do so only after a slash, and do not hyphenate.

12. An article in a journal (Web)

Grady GF. 2007. The here and now of hepatitis B immunization. Today's Med [Internet]. [cited 2007 Dec 7]; 6(2):39-41. Available from: http://www.fmrt.org/todayamedicine/Grady050293.pdf6

12. Grady GF. The here and now of hepatitis B immunization. Today's Med [Internet]. 2007 [cited 2007 Dec 7]; 6(2):39-41. Available from: http://www.fmrt.org/todaysmedicine/Grady050293.pdf6

Give the date of your access, preceded by "cited," in brackets: [cited 2007 Dec 7] in the examples. If the article has no reference numbers (pages, paragraphs, and so on), give your calculation of its length in brackets—for instance, [about 15 p.] or [20 paragraphs]. If the article has a Digital Object Identifier (DOI), you may include the number for readers' convenience. Add it to the end of the entry after a space. (See **APA** p. 474 for more on DOIs.)

13. An article in a database (Web)

McAskill MR, Anderson TJ, Jones RD. 2005. Saccadic adaptation in neurological disorders. Prog Brain Res. 140:417-431. PubMed [database on the Internet]. Bethesda (MD): National Library of Medicine; [cited 2007 Mar 6]. Available from: http://www.ncbi.nlm.nih.gov/PubMed

13. McAskill MR, Anderson TJ, Jones RD. Saccadic adaptation in neurological disorders. Prog Brain Res. 2005;140:417-431. PubMed [database on the Internet]. Bethesda (MD): National Library of Medicine; [cited 2007 Mar 6]. Available from: http://www.ncbi.nlm.nih.gov/PubMed

Provide information on the database: title, [database on the Internet], place of publication, and publisher. (If the database author is different from the publisher, give the author's name before the title.) If you see a date of publication or a copyright date for the database, give it after the publisher's name. Add the date of your access, preceded by cited, in brackets. If the article has a Digital Object Identifier (DOI), you may include the number for readers' convenience. Add it to the end of the entry after a space. (See **APA** p. 474 for more on DOIs.)

14. A book (Web)

Ruch BJ, Ruch DB. 2007. Homeopathy and medicine: resolving the conflict [Internet]. New York (NY): Albert Einstein College of Medicine [cited 2008 Jan 28]. Available from: http://www.einstein.edu/medicine/books/ruch.html

14. Ruch BJ, Ruch DB. Homeopathy and medicine: resolving the conflict [Internet]. New York (NY): Albert Einstein College of Medicine; 2007 [cited 2008 Jan 28]. Available from: http://www.einstein.edu/medicine/books/ruch.html

As with an online journal article, give the date of your access, preceded by cited, in brackets.

15. A Web site

American Medical Association [Internet]. 2008. Chicago (IL): American Medical Association; [cited 2008 Nov 26]. Available from: http://ama-assn.org

15. American Medical Association [Internet]. Chicago (IL): American Medical Association; 2008 [cited 2008 Nov 26]. Available from: http://ama-assn.org

16. A message posted to a discussion list

Stalinsky Q. 2007 Aug 16. Reconsidering the hormone-replacement study. Woman Physicians Congress [discussion list on the Internet]. Chicago (IL): American Medical Association; [cited 2008 Aug 17]. Available from: ama-wpc@ama-assn.org

16. Stalinsky Q. Reconsidering the hormone-replacement study. Woman Physicians Congress [discussion list on the Internet]. Chicago (IL): American Medical Association; 2007 Aug 16 [cited 2008 Aug 17]. Available from: ama-wpc@ama-assn.org

17. A personal online communication (text citation)

At least one member of the research team has expressed reservation about the design of the study (personal communication from L. Kogod, 2008 Feb 6; unreferenced).

A personal letter or e-mail message should be cited in your text, not in your reference list. The format is the same for both the name-year and the number styles.

18. A document on CD-ROM or DVD-ROM

Reich WT, editor. 2008. Encyclopedia of bioethics [DVD-ROM]. New York (NY): Co-Health.

18. Reich WT editor. Encyclopedia of bioethics [DVD-ROM]. New York (NY): Co-Health; 2008.

5 Listing other sources

19. A report written and published by the same organization

Warnock M. 2006. Report of the Committee on Fertilization and Embryology. Waco (TX): Baylor University Department of Embryology. Report No.: BU/DE.4261.

19. Warnock M. Report of the Committee on Fertilization and Embryology. Waco (TX): Baylor University Department of Embryology; 2006. Report No.: BU/DE.4261.

20. A report written and published by different organizations

Hackney, JD (Rancho Los Amigos Hospital, Downey, CA). 2007. Effect of atmospheric pollutants on human physiologic function. Washington (DC): Environmental Protection Agency (US). Report No.: R-801396.

20. Hackney, JD (Rancho Los Amigos Hospital, Downey, CA). Effect of atmospheric pollutants on human physiologic function. Washington (DC): Environmental Protection Agency (US); 2007. Report No.: R-801396.

21. An audio or visual recording

Cell mitosis [DVD-ROM]. 2008. White Plains (NY): Teaching Media.

21. Cell mitosis [DVD-ROM]. White Plains (NY): Teaching Media; 2008.

Glossary of Usage *511*

Index *525*

CULTURE LANGUAGE **Guide** *568*

Glossary of Usage *511*

Index *525*

Guide *568*

Glossary of Usage

This glossary provides notes on words or phrases that often cause problems for writers. The recommendations for standard American English are based on current dictionaries and usage guides. Items labeled **nonstandard** should be avoided in academic and business settings. Those labeled **colloquial** and **slang** occur in speech and in some informal writing but are best avoided in formal college and business writing. (Words and phrases labeled *colloquial* include those labeled by many dictionaries with the equivalent term *informal.*)

a, an Use *a* before words beginning with consonant sounds, including those spelled with an initial pronounced *h* and those spelled with vowels that are sounded as consonants: *a historian, a one-o'clock class, a university.* Use *an* before words that begin with vowel sounds, including those spelled with an initial silent *h: an organism, an L, an honor.*

The article before an abbreviation depends on how the abbreviation is to be read: *She was once an AEC undersecretary* (*AEC* is to be read as three separate letters). *Many Americans opposed a SALT treaty* (*SALT* is to be read as one word, *salt*).

See also **4** pp. 242–43 on the uses of *a/an* versus *the.*

accept, except *Accept* is a verb meaning "receive." *Except* is usually a preposition or conjunction meaning "but for" or "other than"; when it is used as a verb, it means "leave out." *I can accept all your suggestions except the last one. I'm sorry you excepted my last suggestion from your list.*

advice, advise *Advice* is a noun, and *advise* is a verb: *Take my advice; do as I advise you.*

affect, effect Usually *affect* is a verb, meaning "to influence," and *effect* is a noun, meaning "result": *The drug did not affect his driving; in fact, it seemed to have no effect at all.* But *effect* occasionally is used as a verb meaning "to bring about": *Her efforts effected a change.* And *affect* is used in psychology as a noun meaning "feeling or emotion": *One can infer much about affect from behavior.*

agree to, agree with *Agree to* means "consent to," and *agree with* means "be in accord with": *How can they agree to a treaty when they don't agree with each other about the terms?*

all ready, already *All ready* means "completely prepared," and *already* means "by now" or "before now": *We were all ready to go to the movie, but it had already started.*

all right *All right* is always two words. *Alright* is a common error.

all together, altogether *All together* means "in unison" or "gathered in one place." *Altogether* means "entirely." *It's not altogether true that our family never spends vacations all together.*

allusion, illusion An *allusion* is an indirect reference, and an *illusion* is a deceptive appearance: *Paul's constant allusions to Shakespeare created the illusion that he was an intellectual.*

almost, most *Almost* means "nearly"; *most* means "the greater number (or part) of." In formal writing, *most* should not be used as a substitute for *almost: We see each other almost* [not *most*] *every day.*

a lot *A lot* is always two words, used informally to mean "many." *Alot* is a common misspelling.

among, between In general, use *among* for relationships involving more than two people or for comparing one thing to a group to which it belongs. *The four of them agreed among themselves that the choice was between New York and Los Angeles.*

amount, number Use *amount* with a singular noun that names something not countable (a noncount noun): *The amount of food varies.* Use *number* with a plural noun that names more than one of something countable (a plural count noun): *The number of calories must stay the same.*

and/or *And/or* indicates three options: one or the other or both (*The decision is made by the mayor and/or the council*). If you mean all three options, *and/or* is appropriate. Otherwise, use *and* if you mean both, *or* if you mean either.

ante-, anti- The prefix *ante-* means "before" (*antedate, antebellum*); *anti-* means "against" (*antiwar, antinuclear*). Before a capital letter or *i*, *anti-* takes a hyphen: *anti-Freudian, anti-isolationist.*

anxious, eager *Anxious* means "nervous" or "worried" and is usually followed by *about*. *Eager* means "looking forward" and is usually followed by *to*. *I've been anxious about getting blisters. I'm eager* [not *anxious*] *to get new running shoes.*

anybody, any body; anyone, any one *Anybody* and *anyone* are indefinite pronouns; *any body* is a noun modified by *any; any one* is a pronoun or adjective modified by *any*. *How can anybody communicate with any body of government? Can anyone help Amy? She has more work than any one person can handle.*

any more, anymore *Any more* means "no more"; *anymore* means "now." Both are used in negative constructions. *He doesn't want any more. She doesn't live here anymore.*

apt, liable, likely *Apt* and *likely* are interchangeable. Strictly speaking, though, *apt* means "having a tendency to": *Horace is apt to forget his lunch in the morning. Likely means* "probably going to": *Horace is leaving so early today that he's likely to catch the first bus.*

Liable normally means "in danger of" and should be confined to situations with undesirable consequences: *Horace is liable to trip over that hose.* Strictly, *liable* means "responsible" or "exposed to": *The owner will be liable for Horace's injuries.*

are, is Use *are* with a plural subject (*books are*), *is* with a singular subject (*a book is*).

as *As* may be vague or ambiguous when it substitutes for *because, since,* or *while: As the researchers asked more questions, their money ran* *out.* (Does *as* mean "while" or "because"?) *As* should never be used as a substitute for *whether* or *who. I'm not sure whether* [not *as*] *we can make it. That's the man who* [not *as*] *gave me directions.*

as, like In formal speech and writing, *like* should not introduce a full clause (with a subject and a verb) because it is a preposition. The preferred choice is *as* or *as if: The plan succeeded as* [not *like*] *we hoped. It seemed as if* [not *like*] *it might fail. Other plans like it have failed.*

as, than In comparisons, *as* and *than* precede a subjective-case pronoun when the pronoun is a subject: *I love you more than he* [*loves you*]. *As* and *than* precede an objective-case pronoun when the pronoun is an object: *I love you as much as* [*I love*] *him.* (See also **4** p. 239.)

assure, ensure, insure *Assure* means "to promise": *He assured us that we would miss the traffic. Ensure* and *insure* often are used interchangeably to mean "make certain," but some reserve *insure* for matters of legal and financial protection and use *ensure* for more general meanings: *We left early to ensure that we would miss the traffic. It's expensive to insure yourself against floods.*

at The use of *at* after *where* is wordy and should be avoided: *Where are you meeting him?* is preferable to *Where are you meeting him at?*

awful, awfully Strictly speaking, *awful* means "awe-inspiring." As intensifiers meaning "very" or "extremely" (*He tried awfully hard*), *awful* and *awfully* should be avoided in formal speech or writing.

a while, awhile *Awhile* is an adverb; *a while* is an article and a noun. *I will be gone awhile* [not *a while*]. *I will be gone for a while* [not *awhile*].

bad, badly In formal speech and writing, *bad* should be used only as an adjective; the adverb is *badly. He felt bad because his tooth ached badly.* In *He felt bad,* the verb *felt* is a linking verb and the adjective *bad* describes the subject. See also **4** p. 237.

being as, being that Colloquial for *because,* the preferable word in formal speech or writing: *Because* [not *Being as*] *the world is round, Columbus never did fall off the edge.*

beside, besides *Beside* is a preposition meaning "next to." *Besides* is a preposition meaning "except" or "in addition to" as well as an adverb meaning "in addition." *Besides, several other people besides you want to sit beside Dr. Christensen.*

better, had better *Had better* (meaning "ought to") is a verb modified by an adverb. The verb is necessary and should not be omitted: *You had better* [not just *better*] *go.*

between, among See *among, between.*

bring, take Use *bring* only for movement from a farther place to a nearer one and *take* for any other movement. *First take these books to the library for renewal; then take them to Mr. Daniels. Bring them back to me when he's finished.*

but, hardly, scarcely These words are negative in their own right; using *not* with any of them produces a double negative (see **4** pp. 239–40). *We have but* [not *haven't got but*] *an hour before our plane leaves. I could hardly* [not *couldn't hardly*] *make out her face.*

but, however, yet Each of these words is adequate to express contrast. Don't combine them. *He had finished, yet* [not *but yet*] *he continued.*

can, may Strictly, *can* indicates capacity or ability, and *may* indicates permission or possibility: *If I may talk with you a moment, I believe I can solve your problem.*

censor, censure To *censor* is to edit or remove from public view on moral or some other grounds; to *censure* is to give a formal scolding. *The lieutenant was censured by Major Taylor for censoring the letters her soldiers wrote home from boot camp.*

center around *Center on* is more logical than, and preferable to, *center around.*

cite, sight, site *Cite* is a verb usually meaning "quote," "commend," or "acknowledge": *You must cite your sources. Sight* is both a noun meaning "the ability to see" or "a view" and a verb meaning "perceive" or "observe": *What a sight you see when you sight Venus through a strong telescope. Site* is a noun meaning "place" or "location" or a verb meaning "situate": *The builder sited the house on an unlikely site.*

climatic, climactic *Climatic* comes from *climate* and refers to the weather: *Recent droughts may indicate a climatic change. Climactic* comes from *climax* and refers to a dramatic high point: *During the climactic duel between Hamlet and Laertes, Gertrude drinks poisoned wine.*

complement, compliment To *complement* something is to add to, complete, or reinforce it: *Her yellow blouse complemented her black hair.* To *compliment* something is to make a flattering remark about it: *He complimented her on her hair. Complimentary* can also mean "free": *complimentary tickets.*

conscience, conscious *Conscience* is a noun meaning "a sense of right and wrong"; *conscious* is an adjective meaning "aware" or "awake." *Though I was barely conscious, my conscience nagged me.*

contact Often used imprecisely as a verb instead of a more exact word such as *consult, talk with, telephone,* or *write to.*

continual, continuous *Continual* means "constantly recurring": *Most movies on television are continually interrupted by commercials. Continuous* means "unceasing": *Some cable channels present movies continuously without commercials.*

could of See *have, of.*

credible, creditable, credulous *Credible* means "believable": *It's a strange story, but it seems credible to me. Creditable* means "deserving of credit" or "worthy": *Steve gave a creditable performance. Credulous* means "gullible": *The credulous Claire believed Tim's lies.* See also *incredible, incredulous.*

criteria The plural of *criterion* (meaning "standard for judgment"): *Our criteria are strict. The most important criterion is a sense of humor.*

data The plural of *datum* (meaning "fact"). Though *data* is often used as a singular noun, most careful writers still treat it as plural: *The data fail* [not *fails*] *to support the hypothesis.*

device, devise *Device* is the noun, and *devise* is the verb: *Can you devise some device for getting his attention?*

different from, different than *Different from* is preferred: *His purpose is different from mine.* But *different than* is widely accepted when a construction using *from* would be wordy: *I'm a different person now than I used to be* is preferable to *I'm a different person now from the person I used to be.*

differ from, differ with To *differ from* is to be unlike: *The twins differ from each other only in their hairstyles.* To *differ with* is to disagree with: *I have to differ with you on that point.*

discreet, discrete *Discreet* (noun form *discretion*) means "tactful": *What's a discreet way of telling Maud to be quiet? Discrete* (noun form *discreteness*) means "separate and distinct": *Within a computer's memory are millions of discrete bits of information.*

disinterested, uninterested *Disinterested* means "impartial": *We chose Pete, as a disinterested third party, to decide who was right. Uninterested* means "bored" or "lacking interest": *Unfortunately, Pete was completely uninterested in the question.*

don't *Don't* is the contraction for *do not*, not for *does not: I don't care, you don't care, and he doesn't* [not *don't*] *care.*

due to the fact that Wordy for *because.*

eager, anxious See *anxious, eager.*

effect See *affect, effect.*

elicit, illicit *Elicit* is a verb meaning "bring out" or "call forth." *Illicit* is an adjective meaning "unlawful." *The crime elicited an outcry against illicit drugs.*

emigrate, immigrate *Emigrate* means "to leave one place and move to another": *The Chus emigrated from Korea. Immigrate* means "to move into a place where one was not born": *They immigrated to the United States.*

ensure See *assure, ensure, insure.*

enthused Used colloquially as an adjective meaning "showing enthusiasm." The preferred adjective is *enthusiastic: The coach was enthusiastic* [not *enthused*] *about the team's victory.*

et al., etc. Use *et al.*, the Latin abbreviation for "and other people," only in source citations: *Jones et al.* Avoid *etc.*, the Latin abbreviation for "and other things," in formal writing, and do not use it to refer to people or to substitute for precision, as in *The government provides health care, etc.*

everybody, every body; everyone, every one *Everybody* and *everyone* are indefinite pronouns: *Everybody* [*everyone*] *knows Tom steals. Every one* is a pronoun modified by *every*, and *every body* a noun modified by *every*. Both refer to each thing or person of a specific group and are typically followed by *of: The game commissioner has stocked every body of fresh water in the state with fish, and now every one of our rivers is a potential trout stream.*

everyday, every day *Everyday* is an adjective meaning "used daily" or "common"; *every day* is a noun modified by *every: Everyday problems tend to arise every day.*

everywheres Nonstandard for *everywhere.*

except See *accept, except.*

except for the fact that Wordy for *except that.*

explicit, implicit *Explicit* means "stated outright": *I left explicit instructions. Implicit* means "implied, unstated": *We had an implicit understanding.*

farther, further *Farther* refers to additional distance (*How much farther is it to the beach?*), and *further* refers to additional time, amount, or other abstract matters (*I don't want to discuss this any further*).

fewer, less *Fewer* refers to individual countable items (a plural count noun), *less* to general amounts (a noncount noun, always singular). *Skim milk has fewer calories than whole milk. We have less milk left than I thought.*

flaunt, flout *Flaunt* means "show off": *If you have style, flaunt it. Flout* means "scorn" or "defy": *Hester Prynne flouted convention and paid the price.*

flunk A colloquial substitute for *fail.*

fun As an adjective, *fun* is colloquial and should be avoided in most writing: *It was a pleasurable* [not *fun*] *evening.*

further See *farther, further.*

get This common verb is used in many slang and colloquial expressions: *get lost, that really gets me, getting on. Get* is easy to overuse: watch out for it in expressions such as *it's getting better* (substitute *improving*) and *we got done* (substitute *finished*).

good, well *Good* is an adjective, and *well* is nearly always an adverb: *Larry's a good dancer. He and Linda dance well together. Well* is properly used as an adjective only to refer to health: *You look well.* (*You look good,* in contrast, means "Your appearance is pleasing.")

good and Colloquial for "very": *I was very* [not *good and*] *tired.*

had better See *better, had better.*

had ought The *had* is unnecessary and should be omitted: *He ought* [not *had ought*] *to listen to his mother.*

hanged, hung Though both are past-tense forms of *hang, hanged* is used to refer to executions and *hung* is used for all other meanings: *Tom Dooley was hanged* [not *hung*] *from a white oak tree. I hung* [not *hanged*] *the picture you gave me.*

hardly See *but, hardly, scarcely.*

have, of Use *have,* not *of,* after helping verbs such as *could, should, would, may,* and *might: You should have* [not *should of*] *told me.*

he, she; he/she Convention has allowed the use of *he* to mean "he or she": *After the infant learns to creep, he progresses to crawling.* However, many writers today consider this usage inaccurate and unfair because it seems to exclude females. The construction *he/she,* one substitute for *he,* is awkward and objectionable to most readers. The better choice is to make the pronoun plural, to rephrase, or, sparingly, to use *he or she.* For instance: *After infants learn to creep, they progress to crawling. After learning to creep, the infant progresses to crawling. After the infant learns to creep, he or she progresses to crawling.* See also **3** p. 164 and **4** pp. 231–32.

herself, himself See *myself, herself, himself, yourself.*

hisself Nonstandard for *himself.*

hopefully *Hopefully* means "with hope": *Freddy waited hopefully for a glimpse of Eliza.* The use of *hopefully* to mean "it is to be hoped," "I hope," or "let's hope" is now very common; but since many readers continue to object strongly to the usage, try to avoid it. *I hope* [not *Hopefully*] *the law will pass.*

idea, ideal An *idea* is a thought or conception. An *ideal* (noun) is a model of perfection or a goal. *Ideal* should not be used in place of *idea: The idea* [not *ideal*] *of the play is that our ideals often sustain us.*

if, whether For clarity, use *whether* rather than *if* when you are expressing an alternative: *If I laugh hard, people can't tell whether I'm crying.*

illicit See *elicit, illicit.*

illusion See *allusion, illusion.*

immigrate, emigrate See *emigrate, immigrate.*

implicit See *explicit, implicit.*

imply, infer Writers or speakers *imply,* meaning "suggest": *Jim's letter implies he's having a good time.* Readers or listeners *infer,* meaning "conclude": *From Jim's letter I infer he's having a good time.*

incredible, incredulous *Incredible* means "unbelievable"; *incredulous* means "unbelieving": *When Nancy heard Dennis's incredible story, she was frankly incredulous.* See also *credible, creditable, credulous.*

individual, person, party *Individual* should refer to a single human being in contrast to a group or should stress uniqueness: *The US Constitution places strong emphasis on the rights of the individual.* For other meanings *person* is preferable: *What person* [not *individual*] *wouldn't want the security promised in that advertisement? Party* means "group" (*Can you seat a party of four for dinner?*) and should not be used to refer to an individual except in legal documents. See also *people, persons.*

infer See *imply, infer.*

in regards to Nonstandard for *in regard to, as regards,* or *regarding.*

inside of, outside of The *of* is unnecessary when *inside* and *outside* are used as prepositions: *Stay inside* [not *inside of*] *the house. The decision is outside* [not *outside of*] *my authority. Inside of* may refer colloquially to time, though in formal English *within* is preferred: *The law was passed within* [not *inside of*] *a year.*

insure See *assure, ensure, insure.*

irregardless Nonstandard for *regardless.*

is, are See *are, is.*

is because See *reason is because.*

is when, is where These are faulty constructions in sentences that define: *Adolescence is a stage* [not *is when a person is*] *between childhood and adulthood. Socialism is a system in which* [not *is where*] *government owns the means of production.* See also **4** p. 258.

its, it's *Its* is the pronoun *it* in the possessive case: *That plant is losing its leaves. It's* is a contraction for *it is* or *it has: It's* [*It is*] *likely to die. It's* [*It has*] *got a fungus.* Many people confuse *it's* and *its* because possessives are most often formed with *-'s;* but the possessive *its,* like *his* and *hers,* never takes an apostrophe.

-ize, -wise The suffix *-ize* changes a noun or adjective into a verb: *revolutionize, immunize.* The suffix *-wise* changes a noun or adjective into an adverb: *clockwise, otherwise, likewise.* Avoid the two suffixes except in established words: *I'm highly sensitive* [not *sensitized*] *to that kind of criticism. Financially* [not *Moneywise*], *it's a good time to buy real estate.*

kind of, sort of, type of In formal speech and writing, avoid using *kind of* or *sort of* to mean "somewhat": *He was rather* [not *kind of*] *tall.*

Kind, sort, and *type* are singular and take singular modifiers and verbs: *This kind of dog is easily trained.* Agreement errors often occur when these singular nouns are combined with the plural adjectives *these* and *those: These kinds* [not *kind*] *of dogs are easily trained. Kind, sort,* and *type* should be followed by *of* but not by *a: I don't know what type of* [not *type* or *type of a*] *dog that is.*

Use *kind of, sort of,* or *type of* only when the word *kind, sort,* or *type* is important: *That was a strange* [not *strange sort of*] *statement.*

lay, lie *Lay* means "put" or "place" and takes a direct object: *We could lay the tablecloth in the sun.* Its main forms are *lay, laid, laid. Lie* means "recline" or "be situated" and does not take an object: *I lie awake at night. The town lies east of the river.* Its main forms are *lie, lay, lain.* (See also **4** p. 198.)

leave, let *Leave* and *let* are interchangeable only when followed by *alone; leave me alone* is the same as *let me alone.* Otherwise, *leave* means "depart" and *let* means "allow": *Jill would not let Sue leave.*

less See *fewer, less.*

liable See *apt, liable, likely.*

lie, lay See *lay, lie.*

like, as See *as, like.*

like, such as Strictly, *such as* precedes an example that represents a larger subject, whereas *like* indicates that two subjects are comparable. *Steve has recordings of many great saxophonists such as Ben Webster and Lee Konitz. Steve wants to be a great jazz saxophonist like Ben Webster and Lee Konitz.*

likely See *apt, liable, likely.*

literally This word means "actually" or "just as the words say," and it should not be used to qualify or intensify expressions whose words are not to be taken at face value. The sentence *He was literally climbing the walls* describes a person behaving like an insect, not a person who is restless or anxious. For the latter meaning, *literally* should be omitted.

lose, loose *Lose* means "mislay": *Did you lose a brown glove? Loose* means "unrestrained" or "not tight": *Ann's canary got loose. Loose* also can function as a verb meaning "let loose": *They loose the dogs as soon as they spot the bear.*

lots, lots of Colloquial substitutes for *very many, a great many,* or *much.* Avoid *lots* and *lots of* in college or business writing.

may, can See *can, may.*

may be, maybe *May be* is a verb, and *maybe* is an adverb meaning "perhaps": *Tuesday may be a legal holiday. Maybe we won't have classes.*

may of See *have, of.*

media *Media* is the plural of *medium* and takes a plural verb: *All the news media are increasingly visual.* The singular verb is common, even in the media, but many readers prefer the plural verb and it is always correct.

might of See *have, of.*

moral, morale As a noun, *moral* means "ethical conclusion" or "lesson": *The moral of the story escapes me. Morale* means "spirit" or "state of mind": *Victory improved the team's morale.*

most, almost See *almost, most.*

must of See *have, of.*

myself, herself, himself, yourself The *-self* pronouns refer to or intensify another word or words: *Paul helped himself; Jill herself said so.* The *-self* pronouns are often used colloquially in place of personal pronouns, but that use should be avoided in formal speech and writing: *No one except me* [not *myself*] *saw the accident. Our delegates will be Susan and you* [not *yourself*]. See also **4** p. 225 on the unchanging forms of the *-self* pronouns in standard American English.

nowheres Nonstandard for *nowhere.*

number See *amount, number.*

of, have See *have, of.*

off of *Of* is unnecessary. Use *off* or *from* rather than *off of: He jumped off* [or *from,* not *off of*] *the roof.*

OK, O.K., okay All three spellings are acceptable, but avoid this colloquial term in formal speech and writing.

on account of Wordy for *because of.*

on the other hand This transitional expression of contrast should be preceded by its mate, *on the one hand: On the one hand, we hoped for snow. On the other hand, we feared that it would harm the animals.* However, the two combined can be unwieldy, and a simple *but, however, yet,* or *in contrast* often suffices: *We hoped for snow. Yet we feared that it would harm the animals.*

outside of See *inside of, outside of.*

owing to the fact that Wordy for *because.*

party See *individual, person, party.*

people, persons In formal usage, *people* refers to a general group: *We the people of the United States. . . . Persons* refers to a collection of individuals: *Will the person or persons who saw the accident please notify. . . .* Except when emphasizing individuals, prefer *people* to *persons.* See also *individual, person, party.*

per Except in technical writing, an English equivalent is usually preferable to the Latin *per: $10 an* [not *per*] *hour; sent by* [not *per*] *parcel post; requested in* [not *per* or *as per*] *your letter.*

percent (per cent), percentage Both these terms refer to fractions of one hundred. *Percent* always follows a number (*40 percent of the voters*), and the word should be used instead of the symbol (%) in general writing. *Percentage* stands alone (*the percentage of voters*) or follows an adjective (*a high percentage*).

person See *individual, person, party.*

persons See *people, persons.*

phenomena The plural of *phenomenon* (meaning "perceivable fact" or "unusual occurrence"): *Many phenomena are not recorded. One phenomenon is attracting attention.*

plenty A colloquial substitute for *very: The reaction occurred very* [not *plenty*] *fast.*

plus *Plus* is standard as a preposition meaning "in addition to": *His income plus mine is sufficient.* But *plus* is colloquial as a conjunctive adverb: *Our organization is larger than theirs; moreover* [not *plus*], *we have more money.*

precede, proceed The verb *precede* means "come before": *My name precedes yours in the alphabet.* The verb *proceed* means "move on": *We were told to proceed to the waiting room.*

prejudice, prejudiced *Prejudice* is a noun; *prejudiced* is an adjective. Do not drop the *-d* from *prejudiced: I was fortunate that my parents were not prejudiced* [not *prejudice*].

pretty Overworked as an adverb meaning "rather" or "somewhat": *He was somewhat* [not *pretty*] *irked at the suggestion.*

previous to, prior to Wordy for *before.*

principal, principle *Principal* is an adjective meaning "foremost" or "major," a noun meaning "chief official," or, in finance, a noun meaning "capital sum." *Principle* is a noun only, meaning "rule" or "axiom." *Her principal reasons for confessing were her principles of right and wrong.*

proceed, precede See *precede, proceed.*

question of whether, question as to whether Wordy substitutes for *whether.*

raise, rise *Raise* means "lift" or "bring up" and takes a direct object: *The Kirks raise cattle.* Its main forms are *raise, raised, raised. Rise* means "get up" and does not take an object: *They must rise at dawn.* Its main forms are *rise, rose, risen.* (See also **4** p. 198.)

real, really In formal speech and writing, *real* should not be used as an adverb; *really* is the adverb and *real* an adjective. *Popular reaction to the announcement was really* [not *real*] *enthusiastic.*

reason is because Although colloquially common, this expression should be avoided in formal speech and writing. Use a *that* clause after *reason is: The reason he is absent is that* [not *is because*] *he is sick.* Or: *He is absent because he is sick.* (See also **4** p. 259.)

respectful, respective *Respectful* means "full of (or showing) respect": *Be respectful of other people. Respective* means "separate": *The French and the Germans occupied their respective trenches.*

rise, raise See *raise, rise.*

scarcely See *but, hardly, scarcely.*

sensual, sensuous *Sensual* suggests sexuality; *sensuous* means "pleasing to the senses." *Stirred by the sensuous scent of meadow grass and flowers, Cheryl and Paul found their thoughts growing increasingly sensual.*

set, sit *Set* means "put" or "place" and takes a direct object: *He sets the pitcher down.* Its main forms are *set, set, set. Sit* means "be seated" and does not take an object: *She sits on the sofa.* Its main forms are *sit, sat, sat.* (See also **4** p. 198.)

shall, will *Will* is the future-tense helping verb for all persons: *I will go, you will go, they will go.* The main use of *shall* is for first-person questions requesting an opinion or consent: *Shall I order a pizza? Shall we dance? Shall* can also be used for the first person when a formal effect is desired (*I shall expect you around three*), and it is occasionally used with the second or third person to express the speaker's determination (*You shall do as I say*).

should of See *have, of.*

sight, site, cite See *cite, sight, site.*

since *Since* mainly relates to time: *I've been waiting since noon.* But *since* is also often used to mean "because": *Since you ask, I'll tell you.* Revise sentences in which the word could have either meaning, such as *Since I studied physics, I have been planning to major in engineering.*

sit, set See *set, sit.*

site, cite, sight See *cite, sight, site.*

so Avoid using *so* alone or as a vague intensifier: *He was so late. So* needs to be followed by *that* and a clause that states a result: *He was so late that I left without him.*

somebody, some body; someone, some one *Somebody* and *someone* are indefinite pronouns; *some body* is a noun modified by *some;* and *some one* is a pronoun or an adjective modified by *some. Somebody ought to invent a shampoo that will give hair some body. Someone told Janine she should choose some one plan and stick with it.*

sometime, sometimes, some time *Sometime* means "at an indefinite time in the future": *Why don't you come up and see me sometime? Sometimes* means "now and then": *I still see my old friend Joe sometimes. Some time* means "a span of time": *I need some time to make the payments.*

somewheres Nonstandard for *somewhere.*

sort of, sort of a See *kind of, sort of, type of.*

such Avoid using *such* as a vague intensifier: *It was such a cold winter. Such* should be followed by *that* and a clause that states a result: *It was such a cold winter that Napoleon's troops had to turn back.*

such as See *like, such as.*

supposed to, used to In both these expressions, the *-d* is essential: *I used to* [not *use to*] *think so. He's supposed to* [not *suppose to*] *meet us.*

sure Colloquial when used as an adverb meaning *surely: James Madison sure was right about the need for the Bill of Rights.* If you merely want to be emphatic, use *certainly: Madison certainly was right.* If your goal is to convince a possibly reluctant reader, use *surely: Madison surely was right.*

sure and, sure to; try and, try to *Sure to* and *try to* are the correct forms: *Be sure to* [not *sure and*] *buy milk. Try to* [not *Try and*] *find some decent tomatoes.*

take, bring See *bring, take.*

than, as See *as, than.*

than, then *Than* is a conjunction used in comparisons, *then* an adverb indicating time: *Holmes knew then that Moriarty was wilier than he had thought.*

that, which *That* introduces an essential clause: *We should use the lettuce that Susan bought* (*that Susan bought* limits the lettuce to a particular lettuce). *Which* can introduce both essential and nonessential clauses, but many writers reserve *which* only for nonessential clauses: *The leftover lettuce, which is in the refrigerator, would make a good salad* (*which is in the refrigerator* simply provides more information about the lettuce we already know of). Essential clauses (with *that* or *which*) are not set off by commas; nonessential clauses (with *which*) are. See also **5** p. 269.

that, which, who Use *that* for animals, things, and sometimes collective or anonymous people: *The rocket that failed cost millions. Infants that walk need constant tending.* Use *which* only for animals and things: *The river, which flows south, divides two countries.* Use *who* only for people and for animals with names: *Dorothy is the girl who visits Oz. Her dog, Toto, who accompanies her, gives her courage.*

their, there, they're *Their* is the possessive form of *they: Give them their money. There* indicates place (*I saw her standing there*) or functions as an expletive (*There is a hole behind you*). *They're* is a contraction for *they are: They're going fast.*

theirselves Nonstandard for *themselves.*

them In standard American English, *them* does not serve as an adjective: *Those* [not *them*] *people want to know.*

then, than See *than, then.*

these kind, these sort, these type, those kind See *kind of, sort of, type of.*

this, these *This* is singular: *this car* or *This is the reason I left. These* is plural: *these cars* or *These are not valid reasons.*

thru A colloquial spelling of *through* that should be avoided in all academic and business writing.

to, too, two *To* is a preposition; *too* is an adverb meaning "also" or "excessively"; and *two* is a number. *I too have been to Europe two times.*

too Avoid using *too* as a vague intensifier: *Monkeys are too mean.* If you do use *too,* explain the consequences of the excessive quality: *Monkeys are too mean to make good pets.*

toward, towards Both are acceptable, though *toward* is preferred. Use one or the other consistently.

try and, try to See *sure and, sure to; try and, try to.*

type of See *kind of, sort of, type of.* Don't use *type* without *of: It was a family type of* [not *type*] *restaurant.* Or better: *It was a family restaurant.*

uninterested See *disinterested, uninterested.*

unique *Unique* means "the only one of its kind" and so cannot sensibly be modified with words such as *very* or *most: That was a unique* [not *a very unique* or *the most unique*] *movie.*

usage, use *Usage* refers to conventions, most often those of a language: *Is "hadn't ought" proper usage? Usage* is often misused in place of the noun *use: Wise use* [not *usage*] *of insulation can save fuel.*

use, utilize *Utilize* can be used to mean "make good use of": *Many teachers utilize computers for instruction.* But for all other senses of "place in service" or "employ," prefer *use.*

used to See *supposed to, used to.*

wait for, wait on In formal speech and writing, *wait for* means "await" (*I'm waiting for Paul*) and *wait on* means "serve" (*The owner of the store herself waited on us*).

ways Colloquial as a substitute for *way: We have only a little way* [not *ways*] *to go.*

well See *good, well.*

whether, if See *if, whether.*

which, that See *that, which.*

which, who, that See *that, which, who.*

who's, whose *Who's* is the contraction of *who is* or *who has: Who's* [*Who is*] *at the door? Jim is the only one who's* [*who has*] *passed. Whose* is the possessive form of *who: Whose book is that?*

will, shall See *shall, will.*

-wise See *-ize, -wise.*

would be Often used instead of *is* or *are* to soften statements needlessly: *One example is* [not *would be*] *gun-control laws. Would* can combine with other verbs for the same unassertive effect: *would ask, would seem, would suggest,* and so on.

would have Avoid this construction in place of *had* in clauses that begin *if* and state a condition contrary to fact: *If the tree had* [not *would have*] *withstood the fire, it would have been the oldest in town.* See also **4** p. 215.

would of See *have, of.*

you In all but very formal writing, *you* is generally appropriate as long as it means "you, the reader." In all writing, avoid indefinite uses of *you,* such as *In one ancient tribe your first loyalty was to your parents.* See also **4** p. 235.

your, you're *Your* is the possessive form of *you: Your dinner is ready. You're* is the contraction of *you are: You're bound to be late.*

yourself See *myself, herself, himself, yourself.*

Credits

Text and Illustrations

Brooks, Gwendolyn. "The Bean Eaters" by Gwendolyn Brooks, 1991. Reprinted by consent of Brooks Permissions.

Cunningham, John A., and Peter Selby. "Relighting Cigarettes: How Common Is It?" by John A. Cunningham and Peter Selby, *Nicotine and Tobacco Research*, 9.5, 621–23. Copyright © 2007 by Informa Healthcare—Journals. Reproduced with permission of Informa Healthcare—Journals in the format Textbook via Copyright Clearance Center.

Davies, Antony. "Unemployment Rates of High School Graduates and College Graduates, 1984–2004," from *The Economics of College Tuition* by Antony Davies. Copyright © 2005. Reprinted by permission.

Dyson, Freeman J. From *Disturbing the Universe* by Freeman J. Dyson. Copyright © 1979 by Freeman J. Dyson. Reprinted by permission of Basic Books, a member of Perseus Books Group.

EBSCO. From *www.web.ebscohost.com*. Reprinted by permission.

Friedman, Thomas L. "It's a Flat World, After All" *New York Times*, April 3, 2005.

Google. *www.google.com*.

Goreau, Angeline. "Hers: Worthy Women Revisited" by Angeline Goreau. Copyright © 1986 by Angeline Goreau. Originally appeared in *New York Times*, December 11, 1986. Reprinted by permission of Georges Borchardt, Inc., for the author.

Ik, Kim Yong. Excerpt from "A Book-Writing Venture" by Kim Yong Ik. Originally published in *The Writer*, October 1965. Copyright © Kim Yong Ik. Reprinted by permission of Faith M. Leigh, literary heir to the estate of Kim Yong Ik.

Jackson, Tim. "Live Better by Consuming Less?" by Tim Jackson, *Journal of Industrial Ecology*, 9.1–2. Reprinted by permission of Blackwell Publishing Ltd.

Kuralt, Charles. *Dateline America*. Orlando: Harcourt, 1979.

Lahiri, Jhumpa. From *Unaccustomed Earth* by Jhumpa Lahiri, copyright © 2008 by Jhumpa Lahiri. Used by permission of Alfred A. Knopf, a division of Random House, Inc.

Mayer, Lawrence. "The Confounding Enemy of Sleep." *Fortune*, June, 1974.

Molella, Arthur. From "Cultures of Innovation" by Arthur Molella, Lemelson Center, National Museum of American History, Smithsonian Institution, *www.invention.smithsonian.org*. Used by permission.

Muldoon, Annie. Abstract of "Where the Green Is: Examining the Paradox of Environmentally Conscious Consumption" by Annie Muldoon, *Electronic Green Journal*, 23, April 2006, on the EBSCOhost database Web site, *www.web.ebscohost.com*. Reprinted by permission of EBSCO and UCLA Library.

Ouchi, William G. *Theory Z*. Reading: Addison-Wesley, 1981.

Polletta, Francesca. "Just Talk: Public Deliberation after 9/11" by Francesca Polletta, *Journal of Public Deliberation*, 4.1, Article 2, *www.services.bepress.com*. Used by permission.

ProQuest. From "Privilege and Repression in the Digital Era: Rethinking the Sociopolitics of the Digital Divide," *www.proquest.com*. Used by permission.

Rosen, Ruth. "Search for Yesterday" by Ruth Rosen from *Watching Television* edited by Todd Gitlin. New York: Pantheon Books, 1986.

Selwyn, Neil. "The Social Processes of Learning to Use Computers" by Neil Selwyn, *Social Science Computer Review*, 23.1, 122. Copyright © 2005 by Sage Publications Inc. Journals. Reproduced with permission of Sage Publications Inc. Journals in the format Textbook via Copyright Clearance Center.

Sowell, Thomas. "Student Loans" from *Is Reality Optional? and Other Essays* by Thomas Sowell, 1993. Reprinted by permission of Thomas Sowell and Creators Syndicate, Inc.

Stout, David. From "Blind Win Court Ruling on U.S. Currency" by David Stout, *New York Times*, May 21, 2008. All rights reserved. Used by permission and protected by the Copyright Laws of the United States. The printing, copying, redistribution, or retransmission of the Material without express written permission is prohibited.

Tuchman, Barbara. "The Decline of Quality" by Barbara Tuchman, *New York Times*, November 2, 1980. Reprinted by the permission of Russell & Volkening as agents for the author. Copyright © 1980 by Barbara Tuchman.

UNFPA. "AIDS Clock" from the UNFPA.org Web site, *www.unfpa.org*, 2008. Reprinted with permission.

Woolf, Virginia. *The Waves*. New York: Harcourt, 1931.

Photos

Title page, clockwise from top left: Jamie Grill/Iconica/Getty; The Image Bank/Getty; Stone/Getty; Andersen Ross/Blend Images/Getty; David Fischer/Digital Vision/Getty; **1:** Image Source/Getty; **65:** NASA; **67:** Blend Images/Getty; **85:** *Boostup.org;* **109:** Getty; **110 and 113:** Michael Foujols/Corbis; **114:** Lydia Kibiuk/Society for Neuroscience December 2001; **115:** UNICEF; **141:** Photographer's Choice/Getty; **187:** Sabah Arar/AFP/Getty; **295:** Stone/Getty; **345:** Neo Vision/Getty; **369:** Digital Vision/Getty; **435, 461, 519, and 547:** Stone/Getty; **567:** The Image Bank/Getty.

Index

A

a, an
capitalization in titles, **6** 306
choosing between, **Gl** 511
rules for use of, **4** 242–43
Abbreviations
a vs. *an* with, **Gl** 511
acceptable, **6** 310
BC, BCE, AD, CE, AM, PM, no., $, **6** 310
in business names, **6** 311
for calendar designations, **6** 311
in footnotes or endnotes, **Chic** 497, 501
grammar checkers for, **6** 309
Inc., Bros., Co., &, **6** 311
Latin, **6** 310–11, **Chic** 497, 501
for names of people, places, courses, **6** 311
in online communication, **2** 95
period omitted from, **5** 263
plurals of, **5** 285
with specific dates and numbers, **6** 310
spelling checkers for, **6** 309
for titles with names, **6** 310
for units of measurement, **6** 311
abide by, in, **3** 168
Absolute modifiers, **4** 238
Absolute phrases
commas with, **5** 270
defined, **4** 192–93
Absolute statements, **2** 104
Abstracts
documenting: APA style, **APA** 470, 476, 479; MLA style, **MLA** 418, 420, 441
in one's own paper, **APA** 481
as research sources, **7** 323, 334
Abstract words (abstraction)
defined, **3** 167
grammar checkers for, **3** 165
Academic sites, MLA style, **MLA** 434
Academic skills, **2** 69–76
exam preparation, **2** 75–76
listening and note taking, **2** 69–70
reading comprehension, **2** 70–74
Academic writing. *See also* Critical thinking and reading; Research writing
about literature, **2** 94
acknowledging sources in, **2** 74–75
approaches to, **2** 90–91
audience for, **1** 7–8, **2** 93
content and structure of, **2** 93–94
documentation styles for, **7** 374–75
editing of, **2** 74
essay examinations, **2** 75–76
expectations for, **2** 90–96
features of, **2** 94–96
formality in, **2** 94–96
goals and requirements of, **2** 90–96, **8** 381–83
in humanities, **2** 94, **8** 383–95
language for, **2** 94–96
in natural and applied sciences, **2** 94, **8** 399–402
organization in, **2** 94
person and pronouns in, **2** 95–96
purpose in, **2** 92–93
in research writing, **7** 362–67
in response to texts, **2** 91–92
revising of, **2** 74
in social sciences, **2** 94, **8** 396–97
sources for, acknowledging, **2** 74–75
standard American English in, **2** 94–96
structure and content of, **2** 93–94
synthesis in, **2** 74, 92, **7** 356–57, 359–62, 362–67
thesis statement and support in, **2** 93–94
voice in, **2** 94–96
accept, except, **6** 297, **Gl** 511
accordingly, punctuation with, **4** 257
accords with, according to, **3** 168
AccuNet/AP Multimedia Archives, **7** 342
accuse of, **3** 168
accustomed to, **3** 168
Acknowledgment of opposition, **2** 102
Acknowledgment of sources
disciplines' styles for, **7** 374
necessity for, **7** 370–72
style guides for: humanities, **8** 395; natural and applied sciences, **8** 402; social sciences, **8** 398–99
using APA style, **APA** 462–81
using Chicago style, **Chic** 491–501
using CSE style, **CSE** 502–08
using MLA style, **MLA** 404–47
Acronyms
acceptability of, **6** 310
defined, **6** 310
period omitted from, **5** 263, **6** 309
Active reading, **2** 77–81

Active voice
consistency in use of, **4** 217
defined, **3** 145, **4** 216
formation of, **4** 216–17
vs. passive voice, **4** 216–17
as preferred form, **3** 145, 174, **4** 216–17
AD, BC, **6** 310
adapt from, to, **3** 168
Address, direct, comma with, **5** 271
Address (electronic). *See* URL
Address (lecture), MLA style for, **MLA** 447
Address (street, city, state)
in business letters, **2** 129–30
commas in, **5** 273
numerals instead of words in, **6** 313
Adflip, **7** 341
Ad hominem fallacy, **2** 103
Adjective clauses
defined, **4** 193–94
repetition in, **4** 260
Adjective modifiers, **3** 156
Adjectives
vs. adverbs, **4** 183–87
adverbs to modify, **4** 183–87
comma with two or more, **5** 272–73
comparative and superlative forms of, **4** 184, 237–38
coordinate, **5** 272
defined, **4** 236
forms of, **4** 184, 237–38
grammar checkers for, **4** 236
hyphen in compound, **6** 301
irregular, **4** 238
after linking verbs, **4** 237
to modify nouns and pronouns, **4** 183–84
to modify subjects, **4** 237
not to negate, **4** 236
order of, **4** 248
with plural nouns, **4** 236
prepositional phrases as, **4** 191
present vs. past participles as, **4** 240
proper, capitalization of, **6** 304–05
as subject and object complements, **4** 190
subordinate clauses as, **4** 193–94
verbals and verbal phrases as, **4** 191–92
Adverb clauses, **4** 194
Adverbs. *See also* Conjunctive adverbs
vs. adjectives, **4** 236–37
comparative and superlative forms of, **4** 184, 237–38
forms of, **4** 184, 237–38
grammar checkers for, **4** 236
infinitives and infinitive phrases as, **4** 192
irregular, **4** 238
after linking verbs, **4** 237
-ly ending with, **4** 184
to modify verbs, adjectives, adverbs, word groups, **4** 236
placement of, **3** 156–57, **4** 245–48
prepositional phrases as, **4** 191
subordinate clauses as, **4** 193–94
in two-word verbs, **4** 207
verbals and verbal phrases as, **4** 191–92
Advertisements. *See* Illustrations and artworks
advice, advise, **Gl** 511
a few, few, **4** 244
affect, effect, **6** 297, **Gl** 511
afraid of, **3** 168
Afterword, MLA style, **MLA** 428–29
Agreement of pronouns and antecedents
with antecedents joined by *and*, **4** 230
with antecedents joined by *or* or *nor*, **4** 230
with collective nouns, **4** 221–22
grammar checkers for, **4** 229
with indefinite words, **4** 231–32
Agreement of subjects and verbs
with collective nouns, **4** 232
grammar checkers for, **4** 218
with indefinite pronouns, **4** 220–21
with intervening words, **4** 219–20
with inverted word order, **4** 223
with linking verbs, **4** 223
with singular nouns ending in *-s*, **4** 222
with subjects joined by *and*, **4** 220
with subjects joined by *or* or *nor*, **4** 220
with titles, **4** 223
with *who, which*, or *that*, **4** 222
with words being described or defined, **4** 223
agree on, to, with, **3** 168
agree to, agree with, **Gl** 511
Aircraft, italics or underlining for names of, **6** 308
a little, little, **4** 244
all
pronouns with, **4** 231–32
verbs with, **4** 220–21
all ready, already, **6** 297, **Gl** 511
all right, **Gl** 511
AlltheWeb, **7** 336

all together, altogether, **Gl** 511
allusion, illusion, **6** 297, **Gl** 512
Allusions
defined, **2** 86
of illustrations, **2** 86
Almanacs, MLA style, **MLA** 426
almost, most, **Gl** 512
a lot, **Gl** 512
already, all ready, **6** 297, **Gl** 511
AltaVista, **7** 336
altogether, all together, **Gl** 511
AM, PM, **6** 310
American Memory, **7** 341
American Psychological Association style. *See* APA style
among, between, **Gl** 512
amount, number, **Gl** 512
Ampersands (&), **6** 311, **APA** 469
an, a
capitalization in titles, **6** 306
choosing between, **Gl** 511
rules for use of, **4** 242–43
Analysis (division)
in critical reading of literature, **8** 383–91
in critical reading of research sources, **7** 345–56
in critical thinking and reading, **2** 81
of elements of images, **2** 86–87
in essay development, **1** 13
of illustrations, **2** 86–87
of literature, **8** 383–91
in paragraph development, **1** 47
of poetry, **8** 389–91
sample, for images, **2** 87–88
as writing assignment, **1** 6
and
ampersand (&) for, **6** 311, **APA** 469
antecedents of pronouns joined by, **4** 230
commas with, **5** 265, 275
as coordinating conjunction, **3** 147
main clauses not joined by, **4** 255–56
parallelism with, **3** 151–52
semicolons with, **5** 278
subjects joined by, **4** 220, **5** 275
and/or, **Gl** 512
angry with, **3** 168
Annotated bibliographies, **7** 323–25
Anonymous or unsigned works
APA style: parenthetical citations, **APA** 465–66; reference list, **APA** 469, 477
Chicago style, **Chic** 494
CSE style, **CSE** 505
MLA style: parenthetical citations, **MLA** 409; works cited, **MLA** 417, 422, 432
ante-, anti-, **Gl** 512
Antecedents
agreement of pronouns and, **4** 229–32
defined, **4** 222, 229
reference of pronouns to, **4** 233–35
Anthologies or collections
APA style, **APA** 473
Chicago style, **Chic** 496
CSE style, **CSE** 506
MLA style, **MLA** 425
Anthropology, research sources on, **8** 398
anti-, ante-, **Gl** 512
anxious, eager, **Gl** 512
any
pronouns with, **4** 231–32
verbs with, **4** 220–21
any, any other, **4** 239
anybody
vs. *any body,* **Gl** 512
pronouns with, **4** 231–32
verbs with, **4** 220–21
any more, anymore, **Gl** 512
anyone
vs. *any one,* **Gl** 512
pronouns with, **4** 231–32
verbs with, **4** 220–21
anything
pronouns with, **4** 231–32
verbs with, **4** 220–21
anyway, punctuation with, **4** 257
APA style, **APA** 462–87
for document format, **APA** 481–84
indexes to documentation models: parenthetical citations, **APA** 462; reference list, **APA** 462–63
parenthetical citations: index to, **APA** 462; models of, **APA** 464–67
reference list: guidelines for, **APA** 467–81; index to, **APA** 462–63; models of, **APA** 469–81
sample research paper using, **APA** 484–87
Apostrophes
to form contractions, **5** 285
to form plural abbreviations, dates, and words or characters used as words, **5** 283, 285
to form possessives, **4** 181, **5** 282–84
grammar checkers for, **5** 282
misuses of, with plural noun, singular verb, or possessive personal pronoun, **5** 283, 284–85
spaces with, **1** 58

Appeal, of literary works, **8** 386–87
Appeals, in argument
  appropriate, **2** 101–02, 107, 109
  as evidence, **2** 101–02, 107
  inappropriate, **2** 102–04
  in visual arguments, **2** 109
Appositives
  case of pronoun in, **4** 228
  colon to introduce, **5** 280
  defined, **4** 193
  punctuation of, **5** 270
Appropriate language. *See also* Language; Words
  grammar checkers for, **3** 165
  guidelines for, **3** 158–64
apt, liable, likely, **Gl** 512
are, is, **Gl** 512
Arguments, **2** 97–115
  critical thinking and reading for, **2** 77–89
  elements of, **2** 97–99
  fallacies in, **2** 102–04
  finding common ground in, **2** 102
  illustrations, choice of, **2** 110–11
  organization of, **2** 104–05
  reasonableness in, **2** 100–-04
  Rogerian, **2** 102
  sample of, **2** 111–15
  as writing assignment, **1** 7
Art. *See* Illustrations and artworks
Articles (*a, an, the*)
  a vs. *an,* **Gl** 511
  capitalization in titles, **6** 306
  defined, **4** 240
  grammar checkers for, **4** 241
  omission of, **3** 172
  rules for use of, **4** 242–43
Articles in periodicals
  documenting: APA style, **APA** 470–72, 474–77; Chicago style, **Chic** 495, 497–98; CSE style, **CSE** 505–07; MLA style, **MLA** 418–23, 434, 439–42, 443
  finding bibliographic information for, **MLA** 419, 421, 440
  indexes to, **7** 332–35
  in online databases, **7** 332–35, **MLA** 441–43
  peer-reviewed or refereed, **7** 326
  as research sources, **7** 331–35
  titles of, quotation marks for, **5** 288
  in working bibliography, **7** 324
Art Source directory, **7** 341
ARTstor directory, **7** 342
Artworks. *See* Illustrations and artworks
as
  case of pronoun after, **4** 228
  misuse of, **Gl** 512–13
as . . . as, **4** 186
as, like, **Gl** 513
as, than, **Gl** 513
as a result, punctuation with, **4** 257
ascent, assent, **6** 297
Ask.com, **7** 336
Assignments, writing
  in humanities, **8** 392–93
  in literature, **8** 387–88
  narrowing the purpose for, **1** 6–7
  in natural and applied sciences, **8** 399–400
  in social sciences, **8** 396–97
Associations, capitalizing names of, **6** 304
Assumptions
  interpreting, in critical reading, **2** 82
  using, in argument, **2** 99, 108–09
assure, ensure, insure, **Gl** 513
Astronomy, research sources on, **8** 402
at
  vs. *in* and *on,* **3** 169
  with *where,* **Gl** 513
at last, punctuation with, **4** 257
Audience
  for academic writing, **2** 93
  anticipating objections of, **2** 102
  considering, **1** 4, 7–8, **2** 101–02
  for illustrations, **2** 84
  for oral presentations, **2** 124
  for public writing, **2** 137–38
  purpose and, **1** 8
  questions about, **1** 7–8
  vision loss, designing for readers with, **1** 64–65, **2** 119, 123
Audiovisual works. *See* Films, DVDs, and video recordings; Illustrations and artworks; Sound recordings
Authors
  APA style: parenthetical citations, **APA** 464–67; reference list, **APA** 469–81
  Chicago style: endnotes or footnotes, **Chic** 494–501; list of works cited, **Chic** 494–501
  CSE style: name-year text citations, **CSE** 502; numbered text citations, **CSE** 502–03; reference list, **CSE** 503–08
  determining in online sources, **7** 322, 351, 355

MLA style: list of works cited, **MLA** 416–47; parenthetical citations, **MLA** 407–14
providing names of, when introducing borrowed material, **7** 365
Auxiliary verbs. *See* Helping verbs (auxiliary verbs)
aware of, **3** 168
awful, awfully, **Gl** 513
a while, awhile, **Gl** 513

B

bad, badly, **4** 237, **Gl** 513
Bandwagon fallacy, **2** 103
bare, bear, **6** 297
based on, **3** 168
BC, AD, **6** 310
BCE, CE, **6** 310
be
forms of, **3** 144, **4** 182–83
as helping verb, **3** 144, **4** 183, 201–02
illogical equation with, **4** 258
omission of, **4** 251
past participle and forms of, **4** 202, 216–17
present participle and forms of, **4** 201–02
in subjunctive mood, **4** 215
bear, bare, **6** 297
because, avoiding after *reason is*, **4** 259
Begging the question, **2** 103
Beginnings of sentences
for emphasis, **3** 145–47
for variety, **3** 156–57
being as, being that, **Gl** 513
Beliefs, as claims in arguments, **2** 98
belong in, on, to, **3** 168
beside, besides, **Gl** 513
besides, punctuation with, **4** 257
better, had better, **Gl** 513
between, among, **Gl** 512
Biased language, **2** 102, **3** 161–64, **4** 231–32
Bible
capitalization of, **6** 305
MLA style: list of works cited, **MLA** 428; parenthetical citation, **MLA** 412
no italics or underlining for, **6** 308
Biblio, **7** 374
Bibliographies. *See also* APA style; Chicago style; CSE style; MLA style
annotated, **7** 323–25
guides to preparation of, **8** 395, 398–99, 402, **CSE** 502
as research sources in literature, **8** 388–89
working, **7** 323–25
Biology, research sources on, **8** 402
Block quotations
APA style, **APA** 483
MLA style, **MLA** 449
Blogs
collaboration through, **2** 118
documenting: APA style, **APA** 478; Chicago style, **Chic** 499; MLA style, **MLA** 432, 437
evaluating, **7** 354–56
permission for using, **7** 373
as research sources, **7** 339
board, bored, **6** 297
Body
of argument, **2** 104
of business letter, **2** 129
of essay, **1** 16–17, 38–52
Boldface type, **1** 57
Bookmarks/Favorites, **7** 337
Book reviews
documenting: APA style, **APA** 472, 476; Chicago style, **Chic** 495; MLA style, **MLA** 420–21, 434, 440–41
sources for, **8** 389
writing, **8** 388
Books
documenting: APA style, **APA** 469–70, 472–73, 477; Chicago style, **Chic** 494–97, 498; CSE style, **CSE** 504–06, 507; MLA style, **MLA** 423–29, 437–38, 443
finding bibliographic information for, **MLA** 424
as research sources, **7** 330
reviewing, **8** 388
subdivisions of, quotation marks for, **5** 288
titles of: capitalization of, **6** 306; italics or underlining for, **6** 307
in working bibliography, **7** 324
Boolean operators, in keywords, **7** 328–29
bored, board, **6** 297
Borrowed material, integrating in research papers, **7** 362–67
both
pronouns with, **4** 231–32
verbs with, **4** 220–21
both . . . and
as correlative conjunction, **4** 186
parallelism with, **3** 152–53

Brackets
for changes in quotations, **5** 293, 294, **6** 303, **7** 363
grammar checkers for, **5** 290
with *sic*, **5** 294
Brainstorming, **1** 11–12
brake, break, **6** 297
bring, take, **Gl** 513
Brochures
creating, **2** 139
documenting, MLA style, **MLA** 430
Bros., **6** 311
Browsers, **7** 337
BUBL LINK, **1** 6, **7** 336
Bulleted lists, **1** 58
Bureaucratese, **3** 176
Business and economics, research sources on, **8** 398
Business firms, abbreviations for names of, **6** 311
Business writing. *See* Public writing
but
commas with, **5** 265, 275
as coordinating conjunction, **3** 147, **4** 185
main clauses not joined by, **4** 255–56
parallelism with, **3** 151–52
semicolons with, **5** 278
but, hardly, scarcely, **Gl** 513
but, however, yet, **Gl** 514
buy, by, **6** 298

C

can, may, **Gl** 514
capable of, **3** 168
Capitalization
of *a, an, the* in titles, **6** 306
brackets for altered, **6** 303
after colons, **5** 280, **6** 304
of days, months, holidays, **6** 304
of first word in sentence, **6** 303–04
of government agencies, **6** 304
grammar checkers for, **6** 303
of historical events, documents, periods, movements, **6** 304
of languages, **6** 304
in online communication, **2** 95, 117, **6** 306, 309
of organizations and associations, **6** 304
with parentheses, **5** 291–92
of persons, **6** 304
of places, **6** 304
of proper nouns and adjectives, **6** 304–05
of questions in series, **6** 304
in quoted material, **6** 303, **7** 363
of races and nationalities, **6** 305
for readers with vision loss, **1** 65
of religions and religious terms, **6** 305
of titles of persons, **6** 305
of titles of works: APA style, **APA** 468; CSE style, **CSE** 504; general guidelines for, **6** 306
Cartoons. *See* Illustrations and artworks
Case analysis, **8** 396
Case of pronouns, **4** 224–29
in appositives, **4** 228
in compound subjects or objects, **4** 225–26
defined, **4** 224
before gerunds, **4** 229
grammar checkers for, **4** 225
with infinitives, **4** 229
as subject complement, **4** 224
after *than* or *as*, **4** 228
we vs. *us* with nouns, **4** 228
who vs. *whom*, **4** 226–28
Cause-and-effect analysis
in essay development, **1** 13
in paragraph development, **1** 44, 48
transitional expressions for, **1** 44
CD-ROMs
documenting: APA style, **APA** 480; Chicago style, **Chic** 499; CSE style, **CSE** 507; MLA style, **MLA** 443
periodicals on, **MLA** 443
reference works on, **3** 165, **MLA** 443
searching, **7** 328–29
CE, BCE, **6** 310
censor, censure, **Gl** 514
center around, **Gl** 514
certainly, punctuation with, **4** 257
certain of, **3** 168
cf., **6** 310
Characters, in literary works, **8** 385
charge for, with, **3** 168
Charts. *See* Illustrations and artworks
Chat, online, **2** 118
Chemistry, research sources on, **8** 402
Chicago Manual of Style, The. See Chicago style
Chicago style
for footnotes and endnotes: format of, **Chic** 491–501; models of, **Chic** 494–501
index to documentation models, **Chic** 490

for list of works cited: format of, **Chic** 491–501; index to, **Chic** 490; models of, **Chic** 494–501
Chronological organization, **1** 17, 41
Citation of sources, **7** 372–75. *See also* APA style; Chicago style; CSE style; MLA style
cite, sight, site, **6** 298, **Gl** 514
Claims, in argument, **2** 98, 99
Classification
in essay development, **1** 13
in paragraph development, **1** 47
Clauses
adjective, **4** 193–94, 260
adverb, **4** 194
comma splices with, **4** 253–57
commas with, **5** 265, 267–68, 268–71, 276
conjunctive adverbs with, **4** 257, **5** 277–78
coordinating conjunctions with, **4** 256, **5** 265, 275
coordination between, **3** 147
defined, **4** 193
fused sentences with, **4** 253–57
introductory, commas with, **5** 267–68
main. *See* Main (independent) clauses
nonessential vs. essential, **5** 268–71, 276
noun, **4** 194
semicolons with, **4** 257, **5** 277–79
as sentence fragments, **4** 201, 252
simplifying, **3** 175–76
subordinate, **4** 193–94. *See also* Subordinate (dependent) clauses
Clichés
avoiding, **3** 170–71
defined, **3** 170
no quotation marks for, **5** 288–89
style checkers for, **3** 171
Climactic organization, **1** 18, 41
climatic, climactic, **Gl** 514
Close of business letter, **2** 129
Clustering, **1** 12
Co., **6** 311
Coherence. *See also* Consistency; Unity
of essays, **1** 21
of paragraphs, **1** 39–44
Collaboration
in community work, **2** 138
guidelines for, **1** 35–37
using computers for, **1** 35–37, **2** 118
Collections (anthologies). *See* Anthologies or collections
Collective nouns
agreement of pronouns with, **4** 232
agreement of verbs with, **4** 221–22
defined, **4** 181
Colloquial language, **3** 160
Colons
in business letter salutations, **5** 281
capitalization after, **5** 280, **6** 304
vs. dash, **5** 291
grammar checkers for, **5** 279
to introduce, **5** 280
misuse of, **5** 281
with quotation marks, **5** 289
before quotations, **5** 280
vs. semicolon, **5** 280
space with, **1** 58
before subtitles, **5** 281
in time of day, **5** 281
Color
of images, **2** 86
selecting for readers with vision loss, **1** 65
Combining sentences
for conciseness, **3** 176
for variety, **3** 155–56
Comic strips. *See* Illustrations and artworks
Commands. *See also* Imperative mood
exclamation points with, **5** 264
periods with, **5** 263
Commas, **5** 265–76. *See also* Commas, misuse of
with absolute phrases, **5** 270
with adjectives, **5** 272–73
with conjunctive adverbs, **4** 257, **5** 277–78
vs. dashes, **5** 290
in dates, addresses, place names, long numbers, **5** 273
with direct address, **5** 271
grammar checkers for, **5** 265
with interjections, **5** 271
with introductory elements, **5** 267–68
between items in series, **5** 272
with main clauses joined by *and, but,* etc., **5** 265
main uses of, **5** 266
with nonessential elements, **5** 268–71
vs. parentheses, **5** 291
with parenthetical expressions, **5** 270–71, 291
with phrases of contrast, **5** 271
with prepositional phrases, **5** 267
with quotation marks, **5** 289
with *she said* and other signal phrases, **5** 273–74

Commas *(continued)*
space with, **1** 58
splices, **4** 253–57
with subordinate clauses, **5** 267
with tag questions, **5** 271
with verbals or verbal phrases, **5** 267
with *yes* and *no*, **5** 271
Commas, misuse of
around essential elements, **5** 276
around series, **5** 276
in comma splices, **4** 253–57
in compound subjects, predicates, etc., **5** 275
after conjunctions, **5** 275–76
before indirect quotations, **5** 274, 276
with other punctuation in quotations, **5** 274
before a parenthesis, **5** 291
between prepositions and objects, **5** 275
between subjects and verbs, **5** 275
between verbs and objects, **5** 275
Comma splices, **4** 253–57
defined, **4** 254
grammar checkers for, **4** 255
with main clauses not joined by *and*, *but*, etc., **4** 255–56
with main clauses related by *however*, *for example*, etc., **4** 256–57
revision of, **4** 253–57
Comment function, **1** 36
Common knowledge, **7** 370
Common nouns, **4** 180, **6** 305
Community work
audience for, **2** 137–38
brochures, **2** 139
collaboration in, **2** 138
flyers, **2** 137
newsletters, **2** 138
purpose, **2** 137–38
writing for, **2** 136–39
Comparative form of adjectives and adverbs, **4** 184, 237–38
Comparison and contrast
in essay development, **1** 13
organization of, **1** 47–48
in paragraph development, **1** 47–48
transitional expressions for, **1** 43–44
as writing assignment, **1** 6
Comparisons
complete, **4** 238–39
double, **4** 238
forms of, **4** 237–38
logical, **4** 238
parallelism in, **3** 153
Compass directions, capitalization of, **6** 305
complement, *compliment*, **Gl** 514
Complements. *See* Object complements; Subject complements
Complete compounds, **3** 171
Complete predicates, **4** 187–88
Complete sentences, **3** 171–72
Complete subjects, **4** 187
Complex sentences, **4** 195
Compound adjectives, hyphens in, **6** 301
Compound antecedents, agreement of pronouns with, **4** 230
Compound-complex sentences, **4** 195
Compound constructions. *See also specific compounds*
commas with, **5** 265, 275
defined, **3** 171
parallelism in, **3** 151–52
pronoun case in, **4** 225–26
semicolons with, **5** 278
Compound numbers, hyphens in, **6** 302
Compound objects, case of pronouns in, **4** 225–26
Compound predicates
defined, **4** 187
no commas in, **5** 275
Compounds, complete, **3** 171
Compound sentences, **4** 195
Compound subjects
case of pronouns in, **4** 225–26
defined, **4** 187
no commas in, **5** 275
verbs with, **4** 187
Compound words
apostrophes with possessives of, **5** 284
forming plurals of, **6** 301
hyphens in, **6** 301
Computerized databases. *See* Databases, electronic
Computerized sources. *See* Electronic sources
Computers
AutoSummarize function on, **2** 74
brainstorming on, **1** 11–12
collaborating on, **2** 118
Comment function, **1** 36
databases on, **7** 326–27, 330, 334–35
designing documents on, **1** 52–65
drafting on, **1** 22, **2** 118
editing on, **1** 31
finding overused words with, **3** 168
formatting documents on, **1** 52–65
formatting source citations on, **7** 374–75, **Chic** 494

freewriting on, **1** 10–11
grammar and style checkers for, guidelines on, **1** 32. *See also* entries for specific grammar and style issues
hypertext documents on, **2** 119–24
journals on, **1** 9–10
for keeping notes, **1** 10, **7** 358
library catalogs on, **7** 326–27, 330
mixed sentences and, **4** 259
proofreading and, **1** 31–32
research with. *See* Research writing
revising on, **1** 25
saving and backing up documents on, **1** 22
sharing files on, **2** 118
sources on, **7** 325–42, 347, 350–54. *See also* Electronic sources
spelling checkers on, **1** 31–32, **6** 297
summaries using, **2** 74
using the Web on, **7** 335–40
Computer science, research sources on, **8** 402
Computer services. *See* Databases, electronic
Computer software
for documentation of sources, **7** 374–75
italics or underlining for titles of, **6** 307
Conciseness, achieving
combining sentences, **3** 176
cutting empty words and phrases, **3** 174–75
cutting repetition, **3** 175
eliminating expletive constructions, **3** 176
focusing on subjects and verbs, **3** 173–74
reducing clauses and phrases, **3** 175–76
rewriting jargon, **3** 176
using active voice, **3** 174
using strong verbs, **3** 174
Concluding elements, dashes with, **5** 290–91
Conclusions
of arguments, **2** 105
of essays, **1** 16–17, 51–52
guidelines for, **1** 51–52
transitional expressions to indicate, **1** 44
Concrete words, **3** 167–68
concur in, with, **3** 168
Conditional sentences
defined, **4** 213
sequence of verb tenses in, **4** 213–14
subjunctive mood in, **4** 213–14
Conference proceedings, MLA style, **MLA** 428
Conjunctions
adverbial. *See* Conjunctive adverbs
capitalization in titles, **6** 306
coordinating. *See* Coordinating conjunctions
correlative. *See* Correlative conjunctions
subordinating. *See* Subordinating conjunctions
types of, **4** 185–86
Conjunctive adverbs
and comma splices, **4** 257
commas with, **4** 257, **5** 278
vs. coordinating and subordinating conjunctions, **4** 257
list of, **4** 257
semicolons with main clauses related by, **3** 147, **4** 257, **5** 277–78
Connotation
defined, **3** 167
grammar checkers for, **3** 165
conscience, conscious, **Gl** 514
consequently, punctuation with, **4** 257
Consistency. *See also* Agreement of pronouns and antecedents; Agreement of subjects and verbs; Coherence; Unity
paragraph coherence and, **1** 42–43
in pronouns, **4** 235
in verb mood, **4** 215
in verb tense, **4** 211–12
in verb voice, **4** 217
Consonants, final, **6** 300
contact, **Gl** 514
contend for, with, **3** 168
Content of essay, in academic writing, **2** 93–94
Context
determining for online sources, **7** 351–54, 355
determining in critical thinking, **2** 83
of illustrations, **2** 86, 89
of writing situation, **1** 3
continual, continuous, **Gl** 514
Contractions, apostrophes for, **5** 283, 285
Contrary-to-fact sentences
sequence of verb tenses in, **4** 213–14
subjunctive mood for, **4** 214–15
Contrast. *See* Comparison and contrast
Coordinate adjectives
commas with, **5** 272

Coordinate adjectives *(continued)*
defined, **5** 272
tests for, **5** 272–73
Coordinating conjunctions
commas with, **5** 265, 275
vs. conjunctive adverbs and subordinating conjunctions, **4** 257
for correcting comma splices or fused sentences, **4** 256
defined, **3** 147
list of, **4** 185
parallelism with, **3** 151–52
semicolons with, **5** 278
Coordination
defined, **3** 147
effective, **3** 148–49
excessive or faulty, **3** 148–49
grammar checkers for, **3** 148
parallelism with, **3** 151–52
to relate equal ideas, **3** 148
Copyright, Web compositions and, **7** 373
Corporate or group authors
APA style: parenthetical citations, **APA** 465; reference list, **APA** 469
CSE style, **CSE** 508
MLA style: list of works cited, **MLA** 417; parenthetical citations, **MLA** 409
Correlative conjunctions
list of, **3** 147, **4** 186
parallelism with, **3** 152–53
could of, **Gl** 516
Council of Science Editors. *See* CSE style
Count nouns
defined, **4** 181, 241
determiners with, **4** 240–41, 242–44
Country names, abbreviation of, **6** 310
Courses of instruction, abbreviations of, **6** 311
Creativity, for discovering ideas, **1** 8–13
Credentials of source author, providing, **7** 365
credible, creditable, credulous, **Gl** 514
criteria, **Gl** 514
Critical thinking and reading, **2** 77–89
and academic writing, **2** 74–75, 90–92
active reading for, **2** 77–81
analysis in, **2** 81, 86–87
and argument, **2** 97–99
defined, **2** 77
evaluating for, **2** 83, 89, **7** 345–56
with illustrations, **2** 83–89
interpreting for, **2** 82, 87–89
and literature, **8** 383–91
with online discussions and blogs, **7** 354–56
previewing for, **2** 77–80, 84
with research sources, **7** 345–56
for revision, **1** 25–27
summarizing for, **2** 72–74, 80–81
synthesis for, **2** 74, 82–83, 89, 92, **7** 356–57
techniques of, **2** 69–74, 77–81
with Web sites and pages, **7** 347, 350–54
Critique, as research paper, **8** 400
CSE style
vs. APA style, **CSE** 502
for documenting sources, **CSE** 502–08
index to documentation models, **CSE** 491
reference list: index of models, **CSE** 491; name-year style, **CSE** 503–08; number style, **CSE** 503–08
text citations: name-year style, **CSE** 502; number style, **CSE** 502–03
Culture-language issues
a, an, the, **3** 172, **4** 242–43
academic writing, structure of, **2** 93–94
adjectives, order of, **4** 248
adjectives with plural nouns, **4** 236
adverbs, position of, **3** 156–57, **4** 247–48
American vs. British spelling, **6** 299
argument and, **2** 97
articles (*a, an, the*), **3** 172, **4** 242–43
at, in, on, **3** 169
capitalization, **6** 303
collaboration and, **1** 37
collective nouns, **4** 221–22, 232
comma splices, **4** 255
count nouns, **4** 241
critical reading, **1** 37, **2** 77
determiners, **4** 240–44
dialect, **3** 158–59
dictionaries, **3** 166, 169, **4** 241
direct questions, **5** 263
editing, **1** 37
expert opinions, **7** 368
expletive constructions, **3** 176
exploratory writing, **1** 9
for, since, **3** 169, **4** 211
fused sentences, **4** 255
gender of nouns and pronouns, **4** 230
gerunds and infinitives, **4** 192, 205–07
helping verbs and main verbs, **4** 200–05

intellectual property, **7** 368
introductory paragraphs, **1** 50
invisible writing, **1** 11
journal writing, **1** 10
main clauses, **4** 255
modal helping verbs, **4** 203–05
Ms. vs. *Miss* or *Mrs.*, **3** 162
noncount nouns, **4** 221–22, 232, **6** 301
nonstandard dialect, **3** 158–59
no to negate nouns, **4** 237
not to negate verbs or adjectives, **4** 236
noun gender, **4** 230
noun plurals, **4** 232
numbers, periods vs. commas with, **5** 273, **6** 312
omitted helping verbs, **4** 201
omitted *here*, *it*, or *there* in expletive constructions, **3** 176
omitted subjects or verbs, **4** 251
organization of essay, **1** 17
paragraphing, **1** 38
paraphrasing, **7** 361
passive voice, **4** 189, 202
plagiarism, **7** 368
plural nouns after *one of the*, **4** 222
plural nouns and adjectives, **4** 232
prepositions, **3** 168–69, **4** 184–85
present vs. past participles as adjectives, **4** 240
progressive tenses, **4** 211
pronoun-antecedent agreement, **4** 230, 232
pronoun gender, **4** 230
public writing, **2** 128
questions, direct, **5** 263
redundant phrases, **3** 175
repetition of sentence parts, **4** 260
research topic development, **7** 344
revision of comma splices, **4** 255
revision of essays, **1** 37
-s and *-ed* verb endings, **4** 199–200
-s and *-es* subject and verb endings, **4** 219
-self pronouns, **4** 225
standard American English, **3** 158
structure of academic writing, **2** 93–94
subject of sentence, **4** 188
subject-verb agreement, **4** 219, 221–22
subordinating conjunctions, **4** 186
thesis statements, **1** 15–16
titles of address, **3** 162
transitional expressions, **1** 44
transitive vs. intransitive verbs, **4** 188–89, 202
verb forms, **4** 198
verbs plus particles (two-word verbs), **4** 207–08
verbs with *to* or *for*, **4** 190
verb tenses, **4** 208–09
verb tense sequence in conditional sentences, **4** 213–14
vocabulary development, **2** 71–72
voice, **4** 216
wordiness, avoiding, **3** 172
word meanings, **2** 71–72
word order in sentences, **4** 188, 247–48, **5** 263
Cumulative sentences, **3** 146–47

D

-d, *-ed*, verb forms requiring, **4** 182, 192, 200
Dance, research sources on, **8** 394
Dangling modifiers, **4** 248–49
Dashes
vs. colons, **5** 291
vs. commas, **5** 290
with concluding series and explanations, **5** 291
forming and spacing, **1** 58, **5** 290
with introductory series, **5** 291
with nonessential elements, **5** 290
overuse of, **5** 291
vs. parentheses, **5** 290
with parenthetical expressions, **5** 290
with quotation marks, **5** 289
with shifts in tone, **5** 290
Data
empirical, **8** 399
qualitative vs. quantitative, **8** 396
data, **Gl** 514
Databases, electronic
on CD-ROMs, **7** 327
documenting: APA style, **APA** 474–76; Chicago style, **Chic** 498; CSE style, **CSE** 506–07; MLA style, **MLA** 441–43
finding bibliographic information for, **MLA** 441–43
of images, **7** 341–42
kinds of, **7** 326–27
library catalog as, **7** 326–27
listed in annotated working bibliography, **7** 324
list of, **7** 335
periodicals and periodical indexes, **7** 332–35
as research sources, **7** 326–27
vs. search engines, **7** 327
searching, **7** 328–29, 332–35
selection of, **7** 326–27, 332
subscription, **7** 326–27, 332–35, **MLA** 441

Date of access
APA style, **APA** 473
Chicago style, **Chic** 497
CSE style, **CSE** 506–07
MLA style, **MLA** 439
Dates
BC and *AD* with, **6** 310
BCE and *CE* with, **6** 310
commas in, **5** 273
numerals vs. words for, **6** 313
Days of week
abbreviations for, **6** 311
capitalization of, **6** 304
Deadlines, in writing situation, **1** 4
Deduction (deductive reasoning), **2** 100–01
Defined terms
italics or underlining for, **6** 308
singular verbs with, **4** 223
Definition
in essay development, **1** 13
in paragraph development, **1** 46–47
as writing assignment, **1** 6
Demonstrative pronouns, **4** 181
Denotation, **3** 166–67
Dependent clauses. *See* Subordinate (dependent) clauses
dependent on, **3** 168
Description
in essay development, **1** 13
in paragraph development, **1** 45
Descriptive titles, **1** 26–27
Descriptors. *See* Keywords
desert, dessert, **6** 298
Design, document. *See* Document design and format
Details
adding, **3** 157
grammar checkers for, **3** 154
Determiners (*a, an, the*, etc.)
defined, **4** 240
grammar checkers for, **4** 241
uses of, **4** 240–44
Development
computers for, **1** 10–12
of essays, **1** 8–13
of paragraphs, **1** 45–49
device, devise, **Gl** 515
Diagrams. *See* Illustrations and artworks
Dialect. *See also* Culture-language issues
appropriate use of, **3** 158–59
defined, **3** 158–59
nonstandard, **3** 158–59
standard American English as, **2** 94–96, **3** 158
Dialog, format for, **5** 287
Diction, **3** 158–71. *See also under* Words *for specific topics.*
Dictionaries
for adjective and adverb forms, **4** 238
for capitalization, **6** 303
documenting: Chicago style, **Chic** 499; MLA style, **MLA** 426, 435, 443
electronic, **3** 165
ESL, **3** 166, 169, **4** 241
list of, **3** 165–66
for meanings, **3** 165–66
as research sources, **8** 388
sample entry, **3** 165
vs. thesaurus, **3** 166
for verb forms, **4** 196, 198
Dictionary form, of verbs. *See* Plain form, of verbs
differ about, over, from, with, **3** 168
different from, different than, **Gl** 515
differ from, with, **Gl** 515
Digital Object Identifier (DOI)
APA style, **APA** 473–77
CSE style, **CSE** 506–07
in working bibliography, **7** 324
Direct address, comma with, **5** 271
Direct discourse. *See* Quotations, direct
Direct object. *See also* Objects
case of, **4** 224
defined, **4** 188
Direct questions, **5** 264
Direct quotations. *See* Quotations, direct
Disabilities. *See* Vision loss, considering readers with
disappointed by, in, with, **3** 168
Disciplines. *See* Academic writing
discreet, discrete, **6** 298, **Gl** 515
Discussion, as writing assignment, **1** 6
Discussion groups, online
author's permission, obtaining, **7** 373
collaboration through, **2** 118
documenting: APA style, **APA** 478; Chicago style, **Chic** 499; CSE style, **CSE** 507; MLA style, **MLA** 443–44
evaluating, **7** 354–56
for opposing views in argument, **2** 102
as research sources, **7** 339
Discussion lists. *See* Discussion groups, online
disinterested, uninterested, **Gl** 515
Dissertation Abstracts, **MLA** 418, **APA** 479
Dissertations
APA style, **APA** 477, 479
MLA style, **MLA** 418, 430

Division (analysis)
in essay development, **1** 13
in paragraph development, **1** 47
Division of words, hyphens for, **6** 301–02
do, as helping verb, **4** 183, 203
Documentation of sources
APA style, **APA** 462–81
and avoiding plagiarism, **7** 372–75
Chicago style, **Chic** 491–501
computer software for, **7** 374–75
CSE style, **CSE** 502–08
MLA style, **MLA** 404–47
necessity for, **7** 372–75
style guides for, **7** 374, **8** 395, 398–99, 402
Document design and format
for academic papers, **1** 53
APA style: document format, **APA** 481–84; reference-list format, **APA** 487
for brochures, **2** 139
for business letters, **2** 129–30
for business memos, **2** 134–35
for charts, **1** 61–62
Chicago style: document format, **Chic** 491–93; works-cited format, **Chic** 491–501
color in, **1** 59–60, **2** 86
community work, **2** 136–39
computers for, **1** 53–65
CSE style: document format, **CSE** 503–04; reference-list format, **CSE** 502–08
for diagrams, **1** 63–64
effective vs. ineffective, **1** 54–60
elements of, **1** 54–60
for fax transmissions, **2** 133–34
for flyers, **2** 137
for graphs, **1** 62–63
headings: APA style, **APA** 481–83; general, **1** 58–59, **2** 122–23
highlighting, **1** 57
identification, **MLA** 448–49
illustrations, **1** 60–64
lists, **1** 58
margins and spacing: APA style, **APA** 481; general, **1** 56; MLA style, **MLA** 448
MLA style: document format, **MLA** 447–49; works-cited format, **MLA** 415–47
for newsletters, **2** 138
paging: APA style, **APA** 481; MLA style, **MLA** 448
for photographs, **1** 64
for poetry and long prose quotations: APA style, **APA** 483; MLA style, **MLA** 449
principles of, **1** 53–56
for reports, **2** 134–36
for résumés, **2** 131–32
tables, **1** 61
type styles and sizes, **1** 57, **2** 119
for Web compositions, **2** 119–24
white space, **1** 55
Dogpile, **7** 336
DOI. *See* Digital Object Identifier (DOI)
Dollar signs ($), **6** 310
don't, **Gl** 515
Dots
to indicate omission from quotation (ellipsis mark), **1** 58, **5** 292–94, **7** 362
as periods, **5** 263
Double comparisons, **4** 238
Double negatives, **4** 239–40
Double talk or doublespeak, **3** 161
Doubt, question mark for, **5** 264
Downloading research sources, pros and cons, **7** 359
Drafting
computers and, **1** 22
of essays, **1** 21–24
and keeping momentum, **1** 22
of research papers, **7** 376–77
starting, **1** 21–22
Drafts
edited, **1** 28–32, **7** 376
final, **1** 33–35, **7** 376–77
first, **1** 21–24, **7** 376
revised, **1** 25–27, **7** 376–77
due to the fact that, **Gl** 515
DVD-ROMs. *See* Films, DVDs, and video recordings

E

-e, final, **6** 299–300
each
pronouns with, **4** 231–32
verbs with, **4** 220–21
eager, anxious, **Gl** 512
EBSCOhost Academic Search, **7** 335
Economics, research sources on, **8** 398
-ed, *-d*, verb forms requiring, **4** 182, 192, 200
Edited works
APA style, **APA** 472–73
Chicago style, **Chic** 496, 498, 500
CSE style, **CSE** 505, 506, 507
MLA style, **MLA** 423–24
Editing
checklist for, **1** 30
on computers, **1** 31
of essays, **1** 28–32
by peers, **1** 35–37

Editing *(continued)*
of research papers, **7** 376–77
vs. revising, **1** 24
Editions, later
APA style, **APA** 473
Chicago style, **Chic** 496
MLA style, **MLA** 423
Editorials, MLA style, **MLA** 422, 434, 440–41
Education, research sources on, **8** 398
effect, affect, **6** 297, **Gl** 511
e.g., **6** 311
either
as determiner, **4** 244
pronouns with, **4** 231–32
verbs with, **4** 220–21
either . . . or
as correlative conjunction, **4** 186
parallelism with, **3** 152–53
Either/or fallacy, **2** 104
ei vs. *ie,* **6** 299
Electronic addresses. *See* URL
Electronic communication. *See also* Discussion groups, online; E-mail; Internet; Web sites
for collaboration, **2** 118
faxes, **2** 133–34
Electronic mail. *See* E-mail
Electronic sources. *See also* Internet; Sources; Web sites
and copyright, **7** 373
documenting: APA style: parenthetical citations, **APA** 466–67; reference list, **APA** 473–78; Chicago style, **Chic** 497–99; CSE style, **CSE** 506–07; MLA style: list of works cited, **MLA** 431–44; parenthetical citations, **MLA** 409–10
downloading, **7** 359
evaluating, **7** 347, 350–56
finding and tracking, **7** 323–29
finding bibliographic information for, **MLA** 433, 440, 442
gathering information from, **7** 358–59
Internet, **7** 335–42, 347, 350–56
keyword searches for, **7** 328–29
kinds of, **7** 326–27
periodicals and periodical indexes, **7** 332–35
plagiarism of, **7** 358–59, 368–69
reference works, **3** 165, **7** 329–30
as research sources, **7** 325–30, 347, 350–54
and research strategy, **7** 321
searching for, **7** 328–29, 332–40
Web, **7** 330, 335–40, 347, 350–54
in working bibliography, **7** 324
elicit, illicit, **Gl** 515
Ellipsis marks
forming and spacing, **1** 58, **5** 292
to indicate omissions from quotations, **5** 292–94, **7** 362
E-mail
alternatives to italics or underlining in, **6** 309
author's permission, obtaining, **7** 373
capitalization in, **6** 306, 309
collaborating through, **2** 118
composing, **2** 117
documenting: APA style, **APA** 478; Chicago style, **Chic** 499; CSE style, **CSE** 507; MLA style, **MLA** 443
flaming, **2** 117
formal vs. informal language, **2** 116
format for, **2** 116–18
interviews through, **7** 343
proofreading, **2** 116
as research source, **7** 339
responding to, **2** 117–18
revising shortcuts of, **2** 95
signatures in, **2** 117
spamming, **2** 117
tone in, **2** 116, 117
Em dashes, **1** 58, **5** 290
emigrate, immigrate, **Gl** 515
Emotional appeals, **2** 101–02, 109
Emphasis
active voice for, **3** 145
avoiding nouns made from verbs for, **3** 144
coordination for, **3** 147–49
in document design, **1** 57
exclamation points for, **5** 264
grammar checkers for, **3** 143
in illustrations, **2** 86
italics or underlining for, **1** 57, **6** 308
sentence beginnings and endings for, **3** 145–47
strong verbs for, **3** 144–45
subjects and verbs for, **3** 143–45
subordination for, **3** 149–51
Empty words and phrases, **3** 174–75
Encyclopedias
documenting: APA style, **APA** 477; Chicago style, **Chic** 497, 498; MLA style, **MLA** 426, 435, 443
as research sources, **8** 388
Endnote, **7** 374
Endnotes. *See* Footnotes or endnotes
End punctuation marks, **5** 263–64

Engineering, research sources on, **8** 402
English (discipline). *See also* Literature and literary works
  integrating borrowed material in, **7** 366
  Web sources on, **8** 389
English as a second language. *See* Culture-language issues
ensure, insure, assure, **Gl** 513
enthused, **Gl** 515
Envelopes, for business letters, **2** 129–30
Environmental science, research sources on, **8** 402
-er, as adjective or adverb ending, **4** 237–38
ERIC, APA style, **APA** 479
-es. See -s, -es
ESL. *See* Culture-language issues
Essays. *See also* Research writing
  arguments in, **2** 97–115
  audience for, **1** 4, 7–8
  collaborating on, **1** 35–37
  content of, in academic writing, **2** 93–94
  context for, **1** 3
  creativity techniques for, **1** 8–13
  developing topic for, **1** 8 13
  drafting, **1** 21–24
  editing and proofreading, **1** 28–33
  finding subject for, **1** 3–4
  format for, **1** 52–65
  introductions and conclusions for, **1** 49–52
  on literary works, **8** 389–91
  organizing, **1** 16–21
  peer editing of, **1** 35–37
  purpose of, **1** 4, 6–7
  quotation marks for titles of, **5** 288
  responding to texts in, **2** 90–92, **7** 376
  revising, **1** 25–27
  samples of, **1** 33–35, **2** 111–15, **8** 389–91
  thesis of, **1** 14–16
  titling, **1** 25–27
Essential elements
  appositives, **5** 270, 276
  defined, **5** 268
  modifiers, **5** 268–69
  no commas with, **5** 268–69, 276
  vs. nonessential elements, **5** 268–71
  testing for, **5** 269
-est, as adjective or adverb ending, **4** 237–38
et al., **6** 311, **MLA** 408, 417, **CSE** 502, **Gl** 515
etc., **6** 311, **Gl** 515
Ethical appeals, **2** 101
Ethnic studies, research sources on, **8** 398
Euphemisms, **3** 161
Evaluation
  in critical thinking and reading, **2** 83
  of illustrations, **2** 89
  of library sources, **7** 346–48
  of multimedia sources, **7** 354–56
  of online discussions and blogs, **7** 339–40, 354–56
  of research sources, **7** 345–56
  of Web sites and pages, **7** 347, 350–54
  as writing assignment, **1** 7, **8** 393
Evasions, **2** 102–03
even so, punctuation with, **4** 257
every, verb with, **4** 220–21
everybody
  vs. *every body*, **Gl** 515
  pronouns with, **4** 231–32
  verbs with, **4** 220–21
everyday, every day, **Gl** 516
everyone
  vs. *every one*, **Gl** 515
  pronouns with, **4** 231–32
  verbs with, **4** 220–21
everything
  pronouns with, **4** 231–32
  verbs with, **4** 220–21
everywheres, **Gl** 515
Evidence
  in history, **8** 392
  in literature, **8** 387
  in the natural and applied sciences, **8** 399
  in the social sciences, **8** 395–96
  textual, to support arguments, **2** 98–99
  visual, to support arguments, **2** 106–08
Exact language. *See also* Language; Words
  grammar checkers for, **3** 165
  guidelines for, **3** 165–71
Examples
  in essay development, **1** 13
  as evidence in argument, **2** 99, 106
  in paragraph development, **1** 45–46
except, accept, **6** 297, **Gl** 511
except for the fact that, **Gl** 516
Exclamation points
  with quotation marks, **5** 289
  space with, **1** 58
  uses of, **5** 264
Expert opinion, **2** 99, 107, **7** 367–68
Explanation, as writing assignment, **8** 393

Expletive constructions
defined, **3** 176
eliminating, for conciseness, **3** 176
necessity of *here*, *it*, or *there* in, **3** 176
subject-verb agreement in, **4** 223
explicit, *implicit*, **Gl** 516

F

Facts
as claims in arguments, **2** 98
as evidence in arguments, **2** 99, 106
fair, *fare*, **6** 298
Fair use, **7** 373
Fallacies, **2** 102–04, 110
familiar with, **3** 168
farther, *further*, **Gl** 516
Faulty predication, **4** 258–59
Fax transmissions, **2** 133–34
few
pronouns with, **4** 231–32
verbs with, **4** 220–21
few, *a few*, **4** 244
fewer, *less*, **Gl** 516
Fiction, analyzing and writing about, **8** 383–91
Figurative language (figures of speech), **3** 169–70
Figures. *See* Illustrations and artworks
Films, DVDs, and video recordings
documenting: APA style, **APA** 478, 480; Chicago style, **Chic** 499, 500; CSE style, **CSE** 508; MLA style, **MLA** 436, 438, 443, 445
as research sources, **7** 340, 342
research sources on, **8** 394
titles of, italics or underlining for, **6** 307
in Web compositions, **2** 123
Final drafts, **1** 33–35
finally, punctuation with, **4** 257
Finite verbs, **4** 251
First drafts, **1** 21–24, **7** 376
First person (*I*, *we*)
in academic writing, **2** 95–96
and grammatical agreement, **4** 218
point of view, in literary works, **8** 385
Flaming, **2** 118
flaunt, *flout*, **Gl** 516
Flow
in document design, **1** 54
in Web compositions, **2** 122–23
flunk, **Gl** 516
Flyers, **2** 137
Focused freewriting, **1** 11
Folk literature, **7** 370
Fonts, **1** 57, 64–65
Footnotes or endnotes
Chicago style, **Chic** 491–501
MLA style, **MLA** 414–15
for
commas with, **5** 265
as coordinating conjunction, **4** 185
as preposition, **4** 184
vs. *since*, **3** 169, **4** 211
for all that, punctuation with, **4** 257
Foreign words
italics or underlining for, **6** 308
Latin abbreviations, **6** 310–11, **Chic** 497, 501
as source of English words, plurals of, **6** 301
Foreword, MLA style, **MLA** 428–29
for example, punctuation with, **4** 257, **5** 277–78
for instance, punctuation with, **4** 257
Form, in literary works, **8** 386
Formal outlines
constructing, **1** 19–20
for essays, **1** 19–20
for research papers, **MLA** 450–51
for revisions, **1** 25
sentence, **1** 19–20, **MLA** 450–51
topic, **1** 19–20, **MLA** 450–51
Formal vs. informal usage
in academic writing, **2** 94–96, **3** 158–64
in e-mail, **2** 116
in research sources, **7** 356
Format, document. *See* Document design and format
forth, *fourth*, **6** 298
Fractions
hyphens in, **6** 302
numerals vs. words for, **6** 313
Fragments. *See* Sentence fragments
Freewriting, **1** 10–11
Full-text resources, **7** 327, 332
fun, **Gl** 516
further, *farther*, **Gl** 516
further, punctuation with, **4** 257
furthermore, punctuation with, **4** 257
Fused sentences
avoiding, **4** 253–57
grammar checkers for, **4** 255
Future perfect progressive tense, **4** 209, 211
Future perfect tense, **4** 209

Future progressive tense, **4** 209, 211
Future tense, **4** 209

G

Gender
  of pronouns, **4** 230
  and sexist language, **3** 162–64, **4** 231–32, **Gl** 516–17
Gender studies, research sources on, **8** 398
Generalizations
  hasty, **2** 103
  in inductive and deductive reasoning, **2** 100–01
  sweeping, **2** 104
General-to-specific organization, **1** 18, 41
General vs. specific, **1** 18, **3** 167–68
General words, **3** 167–68
Generic *he*, **3** 164, **4** 231–32. *See also* Sexist language
Generic nouns, and pronoun agreement, **4** 231–32
Genre, **2** 90
Geographical names
  abbreviating, **6** 311
  capitalizing, **6** 304
  commas in, **5** 273
Geology, research sources on, **8** 402
Gerunds and gerund phrases
  defined, **4** 192
  grammar checkers for, **4** 205
  possessives before, **4** 229
  after verbs, **4** 205–07
get, **Gl** 516
Glossary of Usage, **Gl** 511–23
good, well, **4** 237, **Gl** 516
good and, **Gl** 516
Google, **7** 336, 337–38, 341–42
Google Scholar, **7** 332
Government agencies, capitalizing names of, **6** 304
Government publications
  documenting: APA style, **APA** 476–77, 479; Chicago style, **Chic** 499–500; CSE style, **CSE** 508; MLA style, **MLA** 409, 417, 429, 435
  as research sources, **7** 340
Grammar, defined, **4** 180
Grammar and style checkers, **1** 32. *See also entries for specific grammar and style issues*
Graphic art. *See* Illustrations and artworks
Graphic narrative works, MLA style, **MLA** 426–27
Graphs. *See* Illustrations and artworks
Grouping, in document design, **1** 55
Group or corporate authors
  APA style: parenthetical citation, **APA** 465; reference list, **APA** 469
  Chicago style, **Chic** 499–500
  CSE style, **CSE** 508
  MLA style: list of works cited, **MLA** 417; parenthetical citation, **MLA** 409
Grove Art Online, **7** 342

H

had better, better, **Gl** 513
had ought, **Gl** 516
Handwritten research notes, pros and cons, **7** 358
hanged, hung, **Gl** 516
hardly, scarcely, but, **Gl** 513
Hasty generalizations, **2** 103
have, as helping verb, **3** 144–45, **4** 183, 200, 203
have, of, **Gl** 516
he
  case forms of, **4** 225–26
  generic, **3** 164, **4** 231–32
  vs. *him*, **4** 224–29
  with indefinite antecedents, **4** 231–32
  and sexist language, **3** 164, **4** 231–32, **Gl** 516–17
he, she: he/she, **4** 231–32, **Gl** 516–17
Headings
  APA style, **APA** 481–83
  in document design, **1** 58–59, **2** 119
  and page breaks, **1** 59
  parallelism in, **3** 153
Health sciences, research sources on, **8** 402
hear, here, **6** 298
heard, herd, **6** 298
Helping verbs (auxiliary verbs)
  combined with main verbs, **4** 200–05
  defined, **3** 144
  grammar checkers for, **4** 200
  list of, **4** 183
  modal, **4** 203–05
  omitted, **4** 201
hence, punctuation with, **4** 257
he or *she*, **3** 164, **4** 231–32
herd, heard, **6** 298
here, hear, **6** 298
here is/are, **3** 176

herself, himself, yourself, myself, **Gl** 519
her vs. *she,* **4** 224–29
himself, yourself, myself, herself, **Gl** 519
him vs. *he,* **4** 224–29
hisself, **Gl** 517
Historical Abstracts, **7** 332
Historical events and periods, capitalization of, **6** 304
History
  integrating borrowed material in, **7** 366
  research sources on, **8** 394
  writing about, **8** 392–95
Hits, in electronic searches, **7** 337–38
hole, whole, **6** 298
Holidays
  abbreviation of, **6** 311
  capitalization of, **6** 304
Homonyms
  defined, **3** 166, **6** 297
  list of, **6** 297–98
hopefully, **Gl** 517
however, punctuation with, **4** 257, **5** 277–78
however, yet, but, **Gl** 514
HTML editors, **2** 119
Humanities, **8** 392–95
  assignments in: literature, **8** 387–88; other disciplines, **8** 392–93
  Chicago style, **Chic** 491–501
  integrating borrowed material in, **7** 366
  methods and evidence in: literature, **8** 384–87; other disciplines, **8** 392
  MLA style: documentation, **MLA** 404–47; document format, **MLA** 447–49; sample paper, **MLA** 452–60
  research sources on: literature, **8** 388–89; other disciplines, **8** 394
  style guides in, **8** 395
  tools and language in: in literature, **8** 388–89; other disciplines, **8** 393–94
  Web sources on, **8** 394
hung, hanged, **Gl** 516
Hypertext documents, **2** 119–24. *See also* Web sites
Hyphens
  in attaching prefixes and suffixes, **6** 302
  in compound adjectives, **6** 301
  in forming dashes, **5** 290
  in fractions and compound numbers, **6** 302
  spacing for, **1** 58
  in URLs (electronic addresses), **MLA** 439, **APA** 473, **Chic** 497, **CSE** 506
  in word division, **6** 301–02
Hypothesis, **8** 395, 399

I

I
  case forms of, **4** 225
  vs. *me,* **4** 225–26
ibid., **Chic** 501
idea, ideal, **Gl** 517
Ideas
  coordination to relate, **3** 148
  discovering, **1** 8–13
  emphasizing, **3** 143–51
  organizing, **1** 16–21
identical with, to, **3** 168
Idioms, **3** 168–69
i.e., **6** 310
ie vs. *ei,* **6** 299
if
  in conditional sentences, **4** 213–14
  subjunctive after, **4** 215
if, whether, **Gl** 517
illicit, elicit, **Gl** 515
illusion, allusion, **6** 297, **Gl** 512
Illustrated books, MLA style, **MLA** 426–27
Illustration or support. *See* Examples
Illustrations and artworks
  acknowledging sources of, **1** 60, 64, **2** 124, **7** 340
  advertisements, MLA style, **MLA** 435, 447
  analyzing context, **2** 86
  cartoons, MLA style, **MLA** 439, 446
  charts: documenting, MLA style, **MLA** 435, 446; using, **1** 61–62, **APA** 484
  comic strips, MLA style, **MLA** 446
  copyrights of, **7** 340
  creating, **1** 60–64
  diagrams: documenting, MLA style, **MLA** 435, 446; using, **1** 63
  in document design, **1** 5, 60–64
  in document format: APA style, **APA** 484; MLA style, **MLA** 454
  documenting: APA style, **APA** 478; Chicago style, **Chic** 498–99, 500; CSE style, **CSE** 508; MLA style, **MLA** 426–27, 435, 439, 444, 446
  evaluating, **7** 354–56

finding online, **7** 340–42
graphs: documenting, MLA style, **MLA** 435, 446; using, **1** 62–63, **APA** 484
images: APA style, **APA** 478; finding, **7** 341–42; MLA style, **MLA** 435, 439, 444
maps, MLA style, **MLA** 435, 446
online databases of, **7** 341–42
in oral presentations, **2** 126
paintings: Chicago style, **Chic** 498, 500; MLA style, **MLA** 446
permission for using, **1** 64, **2** 111, 124, **7** 340, 373
photographs: documenting, MLA style, **MLA** 435, 444, 446; using, **1** 64
as research sources, **7** 340–42, **8** 394
sources of, **2** 124, **7** 340–42
tables: APA style for, **APA** 486; in document design, **1** 61
titles of, italics or underlining for, **6** 307
using, **1** 60–64, **2** 105–11, 123, 126–27, **7** 340–42
viewing critically, **2** 83–89
visual arguments with, **2** 105–11
in Web compositions, **2** 123, **7** 373

Image Resources directory, **7** 341
Imagery, in literary works, **8** 386
Images (photographs, paintings, etc.). *See* Illustrations and artworks
immigrate, emigrate, **Gl** 515
impatient for, with, **3** 168
Imperative mood
defined, **4** 214
omission of *you* with, **4** 214, 251
punctuation and, **5** 263, 264
shifts between indicative and, **4** 215
implicit, explicit, **Gl** 516
Implied nouns, **4** 234–35
imply, infer, **Gl** 517
in, at, on, **3** 169
Inc., **6** 311
incidentally, punctuation with, **4** 257
including, no colon after, **5** 281
Incomplete sentences, grammar checkers for, **3** 171
in contrast, punctuation with, **4** 257
incredible, incredulous, **Gl** 517
indeed, punctuation with, **4** 257
Indefinite pronouns
alternatives to *he* with, **4** 231–32
defined, **4** 181
list of, **4** 221, 231
possessives of, **5** 283
pronoun agreement with, **4** 231–32
verb agreement with, **4** 220–21
Independent clauses. *See* Main (independent) clauses
independent of, **3** 168
Indexes to periodicals. *See* Periodical databases
Indicative mood
defined, **4** 214
shifts between imperative and, **4** 215
Indirect discourse. *See* Indirect quotations
Indirect objects. *See also* Objects
case of, **4** 224–25, 226–28
defined, **4** 190
Indirect questions, **5** 263
Indirect quotations. *See also* Quotations, direct
defined, **5** 287
no commas before, **5** 276
Indirect sources
APA style, **APA** 466
MLA style, **MLA** 411
individual, person, party, **Gl** 517
Individual possession, possessive case to indicate, **5** 284
Induction (inductive reasoning), **2** 100
Inexact language, grammar checkers for, **3** 165
in fact, punctuation with, **4** 257
infer, imply, **Gl** 517
infer from, **3** 168
inferior to, **3** 168
Infinitives and infinitive phrases
case of pronouns with, **4** 229
defined, **4** 192
grammar checkers for, **4** 205
split, **4** 246
subjects or objects of, **4** 229
after verbs, **4** 205–07
Informal (scratch) outlines, **1** 18
Informal vs. formal usage, **2** 94–96, **3** 160
Information gathering
on computers, **7** 358–59
critical reading for, **2** 69–70, 77–89, **7** 344–57
direct quotations in, **7** 361–62
downloading for, **7** 359
handwritten notes for, **7** 358
note taking for, **7** 358–59
paraphrases in, **7** 360–61
photocopying for, **7** 358–59
printing out for, **7** 358–59

Information gathering *(continued)*
- in research process, **7** 326–27, 358–59
- risk of plagiarism during, **7** 359–62
- summaries in, **7** 359–60
- synthesis in, **7** 356–57
- tips for, **2** 69–70
- while reading literature, **8** 384

Information services. *See* Databases, electronic

InfoTrac Expanded Academic, **7** 335

-ing
- in gerunds, **4** 192
- in present participles, **4** 182, 192
- in progressive tenses, **4** 211

in other words, punctuation with, **4** 257

in regards to, **Gl** 517

in short, punctuation with, **4** 257

Inside addresses, of business letters, **2** 129

inside of, *outside of*, **Gl** 517

Instant messaging, revising shortcuts of, **2** 95

instead, punctuation with, **4** 257

insure, *assure*, *ensure*, **Gl** 513

Integrating borrowed material
- in English and some other humanities, **7** 366
- in history and some other humanities, **7** 366
- interpretation and, **7** 363–65
- introduction and, **7** 363
- with signal phrases, **7** 364–67
- in social and natural sciences, **7** 366–67
- verbs and verb tenses for, **7** 363, 366–67

Integrity, in academic writing, **7** 367

Intellectual property, and plagiarism, **7** 367–68

Intensive pronouns, **4** 181

Interjections
- defined, **4** 186
- punctuation of, **5** 264, 271

Internet, **7** 347, 350–56. *See also* Blogs; Discussion groups, online; Electronic sources; E-mail; Web sites
- acknowledging sources found on, **7** 368–69, 372–73
- addresses. *See* URL
- advantages and disadvantages of, **7** 335–36
- collaboration on, **2** 118
- discussion groups on, **7** 339–40, 354–56
- downloading from, **7** 359
- evaluating sources on, **7** 347, 350–56
- reference works on, **7** 329–30
- searching, **7** 328–29, 335–40
- Web forums on, **2** 118

Internet Public Library, **7** 336

Internet Scout Project, **7** 336

Interpretation
- of borrowed material, **7** 363–65
- in critical thinking and reading, **2** 87–89
- of illustrations, **2** 87–89
- as kind of research paper, **8** 393
- as writing assignment, **1** 6

Interrogative pronouns, **4** 181

Interviews
- documenting: APA style, **APA** 480; Chicago style, **Chic** 500; MLA style, **MLA** 422, 434, 440–41, 445
- as research sources, **7** 343

in the meantime, punctuation with, **4** 257

in the past, punctuation with, **4** 257

Intransitive verbs, **4** 188–89, 199

Introductions
- to arguments, **2** 104
- to books and other sources, MLA style, **MLA** 428–29
- to essays, **1** 16–17, 49–51
- guidelines for writing, **1** 49–51

Introductory elements
- commas with, **5** 267–68
- dashes with, **5** 291
- defined, **5** 267

Invention
- computers for, **1** 10–12
- techniques for, **1** 8–13

Inverted word order, subject-verb agreement and, **4** 223

Invisible writing, on computers, **1** 10–11

involved in, *with*, **3** 168

irregardless, **Gl** 517

Irregular adjectives, **4** 238

Irregular adverbs, **4** 238

Irregular verbs
- forms of, **4** 196–98
- grammar checkers for, **4** 196, 198
- list of common, **4** 197–98

is, *are*, **Gl** 512

is because, **4** 259

is when, *is where*, **4** 258, **Gl** 518

it
- case forms of, **4** 225
- reference of, **4** 234

Italics or underlining, **6** 306–09
- for defined words, **6** 308
- for emphasis, **1** 57, **6** 308
- for foreign words, **6** 308
- grammar checkers for, **6** 307
- for names of ships, aircraft, spacecraft, trains, **6** 308

in online communication, **6** 309
for titles of works, **6** 307
for words and characters named as words, **6** 308
it is, as expletive construction
eliminating for conciseness, **3** 176
necessity of *it* in, **3** 176
uses of, **3** 176
it is, *it has*, as contraction *it's*, **5** 285, **Gl** 518
its, *it's*
grammar checkers for, **5** 282
possessive vs. contraction, **6** 298, **Gl** 518
-ize, *-wise*, **Gl** 518

J

Jargon, **3** 176
Job-application letters, **2** 131
Joint possession, possessive case to indicate, **5** 284
Journalist's questions, for essay development, **1** 13
Journals
defined, **1** 9
for essay development, **1** 9–10
reading, **1** 9–10, **7** 318, **8** 384
research, **7** 318, **8** 384, 393, 397, 400–01
scholarly. *See* Articles in periodicals; Periodicals
just because, **4** 259

K

Keywords
Boolean operators in, **7** 328–29
for catalog searches, **7** 328–29
for database searches, **7** 328–29
defined, **7** 326
developing, **7** 328–29
sample search, **7** 337–38
trial and error with, **7** 329
for Web searches, **7** 328–29, 337–38
kind of, *sort of*, *type of*, **Gl** 518
know, *no*, **6** 298

L

Labels
for lists, **5** 292
for people, and biased language, **3** 164
Lab notebooks, **8** 400–01
Laboratory reports, as writing assignment, **8** 400
Language. *See also* Culture-language issues; Words
of academic writing, **2** 94–96, **8** 382–83
appropriate, **3** 158–64
colloquial, **3** 160, **Gl** 511
exact, **3** 165–71
figurative, **3** 169–70
formal vs. informal, **2** 94–96, **3** 160
grammar checkers for, **3** 158, 165
in the humanities, **8** 393–94
in literary analysis, **8** 388
in the natural and applied sciences, **8** 400–02
nonstandard. *See* Culture-language issues
sexist, **3** 162–64
in the social sciences, **8** 397–98
standard. *See* Standard American English
Languages, capitalization of names of, **6** 304
Latin abbreviations, **6** 310–11, **Chic** 497, 501
Law, research sources on, **8** 398
lay, *lie*, **4** 198–99, **Gl** 518
leave, *let*, **Gl** 518
Lectures, documenting using MLA style, **MLA** 447
Legal documents, no italics or underlining for, **6** 308
less, *fewer*, **Gl** 518
let, *leave*, **Gl** 518
Letters (correspondence)
business, **2** 129–30
documenting: APA style, **APA** 478; Chicago style, **Chic** 500; CSE style, **CSE** 507; MLA style, **MLA** 430
e-mail, **7** 339, **MLA** 443, **Chic** 499
faxes, **2** 133–34
job application, **2** 131
Letters (of alphabet)
apostrophes for omission of, **5** 285
in formal outlines, **1** 19–20
forming plurals of, **5** 283
italics or underlining for, **6** 308
Letters to editor, documenting using MLA style, **MLA** 422, 434
LexisNexis Academic, **7** 335
liable, *likely*, *apt*, **Gl** 512
Librarians' Internet Index, **7** 336
Libraries
book catalog in, **7** 326–27, 330
CD-ROMs in, **7** 327
databases from, **7** 326–27, 332–35
electronic sources from, **7** 326–27, 330–35
evaluating sources in, **7** 346–47, 348–49
periodicals in, **7** 332–35

Libraries *(continued)*
  reference librarians in, **7** 327
  reference works in, **7** 334–35
  as Web gateway for research, **7** 326
  Web sites of, **7** 326, 330
Library of Congress Subject Headings, **7** 330
Library subscription services
  documenting: APA style, **APA** 474; Chicago style, **Chic** 498; CSE style, **CSE** 506; MLA style, **MLA** 441–42
  use of, **7** 332
lie, lay, **4** 198–99, **Gl** 518
like, as, **Gl** 513
like, such as, **Gl** 518
likely, apt, liable, **Gl** 512
likewise, punctuation with, **4** 257
Limiting modifiers, **4** 245
Linear text, **2** 119
Line graphs. *See* Illustrations and artworks
Linking verbs
  adjectives vs. adverbs after, **4** 237
  agreement with subjects, **4** 223
  defined, **4** 189–90
  list of, **4** 190
List of works cited. *See also* APA style; Bibliographies; CSE style; Parenthetical text citations
  Chicago style, **Chic** 491–500
  MLA style, **MLA** 415–47
Lists. *See also* Series
  in document design, **1** 58
  format of, **1** 58
  parallelism with, **3** 153
  parentheses with labels for, **5** 292
Listservs. *See* Discussion groups, online
literally, **Gl** 518
Literary analysis, **8** 383–91
Literature and literary works
  analysis of, **8** 383–91
  documenting, in MLA style, **8** 389–91, **MLA** 411–12
  elements of, **8** 385–87
  integrating sources in, **7** 366
  meaning of, **8** 384–85
  reading, **8** 384
  research papers about, **8** 387
  research sources on, **8** 388–89
  sample essay on, **8** 389–91
  titles of: italics or underlining for books, plays, and long poems, **6** 307; quotation marks for stories and short poems, **5** 274
  Web sources on, **8** 389
  writing about, **8** 383–91
little, a little, **4** 244
Location or place, transitional expressions to indicate, **1** 44
Logical comparisons, **4** 238
Logical fallacies, **2** 102–04, 110
Logical thinking, in arguments, **2** 100–01
Long quotations, format of
  in MLA style, **MLA** 449
  no quotation marks with, **APA** 483
loose, lose, **Gl** 519
lots, lots of, **Gl** 519
Lurking, **7** 339
-ly ending, adverbs with and without, **4** 184

M

Magazines. *See* Articles in periodicals; Periodicals
Main (independent) clauses
  comma splices with, **4** 253–57
  defined, **4** 193
  fused, **4** 253–57
  joined by commas and coordinating conjunctions, **5** 266
  for main ideas, **3** 154–56
  related by conjunctive adverb (with semicolon), **4** 257, **5** 277–78
  vs. sentence fragments, **4** 201
  vs. subordinate clauses, **4** 193
Main verbs, **4** 183, 200–05
Manual for Writers of Research Papers, Theses, and Dissertations, A (Turabian). *See* Chicago style
Manuscripts. *See* Document design and format
many
  vs. *much*, **4** 244
  pronouns with, **4** 231–32
  verbs with, **4** 220–21
Maps. *See* Illustrations and artworks
Margins and spacing
  in academic papers: APA style, **APA** 481; MLA style, **MLA** 448
  in business correspondence, **2** 129–30
  in document design, **1** 56, **MLA** 448
Mass nouns. *See* Noncount nouns
Mathematics, reference sources on, **8** 402
may, can, **Gl** 514
may be, maybe, **Gl** 519
may of, **Gl** 516
Meanings of words, connotations and denotations, **3** 166–67
meanwhile, punctuation with, **4** 257

Measurement, units of, **6** 311
meat, meet, **6** 298
media, **Gl** 519
Media files, MLA style, **MLA** 444
Medium of publication, documenting
  APA style, **APA** 480–81
  Chicago style, **Chic** 497
  CSE style, **CSE** 508
  MLA style, **MLA** 416, 432, 434, 438
meet, meat, **6** 298
Memos, business, **2** 134–35
MetaCrawler, **7** 336
Metaphor, **3** 170
Methodology, **8** 381–83
me vs. *I*, **4** 225–26
might of, **Gl** 516
Misplaced modifiers
  defined, **4** 245
  grammar checkers for, **4** 245
  with *only* and other limiting modifiers, **4** 245
  and order of adjectives, **4** 248
  and position of adverbs, **4** 247–48
  with separated subjects and verbs, **4** 246
  and split infinitives, **4** 246
  unclear placement and, **4** 245
Miss, Mrs., Ms., **2** 129, **3** 162
Mixed metaphors, **3** 170
Mixed sentences
  defined, **4** 258
  in grammar, **4** 258–60
  in meaning, **4** 258–59
  with repeated sentence parts, **4** 260
MLA Handbook for Writers of Research Papers. *See* MLA style
MLA style
  for document format, **MLA** 447–49
  for footnotes or endnotes, **MLA** 414–15
  indexes to documentation models: parenthetical citations, **MLA** 404; works cited, **MLA** 404–06
  list of works cited: format of, **MLA** 415–16; index to, **MLA** 404–06; models of, **MLA** 416–47
  parenthetical citations: index to, **MLA** 404; models of, **MLA** 407–12; placement and punctuation of, **MLA** 412–14
  for poetry and long prose quotations, **MLA** 449
  sample paper, **MLA** 452–60
Modal verbs, **4** 203–05. *See also* Helping verbs (auxiliary verbs)
Modern Language Association style. *See* MLA style
Modifiers, **4** 236–49
  absolute, **4** 238
  absolute phrases as, **4** 192–93
  adjectives and adverbs, **4** 236–37
  as antecedents, **4** 234
  dangling, **4** 248–49
  defined, **4** 236
  grammar checkers for, **4** 245
  misplaced, **4** 245–48
  nonessential vs. essential, **5** 268–71, 276
  order of, **4** 246–48
  prepositional phrases as, **4** 191
  reducing, **3** 175–76
  subordinate clauses as, **4** 193–94
  verbals and verbal phrases as, **4** 191–92
Money amounts
  dollar signs with, **6** 310
  numerals vs. words for, **6** 313
Months of year
  abbreviation of, **6** 311
  capitalization of, **6** 304
Mood of verbs
  consistency of, **4** 215
  defined, **4** 214
  forms for, **4** 215
  grammar checkers for, **4** 214
  subjunctive, **4** 214–15
moral, morale, **Gl** 519
more
  in comparative forms, **4** 237–38
  pronouns with, **4** 231–32
  verbs with, **4** 220–21
moreover, punctuation with, **4** 257
most
  pronouns with, **4** 231–32
  in superlative forms, **4** 237–38
  verbs with, **4** 220–21
most, almost, **Gl** 512
Motion pictures or movies. *See* Films, DVDs, and video recordings
Mrs., Miss, Ms., **3** 162, **6** 310
Ms., Miss, Mrs., **3** 162, **6** 310
much
  vs. *many*, **4** 244
  pronouns with, **4** 231–32
  verbs with, **4** 220–21
Multilingual writers, tips for. *See* Culture-language issues
Multimedia sources. *See also* Films, DVDs, and video recordings; Illustrations and artworks; Sound recordings; Web sites

Multimedia sources *(continued)*
  acknowledging in one's own compositions, **2** 124
  creating and using, **1** 60–64, **2** 83–85, 123–24, **7** 340–42, 373
  documenting: APA style, **APA** 478, 480; Chicago style, **Chic** 499, 500; CSE style, **CSE** 508; MLA style, **MLA** 444–45
  evaluating, **2** 105–11, **7** 354–56
  permission for using, **2** 124, **7** 373
  as research sources, **7** 340–42
  in Web compositions, **2** 123–24, **7** 373
Multiple authors. *See* Authors
Multiple works by the same authors. *See* Authors
Multivolume works
  APA style, **APA** 473
  Chicago style, **Chic** 496
  MLA style: list of works cited, **MLA** 427; parenthetical citations, **MLA** 410
Museum Computer Network directory, **7** 341
Musical works. *See also* Sound recordings
  documenting: APA style, **APA** 480; Chicago style, **Chic** 500; MLA style, **MLA** 436, 438, 444, 445
  research sources on, **8** 394
  titles of: italics or underlining for longer works, **6** 307; quotation marks for songs, **5** 288
myself, herself, himself, yourself, **Gl** 519

N

namely, punctuation with, **4** 257, **5** 280
Names of persons
  abbreviating, **6** 311
  capitalizing, **6** 304
  titles before and after, **2** 129, **6** 305, 310
Narration
  in essay development, **1** 13
  in image analysis, **2** 86
  in paragraph development, **1** 45
Narrators, of literary works, **8** 385–86
Nationalities, capitalizing, **6** 304
NB, **6** 311
n.d. (no date)
  APA style, **APA** 477
  MLA style, **MLA** 437
neither
  pronouns with, **4** 231–32
  verbs with, **4** 220–21
neither . . . nor
  as correlative conjunction, **4** 186
  parallelism with, **3** 152–53
Networks, computer. *See* Internet; Web sites
nevertheless, punctuation with, **4** 257
Newsgroups. *See* Discussion groups, online
Newsletters, **2** 138
Newspapers. *See* Articles in periodicals; Periodicals
New York Public Library Digital Gallery, **7** 341
Nicknames, **5** 288
no. (abbreviation), **6** 310
no, know, **6** 298
no, to negate a noun, **4** 237
nobody
  pronouns with, **4** 231–32
  verbs with, **4** 220–21
No city of publication. *See n.p.*
No date. *See n.d.* (no date)
Noncount nouns
  defined, **4** 181, 241
  determiners with, **4** 240–41, 243–44
  list of, **4** 241
  no plurals with, **4** 232, **6** 301
  pronouns with, **4** 232
  verbs with, **4** 221–22
none
  pronouns with, **4** 231–32
  verbs with, **4** 220–21
Nonessential elements
  commas with, **5** 268–71
  dashes with, **5** 290
  defined, **5** 268
  vs. essential elements, **5** 268–71, 276
  parentheses with, **5** 290
  test for, **5** 269
nonetheless, punctuation with, **4** 257
Nonperiodical sources, documenting
  APA style, **APA** 472–73, 477–81
  Chicago style, **Chic** 495–97, 498–500
  CSE style, **CSE** 505–06, 507–08
  MLA style, **MLA** 423–30, 443–47
Nonprint sources
  APA style, **APA** 473–78, 480–81
  Chicago style, **Chic** 497–500
  CSE style, **CSE** 506–08
  MLA style, **MLA** 409–10, 431–47
Nonrestrictive elements. *See* Nonessential elements
Non sequiturs, **2** 103

Nonstandard usage. *See* Culture-language issues; Standard American English
no one
pronouns with, **4** 231–32
verbs with, **4** 220–21
No pagination. *See n.pag.* (no pagination)
No publisher. *See n.p.*
nor
and agreement of pronouns, **4** 230
and agreement of verbs, **4** 220
commas with, **5** 265, 275
as coordinating conjunction, **4** 185
parallelism with, **3** 151–52
not
to negate verbs or adjectives, **4** 236
position of, **4** 248
not . . . but
as correlative conjunction, **4** 186
parallelism with, **3** 152–53
Note cards. *See* Information gathering
Notes. *See* Footnotes or endnotes
Note taking
in class, **2** 69–70
for information gathering, **7** 358–59
nothing
pronouns with, **4** 231–32
verbs with, **4** 220–21
not only . . . but also
as correlative conjunction, **4** 186
parallelism with, **3** 152–53
Noun clauses, **4** 194
Nouns
a, an, the, and other determiners with, **4** 242–44
abstract vs. concrete, **3** 167–68
adjectives to modify, **4** 236–37
apostrophes with possessive, **4** 181, **5** 282–84
capitalization of proper, **6** 304–05
collective, **4** 181, 221–22, 232
common, **4** 180
count, **4** 181, 242–44
derived from verbs, **3** 144, 173
effective use of, **3** 143–44
general vs. specific, **3** 167–68
gerunds and gerund phrases as, **4** 192
implied, **4** 234–35
infinitives and infinitive phrases as, **4** 192
noncount, **4** 181, 241, 243–44
plurals of, **4** 181, **5** 284
proper. *See* Proper nouns
as subject and object complements, **4** 190
subordinate clauses as, **4** 194
types of, **4** 180–81
Novels, MLA style
in list of works cited, **MLA** 438
in parenthetical citations, **MLA** 411
now, punctuation with, **4** 257
nowheres, **Gl** 519
n.p. (no place of publication or publisher), MLA style, **MLA** 429, 436
n. pag. (no pagination)
MLA style, **MLA** 410, 429, 438
Number (singular, plural)
defined, **4** 218
grammar checkers for, **1** 43, **4** 218
pronoun-antecedent agreement in, **4** 229–32
shifts in, **1** 42
subject-verb agreement in, **4** 218–23
number, amount, **Gl** 512
Numbered lists, **1** 58
Numbers
abbreviations with, **6** 310
apostrophes to form plurals of, **5** 283
commas in, **5** 273
hyphens in, **6** 302
numerals vs. words for, **6** 312–13
spelled out at beginnings of sentences, **6** 313
Numerals. *See* Numbers

O

Object complements, **4** 190
Objective case
defined, **4** 224
for objects, **4** 225–26, 226–28
of pronouns, **4** 225
uses of, **4** 225–26
Objective narrators, in literary works, **8** 385
Objects
appositives, identifying, **4** 228
compound, **4** 225–26
direct, **4** 188–89
indirect, **4** 190
of infinitives, **4** 229
objective case for, **4** 225–26
of prepositions, **4** 191
of verbs, **4** 190
Objects of prepositions
case of, **4** 224–25
defined, **4** 191
oblivious of, to, **3** 168

Observation, for essay development, **1** 10, **7** 342–43
occupied by, in, with, **3** 168
of, have, **Gl** 516
of course, punctuation with, **4** 257
off of, **Gl** 519
OK, O.K., okay, **Gl** 519
Omissions
  from comparisons, **4** 239
  from compound constructions, **3** 171
  from contractions, **5** 285
  from direct quotations, **5** 292–94, **7** 362
  of needed words, **3** 171–72
  from *there is, here is,* or *it is* constructions, **3** 176
Omniscient narrators, in literary works, **8** 385
on, at, in, **3** 169
on account of, **Gl** 519
one
  pronouns with, **4** 231–32
  verbs with, **4** 220–21
  vs. *you,* **4** 235
one of the, agreement problems with, **4** 222
Online papers, posted via the Web, **2** 121
Online sources. *See* Electronic sources
only, placement of, **4** 245
on the contrary, punctuation with, **4** 257
on the other hand, **Gl** 519
Opinions, as claims in argument, **2** 98
opposed to, **3** 168
Opposition, acknowledging, in argument, **2** 102
or
  and agreement of pronouns, **4** 230
  and agreement of verbs, **4** 220
  commas with, **5** 265, 275
  as coordinating conjunction, **3** 147, **4** 185
  parallelism with, **3** 151–52
Oral presentations, **2** 124–28. *See also* Speeches
  delivering, **2** 125–28
  documenting, MLA style, **MLA** 447
  organization of, **2** 124–25
  PowerPoint in, **2** 126–27
  purpose and audience for, **2** 124–25
  writing vs. speaking, **2** 125
Organization
  of arguments, **2** 104–05
  of essays, **1** 16–21
  of oral presentations, **2** 124–25
  of paragraphs, **1** 40–41
  of research papers, **7** 375–76
  of science papers, **8** 400
  of social-science papers, **8** 396–97
Organization names
  abbreviating, **6** 310
  capitalizing, **6** 304
otherwise, punctuation with, **4** 257
Outlines
  constructing, **1** 18–20
  of essays, **1** 18–20
  formal, **1** 19–20, **MLA** 450–51
  format for, **MLA** 450–51
  with heading levels, **1** 59
  informal, **1** 18
  parallelism with, **1** 20, **3** 153
  of research papers, **MLA** 450–51
  as revision aids, **1** 20, 25
  sample, **MLA** 450–51
  scratch, **1** 18
  sentence vs. topic, **1** 20, **MLA** 450–51
  tree diagrams, **1** 18–19
outside of, inside of, **Gl** 517
Oversimplification, **2** 103–04
owing to the fact that, **Gl** 519

P

p., pp., **APA** 468
Page numbers
  documenting: APA style, **APA** 464, 467–68; Chicago style, **Chic** 493; CSE style, **CSE** 504, 506; MLA style, **MLA** 407, 418–23, 425–26, 429, 430, 442
  of journals vs. magazines, **7** 331
  none in source: APA style, **APA** 466–67; CSE style, **CSE** 506; MLA style, **MLA** 410, 429, 438, 440
  in one's own papers: APA style, **APA** 481; MLA style, **MLA** 448
  in periodicals: APA style, **APA** 470–72; Chicago style, **Chic** 494, 495; CSE style, **CSE** 505; MLA style, **MLA** 419
Pagination. *See n. pag.;* Page numbers
Paintings. *See* Illustrations and artworks
Pamphlets
  MLA style, **MLA** 430
  titles of, italics or underlining for, **6** 307
par., para., or *pars.* (paragraph)
  APA style, **APA** 464, 466–67
  CSE style, **CSE** 506
  MLA style, **MLA** 411

Paragraph numbers, documenting
APA style, **APA** 464, 466–67
CSE style, **CSE** 506
MLA style, **MLA** 411
Paragraphs, **1** 38–52
central idea in, **1** 38–39
coherence of, **1** 39–44
concluding, **1** 51–52
consistency in, **1** 42–43
development of, **1** 45–49
for dialog, **5** 287
indention of, **1** 38
introductory, **1** 50
length of, **1** 45
organization of, **1** 40–41
parallelism in, **1** 41
pronouns in, **1** 42
related to thesis, **1** 17–18
repetition and restatement in, **1** 41–42, 44
topic sentence of, **1** 39
transitional expressions in and between, **1** 43–44
unity of, **1** 38–39
Parallelism
in compound sentences with semicolon, **3** 147
with coordinating conjunctions, **3** 151–52
with correlative conjunctions, **3** 152–53
defined, **3** 151
grammar checkers for, **3** 151
with lists, headings, and outlines, **1** 58–59, **3** 153
in paragraphs, **1** 41
Paraphrases
avoiding plagiarism with, **7** 371–72, 372–75
checklist for, **7** 361
defined, **7** 360
documenting, **7** 372–75
examples of, **7** 360, 371–72
integrating, in paper, **7** 362–67
vs. summaries and direct quotations, **7** 359–62
vs. translation, **7** 361
Parentheses
around complete sentences, **5** 291–92
capitalization with, **5** 291–92
vs. commas and dashes, **5** 291
grammar checkers for, **5** 290
for labels of lists and outlines, **5** 292
with other punctuation, **5** 291–92
for parenthetical expressions, **5** 291–92
Parenthetical expressions
commas for, **5** 270–71, 291
dashes for, **5** 291
parentheses for, **5** 291–92
Parenthetical text citations
APA style: index to, **APA** 462; models of, **APA** 464–67
Chicago style, **Chic** 501
CSE name-year style, **CSE** 502
footnotes and endnotes with, **Chic** 501
MLA style: index to, **MLA** 404; models of, **MLA** 407–12; placement and punctuation of, **MLA** 412–14
part from, with, **3** 168
Participles and participial phrases. *See also* Past participles; Present participles
as adjectives, **4** 192, 240
defined, **4** 182, 192
of irregular verbs, **4** 196–98
present vs. past, **4** 240
punctuation of, **5** 269
Particles, in two-word verbs, **4** 207–08
Parts of speech, **4** 180–86
party, individual, person, **Gl** 517
passed, past, **6** 298
Passive voice
vs. active voice, **3** 145, 174
consistency in use of, **4** 217
defined, **3** 145
formation of, **4** 202, 216
grammar checkers for, **4** 217
in science writing, **8** 401
transitive verbs for, **4** 188–89, 202
unemphatic, **3** 145
wordiness of, **3** 174
past, passed, **6** 298
Past participles
as adjectives, **4** 192, 240
be forms with, **4** 202
defined, **4** 182
formation of, **4** 182, 196
irregular, **4** 197–98
participial phrases with, **4** 192
with perfect tenses, **4** 210–11
vs. present participles, as adjectives, **4** 240
Past perfect progressive tense, **4** 209, 211
Past perfect tense, **4** 209
Past progressive tense, **4** 209, 211
Past tense
in academic writing, **7** 364, 367, **8** 388, 393–94, 401
defined, **4** 182
formation of, **4** 182, 196, 209
irregular, **4** 197–98
in science writing, **8** 401
and tense sequence, **4** 212–13

patience, patients, **6** 298
Patterns of development
  for essays, **1** 13
  for paragraphs, **1** 45–49
peace, piece, **6** 298
Peer editing, **1** 35–37
Peer-reviewed journals, **7** 334
people, persons, **Gl** 519–20
per, **Gl** 520
percent (*per cent*), *percentage*, **Gl** 520
Perfect tenses
  helping verbs with, **4** 203
  and tense sequence, **4** 212–13
  uses of, **4** 210–11
Performances, MLA style, **MLA** 447
Periodical databases. *See also* Databases, electronic
  determining subject headings, **7** 327
  documenting: Chicago style, **Chic** 498; MLA style, **MLA** 439–42
  keyword searches of, **7** 327–28, 332–34
  for literature and literary analysis, **8** 389
  searching, **7** 332–34
  using, **7** 332–35
Periodicals
  database searches for, **7** 327, 332–35
  documentation of. *See* Articles in periodicals
  finding and using, **7** 327, 332–35
  journals vs. magazines, **7** 331
  kinds of, **7** 331
  pagination of, **MLA** 419, **APA** 470–72, **CSE** 505
  peer-reviewed or refereed, **7** 334
  quotation marks for titles of articles in, **5** 288
  as research sources, **7** 332–35
  titles of, italics or underlining for, **6** 307
Periodic sentences, **3** 147
Periods
  correcting comma splices and fused sentences with, **4** 254–55
  ending sentences with, **5** 263
  with quotation marks, **5** 289
  in some abbreviations, **5** 263
  space with, **5** 292–94
  used in ellipsis marks, **5** 292, **7** 362
Permission
  for material used in a Web composition, **7** 373
  for postings on e-mail, discussion groups, or blogs, **7** 373
  for use of images, **7** 340, 373
person
  pronouns with, **4** 231–32
  vs. *you*, **4** 235
Person (first, second, third)
  in academic writing, **2** 95–96
  defined, **4** 218
  grammar checkers for, **1** 43
  and point of view, in literary works, **8** 385–86
  pronoun-antecedent agreement in, **4** 229–32
  shifts in, **1** 42–43
  subject-verb agreement in, **4** 218
person, party, individual, **Gl** 517
Personal pronouns
  in academic writing, **1** 42–43, **2** 95–96
  agreement with antecedents, **4** 229–32
  cases of, **4** 224–29
  vs. contractions, **5** 285
  defined, **4** 181
  list of, **4** 225
  no apostrophes with possessives of, **5** 285
persons, people, **Gl** 519–20
phenomena, **Gl** 520
Phenomena, in scientific research, **8** 399
Philosophy, research sources on, **8** 394
Photocopying research sources, pros and cons, **7** 358–59
Photographs. *See* Illustrations and artworks
Phrases
  absolute, **4** 192–93, **5** 270
  appositive, **4** 193, **5** 270
  conciseness of, **3** 174–75
  defined, **4** 191–93
  essential vs. nonessential, **5** 268–71, 276
  as modifiers, **4** 191–92
  prepositional. *See* Prepositional phrases
  punctuation of: coordinate, **5** 272, 275; modifying, **5** 268–71
  subordination with, **3** 149–51
  types of, **4** 191–93
  verb, **4** 183, 200–05
  verbal. *See* Verbals and verbal phrases
Physics, research sources on, **8** 402
piece, peace, **6** 298
Place names
  abbreviation of, **6** 311
  capitalization of, **6** 304
  commas in, **5** 273
Plagiarism
  vs. academic integrity, **7** 367–68
  accidental, **7** 368
  avoiding, **7** 367–75
  with computer notes, **7** 358–59

defined, **7** 367
deliberate, **7** 368
detecting, on the Internet, **7** 369
with downloaded sources, **7** 359
with handwritten notes, **7** 358
during information gathering, **7** 358–59
and intellectual property, **7** 367–68
with Internet sources, **7** 368–69
with paraphrases, **7** 371–72
with photocopied or printed-out sources, **7** 358–59
with quotations, **7** 371
with summaries, **2** 81, **7** 371–72
Turnitin to detect, **7** 359
vs. using common knowledge, **7** 370
vs. using your own independent material, **7** 370

plain, plane, **6** 298
Plain form, of verbs
defined, **4** 182
in forming past tense and past participles, **4** 196
in forming simple present tense, **4** 182
forms of *do* with, **4** 203
plane, plain, **6** 298
Plays
acts and scenes of, **MLA** 412, 414
MLA style: list of works cited, **MLA** 447; parenthetical citations, **MLA** 412, 414
research sources on, **8** 394
titles of, italics or underlining for, **6** 307
plenty, **Gl** 520
Plots, of literary works, **8** 385
Plurals. *See also* Agreement of pronouns and antecedents; Agreement of subjects and verbs
of abbreviations, dates, and characters or words named as words, **5** 283, 285
apostrophes misused to form, **5** 283, 284
apostrophes with possessives of, **5** 284
defined, **4** 181
determiners with, **4** 241
formation of, **6** 300–01
grammar checkers for, **5** 282
of nouns, **4** 181, **5** 284
in pronoun-antecedent agreement, **4** 229–32
in subject-verb agreement, **4** 218–23
plus, **Gl** 520
PM, AM, **6** 310
Podcasts
documenting: APA style, **APA** 478; MLA style, **MLA** 437
evaluating, **7** 354–56
as research sources, **7** 340, 342
Poetry
analyzing, **8** 389–91
MLA style: formatting quotations from, **MLA** 449; parenthetical citations for, **MLA** 411–12; works-cited entry for, **MLA** 438
omission of lines of, **5** 294
slashes between lines of, **5** 294, **MLA** 449
titles of: italics or underlining for long, **6** 307; quotation marks for short, **5** 288
writing about, **8** 389–91
Point-by-point comparison and contrast, **1** 48
Point of view
in illustrations, **2** 86
in literary works, **8** 385–86
Point size (type fonts), **1** 57
Political Cartoons, **7** 341
Political science, research sources on, **8** 398
Popular Culture directory, **7** 341
Portfolios, writing, **1** 37
Positive form, of adjectives and adverbs, **4** 184, 237–38
Possessive case
apostrophes to indicate, **4** 181, **5** 282–84
defined, **4** 224
forming, **4** 181, 224–25, **5** 282–84
before gerunds, **4** 229
grammar checkers for, **5** 282
of nouns and indefinite pronouns, **4** 181, **5** 282–84
of personal pronouns, **4** 225, **5** 285
Post hoc fallacy, **2** 104
PowerPoint, **2** 126–27
precede, proceed, **Gl** 520
Predicate adjectives. *See* Subject complements
Predicate nouns. *See* Subject complements
Predicates. *See also* Objects; Subject complements; Verbs
agreement of subjects with, **4** 218–23
complete, **4** 187–88
compound, **4** 187, **5** 275
defined, **4** 186–87
patterns, **4** 188–90
in sentences with mixed grammar, **4** 258–60
in sentences with mixed meaning (faulty predication), **4** 258–59
simple, **4** 187–88

Predication, faulty, **4** 258–59
Preface, MLA style, **MLA** 428–29
Prefixes
  with capitalized words, **6** 302
  hyphens to attach, **6** 302
  spelling with, **6** 300
prejudice, prejudiced, **Gl** 520
Prepositional phrases
  as adjectives or adverbs, **4** 191
  commas with, **5** 267
  defined, **4** 191
  unneeded, **3** 174–75
Prepositions
  at, in, on, **3** 169
  capitalization in titles, **6** 306
  defined, **4** 184
  for, since, **3** 169, **4** 211
  idioms with, **3** 168–69
  list of, **4** 184
  objects of, **4** 191
  in two-word verbs, **4** 207–08
presence, presents, **6** 298
Present participles
  as adjectives, **4** 192, 240
  be forms with, **4** 211
  defined, **4** 182
  formation of, **4** 182, 192
  participial phrases with, **4** 192
  vs. past participles, as adjectives, **4** 240
  with progressive tenses, **4** 211
Present perfect progressive tense, **4** 209, 211
Present perfect tense, **4** 209, 210–11
Present progressive tense, **4** 209, 211
presents, presence, **6** 298
Present tense
  defined, **4** 209
  in literary analysis and other humanities writing, **7** 364, 366
  uses of, **4** 210
Pretentious writing, **3** 161
pretty, **Gl** 520
Previewing, for critical reading or viewing
  of images, **2** 84
  of text, **2** 70–71, 77–80
previous to, prior to, **Gl** 520
Primary sources
  defined, **7** 321, **8** 381
  one's own knowledge as, **7** 320, 342–44
  for research, **7** 321, 339–40
  as research sources, **8** 381
  vs. secondary sources, **7** 321, **8** 381–82
principal, principle, **6** 298, **Gl** 520
Principal parts of verbs, **4** 196
Printing out research sources, pros and cons, **7** 358–59
Prints and Photographs Online Catalog, **7** 341
Print sources, documenting
  APA style, **APA** 470–73, 478–79
  Chicago style, **Chic** 494–97, 499–500
  CSE style, **CSE** 504–06, 508
  MLA style, **MLA** 418–30, 446
prior to, **3** 168
prior to, previous to, **Gl** 520
Problem-solution organization, **1** 18
Problem-solving analysis, **8** 396
proceed, precede, **Gl** 520
Proceedings, MLA style, **MLA** 428
Process
  critical reading and viewing, **2** 77–89
  research writing, **7** 375–77
  writing, **1** 3–65
Process analysis
  in essay development, **1** 13
  in paragraph development, **1** 49
Progressive tenses
  defined, **4** 201
  formation of, **4** 201–02, 211
  uses of, **4** 211
Pronoun-antecedent agreement. *See* Agreement of pronouns and antecedents
Pronouns, **4** 224–35
  adjectives to modify, **4** 236–37
  agreement with antecedents, **4** 229–32
  apostrophes misused with possessives, **5** 285
  cases of, **4** 224–29
  consistency in, **4** 235
  defined, **4** 181, 224
  demonstrative, **4** 181
  gender of, **4** 230
  grammar checkers for, **4** 233
  indefinite. *See* Indefinite pronouns
  intensive, **4** 181
  interrogative, **4** 181
  for paragraph coherence, **1** 42
  personal. *See* Personal pronouns
  reference of, **4** 233–35
  reflexive, **4** 181
  relative. *See* Relative pronouns
  as subject complements, **4** 224
  types of, **4** 181
Pronunciation, spelling and, **6** 297–98
Proofreading
  of direct quotations, **7** 362
  of e-mail, **2** 116

for online communications, **3** 159
as part of writing process, **1** 33, **3** 172
Proper adjectives, capitalization of, **6** 304–05
Proper nouns
articles with, **4** 241, 243
capitalization of, **6** 304–05
common nouns as essential parts of, **6** 305
defined, **4** 181, 241, **6** 304
ProQuest, **7** 332, 335
Prose, formatting long quotations from
APA style, **APA** 483
MLA style, **MLA** 449
proud of, **3** 168
Psychology, research sources on, **8** 398
Publication Manual of the American Psychological Association. See APA style
Publications, government. *See* Government publications
Public writing, **2** 128–39. *See also* Community work
audience for, **1** 7–8
design considerations for, **1** 53–56
e-mail, **2** 116–18, 132–33
fax transmissions, **2** 133–34
introductions in, **1** 49–51
letters, **2** 129–31
memos, **2** 134–35
reports, **2** 134–36
résumés, **2** 131–32
Published proceedings of a conference, MLA style, **MLA** 428
Punctuation. *See also specific punctuation marks*
of absolute phrases, **5** 270
of appositives, **5** 270, 280
with conjunctive adverbs, **4** 257, **5** 277–78
of coordinate elements, **5** 265, 272, 275, 278
at ends of sentences, **5** 263–64
of essential vs. nonessential elements, **5** 268–71, 276
forming and spacing, **1** 58
grammar checkers for, **5** 263, 265, 277, 279, 282, 286, 290
of introductory elements, **5** 267–68
of linked main clauses, **4** 253–57, **5** 265, 277
in online communication, **2** 95
with parenthetical citations, **MLA** 412–14
of parenthetical expressions, **5** 291–92
of possessive case, **5** 282–84
of prepositional phrases, **5** 267
of quotations. *See* Quotations, direct
of series, **5** 272, 279, 280
of subordinate clauses, **5** 267, 268–71, 279
of titles of works, **5** 281, 288
of transitional elements, **5** 267
of verbals and verbal phrases, **5** 268–71
Purpose
in academic writing, **2** 92–93
as component of writing situation, **1** 4, 6–7, **2** 92–93
determining: in evaluating online sources, **7** 351, 355; in viewing illustrations, **2** 84

Q

Qualitative evidence in the social sciences, **8** 396
Quantitative evidence in the social and natural sciences, **8** 396, 399
Question marks
with direct questions, **5** 264
to express doubt, **5** 264
with quotation marks, **5** 289
space with, **1** 58
question of whether, *question as to whether*, **Gl** 520
Questions
about audience, **1** 7–8
capitalization in series, **6** 304
for developing paper subjects, **1** 13, **7** 319–20
direct, **5** 264
indirect, **5** 263
journalist's, **1** 13
for literary analysis, **8** 385–87
for patterns of development, **1** 13
research, **7** 319–20
tag, **5** 271
who vs. *whom* in, **4** 226–28
Quotation marks, **5** 286–89
avoiding unnecessary, **5** 288–89
for dialog, **5** 287
for direct quotations, **5** 286–87, 289, **7** 371
double, **5** 286–87
grammar checkers for, **5** 286
not with quotations set off from one's text: APA style, **APA** 483; MLA style, **MLA** 449
with other punctuation, **5** 289
for quotations within quotations, **5** 287
single, **5** 286

Quotation marks *(continued)*
- spaces with, **1** 58
- for titles of works, **5** 288
- for words used in special senses, **5** 288

Quotations, direct. *See also* Indirect quotations
- accuracy of, **7** 361–62
- avoiding plagiarism with, **7** 371
- brackets for changes in, **5** 294, **6** 303
- capitalization in, **6** 303
- changes in, **5** 292–94, **6** 303, **7** 362
- colons before, **5** 280
- commas with, **5** 274
- and copyright, **7** 372–73
- criteria for using, **7** 361
- defined, **5** 286
- of dialog, **5** 287
- documenting sources of, **7** 372–75
- ellipsis marks for omissions from, **5** 292–94
- fair use of, **7** 373
- integrating, in a paper, **7** 362–67
- of long prose quotations, format of: APA style, **APA** 483; MLA style, **MLA** 449
- omissions from, **5** 292–94
- vs. paraphrases and summaries, **7** 359–62
- of poetry, MLA style, **MLA** 449
- quotation marks with, **5** 287, 289
- within quotations, **5** 287
- *she said* and other signal phrases with, **5** 273–74
- *sic* in, **5** 294
- slashes with, **5** 294
- tests for when to use, **7** 369

Quotations, indirect. *See* Indirect quotations

R

Races of people, capitalization of, **6** 305

Radio programs. *See* Television and radio programs

rain, reign, rein, **6** 298

raise, rise, **4** 198–99, **Gl** 520

Rational appeals, **2** 101–02

Readers. *See* Audience

Reading
- for comprehension, **2** 70–72
- critical, **2** 70–74, 77–89, **7** 344–57
- of illustrations, **2** 84–85
- literature, **8** 384
- previewing for, **2** 70–71
- research sources, **7** 344–57
- for revision, **1** 25–26
- skimming, **2** 70–71

Reading journal, **1** 9–10, **2** 70, 72, **7** 318, **8** 384

Readings (lectures). *See* Oral presentations

real, really, **Gl** 520

Reasonableness, in arguments
- acknowledgment of opposition, **2** 102
- appropriate appeals, **2** 101–02
- fallacies, **2** 102–04
- logical thinking, **2** 100–04

reason is because, **4** 259, **Gl** 520–21

Red herring, **2** 103

Reductive fallacy, **2** 104

Refereed journals, **7** 334

Reference librarians, **7** 327

Reference lists. *See also* Chicago style; MLA style
- APA style, **APA** 469–81
- CSE style, **CSE** 502–08

Reference of pronouns
- appropriate *that, which, who,* **Gl** 522
- appropriate *you,* **4** 235
- to clear antecedents, **4** 222, 233
- to close antecedents, **4** 233–34
- definite *it, they,* **4** 234
- to specific antecedents, **4** 234–35
- vague *this, that, which, it,* **4** 234

References, parenthetical. *See* Parenthetical text citations

Reference works
- documenting: APA style, **APA** 477; Chicago style, **Chic** 497, 498, 499; MLA style, **MLA** 426, 435
- electronic, **3** 165, **7** 329–30
- for the humanities, **8** 394
- for the natural and applied sciences, **8** 401–02
- as research sources, **7** 329–30
- for the social sciences, **8** 398
- style guides, **7** 374, **8** 395, 398–99, 402
- *Wikipedia* as, **7** 330
- for writing about literature, **8** 388–89

Reflexive pronouns, **4** 181

Refworks, **7** 374

Regular verbs
- defined, **4** 196
- vs. irregular verbs, **4** 196

reign, rein, rain, **6** 298

related to, **3** 169

Relative pronouns
- in adjective clauses, **4** 193–94
- defined, **4** 181
- list of, **4** 181, 252
- reference of, **4** 233–34
- in sentence fragments, **4** 252
- verb agreement with, **4** 222

Relevance and reliability
in evaluating sources, **7** 345–46
of evidence, **2** 99
Reliable narrators, in literary works, **8** 385–86
Religion, research sources on, **8** 394
Religious groups and terms, capitalization of, **6** 305
Repetition
for coherence of paragraphs, **1** 41–42
unneeded, **3** 175, **4** 260
Reports
in business writing, **2** 136
documenting: APA style, **APA** 476–77, 479; CSE style, **CSE** 508
as writing assignment, **1** 6, **8** 396, 400
Republished books, documenting using MLA style, **MLA** 427, 438
Research journals, **7** 318, **8** 384, 393, 397
Research proposals, **8** 400
Research writing, **7** 317–77
annotated bibliographies for, **7** 323–25
APA style: documentation, **APA** 462–81; format, **APA** 481–84; parenthetical citations, **APA** 464–67, reference list, **APA** 467–81; sample paper, **APA** 484–87
audio and video for, **7** 342
avoiding plagiarism in, **7** 367–75
bibliographies for. *See subentries here for individual styles*
books for, **7** 330
Chicago style, **Chic** 491–501
citing sources in, **7** 372–75
critical reading of sources for, **7** 344–57
CSE style, **CSE** 502–08; name-year text citations, **CSE** 502; numbered text citations, **CSE** 502–03; reference list, **CSE** 503–08
discussion groups for, **7** 339, 354–56
documentation in, **7** 372–75
drafting, **7** 376
electronic searches for, **7** 325–29, 335–38
electronic sources for, **7** 326–29
evaluating sources for, **7** 345–56
gathering information for, **7** 358–59
goals for, **7** 320–23
government publications for, **7** 340
in humanities, **8** 392–95
images for, **7** 342
integrating borrowed material in, **7** 362–67
interviews for, **7** 343
journal keeping for, **7** 318
keywords for, **7** 328–29
library for, **7** 326–35
literary analysis sources, **8** 388–89
MLA style: documentation, **MLA** 404–47; document format, **MLA** 447–49; list of works cited: format of, **MLA** 415–16; models of, **MLA** 415–47; parenthetical citations, **MLA** 407–14; sample paper, **MLA** 452–60
multimedia sources for, **7** 340–42
in natural and applied sciences, **8** 399–402
one's own sources for, **7** 342–44
organizing, **7** 375–76
outlines for, **MLA** 450–51
paraphrases in, **7** 360–61, 371–72
periodicals for, **7** 332–35
planning, **7** 317–18
primary sources for, **7** 321, 342–44
questions for, **7** 319–20
quotations in, **7** 361–62, 371
revising, **7** 376–77
scheduling, **7** 317–18
secondary sources for, **7** 321, 340, 361–62
in social sciences, **8** 395–99
sources for, **7** 325–44, **8** 388–89
style guides for, **7** 374, **8** 395, 398–99, 402
subjects for, **7** 319–20
summaries in, **7** 359–60
synthesizing sources for, **7** 356–57, 362
thesis statements for, **7** 375
Web sources for, **7** 335–40, 347, 350–54
working bibliographies for, **7** 323–25
writing process for, **7** 317–18
respectful, respective, **Gl** 521
Responding to texts. *See* Academic writing
Restrictive elements. *See* Essential elements
Résumés, **2** 131–32
Return-address heading, **2** 129
Reviews
APA style, **APA** 472, 476
Chicago style, **Chic** 495
MLA style, **MLA** 420–21, 434, 440–41
Revisions
checklists for, **1** 26, 39, **7** 377
collaborating on, **1** 35–37

Revisions *(continued)*
computers for, **1** 25
creating distance for, **1** 25
critical reading for, **1** 25–26
vs. editing, **1** 24
of essays, **1** 25–27, 35–37
outlines for, **1** 20, 25
of paragraphs, **1** 39
of research paper, **7** 376–77
sample of, **1** 27–28
of thesis statements, **1** 15–16
rewarded by, for, with, **3** 169
right, rite, write, **6** 298
rise, raise, **4** 198–99, **Gl** 520
road, rode, **6** 298
Rogerian argument, **2** 102
Run-on sentences (fused sentences), **4** 253–57

S

-s, -es
grammar checkers for, **4** 199
for plural nouns, **4** 181, 218–19
possessive of words ending in, **5** 284
for singular verbs, **4** 182, 199–200, 218–19
and subject-verb agreement, **4** 218–19
-'s
for possessives, **4** 181, **5** 282–84
for some plural dates, abbreviations, and characters or words used as words, **5** 283, 285
Salutations of business letters
colons after, **5** 281
format of, **2** 129
Sans serif type fonts, **1** 57
scarcely, but, hardly, **Gl** 513
scene, seen, **6** 298
Scheduling, of research writing, **7** 317–18
Scholarly projects, MLA style, **MLA** 434
Sciences, natural and applied
assignments in, **8** 399–400
CSE documentation style, **CSE** 502–08; name-year text citations, **CSE** 502; numbered text citations, **CSE** 502–03; reference list, **CSE** 503–08
integrating borrowed material in, **7** 366–67
methods and evidence in, **8** 399
research sources on, **8** 401–02
style guides in, **8** 402, **CSE** 502
tools and language in, **8** 400–02
verb tenses in, **7** 366–67
Sciences, social. *See* Social sciences
Scientific method, **8** 399
Scientific Style and Format: The CSE Manual for Authors, Editors, and Publishers. *See* CSE style
Scratch (informal) outlines, **1** 18
Search engines
vs. databases, **7** 327–28
defined, **7** 336
for finding images, **7** 341
keyword searches of, **7** 328–29
list of, **7** 336
sample search, **7** 337–38
using, **7** 328–29, 335–38
Searches, electronic, **7** 325–29, 335–38
Search histories, **7** 337
Secondary sources
defined, **7** 321, **8** 381
vs. primary sources, **7** 321, **8** 381–82
for research, **7** 321, **8** 381–82
Second person (*you*), **2** 96, **4** 218
seen, scene, **6** 298
-self, -selves, **4** 181
Semicolons, **5** 277–79
vs. colons, **5** 280
correcting comma splices with, **4** 256
grammar checkers for, **5** 277
with *however, for example*, etc., **4** 257, **5** 277–78
misuse of, **5** 279
with quotation marks, **5** 289
to separate main clauses, **5** 277
in series, **5** 279
spaces with, **1** 58
sensual, sensuous, **Gl** 521
Sentence combining
for conciseness, **3** 176
for variety, **3** 155–56
Sentence fragments
acceptable uses of, **4** 252–53
vs. complete sentences, **4** 250–52
defined, **4** 201
grammar checkers for, **4** 250
omitted subjects in, **4** 251–52
omitted verbs in, **4** 201
in online communication, **2** 95
revising, **4** 252
subordinate clauses as, **4** 252
tests for, **4** 250–52
verbal phrases as, **4** 201, 251
Sentence outlines, **1** 20, **MLA** 450–51
Sentences. *See also* Sentence fragments
beginnings of, for emphasis, **3** 145–47
capitalization of first word in, **6** 303–04

completeness of, **3** 171–72
complex, **4** 195
compound, **4** 195
compound-complex, **4** 195
conciseness of, **3** 172–76
conditional. *See* Conditional sentences
coordination in, **3** 147–49
cumulative, **3** 146–47
defined, **4** 186
elements of, **4** 186–90
fused, **4** 253–57
incomplete, grammar checkers for, **3** 171
length of, **3** 154
mixed, **4** 258–60
numbers at beginning of, **6** 313
outlines, **1** 20, **MLA** 450–51
periodic, **3** 147
predicates of, **4** 186–90
punctuation at end of, **5** 263–64
repeated parts in, **4** 260
run-on, **4** 253–57
vs. sentence fragments, **4** 250–52
simple, **4** 195
subjects of, **4** 186–87
subordination in, **3** 149–51
thesis. *See* Thesis and thesis statement
topic, **1** 39
types of, **4** 194–95
variety in, **3** 154–57

Sequence, transitional expressions to indicate, **1** 43
Sequence of tenses
in conditional sentences, **4** 213–14
defined, **4** 212
with past or past perfect tense in main clauses, **4** 212–13
Series
capitalization of questions in, **6** 304
colons to introduce, **5** 280
commas in, **5** 272, 276
dashes before or after, **5** 291
defined, **5** 272
documenting: Chicago style, **Chic** 497; MLA style, **MLA** 422, 427
misuse of commas around, **5** 276
semicolons with, **5** 279
Serif type fonts, **1** 57
Service learning, **2** 136
set, sit, **4** 198–99, **Gl** 521
Setting, in literary works, **8** 386
several
pronouns with, **4** 231–32
verbs with, **4** 220–21
Sexist language
avoiding, **3** 162–64, **4** 231–32, **Gl** 516–17
generic *he* in, **4** 231–32, **Gl** 516–17
shall, will, **Gl** 521
she
case forms of, **4** 225–26
vs. *her*, **4** 224–29
she, he: he/she, **Gl** 516–17
Shifts
grammar checkers for, **1** 43
in mood, **4** 215
in number, **1** 42
paragraph coherence and, **1** 42–43
in person, **1** 42–43
in pronouns, **4** 235
in tense, **4** 211–12
in tone, **5** 290
in voice, **4** 217
Ship names, italics or underlining for, **6** 308
Short stories, quotation marks for titles of, **5** 288
should of, **Gl** 516
sic, **5** 294
sight, site, cite, **6** 298, **Gl** 514
Signal phrases
commas with, **5** 273–74
interrupting quotations with, **5** 274
for introducing and interpreting borrowed material, **7** 364–65
verbs and verb tenses for, **7** 364, 366–67
Signatures, in business letters, **2** 129
similarly, punctuation with, **4** 257
similar to, **3** 169
Similes, **3** 170
Simple future tense, **4** 209
Simple past tense, **4** 209
Simple predicate, **4** 187–88
Simple present tense, **4** 209
Simple sentence, **4** 195
Simple subject, **4** 187
since
vs. *for*, **3** 169, **4** 211
used for *because*, **Gl** 521
Singular
in pronoun-antecedent agreement, **4** 229–32
in subject-verb agreement, **4** 218–23
sit, set, **4** 198–99, **Gl** 521
site, cite, sight, **6** 298, **Gl** 514
Slang
appropriate use of, **3** 160
defined, **3** 160
no quotation marks for, **5** 288–89

Slashes
  between options, **5** 294
  to separate lines of poetry, **5** 294, **MLA** 449
  spaces with, **1** 58, **5** 294
  in URLs, **MLA** 439, **APA** 473, **Chic** 497, **CSE** 506
so
  commas with, **5** 265, 275
  as coordinating conjunction, **4** 185
  as vague intensifier, **Gl** 521
Social sciences
  APA documentation style, **APA** 462–81; document format, **APA** 481–84; parenthetical citations, **APA** 464–67; reference list, **APA** 467–81; sample paper, **APA** 484–87
  assignments in, **8** 396–97
  integrating borrowed material in, **7** 366–67
  methods and evidence in, **8** 395–96
  research sources on, **8** 398–99
  sample paper in, **APA** 484–87
  style guides for, **8** 398–99
  tools and language in, **8** 397–98
  writing for, **8** 395–99
Sociology, research sources on, **8** 398
Software. *See* Computer software
some
  pronouns with, **4** 231–32
  verbs with, **4** 220–21
somebody
  pronouns with, **4** 231–32
  vs. *some body*, **Gl** 521
  verbs with, **4** 220–21
someone
  pronouns with, **4** 231–32
  vs. *some one*, **Gl** 521
  verbs with, **4** 220–21
something
  pronouns with, **4** 231–32
  verbs with, **4** 220–21
sometime, sometimes, some time, **Gl** 521
somewheres, **Gl** 521
Songs, quotation marks for titles of, **5** 288
sorry about, for, **3** 169
sort of, type of, kind of, **Gl** 518
Sound recordings. *See also* Musical works
  acknowledging, **7** 372–73
  documenting: APA style, **APA** 480; Chicago style, **Chic** 499, 500; CSE style, **CSE** 508; MLA style, **MLA** 437, 438, 444, 445
  evaluating, **7** 354–56
  as research sources, **7** 340, 342
  titles of: italics or underlining for longer works, **6** 307; quotation marks for songs, **5** 288
  in Web compositions, **2** 123
Sources. *See also* Electronic sources; Primary sources; Secondary sources
  annotated bibliographies of, **7** 323–25
  audio and video, **7** 340–42
  books, **7** 330
  citing to avoid plagiarism, **7** 367–75
  documentation of: APA style, **APA** 462–81; Chicago style, **Chic** 491–501; CSE style, **CSE** 502–08; MLA style, **MLA** 404–47
  downloading, **7** 359
  electronic searches for, **7** 325–29, 335–38
  evaluating, **2** 77–89, **7** 345–56
  fair use of, **7** 373
  full-text, **7** 327
  gathering information from, **7** 358–59
  goals for, **7** 320–23
  with helpful features, **7** 323
  in humanities, **8** 394
  images, **7** 340–42
  impartial vs. biased, **7** 322
  integrating material from, **7** 362–67
  interviews, **7** 343
  keywords for finding, **7** 328–29
  library vs. Internet, **7** 321, 326
  in literary analysis, **8** 388–89
  multimedia, **2** 123–24, **7** 373
  in natural and applied sciences, **8** 401–02
  older vs. newer, **7** 322
  for online images, **7** 340–42
  paraphrases of, **7** 360–61, 371–72
  periodicals, finding, **7** 332–35
  permission for using, **7** 340, 372–73
  photocopying from, **7** 358–59
  plagiarism vs. acknowledgment of, **7** 367–75
  primary vs. secondary, **7** 321
  quotations from, **7** 361–62, 371
  reference works, **7** 330
  scholarly vs. popular, **7** 322
  searching using Boolean operators, **7** 328–29
  summaries of, **7** 359–60
  synthesizing, **7** 356–57
  using, **7** 344–67
  working bibliographies of, **7** 323–25

SourceWatch, as research source, **7** 336
Spacecraft, italics or underlining for names of, **6** 308
Spamming, **2** 117
Spatial organization, **1** 17, 41
Specific-to-general organization, **1** 18
Specific vs. general, **1** 18, **3** 167–68
Speech, parts of, **4** 180–86
Speeches
  documenting: Chicago style, **Chic** 499; MLA style, **MLA** 447
  published, italics or underlining for titles of, **6** 307
Spelling
  American vs. British, **6** 299
  for different forms of same word, **6** 299
  electronic checkers for, **1** 31–32, **6** 297
  of homonyms, **6** 297–98
  in online communication, **2** 95
  pronunciation and, **6** 297–98
  rules for, **6** 299–301
Split infinitives, **4** 246
Standard American English
  in academic writing, **2** 94–96, **3** 158
  defined, **3** 158, **Gl** 511
  vs. other dialects and languages, **3** 158–59
Standardization, in document design, **1** 56
stationary, stationery, **6** 298
Statistics, as evidence, **2** 99
Stereotypes, eliminating, **2** 104, **3** 162, **4** 231–32
still, punctuation with, **4** 257
Stories
  quotation marks for titles of, **5** 288
  reading and writing about, **8** 384–88
Structure of essays, in academic writing, **2** 93–94
Study skills. *See* Academic skills
Style, writing
  in academic writing, **2** 94–96
  appropriate words for, **3** 158–64
  conciseness for, **3** 172–76
  effective sentences for, **3** 143–57
  exact words for, **3** 165–71
Style and grammar checkers, **1** 32. *See also entries for specific style and grammar issues*
Style guides
  humanities, **8** 395
  literature, **8** 389
  natural and applied sciences, **8** 402, **CSE** 502
  social sciences, **8** 398–99
Subject-by-subject comparison and contrast, **1** 47–48
Subject complements
  adjectives as, **4** 189–90
  defined, **4** 189
  nouns as, **4** 190
  pronouns as, **4** 226
  subjective case for, **4** 226
Subject headings, discovering using keyword searches, **7** 328–29, 332–34
Subjective case
  defined, **4** 224
  of pronouns, **4** 225
  for subject complements, **4** 226
  for subjects, **4** 224–28
Subject of paper
  for arguments, **2** 97
  development of, **1** 8–13
  for essays, **1** 3–4, 5–6
  limiting, **1** 5–6
  for research papers, **7** 319–20
Subject of sentence
  active vs. passive voice and, **4** 216–17
  complement of. *See* Subject complements
  complete, **4** 187
  compound, **4** 225–26, **5** 275
  conciseness and, **3** 173–74
  defined, **3** 143, **4** 186–87
  effective use of, for emphasis, **3** 143–45
  misuse of comma between verb and, **5** 275
  and mixed grammar, **4** 258–60
  and mixed meaning, **4** 258–59
  omission of, **4** 214, 251–52
  repetition of, **4** 260
  separation from verb, **4** 246
  simple, **4** 187
  subjective case for, **4** 224–25, 224–28
  verb with, **4** 218–23
Subject-verb agreement. *See* Agreement of subjects and verbs
Subjunctive mood
  defined, **4** 214
  formation of, **4** 215
  grammar checkers for, **4** 214
  tense sequences with, **4** 213–14
  uses of, **4** 214–15
Subordinate (dependent) clauses
  as adjective or adverb, **4** 193
  commas with, **5** 267, 268–69
  correcting comma splices and fused sentences with, **4** 256
  defined, **4** 193
  excessive use of, **3** 150–51
  vs. main clauses, **4** 193

Subordinate (dependent) clauses *(continued)*
- misuse of semicolon with, **5** 279
- as noun, **4** 194
- relative pronouns and, **4** 193–94, 252
- as sentence fragments, **4** 252
- subordinating conjunctions and, **4** 185, 194, 252
- subordination and, **3** 149–51
- tense sequence with, **4** 213–14
- types of, **4** 194
- *who* vs. *whom* in, **4** 226–28

Subordinating conjunctions
- vs. coordinating conjunctions and conjunctive adverbs, **4** 257
- defined, **4** 185
- list of, **4** 185, 252

Subordination
- defined, **3** 149
- effective, **3** 150–51
- to emphasize main ideas, **3** 150
- excessive or faulty, **3** 150–51
- grammar checkers for, **3** 150
- for variety, **3** 154–57

Subscription services. *See also* Databases, electronic
- documenting: APA style, **APA** 474–75; Chicago style, **Chic** 498; CSE style, **CSE** 506–07; MLA style, **MLA** 441–43
- finding bibliographic information for, **MLA** 442
- for images, **7** 342
- listed in working bibliography, **7** 326
- as research sources, **7** 327, 332–35

Subtitles
- capitalization in, **6** 306
- colons with, **5** 281

such
- as determiner, **4** 244
- as vague intensifier, **Gl** 521

such as, like, **Gl** 518
such as, no colon with, **5** 281
Suffixes, hyphen to attach, **6** 302
Suggestive titles, **1** 27
Summaries
- as aid to exam preparation, **2** 76
- as aid to reading comprehension, **2** 72–74
- avoiding plagiarism with, **7** 371–72
- in critical reading, **2** 80–81
- defined, **7** 359
- documenting, **7** 372–75
- examples of, **2** 73–74, 80–81, **7** 360
- integrating, in paper, **7** 362–67
- organizing for studying, **2** 76
- vs. paraphrase and direct quotation, **7** 359–62
- as research paper, **8** 400
- transitional expressions to indicate, **1** 44
- writing, **1** 6, **2** 72–74, 80–81, **7** 359–60

Summary or review of research reports, **8** 396
Superfluous commas, **5** 274–76. *See also* Commas, misuse of
superior to, **3** 169
Superlative form of adjectives and adverbs, **4** 184, 237–38
supposed to, used to, **Gl** 522
sure, **Gl** 522
sure and, sure to, **Gl** 522
Surveys, conducting, **7** 343–44
Sweeping generalizations, **2** 104
Syllogisms, **2** 101
Symbolism, in literary works, **8** 386
Synonyms, **3** 166
Synthesis, **7** 356–57, 358–62
- in academic writing, **2** 74, 92
- in critical thinking and reading, **2** 82–83, 89
- of illustrations, **2** 89
- of research sources, **7** 356–57, 362
- in research writing, **8** 393
- in responding to texts, **2** 90–92, 94

T

Tables
- APA style: sample, **APA** 486; using, **APA** 484
- creating, **1** 61

Tag questions, commas with, **5** 271
take, bring, **Gl** 513
Taking notes. *See* Information gathering
Technical words, **3** 160–61
Technical writing
- abbreviations in, **6** 311
- brackets in, **5** 294
- capital letters in, **6** 303
- documentation in, **CSE** 502–08
- numbers in, **6** 312–13
- words in, **3** 160–61

Television and radio programs
- documenting: APA style, **APA** 481; MLA style, **MLA** 436, 444–45
- titles of: italics or underlining for programs, **6** 307; quotation marks for episodes, **5** 288

Templates, **1** 56
Tenses
  in conditional sentences, **4** 213–14
  consistency in, **1** 42, **4** 211–12
  defined, **4** 208–09
  grammar checkers for, **1** 43, **4** 208
  in humanities writing, **8** 388, 393–94
  list and forms of, **4** 209
  in natural and applied science writing, **8** 401
  perfect, uses of, **4** 210–11
  present, uses of, **4** 210
  progressive, uses of, **4** 211
  sequence of, **4** 213–14
  shifts in, **1** 42, **4** 211–12
  in writing about literature, **8** 388
Term papers. *See* Research writing
Terms, defined. *See* Defined terms
Text files, MLA style, **MLA** 444
Text messaging, revising shortcuts of, **2** 95
than, as, **3** 153, **Gl** 513
than, case of pronouns after, **4** 228
than, then, **Gl** 522
that
  as demonstrative pronoun, **4** 181
  direct quotation preceded by, **5** 274
  in essential clauses, **5** 269, **Gl** 522
  as relative pronoun, **4** 181, 252
  in sentence fragments, **4** 252
  vague reference of, **4** 234
  verbs with, **4** 215, 222
that, which, **5** 269, **Gl** 522
that, which, who, **Gl** 522
that is, punctuation with, **4** 257, **5** 280
the
  capitalization in titles, **6** 306
  rules for use of, **4** 242–43
Theater. *See also* Plays
  reviews of, **8** 388
  Web sources on, **8** 394
their, there, they're, **5** 282, **6** 298, **Gl** 522
theirselves, **Gl** 522
them
  as adjective, **Gl** 522
  vs. *they*, **4** 225–26
Themes, in literary works, **8** 386
then, punctuation with, **4** 257
then, than, **Gl** 522
the only one of the, agreement problems with, **4** 222
there, they're, their, **5** 282, **6** 298, **Gl** 522
thereafter, punctuation with, **4** 257
therefore, punctuation with, **4** 257
there is/are
  eliminating for conciseness, **3** 176
  necessity of *there* in, **3** 176
  uses of, **3** 176
Thesauruses, **3** 166
these, this, **Gl** 522
Theses. *See* Dissertations
Thesis and thesis statement
  argumentative, **1** 14–16
  as central claim of argument, **2** 98
  conceiving, **1** 14–16
  defined, **1** 14
  of essay, **1** 14–16, 50
  explanatory, **1** 14–15
  functions of, **1** 14 15
  of research paper, **7** 375
  revising, **1** 15–16
they
  to avoid generic *he*, **4** 231–32
  case forms of, **4** 225–26
  indefinite reference of, **4** 234
  vs. *them*, **4** 225–26
they're, their, there, **5** 282, **6** 298, **Gl** 522
Third person (*he, she, it, they*)
  in academic writing, **2** 95–96
  point of view, in literary works, **8** 385–86
  and -s form of verbs, **4** 199–200
  and subject-verb agreement, **4** 218–19
this, these, **Gl** 522
this, vague reference of, **4** 234
thru, **Gl** 522
thus, punctuation with, **4** 257
Time
  AM or *PM* with, **6** 310
  colons used to punctuate, **5** 281
  for or *since* in expressions of, **3** 169, **4** 211
  in, at, on in expressions of, **3** 169
  numerals vs. words for, **6** 313
  organization by, **1** 17, 41
  transitional expressions to indicate, **1** 44
Titles of papers
  capitalization of, **6** 306
  creating, **1** 25–27
  format of: APA style, **APA** 481; MLA style, **MLA** 449
  no quotation marks for, **5** 288
  subject indicated by, **2** 71
Titles of persons
  abbreviations for, **6** 310
  in business letters, **2** 129
  capitalization of, **6** 305
  Ms. vs. *Mrs.* or *Miss*, **2** 129, **3** 162

Titles of works. *See also* Titles of papers
APA style: parenthetical citations, **APA** 465–66; reference list, **APA** 468
capitalization in, **6** 306
Chicago style, **Chic** 493
colons before subtitle in, **5** 281
commas with, **5** 274
CSE style, **CSE** 504
italics or underlining for, **6** 307–08
MLA style: list of works cited, **MLA** 415; parenthetical citations, **MLA** 408–12
providing, when introducing borrowed material, **7** 365
quotation marks for, **5** 288
verb agreement with, **4** 223
Titles within titles, MLA style, **MLA** 428
to
with infinitives, **4** 192
after verbs, **4** 205–07
to, too, two, **6** 298, **Gl** 522
Tone
in argument, **2** 101
dashes for shifts in, **5** 290
in e-mail, **2** 117
evaluating in online sources, **7** 356
of literary works, **8** 386
too, as vague intensifier, **Gl** 522
Topic of paper. *See* Subject of paper
Topic outlines, **1** 19–20, **MLA** 450–51
Topic sentences, **1** 39
Toulmin, Stephen, **2** 97
toward, towards, **Gl** 523
Train names, italics or underlining for, **6** 308
Transitional expressions
for coherence, **1** 43–44
with commas, **5** 267, 270–71
in comma splices, **4** 257
defined, **1** 43
list of, **1** 43–44
with semicolons, **4** 257, **5** 278
Transitive verbs
defined, **4** 188
in passive voice, **4** 202, 216
Translations
APA style, **APA** 473
Chicago style, **Chic** 496
MLA style, **MLA** 425
Tree diagrams, **1** 18–19
Trite expressions, **3** 170–71, **5** 288–89
try and, try to, **Gl** 522
Turabian, *A Manual for Writers of Research Papers, Theses, and Dissertations*. *See* Chicago style
Turnitin, for plagiarism detection, **7** 359
two, too, to, **6** 298, **Gl** 522
Two-word verbs, **4** 207–08
type, type of, **Gl** 523
Type fonts, **1** 57, 64–65
type of, kind of, sort of, **Gl** 518

U

Underlining, **6** 306–09. *See also* Italics or underlining
undoubtedly, punctuation with, **4** 257
Uniform resource locator (URL). *See* URL
uninterested, disinterested, **Gl** 515
unique, **Gl** 523
Unity. *See also* Coherence
defined, **1** 21, 38
of essays, **1** 21
of paragraphs, **1** 38–39
unless, in conditional sentences, **4** 213–14
Unpublished dissertations or theses. *See* Dissertations
Unreliable narrators, in literary works, **8** 385–86
Unsigned works. *See* Anonymous or unsigned works
until now, punctuation with, **4** 257
URL
breaking: APA style, **APA** 473; Chicago style, **Chic** 497; CSE style, **CSE** 506; MLA style, **MLA** 439
documenting: APA style, **APA** 473–78, 480; Chicago style, **Chic** 497–99; CSE style, **CSE** 506; MLA style, **MLA** 431, 439
in evaluating sources, **7** 346
finding, **7** 350
slashes in, **6** 302
and Web sources, **MLA** 431, 439
Usage
biased, **3** 161–64
colloquial, **3** 160, **Gl** 511
and dialects, **3** 158–59
double negatives, **4** 239–40
glossary of, **Gl** 511–23
nonstandard, **3** 158–59, **4** 239–40, **Gl** 511
sexist, **3** 162–64
slang, **3** 160, **Gl** 511
standard American English, **3** 158–59, **Gl** 511
technical, **3** 160–61

use, usage, **Gl** 523
use, utilize, **Gl** 523
used to, supposed to, **Gl** 522
Usenet newsgroups. *See* Discussion groups, online
us vs. *we*, **4** 225–26, 228

V

Variety in sentences
  beginnings for, **3** 156–57
  grammar checkers for, **3** 154
  length for, **3** 154
  subordination for, **3** 154–57
Verbals and verbal phrases
  as adjectives or adverbs, **4** 191–92
  commas with, **5** 267
  defined, **4** 191
  gerunds, **4** 192, 205–07, 229
  infinitives, **4** 192, 205–07, 229, 246
  as nouns, **4** 191–92
  participles, **4** 192, 240
  in sentence fragments, **4** 251
  types of, **4** 191–92
  uses of, **4** 191–92
Verbs, **4** 196–223. *See also* Predicates
  active vs. passive, **4** 202, 216–17
  adverbs to modify, **4** 237
  agreement with subjects, **4** 218–23
  conciseness and, **3** 173–74
  in conditional sentences, **4** 213–14
  -d and *-ed* forms of, **4** 182, 192, 200
  defined, **3** 143, **4** 196
  direct objects of, **4** 188–89, 224
  effective use of, **3** 143–45
  finite vs. nonfinite, **4** 251
  followed by *to* or *for*, **4** 190
  forms of, **4** 182–83, 196–208
  gerunds vs. infinitives after, **4** 192, 205–07
  grammar checkers for, **4** 196, 198, 199, 207
  helping, **3** 144–45, **4** 183, 200–05
  in idioms with prepositions, **3** 168–69
  indirect objects of, **4** 190, 224
  intransitive, **4** 188–89, 199
  for introducing borrowed material, **7** 364
  irregular, **4** 192, 196–98
  linking, **4** 189–90, 223, 237
  main, **4** 183, 200–05
  misuse of apostrophes with, **5** 284
  misuse of commas between subjects and, **5** 275
  modal, **4** 203–05
  mood, **4** 214–15
  nouns made from, **3** 144, 173
  objects of, **4** 190, 224–25, 226–28
  omission of, **4** 201, 251
  with particles, **4** 207–08
  passive, **3** 145, 174, **4** 202, 216–17
  phrases, **4** 183
  plain form of, **4** 182
  principal parts of, **4** 196
  regular, **4** 196
  -s and *-es* forms of, **4** 182, 199–200
  in science writing, **8** 401
  with signal phrases, **7** 364–67
  strong vs. weak, **3** 144–45, 174
  subjunctive mood of, **4** 214–15
  tenses of, **4** 208–14
  transitive, **4** 188–89, 199
  two-word, **4** 207–08
  voice of, **4** 216–17
Video recordings. *See* Films, DVDs, and video recordings
Vision loss, considering readers with, **1** 64–65, **2** 119, 123
Visual argument, using, **2** 105–11
Visual art. *See* Illustrations and artworks
Visual literacy, **2** 83–89, 105–11
Visuals. *See* Illustrations and art works
Voice of verbs
  active vs. passive, **3** 145, 174, **4** 202, 216–17
  avoiding passive, **3** 145, 174, **4** 216–17
  consistency in, **4** 217
  defined, **4** 216
  grammar checkers for, **4** 217
Volumes
  books: APA style, **APA** 473; Chicago style, **Chic** 496; MLA style, **MLA** 410, 427
  periodicals: APA style, **APA** 470–72; Chicago style, **Chic** 495; CSE style, **CSE** 504; MLA style, **MLA** 419

W

waist, waste, **6** 298
wait at, for, in, on, **3** 169
wait for, wait on, **Gl** 523
Warrants. *See* Assumptions
ways, **Gl** 523
we
  case forms of, **4** 225–26, 228
  vs. *us*, **4** 225–26, 228
weak, week, **6** 298
Weasel words, **3** 161

weather, whether, **6** 298
Web. *See* Web sites
Webcasts, **7** 340, 342
Web forums. *See* Discussion groups, online
Web logs. *See* Blogs
Web sites
  acknowledging sources from, **7** 373
  advantages and disadvantages for research, **7** 335–36
  composing, **2** 119–24
  and copyright, **7** 373
  critical reading of, **7** 347, 350–54
  vs. databases, **7** 327–28
  designing, **1** 53
  disabilities, considering, **2** 119
  documenting sources from: APA style, **APA** 473–78; Chicago style, **Chic** 497–99; CSE style, **CSE** 506–07; MLA style, **MLA** 431–41
  downloading material from, **7** 359
  evaluating sources from, **7** 347, 350–54
  finding bibliographic information for, **MLA** 433
  keyword searches of, **7** 328–29, 335–38
  library vs. search engine for access, **7** 326
  original sites, **2** 121–24
  papers posted on, **2** 121
  permission for use of material on, **7** 373
  plagiarism and, **7** 368–69
  resources: for humanities, **8** 394; for natural and applied sciences, **8** 401–02; for social sciences, **8** 398
  searching and search engines, **7** 328–29, 335–40
  sources from, **7** 321, 326
  titles of: italics or underlining for sites, **6** 307; quotation marks for pages or documents, **5** 288
  using and acknowledging sources from, **7** 373
  vision loss, designing for people with, **2** 119
Web sources. *See* Web sites
well, good, **4** 237, **Gl** 516
when, in conditional sentences, **4** 213–14
where, at with, **Gl** 513
whether . . . or, **4** 186
whether, if, **Gl** 517
whether, weather, **6** 298
which
  as interrogative pronoun, **4** 181
  in nonessential and essential clauses, **5** 269, **Gl** 522
  omitted, **4** 260
  as relative pronoun, **4** 181, 252
  in sentence fragments, **4** 252
  vague reference of, **4** 234
  verbs with, **4** 222
which, that, **5** 269, **Gl** 522
which, who, that, **Gl** 522
which, witch, **6** 298
who
  case forms of, **4** 225, 226–28
  as interrogative pronoun, **4** 181
  reference of, **4** 233–34
  as relative pronoun, **4** 181, 252
  in sentence fragments, **4** 252
  verbs with, **4** 222
  vs. *whom*, **4** 226–28
who, that, which, **Gl** 522
whoever, whomever, **4** 181, 226–28, 252
who is, who has, as contraction *who's*, **5** 285, **Gl** 523
whole, hole, **6** 298
whose, who's, **5** 282, **6** 298, **Gl** 523
Wikipedia
  MLA style, **MLA** 437
  as research source, **7** 330, 336
Wikis
  collaborating through, **2** 118
  defined, **7** 330
  documenting: APA style, **APA** 477; MLA style, **MLA** 437
  evaluation of, **7** 351–52
  as research source, **7** 336
will, shall, **Gl** 521
-wise, -ize, **Gl** 518
witch, which, **6** 298
Wizards, **1** 56
Word division, hyphens for, **6** 301–02
Wordiness, avoiding, **3** 172–76
  combining sentences, **3** 176
  cutting repetition, **3** 175
  eliminating jargon, **3** 176
  eliminating *there is, here is*, or *it is*, **3** 176
  for emphasis, **3** 143–45
  grammar checkers for, **3** 172
  nouns made from verbs, **3** 173
  reducing clauses and phrases, **3** 175–76
  rewriting jargon, **3** 176
  using active voice, **3** 174

using effective subjects and verbs, **3** 173–74
using strong verbs, **3** 173–74
Word order
with adjectives, **4** 248
with adverbs, **3** 156–57, **4** 245–48
inverted, and subject-verb agreement, **4** 223
subject-verb pattern, **4** 188–90
variety in, **3** 157
Word processors. *See* Computers
Words
abstract, **3** 167–68
appropriate language, **3** 158–64
in arguments, **2** 102
biased, **2** 102, **3** 161–64, **4** 231–32
clichés, **3** 170–71
colloquial, **3** 160
compound, **5** 284, **6** 301
conciseness of, **3** 172–76
concrete, **3** 167–68
connotations, **3** 167
denotations, **3** 166–67
dialect, **3** 158–59
double talk (doublespeak), **3** 161
emotional, **2** 102
empty, **3** 174–75
euphemisms, **3** 161
exact language, **3** 165–71
figurative language, **3** 169–70
formal vs. informal, **2** 91–96
general, **3** 167–68
homonyms, **3** 166
idioms, **3** 168–69
jargon, **3** 176
nonstandard. *See* Culture-language issues
pretentious, **3** 161
repetitive, **3** 175
sarcastic, **2** 102
sexist, **3** 162–64
slang, **3** 160
standard. *See* Standard American English
strong verbs, **3** 173–74
technical, **3** 160–61
trite, **3** 170–71
weasel, **3** 161
Words used as words
italics or underlining for, **5** 285, **6** 308
plurals of, **5** 283, 285
quotation marks for, **5** 288
subject-verb agreement for, **4** 223
Working bibliographies
annotated, **7** 323–25
information for, **7** 318
Works cited. *See also* APA style; CSE style
Chicago style, **Chic** 494–501
MLA style, **MLA** 415–47
Works of art. *See* Illustrations and artworks
World Wide Web. *See* Electronic sources; Internet; Web sites
would be, **Gl** 523
would have, **Gl** 523
would of, **Gl** 516
write, right, rite, **6** 298
Writing portfolios, **1** 37
Writing process, **1** 3–65
assessment of writing situation, **1** 3–5, **8** 382
collaborating in, **1** 35–37, **2** 118
development, **1** 8–13
drafting, **1** 21–24, **7** 376
editing, **1** 28–32
invention in, **1** 8–13
organization, **1** 16–21
portfolio as result of, **1** 37
proofreading, **1** 33
for research, **7** 375–77
revision, **1** 25–27, **7** 376–77
summarizing for, **2** 72–74
thesis statement, **1** 14–16
types of writing assignments, **8** 387–88
Writing situation, **1** 3–8, **2** 90–96

Y

-y, final, **6** 300
Yahoo!, **7** 336
yet
commas with, **5** 265, 275
as coordinating conjunction, **4** 185
parallelism with, **3** 151–52
yet, but, however, **Gl** 514
you
appropriate use of, in academic writing, **2** 96, **4** 235, **Gl** 523
case of, **4** 224
omission in commands, **4** 251
your, you're, **5** 282, **6** 298, **Gl** 523
yourself, myself, herself, himself, **Gl** 519
YouTube, **7** 342

Z

Zip codes, no commas with, **5** 273
Zotero, **7** 374

Throughout this handbook, the symbol CULTURE LANGUAGE signals topics for students whose first language or dialect is not standard American English. These topics can be tricky because they arise from rules in standard English that are quite different in other languages and dialects. Many of the topics involve significant cultural assumptions as well.

No matter what your language background, as a college student you are learning the culture of US higher education and the language that is used and shaped by that culture. The process is challenging, even for native speakers of standard American English. It requires not just writing clearly and correctly but also mastering conventions of developing, presenting, and supporting ideas. The challenge is greater if, in addition, you are trying to learn standard American English and are accustomed to other conventions. Several habits can help you succeed:

- **Read.** Besides course assignments, read newspapers, magazines, and books in English. The more you read, the more fluently and accurately you'll write.
- **Write.** Keep a journal in which you practice writing in English every day.
- **Talk and listen.** Take advantage of opportunities to hear and use English.
- **Ask questions.** Your instructors, tutors in the writing lab, and fellow students can clarify assignments and help you identify and solve writing problems.
- **Don't try for perfection.** No one writes perfectly, and the effort to do so can prevent you from expressing yourself fluently. View mistakes not as failures but as opportunities to learn.
- **Revise first; then edit.** Focus on each essay's ideas, support, and organization before attending to grammar and vocabulary. See the revision and editing checklists in **1** pp. 26 and 30.
- **Set editing priorities.** Concentrate first on any errors that interfere with clarity, such as problems with word order or subject-verb agreement.

The following index leads you to text discussions of writing topics that you may need help with.

Academic writing, 2 94, 96, **3** 158–59
Adjective(s)
  clauses, repetition in, **4** 260
  no, with a noun, **4** 237
  no plurals for, **4** 236
  order of, **4** 248
  participles as, **4** 240
Adverb(s)
  introductory, word order after, **3** 157
  not, with a verb or adjective, **4** 238, 247
  position of, **4** 247–48
Argument, opinion and evidence in, **2** 97
Articles (*a, an, the*), **4** 240–43
Audience, 1 15, 17, 37, 50, **2** 77, 96, 128
Business writing, 2 128
Capital letters, 6 303

Collaboration, 1 37
Comma splices
revision of, **4** 254
and sentence length, **4** 254
Determiners (*a, an, the, few, a few, many, some,* etc.), **4** 240–44
Dictionaries, ESL, **3** 166
Fluency, in writing, **1** 9, 10
Forms of address (*Mrs., Miss, Ms.*), **3** 162
Idioms, 3 169
Intellectual property, 7 368
Introductions, 1 50
Nonstandard dialect, 2 96, **3** 158–59
Nouns
collective: pronouns with, **4** 233; verbs with, **4** 221
noncount: form of, **4** 241, **6** 301; list of, **4** 241; verbs with, **4** 221
plural: forms of, **4** 242–44, **6** 301; with *one of the,* **4** 224
Numbers, punctuation of, **5** 273, **6** 312
Omissions
helping or linking verb, **4** 200–01, 251
subject of sentence, **4** 252
there, here, or *it* at sentence beginning, **3** 176
Organization, 1 17, **2** 93–94
Paragraphs, 1 17, 38, 44, 50
Paraphrasing, 7 361
Prepositions
for vs. *since,* **3** 169, **4** 211
idioms with, **3** 168–69
in vs. *at* vs. *on,* **3** 169
to or *for* needed after some verbs, **4** 190
Pronouns
with collective nouns, **4** 232
matching antecedent in gender, **4** 230
needless repetition with, **4** 187, 233, 260
-self forms of, **4** 225
Public writing, 2 128
Questions
forming indirect, **5** 263
position of adverbs in, **4** 247
Reading, critical, **2** 71, 77, **7** 344
Redundancy
and implied meaning, **3** 175
in sentence parts, **4** 260
Research writing, originality in, **7** 344, 368
Spelling
British vs. American, **6** 299
noncount nouns, no plurals of, **6** 301
Standard American English, 2 96, **3** 158–59
Subject of sentence
agreement of verb with, **4** 219
needless repetition of, **4** 187, 233, 260
omission in sentence fragments, **4** 251
Subordinating conjunctions, 4 187
Thesis statement, 1 15, **2** 93–94
Transitional expressions, 1 44
Verbs
agreement with subjects, **4** 219
with collective nouns, **4** 221
gerund vs. infinitive with, **4** 205–08
helping (*be, can,* etc.), **4** 200–05
with indirect objects, **4** 190
intransitive, **4** 189
irregular, **4** 196
modal, **4** 203–05
with noncount nouns, **4** 221
omission in sentence fragments, **4** 251
participles of, **4** 240
passive voice of, **4** 189, 202, 216
perfect tenses of, **4** 203, 211
progressive tenses of, **4** 203–04, 211
-s and *-ed* endings of, **4** 199–200
tense formation of, **4** 208
transitive, **4** 189, 202, 216
two-word, particles with, **4** 207–08
Wordiness, vs. incorrect grammar, **3** 173
Word order
adjectives and adverbs, **3** 157, **4** 247–48
questions, **4** 247, **5** 263
subject-verb-object, **4** 190

Contents

Preface for Students vii
Preface for Instructors ix

1 WRITING PROCESS

1 The Writing Situation 3
- a Assessment
- b Subject
- c Purpose
- d Audience

2 Invention 8
- a Journal keeping
- b Observing
- c Freewriting
- d Brainstorming
- e Clustering
- f Asking questions

3 Thesis and Organization 14
- a Thesis statement
- b Organization

4 Drafting 21
- a Starting to draft
- b Maintaining momentum
- c Sample first draft

5 Revising and Editing 24
- a Revising the whole essay
- b Sample revision
- c Editing the revised draft
- d Formatting and proofreading
- e SAMPLE FINAL DRAFT 33
- f Collaborating
- g Preparing a writing portfolio

6 Paragraphs 38
- a Unity
- b Coherence
- c Development
- d Introductions and conclusions

7 Document Design 52
- a Academic papers
- b Principles of design
- c Elements of design
- d Illustrations
- e Readers with vision loss

2 WRITING IN AND OUT OF COLLEGE

8 Academic Skills 69
- a Listening and note taking
- b Reading
- c Becoming an academic writer
- d Preparing for exams

9 Critical Thinking and Reading 77
- a Techniques of critical reading
- b Critical response
- c Viewing images critically

10 Academic Writing 90
- a Responding to texts
- b Purpose
- c Audience
- d Structure and content
- e Language

11 Argument 97
- a Elements of argument
- b Reasonableness
- c Organization
- d Visual arguments
- e SAMPLE ARGUMENT 111

12 Online Writing 115
- a E-mail
- b Collaboration
- c Web compositions

13 Oral Presentations 124
- a Organization
- b Delivery

14 Public Writing 128
- a Business letters and résumés
  SAMPLE LETTER AND RÉSUMÉS 130, 132–33
- b Memos, reports, and proposals
  SAMPLE MEMO AND REPORT 135–36
- c Community work
  SAMPLE FLYER, NEWSLETTER, AND BROCHURE 137–39

3 CLARITY AND STYLE

15 Emphasis 143
- a Effective subjects and verbs
- b Sentence beginnings and endings
- c Coordination
- d Subordination

16 Parallelism 151
- a With *and, but, or, nor, yet*
- b With *both . . . and, not . . . but,* etc.
- c In comparisons
- d With lists, headings, and outlines

17 Variety and Details 154
- a Sentence length
- b Sentence structure
- c Details

18 Appropriate and Exact Language 158
- a Appropriate language
- b Exact language

19 Completeness 171
- a Compounds
- b Needed words

20 Conciseness 172
- a Focusing on subject and verb
- b Cutting empty words
- c Cutting repetition
- d Reducing clauses and phrases
- e Revising *there is, here is, it is*
- f Combining sentences
- g Rewriting jargon

4 SENTENCE PARTS AND PATTERNS

Basic Grammar

21 Parts of Speech 180
- a Nouns
- b Pronouns
- c Verbs
- d Adjectives and adverbs
- e Prepositions and conjunctions
- f Interjections

← CULTURE LANGUAGE Guide on reverse

RC Roanoke College

RC1 The Handbook, 1

RC2 The Liberal Arts, 1
- a Freedom with Purpose, 1
- b Goals for Liberal Learning, 3

RC3 The General Education Program, 5
- a The Intellectual Inquiry Curriculum, 5
- b The Intellectual Inquiry Curriculum Check Sheet, 8

RC4 Writing, 10
- a Intellectual Inquiry and Writing across the Curriculum, 10
- b The Writing Center, 12
- c Goode-Pasfield Center for Learning and Teaching, 13
- d Fintel Library: Research Help and Resources, 13

RC5 Academic Integrity, 15
- a Introduction, 15
- b Violations, 16
- c Penalties, 16
- d Integrity Guidelines for Specific Situations, 17

RC6 Tools, 21
- a Submitting a Paper through Turnitin, 21
- b Mapping the Z: Drive, 22

SEVENTH EDITION

A Writer's Reference

Roanoke College Edition

Diana Hacker

Nancy Sommers
Harvard University

BEDFORD/ST. MARTIN'S Boston ♦ New York

Manufactured in the United States of America.

6 5 4 3 2 1
f e d c b a

For information, write: Bedford/St. Martin's, 75 Arlington Street, Boston, MA 02116 (617-399-4000)

ISBN: 978-1-4576-0022-7

RC

Roanoke College

RC Roanoke College

RC1 The Handbook, 1

RC2 The Liberal Arts, 1
- **a** Freedom with Purpose, 1
- **b** Goals for Liberal Learning, 3

RC3 The General Education Program, 5
- **a** The Intellectual Inquiry Curriculum, 5
- **b** The Intellectual Inquiry Curriculum Check Sheet, 8

RC4 Writing, 10
- **a** Intellectual Inquiry and Writing across the Curriculum, 10
- **b** The Writing Center, 12
- **c** Goode-Pasfield Center for Learning and Teaching, 13
- **d** Fintel Library: Research Help and Resources, 13

RC5 Academic Integrity, 15
- **a** Introduction, 15
- **b** Violations, 16
- **c** Penalties, 16
- **d** Integrity Guidelines for Specific Situations, 17

RC6 Tools, 21
- **a** Submitting a Paper through Turnitin, 21
- **b** Mapping the Z: Drive, 22

RC1 The Handbook

This edition of *A Writer's Reference* has been customized for your use at Roanoke College. It is yours to use in all of your courses throughout your years here. Though your instructors may provide you with additional writing guides and specific style sheets for their courses, this handbook will provide all of us with a common vocabulary and a common reference.

To get the most out of this resource, take a quick look at "How to Use This Book" on pages vii–xv. The handbook is tabbed and organized to be a concise, user-friendly tool for writers. With just a little practice, you will find that it answers most of your writing questions and helps you get the most out of your writing time.

This introductory section of your custom edition of *A Writer's Reference* provides you with key information about your education at Roanoke College and our approach to writing, and helpful tips to make your work easier and more rewarding. It includes descriptions of the Intellectual Inquiry Curriculum and a variety of academic resources available to support your work. Please take a few minutes to read this section. It is part of your introduction to the community of Roanoke College.

RC2 The Liberal Arts at Roanoke College

RC2-a Freedom with Purpose

Education in the Liberal Arts is education for liberation. The term "liberal arts" derives from the Latin *artes liberales* and means, literally, the subjects of study appropriate to free persons. And the verb "to educate" means, in its Latin root, "to lead." A liberal arts education, then, is one that leads out from small worlds into larger ones.

It leads us out from small, safe worlds into larger, more interesting ones by training us to be dissatisfied with partial knowledge, with sloganeering, and with fixed ideologies. It instills in us instead an appreciation for the true complexity of things and a lifelong commitment to learning. A mind so trained respects facts, employs apt methods, and engages in creative problem solving. It examines alternatives; it does not fear tension or paradox. It welcomes the stubborn "misfit" fact that cracks open a too-small view and releases us into a wider play of thought. And it encounters this liberating openness in the vision of artists; in the venturesome thought of philosophers, theologians, and mathematicians; in the observation and experimentation of scientists; in the insights of social scientists; and in the experience of living in community.

A liberal arts education at a small, residential college frees us from isolation within ourselves into a community of learners and sharers, a community of discovery and collaboration in which we can grow as individuals in constructive engagement with others.

A liberal arts education frees us from reliance upon received opinion into an achieved personal authority by training the skills of critical thought, sound research, and informed and reasoned debate. At Roanoke College, this freedom grows out of a tradition of debating societies within a community of open discourse.

A liberal arts education frees us from entrapment within the conventions of our present place and time into a wider perspective that comprehends our own legacies, the breadth of human history, and the variety of human cultures. To support this work, Roanoke College commits itself to the work of building a diverse and tolerant college community.

A liberal arts education frees us from superficiality and distraction into the satisfactions of knowledge in depth, in which depth of learning leads to useful understanding—and to pleasure, wonder, and awe. At the same time, a liberal education frees us from mere specialization into a wider dialogue, in which depth of knowledge is shared and debated to clarify distinctions, to discover patterns, and to integrate human knowledge into an ever larger and more adequate view.

A liberal arts education engages ethics and questions of ultimate meaning. It does not offer pat moral answers. Instead, it provides the basis of all moral behavior—it helps us to imagine the reality of other lives. In matters of ethical living, it does not limit itself to the human, social world, but includes thoughtful consideration of our place within the natural world. At Roanoke College, these inquiries are informed, in part, by a tradition of Lutheran education that encourages a dialogue between faith and learning.

Education in the liberal arts frees us from purposelessness into productive careers and lives of service, in which our work to discover what is good, true, and beautiful leads on to work for good in the world.

The effects of a liberal arts education—an education for liberation—are a love of learning; an openness within the vastness of what we do not know; and a desire to use what we do know in ethical living, engaged citizenship, and service for the general good. The broad aim of such an education, therefore, is to produce resourceful, informed, and responsible citizens.

RC2-b Goals for Liberal Learning at Roanoke College

At Roanoke College a liberal arts education prepares students for lives of freedom with purpose. The college aims to produce resourceful, informed, and responsible citizens prepared for productive careers and for leadership in community, with an understanding of community appropriate to American diversity and to the increasingly global experience of the twenty-first century. To that end, the college's curricular and cocurricular programs together pursue the following goals. ***Traditionally, the liberal arts are the skills of freedom***. A liberal education at Roanoke College aims to produce resourceful citizens by developing these skills and habits of mind, including:

- the ability to read, listen, and observe carefully
- the ability to access information from disparate sources, to assess it appropriately, and to develop information into useful knowledge
- the ability to think critically, analytically, and creatively; to apply apt methods; to reason with rigor; and to use effective problem-solving skills
- the ability to use writing as a tool of thought and to communicate effectively in a variety of written and oral forms
- the ability to construct, understand, and evaluate arguments that use quantitative reasoning
- the ability to understand scientific discovery and to appraise it wisely
- the ability to make judicious use of new technologies

- the ability to work independently and collaboratively and to participate in experiential learning

Knowledge is essential to freedom. A liberal education at Roanoke College aims to produce citizens informed by:

- the cardinal achievements of human imagination as expressed in the arts and humanities, in the sciences, and in the social sciences
- depth of knowledge in at least one academic field of study, complemented by a breadth of experience across the traditional divisions of knowledge sufficient to enable integrative learning and thinking
- knowledge of the histories, values, and achievements of both Western and non-Western cultures in depth sufficient for the appreciation of disparate values and perspectives; this knowledge includes the cultural insight gained through language study
- knowledge of the values and histories that gave rise to liberal democracy in the United States and an understanding of contemporary issues from a variety of perspectives

Freedom, according to Martin Luther, includes both "freedom from" varieties of oppression and "freedom for" service in community. A liberal arts education at Roanoke College aims to produce responsible citizens by cultivating in its students:

- a commitment to academic integrity and intellectual freedom
- a lifelong commitment to learning and to using that learning in active engagement with others
- a sense of responsibility in which individual identity is honored within a diverse community characterized by mutual understanding and respect
- a commitment to engage in contemplation and reflection as a prelude to action, to make principled and ethical decisions, and to participate in deliberative public discourse

- a commitment to health in its largest sense: the physical and emotional well-being of self within a community that balances intellectual, ethical, spiritual, and personal growth
- a willingness to understand and respond to the needs and challenges of our time, both as individuals and as members of wide, inclusive communities
- a desire to contribute to the common good at Roanoke College, in the Roanoke Valley, and beyond

Adopted by the faculty on May 5, 2005.
Adopted by the Board of Trustees on October 27, 2005.

RC3 The Roanoke College General Education Program

RC3-a The Intellectual Inquiry Curriculum

The Intellectual Inquiry Curriculum flows from the Roanoke College Goals for Liberal Learning, "Freedom with Purpose." It is built around critical inquiry into questions that are important to us as individuals, citizens, and members of a global community. By engaging students in rigorous inquiry and developing abilities in communication and critical thinking across the curriculum, it furthers the college's mission of developing the skills students need to live as informed, resourceful, and responsible citizens. Combined with students' majors, the Intellectual Inquiry Curriculum gives students the resources for building an integrated body of knowledge concerning themselves and their world.

Of the 33 ½ course units required for a degree at Roanoke College, roughly one third of them will be taken within the Intellectual Inquiry Curriculum.

First-Year Seminars

The Intellectual Inquiry core courses (INQ courses) begin with two first-year seminars that introduce students to the fundamentals of liberal arts education. The first of these courses, entitled "Intellectual Inquiry," introduces students to critical thinking in higher education. INQ 110 helps students develop their skills in academic argumentation and writing. The second, "Living an Examined Life," is a disciplined reflection on basic questions of ethics and values. INQ 120 introduces oral communication skills and continues the emphasis on writing.

Intensive Learning

The objectives of the Intensive Learning Program are to foster intense and purposeful faculty-student interchange and to encourage thoughtful, creative exploration of a focused topic during a time when students are enrolled in one and only one course. The college provides a wide array of Intensive Learning opportunities during May, including travel courses as well as on-campus courses.

The Intellectual Inquiry Perspectives Courses

Students also take a series of courses that calls upon them to inquire into questions about Western civilization, global perspectives, and the natural world. At the same time, these Perspectives courses train students to use the different ways of knowing employed in the humanities and fine arts, the social sciences, and the natural sciences and mathematics.

There are seven different Intellectual Inquiry (INQ) Perspectives courses.

HUMANITIES AND FINE ARTS DIVISION

INQ 270: Human Heritage I
INQ 271: Human Heritage II

SOCIAL SCIENCES DIVISION

INQ 260: Social Scientific Reasoning

NATURAL SCIENCES AND MATHEMATICS DIVISION

INQ 240: Statistical Reasoning
INQ 241: Mathematical Reasoning (Math/Stat/CS)

INQ 250: Scientific Reasoning I (with lab)
INQ 251: Scientific Reasoning II (without lab)

Students take seven of these courses: two in the Humanities and Fine Arts Division, two in the Social Sciences Division, and three in the Natural Sciences and Mathematics Division. For a detailed description of the curriculum and its requirements, students should consult the Academic Catalog.

The Capstone: Contemporary Issues

Having seen ways in which different disciplines address questions, students complete the INQ courses with a capstone seminar entitled "Contemporary Issues." The course asks them to look back on their experiences and their work in the Intellectual Inquiry Curriculum and to synthesize diverse disciplinary approaches in a collaborative investigation of a contemporary issue.

Foreign Language

Students are required to complete the study of a foreign language through the first semester of the intermediate level (through the 201-level). Study of a foreign language is part of a well-rounded education, and it is a key component in meeting many of the Roanoke College Goals for Liberal Learning. See the Academic Catalog for details on placement exams and competency standards.

Health and Human Performance

Because a Roanoke College education addresses the whole person, students are required to complete two Health and Human Performance courses. "Fitness for Life," along with an activities course, supports the college goal of instilling in students "a commitment to health in its largest sense."

More Information on the Intellectual Inquiry Core

Details of core requirements are described in the college catalog and on the Web site under Academics/Core Curriculum.

RC3-b The Intellectual Inquiry Curriculum Check Sheet

First Year (2 units)

INQ 110: Intellectual Inquiry — Grade Received ______

INQ 120: Living an Examined Life — Grade Received ______

Perspectives Courses (7 units)

- Students must take at least one course from each Perspective (Western, Global, and Natural World).
- Students may substitute up to three disciplinary courses outside INQ for INQ courses in the divisions of those disciplines. However, students must still take at least one INQ course from each Perspective (Western, Global, Natural World) and at least one course from each division (Humanities and Fine Arts, Social Sciences, and Natural Sciences and Mathematics).
- See Table 1 for a checklist.

The Capstone (1 unit)

INQ 300: Contemporary Issues — Grade Received ______

Intensive Learning (1 unit)

INQ 177/277/377/477 — Grade Received ______

Foreign Language (through 201)

101 (if needed)
102 or 150 (if needed)
201 (if needed)

Health and Human Performance (0.5 units)

HHP 160: Fitness for Life
HHP Activity Course

Table 1: Perspectives Checklist

<table>
<tr><th rowspan="2" colspan="2"></th><th colspan="3">Content Perspectives</th><th rowspan="2">Disciplinary Course Alternative (up to 3)</th><th rowspan="2">Grade Rec'd</th></tr>
<tr><th>W</th><th>G</th><th>N</th></tr>
<tr><td rowspan="2">Humanities and Fine Arts Division</td><td>INQ 270 Human Heritage I</td><td></td><td></td><td></td><td></td><td></td></tr>
<tr><td>INQ 271 Human Heritage II</td><td></td><td></td><td></td><td></td><td></td></tr>
<tr><td rowspan="2">Social Sciences Division</td><td>INQ 260 Social Scientific Reasoning (1st discipline)</td><td></td><td></td><td></td><td></td><td></td></tr>
<tr><td>INQ 260 Social Scientific Reasoning (2nd discipline)</td><td></td><td></td><td></td><td></td><td></td></tr>
<tr><td rowspan="3">Natural Sciences and Mathematics Division</td><td>INQ 240 Statistical Reasoning</td><td></td><td></td><td></td><td></td><td></td></tr>
<tr><td>INQ 250 Scientific Reasoning I (Lab Science)</td><td></td><td></td><td></td><td></td><td></td></tr>
<tr><td>INQ 241 Mathematical Reasoning
or
INQ 251 Scientific Reasoning II (Non-lab Science)</td><td></td><td></td><td></td><td></td><td></td></tr>
</table>

How to decipher a course number: 200-level Perspectives courses are coded as W (Western), G (Global), or N (Natural World). Some sections are also coded by discipline. Within the sciences, disciplines are codes are as follows: AS (astronomy), BI (biology), CH (chemistry), and PH (physics). Within the social sciences, codes are AN (anthropology), EC (economics), PS (political science), PY (psychology), and SO (sociology). So, INQ 260 PS-GA is section A of INQ 260 from political science with a global perspective.

RC4 Writing at Roanoke College

RC4-a Intellectual Inquiry and Writing across the Curriculum

The Intellectual Inquiry program employs a "writing-across-the-curriculum" approach to writing instruction. This simply means that, at Roanoke College, you will develop your writing skills in a variety of courses taught by professors in many fields all across the college. The college has adopted this philosophy because, over time, students and teachers have discovered that writing is learned best when:

- students practice writing steadily throughout their college years, and
- students use writing as a tool of thought to explore significant content in a variety of courses.

Point 1. *Students grow as writers most quickly and steadily when they practice writing throughout their college years.* The standards of writing you encounter in college cannot be taught in a single semester, or even a year. Rather, they are best learned over time, through repeated practice in a variety of contexts. In these contexts, you will learn with the help of frequent feedback–in the form of paper conferences with instructors, written comments on papers, or other forms of response. Given these types of ongoing responses, you will come to recognize your strengths and be able to improve upon your weaknesses.

With practice, you will learn processes and techniques that will help you to discover your ideas for yourself and to communicate them effectively to your audiences. And because you will be developing and using these skills constantly, you will be less likely to forget the successful ways of writing that you discover.

As you practice writing across the curriculum, professors in different departments will train you in the forms and expectations of their fields. Lab reports, personal essays, and research essays, for instance, take different forms. And as you write in different classes, you will learn new ways of presenting information, building arguments, and citing evidence. Also, as you write for a variety of professors you will be exposed to different writing tips and methods, adding to your writing "toolkit."

After college, in work and in life, you will write for different reasons and for different audiences. Therefore, in your years at Roanoke College, you will practice writing continually in many contexts in order to develop skill, confidence, and flexibility.

Point 2. *Student writers grow most quickly and steadily when they use writing as a tool of thought to explore significant content.* In the Intellectual Inquiry Curriculum, you will not take a course dedicated solely to writing; you will not take an "English composition" course. Instead, in the writing-across-the-curriculum approach employed within the INQ curriculum, you will write to explore questions and find answers in the context of your regular content-based courses. All of your courses in the Intellectual Inquiry program will ask you to use writing as a tool of thought as you probe their questions and issues.

Consider this analogy: Students living abroad learn a foreign language more quickly than students who only study the language in a classroom. This is true partly because students overseas use the language in settings that matter, achieving daily goals like traveling and shopping that are important to their success and survival. If they practice for an extended time and gain fluency in their new language, they will be able to think, solve problems, and live with this new skill as a reliable ability.

Writing in the context of your content-based courses is like learning a language while immersed in the culture that uses it. That is why the INQ curriculum contains no stand-alone composition courses in which writing is assigned merely as an exercise in writing. Instead, you will use writing as a tool of thought to explore significant questions in fields like biology, history, sociology, English, and art. As you write in your INQ courses, you will work to answer real questions on substantive topics. And as you do, we expect you to invest in your writing, recognizing its importance in achieving something valuable—namely, a better understanding of the world and yourself.

RC4-b The Writing Center @ Roanoke College

The Writing Center, located in Fintel Library, is a place where writers, working in any academic field, at any level of competence, and at any stage of the writing process, meet with trained peer writing tutors in informal, one-on-one tutoring sessions. In other words, we talk with writers about their writing.

Scheduled appointments and walk-ins are available. The Writing Center is typically open for tutorials from 4:00 p.m. to 9:00 p.m., Sunday through Thursday, and tutoring is free. The Writing Center also offers a slate of fun and informative writing workshops, creative writing playshops, and grammar crammers each semester. Topics range from beating writer's block to developing proofreading strategies to reviewing comma usage guidelines.

We actively encourage struggling writers, advanced writers, *and* creative writers to make use of our services, because even professional writers benefit from having a conversation about their writing with someone before they publish it.

Students who wish to work in the Writing Center as tutors should contact the Director; applications are accepted each spring.

TUTORIAL HOURS

Sunday–Thursday, 4:00 p.m. – 9:00 p.m.

CONTACT

Phone: (540) 375-2247
E-mail: **writingcenter@roanoke.edu**
Web site: **www.roanoke.edu/writingcenter**
Online scheduling is available at **MyRC: Academics: Writing Center Scheduling**, or by telephone.

RC4-c Goode-Pasfield Center for Learning and Teaching

The Writing Center @ Roanoke College, in Fintel Library, is part of the Goode-Pasfield Center for Learning and Teaching. The Goode-Pasfield Center provides students with a comfortable, welcoming place where they can realize their academic potential as independent and resourceful learners.

In addition to the Writing Center, the Goode-Pasfield Center offers peer mentoring, subject tutoring, success skills workshops, and special services for students with disabilities that may affect academic performance. It also offers ongoing support in pedagogical development to members of the Roanoke College Community.

Professional staff members and testing services are available from 8:00 a.m. to 4:30 p.m., Monday through Friday.

Subject tutoring is available from 3:00 p.m. to 9:00 p.m. Sunday through Thursday. Subject tutors are available on a walk-in basis.

CONTACT

Fintel Library
220 High Street
Salem, VA 24153
Phone: (540) 375-2247
FAX: (540) 375-2485
E-mail: **CLT@roanoke.edu**

RC4-d Fintel Library: Research Help and Resources

Fintel Library is a vital center of learning at the college and a student-friendly environment. One of your first priorities as a new college student should be to get to know the library, its many resources, and the many people who can help you there. The Goode-Pasfield Center for Learning and Teaching is located in the library, as is the Writing Center, but you will also find willing helpers behind the circulation desk and among the skilled and friendly research assistants.

There is no replacement for a trip to the library to explore its services and to meet people, but the library staff has also placed invaluable research help on its Web pages. When conducting research, be sure to consult these resources.

Click on Quick Links at the top of the college's homepage. Choose Library, and then follow the link on the left for "Research Assistance." In addition to the information found on the "Research Assistance" page, you will find links to additional information, including:

- How to Cite Full-Text Articles
- How to Cite and Evaluate Web Sources
- How to Connect from Off-Campus
- How to Locate Library Materials

You will also be able to schedule a reference appointment from this site. While you will find these pages enormously helpful, you don't have to feel alone in your research. The research librarians are there to give you personal, individual assistance. You can simply walk in and ask for help or make an appointment. On the "Research Help" Web page, you will find the following invitation:

> "Reference librarians are available to help!! Don't spend hours searching. We can usually help you in a matter of minutes! x2295"

During the school year, reference librarians are available as follows:

Monday–Friday, 9:00 a.m. –4:30 p.m.
Sunday–Wednesday, 7:00 p.m. –9:00 p.m.

During May term, summer school, and interim, reference librarians are available as follows:

Monday–Friday, 9:00 a.m. –4:30 p.m.

Don't be afraid to ask for assistance!

RC5 Academic Integrity at Roanoke College

What follows is a brief description of the Roanoke College Academic Integrity system, excerpted and adapted from the AI Handbook, *Academic Integrity at Roanoke College*. Students are bound by and responsible for all material in the AI Handbook and should refer to it for complete information.

RC5-a Introduction

Roanoke College is a collection of learners–students, faculty, and staff alike. We have gathered to provide mutual support in our search for truth. Our Statement of Purpose says that we are "dedicated to educating men and women in high standards of scholarship to prepare them for responsible lives of learning, service and leadership"; we are "committed to an integrative approach to education that strives to balance intellectual, ethical, spiritual, and personal growth." In order for this to be possible, we are all responsible for ensuring both an atmosphere conducive to learning and systems to safeguard the learning process. Two of those safeguards are *academic freedom* and *academic integrity*.

Roanoke College has adopted and vigorously defends a statement on *academic freedom* that is published in the *Faculty Handbook*. That statement ensures each of us the right to speak and write the truth as we see it. We cannot be censured for religious, political, or philosophical beliefs, and we cannot be discouraged from publishing the results of our work. We protect each other's rights and responsibilities in learning for ourselves and sharing with others the truth as we discover it.

The other side of this freedom is a responsibility to learn for ourselves. We are responsible as honorable members of a learning community to maintain the highest standards of intellectual scholarship and to insist that others do so as well. We must teach each other what it means to be intellectually honest by our own actions; by what we teach and learn in the classroom, laboratory, and library; and by our institutionalized system of academic integrity.

RC5-b Violations

The following offenses constitute academic integrity violations at Roanoke College:

- cheating,
- lying,
- plagiarizing,
- impeding an investigation,
- denying access to academic materials, and
- any other actions that violate student regulations, as outlined in the *Student Handbook* or public statutes, for the purpose of leading to or supporting an academic integrity violation as outlined above.

Please refer to the AI Handbook for descriptions of these violations and additional information.

RC5-c Penalties

The usual minimum penalty for a student found to be in violation of academic integrity is an F in the course. A violation that is found to warrant a more severe penalty, including but not limited to a second violation, will receive an XF, possibly accompanied by academic integrity suspension or expulsion. Academic integrity probation and/or restitution may accompany other penalties as appropriate.

Please refer to the AI Handbook for descriptions of these penalties and additional information.

RC5-d Integrity Guidelines for Specific Situations

Assistance with Preparing Papers

If students have a term paper or any written material typed or word processed by another person, they must give precise instructions to the person assisting them that the material is to be typed in accordance with the academic integrity policies of the course as outlined by the professor. In general, if the typed or word-processed version of the term paper is not the student's own work, the student has violated academic integrity policy.

Students may or may not be permitted to receive other forms of assistance when researching and preparing their papers. The policy may well vary from course to course and from instructor to instructor. *It is the student's responsibility to understand and abide by the academic integrity policies of the course and the instructor for which the work is being prepared.*

Group Assignments

Unless otherwise specified by the professor, all work presented by a student is assumed to be that student's original work, created or prepared by that student while working alone. For some course assignments, students may be expected to work together, in pairs, in teams, or as a class.

The professor has an obligation to make clear the expectations for the work required by each student in such a group assignment. Students are expected to contribute their assigned share. Any violation of the guidelines established by the professor will constitute a violation of academic integrity. In supervising such work, students themselves, along with the professor, have a clear responsibility for ensuring academic integrity.

Science Laboratory Assignments

Academic integrity rules apply to the laboratory setting just as they do to lecture and discussion courses. However, because laboratory experiments, projects, and reports are often done in a public setting, students sometimes have a more difficult time judging what conduct is and is not allowed.

Although some instructors permit homework or laboratory reports to be group projects, others do not. *It is the student's responsibility to know and abide by the rules of the instructor.* Unless otherwise permitted, all graded laboratory problems and reports must be completed individually, without collaboration. In general, there should never be any reason for you to look at another student's laboratory report, or for you to allow another student to look at your report.

Unless specifically directed to do so by an instructor, a student may not work with a partner or share laboratory data. Laboratory reports are always to be written as an individual effort and never as a group project. Data should *not* be altered after an experiment has been completed. It is also a violation of academic integrity to falsify data or to discard data without the prior consent of the instructor.

Students may *not* receive help that amounts to another student directly supplying them with an answer to an assignment or to another student working through the material such that the answers become a product of a joint effort. Giving aid in violation of academic integrity rules is just as much a violation of the system as is receiving aid.

Falsification

Any material used in the preparation of an assignment must be verifiable by the professor. If the student falsifies data or materials gained in laboratories, interviews, or research, that student has violated the college's academic integrity policy.

Lying

Telling a lie in an academic situation is a violation of integrity. For example, if a student lies to a professor about the reason for missing a test or for the lateness of a paper, that student has committed a violation of academic integrity. In fact, if a student lies about another student's alleged violation, that constitutes a violation as well.

Aiding and Abetting

When a student assists another student in committing a violation of academic integrity, that student (i.e., the one providing the assistance) is equally culpable and can be charged with and prosecuted for an academic integrity violation.

Quizzes, Tests, and Examinations

Professors should provide clear guidelines to their students for testing situations. It is important, however, for students to guarantee their own integrity in these situations. During tests and examinations, students should keep attention on their own work at all times. No books, notes, or other materials, except those that are explicitly allowed, should be brought into a testing area or should otherwise be accessible during the testing period. Unless otherwise expressly permitted by the instructor, the use of any electronic device during a quiz, exam, or any other graded assignment in class is prohibited and will be considered a breach of academic integrity.

Guidelines for Computer Use

Computers have made great technological contributions to the academic world. Unfortunately, they have also given rise to new problems in integrity. The general rule is that a student's work done on a computer, or for execution by a computer, must be an original production of the student unless otherwise specified by the professor. See the AI Handbook for additional guidelines.

Use of Previously Submitted Work

An assignment prepared for one professor cannot be simultaneously, or subsequently, submitted to another professor unless both professors agree to such a submission. Likewise, an assignment done in secondary school or at another college cannot be submitted without the professor's knowledge and permission.

Plagiarism

Plagiarism is a very serious violation of academic integrity. It can also be a complex problem for students to understand and to avoid. In an academic setting, plagiarism occurs when the words, ideas, or data of another writer, speaker, or researcher—whether published or unpublished—are presented as one's own. Such an act of misrepresentation without proper acknowledgement is a violation of academic integrity at Roanoke College. Students are therefore expected to submit their own work, in their own words, and in their own original format.

Any sources used in the preparation and presentation of a student's work must be carefully and thoroughly acknowledged with the proper documentation. Merely to copy a passage, however brief, without proper documentation or acknowledgement and without quotation marks is a flagrant form of plagiarism.

Plagiarism is abhorred by the academic community because it is antithetical to the principles of liberal education and intellectual freedom, and also because it is immoral behavior that deceives the reader regarding the actual authorship of the work being presented.

Students will, of course, find it necessary to "borrow" words and ideas with proper acknowledgement from written materials and other sources. That borrowing will generally take one of two forms: direct quotation or paraphrasing. A paraphrase is a complete restatement, rewriting, or restructuring of a borrowed idea in one's own words. Since the idea is not original, however, there must also be appropriate documentation to acknowledge that borrowing.

Here are some important guidelines on plagiarism:

- Quotation marks should always be used to set off words that are borrowed directly, even though only one or two words are involved.
- The source of words or ideas should always be acknowledged in the text of the presentation, in an appropriate footnote or endnote, or in both.
- Students must use quotation marks when required and citations to indicate sources of material on all work submitted to their instructor for evaluation and grading. This includes drafts unless otherwise explicitly communicated by the instructor.
- As a rule, anything students learn while they are preparing an assignment should be considered as material that must be documented, even if this material is paraphrased. It is important to remember that adequate documentation must include exact page numbers.
- A bibliography by itself is *not* sufficient documentation because it does not inform the reader of the specific uses of the works in it. Some textual or notational system, such as footnotes, endnotes, or the author-date method, must be employed to cite when and how specific portions of

sources are used. *Most* systems of documentation require page numbers for all citations. *All* systems of documentation require page numbers for direct quotations.

Additional guidelines can be found in the AI Handbook, *Academic Integrity at Roanoke College*. Section R3 of the writing handbook you are holding (pp. 357–65) contains more information on paraphrasing, summarizing, and other elements of writing that require citation. MLA, APA, and CMS styles are described in this section; your instructor may specify that you use one of these styles or may provide information about a different style.

RC6 Tools

RC6-a Submitting a Paper through Turnitin

Turnitin is a plagiarism prevention service offered through Inquire. Some of your instructors may require that you submit papers through Turnitin. Instructions for doing so are provided on the following page.

The Roanoke College Information Technology department recommends that you only submit Microsoft Word Documents to Turnitin. These documents end with the ".doc" or ".docx" extension. If you do not have Microsoft Word, you may pick up your free copy at the HelpDesk (Trexler 369). Microsoft Word is available on all campus lab computers. Word Perfect or Microsoft Works files are not acceptable.

Note for Mac Users

To properly submit your work to Turnitin and ensure that your professor can read your files, you must use Microsoft Word Mac 2011 and add ".doc" to the end of your file name. When submitting to Turnitin, use Firefox as your Web browser instead of Safari.

If you do not have Microsoft Word Mac 2011, you may pick up your free copy at the HelpDesk (Trexler 369). TextEdit or Apple Pages files are not acceptable.

Follow these steps to submit your paper for grading.

1. Put the entire paper in one file, including the body and citations.
2. Save your file in any common format such as a Word (.doc or .docx), PDF, RTF, or TXT file.
3. Go to the course Inquire site and find the area where the instructor has placed the assignment.
4. Click on the name of the assignment.
5. Click “Submit.”
6. You will see a screen with several fields to fill in. (The submission method should be “single file upload.”)
   a. Enter a submission title for your paper.
   b. Browse to find the file you want to upload.
   c. Click “Upload.”
7. You will see a submission preview page. Don’t worry if formatting appears to change in the preview box.
   a. Make sure the file you submitted looks like the paper you meant to submit.
   b. Click “Submit.”
8. You will see a digital receipt on your screen, and then you will receive an e-mail confirming that your paper was successfully submitted.
9. If Turnitin does not accept your file format, you can copy and paste your entire paper into the window provided when you go back to Step 5 (above) and choose the copy/paste submission method.

RC6-b Mapping the Z: Drive

The Z: drive is a personal network drive available to Roanoke College students, faculty and staff. Students who wish to access this drive from their dorm rooms can map it using the instructions on the following page. The Z: drive will already be available when students log on to lab computers.

Windows 7

Follow these steps to map your Z drive from a Windows 7 computer.

- Double click on "Computer."
- Select "Map Network Drive."
- Choose "Z:" for the "Drive" field.
- Type the following under the "Folder" field, replacing "yourusername" in both places with your personal username: **\\studentfiles\yourusername$<file:///\\studentfiles\yourusername$>**. Retain the "$" sign.
- Make sure the "Reconnect at logon" box is checked.
- Click "Finish."

Note: If prompted for your username and password, use **academic\yourusername** for your username with your regular RC password.

Mac

Follow these steps to map your Z: drive from a Mac computer.

- From the Finder, find "Go" at the top of the screen.
- Scroll down to "Connect to Server."
- Type in **smb://studentfiles/yourusername$**, where "yourusername" is your RC username. Retain the "$" sign.
- When prompted, type in your RC username and password, and the drive will then be mounted.

A Writer's Reference

For Bedford/St. Martin's

Executive Editor: Michelle M. Clark
Senior Development Editor: Barbara G. Flanagan
Development Editor: Mara Weible
Associate Editor: Alicia Young
Senior Production Editor: Rosemary R. Jaffe
Assistant Production Editor: Lindsay DiGianvittorio
Assistant Production Manager: Joe Ford
Marketing Manager: Marjorie Adler
Editorial Assistant: Kylie Paul
Copyeditor: Linda McLatchie
Indexer: Ellen Kuhl Repetto
Permissions Manager: Kalina Ingham Hintz
Senior Art Director: Anna Palchik
Text Design: Claire Seng-Niemoeller
Cover Design: Donna Lee Dennison
Composition: Nesbitt Graphics, Inc.
Printing and Binding: RR Donnelley and Sons

President: Joan E. Feinberg
Editorial Director: Denise B. Wydra
Editor in Chief: Karen S. Henry
Director of Marketing: Karen R. Soeltz
Director of Production: Susan W. Brown
Associate Director, Editorial Production: Elise S. Kaiser
Managing Editor: Elizabeth M. Schaaf

Library of Congress Control Number: 2010920402

Manufactured in the United States of America.

6 5 4 3
g f e

For information, write: Bedford/St. Martin's, 75 Arlington Street,
Boston, MA 02116 (617-399-4000)

ISBN-10: 0-312-60143-3 ISBN-13: 978-0-312-60143-0 (Student Edition)
0-312-60146-8 978-0-312-60146-1 (Instructor's Edition)

How to use this book and its companion Web site

A Writer's Reference is designed to save you time and will answer most of the questions you are likely to ask as you plan, draft, revise, and edit a piece of writing: How do I choose and narrow a topic? How do I know when to begin a new paragraph? Should I write *each was* or *each were*? When should I place a comma before *and*? What is counterargument? How do I cite a source from the Web?

The book's companion Web site extends the book beyond its covers. See pages x–xi for details.

How to find information with an instructor's help

When you are revising an essay that your instructor has marked, tracking down information is simple. If your instructor uses a code such as S1-a or MLA-2b to indicate a problem, you can turn directly to the appropriate section of the handbook. Just flip through the tabs at the tops of the pages until you find the code in question.

If your instructor uses an abbreviation such as *w* or *dm*, consult the list of abbreviations and revision symbols on the next-to-last page of the book. There you will find the name of the problem (*wordy*; *dangling modifier*) and the number of the section to consult.

If your instructor provides advice without codes or abbreviations, use the index at the back of the book to look up specific terms. (See pp. ix and xii for more about the index.)

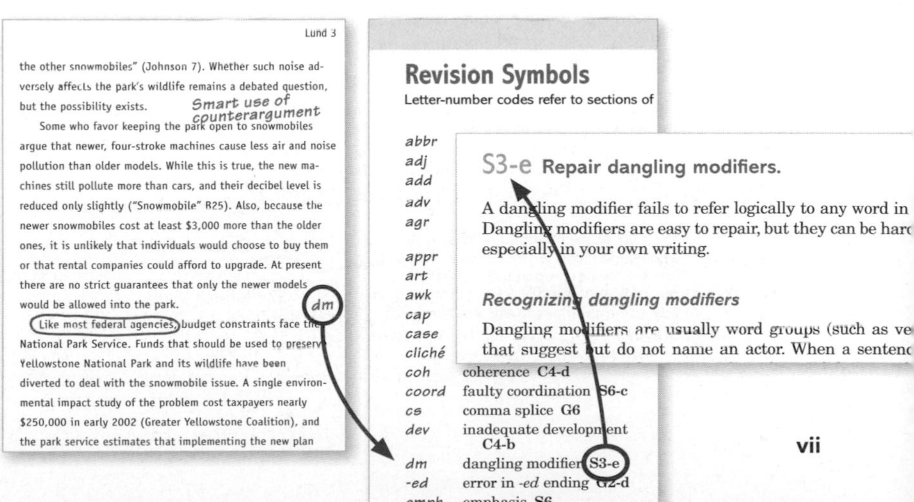

Lund 3

the other snowmobiles" (Johnson 7). Whether such noise adversely affects the park's wildlife remains a debated question, but the possibility exists.

Some who favor keeping the park open to snowmobiles argue that newer, four-stroke machines cause less air and noise pollution than older models. While this is true, the new machines still pollute more than cars, and their decibel level is reduced only slightly ("Snowmobile" B25). Also, because the newer snowmobiles cost at least $3,000 more than the older ones, it is unlikely that individuals would choose to buy them or that rental companies could afford to upgrade. At present there are no strict guarantees that only the newer models would be allowed into the park.

Like most federal agencies, budget constraints face the National Park Service. Funds that should be used to preserve Yellowstone National Park and its wildlife have been diverted to deal with the snowmobile issue. A single environmental impact study of the problem cost taxpayers nearly $250,000 in early 2002 (Greater Yellowstone Coalition), and the park service estimates that implementing the new plan

Revision Symbols

Letter-number codes refer to sections of

abbr
adj
add
adv
agr
appr
art
awk
cap
case
cliché
coh coherence C4-d
coord faulty coordination S6-c
cs comma splice G6
dev inadequate development C4-b
dm dangling modifier S3-e
-ed error in -*ed* ending G2-d
emph emphasis S6
ESL ESL grammar M1, M2, M3, M4, M5

S3-e **Repair dangling modifiers.**

A dangling modifier fails to refer logically to any word in
Dangling modifiers are easy to repair, but they can be hard
especially in your own writing.

Recognizing dangling modifiers

Dangling modifiers are usually word groups (such as ve
that suggest but do not name an actor. When a sentenc

How to find information on your own

This handbook is designed to allow you to find information quickly without an instructor's help—usually by consulting the main menu inside the front cover. At times, you may also consult the detailed menu inside the back cover, the index, the glossary of usage, the list of revision symbols, or one of the directories to documentation models. The tutorials on pages xii–xv give you opportunities to practice finding information in different ways.

THE MAIN MENU The main menu inside the front cover displays the handbook's contents briefly and simply. Each of the twelve sections in the main menu leads you to a color-coded tabbed divider (such as C/Composing and Revising), where you can find a more detailed menu.

Let's say that you want to find out how to make your sentences parallel. Your first step is to scan the main menu for the appropriate topic—in this case, S1, "Parallelism." Then you can browse the section numbers at the tops of the pages to find section S1.

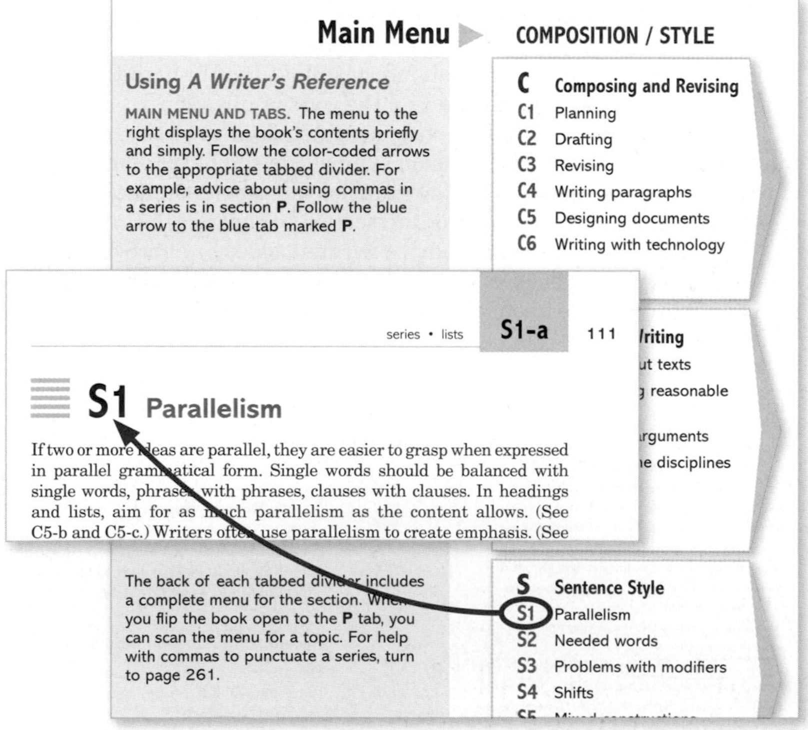

THE DETAILED MENU The detailed menu appears inside the back cover. When the section you're looking for is broken up into quite a few subsections, try consulting this menu. For instance, if you have a question about the proper use of commas after introductory elements, this menu will quickly lead you from P/Punctuation to P1, "The comma" to P1-b, "Introductory elements."

Once you find the right subsection in the book, you will see three kinds of advice to help you edit your writing—a rule, an explanation, and one or more examples that show editing.

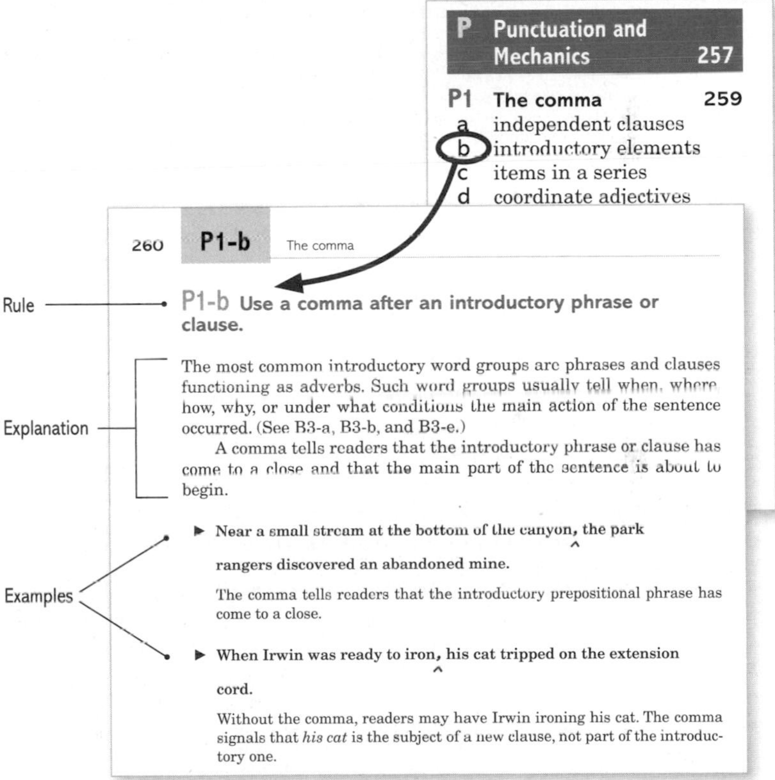

P Punctuation and Mechanics 257

P1 The comma 259
a independent clauses
b introductory elements
c items in a series
d coordinate adjectives

260 **P1-b** The comma

P1-b Use a comma after an introductory phrase or clause.

The most common introductory word groups are phrases and clauses functioning as adverbs. Such word groups usually tell when, where, how, why, or under what conditions the main action of the sentence occurred. (See B3-a, B3-b, and B3-e.)

A comma tells readers that the introductory phrase or clause has come to a close and that the main part of the sentence is about to begin.

▶ **Near a small stream at the bottom of the canyon, the park rangers discovered an abandoned mine.**

The comma tells readers that the introductory prepositional phrase has come to a close.

▶ **When Irwin was ready to iron, his cat tripped on the extension cord.**

Without the comma, readers may have Irwin ironing his cat. The comma signals that *his cat* is the subject of a new clause, not part of the introductory one.

THE INDEX If you aren't sure which topic to choose from one of the menus, consult the index at the back of the book. For example, you may not realize that the question of whether to use *have* or *has* is a matter of subject-verb agreement (section G1). In that case, simply look up "*has* vs. *have*" in the index. You will be directed to specific pages covering subject-verb agreement.

MAKING THE MOST OF YOUR HANDBOOK You will find your way to helpful advice by using the index, the menus, or the tabbed dividers. Once you get to the page with the advice you are looking for, you may also find a "Making the most of your handbook" box that pulls together additional related advice and models for your assignment.

drilling, for example, imagine a jury that represents those who have a stake in the matter: environmentalists, policymakers, oil company executives, and consumers.

At times, you can deliberately narrow your audience. If you are working within a word limit, for example, you might not have the space in which to address all the concerns surrounding the offshore drilling debate. Or you might be primarily interested in reaching one segment of a general

Making the most of your handbook

You may need to consider a specific audience for your argument.

- ▶ Writing in a particular discipline, such as business or psychology: A4

THE GLOSSARY OF USAGE When in doubt about the correct use of a particular word (such as *affect* and *effect*), consult the glossary of usage, section W1. This glossary explains the difference between commonly confused words; it also includes words that are inappropriate in formal written English.

MORE ONLINE

Using the book's companion Web site: hackerhandbooks.com/writersref

Throughout *A Writer's Reference,* Seventh Edition, you will see references to more advice and help on the book's Web site. These are labeled PRACTICE (for interactive exercises), MODELS (for model papers and other documents), and THE WRITING CENTER (for tips on getting help with your assignments). Here is a complete list of resources on the site. Your instructor may use some of this material in class; each area of the site, however, has been developed for you to use on your own whenever you need it.

> Practice exercises
More than 1,800 interactive writing, grammar, and research/documentation exercise items, all with immediate feedback. Research exercises include topics such as integrating quotations and documenting sources in MLA, APA, and CMS (*Chicago*) styles.

> Model papers
Annotated sample papers, organized by style (MLA, APA, CMS [*Chicago*], CSE) and by genre (research paper, argument paper, review of the literature, and so on)

> *Research and Documentation Online*
Advice on finding sources in a variety of academic disciplines and up-to-date guidelines for documenting print and online sources in MLA, APA, CMS (*Chicago*), and CSE styles

DIRECTORIES TO DOCUMENTATION MODELS When you are documenting sources in a research paper with MLA, APA, or CMS (*Chicago*) style, you can find documentation models by consulting the appropriate color-coded directories.

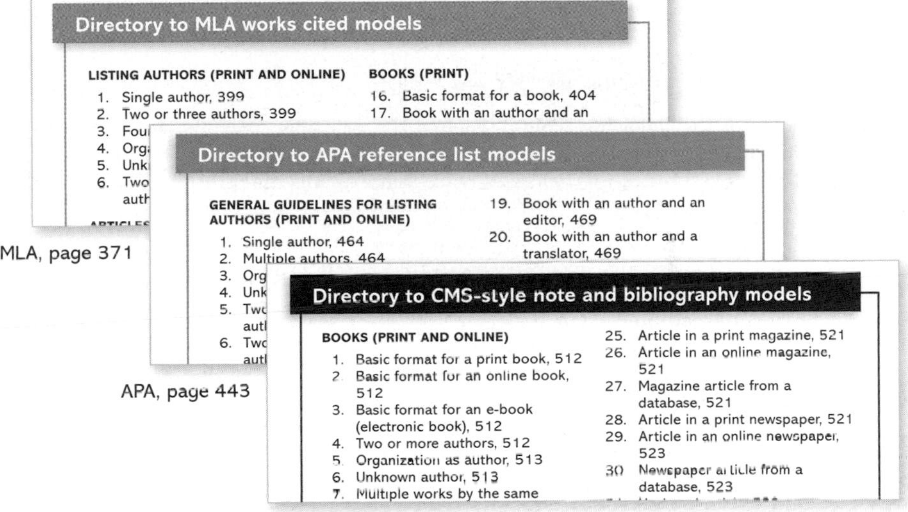

Directory to MLA works cited models
LISTING AUTHORS (PRINT AND ONLINE)
1. Single author, 399
2. Two or three authors, 399
BOOKS (PRINT)
16. Basic format for a book, 404
17. Book with an author and an
Directory to APA reference list models
GENERAL GUIDELINES FOR LISTING AUTHORS (PRINT AND ONLINE)
1. Single author, 464
19. Book with an author and an editor, 469
20. Book with an author and a translator, 469
Directory to CMS-style note and bibliography models
BOOKS (PRINT AND ONLINE)
1. Basic format for a print book, 512
2. Basic format for an online book, 512
3. Basic format for an e-book (electronic book), 512
4. Two or more authors, 512
5. Organization as author, 513
6. Unknown author, 513
7. Multiple works by the same
25. Article in a print magazine, 521
26. Article in an online magazine, 521
27. Magazine article from a database, 521
28. Article in a print newspaper, 521
29. Article in an online newspaper, 523
30. Newspaper article from a database, 523

MLA, page 371

APA, page 443

CMS (*Chicago*), page 498

> Multilingual/ESL
Resources, strategies, model papers, and exercises to help multilingual students improve their college writing skills

> Revision
Papers in progress and models of global and sentence-level revisions

> Writing center resources
Revision checklists and helpsheets for common writing problems

> Language Debates
Mini-essays exploring controversial issues of grammar and usage

> Exercise PDFs, diagnostics, and test prep
Print-format practice exercises, interactive diagnostic tests, and links to additional online resources for every part of the book

> Nancy Sommers videos
From the book's coauthor, advice on revising, reading and responding to texts, working with teacher comments, and developing an argument

> *Re:Writing*
A free collection of resources for composition and other college classes: help with preparing presentation slides, avoiding plagiarism, evaluating online sources, and more

> E-book
An online version of the book with interactive exercises, audio commentary on model papers, and short movies that teach essential college skills such as integrating sources in a research paper and revising with peer comments (This area of the Web site requires an activation code.)

Tutorials

The following tutorials will give you practice using the book's menus, index, glossary of usage, and MLA directory. Answers to the tutorials begin on page xiv.

TUTORIAL 1: Using the menus

Each of the following "rules" violates the principle it expresses. Using the main menu inside the front cover or the detailed menu inside the back cover, find the section in *A Writer's Reference* that explains the principle. Then fix the problem. Example:

Tutors in
▶ ~~In~~ the writing center/ ~~they~~ say that vague pronoun reference is unacceptable. *G3-b*

1. A verb have to agree with its subject.
2. About sentence fragments. You should avoid them.
3. Its important to use apostrophe's correctly.
4. If your sentence begins with a long introductory word group use a comma to separate the word group from the rest of the sentence.

TUTORIAL 2: Using the index

Assume that you have written the following sentences and want to know the answers to the questions in brackets. Use the index at the back of the book to locate the information you need, and edit the sentences if necessary.

1. Each of the candidates have decided to participate in tonight's debate. [Should the verb be *has* or *have* to agree with *Each*?]
2. We had intended to go surfing but spent most of our vacation lying on the beach. [Should I use *lying* or *laying*?]
3. In some cultures, it is considered ill mannered for you to accept a gift. [Is it OK to use *you* to mean "anyone in general"?]
4. In Canada, Joanne picked up several bottles of maple syrup for her sister and me. [Should I write *for her sister and I*?]

TUTORIAL 3: Using the menus or the index

Imagine that you are in the following situations. Using either the menus or the index, find the information you need.

1. You are a student studying health administration, and you're editing a report you've just written on the benefits of community-based urgent

care clinics. You recall learning to put a comma between all items in a series except the last two. But you have noticed that most writers use a comma between all items. You're curious about the rule. Which section of *A Writer's Reference* will you consult?

2. You are tutoring in your university's writing center. A composition student comes to you for help with her first college essay. She is revising a draft and struggling with her use of articles (*a*, *an*, and *the*). You know how to use articles, but you aren't able to explain the complicated rules on their correct use. Which section in *A Writer's Reference* will you and the student, a multilingual writer, consult?
3. You have been assigned to write a response to an essay you read for your composition class. Your instructor has asked that you use at least three quotations from the text in your response, which must be written in MLA style. You aren't quite sure how to integrate words from another source in your own writing. Which section in this handbook will help?
4. You supervise interns at a housing agency. Two of your interns have trouble with the *-s* endings on verbs. One tends to drop *-s* endings; the other tends to add them where they don't belong. You suspect that both problems stem from dialects spoken at home. The interns are in danger of losing their jobs because your boss thinks that anyone who writes "the tenant refuse . . ." or "the landlords insists . . ." is beyond hope. You disagree. Where can you direct your interns for help in *A Writer's Reference*?

TUTORIAL 4: Using the glossary of usage

Consult the glossary of usage to see if the italicized words are used correctly. Then edit any sentences containing incorrect usage. Example:

► **The pediatrician gave my daughter ~~a~~ an injection for her allergy.**

1. Changing attitudes toward alcohol have *effected* the beer industry.
2. It is *mankind's* nature to think wisely and act foolishly.
3. Our goal this year is to *grow* our profits by 9 percent.
4. Most sleds are pulled by no *less* than two dogs and no more than ten.

TUTORIAL 5: Using the directory to MLA works cited models

Let's say that you have written a short research essay on the origins of hip-hop music. You have cited the following four sources in your essay, using MLA style, and you are ready to type your list of works cited. Turn to pages 371–72 and use the MLA directory to locate the appropriate models. Then write a correct entry for each source and arrange the entries in a properly formatted list of works cited.

> A book by Jeff Chang titled *Can't Stop, Won't Stop: A History of the Hip-Hop Generation*. The book was published in New York by St. Martin's Press in 2005.

An online article by Kay Randall called "Studying a Hip Hop Nation." The article appeared on the University of Texas at Austin Web site. The title of the site is *University of Texas at Austin*. You accessed the site on April 13, 2010; the last update was October 9, 2008.

A sound recording entitled "Rapper's Delight" performed by the Sugarhill Gang on the CD *Sugarhill Gang*. The CD was released in 2008 by DBK Works.

A magazine article accessed online through the database *Expanded Academic ASAP*. The article, "The Roots Redefine Hip-Hop's Past," was written by Kimberly Davis and published in *Ebony* magazine in June 2003. The article appears on pages 162–64. You found this article on April 13, 2010.

Answers to the Tutorials

TUTORIAL 1

1. A verb has to agree with its subject. (G1-a)
2. Avoid sentence fragments. (G5)
3. It's important to use apostrophes correctly. (P4)
4. If your sentence begins with a long introductory word group, use a comma to separate the word group from the rest of the sentence. (P1-b)

TUTORIAL 2

1. The index entry "*each*" mentions that the word is singular, so you might not need to look further to realize that the verb should be *has*, not *have*. The first page reference takes you to the entry for *each* in the glossary of usage (W1), which directs you to G1-e and G3-a for details about why *has* is correct. The index entry "*has* vs. *have*" leads you to the chart in G1.
2. The index entry "*lying* vs. *laying*" takes you to section G2-b, where you will learn that *lying* (meaning "reclining or resting on a surface") is correct.
3. Looking up "*you*, inappropriate use of" leads you to the glossary of usage (W1) and section G3-b, which explain that *you* should not be used to mean "anyone in general." You can revise the sentence by using *a person* or *one* instead of *you*, or you can restructure the sentence completely: *In some cultures, accepting a gift is considered ill mannered.*
4. The index entries "*I* vs. *me*" and "*me* vs. *I*" take you to section G3-c, which explains why *for her sister and me* is correct.

TUTORIAL 3

1. Section P1-c states that, although usage varies, most experts advise using a comma between all items in a series—to prevent possible misreadings or ambiguities. To find this section, you would probably use the menu system.
2. You and the student would consult section M2, on articles. This section is easy to locate in the menu system.

3. In the menu system, you will find “MLA papers” and then section MLA-3, “Integrating sources.”
4. You can send your interns to sections G1 and G2-c, which you can find in the menu system if you know to look under “Subject-verb agreement” or “Verb forms, tenses, and moods.” If you aren’t sure about the grammatical terminology, you can look in the index under “*-s*, as verb ending” or “Verbs, *-s* form of.”

TUTORIAL 4

1. Changing attitudes toward alcohol have *affected* the beer industry.
2. It is *human* nature to think wisely and act foolishly.
3. Our goal this year is to *increase* our profits by 9 percent.
4. Most sleds are pulled by no *fewer* than two dogs and no more than ten.

TUTORIAL 5

Chang, Jeff. *Can’t Stop, Won’t Stop: A History of the Hip-Hop Generation*. New York: St. Martin’s, 2005. Print.

Davis, Kimberly. “The Roots Redefine Hip-Hop’s Past.” *Ebony* June 2003: 162-64. *Expanded Academic ASAP*. Web. 13 Apr. 2010.

Randall, Kay. “Studying a Hip Hop Nation.” *University of Texas at Austin*. U of Texas at Austin, 9 Oct. 2008. Web. 13 Apr. 2010.

Sugarhill Gang. “Rapper’s Delight.” *Sugarhill Gang*. DBK Works, 2008. CD.

Preface for instructors

Everywhere I travel, instructors tell me that they love *A Writer's Reference*—its clear, concise explanations and respectful tone and its ease of use inside and outside the classroom. I understand why *A Writer's Reference* inspires such affection; it is the book I too have always loved, the book my students trust and keep, and the one that teaches one patient lesson at a time. Over the last six editions, millions of students and instructors have turned to *A Writer's Reference* for the straightforward, reliable, and comprehensive support that Diana Hacker always offered. It has been one of the great pleasures of my own teaching career to build on that foundation as the coauthor of *A Writer's Reference*.

Many people have asked, *How do you revise the most successful handbook in the country—the handbook that everyone loves?* To prepare for the seventh edition, I traveled to more than forty-five colleges and universities to learn how students use their handbooks and how instructors teach from them. I listened, everywhere, for clues about how to make the handbook an even more helpful companion for students throughout their academic careers and an even stronger resource for the teachers guiding their development as writers. Throughout my travels, I heard students puzzle out the unfamiliar elements of academic writing, particularly those related to working with sources. I watched creative instructors show their students how to build arguments, synthesize sources, and strengthen their ideas through revision. I observed writing center tutors responding to students' questions about thesis statements and counterargument. And I listened to librarians expertly explain how to approach research assignments and evaluate sources. I wanted the seventh edition to capture the vibrant energy and creativity that surround conversations about student writing, wherever they take place.

As you look through the seventh edition, you'll discover many innovations inspired by these conversations. One of the new features I'm most excited about is "Revising with comments." During my travels, I asked students about the comments they receive most frequently and asked instructors to show me the comments they write most frequently on their students' drafts. The answers to these questions, combined with my own research on responding to student writers, shaped this feature, which helps students and instructors make the most of reviewing and commenting. In keeping with the Hacker tradition, this new feature teaches one lesson at a time—how to revise an unclear thesis or how to consider opposing viewpoints, for instance—and directs students to specific sections of the handbook to guide their revision strategies.

In *A Writer's Reference*, Diana Hacker created the most innovative and practical college reference—the one that responds most directly to student writers' questions and challenges. The seventh edition carries on that tradition. You'll find that the book you've always loved now includes a new argument paper, a stepped-out approach to writing and revising thesis statements, new coverage of synthesizing sources, expanded attention to writing assignments across the disciplines, and many more practical innovations. As a classroom teacher, I know how much a trusted and reliable handbook can help students make the most of their writing experiences in college and beyond. And now as the coauthor of the seventh edition, I am eager to share this book with you, knowing that you'll find everything you and your students love and trust about *A Writer's Reference*.

Nancy Sommers

Features of the seventh edition

What's new

TARGETED CONTENT FOR TODAY'S STUDENTS: ACADEMIC WRITING AND RESEARCH

- ***Synthesis.*** Many of today's college writing assignments require that students synthesize—analyze sources and work them into a conversation that helps develop an argument. New coverage of synthesis, with annotated examples in MLA and APA styles, helps students work with sources to meet the demands of academic writing. (See MLA-3c and APA-3c.)

- ***A new sample argument paper*** shows students how to state and support an argumentative thesis, address counterarguments, integrate visuals, and document sources. (See pp. 87–91.)
- ***A new annotated advertisement*** illustrates how one student analyzes key elements of a visual to begin building an interpretation. (See p. 70.)
- ***A new case study*** follows one student's research and writing process, providing an illustrated model for strategizing about a research assignment, using search tools and techniques, evaluating search results and sources, taking notes, thinking critically about how best to use sources in a paper, and integrating a source responsibly. This self-contained section (MLA-5b) directs students to more detailed information throughout the book. (See pp. 432–35.)
- ***New advice for distinguishing scholarly and popular sources.*** (See pp. 350–51.)
- ***Integrating evidence in analytical papers.*** New coverage in section A1-d, "Using interpretation in an analysis," shows—at the sentence level—how to introduce, include, and interpret a passage in an analytical paper. (See p. 74.)
- ***More help with writing assignments in other disciplines and in various genres.*** For students who work with evidence in disciplines other than English, we have included annotated assignments and excerpts from model papers in psychology, business, biology, and nursing. (See pp. 105-08.)
- ***New documentation models, many annotated.*** Eighty-six new models across the three styles (MLA, APA, CMS [*Chicago*]) include sources students are using today—podcasts, online videos, blogs, and DVD features. Detailed annotations for many models help students see at a glance how to gather information about their sources and format their citations. (See p. 419 for an example.)
- ***New chart on avoiding plagiarism.*** (See pp. 364–65.)

CONCRETE STRATEGIES FOR REVISING

- ***New coverage of portfolio keeping.*** For students who are asked to maintain and submit a writing portfolio, a new section, C3-e, "Prepare a portfolio; reflect on your writing," covers types of portfolios, offers tips for writing a reflective cover document, and provides a sample reflective essay. (See pp. 28-31.)

- ***Revising with comments.*** Based on research with sixty-five students at colleges and universities across the country, this new feature helps students understand common instructor comments such as "unclear thesis," "develop more," or "cite your source" and gives students revision strategies they can apply to their own work. (See pp. 23–27.)
- ***Specific strategies for revising thesis statements.*** We know that college writers often need help reworking thesis statements, in whatever discipline they are writing. A new stepped-out approach helps students identify a problem in a draft thesis, ask relevant questions, and use their own responses to revise. (See pp. 16–18.)

NEW EXAMPLES, RELEVANT GRAMMAR COVERAGE

- ***Academic examples that reflect the types of sentences students are expected to write in college.*** A new type of hand-edited example ("Writing with sources") shows typical errors students make—and how they can correct them—when they integrate sources in MLA, APA, and CMS (*Chicago*) papers. (See p. 270 for an example.)
- ***More ESL coverage.*** Part M, Multilingual Writers and ESL Challenges, offers more accessible advice and more support for multilingual writers across the disciplines.
- ***Basic grammar content that is more straightforward than ever.*** Tabbed section B, Basic Grammar, the handbook's reference within a reference, now teaches with everyday example sentences.

NAVIGATION HELP THAT MAKES SENSE TO STUDENTS

- ***Making the most of your handbook.*** These new boxes, running throughout the book, help students pull together the advice they need to complete writing assignments in any class. The boxes teach students to use their handbook as a reference by prompting them to consult related advice and examples from different parts of the book as they write and revise. (See p. 347 for an example.)
- ***Plain-language navigation for quick and easy reference.*** In the upper right-hand corner of every page, terms like *main idea*, *flow*, and *presenting the other side* will help students see at a glance the exact page they need.

A NEW COLLECTION OF RESOURCES THAT HELPS INSTRUCTORS MAKE THE MOST OF THEIR HANDBOOK

- ***Teaching with Hacker Handbooks***, by Marcy Carbajal Van Horn, offers practical advice on common topics such as designing a composition course, crafting writing assignments, and teaching multilingual writers. Ten lesson plans, each including strategies and materials that are ready to use or customize, support common course goals, like teaching argument, teaching paragraphs, and teaching with peer review. The collection also includes a wealth of handouts, syllabi, and other resources for integrating a Hacker handbook into your course. Available in print and online (hackerhandbooks.com/teaching).

What's the same

The features that have made *A Writer's Reference* work so well for so many students and instructors are still here.

Color-coded main menu and tabbed dividers. The main menu directs students to yellow, blue, and green tabbed dividers; the color coding makes it easy for students to identify and flip to the section they need. The documentation sections are further color-coded: orange for MLA, dark green for APA, and purple for CMS (*Chicago*).

User-friendly index. Even students who are unsure of grammar terminology will find help fast by consulting the user-friendly index. When facing a choice between *I* and *me*, for example, students may not know to look for "Case" or "Pronoun case." They are more likely to look up "*I*" or "*me*," so the index includes entries for "*I* vs. *me*" and "*me* vs. *I*." Similar entries appear throughout the index.

Citation at a glance. Annotated visuals show students where to find the publication information they need to cite common types of sources in MLA, APA, and CMS (*Chicago*) styles. (See p. 416 for an example.)

Quick-access charts and an uncluttered design. The seventh edition has what instructors and students have come to expect of a Hacker handbook: a clear and navigable presentation of information, with charts that summarize key content.

What's on the companion Web site?

hackerhandbooks.com/writersref

See page xxi for a list of resources available on the handbook's companion Web site.

Grammar, writing, and research exercises with feedback for every item. More than 1,800 items offer students plenty of extra practice, and our new scorecard gives instructors flexibility in viewing students' results.

Annotated model papers in MLA, APA, CMS (*Chicago*), and CSE styles. Student writers can see formatting conventions and effective writing in traditional college essays and in other common genres: annotated bibliographies, literature reviews, lab reports, business proposals, and clinical documents.

Research and Documentation Online. Written by a college librarian, this award-winning resource gives students a jump start with research in thirty academic disciplines. In addition to coverage of MLA, APA, and CMS (*Chicago*) styles of documentation, the site includes complete documentation advice for writing in the sciences (CSE style).

Resources for writers and tutors. Checklists, hints, tips, and helpsheets are available in downloadable format.

Resources for multilingual writers and ESL. Writers will find advice and strategies for understanding college expectations and completing writing assignments. Also included are charts, exercises, activities, and an annotated student essay in draft and final form.

Language Debates. Twenty-two brief essays provide opportunities for critical thinking about grammar and usage issues.

Access to premium content. New copies of the print handbook can be packaged with a free activation code for premium content: the e-book, a series of online video tutorials, and a collection of games, activities, readings, guides, and more.

Supplements for instructors

PRACTICAL

Teaching with Hacker Handbooks (in print and online at hackerhandbooks.com/teaching)

A Writer's Reference instructor resources (on the companion Web site at hackerhandbooks.com/writersref)

PROFESSIONAL

Teaching Composition: Background Readings

The Bedford Guide for Writing Tutors, Fifth Edition

The Bedford Bibliography for Teachers of Writing, Sixth Edition

Supplements for students

PRINT

Exercises for A Writer's Reference

Developmental Exercises for A Writer's Reference

Working with Sources: Exercises for A Writer's Reference

Research and Documentation in the Electronic Age

Resources for Multilingual Writers and ESL

Writing in the Disciplines: Advice and Models

Writing about Literature

Strategies for Online Learners

ONLINE

A Writer's Reference e-Book

CompClass for A Writer's Reference

Acknowledgments

I am grateful for the expertise, enthusiasm, and classroom wisdom that so many individuals brought to the seventh edition.

Reviewers

For their participation in a focus group on *A Writer's Reference* at the 2010 Conference on College Composition and Communication, I would like to thank Jennifer Cellio, Northern Kentucky University; Robert Cummings, University of Mississippi; Karen Gardiner, University of Alabama; Letizia Guglielmo, Kennesaw State College; Liz Kleinfeld, Metropolitan State College of Denver; and Melinda Knight, Montclair State University.

I thank those professors whose meticulous feedback helped shape *Strategies for Online Learners*: Jill Dahlman, University of Hawaii; Dana Del George, Santa Monica College; Larry Giddings, Pikes Peak Community College; David Hennessy, Broward College; Neil Plakcy, Broward College; and Rolando Regino, Riverside Community College.

I am indebted to the members of our Librarian Advisory Board: Barbara Fister, Gustavus Adolphus College; Susan Gilroy, Harvard University; John Kupersmith, University of California, Berkeley; and Monica Wong, El Paso Community College.

For their invaluable input, I would like to thank an insightful group of reviewers who answered detailed questionnaires about the sixth edition: Susan Achziger, Community College of Aurora; Michelle Adkerson, Nashville State Community College; Chanon Adsanatham, Community College of Aurora; Martha Ambrose, Edison Community College; Kimberley Aslett, Lake Superior State University; Laurel Barlow, Weber State University; Cynthia Bates, University of California, Davis; Fiona C. Brantley, Kennesaw State University; Max Brzezinski, Wake Forest University; Ken A. Bugajski, University of Saint Francis; Jeff Calkins, Tacoma Community College; Erin E. Campbell, Abraham Baldwin Agricultural College; Elizabeth Canfield, Virginia Commonwealth University; Eric Cash, Abraham Baldwin College; Michael Chamberlain, Azusa Pacific University; Deborah Chedister, SUNY Orange County Community College; Rong Chen, SUNY at Stony Brook; Michele J. Cheung, University of Southern Maine; Denise-Marie Coulter, Atlantic Cape Community College; Meriah Crawford, Virginia Commonwealth University; Tony Cruz, SUNY Orange County Community College; Janet Dean, Bryant College; Jeffrey L. Decker, University of California, Los Angeles; Sarah Doetschman, University of Alaska, Fairbanks; Elizabeth Evans, Wake Forest University; Martin Fertig, Montgomery County Community College; Christina D. French, Diablo Valley College; Marilyn Gilbert, The Art Institute of Seattle; William Gorski, West Los Angeles College; Ann H. Gray, Scott Community College; Jeanette Gregory, Cloud County Community College; Wendy Harrison, Abraham Baldwin Agricultural College; Catherine Hutcheson, Troy University; Melissa Jenkins, Wake Forest University; Elizabeth C. Jones, Wor-Wic Community College; Kristen Katzin-Nystrom, SUNY Orange County Community College; Lolann A. King, Trinity Valley Community College; Jamison Klagmann, University of Alaska, Fairbanks; Cheryl Laz, University of Southern Maine; Mark Leidner, Abraham Baldwin Agricultural College; Lindsay Lewan, Arapahoe Community College; Keming Liu, Medgar Evers College; Jeanette Lonia, Delaware Technical & Community College; Stefanie Low, Brooklyn College; Angie Macri, Pulaski Technical College; Edward W. Maine, California State University, Fullerton; Diane McDonald, Montgomery County Community College; Vickie Melograno, Atlantic Cape Community College; Priya Menon, Troy University; Gayla Mills, Randolph-Macon College; Frank Nigro, Shasta College; Diana Palmer, Montgomery County Community College; Peter J. Pellegrin, Cloud County Community College; Brenton Phillips, Cloud County Community College; J. Andrew Prall, University of Saint Francis; Mary Jean Preston, Carthage College; Molly Pulda, Brooklyn College; Tiffany A. Rayl, Montgomery County Community College; Jessica Richard, Wake Forest University; S. Randall Rightmire, University of California, Santa Barbara; Charles Riley, Baruch College/CUNY;

Rekha Rosha, Wake Forest University; Mitchell Rowat, University of Western Ontario; Kirsti Sandy, Keene State College; Robert M. Sanford, University of Southern Maine; Su Senapati, Abraham Baldwin Agricultural College; Shant Shahoian, Glendale Community College; Michele Singletary, Nashville State Community College; Michel Small, Shasta College; Matt Smith, University of Saint Francis; Marcia A. Sol, Cloud Community College; Stephen E. Sullivan, University of Saint Francis; Judith K. Taylor, Northern Kentucky University; Matt Theado, Gardner-Webb University; Jennifer Thomas, Azusa Pacific University; Matthew A. Thomas, Azusa Pacific University; Katherine E. Tirabassi, Keene State College; Cliff Toliver, Missouri Southern State University; Elaine Torda, SUNY Orange County Community College; Monica Trent, Montgomery College, Rockville; Ellen Vance, Art Institute of Seattle; Travis Wagner, University of Southern Maine; Karen Woods Weierman, Worcester State College; and Kelli Wood, El Paso Community College. We would also like to thank our anonymous reviewers from Brooklyn College, the University of Colorado at Denver, Glendale Community College, Ithaca College, Northern Kentucky University, Pulaski Technical College, and Wake Forest University.

Contributors

I am grateful to the following individuals, fellow teachers of writing, for their smart revisions of two key supplements: Joe Bizup, Boston University, updated *Writing about Literature* with fresh selections and relevant advice; and Jon Cullick, Northern Kentucky University, and Terry Myers Zawacki, George Mason University, tackled *Writing in the Disciplines*, expanding the advice to cover nine disciplines with the addition of music, engineering, and criminology. I am enormously grateful to Marcy Carbajal Van Horn, ESL specialist, experienced composition instructor, and former online writing lab director, who lent her expertise on several projects: She served as lead author for two brand-new resources, *Teaching with Hacker Handbooks* and *Strategies for Online Learners*, and she improved our coverage for multilingual writers both in the handbook and on the companion Web site.

Student contributors

A number of bright and willing students helped identify which instructor comments provide the best guidance for revision. From Green River Community College: Kyle Baskin, Josué Cardona, Emily Dore, Anthony Hines, Stephanie Humphries, Joshua Kin, Jessica Llapitan, James Mitchell, Derek Pegram, Charlie Piehler, Lindsay

Allison Rae Richards, Kristen Saladis, Jacob Simpson, Christina Starkey, Ariana Stone, and Joseph Vreeburg. From Northern Kentucky University: Sarah Freidhoff, Marisa Hempel, Sarah Laughlin, Sean Moran, Laren Reis, and Carissa Spencer. From Palm Beach Community College: Alexis Day, Shawn Gibbons, Zachary Jennison, Jean Lacz, Neshia Neal, Sarah Reich, Jude Rene, and Sam Smith. And from the University of Maine at Farmington: Nicole Carr, Hannah Courtright, Timothy Doyle, Janelle Gallant, Amy Hobson, Shawn Menard, Jada Molton, Jordan Nicholas, Nicole Phillips, Tessa Rockwood, Emily Rose, Nicholas Tranten, and Ashley Wyman. I also thank the students who have let us use and adapt their papers as models in the handbook and on its companion Web site: Ned Bishop, Lucy Bonilla, Jamal Hammond, Sam Jacobs, Albert Lee, Luisa Mirano, Anna Orlov, Emilia Sanchez, and Matt Watson.

Bedford/St. Martin's

A handbook is truly a collaborative writing project, and it is a pleasure to acknowledge and thank the enormously talented Bedford/St. Martin's editorial team, whose deep commitment to students informs each new feature of *A Writer's Reference.* Joan Feinberg, Bedford's president and Diana Hacker's first editor, offers her superb judgment on every aspect of the book. Joan's graceful and generous leadership, both within Bedford and in the national composition community, is a never-ending source of inspiration for those who work closely with her. Michelle Clark, executive editor; Mara Weible, lead development editor; and Barbara Flanagan, senior editor, are treasured friends and colleagues, the kind of editors every author dreams of having. Michelle, an endless source of creativity and joy, combines wisdom with patience, imagination with practicality, and hard work with good cheer. Mara's brilliant, close, and careful attention to each detail of the handbook comes from her teacher's sensibility and editor's unerring eye. And Barbara, who has worked on Diana Hacker's handbooks for more than twenty-five years, brings to the seventh edition her unrelenting insistence on both clarity and precision as well as her editorial patience and perseverance. Thanks to Alicia Young, associate editor, for expertly managing the review process, preparing documents, and editing several ancillaries. Thanks also to Kylie Paul, editorial assistant and newest member of the handbook team, for managing many small details related to both our Web and print projects.

The passionate commitment to *A Writer's Reference* of many Bedford colleagues—Denise Wydra, editorial director; Karen Henry, editor in chief; Marjorie Adler, marketing manager; and John Swanson, senior executive marketing manager—ensures that the seventh edition remains the most innovative and practical handbook on the market. Special thanks go to Jimmy Fleming, senior English specialist, for his abundant contributions, always wise and judicious, and for his enthusiasm and support as we traveled to colleges near and far. Many thanks to Rosemary Jaffe, senior production editor, who kept us on schedule and efficiently and gracefully turned a manuscript into a handbook. And thanks to Linda McLatchie, copyeditor, for her thoroughness and attention to detail; to Claire Seng-Niemoeller, text designer, who always has clarity and ease of use in mind as she designs *A Writer's Reference*; to Donna Dennison, art director, who has given the book a strikingly beautiful cover; and to Sarah Ferguson, new media editor, who developed the book's companion Web site and e-book.

Most important, I want to thank Diana Hacker. To create the best writing help for her students at Prince George's Community College, she studied their practices and puzzled out their challenges. What she learned inspired her to create the best reference for all students of academic writing. I'm honored to acknowledge her work, her legacy, and her innovative spirit—and pleased to continue in the tradition of this brilliant teacher and writer.

And last, but never least, I offer thanks to Maxine Rodburg, Laura Saltz, and Kerry Walk, friends and colleagues, for sustaining conversations about teaching writing; to Joshua Alper, an attentive reader of life and literature, for his steadfastness across the drafts; to Sam and Kate for lively conversations about writing; and to Rachel and Alexandra, whose good-natured and humorous observations about their real lives as college writers are a constant source of instruction and inspiration.

Nancy Sommers

C

Composing and Revising

C Composing and Revising

C1 Planning, 3

- **a** Assessing the writing situation, 3
- **b** Exploring ideas, 4
- **c** Drafting a working thesis, 10
- **d** Sketching a plan, 12

C2 Drafting, 14

- **a** Introduction and thesis, 14
- **b** Body, 18
- **c** Conclusion, 19

C3 Revising, 20

- **a** Making global revisions, 20
- **b** Revising and editing sentences, 21
- **c** Revising with comments, 23
- **d** Proofreading, 28
- **e** Preparing a portfolio; reflecting on your writing, 28

C4 Writing paragraphs, 32

- **a** Focusing on a main point, 32
- **b** Developing the point, 33
- **c** Using patterns of organization, 34
- **d** Improving coherence, 39
- **e** Adjusting paragraph length, 44

C5 Designing documents, 45

- **a** Layout and format, 46
- **b** Headings, 47
- **c** Lists, 49
- **d** Visuals, 50
- **e** Academic formatting, 54
- **f** Business formatting, 57

C6 Writing with technology, 62

- **a** Using software tools wisely, 62
- **b** Managing your files, 63

Writing is a process of figuring out what you think, not a matter of recording already developed thoughts. Since it's not possible to think about everything all at once, most experienced writers handle a piece of writing in stages. You will generally move from planning to drafting to revising, but be prepared to return to earlier stages as your ideas develop.

C1 Planning

C1-a Assess the writing situation.

Begin by taking a look at your writing situation. Consider your subject, your purpose, your audience, available sources of information, and any assignment requirements such as length, document design, and deadlines (see the checklist on p. 6). It is likely that you will make final decisions about all of these matters later in the writing process—after a first draft, for example—but you can save yourself time by thinking about as many of them as possible in advance.

In many writing situations, part of your challenge will be determining your purpose, or your reason, for writing. The wording of an assignment may suggest its purpose. If no guidelines are given, you may need to ask yourself, "Why am I communicating with my readers?" or "What do I want to accomplish?" College writers most often write for the following purposes:

to inform
to explain
to summarize
to recommend
to evaluate
to persuade
to analyze
to synthesize
to propose
to call readers to action
to change attitudes
to express feelings

Audience analysis can often help you determine how to accomplish your purpose—how much detail or explanation to provide, what kind of tone and language to use, and what potential objections to address. You may need to consider multiple audiences. The audience for a business report, for example, might include readers who want details and those who prefer a quick overview. For a service learning course, the audience for a proposal might include both your instructor and the supervisor at the organization at which you volunteered. The checklist

PRACTICE **hackerhandbooks.com/writersref**
> Composing and revising > C1–3

on page 6 includes questions that will help you analyze your audience and develop an effective strategy for reaching your readers.

Academic English What counts as good writing varies from culture to culture and even among groups within cultures. In some situations, you will need to become familiar with the writing styles—such as direct or indirect, personal or impersonal, plain or embellished—that are valued by the culture or discipline for which you are writing.

C1-b Experiment with ways to explore your subject.

Instead of just plunging into a first draft, experiment with one or more techniques for exploring your subject: talking and listening, reading and annotating texts, listing, clustering, freewriting, asking questions, keeping a journal, blogging. Whatever technique you turn to, the goal is the same: to generate ideas that will lead you to a question, a problem, or a topic that you want to explore. At this early stage of the writing process, don't censor yourself. Sometimes an idea that initially seems trivial or far-fetched will turn out to be worthwhile.

Talking and listening

Because writing is a process of figuring out what you think about a subject, it can be useful to try out your ideas on other people. Conversation can deepen and refine your ideas before you even begin to set them down on paper. By talking and listening to others, you can also discover what they find interesting, what they are curious about, and where they disagree with you. If you are planning to advance an argument, you can try it out on listeners with other points of view.

Many writers begin a writing project by brainstorming ideas in a group, debating a point with friends, or chatting with an instructor. Others prefer to record themselves talking through their own thoughts. Some writers exchange ideas by sending e-mails or instant messages or by posting to discussion boards or blogs. You may be encouraged to share ideas with your classmates and instructor in an online workshop, where you can begin to refine your thoughts before starting a draft.

THE WRITING CENTER **hackerhandbooks.com/writersref**
> Resources for writers and tutors > Tips from writing tutors: Invention strategies

Understanding an assignment

Determining the purpose of the assignment

Usually the wording of an assignment will suggest its purpose. You might be expected to do one of the following in a college writing assignment:

- summarize information from books, lectures, or research (See A1-c.)
- analyze ideas and concepts (See A1-d.)
- take a position and defend it with evidence (See A2.)
- synthesize (combine ideas from) several sources and create an original argument (See MLA-3.)

Understanding how to answer an assignment's questions

Many assignments will ask you to answer a *how* or *why* question. Such questions cannot be answered using only facts; instead, you will need to take a position. For example, the question "*What* are the survival rates for leukemia patients?" can be answered by reporting facts. The question "*Why* are the survival rates for leukemia patients in one state lower than they are in a neighboring state?" must be answered with both facts and interpretation.

If a list of prompts appears in the assignment, be careful—instructors rarely expect you to answer all of the questions in order. Look instead for topics, themes, or ideas that will help you ask your own questions.

Recognizing implied questions

When you are asked to *discuss*, *analyze*, *argue*, or *consider*, your instructor will often expect you to answer a *how* or *why* question.

Discuss the effects of the No Child Left Behind Act on special education programs.	=	How has the No Child Left Behind Act affected special education programs?
Consider the recent rise of autism diagnoses.	=	Why are diagnoses of autism rising?

Recognizing disciplinary expectations

When you are asked to write in a specific discipline, pay attention to the expectations and features of the writing in that discipline. Look closely at the key terms and specialized vocabulary of the assignment and the kinds of evidence and citation style your instructor expects. (See A4.)

Checklist for assessing the writing situation

Subject

- Has the subject (or a range of possible subjects) been given to you, or are you free to choose your own?
- What interests you about your subject? What questions would you like to explore?
- Why is your subject worth writing about? How might readers benefit from reading about it?
- Do you need to narrow your subject to a more specific topic (because of length restrictions, for instance)?

Purpose and audience

- Why are you writing: To inform readers? To persuade them? To entertain them? To call them to action? Some combination of these?
- Who are your readers? How well informed are they about the subject? What do you want them to learn?
- How interested and attentive are they likely to be? Will they resist any of your ideas?
- What is your relationship to your readers: Student to instructor? Employee to supervisor? Citizen to citizen? Expert to novice?

Sources of information

- Where will your information come from: Reading? Personal experience? Research? Direct observation? Interviews? Questionnaires?
- What kinds of evidence will best serve your subject, purpose, and audience?
- What sort of documentation style is required: MLA? APA? CMS?

Length and document design

- Do you have any length specifications? If not, what length seems appropriate, given your subject, purpose, and audience?
- Does the assignment call for a particular kind of paper: A report? A proposal? An essay? An analysis of data? A reflection?
- Is a particular format required? If so, do you have guidelines to follow or examples to consult?
- How might visuals—charts, graphs, tables, images—help you convey information?

Reviewers and deadlines

- Who will be reviewing your draft in progress: Your instructor? A writing center tutor? Your classmates?
- What are your deadlines? How much time will you need for each stage, including proofreading and printing the final draft?

Reading and annotating texts

Reading is an important way to deepen your understanding of a topic and expand your perspective. Annotating a text, written or visual, encourages you to read actively—to highlight key concepts, to note possible contradictions in an argument, or to raise questions for further research and investigation. Here, for example, is a paragraph from an essay on medical ethics as one student annotated it:

Making the most of your handbook

Read critically and take notes before you write.

▶ Guidelines for active reading: page 68
▶ Taking notes: R3-c
▶ Analyzing texts: A1-d

What breakthroughs? Do all breakthroughs have the same consequences?

Stem cell research

Is everyone really uneasy? Is something a breakthrough if it creates a predicament?

Breakthroughs in genetics present us with a promise and a predicament. The promise is that we may soon be able to treat and prevent a host of debilitating diseases. The predicament is that our newfound genetic knowledge may also enable us to manipulate our own nature—to enhance our muscles, memories, and moods; to choose the sex, height, and other genetic traits of our children; to make ourselves "better than well." When science moves faster than moral understanding, as it does today, men and women struggle to articulate their unease. In liberal societies they reach first for the language of autonomy, fairness, and individual rights. But this part of our moral vocabulary is ill equipped to address the hardest questions posed by genetic engineering. The genomic revolution has induced a kind of moral vertigo.

—Michael Sandel, "The Case against Perfection"

Sandel's key dilemma

What does he mean by "moral understanding"?

Which questions? He doesn't seem to be taking sides.

Listing

Listing ideas—a technique sometimes known as *brainstorming*—is a good way to figure out what you know and what questions you have.

Here is a list one student jotted down for an essay about community service requirements for college students:

- Volunteered in high school.
- Teaching adults to read motivated me to study education.
- "The best way to find yourself is to lose yourself in the service of others." —Gandhi

- Volunteering helps students find interests and career paths.
- Volunteering as requirement? Contradiction?
- Many students need to work to pay college tuition.
- Enough time to study, work, and volunteer?
- Can't students volunteer for their own reasons?
- What schools have community service requirements?
- What do students say about community service requirements?

Listing questions and ideas helped the writer narrow her subject and identify her position. In other words, she treated her early list as a record of her thoughts and a springboard to new ideas, not as an outline.

Clustering

Unlike listing, clustering highlights relationships among ideas. To cluster ideas, write your subject in the center of a sheet of paper, draw a circle around it, and surround the circle with related ideas connected to it with lines. If some of the satellite ideas lead to more specific clusters, write them down as well. The writer of the following cluster diagram was exploring ideas for an essay on obesity in children.

CLUSTER DIAGRAM

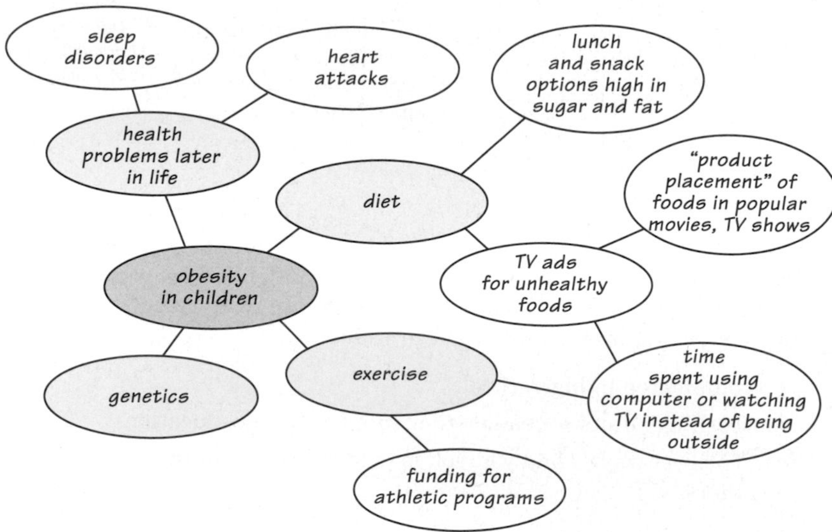

Freewriting

In its purest form, freewriting is simply nonstop writing. You set aside ten minutes or so and write whatever comes to mind, without pausing to think about word choice, spelling, or even meaning. If you get stuck, you can write about being stuck, but you should keep your fingers moving. If nothing much happens, you have lost only ten minutes. It's more likely, though, that something interesting will emerge—perhaps an eloquent sentence, a genuine expression of curiosity, or an idea worth further investigation.

To explore ideas on a particular topic, consider using a technique called *focused freewriting.* Again, you write quickly and freely, but this time you focus on a subject and pay attention to the connections among your ideas.

Asking questions

When gathering material for a story, journalists routinely ask themselves Who? What? When? Where? Why? and How? In addition to helping journalists get started, these questions ensure that they will not overlook an important fact.

Whenever you are writing about events, whether current or historical, asking the journalist's questions is one way to get started. One student, whose topic was the negative reaction in 1915 to D. W. Griffith's silent film *The Birth of a Nation*, began exploring her topic with this set of questions:

Who objected to the film?

What were the objections?

When were the protests first voiced?

Where were protests most strongly expressed?

Why did protesters object to the film?

How did protesters make their views known?

In the academic world, scholars often generate ideas by posing questions related to a specific discipline: one set of questions for analyzing short stories, another for evaluating experiments in social psychology, still another for reporting field experiences in criminal justice.

If you are writing in a particular discipline, you might begin your writing process by finding out which questions scholars in that discipline typically explore.

Making the most of your handbook

Effective college writers begin by asking questions.

▶ Asking questions in academic disciplines: A4-b

Keeping a journal

A journal is a collection of informal, exploratory, sometimes experimental writing. In a journal, often meant for your eyes only, you can take risks. You might freewrite, pose questions, comment on an interesting idea from one of your classes, or keep a list of questions that occur to you while reading and researching. You might imagine a conversation between yourself and your readers or stage a debate to understand opposing positions. A journal can also serve as a sourcebook of ideas to draw on in future essays.

Blogging

Although a blog (Weblog) is a type of journal, it is a public writing space rather than a private one. In a blog, you might express opinions, make observations, recap events, have fun with language, or interpret an image. Since most blogs have a commenting feature, you can create a conversation by inviting readers to give you feedback—ask questions, pose counterarguments, or suggest other readings on a topic.

C1-c Draft a working thesis.

As you explore your topic and identify questions to investigate, you will begin to see possible ways to focus your material. At this point, try to settle on a tentative central idea. The more complex your topic, the more your focus will change as your drafts evolve. For many types of writing, you will be able to assert your central idea in a sentence or two. Such a statement, which ordinarily appears in the opening paragraph of your finished essay, is called a *thesis statement* (see also C2-a).

A thesis is often one or more of the following:

- the answer to a question you have posed
- the solution for a problem you have identified
- a statement that takes a position on a debatable topic

A tentative or working thesis will help you organize your draft. Don't worry about the exact wording because your main point may change as you refine and focus your ideas. Here, for example, are one student's efforts to pose a question and draft a thesis statement for an essay in his film course.

QUESTION

In *Rebel without a Cause,* how does the filmmaker show that the main character becomes alienated from his family and friends?

Testing a working thesis

Once you have come up with a working thesis, you can use the following questions to evaluate it.

- Does your thesis answer a question, propose a solution to a problem, or take a position in a debate?
- Does the thesis require an essay's worth of development? Or will you run out of points too quickly?
- Is the thesis too obvious? If you cannot come up with interpretations that oppose your own, consider revising your thesis.
- Can you support your thesis with the evidence available?
- Can you explain why readers will want to read an essay with this thesis? Can you respond when a reader asks "So what?"

WORKING THESIS

In *Rebel without a Cause*, Jim Stark, the main character, is often seen literally on the edge of physical danger, suggesting that he is becoming more and more agitated by family and society.

The working thesis will need to be revised as the student thinks through and revises his paper, but it provides a useful place to start writing.

Here another student identifies a problem to focus an argument paper.

PROBLEM

Americans who earn average incomes cannot run effective national political campaigns.

WORKING THESIS

Congress should pass legislation that would make it possible for Americans who are not wealthy to be viable candidates in national political campaigns.

The student has roughed out language for how to solve the problem—enacting federal legislation. As she learns more about her topic, she will be able to refine her thesis and suggest a more specific solution, such as federal restriction of campaign spending.

Keep in mind as you draft your working thesis that an effective thesis is a promise to a reader; it points both the writer and the reader in a definite direction. For a more detailed discussion of thesis, see C2-a.

C1-d Sketch a plan.

Once you have drafted a working thesis, listing and organizing your supporting ideas is a good next step. Creating outlines, whether formal or informal, can help you make sure your writing is credible and logical.

When to use an informal outline

You might want to sketch an informal outline to see how you will support your thesis and to figure out a tentative structure for your ideas. Informal outlines can take many forms. Perhaps the most common is simply the thesis followed by a list of major ideas.

> Working thesis: Television advertising should be regulated to help prevent childhood obesity.
>
> - Children watch more television than ever.
> - Snacks marketed to children are often unhealthy and fattening.
> - Childhood obesity can cause sleeping disorders and other health problems.
> - Addressing these health problems costs taxpayers billions of dollars.
> - Therefore, these ads are actually costing the public money.
> - But if advertising is free speech, do we have the right to regulate it?
> - We regulate alcohol and cigarette ads on television, so why not advertisements for soda and junk food?

If you began by jotting down a list of ideas (see pp. 7–8), you can turn that list into a rough outline by crossing out some ideas, adding others, and putting the ideas in a logical order.

When to use a formal outline

Early in the writing process, rough outlines have certain advantages: They can be produced quickly, they are obviously tentative, and they can be revised easily. However, a formal outline may be useful later in the writing process, after you have written a rough draft, especially if your topic is complex. It can help you see whether the parts of your essay work together and whether your essay's structure is logical.

The following formal outline brought order to the research paper that appears in MLA-5c, on Internet surveillance in the workplace. The student's thesis is an important part of the outline. Everything else in the outline supports it, directly or indirectly.

FORMAL OUTLINE

Thesis: Although companies often have legitimate concerns that lead them to monitor employees' Internet usage—from expensive security breaches to reduced productivity—the benefits of electronic surveillance are outweighed by its costs to employees' privacy and autonomy.

I. Although employers have always monitored employees, electronic surveillance is more efficient.
   - A. Employers can gather data in large quantities.
   - B. Electronic surveillance can be continuous.
   - C. Electronic surveillance can be conducted secretly, with keystroke logging programs.

II. Some experts argue that employers have legitimate reasons to monitor employees' Internet usage.
   - A. Unmonitored employees could accidentally breach security.
   - B. Companies are legally accountable for the online actions of employees.

III. Despite valid concerns, employers should value employee morale and autonomy and avoid creating an atmosphere of distrust.
   - A. Setting the boundaries for employee autonomy is difficult in the wired workplace.
      1. Using the Internet is the most popular way of wasting time at work.
      2. Employers can't tell easily if employees are working or surfing the Web.
   - B. Surveillance can create resentment among employees.
      1. Web surfing can relieve stress, and restricting it can generate tension between managers and workers.
      2. Enforcing Internet usage can seem arbitrary.

IV. Surveillance may not increase employee productivity, and trust may benefit productivity.
   - A. A company shouldn't care how many hours salaried employees work as long as they get the job done.
   - B. Casual Internet use can actually benefit companies.
      1. The Internet may spark business ideas.
      2. The Internet may suggest ideas about how to operate more efficiently.

V. Employees' rights to privacy are not well defined by the law.
   - A. Few federal guidelines on electronic surveillance exist.
   - B. Employers and employees are negotiating the boundaries without legal guidance.
   - C. As technological capabilities increase, the need to define boundaries will also increase.

Guidelines for constructing an outline

1. Put the thesis at the top.
2. Make items at the same level parallel grammatically (see S1).
3. Use sentences unless phrases are clear.
4. Use the conventional system of numbers, letters, and indents:

   I.
      A.
      B.
         1.
         2.
            a.
            b.
   II.
      A.
      B.
         1.
         2.
            a.
            b.

5. Always include at least two items at each level.
6. Limit the number of major sections in the outline; if the list of roman numerals (at the first level) gets too long, try clustering the items into fewer major categories with more subcategories.

C2 Drafting

Generally, the introduction to a piece of writing announces the main point; the body develops it, usually in several paragraphs; the conclusion drives it home. You can begin drafting, however, at any point. If you find it difficult to introduce a paper that you have not yet written, try drafting the body first and saving the introduction for later.

C2-a For most types of writing, draft an introduction that includes a thesis.

Drafting an introduction

Your introduction will usually be a paragraph of 50 to 150 words (in a longer paper, it may be more than one paragraph). Perhaps the most common strategy is to open the paragraph with a few sentences that

THE WRITING CENTER **hackerhandbooks.com/writersref**
> Resources for writers and tutors > Tips from writing tutors: Writing introductions and conclusions

engage the reader and establish your purpose for writing and then state your main point. The statement of your main point is called the *thesis*. (See also C1-c.)

In the following introductions, the thesis is highlighted.

> Credit card companies love to extend credit to college students, especially those just out of high school. Ads for credit cards line campus bulletin boards, flash across commercial Web sites for students, and get stuffed into shopping bags at college bookstores. Why do the companies market their product so vigorously to a population that lacks a substantial credit history and often has no steady source of income? The answer is that significant profits can be earned through high interest rates and assorted penalties and fees. By granting college students liberal lending arrangements, credit card companies often hook them on a cycle of spending that can ultimately lead to financial ruin. —Matt Watson, student

> As the United States industrialized in the nineteenth century, using immigrant labor, social concerns took a backseat to the task of building a prosperous nation. The government did not regulate industries and did not provide an effective safety net for the poor or for those who became sick or injured on the job. Immigrants and the poor did have a few advocates, however. Settlement houses such as Hull-House in Chicago provided information, services, and a place for reform-minded individuals to gather and work to improve the conditions of the urban poor. Alice Hamilton was one of these reformers. Hamilton's efforts helped to improve the lives of immigrants and drew attention and respect to the problems and people that until then had been ignored. —Laurie McDonough, student

Ideally, the introductory sentences leading to the thesis should hook the reader, perhaps with one of the following:

- a startling statistic or an unusual fact
- a vivid example
- a description or an image
- a paradoxical statement
- a quotation or a bit of dialogue
- a question
- an analogy
- an anecdote

Whether you are writing for a scholarly audience, a professional audience, or a general audience, you cannot assume your readers' interest in the topic. The hook should spark curiosity and offer readers a reason to continue.

PRACTICE **hackerhandbooks.com/writersref**
> Composing and revising > C2–2 to C2–4

Although the thesis frequently appears at the end of the introduction, it can also appear at the beginning. Much work-related writing, for example, requires a straightforward approach and commonly begins with the thesis.

> Flextime scheduling, which has proved effective at the Library of Congress, should be introduced on a trial basis at the main branch of the Montgomery County Public Library. By offering flexible work hours, the library can boost employee morale, cut down on absenteeism, and expand its hours of operation. —David Warren, student

For some types of writing, it may be difficult or impossible to express the central idea in a thesis statement; or it may be unwise or unnecessary to include a thesis statement in the essay. A personal narrative, for example, may have a focus that is too subtle to be distilled in a single statement. Strictly informative writing, like that found in many business memos, may be difficult to summarize in a thesis. In such instances, do not try to force the central idea into a thesis sentence. Instead, think in terms of an overriding purpose, which may or may not be stated directly.

Making the most of your handbook

The thesis statement is central to many types of writing.

▶ Writing about texts: A1
▶ Constructing reasonable arguments: A2
▶ Writing research papers: MLA-1, APA-1, CMS-1

Academic English If you come from a culture that prefers an indirect approach in writing, you may feel that asserting a thesis early in an essay sounds unrefined or even rude. In the United States, however, readers appreciate a direct approach; when you state your point as directly as possible, you show that you understand your topic and value your readers' time.

Writing effective thesis statements

An effective thesis statement is a central idea that requires supporting evidence; its scope is appropriate for the required length of the essay; and it is sharply focused. It should answer a question you have posed, resolve a problem you have identified, or take a position in a debate.

When constructing a thesis statement, ask yourself whether you can successfully develop it with the sources available to you and for the purposes you've identified. Also ask if you can explain why readers should be interested in reading an essay that explores this thesis.

A thesis must require proof or further development through facts and details; it cannot itself be a fact or a description.

DRAFT THESIS The first polygraph was developed by Dr. John A. Larson in 1921.

PROBLEM The thesis is *too factual.* A reader could not disagree with it or debate it; no further development of this idea is required.

STRATEGY *Enter a debate* by posing a question about your topic that has more than one possible answer. For example: Should the polygraph be used by private employers? Your thesis should be your answer to the question.

REVISED THESIS Because the polygraph has not been proved reliable, even under controlled conditions, its use by employers should be banned.

A thesis should be an answer to a question, not a question itself.

DRAFT THESIS Would John F. Kennedy have continued to escalate the war in Vietnam if he had lived?

PROBLEM The thesis is a *question*, not an answer to a question.

STRATEGY *Take a position* on your topic by answering the question you have posed. Your thesis should be your answer to the question.

REVISED THESIS Although John F. Kennedy sent the first American troops to Vietnam before he died, an analysis of his foreign policy suggests that he would not have escalated the war had he lived.

A thesis should be of sufficient scope for your assignment; it should not be too broad.

DRAFT THESIS Mapping the human genome has many implications for health and science.

PROBLEM The thesis is *too broad.* Even in a very long research paper, you would not be able to discuss all the implications of mapping the human genome.

STRATEGY *Consider subtopics of your original topic.* Once you have chosen a subtopic, take a position in an ongoing debate and pose a question that has more than one answer. For example: Should people be tested for genetic diseases? Your thesis should be your answer to the question.

REVISED THESIS Although scientists can now detect genetic predisposition for specific diseases, policymakers should establish guidelines about whom to test and under what circumstances.

A thesis also should not be too narrow.

DRAFT THESIS A person who carries a genetic mutation linked to a particular disease might or might not develop that disease.

PROBLEM The thesis is *too narrow.* It does not suggest any argument or debate about the topic.

STRATEGY *Identify challenging questions* that readers might have about your topic. Then pose a question that has more than one answer. For example: Do the risks of genetic testing outweigh its usefulness? Your thesis should be your answer to this question.

REVISED THESIS Though positive results in a genetic test do not guarantee that the disease will develop, such results can cause psychological trauma; genetic testing should therefore be avoided in most cases.

A thesis should be sharply focused, not too vague. Avoid fuzzy, hard-to-define words such as *interesting, good,* or *disgusting*.

DRAFT THESIS The Vietnam Veterans Memorial is an interesting structure.

PROBLEM This thesis is *too fuzzy and unfocused.* It's difficult to define *interesting*, and the sentence doesn't give the reader any cues about where the essay is going.

STRATEGY *Focus your thesis with concrete language and a clear plan.* Pose a question about the topic that has more than one answer. For example: How does the physical structure of the Vietnam Veterans Memorial shape the experience of visitors? Your thesis—your answer to the question—should use specific language that engages readers to follow your argument.

REVISED THESIS By inviting visitors to see their own reflections in the wall, the Vietnam Veterans Memorial creates a link between the present and the past.

C2-b Draft the body.

The body of your essay develops support for your thesis, so it's important to have at least a working thesis before you start writing. What does your thesis promise readers? Try to keep your response to that question in mind as you draft the body.

You may already have written an introduction that includes your working thesis. If not, as long as you have a draft thesis, you can begin developing the body and return later to the introduction. If your thesis suggests a plan or if you have sketched a preliminary outline, try to block out your paragraphs accordingly. Draft the body of your essay by writing at least a paragraph about each supporting point you listed in the planning stage. If you do not have a plan, pause for a few moments and sketch one (see C1-d).

Keep in mind that often you might not know what you want to say until you have written a draft. It is possible to begin without a plan—assuming you are prepared to treat your first attempt as a "discovery draft" that will be radically rewritten once you discover what you really want to say. Whether or not you have a plan when you begin drafting, you can often figure out a workable order for your ideas by stopping each time you start a new paragraph, to think about what your readers will need to know to follow your train of thought.

For more detailed advice about paragraphs in the body of an essay, see C4. For specific help with drafting paragraphs, see C4-b.

TIP: As you draft, keep careful notes and records of any sources you read and consult. (See R3.) If you quote, paraphrase, or summarize a source, include a citation, even in your draft. You will save time and avoid plagiarism if you follow the rules of citation and documentation while drafting.

C2-c Draft a conclusion.

A conclusion should remind readers of the essay's main idea without repeating it. Often the concluding paragraph can be relatively short. By the end of the essay, readers should already understand your main point; your conclusion drives it home and, perhaps, gives readers something larger to consider.

In addition to echoing your main idea, a conclusion might

- briefly summarize your essay's key points
- propose a course of action
- offer a recommendation
- discuss the topic's wider significance or implications
- pose a question for future study

To conclude an essay analyzing the shifting roles of women in the military services, one student discusses her topic's implications for society as a whole:

> As the military continues to train women in jobs formerly reserved for men, our understanding of women's roles in society will no doubt continue to change. As news reports of women training for and taking part in combat operations become commonplace, reports of women becoming CEOs, police chiefs, and even president of the United States will cease to surprise us. Or perhaps we have already reached this point.
>
> —Rosa Broderick, student

To make the conclusion memorable, you might include a detail, an example, or an image from the introduction to bring readers full circle; a quotation or a bit of dialogue; an anecdote; or a witty or ironic comment.

Whatever concluding strategy you choose, keep in mind that an effective conclusion is decisive and unapologetic. Avoid introducing wholly new ideas at the end of an essay. And because the conclusion is so closely tied to the rest of the essay in both content and tone, be prepared to rework it (or even replace it) as you revise your draft.

C3 Revising

Revising is rarely a one-step process. Global matters—focus, purpose, organization, content, and overall strategy—generally receive attention first. Improvements in sentence structure, word choice, grammar, punctuation, and mechanics come later.

C3-a Make global revisions.

Many of us resist global revisions because we find it difficult to view our work from our audience's perspective. To distance yourself from a draft, put it aside for a while, preferably overnight or even longer. When you return to it, try to play the role of your audience as you read. If possible, enlist friends or family to be the audience for your draft. Or visit your school's writing center to go over your draft with a writing tutor. Ask your reviewers to focus on the larger issues of writing, such as purpose and organization, not on word- or sentence-level issues. The checklist for global revision on the next page may help you and your reviewers get started.

Making the most of your handbook

Seeking and using feedback are critical steps in revising a college paper.

- ▶ Guidelines for peer reviewers: **page 22**
- ▶ Revising with comments: C3-c

PRACTICE AND MODELS **hackerhandbooks.com/writersref**

> Composing and revising > C3–1 and C3–2
> Revising > Sample global revision
> Sample sentence-level revision

Checklist for global revision

Purpose and audience

- Does the draft address a question, a problem, or an issue that readers care about?
- Is the draft appropriate for its audience? Does it account for the audience's knowledge of and possible attitudes toward the subject?

Focus

- Is the thesis clear? Is it prominently placed?
- If there is no thesis, is there a good reason for omitting one?
- Are any ideas obviously off the point?

Organization and paragraphing

- Are there enough organizational cues for readers (such as topic sentences or headings)?
- Are ideas presented in a logical order?
- Are any paragraphs too long or too short for easy reading?

Content

- Is the supporting material relevant and persuasive?
- Which ideas need further development?
- Are the parts proportioned sensibly? Do major ideas receive enough attention?
- Where might material be deleted?

Point of view

- Is the dominant point of view—first person (*I* or *we*), second person (*you*), or third person (*he, she, it, one,* or *they*)—appropriate for your purpose and audience? (See S4-a.)

C3-b Revise and edit sentences.

Much of this book offers advice on revising sentences for clarity and on editing them for grammar, punctuation, and mechanics. Some writers handle sentence-level revisions directly at the computer, experimenting with a variety of possible improvements. Other writers prefer to print out a hard copy of the draft and mark it up before

THE WRITING CENTER **hackerhandbooks.com/writersref**
> Resources for writers and tutors > Tips from writing tutors: Revising and editing

Guidelines for peer reviewers

- View yourself as a coach, not a judge. Work with the writer to identify the draft's strengths and areas for improvement.
- Restate the writer's main ideas to check that they are clearly expressed.
- Where possible, give specific compliments. Let the writer know which of his or her strategies are successful.
- Ask to hear more about passages you find confusing or interesting.
- Express interest in reading the next draft.

making changes in the file. Here is a rough-draft paragraph as one student edited it on-screen for a variety of sentence-level problems.

> Although some cities have found creative ways to improve access to public transportation for passengers with physical disabilities, ~~and to fund other programs, there have been problems in~~ our city has struggled with ~~due to the need to address~~ budget constraints and competing ~~needs~~ priorities. ~~This~~ The budget crunch has led citizens to question how funds are distributed.~~?~~ For example, last year ~~when~~ city officials voted to use available funds to support ~~had to choose between allocating funds for accessible transportation or allocating funds to~~ after-school programs rather than transportation upgrades. ~~, they voted for the after school programs.~~ It is not clear to some citizens why ~~these~~ after-school programs are more important.

The original paragraph was flawed by wordiness, a problem that can be addressed through any number of revisions. The following revision would also be acceptable:

> Some cities have funded improved access to public transportation for passengers with physical disabilities. Because of budget constraints, our city chose to fund after-school programs rather than transportation programs. As a result, citizens have begun to question how funds are distributed and why certain programs are more important than others.

Some of the paragraph's improvements do not involve choice and must be fixed in any revision. The hyphen in *after-school programs* is necessary; a noun must be substituted for the pronoun *these* in the last sentence; and the question mark in the second sentence must be changed to a period.

C3-c Revising with comments

To revise is to "re-see," and the comments you receive from your instructors, peers, and writing center tutors will help you re-see your draft from your readers' point of view. Sometimes these comments are written as shorthand commands—"Be specific!"—and sometimes as questions—"What is your main point?" Such comments don't immediately show you *how* to revise, but they do identify places where global and sentence-level revisions can improve your draft.

When instructors, peers, and writing tutors comment on your work, you won't be able to incorporate everyone's advice. Sort through the comments you receive with your purpose and audience in mind.

You may also want to keep a revision and editing log, a list of the global and sentence-level concerns that come up repeatedly in your reviewers' comments. When you apply lessons from one assignment to another, comments can help you become a more effective writer.

Remember not to take criticism personally. Your readers are responding to your essay, not to you. It may be frustrating to hear that you still have more work to do, but taking feedback seriously—and revising accordingly—will make your essay stronger. This section addresses common types of comments an instructor or peer might make in response to your writing.

THE COMMENT: **Unclear thesis**

SIMILAR COMMENTS: **Vague thesis · State your position · What is your main point?**

the mother or other relatives.
drives to dance lessons,
eball team, hosts birthday
omework help. Do more **Unclear thesis**
r hinder the development of

UNDERSTANDING THE COMMENT When readers point out that your thesis is unclear, the comment often signals that they have a hard time identifying your essay's main point.

STRATEGIES FOR REVISING

- *Ask questions.* What is the thesis, position, or main point of the draft? Can you support it with the available evidence? (See C1-c, A2-c, and A2-d.)
- *Reread your entire draft.* Because ideas develop as you write, you may find that your conclusion contains a clearer statement of your main point than does your working thesis. Or you may find your thesis elsewhere in your draft. (See C-2a.)
- *Try framing your thesis* as an answer to a question you pose, the resolution of a problem you identify, or a position you take in a

debate. And put your thesis to the "So what?" test: Why would a reader be interested in this thesis? (See C1-c and p. 11.)

THE COMMENT: **Narrow your introduction**

SIMILAR COMMENTS: **Unfocused intro · Too broad**

UNDERSTANDING THE COMMENT When readers point out that your introduction needs to be "narrowed," the comment often signals that the beginning sentences of your essay are not specific or focused.

even believe that rituals
actions influence the outcome
fans go beyond cheering, and
ssment, and chanted slurs
orts.
Narrow your introduction

STRATEGIES FOR REVISING

- *Reread your introduction and ask questions.* Are the sentences leading to your thesis specific enough to engage readers and communicate your purpose? Do these sentences lead logically to your thesis? Do they spark your readers' curiosity and offer them a reason to continue reading? (See C-2a.)
- *Try engaging readers with a "hook"* in your introduction—a question, quotation, paradoxical statement, vivid example, or an image. (See p. 15.)

THE COMMENT: **Develop more**

SIMILAR COMMENTS: **Undeveloped · Give examples · Explain**

UNDERSTANDING THE COMMENT When readers suggest that you "develop more," the comment often signals that you stopped short of providing a full and detailed discussion of your idea.

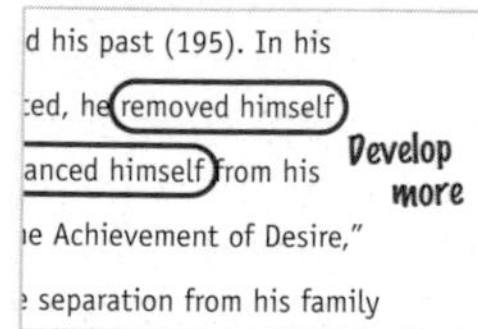

STRATEGIES FOR REVISING

- *Read your paragraph to a peer or a tutor* and ask specific questions. What's missing? Do readers need more background information or examples to understand your point? Do they need more evidence to be convinced? Is it clear what point you're making with your details? (See A2-d.)
- *Keep your purpose in mind.* Your assignment probably asks you to do more than summarize sources or list examples and evidence. Make sure you discuss the examples and illustrations you provide and analyze your evidence. (See A2-e.)

- *Think about why your main point matters to your readers.* Take another look at your points and support and answer the question "So what?" (See p. 11.)

THE COMMENT: **Be specific**

SIMILAR COMMENTS: **Need examples • Evidence?**

UNDERSTANDING THE COMMENT When readers say that you need to "be specific," the comment often signals that you could strengthen your writing with additional details.

cultural differences between the
Italy. Italian citizens do not share
attitudes or values as American
rences make it hard for some
feel comfortable coming to the
Be specific

STRATEGIES FOR REVISING

- *Reread your topic sentence* to understand the focus of the paragraph. (See C4-a.)
- *Ask questions.* Does the paragraph contain claims that need support? Have you provided evidence—specific examples, vivid details and illustrations, statistics and facts—to help readers understand your ideas and find them persuasive? (See A2-e.)
- *Interpret your evidence.* Remember that details and examples don't speak for themselves. You'll need to show readers how evidence supports your claims. (See A1-d and A2-e.)

THE COMMENT: **Consider opposing viewpoints**

SIMILAR COMMENTS: **What about the other side? • Counterargument?**

UNDERSTANDING THE COMMENT When readers suggest that you "consider opposing viewpoints," the comment often signals that you need to recognize and respond to possible objections to your argument.

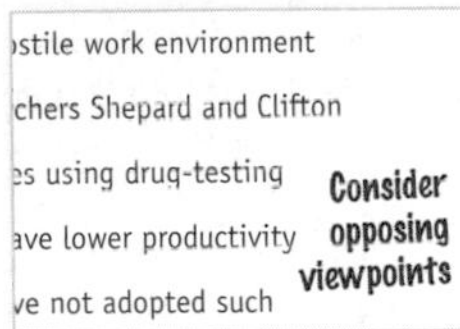

stile work environment
chers Shepard and Clifton
es using drug-testing
ave lower productivity
ve not adopted such
Consider opposing viewpoints

STRATEGIES FOR REVISING

- *Read more* to learn about the debates surrounding the topic. (See p. 7.)
- *Ask questions:* Are there other sides to the issue? Would a reasonable person offer an alternative explanation for the evidence or provide counterevidence? (See p. 85.)
- *Be open-minded.* Although it might seem illogical to introduce opposing arguments, you'll show your knowledge of the topic by

recognizing that not everyone draws the same conclusion. (See A2-f, A2-g, and p. 376.)

- *Introduce and counter objections* with phrases like these: "Some readers might point out that . . ." or "Critics of this view argue that. . . . " (See p. 85.)
- *Revise your thesis*, if necessary, to account for other points of view.

THE COMMENT: **Summarize less, analyze more**

SIMILAR COMMENTS: **Too much summary · Show, don't tell · Go deeper**

UNDERSTANDING THE COMMENT When readers point out that you need to include more analysis and less summary, the comment often signals that they are looking for your interpretation of the text.

ıages she speaks with
For example, she speaks
:ano Texas Spanish with her
; English at school (327).
r experience with speaking
Summarize less, analyze more

STRATEGIES FOR REVISING

- *Reread your paragraph and highlight the sentences that summarize.* Then, in a different color, highlight the sentences that contain your analysis. (Summary describes what the text says; analysis offers a judgment or interpretation of the text.) (See A1-c and A1-d.)
- *Reread the text* (or passages of the text) that you are analyzing. Pay attention to how the language and structure of the text contribute to its meaning. (See A1-a.)
- *Ask questions.* What strategies does the author use and how do those strategies help convey the author's message? What insights about the text can you share with your readers? How can you deepen your reader's understanding of the author's main points? (See A3 and A1-d.)

THE COMMENT: **More than one point in this paragraph**

SIMILAR COMMENTS: **Unfocused · Lacks unity · Hard to follow**

UNDERSTANDING THE COMMENT When readers tell you that you have "more than one point in this paragraph," the comment often signals that not all sentences in your paragraph support the topic sentence.

he believes the social
omic benefits. Many
Most important, casino
reas of the state that
ecent years.
More than one point in this paragraph

STRATEGIES FOR REVISING

- *Reread your paragraph and ask questions.* What is the main point of the paragraph? Is there a topic sentence that signals to readers what to expect in the rest of the paragraph? Have you included sentences that perhaps belong elsewhere in your draft? (See C4-a.)
- *Revisit your topic sentence.* It should serve as an important signpost for readers. Make sure the wording of your topic sentence is precise and that you have enough evidence to support it in the paragraph. (See C4-b.)

THE COMMENT: **Your words?**

SIMILAR COMMENTS: **Source? · Who's talking here?**

UNDERSTANDING THE COMMENT When readers ask "Your words?" the comment often signals that it is unclear whether you are using only your own words or are mixing in some words of your sources.

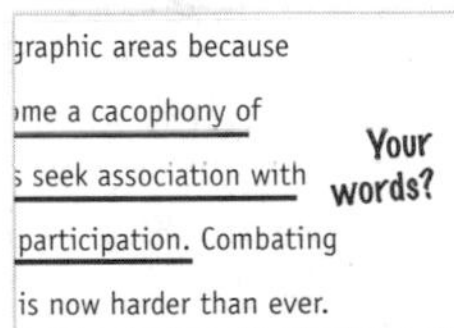

STRATEGIES FOR REVISING

- *Check that you have clearly marked the boundaries* between your source material and your own words. Have you borrowed words from sources without properly acknowledging them? (See MLA-2, APA-2, and CMS-2.)
- *Use a signal phrase* to introduce each source and provide context. Doing so prepares readers for a source's words. (See MLA-3b, APA-3b, and CMS-3b.)
- *Use quotation marks* to enclose language that you borrow word-for-word from a source and follow each quotation with a parenthetical citation. (See MLA-2b, APA-2b, and CMS-2b.)
- *Put summaries and paraphrases in your own words* and always cite your sources. (See MLA-2c, APA-2c, and CMS-2c.)

As you revise your paper, you might request feedback or clarification from instructors or peers by e-mail. Because e-mail communication can be quick and convenient, it's natural to think of it as informal, but be sure to keep your audience in mind. You should usually use a formal greeting for an instructor (*Dear Professor Brink*) instead of a casual one (*Hey!*) and use standard formatting and language (avoiding emoticons, abbreviations like *LOL,* and unconventional capitalization). You can often be more flexible with peers, but use a more formal style at the beginning of the semester, until you get to know them. And make sure you have a clear purpose in mind: Are you trying to share an observation? Asking for another perspective on your topic? Requesting feedback on a particular paragraph? For more on using e-mail in business and academic contexts, see C5-f.

C3-d Proofread the final manuscript.

After revising and editing, you are ready to prepare the final manuscript. (See C5-e for guidelines.) Make sure to allow yourself enough time for proofreading—the final and most important step in manuscript preparation.

Proofreading is a special kind of reading: a slow and methodical search for misspellings, typographical mistakes, and omitted words or word endings. Such errors can be difficult to spot in your own work because you may read what you intended to write, not what is actually on the page. To fight this tendency, try proofreading out loud, articulating each word as it is actually written. You might also try proofreading your sentences in reverse order, a strategy that takes your attention away from the meanings you intended and forces you to focus on one word at a time.

Although proofreading may be slow, it is crucial. Errors strewn throughout an essay are distracting and annoying. If the writer doesn't care about this piece of writing, the reader might wonder, why should I? A carefully proofread essay, however, sends a positive message that you value your writing and respect your readers.

C3-e Prepare a portfolio; reflect on your writing.

At the end of the semester, your instructor may ask you to submit a portfolio, or collection, of your writing. A writing portfolio often consists of drafts, revisions, and reflections that demonstrate a writer's thinking and learning processes or showcase the writer's best work. Your instructor may give you the choice of submitting a paper portfolio or an e-portfolio.

Reflection—the process of stepping back periodically to examine your decisions, preferences, strengths, and challenges as a writer—is the backbone of portfolio keeping. Your instructor may ask you to submit a reflective document in which you introduce or comment on the pieces in your portfolio and discuss your development as a writer throughout the course. This reflection may take the form of an essay, a cover letter, or some other kind of statement—often, but not always, placed as an introductory piece. You might try one or more of the following strategies:

- Discuss, in depth, your best entry. Explain why it is your best and how it represents what you learned in the course.
- Describe in detail the revisions you've made to one key piece and the improvements and changes you want readers to notice. Include specific passages from the piece.
- Demonstrate what this portfolio illustrates about you as a writer, student, researcher, or critical thinker.
- Reflect on what you've learned about writing and reading throughout the course.
- Reflect on how you plan to use the skills and experiences from your writing course in other courses where writing will be assigned.

SAMPLE REFLECTIVE LETTER FOR A PORTFOLIO

December 11, 2010
Professor Todd Andersen
Humanities Department
Johnson State College

Dear Professor Andersen,

This semester has been more challenging than I had anticipated. I have always been a good writer, but I discovered this semester that I had to stretch myself in ways that weren't always comfortable. I learned that if I wanted to reach my readers, I needed to understand that not everyone sees the world the way I do. I needed to work with my peers and write multiple drafts to understand that a first draft is just a place to start. I have chosen three pieces of writing for my portfolio: "Negi and the Other Girl: Nicknames and Identity," "School Choice Is a Bad Choice," and "Flat-footed Advertising." Each shows my growth as a writer in different ways, and the final piece was my favorite assignment of the semester.

Reflective writing can take various forms. Bonilla wrote her reflection as a letter.

Reflective writing often calls for first person ("I").

Bonilla lists the pieces included in her portfolio by title.

The peer review sessions that our class held in October helped me with my analytical response paper. My group and I chose to write about

"Jíbara," by Esmeralda Santiago, for the Identity unit. My first and second drafts were unfocused. I spent my first draft basically retelling the events of the essay. I think I got stuck doing that because the details of Santiago's essay are so interesting—the biting termites, the burning metal, and the *jíbara* songs on the radio—and because I didn't understand the differences between summary and analysis. My real progress came when I decided to focus the essay on one image—the mirror hanging in Santiago's small house, a mirror that was hung too high for her to look into. Finding a focus helped me move from listing the events of the essay to interpreting those events. I thought my peers would love my first draft, but they found it confusing. Some of their comments were hard to take, but their feedback (and all the peer feedback I received this semester) helped me see my words through a reader's eyes.

Bonilla comments on a specific area of growth.

While my Identity paper shows my struggle with focus, my next paper shows my struggle with argument. For my argument essay, I wrote about charter schools. My position is that the existence of charter schools weakens the quality of public schools. In my first draft, my lines of argument were not in the best order. When I revised, I ended the paper with my most powerful argument: Because they refuse to adopt open enrollment policies and are unwilling to admit students with severe learning or behavior problems, charter schools are elitist. While revising, I also introduced a counterargument in my final draft because our class discussion showed me that many of my peers disagree with me. To persuade them, I needed to address their arguments in favor of charter schools. My essay is stronger because I acknowledged that both the proponents and opponents of abandoning charters want improved education for America's children. It took me a while to understand that including counterarguments would actually make my argument more convincing, especially to readers who don't already agree with me. Understanding the importance of counterargument helped me with other writing I did in this course, and it will help me in the writing I do for my major, political science.

Even in the reflective document, Bonilla includes elements of good college writing, such as using transitions.

Bonilla reflects on how skills from her writing course will carry over to other courses.

Another stretch for me this semester was seeing visuals as texts that are worth more than a five-second response. The final assignment was my favorite because it involved a number of surprises. I wasn't so much surprised by the idea that ads make arguments because I understand that they are designed to persuade. What was surprising was being able to see all the elements of a visual and write about how they work together to convey a clear message. For my essay "Flat-footed Advertising," I chose the EAS Performance Nutrition ad "The New Theory of Evolution for Women." In my summary of the ad, I noted that the woman who follows the EAS program for twelve weeks and "evolves" is compared to modern humans and our evolution from apes as shown in the classic 1966 *March of Progress* illustration (Howell 41). It was these familiar poses of "Nicolle," the woman in the image, that drew me to study this ad. In my first draft, I made all of the obvious points, looking only literally at the comparison and almost congratulating the company on such a clever use of a classic scientific drawing. Your comments on my draft were a little unsettling because you asked me "So what?"—why would my ideas matter to a reader? You pushed me to consider the ad's assumptions and to question the meaning of the word *evolve*. In my revised essay, I argue that even though Nicolle is portrayed as powerful, satisfied, and "fully evolved," the ad campaign rests on the assumption that performance is best measured by physical milestones. In the end, an ad that is meant to pay homage to woman's strength is in fact demeaning. My essay evolved from draft to draft because I allowed my thinking to change and develop as I revised. I've never revised as much as I did with this final assignment. I cared about this paper and wanted to show my readers why my argument mattered.

Bonilla mentions how comments on her draft helped her revise.

The expectations for college writing are different from those for high school writing. I believe that my portfolio pieces show that I finished this course as a stronger writer. I have learned to take risks in my writing and to use the feedback from you and my peers, and now I know how to acknowledge the points of view of my audience to be more persuasive. I'm glad to have had the chance to write a reflection at the end of the course. I hope you enjoy reading this portfolio and seeing the evolution of my work this semester.

In her conclusion, Bonilla summarizes her growth in the course.

Sincerely,

Lucy Bonilla

Lucy Bonilla

C4 Writing paragraphs

Except for special-purpose paragraphs, such as introductions and conclusions (see C2-a and C2-c), paragraphs are clusters of information supporting an essay's main point (or advancing a story's action). Aim for paragraphs that are clearly focused, well developed, organized, coherent, and neither too long nor too short for easy reading.

C4-a Focus on a main point.

A paragraph should be unified around a main point. The main point should be clear to readers, and every sentence in the paragraph should relate to it.

Stating the main point in a topic sentence

As a rule, you should state the main point of a paragraph in a topic sentence—a one-sentence summary that tells readers what to expect as they read on. Usually the topic sentence (highlighted in the following example) comes first in the paragraph.

> All living creatures manage some form of communication. The dance patterns of bees in their hive help to point the way to distant flower fields or announce successful foraging. Male stickleback fish regularly swim upside-down to indicate outrage in a courtship contest. Male deer and lemurs mark territorial ownership by rubbing their own body secretions on boundary stones or trees. Everyone has seen a frightened dog put his tail between his legs and run in panic. We, too, use gestures, expressions, postures, and movement to give our words point. —Olivia Vlahos, *Human Beginnings*

In college writing, topic sentences are often necessary for advancing or clarifying the lines of an argument or reporting the research in a field. In business writing, topic sentences (along with headings) are essential because readers often scan for information and summary statements. Sometimes the topic sentence is introduced by a transitional sentence linking the paragraph to earlier material, and occasionally the topic sentence is withheld until the end of the paragraph.

Making the most of your handbook

Topic sentences let your reader know how a body paragraph relates to your essay's thesis.

▶ Effective thesis statements: page 16

PRACTICE hackerhandbooks.com/writersref
> Composing and revising > C4–2

Sticking to the point

Sentences that do not support the topic sentence destroy the unity of a paragraph. If the paragraph is otherwise focused, such sentences can simply be deleted or perhaps moved elsewhere. In the following paragraph describing the inadequate facilities in a high school, the information about the chemistry instructor (highlighted) is clearly off the point.

> As the result of tax cuts, the educational facilities of Lincoln High School have reached an all-time low. Some of the books date back to 1990 and have long since shed their covers. The few computers in working order must share one printer. The lack of lab equipment makes it necessary for four or five students to work at one table, with most watching rather than performing experiments. Also, the chemistry instructor left to have a baby at the beginning of the semester, and most of the students don't like the substitute. As for the furniture, many of the upright chairs have become recliners, and the desk legs are so unbalanced that they play seesaw on the floor.

Sometimes the solution for a disunified paragraph is not as simple as deleting or moving material. Writers often wander into uncharted territory because they cannot think of enough evidence to support a topic sentence. Feeling that it is too soon to break into a new paragraph, they move on to new ideas for which they have not prepared the reader. When this happens, the writer is faced with a choice: Either find more evidence to support the topic sentence or adjust the topic sentence to mesh with the evidence that is available.

C4-b Develop the main point.

Though an occasional short paragraph is fine, particularly if it functions as a transition or emphasizes a point, a series of brief paragraphs suggests inadequate development. How much development is enough? That varies, depending on the writer's purpose and audience.

For example, when health columnist Jane Brody wrote a paragraph attempting to convince readers that it is impossible to lose fat quickly, she knew that she would have to present a great deal of evidence because many dieters want to believe the opposite. She did *not* write only the following:

> When you think about it, it's impossible to lose—as many diets suggest—10 pounds of *fat* in ten days, even on a total fast. Even a moderately active person cannot lose so much weight so fast. A less active person hasn't a prayer.

This three-sentence paragraph is too skimpy to be convincing. But the paragraph that Brody did write contains enough evidence to convince even skeptical readers.

> When you think about it, it's impossible to lose—as many . . . diets suggest—10 pounds of *fat* in ten days, even on a total fast. A pound of body fat represents 3,500 calories. To lose 1 pound of fat, you must expend 3,500 more calories than you consume. Let's say you weigh 170 pounds and, as a moderately active person, you burn 2,500 calories a day. If your diet contains only 1,500 calories, you'd have an energy deficit of 1,000 calories a day. In a week's time that would add up to a 7,000-calorie deficit, or 2 pounds of real fat. In ten days, the accumulated deficit would represent nearly 3 pounds of lost body fat. Even if you ate nothing at all for ten days and maintained your usual level of activity, your caloric deficit would add up to 25,000 calories. . . . At 3,500 calories per pound of fat, that's still only 7 pounds of lost fat.
>
> —Jane Brody, *Jane Brody's Nutrition Book*

C4-c Choose a suitable pattern of organization.

Although paragraphs (and indeed whole essays) may be patterned in any number of ways, certain patterns of organization occur frequently, either alone or in combination:

- examples and illustrations (p. 34)
- narration (p. 35)
- description (p. 36)
- process (p. 36)
- comparison and contrast (p. 36)
- analogy (p. 37)
- cause and effect (p. 38)
- classification and division (p. 38)
- definition (p. 39)

These patterns (sometimes called *methods of development*) have different uses, depending on the writer's subject and purpose.

Examples and illustrations

Providing examples, perhaps the most common method of development, is appropriate whenever the reader might be tempted to ask, "For example?"

Normally my parents abided scrupulously by "The Budget," but several times a year Dad would dip into his battered black strongbox and splurge on some irrational, totally satisfying luxury. Once he bought over a hundred comic books at a flea market, doled out to us thereafter at the tantalizing rate of two a week. He always got a whole flat of pansies, Mom's favorite flower, for us to give her on Mother's Day. One day a boy stopped at our house selling fifty-cent raffle tickets on a sailboat, and Dad bought every ticket the boy had left—three books' worth. —Connie Hailey, student

Illustrations are extended examples, frequently presented in story form. When well selected, they can be a vivid and effective means of developing a point.

Part of [Harriet Tubman's] strategy of conducting was, as in all battle-field operations, the knowledge of how and when to retreat. Numerous allusions have been made to her moves when she suspected that she was in danger. When she feared the party was closely pursued, she would take it for a time on a train southward bound. No one seeing Negroes going in this direction would for an instant suppose them to be fugitives. Once on her return she was at a railroad station. She saw some men reading a poster and she heard one of them reading it aloud. It was a description of her, offering a reward for her capture. She took a southbound train to avert suspicion. At another time when Harriet heard men talking about her, she pretended to read a book which she carried. One man remarked, "This can't be the woman. The one we want can't read or write." Harriet devoutly hoped the book was right side up.

—Earl Conrad, *Harriet Tubman*

Narration

A paragraph of narration tells a story or part of a story. The following paragraph recounts one of the author's experiences in the African wild.

One evening when I was wading in the shallows of the lake to pass a rocky outcrop, I suddenly stopped dead as I saw the sinuous black body of a snake in the water. It was all of six feet long, and from the slight hood and the dark stripes at the back of the neck I knew it to be a Storm's water cobra—a deadly reptile for the bite of which there was, at that time, no serum. As I stared at it an incoming wave gently deposited part of its body on one of my feet. I remained motionless, not even breathing, until the wave rolled back into the lake, drawing the snake with it. Then I leaped out of the water as fast as I could, my heart hammering.

—Jane Goodall, *In the Shadow of Man*

Description

A descriptive paragraph sketches a portrait of a person, place, or thing by using concrete and specific details that appeal to one or more of the senses—sight, sound, smell, taste, and touch. Consider, for example, the following description of the grasshopper invasions that devastated the midwestern landscape in the late 1860s.

> They came like dive bombers out of the west. They came by the millions with the rustle of their wings roaring overhead. They came in waves, like the rolls of the sea, descending with a terrifying speed, breaking now and again like a mighty surf. They came with the force of a williwaw and they formed a huge, ominous, dark brown cloud that eclipsed the sun. They dipped and touched earth, hitting objects and people like hailstones. But they were not hail. These were *live* demons. They popped, snapped, crackled, and roared. They were dark brown, an inch or longer in length, plump in the middle and tapered at the ends. They had transparent wings, slender legs, and two black eyes that flashed with a fierce intelligence.
>
> —Eugene Boe, "Pioneers to Eternity"

Process

A process paragraph is structured in chronological order. A writer may choose this pattern either to describe how something is made or done or to explain to readers, step by step, how to do something. The following paragraph explains how to perform a "roll cast," a popular fly-fishing technique.

> Begin by taking up a suitable stance, with one foot slightly in front of the other and the rod pointing down the line. Then begin a smooth, steady draw, raising your rod hand to just above shoulder height and lifting the rod to the 10:30 or 11:00 position. This steady draw allows a loop of line to form between the rod top and the water. While the line is still moving, raise the rod slightly, then punch it rapidly forward and down. The rod is now flexed and under maximum compression, and the line follows its path, bellying out slightly behind you and coming off the water close to your feet. As you power the rod down through the 3:00 position, the belly of line will roll forward. Follow through smoothly so that the line unfolds and straightens above the water.
>
> —*The Dorling Kindersley Encyclopedia of Fishing*

Comparison and contrast

To compare two subjects is to draw attention to their similarities, although the word *compare* also has a broader meaning that includes a consideration of differences. To contrast is to focus only on differences.

Whether a paragraph stresses similarities or differences, it may be patterned in one of two ways. The two subjects may be presented one at a time, as in the following paragraph of contrast.

> So Grant and Lee were in complete contrast, representing two diametrically opposed elements in American life. Grant was the modern man emerging; beyond him, ready to come on the stage, was the great age of steel and machinery, of crowded cities and a restless, burgeoning vitality. Lee might have ridden down from the old age of chivalry, lance in hand, silken banner fluttering over his head. Each man was the perfect champion of his cause, drawing both his strengths and his weaknesses from the people he led.
>
> —Bruce Catton, "Grant and Lee: A Study in Contrasts"

Or a paragraph may proceed point by point, treating the two subjects together, one aspect at a time. The following paragraph uses the point-by-point method to contrast speeches given by Abraham Lincoln in 1860 and Barack Obama in 2008.

> Two men, two speeches. The men, both lawyers, both from Illinois, were seeking the presidency, despite what seemed their crippling connection with extremists. Each was young by modern standards for a president. Abraham Lincoln had turned fifty-one just five days before delivering his speech. Barack Obama was forty-six when he gave his. Their political experience was mainly provincial, in the Illinois legislature for both of them, and they had received little exposure at the national level—two years in the House of Representatives for Lincoln, four years in the Senate for Obama. Yet each was seeking his party's nomination against a New York senator of longer standing and greater prior reputation—Lincoln against Senator William Seward, Obama against Senator Hillary Clinton. They were both known for having opposed an initially popular war—Lincoln against President Polk's Mexican War, raised on the basis of a fictitious provocation; Obama against President Bush's Iraq War, launched on false claims that Saddam Hussein possessed WMDs [weapons of mass destruction] and had made an alliance with Osama bin Laden.
>
> —Garry Wills, "Two Speeches on Race"

Analogy

Analogies draw comparisons between items that appear to have little in common. Writers can use analogies to make something abstract or unfamiliar easier to grasp or to provoke fresh thoughts about a common subject. In the following paragraph, physician Lewis Thomas draws an analogy between the behavior of ants and that of humans.

> Ants are so much like human beings as to be an embarrassment. They farm fungi, raise aphids as livestock, launch armies into wars, use chemical sprays to alarm and confuse enemies, capture slaves. The families of weaver ants engage in child labor, holding their larvae like shuttles to spin out the thread that sews the leaves together for their fungus gardens. They exchange information ceaselessly. They do everything but watch television.
>
> —Lewis Thomas, "On Societies as Organisms"

Cause and effect

A paragraph may move from cause to effects or from an effect to its causes. The topic sentence in the following paragraph mentions an effect; the rest of the paragraph lists several causes.

> The fantastic water clarity of the Mount Gambier sinkholes results from several factors. The holes are fed from aquifers holding rainwater that fell decades—even centuries—ago, and that has been filtered through miles of limestone. The high level of calcium that limestone adds causes the silty detritus from dead plants and animals to cling together and settle quickly to the bottom. Abundant bottom vegetation in the shallow sinkholes also helps bind the silt. And the rapid turnover of water prohibits stagnation.
>
> — Hillary Hauser, "Exploring a Sunken Realm in Australia"

Classification and division

Classification is the grouping of items into categories according to some consistent principle. The following paragraph classifies species of electric fish.

> Scientists sort electric fishes into three categories. The first comprises the strongly electric species like the marine electric rays or the freshwater African electric catfish and South American electric eel. Known since the dawn of history, these deliver a punch strong enough to stun a human. In recent years, biologists have focused on a second category: weakly electric fish in the South American and African rivers that use tiny voltages for communication and navigation. The third group contains sharks, nonelectric rays, and catfish, which do not emit a field but possess sensors that enable them to detect the minute amounts of electricity that leak out of other organisms.
>
> —Anne and Jack Rudloe, "Electric Warfare: The Fish That Kill with Thunderbolts"

Division takes one item and divides it into parts. As with classification, division should be made according to some consistent principle.

The following paragraph describes the components that make up a baseball.

> Like the game itself, a baseball is composed of many layers. One of the delicious joys of childhood is to take apart a baseball and examine the wonders within. You begin by removing the red cotton thread and peeling off the leather cover—which comes from the hide of a Holstein cow and has been tanned, cut, printed, and punched with holes. Beneath the cover is a thin layer of cotton string, followed by several hundred yards of woolen yarn, which makes up the bulk of the ball. Finally, in the middle is a rubber ball, or "pill," which is a little smaller than a golf ball. Slice into the rubber and you'll find the ball's heart—a cork core. The cork is from Portugal, the rubber from southeast Asia, the covers are American, and the balls are assembled in Costa Rica.
>
> —Dan Gutman, *The Way Baseball Works*

Definition

A definition puts a word or concept into a general class and then provides enough details to distinguish it from other members in the same class. In the following paragraph, the writer defines *envy* as a special kind of desire.

> Envy is so integral and so painful a part of what animates behavior in market societies that many people have forgotten the full meaning of the word, simplifying it into one of the synonyms of desire. It is that, which may be why it flourishes in market societies: democracies of desire, they might be called, with money for ballots, stuffing permitted. But envy is more or less than desire. It begins with an almost frantic sense of emptiness inside oneself, as if the pump of one's heart were sucking on air. One has to be blind to perceive the emptiness, of course, but that's just what envy is, a selective blindness. *Invidia*, Latin for envy, translates as "non-sight," and Dante has the envious plodding along under cloaks of lead, their eyes sewn shut with leaden wire. What they are blind to is what they have, God-given and humanly nurtured, in themselves.
>
> —Nelson W. Aldrich Jr., *Old Money*

C4-d Make paragraphs coherent.

When sentences and paragraphs flow from one to another without discernible bumps, gaps, or shifts, they are said to be coherent. Coherence can be improved by strengthening the ties between old information and new. A number of techniques for strengthening those ties are detailed in this section.

Linking ideas clearly

Readers expect to learn a paragraph's main point in a topic sentence early in the paragraph. Then, as they move into the body of the paragraph, they expect to encounter specific details, facts, or examples that support the topic sentence—either directly or indirectly. In the following paragraph, all of the sentences following the topic sentence directly support it.

> A passenger list of the early years [of the Orient Express] would read like a *Who's Who of the World*, from art to politics. Sarah Bernhardt and her Italian counterpart Eleonora Duse used the train to thrill the stages of Europe. For musicians there were Toscanini and Mahler. Dancers Nijinsky and Pavlova were there, while lesser performers like Harry Houdini and the girls of the Ziegfeld Follies also rode the rails. Violinists were allowed to practice on the train, and occasionally one might see trapeze artists hanging like bats from the baggage racks. —Barnaby Conrad III, "Train of Kings"

If a sentence does not support the topic sentence directly, readers expect it to support another sentence in the paragraph and therefore to support the topic sentence indirectly. The following paragraph begins with a topic sentence. The highlighted sentences are direct supports, and the rest of the sentences are indirect supports.

> Though the open-space classroom works for many children, it is not practical for my son, David. First, David is hyperactive. When he was placed in an open-space classroom, he became distracted and confused. He was tempted to watch the movement going on around him instead of concentrating on his own work. Second, David has a tendency to transpose letters and numbers, a tendency that can be overcome only by individual attention from the instructor. In the open classroom, he was moved from teacher to teacher, with each one responsible for a different subject. No single teacher worked with David long enough to diagnose the problem, let alone help him with it. Finally, David is not a highly motivated learner. In the open classroom, he was graded "at his own level," not by criteria for a certain grade. He could receive a B in reading and still be a grade level behind, because he was doing satisfactory work "at his own level."
> —Margaret Smith, student

Repeating key words

Repetition of key words is an important technique for gaining coherence. To prevent repetitions from becoming dull, you can use variations of the key word (*hike, hiker, hiking*), pronouns referring to the word (*gamblers . . . they*), and synonyms (*run, spring, race, dash*). In the following paragraph describing plots among indentured servants in the seventeenth century, historian Richard Hofstadter binds sentences together by repeating the key word *plots* and echoing it with a variety of synonyms (which are highlighted).

> Plots hatched by several servants to run away together occurred mostly in the plantation colonies, and the few recorded servant uprisings were entirely limited to those colonies. Virginia had been forced from its very earliest years to take stringent steps against mutinous plots, and severe punishments for such behavior were recorded. Most servant plots occurred in the seventeenth century: a contemplated uprising was nipped in the bud in York County in 1661; apparently led by some left-wing offshoots of the Great Rebellion, servants plotted an insurrection in Gloucester County in 1663, and four leaders were condemned and executed; some discontented servants apparently joined Bacon's Rebellion in the 1670's. In the 1680's the planters became newly apprehensive of discontent among the servants "owing to their great necessities and want of clothes," and it was feared they would rise up and plunder the storehouses and ships; in 1682 there were plant-cutting riots in which servants and laborers, as well as some planters, took part.
>
> —Richard Hofstadter, *America at 1750*

Using parallel structures

Parallel structures are frequently used within sentences to underscore the similarity of ideas (see S1). They may also be used to bind together a series of sentences expressing similar information. In the following passage describing folk beliefs, anthropologist Margaret Mead presents similar information in parallel grammatical form.

> Actually, almost every day, even in the most sophisticated home, something is likely to happen that evokes the memory of some old folk belief. The salt spills. A knife falls to the floor. Your nose tickles. Then perhaps, with a slightly embarrassed smile, the person who spilled the salt tosses a pinch over his left shoulder. Or someone recites the old rhyme, "Knife falls, gentleman calls." Or as you rub your nose you think, That means a letter. I wonder who's writing?
>
> —Margaret Mead, "New Superstitions for Old"

Maintaining consistency

Coherence suffers whenever a draft shifts confusingly from one point of view to another or from one verb tense to another. In addition, coherence can suffer when new information is introduced with the subject of each sentence. For advice on avoiding shifts, see S4.

Providing transitions

Transitions are bridges between what has been read and what is about to be read. Transitions help readers move from sentence to sentence; they also alert readers to more global connections of ideas—those between paragraphs or even larger blocks of text.

Academic English Choose transitions carefully and vary them appropriately. Each transition has a different meaning; if you use a transition with an inappropriate meaning, you might confuse your reader.

- ▶ **Although taking eight o'clock classes may seem unappealing, coming to school early has its advantages. ~~Moreover~~** *For example,* **students who arrive early typically avoid the worst traffic and find the best parking spaces.**

SENTENCE-LEVEL TRANSITIONS Certain words and phrases signal connections between (or within) sentences. Frequently used transitions are included in the chart on page 43.

Skilled writers use transitional expressions with care, making sure, for example, not to use *consequently* when *also* would be more precise. They are also careful to select transitions with an appropriate tone, perhaps preferring *so* to *thus* in an informal piece, *in summary* to *in short* for a scholarly essay.

In the following paragraph, an excerpt from an argument that dinosaurs had the "'right-sized' brains for reptiles of their body size," biologist Stephen Jay Gould uses transitions (highlighted) to guide readers from one idea to the next.

> I don't wish to deny that the flattened, minuscule head of large bodied Stegosaurus houses little brain from our subjective, top-heavy perspective, but I do wish to assert that we should not expect more of the beast. First of all, large animals have relatively smaller brains than related, small animals. The correlation of brain size with body size among kindred animals (all reptiles, all mammals, for example) is remarkably regular. As we move from small to large

PRACTICE hackerhandbooks.com/writersref
> Composing and revising > C4–3

Common transitions

TO SHOW ADDITION	and, also, besides, further, furthermore, in addition, moreover, next, too, first, second
TO GIVE EXAMPLES	for example, for instance, to illustrate, in fact, specifically
TO COMPARE	also, similarly, likewise
TO CONTRAST	but, however, on the other hand, in contrast, nevertheless, still, even though, on the contrary, yet, although
TO SUMMARIZE OR CONCLUDE	in other words, in short, in conclusion, to sum up, therefore
TO SHOW TIME	after, as, before, next, during, later, finally, meanwhile, since, then, when, while, immediately
TO SHOW PLACE OR DIRECTION	above, below, beyond, farther on, nearby, opposite, close, to the left
TO INDICATE LOGICAL RELATIONSHIP	if, so, therefore, consequently, thus, as a result, for this reason, because, since

animals, from mice to elephants or small lizards to Komodo dragons, brain size increases, but not so fast as body size. In other words, bodies grow faster than brains, and large animals have low ratios of brain weight to body weight. In fact, brains grow only about two-thirds as fast as bodies. Since we have no reason to believe that large animals are consistently stupider than their smaller relatives, we must conclude that large animals require relatively less brain to do as well as smaller animals. If we do not recognize this relationship, we are likely to underestimate the mental power of very large animals, dinosaurs in particular.

—Stephen Jay Gould, "Were Dinosaurs Dumb?"

PARAGRAPH-LEVEL TRANSITIONS Paragraph-level transitions usually link the *first* sentence of a new paragraph with the *first* sentence of the previous paragraph. In other words, the topic sentences signal global connections.

Look for opportunities to allude to the subject of a previous paragraph (as summed up in its topic sentence) in the topic sentence of the next one. In his essay "Little Green Lies," Jonathan H. Alder uses this strategy in the topic sentences of the following paragraphs, which appear in a passage describing the benefits of plastic packaging.

> Consider aseptic packaging, the synthetic packaging for the "juice boxes" so many children bring to school with their lunch. One criticism of aseptic packaging is that it is nearly impossible to recycle, yet on almost every other count, aseptic packaging is environmentally preferable to the packaging alternatives. Not only do aseptic containers not require refrigeration to keep their contents from spoiling, but their manufacture requires less than one-10th the energy of making glass bottles.
>
> What is true for juice boxes is also true for other forms of synthetic packaging. The use of polystyrene, which is commonly (and mistakenly) referred to as "Styrofoam," can reduce food waste dramatically due to its insulating properties. (Thanks to these properties, polystyrene cups are much preferred over paper for that morning cup of coffee.) Polystyrene also requires significantly fewer resources to produce than its paper counterpart.

TRANSITIONS BETWEEN BLOCKS OF TEXT In long essays, you will need to alert readers to connections between blocks of text that are more than one paragraph long. You can do this by inserting transitional sentences or short paragraphs at key points in the essay. Here, for example, is a transitional paragraph from a student research paper. It announces that the first part of the paper has come to a close and the second part is about to begin.

> Although the great apes have demonstrated significant language skills, one central question remains: Can they be taught to use that uniquely human language tool we call grammar, to learn the difference, for instance, between "ape bite human" and "human bite ape"? In other words, can an ape create a sentence?

C4-e If necessary, adjust paragraph length.

Most readers feel comfortable reading paragraphs that range between one hundred and two hundred words. Shorter paragraphs can require too much starting and stopping, and longer ones can strain the reader's attention span. There are exceptions to this guideline, however. Paragraphs longer than two hundred words frequently appear in scholarly writing, where writers explore complex ideas. Paragraphs shorter than one hundred words occur in business writing and on Web sites, where readers routinely skim for main ideas; in newspapers because of narrow columns; and in informal essays to quicken the pace.

In an essay, the first and last paragraphs will ordinarily be the introduction and the conclusion. These special-purpose paragraphs are likely to be shorter than those in the body of the essay. Typically, the body paragraphs will follow the essay's outline: one paragraph per point in short essays, several per point in longer ones. Some ideas require more development than others, however, so it is best to be flexible. If an idea stretches to a length unreasonable for a paragraph, you should divide the paragraph, even if you have presented comparable points in the essay in single paragraphs.

Paragraph breaks are not always made for strictly logical reasons. Writers use them for all of the following reasons.

REASONS FOR BEGINNING A NEW PARAGRAPH

- to mark off the introduction and the conclusion
- to signal a shift to a new idea
- to indicate an important shift in time or place
- to emphasize a point (by placing it at the beginning or the end, not in the middle, of a paragraph)
- to highlight a contrast
- to signal a change of speakers (in dialogue)
- to provide readers with a needed pause
- to break up text that looks too dense

Beware of using too many short, choppy paragraphs, however. Readers want to see how your ideas connect, and they become irritated when you break their momentum by forcing them to pause every few sentences. Here are some reasons you might have for combining some of the paragraphs in a rough draft.

REASONS FOR COMBINING PARAGRAPHS

- to clarify the essay's organization
- to connect closely related ideas
- to bind together text that looks too choppy

C5 Designing documents

The term *document* is broad enough to describe anything you might write in a college class, in the business world, or in everyday life. How you design a document (format it for the printed page or for a computer screen) will affect how readers respond to it.

Good document design promotes readability, but what *readability* means depends on your purpose and audience and perhaps on other elements of your writing situation, such as your subject and any length restrictions. All of your design choices—formatting options, headings, and lists—should be made with your writing situation in mind. Likewise, visuals—tables, charts, and images—can support your writing if they are used appropriately.

C5-a Determine layout and format to suit your purpose and audience.

Similar documents share common design features. Together, these features—layout, margins and line spacing, alignment, fonts, and font styles—can help guide readers through a document.

Layout

Most readers have set ideas about how different kinds of documents should look. Advertisements, for example, have a distinctive appearance, as do newsletters and brochures. Instructors have expectations about how a college paper should look (see C5-e). Employers, too, expect documents such as letters, résumés, memos, and e-mail messages to be presented in standard ways (see C5-f).

Unless you have a compelling reason to stray from convention, it's best to choose a document layout that conforms to your readers' expectations. If you're not sure what readers expect, look at examples of the kind of document you are producing.

Margins and line spacing

Margins help control the look of a page. For most academic and business documents, leave a margin of one to one and a half inches on all sides. These margins create a visual frame for the text and provide room for annotations, such as an instructor's comments or a peer's suggestions. Tight margins generally make a page crowded and difficult to read.

Most manuscripts in progress are double-spaced to allow room for editing. Final copy is often double-spaced as well, since single-spaced text is less inviting to read. If you are unsure about margin and spacing requirements for your document, check with your instructor or consult documents similar to the one you are writing. At times, the advantages of wide margins and double-spaced lines are offset by other considerations. For example, most business and technical documents are single-spaced, with double-spacing between paragraphs, to save paper and to promote quick scanning. Keep your purpose and audience in mind as you determine appropriate margins and line spacing for your document.

Planning a document: Design checklist for purpose and audience

- What is the purpose of your document? How can your document design help you achieve this purpose?
- Who are your readers? What are their expectations?
- What format is required? What format options—layout, margins, line spacing, and font styles—will readers expect?
- How can you use visuals—charts, graphs, tables, images—to help you convey information and achieve your purpose?

Fonts

If you have a choice, select a font that fits your writing situation in an easy-to-read size (usually 10–12 points). Although offbeat fonts may seem attractive, they slow readers down and can distract them from your ideas. For example, using Comic Sans, a font with a handwritten, childish feel, can make an essay seem too informal or unpolished, regardless of how well it's written. Fonts that are easy to read and appropriate for college and workplace documents include the following: Arial, Courier, Georgia, Times New Roman, and Verdana. Check with your instructor; he or she may expect or prefer a particular font.

Font styles

Font styles—such as **boldface,** *italics,* and underlining—can be useful for calling attention to parts of a document. On the whole, it is best to use restraint when selecting styles. Applying too many different styles within a document can result in busy-looking pages and can confuse readers.

TIP: Never write an academic document in all capital or all lowercase letters. Although some readers have become accustomed to instant messages and e-mails that omit capital letters entirely, their absence makes a piece of writing too informal and difficult to read.

C5-b Use headings when appropriate.

In short essays, you will have little need for headings, especially if you use paragraphing and clear topic sentences to guide readers. In more complex documents, however, such as longer essays, research papers, business reports, and Web sites, headings can be a useful visual cue for readers.

Headings help readers see at a glance the organization of a document. If more than one level of heading is used, the headings also indicate the hierarchy of ideas—as they do throughout this book.

Headings serve a number of functions for your readers, depending on the needs of different readers. When readers are looking for specific information and don't want to read the entire document, headings can guide them to the right place quickly. When readers are scanning, hoping to pick up a document's meaning or message, headings can provide an overview. Even when readers are committed enough to read every word, headings can help them preview a document before they begin reading or easily revisit a specific section after they've read through the document once.

Making the most of your handbook

Headings can help writers plan and readers understand a document.

▶ Papers organized with headings: **pages 485** and **530**

TIP: While headings can be useful, they cannot substitute for transitions between paragraphs (see p. 43).

Phrasing headings

Headings should be as brief and as informative as possible. Certain styles of headings—the most common being *-ing* phrases, noun phrases, questions, and imperative sentences—work better for some purposes, audiences, and subjects than for others.

Whatever style you choose, use it consistently. Headings on the same level of organization should be written in parallel structure (see S1), as in the following examples from a report, a history textbook, a financial brochure, and a nursing manual, respectively.

-ING **PHRASES AS HEADINGS**

Safeguarding Earth's atmosphere
Charting the path to sustainable energy
Conserving global forests

NOUN PHRASES AS HEADINGS

The civil rights movement
The antiwar movement
The feminist movement

QUESTIONS AS HEADINGS

How do I buy shares?
How do I redeem shares?
How has the fund performed in the past three years?

IMPERATIVE SENTENCES AS HEADINGS

Ask the patient to describe current symptoms.
Take a detailed medical history.
Record the patient's vital signs.

Placing and formatting headings

Headings on the same level of organization should be placed and formatted in a consistent way. If you have more than one level of heading, you might center your first-level headings and make them boldface; then you might make the second-level headings left-aligned and italicized, like this:

First-level heading

Second-level heading

A college paper with headings typically has only one level, and the headings are often centered, as in the sample paper on pages 488–96. In a report or a brochure, important headings can be highlighted by using white space above and below them. Less important headings can be downplayed by using less white space or by running them into the text.

C5-c Use lists to guide readers.

Lists are easy to read or scan when they are displayed, item by item, rather than run into your text. You might choose to display the following kinds of lists:

- steps in a process
- advice or recommendations
- items to be discussed
- criteria for evaluation (as in checklists)
- parts of an object

Lists are usually introduced with an independent clause followed by a colon (*All mammals share the following five characteristics:*).

Periods are not used after items in a list unless the items are complete sentences. Lists should be in parallel grammatical form (see S1).

Use bullets (circles or squares) or dashes to draw readers' eyes to a list and to emphasize individual items. If you are describing a sequence or a set of steps, number your list with arabic numerals (1, 2, 3) followed by periods.

Although lists can be useful visual cues, don't overdo them. Too many will clutter a document.

C5-d Add visuals to support your purpose.

Visuals can convey information concisely and powerfully. Charts, graphs, and tables, for example, can simplify complex numerical information. Images—including photographs and diagrams—often express an idea more vividly than words can. With access to the Internet, digital photography, and word processing or desktop publishing software, you can download or create your own visuals to enhance your document. Keep in mind that if you download a visual—or use published information to create your own visual—you must credit your source (see R3).

Choosing appropriate visuals

Use visuals to supplement your writing, not to substitute for it. Always consider how a visual supports your purpose and how your audience might respond to it. A student writing about online news used two screen shots to illustrate a point about hyperlinked text (see A2-h). Another student, writing about treatments for childhood obesity, created a table to display data she had found in two different sources and discussed in her paper (see APA-5b).

In many cases, the same information can be presented visually in different formats. When deciding whether to display data in a table or a graph, for example, think about the message you want to convey and the information your readers need. (See the examples on p. 51.) If your discussion refers to specific numbers, a table will be more useful to readers. If, however, you want readers to grasp at a glance that sales of hybrid electric vehicles increased from 2001 to 2007 and then declined, a line graph will be more effective.

As you draft and revise a document, carefully choose the visuals that support your main point, and avoid overloading your text with too many images. The chart on pages 52–53 describes eight types of visuals and their purposes.

INFORMATION DISPLAYED IN TWO TYPES OF VISUALS These visuals present the same information in two different ways. The table provides exact numbers for comparison. The line graph allows readers to see the trend in sales.

Hybrid electric vehicle sales by year in the United States

Year	Number of vehicles sold
2001	20,282
2002	36,035
2003	47,600
2004	84,199
2005	209,711
2006	252,636
2007	352,274
2008	312,386

Source: US Dept. of Energy (2009).

Hybrid electric vehicle sales by year in the United States

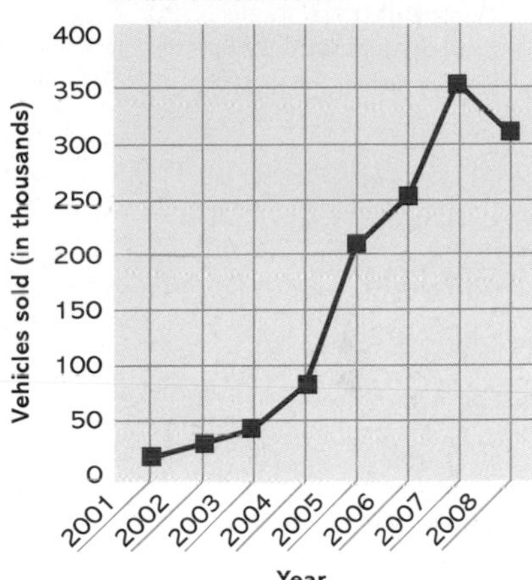

Placing and labeling visuals

A visual may be placed in the text of a document, near a discussion to which it relates, or it can be put in an appendix, labeled, and referred to in the text. Placing visuals in the text of a document can be tricky. Usually you will want a visual to appear close to the sentences that relate to it, but page breaks won't always allow this placement. At times, you may need to insert the visual at a later point and tell readers where it can be found; sometimes you can make the text flow, or wrap, around the visual. No matter where you place a visual, refer to it in your text. Don't expect visuals to speak for themselves.

Making the most of your handbook

Guidelines for using visuals may vary by academic discipline.

▶ English and other humanities: MLA-5a
▶ Social sciences: APA-5a
▶ History: CMS-5a

Most of the visuals you include in a document will require some sort of label. A label, which is typically placed above or below the visual, should be brief but descriptive. Most commonly, a visual is labeled with the word "Figure" or the abbreviation "Fig.," followed by a number: *Fig. 4*. Sometimes a title might be included to explain how the visual relates to the text: *Fig. 4. Voter turnout by age.*

Choosing visuals to suit your purpose

Pie chart

Pie charts compare a part or parts to the whole. Segments of the pie represent percentages of the whole (and always total 100 percent).

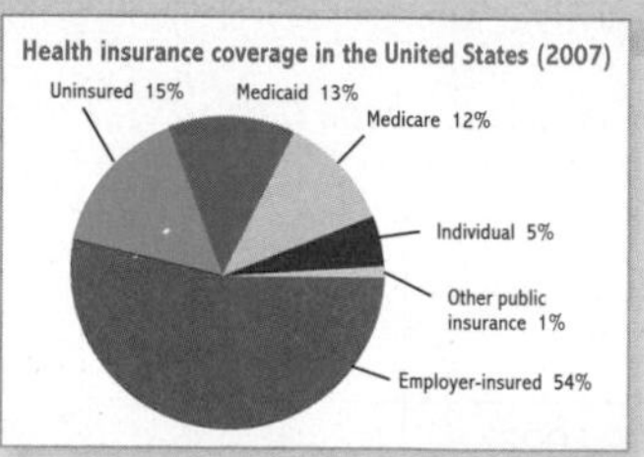

Line graph

Line graphs highlight trends over a period of time or compare numerical data.

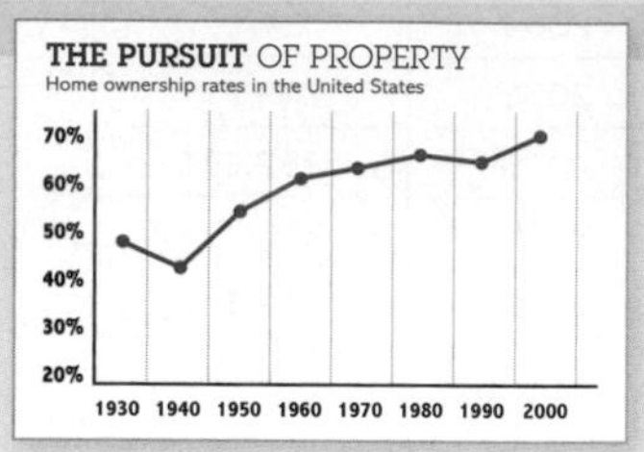

Bar graph

Bar graphs, like line graphs, show trends or comparisons at a glance. This bar graph displays the same data as in the line graph above.

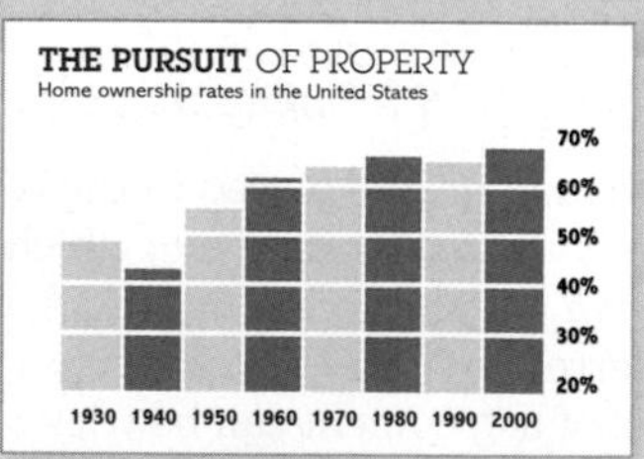

Table

Tables display numbers and words in columns and rows. They can be used to organize complicated numerical information into an easily understood format.

Prices of daily doses of AIDS drugs
($US)

Drug	*Brazil*	*Uganda*	*Côte d'Ivoire*	*US*
3TC (Lamuvidine)	1.66	3.28	2.95	8.70
ddC (Zalcitabine)	0.24	4.17	3.75	8.80
Didanosine	2.04	5.26	3.48	7.25
Efavirenz	6.96	n/a	6.41	13.13
Indinavir	10.32	12.79	9.07	14.93
Nelfinavir	4.14	4.45	4.39	6.47
Nevirapine	5.04	n/a	n/a	8.48
Saquinavir	6.24	7.37	5.52	6.50
Stavudine	0.56	6.19	4.10	9.07
ZDV/3TC	1.44	7.34	n/a	18.78
Zidovudine	1.08	4.34	2.43	10.12

Source: UNAIDS, 2000

Sources [top to bottom]: Kaiser Foundation; US Census Bureau; US Census Bureau; UNAIDS.

Photograph

Photographs can be used to vividly depict people, scenes, or objects discussed in a text.

Diagram

Diagrams, useful in scientific and technical writing, concisely illustrate processes, structures, or interactions.

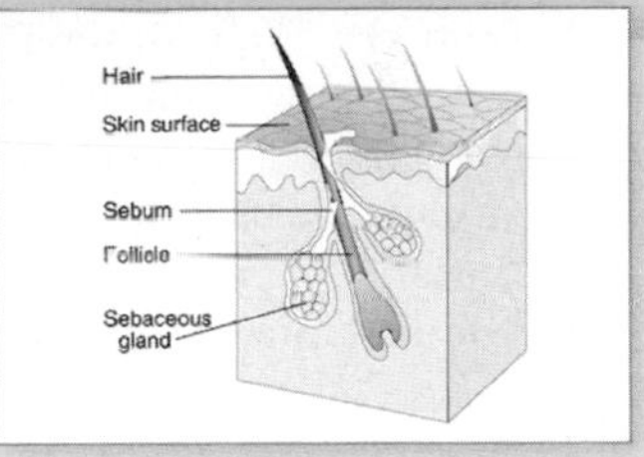

Flowchart

Flowcharts show structures (the hierarchy of employees at a company, for example) or steps in a process and their relation to one another. (For another example, see p. 122.)

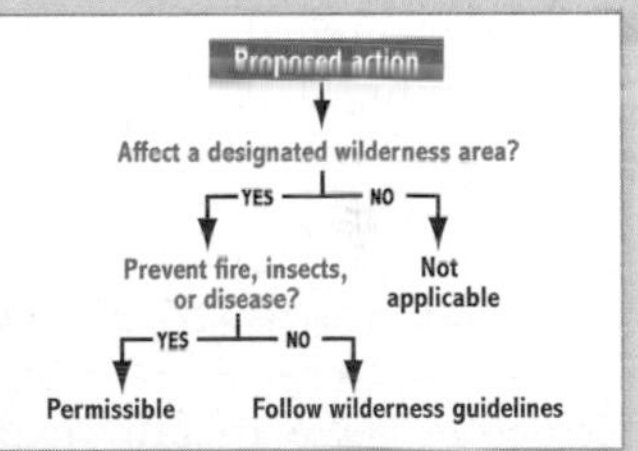

Map

Maps illustrate distances, historical information, or demographics and often use symbols for geographic features and points of interest.

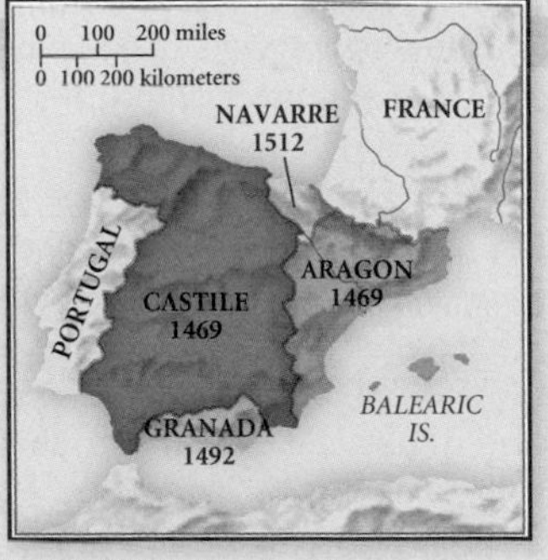

Sources [top to bottom]: Fred Zwicky; NIAMS; Arizona Board of Regents; Lynn Hunt et al.

Using visuals responsibly

Most word processing and spreadsheet software will allow you to produce your own visuals. If you create a chart, a table, or a graph using information from your research, you must cite the source of the information even though the visual is your own. The visual at the right credits the source of its data.

VISUAL WITH A SOURCE CREDITED

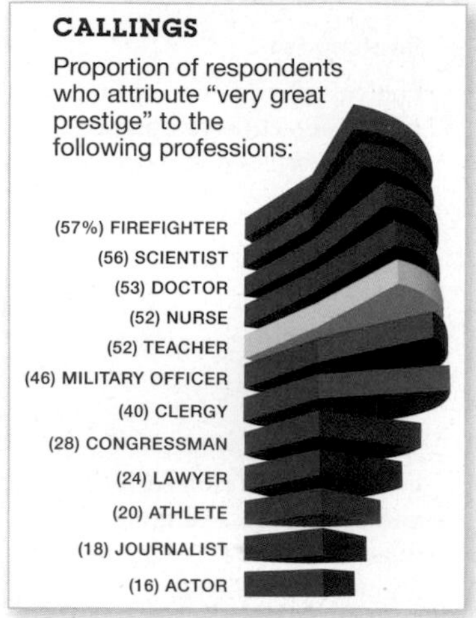

Source: The New York Times Company, September 21, 2008, from data by the Harris Poll, July 2008.

If you download a photograph from the Web or scan an image from a magazine or book, you must credit the person or organization that created it, just as you would cite any other source you use in a college paper (see R3). Make sure any cropping or other changes you make to the visual do not distort the meaning of the original. If your document is written for publication outside the classroom, you will need to request permission to use any visual you borrow.

C5-e Use standard academic formatting.

Instructors have certain expectations about how a college paper should look. If your instructor provides guidelines for formatting an essay, a report, a research paper, or another document, you should follow them. Otherwise, use the manuscript format that is recommended for your academic discipline.

In most English and other humanities classes, you will be asked to use MLA (Modern Language Association) format (see pp. 55–56 and MLA-5). In most social science classes, such as psychology and sociology, and in most education, business, and health-related classes, you will be asked to use APA (American Psychological Association) format (see APA-5). In history and some other humanities classes, you will be asked to use CMS (*Chicago*) format (see CMS-5).

MLA PAPER FORMAT

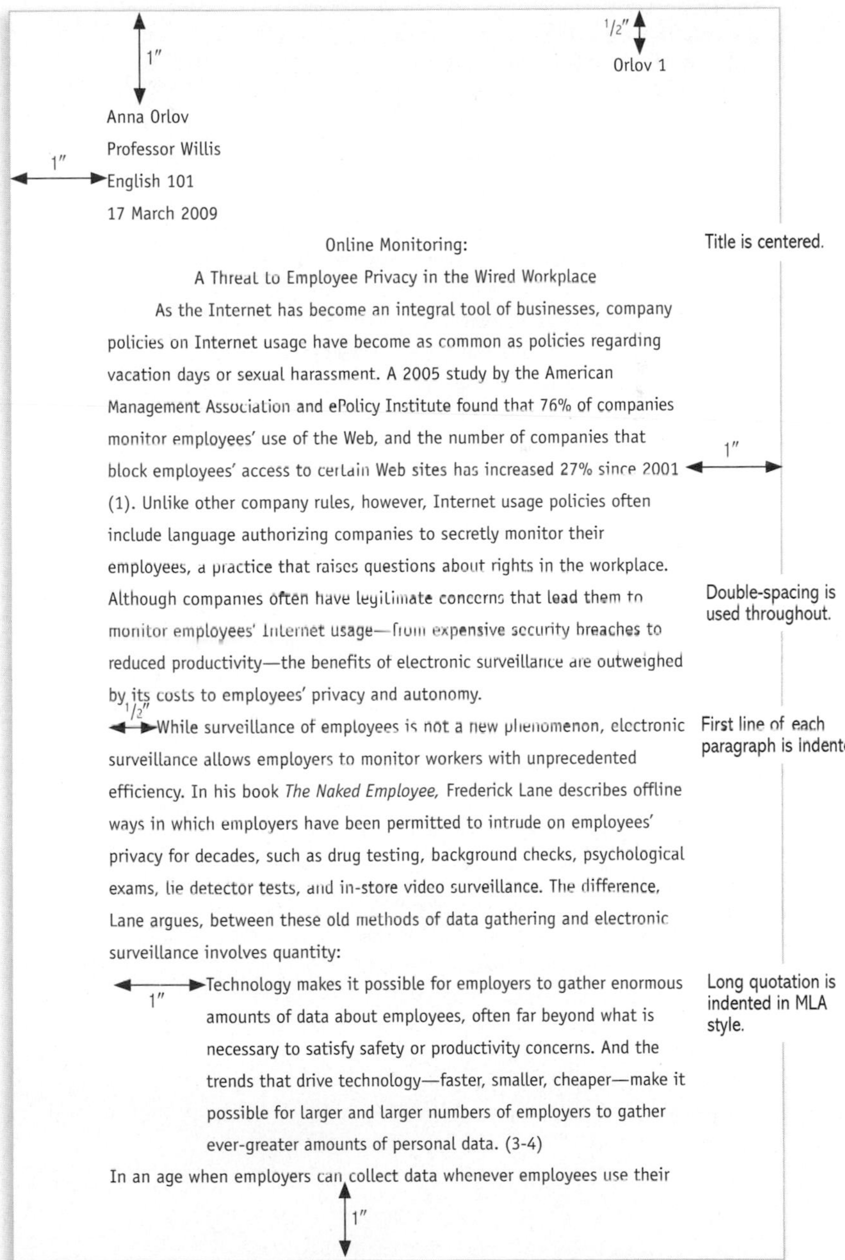

Orlov 1

Anna Orlov

Professor Willis

English 101

17 March 2009

Online Monitoring:

A Threat to Employee Privacy in the Wired Workplace

As the Internet has become an integral tool of businesses, company policies on Internet usage have become as common as policies regarding vacation days or sexual harassment. A 2005 study by the American Management Association and ePolicy Institute found that 76% of companies monitor employees' use of the Web, and the number of companies that block employees' access to certain Web sites has increased 27% since 2001 (1). Unlike other company rules, however, Internet usage policies often include language authorizing companies to secretly monitor their employees, a practice that raises questions about rights in the workplace. Although companies often have legitimate concerns that lead them to monitor employees' Internet usage—from expensive security breaches to reduced productivity—the benefits of electronic surveillance are outweighed by its costs to employees' privacy and autonomy.

While surveillance of employees is not a new phenomenon, electronic surveillance allows employers to monitor workers with unprecedented efficiency. In his book *The Naked Employee,* Frederick Lane describes offline ways in which employers have been permitted to intrude on employees' privacy for decades, such as drug testing, background checks, psychological exams, lie detector tests, and in-store video surveillance. The difference, Lane argues, between these old methods of data gathering and electronic surveillance involves quantity:

> Technology makes it possible for employers to gather enormous amounts of data about employees, often far beyond what is necessary to satisfy safety or productivity concerns. And the trends that drive technology—faster, smaller, cheaper—make it possible for larger and larger numbers of employers to gather ever-greater amounts of personal data. (3-4)

In an age when employers can collect data whenever employees use their

Marginal annotations indicate MLA-style formatting.

MLA PAPER FORMAT (continued)

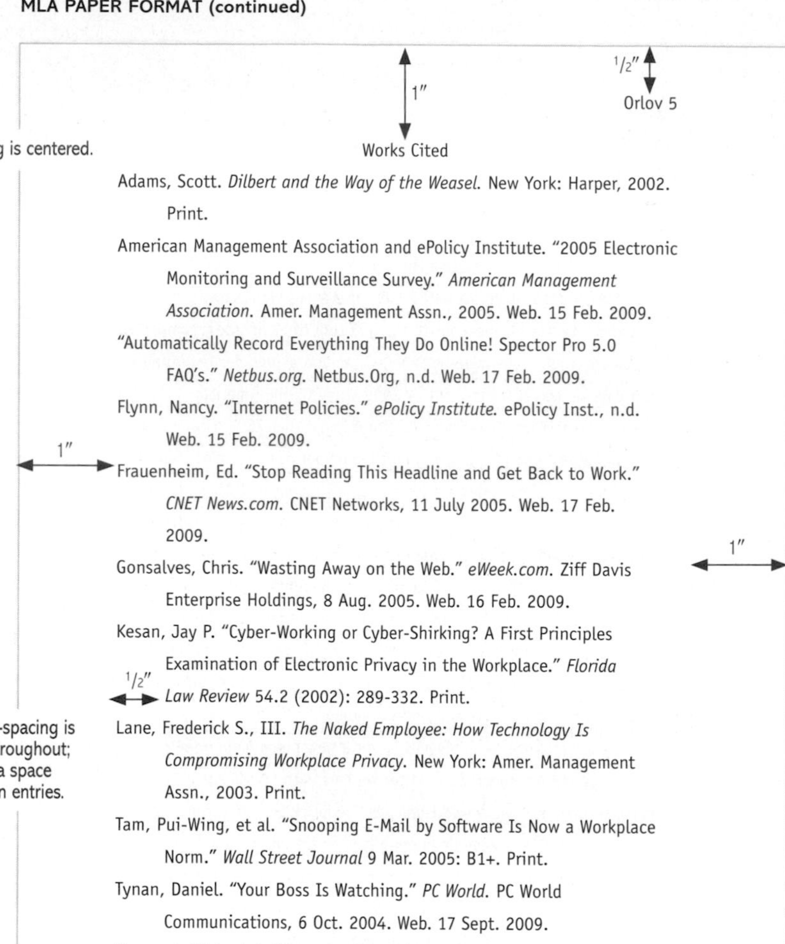
1/2"
1"
Orlov 5
Heading is centered.
Works Cited
Adams, Scott. *Dilbert and the Way of the Weasel.* New York: Harper, 2002. Print.
American Management Association and ePolicy Institute. "2005 Electronic Monitoring and Surveillance Survey." *American Management Association.* Amer. Management Assn., 2005. Web. 15 Feb. 2009.
"Automatically Record Everything They Do Online! Spector Pro 5.0 FAQ's." *Netbus.org.* Netbus.Org, n.d. Web. 17 Feb. 2009.
Flynn, Nancy. "Internet Policies." *ePolicy Institute.* ePolicy Inst., n.d. Web. 15 Feb. 2009.
1"
Frauenheim, Ed. "Stop Reading This Headline and Get Back to Work." *CNET News.com.* CNET Networks, 11 July 2005. Web. 17 Feb. 2009.
1"
Gonsalves, Chris. "Wasting Away on the Web." *eWeek.com.* Ziff Davis Enterprise Holdings, 8 Aug. 2005. Web. 16 Feb. 2009.
Kesan, Jay P. "Cyber-Working or Cyber-Shirking? A First Principles Examination of Electronic Privacy in the Workplace." *Florida Law Review* 54.2 (2002): 289-332. Print.
1/2"
Double-spacing is used throughout; no extra space between entries.
Lane, Frederick S., III. *The Naked Employee: How Technology Is Compromising Workplace Privacy.* New York: Amer. Management Assn., 2003. Print.
Tam, Pui-Wing, et al. "Snooping E-Mail by Software Is Now a Workplace Norm." *Wall Street Journal* 9 Mar. 2005: B1+. Print.
Tynan, Daniel. "Your Boss Is Watching." *PC World.* PC World Communications, 6 Oct. 2004. Web. 17 Sept. 2009.
Verespej, Michael A. "Inappropriate Internet Surfing." *Industry Week.* Penton Media, 7 Feb. 2000. Web. 16 Feb. 2009.

C5-f Use standard business formatting.

This section provides guidelines for preparing business letters, résumés, and memos.

BUSINESS LETTER IN FULL BLOCK STYLE

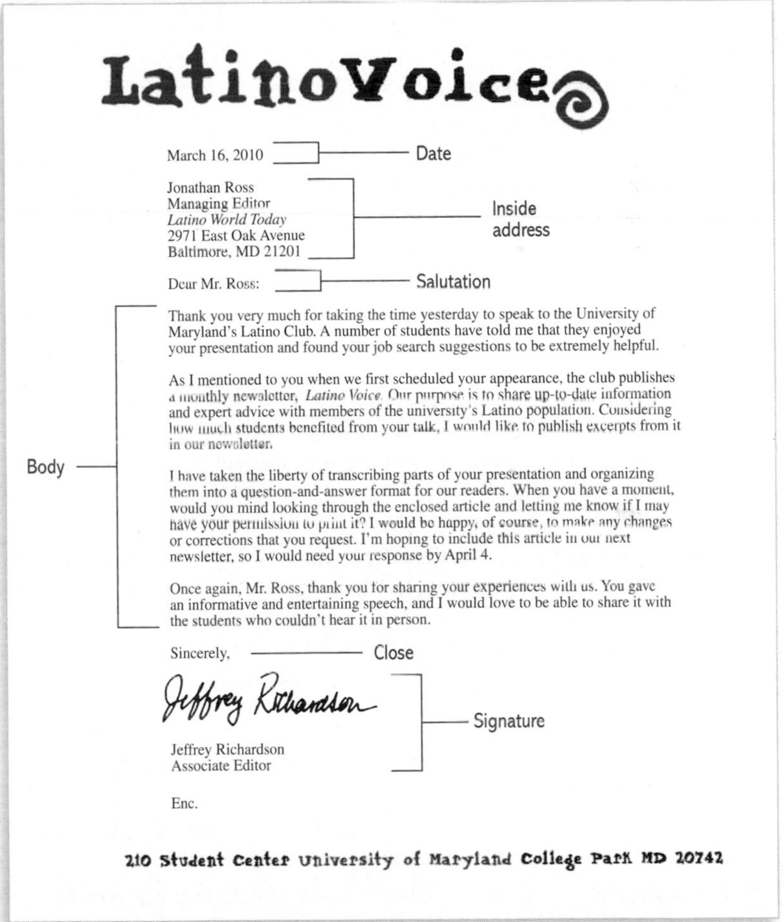

LatinoVoice

March 16, 2010

Jonathan Ross
Managing Editor
Latino World Today
2971 East Oak Avenue
Baltimore, MD 21201

Dear Mr. Ross:

Thank you very much for taking the time yesterday to speak to the University of Maryland's Latino Club. A number of students have told me that they enjoyed your presentation and found your job search suggestions to be extremely helpful.

As I mentioned to you when we first scheduled your appearance, the club publishes a monthly newsletter, *Latino Voice*. Our purpose is to share up-to-date information and expert advice with members of the university's Latino population. Considering how much students benefited from your talk, I would like to publish excerpts from it in our newsletter.

I have taken the liberty of transcribing parts of your presentation and organizing them into a question-and-answer format for our readers. When you have a moment, would you mind looking through the enclosed article and letting me know if I may have your permission to print it? I would be happy, of course, to make any changes or corrections that you request. I'm hoping to include this article in our next newsletter, so I would need your response by April 4.

Once again, Mr. Ross, thank you for sharing your experiences with us. You gave an informative and entertaining speech, and I would love to be able to share it with the students who couldn't hear it in person.

Sincerely,

Jeffrey Richardson

Jeffrey Richardson
Associate Editor

Enc.

210 Student Center University of Maryland College Park MD 20742

MODELS hackerhandbooks.com/writersref
> Model papers > Résumés and cover letters

Business letters

In writing a business letter, be direct, clear, and courteous. State your purpose or request at the beginning of the letter and include only relevant information in the body. By being as direct and concise as possible, you show that you value your reader's time.

For the format of the letter, use established business conventions. A sample business letter in full block style appears on page 57.

Résumés and cover letters

An effective résumé gives relevant information in a clear, concise form. You may be asked to produce a traditional résumé, a scannable résumé, or a Web résumé. The cover letter gives a prospective employer a reason to look at your résumé. The goal is to present yourself in a favorable light without including unnecessary details.

COVER LETTERS Always include a cover letter to introduce yourself, state the position you seek, and tell where you learned about it. The letter should also highlight past experiences that qualify you for the position and emphasize what you can do for the employer (not what the job will do for you). End the letter with a suggestion for a meeting, and tell your prospective employer when you will be available.

TRADITIONAL RÉSUMÉS Traditional résumés are produced on paper, and they are screened by people, not by computers. Because screeners often face stacks of applications, they may spend very little time looking at each résumé. Therefore, you need to make your résumé as reader-friendly as possible. Here are a few guidelines:

- Limit your résumé to one page if possible, two pages at most.
- Organize your information into clear categories—Education, Experience, and so on.
- Present the information in each category in reverse chronological order to highlight your most recent accomplishments.
- Use bulleted lists or some other simple, clear visual device to organize information.
- Use strong, active verbs to emphasize your accomplishments. For current activities, use present-tense verbs, such as *manage*; for past activities, use past-tense verbs, such as *managed*.

TRADITIONAL RÉSUMÉ

Jeffrey Richardson
121 Knox Road, #6
College Park, MD 20740
301-555-2651
jrichardson@example.net

OBJECTIVE	To obtain an editorial internship with a magazine
EDUCATION	
Fall 2007–present	University of Maryland • BA expected in June 2011 • Double major: English and Latin American studies • GPA: 3.7 (on a 4-point scale)
EXPERIENCE	
Fall 2009–present	Associate editor, *Latino Voice*, newsletter of Latino Club • Assign and edit feature articles • Coordinate community outreach
Fall 2008–present	Photo editor, *The Diamondback*, college paper • Shoot and organize photos for print and online publication • Oversee photo staff assignments; evaluate photos
Summer 2009	Intern, *The Globe,* Fairfax, Virginia • Wrote stories about local issues and personalities • Interviewed political candidates • Edited and proofread copy • Coedited "The Landscapes of Northern Virginia: A Photoessay"
Summers 2008, 2009	Tutor, Fairfax County ESL Program • Tutored Latino students in English as a Second Language • Trained new tutors
ACTIVITIES	Photographers' Workshop, Latino Club
PORTFOLIO	Available at http://jrichardson.example.net/jrportfolio.htm
REFERENCES	Available on request

SCANNABLE RÉSUMÉS Scannable résumés can be submitted on paper, by e-mail, or through an online employment service. The résumés are scanned and searched electronically, and a database matches keywords in the employer's job description with keywords in the résumés. A human screener then looks through the résumés selected by the database.

A scannable résumé must be formatted simply so that the scanner can accurately pick up its content. In general, follow these guidelines when preparing a scannable résumé:

- Include a Keywords section that lists words likely to be searched by a scanner. Use nouns, such as *manager*, not verbs, such as *manage*.
- Use standard résumé headings (for example, Education, Experience, References).
- Avoid special characters, graphics, or font styles.
- Avoid formatting such as tabs, indents, columns, or tables.

WEB RÉSUMÉS Posting your résumé on a Web site is an easy way to provide recent information about your employment goals and accomplishments. Most guidelines for traditional résumés apply to Web résumés. You may want to include a downloadable version of your résumé and link to an electronic portfolio. Always list the date that you last updated your résumé.

Memos

Usually brief and to the point, a memo reports information, makes a request, or recommends an action. The format of a memo, which varies from company to company, is designed for easy distribution, quick reading, and efficient filing.

Most memos display the date, the name of the recipient, the name of the sender, and the subject on separate lines at the top of the page. Many companies have preprinted forms for memos, and most word processing programs have memo templates.

The subject line of a memo should describe the topic as clearly and concisely as possible, and the introductory paragraph should get right to the point. In addition, the body of the memo should be well organized and easy to skim. To promote skimming, use headings where possible and set off any items that deserve special attention (in a list, for example, or in boldface).

E-mail

In business and academic contexts, you will want to show readers that you value their time. Your e-mail message may be just one of many that your readers have to wade through. Here are some strategies for writing effective e-mails:

- Use a meaningful, concise subject line to help readers sort through messages and set priorities.

BUSINESS MEMO

Commonwealth Press

MEMORANDUM

February 25, 2010

To: Editorial assistants, Advertising Department

cc: Stephen Chapman

From: Helen Brown

Subject: New database software

The new database software will be installed on your computers next week. I have scheduled a training program to help you become familiar with the software and with our new procedures for data entry and retrieval.

Training program

A member of our IT staff will teach in-house workshops on how to use the new software. If you try the software before the workshop, please be prepared to discuss any problems you encounter.

We will keep the training groups small to encourage hands-on participation and to provide individual attention. The workshops will take place in the training room on the third floor from 10:00 a.m. to 2:00 p.m.

Lunch will be provided in the cafeteria.

Sign-up

Please sign up by March 1 for one of the following dates by adding your name in the department's online calendar:

- Wednesday, March 3
- Friday, March 5
- Monday, March 8

If you will not be in the office on any of those dates, please let me know by March 1.

- Put the most important part of your message at the beginning so that your reader sees it without scrolling.
- For long, detailed messages, provide a summary at the beginning.
- Write concisely, and keep paragraphs fairly short.
- Avoid writing in all capital letters or all lowercase letters.
- Be sparing with boldface, italics, and special characters; not all e-mail systems handle such elements consistently.
- Proofread for typos and obvious errors that are likely to slow down readers.

You will also want to use e-mail responsibly by following conventions of good etiquette and not violating standards of academic integrity. Here are some strategies for writing responsible e-mails:

- Remember that your messages can easily be forwarded to others and reproduced. Do not write anything that you would not want attributed to you. And do not forward another person's message without asking his or her consent.
- If you write an e-mail message that includes someone else's words—opinions, statistics, song lyrics, and so forth—it's best to let your reader know where any borrowed material begins and ends and the source for that material.
- Remember to choose your words carefully and judiciously because e-mail messages can easily be misread. Without your voice, facial gestures, or body language, a message can be misunderstood. Pay careful attention to tone and avoid writing anything that you wouldn't be comfortable saying directly to a reader.

C6 Writing with technology

C6-a Use software tools wisely.

Grammar checkers, spell checkers, and autoformatting are software tools designed to help you avoid errors and save time. These tools can alert you to possible errors in words, sentence structures, or formatting. But they're not always right. If a program suggests or makes a change, be sure the change is one you really want to make. Familiarizing yourself with your software's settings can help you use these tools effectively.

Grammar checkers

Grammar checkers can help with some of the sentence-level problems in a typical draft. But they will often misdiagnose errors, especially because they cannot account for your intended meaning. When the grammar checker makes a suggestion for revision, you must decide whether the change is more effective than your original.

It's just as important to be aware of what your grammar checker isn't picking up on. If you count on your grammar checker to identify trouble spots, you might overlook problems with coordination and subordination (see S6), sentence variety (see S7), sexist language (see W4-e), and passive verbs (see W3-a), for example.

Spell checkers

Spell checkers flag words not found in their dictionaries; they will suggest a replacement for any word they don't recognize. They can help you spot many errors, but don't let them be your only proofreader. If you're writing about the health benefits of a Mediterranean diet, for example, don't let your software change *briam* (a vegetable dish) to *Brian*. Even if your spell checker identifies a real misspelling, the replacement word it suggests might carry a different connotation or even be nonsensical. After misspelling *probably*, you might end up with *portly*. Consider changes carefully before accepting them. If you're not sure what word or spelling you need, consult a dictionary, such as *Merriam-Webster's Collegiate Dictionary*. (See also W6-a.)

Because spell checkers flag only unrecognized words, they won't catch misused words, such as *accept* when you mean *except*. For help with commonly confused or misused words and with avoiding informal speech and jargon, consult the glossary of usage (W1).

Autoformatting

As you write, your software may attempt to save you effort with autoformatting. It might recognize that you've typed a URL and turn it into a link. Or if you're building a list, it might add numbering for you. Be aware of such changes and make sure they are appropriate for your paper and applied to the right text.

C6-b Manage your files.

Your instructor may ask you to complete assignments in stages, including notes, outlines, annotated bibliographies, rough drafts, and a final draft. Keeping track of all of these documents can be challenging. Be sure to give your files distinct names that reflect the appropriate stage of your writing process, and store them in a logical place.

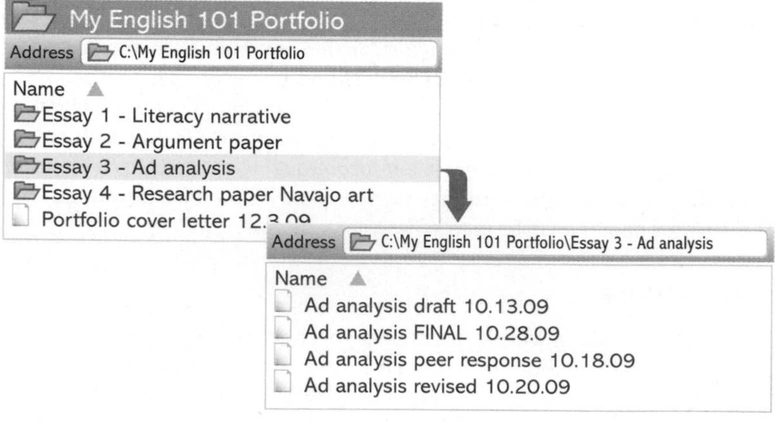

Writing online or in a word processing program can make writing and revising easier. You can undo changes or return to an earlier draft if a revision misfires. Applying the following steps can help you explore revision possibilities with little risk.

- Create folders and subfolders for each assignment. Save notes, outlines, and drafts together.
- Label revised drafts with different file names and dates.
- Print hard copies, make backup copies, and press the Save button early and often. Save work every five to ten minutes.
- Always record complete bibliographic information about sources, including images.
- Use a comment function to make notes to yourself or to respond to the drafts of peers.

A

Academic Writing

Academic Writing

A1 Writing about texts, 67

- **a** Reading actively: Annotating the text, 67
- **b** Sketching an outline, 71
- **c** Summarizing, 72
- **d** Analyzing, 74
- **e** Sample analysis paper, 74

A2 Constructing reasonable arguments, 78

- **a** Examining an issue's contexts, 79
- **b** Viewing the audience as a jury, 79
- **c** Establishing credibility; stating a position, 80
- **d** Backing up the thesis, 81
- **e** Supporting claims with evidence, 82
- **f** Countering opposing arguments, 85
- **g** Building common ground, 86
- **h** Sample argument paper, 86

A3 Evaluating arguments, 92

- **a** Distinguishing between reasonable and fallacious tactics, 92
- **b** Distinguishing between legitimate and unfair emotional appeals, 97
- **c** Judging how fairly a writer handles opposing views, 98

A4 Writing in the disciplines, 100

- **a** Finding commonalities, 100
- **b** Recognizing questions, 100
- **c** Understanding evidence, 102
- **d** Noting language conventions, 102
- **e** Using a discipline's citation style, 103
- **f** Understanding writing assignments, 104

When you write in college, you pose questions, explore ideas, and engage in scholarly debates and conversations. To join in those conversations, you will analyze and respond to texts, evaluate other people's arguments, and put forth your own ideas.

A1 Writing about texts

The word *texts* can refer to a variety of works, including essays, articles, government reports, books, Web sites, advertisements, and photographs. Most assignments that ask you to respond to a text call for a summary or an analysis or both.

A summary is neutral in tone and demonstrates that you have understood the author's key ideas. Assignments calling for an analysis of a text vary widely, but they usually ask you to look at how the text's parts contribute to its central argument or purpose, often with the aim of judging its evidence or overall effect.

When you write about a text, you will need to read it—or, in the case of a visual text, view it—several times to discover meaning. Two techniques will help you move beyond a superficial first reading: (1) annotating the text with your observations and questions and (2) outlining the text's key points. These techniques will help you analyze both written and visual texts.

Making the most of your handbook

Knowing the expectations for a writing assignment is a key first step in drafting.

▶ Understanding writing assignments: A4-f

A1-a Read actively: Annotate the text.

Read actively by jotting down your questions and thoughts in a notebook or in the margins of the text or visual. Use a pencil instead of a highlighter; with a pencil you can underline key concepts, mark points, or circle elements that intrigue you. If you change your mind, you can erase your early annotations and replace them with new ones. To annotate an electronic document, take notes in a separate file or use software features to highlight, underline, or insert comments.

Guidelines for active reading

Familiarize yourself with the basic features and structure of a text.

- What kind of text are you reading: An essay? An editorial? A scholarly article? An advertisement? A photograph? A Web site?
- What is the author's purpose: To inform? To persuade? To call to action?
- Who is the audience? How does the author appeal to the audience?
- What is the author's thesis? What question does the text attempt to answer?
- What evidence does the author provide to support the thesis?
- What key terms does the author define?

Note details that surprise, puzzle, or intrigue you.

- Has the author revealed a fact or made a point that counters your assumptions? Is anything surprising?
- Has the author made a generalization you disagree with? Can you think of evidence that would challenge the generalization?
- Do you see any contradictions or inconsistencies in the text?
- Does the text contain words, statements, or phrases that you don't understand? If so, what reference materials do you need to consult?

Read and reread to discover meaning.

- What do you notice on a second or third reading that you didn't notice earlier?
- Does the text raise questions that it does not resolve?
- If you could address the author directly, what questions would you pose? Where do you agree and disagree with the author? Why?

Apply additional critical thinking strategies to visual texts.

- What first strikes you about the visual text? What elements do you notice immediately?
- Who or what is the main subject of the visual text?
- What colors and textures dominate?
- What is in the background? In the foreground?
- What role, if any, do words or numbers play in the text?
- When was the visual created or the information collected?

On this page and on page 70 are an article from *CQ Researcher*, a newsletter about social and political issues, and an advertisement, both annotated by students. The students, Emilia Sanchez and Ren Yoshida, were assigned to analyze these texts. They began by reading actively.

ANNOTATED ARTICLE

Big Box Stores Are Bad for Main Street

BETSY TAYLOR

There is plenty of reason to be concerned about the proliferation of Wal-Marts and other so-called "big box" stores. The question, however, is not whether or not these types of stores create jobs (although several studies claim they produce a net job loss in local communities) or whether they ultimately save consumers money. The real concern about having a 25-acre slab of concrete with a 100,000 square foot box of stuff land on a town is whether it's good for a community's soul.

Opening strategy— the problem is not x, it's y.

Sentimental— what is a community's soul?

The worst thing about "big boxes" is that they have a tendency to produce Ross Perot's famous "big sucking sound"—sucking the life out of cities and small towns across the country. On the other hand, small businesses are great for a community. They offer more personal service; they won't threaten to pack up and leave town if they don't get tax breaks, free roads and other blandishments; and small-business owners are much more responsive to a customer's needs. (Ever try to complain about bad service or poor quality products to the president of Home Depot?)

Lumps all big boxes together.

Assumes all small businesses are attentive.

Logic problem? Why couldn't customer complain to store manager?

Yet, if big boxes are so bad, why are they so successful? One glaring reason is that we've become a nation of hyper-consumers, and the big-box boys know this. Downtown shopping districts comprised of small businesses take some of the efficiency out of overconsumption. There's all that hassle of having to travel from store to store, and having to pull out your credit card so many times. Occasionally, we even find ourselves chatting with the shopkeeper, wandering into a coffee shop to visit with a friend or otherwise wasting precious time that could be spent on acquiring more stuff.

True?

Taylor wishes for a time that is long gone or never was.

But let's face it—bustling, thriving city centers are fun. They breathe life into a community. They allow cities and towns to stand out from each other. They provide an atmosphere for people to interact with each other that just cannot be found at Target, or Wal-Mart or Home Depot.

Community vs. economy. What about prices?

Is it anti-American to be against having a retail giant set up shop in one's community? Some people would say so. On the other hand, if you board up Main Street, what's left of America?

Ends with emotional appeal.

ANNOTATED ADVERTISEMENT

What is being exchanged?

empowering
FARMERS

"Empowering"—why in an elegant font? Who is empowering farmers?

"Farmers" in all capital letters—shows strength?

Straightforward design and not much text.

Outstretched hands. Is she giving a gift? Inviting a partnership?

Raw coffee is red: earthy, natural, warm.

When you choose Equal Exchange fairly traded coffee, tea or chocolate, you join a network that empowers farmers in Latin America, Africa, and Asia to:

- **Stay on their land**
- **Care for the environment**
- **Farm organically**
- **Support their family**
- **Plan for the future**

www.equalexchange.coop

Photo: Jesus Choqueheranca de Quevero,
Coffee farmer & CEPICAFE Cooperative member, Peru

Positive verbs: consumers choose, join, empower; farmers stay, care, farm, support, plan.

Source: Equal Exchange.

A1-b Sketch a brief outline of the text.

After reading, rereading, and annotating a text, try to outline it. Seeing how the author has constructed a text can help you understand it. As you sketch an outline, pay special attention to the text's thesis (central idea) and its topic sentences. The thesis of a written text usually appears in the introduction, often in the first or second paragraph. Topic sentences can be found at the beginnings of most body paragraphs, where they announce a shift to a new topic. (See C2-a and C4-a.)

In your outline, put the author's thesis and key points in your own words. Here, for example, is the outline that Emilia Sanchez developed as she prepared to write her summary and analysis of the text on page 69. Notice that Sanchez's informal outline does not trace the author's ideas paragraph by paragraph; instead, it sums up the article's central points.

OUTLINE OF "BIG BOX STORES ARE BAD FOR MAIN STREET"

Thesis: Whether or not they take jobs away from a community or offer low prices to consumers, we should be worried about "big-box" stores like Wal-Mart, Target, and Home Depot because they harm communities by taking the life out of downtown shopping districts.

I. Small businesses are better for cities and towns than big box stores are.
   A. Small businesses offer personal service, but big-box stores do not.
   B. Small businesses don't make demands on community resources as big-box stores do.
   C. Small businesses respond to customer concerns, but big-box stores do not.

II. Big-box stores are successful because they cater to consumption at the expense of benefits to the community.
   A. Buying everything in one place is convenient.
   B. Shopping at small businesses may be inefficient, but it provides opportunities for socializing.
   C. Downtown shopping districts give each city or town a special identity.

Conclusion: Although some people say that it's anti-American to oppose big-box stores, actually these stores threaten the communities that make up America by encouraging buying at the expense of the traditional interactions of Main Street.

A visual often doesn't state an explicit thesis or an explicit line of reasoning. Instead, you must sometimes infer the meaning beneath the image's surface and interpret its central point and supporting ideas from the elements of its design. One way to outline a visual text is to try to define its purpose and sketch a list of its key elements. Here, for example, are the key features that Ren Yoshida identified for the advertisement printed on page 70.

OUTLINE OF EQUAL EXCHANGE ADVERTISEMENT

Purpose: To persuade readers that they can improve the lives of organic farmers and their families by purchasing Equal Exchange coffee.

Key features:

- The farmer's heart-shaped hands are outstretched, offering the viewer partnership and the product of her hard work.
- The coffee beans are surprisingly red, fruitlike, and fresh—natural and healthy looking.
- Words above and below the photograph describe the equal exchange between farmers and consumers.
- Consumer support leads to a higher quality of life for the farmers and for all people, since these farmers care for the environment and plan for the future.
- The simplicity of the design echoes the simplicity of the exchange. The consumer only has to buy a cup of coffee to make a difference.
- Equal Exchange is selling more than a product—coffee. It is selling the idea that together farmers and consumers hold the future of land, environment, farms, and family in their hands.

A1-c Summarize to demonstrate your understanding.

Your goal in summarizing a text is to state the work's main ideas and key points simply, briefly, and accurately in your own words. Writing a summary does not require you to judge the author's ideas. If you have sketched a brief outline of the text (see A1-b), refer to it as you draft your summary.

To summarize a written text, first find the author's central idea—the thesis. Then divide the whole piece into a few major and perhaps minor ideas. Since a summary

Making the most of your handbook

Summarizing is a key research skill.

- Summarizing without plagiarizing: R3-c
- Putting summaries and paraphrases in your own words: MLA-2c, APA-2c, CMS-2c

Guidelines for writing a summary

- In the first sentence, mention the title of the text, the name of the author, and the author's thesis or the visual's central point.
- Maintain a neutral tone; be objective.
- Use the third-person point of view and the present tense: *Taylor argues. . . .*
- Keep your focus on the text. Don't state the author's ideas as if they were your own.
- Put all or most of your summary in your own words; if you borrow a phrase or a sentence from the text, put it in quotation marks and give the page number in parentheses.
- Limit yourself to presenting the text's key points.
- Be concise; make every word count.

must be fairly short, you must make judgments about what is most important.

To summarize a visual text, begin with essential information such as who created the visual, who the intended audience is, where the visual appeared, and when it was created. Briefly explain the visual's main point or purpose and identify its key features (see p. 72).

Following is Emilia Sanchez's summary of the article that is printed on page 69.

> In her essay "Big Box Stores Are Bad for Main Street," Betsy Taylor argues that chain stores harm communities by taking the life out of downtown shopping districts. Explaining that a community's "soul" is more important than low prices or consumer convenience, she argues that small businesses are better than stores like Home Depot and Target because they emphasize personal interactions and don't place demands on a community's resources. Taylor asserts that big-box stores are successful because "we've become a nation of hyper-consumers" (1011), although the convenience of shopping in these stores comes at the expense of benefits to the community. She concludes by suggesting that it's not "anti-American" to oppose big-box stores because the damage they inflict on downtown shopping districts extends to America itself.
>
> —Emilia Sanchez, student

A1-d Analyze to demonstrate your critical thinking.

Whereas a summary most often answers the question of *what* a text says, an analysis looks at *how* a text makes its point.

Typically, an analysis takes the form of an essay that makes its own argument about a text. Include an introduction that briefly summarizes the text, a thesis that states your own judgment about the text, and body paragraphs that support your thesis with evidence. If you are analyzing a visual, examine it as a whole and then reflect on how the individual elements contribute to its overall meaning. If you have written a summary of the text or visual, you may find it useful to refer to the main points of the summary as you write your analysis.

Making the most of your handbook

When you analyze a text, you weave words and ideas from the source into your own writing.

- Guidelines for using quotation marks: R3-c
- Quoting or paraphrasing: MLA-2, APA-2, CMS-2
- Using signal phrases: MLA-3b, APA-3b, CMS-3b

Using interpretation in an analysis

Student writer Emilia Sanchez begins her essay about Betsy Taylor's article (see p. 69) by summarizing Taylor's argument. She then states her own thesis, or claim, which offers her judgment of Taylor's article, and begins her analysis. In her first body paragraph, Sanchez interprets Taylor's use of language.

Topic sentence includes Sanchez's claim.

Quoted material shows Taylor's language and is placed in quotation marks.

Transition to Sanchez's next point.

Taylor's use of colorful language reveals that she has a sentimental view of American society and does not understand economic realities. In her first paragraph, Taylor refers to a big-box store as a "25-acre slab of concrete with a 100,000 square foot box of stuff" that "land[s] on a town," evoking images of a powerful monster crushing the American way of life (1011). But she oversimplifies a complex issue. Taylor does not consider. . . .

Signal phrase introduces a quotation from the text.

Quotation is followed by Sanchez's interpretation of Taylor's language.

A1-e Sample student essay: Analysis of an article

Beginning on the next page is Emilia Sanchez's analysis of the article by Betsy Taylor (see p. 69). Sanchez used Modern Language Association (MLA) style to format her paper and cite the source.

MODELS **hackerhandbooks.com/bedhandbook**
> Model papers > MLA analysis papers: Sanchez; Lee; Lopez

Sanchez 1

Emilia Sanchez

Professor Goodwin

English 10

23 October 2009

Rethinking Big-Box Stores

In her essay "Big Box Stores Are Bad for Main Street," Betsy Taylor focuses not on the economic effects of large chain stores but on the effects these stores have on the "soul" of America. She argues that stores like Home Depot, Target, and Wal-Mart are bad for America because they draw people out of downtown shopping districts and cause them to focus on consumption. In contrast, she believes that small businesses are good for America because they provide personal attention, encourage community interaction, and make each city and town unique. But Taylor's argument is unconvincing because it is based on sentimentality—on idealized images of a quaint Main Street—rather than on the roles that businesses play in consumers' lives and communities. By ignoring the complex economic relationship between large chain stores and their communities, Taylor incorrectly assumes that simply getting rid of big-box stores would have a positive effect on America's communities.

Opening briefly summarizes the article's purpose and thesis.

Sanchez begins to analyze Taylor's argument.

Thesis expresses Sanchez's judgment of Taylor's article.

Taylor's use of colorful language reveals that she has a sentimental view of American society and does not understand economic realities. In her first paragraph, Taylor refers to a big-box store as a "25-acre slab of concrete with a 100,000 square foot box of stuff" that "land[s] on a town," evoking images of a powerful monster crushing the American way of life (1011). But she oversimplifies a complex issue. Taylor does not consider that many downtown business districts failed long before chain stores moved in, when factories and mills closed and workers lost their jobs. In cities with struggling economies, big-box stores can actually provide much-needed jobs. Similarly, while Taylor blames big-box stores for harming local economies by asking for tax breaks, free roads, and other perks, she doesn't acknowledge that these stores also enter into economic partnerships with the surrounding communities by offering financial benefits to schools and hospitals.

Signal phrase introduces quotations from the source; Sanchez uses an MLA in-text citation.

Sanchez begins to identify and challenge Taylor's assumptions.

Transition to another point in Sanchez's analysis.

Marginal annotations indicate MLA-style formatting and effective writing.

Sanchez 2

Clear topic sentence announces a shift to a new topic.

Taylor's assumption that shopping in small businesses is always better for the customer also seems driven by nostalgia for an old-fashioned Main Street rather than by the facts. While she may be right that many small businesses offer personal service and are responsive to customer complaints, she does not consider that many customers appreciate the service at big-box stores. Just as customer service is better at some small businesses than at others, it is impossible to generalize about service at all big-box stores. For example, customers depend on the lenient return policies and the wide variety of products at stores like Target and Home Depot.

Sanchez refutes Taylor's claim.

Taylor blames big-box stores for encouraging American "hyper-consumerism," but she oversimplifies by equating big-box stores with bad values and small businesses with good values. Like her other points, this claim ignores the economic and social realities of American society today. Big-box stores do not force Americans to buy more. By offering lower prices in a convenient setting, however, they allow consumers to save time and purchase goods they might not be able to afford from small businesses. The existence of more small businesses would not change what most Americans can afford, nor would it reduce their desire to buy affordable merchandise.

Sanchez treats the author fairly.

Conclusion returns to the thesis and shows the wider significance of Sanchez's analysis.

Taylor may be right that some big-box stores have a negative impact on communities and that small businesses offer certain advantages. But she ignores the economic conditions that support big-box stores as well as the fact that Main Street was in decline before the big-box store arrived. Getting rid of big-box stores will not bring back a simpler America populated by thriving, unique Main Streets; in reality, Main Street will not survive if consumers cannot afford to shop there.

Sanchez 3

Work Cited

Work cited page is in MLA style.

Taylor, Betsy. "Big Box Stores Are Bad for Main Street." *CQ Researcher* 9.44 (1999): 1011. Print.

Guidelines for analyzing a text

Written texts

Instructors who ask you to analyze an essay or an article often expect you to address some of the following questions.

- What is the author's thesis or central idea? Who is the audience?
- What questions (stated or unstated) does the author address?
- How does the author structure the text? What are the key parts, and how do they relate to one another and to the thesis?
- What strategies has the author used to generate interest in the argument and to persuade readers of its merit?
- What evidence does the author use to support the thesis? How persuasive is the evidence? (See A2-d and A2-e.)
- Does the author anticipate objections and counter opposing views? (See A2-f.)
- Does the author use any faulty reasoning? (See A3-a.)

Visual texts

If you are analyzing a visual text, the following additional questions will help you evaluate an image's purpose and meaning.

- What confuses, surprises, or intrigues you about the image?
- What is the source of the visual, and who created it? What is its purpose?
- What clues suggest the visual text's intended audience? How does the image appeal to its audience?
- If the text is an advertisement, what product is it selling? Does it attempt to sell an idea or a message as well?
- If the visual text includes words, how do the words contribute to the meaning?
- How do design elements—colors, shapes, perspective, background, foreground—help convey the visual text's meaning or serve its purpose?

A2 Constructing reasonable arguments

In writing an argument, you take a stand on a debatable issue. The question being debated might be a matter of public policy:

> Should religious groups be allowed to meet on public school property?
>
> What is the least dangerous way to dispose of hazardous waste?
>
> Should motorists be banned from texting while driving?
>
> Should a state limit the number of charter schools?

On such questions, reasonable people may disagree.

Reasonable men and women also disagree about many scholarly issues. Psychologists debate the role of genes and environment in determining behavior; historians interpret the causes of the Civil War quite differently; biologists challenge one another's predictions about the effects of global warming.

When you construct a *reasonable* argument, your goal is not simply to win or to have the last word. Your aim is to explain your understanding of the truth about a subject or to propose the best solution to

Academic English Some cultures value writers who argue with force; other cultures value writers who argue subtly or indirectly. Academic audiences in the United States will expect your writing to be assertive and confident—neither aggressive nor passive. You can create an assertive tone by acknowledging different positions and supporting your ideas with specific evidence.

TOO AGGRESSIVE	Of course only registered organ donors should be eligible for organ transplants. It's selfish and shortsighted to think otherwise.
TOO PASSIVE	I might be wrong, but I think that maybe people should have to register as organ donors if they want to be considered for a transplant.
ASSERTIVE	If only registered organ donors are eligible for transplants, more people will register as donors.

If you are uncertain about the tone of your work, ask for help at your school's writing center.

a problem—without being needlessly combative. In constructing your argument, you join a conversation with other writers and readers. Your aim is to convince readers to reconsider their positions by offering new reasons to question existing viewpoints.

A2-a Examine your issue's social and intellectual contexts.

Arguments appear in social and intellectual contexts. Public policy debates arise in social contexts and are conducted among groups with competing values and interests. For example, the debate over offshore oil drilling has been renewed in the United States in light of skyrocketing energy costs and terrorism concerns—with environmentalists, policymakers, oil company executives, and consumers all weighing in on the argument. Most public policy debates also have intellectual dimensions that address scientific or theoretical questions. In the case of the drilling issue, geologists, oceanographers, and economists all contribute their expertise.

Scholarly debates play out in intellectual contexts, but they have a social dimension as well. For example, scholars respond to the contributions of other specialists in the field, often building on others' views and refining them, but at times challenging them.

Because many of your readers will be aware of the social and intellectual contexts in which your issue is grounded, you will be at a disadvantage if you are not informed. That's why it is a good idea to conduct some research before preparing your argument; consulting even a few sources can deepen your understanding of the debates surrounding your topic. For example, the student whose paper appears on pages 87–91 became more knowledgeable about his issue—the shift from print to online news—after reading and annotating a few sources.

Making the most of your handbook

Supporting your claims with evidence from sources can strengthen your argument.

▶ Conducting research: R1

A2-b View your audience as a panel of jurors.

Do not assume that your audience already agrees with you; instead, envision skeptical readers who, like a panel of jurors, will make up their minds after listening to all sides of the argument. If you are arguing a public policy issue, aim your paper at readers who represent a variety of positions. In the case of the debate over offshore drilling, for example, imagine a jury that represents those who have a stake in the matter: environmentalists, policymakers, oil company executives, and consumers.

Making the most of your handbook

You may need to consider a specific audience for your argument.

▶ Writing in a particular discipline, such as business or psychology: A4

At times, you can deliberately narrow your audience. If you are working within a word limit, for example, you might not have the space in which to address all the concerns surrounding the offshore drilling debate. Or you might be primarily interested in reaching one segment of a general audience, such as consumers. In such instances, you can still view your audience as a panel of jurors; the jury will simply be a less diverse group.

In the case of scholarly debates, you will be addressing readers who share your interest in a discipline, such as literature or psychology. Such readers belong to a group with an agreed-upon way of investigating and talking about issues. Though they generally agree about disciplinary methods of asking questions and share specialized vocabulary, scholars in an academic discipline often disagree about particular issues. Once you see how they disagree about your issue, you should be able to imagine a jury that reflects the variety of positions they hold.

A2-c In your introduction, establish credibility and state your position.

When you are constructing an argument, make sure your introduction contains a thesis that states your position on the issue you have chosen to debate (see also C2-a). In the sentences leading up to the thesis, establish your credibility with readers by showing that you are knowledgeable and fair-minded. If possible, build common ground with readers who may not at first agree with your views and show them why they should consider your thesis.

Making the most of your handbook

When you write an argument, you state your position in a thesis.

▶ Writing effective thesis statements: C1-c, C2-a

In the following introduction, student Kevin Smith presents himself as someone worth listening to. Because Smith introduces both sides of the debate, readers are likely to approach his essay with an open mind.

Smith shows that he is familiar with the legal issues surrounding school prayer.

Although the Supreme Court has ruled against prayer in public schools on First Amendment grounds, many people still feel that prayer should be allowed. Such people value prayer as a practice central to their faith and believe that prayer is a way for schools to reinforce moral principles. They also compellingly point out a paradox in the First Amendment itself: at what point does the separation of church and state restrict the freedom of those who wish to practice their religion? What proponents of school prayer fail to realize, however, is that the Supreme Court's decision, although it was made on legal grounds, makes sense on religious grounds as well. Prayer is too important to be trusted to our public schools.

—Kevin Smith, student

Smith is fair-minded, presenting the views of both sides.

Smith's thesis builds common ground.

TIP: A good way to test a thesis while drafting and revising is to imagine a counterargument to your argument (see A2-f). If you can't think of an opposing point of view, rethink your thesis and ask a classmate or writing center tutor to respond to your argument.

A2-d Back up your thesis with persuasive lines of argument.

Arguments of any complexity contain lines of argument that, when taken together, might reasonably persuade readers that the thesis has merit. The following, for example, are the main lines of argument that Sam Jacobs used in his paper about the shift from print to online news (see pp. 87–91).

CENTRAL CLAIM	Thesis: The shift from print to online news provides unprecedented opportunities for readers to become more engaged with the news, to hold journalists accountable, and to participate as producers, not simply as consumers.
SUPPORTING CLAIMS	• Print news has traditionally had a one-sided relationship with its readers, delivering information for passive consumption.

(continued)

THE WRITING CENTER **hackerhandbooks.com/writersref**
> Resources for writers and tutors > Tips from writing tutors: Writing assignments; Writing essays in English

SUPPORTING CLAIMS (continued)

- Online news invites readers to participate in a collaborative process—to question and even contribute to the content.
- Links within news stories provide transparency, allowing readers to move easily from the main story to original sources, related articles, or background materials.
- Technology has made it possible for readers to become news producers—posting text, audio, images, and video of news events.
- Citizen journalists can provide valuable information, sometimes more quickly than traditional journalists can.

If you sum up your main lines of argument, as Jacobs did, you will have a rough outline of your essay. In your paper, you will provide evidence for each of your claims.

A2-e Support your claims with specific evidence.

You will need to support your central claim and any subordinate claims with evidence: facts, statistics, examples and illustrations, visuals, expert opinion, and so on. Most debatable topics require that you consult some written sources. As you read through the sources, you will learn more about the arguments and counterarguments at the center of your debate.

Remember that you must document your sources. Documentation gives credit to the authors and shows readers how to locate a source in case they want to assess its credibility or explore the issues further.

Making the most of your handbook

Sources, when used responsibly, can provide evidence to support an argument.

- ▶ Paraphrasing, summarizing, and quoting sources: R3-c
- ▶ Punctuating direct quotations: P5-a
- ▶ Citing sources: MLA-2, APA-2, CMS-2

Using facts and statistics

A fact is something that is known with certainty because it has been objectively verified: The capital of Wyoming is Cheyenne. Carbon has an atomic weight of 12. John F. Kennedy was assassinated on

November 22, 1963. Statistics are collections of numerical facts: Alcohol abuse is a factor in nearly 40 percent of traffic fatalities. More than four in ten businesses in the United States are owned by women.

Most arguments are supported at least to some extent by facts and statistics. For example, in the following passage the writer uses statistics to show that college students are granted unreasonably high credit limits.

> A 2009 study by Sallie Mae revealed that undergraduates are carrying record-high credit card balances and are relying on credit cards more than ever, especially in the economic downturn. The average credit card debt per college undergraduate is $3,173, and 82 percent of undergraduates carry balances and incur finance charges each month (Sallie Mae).

Writers often use statistics in selective ways to bolster their own positions. If you suspect that a writer's handling of statistics is not quite fair, track down the original sources for those statistics or read authors with opposing views, who may give you a fuller understanding of the numbers.

Using examples and illustrations

Examples and illustrations (extended examples, often in story form) rarely prove a point by themselves, but when used in combination with other forms of evidence they flesh out an argument with details and specific instances and bring it to life. Because examples are often concrete and sometimes vivid, they can reach readers in ways that statistics and abstract ideas cannot.

In a paper arguing that online news provides opportunities for readers that print news does not, Sam Jacobs describes how regular citizens armed with only cell phones and laptops helped save lives during Hurricane Katrina by relaying critical news updates.

Using visuals

Visuals—charts, graphs, diagrams, photographs—can support your argument by providing vivid and detailed evidence and by capturing your readers' attention. Bar or line graphs, for instance, describe and organize complex statistical data; photographs can immediately and evocatively convey abstract ideas. Writers in almost every academic field use visual evidence to support their arguments or to counter opposing arguments. For example, to explain a conflict among Southeast Asian countries, a historian might choose a map to illustrate the geographical situation and highlight particular issues. Or to refute another scholar's hypothesis about the dangers of a vegetarian diet, a nutritionist might support her claims by using a table to organize and highlight detailed numerical information. (See C5-d.)

As you consider using visual evidence, ask yourself the following questions:

- Is the visual accurate, credible, and relevant?
- How will the visual appeal to readers? Logically? Ethically? Emotionally?
- How will the visual evidence function? Will it provide background information? Present complex numerical information or an abstract idea? Lend authority? Anticipate or refute counterarguments?

Making the most of your handbook

Integrating visuals can strengthen your writing.

▶ Choosing appropriate visuals: **page 50**
▶ Placing and labeling visuals: **page 51**
▶ Using visuals responsibly: **page 54**

Like all forms of evidence, visuals don't speak for themselves; you'll need to analyze and interpret the evidence to show readers how the visuals inform and support your argument.

Citing expert opinion

Although they are no substitute for careful reasoning of your own, the views of an expert can contribute to the force of your argument. For example, to help him make the case that print journalism has a one-sided relationship with its readers, Sam Jacobs integrates an expert's key description:

> With the rise of the Internet, however, this one-sided relationship has been criticized by journalists such as Dan Gillmor, founder of the Center for Citizen Media, who argues that traditional print journalism treats "news as a lecture," whereas online news is "more of a conversation" (xxiv).

When you rely on expert opinion, make sure that your source is an expert in the field you are writing about. In some cases, you may need to provide credentials showing why your source is worth listening to. When including expert testimony in your paper, you can summarize or paraphrase the expert's opinion or you can quote the expert's exact words. You will of course need to document the source, as Jacobs did in the example just given.

Anticipating and countering opposing arguments

To anticipate a possible objection to your argument, consider the following questions:

- Could a reasonable person draw a different conclusion from your facts or examples?
- Might a reader question any of your assumptions?
- Could a reader offer an alternative explanation of this issue?
- Is there any evidence that might weaken your position?

The following questions may help you respond to a reader's potential objection:

- Can you concede the point to the opposition but challenge the point's importance or usefulness?
- Can you explain why readers should consider a new perspective or question a piece of evidence?
- Should you explain how your position responds to contradictory evidence?
- Can you suggest a different interpretation of the evidence?

When you write, use phrasing to signal to readers that you're about to present an objection. Often the signal phrase can go in the lead sentence of a paragraph:

Critics of this view argue that. . . .
Some readers might point out that. . . .
Researchers challenge these claims by. . . .

A2-f Anticipate objections; counter opposing arguments.

Readers who already agree with you need no convincing, but indifferent or skeptical readers may resist your arguments. To be willing to give up a position that seems reasonable, a reader has to see that there is an even more reasonable one. In addition to presenting your own case, therefore, you should consider the opposing arguments and attempt to counter them.

It might seem at first that drawing attention to an opposing point of view or contradictory evidence would weaken your argument. But by anticipating and countering objections, you show yourself as a reasonable and well-informed writer. You also establish your purpose, demonstrate the significance of the issue you are debating, and ultimately strengthen your argument.

There is no best place in an essay to deal with opposing views. Often it is useful to summarize the opposing position early in your essay. After stating your thesis but before developing your own arguments, you might have a paragraph that addresses the most important counterargument. Or you can anticipate objections paragraph by paragraph as you develop your case. Wherever you decide to address opposing arguments, you will enhance your credibility if you explain the arguments of others accurately and fairly.

A2-g Build common ground.

As you counter opposing arguments, try to seek out one or two assumptions you might share with readers who do not initially agree with your views. If you can show that you share their concerns, your readers may be more likely to acknowledge the validity of your argument. For example, to persuade people opposed to controlling the deer population with a regulated hunting season, a state wildlife commission would have to show that it too cares about preserving deer and does not want them to die needlessly. Having established these values in common, the commission might be able to persuade critics that reducing the total number of deer prevents starvation caused by overpopulation.

People believe that intelligence and decency support their side of an argument. To be persuaded, they must see these qualities in your argument. Otherwise they will persist in their opposition.

A2-h Sample argument paper

In the paper that begins on the next page, student Sam Jacobs argues that the shift from print to online news benefits readers by providing them with opportunities to become more engaged with the news, to hold journalists accountable, and to participate as producers, not simply as consumers. Notice that he is careful to present opposing views fairly before providing his counterarguments.

In writing the paper, Jacobs consulted both print and online sources. When he quotes or uses information from a source, he cites the source with an MLA (Modern Language Association) in-text citation. Citations in the paper refer readers to the list of works cited at the end of the paper. (For more details about citing sources, see MLA-4.)

MODELS **hackerhandbooks.com/writersref**

> Model papers > MLA argument papers: Jacobs; Hammond; Lund; Sanghvi

> MLA papers: Orlov; Daly; Levi

Jacobs 1

Sam Jacobs

Professor Alperini

English 101

March 19, 2010

From Lecture to Conversation: Redefining What's "Fit to Print"

"All the news that's fit to print," the motto of the *New York Times* since 1896, plays with the word *fit*, asserting that a news story must be newsworthy and must not exceed the limits of the printed page. The increase in online news consumption, however, challenges both meanings of the word *fit*, allowing producers and consumers alike to rethink who decides which topics are worth covering and how extensive that coverage should be. Any cultural shift usually means that something is lost, but in this case there are clear gains. The shift from print to online news provides unprecedented opportunities for readers to become more engaged with the news, to hold journalists accountable, and to participate as producers, not simply as consumers.

Jacobs provides background in opening sentences for his thesis.

Thesis states the main point.

Guided by journalism's code of ethics—accuracy, objectivity, and fairness—print news reporters have gathered and delivered stories according to what editors decide is fit for their readers. Except for op-ed pages and letters to the editor, print news has traditionally had a one-sided relationship with its readers. The print news media's reputation for objective reporting has been held up as "a stop sign" for readers, sending a clear message that no further inquiry is necessary (Weinberger). With the rise of the Internet, however, this model has been criticized by journalists such as Dan Gillmor, founder of the Center for Citizen Media, who argues that traditional print journalism treats "news as a lecture," whereas online news is "more of a conversation" (xxiv). Print news arrives on the doorstep every morning as a fully formed lecture, a product created without participation from its readership. By contrast, online news invites readers to participate in a collaborative process—to question and even help produce the content.

Jacobs does not need a citation for common knowledge.

One of the most important advantages online news offers over print news is the presence of built-in hyperlinks, which carry readers from one electronic document to another. If readers are curious about the definition of a term, the roots of a story, or other perspectives on a topic, links provide a path. Links help readers become more critical consumers of

Transition moves from Jacobs's main argument to specific examples.

Marginal annotations indicate MLA-style formatting and effective writing.

information by engaging them in a totally new way. For instance, the link embedded in the story "Window into Fed Debate over a Crucial Program" (Healy) allows readers to find out more about the trends in consumer spending and to check the journalist's handling of an original source (see Fig. 1). This kind of link gives readers the opportunity to conduct their own evaluation of the evidence and verify the journalist's claims.

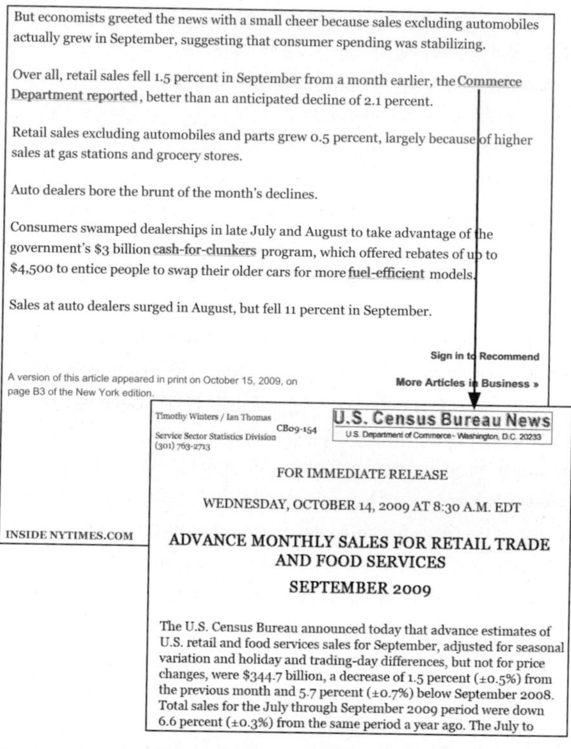

But economists greeted the news with a small cheer because sales excluding automobiles actually grew in September, suggesting that consumer spending was stabilizing.

Over all, retail sales fell 1.5 percent in September from a month earlier, the Commerce Department reported, better than an anticipated decline of 2.1 percent.

Retail sales excluding automobiles and parts grew 0.5 percent, largely because of higher sales at gas stations and grocery stores.

Auto dealers bore the brunt of the month's declines.

Consumers swamped dealerships in late July and August to take advantage of the government's $3 billion cash-for-clunkers program, which offered rebates of up to $4,500 to entice people to swap their older cars for more fuel-efficient models.

Sales at auto dealers surged in August, but fell 11 percent in September.

Sign in to Recommend

A version of this article appeared in print on October 15, 2009, on page B3 of the New York edition.

More Articles in Business »

INSIDE NYTIMES.COM

Timothy Winters / Ian Thomas
Service Sector Statistics Division
(301) 763-2713

CB09-154

U.S. Census Bureau News
U.S. Department of Commerce • Washington, D.C. 20233

FOR IMMEDIATE RELEASE

WEDNESDAY, OCTOBER 14, 2009 AT 8:30 A.M. EDT

ADVANCE MONTHLY SALES FOR RETAIL TRADE AND FOOD SERVICES

SEPTEMBER 2009

The U.S. Census Bureau announced today that advance estimates of U.S. retail and food services sales for September, adjusted for seasonal variation and holiday and trading-day differences, but not for price changes, were $344.7 billion, a decrease of 1.5 percent (±0.5%) from the previous month and 5.7 percent (±0.7%) below September 2008. Total sales for the July through September 2009 period were down 6.6 percent (±0.3%) from the same period a year ago. The July to

Fig. 1. Links embedded in online news articles allow readers to move from the main story to original sources, related articles, or background materials. The link in this online article (Healy) points to a government report, the original source of the author's data on consumer spending.

Jacobs 3

Links provide a kind of transparency impossible in print because they allow readers to see through online news to the "sources, disagreements, and the personal assumptions and values" that may have influenced a news story (Weinberger). The International Center for Media and the Public Agenda underscores the importance of news organizations letting "customers in on the often tightly held little secrets of journalism." To do so, they suggest, will lead to "accountability and accountability leads to credibility" ("Openness"). These tools alone don't guarantee that news producers will be responsible and trustworthy, but they encourage an open and transparent environment that benefits news consumers.

Jacobs clarifies key terms (*transparency* and *accountability*).

Source is cited in MLA style.

Not only has technology allowed readers to become more critical news consumers, but it also has helped some to become news producers. The Web gives ordinary people the power to report on the day's events. Anyone with an Internet connection can publish on blogs and Web sites, engage in online discussion forums, and contribute video and audio recordings. Citizen journalists with laptops, cell phones, and digital camcorders have become news producers alongside large news organizations.

Jacobs develops the thesis.

Not everyone embraces the spread of unregulated news reporting online. Critics point out that citizen journalists are not necessarily trained to be fair or ethical, for example, nor are they subject to editorial oversight. Acknowledging that citizen reporting is more immediate and experimental, critics also question its accuracy and accountability: "While it has its place . . . it really isn't journalism at all, and it opens up information flow to the strong probability of fraud and abuse. . . . Information without journalistic standards is called gossip," writes David Hazinski in the *Atlanta Journal-Constitution* (23A). In his book *Losing the News*, media specialist Alex S. Jones argues that what passes for news today is in fact "pseudo news" and is "far less reliable" than traditional print news (27). Even a supporter like Gillmor is willing to agree that citizen journalists are "nonexperts," but he argues that they are "using technology to make a profound contribution, and a real difference" (140).

Opposing views are presented fairly.

Jacobs counters opposing arguments.

Citizen reporting made a difference in the wake of Hurricane Katrina in 2005. Armed with cell phones and laptops, regular citizens relayed critical news updates in a rapidly developing crisis, often before traditional journalists were even on the scene. In 2006, the enormous contributions of

A vivid example helps Jacobs make his point.

Jacobs 4

Jacobs uses specific evidence for support.

citizen journalists were recognized when the New Orleans *Times-Picayune* received the Pulitzer Prize in public service for its online coverage—largely citizen-generated—of Hurricane Katrina. In recognizing the paper's "meritorious public service," the Pulitzer Prize board credited the newspaper's blog for "heroic, multi-faceted coverage of [the storm] and its aftermath" ("2006 Pulitzer"). Writing for the *Online Journalism Review*, Mark Glaser emphasizes the role that blog updates played in saving storm victims' lives. Further, he calls the *Times-Picayune*'s partnership with citizen journalists a "watershed for online journalism."

Conclusion echoes the thesis without dully repeating it.

The Internet has enabled consumers to participate in a new way in reading, questioning, interpreting, and reporting the news. Decisions about appropriate content and coverage are no longer exclusively in the hands of news editors. Ordinary citizens now have a meaningful voice in the conversation—a hand in deciding what's "fit to print." Some skeptics worry about the apparent free-for-all and loss of tradition. But the expanding definition of news provides opportunities for consumers to be more engaged with events in their communities, their nations, and the world.

Jacobs 5

Works Cited

Gillmor, Dan. *We the Media: Grassroots Journalism by the People, for the People*. Sebastopol: O'Reilly, 2006. Print.

Glaser, Mark. "NOLA.com Blogs and Forums Help Save Lives after Katrina." *OJR: The Online Journalism Review*. Knight Digital Media Center, 13 Sept. 2005. Web. 2 Mar. 2010.

Hazinski, David. "Unfettered 'Citizen Journalism' Too Risky." *Atlanta Journal-Constitution* 13 Dec. 2007: 23A. *General OneFile*. Web. 2 Mar. 2010.

Healy, Jack. "Window into Fed Debate over a Crucial Program." *New York Times*. New York Times, 14 Oct. 2009. Web. 4 Mar. 2010.

Jones, Alex S. *Losing the News: The Future of the News That Feeds Democracy*. New York: Oxford UP, 2009. Print.

"Openness and Accountability: A Study of Transparency in Global Media Outlets." *ICMPA: International Center for Media and the Public Agenda*. Intl. Center for Media and the Public Agenda, 2006. Web. 26 Feb. 2010.

"The 2006 Pulitzer Prize Winners: Public Service." *The Pulitzer Prizes*. Columbia U, n.d. Web. 2 Mar. 2010.

Weinberger, David. "Transparency Is the New Objectivity." *Joho the Blog*. David Weinberger, 19 July 2009. Web. 26 Feb. 2010.

Works cited page uses MLA style.

List is alphabetized by authors' last names (or by title when a work has no author).

Abbreviation "n.d." indicates that the online source has no update date.

A3 Evaluating arguments

In your reading and in your own writing, evaluate all arguments for logic and fairness. Many arguments can stand up to critical scrutiny. Sometimes, however, a line of argument that at first seems reasonable turns out to be illogical, unfair, or both.

A3-a Distinguish between reasonable and fallacious argumentative tactics.

A number of unreasonable argumentative tactics are known as *logical fallacies*. Most of the fallacies—such as hasty generalizations and false analogies—are misguided or dishonest uses of legitimate argumentative strategies. The examples in this section suggest when such strategies are reasonable and when they are not.

Generalizing (inductive reasoning)

Writers and thinkers generalize all the time. We look at a sample of data and conclude that data we have not observed will most likely conform to what we have seen. From a spoonful of soup, we conclude just how salty the whole bowl will be. After numerous unpleasant experiences with an airline, we decide to book future flights with a competitor.

When we draw a conclusion from an array of facts, we are engaged in inductive reasoning. Such reasoning deals in probability, not certainty. For a conclusion to be highly probable, it must be based on evidence that is sufficient, representative, and relevant. (See the chart on p. 94.)

The fallacy known as *hasty generalization* is a conclusion based on insufficient or unrepresentative evidence.

HASTY GENERALIZATION

> In a single year, scores on standardized tests in California's public schools rose by ten points. Therefore, more children than ever are succeeding in America's public school systems.

Data from one state do not justify a conclusion about the whole United States.

A *stereotype* is a hasty generalization about a group. Here are a few examples.

STEREOTYPES

Women are bad bosses.

All politicians are corrupt.

Athletes are never strong students.

Stereotyping is common because of our tendency to perceive selectively. We tend to see what we want to see; we notice evidence confirming our already formed opinions and fail to notice evidence to the contrary. For example, if you have concluded that all politicians are corrupt, this stereotype will be confirmed by news reports of legislators being indicted—even though every day the media describe conscientious officials serving the public honestly and well.

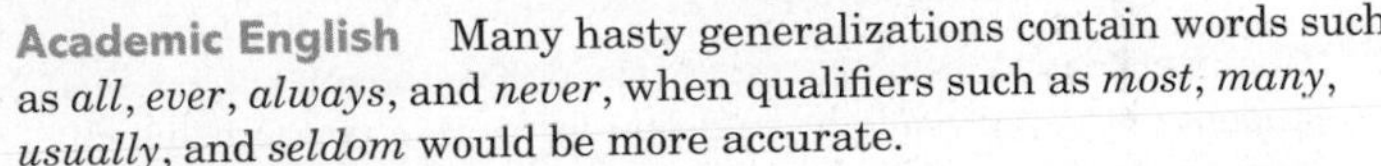

Academic English Many hasty generalizations contain words such as *all*, *ever*, *always*, and *never*, when qualifiers such as *most*, *many*, *usually*, and *seldom* would be more accurate.

Drawing analogies

An analogy points out a similarity between two things that are otherwise different. Analogies can be an effective means of arguing a point. Our system of judicial decision making, or case law, which relies heavily on previous decisions, makes extensive use of reasoning by analogy. One lawyer may point out, for example, that specific facts or circumstances resemble those from a previous case and will thus argue for a similar result or decision. In response, the opposing lawyer may maintain that such facts or circumstances bear only a superficial resemblance to those in the previous case and that in legally relevant respects they are quite different and thus require a different result or decision.

It is not always easy to draw the line between a reasonable and an unreasonable analogy. At times, however, an analogy is clearly off base, in which case it is called a *false analogy*.

FALSE ANALOGY

If we can send a spacecraft to Pluto, we should be able to find a cure for the common cold.

The writer has falsely assumed that because two things are alike in one respect, they must be alike in others. Exploring the outer reaches of the solar system and finding a cure for the common cold are both scientific challenges, but the problems confronting medical researchers are quite different from those solved by space scientists.

Testing inductive reasoning

Though inductive reasoning leads to probable and not absolute truth, you can assess a conclusion's likely probability by asking three questions. This chart shows how to apply those questions to a sample conclusion based on a survey.

CONCLUSION The majority of students on our campus would volunteer at least five hours a week in a community organization if the school provided a placement service for volunteers.

EVIDENCE In a recent survey, 723 of 1,215 students questioned said they would volunteer at least five hours a week in a community organization if the school provided a placement service for volunteers.

1. Is the evidence sufficient?

   That depends. On a small campus (say, 3,000 students), the pool of students surveyed would be sufficient for market research, but on a large campus (say, 30,000), 1,215 students are only 4 percent of the population. If that 4 percent were known to be truly representative of the other 96 percent, however, even such a small sample would be sufficient (see question 2).

2. Is the evidence representative?

   The evidence is representative if those responding to the survey reflect the characteristics of the entire student population: age, sex, race, field of study, overall number of extracurricular commitments, and so on. If most of those surveyed are majors in a field like social work, however, the researchers would be wise to question the survey's conclusion.

3. Is the evidence relevant?

   Yes. The results of the survey are directly linked to the conclusion. Evidence based on a survey about the number of hours students work for pay, by contrast, would not be relevant because it would not be about *choosing to volunteer*.

Tracing causes and effects

Demonstrating a connection between causes and effects is rarely simple. For example, to explain why a chemistry course has a high failure rate, you would begin by listing possible causes: inadequate preparation of students, poor teaching, lack of qualified tutors, and so on. Next you would investigate each possible cause. Only after investigating the possible causes would you be able to weigh the relative impact of each cause and suggest appropriate remedies.

Because cause-and-effect reasoning is so complex, it is not surprising that writers frequently oversimplify it. In particular, writers sometimes assume that because one event follows another, the first is the cause of the second. This common fallacy is known as *post hoc*, from the Latin *post hoc, ergo propter hoc*, meaning "after this, therefore because of this."

POST HOC FALLACY

Since Governor Cho took office, unemployment of minorities in the state has decreased by 7 percent. Governor Cho should be applauded for reducing unemployment among minorities.

The writer must show that Governor Cho's policies are responsible for the decrease in unemployment; it is not enough to show that the decrease followed the governor's taking office.

Weighing options

Especially when reasoning about problems and solutions, writers must weigh options. To be fair, a writer should mention the full range of options, showing why one is superior to the others or might work well in combination with others.

It is unfair to suggest that there are only two alternatives when in fact there are more. When writers set up a false choice between their preferred option and one that is clearly unsatisfactory, they create an *either . . . or* fallacy.

***EITHER . . . OR* FALLACY**

Our current war against drugs has not worked. Either we should legalize drugs or we should turn the drug war over to our armed forces and let them fight it.

Clearly there are other options, such as increased funding for drug abuse prevention and treatment.

Making assumptions

An assumption is a claim that is taken to be true—without the need of proof. Most arguments are based to some extent on assumptions, since writers rarely have the time and space to prove all the conceivable claims on which an argument is based. For example, someone arguing about the best means of limiting population growth in developing countries might well assume that the goal of limiting population growth is worthwhile. For most audiences, there would be no need to articulate this assumption or to defend it.

There is a danger, however, in failing to spell out and prove a claim that is clearly controversial. Consider the following short argument, in which a key claim is missing.

ARGUMENT WITH MISSING CLAIM

Violent crime is increasing. Therefore, we should vigorously enforce the death penalty.

The writer seems to be assuming that the death penalty deters violent criminals—and that most audiences will agree. The writer also assumes that the death penalty is a fair punishment for violent crimes. These are not safe assumptions; the writer will need to state and support both claims.

When a missing claim is an assertion that few would agree with, we say that a writer is guilty of a *non sequitur* (Latin for "it does not follow").

NON SEQUITUR

Leah loves good food; therefore, she will be an excellent chef.

Few people would agree with the missing claim—that lovers of good food always make excellent chefs.

Deducing conclusions (deductive reasoning)

When we deduce a conclusion, we—like Sherlock Holmes—put things together. We establish that a general principle is true, that a specific case is an example of that principle, and that therefore a particular conclusion about that case is a certainty. In real life, such absolute reasoning rarely happens. Approximations of it, however, sometimes occur.

Deductive reasoning can often be structured in a three-step argument called a *syllogism*. The three steps are the major premise, the minor premise, and the conclusion.

1. Anything that increases radiation in the environment is dangerous to public health. (Major premise)
2. Nuclear reactors increase radiation in the environment. (Minor premise)
3. Therefore, nuclear reactors are dangerous to public health. (Conclusion)

The major premise is a generalization. The minor premise is a specific case. The conclusion follows from applying the generalization to the specific case.

Deductive arguments break down if one of the premises is not true or if the conclusion does not logically follow from the premises. In the following argument, the major premise is very likely untrue.

UNTRUE PREMISE

The police do not give speeding tickets to people driving less than five miles per hour over the limit. Dominic is driving fifty-nine miles per hour in a fifty-five-mile-per-hour zone. Therefore, the police will not give Dominic a speeding ticket.

The conclusion is true only if the premises are true. If the police sometimes give speeding tickets for driving less than five miles per hour over the limit, Dominic cannot safely conclude that he will avoid a ticket.

In the following argument, both premises might be true, but the conclusion does not follow logically from them.

CONCLUSION DOES NOT FOLLOW

All members of our club ran in this year's Boston Marathon. Jay ran in this year's Boston Marathon. Therefore, Jay is a member of our club.

The fact that Jay ran the marathon is no guarantee that he is a member of the club. Presumably, many marathon runners are nonmembers.

Assuming that both premises are true, the following argument holds up.

CONCLUSION FOLLOWS

All members of our club ran in this year's Boston Marathon. Jay is a member of our club. Therefore, Jay ran in this year's Boston Marathon.

A3-b Distinguish between legitimate and unfair emotional appeals.

There is nothing wrong with appealing to readers' emotions. After all, many issues worth arguing about have an emotional as well as a logical dimension. Even the Greek logician Aristotle lists *pathos* (emotion) as a legitimate argumentative tactic. For example, in an essay criticizing big-box stores, writer Betsy Taylor has a good reason for tugging at readers' emotions: Her subject is the decline of city and town life. In her conclusion, Taylor appeals to readers' emotions by invoking their national pride.

LEGITIMATE EMOTIONAL APPEAL

Is it anti-American to be against having a retail giant set up shop in one's community? Some people would say so. On the other hand, if you board up Main Street, what's left of America?

As we all know, however, emotional appeals are frequently misused. Many of the arguments we see in the media, for instance, strive to win our sympathy rather than our intelligent agreement. A TV commercial suggesting that you will be thin and sexy if you drink a certain diet beverage is making a pitch to emotions. So is a political speech that recommends electing a candidate because he is a devoted husband and father who serves as a volunteer firefighter.

The following passage illustrates several types of unfair emotional appeals.

UNFAIR EMOTIONAL APPEALS

This progressive proposal to build a ski resort in the state park has been carefully researched by Western Trust, the largest bank in the state; furthermore, it is favored by a majority of the local merchants. The only opposition comes from narrow-minded, hippie environmentalists who care more about trees than they do about people; one of their leaders was actually arrested for disturbing the peace several years ago.

Words with strong positive or negative connotations, such as *progressive* and *hippie,* are examples of *biased language*. Attacking the people who hold a belief (environmentalists) rather than refuting their argument is called *ad hominem*, a Latin term meaning "to the man." Associating a prestigious name (Western Trust) with the writer's side is called *transfer*. Claiming that an idea should be accepted because a large number of people (the majority of merchants) are in favor is called the *bandwagon appeal*. Bringing in irrelevant issues (the arrest) is a *red herring*, named after a trick used in fox hunts to mislead the dogs by dragging a smelly fish across the trail.

A3-c Judge how fairly a writer handles opposing views.

The way in which a writer deals with opposing views is revealing. Some writers address the arguments of the opposition fairly, conceding points when necessary and countering others, all in a civil spirit. Other writers will do almost anything to win an argument: either ignoring opposing views altogether or misrepresenting such views and attacking their proponents.

In your own writing, you build credibility by addressing opposing arguments fairly. (See also A2-f.) In your reading, you can assess the credibility of your sources by looking at how they deal with views not in agreement with their own.

Describing the views of others

Writers and politicians often deliberately misrepresent the views of others. One way they do this is by setting up a "straw man," a character so weak that he is easily knocked down. The *straw man* fallacy consists of an oversimplification or outright distortion of opposing views. For example, in a California debate over attempts to control the mountain lion population, pro-lion groups characterized their opponents as trophy hunters bent on shooting harmless lions and sticking them on the walls of their dens. In truth, such hunters were only one faction of those who saw a need to control the lion population.

During the District of Columbia's struggle for voting representation, some politicians set up a straw man, as shown in the following example.

STRAW MAN FALLACY

> Washington, DC, residents are lobbying for statehood. Giving a city such as the District of Columbia the status of a state would be unfair.

The straw man wanted statehood. In fact, most District citizens lobbied for voting representation in any form, not necessarily through statehood.

Quoting opposing views

Writers often quote the words of writers who hold opposing views. In general, this is a good idea, for it assures some level of fairness and accuracy. At times, though, both the fairness and the accuracy are an illusion.

A source may be misrepresented when it is quoted out of context. All quotations are to some extent taken out of context, but a fair writer will explain the context to readers. To select a provocative sentence from a source and to ignore the more moderate sentences surrounding it is both unfair and misleading. Sometimes a writer deliberately distorts a source through the device of ellipsis dots. Ellipsis dots tell readers that words have been omitted from the original source. When those words are crucial to an author's meaning, omitting them is obviously unfair. (See P6-c.)

ORIGINAL SOURCE

Johnson's *History of the American West* is riddled with inaccuracies and astonishing in its blatantly racist description of the Indian wars.

—B. R., reviewer

MISLEADING QUOTATION

According to B. R., Johnson's *History of the American West* is "astonishing in its . . . description of the Indian wars."

A4 Writing in the disciplines

College courses expose you to the thinking of scholars in many disciplines, such as the humanities (literature, music, art), the social sciences (psychology, anthropology, sociology), the sciences (biology, physics, chemistry), and the professions and applied sciences (nursing, education, forestry). Writing in any discipline provides opportunities to practice the methods used by scholars in these fields and to enter into their debates. Each field has its own questions, evidence, language, and conventions, but all disciplines share certain expectations for good writing.

A4-a Find commonalities across disciplines.

A good paper in any field needs to communicate a writer's purpose to an audience and to explore an engaging question about a subject. Effective writers make an argument and support their claims with evidence. Writers in most fields need to show the thesis they're developing (or, in the sciences, the hypothesis they're testing) and counter opposition from other writers. All disciplines require writers to document where they found their evidence and from whom they borrowed ideas.

A4-b Recognize the questions writers in a discipline ask.

Disciplines are characterized by the kinds of questions their scholars attempt to answer. Historians, for example, often ask questions about the causes and effects of events and about the connections between current and past events. One way to understand how disciplines ask different questions is to look at assignments on the same subject in

Writing advice for all your college courses

When writing for any course in any discipline, keeping the following steps in mind can help you write a strong academic paper. Consult sections of this handbook that are appropriate to your assignment.

- Understand the writing assignment: C1-b, A4-f
- Determine and communicate a purpose: C1-a, C1-b
- Consider your audience: C1-a, C1-b
- Ask questions appropriate to the field: A4-b
- Formulate a thesis: C2-a, MLA-1a, APA-1a, CMS-1a
- Determine what types of evidence to gather: A4-c, C5-d
- Conduct research: R1
- Support your claim: A2-d, A2-e, MLA-1c, APA-1c, CMS-1c
- Counter opposing arguments or objections: A2-f
- Identify the appropriate documentation style: A4-e, R4
- Integrate sources: MLA-3, APA-3, CMS-3
- Document your sources: MLA-4, APA-4, CMS-4
- Design and format your document: C5, MLA-5a, APA-5a, CMS-5a

various fields. In many disciplines, for example, writers might discuss disasters. The following are some questions that writers in different fields might ask about this subject.

EDUCATION	Should the elementary school curriculum teach students how to cope in disasters?
FILM	How has the disaster film genre changed since the advent of computer-generated imagery (CGI) in the early 1970s?
HISTORY	How did the formation of the American Red Cross reshape disaster relief in the United States?
ENGINEERING	What recent innovations in levee design are most promising?
PSYCHOLOGY	What are the most effective ways to identify and treat post-traumatic stress disorder (PTSD) in disaster survivors?

The questions you ask in any discipline will form the basis of the thesis for your paper. The questions themselves don't communicate a central idea, but they may lead you to one. For an education paper, for example, you might begin with the question "Should the elementary school curriculum teach students how to cope in disasters?" After considering the issues involved, you might draft the following working thesis.

> School systems should adopt age-appropriate curriculum units that introduce children to the risks of natural and human-made disasters and that allow children to practice coping strategies.

Whenever you write for a college course, try to determine the kinds of questions scholars in the field might ask about a topic. You can find clues in assigned readings, lecture or discussion topics, e-mail discussion groups, and the paper assignment itself.

A4-c Understand the kinds of evidence writers in a discipline use.

Regardless of the discipline in which you're writing, you must support any claims you make with evidence—facts, statistics, examples and illustrations, visuals, expert opinion, and so on.

The kinds of evidence used in different disciplines commonly overlap. Students of geography, media studies, and political science, for example, might use census data to explore different topics. The evidence that one discipline values, however, might not be sufficient to support an interpretation or a conclusion in another field. You might use anecdotes or interviews in an anthropology paper, for example, but such evidence would be irrelevant in a biology lab report. The chart on page 103 lists the kinds of evidence typically used in various disciplines.

A4-d Become familiar with a discipline's language conventions.

Every discipline has a specialized vocabulary. As you read the articles and books in a field, you'll notice certain words and phrases that come up repeatedly. Sociologists, for example, use terms such as *independent variables*, *political opportunity resources*, and *dyads* to describe social phenomena; computer scientists might refer to *algorithm design* and *loop invariants* to describe programming methods. Practitioners in health fields such as nursing use terms like *treatment plan* and *systemic assessment* to describe patient care. Use discipline-specific terms only when you are certain that you and your readers fully understand their meaning.

In addition to vocabulary, many fields of study have developed specialized conventions for point of view and verb tense. See the chart on page 104.

Evidence typically used in various disciplines

Humanities: Literature, art, film, music, philosophy

- Passages of text or lines of a poem
- Details from an image, a film, or a work of art
- Passages of a musical composition
- Critical essays that analyze original works

Humanities: History

- Primary sources such as photographs, letters, maps, and government documents
- Scholarly books and articles that interpret evidence

Social sciences: Psychology, sociology, political science, anthropology

- Data from original experiments
- Results of field research such as interviews, observations, or surveys
- Statistics from government agencies
- Scholarly books and articles that interpret data from original experiments and from other researchers' studies

Sciences: Biology, chemistry, physics

- Data from original experiments
- Scholarly articles that report findings from experiments

A4-e Use a discipline's preferred citation style.

In any discipline, you must give credit to those whose ideas or words you have borrowed. Avoid plagiarism by citing sources honestly and accurately (see R3).

While all disciplines emphasize careful documentation, each follows a particular system of citation that its members have agreed on. Writers in the humanities usually use the system established by the Modern Language Association (MLA). Scholars in some social sciences, such as psychology and anthropology, follow the style guidelines of the American Psychological Association (APA); scholars in history and some humanities typically follow *The Chicago Manual of Style*. For guidance on using the MLA, APA, or *Chicago* (CMS) format, see MLA-4, APA-4, or CMS-4, respectively. (For CSE [Council of Science Editors] style, see hackerhandbooks.com/resdoc.)

Point of view and verb tense in academic writing

Point of view

- Writers of analytical or research essays in the humanities usually use the third-person point of view: *Austen presents* . . . or *Castel describes the battle as*. . . .
- Scientists and most social scientists, who depend on quantitative research to present findings, tend to use the third-person point of view: *The results indicated*. . . .
- Writers in the humanities and in some social sciences occasionally use the first person in discussing their own experience or in writing a personal narrative: *After spending two years interviewing families affected by the war, I began to understand that* . . . or *Every July as we approached the Cape Cod Canal, we could sense*. . . .

Present or past tense

- Literature scholars use the present tense to discuss a text: *Hughes effectively dramatizes different views of minority assertiveness*. (See MLA-3.)
- Science and social science writers use the past tense to describe experiments and the present tense to discuss the findings: *In 2003, Berkowitz released the first double-blind placebo study*. . . . *These results paint a murky picture*. (See APA-3.)
- Writers in history use the present tense or the present perfect tense to discuss a text: *Shelby Foote describes the scene like this* . . . or *Shelby Foote has described the scene like this*. . . . (See CMS-3.)

A4-f Understand writing assignments in the disciplines.

When you are asked to write in a specific discipline, become familiar with the distinctive features of the writing in that discipline. Then read the assignment carefully and identify the purpose of the assignment and the types of evidence you are expected to use.

On the following pages are examples of assignments in four disciplines—psychology, business, biology, and nursing—along with excerpts from student papers that were written in response to the assignments.

MODELS **hackerhandbooks.com/writersref**
> Model papers > APA literature review: Charat
> APA business proposal: Ratajczak
> CSE laboratory report: Johnson and Arnold
> APA nursing practice paper: Riss

Psychology

ASSIGNMENT: LITERATURE REVIEW

Write a literature review in which you report on and evaluate the published research on a behavioral disorder.

1 Key terms
2 Purpose: to report on and evaluate a body of evidence
3 Evidence: research of other psychologists

ADHD IN BOYS VS. GIRLS 3

Always Out of Their Seats (and Fighting):
Why Are Boys Diagnosed with ADHD More Often Than Girls?

Attention deficit hyperactivity disorder (ADHD) is a commonly diagnosed disorder in children that affects social, academic, or occupational functioning. As the name suggests, its hallmark characteristics are hyperactivity and lack of attention as well as impulsive behavior. For decades, studies have focused on the causes, expression, prevalence, and outcome of the disorder, but until recently very little research investigated gender differences. In fact, until the early 1990s most research focused exclusively on boys (Brown, Madan-Swain, & Baldwin, 1991), perhaps because many more boys than girls are diagnosed with ADHD. Researchers have speculated on the possible explanations for the disparity, citing reasons such as true sex differences in the manifestation of the disorder's symptoms, gender biases in those who refer children to clinicians, and possibly even the diagnostic procedures themselves (Gaub & Carlson, 1997). But the most persuasive reason is that ADHD is often a comorbid condition—that is, it coexists with other behavior disorders that are not diagnosed properly and that do exhibit gender differences.

It has been suggested that in the United States children are often misdiagnosed as having ADHD when they actually suffer from a behavior disorder such as conduct disorder (CD) or a combination of ADHD and another behavior disorder (Disney, Elkins, McGue, & Iancono, 1999; Lilienfeld & Waldman, 1990). Conduct disorder is characterized by negative and criminal behavior in children and is highly correlated with adult diagnoses of antisocial personality disorder (ASPD). This paper first considers research that has dealt only with gender difference in the

Background and explanation of writer's purpose.

Evidence from research the writer has reviewed.

APA citations and specialized language (*ADHD*, *comorbid*).

Thesis: writer's argument.

Two sources in one parenthetical citation are separated by a semicolon.

Marginal annotations indicate appropriate formatting and effective writing.

Business

ASSIGNMENT: PROPOSAL

Write a proposal, as a memo, for improving or adding a service at a company where you have worked. Address the pros and cons of your proposal; draw on relevant studies, research, and your knowledge of the company.

1 Key terms
2 Purpose: to analyze certain evidence and make a proposal based on that analysis
3 Appropriate evidence: relevant studies, research, personal experience

MEMORANDUM

To: Jay Crosson, Senior Vice President, Human Resources
From: Kelly Ratajczak, Intern, Purchasing Department
Subject: Proposal to Add a Wellness Program
Date: April 24, 2009

Writer's main idea.

Health care costs are rising. In the long run, implementing a wellness program in our corporate culture will decrease the company's health care costs.

Data from recent study as support for claim.

APA citation style, typical in business.

Business terms familiar to readers (*costs, productivity, absenteeism*).

Research indicates that nearly 70% of health care costs are from common illnesses related to high blood pressure, overweight, lack of exercise, high cholesterol, stress, poor nutrition, and other preventable health issues (Hall, 2006). Health care costs are a major expense for most businesses, and they do not reflect costs due to the loss of productivity or absenteeism. A wellness program would address most, if not all, of these health care issues and related costs.

Headings define sections of proposal.

Benefits of Healthier Employees

Not only would a wellness program substantially reduce costs associated with employee health care, but our company would prosper through many other benefits. Businesses that have wellness programs show a lower cost in production, fewer sick days, and healthier employees ("Workplace Health," 2006). Our healthier employees will help to cut not only our production and absenteeism costs but also potential costs such as higher

Biology

ASSIGNMENT: LABORATORY REPORT

Write a report[1] on an experiment[1] you conduct on the distribution pattern[1] of a plant species indigenous[1] to the Northeast. Describe your methods[2] for collecting data[3] and interpret your experiment's results[2].

1 Key terms
2 Purpose: to describe and interpret the results of an experiment
3 Evidence: data collected during the experiment

Distribution Pattern of Dandelion 1

CSE style, typical in sciences.

Distribution Pattern of Dandelion (*Taraxacum officinale*)
on an Abandoned Golf Course

ABSTRACT

Abstract: an overview of hypothesis, experiment, and results.

This paper reports our study of the distribution pattern of the common dandelion (*Taraxacum officinale*) on an abandoned golf course in Hilton, NY, on 10 July 2005. An area of 6 ha was sampled with 111 randomly placed 1 × 1 m^2 quadrats. The dandelion count from each quadrat was used to test observed frequencies against expected frequencies based on a hypothesized random distribution. [Abstract continues.]

Specialized language (*aggregated*, *random*, *uniformly distributed*).

INTRODUCTION

Theoretically, plants of a particular species may be aggregated, random, or uniformly distributed in space [1]. The distribution type may be determined by many factors, such as availability of nutrients, competition, distance of seed dispersal, and mode of reproduction [2].

The purpose of this study was to determine if the distribution pattern of the common dandelion (*Taraxacum officinale*) on an abandoned golf course was aggregated, random, or uniform.

Introduction: context and purpose of experiment. Instead of a thesis in the introduction, a lab report interprets the data in a later Discussion section.

METHODS

The study site was an abandoned golf course in Hilton, NY. The vegetation was predominantly grasses, along with dandelions, broad-leaf plantain (*Plantago major*), and bird's-eye speedwell (*Veronica chamaedrys*). We sampled an area of approximately 6 ha on 10 July 2005, approximately two weeks after the golf course had been mowed.

Scientific names for plant species.

Nursing

ASSIGNMENT: NURSING PRACTICE PAPER

Write a client history, a nursing diagnosis, recommendations for care, your rationales, and expected and actual outcomes. Use interview notes, the client's health records, and relevant research findings.

1 Key terms
2 Purpose: to provide client history, diagnosis, recommendations, and outcomes
3 Evidence: interviews, health records, and research findings

ALL AND HTN IN ONE CLIENT 1

Acute Lymphoblastic Leukemia and Hypertension in One Client:
A Nursing Practice Paper

Physical History

Evidence from client's medical chart for overall assessment.

E.B. is a 16-year-old white male 5′10″ tall weighing 190 lb. He was admitted to the hospital on April 14, 2006, due to decreased platelets and a need for a PRBC transfusion. He was diagnosed in October 2005 with T-cell acute lymphoblastic leukemia (ALL), after a 2-week period of decreased energy, decreased oral intake, easy bruising, and petechia. The client had experienced a 20-lb weight loss in the previous 6 months. At the time of diagnosis, his CBC showed a WBC count of 32, an H & H of 13/38, and a platelet count of 34,000. His initial chest X-ray showed an anterior mediastinal mass. Echocardiogram showed a structurally normal heart. He began induction chemotherapy on October 12, 2005, receiving vincristine, 6-mercaptopurine, doxorubicin, intrathecal methotrexate, and then high-dose methotrexate per protocol. During his hospital stay, he required packed red cells and platelets on two different occasions. He was diagnosed with hypertension (HTN) due to systolic blood pressure readings consistently ranging between 130s and 150s and was started on nifedipine. E.B. has a history of mild ADHD, migraines, and deep vein thrombosis (DVT). He has tolerated the induction and consolidation phases of chemotherapy well and is now in the maintenance phase, in which he receives a daily dose of mercaptopurine, weekly doses of methotrexate, and intermittent doses of steroids.

Specialized nursing language (*echocardiogram*, *chemotherapy*, and so on).

Instead of a thesis, or main claim, the writer gives a diagnosis, recommendations for care, and expected outcomes, all supported by evidence from observations and client records.

S

Sentence Style

S Sentence Style

S1 Parallelism, 111

- **a** With items in a series, 111
- **b** With paired ideas, 112
- **c** Repeated words, 113

S2 Needed words, 114

- **a** In compound structures, 114
- **b** *that*, 115
- **c** In comparisons, 115
- **d** *a*, *an*, and *the*, 117

S3 Problems with modifiers, 117

- **a** Limiting modifiers such as *only*, *even*, 117
- **b** Misplaced phrases and clauses, 118
- **c** Awkwardly placed modifiers, 119
- **d** Split infinitives, 120
- **e** Dangling modifiers, 120

S4 Shifts, 123

- **a** Point of view, 123
- **b** Verb tense, 124
- **c** Verb mood and voice, 124
- **d** Indirect to direct questions or quotations, 125

S5 Mixed constructions, 126

- **a** Mixed grammar, 126
- **b** Illogical connections, 128
- **c** *is when*, *is where*, *reason . . . is because*, 128

S6 Sentence emphasis, 129

- **a** Coordination and subordination, 129
- **b** Choppy sentences, 130
- **c** Ineffective coordination, 132
- **d** Ineffective subordination, 132
- **e** Excessive subordination, 133
- **f** Special techniques, 133

S7 Sentence variety, 134

- **a** Sentence structures, 134
- **b** Sentence openings, 135
- **c** Inverted order, 135

S1 Parallelism

If two or more ideas are parallel, they are easier to grasp when expressed in parallel grammatical form. Single words should be balanced with single words, phrases with phrases, clauses with clauses. In headings and lists, aim for as much parallelism as the content allows. (See C5-b and C5-c.) Writers often use parallelism to create emphasis. (See p. 134.)

> A kiss can be a comma, a question mark, or an exclamation point.
> —Mistinguett

> This novel is not to be tossed lightly aside, but to be hurled with great force.
> —Dorothy Parker

> In matters of principle, stand like a rock; in matters of taste, swim with the current.
> —Thomas Jefferson

S1-a Balance parallel ideas in a series.

Readers expect items in a series to appear in parallel grammatical form. When one or more of the items violate readers' expectations, a sentence will be needlessly awkward.

▶ **Children who study music also learn confidence, discipline, and ~~they are creative.~~** *creativity.*

The revision presents all the items in the series as nouns: *confidence*, *discipline*, and *creativity*.

▶ **Impressionist painters believed in focusing on ordinary subjects, capturing the effects of light on those subjects, and ~~to use~~** *using* **short brushstrokes.**

The revision uses *-ing* forms for all the items in the series: *focusing*, *capturing*, and *using*.

PRACTICE **hackerhandbooks.com/writersref**
> Sentence style > S1–2 to S1–5

▶ **Racing to get to work on time, Sam drove down the middle of the road, ran one red light, and** *ignored* **two stop signs.**

The revision adds a verb to make the three items parallel: *drove*, *ran*, and *ignored*.

S1-b Balance parallel ideas presented as pairs.

When pairing ideas, underscore their connection by expressing them in similar grammatical form. Paired ideas are usually connected in one of these ways:

- with a coordinating conjunction such as *and*, *but*, or *or*
- with a pair of correlative conjunctions such as *either . . . or* or *not only . . . but also*
- with a word introducing a comparison, usually *than* or *as*

Parallel ideas linked with coordinating conjunctions

Coordinating conjunctions (*and*, *but*, *or*, *nor*, *for*, *so*, and *yet*) link ideas of equal importance. When those ideas are closely parallel in content, they should be expressed in parallel grammatical form.

▶ **Emily Dickinson's poetry features the use of dashes and** ~~capitalizing~~ *the capitalization of* **common words.**

The revision balances the nouns *use* and *capitalization*.

▶ **Many states are reducing property taxes for home owners and** ~~extend~~ *extending* **financial aid in the form of tax credits to renters.**

The revision balances the verb *reducing* with the verb *extending*.

Parallel ideas linked with correlative conjunctions

Correlative conjunctions come in pairs: *either . . . or*, *neither . . . nor*, *not only . . . but also*, *both . . . and*, *whether . . . or*. Make sure that the grammatical structure following the second half of the pair is the same as that following the first half.

▶ **Thomas Edison was not only a prolific inventor but also ~~was~~ a successful entrepreneur.**

The words *a prolific inventor* immediately follow *not only*, so *a successful entrepreneur* should follow *but also*. Repeating *was* after *also* creates an unbalanced effect.

▶ **The clerk told me either to change my flight or** *to* **take the train.**

To change, which follows *either*, should be balanced with *to take*, which follows *or*.

Comparisons linked with than *or* as

In comparisons linked with *than* or *as*, the elements being compared should be expressed in parallel grammatical structure.

▶ **It is easier to speak in abstractions than** *to ground* **~~grounding~~ one's thoughts in reality.**

To speak is balanced with *to ground.*

▶ **In Pueblo culture, according to Silko,** *writing* **~~to write~~ down the stories of a tribe is not the same as "keeping track of all the stories" (290).**

Writing with sources
MLA-style citation

When you are quoting from a source, parallel grammatical structure—such as *writing . . . keeping*—helps create continuity between your sentence and the words from the source.

Comparisons should also be logical and grammatically complete. (See S2-c.)

S1-c Repeat function words to clarify parallels.

Function words such as prepositions (*by*, *to*) and subordinating conjunctions (*that*, *because*) signal the grammatical nature of the word groups to follow. Although you can sometimes omit such function words, be sure to include them whenever they signal parallel structures that readers might otherwise miss.

▶ **Our study revealed that left-handed students were more likely to have trouble with classroom desks and** ^*that* **rearranging desks for exam periods was useful.**

A second subordinating conjunction helps readers sort out the two parallel ideas: *that* left-handed students have trouble with classroom desks and *that* rearranging desks was useful.

S2 Needed words

Sometimes writers leave out words intentionally, and the meaning of the sentence is not affected. But leaving out words can occasionally cause confusion for readers or make the sentence ungrammatical. Readers need to see at a glance how the parts of a sentence are connected.

ESL Languages sometimes differ in the need for certain words. In particular, be alert for missing articles, verbs, subjects, or expletives. See M2, M3-a, and M3-b.

S2-a Add words needed to complete compound structures.

In compound structures, words are often left out for economy: *Tom is a man who means what he says and* [*who*] *says what he means.* Such omissions are acceptable as long as the omitted words are common to both parts of the compound structure.

If a sentence defies grammar or idiom because an omitted word is not common to both parts of the compound structure, the simplest solution is to put the word back in.

▶ **Successful advertisers target customers whom they identify through demographic research or** ^*who* **have purchased their product in the past.**

The word *who* must be included because *whom . . . have purchased* is not grammatically correct.

▶ **Mayor Davis never has** ^*accepted* **and never will accept a bribe.**

Has . . . accept is not grammatically correct.

PRACTICE **hackerhandbooks.com/writersref**
> Sentence style > S2–2 to S2–4

► **Many South Pacific islanders still believe** ~~^~~ *in* **and live by ancient laws.**

Believe . . . by is not idiomatic in English. (For a list of common idioms, see W5-d.)

NOTE: Even when the omitted word is common to both parts of the compound structure, occasionally it must be repeated to avoid ambiguity.

My favorite *professor* and *mentor* influenced my choice of a career. [Professor and mentor are the same person.]

My favorite *professor* and *my mentor* influenced my choice of a career. [Professor and mentor are two different people; *my* must be repeated.]

S2-b Add the word *that* if there is any danger of misreading without it.

If there is no danger of misreading, the word *that* may be omitted when it introduces a subordinate clause. *The value of a principle is the number of things [that] it will explain.* Occasionally, however, a sentence might be misread without *that.*

► **In his famous obedience experiments, psychologist Stanley Milgram discovered** ^ *that* **ordinary people were willing to inflict physical pain on strangers.**

Milgram didn't discover ordinary people; he discovered that ordinary people were willing to inflict pain on strangers. The word *that* tells readers to expect a clause, not just *ordinary people*, as the direct object of *discovered.*

S2-c Add words needed to make comparisons logical and complete.

Comparisons should be made between items that are alike. To compare unlike items is illogical and distracting.

► **The forests of North America are much more extensive than** ^ *those of* **Europe.**

Forests must be compared with forests, not with all of Europe.

▶ **~~The death rate of~~ I~~i~~nfantry soldiers in the Vietnam War ~~was~~** *died* *at a* **much higher** *rate* **than the other combat troops.**

The death rate cannot logically be compared with troops. The writer could revise the sentence by inserting *that of* after *than*, but the revision shown here is more concise.

▶ **Some say that Ella Fitzgerald's renditions of Cole Porter's songs are better than any other ~~singer.~~** *singer's.*

Ella Fitzgerald's renditions cannot logically be compared with a singer. The revision uses the possessive form *singer's*, with the word *renditions* being implied.

Sometimes the word *other* must be inserted to make a comparison logical.

▶ **Jupiter is larger than any** *other* **planet in our solar system.**

Jupiter is a planet, and it cannot be larger than itself.

Sometimes the word *as* must be inserted to make a comparison grammatically complete.

▶ **The city of Lowell is as old,** *as* **if not older than, the neighboring city of Lawrence.**

The construction *as old* is not complete without a second *as*: *as old as . . . the neighboring city of Lawrence.*

Comparisons should be complete enough to ensure clarity. The reader should understand what is being compared.

INCOMPLETE Brand X is less salty.

COMPLETE Brand X is less salty than Brand Y.

Finally, comparisons should leave no ambiguity for readers. If more than one interpretation is possible, revise the sentence to state clearly which interpretation you intend. In the following ambiguous sentence, two interpretations are possible.

AMBIGUOUS Ken helped me more than my roommate.

CLEAR Ken helped me more than *he helped* my roommate.

CLEAR Ken helped me more than my roommate *did.*

S2-d Add the articles *a*, *an*, and *the* where necessary for grammatical completeness.

It is not always necessary to repeat articles with paired items: *We bought a computer and printer.* However, if one of the items requires *a* and the other requires *an*, both articles must be included.

an
▶ **We bought a computer and ^ antivirus program.**

Articles are sometimes omitted in recipes and other instructions that are meant to be followed while they are being read. In nearly all other forms of writing, whether formal or informal, such omissions are inappropriate.

ESL Choosing and using articles can be challenging for multilingual writers. See M2.

S3 Problems with modifiers

Modifiers, whether they are single words, phrases, or clauses, should point clearly to the words they modify. As a rule, related words should be kept together.

S3-a Put limiting modifiers in front of the words they modify.

Limiting modifiers such as *only*, *even*, *almost*, *nearly*, and *just* should appear in front of a verb only if they modify the verb: *At first, I couldn't even touch my toes, much less grasp them.* If modifiers limit the meaning of some other word in the sentence, they should be placed in front of that word.

▶ **St. Vitus Cathedral, commissioned by Charles IV in the**
almost
mid-fourteenth century, ~~almost~~ took ^ six centuries to complete.

Almost limits the meaning of *six centuries*, not *took*.

PRACTICE hackerhandbooks.com/writersref
> Sentence style > S3–3 to S3–5

▶ **If you ~~just~~ interview ^just chemistry majors, your picture of the student body's response to the new grading policies will be incomplete.**

The adverb *just* limits the meaning of *chemistry majors*, not *interview.*

When the limiting modifier *not* is misplaced, the sentence usually suggests a meaning the writer did not intend.

▶ **In the United States in 1860, ^not all black southerners were ~~not~~ slaves.**

The original sentence says that no black southerners were slaves. The revision makes the writer's real meaning clear: Some (but not all) black southerners were slaves.

S3-b Place phrases and clauses so that readers can see at a glance what they modify.

Although phrases and clauses can appear at some distance from the words they modify, make sure your meaning is clear. When phrases or clauses are oddly placed, absurd misreadings can result.

MISPLACED	The soccer player returned to the clinic where he had undergone emergency surgery in 2009 in a limousine sent by Adidas.
REVISED	Traveling in a limousine sent by Adidas, the soccer player returned to the clinic where he had undergone emergency surgery in 2009.

The revision corrects the false impression that the soccer player underwent emergency surgery in a limousine.

▶ **^On the walls ~~There~~ are many pictures of comedians who have performed at Gavin's^. ~~on the walls.~~**

The comedians weren't performing on the walls; the pictures were on the walls.

▶ **The robber was described as a ^170-pound, six-foot-tall man with a heavy mustache^. ~~weighing 170 pounds.~~**

The robber, not the mustache, weighed 170 pounds.

Occasionally the placement of a modifier leads to an ambiguity—a squinting modifier. In such a case, two revisions will be possible, depending on the writer's intended meaning.

AMBIGUOUS The exchange students we met for coffee occasionally questioned us about our latest slang.

CLEAR The exchange students we occasionally met for coffee questioned us about our latest slang.

CLEAR The exchange students we met for coffee questioned us occasionally about our latest slang.

In the original version, it was not clear whether the meeting or the questioning happened occasionally. Both revisions eliminate the ambiguity.

S3-c Move awkwardly placed modifiers.

As a rule, a sentence should flow from subject to verb to object, without lengthy detours along the way. When a long adverbial word group separates a subject from its verb, a verb from its object, or a helping verb from its main verb, the result is often awkward.

▶ ~~Hong Kong,~~ ~~a~~fter more than 150 years of British rule, was transferred back to Chinese control in 1997. [Edits: "A" inserted at "after"; "Hong Kong" inserted before "was"]

There is no reason to separate the subject, *Hong Kong*, from the verb, *was transferred*, with a long phrase.

▶ ~~Jeffrey Meyers discusses,~~ ~~i~~n his biography of F. Scott Fitzgerald, the writer's "fascination with the superiority, the selfishness, and the emptiness of the rich" (166). [Edits: "I" inserted at "in"; "Jeffrey Meyers discusses" inserted after "Fitzgerald,"]

Writing with sources
MLA-style citation

When you quote from a source, the phrase or clause that you use to introduce the source should be as straightforward as possible. There is no reason to separate the verb, *discusses*, from its object, *fascination*, with two prepositional phrases.

ESL English does not allow an adverb to appear between a verb and its object. See M3-f.

▶ Yolanda lifted ~~easily~~ the fifty-pound weight. [Edit: "easily" inserted after "Yolanda"]

S3-d Avoid split infinitives when they are awkward.

An infinitive consists of *to* plus the base form of a verb: *to think*, *to run*, *to dance.* When a modifier appears between *to* and the verb, an infinitive is said to be "split": *to carefully balance*, *to completely understand.*

When a long word or a phrase appears between the parts of the infinitive, the result is usually awkward.

If possible, the
▶ **~~The~~ patient should try to ~~if possible~~ avoid putting weight on his foot.**

Attempts to avoid split infinitives can result in equally awkward sentences. When alternative phrasing sounds unnatural, most experts allow—and even encourage—splitting the infinitive.

AWKWARD We decided actually to enforce the law.

BETTER We decided to actually enforce the law.

At times, neither the split infinitive nor its alternative sounds particularly awkward. In such situations, it is usually better to unsplit the infinitive, especially in formal writing.

▶ **Nursing students learn to ~~accurately~~ record a patient's vital signs~~.~~** *accurately.*

S3-e Repair dangling modifiers.

A dangling modifier fails to refer logically to any word in the sentence. Dangling modifiers are easy to repair, but they can be hard to recognize, especially in your own writing.

Recognizing dangling modifiers

Dangling modifiers are usually word groups (such as verbal phrases) that suggest but do not name an actor. When a sentence opens with such a modifier, readers expect the subject of the next clause to name the actor. If it doesn't, the modifier dangles.

▶ **Understanding the need to create checks and balances on power,** *the framers of* **the Constitution divided the government into three branches.**

PRACTICE hackerhandbooks.com/writersref
> Sentence style > S3–6 to S3–8

The framers of the Constitution (not the document itself) understood the need for checks and balances.

▶ **After completing seminary training, ~~women's~~ *women have often been denied* access to the priesthood. ~~has often been denied.~~**

Women (not their access to the priesthood) complete the training.

The following sentences illustrate four common kinds of dangling modifiers.

DANGLING *Deciding to join the navy*, the recruiter enthusiastically pumped Joe's hand. [Participial phrase]

DANGLING *Upon entering the doctor's office*, a skeleton caught my attention. [Preposition followed by a gerund phrase]

DANGLING *To satisfy her mother*, the piano had to be practiced every day. [Infinitive phrase]

DANGLING *Though not eligible for the clinical trial*, the doctor was willing to prescribe the drug for Ethan on compassionate grounds. [Elliptical clause with an understood subject and verb]

These dangling modifiers falsely suggest that the recruiter decided to join the navy, that the skeleton entered the doctor's office, that the piano intended to satisfy the mother, and that the doctor was not eligible for the clinical trial.

Although most readers will understand the writer's intended meaning in such sentences, the inadvertent humor can be distracting.

Repairing dangling modifiers

To repair a dangling modifier, you can revise the sentence in one of two ways:

- Name the actor in the subject of the sentence.
- Name the actor in the modifier.

Depending on your sentence, one of these revision strategies may be more appropriate than the other.

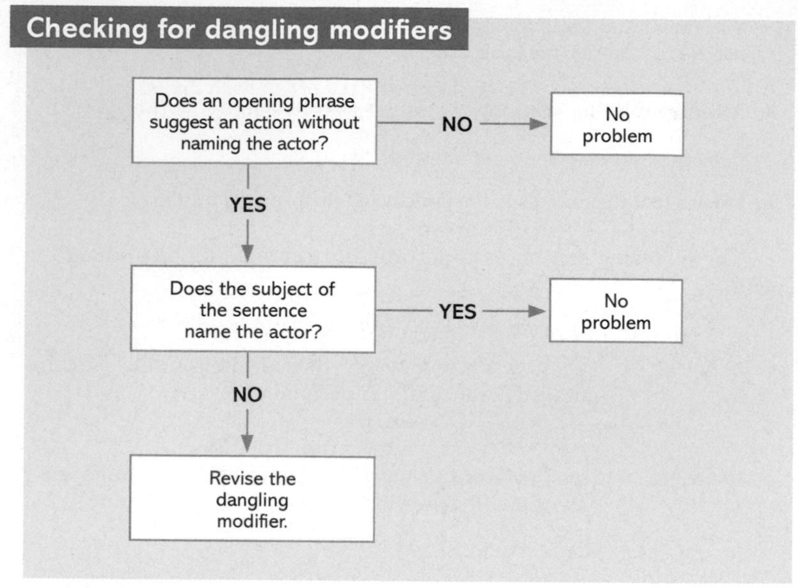

ACTOR NAMED IN SUBJECT

▶ Upon entering the doctor's office, a skeleton. ~~caught my attention.~~ [inserted: I noticed ^ ... ^]

▶ To satisfy her mother, [inserted: Jing-mei] the piano ~~had to be practiced~~ [inserted: had to practice] every day.

ACTOR NAMED IN MODIFIER

▶ ~~Deciding~~ [inserted: When Joe decided] to join the navy, the recruiter enthusiastically pumped ~~Joe's~~ [inserted: his] hand.

▶ Though [inserted: Ethan was] not eligible for the clinical trial, the doctor was willing to prescribe the drug for ~~Ethan~~ [inserted: him] on compassionate grounds.

NOTE: You cannot repair a dangling modifier just by moving it. Consider, for example, the sentence about the skeleton. If you put the modifier at the end of the sentence (*A skeleton caught my attention upon entering the doctor's office*), you are still suggesting—absurdly, of course—that the skeleton entered the office. The only way to avoid the problem is to put the word *I* in the sentence, either as the subject or in the modifier.

I noticed
▶ **Upon entering the doctor's office, a skeleton. ~~caught my attention.~~**

As I entered
▶ **~~Upon entering~~ the doctor's office, a skeleton caught my attention.**

S4 Shifts

The following sections can help you avoid unnecessary shifts that might distract or confuse your readers: shifts in point of view, in verb tense, in mood or voice, or from indirect to direct questions or quotations.

S4-a Make the point of view consistent in person and number.

The point of view of a piece of writing is the perspective from which it is written: first person (*I* or *we*), second person (*you*), or third person (*he, she, it, one, they*, or any noun).

The *I* (or *we*) point of view, which emphasizes the writer, is a good choice for informal letters and writing based primarily on personal experience. The *you* point of view, which emphasizes the reader, works well for giving advice or explaining how to do something. The third-person point of view, which emphasizes the subject, is appropriate in formal academic and professional writing.

Writers who are having difficulty settling on an appropriate point of view sometimes shift confusingly from one to another. The solution is to choose a suitable perspective and then stay with it.

▶ **Our class practiced rescuing a victim trapped in a wrecked car. We learned to dismantle the car with the essential tools.** We **~~You~~ were graded on** our **~~your~~ speed and** our **~~your~~ skill in freeing the victim.**

The writer should have stayed with the *we* point of view. *You* is inappropriate because the writer is not addressing readers directly. *You* should not be used in a vague sense meaning "anyone." (See G3-b.)

You need
▶ **~~One needs~~ a password and a credit card number to access the database. You will be billed at an hourly rate.**

You is appropriate because the writer is giving advice directly to readers.

PRACTICE **hackerhandbooks.com/writersref**
> Sentence style > S4–5

Writing with sources

APA-style citation

▶ According to the National Institute of Mental Health (2007), ~~a child~~ *children* with attention deficit hyperactivity disorder may have trouble sitting still and may gradually stop paying attention to their teachers (Symptoms section, para. 2).

In describing reports or results of studies, writers are often tempted to generalize with singular nouns, such as *child*, and then later in the passage find themselves shifting from singular to plural. Here the writer might have changed *their* to the singular *his or her* to agree with *child*, but the revision making both terms plural is more concise. (See also W4-e and G3-a.)

S4-b Maintain consistent verb tenses.

Consistent verb tenses clearly establish the time of the actions being described. When a passage begins in one tense and shifts without warning and for no reason to another, readers are distracted and confused.

▶ There was no way I could fight the current and win. Just as I was losing hope, a stranger ~~jumps~~ *jumped* off a passing boat and ~~swims~~ *swam* toward me.

The writer thought that the present tense (*jumps*, *swims*) would convey immediacy and drama. But having begun in the past tense (*could fight*, *was losing*), the writer should follow through in the past tense.

Writers often encounter difficulty with verb tenses when writing about literature. Because fictional events occur outside the time frames of real life, the past tense and the present tense may seem equally appropriate. The literary convention, however, is to describe fictional events consistently in the present tense. (See p. 192.)

▶ The scarlet letter is a punishment sternly placed on Hester's breast by the community, and yet it ~~was~~ *is* a fanciful and imaginative product of Hester's own needlework.

S4-c Make verbs consistent in mood and voice.

Unnecessary shifts in the mood of a verb can be distracting and confusing to readers. There are three moods in English: the *indicative*, used for facts, opinions, and questions; the *imperative*, used for orders or advice; and the *subjunctive*, used in certain contexts to express wishes or conditions contrary to fact (see G2-g).

The following passage shifts confusingly from the indicative to the imperative mood.

▶ **The counselor advised us to spread out our core requirements over two or three semesters. ~~Also,~~** *She also suggested that we* **pay attention to prerequisites for elective courses.**

The writer began by reporting the counselor's advice in the indicative mood (*counselor advised*) and switched to the imperative mood (*pay attention*); the revision puts both sentences in the indicative.

A verb may be in either the active voice (with the subject doing the action) or the passive voice (with the subject receiving the action). (See W3-a.) If a writer shifts without warning from one to the other, readers may be left wondering why.

▶ **Each student completes a self-assessment, ~~The self-assessment is then given~~** *gives it* **to the teacher, and a copy ~~is exchanged~~** *exchanges* **with a classmate.**

Because the passage began in the active voice (*student completes*) and then switched to the passive (*self-assessment is given, copy is exchanged*), readers are left wondering who gives the self-assessment to the teacher and the classmate. The active voice, which is clearer and more direct, leaves no ambiguity.

S4-d Avoid sudden shifts from indirect to direct questions or quotations.

An indirect question reports a question without asking it: *We asked whether we could visit Miriam.* A direct question asks directly: *Can we visit Miriam?* Sudden shifts from indirect to direct questions are awkward. In addition, sentences containing such shifts are impossible to punctuate because indirect questions must end with a period and direct questions must end with a question mark. (See P6-a.)

▶ **I wonder whether Karla knew of the theft and, if so, ~~did she report~~** *whether she reported* **it to the police~~?~~.**

PRACTICE hackerhandbooks.com/writersref
> Sentence style > S4–7 to S4–9

The revision poses both questions indirectly. The writer could also ask both questions directly: *Did Karla know of the theft, and, if so, did she report it to the police?*

An indirect quotation reports someone's words without quoting word for word: *Annabelle said that she is a Virgo.* A direct quotation presents the exact words of a speaker or writer, set off with quotation marks: *Annabelle said, "I am a Virgo."* Unannounced shifts from indirect to direct quotations are distracting and confusing, especially when the writer fails to insert the necessary quotation marks, as in the following example.

▶ **The patient said she had been experiencing heart palpitations and ~~please~~ *asked me to* run as many tests as possible to find out what~~'s~~ *was* wrong.**

The revision reports the patient's words indirectly. The writer also could quote the words directly: *The patient said, "I have been experiencing heart palpitations. Please run as many tests as possible to find out what's wrong."*

S5 Mixed constructions

A mixed construction contains sentence parts that do not sensibly fit together. The mismatch may be a matter of grammar or of logic.

S5-a Untangle the grammatical structure.

Once you begin a sentence, your choices are limited by the range of grammatical patterns in English. (See B2 and B3.) You cannot begin with one grammatical plan and switch without warning to another. Often you must rethink the purpose of the sentence and revise.

MIXED For most drivers who have a blood alcohol level of .05 percent double their risk of causing an accident.

The writer begins the sentence with a long prepositional phrase and makes it the subject of the verb *double.* But a prepositional phrase can serve only as a modifier; it cannot be the subject of a sentence.

REVISED For most drivers who have a blood alcohol level of .05 percent, the risk of causing an accident is doubled.

REVISED Most drivers who have a blood alcohol level of .05 percent double their risk of causing an accident.

PRACTICE hackerhandbooks.com/writersref
> Sentence style > S5–2 to S5–4

In the first revision, the writer begins with the prepositional phrase and finishes the sentence with a proper subject and verb (*risk . . . is doubled*). In the second revision, the writer stays with the original verb (*double*) and heads into the sentence another way, making *drivers* the subject of *double.*

Electing
▶ **~~When the country elects~~ a president is the most important responsibility in a democracy.**

The adverb clause *When the country elects a president* cannot serve as the subject of the verb *is.* The revision replaces the adverb clause with a gerund phrase, a word group that can function as a subject. (See B3-e and B3-b.)

▶ **Although the United States is one of the wealthiest nations in the world, ~~but~~ more than twelve million of our children live in poverty.**

The coordinating conjunction *but* cannot link a subordinate clause (*Although the United States . . .*) with an independent clause (*more than twelve million of our children live in poverty*).

Occasionally a mixed construction is so tangled that it defies grammatical analysis. When this happens, back away from the sentence, rethink what you want to say, and then rewrite the sentence.

MIXED In the whole-word method, children learn to recognize entire words rather than by the phonics method in which they learn to sound out letters and groups of letters.

REVISED The whole-word method teaches children to recognize entire words; the phonics method teaches them to sound out letters and groups of letters.

ESL English does not allow double subjects, nor does it allow an object or an adverb to be repeated in an adjective clause. Unlike some other languages, English does not allow a noun and a pronoun to be repeated in a sentence if they have the same grammatical function. See M3-c and M3-d.

▶ **My father ~~he~~ moved to Peru before he met my mother.**

▶ **~~The final exam~~ I should really study for ~~it~~ *the final exam* to pass the course.**

S5-b Straighten out the logical connections.

The subject and the predicate (the verb and its modifiers) should make sense together; when they don't, the error is known as *faulty predication.*

▶ **We decided that ~~Tiffany's welfare~~** *Tiffany* **would not be safe living with her mother.**

Tiffany, not her welfare, would not be safe.

▶ **Under the revised plan, the** *double personal exemption for the* **elderly/~~who now receive a double personal exemption,~~ will be abolished.**

The exemption, not the elderly, will be abolished.

An appositive is a noun that renames a nearby noun. When an appositive and the noun it renames are not logically equivalent, the error is known as *faulty apposition.* (See B3-c.)

▶ *Tax accounting,* **~~The tax accountant,~~ a very lucrative profession, requires intelligence, patience, and attention to mathematical detail.**

The tax accountant is a person, not a profession.

S5-c Avoid *is when*, *is where*, and *reason . . . is because* constructions.

In formal English, readers sometimes object to *is when*, *is where*, and *reason . . . is because* constructions on grammatical or logical grounds.

▶ **The ~~reason the~~ experiment failed ~~is~~ because conditions in the lab were not sterile.**

Grammatically, the verb *is* should not be followed by an adverb clause beginning with *because.* (See B2-b and B3-e.) The writer might have changed *because* to *that* (*The reason the experiment failed is that conditions in the lab were not sterile*), but the preceding revision is more concise.

▶ **Anorexia nervosa is ~~where people~~** *a disorder suffered by people who* **think they are too fat and diet to the point of starvation.**

Where refers to places. Anorexia nervosa is a disorder, not a place.

S6 Sentence emphasis

Within each sentence, emphasize your point by expressing it in the subject and verb of an independent clause, the words that receive the most attention from readers (see S6-a to S6-e).

Within longer stretches of prose, you can draw attention to ideas that deserve special emphasis by using a variety of techniques, often involving an unusual twist or some element of surprise (see S6-f).

S6-a Coordinate equal ideas; subordinate minor ideas.

When combining two or more ideas in one sentence, you have two choices: coordination or subordination. Choose coordination to indicate that the ideas are equal or nearly equal in importance. Choose subordination to indicate that one idea is less important than another.

Coordination

Coordination draws attention equally to two or more ideas. To coordinate single words or phrases, join them with a coordinating conjunction or with a pair of correlative conjunctions: bananas *and* strawberries; *not only* a lackluster plot *but also* inferior acting (see B1-g).

To coordinate independent clauses—word groups that express a complete thought and that can stand alone as a sentence—join them with a comma and a coordinating conjunction (*and*, *but*, *or*, *nor*, *for*, *so*, *yet*) or with a semicolon. The semicolon is often accompanied by a conjunctive adverb such as *moreover*, *furthermore*, *therefore*, or *however* or by a transitional phrase such as *for example*, *in other words*, or *as a matter of fact*. (For longer lists, see P3-a.)

> Social networking Web sites offer ways for people to connect in the virtual world, but they do not replace face-to-face social interaction.

> Social networking Web sites offer ways for people to connect in the virtual world; however, they do not replace face-to-face social interaction.

Subordination

To give unequal emphasis to two or more ideas, express the major idea in an independent clause and place any minor ideas in subordinate clauses or phrases. (See B3.) Subordinate clauses, which cannot stand alone, typically begin with one of the following subordinating conjunctions or relative pronouns.

after	since	whether
although	so that	which
as	that	while
as if	though	who
because	unless	whom
before	until	whose
even though	when	
if	where	

Let your intended meaning determine which idea you emphasize. Consider the two ideas about social networking Web sites.

> Social networking Web sites offer ways for people to connect in the virtual world. They do not replace face-to-face social interaction.

If your purpose is to stress the ways that people can connect in the virtual world rather than the limitations of these connections, subordinate the idea about the limitations.

> Although they do not replace face-to-face social interaction, social networking Web sites offer ways for people to connect in the virtual world.

To focus on the limitations of the virtual world, subordinate the idea about the Web sites.

> Although social networking Web sites offer ways for people to connect in the virtual world, they do not replace face-to-face social interaction.

S6-b Combine choppy sentences.

Short sentences demand attention, so you should use them primarily for emphasis. Too many short sentences, one after the other, make for a choppy style.

If an idea is not important enough to deserve its own sentence, try combining it with a sentence close by. Put any minor ideas in subordinate structures such as phrases or subordinate clauses. (See B3.)

▶ **The Parks Department keeps the use of insecticides to a minimum/** *because the* **~~The~~ city is concerned about the environment.**

The writer wanted to emphasize that the Parks Department minimizes its use of chemicals, so she put the reason in a subordinate clause beginning with *because.*

▶ **The Chesapeake and Ohio Canal, ~~is~~ a 184-mile waterway constructed in the 1800s/, ~~It~~ was a major source of transportation for goods during the Civil War.**

A minor idea is now expressed in an appositive phrase (*a 184-mile waterway constructed in the 1800s*).

▶ **~~Sister Consilio was~~ E/nveloped in a black robe with only her face and hands visible/, Sister Consilio ~~She~~ was an imposing figure.**

Because Sister Consilio's overall impression was more important to the writer's purpose, the writer put the description of the clothing in a participial phrase beginning with *Enveloped.*

Although subordination is ordinarily the most effective technique for combining short, choppy sentences, coordination is appropriate when the ideas are equal in importance.

▶ **At 3:30 p.m., Forrest displayed a flag of truce/ and ~~Forrest~~ sent in a demand for unconditional surrender.**

Combining two short sentences by joining their predicates (*displayed . . . sent*) is an effective coordination technique.

ESL Unlike some other languages, English does not repeat objects or adverbs in adjective clauses. The relative pronoun (*that, which, whom*) or relative adverb (*where*) in the adjective clause represents the object or adverb. See M3-d.

▶ **The apartment that we rented ~~it~~ needed repairs.**

The pronoun *it* cannot repeat the relative pronoun *that.*

▶ **The small town where my grandfather was born ~~there~~ is now a big city.**

The adverb *there* cannot repeat the relative adverb *where.*

S6-c Avoid ineffective or excessive coordination.

Coordinate structures are appropriate only when you intend to draw readers' attention equally to two or more ideas: *Professor Sakellarios praises loudly, and she criticizes softly.* If one idea is more important than another—or if a coordinating conjunction does not clearly signal the relationship between the ideas—you should subordinate the less important idea.

INEFFECTIVE COORDINATION	Closets were taxed as rooms, and most colonists stored their clothes in chests or clothespresses.
IMPROVED WITH SUBORDINATION	Because closets were taxed as rooms, most colonists stored their clothes in chests or clothespresses.

Because it is so easy to string ideas together with *and*, writers often rely too heavily on coordination in their rough drafts. Revising for excessive coordination is important: Look for opportunities to tuck minor ideas into subordinate clauses or phrases.

After four hours,
▶ **~~Four hours went by, and~~ a rescue truck finally arrived, but by that time we had been evacuated in a helicopter.**

Three independent clauses were excessive. The least important idea has become a prepositional phrase.

S6-d Do not subordinate major ideas.

If a sentence buries its major idea in a subordinate construction, readers may not give the idea enough attention. Make sure to express your major idea in an independent clause and to subordinate any minor ideas.

defeated Thomas E. Dewey,
▶ **Harry S. Truman, who was the unexpected winner of the 1948 presidential election/. ~~defeated Thomas E. Dewey.~~**

The writer wanted to focus on Truman's unexpected victory, but the original sentence buried this information in an adjective clause. The revision puts the more important idea in an independent clause and tucks the less important idea into an adjective clause (*who defeated Thomas E. Dewey*).

As
▶ **I was driving home from my new job, heading down Ranchitos Road, ~~when~~ my car suddenly overheated.**

PRACTICE hackerhandbooks.com/writersref
> Sentence style > S6–7 and S6–8

The writer wanted to emphasize that the car overheated, not the fact of driving home. The revision expresses the major idea in an independent clause and places the less important idea in an adverb clause (*As I was driving home from my new job*).

S6-e Do not subordinate excessively.

In attempting to avoid short, choppy sentences, writers sometimes go to the opposite extreme, putting more subordinate ideas into a sentence than its structure can bear. Sentences that become too complicated can sometimes be restructured. More often, however, such sentences must be divided.

▶ **In *Animal Liberation*, Peter Singer argues that animals possess nervous systems and can feel pain. ~~and that~~ He therefore believes that "the ethical principle on which human equality rests requires us to extend equal consideration to animals" (1).**

Writing with sources
MLA-style citation

Excessive subordination makes it difficult for the reader to focus on the quoted passage. By splitting the original sentence into two separate sentences, the writer draws attention to Peter Singer's main claim, that animals should be given "equal consideration" to humans.

S6-f Experiment with techniques for gaining special emphasis.

By experimenting with certain techniques, usually involving some element of surprise, you can draw attention to ideas that deserve special emphasis. Use such techniques sparingly, however, or they will lose their punch. The writer who tries to emphasize everything ends up emphasizing nothing.

Using sentence endings for emphasis

You can highlight an idea simply by withholding it until the end of a sentence. The technique works something like a punch line. In the following example, the sentence's meaning is not revealed until its very last word.

The only completely consistent people are the dead.
— Aldous Huxley

Using parallel structure for emphasis

Parallel grammatical structure draws special attention to paired ideas or to items in a series. (See S1.) When parallel ideas are paired, the emphasis falls on words that underscore comparisons or contrasts, especially when they occur at the end of a phrase or clause.

> We must *stop talking* about the *American dream* and *start listening* to the *dreams of Americans.* —Reubin Askew

In a parallel series, the emphasis falls at the end, so it is generally best to end with the most dramatic or climactic item in the series.

> Sister Charity enjoyed passing out writing punishments: translate the Ten Commandments into Latin, type a thousand-word essay on good manners, copy the New Testament with a quill pen.
> —Marie Visosky, student

Using an occasional short sentence for emphasis

Too many short sentences in a row will fast become monotonous (see S6-b), but an occasional short sentence, when played off against longer sentences in the same passage, will draw attention to an idea.

> The great secret, known to internists and learned early in marriage by internists' wives [or husbands], but still hidden from the general public, is that most things get better by themselves. Most things, in fact, are better by morning. —Lewis Thomas

S7 Sentence variety

When a rough draft is filled with too many sentences that begin the same way or have the same structure, try injecting some variety—as long as you can do so without sacrificing clarity or ease of reading.

S7-a Use a variety of sentence structures.

A writer should not rely too heavily on simple sentences and compound sentences, for the effect tends to be both monotonous and choppy. (See S6-b and S6-c.) Too many complex or compound-complex sentences, however, can be equally monotonous. If your style tends to one or the other extreme, try to achieve a better mix of sentence types.

For a discussion of sentence types, see B4-a.

S7-b Vary your sentence openings.

Most sentences in English begin with the subject, move to the verb, and continue to the object, with modifiers tucked in along the way or put at the end. For the most part, such sentences are fine. Put too many of them in a row, however, and they become monotonous.

Adverbial modifiers are easily movable when they modify verbs; they can often be inserted ahead of the subject. Such modifiers might be single words, phrases, or clauses.

Eventually a
▶ ~~A~~ few drops of sap ~~eventually~~ began to trickle into the bucket.

Like most adverbs, *eventually* does not need to appear close to the verb it modifies (*began*).

Just as the sun was coming up, a
▶ ~~A~~ pair of black ducks flew over the pond. ~~just as the sun was coming up.~~

The adverb clause, which modifies the verb *flew*, is as clear at the beginning of the sentence as it is at the end.

Adjectives and participial phrases can frequently be moved to the beginning of a sentence without loss of clarity.

Dejected and withdrawn,
▶ Edward/~~dejected and withdrawn,~~ nearly gave up his search for a job.

A *John and I*
▶ ~~John and I,~~ ~~a~~nticipating a peaceful evening, sat down at the campfire to brew a cup of coffee.

TIP: When beginning a sentence with an adjective or a participial phrase, make sure that the subject of the sentence names the person or thing described in the introductory phrase. If it doesn't, the phrase will dangle. (See S3-e.)

S7-c Try inverting sentences occasionally.

A sentence is inverted if it does not follow the normal subject-verb-object pattern. Many inversions sound artificial and should be avoided except in the most formal contexts. But if an inversion sounds natural, it can provide a welcome touch of variety.

Opposite the produce section is a
▶ ~~A~~ refrigerated case of cheeses. ~~is opposite the produce section.~~

The revision inverts the normal subject-verb order by moving the verb, *is*, ahead of its subject, *case*.

Placed at the top two corners of the stage were huge
▶ ~~Huge~~ lavender hearts outlined in bright white lights. ~~were at the top two corners of the stage.~~

In the revision, the subject, *hearts*, appears after the verb, *were placed*. The two parts of the verb are also inverted—and separated from each other (*Placed* . . . *were*)—without any awkwardness or loss of meaning.

Inverted sentences are used for emphasis as well as for variety (see S6-f).

W

Word Choice

W Word Choice

W1 **Glossary of usage, 139**

W2 **Wordy sentences, 153**

- **a** Redundancies, 153
- **b** Unnecessary repetition, 153
- **c** Empty or inflated phrases, 154
- **d** Simplified structure, 155
- **e** Reducing clauses to phrases, phrases to single words, 156

W3 **Active verbs, 156**

- **a** Active versus passive verbs, 157
- **b** Active versus *be* verbs, 158

W4 **Appropriate language, 159**

- **a** Jargon, 159
- **b** Pretentious language, euphemisms, "doublespeak," 159
- **c** Slang, regionalisms, nonstandard English, 160
- **d** Levels of formality, 162
- **e** Sexist language, 162
- **f** Offensive language, 164

W5 **Exact language, 165**

- **a** Connotations, 165
- **b** Concrete nouns, 165
- **c** Misused words, 166
- **d** Standard idioms, 167
- **e** Clichés, 167
- **f** Figures of speech, 168

W6 **The dictionary and thesaurus, 169**

- **a** The dictionary, 169
- **b** The thesaurus, 172

W1 Glossary of usage

This glossary includes words commonly confused (such as *accept* and *except*), words commonly misused (such as *aggravate*), and words that are nonstandard (such as *hisself*). It also lists colloquialisms and jargon. Colloquialisms are casual expressions that may be appropriate in informal speech but are inappropriate in formal writing. Jargon is needlessly technical or pretentious language that is inappropriate in most contexts. If an item is not listed here, consult the index. For irregular verbs (such as *sing, sang, sung*), see G2-a. For idiomatic use of prepositions, see W5-d.

a, an Use *an* before a vowel sound, *a* before a consonant sound: *an apple, a peach.* Problems sometimes arise with words beginning with *h* or *u*. If the *h* is silent, the word begins with a vowel sound, so use *an*: *an hour, an honorable deed.* If the *h* is pronounced, the word begins with a consonant sound, so use *a*: *a hospital, a historian, a hotel.* Words such as *university* and *union* begin with a consonant sound (a *y* sound), so use *a*: *a union.* Words such as *uncle* and *umbrella* begin with a vowel sound, so use *an*: *an underground well.* When an abbreviation or an acronym begins with a vowel sound, use *an*: *an EKG, an MRI, an AIDS prevention program.*

accept, except *Accept* is a verb meaning "to receive." *Except* is usually a preposition meaning "excluding." *I will accept all the packages except that one.* *Except* is also a verb meaning "to exclude." *Please except that item from the list.*

adapt, adopt *Adapt* means "to adjust or become accustomed"; it is usually followed by *to*. *Adopt* means "to take as one's own." *Our family adopted a Vietnamese child, who quickly adapted to his new life.*

adverse, averse *Adverse* means "unfavorable." *Averse* means "opposed" or "reluctant"; it is usually followed by *to*. *I am averse to your proposal because it could have an adverse impact on the economy.*

advice, advise *Advice* is a noun, *advise* a verb. *We advise you to follow John's advice.*

affect, effect *Affect* is usually a verb meaning "to influence." *Effect* is usually a noun meaning "result." *The drug did not affect the disease, and it had adverse side effects.* *Effect* can also be a verb meaning "to bring about." *Only the president can effect such a dramatic change.*

aggravate *Aggravate* means "to make worse or more troublesome." *Overgrazing aggravated the soil erosion.* In formal writing, avoid the use of *aggravate* meaning "to annoy or irritate." *Her babbling annoyed* (not *aggravated*) *me.*

agree to, agree with *Agree to* means "to give consent to." *Agree with* means "to be in accord with" or "to come to an understanding with." *He agrees with me about the need for change, but he won't agree to my plan.*

ain't *Ain't* is nonstandard. Use *am not, are not (aren't),* or *is not (isn't). I am not* (not *ain't*) *going home for spring break.*

all ready, already *All ready* means "completely prepared." *Already* means "previously." *Susan was all ready for the concert, but her friends had already left.*

all right *All right* is written as two words. *Alright* is nonstandard.

all together, altogether *All together* means "everyone or everything in one place." *Altogether* means "entirely." *We were not altogether certain that we could bring the family all together for the reunion.*

allude To *allude* to something is to make an indirect reference to it. Do not use *allude* to mean "to refer directly." *In his lecture, the professor referred* (not *alluded*) *to several pre-Socratic philosophers.*

allusion, illusion An *allusion* is an indirect reference. An *illusion* is a misconception or false impression. *Did you catch my allusion to Shakespeare? Mirrors give the room an illusion of depth.*

a lot *A lot* is two words. Do not write *alot. Sam lost a lot of weight.* See also *lots, lots of.*

among, between See *between, among.*

amongst In American English, *among* is preferred.

amoral, immoral *Amoral* means "neither moral nor immoral"; it also means "not caring about moral judgments." *Immoral* means "morally wrong." *Until recently, most business courses were taught from an amoral perspective. Murder is immoral.*

amount, number Use *amount* with quantities that cannot be counted; use *number* with those that can. *This recipe calls for a large amount of sugar. We have a large number of toads in our garden.*

an See *a, an.*

and etc. *Et cetera* (*etc.*) means "and so forth"; *and etc.* is redundant. See also *etc.*

and/or Avoid the awkward construction *and/or* except in technical or legal documents.

angry at, angry with Use *angry with,* not *angry at,* when referring to a person. *The coach was angry with the referee.*

ante-, anti- The prefix *ante-* means "earlier" or "in front of"; the prefix *anti-* means "against" or "opposed to." *William Lloyd Garrison was a leader of the antislavery movement during the antebellum period. Anti-* should be used with a hyphen when it is followed by a capital letter or a word beginning with *i*.

anxious *Anxious* means "worried" or "apprehensive." In formal writing, avoid using *anxious* to mean "eager." *We are eager* (not *anxious*) *to see your new house.*

anybody, anyone *Anybody* and *anyone* are singular. (See G1-e and G3-a.)

anymore Use the adverb *anymore* in a negative context to mean "any longer" or "now." *The factory isn't producing shoes anymore.* Using *anymore* in a positive context is colloquial; in formal writing, use *now* instead. *We order all our food online now* (not *anymore*).

anyone See *anybody, anyone.*

anyone, any one *Anyone*, an indefinite pronoun, means "any person at all." *Any one*, the pronoun *one* preceded by the adjective *any*, refers to a particular person or thing in a group. *Anyone from the winning team may choose any one of the games on display.*

anyplace In formal writing, use *anywhere.*

anyways, anywheres *Anyways* and *anywheres* are nonstandard. Use *anyway* and *anywhere.*

as Do not use *as* to mean "because" if there is any chance of ambiguity. *We canceled the picnic because* (not *as*) *it began raining. As* here could mean either "because" or "when."

as, like See *like, as.*

as to *As to* is jargon for *about. He inquired about* (not *as to*) *the job.*

averse See *adverse, averse.*

awful The adjective *awful* and the adverb *awfully* are not appropriate in formal writing.

awhile, a while *Awhile* is an adverb; it can modify a verb, but it cannot be the object of a preposition such as *for*. The two-word form *a while* is a noun preceded by an article and therefore can be the object of a preposition. *Stay awhile. Stay for a while.*

back up, backup *Back up* is a verb phrase. *Back up the car carefully. Be sure to back up your hard drive. Backup* is a noun meaning "a copy of electronically stored data." *Keep your backup in a safe place. Backup* can also be used as an adjective. *I regularly create backup disks.*

bad, badly *Bad* is an adjective, *badly* an adverb. *They felt bad about ruining the surprise. Her arm hurt badly after she slid into second base.* (See G4-a and G4-b.)

being as, being that *Being as* and *being that* are nonstandard expressions. Write *because* instead. *Because* (not *Being as*) *I slept late, I had to skip breakfast.*

USAGE **hackerhandbooks.com/writersref**
> Language Debates > Pronoun-antecedent agreement
> *bad* versus *badly*

beside, besides *Beside* is a preposition meaning "at the side of" or "next to." *Annie Oakley slept with her gun beside her bed. Besides* is a preposition meaning "except" or "in addition to." *No one besides Terrie can have that ice cream. Besides* is also an adverb meaning "in addition." *I'm not hungry; besides, I don't like ice cream.*

between, among Ordinarily, use *among* with three or more entities, *between* with two. *The prize was divided among several contestants. You have a choice between carrots and beans.*

bring, take Use *bring* when an object is being transported toward you, *take* when it is being moved away. *Please bring me a glass of water. Please take these forms to Mr. Scott.*

burst, bursted; bust, busted *Burst* is an irregular verb meaning "to come open or fly apart suddenly or violently." Its past tense is *burst*. The past-tense form *bursted* is nonstandard. *Bust* and *busted* are slang for *burst* and, along with *bursted*, should not be used in formal writing.

can, may The distinction between *can* and *may* is fading, but some writers still observe it in formal writing. *Can* is traditionally reserved for ability, *may* for permission. *Can you speak French? May I help you?*

capital, capitol *Capital* refers to a city, *capitol* to a building where lawmakers meet. *Capital* also refers to wealth or resources. *The residents of the state capital protested plans to close the streets surrounding the capitol.*

censor, censure *Censor* means "to remove or suppress material considered objectionable." *Censure* means "to criticize severely." *The administration's policy of censoring books has been censured by the media.*

cite, site *Cite* means "to quote as an authority or example." *Site* is usually a noun meaning "a particular place." *He cited the zoning law in his argument against the proposed site of the gas station.* Locations on the Internet are usually referred to as *sites. The library's Web site improves every week.*

climactic, climatic *Climactic* is derived from *climax*, the point of greatest intensity in a series or progression of events. *Climatic* is derived from *climate* and refers to meteorological conditions. *The climactic period in the dinosaurs' reign was reached just before severe climatic conditions brought on an ice age.*

coarse, course *Coarse* means "crude" or "rough in texture." *The coarse weave of the wall hanging gave it a three-dimensional quality. Course* usually refers to a path, a playing field, or a unit of study; the expression *of course* means "certainly." *I plan to take a course in car repair this summer. Of course, you are welcome to join me.*

compare to, compare with *Compare to* means "to represent as similar." *She compared him to a wild stallion. Compare with* means "to examine similarities and differences." *The study compared the language ability of apes with that of dolphins.*

complement, compliment *Complement* is a verb meaning "to go with or complete" or a noun meaning "something that completes." As a verb, *compliment* means "to flatter"; as a noun, it means "flattering remark." *Her skill at rushing the net complements his skill at volleying. Martha's flower arrangements receive many compliments.*

conscience, conscious *Conscience* is a noun meaning "moral principles." *Conscious* is an adjective meaning "aware or alert." *Let your conscience be your guide. Were you conscious of his love for you?*

continual, continuous *Continual* means "repeated regularly and frequently." *She grew weary of the continual telephone calls. Continuous* means "extended or prolonged without interruption." *The broken siren made a continuous wail.*

could care less *Could care less* is nonstandard. Write *couldn't care less* instead. *He couldn't* (not *could*) *care less about his psychology final.*

could of *Could of* is nonstandard for *could have. We could have* (not *could of*) *taken the train.*

council, counsel A *council* is a deliberative body, and a *councilor* is a member of such a body. *Counsel* usually means "advice" and can also mean "lawyer"; a *counselor* is one who gives advice or guidance. *The councilors met to draft the council's position paper. The pastor offered wise counsel to the troubled teenager.*

criteria *Criteria* is the plural of *criterion*, which means "a standard or rule or test on which a judgment or decision can be based." *The only criterion for the scholarship is ability.*

data *Data* is a plural noun technically meaning "facts or results." But *data* is increasingly being accepted as a singular noun. *The new data suggest* (or *suggests*) *that our theory is correct.* (The singular *datum* is rarely used.)

different from, different than Ordinarily, write *different from. Your sense of style is different from Jim's.* However, *different than* is acceptable to avoid an awkward construction. *Please let me know if your plans are different than* (to avoid *from what*) *they were six weeks ago.*

differ from, differ with *Differ from* means "to be unlike"; *differ with* means "to disagree with." *My approach to the problem differed from hers. She differed with me about the wording of the agreement.*

disinterested, uninterested *Disinterested* means "impartial, objective"; *uninterested* means "not interested." *We sought the advice of a disinterested counselor to help us solve our problem. Mark was uninterested in anyone's opinion but his own.*

don't *Don't* is the contraction for *do not. I don't want any. Don't* should not be used as the contraction for *does not*, which is *doesn't. He doesn't* (not *don't*) *want any.*

due to *Due to* is an adjective phrase and should not be used as a preposition meaning "because of." *The trip was canceled because of* (not *due to*) *lack of interest. Due to* is acceptable as a subject complement and usually follows a form of the verb *be. His success was due to hard work.*

each *Each* is singular. (See G1-e and G3-a.)

effect See *affect, effect.*

e.g. In formal writing, replace the Latin abbreviation *e.g.* with its English equivalent: *for example* or *for instance.*

either *Either* is singular. (See G1-e and G3-a.) For *either . . . or* constructions, see G1-d and G-3a.

elicit, illicit *Elicit* is a verb meaning "to bring out" or "to evoke." *Illicit* is an adjective meaning "unlawful." *The reporter was unable to elicit any information from the police about illicit drug traffic.*

emigrate from, immigrate to *Emigrate* means "to leave one country or region to settle in another." *In 1903, my great-grandfather emigrated from Russia to escape the religious pogroms. Immigrate* means "to enter another country and reside there." *More than fifty thousand Bosnians immigrated to the United States in the 1990s.*

eminent, imminent *Eminent* means "outstanding" or "distinguished." *We met an eminent professor of Greek history. Imminent* means "about to happen." *The snowstorm is imminent.*

enthused Many people object to the use of *enthused* as an adjective. Use *enthusiastic* instead. *The children were enthusiastic* (not *enthused*) *about going to the circus.*

etc. Avoid ending a list with *etc.* It is more emphatic to end with an example, and in most contexts readers will understand that the list is not exhaustive. When you don't wish to end with an example, *and so on* is more graceful than *etc.* (See also *and etc.*)

eventually, ultimately Often used interchangeably, *eventually* is the better choice to mean "at an unspecified time in the future," and *ultimately* is better to mean "the furthest possible extent or greatest extreme." *He knew that eventually he would complete his degree. The existentialists considered suicide the ultimately rational act.*

everybody, everyone *Everybody* and *everyone* are singular. (See G1-e and G3-a.)

everyone, every one *Everyone* is an indefinite pronoun. *Every one*, the pronoun *one* preceded by the adjective *every*, means "each individual or thing in a particular group." *Every one* is usually followed by *of. Everyone wanted to go. Every one of the missing books was found.*

except See *accept, except*.

expect Avoid the informal use of *expect* meaning "to believe, think, or suppose." *I think* (not *expect*) *it will rain tonight*.

explicit, implicit *Explicit* means "expressed directly" or "clearly defined"; *implicit* means "implied, unstated." *I gave him explicit instructions not to go swimming. My mother's silence indicated her implicit approval.*

farther, further *Farther* usually describes distances. *Further* usually suggests quantity or degree. *Chicago is farther from Miami than I thought. I would be grateful for further suggestions.*

fewer, less Use *fewer* for items that can be counted; use *less* for items that cannot be counted. *Fewer people are living in the city. Please put less sugar in my tea.*

finalize *Finalize* is jargon meaning "to make final or complete." Use ordinary English instead. *The architect prepared final drawings* (not *finalized the drawings*).

firstly *Firstly* sounds pretentious, and it leads to the ungainly series *firstly, secondly, thirdly,* and so on. Write *first, second, third* instead.

further See *farther, further*.

get *Get* has many colloquial uses. In writing, avoid using *get* to mean the following: "to evoke an emotional response" (*That music always gets to me*); "to annoy" (*After a while his sulking got to me*); "to take revenge on" (*I got back at her by leaving the room*); "to become" (*He got sick*); "to start or begin" (*Let's get going*). Avoid using *have got to* in place of *must*. *I must* (not *have got to*) *finish this paper tonight*.

good, well *Good* is an adjective, *well* an adverb. (See G4-a and G4-b.) *He hasn't felt good about his game since he sprained his wrist last season. She performed well on the uneven parallel bars.*

graduate Both of the following uses of *graduate* are standard: *My sister was graduated from UCLA last year. My sister graduated from UCLA last year*. It is nonstandard, however, to drop the word *from*: *My sister graduated UCLA last year*. Though this usage is common in informal English, many readers object to it.

grow Phrases such as *to grow the economy* and *to grow a business* are jargon. Usually the verb *grow* is intransitive (it does not take a direct object). *Our business has grown very quickly*. Use *grow* in a transitive sense, with a direct object, to mean "to cultivate" or "to allow to grow." *We plan to grow tomatoes this year. John is growing a beard.*

hanged, hung *Hanged* is the past-tense and past-participle form of the verb *hang* meaning "to execute." *The prisoner was hanged at dawn. Hung* is the past-tense and past-participle form of the verb *hang* meaning "to fasten or suspend." *The stockings were hung by the chimney with care.*

hardly Avoid expressions such as *can't hardly* and *not hardly*, which are considered double negatives. *I can* (not *can't*) *hardly describe my surprise at getting the job*. (See G4-d.)

has got, have got *Got* is unnecessary and awkward in such constructions. It should be dropped. *We have* (not *have got*) *three days to prepare for the opening*.

he At one time *he* was commonly used to mean "he or she." Today such usage is inappropriate. (See W4-e and G3-a.)

he/she, his/her In formal writing, use *he or she* or *his or her*. For alternatives to these wordy constructions, see W4-e and G3-a.

hisself *Hisself* is nonstandard. Use *himself*.

hopefully *Hopefully* means "in a hopeful manner." *We looked hopefully to the future*. Some usage experts object to the use of *hopefully* as a sentence adverb, apparently on grounds of clarity. To be safe, avoid using *hopefully* in sentences such as the following: *Hopefully, your son will recover soon*. Instead, indicate who is doing the hoping: *I hope that your son will recover soon*.

however In the past, some writers objected to the conjunctive adverb *however* at the beginning of a sentence, but current experts allow placing the word according to the intended meaning and emphasis. All of the following sentences are correct. *Pam decided, however, to attend the lecture. However, Pam decided to attend the lecture.* (She had been considering other activities.) *Pam, however, decided to attend the lecture*. (Unlike someone else, Pam chose to attend the lecture.) (See P1-f.)

hung See *hanged, hung*.

i.e. In formal writing, replace the Latin abbreviation *i.e.* with its English equivalent: *that is*.

if, whether Use *if* to express a condition and *whether* to express alternatives. *If you go on a trip, whether to Nebraska or Italy, remember to bring traveler's checks*.

illusion See *allusion, illusion*.

immigrate See *emigrate from, immigrate to*.

imminent See *eminent, imminent*.

immoral See *amoral, immoral*.

implement *Implement* is a pretentious way of saying "do," "carry out," or "accomplish." Use ordinary language instead. *We carried out* (not *implemented*) *the director's orders*.

imply, infer *Imply* means "to suggest or state indirectly"; *infer* means "to draw a conclusion." *John implied that he knew all about computers, but the interviewer inferred that John was inexperienced*.

USAGE **hackerhandbooks.com/writersref**
> Language Debates > Sexist language
> *however* at the beginning of a sentence

in, into *In* indicates location or condition; *into* indicates movement or a change in condition. *They found the lost letters in a box after moving into the house.*

in regards to *In regards to* confuses two different phrases: *in regard to* and *as regards*. Use one or the other. *In regard to* (or *As regards*) *the contract, ignore the first clause.*

irregardless *Irregardless* is nonstandard. Use *regardless*.

is when, is where These mixed constructions are often incorrectly used in definitions. *A run-off election is a second election held to break a tie* (not *is when a second election is held to break a tie*). (See S5-c.)

its, it's *Its* is a possessive pronoun; *it's* is a contraction for *it is*. (See P4-a and P4-b.) *It's always fun to watch a dog chase its tail.*

kind(s) *Kind* is singular and should be treated as such. Don't write *These kind of chairs are rare*. Write instead *This kind of chair is rare*. *Kinds* is plural and should be used only when you mean more than one kind. *These kinds of chairs are rare.*

kind of, sort of Avoid using *kind of* or *sort of* to mean "somewhat." *The movie was somewhat* (not *sort of*) *boring*. Do not put *a* after either phrase. *That kind of* (not *kind of a*) *salesclerk annoys me.*

lay, lie See *lie, lay*.

lead, led *Lead* is a metallic element; it is a noun. *Led* is the past tense of the verb *lead*. *He led me to the treasure.*

learn, teach *Learn* means "to gain knowledge"; *teach* means "to impart knowledge." *I must teach* (not *learn*) *my sister to read.*

leave, let *Leave* means "to exit." Avoid using it with the nonstandard meaning "to permit." *Let* (not *Leave*) *me help you with the dishes.*

less See *fewer, less*.

let, leave See *leave, let*.

liable *Liable* means "obligated" or "responsible." Do not use it to mean "likely." *You're likely* (not *liable*) *to trip if you don't tie your shoelaces.*

lie, lay *Lie* is an intransitive verb meaning "to recline or rest on a surface." Its forms are *lie*, *lay*, *lain*. *Lay* is a transitive verb meaning "to put or place." Its forms are *lay*, *laid*, *laid*. (See G2-b.)

like, as *Like* is a preposition, not a subordinating conjunction. It can be followed only by a noun or a noun phrase. *As* is a subordinating conjunction that introduces a subordinate clause. In casual speech, you may say *She looks like she hasn't slept* or *You don't know her like I do*. But in formal writing, use *as*. *She looks as if she hasn't slept. You don't know her as I do*. (See also B1-f and B1-g.)

USAGE **hackerhandbooks.com/writersref**
> Language Debates > *lie* versus *lay*

loose, lose *Loose* is an adjective meaning "not securely fastened." *Lose* is a verb meaning "to misplace" or "to not win." *Did you lose your only loose pair of work pants?*

lots, lots of *Lots* and *lots of* are informal substitutes for *many*, *much*, or *a lot*. Avoid using them in formal writing.

mankind Avoid *mankind* whenever possible. It offends many readers because it excludes women. Use *humanity*, *humans*, *the human race*, or *humankind* instead. (See W4-e.)

may See *can, may.*

maybe, may be *Maybe* is an adverb meaning "possibly." *Maybe the sun will shine tomorrow. May be* is a verb phrase. *Tomorrow may be brighter.*

may of, might of *May of* and *might of* are nonstandard for *may have* and *might have*. *We might have* (not *might of*) *had too many cookies.*

media, medium *Media* is the plural of *medium*. *Of all the media that cover the Olympics, television is the medium that best captures the spectacle of the events.*

most *Most* is informal when used to mean "almost" and should be avoided. *Almost* (not *Most*) *everyone went to the parade.*

must of See *may of.*

myself *Myself* is a reflexive or intensive pronoun. Reflexive: *I cut myself.* Intensive: *I will drive you myself.* Do not use *myself* in place of *I* or *me*. *He gave the flowers to Melinda and me* (not *myself*). (See also G3-c.)

neither *Neither* is singular. (See G1-e and G3-a.) For *neither . . . nor* constructions, see G1-d and G3-a.

none *None* may be singular or plural. (See G1-e.)

nowheres *Nowheres* is nonstandard. Use *nowhere* instead.

number See *amount, number.*

of Use the verb *have*, not the preposition *of*, after the verbs *could*, *should*, *would*, *may*, *might*, and *must*. *They must have* (not *must of*) *left early.*

off of *Off* is sufficient. Omit *of*. *The ball rolled off* (not *off of*) *the table.*

OK, O.K., okay All three spellings are acceptable, but avoid these expressions in formal speech and writing.

parameters *Parameter* is a mathematical term that has become jargon for "fixed limit," "boundary," or "guideline." Use ordinary English instead. *The task force worked within certain guidelines* (not *parameters*).

passed, past *Passed* is the past tense of the verb *pass*. *Ann passed me another slice of cake. Past* usually means "belonging to a former time" or

USAGE **hackerhandbooks.com/writersref**
> Language Debates > *myself*
> *none*

"beyond a time or place." *Our past president spoke until past midnight. The hotel is just past the next intersection.*

percent, per cent, percentage *Percent* (also spelled *per cent*) is always used with a specific number. *Percentage* is used with a descriptive term such as *large* or *small*, not with a specific number. *The candidate won 80 percent of the primary vote. A large percentage of registered voters turned out for the election.*

phenomena *Phenomena* is the plural of *phenomenon*, which means "an observable occurrence or fact." *Strange phenomena occur at all hours of the night in that house, but last night's phenomenon was the strangest of all.*

plus *Plus* should not be used to join independent clauses. *This raincoat is dirty; moreover* (not *plus*), *it has a hole in it.*

precede, proceed *Precede* means "to come before." *Proceed* means "to go forward." *As we proceeded up the mountain path, we noticed fresh tracks in the mud, evidence that a group of hikers had preceded us.*

principal, principle *Principal* is a noun meaning "the head of a school or an organization" or "a sum of money." It is also an adjective meaning "most important." *Principle* is a noun meaning "a basic truth or law." *The principal expelled her for three principal reasons. We believe in the principle of equal justice for all.*

proceed, precede See *precede, proceed.*

quote, quotation *Quote* is a verb; *quotation* is a noun. Avoid using *quote* as a shortened form of *quotation*. *Her quotations* (not *quotes*) *from current movies intrigued us.*

raise, rise *Raise* is a transitive verb meaning "to move or cause to move upward." It takes a direct object. *I raised the shades. Rise* is an intransitive verb meaning "to go up." *Heat rises.*

real, really *Real* is an adjective; *really* is an adverb. *Real* is sometimes used informally as an adverb, but avoid this use in formal writing. *She was really* (not *real*) *angry.* (See G4-b.)

reason . . . is because Use *that* instead of *because. The reason she's cranky is that* (not *because*) *she didn't sleep last night.* (See S5-c.)

reason why The expression *reason why* is redundant. *The reason* (not *The reason why*) *Jones lost the election is clear.*

relation, relationship *Relation* describes a connection between things. *Relationship* describes a connection between people. *There is a relation between poverty and infant mortality. Our business relationship has cooled over the years.*

respectfully, respectively *Respectfully* means "showing or marked by respect." *Respectively* means "each in the order given." *He respectfully* *submitted his opinion to the judge. John, Tom, and Larry were a butcher, a baker, and a lawyer, respectively.*

sensual, sensuous *Sensual* means "gratifying the physical senses," especially those associated with sexual pleasure. *Sensuous* means "pleasing to the senses," especially those involved in the experience of art, music, and nature. *The sensuous music and balmy air led the dancers to more sensual movements.*

set, sit *Set* is a transitive verb meaning "to put" or "to place." Its past tense is *set*. *Sit* is an intransitive verb meaning "to be seated." Its past tense is *sat*. *She set the dough in a warm corner of the kitchen. The cat sat in the doorway.*

shall, will *Shall* was once used in place of the helping verb *will* with *I* or *we*: *I shall, we shall*. Today, however, *will* is generally accepted even when the subject is *I* or *we*. The word *shall* occurs primarily in polite questions (*Shall I find you a pillow?*) and in legalistic sentences suggesting duty or obligation (*The applicant shall file form A by December 31*).

should of *Should of* is nonstandard for *should have*. *They should have* (not *should of*) *been home an hour ago.*

since Do not use *since* to mean "because" if there is any chance of ambiguity. *Because* (not *Since*) *we won the game, we have been celebrating with a pitcher of root beer*. *Since* here could mean "because" or "from the time that."

sit See *set, sit*.

site See *cite, site*.

somebody, someone *Somebody* and *someone* are singular. (See G1-e and G3-a.)

something *Something* is singular. (See G1-e.)

sometime, some time, sometimes *Sometime* is an adverb meaning "at an indefinite or unstated time." *Some time* is the adjective *some* modifying the noun *time* and means "a period of time." *Sometimes* is an adverb meaning "at times, now and then." *I'll see you sometime soon. I haven't lived there for some time. Sometimes I see him at the library.*

suppose to Write *supposed to*.

sure and Write *sure to*. *We were all taught to be sure to* (not *sure and*) *look both ways before crossing a street.*

take See *bring, take*.

than, then *Than* is a conjunction used in comparisons; *then* is an adverb denoting time. *That pizza is more than I can eat. Tom laughed, and then we recognized him.*

that See *who, which, that*.

that, which Many writers reserve *that* for restrictive clauses, *which* for nonrestrictive clauses. (See P1-e.)

theirselves *Theirselves* is nonstandard for *themselves. The crash victims pushed the car out of the way themselves* (not *theirselves*).

them The use of *them* in place of *those* is nonstandard. *Please take those* (not *them*) *flowers to the patient in room 220.*

then, than See *than, then.*

there, their, they're *There* is an adverb specifying place; it is also an expletive (placeholder). Adverb: *Sylvia is lying there unconscious.* Expletive: *There are two plums left. Their* is a possessive pronoun. *Fred and Jane finally washed their car. They're* is a contraction of *they are. They're later than usual today.*

they The use of *they* to indicate possession is nonstandard. Use *their* instead. *Cindy and Sam decided to sell their* (not *they*) *1975 Corvette.*

they, their The use of the plural pronouns *they* and *their* to refer to singular nouns or pronouns is nonstandard. *No one handed in his or her* (not *their*) *draft on time.* (See G3-a.)

this kind See *kind(s).*

to, too, two *To* is a preposition; *too* is an adverb; *two* is a number. *Too many of your shots slice to the left, but the last two were just right.*

toward, towards *Toward* and *towards* are generally interchangeable, although *toward* is preferred in American English.

try and *Try and* is nonstandard for *try to. The teacher asked us all to try to* (not *try and*) *write an original haiku.*

ultimately, eventually See *eventually, ultimately.*

unique Avoid expressions such as *most unique, more straight, less perfect, very round.* Either something is unique or it isn't. It is illogical to suggest degrees of uniqueness. (See G4-c.)

usage The noun *usage* should not be substituted for *use* when the meaning is "employment of." *The use* (not *usage*) *of insulated shades has cut fuel costs dramatically.*

use to Write *used to.*

utilize *Utilize* means "to make use of." It often sounds pretentious; in most cases, *use* is sufficient. *I used* (not *utilized*) *the laser printer.*

wait for, wait on *Wait for* means "to be in readiness for" or "to await." *Wait on* means "to serve." *We're only waiting for* (not *waiting on*) *Ruth to take us to the museum.*

ways *Ways* is colloquial when used to mean "distance." *The city is a long way* (not *ways*) *from here.*

USAGE **hackerhandbooks.com/writersref**
> Language Debates > *that* versus *which*
> Absolute concepts such as *unique*

weather, whether The noun *weather* refers to the state of the atmosphere. *Whether* is a conjunction referring to a choice between alternatives. *We wondered whether the weather would clear.*

well, good See *good, well.*

where Do not use *where* in place of *that. I heard that* (not *where*) *the crime rate is increasing.*

which See *that, which* and *who, which, that.*

while Avoid using *while* to mean "although" or "whereas" if there is any chance of ambiguity. *Although* (not *While*) *Gloria lost money in the slot machine, Tom won it at roulette.* Here *While* could mean either "although" or "at the same time that."

who, which, that Do not use *which* to refer to persons. Use *who* instead. *That*, though generally used to refer to things, may be used to refer to a group or class of people. *The player who* (not *that* or *which*) *made the basket at the buzzer was named MVP. The team that scores the most points in this game will win the tournament.*

who, whom *Who* is used for subjects and subject complements; *whom* is used for objects. (See G3-d.)

who's, whose *Who's* is a contraction of *who is*; *whose* is a possessive pronoun. *Who's ready for more popcorn? Whose coat is this?* (See P4-b and P4-a.)

will See *shall, will.*

would of *Would of* is nonstandard for *would have. She would have* (not *would of*) *had a chance to play if she had arrived on time.*

you In formal writing, avoid *you* in an indefinite sense meaning "anyone." (See G3-b.) *Any spectator* (not *You*) *could tell by the way John caught the ball that his throw would be too late.*

your, you're *Your* is a possessive pronoun; *you're* is a contraction of *you are. Is that your new bike? You're in the finals.* (See P4-a and P4-b.)

USAGE **hackerhandbooks.com/writersref**
> Language Debates > *who* versus *which* or *that*
> *who* versus *whom*
> *you*

W2 Wordy sentences

Long sentences are not necessarily wordy, nor are short sentences always concise. A sentence is wordy if it can be tightened without loss of meaning.

W2-a Eliminate redundancies.

Writers often repeat themselves unnecessarily, thinking that expressions such as *cooperate together*, *yellow in color*, or *basic essentials* add emphasis to their writing. In reality, such redundancies do just the opposite. There is no need to say the same thing twice.

▶ **Daniel ~~is now employed~~ *works* at a private rehabilitation center ~~working~~ as a registered physical therapist.**

Though modifiers ordinarily add meaning to the words they modify, occasionally they are redundant.

▶ **Sylvia ~~very hurriedly~~ scribbled her name, address, and phone number on a greasy napkin.**

The word *scribbled* already suggests that Sylvia wrote very hurriedly

▶ **Gabriele Muccino's film *The Pursuit of Happyness* tells the story of a single father determined ~~in his mind~~ to pull himself and his son out of homelessness.**

The word *determined* contains the idea that his resolution formed in his mind.

W2-b Avoid unnecessary repetition of words.

Though words may be repeated deliberately, for effect, repetitions will seem awkward if they are clearly unnecessary. When a more concise version is possible, choose it.

PRACTICE hackerhandbooks.com/writersref
> Word choice > W2–3 to W2–6

► Our fifth patient, in room six, is ~~a~~ mentally ill. ~~patient~~.

Writing with sources
APA-style citation

► A study by the Henry J. Kaiser Family Foundation (2004) *measured* ~~studied~~ the effects of diet and exercise on childhood obesity.

The repetition of *study . . . studied* is awkward and redundant. By using the descriptive verb *measured* instead, the writer conveys more precisely the purpose of the study and suggests its function in the paper.

W2-c Cut empty or inflated phrases.

An empty phrase can be cut with little or no loss of meaning. Common examples are introductory word groups that weaken the writer's authority by apologizing or hedging: *in my opinion*, *I think that*, *it seems that*, *one must admit that*, and so on.

► ~~In my opinion,~~ O~~o~~ur current immigration policy is misguided.

Inflated phrases can be reduced to a word or two without loss of meaning.

INFLATED	CONCISE
along the lines of	like
as a matter of fact	in fact
at all times	always
at the present time	now, currently
at this point in time	now, currently
because of the fact that	because
by means of	by
by virtue of the fact that	because
due to the fact that	because
for the purpose of	for
for the reason that	because
have the ability to	be able to, can
in light of the fact that	because
in order to	to
in spite of the fact that	although, though
in the event that	if
in the final analysis	finally
in the nature of	like
in the neighborhood of	about
until such time as	until

▶ **We are unable to provide funding ~~at this point in time.~~** *now.*

W2-d Simplify the structure.

If the structure of a sentence is needlessly indirect, try simplifying it. Look for opportunities to strengthen the verb.

▶ **The financial analyst claimed that because of volatile market conditions she could not ~~make an~~ estimate ~~of~~ the company's future profits.**

The verb *estimate* is more vigorous and concise than *make an estimate of.*

The colorless verbs *is*, *are*, *was*, and *were* frequently generate excess words. (See also W3-b.)

▶ **Investigators** *examined* **~~were involved in examining~~ the effect of classical music on unborn babies.**

The revision is more direct and concise. The action (*examining*), originally appearing in a subordinate structure, has become a strong verb, *examined.*

The expletive constructions *there is* and *there are* (or *there was* and *there were*) can also generate excess words. The same is true of expletive constructions beginning with *it*.

▶ **~~There is~~** *A* **~~a~~nother module ~~that~~ tells the story of Charles Darwin and introduces the theory of evolution.**

▶ **~~It is imperative that~~** *A* **~~a~~ll night managers** *must* **follow strict procedures when locking the safe.**

Finally, verbs in the passive voice may be needlessly indirect. When the active voice expresses your meaning as effectively, use it. (See also W3-a.)

▶ **All too often,** *our coaches have recruited* **athletes with marginal academic skills. ~~have been recruited by our coaches.~~**

W2-e Reduce clauses to phrases, phrases to single words.

Word groups functioning as modifiers can often be made more compact. Look for any opportunities to reduce clauses to phrases or phrases to single words.

► We took a side trip to Monticello, ~~which was~~ the home of Thomas Jefferson.

► In ~~the~~ *this* essay, ~~that follows,~~ I argue against Immanuel Kant's *problematic* claim that we should not lie under any circumstances. ~~which is a problematic assertion.~~

W3 Active verbs

As a rule, choose an active verb and pair it with a subject that names the person or thing doing the action. Active verbs express meaning more emphatically and vigorously than their weaker counterparts—forms of the verb *be* or verbs in the passive voice.

PASSIVE The pumps *were destroyed* by a surge of power.

BE VERB A surge of power *was* responsible for the destruction of the pumps.

ACTIVE A surge of power *destroyed* the pumps.

Verbs in the passive voice lack strength because their subjects receive the action instead of doing it. Forms of the verb *be* (*be*, *am*, *is*, *are*, *was*, *were*, *being*, *been*) lack vigor because they convey no action.

Although passive verbs and the forms of *be* have legitimate uses, choose an active verb if it can carry your meaning. Even among active verbs, some convey action more vigorously than others. Carefully selected verbs can energize a piece of writing.

► The goalie crouched low, ~~reached~~ *swept* out his stick, and ~~sent~~ *hooked* the rebound away from the mouth of the net.

PRACTICE **hackerhandbooks.com/writersref**
> Word choice > W3–2 to W3–5

Academic English Although you may be tempted to avoid the passive voice completely, keep in mind that some writing situations call for it, especially scientific writing. For appropriate uses of the passive voice, see pages 157 and 158; for advice about forming the passive voice, see M1-b and B2-b.

W3-a Use the active voice unless you have a good reason for choosing the passive.

In the active voice, the subject of the sentence does the action; in the passive voice, the subject receives the action. Although both voices are grammatically correct, the active voice is usually more effective because it is clearer and more direct.

ACTIVE Hernando *caught* the fly ball.

PASSIVE The fly ball *was caught* by Hernando.

Passive sentences often identify the actor in a phrase beginning with *by*, as in the preceding example. Sometimes, however, that phrase is omitted, and who or what is responsible for the action becomes unclear: *The fly ball was caught.*

Most of the time, you will want to emphasize the actor, so you should use the active voice. To replace a passive verb with an active one, make the actor the subject of the sentence.

The settlers stripped the land of timber before realizing
▶ ~~The land was stripped of timber before the settlers realized~~ ^ **the consequences of their actions.**

The revision emphasizes the actors (*settlers*) by naming them in the subject.

The contractor removed the
▶ ~~The~~ **debris** ~~was removed~~ **from the construction site.** ^

Sometimes the actor does not appear in a passive-voice sentence. To turn such a sentence into the active voice, the writer must determine an appropriate subject, in this case *contractor*.

The passive voice is appropriate if you wish to emphasize the receiver of the action or to minimize the importance of the actor.

APPROPRIATE PASSIVE	Many Hawaiians *were forced* to leave their homes after the earthquake.
APPROPRIATE PASSIVE	As the time for harvest approaches, the tobacco plants *are sprayed* with a chemical to retard the growth of suckers.

The writer of the first sentence wished to emphasize the receiver of the action, *Hawaiians*. The writer of the second sentence wished to focus on the tobacco plants, not on the people spraying them.

In much scientific writing, the passive voice properly emphasizes the experiment or process being described, not the researcher. Check with your instructor for the preference in your discipline.

APPROPRIATE PASSIVE	The solution *was heated* to the boiling point, and then it was reduced in volume by 50%.

W3-b Replace *be* verbs that result in dull or wordy sentences.

Not every *be* verb needs replacing. The forms of *be* (*be*, *am*, *is*, *are*, *was*, *were*, *being*, *been*) work well when you want to link a subject to a noun that clearly renames it or to an adjective that describes it: *Orchard House was the home of Louisa May Alcott. The harvest will be bountiful after the summer rains*. And *be* verbs are essential as helping verbs before present participles (*is flying, are disappearing*) to express ongoing action: *Derrick was fighting the fire when his wife went into labor*. (See G2-f.)

If using a *be* verb makes a sentence needlessly dull and wordy, however, consider replacing it. Often a phrase following the verb will contain a noun or an adjective (such as *violation*, *resistant*) that suggests a more vigorous, active verb (*violate*, *resist*).

▶ **Burying nuclear waste in Antarctica would ~~be in violation of~~ [violate] an international treaty.**

Violate is less wordy and more vigorous than *be in violation of*.

▶ **When Rosa Parks ~~was resistant to~~ [resisted] giving up her seat on the bus, she became a civil rights hero.**

Resisted is stronger than *was resistant to*.

W4 Appropriate language

Language is appropriate when it suits your subject, engages your audience, and blends naturally with your own voice.

W4-a Stay away from jargon.

Jargon is specialized language used among members of a trade, profession, or group. Use jargon only when readers will be familiar with it; even then, use it only when plain English will not do as well.

JARGON We outsourced the work to a firm in Ohio because we didn't have the bandwidth to tackle it in-house.

REVISED We hired a company in Ohio because we had too few employees to do the work.

Broadly defined, jargon includes puffed-up language designed more to impress readers than to inform them. The following are common examples from business, government, higher education, and the military, with plain English alternatives in parentheses.

ameliorate (improve)
commence (begin)
components (parts)
endeavor (try)
facilitate (help)
impact (v.) (affect)

indicator (sign)
optimal (best, most favorable)
parameters (boundaries, limits)
peruse (read, look over)
prior to (before)
utilize (use)

Sentences filled with jargon are hard to read and often wordy.

▶ All ~~employees functioning in the capacity of~~ work-study students *must prove that they are currently enrolled.* ~~are required to give evidence of current enrollment.~~

▶ The CEO should *talk* ~~dialogue~~ with investors about *working* ~~partnering~~ with clients to buy land in *poor neighborhoods.* ~~economically deprived zones.~~

W4-b Avoid pretentious language, most euphemisms, and "doublespeak."

Hoping to sound profound or poetic, some writers embroider their thoughts with large words and flowery phrases. Such pretentious language is so ornate and wordy that it obscures the writer's meaning.

PRACTICE **hackerhandbooks.com/writersref**
> Word choice > W4–5

▶ Taylor's ~~employment of multihued means of expression draws back the curtains and lets slip the~~ *use of colorful language reveals that she has a* sentimental ~~vantage point from which she observes~~ *view of* American society ~~as well as her lack of comprehension of~~ *and does not understand* economic realities.

Euphemisms—nice-sounding words or phrases substituted for words thought to sound harsh or ugly—are sometimes appropriate. Many cultures, for example, accept euphemisms when speaking or writing about excretion (*I have to go to the bathroom*), sexual intercourse (*They did not sleep together*), and the like.

Most euphemisms, however, are needlessly evasive or even deceitful. Like pretentious language, they obscure the intended meaning.

EUPHEMISM	PLAIN ENGLISH
adult entertainment	pornography
preowned automobile	used car
economically deprived	poor
strategic withdrawal	retreat or defeat
revenue enhancers	taxes
chemical dependency	drug addiction
downsize	lay off, fire
correctional facility	prison

The term *doublespeak* applies to any deliberately evasive or deceptive language, including euphemisms. Doublespeak is especially common in politics and business. A military retreat is described as *tactical redeployment*, *enhanced interrogation* is a euphemism for "torture," and *downsizing* really means "firing employees."

W4-c In most contexts, avoid slang, regional expressions, and nonstandard English.

Slang is an informal and sometimes private vocabulary that expresses the solidarity of a group such as teenagers, rock musicians, or football fans; it is subject to more rapid change than standard English. For example, the slang teenagers use to express approval changes every few years; *cool*, *groovy*, *neat*, *awesome*, *phat*, and *sick* have replaced one another within the last four decades. Sometimes slang becomes so widespread that it is accepted as standard vocabulary. *Jazz*, for example, started out as slang but is now a standard term for a style of music.

Although slang has a certain vitality, it is a code that not everyone understands, and it is very informal. Therefore, it is inappropriate in most written work.

▶ When the server crashed unexpectedly, *we lost* three hours of unsaved data. ~~went down the tubes.~~

▶ The government's "filth" guidelines for food will *disgust you.* ~~gross you out.~~

Regional expressions are common to a group in a geographic area. *Let's talk with the bark off* (for *Let's speak frankly*) is an expression in the southern United States, for example. Regional expressions have the same limitations as slang and are therefore inappropriate in most writing.

▶ John was four blocks from the house before he remembered to *turn on* ~~out~~ the headlights. ~~on.~~

▶ Seamus wasn't ~~for~~ sure, but he thought the whales might be migrating during his visit to Oregon.

Standard English is the language used in all academic, business, and professional fields. Nonstandard English is spoken by people with a common regional or social heritage. Although nonstandard English may be appropriate when spoken within a close group, it is out of place in most formal and informal writing.

▶ The governor said he *doesn't* ~~don't~~ know if he will approve the budget without the clean air provision.

If you speak a nonstandard dialect, try to identify the ways in which your dialect differs from standard English. Look especially for the following features of nonstandard English, which commonly cause problems in writing.

Misusing verb forms such as *began* and *begun* (See G2-a.)
Leaving *-s* endings off verbs (See G2-c.)
Leaving *-ed* endings off verbs (See G2-d.)
Leaving out necessary verbs (See G2-e.)
Using double negatives (See G4-d.)

W4-d Choose an appropriate level of formality.

In deciding on a level of formality, consider both your subject and your audience. Does the subject demand a dignified treatment, or is a relaxed tone more suitable? Will readers be put off if you assume too close a relationship with them, or might you alienate them by seeming too distant?

For most college and professional writing, some degree of formality is appropriate. In a job application letter, for example, it is a mistake to sound too breezy and informal.

TOO INFORMAL	I'd like to get that sales job you've got in the paper.
MORE FORMAL	I would like to apply for the position of sales associate advertised in the *Peoria Journal Star*.

Informal writing is appropriate for private letters, personal e-mail and text messages, and business correspondence between close associates. In choosing a level of formality, above all be consistent. When a writer's voice shifts from one level of formality to another, readers receive mixed messages.

► **Once a pitcher for the Blue Jays, Jorge shared with me the secrets of his trade. His lesson ~~commenced~~ *began* with his famous curveball, ~~implemented~~ *thrown* by tucking the little finger behind the ball. Next he ~~elucidated~~ *revealed* the mysteries of the sucker pitch, a slow ball coming behind a fast windup.**

Commenced and *elucidated* are inappropriate for the subject, and they clash with informal terms such as *sucker pitch* and *fast windup*.

W4-e Avoid sexist language.

Sexist language is language that stereotypes, excludes, or demeans women or men. Using nonsexist language is a matter of courtesy—of respect for and sensitivity to the feelings of others.

Recognizing sexist language

Some sexist language is easy to recognize because it reflects genuine contempt for women: referring to a woman as a "chick," for example, or calling a lawyer a "lady lawyer."

PRACTICE **hackerhandbooks.com/writersref**
> Word choice > W4–6 and W4–7

Other forms of sexist language are less blatant. The following practices, while they may not result from conscious sexism, reflect stereotypical thinking: referring to members of one profession as exclusively male or exclusively female (teachers as women or computer engineers as men, for instance) or using different conventions when naming or identifying women and men.

STEREOTYPICAL LANGUAGE

After a nursing student graduates, *she* must face a difficult state board examination. [Not all nursing students are women.]

Running for city council are Boris Stotsky, an attorney, and *Mrs.* Cynthia Jones, a professor of English and *mother of three*. [The title *Mrs.* and the description *mother of three* are irrelevant.]

Still other forms of sexist language result from outdated traditions. The pronouns *he*, *him*, and *his*, for instance, were traditionally used to refer generically to persons of either sex. Some writers now use *she*, *her*, and *hers* generically or substitute the female pronouns alternately with the male pronouns.

GENERIC PRONOUNS

A journalist is motivated by *his* deadline.

A good interior designer treats *her* clients' ideas respectfully.

But both forms are sexist—for excluding one sex entirely and for making assumptions about the members of particular professions.

Similarly, the nouns *man* and *men* were once used to refer generically to persons of either sex. Current usage demands gender-neutral terms for references to both men and women.

INAPPROPRIATE	APPROPRIATE
chairman	chairperson, moderator, chair, head
congressman	member of Congress, representative, legislator
fireman	firefighter
foreman	supervisor
mailman	mail carrier, postal worker, letter carrier
to man	to operate, to staff
mankind	people, humans
manpower	personnel, staff
policeman	police officer
weatherman	forecaster, meteorologist

Revising sexist language

When revising sexist language, you may be tempted to substitute *he or she* and *his or her*. These terms are inclusive but wordy; fine in small doses, they can become awkward when repeated throughout an essay. A better revision strategy is to write in the plural; yet another strategy is to recast the sentence so that the problem does not arise.

SEXIST

A journalist is motivated by *his* deadline.

A good interior designer treats *her* clients' ideas respectfully.

ACCEPTABLE BUT WORDY

A journalist is motivated by *his or her* deadline.

A good interior designer treats *his or her* clients' ideas respectfully.

BETTER: USING THE PLURAL

Journalists are motivated by *their* deadlines.

Good interior designers treat *their* clients' ideas respectfully.

BETTER: RECASTING THE SENTENCE

A journalist is motivated by *a* deadline.

A good interior designer treats clients' ideas respectfully.

For more examples of these revision strategies, see G3-a.

W4-f Revise language that may offend groups of people.

Obviously it is impolite to use offensive terms such as *Polack* and *redneck*, but biased language can take more subtle forms. Because language evolves over time, names once thought acceptable may become offensive. When describing groups of people, choose names that the groups currently use to describe themselves.

▶ **North Dakota takes its name from the ~~Indian~~ *Lakota* word meaning "friend" or "ally."**

▶ **Many ~~Oriental~~ *Asian* immigrants have recently settled in our town.**

Negative stereotypes (such as "drives like a teenager" or "sour as a spinster") are of course offensive. But you should avoid stereotyping a person or a group even if you believe your generalization to be positive.

▶ **It was no surprise that Greer, ~~a Chinese American,~~ *an excellent math and science student,* was selected for the honors chemistry program.**

W5 Exact language

Two reference works will help you find words to express your meaning exactly: a good dictionary, such as *Merriam-Webster's Online Dictionary* or *The American Heritage Dictionary*, and a thesaurus, such as *Roget's International Thesaurus*. (See W6.)

TIP: Do not turn to a thesaurus in search of flowery or impressive language. Look instead for words that exactly express your meaning.

W5-a Select words with appropriate connotations.

In addition to their strict dictionary meanings (or *denotations*), words have *connotations*, emotional colorings that affect how readers respond to them. The word *steel* denotes "commercial iron that contains carbon," but it also calls up a cluster of images associated with steel. These associations give the word its connotations—cold, hard, smooth, unbending.

If the connotation of a word does not seem appropriate for your purpose, your audience, or your subject matter, you should change the word. When a more appropriate synonym does not come quickly to mind, consult a dictionary or a thesaurus. (See W6.)

▶ **When American soldiers returned home after World War II, many women ~~abandoned~~ *left* their jobs in favor of marriage.**

The word *abandoned* is too negative for the context.

W5-b Prefer specific, concrete nouns.

Unlike general nouns, which refer to broad classes of things, specific nouns point to particular items. *Film*, for example, names a general class, *fantasy film* names a narrower class, and *The Golden Compass* is more specific still.

Unlike abstract nouns, which refer to qualities and ideas (*justice*, *beauty*, *realism*, *dignity*), concrete nouns point to immediate, often sensory experience and to physical objects (*steeple*, *asphalt*, *lilac*, *stone*, *garlic*).

Specific, concrete nouns express meaning more vividly than general or abstract ones. Although general and abstract language is sometimes necessary to convey your meaning, use specific, concrete words whenever possible.

► **The senator spoke about the challenges of our state's future:** *pollution, dwindling natural resources, and overcrowded prisons.* ~~**the environment and crime.**~~

Nouns such as *thing*, *area*, *aspect*, *factor*, and *individual* are especially dull and imprecise.

► **Toni Morrison's *Beloved* is about slavery,** *motherhood, and memory.* ~~**among other things.**~~

► **Try pairing a new employee with an** *experienced technician.* ~~**individual with technical experience.**~~

W5-c Do not misuse words.

If a word is not in your active vocabulary, you may find yourself misusing it, sometimes with embarrassing consequences. When in doubt, check the dictionary.

► **Fans who arrived late were** *climbing* ~~**migrating**~~ **up the bleachers in search of seats.**

Writing with sources
MLA-style citation

► **Marie Winn** *argues* ~~**quarrels**~~ **that television viewing is bad for families because it "serves to anesthetize parents into accepting their family's diminished state" (357).**

When you are introducing a quotation with a signal phrase, be sure to choose a verb that clearly reflects the source's intention. *Quarrel* suggests a heated or angry dispute; *argue* is a more neutral word. (See also MLA-3b on using signal phrases.)

Be especially alert for misused word forms—using a noun such as *absence*, *significance*, or *persistence*, for example, when your meaning requires the adjective *absent*, *significant*, or *persistent*.

► **Most dieters are not** *persistent* ~~**persistence**~~ **enough to make a permanent change in their eating habits.**

PRACTICE **hackerhandbooks.com/writersref**
> Word choice > W5–5 and W5–6

W5-d Use standard idioms.

Idioms are speech forms that follow no easily specified rules. The English say "Bernadette went *to hospital*," an idiom strange to American ears, which are accustomed to hearing *to the hospital*. Native speakers of a language seldom have problems with idioms, but prepositions (such as *with*, *to*, *at*, and *of*) sometimes cause trouble, especially when they follow certain verbs and adjectives. When in doubt, consult a dictionary.

UNIDIOMATIC	IDIOMATIC
abide with (a decision)	abide by (a decision)
according with	according to
agree to (an idea)	agree with (an idea)
angry at (a person)	angry with (a person)
capable to	capable of
comply to	comply with
desirous to	desirous of
different than (a person or thing)	different from (a person or thing)
intend on doing	intend to do
off of	off
plan on doing	plan to do
preferable than	preferable to
prior than	prior to
similar than	similar to
superior than	superior to
sure and	sure to
think on	think of, about
try and	try to
type of a	type of

ESL Because idioms follow no particular rules, you must learn them individually. You may find it helpful to keep a list of idioms that you frequently encounter in conversation and in reading. See M5.

W5-e Do not rely heavily on clichés.

The pioneer who first announced that he had "slept like a log" no doubt amused his companions with a fresh, unlikely comparison. Today, however, that comparison is a cliché, a saying that can no longer add emphasis or surprise.

To see just how dully predictable clichés are, put your hand over the right-hand column in the following list and then finish the phrases on the left.

cool as a	cucumber
beat around	the bush
blind as a	bat
busy as a	bee, beaver
crystal	clear
out of the frying pan and	into the fire
light as a	feather
like a bull	in a china shop
playing with	fire
nutty as a	fruitcake
selling like	hotcakes
starting out at the bottom	of the ladder
water under the	bridge
white as a	sheet, ghost
avoid clichés like the	plague

The solution for clichés is simple: Just delete them or rewrite them.

► **When I received a full scholarship from my second-choice school,** *felt squeezed to settle for second best.*
I ~~found myself between a rock and a hard place.~~ ^

Sometimes you can write around a cliché by adding an element of surprise. One student, for example, who had written that she had butterflies in her stomach, revised her cliché like this:

> If all of the action in my stomach is caused by butterflies, there must be a horde of them, with horseshoes on.

The image of butterflies wearing horseshoes is fresh and unlikely, not predictable like the original cliché.

W5-f Use figures of speech with care.

A figure of speech is an expression that uses words imaginatively (rather than literally) to make abstract ideas concrete. Most often, figures of speech compare two seemingly unlike things to reveal surprising similarities.

In a *simile*, the writer makes the comparison explicitly, usually by introducing it with *like* or *as*: *By the time cotton had to be picked, Grandfather's neck was as red as the clay he plowed*. In a *metaphor*, the *like* or *as* is omitted, and the comparison is implied. For example, in the Old Testament Song of Solomon, a young woman compares the man she loves to a fruit tree: *With great delight I sat in his shadow, and his fruit was sweet to my taste.*

Although figures of speech are useful devices, writers sometimes use them without thinking through the images they evoke. The result is sometimes a *mixed metaphor*, the combination of two or more images that don't make sense together.

▶ **Our manager decided to put all controversial issues ~~in a holding pattern~~ on a back burner until after the annual meeting.**

Here the writer is mixing airplanes (*holding pattern*) and stoves (*back burner*). Simply deleting one of the images corrects the problem.

W6 The dictionary and thesaurus

W6-a The dictionary

A good dictionary, whether print or online—such as *The American Heritage Dictionary of the English Language, The Random House College Dictionary*, or *Merriam-Webster's Collegiate Dictionary*—is an indispensable writer's aid.

A sample print dictionary entry, taken from *The American Heritage Dictionary*, appears on page 170. Labels show where various kinds of information about a word can be found in that dictionary.

A sample online dictionary entry, taken from *Merriam-Webster Online Dictionary*, appears on page 171.

Spelling, word division, and pronunciation

The main entry (*re•gard* in the sample entries) shows the correct spelling of the word. When there are two correct spellings of a word (as in *collectible*, *collectable*, for example), both are given, with the preferred spelling usually appearing first.

The main entry also shows how the word is divided into syllables. The dot between *re* and *gard* separates the two syllables and indicates where the word should be divided if it can't fit at the end of a line of type (see P7-h). When a word is compound, the main entry shows how to write it: as one word (*crossroad*), as a hyphenated word (*cross-stitch*), or as two words (*cross section*).

The word's pronunciation is given just after the main entry. The accents indicate which syllables are stressed; the other marks are explained in the dictionary's pronunciation key. In print dictionaries, this key usually appears at the bottom of every page or every other page. Many online entries include an audio link to a person's voice pronouncing the word. And most online dictionaries have an audio pronunciation guide.

PRINT DICTIONARY ENTRY

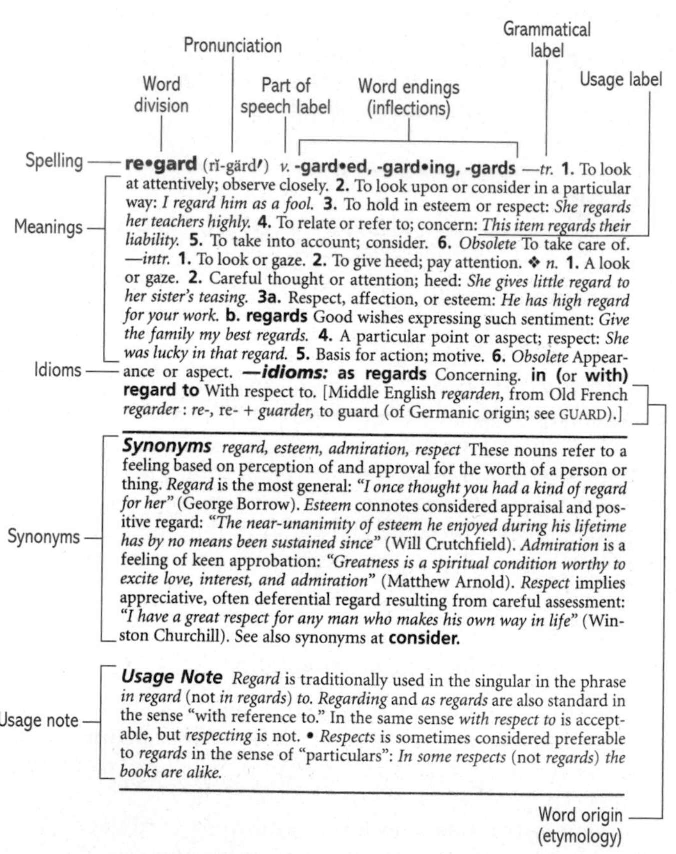

re•gard (rĭ-gärd′) *v.* **-gard•ed, -gard•ing, -gards** —*tr.* **1.** To look at attentively; observe closely. **2.** To look upon or consider in a particular way: *I regard him as a fool.* **3.** To hold in esteem or respect: *She regards her teachers highly.* **4.** To relate or refer to; concern: *This item regards their liability.* **5.** To take into account; consider. **6.** *Obsolete* To take care of. —*intr.* **1.** To look or gaze. **2.** To give heed; pay attention. ❖ *n.* **1.** A look or gaze. **2.** Careful thought or attention; heed: *She gives little regard to her sister's teasing.* **3a.** Respect, affection, or esteem: *He has high regard for your work.* **b. regards** Good wishes expressing such sentiment: *Give the family my best regards.* **4.** A particular point or aspect; respect: *She was lucky in that regard.* **5.** Basis for action; motive. **6.** *Obsolete* Appearance or aspect. ***—idioms:*** **as regards** Concerning. **in** (or **with**) **regard to** With respect to. [Middle English *regarden,* from Old French *regarder* : *re-,* re- + *guarder,* to guard (of Germanic origin; see GUARD).]

Synonyms *regard, esteem, admiration, respect* These nouns refer to a feeling based on perception of and approval for the worth of a person or thing. *Regard* is the most general: "*I once thought you had a kind of regard for her*" (George Borrow). *Esteem* connotes considered appraisal and positive regard: "*The near-unanimity of esteem he enjoyed during his lifetime has by no means been sustained since*" (Will Crutchfield). *Admiration* is a feeling of keen approbation: "*Greatness is a spiritual condition worthy to excite love, interest, and admiration*" (Matthew Arnold). *Respect* implies appreciative, often deferential regard resulting from careful assessment: "*I have a great respect for any man who makes his own way in life*" (Winston Churchill). See also synonyms at **consider.**

Usage Note *Regard* is traditionally used in the singular in the phrase *in regard* (not *in regards*) *to. Regarding* and *as regards* are also standard in the sense "with reference to." In the same sense *with respect to* is acceptable, but *respecting* is not. • *Respects* is sometimes considered preferable to *regards* in the sense of "particulars": *In some respects* (not *regards*) *the books are alike.*

Word endings and grammatical labels

When a word takes endings to indicate grammatical functions (called *inflections*), the endings are listed in boldface, as with *-garded*, *-garding*, and *-gards* in the sample print entry (p. 170).

Labels for the parts of speech and for other grammatical terms are sometimes abbreviated, as they are in the print entry. The most commonly used abbreviations are these:

n.	noun	adj.	adjective
pl.	plural	adv.	adverb
sing.	singular	pron.	pronoun
v.	verb	prep.	preposition
tr.	transitive verb	conj.	conjunction
intr.	intransitive verb	interj.	interjection

ONLINE DICTIONARY ENTRY

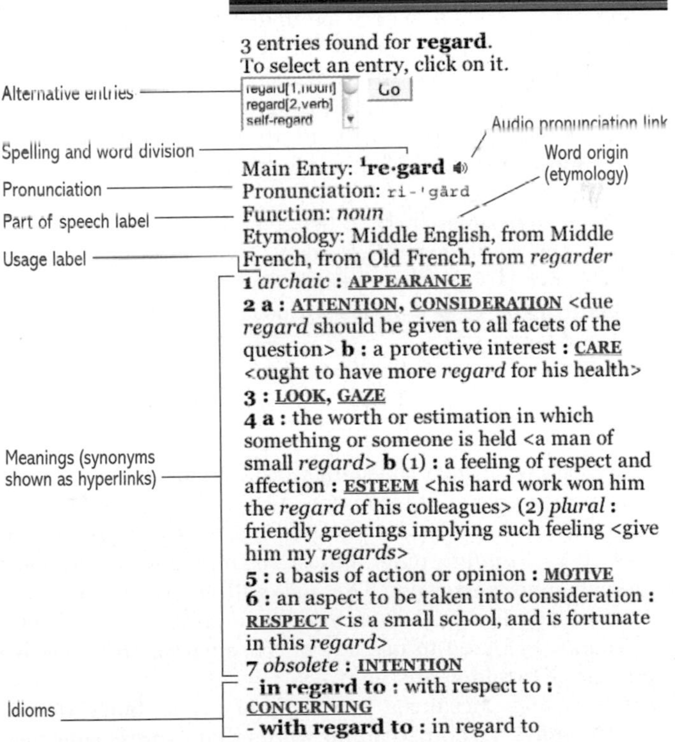

Merriam-Webster Online Dictionary
3 entries found for **regard**.
To select an entry, click on it.
regard[1,noun]
regard[2,verb]
self-regard
Go
Alternative entries
Spelling and word division
Pronunciation
Part of speech label
Usage label
Audio pronunciation link
Word origin (etymology)
Main Entry: **¹re·gard**
Pronunciation: ri-ˈgärd
Function: *noun*
Etymology: Middle English, from Middle French, from Old French, from *regarder*
1 *archaic* **:** APPEARANCE
2 a : ATTENTION, CONSIDERATION <due *regard* should be given to all facets of the question> **b :** a protective interest **:** CARE <ought to have more *regard* for his health>
3 : LOOK, GAZE
4 a : the worth or estimation in which something or someone is held <a man of small *regard*> **b** (1) **:** a feeling of respect and affection **:** ESTEEM <his hard work won him the *regard* of his colleagues> (2) *plural* **:** friendly greetings implying such feeling <give him my *regards*>
5 : a basis of action or opinion **:** MOTIVE
6 : an aspect to be taken into consideration **:** RESPECT <is a small school, and is fortunate in this *regard*>
7 *obsolete* **:** INTENTION
- in regard to : with respect to **:** CONCERNING
- with regard to : in regard to
Meanings (synonyms shown as hyperlinks)
Idioms

Meanings, word origin, synonyms, and antonyms

Each meaning for the word is given a number. Occasionally a word's use is illustrated in a quoted sentence. Sometimes a word can be used as more than one part of speech (*regard*, for instance, can be used as either a verb or a noun). In such a case, all the meanings for one part of speech are given before all the meanings for another, as in the sample entries. The entries also give idiomatic uses of the word.

The origin of the word, called its *etymology*, appears in brackets after all the meanings in the print version; in the online version, it appears before the meanings.

Synonyms, words similar in meaning to the main entry, are frequently listed. In the sample print entry (p. 170), the dictionary draws distinctions in meaning among the various synonyms. In the online entry (p. 171), synonyms appear as hyperlinks. Antonyms, which do not appear in the sample entries, are words having a meaning opposite from that of the main entry.

Usage

Usage labels indicate when, where, or under what conditions a particular meaning for a word is appropriately used. Common labels are *informal* (or *colloquial*), *slang*, *archaic*, *poetic*, *nonstandard*, *dialect*, *obsolete*, and *British*. In the sample print entry (p. 170), two meanings of *regard* are labeled *obsolete* because they are no longer in use. The sample online entry (p. 171) has meanings labeled both *archaic* and *obsolete*.

Dictionaries sometimes include usage notes as well. In the sample print entry, the dictionary offers advice on several uses of *regard* not specifically covered by the meanings. Such advice is based on the opinions of many experts and on actual usage in current magazines, newspapers, and books.

W6-b The thesaurus

When you are looking for just the right word, you may want to consult a collection of synonyms and antonyms such as *Roget's International Thesaurus*. Look up the adjective *still*, for example, and you will find synonyms such as *tranquil*, *quiet*, *quiescent*, *reposeful*, *calm*, *pacific*, *halcyon*, *placid*, and *unruffled*. The list will likely contain words you've never heard of or with which you are only vaguely familiar. Whenever you are tempted to use one of these words, first look it up in the dictionary to avoid misusing it.

Do not turn to a thesaurus in search of exotic, fancy words to embellish your essays. Look instead for words that express your meaning exactly and that are familiar to both you and your readers.

G

Grammatical Sentences

G Grammatical Sentences

G1 Subject-verb agreement, 175

love or *loves*?
have or *has*?
do or *does*?
is or *are*?
was or *were*?

- **a** Standard subject-verb combinations, 175
- **b** Words between subject and verb, 175
- **c** Subjects with *and*, 178
- **d** Subjects with *or*, *nor*, 178
- **e** Indefinite pronouns such as *someone*, *each*, 179
- **f** Collective nouns such as *jury*, *class*, 179
- **g** Subject after verb, 180
- **h** Subject complement, 181
- **i** *who*, *which*, *that*, 181
- **j** Plural form, singular meaning, 182
- **k** Titles, company names, words as words, gerund phrases, 182

G2 Verb forms, tenses, and moods, 183

- **a** Irregular verbs, 183
- **b** *lie* and *lay*, 186
- **c** *-s* endings, 187
- **d** *-ed* endings, 188
- **e** Omitted verbs, 190
- **f** Tense, 190
- **g** Subjunctive mood, 195

G3 Pronouns, 196

- **a** Pronoun-antecedent agreement, 197
- **b** Pronoun reference, 199
- **c** Pronoun case (*I* vs. *me*, etc.), 201
- **d** *who* and *whom*, 205

G4 Adjectives and adverbs, 207

- **a** Adjectives, 208
- **b** Adverbs, 209
- **c** Comparatives and superlatives, 210
- **d** Double negatives, 212

G5 Sentence fragments, 212

- **a** Subordinate clauses, 215
- **b** Phrases, 215
- **c** Other word groups, 216
- **d** Acceptable fragments, 218

G6 Run-on sentences, 218

- **a** Revision with coordinating conjunction, 220
- **b** Revision with semicolon, 220
- **c** Revision by separating sentences, 222
- **d** Revision by restructuring, 222

G1 Subject-verb agreement

In the present tense, verbs agree with their subjects in number (singular or plural) and in person (first, second, or third): *I sing*, *you sing*, *he sings*, *she sings*, *we sing*, *they sing*. Even if your ear recognizes the standard subject-verb combinations presented in G1-a, you will no doubt encounter tricky situations such as those described in G1-b to G1-k.

G1-a Consult this section for standard subject-verb combinations.

This section describes the basic guidelines for making present-tense verbs agree with their subjects. The present-tense ending *-s* (or *-es*) is used on a verb if its subject is third-person singular (*he*, *she*, *it*, and singular nouns); otherwise the verb takes no ending. Consider, for example, the present-tense forms of the verbs *love* and *try*, given at the beginning of the chart on the following page.

The verb *be* varies from this pattern; unlike any other verb, it has special forms in *both* the present and the past tense. These forms appear at the end of the chart on page 176.

If you aren't confident that you know the standard forms, use the charts on pages 176 and 177 as you proofread for subject-verb agreement. You may also want to look at G2-c on *-s* endings of regular and irregular verbs.

G1-b Make the verb agree with its subject, not with a word that comes between.

Word groups often come between the subject and the verb. Such word groups, usually modifying the subject, may contain a noun that at first appears to be the subject. By mentally stripping away such modifiers, you can isolate the noun that is in fact the subject.

The *samples* on the tray in the lab *need* testing.

▶ **High levels of air pollution causes damage to the respiratory tract.**

The subject is *levels*, not *pollution*. Strip away the phrase *of air pollution* to hear the correct verb: *levels cause*.

PRACTICE **hackerhandbooks.com/writersref**
> Grammatical sentences > G1–3 to G1–5

Subject-verb agreement at a glance

Present-tense forms of *love* and *try* (typical verbs)

	SINGULAR		PLURAL	
FIRST PERSON	I	love	we	love
SECOND PERSON	you	love	you	love
THIRD PERSON	he/she/it*	loves	they**	love

	SINGULAR		PLURAL	
FIRST PERSON	I	try	we	try
SECOND PERSON	you	try	you	try
THIRD PERSON	he/she/it*	tries	they**	try

Present-tense forms of *have*

	SINGULAR		PLURAL	
FIRST PERSON	I	have	we	have
SECOND PERSON	you	have	you	have
THIRD PERSON	he/she/it*	has	they**	have

Present-tense forms of *do* (including negative forms)

	SINGULAR		PLURAL	
FIRST PERSON	I	do/don't	we	do/don't
SECOND PERSON	you	do/don't	you	do/don't
THIRD PERSON	he/she/it*	does/doesn't	they**	do/don't

Present-tense and past-tense forms of *be*

	SINGULAR		PLURAL	
FIRST PERSON	I	am/was	we	are/were
SECOND PERSON	you	are/were	you	are/were
THIRD PERSON	he/she/it*	is/was	they**	are/were

*And singular nouns (*child, Roger*)
**And plural nouns (*children, the Mannings*)

▶ **The slaughter of pandas for their pelts ~~have~~ *has* caused the panda population to decline drastically.**

The subject is *slaughter*, not *pandas* or *pelts.*

NOTE: Phrases beginning with the prepositions *as well as, in addition to, accompanied by, together with*, and *along with* do not make a singular subject plural.

When to use the -*s* (or -*es*) form of a present-tense verb

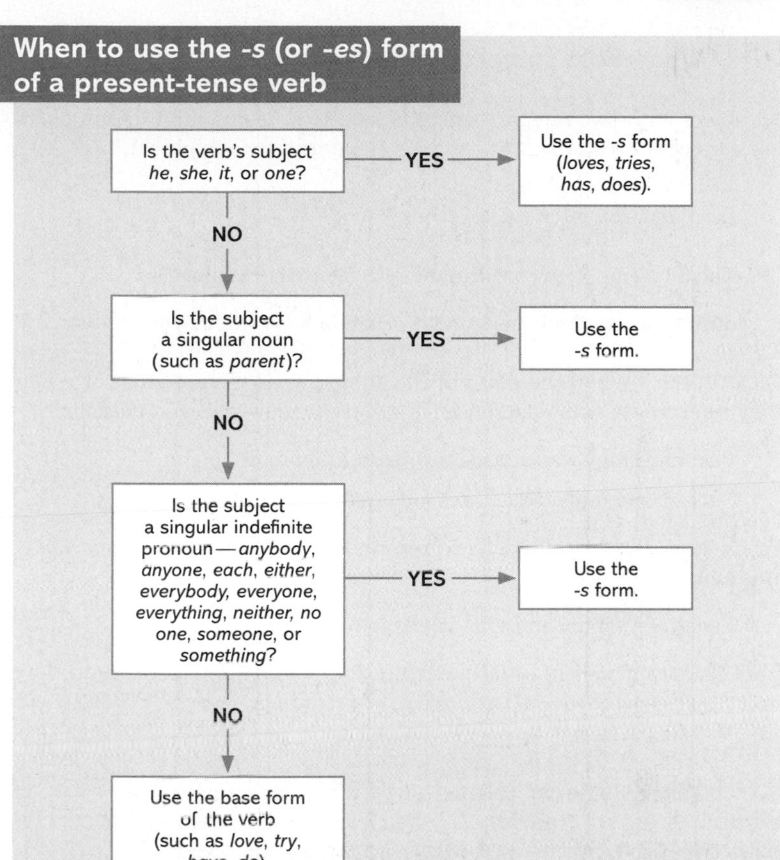
Is the verb's subject *he*, *she*, *it*, or *one*?
YES
Use the -*s* form (*loves*, *tries*, *has*, *does*).
NO
Is the subject a singular noun (such as *parent*)?
YES
Use the -*s* form.
NO
Is the subject a singular indefinite pronoun—*anybody*, *anyone*, *each*, *either*, *everybody*, *everyone*, *everything*, *neither*, *no one*, *someone*, or *something*?
YES
Use the -*s* form.
NO
Use the base form of the verb (such as *love*, *try*, *have*, *do*).

EXCEPTION: Choosing the correct present-tense form of *be* (*am*, *is*, or *are*) is not always so simple. See the chart on the previous page for both present- and past-tense forms of *be*.

ESL TIP: Do not use the -*s* form of a verb if it follows a modal verb such as *can*, *must*, or *should* or another helping verb. (See M1-c.)

▶ **The governor as well as his press secretary ~~were~~ *was* on the plane.**

To emphasize that two people were on the plane, the writer could use *and* instead: *The governor and his press secretary were on the plane.*

G1-c Treat most subjects joined with *and* as plural.

A subject with two or more parts is said to be compound. If the parts are connected with *and*, the subject is nearly always plural.

Leon and Jan often *jog* together.

▶ **The Supreme Court's willingness to hear the case and its affirmation of the lower court's decision ~~has~~ *have* set a new precedent.**

EXCEPTIONS: When the parts of the subject form a single unit or when they refer to the same person or thing, treat the subject as singular.

Fish and chips was a last-minute addition to the menu.

Sue's friend and adviser was surprised by her decision.

When a compound subject is preceded by *each* or *every*, treat it as singular.

Each tree, shrub, and vine needs to be sprayed.

This exception does not apply when a compound subject is followed by *each*: *Alan and Marcia each have different ideas.*

G1-d With subjects joined with *or* or *nor* (or with *either . . . or* or *neither . . . nor*), make the verb agree with the part of the subject nearer to the verb.

A driver's *license* or credit *card is* required.

A driver's *license* or two credit *cards are* required.

▶ **If an infant or a child ~~are~~ *is* having difficulty breathing, seek medical attention immediately.**

▶ **Neither the chief financial officer nor the marketing managers ~~was~~ *were* able to convince the client to reconsider.**

The verb must be matched with the part of the subject closer to it: *child is* in the first sentence, *managers were* in the second.

NOTE: If one part of the subject is singular and the other is plural, put the plural one last to avoid awkwardness.

G1-e Treat most indefinite pronouns as singular.

Indefinite pronouns are pronouns that do not refer to specific persons or things. The following commonly used indefinite pronouns are singular.

anybody	each	everyone	nobody	somebody
anyone	either	everything	no one	someone
anything	everybody	neither	nothing	something

Many of these words appear to have plural meanings, and they are often treated as plural in casual speech. In formal written English, however, they are nearly always treated as singular.

Everyone on the team *supports* the coach.

▶ **Each of the furrows ~~have~~ *has* been seeded.**

▶ **Nobody who participated in the clinical trials ~~were~~ *was* given a placebo.**

The subjects of these sentences are *Each* and *Nobody*. These indefinite pronouns are third-person singular, so the verbs must be *has* and *was*.

A few indefinite pronouns (*all*, *any*, *none*, *some*) may be singular or plural depending on the noun or pronoun they refer to.

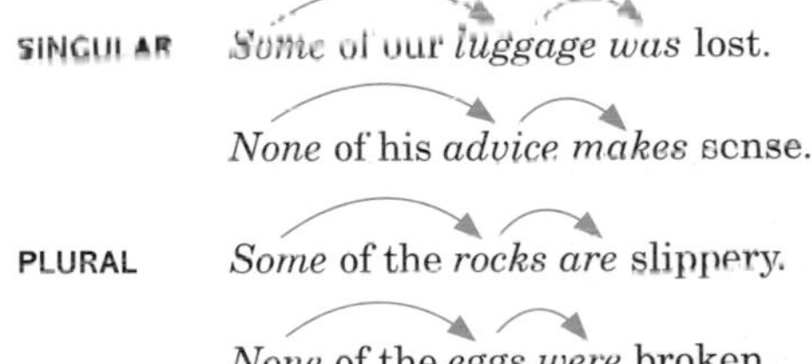

SINGULAR *Some* of our *luggage was* lost.
None of his *advice makes* sense.
PLURAL *Some* of the *rocks are* slippery.
None of the *eggs were* broken.

NOTE: When the meaning of *none* is emphatically "not one," *none* may be treated as singular: *None* [meaning "Not one"] *of the eggs was broken*. Using *not one* instead is sometimes clearer: *Not one of the eggs was broken.*

G1-f Treat collective nouns as singular unless the meaning is clearly plural.

Collective nouns such as *jury*, *committee*, *audience*, *crowd*, *troop*, *family*, and *couple* name a class or a group. In American English, collective nouns are nearly always treated as singular: They emphasize the group as a unit. Occasionally, when there is some reason to draw attention to the individual members of the group, a collective noun may be treated as plural. (See also p. 198.)

SINGULAR The *class respects* the teacher.

PLURAL The *class are* debating among themselves.

To emphasize the notion of individuality in the second sentence, many writers would add a clearly plural noun.

PLURAL The class *members are* debating among themselves.

▶ **The board of trustees ~~meet~~ *meets* in Denver twice a year.**

The board as a whole meets; there is no reason to draw attention to its individual members.

▶ **A young couple ~~was~~ *were* arguing about politics while holding hands.**

The meaning is clearly plural. Only separate individuals can argue and hold hands.

NOTE: The phrase *the number* is treated as singular, *a number* as plural.

SINGULAR *The number* of school-age children *is* declining.

PLURAL *A number* of children *are* attending the wedding.

NOTE: In general, when fractions or units of measurement are used with a singular noun, treat them as singular; when they are used with a plural noun, treat them as plural.

SINGULAR *Three-fourths* of the salad *has* been eaten.

Twenty *inches* of wallboard *was* covered with mud.

PLURAL *One-fourth* of the drivers *were* texting.

Two *pounds* of blueberries *were* used to make the pie.

G1-g Make the verb agree with its subject even when the subject follows the verb.

Verbs ordinarily follow subjects. When the normal order is reversed, it is easy to be confused. Sentences beginning with *there is* or *there are* (or *there was, there were*) are inverted; the subject follows the verb.

There *are* surprisingly few *honeybees* left in southern China.

▶ **There ~~was~~ were a social worker and a neighbor at the scene of the crash.**

The subject, *worker and neighbor*, is plural, so the verb must be *were*.

Occasionally you may invert a sentence for variety or effect. If you do, check to make sure that your subject and verb agree.

▶ **Of particular concern ~~is~~ are penicillin and tetracycline, antibiotics used to make animals more resistant to disease.**

The subject, *penicillin and tetracycline*, is plural, so the verb must be *are*.

G1-h Make the verb agree with its subject, not with a subject complement.

One basic sentence pattern in English consists of a subject, a linking verb, and a subject complement: *Jack is a lawyer.* Because the subject complement (*lawyer*) names or describes the subject (*Jack*), it is sometimes mistaken for the subject. (See B2-b on subject complements.)

▶ **A major force in today's economy ~~are~~ is children—as consumers, decision makers, and trend spotters.**

Force is the subject, not *children*. If the corrected version seems too awkward, make *children* the subject: *Children are a major force in today's economy—as consumers, decision makers, and trend spotters.*

▶ **A tent and a sleeping bag ~~is~~ are the required equipment for all campers.**

Tent and bag is the subject, not *equipment*.

G1-i *Who, which,* and *that* take verbs that agree with their antecedents.

Like most pronouns, the relative pronouns *who*, *which*, and *that* have antecedents, nouns or pronouns to which they refer. Relative pronouns used as subjects of subordinate clauses take verbs that agree with their antecedents.

ANT PN V

Take a *course that prepares* you for classroom management.

One of the

Constructions such as *one of the students who* [or *one of the things that*] may cause problems for writers. Do not assume that the antecedent must be *one*. Instead, consider the logic of the sentence.

► **Our ability to use language is one of the things that set~~s~~ us apart from animals.**

The antecedent of *that* is *things*, not *one*. Several things set us apart from animals.

Only one of the

When the word *only* comes before *one*, you are safe in assuming that *one* is the antecedent of the relative pronoun.

► **Veronica was the only one of the first-year Spanish students who ~~were~~ *was* fluent enough to apply for the exchange program.**

The antecedent of *who* is *one*, not *students*. Only one student was fluent enough.

G1-j Words such as *athletics*, *economics*, *mathematics*, *physics*, *politics*, *statistics*, *measles*, and *news* are usually singular, despite their plural form.

► **Politics ~~are~~ *is* among my mother's favorite pastimes.**

EXCEPTION: Occasionally some of these words, especially *economics*, *mathematics*, *politics*, and *statistics*, have plural meanings:

Office politics often sway decisions about hiring and promotion.

The economics of the building plan are prohibitive.

G1-k Titles of works, company names, words mentioned as words, and gerund phrases are singular.

► ***Lost Cities* ~~describe~~ *describes* the discoveries of fifty ancient civilizations.**

► **Delmonico Brothers ~~specialize~~ *specializes* in organic produce and additive-free meats.**

▶ ***Controlled substances*** ~~**are**~~ *is* **a euphemism for illegal drugs.**

A gerund phrase consists of an *-ing* verb form followed by any objects, complements, or modifiers (see B3-b). Treat gerund phrases as singular.

▶ **Encountering long hold times** ~~**make**~~ *makes* **customers impatient with telephone tech support.**

G2 Verb forms, tenses, and moods

Section G-1 deals with subject-verb agreement, and section W3 offers advice on active and passive verbs. This section describes other potential challenges with verbs:

a. irregular verb forms (such as *drive, drove, driven*)
b. *lie* and *lay*
c. *-s* (or *-es*) endings on verbs
d. *-ed* endings on verbs
e. omitted verbs
f. tense
g. subjunctive mood

ESL If English is not your native language, see also M1 for more help with verbs.

G2-a Choose standard English forms of irregular verbs.

Except for the verb *be*, all verbs in English have five forms. The following list shows the five forms and provides a sample sentence in which each might appear.

BASE FORM	Usually I (*walk, ride*).
PAST TENSE	Yesterday I (*walked, rode*).
PAST PARTICIPLE	I have (*walked, ridden*) many times before.
PRESENT PARTICIPLE	I am (*walking, riding*) right now.
-S FORM	He/she/it (*walks, rides*) regularly.

PRACTICE **hackerhandbooks.com/writersref**
> Grammatical sentences > G2–4 and G2–5

The verb *be* has eight forms instead of the usual five: *be*, *am*, *is*, *are*, *was*, *were*, *being*, *been*.

For all regular verbs, the past-tense and past-participle forms are the same (ending in *-ed* or *-d*), so there is no danger of confusion. This is not true, however, for irregular verbs, such as the following.

BASE FORM	PAST TENSE	PAST PARTICIPLE
go	went	gone
break	broke	broken
fly	flew	flown
sing	sang	sung

The past-tense form always occurs alone, without a helping verb. It expresses action that occurred entirely in the past: *I rode to work yesterday. I walked to work last Tuesday.* The past participle is used with a helping verb. It forms the perfect tenses with *has*, *have*, or *had*; it forms the passive voice with *be*, *am*, *is*, *are*, *was*, *were*, *being*, or *been*. (See B1-c for a complete list of helping verbs and G2-f for a survey of tenses.)

PAST TENSE	Last July, we *went* to Paris.
HELPING VERB + PAST PARTICIPLE	We *have gone* to Paris twice.

The list of common irregular verbs beginning at the bottom of this page will help you distinguish between the past tense and the past participle. Choose the past-participle form if the verb in your sentence requires a helping verb; choose the past-tense form if the verb does not require a helping verb. (See verb tenses in G2-f.)

▶ **Yesterday we ~~seen~~ *saw* a documentary about Isabel Allende.**

The past-tense *saw* is required because there is no helping verb.

▶ **The truck was apparently ~~stole~~ *stolen* while the driver ate lunch.**

▶ **By Friday, the stock market had ~~fell~~ *fallen* two hundred points.**

Because of the helping verbs *was* and *had*, the past-participle forms are required: *was stolen*, *had fallen.*

Common irregular verbs

BASE FORM	PAST TENSE	PAST PARTICIPLE
arise	arose	arisen
awake	awoke, awaked	awaked, awoke, awoken
be	was, were	been

BASE FORM	PAST TENSE	PAST PARTICIPLE
beat	beat	beaten, beat
become	became	become
begin	began	begun
bend	bent	bent
bite	bit	bitten, bit
blow	blew	blown
break	broke	broken
bring	brought	brought
build	built	built
burst	burst	burst
buy	bought	bought
catch	caught	caught
choose	chose	chosen
cling	clung	clung
come	came	come
cost	cost	cost
deal	dealt	dealt
dig	dug	dug
dive	dived, dove	dived
do	did	done
drag	dragged	dragged
draw	drew	drawn
dream	dreamed, dreamt	dreamed, dreamt
drink	drank	drunk
drive	drove	driven
eat	ate	eaten
fall	fell	fallen
fight	fought	fought
find	found	found
fly	flew	flown
forget	forgot	forgotten, forgot
freeze	froze	frozen
get	got	gotten, got
give	gave	given
go	went	gone
grow	grew	grown
hang (execute)	hanged	hanged
hang (suspend)	hung	hung
have	had	had
hear	heard	heard
hide	hid	hidden
hurt	hurt	hurt
keep	kept	kept
know	knew	known
lay (put)	laid	laid
lead	led	led
lend	lent	lent
let (allow)	let	let

BASE FORM	PAST TENSE	PAST PARTICIPLE
lie (recline)	lay	lain
lose	lost	lost
make	made	made
prove	proved	proved, proven
read	read	read
ride	rode	ridden
ring	rang	rung
rise (get up)	rose	risen
run	ran	run
say	said	said
see	saw	seen
send	sent	sent
set (place)	set	set
shake	shook	shaken
shoot	shot	shot
shrink	shrank	shrunk
sing	sang	sung
sink	sank	sunk
sit (be seated)	sat	sat
slay	slew	slain
sleep	slept	slept
speak	spoke	spoken
spin	spun	spun
spring	sprang	sprung
stand	stood	stood
steal	stole	stolen
sting	stung	stung
strike	struck	struck, stricken
swear	swore	sworn
swim	swam	swum
swing	swung	swung
take	took	taken
teach	taught	taught
throw	threw	thrown
wake	woke, waked	waked, woken
wear	wore	worn
wring	wrung	wrung
write	wrote	written

G2-b Distinguish among the forms of *lie* and *lay*.

Writers and speakers frequently confuse the various forms of *lie* (meaning "to recline or rest on a surface") and *lay* (meaning "to put or place something"). *Lie* is an intransitive verb; it does not take a direct object: *The tax forms lie on the table*. The verb *lay* is transitive; it takes a direct object: *Please lay the tax forms on the table*. (See B2-b.)

In addition to confusing the meaning of *lie* and *lay*, writers and speakers are often unfamiliar with the standard English forms of these verbs.

BASE FORM	PAST TENSE	PAST PARTICIPLE	PRESENT PARTICIPLE
lie ("recline")	lay	lain	lying
lay ("put")	laid	laid	laying

▶ **Sue was so exhausted that she ~~laid~~ *lay* down for a nap.**

The past-tense form of *lie* ("to recline") is *lay*.

▶ **The patient had ~~laid~~ *lain* in an uncomfortable position all night.**

The past-participle form of *lie* ("to recline") is *lain*. If the correct English seems too stilted, recast the sentence: *The patient had been lying in an uncomfortable position all night.*

▶ **The prosecutor ~~lay~~ *laid* the pistol on a table close to the jurors.**

The past-tense form of *lay* ("to place") is *laid*.

▶ **Letters dating from the Civil War were ~~laying~~ *lying* in the corner of the chest.**

The present participle of *lie* ("to rest on a surface") is *lying*.

G2-c Use *-s* (or *-es*) endings on present-tense verbs that have third-person singular subjects.

All singular nouns (*child*, *tree*) and the pronouns *he*, *she*, and *it* are third-person singular; indefinite pronouns such as *everyone* and *neither* are also third-person singular. When the subject of a sentence is third-person singular, its verb takes an *-s* or *-es* ending in the present tense. (See also G1.)

	SINGULAR		PLURAL	
FIRST PERSON	I	know	we	know
SECOND PERSON	you	know	you	know
THIRD PERSON	he/she/it	knows	they	know
	child	knows	parents	know
	everyone	knows		

PRACTICE **hackerhandbooks.com/writersref**
> Grammatical sentences > G2–6 and G2–7

▶ **My neighbor ~~drive~~ *drives* to Marco Island every weekend.**

▶ **Sulfur dioxide ~~turn~~ *turns* leaves yellow, ~~dissolve~~ *dissolves* marble, and ~~eat~~ *eats* away iron and steel.**

The subjects *neighbor* and *sulfur dioxide* are third-person singular, so the verbs must end in *-s*.

TIP: Do not add the *-s* ending to the verb if the subject is not third-person singular. The writers of the following sentences, knowing they sometimes dropped *-s* endings from verbs, overcorrected by adding the endings where they don't belong.

▶ **I prepare~~s~~ program specifications and logic diagrams.**

The writer mistakenly concluded that the *-s* ending belongs on present-tense verbs used with *all* singular subjects, not just *third-person* singular subjects. The pronoun *I* is first-person singular, so its verb does not require the *-s*.

▶ **The dirt floors require~~s~~ continual sweeping.**

The writer mistakenly thought that the verb needed an *-s* ending because of the plural subject. But the *-s* ending is used only on present-tense verbs with third-person *singular* subjects.

In nonstandard speech, the *-s* verb form *has*, *does*, or *doesn't* is sometimes replaced with *have*, *do*, or *don't*. In standard English, use *has*, *does*, or *doesn't* with a third-person singular subject. (See also G1-a.)

▶ **This respected musician always ~~have~~ *has* a message in his work.**

▶ **~~Do~~ *Does* she know the correct procedure for the experiment?**

▶ **My uncle ~~don't~~ *doesn't* want to change jobs right now.**

G2-d Do not omit *-ed* endings on verbs.

Speakers who do not fully pronounce *-ed* endings sometimes omit them unintentionally in writing. Leaving off *-ed* endings is common in many dialects and in informal speech even in standard English. In the following frequently used words and phrases, for example, the *-ed* ending is not always fully pronounced.

advised developed prejudiced supposed to
asked fixed pronounced used to
concerned frightened stereotyped

When a verb is regular, both the past tense and the past participle are formed by adding *-ed* (or *-d*) to the base form of the verb.

Past tense

Use the ending *-ed* or *-d* to express the past tense of regular verbs. The past tense is used when the action occurred entirely in the past.

▶ **Over the weekend, Ed ~~fix~~ *fixed* his brother's skateboard and tuned up his mother's 1991 Fiat.**

▶ **Last summer, my counselor ~~advise~~ *advised* me to ask my chemistry instructor for help.**

Past participles

Past participles are used in three ways: (1) following *have*, *has*, or *had* to form one of the perfect tenses; (2) following *be*, *am*, *is*, *are*, *was*, *were*, *being*, or *been* to form the passive voice; and (3) as adjectives modifying nouns or pronouns. The perfect tenses are listed on page 191, and the passive voice is discussed in W3. For a discussion of participles as adjectives, see B3-b.

▶ **Robin has ~~ask~~ *asked* for more housing staff for next year.**

Has asked is present perfect tense (*have* or *has* followed by a past participle).

▶ **Though it is not a new phenomenon, domestic violence is now ~~publicize~~ *publicized* more than ever.**

Is publicized is a verb in the passive voice (a form of *be* followed by a past participle).

▶ **All kickboxing classes end in a cool-down period to stretch ~~tighten~~ *tightened* muscles.**

The past participle *tightened* functions as an adjective modifying the noun *muscles*.

G2-e Do not omit needed verbs.

Although standard English allows some linking verbs and helping verbs to be contracted in informal contexts, it does not allow them to be omitted.

Linking verbs, used to link subjects to subject complements, are frequently a form of *be*: *be*, *am*, *is*, *are*, *was*, *were*, *being*, *been*. (See B2-b.) Some of these forms may be contracted (*I'm*, *she's*, *we're*, *you're*, *they're*), but they should not be omitted altogether.

▶ **When we** ^*are* **quiet in the evening, we can hear crickets in the woods.**

Helping verbs, used with main verbs, include forms of *be*, *do*, and *have* and the modal verbs *can*, *will*, *shall*, *could*, *would*, *should*, *may*, *might*, and *must*. (See B1-c.) Some helping verbs may be contracted (*he's leaving*, *we'll celebrate*, *they've been told*), but they should not be omitted altogether.

▶ **We** ^*have* **been in Chicago since last Thursday.**

ESL Some languages do not require a linking verb between a subject and its complement. English, however, requires a verb in every sentence. See M3-a.

▶ **Every night, I read a short book to my daughter. When I** ^*am* **too busy, my husband reads to her.**

G2-f Choose the appropriate verb tense.

Tenses indicate the time of an action in relation to the time of the speaking or writing about that action.

The most common problem with tenses—shifting confusingly from one tense to another—is discussed in section S4. Other problems with tenses are detailed in this section, after the following survey of tenses.

Survey of tenses

Tenses are classified as present, past, and future, with simple, perfect, and progressive forms for each.

PRACTICE **hackerhandbooks.com/writersref**
> Grammatical sentences > G2–8 and G2–9

SIMPLE TENSES The simple tenses indicate relatively simple time relations. The *simple present* tense is used primarily for actions occurring at the same time they are being discussed or for actions occurring regularly. The *simple past* tense is used for actions completed in the past. The *simple future* tense is used for actions that will occur in the future. In the following table, the simple tenses are given for the regular verb *walk*, the irregular verb *ride*, and the highly irregular verb *be*.

SIMPLE PRESENT

SINGULAR		PLURAL	
I	walk, ride, am	we	walk, ride, are
you	walk, ride, are	you	walk, ride, are
he/she/it	walks, rides, is	they	walk, ride, are

SIMPLE PAST

SINGULAR		PLURAL	
I	walked, rode, was	we	walked, rode, were
you	walked, rode, were	you	walked, rode, were
he/she/it	walked, rode, was	they	walked, rode, were

SIMPLE FUTURE

I, you, he/she/it, we, they	will walk, ride, be

PERFECT TENSES More complex time relations are indicated by the perfect tenses. A verb in one of the perfect tenses (a form of *have* plus the past participle) expresses an action that was or will be completed at the time of another action.

PRESENT PERFECT

I, you, we, they	have walked, ridden, been
he/she/it	has walked, ridden, been

PAST PERFECT

I, you, he/she/it, we, they	had walked, ridden, been

FUTURE PERFECT

I, you, he/she/it, we, they	will have walked, ridden, been

PROGRESSIVE FORMS The simple and perfect tenses have progressive forms that describe actions in progress. A progressive verb consists of a form of *be* followed by a present participle. The progressive forms are not normally used with certain verbs, such as *believe*, *know*, *hear*, *seem*, and *think*.

PRESENT PROGRESSIVE

I	am walking, riding, being
he/she/it	is walking, riding, being
you, we, they	are walking, riding, being

PAST PROGRESSIVE

I, he/she/it	was walking, riding, being
you, we, they	were walking, riding, being

FUTURE PROGRESSIVE

I, you, he/she/it, we, they	will be walking, riding, being

PRESENT PERFECT PROGRESSIVE

I, you, we, they	have been walking, riding, being
he/she/it	has been walking, riding, being

PAST PERFECT PROGRESSIVE

I, you, he/she/it, we, they	had been walking, riding, being

FUTURE PERFECT PROGRESSIVE

I, you, he/she/it, we, they	will have been walking, riding, being

ESL See M1-a for more specific examples of verb tenses that can be challenging for multilingual writers.

Special uses of the present tense

Use the present tense when expressing general truths, when writing about literature, and when quoting, summarizing, or paraphrasing an author's views.

General truths or scientific principles should appear in the present tense unless such principles have been disproved.

► **Galileo taught that the earth ~~revolved~~ *revolves* around the sun.**

Because Galileo's teaching has not been discredited, the verb should be in the present tense. The following sentence, however, is acceptable: *Ptolemy taught that the sun revolved around the earth.*

When writing about a work of literature, you may be tempted to use the past tense. The convention, however, is to describe fictional events in the present tense.

▶ **In Masuji Ibuse's *Black Rain*, a child ~~reached~~ *reaches* for a pomegranate in his mother's garden, and a moment later he ~~was~~ *is* dead, killed by the blast of the atomic bomb.**

When you are quoting, summarizing, or paraphrasing the author of a nonliterary work, use present-tense verbs such as *writes*, *reports*, *asserts*, and so on to introduce the source. This convention is usually followed even when the author is dead (unless a date or the context specifies the time of writing).

▶ **Dr. Jerome Groopman ~~argued~~ *argues* that doctors are "susceptible to the subtle and not so subtle efforts of the pharmaceutical industry to sculpt our thinking" (9).**

Writing with sources
MLA-style citation

In MLA style, signal phrases are written in the present tense, not the past tense. (See also MLA-3b.)

APA NOTE: When you are documenting a paper with the APA (American Psychological Association) style of in-text citations, use past tense verbs such as *reported* or *demonstrated* or present perfect verbs such as *has reported* or *has demonstrated* to introduce the source.

E. Wilson (1994) reported that positive reinforcement alone was a less effective teaching technique than a mixture of positive reinforcement and constructive criticism.

The past perfect tense

The past perfect tense consists of a past participle preceded by *had* (*had worked*, *had forgotten*). This tense is used for an action already completed by the time of another past action or for an action already completed at some specific past time.

Everyone *had spoken* by the time I arrived.

I pleaded my case, but Paula *had made up* her mind.

Writers sometimes use the simple past tense when they should use the past perfect.

▶ **We built our cabin high on a pine knoll, forty feet above an abandoned quarry that ~~was~~ *had been* flooded in 1920 to create a lake.**

The building of the cabin and the flooding of the quarry both occurred in the past, but the flooding was completed before the time of building.

▶ **By the time dinner was served, the guest of honor ^had^ left.**

The past perfect tense is needed because the action of leaving was already completed at a specific past time (when dinner was served).

Some writers tend to overuse the past perfect tense. Do not use the past perfect if two past actions occurred at the same time.

▶ **When Ernest Hemingway lived in Cuba, he ~~had written~~ ^wrote^ *For Whom the Bell Tolls.***

Sequence of tenses with infinitives and participles

An infinitive is the base form of a verb preceded by *to*. (See B3-b.) Use the present infinitive to show action occurring at the same time as or later than the action of the verb in the sentence.

▶ **The club had hoped to ~~have raised~~ ^raise^ fifteen thousand dollars by April 1.**

The action expressed in the infinitive (*to raise*) occurred later than the action of the sentence's verb (*had hoped*).

Use the perfect form of an infinitive (*to have* followed by the past participle) for an action occurring earlier than that of the verb in the sentence.

▶ **Dan would like to ~~join~~ ^have joined^ the navy, but he did not pass the physical.**

The liking occurs in the present; the joining would have occurred in the past.

Like the tense of an infinitive, the tense of a participle is governed by the tense of the sentence's verb. Use the present participle (ending in *-ing*) for an action occurring at the same time as that of the sentence's verb.

Hiking the Appalachian Trail in early spring, we spotted many wildflowers.

Use the past participle (such as *given* or *helped*) or the present perfect participle (*having* plus the past participle) for an action occurring before that of the verb.

Discovered off the coast of Florida, the Spanish galleon yielded many treasures.

Having worked her way through college, Lee graduated debt-free.

G2-g Use the subjunctive mood in the few contexts that require it.

There are three moods in English: the *indicative*, used for facts, opinions, and questions; the *imperative*, used for orders or advice; and the *subjunctive*, used in certain contexts to express wishes, requests, or conditions contrary to fact. For many writers, the subjunctive causes the most problems.

Forms of the subjunctive

In the subjunctive mood, present-tense verbs do not change form to indicate the number and person of the subject (see G1-a). Instead, the subjunctive uses the base form of the verb (*be*, *drive*, *employ*) with all subjects.

It is important that you *be* [not *are*] prepared for the interview.

We asked that she *drive* [not *drives*] more slowly.

Also, in the subjunctive mood, there is only one past-tense form of *be*: *were* (never *was*).

If I *were* [not *was*] you, I'd try a new strategy.

Uses of the subjunctive

The subjunctive mood appears in only a few contexts: in contrary-to-fact clauses beginning with *if* or expressing a wish; in *that* clauses following verbs such as *ask*, *insist*, *recommend*, *request*, and *suggest*; and in certain set expressions.

IN CONTRARY-TO-FACT CLAUSES BEGINNING WITH *IF* When a subordinate clause beginning with *if* expresses a condition contrary to fact, use the subjunctive *were* in place of *was*.

► **The astronomers would be able to see the moons of Jupiter tonight if the weather ~~was~~ *were* clearer.**

The verb in the subordinate clause expresses a condition that does not exist: The weather is not clear.

▶ **If I ~~was~~** *were* **a member of Congress, I would vote for that bill.**

The writer is not a member of Congress, so the verb in the *if* clause must be *were*.

Do not use the subjunctive mood in *if* clauses expressing conditions that exist or may exist.

If Dana *wins* the contest, she will leave for Barcelona in June.

IN CONTRARY-TO-FACT CLAUSES EXPRESSING A WISH In formal English, use the subjunctive *were* in clauses expressing a wish or desire. While use of the indicative is common in informal speech, it is not appropriate in academic writing.

INFORMAL I wish that Dr. Vaughn *was* my professor.

FORMAL I wish that Dr. Vaughn *were* my professor.

IN *THAT* CLAUSES FOLLOWING VERBS SUCH AS *ASK*, *INSIST*, *REQUEST*, AND *SUGGEST* Because requests have not yet become reality, they are expressed in the subjunctive mood.

▶ **Professor Moore insists that her students ~~are~~** *be* **on time.**

▶ **We recommend that Lambert ~~files~~** *file* **form 1050 soon.**

IN CERTAIN SET EXPRESSIONS The subjunctive mood appears in certain expressions: *be that as it may*, *as it were*, *far be it from me*, and so on.

G3 Pronouns

Pronouns are words that substitute for nouns (see B1-b). Pronoun errors are typically related to the four topics discussed in this section:

a. pronoun-antecedent agreement (singular vs. plural)
b. pronoun reference (clarity)
c. pronoun case (personal pronouns such as *I* vs. *me*, *she* vs. *her*)
d. pronoun case (*who* vs. *whom*)

For more help with pronouns, consult the glossary of usage (W1).

G3-a Make pronouns and antecedents agree.

Many pronouns have antecedents, nouns or pronouns to which they refer. A pronoun and its antecedent agree when they are both singular or both plural.

SINGULAR *Dr. Ava Berto* finished *her* rounds.

PLURAL The hospital *interns* finished *their* rounds.

ESL The pronouns *he*, *his*, *she*, *her*, *it*, and *its* must agree in gender (masculine, feminine, or neuter) with their antecedents, not with the words they modify.

Steve visited *his* [not *her*] sister in Seattle.

Indefinite pronouns

Indefinite pronouns refer to nonspecific persons or things. Even though some of the following indefinite pronouns may seem to have plural meanings, treat them as singular in formal English.

anybody	each	everyone	nobody	somebody
anyone	either	everything	no one	someone
anything	everybody	neither	nothing	something

Everyone performs at *his or her* [not *their*] own fitness level.

When a plural pronoun refers mistakenly to a singular indefinite pronoun, you can usually choose one of three options for revision:

1. Replace the plural pronoun with *he or she* (or *his or her*).
2. Make the antecedent plural.
3. Rewrite the sentence so that no agreement problem exists.

▶ **When someone travels outside the United States for the first time, ~~they need~~ *he or she needs* to apply for a passport.**

▶ **When ~~someone travels~~ *people travel* outside the United States for the first time, they need to apply for a passport.**

PRACTICE **hackerhandbooks.com/writersref**
> Grammatical sentences > G3–8 to G3–10

▶ ~~When someone~~ *Anyone who* travels outside the United States for the first time/ ~~they need~~ *needs* to apply for a passport.

Because the *he or she* construction is wordy, often the second or third revision strategy is more effective. Using *he* (or *his*) to refer to persons of either sex, while less wordy, is considered sexist, as is using *she* (or *her*) for all persons. See W4-e for strategies that avoid sexist usage.

NOTE: If you change a pronoun from singular to plural (or vice versa), check to be sure that the verb agrees with the new pronoun (see G1-e).

Generic nouns

A generic noun represents a typical member of a group, such as a typical student, or any member of a group, such as any lawyer. Although generic nouns may seem to have plural meanings, they are singular.

Every *runner* must train rigorously if *he or she wants* [not *they want*] to excel.

When a plural pronoun refers mistakenly to a generic noun, you will usually have the same revision options as on page 197.

▶ A medical student must study hard if ~~they want~~ *he or she wants* to succeed.

▶ ~~A medical student~~ *Medical students* must study hard if they want to succeed.

▶ A medical student must study hard ~~if they want~~ to succeed.

Collective nouns

Collective nouns such as *jury*, *committee*, *audience*, *crowd*, *class*, *troop*, *family*, *team*, and *couple* name a group. Ordinarily the group functions as a unit, so the noun should be treated as singular; if the members of the group function as individuals, however, the noun should be treated as plural. (See also G1-f.)

AS A UNIT The *committee* granted *its* permission to build.

AS INDIVIDUALS The *committee* put *their* signatures on the letter.

When treating a collective noun as plural, many writers prefer to add a clearly plural antecedent such as *members* to the sentence: *The members of the committee put their signatures on the letter.*

► **Defense attorney Clarence Darrow urged the jury to find his client, John Scopes, guilty so that he could appeal the case to a higher court. The jury complied, returning ~~their~~ *its* verdict in nine minutes.**

There is no reason to draw attention to the individual members of the jury, so *jury* should be treated as singular.

Compound antecedents

Treat most compound antecedents joined with *and* as plural.

In 1987, *Reagan and Gorbachev* held a summit where *they* signed the Intermediate-Range Nuclear Forces Treaty.

With compound antecedents joined with *or* or *nor* (or with *either . . . or* or *neither . . . nor*), make the pronoun agree with the nearer antecedent.

Either *Bruce* or *Tom* should receive first prize for *his* poem.

Neither the *mouse* nor the *rats* could find *their* way through the maze.

NOTE: If one of the antecedents is singular and the other plural, as in the second example, put the plural one last to avoid awkwardness.

EXCEPTION: If one antecedent is male and the other female, do not follow the traditional rule. The sentence *Either Bruce or Elizabeth should receive first prize for her short story* makes no sense. A better solution is to recast the sentence: *The prize for best short story should go to either Bruce or Elizabeth.*

G3-b Make pronoun references clear.

In a sentence like *After Andrew intercepted the ball, he kicked it as hard as he could*, the pronouns *he* and *it* substitute for the nouns *Andrew* and *ball*. The word a pronoun refers to is called its *antecedent*.

Ambiguous reference

Ambiguous pronoun reference occurs when a pronoun could refer to two possible antecedents.

PRACTICE **hackerhandbooks.com/writersref**
> Grammatical sentences > G3-11 to G3-13

The pitcher broke when Gloria set it
▶ **~~When Gloria set the pitcher~~ on the glass-topped table/. ~~it broke.~~**

"You have
▶ **Tom told James, ~~that he had~~ won the lottery."**

What broke—the pitcher or the table? Who won the lottery—Tom or James? The revisions eliminate the ambiguity.

Implied reference

A pronoun should refer to a specific antecedent, not to a word that is implied but not present in the sentence.

the braids
▶ **After braiding Ann's hair, Sue decorated ~~them~~ with colorful silk ribbons.**

The pronoun *them* referred to Ann's braids (implied by the term *braiding*), but the word *braids* did not appear in the sentence.

Modifiers, such as possessives, cannot serve as antecedents. A modifier may strongly imply the noun that a pronoun might logically refer to, but it is not itself that noun.

Writing with sources
MLA-style citation

Jamaica Kincaid
▶ **In ~~Jamaica Kincaid's~~ "Girl," ~~she~~ describes the advice a mother gives her daughter, including the mysterious warning not to be "the kind of woman who the baker won't let near the bread" (454).**

Using the possessive form of an author's name to introduce a source leads to a problem later in this sentence: The pronoun *she* cannot refer logically to a possessive modifier (*Jamaica Kincaid's*). The revision substitutes the noun *Jamaica Kincaid* for the pronoun *she*, thereby eliminating the problem.

Broad reference of this, that, which, *and* it

For clarity, the pronouns *this*, *that*, *which*, and *it* should ordinarily refer to specific antecedents rather than to whole ideas or sentences. When a pronoun's reference is needlessly broad, either replace the pronoun with a noun or supply an antecedent to which the pronoun clearly refers.

▶ **By advertising on television, pharmaceutical companies gain exposure for their prescription drugs. Patients respond**
the ads
to ~~this~~ by requesting drugs they might not need.

For clarity, the writer substituted the noun *ads* for the pronoun *this*, which referred broadly to the idea expressed in the preceding sentence.

▶ **Romeo and Juliet were both too young to have acquired much wisdom, ~~and~~ *a fact* that accounts for their rash actions.**

The writer added an antecedent (*fact*) that the pronoun *that* clearly refers to.

Indefinite use of they, it, *and* you

Do not use the pronoun *they* to refer indefinitely to persons who have not been specifically mentioned. *They* should always refer to a specific antecedent.

▶ **In June, ~~they~~ *the board* announced that parents would have to pay a fee for their children to participate in sports and music programs starting in September.**

The word *it* should not be used indefinitely in constructions such as *It is said on television* . . . or *In the article, it says that*. . . .

▶ **~~In the encyclopedia it states~~ *The encyclopedia states* that male moths can smell female moths from several miles away.**

The pronoun *you* is appropriate only when the writer is addressing the reader directly: *Once you have kneaded the dough, let it rise in a warm place.* Except in informal contexts, however, *you* should not be used to mean "anyone in general." Use a noun instead.

▶ **Ms. Pickersgill's *Guide to Etiquette* stipulates that ~~you~~ *a guest* should not arrive at a party too early or leave too late.**

G3-c Distinguish between pronouns such as *I* and *me*.

The personal pronouns in the following chart change what is known as *case form* according to their grammatical function in a sentence. Pronouns functioning as subjects or subject complements appear in the *subjective* case; those functioning as objects appear in the *objective* case; and those showing ownership appear in the *possessive* case.

PRACTICE **hackerhandbooks.com/writersref**
> Grammatical sentences > G3–14 and G3–15
> G3–17 and G3–18 (pronoun review)

	SUBJECTIVE CASE	OBJECTIVE CASE	POSSESSIVE CASE
SINGULAR	I	me	my
	you	you	your
	he/she/it	him/her/it	his/her/its
PLURAL	we	us	our
	you	you	your
	they	them	their

Pronouns in the subjective and objective cases are frequently confused. Most of the rules in this section specify when to use one or the other of these cases (*I* or *me*, *he* or *him*, and so on). See page 205 for a special use of pronouns and nouns in the possessive case.

Subjective case (I, you, he, she, it, we, they)

When a pronoun functions as a subject or a subject complement, it must be in the subjective case.

SUBJECT	Sylvia and *he* shared the award.
SUBJECT COMPLEMENT	Greg announced that the winners were Sylvia and *he*.

Subject complements—words following linking verbs that complete the meaning of the subject—frequently cause problems for writers, since we rarely hear the correct form in casual speech. (See B2-b.)

► **During the Lindbergh trial, Bruno Hauptmann repeatedly denied that the kidnapper was ~~him.~~** *he.* ^

If *kidnapper was he* seems too stilted, rewrite the sentence: *During the Lindbergh trial, Bruno Hauptmann repeatedly denied that he was the kidnapper.*

Objective case (me, you, him, her, it, us, them)

When a personal pronoun is used as a direct object, an indirect object, or the object of a preposition, it must be in the objective case.

DIRECT OBJECT	Bruce found Tony and brought *him* home.
INDIRECT OBJECT	Alice gave *me* a surprise party.
OBJECT OF A PREPOSITION	Jessica wondered if the call was for *her*.

Compound word groups

When a subject or an object appears as part of a compound structure, you may occasionally become confused. To test for the correct pronoun, mentally strip away all of the compound word group except the pronoun in question.

▶ **Joel ran away from home because his stepfather and ~~him~~ *he* had quarreled.**

His stepfather and he is the subject of the verb *had quarreled*. If we strip away the words *his stepfather and*, the correct pronoun becomes clear: *he had quarreled* (not *him had quarreled*).

▶ **The most traumatic experience for her father and ~~I~~ *me* occurred long after her operation.**

Her father and me is the compound object of the preposition *for*. Strip away the words *her father and* to test for the correct pronoun: *for me* (not *for I*).

When in doubt about the correct pronoun, some writers try to avoid making the choice by using a reflexive pronoun such as *myself*. Using a reflexive pronoun in such situations is nonstandard.

▶ **The Indian cab driver gave my cousin and ~~myself~~ *me* some good tips on traveling in New Delhi.**

My cousin and me is the indirect object of the verb *gave*. For correct uses of *myself*, see the glossary of usage (W1).

Appositives

Appositives are noun phrases that rename nouns or pronouns. A pronoun used as an appositive has the same function (usually subject or object) as the word(s) it renames.

▶ **The chief strategists, Dr. Bell and ~~me,~~ *I,* could not agree on a plan.**

The appositive *Dr. Bell and I* renames the subject, *strategists*. Test: *I could not agree* (not *me could not agree*).

▶ **The newspaper reporter interviewed only two witnesses, the bicyclist and ~~I.~~ *me.***

The appositive *the bicyclist and me* renames the direct object, *witnesses*. Test: *interviewed me* (not *interviewed I*).

We or *us* before a noun

When deciding whether *we* or *us* should precede a noun, choose the pronoun that would be appropriate if the noun were omitted.

- ▶ ~~Us~~ We tenants would rather fight than move.
- ▶ Management is shortchanging ~~we~~ us tenants.

No one would say *Us would rather fight than move* or *Management is shortchanging we.*

Comparisons with *than* or *as*

When a comparison begins with *than* or *as*, your choice of a pronoun will depend on your meaning. To test for the correct pronoun, mentally complete the sentence: *My roommate likes football more than I* [*do*].

- ▶ In our position paper supporting nationalized health care in the United States, we argued that Canadians are much better off than ~~us.~~ we.

We is the subject of the verb *are*, which is understood: *Canadians are much better off than we* [*are*]. If the correct English seems too formal, you can always add the verb.

- ▶ We respected no other candidate for the city council as much as ~~she.~~ her.

This sentence means that we respected no other candidate as much as *we respected her*. *Her* is the direct object of the understood verb *respected*.

Subjects and objects of infinitives

An infinitive is the word *to* followed by the base form of a verb. (See B3-b.) Subjects of infinitives are an exception to the rule that subjects must be in the subjective case. Whenever an infinitive has a subject, it must be in the objective case. Objects of infinitives also are in the objective case.

- ▶ Ms. Wilson asked John and ~~I~~ me to drive the senator and ~~she~~ her to the airport.

John and me is the subject of the infinitive *to drive*; *senator and her* is the direct object of the infinitive.

Possessive case to modify a gerund

A pronoun that modifies a gerund or a gerund phrase should be in the possessive case (*my*, *your*, *his*, *her*, *its*, *our*, *their*). A gerund is a verb form ending in *-ing* that functions as a noun. Gerunds frequently appear in phrases; when they do, the whole gerund phrase functions as a noun. (See B3-b.)

▶ **The chances of ~~you~~ *your* being hit by lightning are about two million to one.**

Your modifies the gerund phrase *being hit by lightning.*

Nouns as well as pronouns may modify gerunds. To form the possessive case of a noun, use an apostrophe and an *-s* (*victim's*) or just an apostrophe (*victims'*). (See P4-a.)

▶ **The old order in France paid a high price for the ~~aristocracy~~ *aristocracy's* exploiting the lower classes.**

The possessive noun *aristocracy's* modifies the gerund phrase *exploiting the lower classes.*

G3-d Distinguish between *who* and *whom*.

The choice between *who* and *whom* (or *whoever* and *whomever*) occurs primarily in subordinate clauses and in questions. *Who* and *whoever*, subjective-case pronouns, are used for subjects and subject complements. *Whom* and *whomever*, objective-case pronouns, are used for objects.

An exception to this general rule occurs when the pronoun functions as the subject of an infinitive (see p. 207).

In subordinate clauses

When *who* and *whom* (or *whoever* and *whomever*) introduce subordinate clauses, their case is determined by their function within the clause they introduce.

PRACTICE hackerhandbooks.com/writersref
> Grammatical sentences > G3–16
> G3–17 and G3–18 (pronoun review)

In the following two examples, the pronouns *who* and *whoever* function as the subjects of the clauses they introduce.

- ▶ **First prize goes to the runner ~~whom~~ who earns the most points.**

  The subordinate clause is *who earns the most points*. The verb of the clause is *earns*, and its subject is *who*.

- ▶ **Maya Angelou's *I Know Why the Caged Bird Sings* should be read by ~~whomever~~ whoever is interested in the effects of racial prejudice on children.**

  The writer selected the pronoun *whomever*, thinking that it was the object of the preposition *by*. However, the object of the preposition is the entire subordinate clause *whoever is interested in the effects of racial prejudice on children*. The verb of the clause is *is*, and the subject of the verb is *whoever*.

When functioning as an object in a subordinate clause, *whom* (or *whomever*) appears out of order, before the subject and verb. To choose the correct pronoun, you can mentally restructure the clause.

- ▶ **You will work with our senior traders, ~~who~~ whom you will meet after your orientation.**

  The subordinate clause is *whom you will meet after your orientation*. The subject of the clause is *you*, and the verb is *will meet*. *Whom* is the direct object of the verb. The correct choice becomes clear if you mentally restructure the clause: *you will meet whom*.

When functioning as the object of a preposition in a subordinate clause, *whom* is often separated from its preposition.

- ▶ **The tutor ~~who~~ whom I was assigned to was very supportive.**

  Whom is the object of the preposition to. In this sentence, the writer might choose to drop *whom*: *The tutor I was assigned to was very supportive*.

NOTE: Inserted expressions such as *they know*, *I think*, and *she says* should be ignored in determining whether to use *who* or *whom*.

- ▶ **The speech pathologist reported a particularly difficult session with a stroke patient ~~whom~~ who she knew was suffering from aphasia.**

  Who is the subject of *was suffering*, not the object of *knew*.

In questions

The case of an interrogative pronoun is determined by its function within the question.

▶ **~~Whom~~** *Who* **was responsible for creating that computer virus?**

Who is the subject of the verb *was*.

When *whom* functions as the object in a question, it appears out of normal order. To choose the correct pronoun, you can mentally restructure the question.

▶ **~~Who~~** *Whom* **did the Democratic Party nominate in 2004?**

Whom is the direct object of the verb *did nominate*. This becomes clear if you restructure the question: *The Democratic Party did nominate whom in 2004?*

For subjects or objects of infinitives

An infinitive is the word *to* followed by the base form of a verb. (See B3-b.) Subjects of infinitives are an exception to the rule that subjects must be in the subjective case. The subject of an infinitive must be in the objective case. Objects of infinitives also are in the objective case. (See also p. 204.)

▶ **When it comes to money, I know ~~who~~** *whom* **to believe.**

The infinitive phrase *whom to believe* is the direct object of the verb *know*, and *whom* is the subject of the infinitive *to believe*.

G4 Adjectives and adverbs

Adjectives modify nouns or pronouns. They usually come before the word they modify; occasionally they function as complements following the word they modify. Adverbs modify verbs, adjectives, or other adverbs. (See B1-d and B1-e.)

Many adverbs are formed by adding *-ly* to adjectives (*normal*, *normally*; *smooth*, *smoothly*). But don't assume that all words ending in *-ly* are adverbs or that all adverbs end in *-ly*. Some adjectives end in *-ly* (*lovely*, *friendly*), and some adverbs don't (*always*, *here*, *there*). When in doubt, consult a dictionary.

PRACTICE **hackerhandbooks.com/writersref**
> Grammatical sentences > G4–3 and G4–4

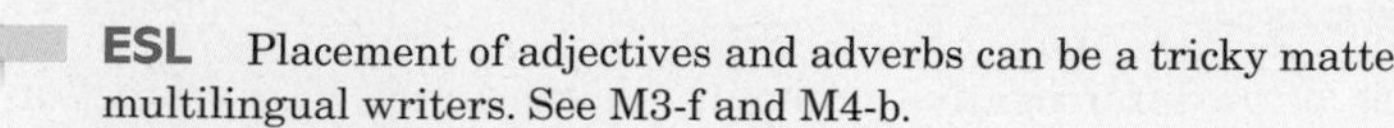

ESL Placement of adjectives and adverbs can be a tricky matter for multilingual writers. See M3-f and M4-b.

G4-a Use adjectives to modify nouns.

Adjectives ordinarily precede the nouns they modify. But they can also function as subject complements or object complements, following the nouns they modify.

ESL In English, adjectives are not pluralized to agree with the words they modify: *The red* [not *reds*] *roses were a surprise.*

Subject complements

A subject complement follows a linking verb and completes the meaning of the subject. (See B2-b.) When an adjective functions as a subject complement, it describes the subject.

Justice is *blind.*

Problems can arise with verbs such as *smell*, *taste*, *look*, and *feel*, which sometimes, but not always, function as linking verbs. If the word following one of these verbs describes the subject, use an adjective; if the word following the verb modifies the verb, use an adverb.

ADJECTIVE The detective looked *cautious*.

ADVERB The detective looked *cautiously* for fingerprints.

The adjective *cautious* describes the detective; the adverb *cautiously* modifies the verb *looked*.

Linking verbs suggest states of being, not actions. Notice, for example, the different meanings of *looked* in the preceding examples. To look cautious suggests the state of being cautious; to look cautiously is to perform an action in a cautious way.

▶ **The lilacs in our backyard smell especially ~~sweetly~~ *sweet* this year.**

The verb *smell* suggests a state of being, not an action. Therefore, it should be followed by an adjective, not an adverb.

▶ **The drawings looked ~~well~~ *good* after the architect made a few changes.**

The verb *looked* is a linking verb suggesting a state of being, not an action. The adjective *good* is appropriate following the linking verb to describe *drawings*. (See also the note on p. 210.)

When the verb *feel* refers to the state of a person's health or emotions, it is a linking verb and should be followed by an adjective (such as *bad*) instead of an adverb (such as *badly*).

▶ We felt ~~badly~~ *bad* when we heard of your grandmother's death.

Object complements

An object complement follows a direct object and completes its meaning. (See B2-b.) When an adjective functions as an object complement, it describes the direct object.

Sorrow makes *us wise*.

Object complements occur with verbs such as *call*, *consider*, *create*, *find*, *keep*, and *make*. When a modifier follows the direct object of one of these verbs, use an adjective to describe the direct object; use an adverb to modify the verb.

ADJECTIVE The referee called the plays *perfect*.

ADVERB The referee called the plays *perfectly*.

The first sentence means that the referee considered the plays to be perfect; the second means that the referee did an excellent job of calling the plays.

G4-b Use adverbs to modify verbs, adjectives, and other adverbs.

When adverbs modify verbs (or verbals), they nearly always answer the question When? Where? How? Why? Under what conditions? How often? or To what degree? When adverbs modify adjectives or other adverbs, they usually qualify or intensify the meaning of the word they modify. (See B1-e.)

Adjectives are often used incorrectly in place of adverbs in casual or nonstandard speech.

▶ The transportation arrangement worked out ~~perfect~~ *perfectly* for everyone.

▶ The manager must see that the office runs ~~smooth~~ *smoothly* and ~~efficient.~~ *efficiently.*

The adverb *perfectly* modifies the verb *worked out*; the adverbs *smoothly* and *efficiently* modify the verb *runs*.

▶ **The chance of recovering any property lost in the fire looks** *really* ~~**real**~~ **slim.**

Only adverbs can modify adjectives or other adverbs. *Really* intensifies the meaning of the adjective *slim*.

NOTE: The incorrect use of the adjective *good* in place of the adverb *well* to modify a verb is especially common in casual and nonstandard speech. Use *well*, not *good*, to modify a verb in your writing.

▶ **We were glad that Sanya had done** *well* ~~**good**~~ **on the CPA exam.**

The adverb *well* should be used to modify the verb *had done*.

The word *well* is an adjective, however, when it means "healthy," "satisfactory," or "fortunate": *I feel very well today. All is well. It is just as well.*

For more help with *well* and *good*, consult the glossary of usage (W1).

ESL The placement of adverbs varies from language to language. Unlike some languages, such as French and Spanish, English does not allow an adverb between a verb (*poured*) and its direct object (*the liquid*). See M3-f.

▶ **In the last stage of our experiment, we poured** ~~**slowly**~~ **the** *slowly* **liquid into the container.**

G4-c Use comparatives and superlatives with care.

Most adjectives and adverbs have three forms: the positive, the comparative, and the superlative.

POSITIVE	COMPARATIVE	SUPERLATIVE
soft	softer	softest
fast	faster	fastest
careful	more careful	most careful
bad	worse	worst
good	better	best

Comparative versus superlative

Use the comparative to compare two things, the superlative to compare three or more.

▶ **Which of these two low-carb drinks is ~~best?~~** *better?*

▶ **Though Shaw and Jackson are impressive, Hobbs is the ~~more~~** *most* **qualified of the three candidates running for mayor.**

Forming comparatives and superlatives

To form comparatives and superlatives of one-syllable adjectives, use the endings *-er* and *-est*: *smooth, smoother, smoothest; dark, darker, darkest*. For adjectives with three or more syllables, use *more* and *most* (or *less* and *least* for downward comparisons): *exciting, more exciting, most exciting; interesting, less interesting, least interesting.* Two-syllable adjectives form comparatives and superlatives in both ways: *lovely, lovelier, loveliest; helpful, more helpful, most helpful.*

Some one-syllable adverbs take the endings *-er* and *-est* (*fast, faster, fastest*), but longer adverbs and all of those ending in *-ly* form the comparative and superlative with *more* and *most* (or *less* and *least*).

The comparative and superlative forms of some adjectives and adverbs are irregular: *good, better, best; well, better, best; bad, worse, worst; badly, worse, worst.*

▶ **The Kirov is the ~~talentedest~~** *most talented* **ballet company we have seen.**

▶ **According to our projections, sales at local businesses will be ~~worser~~** *worse* **than those at the chain stores this winter.**

Double comparatives or superlatives

Do not use double comparatives or superlatives. When you have added *-er* or *-est* to an adjective or adverb, do not also use *more* or *most* (or *less* or *least*).

▶ **Of all her family, Julia is the ~~most~~ happiest about the move.**

▶ **All the polls indicated that Gore was more ~~likelier~~** *likely* **to win than Bush.**

Absolute concepts

Avoid expressions such as *more straight*, *less perfect*, *very round*, and *most unique.* Either something is unique or it isn't. It is illogical to suggest that absolute concepts come in degrees.

- ▶ **That is the most ~~unique~~ *unusual* wedding gown I have ever seen.**
- ▶ **The painting would have been even more ~~priceless~~ *valuable* had it been signed.**

G4-d Avoid double negatives.

Standard English allows two negatives only if a positive meaning is intended: *The orchestra was not unhappy with its performance* (meaning that the orchestra was happy). Using a double negative to emphasize a negative meaning is nonstandard.

Negative modifiers such as *never*, *no*, and *not* should not be paired with other negative modifiers or with negative words such as *neither*, *none*, *no one*, *nobody*, and *nothing*.

- ▶ **Management is not doing ~~nothing~~ *anything* to see that the trash is picked up.**

  The double negative *not . . . nothing* is nonstandard.

The modifiers *hardly*, *barely*, and *scarcely* are considered negatives in standard English, so they should not be used with negatives such as *not*, *no one*, or *never*.

- ▶ **Maxine is so weak that she ~~can't~~ *can* hardly climb stairs.**

G5 Sentence fragments

A sentence fragment is a word group that pretends to be a sentence. Sentence fragments are easy to recognize when they appear out of context, like these:

When the cat leaped onto the table.

Running for the bus.

And immediately popped their flares and life vests.

PRACTICE hackerhandbooks.com/writersref
> Grammatical sentences > G5–3 to G5–6

Test for fragments

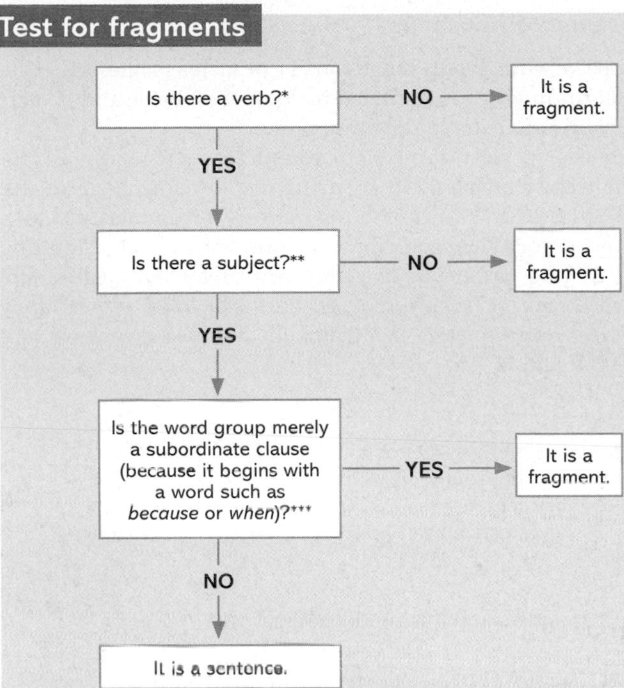

*Do not mistake verbals for verbs. A verbal is a verb form (such as *walking, to act*) that does not function as a verb of a clause. (See B3-b.)
**The subject of a sentence may be *you*, understood. (See B2-b.)
***A sentence may open with a subordinate clause, but the sentence must also include an independent clause. (See G5-a and B4-a.)

If you find any fragments, try one of these methods of revision (see G5-a to G5-c):

1. Attach the fragment to a nearby sentence.
2. Rewrite the fragment as a complete sentence.

When fragments appear next to related sentences, however, they are harder to spot.

> We had just sat down to dinner. When the cat leaped onto the table.
>
> I tripped and twisted my ankle. Running for the bus.
>
> The pilots ejected from the burning plane, landing in the water not far from the ship. And immediately popped their flares and life vests.

Recognizing sentence fragments

To be a sentence, a word group must consist of at least one full independent clause. An independent clause includes a subject and a verb, and it either stands alone or could stand alone.

To test whether a word group is a complete sentence or a fragment, use the flowchart on page 213. By using the flowchart, you can see exactly why *When the cat leaped onto the table* is a fragment: It has a subject (*cat*) and a verb (*leaped*), but it begins with a subordinating word (*When*). *Running for the bus* is a fragment because it lacks a subject and a verb (*Running* is a verbal, not a verb). *And immediately popped their flares and life vests* is a fragment because it lacks a subject. (See also B3-b and B3-e.)

> **ESL** Unlike some other languages, English requires a subject and a verb in every sentence (except in commands, where the subject *you* is understood but not present: *Sit down*). See M3-a and M3-b.
>
> ▶ *It is* ~~Is~~ often hot and humid during the summer.
>
> ▶ Students *are* usually very busy at the end of the semester.

Repairing sentence fragments

You can repair most fragments in one of two ways:

1. Pull the fragment into a nearby sentence.
2. Rewrite the fragment as a complete sentence.

▶ We had just sat down to dinner/ *when* ~~When~~ the cat leaped onto the table.

▶ *Running for the bus,* I tripped and twisted my ankle. ~~Running for the bus.~~

▶ The pilots ejected from the burning plane, landing in the water not far from the ship. *They* ~~And~~ immediately popped their flares and life vests.

G5-a Attach fragmented subordinate clauses or turn them into sentences.

A subordinate clause is patterned like a sentence, with both a subject and a verb, but it begins with a word that marks it as subordinate. The following words commonly introduce subordinate clauses.

after	before	so that	until	while
although	even though	than	when	who
as	how	that	where	whom
as if	if	though	whether	whose
because	since	unless	which	why

Subordinate clauses function within sentences as adjectives, as adverbs, or as nouns. They cannot stand alone. (See B3-e.)

Most fragmented clauses beg to be pulled into a sentence nearby.

► **Americans have come to fear the West Nile virus/ ~~Because~~** *because* **it is transmitted by the common mosquito.**

Because introduces a subordinate clause, so it cannot stand alone. (For punctuation of subordinate clauses at the end of a sentence, see P2-f.)

If a fragmented clause cannot be attached to a nearby sentence or if you feel that attaching it would be awkward, try turning the clause into a sentence. The simplest way to do this is to delete the opening word or words that mark it as subordinate.

► **Population increases and uncontrolled development are taking a deadly toll on the environment. ~~So that across~~** *Across* **the globe, fragile ecosystems are collapsing.**

G5-b Attach fragmented phrases or turn them into sentences.

Like subordinate clauses, phrases function within sentences as adjectives, as adverbs, or as nouns. They cannot stand alone. Fragmented phrases are often prepositional or verbal phrases; sometimes they are appositives, words or word groups that rename nouns or pronouns. (See B3-a, B3-b, and B3-c.)

Often a fragmented phrase may simply be pulled into a nearby sentence.

▶ **The archaeologists worked slowly/, ~~Examining~~ *examining* and labeling every pottery shard they uncovered.**

The word group beginning with *Examining* is a verbal phrase.

▶ **The patient displayed symptoms of ALS/, ~~A~~ *a* neurodegenerative disease.**

A neurodegenerative disease is an appositive renaming the noun *ALS*. (For punctuation of appositives, see P1-e.)

If a fragmented phrase cannot be pulled into a nearby sentence effectively, turn the phrase into a sentence. You may need to add a subject, a verb, or both.

▶ **Jamie explained how to access our new database. ~~Also~~ *She also taught us* how to submit expense reports and request vendor payments.**

The revision turns the fragmented phrase into a sentence by adding a subject and a verb.

G5-c Attach other fragmented word groups or turn them into sentences.

Other word groups that are commonly fragmented include parts of compound predicates, lists, and examples introduced by *for example*, *in addition*, or similar expressions.

Parts of compound predicates

A predicate consists of a verb and its objects, complements, and modifiers (see B2-b). A compound predicate includes two or more predicates joined with a coordinating conjunction such as *and*, *but*, or *or*. Because the parts of a compound predicate have the same subject, they should appear in the same sentence.

▶ **The woodpecker finch of the Galápagos Islands carefully selects a twig of a certain size and shape/ ~~And~~ *and* then uses this tool to pry out grubs from trees.**

The subject is *finch*, and the compound predicate is *selects . . . and . . . uses*. (For punctuation of compound predicates, see P2-a.)

Lists

To correct a fragmented list, often you can attach it to a nearby sentence with a colon or a dash. (See P3-d and P6-b.)

> ▶ **It has been said that there are only three indigenous American art forms~~.~~: ~~Musical~~** *musical* **comedy, jazz, and soap opera.**

Sometimes terms like *especially*, *like*, and *such as* introduce fragmented lists. Such fragments can usually be attached to the preceding sentence.

> ▶ **In the twentieth century, the South produced some great American writers~~.~~, ~~Such~~** *such* **as Flannery O'Connor, William Faulkner, Alice Walker, and Tennessee Williams.**

Examples introduced by for example, in addition, *or similar expressions*

Expressions that introduce examples or explanations can lead to fragments. Although a sentence may begin with a word or phrase like the following, the rest of the sentence must include a subject and a verb.

also	for example	mainly
and	for instance	or
but	in addition	that is

Often the easiest solution is to turn the fragment into a sentence.

> ▶ **A streaming gauge is useful for measuring a river's height and flow. In addition, ~~providing~~** *it provides* **residents with early flood warnings.**

The writer corrected this fragment by adding a subject—*it*—and substituting the verb *provides* for the verbal *providing*.

/riting
/ith
ources
ILA-style
itation

> ▶ **Tannen claims that men and women have different ideas about communication. For example,** *she explains* **that a woman "expects her husband to be a new and improved version of her best friend" (441).**

A quotation must be part of a complete sentence. *That a woman "expects her husband to be a new and improved version of her best friend"* is a fragment—a subordinate clause. Adding a signal phrase that includes a subject and a verb (*she explains*) corrects the fragment.

G5-d Exception: A fragment may be used for effect.

Writers occasionally use sentence fragments for special purposes.

FOR EMPHASIS	Following the dramatic Americanization of their children, even my parents grew more publicly confident. *Especially my mother.* —Richard Rodriguez
TO ANSWER A QUESTION	Are these new drug tests 100 percent reliable? *Not in the opinion of most experts.*
TRANSITIONS	*And now the opposing arguments.*
EXCLAMATIONS	*Not again!*
IN ADVERTISING	*Fewer carbs. Improved taste.*

Although fragments are sometimes effective, writers and readers do not always agree on when they are appropriate. That's why you will find it safer to write in complete sentences.

G6 Run-on sentences

Run-on sentences are independent clauses that have not been joined correctly. An independent clause is a word group that can stand alone as a sentence. (See B4-a.) When two independent clauses appear in one sentence, they must be joined in one of these ways:

- with a comma and a coordinating conjunction (*and*, *but*, *or*, *nor*, *for*, *so*, *yet*)
- with a semicolon (or occasionally with a colon or a dash)

Recognizing run-on sentences

There are two types of run-on sentences. When a writer puts no mark of punctuation and no coordinating conjunction between independent clauses, the result is called a *fused sentence.*

INDEPENDENT CLAUSE — INDEPENDENT CLAUSE

FUSED Air pollution poses risks to all humans it can be deadly for asthma sufferers.

A far more common type of run-on sentence is the *comma splice*—two or more independent clauses joined with a comma but without a coordinating conjunction. In some comma splices, the comma appears alone.

PRACTICE **hackerhandbooks.com/writersref**
> Grammatical sentences > G6–4 to G6–7

COMMA SPLICE Air pollution poses risks to all humans, it can be deadly for asthma sufferers.

In other comma splices, the comma is accompanied by a joining word that is *not* a coordinating conjunction (*and*, *but*, *or*, *nor*, *for*, *so*, and *yet*).

COMMA SPLICE Air pollution poses risks to all humans, however, it can be deadly for asthma sufferers.

However is a transitional expression and cannot be used with only a comma to join two independent clauses (see G6-b).

Revising run-on sentences

To revise a run-on sentence, you have four choices.

1. Use a comma and a coordinating conjunction (*and*, *but*, *or*, *nor*, *for*, *so*, *yet*).

▶ **Air pollution poses risks to all humans, *but* it can be deadly for asthma sufferers.**

2. Use a semicolon (or, if appropriate, a colon or a dash). A semicolon may be used alone or with a transitional expression.

▶ **Air pollution poses risks to all humans; it can be deadly for asthma sufferers.**

▶ **Air pollution poses risks to all humans; *however,* it can be deadly for asthma sufferers.**

3. Make the clauses into separate sentences.

▶ **Air pollution poses risks to all humans. ~~it~~ *It* can be deadly for asthma sufferers.**

4. Restructure the sentence, perhaps by subordinating one of the clauses.

▶ **~~Air~~ *Although air* pollution poses risks to all humans, it can be deadly for asthma sufferers.**

One of these revision techniques usually works better than the others for a particular sentence. The fourth technique, the one requiring the most extensive revision, is often the most effective.

G6-a Consider separating the clauses with a comma and a coordinating conjunction.

There are seven coordinating conjunctions in English: *and*, *but*, *or*, *nor*, *for*, *so*, and *yet*. When a coordinating conjunction joins independent clauses, it is usually preceded by a comma. (See P1-a.)

▶ **Some lesson plans include exercises, ^but completing them should not be the focus of all class periods.**

G6-b Consider separating the clauses with a semicolon (or, if appropriate, with a colon or a dash).

When the independent clauses are closely related and their relation is clear without a coordinating conjunction, a semicolon is an acceptable method of revision. (See P3-a.)

▶ **Tragedy depicts the individual confronted with the fact of death/^; comedy depicts the adaptability of human society.**

A semicolon is required between independent clauses that have been linked with a transitional expression (such as *however*, *therefore*, *moreover*, *in fact*, or *for example*). For a longer list, see P3-a.

▶ **In his film adaptation of the short story "Killings," director Todd Field changed key details of the plot/^; as a matter of fact, he added whole scenes that do not appear in the story.**

A colon or a dash may be more appropriate if the first independent clause introduces the second or if the second clause summarizes or explains the first. (See P3-d and P6-b.) In formal writing, the colon is usually preferred to the dash.

▶ **Nuclear waste is hazardous^: ~~this~~ This is an indisputable fact.**

▶ **The female black widow spider is often a widow of her own making/^— she has been known to eat her partner after mating.**

Recognizing run-on sentences

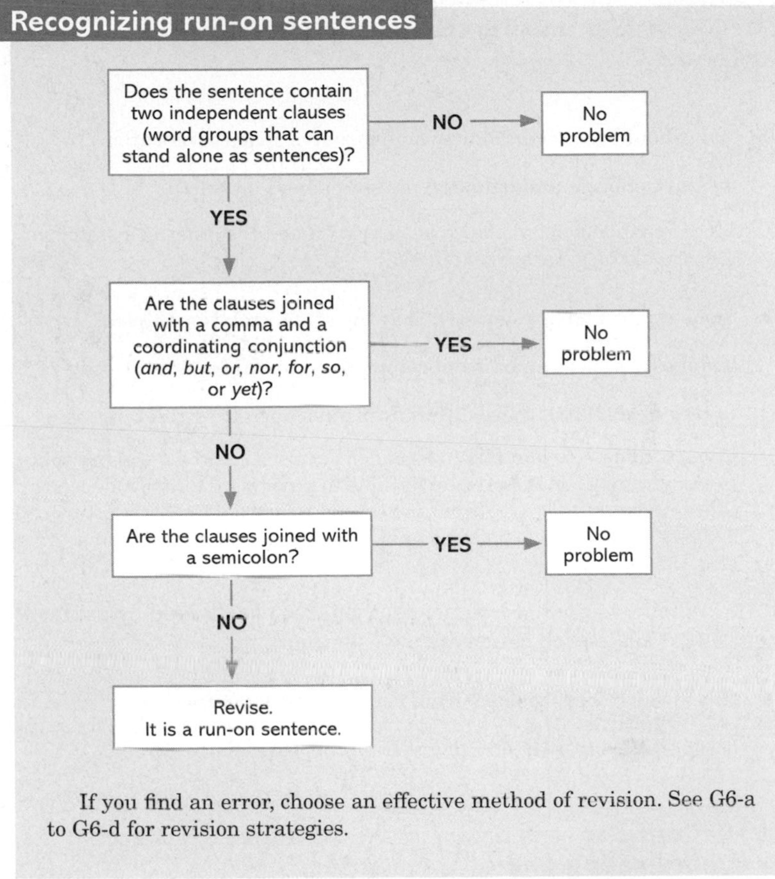

If you find an error, choose an effective method of revision. See G6-a to G6-d for revision strategies.

A colon is an appropriate method of revision if the first independent clause introduces a quoted sentence.

▶ **Nobel Peace Prize winner Al Gore had this to say about climate change/: "The truth is that our circumstances are not only new; they are completely different than they have ever been in all of human history."**

G6-c Consider making the clauses into separate sentences.

▶ **Why should we spend money on expensive space exploration/? We ~~we~~ have enough underfunded programs here on Earth.**

Since one independent clause is a question and the other is a statement, they should be separate sentences.

Writing with sources
APA-style citation

▶ **Some studies have suggested that the sexual relationships of bonobos set them apart from common chimpanzees/. A ~~a~~ccording to Stanford (1998), these differences have been exaggerated.**

Using a comma to join two independent clauses creates a comma splice. In this example, an effective revision is to separate the first independent clause (*Some studies* . . .) from the second independent clause (*these differences* . . .) and to keep the signal phrase with the second clause. (See also APA-3.)

NOTE: When two quoted independent clauses are divided by explanatory words, make each clause its own sentence.

▶ **"It's always smart to learn from your mistakes," quipped my boss/. "It's ~~"it's~~ even smarter to learn from the mistakes of others."**

G6-d Consider restructuring the sentence, perhaps by subordinating one of the clauses.

If one of the independent clauses is less important than the other, turn it into a subordinate clause or a phrase. (For more about subordination, see S6, especially the list on p. 130.)

▶ **One of the most famous advertising slogans is Wheaties cereal's "Breakfast of Champions," which ~~it~~ was penned in 1933.**

▶ **Mary McLeod Bethune, ~~was~~ the seventeenth child of former slaves, ~~she~~ founded the National Council of Negro Women in 1935.**

M

Multilingual Writers and ESL Challenges

M Multilingual Writers and ESL Challenges

M1 Verbs, 225

- **a** Appropriate form and tense, 225
- **b** Passive voice, 226
- **c** Base form after a modal, 230
- **d** Negative verb forms, 230
- **e** Verbs in conditional sentences, 231
- **f** Verbs followed by gerunds or infinitives, 235

M2 Articles, 237

- **a** Articles and other noun markers, 237
- **b** When to use *the*, 240
- **c** When to use *a* or *an*, 241
- **d** When not to use *a* or *an*, 243
- **e** No articles with general nouns, 244
- **f** Articles with proper nouns, 244

M3 Sentence structure, 245

- **a** Linking verb between a subject and its complement, 246
- **b** A subject in every sentence, 246
- **c** Repeated nouns or pronouns with the same grammatical function, 247
- **d** Repeated objects, adverbs in adjective clauses, 248
- **e** Mixed constructions with *although* or *because*, 249
- **f** Placement of adverbs, 249

M4 Using adjectives, 250

- **a** Present participles and past participles, 250
- **b** Order of cumulative adjectives, 251

M5 Prepositions and idiomatic expressions, 252

- **a** Prepositions showing time and place, 252
- **b** Noun (including *-ing* form) after a preposition, 253
- **c** Common adjective + preposition combinations, 254
- **d** Common verb + preposition combinations, 255

This section of *A Writer's Reference* is primarily for multilingual writers. You may find this section helpful if you learned English as a second language (ESL) or if you speak a language other than English with your friends and family.

M1 Verbs

Both native and nonnative speakers of English encounter challenges with verbs. Section M1 focuses on specific challenges that multilingual writers sometimes face. You can find more help with verbs in other sections in the book:

making subjects and verbs agree (G1)
using irregular verb forms (G2-a, G2-b)
leaving off verb endings (G2-c, G2-d)
choosing the correct verb tense (G2-f)
avoiding inappropriate uses of the passive voice (W3-a)

M1-a Use the appropriate verb form and tense.

This section offers a brief review of English verb forms and tenses. For additional help, see G2-f and B1-c.

Basic verb forms

Every main verb in English has five forms, which are used to create all of the verb tenses in standard English. The chart on page 226 shows these forms for the regular verb *help* and the irregular verbs *give* and *be*. See G2-a for the forms of other common irregular verbs.

Verb tenses

Section G2-f describes all the verb tenses in English, showing the forms of a regular verb, an irregular verb, and the verb *be* in each tense. The chart on pages 227–28 provides more details about the tenses commonly used in the active voice in writing; the chart on page 229 gives details about tenses commonly used in the passive voice.

PRACTICE AND MODELS **hackerhandbooks.com/writersref**
> Multilingual/ESL > Charts and study help
> Sample student paper (draft and final)
> Exercises
> Links to online resources

Basic verb forms

	REGULAR VERB *HELP*	IRREGULAR VERB *GIVE*	IRREGULAR VERB *BE**
BASE FORM	help	give	be
PAST TENSE	helped	gave	was, were
PAST PARTICIPLE	helped	given	been
PRESENT PARTICIPLE	helping	giving	being
-*S* FORM	helps	gives	is

**Be* also has the forms *am* and *are*, which are used in the present tense.

M1-b To write a verb in the passive voice, use a form of *be* with the past participle.

When a sentence is written in the passive voice, the subject receives the action instead of doing it. (See B2-b.)

The solution *was measured* by the lab assistant.

Melissa *was taken* to the hospital.

To form the passive voice, use a form of *be*—*am, is, are, was, were, being, be,* or *been*—followed by the past participle of the main verb: *was chosen, are remembered.* (Sometimes a form of *be* follows another helping verb: *will be stopped, could have been broken.*)

For details on forming the passive in various tenses, consult the chart on page 229. (For appropriate uses of the passive voice, see W3-a.)

▶ ***Dreaming in Cuban*** **was ~~writing~~ *written* by Cristina García.**

In the passive voice, the past participle *written*, not the present participle *writing*, must follow *was* (the past tense of *be*).

▶ **Senator Dixon will *be* defeated.**

The passive voice requires a form of *be* before the past participle.

▶ **The child was being ~~tease.~~ *teased.***

The past participle *teased*, not the base form *tease*, must be used with *was being* to form the passive voice.

PRACTICE **hackerhandbooks.com/writersref**
> Multilingual/ESL > M1–5

Verb tenses commonly used in the active voice

For descriptions and examples of all verb tenses, see G2-f. For verb tenses commonly used in the passive voice, see the chart on page 229.

Simple tenses
For general facts, states of being, habitual actions

Simple present	**Base form or *-s* form**
▪ general facts	College students often *study* late at night.
▪ states of being	Water *becomes* steam at 100° centigrade.
▪ habitual, repetitive actions	We *donate* to a different charity each year.
▪ scheduled future events	The train *arrives* tomorrow at 6:30 p.m.

NOTE: For advice about using the present tense in writing about literature, see page 192.

Simple past	**Base form + *-ed* or *-d* or irregular form**
▪ completed actions at a specific time in the past	The storm *destroyed* their property. She *drove* to Montana three years ago.
▪ facts or states of being in the past	When I *was* young, I usually *walked* to school with my sister.

Simple future	***will* + base form**
▪ future actions, promises, or predictions	I *will exercise* tomorrow. The snowfall *will begin* around midnight.

Simple progressive forms
For continuing actions

Present progressive	***am, is, are* + present participle**
▪ actions in progress at the present time, not continuing indefinitely	The students *are taking* an exam in Room 105. Jonathan *is parking* the car.
▪ future actions (with *go, leave, come, move*, etc.)	I *am leaving* tomorrow morning.

Past progressive	***was, were* + present participle**
▪ actions in progress at a specific time in the past	They *were swimming* when the storm struck.
▪ *was going to, were going to* for past plans that did not happen	We *were going to* drive to Florida for spring break, but the car broke down.

→

Verb tenses commonly used in the active voice (continued)

NOTE: Some verbs are not normally used in the progressive: *appear*, *believe*, *belong*, *contain*, *have*, *hear*, *know*, *like*, *need*, *see*, *seem*, *taste*, *understand*, and *want*.

▶ I ~~am wanting~~ [want] to see August Wilson's *Radio Golf.*

Perfect tenses
For actions that happened or will happen before another time

Present perfect	***has, have* + past participle**
▪ repetitive or constant actions that began in the past and continue to the present	I *have loved* cats since I was a child. Alicia *has worked* in Kenya for ten years.
▪ actions that happened at an unknown or unspecific time in the past	Stephen *has visited* Wales three times.
Past perfect	***had* + past participle**
▪ actions that began or occurred before another time in the past	She *had* just *crossed* the street when the runaway car crashed into the building.

NOTE: For more discussion of uses of the past perfect tense, see G2-f. For advice about using the past perfect in conditional sentences, see M1-e.

Perfect progressive forms
For continuous past actions before another time

Present perfect progressive	***has, have* + *been* + present participle**
▪ continuous actions that began in the past and continue to the present	Yolanda *has been trying* to get a job in Boston for five years.
Past perfect progressive	***had* + *been* + present participle**
▪ actions that began and continued in the past until some other past action	By the time I moved to Georgia, I *had been supporting* myself for five years.

Verb tenses commonly used in the passive voice

For details about verb tenses in the active voice, see pages 227–28.

Simple tenses (passive voice)

Simple present	***am, is, are* + past participle**
▪ general facts	Breakfast *is served* daily.
▪ habitual, repetitive actions	The receipts *are counted* every night.
Simple past	***was, were* + past participle**
▪ completed past actions	He *was punished* for being late.
Simple future	***will be* + past participle**
▪ future actions, promises, or predictions	The decision *will be made* by the committee next week.

Simple progressive forms (passive voice)

Present progressive	***am, is, are* + *being* + past participle**
▪ actions in progress at the present time	The new stadium *is being built* with private money.
▪ future actions (with *go, leave, come, move,* etc.)	Jo *is being moved* to a new class next month.
Past progressive	***was, were* + *being* + past participle**
▪ actions in progress at a specific time in the past	We thought we *were being followed*.

Perfect tenses (passive voice)

Present perfect	***has, have* + *been* + past participle**
▪ actions that began in the past and continue to the present	The flight *has been delayed* because of violent storms in the Midwest.
▪ actions that happened at an unknown or unspecific time in the past	Wars *have been fought* throughout history.
Past perfect	***had* + *been* + past participle**
▪ actions that began or occurred before another time in the past	He *had been given* all the hints he needed to complete the puzzle.

NOTE: The future progressive, future perfect, and perfect progressive forms are not used in the passive voice.

NOTE: Only transitive verbs, those that take direct objects, may be used in the passive voice. Intransitive verbs such as *occur*, *happen*, *sleep*, *die*, *become*, and *fall* are not used in the passive. (See B2-b.)

▶ **The accident ~~was~~ happened suddenly.**

▶ **Stock prices ~~were fallen~~** *fell* **all week.**

M1-c Use the base form of the verb after a modal.

The modal verbs are *can*, *could*, *may*, *might*, *must*, *shall*, *should*, *will*, and *would*. (*Ought to* is also considered a modal verb.) The modals are used with the base form of a verb to show certainty, necessity, or possibility.

Modals and the verbs that follow them do not change form to indicate tense. For a summary of modals and their meanings, see the chart on pages 232–33. (See also G2-e.)

▶ **The art museum will ~~launches~~** *launch* **its fundraising campaign next month.**

The modal *will* must be followed by the base form *launch*, not the present tense *launches*.

▶ **The translator could ~~spoke~~** *speak* **many languages, so the ambassador hired her for the European tour.**

The modal *could* must be followed by the base form *speak*, not the past tense *spoke*.

TIP: Do not use *to* in front of a main verb that follows a modal.

▶ **Gina can ~~to~~ drive us home if we miss the last train.**

For the use of modals in conditional sentences, see M1-e.

M1-d To make negative verb forms, add *not* in the appropriate place.

If the verb is the simple present or past tense of *be* (*am*, *is*, *are*, *was*, *were*), add *not* after the verb.

Mario *is not* a member of the club.

PRACTICE **hackerhandbooks.com/writersref**
> Multilingual/ESL > M1–6

For simple present-tense verbs other than *be*, use *do* or *does* plus *not* before the base form of the verb. (For the correct forms of *do* and *does*, see the chart in G1-a.)

▶ **Mariko ~~no~~ *does not* want more dessert.**

▶ **Mariko does not want~~s~~ more dessert.**

For simple past-tense verbs other than *be*, use *did* plus *not* before the base form of the verb.

▶ **They did not ~~planted~~ *plant* corn this year.**

In a verb phrase consisting of one or more helping verbs and a present or past participle (*is watching, were living, has played, could have been driven*), use the word *not* after the first helping verb.

▶ **Inna should *not* have ~~not~~ gone dancing last night.**

▶ **Bonnie is ~~no~~ *not* singing this weekend.**

NOTE: English allows only one negative in an independent clause to express a negative idea, using more than one is an error known as a *double negative* (see G4-d).

▶ **We could not find ~~no~~ *any* books about the history of our school in the public library.**

M1-e In a conditional sentence, choose verb tenses according to the type of condition expressed in the sentence.

Conditional sentences contain two clauses: a subordinate clause (usually starting with *if, when,* or *unless*) and an independent clause. The subordinate clause (sometimes called the *if* or *unless* clause) states the condition or cause; the independent clause states the result or effect. In each example in this section, the subordinate clause (*if* clause) is marked SUB, and the independent clause is marked IND. (See B3-e on clauses.)

PRACTICE hackerhandbooks.com/writersref
> Multilingual/ESL > M1–7

Modals and their meanings

can

▪ general ability (present)	Ants *can survive* anywhere, even in space. Jorge *can run* a marathon faster than his brother.
▪ informal requests or permission	*Can* you *tell* me where the light is? Sandy *can borrow* my calculator.

could

▪ general ability (past)	Lea *could read* when she was only three years old.
▪ polite, informal requests or permission	*Could* you *give* me that pen?

may

▪ formal requests or permission	*May* I *see* the report? Students *may park* only in the yellow zone.
▪ possibility	I *may try* to finish my homework tonight, or I *may wake up* early and *finish* it tomorrow.

might

▪ possibility	Funding for the language lab *might double* by 2017.

NOTE: *Might* usually expresses a stronger possibility than *may*.

must

▪ necessity (present or future)	To be effective, welfare-to-work programs *must provide* access to job training.
▪ strong probability	Amy *must be* sick. [She is probably sick.]
▪ near certainty (present or past)	I *must have left* my wallet at home. [I almost certainly left my wallet at home.]

should

▪ suggestions or advice	Diabetics *should drink* plenty of water every day.
▪ obligations or duties	The government *should protect* citizens' rights.
▪ expectations	The books *should arrive* soon. [We expect the books to arrive soon.]

→

will	
▪ certainty	If you don't leave now, you *will be* late.
▪ requests	*Will* you *help* me study for my test?
▪ promises and offers	Jonah *will arrange* the carpool.
would	
▪ polite requests	*Would* you *help* me carry these books? I *would like* some coffee. [*Would like* is more polite than *want*.]
▪ habitual or repeated actions (past)	Whenever Elena needed help with sewing, she *would call* her aunt.

Factual

Factual conditional sentences express relations based on fact. If the relationship is a scientific truth, use the present tense in both clauses.

SUB — IND

If water *cools* to 32° Fahrenheit, it *freezes*.

If the sentence describes a condition that is or was habitually true, use the same tense in both clauses.

SUB — IND

When Sue *jogs* along the canal, her dog *runs* ahead of her.

SUB — IND

Whenever the coach *asked* for help, I *volunteered*.

Predictive

Predictive conditional sentences are used to predict the future or to express future plans or possibilities. To form a predictive sentence, use a present-tense verb in the subordinate clause; in the independent clause, use the modal *will*, *can*, *may*, *should*, or *might* plus the base form of the verb.

SUB — IND

If you *practice* regularly, your tennis game *should improve*.

IND — SUB

We *will lose* our remaining wetlands unless we *act* now.

TIP: In all types of conditional sentences (factual, predictive, and speculative), *if* or *unless* clauses do not use the modal verb *will*.

▶ **If Jenna ~~will pass~~ *passes* her history test, she will graduate this year.**

Speculative

Speculative conditional sentences express unlikely, contrary-to-fact, or impossible conditions. English uses the past or past perfect tense in the *if* clause, even for conditions in the present or the future.

UNLIKELY POSSIBILITIES If the condition is possible but unlikely in the present or the future, use the past tense in the subordinate clause; in the independent clause, use *would*, *could*, or *might* plus the base form of the verb.

> SUB — IND
> If I *won* the lottery, I *would travel* to Egypt.

The writer does not expect to win the lottery. Because this is a possible but unlikely present or future situation, the subordinate clause uses the past tense.

CONDITIONS CONTRARY TO FACT In conditions that are currently unreal or contrary to fact, use the past-tense verb *were* (not *was*) in the *if* clause for all subjects. (See also G2-g, on the subjunctive mood.)

▶ **If I ~~was~~ *were* president, I would make children's issues a priority.**

The writer is not president, so *were* is correct in the *if* clause.

EVENTS THAT DID NOT HAPPEN In a conditional sentence that speculates about an event that did not happen or was impossible in the past, use the past perfect tense in the *if* clause; in the independent clause, use *would have*, *could have*, or *might have* with the past participle. (See also past perfect tense, p. 228.)

> SUB — IND
> If I *had saved* more money, I *would have visited* Laos last year.

The writer did not save more money and did not travel to Laos. This sentence shows a possibility that did not happen.

> SUB — IND
> If Aunt Grace *had been* alive for your graduation, she *would have been* very proud.

Aunt Grace was not alive at the time of the graduation. This sentence shows an impossible situation in the past.

M1-f Become familiar with verbs that may be followed by gerunds or infinitives.

A gerund is a verb form that ends in *-ing* and is used as a noun: *sleeping, dreaming*. (See B3-b.) An infinitive is the word *to* plus the base form of the verb: *to sleep, to dream*. (The word *to* is an infinitive marker, not a preposition, in this use.)

A few verbs may be followed by either a gerund or an infinitive; others may be followed by a gerund but not by an infinitive; still others may be followed by an infinitive but not by a gerund.

Verb + gerund or infinitive (no change in meaning)

The following commonly used verbs may be followed by a gerund or an infinitive, with little or no difference in meaning:

begin	hate	love
continue	like	start

I love *skiing*. I love *to ski*.

Verb + gerund or infinitive (change in meaning)

With a few verbs, the choice of a gerund or an infinitive changes the meaning dramatically:

forget	remember	stop	try

She stopped *speaking* to Lucia. [She no longer spoke to Lucia.]

She stopped *to speak* to Lucia. [She paused so that she could speak to Lucia.]

Verb + gerund

These verbs may be followed by a gerund but not by an infinitive:

admit	enjoy	postpone	resist
appreciate	escape	practice	risk
avoid	finish	put off	suggest
deny	imagine	quit	tolerate
discuss	miss	recall	

Bill enjoys *playing* [not *to play*] the piano.

Jamie quit *smoking*.

PRACTICE **hackerhandbooks.com/writersref**
> Multilingual/ESL > M1–8 and M1–9

Verb + infinitive

These verbs may be followed by an infinitive but not by a gerund:

agree	expect	need	refuse
ask	help	offer	wait
beg	hope	plan	want
claim	manage	pretend	wish
decide	mean	promise	would like

Jill has offered *to water* [not *watering*] the plants while we are away.

Joe finally managed *to find* a parking space.

The man refused *to join* the rebellion.

A few of these verbs may be followed either by an infinitive directly or by a noun or pronoun plus an infinitive:

ask	help	promise	would like
expect	need	want	

We asked *to speak* to the congregation.

We asked *Rabbi Abrams to speak* to our congregation.

Alex expected *to get* the lead in the play.

Ira expected *Alex to get* the lead in the play.

Verb + noun or pronoun + infinitive

With certain verbs in the active voice, a noun or pronoun must come between the verb and the infinitive that follows it. The noun or pronoun usually names a person who is affected by the action of the verb.

advise	convince	order	tell
allow	encourage	persuade	urge
cause	have ("own")	remind	warn
command	instruct	require	

V N ┌ INF ┐

The class encouraged Luis to tell the story of his escape.

The counselor *advised Haley to take* four courses instead of the usual five.

Professor Howlett *instructed us to write* our names on the left side of the paper.

Verb + noun or pronoun + unmarked infinitive

An unmarked infinitive is an infinitive without *to*. A few verbs (often called *causative verbs*) may be followed by a noun or pronoun and an unmarked infinitive.

have ("cause")	let ("allow")
help	make ("force")

Jorge *had the valet park* his car.

▶ **Please let me ~~to~~ pay for the tickets.**

▶ **Frank made me ~~to~~ carry his book for him.**

NOTE: *Help* can be followed by a noun or pronoun and either an unmarked or a marked infinitive:

Emma *helped Brian wash* the dishes.

Emma *helped Brian to wash* the dishes.

M2 Articles

Articles (*a, an, the*) are part of a category of words known as *noun markers* or *determiners*.

M2-a Be familiar with articles and other noun markers.

Standard English uses noun markers to help identify the nouns that follow. In addition to articles (*a, an,* and *the*), noun markers include

- possessive nouns, such as *Elena's* (See P4-a.)
- possessive pronoun/adjectives: *my, your, his, her, its, our, their* (See B1-b.)
- demonstrative pronoun/adjectives: *this, that, these, those* (See B1-b.)
- quantifiers: *all, any, each, either, every, few, many, more, most, much, neither, several, some,* and so on (See M2-d.)
- numbers: *one, twenty-three,* and so on

PRACTICE **hackerhandbooks.com/writersref**
> Multilingual/ESL > M2–3 to M2–5

Types of nouns

Common or proper

Common nouns	Examples	
▪ name general persons, places, things, or ideas ▪ begin with lowercase	religion knowledge rain	beauty student country

Proper nouns	Examples	
▪ name specific persons, places, things, or ideas ▪ begin with capital letter	Hinduism Philip Vietnam	President Adams Washington Monument Renaissance

Count or noncount (common nouns only)

Count nouns	Examples
▪ name persons, places, things, or ideas that can be counted ▪ have plural forms	girl, girls city, cities goose, geese philosophy, philosophies

Noncount nouns	Examples	
▪ name things or abstract ideas that cannot be counted ▪ cannot be made plural	dirt silver furniture	patience knowledge air

NOTE: See the chart on page 243 for commonly used noncount nouns.

Singular or plural (both common and proper)

Singular nouns (count and noncount)	Examples	
▪ represent one person, place, thing, or idea	backpack country woman achievement	rain beauty Nile River Block Island

Plural nouns (count only)	Examples	
▪ represent more than one person, place, thing, or idea ▪ must be count nouns	backpacks countries women	Ural Mountains Falkland Islands achievements

Specific (definite) or general (indefinite) (count and noncount)

Specific nouns	**Examples**
▪ name persons, places, things, or ideas that can be identified within a group of the same type	*The students* in *Professor Martin's class* should study. *The airplane* carrying *the senator* was late. *The furniture* in *the truck* was damaged.
General nouns	**Examples**
▪ name categories of persons, places, things, or ideas (often plural)	*Students* should study. *Books* help *cultures* connect. *The airplane* has made commuting between *cities* easy.

Using articles and other noun markers

Articles and other noun markers always appear before nouns; sometimes other modifiers, such as adjectives, come between a noun marker and a noun.

ART N
Felix is reading a book about mythology.

ART ADJ N
We took an exciting trip to Alaska last summer.

NOUN MARKER ADV ADJ N
That very delicious meal was expensive.

In most cases, do not use an article with another noun marker.

▶ ~~The my~~ *My* older brother lives in Wisconsin.

Expressions like *a few*, *the most*, and *all the* are exceptions: *a few potatoes*, *all the rain*. See also M2-d.

Types of articles and types of nouns

To choose an appropriate article for a noun, you must first determine whether the noun is *common* or *proper*, *count* or *noncount*, *singular* or *plural*, and *specific* or *general*. The chart on pages 238–39 describes the types of nouns.

Articles are classified as *indefinite* and *definite*. The indefinite articles, *a* and *an*, are used with general nouns. The definite article, *the*, is used with specific nouns. (The last section of the chart, on p. 239, explains general and specific nouns.)

A and *an* both mean "one" or "one among many." Use *a* before a consonant sound: *a banana, a tree, a picture, a happy child, a united family*. Use *an* before a vowel sound: *an eggplant, an occasion, an uncle, an honorable person*. (See also *a, an* in W1.)

The shows that a noun is specific; use *the* with one or more than one specific thing: *the newspaper, the soldiers*.

M2-b Use *the* with most specific common nouns.

The definite article, *the*, is used with most nouns—both count and noncount—that the reader can identify specifically. Usually the identity will be clear to the reader for one of the following reasons. (See also the chart on p. 242.)

1. The noun has been previously mentioned.

► **A truck cut in front of our van. When ^the truck skidded a few seconds later, we almost crashed into it.**

The article *A* is used before *truck* when the noun is first mentioned. When the noun is mentioned again, it needs the article *the* because readers can now identify which truck skidded—the one that cut in front of the van.

2. A phrase or clause following the noun restricts its identity.

► **Bryce warned me that ^the computer on his desk had just crashed.**

The phrase *on his desk* identifies the specific computer.

NOTE: Descriptive adjectives do not necessarily make a noun specific. A specific noun is one that readers can identify within a group of nouns of the same type.

► **If I win the lottery, I will buy ~~the~~ ^a brand-new bright red sports car.**

The reader cannot identify which specific brand-new bright red sports car the writer will buy. Even though *car* has several adjectives in front of it, it is a general noun in this sentence.

3. A superlative adjective such as *best* or *most intelligent* makes the noun's identity specific. (See also G4-c on comparatives and superlatives.)

▶ **Our petite daughter dated ^the tallest boy in her class.**

The superlative *tallest* makes the noun *boy* specific. Although there might be several tall boys, only one boy can be the tallest.

4. The noun describes a unique person, place, or thing.

▶ **During an eclipse, one should not look directly at ^the sun.**

There is only one sun in our solar system, so its identity is clear.

5. The context or situation makes the noun's identity clear.

▶ **Please don't slam ^the door when you leave.**

Both the speaker and the listener know which door is meant.

6. The noun is singular and refers to a scientific class or category of items (most often animals, musical instruments, and inventions).

▶ ^The tin ~~**Tin**~~ **whistle is common in traditional Irish music.**

The writer is referring to the tin whistle as a class of musical instruments.

M2-c Use *a* (or *an*) with common singular count nouns that refer to "one" or "any."

If a count noun refers to one unspecific item (not a whole category), use the indefinite article, *a* or *an*. *A* and *an* usually mean "one among many" but can also mean "any one." (See the chart on p. 242.)

▶ **My English professor asked me to bring ^a dictionary to class.**

The noun *dictionary* refers to "one unspecific dictionary" or "any dictionary."

▶ **We want to rent ^an apartment close to the lake.**

The noun *apartment* refers to "any apartment close to the lake," not a specific apartment.

Choosing articles for common nouns

Use *the*

▪ if the reader has enough information to identify the noun specifically	**COUNT:** Please turn on *the lights*. We're going to *the beach* tomorrow. **NONCOUNT:** *The food* throughout Italy is excellent.

Use *a* or *an*

▪ if the noun refers to one item *and* ▪ if the item is singular but not specific	**COUNT:** Bring *a pencil* to class. Charles wrote *an essay* about his first job.

NOTE: Do not use *a* or *an* with plural or noncount nouns.

Use a quantifier (*enough*, *many*, *some*, etc.)

▪ if the noun represents an unspecified amount of something ▪ if the amount is more than one but not all items in a category	**COUNT (PLURAL):** Amir showed us *some photos* of his trip to India. *Many turtles* return to the same nesting site each year. **NONCOUNT:** We didn't get *enough rain* this summer.

NOTE: Sometimes no article conveys an unspecified amount: *Amir showed us photos of his trip to India.*

Use no article

▪ if the noun represents all items in a category	**COUNT (PLURAL):** *Students* can attend the show for free. *Runners* must report to the officials' table at 7:00 a.m.
▪ if the noun represents a category in general	**NONCOUNT:** *Coal* is a natural resource.

NOTE: *The* is occasionally used when a singular count noun refers to all items in a class or a specific category: *The bald eagle is no longer endangered in the United States.*

Commonly used noncount nouns

Food and drink

beef, bread, butter, candy, cereal, cheese, cream, meat, milk, pasta, rice, salt, sugar, water, wine

Nonfood substances

air, cement, coal, dirt, gasoline, gold, paper, petroleum, plastic, rain, silver, snow, soap, steel, wood, wool

Abstract nouns

advice, anger, beauty, confidence, courage, employment, fun, happiness, health, honesty, information, intelligence, knowledge, love, poverty, satisfaction, wealth

Other

biology (and other areas of study), clothing, equipment, furniture, homework, jewelry, luggage, machinery, mail, money, news, poetry, pollution, research, scenery, traffic, transportation, violence, weather, work

NOTE: A few noncount nouns (such as *love*) can also be used as count nouns: *He had two loves: music and archery.*

M2-d Use a quantifier such as *some* or *more*, not *a* or *an*, with a noncount noun to express an approximate amount.

Do not use *a* or *an* with noncount nouns. Also do not use numbers or words such as *several* or *many* because they must be used with plural nouns, and noncount nouns do not have plural forms. (See the chart on this page for a list of commonly used noncount nouns.)

► **Dr. Snyder gave us ~~an~~ information about the Peace Corps.**

► **Do you have ~~many~~ money with you?**

You can use quantifiers such as *enough*, *less*, and *some* to suggest approximate amounts or nonspecific quantities of noncount nouns: *any homework*, *enough wood*, *less information*, *much pollution*.

► **Vincent's mother told him that she had ~~a~~ ^some^ news that would surprise him.**

M2-e Do not use articles with nouns that refer to all of something or something in general.

When a noncount noun refers to all of its type or to a concept in general, it is not marked with an article.

Kindness
▶ ~~The kindness~~ is a virtue.
^

The noun represents kindness in general; it does not represent a specific type of kindness.

▶ **In some parts of the world, ~~the~~ rice is preferred to all other grains.**

The noun *rice* represents rice in general, not a specific type or portion of rice.

In most cases, when you use a count noun to represent a general category, make the noun plural. Do not use unmarked singular count nouns to represent whole categories.

Fountains are
▶ **~~Fountain is~~ an expensive element of landscape design.**
^

Fountains is a count noun that represents fountains in general.

EXCEPTION: In some cases, *the* can be used with singular count nouns to represent a class or specific category: *The Chinese alligator is smaller than the American alligator*. See also number 6 in M2-b.

M2-f Do not use articles with most singular proper nouns. Use *the* with most plural proper nouns.

Since singular proper nouns are already specific, they typically do not need an article: *Prime Minister Cameron*, *Jamaica*, *Lake Huron*, *Mount Etna*.

There are, however, many exceptions. In most cases, if the proper noun consists of a common noun with modifiers (adjectives or an *of* phrase), use *the* with the proper noun.

the
▶ **We visited Great Wall of China last year.**
^

the
▶ **Rob wants to be a translator for Central Intelligence Agency.**
^

The is used with most plural proper nouns: *the McGregors*, *the Bahamas*, *the Finger Lakes*, *the United States*.

Using *the* with geographic nouns

When to omit *the*	
streets, squares, parks	Ivy Street, Union Square, Denali National Park
cities, states, counties	Miami, New Mexico, Bee County
most countries, continents	Italy, Nigeria, China, South America, Africa
bays, single lakes	Tampa Bay, Lake Geneva
single mountains, islands	Mount Everest, Crete
When to use *the*	
country names with *of* phrase	the United States (of America), the People's Republic of China
large regions, deserts	the East Coast, the Sahara
peninsulas	the Baja Peninsula, the Sinai Peninsula
oceans, seas, gulfs	the Pacific Ocean, the Dead Sea, the Persian Gulf
canals and rivers	the Panama Canal, the Amazon
mountain ranges	the Rocky Mountains, the Alps
groups of islands	the Solomon Islands

Geographic names create problems because there are so many exceptions to the rules. When in doubt about whether or not to use an article, consult the chart on this page, check a dictionary, or ask a native speaker.

M3 Sentence structure

Although their structure can vary widely, sentences in English generally flow from subject to verb to object or complement: *Bears eat fish.* This section focuses on the major challenges that multilingual students face when writing sentences in English. For more details on the parts of speech and the elements of sentences, consult sections B1–B4.

M3-a Use a linking verb between a subject and its complement.

Some languages, such as Russian and Turkish, do not use linking verbs (*is*, *are*, *was*, *were*) between subjects and complements (nouns or adjectives that rename or describe the subject). Every English sentence, however, must include a verb. For more on linking verbs, see G2-e.

is
▶ **Jim ^ intelligent.**

are
▶ **Many streets in San Francisco ^ very steep.**

M3-b Include a subject in every sentence.

Some languages, such as Spanish and Japanese, do not require a subject in every sentence. Every English sentence, however, must have a subject. Commands are an exception: The subject *you* is understood but not present ([*You*] *Give me the book*).

She seems
▶ **Your aunt is very energetic. ~~Seems~~ ^ young for her age.**

The word *it* is used as the subject of a sentence describing the weather or temperature, stating the time, indicating distance, or suggesting an environmental fact.

It is
▶ **^ ~~Is~~ raining in the valley and snowing in the mountains.**

It is
▶ **^ ~~Is~~ 9:15 a.m.**

It is
▶ **^ ~~Is~~ three hundred miles to Chicago.**

In most English sentences, the subject appears before the verb. Some sentences, however, are inverted: The subject comes after the verb. In these sentences, a placeholder called an *expletive* (*there* or *it*) often comes before the verb.

EXP V S S V
There are many people here today. (Many people are here today.)

There is
▶ **^ ~~Is~~ an apple in the refrigerator.**

there are
▶ **As you know, ^ many religious sects in India.**

PRACTICE **hackerhandbooks.com/writersref**
> Multilingual/ESL > M3–3

Notice that the verb agrees with the subject that follows it: *apple is, sects are*. (See G1-g.)

Sometimes an inverted sentence has an infinitive (*to work*) or a noun clause (*that she is intelligent*) as the subject. In such sentences, the placeholder *it* is needed before the verb. (Also see B3-b and B3-e.)

EXP V — S — — S — V

It is important to study daily. (To study daily is important.)

▶ **Because the road is flooded, ^it is necessary to change our route.**

The placeholder *it* is required before the verb *is* because the subject *to change our route* follows the verb.

TIP: The words *here* and *there* are not used as subjects. When they mean "in this place" (*here*) or "in that place" (*there*), they are adverbs, not nouns.

▶ **I just returned from a vacation in Japan. ~~There~~ ^It is very beautiful ^there.**

▶ **~~Here~~ ^This school offers a master's degree; ~~there~~ ^that school has only a bachelor's program.**

M3-c Do not use both a noun and a pronoun to perform the same grammatical function in a sentence.

English does not allow a subject to be repeated in its own clause.

▶ **The doctor ~~she~~ advised me to cut down on salt.**

The pronoun *she* cannot repeat the subject, *doctor*.

Do not add a pronoun even when a word group comes between the subject and the verb.

▶ **The watch that I bought on vacation ~~it~~ was not expensive.**

The pronoun *it* cannot repeat the subject, *watch*.

Some languages allow "topic fronting," placing a word or phrase (a "topic") at the beginning of a sentence and following it with an independent clause that explains something about the topic. This form is not allowed in English because the sentence seems to start with one subject but then introduces a new subject in an independent clause.

— TOPIC — — IND CLAUSE —

INCORRECT The seeds I planted them last fall.

The sentence can be corrected by bringing the topic (*seeds*) into the independent clause.

▶ ~~The seeds~~ I planted ~~them~~ ^the seeds^ last fall.

M3-d Do not repeat an object or an adverb in an adjective clause.

Adjective clauses begin with relative pronouns (*who*, *whom*, *whose*, *which*, *that*) or relative adverbs (*when*, *where*). Relative pronouns usually serve as subjects or objects in the clauses they introduce; another word in the clause cannot serve the same function. Relative adverbs should not be repeated by other adverbs later in the clause.

The cat ran under the car [that was parked on the street.]ADJ CLAUSE

▶ **The cat ran under the car that ~~it~~ was parked on the street.**

The relative pronoun *that* is the subject of the adjective clause, so the pronoun *it* cannot be added as a subject.

▶ **Myrna enjoyed the investment seminars that she attended ~~them~~ last week.**

The relative pronoun *that* is the object of the verb *attended*. The pronoun *them* cannot also serve as an object.

Sometimes the relative pronoun is understood but not present in the sentence. In such cases, do not add another word with the same function as the understood pronoun.

▶ **Myrna enjoyed the investment seminars she attended ~~them~~ last week.**

The relative pronoun *that* is understood after *seminars* even though it is not present in the sentence.

If the clause begins with a relative adverb, do not use another adverb with the same meaning later in the clause.

▶ **The office where I work ~~there~~ is one hour from the city.**

The adverb *there* cannot repeat the relative adverb *where*.

M3-e Avoid mixed constructions beginning with *although* or *because*.

A word group that begins with *although* cannot be linked to a word group that begins with *but* or *however*. The result is an error called a *mixed construction* (see also S5-a). Similarly, a word group that begins with *because* cannot be linked to a word group that begins with *so* or *therefore*.

If you want to keep *although* or *because*, drop the other linking word.

▶ **Although Nikki Giovanni is best known for her poetry for adults, ~~but~~ she has written several books for children.**

▶ **Because German and Dutch are related languages, ~~therefore~~ tourists from Berlin can usually read a few signs in Amsterdam.**

If you want to keep the other linking word, omit *although* or *because*.

▶ **~~Although~~ Nikki Giovanni is best known for her poetry for adults, but she has written several books for children.**

▶ **~~Because~~ German and Dutch are related languages/; therefore, tourists from Berlin can usually read a few signs in Amsterdam.**

For advice about using commas and semicolons with linking words, see P1-a, P1-b, and P3-a.

M3-f Do not place an adverb between a verb and its direct object.

Adverbs modifying verbs can appear in various positions: at the beginning or end of a sentence, before or after a verb, or between a helping verb and the main verb.

Slowly, we drove along the rain-slick road.

Mia handled the teapot *very carefully*.

Martin *always* wins our tennis matches.

Christina is *rarely* late for our lunch dates.

My daughter has *often* spoken of you.

The election results were being *closely* followed by analysts.

An adverb cannot appear between a verb and its direct object.

▶ **Mother ^carefully wrapped ~~carefully~~ the gift.**

The adverb *carefully* cannot appear between the verb, *wrapped*, and its direct object, *the gift*.

M4 Using adjectives

M4-a Distinguish between present participles and past participles used as adjectives.

Both present and past participles may be used as adjectives. The present participle always ends in *-ing*. Past participles usually end in *-ed*, *-d*, *-en*, *-n*, or *-t*. (See G2-a.)

PRESENT PARTICIPLES	confusing, speaking, boring
PAST PARTICIPLES	confused, spoken, bored

Like all other adjectives, participles can come before nouns; they also can follow linking verbs, in which case they describe the subject of the sentence. (See B2-b.)

Use a present participle to describe a person or thing *causing or stimulating an experience.*

The printer came with *confusing instructions*. [The instructions caused confusion.]

Use a past participle to describe a person or thing *undergoing an experience.*

Rachel was *confused* by the instructions. [Rachel experienced confusion.]

PRACTICE **hackerhandbooks.com/writersref**
> Multilingual/ESL > M4–3

Participles that describe emotions or mental states often cause the most confusion.

annoying/annoyed	exhausting/exhausted
boring/bored	fascinating/fascinated
confusing/confused	frightening/frightened
depressing/depressed	satisfying/satisfied
exciting/excited	surprising/surprised

▶ Our hike was ~~exhausted.~~ ^exhausting.

Exhausting suggests that the hike caused exhaustion.

▶ The ~~exhausting~~ ^exhausted hikers reached the campground just before sunset.

Exhausted describes how the hikers felt.

M4-b Place cumulative adjectives in an appropriate order.

Adjectives usually come before the nouns they modify and may also come after linking verbs. (See B1-d and B2-b.)

Janine wore new (ADJ) shoes (N). Janine's shoes were (V) new (ADJ).

Cumulative adjectives, which cannot be joined by the word *and* or separated by commas, must come in a particular order. If you use cumulative adjectives before a noun, the chart on page 252 can help you determine their order. The chart is only a guide; don't be surprised if you encounter exceptions. (See also P2-d.)

▶ My dorm room has only a small desk and a ~~plastic red smelly~~ ^smelly red plastic chair.

▶ Nice weather, ~~blue clear~~ ^clear blue water, and ancient monuments attract many people to Italy.

PRACTICE **hackerhandbooks.com/writersref**
> Multilingual/ESL > M4–4

Order of cumulative adjectives

FIRST

ARTICLE OR OTHER NOUN MARKER a, an, the, her, this, my, Joe's, two, many, some

EVALUATIVE WORD attractive, dedicated, delicious, ugly, disgusting

SIZE large, enormous, small, little

LENGTH OR SHAPE long, short, round, square

AGE new, old, young, antique

COLOR yellow, blue, crimson

NATIONALITY French, Peruvian, Vietnamese

RELIGION Catholic, Protestant, Jewish, Muslim

MATERIAL silver, walnut, wool, marble

LAST

NOUN/ADJECTIVE tree (as in *tree* house), kitchen (as in *kitchen* table)

THE NOUN MODIFIED house, coat, bicycle, bread, woman, coin

My large blue wool coat is in the attic.

Joe's collection includes *two small antique silver* coins.

M5 Prepositions and idiomatic expressions

M5-a Become familiar with prepositions that show time and place.

The most frequently used prepositions in English are *at*, *by*, *for*, *from*, *in*, *of*, *on*, *to*, and *with*. Prepositions can be difficult to master because the differences among them are subtle and idiomatic. The chart on page 253 is limited to three troublesome prepositions that show time and place: *at*, *on*, and *in*.

Not every possible use is listed in the chart, so don't be surprised when you encounter exceptions and idiomatic uses that you must learn one at a time. For example, in English a person rides *in* a car but *on* a bus, plane, train, or subway.

PRACTICE **hackerhandbooks.com/writersref**
> Multilingual/ESL > M5–2

At, on, and *in* to show time and place

Showing time

AT	*at* a specific time: *at* 7:20, *at* dawn, *at* dinner
ON	*on* a specific day or date: *on* Tuesday, *on* June 4
IN	*in* a part of a 24-hour period: *in* the afternoon, *in* the daytime [but *at* night]
	in a year or month: *in* 1999, *in* July
	in a period of time: finished *in* three hours

Showing place

AT	*at* a meeting place or location: *at* home, *at* the club
	at the edge of something: sitting *at* the desk
	at the corner of something: turning *at* the intersection
	at a target: throwing the snowball *at* Lucy
ON	*on* a surface: placed *on* the table, hanging *on* the wall
	on a street: the house *on* Spring Street
	on an electronic medium: *on* television, *on* the Internet
IN	*in* an enclosed space: *in* the garage, *in* an envelope
	in a geographic location: *in* San Diego, *in* Texas
	in a print medium: *in* a book, *in* a magazine

▶ My first class starts ~~on~~ *at* 8:00 a.m.

▶ The farmers go to market ~~in~~ *on* Wednesday.

▶ I want to work at one of the biggest companies ~~on~~ *in* the world.

M5-b Use nouns (including *-ing* forms) after prepositions.

In a prepositional phrase, use a noun (not a verb) after the preposition. Sometimes the noun will be a gerund, the *-ing* verb form that functions as a noun (see B3-b).

▶ Our student government is good at ~~save~~ *saving* money.

Distinguish between the preposition *to* and the infinitive marker *to*. If *to* is a preposition, it should be followed by a noun or a gerund.

▶ **We are dedicated to ~~help~~ *helping* the poor.**

If *to* is an infinitive marker, it should be followed by the base form of the verb.

▶ **We want to ~~helping~~ *help* the poor.**

To test whether *to* is a preposition or an infinitive marker, insert a word that you know is a noun after the word *to*. If the noun makes sense in that position, *to* is a preposition. If the noun does not make sense after *to*, then *to* is an infinitive marker.

Zoe is addicted *to* ____________________.

They are planning *to* ____________________.

In the first sentence, a noun (such as *magazines*) makes sense after *to*, so *to* is a preposition and should be followed by a noun or a gerund: Zoe is addicted *to magazines*. Zoe is addicted *to running*.

In the second sentence, a noun (such as *magazines*) does not make sense after *to*, so *to* is an infinitive marker and must be followed by the base form of the verb: They are planning *to build* a new school.

M5-c Become familiar with common adjective + preposition combinations.

Some adjectives appear only with certain prepositions. These expressions are idiomatic and may be different from the combinations used in your native language.

▶ **Paula is married ~~with~~ *to* Jon.**

Check an ESL dictionary for combinations that are not listed in the chart on page 255.

M5-d Become familiar with common verb + preposition combinations.

Many verbs and prepositions appear together in idiomatic phrases. Pay special attention to the combinations that are different from the combinations used in your native language.

▶ **Your success depends ~~of~~ *on* your effort.**

Check an ESL dictionary for combinations that are not listed in the chart below.

Adjective + preposition combinations

accustomed to	connected to	guilty of	preferable to
addicted to	covered with	interested in	proud of
afraid of	dedicated to	involved in	responsible for
angry with	devoted to	involved with	satisfied with
ashamed of	different from	known as	scared of
aware of	engaged in	known for	similar to
committed to	engaged to	made of (*or* made from)	tired of
concerned about	excited about	married to	worried about
concerned with	familiar with	opposed to	
	full of		

Verb + preposition combinations

agree with	compare with	forget about	speak to (*or* speak with)
apply to	concentrate on	happen to	stare at
approve of	consist of	hope for	succeed at
arrive at	count on	insist on	succeed in
arrive in	decide on	listen to	take advantage of
ask for	depend on	participate in	take care of
believe in	differ from	rely on	think about
belong to	disagree with	reply to	think of
care about	dream about	respond to	wait for
care for	dream of	result in	wait on
compare to	feel like	search for	

P

Punctuation and Mechanics

P Punctuation and Mechanics

P1 The comma, 259

- a Clauses with *and*, *but*, etc., 259
- b Introductory elements, 260
- c Items in a series, 261
- d Coordinate adjectives, 261
- e Nonrestrictive elements, 262
- f Transitions, parenthetical expressions, etc., 265
- g Conventional uses, 267
- h To prevent confusion, 269

P2 Unnecessary commas, 269

- a Compound elements, 269
- b Between verb and subject or object, 270
- c Before or after a series, 270
- d Cumulative adjectives, 271
- e Restrictive elements, 271
- f Concluding clauses, 272
- g Inverted sentences, 272
- h Other misuses, 273

P3 The semicolon and the colon, 274

- a Semicolon with independent clauses, 274
- b Semicolon with series, 275
- c Misuses of the semicolon, 276
- d Colon with list, appositive, quotation, summary, 276
- e Conventional uses of the colon, 277
- f Misuses of the colon, 277

P4 The apostrophe, 278

- a Possessive nouns, indefinite pronouns, 278
- b Contractions, 279
- c Plurals of numbers, letters, etc., 279
- d Misuses, 280

P5 Quotation marks, 281

- a Direct quotations, 281
- b Quotation within quotation, 282
- c Titles, 283
- d Words as words, 283
- e With other punctuation, 283
- f Misuses, 285

P6 Other punctuation marks, 286

- a End punctuation, 286
- b Dash, parentheses, brackets, 288
- c Ellipsis mark, 290
- d Slash, 291

P7 Spelling and hyphenation, 291

- a Spelling rules, 291
- b Words that sound alike, 293
- c Compound words, 294
- d Hyphenated adjectives, 294
- e Fractions and numbers, 295
- f With prefixes and suffixes, 295
- g To avoid ambiguity, 295
- h End-of-line breaks, 296

P8 Capitalization, 296

- a Proper versus common nouns, 296
- b Titles with names, 298
- c Titles of works, 298
- d First word of sentence, 298
- e First word after colon, 299
- f Abbreviations, 299

P9 Abbreviations and numbers, 300

- a Titles with names, 300
- b Familiar abbreviations, 300
- c *BC*, *a.m.*, *No.*, etc., 301
- d Latin abbreviations, 301
- e Misuses, 302
- f Spelling out numbers, 302
- g Using numerals, 303

P10 Italics, 304

- a Titles of works, 304
- b Other terms, 305

P1 The comma

The comma was invented to help readers. Without it, sentence parts can collide into one another unexpectedly, causing misreadings.

CONFUSING If you cook Elmer will do the dishes.

CONFUSING While we were eating a rattlesnake approached our campsite.

Add commas in the logical places (after *cook* and *eating*), and suddenly all is clear. No longer is Elmer being cooked, the rattlesnake being eaten.

Various rules have evolved to prevent such misreadings and to speed readers along through complex grammatical structures. Those rules are detailed in this section. (P2 explains when not to use commas.)

P1-a Use a comma before a coordinating conjunction joining independent clauses.

When a coordinating conjunction connects two or more independent clauses—word groups that could stand alone as separate sentences—a comma must precede the conjunction. There are seven coordinating conjunctions in English: *and*, *but*, *or*, *nor*, *for*, *so*, and *yet*.

A comma tells readers that one independent clause has come to a close and that another is about to begin.

▶ **The department sponsored a seminar on college survival skills, and it also hosted a barbecue for new students.**

EXCEPTION: If the two independent clauses are short and there is no danger of misreading, the comma may be omitted.

The plane took off and we were on our way.

TIP: As a rule, do *not* use a comma to separate compound elements that are not independent clauses. (See P2-a.)

▶ **A good money manager controls expenses/ and invests surplus dollars to meet future needs.**

The word group following *and* is not an independent clause; it is the second half of a compound predicate (*controls . . . and invests*).

PRACTICE **hackerhandbooks.com/writersref**
> Punctuation and mechanics > P1–8 to P1–10

P1-b Use a comma after an introductory phrase or clause.

The most common introductory word groups are phrases and clauses functioning as adverbs. Such word groups usually tell when, where, how, why, or under what conditions the main action of the sentence occurred. (See B3-a, B3-b, and B3-e.)

A comma tells readers that the introductory phrase or clause has come to a close and that the main part of the sentence is about to begin.

▶ **Near a small stream at the bottom of the canyon, the park rangers discovered an abandoned mine.**

The comma tells readers that the introductory prepositional phrase has come to a close.

▶ **When Irwin was ready to iron, his cat tripped on the extension cord.**

Without the comma, readers may have Irwin ironing his cat. The comma signals that *his cat* is the subject of a new clause, not part of the introductory one.

EXCEPTION: The comma may be omitted after a short adverb clause or phrase if there is no danger of misreading.

In no time we were at 2,800 feet.

Sentences also frequently begin with participial phrases describing the noun or pronoun immediately following them. The comma tells readers that they are about to learn the identity of the person or thing described; therefore, the comma is usually required even when the phrase is short. (See B3-b.)

▶ **Thinking his motorcade drive through Dallas was routine, President Kennedy smiled and waved at the crowds.**

▶ **Buried under layers of younger rocks, the earth's oldest rocks contain no fossils.**

NOTE: Other introductory word groups include transitional expressions and absolute phrases (see P1-f).

P1-c Use a comma between all items in a series.

When three or more items are presented in a series, those items should be separated from one another with commas. Items in a series may be single words, phrases, or clauses.

▶ **Bubbles of air, leaves, ferns, bits of wood, and insects are often found trapped in amber.**

▶ **Langston Hughes's poetry is concerned with racial pride, social justice, and the diversity of the African American experience.**

Although some writers view the comma between the last two items as optional, most experts advise using the comma because its omission can result in ambiguity or misreading.

▶ **David willed his oldest niece all of his property, houses, and warehouses.**

Did Uncle David will his property *and* houses *and* warehouses—or simply his property, consisting of houses and warehouses? If the former meaning is intended, a comma is necessary to prevent ambiguity.

▶ **The activities include touring the White House, visiting the Air and Space Museum, attending a lecture about the Founding Fathers, and kayaking on the Potomac River.**

Without the comma, the activities might seem to include a lecture about kayaking, not participating in kayaking. The comma makes it clear that *kayaking on the Potomac River* is a separate item in the series.

P1-d Use a comma between coordinate adjectives not joined with *and*. Do not use a comma between cumulative adjectives.

When two or more adjectives each modify a noun separately, they are coordinate.

Roberto is a *warm, gentle, affectionate* father.

TEST: If the adjectives can be joined with *and*, the adjectives are coordinate, so you should use commas: *warm* and *gentle* and *affectionate* (*warm*, *gentle*, *affectionate*).

Adjectives that do not modify the noun separately are cumulative.

Three large gray shapes moved slowly toward us.

Beginning with the adjective closest to the noun *shapes*, these modifiers lean on one another, piggyback style, with each modifying a larger word group. *Gray* modifies *shapes*, *large* modifies *gray shapes*, and *three* modifies *large gray shapes*. Cumulative adjectives cannot be joined with *and* (not *three* and *large* and *gray shapes*).

COORDINATE ADJECTIVES

▶ **Should patients with severe, irreversible brain damage be put on life support systems?**

CUMULATIVE ADJECTIVES

▶ **Ira ordered a rich/ chocolate,/ layer cake.**

P1-e Use commas to set off nonrestrictive elements. Do not use commas to set off restrictive elements.

Certain word groups that modify nouns or pronouns can be restrictive or nonrestrictive—that is, essential or not essential to the meaning of a sentence. These word groups are usually adjective clauses, adjective phrases, or appositives.

Restrictive elements

A restrictive element defines or limits the meaning of the word it modifies; it is therefore essential to the meaning of the sentence and is not set off with commas. If you remove a restrictive modifier from a sentence, the meaning changes significantly, becoming more general than you intended.

RESTRICTIVE (NO COMMAS)

The campers need clothes *that are durable.*

Scientists *who study the earth's structure* are called geologists.

The first sentence does not mean that the campers need clothes in general. The intended meaning is more limited: The campers need durable clothes. The second sentence does not mean that scientists in general are called geologists; only those scientists who specifically study the earth's structure are called geologists. The italicized word groups are essential and are therefore not set off with commas.

Nonrestrictive elements

A nonrestrictive modifier describes a noun or pronoun whose meaning has already been clearly defined or limited. Because the modifier contains nonessential or parenthetical information, it is set off with commas. If you remove a nonrestrictive element from a sentence, the meaning does not change dramatically. Some meaning may be lost, but the defining characteristics of the person or thing described remain the same.

NONRESTRICTIVE (WITH COMMAS)

The campers need sturdy shoes, *which are expensive.*

The scientists, *who represented eight different universities*, met to review applications for the prestigious O'Hara Award.

In the first sentence, the campers need sturdy shoes, and the shoes happen to be expensive. In the second sentence, the scientists met to review applications for the O'Hara Award; that they represented eight different universities is informative but not critical to the meaning of the sentence. The nonessential information in both sentences is set off with commas.

NOTE: Often it is difficult to tell whether a word group is restrictive or nonrestrictive without seeing it in context and considering the writer's meaning. Both of the following sentences are grammatically correct, but their meanings are slightly different.

The dessert made with fresh raspberries was delicious.

The dessert, made with fresh raspberries, was delicious.

In the first example, the phrase *made with fresh raspberries* tells readers which of two or more desserts the writer is referring to. In the example with commas, the phrase merely adds information about the dessert.

Adjective clauses

Adjective clauses are patterned like sentences, containing subjects and verbs, but they function within sentences as modifiers of nouns or pronouns. They always follow the word they modify, usually immediately. Adjective clauses begin with a relative pronoun (*who*, *whom*, *whose*, *which*, *that*) or with a relative adverb (*where*, *when*). (See B3-e.)

Nonrestrictive adjective clauses are set off with commas; restrictive adjective clauses are not.

NONRESTRICTIVE CLAUSE (WITH COMMAS)

▶ **Ed's house, which is located on thirteen acres, was completely furnished with bats in the rafters and mice in the kitchen.**

The adjective clause *which is located on thirteen acres* does not restrict the meaning of *Ed's house*; the information is nonessential and is therefore enclosed in commas.

RESTRICTIVE CLAUSE (NO COMMAS)

▶ **The giant panda/ that was born at the San Diego Zoo in 2003/ was sent to China in 2007.**

Because the adjective clause *that was born at the San Diego Zoo in 2003* identifies one particular panda out of many, the information is essential and is therefore not enclosed in commas.

NOTE: Use *that* only with restrictive (essential) clauses. Many writers prefer to use *which* only with nonrestrictive (nonessential) clauses, but usage varies.

Adjective phrases

Prepositional or verbal phrases functioning as adjectives may be restrictive or nonrestrictive. (See B3-a and B3-b.) Nonrestrictive phrases are set off with commas; restrictive phrases are not.

NONRESTRICTIVE PHRASE (WITH COMMAS)

▶ **The helicopter, with its million-candlepower spotlight illuminating the area, circled above.**

The *with* phrase is nonessential because its purpose is not to specify which of two or more helicopters is being discussed.

RESTRICTIVE PHRASE (NO COMMAS)

▶ **One corner of the attic was filled with newspapers/ dating from the early 1900s.**

Dating from the early 1900s restricts the meaning of *newspapers*, so the comma should be omitted.

▶ **The bill/ proposed by the Illinois representative/ would lower taxes and provide services for middle-income families.**

Proposed by the Illinois representative identifies exactly which bill is meant.

Appositives

An appositive is a noun or noun phrase that renames a nearby noun. Nonrestrictive appositives are set off with commas; restrictive appositives are not.

NONRESTRICTIVE APPOSITIVE (WITH COMMAS)

▶ **Darwin's most important book, *On the Origin of Species,* was the result of many years of research.**

Most important restricts the meaning to one book, so the appositive *On the Origin of Species* is nonrestrictive and should be set off with commas.

RESTRICTIVE APPOSITIVE (NO COMMAS)

▶ **The song/ "Viva la Vida/" was blasted out of huge amplifiers at the concert.**

Once they've read *song*, readers still don't know precisely which song the writer means. The appositive following *song* restricts its meaning, so the appositive should not be enclosed in commas.

P1-f Use commas to set off transitional and parenthetical expressions, absolute phrases, and word groups expressing contrast.

Transitional expressions

Transitional expressions serve as bridges between sentences or parts of sentences. They include conjunctive adverbs such as *however*, *therefore*, and *moreover* and transitional phrases such as *for example*, *as a matter of fact*, and *in other words*. (For complete lists of these expressions, see P3-a.)

When a transitional expression appears between independent clauses in a compound sentence, it is preceded by a semicolon and is usually followed by a comma. (See P3-a.)

► **Minh did not understand our language; moreover, he was unfamiliar with our customs.**

When a transitional expression appears at the beginning of a sentence or in the middle of an independent clause, it is usually set off with commas.

► **As a matter of fact, American football was established by fans who wanted to play a more organized game of rugby.**

► **Natural foods are not always salt free; celery, for example, contains more sodium than most people would imagine.**

EXCEPTION: If a transitional expression blends smoothly with the rest of the sentence, calling for little or no pause in reading, it does not need to be set off with a comma. Expressions such as *also*, *at least*, *certainly*, *consequently*, *indeed*, *of course*, *moreover*, *no doubt*, *perhaps*, *then*, and *therefore* do not always call for a pause.

Alice's bicycle is broken; *therefore* you will need to borrow Sue's.

Parenthetical expressions

Expressions that are distinctly parenthetical, providing only supplemental information, should be set off with commas.

► **Evolution, as far as we know, doesn't work this way.**

► **The bass weighed about twelve pounds, give or take a few ounces.**

Absolute phrases

An absolute phrase, which modifies the whole sentence, usually consists of a noun followed by a participle or participial phrase. (See B3-d.) Absolute phrases may appear at the beginning or at the end of a sentence. Wherever they appear, they should be set off with commas.

ABSOLUTE PHRASE
N PARTICIPLE
The sun appearing for the first time in a week, we were at last able to begin the archaeological dig.

▶ **Elvis Presley made music industry history in the 1950s, his records having sold more than ten million copies.**

NOTE: Do not insert a comma between the noun and the participle in an absolute construction.

▶ **The next contestant/ being five years old, the emcee adjusted the height of the microphone.**

Word groups expressing contrast

Sharp contrasts beginning with words such as *not*, *never*, and *unlike* are set off with commas.

▶ **The Epicurean philosophers sought mental, not bodily, pleasures.**

▶ **Unlike Robert, Celia loved dance contests.**

P1-g Use commas to set off words and phrases according to convention.

Direct address, yes and no

▶ **Forgive me, Angela, for forgetting your birthday.**

▶ **Yes, the loan will probably be approved.**

Interrogative tags, mild interjections

▶ **The film was faithful to the book, wasn't it?**

▶ **Well, cases like these are difficult to decide.**

Direct quotations

▶ **In his "Letter from Birmingham Jail," Martin Luther King Jr. wrote, "We know through painful experience that freedom is never voluntarily given by the oppressor; it must be demanded by the oppressed" (225).**

► **"Happiness in marriage is entirely a matter of chance," says Charlotte Lucas in *Pride and Prejudice*, a novel that ends with two happy marriages (69; ch. 6).**

See P5-a on the use of quotation marks and pages 397–98 on citing literary sources in MLA style.

Dates

In dates, the year is set off from the rest of the sentence with a pair of commas.

► **On December 12, 1890, orders were sent out for the arrest of Sitting Bull.**

EXCEPTIONS: Commas are not necessary if the date is inverted or if only the month and year are given.

The security alert system went into effect on 15 April 2009.

January 2008 was an extremely cold month.

Addresses

The elements of an address or a place name are separated with commas. A zip code, however, is not preceded by a comma.

► **John Lennon was born in Liverpool, England, in 1940.**

► **Please send the package to Greg Tarvin at 708 Spring Street, Washington, IL 61571.**

Personal titles

If a title follows a name, separate the title from the rest of the sentence with a pair of commas.

► **Sandra Belinsky, MD, has been appointed to the hospital board.**

Numbers

In numbers more than four digits long, use commas to separate the numbers into groups of three, starting from the right. In numbers four digits long, a comma is optional.

3,500 [*or* 3500]
100,000
5,000,000

EXCEPTIONS: Do not use commas in street numbers, zip codes, telephone numbers, or years with four or fewer digits.

P1-h Use a comma to prevent confusion.

In certain situations, a comma is necessary to prevent confusion. If the writer has intentionally left out a word or phrase, for example, a comma may be needed to signal the omission.

▶ **To err is human; to forgive, divine.**

If two words in a row echo each other, a comma may be needed for ease of reading.

▶ **All of the catastrophes that we had feared might happen, happened.**

Sometimes a comma is needed to prevent readers from grouping words in ways that do not match the writer's intention.

▶ **Patients who can, walk up and down the halls several times a day.**

P2 Unnecessary commas

Many common misuses of the comma result from misunderstanding of the major comma rules presented in P1.

P2-a Do not use a comma between compound elements that are not independent clauses.

Though a comma should be used before a coordinating conjunction joining independent clauses (see P1-a), this rule should not be extended to other compound word groups.

PRACTICE **hackerhandbooks.com/writersref**
> Punctuation and mechanics > P2–3 and P2–4

▶ **Marie Curie discovered radium/ and later applied her work on radioactivity to medicine.**

And links two verbs in a compound predicate: *discovered* and *applied.*

▶ **Jake told us that his illness is serious/ but that changes in his lifestyle can improve his chances for survival.**

The coordinating conjunction *but* links two subordinate clauses, each beginning with *that*: *that his illness is serious* and *that changes in his lifestyle. . . .*

P2-b Do not use a comma to separate a verb from its subject or object.

A sentence should flow from subject to verb to object without unnecessary pauses. Commas may appear between these major sentence elements only when a specific rule calls for them.

▶ **Zoos large enough to give the animals freedom to roam/ are becoming more popular.**

The comma should not separate the subject, *Zoos*, from the verb, *are becoming.*

Writing with sources
MLA-style citation

▶ **Maxine Hong Kingston writes/ that many Chinese American families struggle "to figure out how the invisible world the emigrants built around our childhoods fits in solid America" (107).**

The comma should not separate the verb, *writes*, from its object, the subordinate clause beginning with *that*. A signal phrase ending in a word like *writes* or *says* is followed by a comma only when a direct quotation immediately follows: *Kingston writes, "Those of us in the first American generations have had to figure out how the invisible world . . ." (107)*. (See also P5-e.)

P2-c Do not use a comma before the first or after the last item in a series.

Though commas are required between items in a series (P1-c), do not place them either before or after the whole series.

▶ **Other causes of asthmatic attacks are/ stress, change in temperature, and cold air.**

▶ **Ironically, even novels that focus on horror, evil, and alienation/ often have themes of spiritual renewal and redemption.**

P2-d Do not use a comma between cumulative adjectives, between an adjective and a noun, or between an adverb and an adjective.

Commas are required between coordinate adjectives (those that can be joined with *and*), but they do not belong between cumulative adjectives (those that cannot be joined with *and*). (For a full discussion, see P1-d.)

▶ **In the corner of the closet, we found an old/ maroon hatbox.**

A comma should never be used between an adjective and the noun that follows it.

▶ **It was a senseless, dangerous/ mission.**

Nor should a comma be used between an adverb and an adjective that follows it.

▶ **The Hillside is a good home for severely/ disturbed youths.**

P2-e Do not use commas to set off restrictive or mildly parenthetical elements.

Restrictive elements are modifiers or appositives that restrict the meaning of the nouns they follow. Because they are essential to the meaning of the sentence, they are not set off with commas. (For a full discussion of restrictive and nonrestrictive elements, see P1-e.)

▶ **Drivers/ who think they own the road/ make cycling a dangerous sport.**

The modifier *who think they own the road* restricts the meaning of *Drivers* and is therefore essential to the meaning of the sentence. Putting commas around the *who* clause falsely suggests that all drivers think they own the road.

▶ **Margaret Mead's book/ *Coming of Age in Samoa*/ stirred up considerable controversy when it was published in 1928.**

Since Mead wrote more than one book, the appositive contains information essential to the meaning of the sentence.

Although commas should be used with distinctly parenthetical expressions (see P1-f), do not use them to set off elements that are only mildly parenthetical.

▶ **Texting has/ essentially/ replaced e-mail for casual communication.**

P2-f Do not use a comma to set off a concluding adverb clause that is essential to the meaning of the sentence.

When adverb clauses introduce a sentence, they are nearly always followed by a comma (see P1-b). When they conclude a sentence, however, they are not set off by commas if their content is essential to the meaning of the earlier part of the sentence. Adverb clauses beginning with *after*, *as soon as*, *because*, *before*, *if*, *since*, *unless*, *until*, and *when* are usually essential.

▶ **Don't visit Paris at the height of the tourist season/ unless you have booked hotel reservations.**

Without the *unless* clause, the meaning of the sentence might at first seem broader than the writer intended.

When a concluding adverb clause is nonessential, it should be preceded by a comma. Clauses beginning with *although*, *even though*, *though*, and *whereas* are usually nonessential.

▶ **The lecture seemed to last only a short time, although the clock said it had gone on for more than an hour.**

P2-g Do not use a comma after a phrase that begins an inverted sentence.

Though a comma belongs after most introductory phrases (see P1-b), it does not belong after phrases that begin an inverted sentence. In an inverted sentence, the subject follows the verb, and a phrase that ordinarily would follow the verb is moved to the beginning.

▶ At the bottom of the hill/ sat the stubborn mule.

P2-h Avoid other common misuses of the comma.

Do not use a comma in the following situations.

AFTER A COORDINATING CONJUNCTION (*AND*, *BUT*, *OR*, *NOR*, *FOR*, *SO*, *YET*)

▶ Occasionally TV talk shows are performed live, but/ more often they are taped.

AFTER *SUCH AS* OR *LIKE*

▶ Shade-loving plants such as/ begonias, impatiens, and coleus can add color to a shady garden.

BEFORE *THAN*

▶ Touring Crete was more thrilling for us/ than visiting the Greek islands frequented by the rich.

AFTER *ALTHOUGH*

▶ Although/ the air was balmy, the water was too cold for swimming.

BEFORE A PARENTHESIS

▶ At InterComm, Sylvia began at the bottom/ (with only three and a half walls and a swivel chair), but within three years she had been promoted to supervisor.

TO SET OFF AN INDIRECT (REPORTED) QUOTATION

▶ Samuel Goldwyn once said/ that a verbal contract isn't worth the paper it's written on.

WITH A QUESTION MARK OR AN EXCLAMATION POINT

▶ "Why don't you try it?/" she coaxed. "You can't do any worse than the rest of us."

P3 The semicolon and the colon

The semicolon is used to connect major sentence elements of equal grammatical rank (see P3-a and P3-b). The colon is used primarily to call attention to the words that follow it (see P3-d). In addition, the colon has some conventional uses (see P3-e).

P3-a Use a semicolon with independent clauses.

Between independent clauses with no coordinating conjunction

When two independent clauses appear in one sentence, they are usually linked with a comma and a coordinating conjunction (*and*, *but*, *or*, *nor*, *for*, *so*, *yet*). The coordinating conjunction signals the relation between the clauses. If the clauses are closely related and the relation is clear without a conjunction, they may be linked with a semicolon instead.

> In film, a low-angle shot makes the subject look powerful; a high-angle shot does just the opposite.

A semicolon must be used whenever a coordinating conjunction has been omitted between independent clauses. To use merely a comma creates a type of run-on sentence known as a *comma splice*. (See G6.)

▶ **In 1800, a traveler needed six weeks to get from New York City to Chicago/; in 1860, the trip by railroad took as little as two days.**

Between independent clauses with a transitional expression

Transitional expressions include conjunctive adverbs and transitional phrases.

CONJUNCTIVE ADVERBS

accordingly	furthermore	moreover	still
also	hence	nevertheless	subsequently
anyway	however	next	then
besides	incidentally	nonetheless	therefore
certainly	indeed	now	thus
consequently	instead	otherwise	
conversely	likewise	similarly	
finally	meanwhile	specifically	

PRACTICE **hackerhandbooks.com/writersref**
> Punctuation and mechanics > P3–4 and P3–5

TRANSITIONAL PHRASES

after all	even so	in fact
as a matter of fact	for example	in other words
as a result	for instance	in the first place
at any rate	in addition	on the contrary
at the same time	in conclusion	on the other hand

When a transitional expression appears between independent clauses, it is preceded by a semicolon and usually followed by a comma.

► **Many corals grow very gradually/; in fact, the creation of a coral reef can take centuries.**

When a transitional expression appears in the middle or at the end of the second independent clause, the semicolon goes *between the clauses.*

► **Biologists have observed laughter in primates other than humans/; chimpanzees, however, sound more like they are panting than laughing.**

Transitional expressions should not be confused with the coordinating conjunctions *and*, *but*, *or*, *nor*, *for*, *so*, and *yet*, which are preceded by a comma when they link independent clauses. (See P1-a.)

P3-b Use a semicolon between items in a series containing internal punctuation.

► **Classic science fiction sagas include *Star Trek*, with Captain Kirk, Dr. McCoy, and Mr. Spock/; *Battlestar Galactica*, with its Cylons/; and *Star Wars*, with Han Solo, Luke Skywalker, and Darth Vader.**

Without the semicolons, the reader would have to sort out the major groupings, distinguishing between important and less important pauses according to the logic of the sentence. By inserting semicolons at the major breaks, the writer does this work for the reader.

P3-c Avoid common misuses of the semicolon.

Do not use a semicolon in the following situations.

BETWEEN A SUBORDINATE CLAUSE AND THE REST OF THE SENTENCE

► **Although children's literature was added to the National Book Awards in 1969~~;~~, it has had its own award, the Newbery Medal, since 1922.**

BETWEEN AN APPOSITIVE AND THE WORD IT REFERS TO

► **The scientists were fascinated by the species *Argyroneta aquatica*~~;~~, a spider that lives underwater.**

TO INTRODUCE A LIST

► **Some of my favorite celebrities have their own blogs~~;~~: Lindsay Lohan, Rosie O'Donnell, and Zach Braff.**

BETWEEN INDEPENDENT CLAUSES JOINED BY *AND*, *BUT*, *OR*, *NOR*, *FOR*, *SO*, OR *YET*

► **Five of the applicants had worked with spreadsheets~~;~~, but only one was familiar with database management.**

P3-d Use a colon after an independent clause to direct attention to a list, an appositive, a quotation, or a summary or an explanation.

A LIST

The daily routine should include at least the following: twenty knee bends, fifty sit-ups, fifteen leg lifts, and five minutes of running in place.

AN APPOSITIVE

My roommate is guilty of two of the seven deadly sins: gluttony and sloth.

A QUOTATION

Consider the words of Benjamin Franklin: "There never was a good war or a bad peace."

PRACTICE hackerhandbooks.com/writersref
> Punctuation and mechanics > P3–6

A SUMMARY OR AN EXPLANATION

Faith is like love: It cannot be forced.

The novel is clearly autobiographical: The author even gives his own name to the main character.

NOTE: For other ways of introducing quotations, see "Introducing quoted material" on pages 284–85. When an independent clause follows a colon, it may begin with a capital or a lowercase letter (see P8-e).

P3-e Use a colon according to convention.

SALUTATION IN A LETTER Dear Sir or Madam:

HOURS AND MINUTES 5:30 p.m.

PROPORTIONS The ratio of women to men was 2:1.

TITLE AND SUBTITLE *The Glory of Hera: Greek Mythology and the Greek Family*

BIBLIOGRAPHIC ENTRIES Boston: Bedford, 2011

NOTE: In biblical references, a colon is ordinarily used between chapter and verse (Luke 2:14). The Modern Language Association (MLA) recommends a period instead (Luke 2.14).

P3-f Avoid common misuses of the colon.

A colon must be preceded by a full independent clause. Therefore, avoid using it in the following situations.

BETWEEN A VERB AND ITS OBJECT OR COMPLEMENT

▶ Some important vitamins found in vegetables are: vitamin A, thiamine, niacin, and vitamin C.

BETWEEN A PREPOSITION AND ITS OBJECT

▶ The heart's two pumps each consist of: an upper chamber, or atrium, and a lower chamber, or ventricle.

AFTER *SUCH AS*, *INCLUDING*, OR *FOR EXAMPLE*

▶ The NCAA regulates college athletic teams, including: basketball, baseball, softball, and football.

P4 The apostrophe

P4-a Use an apostrophe to indicate that a noun or an indefinite pronoun is possessive.

The possessive form of a noun or an indefinite pronoun usually indicates ownership, as in *Tim's hat*, *the lawyer's desk*, or *someone's glove*. Frequently, however, ownership is only loosely implied: *the tree's roots*, *a day's work*. If you are not sure whether a word is possessive, try turning it into an *of* phrase: the roots *of the tree*, the work *of a day*.

When to add -'s to a noun

1. If the noun does not end in *-s*, add *-'s*.

   Luck often propels a rock musician's career.

   The Children's Defense Fund is a nonprofit organization that supports programs for poor and minority children.

2. If the noun is singular and ends in *-s* or an *s* sound, add *-'s*.

   Lois's sister spent last year in India.

   Her article presents an overview of Marx's teachings.

NOTE: To avoid potentially awkward pronunciation, some writers use only the apostrophe with a singular noun ending in *-s*: *Sophocles'*.

When to add only an apostrophe to a noun

If the noun is plural and ends in *-s*, add only an apostrophe.

> Both diplomats' briefcases were searched by guards.

Joint possession

To show joint possession, use *-'s* or (*-s'*) with the last noun only; to show individual possession, make all nouns possessive.

> Have you seen Joyce and Greg's new camper?
>
> John's and Marie's expectations of marriage couldn't have been more different.

Joyce and Greg jointly own one camper. John and Marie individually have different expectations.

PRACTICE **hackerhandbooks.com/writersref**
> Punctuation and mechanics > P4–3 and P4–4

Compound nouns

If a noun is compound, use *-'s* (or *-s'*) with the last element.

> My father-in-law's memoir about his childhood in Sri Lanka was published in October.

Indefinite pronouns

Indefinite pronouns refer to no specific person or thing: *everyone*, *someone*, *no one*, *something*. (See B1-b.)

> Someone's raincoat has been left behind.

P4-b Use an apostrophe to mark omissions in contractions and numbers.

In a contraction, the apostrophe takes the place of one or more missing letters.

> It's a shame that Frank can't go on the tour.

It's stands for *it is*, *can't* for *cannot*.

The apostrophe is also used to mark the omission of the first two digits of a year (*the class of '08*) or years (*the '60s generation*).

P4-c Do not use an apostrophe to form the plural of numbers, letters, abbreviations, and words mentioned as words.

An apostrophe typically is not used to pluralize numbers, letters, abbreviations, and words mentioned as words. Note the few exceptions and be consistent throughout your paper.

Plural of numbers

Do not use an apostrophe in the plural of any numbers, including decades.

> Oksana skated nearly perfect figure 8s.
>
> The 1920s are known as the Jazz Age.

Plural of letters

Italicize the letter and use roman (regular) font style for the *-s* ending. Do not italicize academic grades.

Two large *J*s were painted on the door.

He received two Ds for the first time in his life.

EXCEPTIONS: To avoid misreading, use an apostrophe to form the plural of lowercase letters and the capital letters *A* and *I*: *p*'s, *A*'s.

Beginning readers often confuse *b*'s and *d*'s.

MLA NOTE: The Modern Language Association recommends using an apostrophe for the plural of both capital and lowercase letters: *J*'s, *p*'s.

Plural of abbreviations

Do not use an apostrophe to pluralize an abbreviation.

Harriet has thirty DVDs on her desk.

Marco earned two PhDs before his thirtieth birthday.

Plural of words mentioned as words

Generally, omit the apostrophe to form the plural of words mentioned as words. If the word is italicized, the *-s* ending appears in roman (regular) type.

We've heard enough *maybe*s.

Words mentioned as words may also appear in quotation marks. When you choose this option, use the apostrophe.

We've heard enough "maybe's."

P4-d Avoid common misuses of the apostrophe.

Do not use an apostrophe in the following situations.

WITH NOUNS THAT ARE NOT POSSESSIVE

outpatients
► **Some ~~outpatient's~~ have special parking permits.**

IN THE POSSESSIVE PRONOUNS *ITS, WHOSE, HIS, HERS, OURS, YOURS,* AND *THEIRS*

its
► **Each area has ~~it's~~ own conference room.**

It's means "it is." The possessive pronoun *its* contains no apostrophe despite the fact that it is possessive.

▶ *The House on Mango Street* was written by Sandra Cisneros, ~~who's~~ whose work focuses on the Latino community in the United States.

Who's means "who is." The possessive pronoun is *whose*.

P5 Quotation marks

Writers use quotation marks primarily to enclose direct quotations of another person's spoken or written words. You will also find these other uses and exceptions:

- for quotations within quotations (single quotation marks: P5-b)
- for titles of short works (P5-c)
- for words used as words (P5-d)
- with other marks of punctuation (P5-e)
- with brackets and ellipsis marks (P6-b, P6-c)
- no quotation marks for long quotations (P5-a)
- no quotation marks for indirect quotations, summaries, and paraphrases (P5-a, MLA-2c, APA-2c, CMS-2c)

P5-a Use quotation marks to enclose direct quotations.

Direct quotations of a person's words, whether spoken or written, must be in quotation marks.

> "The contract negotiations are stalled," the airline executive told reporters, "but I am prepared to work night and day to bring both sides together."

In dialogue, begin a new paragraph to mark a change in speaker.

> "Mom, his name is Willie, not William. A thousand times I've told you, it's *Willie*."
>
> "Willie is a derivative of William, Lester. Surely his birth certificate doesn't have Willie on it, and I like calling people by their proper names."
>
> "Yes, it does, ma'am. My mother named me Willie K. Mason."
>
> — Gloria Naylor

PRACTICE hackerhandbooks.com/writersref
> Punctuation and mechanics > P5–3 and P5–4

If a single speaker utters more than one paragraph, introduce each paragraph with a quotation mark, but do not use a closing quotation mark until the end of the speech.

Exception: indirect quotations

Do not use quotation marks around indirect quotations. An indirect quotation reports someone's ideas without using that person's exact words. In academic writing, indirect quotation is called *paraphrase* or *summary*. (See R3-c.)

> The airline executive told reporters that although contract negotiations were at a standstill, she was prepared to work hard with both labor and management to bring about a settlement.

Exception: long quotations

Long quotations of prose or poetry are generally set off from the text by indenting. Quotation marks are not used because the indented format tells readers that the quotation is taken word-for-word from the source.

> After making an exhaustive study of the historical record, James Horan evaluates Billy the Kid like this:
>
> > The portrait that emerges of [the Kid] from the thousands of pages of affidavits, reports, trial transcripts, his letters, and his testimony is neither the mythical Robin Hood nor the stereotyped adenoidal moron and pathological killer. Rather Billy appears as a disturbed, lonely young man, honest, loyal to his friends, dedicated to his beliefs, and betrayed by our institutions and the corrupt, ambitious, and compromising politicians in his time. (158)

The number in parentheses is a citation handled according to MLA style. (See MLA-4a.)

MLA, APA, and CMS (*Chicago*) have specific guidelines for what constitutes a long quotation and how it should be indented (see pp. 381, 485, and 506, respectively).

P5-b Use single quotation marks to enclose a quotation within a quotation.

> Megan Marshall notes that what Elizabeth Peabody "hoped to accomplish in her school was not merely 'teaching' but 'educating children morally and spiritually as well as intellectually from the first'" (107).

P5-c Use quotation marks around the titles of short works.

Short works include newspaper and magazine articles, poems, short stories, songs, episodes of television and radio programs, and chapters or subdivisions of books.

> James Baldwin's story "Sonny's Blues" tells the story of two brothers who come to understand each other's suffering.

NOTE: Titles of books, plays, Web sites, television and radio programs, films, magazines, and newspapers are put in italics. (See P10-a.)

P5-d Quotation marks may be used to set off words used as words.

Although words used as words are ordinarily italicized (see P10-b), quotation marks are also acceptable. Be consistent throughout your paper.

> The words "accept" and "except" are frequently confused.
>
> The words *accept* and *except* are frequently confused.

P5-e Use punctuation with quotation marks according to convention.

This section describes the conventions American publishers use in placing various marks of punctuation inside or outside quotation marks. It also explains how to punctuate when introducing quoted material.

Periods and commas

Place periods and commas inside quotation marks.

> "I'm here as part of my service-learning project," I told the classroom teacher. "I'm hoping to become a reading specialist."

This rule applies to single quotation marks as well as double quotation marks. (See P5-b.) It also applies to all uses of quotation marks: for quoted material, for titles of works, and for words used as words.

EXCEPTION: In the Modern Language Association's style of parenthetical in-text citations (see MLA-4a), the period follows the citation in parentheses. (See the example on p. 284.)

James M. McPherson comments, approvingly, that the Whigs "were not averse to extending the blessings of American liberty, even to Mexicans and Indians" (48).

Colons and semicolons

Put colons and semicolons outside quotation marks.

Harold wrote, "I regret that I am unable to attend the fundraiser for AIDS research"; his letter, however, came with a substantial contribution.

Question marks and exclamation points

Put question marks and exclamation points inside quotation marks unless they apply to the whole sentence.

Contrary to tradition, bedtime at my house is marked by "Mommy, can I tell you a story now?"

Have you heard the old proverb "Do not climb the hill until you reach it"?

In the first sentence, the question mark applies only to the quoted question. In the second sentence, the question mark applies to the whole sentence.

NOTE: In MLA style for a quotation that ends with a question mark or an exclamation point, the parenthetical citation and a period should follow the entire quotation.

Rosie Thomas asks, "Is nothing in life ever straight and clear, the way children see it?" (77).

Introducing quoted material

After a word group introducing a quotation, choose a colon, a comma, or no punctuation at all, whichever is appropriate in context.

FORMAL INTRODUCTION If a quotation is formally introduced, a colon is appropriate. A formal introduction is a full independent clause, not just an expression such as *he said* or *she remarked.*

Thomas Friedman provides a challenging yet optimistic view of the future: "We need to get back to work on our country and on our planet. The hour is late, the stakes couldn't be higher, the project couldn't be harder, the payoff couldn't be greater" (25).

EXPRESSION SUCH AS *HE SAID* If a quotation is introduced with an expression such as *he said* or *she remarked*—or if it is followed by such an expression—a comma is needed.

> About New England's weather, Mark Twain once declared, "In the spring I have counted one hundred and thirty-six different kinds of weather within four and twenty hours" (55).

> "Unless another war is prevented it is likely to bring destruction on a scale never before held possible and even now hardly conceived," Albert Einstein wrote in the aftermath of the atomic bomb (29).

BLENDED QUOTATION When a quotation is blended into the writer's own sentence, either a comma or no punctuation is appropriate, depending on the way in which the quotation fits into the sentence structure.

> The future champion could, as he put it, "float like a butterfly and sting like a bee."

> Virginia Woolf wrote in 1928 that "a woman must have money and a room of her own if she is to write fiction" (4).

BEGINNING OF SENTENCE If a quotation appears at the beginning of a sentence, use a comma after it unless the quotation ends with a question mark or an exclamation point.

> "I've always thought of myself as a reporter," claimed American poet Gwendolyn Brooks (162).

> "What is it?" she asked, bracing herself.

INTERRUPTED QUOTATION If a quoted sentence is interrupted by explanatory words, use commas to set off the explanatory words.

> "With regard to air travel," Stephen Ambrose notes, "Jefferson was a full century ahead of the curve" (53).

If two successive quoted sentences from the same source are interrupted by explanatory words, use a comma before the explanatory words and a period after them.

> "Everyone agrees journalists must tell the truth," Bill Kovach and Tom Rosenstiel write. "Yet people are befuddled about what 'the truth' means" (37).

P5-f Avoid common misuses of quotation marks.

Do not use quotation marks to draw attention to familiar slang, to disown trite expressions, or to justify an attempt at humor.

► **The economist estimated that single-family home prices would decline another 5 percent by the end of the year, emphasizing that this was only a "ballpark figure."**

Do not use quotation marks around the title of your own essay.

P6 Other punctuation marks

P6-a End punctuation

The period

Use a period to end all sentences except direct questions or genuine exclamations. Also use periods in abbreviations according to convention.

TO END SENTENCES Most sentences should end with a period. Problems sometimes arise when a writer must choose between a period and a question mark or between a period and an exclamation point.

If a sentence reports a question instead of asking it directly, it should end with a period, not a question mark.

► **The professor asked whether talk therapy was more beneficial than antidepressants?.**

If a sentence is not a genuine exclamation, it should end with a period, not an exclamation point. (See also p. 287.)

► **After years of working her way through school, Geeta finally graduated with high honors!.**

IN ABBREVIATIONS A period is conventionally used in abbreviations of titles and Latin words or phrases, including the time designations for morning and afternoon.

Mr.	i.e.	a.m. (or AM)
Ms.	e.g.	p.m. (or PM)
Dr.	etc.	

NOTE: If a sentence ends with a period marking an abbreviation, do not add a second period.

Do not use a period with US Postal Service abbreviations for states: MD, TX, CA.

Current usage is to omit the period in abbreviations of organization and country names, academic degrees, and designations for eras.

NATO	UNESCO	UCLA	BS	BC
IRS	AFL-CIO	NIH	PhD	BCE

The question mark

A direct question should be followed by a question mark.

What is the horsepower of a 777 engine?

If a polite request is written in the form of a question, it may be followed by a period.

Would you please send me your catalog of lilies.

TIP: Do not use a question mark after an indirect question, one that is reported rather than asked directly. Use a period instead.

▶ **He asked me who was teaching the mythology course this year~~?~~.**

NOTE: Questions in a series may be followed by question marks even when they are not complete sentences.

We wondered where Calamity had hidden this time. Under the sink? Behind the furnace? On top of the bookcase?

The exclamation point

Use an exclamation point after a word group or sentence to express exceptional feeling or to provide special emphasis. The exclamation point is rarely appropriate in academic writing.

When Gloria entered the room, I switched on the lights, and we all yelled, "Surprise!"

TIP: Do not overuse the exclamation point.

▶ **In the fisherman's memory, the fish lives on, increasing in length and weight with each passing year, until at last it is big enough to shade a fishing boat~~!~~.**

This sentence doesn't need to be pumped up with an exclamation point. It is emphatic enough without it.

► **Whenever I see my favorite hitter, Derrek Lee, in the batter's box, I dream of making it to the big leagues!. My team would win every time!**

The first exclamation point should be deleted so that the second one will have more force.

P6-b The dash, parentheses, and brackets

The dash

When typing, use two hyphens to form a dash (--). Do not put spaces before or after the dash. If your word processing program has what is known as an "em-dash" (—), you may use it instead, with no space before or after it.

A dash can be used to set off parenthetical material that deserves emphasis.

Everything that went wrong—from the peeping Tom at Theodora's window last night to my head-on collision today—we blamed on our move.

A pair of dashes is useful to enclose an appositive that contains commas. An appositive is a noun or noun phrase that renames a nearby noun. Ordinarily appositives are set off with commas (see P1-e), but when the appositive itself contains commas, a pair of dashes helps readers see the relative importance of all the pauses.

In my hometown, the basic needs of people—food, clothing, and shelter—are less costly than in a big city like Los Angeles.

A dash is a dramatic, somewhat informal way to introduce a list, a restatement, an amplification, or a striking shift in tone or thought.

Along the wall are the bulk liquids—sesame seed oil, honey, safflower oil, and that half-liquid "peanuts only" peanut butter.

In his last semester, Peter tried to pay more attention to his priorities—applying to graduate school, getting financial aid, and finding a roommate.

Everywhere we looked there were little kids—a box of Cracker Jacks in one hand and Mommy or Daddy's sleeve in the other.

Kiere took a few steps back, came running full speed, kicked a mighty kick—and missed the ball.

PRACTICE **hackerhandbooks.com/writersref**
> Punctuation and mechanics > P6–3

In the first two examples, the writer could also use a colon. (See P3-d.) The colon is more formal than the dash and not quite as dramatic.

TIP: Unless there is a specific reason for using the dash, avoid it. Unnecessary dashes create a choppy effect.

▶ **Insisting that students use computers as instructional tools~~—~~for information retrieval~~—~~makes good sense. Herding them~~—~~sheeplike~~—~~into computer technology does not.**

Parentheses

Use parentheses to enclose supplemental material, minor digressions, and afterthoughts.

> Nurses record patients' vital signs (temperature, pulse, and blood pressure) several times a day.

Use parentheses to enclose letters or numbers labeling items in a series.

> Regulations stipulated that only the following equipment could be used on the survival mission: (1) a knife, (2) thirty feet of parachute line, (3) a book of matches, (4) a poncho, (5) an E tool, and (6) a signal flare.

TIP: Do not overuse parentheses. Rough drafts are likely to contain more afterthoughts than necessary. As writers head into a sentence, they often think of additional details, occasionally working them in as best they can with parentheses. Usually such sentences should be revised so that the additional details no longer seem to be afterthoughts.

▶ **Researchers have said that** *from* **seventeen million ~~(estimates run as high as~~** *to* **twenty-three million~~)~~ Americans have diabetes.**

Brackets

Use brackets to enclose any words or phrases that you have inserted into an otherwise word-for-word quotation.

> *Audubon* reports that "if there are not enough young to balance deaths, the end of the species [California condor] is inevitable" (4).

The sentence quoted from the *Audubon* article did not contain the words *California condor* (since the context of the full article made clear what species was meant), so the writer needed to add the name in brackets.

The Latin word "sic" in brackets indicates that an error in a quoted sentence appears in the original source.

> According to the review, Nelly Furtado's performance was brilliant, "exceding [sic] the expectations of even her most loyal fans."

Do not overuse "sic," however, since calling attention to others' mistakes can appear snobbish. The preceding quotation, for example, might have been paraphrased instead: *According to the review, even Nelly Furtado's most loyal fans were surprised by the brilliance of her performance.*

P6-c The ellipsis mark

The ellipsis mark consists of three spaced periods. Use an ellipsis mark to indicate that you have deleted words from an otherwise word-for-word quotation.

> Reuben reports that "when the amount of cholesterol circulating in the blood rises over . . . 300 milligrams per 100, the chances of a heart attack increase dramatically."

If you delete a full sentence or more in the middle of a quoted passage, use a period before the three ellipsis dots.

> "Most of our efforts," writes Dave Erikson, "are directed toward saving the bald eagle's wintering habitat along the Mississippi River. . . . It's important that the wintering birds have a place to roost, where they can get out of the cold wind."

TIP: Ordinarily, do not use the ellipsis mark at the beginning or at the end of a quotation. Readers will understand that the quoted material is taken from a longer passage. If you have cut some words from the end of the final quoted sentence, however, MLA requires an ellipsis mark, as in the first example on page 381.

In quoted poetry, use a full line of ellipsis dots to indicate that you have dropped a line or more from the poem, as in this example from "To His Coy Mistress" by Andrew Marvell:

> Had we but world enough, and time,
> This coyness, lady, were no crime.
> . . . .
> But at my back I always hear
> Time's wingèd chariot hurrying near; (1-2, 21-22)

The ellipsis mark may also be used to indicate a hesitation or an interruption in speech or to suggest unfinished thoughts.

> "The apartment building next door . . . it's going up in flames!" yelled Marcia.
>
> Before falling into a coma, the victim whispered, "It was a man with a tattoo on his . . . "

P6-d The slash

Use the slash to separate two or three lines of poetry that have been run into your text. Add a space both before and after the slash.

> In the opening lines of "Jordan," George Herbert pokes gentle fun at popular poems of his time: "Who says that fictions only and false hair / Become a verse? Is there in truth no beauty?" (1-2).

More than three lines of poetry should be handled as an indented quotation. (See p. 282.)

The slash may occasionally be used to separate paired terms such as *pass/fail* and *producer/director*. Do not use a space before or after the slash. Be sparing in this use of the slash. In particular, avoid the use of *and/or*, *he/she*, and *his/her*. Instead of using *he/she* and *his/her* to solve sexist language problems, you can usually find more graceful alternatives. (See W4-e and G3-a.)

P7 Spelling and hyphenation

You learned to spell from repeated experience with words in both reading and writing, but especially writing. Words have a look, a sound, and even a feel to them as the hand moves across the page. As you proofread, you can probably tell if a word doesn't look quite right. In such cases, the solution is obvious: Look up the word in the dictionary. (See W6-a.)

P7-a Become familiar with the major spelling rules.

i *before* e *except after* c

Use *i* before *e* except after *c* or when sounded like *ay*, as in *neighbor* and *weigh*.

I* BEFORE *E	relieve, believe, sieve, niece, fierce, frieze
E* BEFORE *I	receive, deceive, sleigh, freight, eight
EXCEPTIONS	seize, either, weird, height, foreign, leisure

Suffixes

FINAL SILENT *-E* Generally, drop a final silent *-e* when adding a suffix that begins with a vowel. Keep the final *-e* if the suffix begins with a consonant.

combine, combination	achieve, achievement
desire, desiring	care, careful
prude, prudish	entire, entirety
remove, removable	gentle, gentleness

Words such as *changeable*, *acknowledgment*, *judgment*, *argument*, and *truly* are exceptions.

FINAL *-Y* When adding *-s* or *-d* to words ending in *-y*, ordinarily change *-y* to *-ie* when the *-y* is preceded by a consonant but not when it is preceded by a vowel.

comedy, comedies	monkey, monkeys
dry, dried	play, played

With proper names ending in *-y*, however, do not change the *-y* to *-ie* even if it is preceded by a consonant: *the Dougherty family, the Doughertys*.

FINAL CONSONANTS If a final consonant is preceded by a single vowel *and* the consonant ends a one-syllable word or a stressed syllable, double the consonant when adding a suffix beginning with a vowel.

bet, betting	occur, occurrence
commit, committed	

Plurals

-S* OR *-ES Add *-s* to form the plural of most nouns; add *-es* to singular nouns ending in *-s*, *-sh*, *-ch*, and *-x*.

table, tables	church, churches
paper, papers	dish, dishes

Ordinarily add *-s* to nouns ending in *-o* when the *-o* is preceded by a vowel. Add *-es* when it is preceded by a consonant.

radio, radios	hero, heroes
video, videos	tomato, tomatoes

OTHER PLURALS To form the plural of a hyphenated compound word, add *-s* to the chief word even if it does not appear at the end.

mother-in-law, mothers-in-law

English words derived from other languages such as Latin, Greek, or French sometimes form the plural as they would in their original language.

medium, media   chateau, chateaux
criterion, criteria

ESL Spelling varies slightly among English-speaking countries. This can be particularly confusing for multilingual students in the United States, who may have learned British English. Following is a list of some common words spelled differently in American and British English. Consult a dictionary for others.

AMERICAN	BRITISH
canceled, traveled	cancelled, travelled
color, humor	colour, humour
judgment	judgement
check	cheque
realize, apologize	realise, apologise
defense	defence
anemia, anesthetic	anaemia, anaesthetic
theater, center	theatre, centre
fetus	foetus
mold, smolder	mould, smoulder
civilization	civilisation
connection, inflection	connexion, inflexion
licorice	liquorice

P7-b Discriminate between words that sound alike but have different meanings.

Words that sound alike or nearly alike but have different meanings and spellings are called *homophones*. The following sets of words are so commonly confused that a good writer will double-check their every use.

affect (verb: to exert an influence)
effect (verb: to accomplish; noun: result)

its (possessive pronoun: of or belonging to it)
it's (contraction for *it is* or *it has*)

loose (adjective: free, not securely attached)
lose (verb: to fail to keep, to be deprived of)

principal (adjective: most important; noun: head of a school)
principle (noun: a fundamental guideline or truth)

their (possessive pronoun: belonging to them)
they're (contraction for *they are*)
there (adverb: that place or position)

who's (contraction for *who is* or *who has*)
whose (possessive form of *who*)

your (possessive pronoun: belonging to you)
you're (contraction for *you are*)

To check for correct use of these and other commonly confused words, consult the glossary of usage (W1).

P7-c Consult the dictionary to determine whether to hyphenate a compound word.

The dictionary will tell you whether to treat a compound word as a hyphenated compound (*water-repellent*), one word (*waterproof*), or two words (*water table*). If the compound word is not in the dictionary, treat it as two words.

▶ **The prosecutor chose not to cross-examine any witnesses.**

▶ **All students are expected to record their data in a small note book.**

▶ **Alice walked through the looking/glass into a backward world.**

P7-d Hyphenate two or more words used together as an adjective before a noun.

▶ **Mrs. Douglas gave Toshiko a seashell and some newspaper-wrapped fish to take home to her mother.**

▶ **Richa Gupta is not yet a well-known candidate.**

Newspaper-wrapped and *well-known* are adjectives used before the nouns *fish* and *candidate.*

Generally, do not use a hyphen when such compounds follow the noun.

PRACTICE **hackerhandbooks.com/writersref**
> Punctuation and mechanics > P7–3

▶ **After our television campaign, Richa Gupta will be well/known.**

Do not use a hyphen to connect *-ly* adverbs to the words they modify.

▶ **A slowly/moving truck tied up traffic.**

NOTE: When two or more hyphenated adjectives in a row modify the same noun, you can suspend the hyphens.

Do you prefer first-, second-, or third-class tickets?

P7-e Hyphenate fractions and certain numbers when they are spelled out.

For numbers written in words, use a hyphen in all fractions and in compound numbers from twenty-one to ninety-nine.

▶ **One-fourth of my income pays for child care, and one-third pays the rent.**

P7-f Use a hyphen with the prefixes *all-*, *ex-* (meaning "former"), and *self-* and with the suffix *-elect*.

▶ **The private foundation is funneling more money into self-help projects.**

▶ **The Student Senate bylaws require the president-elect to attend all senate meetings between the election and the official transfer of office.**

P7-g Use a hyphen in certain words to avoid ambiguity or to separate awkward double or triple letters.

Without the hyphen, there would be no way to distinguish between words such as *re-creation* and *recreation.*

Bicycling in the city is my favorite form of recreation.

The film was praised for its astonishing re-creation of nineteenth-century London.

Hyphens are sometimes used to separate awkward double or triple letters in compound words (*anti-intellectual*, *cross-stitch*). Always check a dictionary for the standard form of the word.

P7-h Check for correct hyphenation at the ends of lines.

Some word processing programs and other computer applications automatically generate word breaks at the ends of lines. When you're writing an academic paper, it's best to set your computer application not to hyphenate automatically. This setting will ensure that only words already containing a hyphen (such as *long-distance*, *pre-Roman*) will be hyphenated at the ends of lines. (See also C6.)

E-mail addresses, URLs, and other electronic addresses need special attention when they occur at the end of a line of text or in bibliographic citations. You can't rely on your computer application to divide these terms correctly, so you must make a decision in each case. Do not insert a hyphen to divide electronic addresses. Instead, break an e-mail address after the @ symbol or before a period. Break a URL after a slash or a double slash or before any other punctuation mark.

> I repeatedly e-mailed Janine at janine.r.rose@dunbaracademy
> .org before I gave up and called her cell phone.

> To find a zip code quickly, I always use the United States
> Postal Service Web site at http://zip4.usps.com/zip4/
> welcome.jsp.

For breaks in URLs in MLA, APA, and CMS (*Chicago*) documentation styles, see MLA-5a, APA-5a, and CMS-5a, respectively.

P8 Capitalization

In addition to the rules in this section, a good dictionary can tell you when to use capital letters.

P8-a Capitalize proper nouns and words derived from them; do not capitalize common nouns.

Proper nouns are the names of specific persons, places, and things. All other nouns are common nouns. The following types of words are usually capitalized: names of deities, religions, religious followers, sacred books; words of family relationship used as names; particular places;

PRACTICE **hackerhandbooks.com/writersref**
> Punctuation and mechanics > P8–2

nationalities and their languages, races, tribes; educational institutions, departments, degrees, particular courses; government departments, organizations, political parties; historical movements, periods, events, documents; specific electronic sources; and trade names.

PROPER NOUNS	COMMON NOUNS
God (used as a name)	a god
Book of Common Prayer	a sacred book
Uncle Pedro	my uncle
Father (used as a name)	my father
Lake Superior	a picturesque lake
the Capital Center	a center for advanced studies
the South	a southern state
Wrigley Field	a baseball stadium
University of Wisconsin	a state university
Geology 101	geology
Environmental Protection Agency	a federal agency
Phi Kappa Psi	a fraternity
a Democrat	an independent
the Enlightenment	the eighteenth century
the Treaty of Versailles	a treaty
the World Wide Web, the Web	a home page
the Internet, the Net	a computer network
Advil	a painkiller

Months, holidays, and days of the week are treated as proper nouns; the seasons and numbers of the days of the month are not.

> Our academic year begins on a Tuesday in early September, right after Labor Day.
>
> Graduation is in early summer, on the second of June.

EXCEPTION: Capitalize Fourth of July (or July Fourth) when referring to the holiday.

Names of school subjects are capitalized only if they are names of languages. Names of particular courses are capitalized.

> This semester Austin is taking math, geography, geology, French, and English.
>
> Professor Obembe offers Modern American Fiction 501 to graduate students.

CAUTION: Do not capitalize common nouns to make them seem important: *Our company is currently hiring computer programmers* (not *Company*, *Computer Programmers*).

P8-b Capitalize titles of persons when used as part of a proper name but usually not when used alone.

Professor Margaret Barnes; Dr. Sinyee Sein; John Scott Williams Jr.

District Attorney Marshall was reprimanded for badgering the witness.

The district attorney was elected for a two-year term.

Usage varies when the title of an important public figure is used alone: *The president* [or *President*] *vetoed the bill.*

P8-c Capitalize the first, last, and all major words in titles and subtitles of works.

In both titles and subtitles of works (books, articles, songs, artwork, and online documents) major words—nouns, pronouns, verbs, adjectives, and adverbs—should be capitalized. Minor words—articles, prepositions, and coordinating conjunctions—are not capitalized unless they are the first or last word of a title or subtitle.

Capitalize the second part of a hyphenated term in a title if it is a major word but not if it is a minor word. Capitalize chapter titles and the titles of other major divisions of a work following the same guidelines used for titles of complete works.

Seizing the Enigma: The Race to Break the German U-Boat Codes
A River Runs through It
"I Want to Hold Your Hand"
The Canadian Green Page

To learn why some of the titles in the list are italicized and some are put in quotation marks, see P10-a and P5-c.

P8-d Capitalize the first word of a sentence.

The first word of a sentence should be capitalized. When a sentence appears within parentheses, capitalize its first word unless the parentheses appear within another sentence.

Early detection of breast cancer significantly increases survival rates. (See table 2.)

Early detection of breast cancer significantly increases survival rates (see table 2).

Capitalize the first word of a quoted sentence but not a quoted phrase.

> Robert Hughes writes, "There are only about sixty Watteau paintings on whose authenticity all experts agree" (102).

> Russell Baker has written that in this country, sports are "the opiate of the masses" (46).

If a quoted sentence is interrupted by explanatory words, do not capitalize the first word after the interruption. (See P5-e.)

> "If you want to go out," he said, "tell me now."

When quoting poetry, copy the poet's capitalization exactly. Many poets capitalize the first word of every line of poetry; a few contemporary poets dismiss capitalization altogether.

> it was the week   that
> i felt the city's narrow breezes rush about
> me
> —Don L. Lee

P8-e Capitalize the first word after a colon if it begins an independent clause.

If a word group following a colon could stand on its own as a complete sentence, capitalize the first word.

> Clinical trials called into question the safety profile of the drug: A high percentage of participants reported hypertension and kidney problems.

Preferences vary among academic disciplines. See MLA-5a, APA-5a, and CMS-5a for MLA, APA, and CMS (*Chicago*) style, respectively.

Always use lowercase for a list or an appositive that follows a colon.

> Students were divided into two groups: residents and commuters.

P8-f Capitalize abbreviations according to convention.

Abbreviations for government agencies, companies, and other organizations as well as call numbers for radio and television stations are capitalized.

> EPA, FBI, DKNY, IBM, WCRB, KNBC-TV

P9 Abbreviations and numbers

P9-a Use standard abbreviations for titles immediately before and after proper names.

TITLES BEFORE PROPER NAMES	TITLES AFTER PROPER NAMES
Mr. Rafael Zabala	William Albert Sr.
Ms. Nancy Linehan	Thomas Hines Jr.
Mrs. Edward Horn	Anita Lor, PhD
Dr. Margaret Simmons	Robert Simkowski, MD
Rev. John Stone	Margaret Chin, LLD
Prof. James Russo	Polly Stein, DDS

Abbreviate a title only if it is used with a proper name.

► **My history ~~prof.~~ *professor* is an expert on twentieth-century race relations in South Africa.**

Avoid redundant titles such as *Dr. Amy Day, MD*. Choose one title or the other: *Dr. Amy Day* or *Amy Day, MD*.

P9-b Use abbreviations only when you are sure your readers will understand them.

Familiar abbreviations, written without periods, are acceptable.

CIA	FBI	MD	NAACP
NBA	NEA	PhD	CD-ROM
YMCA	CBS	USA	ESL

Talk show host Conan O'Brien is a Harvard graduate with a BA in history.

The YMCA has opened a new gym close to my office.

NOTE: When using an unfamiliar abbreviation (such as NASW for National Association of Social Workers) throughout a paper, write the full name followed by the abbreviation in parentheses at the first mention of the name. Then use just the abbreviation throughout the rest of the paper.

PRACTICE **hackerhandbooks.com/writersref**
> Punctuation and mechanics > P9–3

P9-c Use *BC, AD, a.m., p.m., No.,* and *$* only with specific dates, times, numbers, and amounts.

The abbreviation *BC* ("before Christ") follows a date, and *AD* ("*anno Domini*") precedes a date. Acceptable alternatives are *BCE* ("before the common era") and *CE* ("common era"), both of which follow a date.

40 BC (or 40 BCE)	4:00 a.m. (or AM)	No. 12 (or no. 12)
AD 44 (or 44 CE)	6:00 p.m. (or PM)	$150

Avoid using *a.m., p.m., No.,* or *$* when not accompanied by a specific figure.

▶ **The governor argued that the new sales tax would raise much-needed ~~$~~ *money* for the state.**

P9-d Be sparing in your use of Latin abbreviations.

Latin abbreviations are acceptable in footnotes and bibliographies and in informal writing for comments in parentheses.

cf. (Latin *confer*, "compare")

e.g. (Latin *exempli gratia*, "for example")

et al. (Latin *et alia*, "and others")

etc. (Latin *et cetera*, "and so forth")

i.e. (Latin *id est*, "that is")

N.B. (Latin *nota bene*, "note well")

The text for our sociology class is Harold Simms et al., *Introduction to Social Systems*.

Alfred Hitchcock directed many classic thrillers (e.g., *Psycho*, *Rear Window*, and *Vertigo*).

In formal writing, use the appropriate English phrases.

▶ **Many obsolete laws remain on the books; ~~e.g.,~~ *for example,* a law in Vermont forbids an unmarried man and woman to sit closer than six inches apart on a park bench.**

P9-e Avoid inappropriate abbreviations.

In formal writing, abbreviations for the following are not commonly accepted.

PERSONAL NAMES Charles (not Chas.)

UNITS OF MEASUREMENT feet (not ft.)

DAYS OF THE WEEK Monday (not Mon.)

HOLIDAYS Christmas (not Xmas)

MONTHS January, February, March (not Jan., Feb., Mar.)

COURSES OF STUDY political science (not poli. sci.)

DIVISIONS OF WRITTEN WORKS chapter, page (not ch., p.)

STATES AND COUNTRIES Massachusetts (not MA or Mass.)

PARTS OF A BUSINESS NAME Adams Lighting Company (not Adams Lighting Co.); Kim and Brothers (not Kim and Bros.)

▶ The American Red Cross requires that blood donors be at least seventeen ~~yrs.~~ *years* old, weigh at least 110 ~~lb.,~~ *pounds,* and not have given blood in the past eight ~~wks.~~ *weeks.*

EXCEPTION: Abbreviate states and provinces in complete addresses, and always abbreviate DC when used with Washington.

P9-f Follow the conventions in your discipline for spelling out or using numerals to express numbers.

In the humanities, which generally follow either Modern Language Association (MLA) style or CMS (*Chicago*) style, use numerals only for specific numbers above one hundred: *353*; *1,020*. Spell out numbers one hundred and below and large round numbers: *eleven*, *thirty-five*, *sixty*, *fifteen million*.

The social sciences and sciences, which follow the style guidelines of the American Psychological Association (APA) or the Council of Science Editors (CSE), use numerals for all but the numbers one through nine.

In all fields, treat related numbers in a passage consistently: *The survey found that 89 of 157 respondents had not taken any courses related to alcohol use.*

PRACTICE **hackerhandbooks.com/writersref**
> Punctuation and mechanics > P9–4

When one number immediately follows another, spelling out one number and using numerals for the other is usually effective: *three 100-meter events, 25 four-poster beds.*

▶ **It's been ~~8~~ *eight* years since I visited Peru.**

▶ **Enrollment in the charter school in its first year will be limited to ~~three hundred forty~~ *340* students.**

If a sentence begins with a number, spell out the number or rewrite the sentence.

▶ **~~150~~ *One hundred fifty* children in our program need expensive dental treatment.**

Rewriting the sentence will also correct the error and may be less awkward if the number is long: *In our program, 150 children need expensive dental treatment.*

P9-g Use numerals according to convention in dates, addresses, and so on.

DATES July 4, 1776; 56 BC

ADDRESSES 77 Latches Lane, 519 West 42nd Street

PERCENTAGES 55 percent (or 55%)

FRACTIONS, DECIMALS ½, 0.047

SCORES 7 to 3, 21–18

STATISTICS average age 37, average weight 180

SURVEYS 4 out of 5

EXACT AMOUNTS OF MONEY $105.37, $106,000

DIVISIONS OF BOOKS volume 3, chapter 4, page 189

DIVISIONS OF PLAYS act 3, scene 3 (or act III, scene iii)

IDENTIFICATION NUMBERS serial number 10988675

TIME OF DAY 4:00 p.m., 1:30 a.m.

▶ **The foundation raised ~~four hundred thirty thousand dollars~~ *$430,000* for cancer research.**

NOTE: When not using *a.m.* or *p.m.*, write out the time in words (*two o'clock in the afternoon, twelve noon, seven in the morning*).

P10 Italics

This section describes conventional uses for italics. While italics is recommended by all three style guides covered in this book (MLA, APA, and CMS), some instructors may prefer underlining in student papers. If that is the case in your course, simply substitute underlining for italics in the examples in this section.

Some computer and online applications do not allow for italics. To indicate words that should be italicized, you can use underscore marks or asterisks before and after the italic words.

> I am planning to write my senior thesis on _Memoirs of a Geisha_.

NOTE: Excessive use of italics to emphasize words or ideas, especially in academic writing, is distracting and should be avoided.

P10-a Italicize the titles of works according to convention.

Titles of the following types of works, including electronic works, should be italicized.

TITLES OF BOOKS *The Known World*, *Middlesex*, *Encarta*

MAGAZINES *Time*, *Scientific American*, *Salon.com*

NEWSPAPERS the *Baltimore Sun*, the *Orlando Sentinel Online*

PAMPHLETS *Common Sense*, *Facts about Marijuana*

LONG POEMS *The Waste Land*, *Beowulf*

PLAYS *'Night Mother*, *Wicked*

FILMS *Casablanca*, *The Hurt Locker*

TELEVISION PROGRAMS *American Idol*, *Frontline*

RADIO PROGRAMS *All Things Considered*

MUSICAL COMPOSITIONS *Porgy and Bess*

CHOREOGRAPHIC WORKS *Brief Fling*

WORKS OF VISUAL ART *American Gothic*

ELECTRONIC DATABASES *ProQuest*

WEB SITES *ZDNet*, *Google*

ELECTRONIC GAMES *Everquest*, *Call of Duty*

PRACTICE **hackerhandbooks.com/writersref**
> Punctuation and mechanics > P10–2

The titles of other works, such as short stories, essays, episodes of radio and television programs, songs, and short poems, are enclosed in quotation marks. (See P5-c.)

NOTE: Do not use italics when referring to the Bible, titles of books in the Bible (Genesis, not *Genesis*), or titles of legal documents (the Constitution, not the *Constitution*). Do not italicize the titles of computer software (Keynote, Photoshop). Do not italicize the title of your own paper.

P10-b Italicize other terms according to convention.

SPACECRAFT, SHIPS, AIRCRAFT

Challenger, *Queen Mary 2*, *Spirit of St. Louis*

The success of the Soviets' *Sputnik* energized the US space program.

FOREIGN WORDS

Shakespeare's Falstaff is a comic character known for both his excessive drinking and his general *joie de vivre*.

EXCEPTION: Do not italicize foreign words that have become a standard part of the English language—"laissez-faire," "fait accompli," "modus operandi," and "per diem," for example.

WORDS, LETTERS, NUMBERS AS THEMSELVES

Tomás assured us that the chemicals could probably be safely mixed, but his *probably* stuck in our minds.

Some toddlers have trouble pronouncing the letter *s*.

A big *3* was painted on the stage door.

NOTE: Quotation marks may be used instead of italics to set off words mentioned as words. (See P5-d.)

B

Basic Grammar

B Basic Grammar

B1 Parts of speech, 309

- **a** Nouns, 309
- **b** Pronouns, 309
- **c** Verbs, 311
- **d** Adjectives, 313
- **e** Adverbs, 314
- **f** Prepositions, 314
- **g** Conjunctions, 315
- **h** Interjections, 316

B2 Parts of sentences, 316

- **a** Subjects, 316
- **b** Verbs, objects, and complements, 318

B3 Subordinate word groups, 320

- **a** Prepositional phrases, 320
- **b** Verbal phrases, 321
- **c** Appositive phrases, 323
- **d** Absolute phrases, 323
- **e** Subordinate clauses, 323

B4 Sentence types, 325

- **a** Sentence structures, 326
- **b** Sentence purposes, 327

B1 Parts of speech

Traditional grammar recognizes eight parts of speech: noun, pronoun, verb, adjective, adverb, preposition, conjunction, and interjection. Many words can function as more than one part of speech. For example, depending on its use in a sentence, the word *paint* can be a noun (*The paint is wet*) or a verb (*Please paint the ceiling next*).

B1-a Nouns

A noun is the name of a person, place, thing, or concept.

N N N
The *lion* in the *cage* growled at the *zookeeper*.

Nouns sometimes function as adjectives modifying other nouns. Because of their dual roles, nouns used in this manner may be called *noun/adjectives*.

N/ADJ N/ADJ
The *leather* notebook was tucked in the *student's* backpack.

Nouns are classified in a variety of ways. *Proper* nouns are capitalized, but *common* nouns are not (see P8-a). For clarity, writers choose between *concrete* and *abstract* nouns (see W5-b). The distinction between *count* nouns and *noncount* nouns can be especially helpful to multilingual writers (see M2-a). Most nouns have singular and plural forms; *collective* nouns may be either singular or plural, depending on how they are used (see G1-f and G3-a). *Possessive* nouns require an apostrophe (see P4-a).

B1-b Pronouns

A pronoun is a word used in place of a noun. Usually the pronoun substitutes for a specific noun, known as its *antecedent*.

When the *battery* wears down, we recharge *it*.

Although most pronouns function as substitutes for nouns, some can function as adjectives modifying nouns. Because they have the form of a pronoun and the function of an adjective, such pronouns may be called *pronoun/adjectives*.

PN/ADJ
This bird was at the same window yesterday morning.

Pronouns are classified as personal, possessive, intensive and reflexive, relative, interrogative, demonstrative, indefinite, and reciprocal.

PERSONAL PRONOUNS Personal pronouns refer to specific persons or things. They always function as noun equivalents.

Singular: I, me, you, she, her, he, him, it

Plural: we, us, you, they, them

POSSESSIVE PRONOUNS Possessive pronouns indicate ownership.

Singular: my, mine, your, yours, her, hers, his, its

Plural: our, ours, your, yours, their, theirs

Some of these possessive pronouns function as adjectives modifying nouns: *my*, *your*, *her*, *his*, *its*, *our*, *their*.

INTENSIVE AND REFLEXIVE PRONOUNS Intensive pronouns emphasize a noun or another pronoun (The senator *herself* met us at the door). Reflexive pronouns, which have the same form as intensive pronouns, name a receiver of an action identical with the doer of the action (Paula cut *herself*).

Singular: myself, yourself, himself, herself, itself

Plural: ourselves, yourselves, themselves

RELATIVE PRONOUNS Relative pronouns introduce subordinate clauses functioning as adjectives (The writer *who won the award* refused to accept it). In addition to introducing the clause, the relative pronoun (in this case *who*) points back to a noun or pronoun that the clause modifies (*writer*). (See B3-e.)

who, whom, whose, which, that

INTERROGATIVE PRONOUNS Interrogative pronouns introduce questions (*Who* is expected to win the election?).

who, whom, whose, which, what

DEMONSTRATIVE PRONOUNS Demonstrative pronouns identify or point to nouns. Frequently they function as adjectives (*This* chair is my favorite), but they may also function as noun equivalents (*This* is my favorite chair).

this, that, these, those

INDEFINITE PRONOUNS Indefinite pronouns refer to nonspecific persons or things. Most are always singular (*everyone*, *each*); some are always plural (*both*, *many*); a few may be singular or plural (see G1-e). Most indefinite pronouns function as noun equivalents (*Something* is burning), but some can also function as adjectives (*All* campers must check in at the lodge).

all	anything	everyone	nobody	several
another	both	everything	none	some
any	each	few	no one	somebody
anybody	either	many	nothing	someone
anyone	everybody	neither	one	something

RECIPROCAL PRONOUNS Reciprocal pronouns refer to individual parts of a plural antecedent (By turns, the penguins fed *one another*).

each other, one another

NOTE: Using pronouns correctly can be challenging. See pronoun-antecedent agreement (G3-a), pronoun reference (G3-b), distinguishing between pronouns such as *I* and *me* (G3-c), and distinguishing between *who* and *whom* (G3-d).

B1-c Verbs

The verb of a sentence usually expresses action (*jump*, *think*) or being (*is*, *become*). It is composed of a main verb possibly preceded by one or more helping verbs.

The horses *exercise* [MV] every day.

The task force report *was* [HV] not *completed* [MV] on schedule.

Notice that words, usually adverbs, can intervene between the helping verb and the main verb (was *not* completed). (See B1-e.)

PRACTICE **hackerhandbooks.com/writersref**
> Basic grammar > B1–9 and B1–10

Helping verbs

There are twenty-three helping verbs in English: forms of *have*, *do*, and *be*, which may also function as main verbs; and nine modals, which function only as helping verbs. *Have*, *do*, and *be* change form to indicate tense; the nine modals do not.

FORMS OF *HAVE*, *DO*, AND *BE*

have, has, had

do, does, did

be, am, is, are, was, were, being, been

MODALS

can, could, may, might, must, shall, should, will, would

The verb phrase *ought to* is often classified as a modal as well.

Main verbs

The main verb of a sentence is always the kind of word that would change form if put into these test sentences:

BASE FORM	Usually I (*walk*, *ride*).
PAST TENSE	Yesterday I (*walked*, *rode*).
PAST PARTICIPLE	I have (*walked*, *ridden*) many times before.
PRESENT PARTICIPLE	I am (*walking*, *riding*) right now.
-*S* FORM	Usually he/she/it (*walks*, *rides*).

If a word doesn't change form when slipped into the test sentences, you can be certain that it is not a main verb. For example, the noun *revolution*, though it may seem to suggest an action, can never function as a main verb. Just try to make it behave like one (*Today I revolution* . . . *Yesterday I revolutioned* . . .) and you'll see why.

When both the past-tense and the past-participle forms of a verb end in *-ed*, the verb is regular (*walked*, *walked*). Otherwise, the verb is irregular (*rode*, *ridden*). (See G2-a.)

The verb *be* is highly irregular, having eight forms instead of the usual five: the base form *be*; the present-tense forms *am*, *is*, and *are*; the past-tense forms *was* and *were*; the present participle *being*; and the past participle *been*.

Helping verbs combine with the various forms of main verbs to create tenses. For a survey of tenses, see G2-f.

NOTE: Some verbs are followed by words that look like prepositions but are so closely associated with the verb that they are a part of its meaning. These words are known as *particles*. Common verb-particle combinations include *bring up*, *call off*, *drop off*, *give in*, *look up*, *run into*, and *take off*.

Sharon *packed up* her broken laptop and *sent* it *off* to the repair shop.

TIP: You can find more information about using verbs in other sections of the handbook: active verbs (W3), subject-verb agreement (G1), standard English verb forms (G2-a to G2-d), verb tense and mood (G2-f and G2-g), and multilingual/ESL challenges with verbs (M1).

B1-d Adjectives

An adjective is a word used to modify, or describe, a noun or pronoun. An adjective usually answers one of these questions: Which one? What kind of? How many?

ADJ
the *frisky* horse [Which horse?]

ADJ ADJ
cracked old plates [What kind of plates?]

ADJ
nine months [How many months?]

Adjectives usually precede the words they modify. They may also follow linking verbs, in which case they describe the subject. (See B2-b.)

ADJ
The decision was *unpopular*.

The definite article *the* and the indefinite articles *a* and *an* are also classified as adjectives.

ART ART ART
A defendant should be judged on *the* evidence provided to *the* jury, not on hearsay.

Some possessive, demonstrative, and indefinite pronouns can function as adjectives: *their*, *its*, *this*, *all*, and so on (see B1-b). And nouns can function as adjectives when they modify other nouns: *apple pie* (the noun *apple* modifies the noun *pie*; see B1-a).

TIP: You can find more details about using adjectives in G4. If you are a multilingual writer, you may also find help with articles and specific uses of adjectives in M2 and M4.

PRACTICE **hackerhandbooks.com/writersref**
> Basic grammar > B1–11 to B1–14
> B1–15 and B1–16 (all parts of speech)

B1-e Adverbs

An adverb is a word used to modify, or qualify, a verb (or verbal), an adjective, or another adverb. It usually answers one of these questions: When? Where? How? Why? Under what conditions? To what degree?

Pull *firmly* on the emergency handle. [Pull how?]

Read the text *first* and *then* work the exercises. [Read when? Work when?]

Adverbs modifying adjectives or other adverbs usually intensify or limit the intensity of the word they modify.

ADV ADV
Be *extremely* kind, and you will *probably* have many friends.

The words *not* and *never* are classified as adverbs.

B1-f Prepositions

A preposition is a word placed before a noun or pronoun to form a phrase modifying another word in the sentence. The prepositional phrase nearly always functions as an adjective or as an adverb.

P P P
The road *to* the summit travels *past* craters *from* an extinct volcano.

To the summit functions as an adjective modifying the noun *road*; *past craters* functions as an adverb modifying the verb *travels*; *from an extinct volcano* functions as an adjective modifying the noun *craters*. (For more on prepositional phrases, see B3-a.)

English has a limited number of prepositions. The most common are included in the following list.

about	beside	from	outside	toward
above	besides	in	over	under
across	between	inside	past	underneath
after	beyond	into	plus	unlike
against	but	like	regarding	until
along	by	near	respecting	unto
among	concerning	next	round	up
around	considering	of	since	upon
as	despite	off	than	with
at	down	on	through	within
before	during	onto	throughout	without
behind	except	opposite	till	
below	for	out	to	

Some prepositions are more than one word long. *Along with, as well as, in addition to, next to,* and *rather than* are common examples.

TIP: Prepositions are used in idioms such as *capable of* and *dig up* (see W5-d). For a discussion of specific issues for multilingual writers, see M5.

B1-g Conjunctions

Conjunctions join words, phrases, or clauses, and they indicate the relation between the elements they join.

COORDINATING CONJUNCTIONS A coordinating conjunction is used to connect grammatically equal elements. (See S1-b and S6.) The coordinating conjunctions are *and, but, or, nor, for, so,* and *yet.*

CORRELATIVE CONJUNCTIONS Correlative conjunctions come in pairs. Like coordinating conjunctions, they connect grammatically equal elements. (See S1-b.)

either . . . or
neither . . . nor
not only . . . but also
whether . . . or
both . . . and

SUBORDINATING CONJUNCTIONS A subordinating conjunction introduces a subordinate clause and indicates the relation of the clause to the rest of the sentence. (See B3-e.) The most common subordinating conjunctions are *after, although, as, as if, because, before, if, in order that, once, since, so that, than, that, though, unless, until, when, where, whether,* and *while.* (For a complete list, see p. 325.)

CONJUNCTIVE ADVERBS Conjunctive adverbs connect independent clauses and indicate the relation between the clauses. The most common conjunctive adverbs are *finally, furthermore, however, moreover, nevertheless, similarly, then, therefore,* and *thus.* (See P3-a for a complete list.)

TIP: The ability to distinguish between conjunctive adverbs and coordinating conjunctions will help you avoid run-on sentences and make punctuation decisions (see G6, P1-a, and P1-b). The ability to recognize subordinating conjunctions will help you avoid sentence fragments (see G5).

B1-h Interjections

An interjection is a word used to express surprise or emotion (*Oh! Hey! Wow!*).

B2 Parts of sentences

Most English sentences flow from subject to verb to any objects or complements. The part of the sentence containing the verb plus its objects, complements, and modifiers is called the *predicate*.

B2-a Subjects

The subject of a sentence names who or what the sentence is about. The simple subject is always a noun or a pronoun; the complete subject consists of the simple subject and any words or word groups modifying the simple subject.

The complete subject

To find the complete subject, ask Who? or What?, insert the verb, and finish the question. The answer is the complete subject.

COMPLETE SUBJECT
The devastating effects of famine can last for many years.

Who or what lasts for many years? *The devastating effects of famine.*

COMPLETE SUBJECT
Adventure novels that contain multiple subplots are often made into successful movies.

Who or what are made into movies? *Adventure novels that contain multiple subplots.*

COMPLETE SUBJECT
In our program, student teachers work full-time for ten months.

What or who works full-time for ten months? *Student teachers.* Notice that *In our program, student teachers* is not a sensible answer to the question. (It is not safe to assume that the subject must always appear first in a sentence.)

PRACTICE hackerhandbooks.com/writersref
> Basic grammar > B2–4 and B2–5

The simple subject

To find the simple subject, strip away all modifiers in the complete subject. This includes single-word modifiers such as *the* and *devastating*, phrases such as *of famine*, and subordinate clauses such as *that contain multiple subplots.*

SS

The devastating effects of famine can last for many years.

A sentence may have a compound subject containing two or more simple subjects joined with a coordinating conjunction such as *and*, *but*, or *or*.

SS SS

Great commitment and a little luck make a successful actor.

Understood subjects

In imperative sentences, which give advice or issue commands, the subject is understood to be *you*.

[*You*] Put your clothes in the hamper.

Subject after the verb

Although the subject ordinarily comes before the verb (*The planes took off*), occasionally it does not. When a sentence begins with *There is* or *There are* (or *There was* or *There were*), the subject follows the verb. In such inverted constructions, the word *There* is an expletive, an empty word serving merely to get the sentence started.

SS

There are *eight planes waiting to take off.*

Occasionally a writer will invert a sentence for effect.

SS

Joyful is *the child whose school closes for snow*.

In questions, the subject frequently appears between the helping verb and the main verb.

HV SS MV

Do *Kenyan marathoners* train year-round?

TIP: The ability to recognize the subject of a sentence will help you edit for a variety of problems: sentence fragments (G5), subject-verb agreement (G1), choice of pronouns such as *I* and *me* (G3-c), missing subjects (M3-b), and repeated subjects (M3-c).

B2-b Verbs, objects, and complements

Section B1-c explains how to find the verb of a sentence. A sentence's verb is classified as linking, transitive, or intransitive, depending on the kinds of objects or complements the verb can (or cannot) take.

Linking verbs and subject complements

Linking verbs connect the subject to a subject complement, a word or word group that completes the meaning of the subject by renaming or describing it.

If the subject complement renames the subject, it is a noun or noun equivalent (sometimes called a *predicate noun*).

S V SC
An e-mail requesting personal information may be a scam.

If the subject complement describes the subject, it is an adjective or adjective equivalent (sometimes called a *predicate adjective*).

S V SC
Last month's temperatures were mild.

Whenever they appear as main verbs (rather than helping verbs), the forms of *be*—*be*, *am*, *is*, *are*, *was*, *were*, *being*, *been*—usually function as linking verbs. In the preceding examples, for instance, the main verbs are *be* and *were*.

Verbs such as *appear*, *become*, *feel*, *grow*, *look*, *make*, *seem*, *smell*, *sound*, and *taste* are linking when they are followed by a word group that renames or describes the subject.

S V SC
As it thickens, the sauce will look unappealing.

Transitive verbs and direct objects

A transitive verb takes a direct object, a word or word group that names a receiver of the action.

S V DO
The hungry cat clawed the bag of dry food.

The simple direct object is always a noun or pronoun, in this case *bag*. To find it, simply strip away all modifiers.

Transitive verbs usually appear in the active voice, with the subject doing the action and a direct object receiving the action. Active-voice

PRACTICE **hackerhandbooks.com/writersref**
> Basic grammar > B2–6 to B2–9

sentences can be transformed into the passive voice, with the subject receiving the action instead. (See also W3-a.)

ACTIVE VOICE	Volunteers distributed food and clothing.
PASSIVE VOICE	Food and clothing were distributed by volunteers.

Transitive verbs, indirect objects, and direct objects

The direct object of a transitive verb is sometimes preceded by an indirect object, a noun or pronoun telling to whom or for whom the action of the sentence is done.

S V IO DO S V IO DO
You give her some yarn, and she will knit you a scarf.

Transitive verbs, direct objects, and object complements

The direct object of a transitive verb is sometimes followed by an object complement, a word or word group that renames or describes the object.

S V DO OC
People often consider chivalry a thing of the past.

S V DO OC
The kiln makes clay firm and strong.

When the object complement renames the direct object, it is a noun or pronoun (such as *thing*). When it describes the direct object, it is an adjective (such as *firm* and *strong*).

Intransitive verbs

Intransitive verbs take no objects or complements.

S V
The audience laughed.

S V
The driver accelerated in the straightaway.

Nothing receives the actions of laughing and accelerating in these sentences, so the verbs are intransitive. Notice that such verbs may or may not be followed by adverbial modifiers. In the second sentence, *in the straightaway* is an adverbial prepositional phrase modifying *accelerated*.

NOTE: The dictionary will tell you whether a verb is transitive or intransitive. Some verbs have both transitive and intransitive functions.

TRANSITIVE Sandra *flew* her small plane over the canyon.

INTRANSITIVE A flock of geese *flew* overhead.

In the first example, *flew* has a direct object that receives the action: *her small plane*. In the second example, the verb is followed by an adverb (*overhead*), not by a direct object.

B3 Subordinate word groups

Subordinate word groups include phrases and clauses. Phrases are subordinate because they lack a subject and a verb; they are classified as prepositional, verbal, appositive, and absolute (see B3-a to B3-d). Subordinate clauses have a subject and a verb, but they begin with a word (such as *although*, *that*, or *when*) that marks them as subordinate (see B3-e; see also B4-a).

B3-a Prepositional phrases

A prepositional phrase begins with a preposition such as *at*, *by*, *for*, *from*, *in*, *of*, *on*, *to*, or *with* (see B1-f) and usually ends with a noun or noun equivalent: *on the table*, *for him*, *by sleeping late*. The noun or noun equivalent is known as the *object of the preposition*.

Prepositional phrases function either as adjectives or as adverbs. When functioning as an adjective, a prepositional phrase nearly always appears immediately following the noun or pronoun it modifies.

The hut had *walls of mud*.

Adjective phrases usually answer one or both of the questions Which one? and What kind of? If we ask Which walls? or What kind of walls? we get a sensible answer: *walls of mud*.

Adverbial prepositional phrases usually modify the verb, but they can also modify adjectives or other adverbs. When a prepositional phrase modifies the verb, it can appear nearly anywhere in a sentence.

James *walked* his dog *on a leash*.

PRACTICE hackerhandbooks.com/writersref
> Basic grammar > B3–4 to B3–6

Sabrina *will in time adjust* to life in Ecuador.

During a mudslide, the terrain *can change* drastically.

Adverbial word groups usually answer one of these questions: When? Where? How? Why? Under what conditions? To what degree?

James walked his dog *how*? *On a leash*.

Sabrina will adjust to life in Ecuador *when*? *In time*.

The terrain can change drastically *under what conditions*? *During a mudslide*.

B3-b Verbal phrases

A verbal is a verb form that does not function as the verb of a clause. Verbals include infinitives (the word *to* plus the base form of the verb), present participles (the *-ing* form of the verb), and past participles (the verb form usually ending in *-d*, *-ed*, *-n*, *-en*, or *-t*). (See G2-a.) Instead of functioning as the verb of a clause, a verbal functions as an adjective, a noun, or an adverb.

ADJECTIVE	*Broken* promises cannot be fixed.
NOUN	Constant *complaining* becomes wearisome.
ADVERB	Can you wait *to celebrate*?

Verbals with objects, complements, or modifiers form verbal phrases. Like verbals, verbal phrases function as adjectives, nouns, or adverbs. Verbal phrases are ordinarily classified as participial, gerund, and infinitive.

Participial phrases

Participial phrases always function as adjectives. Their verbals are either present participles (such as *dreaming*, *asking*) or past participles (such as *stolen*, *reached*).

Participial phrases frequently appear immediately following the noun or pronoun they modify.

Congress shall make no *law abridging the freedom of speech or of the press*.

PRACTICE hackerhandbooks.com/writersref
> Basic grammar > B3–7 and B3–8

Unlike other word groups that function as adjectives (prepositional phrases, infinitive phrases, adjective clauses), which must always follow the noun or pronoun they modify, participial phrases are often movable. They can precede the word they modify.

Being a weight-bearing joint, the *knee* is among the most often injured.

They may also appear at some distance from the word they modify.

Last night we saw a *play* that affected us deeply, *written with profound insight into the lives of immigrants*.

Gerund phrases

Gerund phrases are built around present participles (verb forms that end in *-ing*), and they always function as nouns: usually as subjects, subject complements, direct objects, or objects of a preposition.

Lizards usually enjoy sunning themselves. [DO: sunning themselves]

Infinitive phrases

Infinitive phrases, usually constructed around *to* plus the base form of the verb (*to call*, *to drink*), can function as nouns, as adjectives, or as adverbs. When functioning as a noun, an infinitive phrase may appear in almost any noun slot in a sentence, usually as a subject, subject complement, or direct object.

To live without health insurance is risky. [S: To live without health insurance]

Infinitive phrases functioning as adjectives usually appear immediately following the noun or pronoun they modify.

The Twentieth Amendment gave women the *right to vote*.

Adverbial infinitive phrases usually qualify the meaning of the verb, telling when, where, how, why, under what conditions, or to what degree an action occurred.

Volunteers *rolled up* their pants *to wade through the flood waters.*

NOTE: In some constructions, the infinitive is unmarked; in other words, the *to* does not appear. (See also M1-f.)

Graphs and charts can help researchers [*to*] *present complex data.*

B3-c Appositive phrases

Appositive phrases describe nouns or pronouns. Instead of modifying nouns or pronouns, however, appositive phrases rename them. In form they are nouns or noun equivalents.

Bloggers, *conversationalists at heart*, are the online equivalent of radio talk show hosts.

B3-d Absolute phrases

An absolute phrase modifies a whole clause or sentence, not just one word. It consists of a noun or noun equivalent usually followed by a participial phrase.

Her words reverberating in the hushed arena, the senator urged the crowd to support her former opponent.

B3-e Subordinate clauses

Subordinate clauses are patterned like sentences, having subjects and verbs and sometimes objects or complements. But they function within sentences as adjectives, adverbs, or nouns. They cannot stand alone as complete sentences.

Adjective clauses

Adjective clauses modify nouns or pronouns, usually answering the question Which one? or What kind of? They begin with a relative pronoun (*who*, *whom*, *whose*, *which*, or *that*) or occasionally with a relative adverb (usually *when*, *where*, or *why*). (See p. 325.)

The coach chose *players who would benefit from intense drills.*

PRACTICE **hackerhandbooks.com/writersref**
> Basic grammar > B3–9 to B3–12

In addition to introducing the clause, the relative pronoun points back to the noun that the clause modifies.

A *book that goes unread* is a writer's worst nightmare.

Relative pronouns are sometimes "understood."

The things [*that*] *we cherish most* are the things [*that*] *we might lose*.

The parts of an adjective clause are often arranged as in sentences (subject/verb/object or complement).

S V DO
Sometimes it is our closest friends who disappoint us.

Frequently, however, the object or complement appears first.

DO S V
They can be the very friends whom we disappoint.

TIP: For punctuation of adjective clauses, see P1-e and P2-e. For advice about avoiding repeated words in adjective clauses, see M3-d.

Adverb clauses

Adverb clauses modify verbs, adjectives, or other adverbs, usually answering one of these questions: When? Where? Why? How? Under what conditions? To what degree? They always begin with a subordinating conjunction (such as *after*, *although*, *because*, *that*, *though*, *unless*, or *when*). (For a complete list, see p. 325.)

When the sun went down, the hikers *prepared* their camp.

Kate *would have made* the team *if she hadn't broken her ankle*.

Noun clauses

A noun clause functions just like a single-word noun, usually as a subject, a subject complement, a direct object, or an object of a preposition. It usually begins with one of the following words: *how*, *if*, *that*, *what*, *whatever*, *when*, *where*, *whether*, *which*, *who*, *whoever*, *whom*, *whomever*, *whose*, *why*. (For a complete list, see p. 325.)

Words that introduce subordinate clauses

Words introducing adverb clauses

Subordinating conjunctions: after, although, as, as if, because, before, even though, if, in order that, since, so that, than, that, though, unless, until, when, where, whether, while

Words introducing adjective clauses

Relative pronouns: that, which, who, whom, whose

Relative adverbs: when, where, why

Words introducing noun clauses

Relative pronouns: that, which, who, whom, whose

Other pronouns: what, whatever, whichever, whoever, whomever

Other subordinating words: how, if, when, whenever, where, wherever, whether, why

S
Whoever leaves the house last must double-lock the door.

DO
Copernicus argued that the sun is the center of the universe.

The subordinating word introducing the clause may not play a significant role in the clause. In the preceding example sentences, *Whoever* is the subject of its clause, but *that* does not perform a function in its clause.

As with adjective clauses, the parts of a noun clause may appear in normal order (subject/verb/object or complement) or out of normal order.

S V DO
Loyalty is what keeps a friendship strong.

DO S V
New Mexico is where we live.

B4 Sentence types

Sentences are classified in two ways: according to their structure (simple, compound, complex, and compound-complex) and according to their purpose (declarative, imperative, interrogative, and exclamatory).

B4-a Sentence structures

Depending on the number and types of clauses they contain, sentences are classified as simple, compound, complex, or compound-complex.

Clauses come in two varieties: independent and subordinate. An independent clause contains a subject and a predicate, and it either stands alone or could stand alone as a sentence. A subordinate clause also contains a subject and a predicate, but it functions within a sentence as an adjective, an adverb, or a noun; it cannot stand alone. (See B3-e.)

Simple sentences

A simple sentence is one independent clause with no subordinate clauses.

INDEPENDENT CLAUSE
Without a passport, Eva could not visit her parents in Lima.

A simple sentence may contain compound elements—a compound subject, verb, or object, for example—but it does not contain more than one full sentence pattern. The following sentence is simple because its two verbs (*comes in* and *goes out*) share a subject (*Spring*).

INDEPENDENT CLAUSE
Spring comes in like a lion and goes out like a lamb.

Compound sentences

A compound sentence is composed of two or more independent clauses with no subordinate clauses. The independent clauses are usually joined with a comma and a coordinating conjunction (*and*, *but*, *or*, *nor*, *for*, *so*, *yet*) or with a semicolon. (See P1-a and P3-a.)

INDEPENDENT CLAUSE — INDEPENDENT CLAUSE
The car broke down, but a rescue van arrived within minutes.

INDEPENDENT CLAUSE — INDEPENDENT CLAUSE
A shark was spotted near shore; people left immediately.

PRACTICE **hackerhandbooks.com/writersref**
> Basic grammar > B4–2

Complex sentences

A complex sentence is composed of one independent clause with one or more subordinate clauses. (See B3-e.)

SUBORDINATE CLAUSE
If you leave late, take a cab home.

SUBORDINATE CLAUSE
What matters most to us is a quick commute.

Compound-complex sentences

A compound-complex sentence contains at least two independent clauses and at least one subordinate clause. The following sentence contains two independent clauses, each of which contains a subordinate clause.

INDEPENDENT CLAUSE — SUB CL — INDEPENDENT CLAUSE — SUB CL
Tell the doctor how you feel, and she will decide whether you can go home.

B4-b Sentence purposes

Writers use declarative sentences to make statements, imperative sentences to issue requests or commands, interrogative sentences to ask questions, and exclamatory sentences to make exclamations.

DECLARATIVE	The echo sounded in our ears.
IMPERATIVE	Love your neighbor.
INTERROGATIVE	Did the better team win tonight?
EXCLAMATORY	We're here to save you!

R

Researching

R Researching

R1 Conducting research, 332

- **a** Posing questions worth exploring, 332
- **b** Mapping out a search strategy, 334
- **c** Finding articles through databases or indexes, 336
- **d** Finding books through a library's catalog, 340
- **e** Finding Web sources, 341
- **f** Using other search tools, 345
- **g** Conducting field research, 346

R2 Evaluating sources, 346

- **a** Determining how sources support your purpose, 347
- **b** Selecting sources worth your time, 347
- **c** Reading critically, 353
- **d** Assessing Web sources, 355

R3 Managing information; avoiding plagiarism, 357

- **a** Maintaining a working bibliography, 358
- **b** Keeping track of sources, 359
- **c** Taking notes without plagiarizing, 359

R4 Choosing a documentation style, 366

- **a** Selecting a style appropriate for your discipline, 366

College research assignments ask you to pose a question worth exploring, to read widely in search of possible answers, to interpret what you read, to draw reasoned conclusions, and to support those conclusions with valid and well-documented evidence. The process takes time—for researching and for drafting, revising, and documenting the paper in the style recommended by your instructor (see the tabbed dividers marked MLA and APA/CMS). Before beginning a research project, set a realistic schedule of deadlines.

One student created a calendar to map out her tasks for a paper assigned on October 3 and due October 31, keeping in mind that some tasks might overlap or need to be repeated.

RESEARCH TIP: Think of research as a process. As your topic evolves, you may find new questions arising that require you to create a new

SAMPLE CALENDAR FOR A RESEARCH ASSIGNMENT

2	3 **Receive and analyze the assignment.**	4 Pose questions you might explore →	5 Talk with a reference librarian; plan a search strategy. →	6	7 Settle on a topic; narrow the focus.	8 Revise research questions. Locate sources. →
9 Read, take notes, and compile a working bibliography. →	10	11	12	13 Draft a working thesis and an outline.	14 Draft the paper. →	15
16 Draft the paper. →	17	18	19 Visit the writing center for feedback.	20 Do additional research if needed. →	21	22
23 Ask peers for feedback. Revise the paper; if necessary, revise the thesis. →	24	25	26	27 Prepare a list of works cited. →	28	29 Proofread the final draft. →
30 Proofread the final draft. →	31 **Submit the final draft.**					

search strategy, find additional sources, and challenge your initial assumptions. Keep an open mind throughout the process, be curious, and enjoy the detective work.

R1 Conducting research

Throughout this tabbed section, you will encounter examples related to three sample research papers:

- A paper on Internet surveillance in the workplace, written by a student in an English composition class (see pp. 436–40). The student, Anna Orlov, uses the MLA (Modern Language Association) style of documentation. (See highlights of Orlov's research process on pp. 432–35.)
- A paper on the limitations of medications to treat childhood obesity, written by a student in a psychology class (see pp. 488–96). The student, Luisa Mirano, uses the APA (American Psychological Association) style of documentation.
- A paper on the extent to which Civil War general Nathan Bedford Forrest can be held responsible for the Fort Pillow massacre, written by a student in a history class (see pp. 532–37). The student, Ned Bishop, uses the CMS (*Chicago Manual of Style*) documentation system.

R1-a Pose questions worth exploring.

Working within the guidelines of your assignment, pose a few questions that seem worth researching—questions that you want to explore, that you feel would interest your audience, and about which there is a substantial debate. Here, for example, are some preliminary questions jotted down by students enrolled in a variety of courses in different disciplines.

- Should the FCC broaden its definition of indecency to include violence?
- Which geological formations are the safest repositories for nuclear waste?
- What was Marcus Garvey's contribution to the fight for racial equality?
- How can governments and zoos help preserve Asia's endangered snow leopard?

- Why was amateur archaeologist Heinrich Schliemann such a controversial figure in his own time?

Approaching your topic with a series of worthwhile questions can help you focus your research and guide you toward developing an answer. As you think about possible questions, make sure that they are appropriate lines of inquiry for a research paper. Choose questions that are narrow (not too broad), challenging (not too bland), and grounded (not too speculative).

Choosing a narrow question

If your initial question is too broad, given the length of the paper you plan to write, look for ways to restrict your focus. Here, for example, is how two students narrowed their initial questions.

TOO BROAD	NARROWER
What are the hazards of fad diets?	Why are low-carbohydrate diets hazardous?
What are the benefits of stricter auto emissions standards?	How will stricter auto emissions standards create new, more competitive auto industry jobs?

Choosing a challenging question

Your research paper will be more interesting to both you and your audience if you base it on an intellectually challenging line of inquiry. Draft questions that provoke thought or engage readers in a debate.

TOO BLAND	CHALLENGING
What is obsessive-compulsive disorder?	Why is obsessive-compulsive disorder so difficult to treat?
How does DNA testing work?	How reliable is DNA testing?

You may need to address a bland question in the course of answering a more challenging one. For example, if you were writing about promising treatments for obsessive-compulsive disorder, you would no doubt answer the question "What is obsessive-compulsive disorder?" at some point in your paper. It would be a mistake, however, to use the bland question as the focus for the whole paper.

Choosing a grounded question

Finally, you will want to make sure that your research question is grounded, not too speculative. Although speculative questions—such as those that address morality or beliefs—are worth asking and may receive some attention in a research paper, they are inappropriate central questions. For most college courses, the central argument of a research paper should be grounded in facts.

TOO SPECULATIVE	GROUNDED
Is it wrong to share pornographic personal photos by cell phone?	What role should the US government play in regulating mobile content?
Do medical scientists have the right to experiment on animals?	How have technology breakthroughs made medical experiments on animals increasingly unnecessary?

R1-b Map out a search strategy.

A search strategy is a systematic plan for tracking down sources. To create a search strategy appropriate for your research question, consult a reference librarian and take a look at your library's Web site, which will give you an overview of available resources.

Including the library in your plan

Reference librarians are information specialists who can save you time by steering you toward relevant and reliable sources. With the help of an expert, you can make the best use of electronic databases, Web search engines, your library's catalog, and other reference tools.

Before you ask a reference librarian for help, be sure you have thought through the following questions:

- What is your assignment?
- In which academic discipline are you writing?
- What is your tentative research question?
- How long will the paper be?
- How much time can you spend on the project?

It's a good idea to bring a copy of the assignment with you.

In addition to speaking with a reference librarian, take some time to explore your library's Web site. You will typically find links to the library's catalog and to a variety of databases and electronic sources. You may also find resources listed by subject, research guides, information about interlibrary loans, and links to Web sites selected by librarians for their quality. Many libraries also offer online reference assistance to help you locate information and refine your search strategy.

NOTE FOR ONLINE STUDENTS: Even if you are unable to visit the library, as an enrolled student you can still use its resources. Most libraries offer chat reference services and remote access to online databases, though you may have to follow special procedures to use them. Check your library's Web site for information for distance learners.

Starting with your library's databases

You may be tempted to go straight to the Internet and ignore your library's resources, but using them early and often in the research process can save you time in the end. Libraries make a wide range of quality materials readily available, and they weed out questionable sources.

While a general Internet search might seem quick and convenient, it is often more time-consuming and can be less reliable than a search in a library's databases. Initial Internet searches may generate thousands of results. Figuring out which of these are credible, relevant, and worth further investigation can require many additional steps:

- Refining search terms (See the chart on refining keyword searches on p. 338.)
- Narrowing the domain name to include only .org, .gov, or .edu sites
- Weeding out any advertisements associated with results
- Scanning titles and sometimes content for relevant results
- Combing through sites to determine their currency and relevance as well as the credibility of their authors

Starting with your library's collection of databases can save time and effort. Because you can limit library database searches to only academic databases, you can count on finding reliable sources. Not all of the results will be worth examining in detail, but many library searches automatically sort them into subject categories that allow you to view narrowed results with just one click.

Choosing an appropriate search strategy

No single search strategy works for every topic. For some topics, it may be appropriate to search for information in newspapers, magazines, and Web sites. For others, the best sources might be found in scholarly journals and books and specialized reference works. Still other topics might be enhanced by field research—interviews, surveys, or direct observation.

With the help of a reference librarian, each of the students mentioned on page 332 constructed a search strategy appropriate for his or her research question.

ANNA ORLOV Anna Orlov's topic, Internet surveillance in the workplace, was current and influenced by technological changes, so she relied heavily on recent sources, especially those online. To find information on her topic, Orlov decided to

- search her library's general database for articles in magazines, newspapers, and journals
- check the library's catalog for recently published books
- use Web search engines, such as *Google*, to locate articles and government publications that might not show up in a database search

LUISA MIRANO Luisa Mirano's topic, the limitations of medications for childhood obesity, is the subject of psychological studies as well as articles in newspapers and magazines aimed at the general public. Thinking that both scholarly and popular works would be appropriate, Mirano decided to

- locate books through the library's online catalog
- check a specialized encyclopedia, *Encyclopedia of Psychology*
- search a specialized database, *PsycINFO*, for scholarly articles
- search her library's general database for popular articles

NED BISHOP Ned Bishop's topic, Nathan Bedford Forrest's role in the Fort Pillow massacre, has been investigated and debated by professional historians. Given the nature of his historical topic, Ned Bishop decided to

- locate books through the library's online catalog
- locate scholarly articles by searching a specialized database, *America: History and Life*
- locate newspaper articles from 1864 by searching the historical archive at the *New York Times* Web site
- search the Web for other historical primary sources (See p. 353.)

R1-c To locate articles, search a database or consult a print index.

Libraries subscribe to a variety of electronic databases (sometimes called *periodical* or *article databases*) that give students access to articles and other materials without charge. Because many databases are limited to relatively recent works, you may need to consult a print index as well.

What databases offer

Your library has access to databases that can lead you to articles in periodicals such as newspapers, magazines, and scholarly or technical journals. General databases cover several subject areas; subject-specific databases cover one subject area in depth.

Many databases, especially general databases, include the full text of at least some articles; others list only citations or citations with short summaries called *abstracts* (see also p. 352). When the full text is not available, a citation usually will give you enough information to track down an article. Your library's Web site will help you determine which articles are available in your library, either in print or in electronic form.

Your library might subscribe to some of the following databases.

GENERAL DATABASES

The information in general databases is not restricted to a specific discipline or subject area. You may find searching a general database helpful in the early stages of your research process.

Academic Search Premier. An interdisciplinary database that indexes thousands of popular and scholarly journals on all subjects.

Expanded Academic ASAP. An interdisciplinary database that indexes the contents of magazines, newspapers, and scholarly journals in all subject areas.

JSTOR. A full-text archive of scholarly journals from many disciplines; unlike most databases, it includes articles published decades ago but does not include articles from the most recent issues of publications.

LexisNexis. A database that is particularly strong in coverage of news, business, legal, and political topics.

ProQuest. A database of periodical articles. Through *ProQuest*, your library may subscribe to databases in subjects such as nursing, biology, and psychology.

SUBJECT-SPECIFIC DATABASES

Libraries have access to dozens of specialized databases, each of which covers a specific area of research. To find out what's available, consult your library's Web site or ask your reference librarian. The following are examples of subject-specific databases.

ERIC. A database offering education-related documents and abstracts of articles published in education journals.

Refining keyword searches in databases and search engines

Although command terms and characters vary in electronic databases and Web search engines, some common functions are listed here.

- Use quotation marks around words that are part of a phrase: "gateway drug".
- Use AND to connect words that must appear in a document: hyperactivity AND children. In some search engines—*Google*, for example—AND is assumed, so typing it is unnecessary. Other search engines require a plus sign instead: hyperactivity + children.
- Use NOT in front of words that must not appear in a document: Persian Gulf NOT war. Some search engines require a minus sign (hyphen) instead: Persian Gulf -war.
- Use OR if only one of the terms must appear in a document: "mountain lion" OR cougar.
- Use an asterisk as a substitute for letters that might vary: "marine biolog*" (to find *marine biology* or *marine biologist*, for example).
- Use parentheses to group a search expression and combine it with another: (standard OR student OR test*) AND reform.

NOTE: Many search engines and databases offer an advanced search option for refining your search with filters for exact phrases that must appear, specific words that should not appear, date restrictions, and so on.

MLA Bibliography. A database of literary criticism, with citations to help researchers find articles, books, and dissertations.

PsycINFO. A comprehensive database of psychology research, including abstracts of articles in journals and books.

Public Affairs Information Service (PAIS). A database that indexes books, journals, government documents, statistical directories, and research reports in the social sciences.

PubMed. A database offering millions of abstracts of medical research studies.

How to search a database

To find articles on your topic in a database, start by searching with keywords, terms that describe the information you need. If the first keyword you try results in too few or no matches, experiment with synonyms or ask a librarian for suggestions. For example, if you're searching for sources on a topic related to education, you might also want to try the terms *teaching*, *learning*, and *curriculum*. If your keyword search results in too many matches, narrow it by using one of the strategies in the chart on page 338.

For her paper on Internet surveillance in the workplace, Anna Orlov conducted a keyword search in a general database. She typed in *"internet use"* and *employee* and *surveillance* (see the database screen on this page). This search brought up twenty possible articles, some of which looked promising. (See p. 433 for Orlov's annotated list of search results.) Orlov e-mailed several full-text articles to herself and printed citations to other sources so that she could locate them in the library.

Making the most of your handbook

Freewriting, listing, and clustering can help you come up with additional search terms.

▶ Ways to explore your subject: C1-b

When to use a print index

A print index to periodical articles is a useful tool when you are researching a historical topic, especially from the early to mid-twentieth century. *The Readers' Guide to Periodical Literature* and *Poole's Index to Periodical Literature* index magazine articles beginning around

DATABASE SCREEN: KEYWORD SEARCH

1900, many of which are too old to appear in electronic databases. You can usually access the print articles themselves in your library's shelves or on microfilm.

R1-d To locate books, consult the library's catalog.

The books your library owns are listed along with other resources in its catalog. You can search the catalog by author, title, or subject.

If your first search calls up too few results, try different keywords or search for books on broader topics. If your search gives you too many results, use the strategies in the chart on page 338 or try an advanced search tool to combine concepts and limit your results. If those strategies don't work, ask a librarian for suggestions.

When Luisa Mirano, whose topic was childhood obesity, entered the term *obesity* into the library's catalog, she was faced with an unmanageable number of hits. She narrowed her search by adding two more specific terms to *obesity*: *child** (to include the terms *child*, *children*, and *childhood*) and *treatment*. When she still got too many results, she limited the first two terms to subject searches to find books that had obesity in children as their primary subject (see screen 1). Screen 2 shows the complete record for one of the books she found. The call number, listed beside *Availability*, is the book's address on the shelf. When you're retrieving a book from the shelf, take time to scan other books in the area since they are likely to be on the same topic.

RESEARCH TIP: The catalog record for a book lists related subject headings. These headings are a good way to locate other books on your

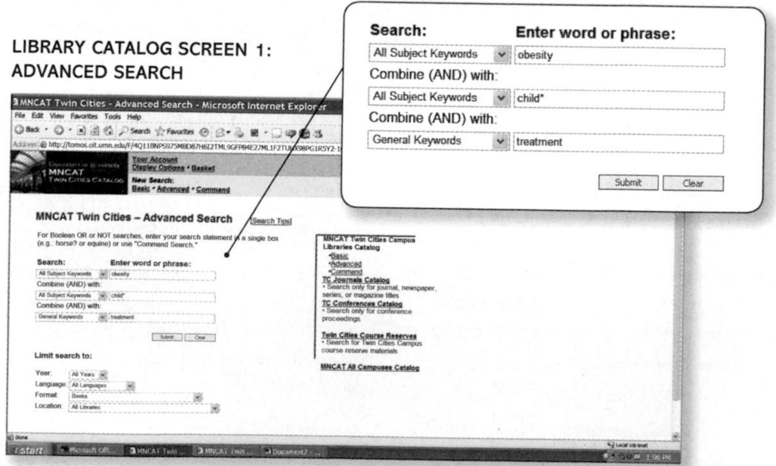

LIBRARY CATALOG SCREEN 1: ADVANCED SEARCH

LIBRARY CATALOG SCREEN 2: COMPLETE RECORD FOR A BOOK

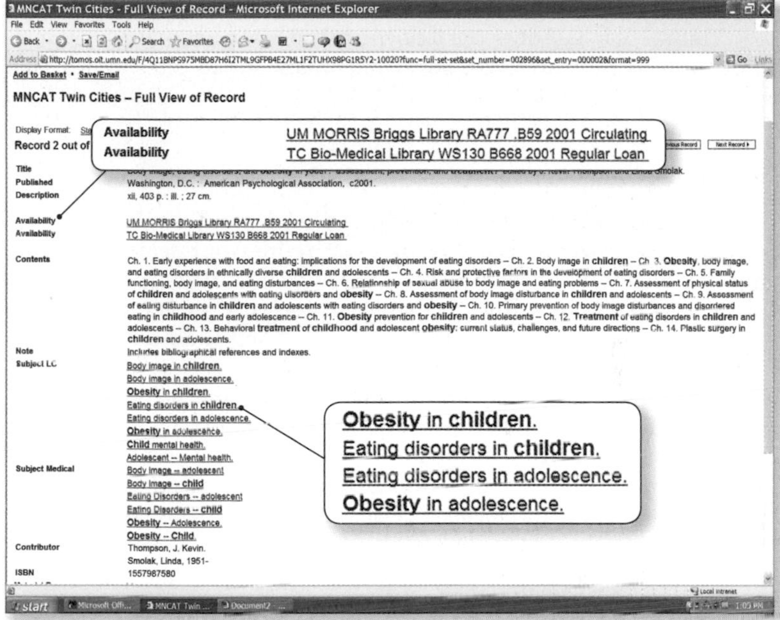

subject. For example, the record in screen 2 lists the terms *obesity in children* and *obesity in adolescence* as related subject headings. By clicking on these new terms, Mirano found more books on her subject. Subject headings can be useful terms for a database search as well.

R1-e To locate other sources, use a variety of online tools.

You can find a variety of reliable sources by using online tools beyond those offered by your library. For example, most government agencies post information on their Web sites, and federal and state governments use Web sites to communicate with citizens. The sites of many private organizations, such as Doctors without Borders and the Sierra Club, contain useful information about current issues. Museums and libraries often post digital versions of primary sources, such as photographs, political speeches, and classic literary texts.

Although the Internet at large can be a rich source of information, some of which can't be found anywhere else, it lacks quality control. The material on many sites has not necessarily been reviewed by experts. So when you're not working with your library's tools to locate online sources, carefully evaluate what you find (see R2).

This section describes the following Web resources: search engines, directories, digital archives, government and news sites, blogs, and wikis.

Search engines

When using a search engine, such as *Google* or *Yahoo!*, focus your search as narrowly as possible. You can refine your search by using many of the tips in the chart on page 338 or by using the search engine's advanced search form. For her paper on Internet surveillance in the workplace, Anna Orlov had difficulty restricting the number of hits. When she typed the words *Internet*, *surveillance*, *workplace*, and *privacy* into a search engine, she received more than 80,000 matches. After examining the first page of her results and viewing some that looked promising, Orlov grouped her search terms into the phrases *"Internet surveillance"* and *"workplace privacy"* and added the term *employee* to narrow the focus. The result was 422 matches. To refine her search further, Orlov clicked on Advanced Search and restricted her search to sites with URLs ending in *.org* and to those updated in the last three months. (See the results screen on p. 343.)

Directories

If you want to find good resources on topics too broad for a search engine, try a directory. Unlike search engines, directories are put together by information specialists who choose reputable sites and arrange them by topic: education, health, politics, and so on.

Try the following directories for scholarly research.

Internet Scout Project: http://scout.wisc.edu/Archives

Librarian's Internet Index: http://www.lii.org

Open Directory Project: http://www.dmoz.org

WWW Virtual Library: http://www.vlib.org

Digital archives

Archives are a good place to find primary sources: the texts of poems, books, speeches, and historically significant documents; photographs; and political cartoons. (See p. 353.)

The materials in these sites are usually limited to official documents and older works because of copyright laws.

SEARCH ENGINE SCREEN: RESULTS OF AN ADVANCED SEARCH

Web Results **1** - **5** of about **9** over the **past 3 months** for **"Internet surveillance" employee "workplace privacy"**

Web Results **1** - **5** of about **9** over the **past 3 months** for **"Internet surveillance" employee "workplace privacy" site:.org** (**0.44** seconds)

Tip: Try removing quotes from your search to get more results.

EPIC/PI - Privacy & Human Rights 2000
Now the supervision of **employee**'s performance, behavior and... [89]Information and Privacy Commissioner/Ontario, **Workplace Privacy**: The Need for a..
www.privacyinternational.org/survey/phr2000/threats.html - 131k Cached - Similar pages

Privacy and Human Rights 2003: Threats to Privacy
Other issues that raise **workplace privacy** concerns are employer requirements that **employees** complete medical tests, questionnaires, and polygraph tests..
www.privacyinternational.org/survey/phr2003/threats.htm - 279k Cached - Similar pages
[More results from www.privacyinternational.org]

[PDF] Monitoring Employee E-Mail And Internet Usage: Avoiding The..
File Format: PDF/Adobe Acrobat - View as HTML
Internet surveillance by employers in the American workplace. At present, US **employees** in the private workplace have no constitutional, common law or statu
lsr.nellco.org/cgi/viewcontent.cgi?article=1006&context=suffolk/ip - Similar pages

Previous EPIC Top News
The agencies plan to use RFID to track **employees**' movements and in ID cards... For more information on **workplace privacy**, see the EPIC **Workplace Privacy**...
www.epic.org/news/2005.html - 163k - Cached - Similar pages

American Memory: http://memory.loc.gov

Avalon Project: http://www.yale.edu/lawweb/avalon/avalon.htm

Eurodocs: http://eudocs.lib.byu.edu

Google Books: http://books.google.com

Google Scholar: http://scholar.google.com

The Making of America: http://quod.lib.umich.edu/m/moagrp

The New York Public Library Digital Collections: http://www.nypl.org/digital

Online Books Page: http://digital.library.upenn.edu/books

Government and news sites

For current topics, both government and news sites can prove useful. Many government agencies at every level provide online information. Government-maintained sites include resources such as legal texts, facts and statistics, government reports, and searchable reference databases. Here are just a few government sites:

Fedstats: http://www.fedstats.gov

GPO Access: http://www.gpoaccess.gov

United Nations: http://www.un.org

University of Michigan Documents Center: http://www.lib.umich.edu/m/moagrp

US Census Bureau: http://www.census.gov

Many news organizations offer up-to-date information on the Web. Some require registration and may charge fees for some articles. (Find out if your library subscribes to news sites so that you can access them at no charge.) The following news sites offer many free resources.

BBC: http://www.bbc.co.uk

Google News: http://news.google.com

Kidon Media-Link: http://www.kidon.com/media-link

New York Times: http://nytimes.com

Reuters: http://www.reuters.com

Blogs

A blog (short for *Weblog*) is a site that contains text or multimedia entries usually written and maintained by one person, with comments contributed by readers. Though some blogs are personal diaries and others are devoted to partisan politics, many journalists and academics maintain blogs that cover topics of interest to researchers. Some blogs feature short essays that provide useful insights or analysis; others point to new developments in a particular area of interest. The following Web sites can lead you to a wide range of blogs.

Academic Blog Portal: http://academicblogs.org

Google Blog Search: http://www.google.com/blogsearch

Science Blogs: http://scienceblogs.com

Technorati: http://technorati.com

Wikis

A wiki is a collaborative Web site with many contributions and with content that may change frequently. *Wikipedia*, the collaborative online encyclopedia, is one of the most frequently consulted wikis.

In general, *Wikipedia* may be helpful if you're checking for something that is common knowledge (facts available in multiple sources, such as dates and well-known historical events) or looking for current information about a topic in contemporary culture that isn't covered elsewhere. However, many scholars do not consider *Wikipedia* and wikis in general to be appropriate sources for college research. Authorship is not limited to experts; articles may be written by amateurs who are not well informed. And because the articles can be changed by anyone, controversial texts are often altered to reflect a particular perspective and are susceptible to bias. When possible, locate and cite another, more reliable source for any useful information you find in a wiki.

R1-f Use other search tools.

In addition to articles, books, and online sources, you may want to consult references such as encyclopedias and almanacs. Citations in scholarly works can also lead you to additional sources.

Reference works

The reference section of the library holds both general and specialized encyclopedias, dictionaries, almanacs, atlases, and biographical references, some available in electronic form through the library's Web site. Such works often provide a good overview of your subject and include references to the most significant works on a topic. Check with a reference librarian to see which works are most appropriate for your project.

GENERAL REFERENCE WORKS General reference works are good places to check facts and get basic information. Here are a few frequently used general references:

American National Biography
National Geographic Atlas of the World
The New Encyclopaedia Britannica
The Oxford English Dictionary
Statistical Abstract of the United States

Although general encyclopedias are often a good place to find background for your topic, you should rarely use them in your final paper. Most instructors expect you to rely on more specialized sources.

SPECIALIZED REFERENCE WORKS Specialized reference works often explore a topic in depth, usually in the form of articles written by leading authorities. They offer a quick way to gain an expert's overview of a complex topic. Many specialized works are available, including these:

Contemporary Authors
Encyclopedia of Bioethics
Encyclopedia of Crime and Justice
Encyclopedia of Psychology
Encyclopedia of World Environmental History
International Encyclopedia of Communication
New Encyclopedia of Africa

Bibliographies and scholarly citations as shortcuts

Scholarly books and articles list the works the author has cited, usually at the end. These lists can be useful shortcuts to additional reliable sources on your topic. For example, most of the scholarly articles Luisa Mirano consulted contained citations to related research studies; through these citations, she quickly located other sources related to her topic, treatments for childhood obesity.

R1-g Conduct field research, if appropriate.

Your own field research can enhance or be the focus of a writing project. For a composition class, for example, you might want to interview a local politician about a current issue, such as the use of alternative energy sources. For a sociology class, you might decide to conduct a survey regarding campus trends in community service. At work, you might need to learn how food industry executives have responded to reports that their products are contributing to health problems.

NOTE: Colleges and universities often require researchers to submit projects to an institutional review board (IRB) if the research involves human subjects outside of a classroom setting. Before administering a survey or conducting other fieldwork, check with your instructor to see if IRB approval is required.

R2 Evaluating sources

You can often locate dozens or even hundreds of potential sources for your topic—far more than you will have time to read. Your challenge will be to determine what kinds of sources you need and to zero in on a reasonable number of quality sources, those truly worthy of your time and attention.

Later, once you have decided on some sources worth consulting, your challenge will be to read them with an open mind and a critical eye.

R2-a Think about how sources might contribute to your writing.

How you plan to use sources will affect how you evaluate them. Not every source must directly support your thesis; sources can have other functions in a paper. They can

- provide background information or context for your topic
- explain terms or concepts that your readers might not understand
- provide evidence for your argument
- lend authority to your argument
- offer alternative interpretations and counterevidence to your argument

For examples of how student writers use sources for a variety of purposes, see MLA 1c, APA-1c, and CMS-1c.

R2-b Select sources worth your time and attention.

Sections R1-c through R1-e show how to refine your searches in databases, in the library's catalog, and in search engines. This section explains how to scan through the results for the most promising sources and how to preview them to see whether they are likely to live up to your expectations and meet your needs.

Making the most of your handbook

Annotating bibliography entries can help you evaluate sources.

- ▶ Maintain a working bibliography: R3-a
- ▶ Summarize sources: A1-c
- ▶ Analyze sources: A1-d
- ▶ Consider how sources inform your argument: MLA-1c, APA-1c, CMS-1c

Scanning search results

As you scan through a list of search results, watch for clues indicating whether a source might be useful for your purposes or is not worth pursuing. (For an annotated list of one student's search results, see p. 433.) You will need to use somewhat different strategies when scanning search results from a database, a library catalog, and a Web search engine.

DATABASES Most databases (see p. 337) list at least the following information, which can help you decide if a source is relevant, current, scholarly enough (see the chart on p. 352), and a suitable length for your purposes.

Title and brief description (How relevant?)

Date (How current?)

Name of periodical (How scholarly?)

Length (How extensive in coverage?)

At the bottom of this page are just a few of the hits Ned Bishop came up with when he consulted a general database for articles on the Fort Pillow massacre, using the search term *Fort Pillow*.

Many databases allow you to sort your list of results by relevance or date; sorting may help you scan the information more efficiently. By scanning the titles in his search results, Bishop saw that only one contained the words *Fort Pillow*. The name of the periodical in which it appeared, *Journal of American History*, suggested that the source was scholarly. The 1989 publication date was not a problem, since currency is not necessarily a criterion for historical sources. The article's length (eight pages) is given in parentheses at the end of the citation. While the article may seem short, the topic—a statistical note—is narrow enough to ensure adequate depth of coverage. Bishop decided that the article was worth consulting. Because the other sources were irrelevant or too broad, he decided not to consult them.

LIBRARY CATALOGS A library's catalog usually lists enough basic information about books, periodicals, DVDs, and other material to give you a first impression. A book's title and date of publication, for example, will often be your first clues as to whether the book is worth consulting. If a title looks interesting, you can click on it for further information about

EVALUATING SEARCH RESULTS: LIBRARY DATABASE

Popular magazine. Not relevant.	☐ Mark **Black, blue and gray: the other Civil War; African-American soldiers, sailors and spies were the unsung heroes.** *Ebony* Feb 1991 v46 n4 p96(6) View text and retrieval choices
Movie review. Not relevant.	☐ Mark **The Civil War.** (movie reviews) Lewis Cole. *The Nation* Dec 3, 1990 v251 n19 p694(5) View text and retrieval choices
Subject too broad.	☐ Mark **The hard fight was getting into the fight at all.** (black soldiers in the Civil War) Jack Fincher. *Smithsonian* Oct 1990 v21 n7 p46(13) View text and retrieval choices
Brief scholarly article. Matches the student's topic. Promising.	☑ Mark **The Fort Pillow massacre: a statistical note.** John Cimprich, Robert C. Mainfort Jr.. *Journal of Ameri History* Dec 1989 v76 n3 p830(8) View extended citation and retrieval choices

EVALUATING SEARCH RESULTS: INTERNET SEARCH ENGINE

American **Obesity** Association - **Childhood Obesity** **Childhood Obesity**. **Obesity** in **children** ... Note: The term "**childhood obesity**" may refer to both **children** and adolescents. In general, we ... www.**obesity**.org/subs/**childhood**/ - 17k - Jan 8, 2005 - Cached - Similar pages	Content from a research-based organization. Promising.
Childhood Obesity KS Logo, **Childhood Obesity**. advertisement. Source. ERIC Clearinghouse on Teaching and Teacher Education. Contents. ... Back to the Top Causes of **Childhood Obesity**. ... www.kidsource.com/kidsource/content2/**obesity**.html - 18k - Cached - Similar pages	Popular rather than scholarly source. Not relevant.
Childhood Obesity, June 2002 Word on Health - National Institutes ... **Childhood Obesity** on the Rise, an article in the June 2002 edition of The NIH Word on Health - Consumer Information Based on Research from the National ... www.nih.gov/news/WordonHealth/ jun2002/**childhoodobesity**.htm - 22k - Cached - Similar pages	Content too general. Not relevant.
MayoClinic.com - **Childhood obesity**: Parenting advice ... **Childhood obesity**: Parenting advice By Mayo Clinic staff. ... Here are some other tips to help your **obese child** — and yourself: Be a positive role model. ... www.mayoclinic.com/invoke.cfm?id=FL00058 - 42k - Jan 8, 2005 - Cached - Similar pages	Popular and too general. Not relevant.

the book's subject matter and its length. The table of contents may also be available, offering a glimpse of what's inside. (See also p. 341.)

WEB SEARCH ENGINES Because anyone can publish a Web site, legitimate sources and unreliable sources live side by-side online. As you scan through search results, look for the following clues about the probable relevance, currency, and reliability of a site—but be aware that the clues are by no means foolproof.

The title, keywords, and lead-in text (How relevant?)

A date (How current?)

An indication of the site's sponsor or purpose (How reliable?)

The URL, especially the domain name extension: for example, .com, .edu, .gov, or .org (How relevant? How reliable?)

At the top of this page are a few of the results that Luisa Mirano retrieved after typing the keywords *childhood obesity* into a search engine; she limited her search to works with those words in the title.

Mirano found the first site, sponsored by a research-based organization, promising enough to explore for her paper. The second and fourth sites held less promise because they seemed to offer popular rather than scholarly information. In addition, the second site was full of distracting commercial advertisements. Mirano rejected the third source not because she doubted its reliability—in fact, research from the National Institutes of Health was what she hoped to find—but because a skim of its contents revealed that the information was too general for her purposes.

COMMON FEATURES OF A SCHOLARLY SOURCE

1 Formal presentation includes abstract and research methods.
2 Includes review of previous research studies.
3 Reports original research.
4 Includes references.
5 Often has multiple authors who are academics.

Cyberbullying: Using Virtual Scenarios to Educate and Raise Awareness

Vivian H. Wright, Joy J. Burnham, Christopher T. Inman, and Heather N. Ogorchock

Abstract

This study examined cyberbullying in three distinct phases to facilitate a multifaceted understanding of cyberbullying. The phases included (a) a quantitative survey, (b) a qualitative focus group, and (c) development of educational scenarios/simulations (within the Second Life virtual environment). Phase III was based on adolescent feedback about cyberbullying from Phases I and II of this study. In all three phases, adolescent reactions to cyberbullying were examined and reported to raise awareness and to educate others about cyberbullying. Results from scenario development indicate that simulations created in a virtual environment are engaging and have the potential to be powerful tools in helping schools address problems such as cyberbullying education and prevention. (Keywords: cyberbullying, virtual worlds, Second Life, teacher education, counselor education)

Introduction

Cyberbullying has gained attention and recognition in recent years (Beale & Hall, 2007; Carney, 2008; Casey-Canon, Hayward, & Gowen, 2001; Kowalski & Limber, 2007; Li, 2007; Shariff, 2005). The increased interest and awareness of cyberbullying relates to such factors as the national media attention after several publicized cyberbullying tragedies (Maag, 2007; Stelter, 2008; Zifcak, 2006), the attenuation of communication boundaries (i.e., cell phones, the Internet, and computer network connections), and the exponential increases in technology use among youth. Nonetheless, with the escalation of technology and the easy access and popularity of technological devices among youth, presently there remains a critical gap in the literature related to cyberbullying and its possible effects on school-aged children and adolescents. Because cyberbullying has the potential to impact youth across systems (i.e., home, school, and the community), we believe that parents, "school professionals" (Li, 2007, p. 1778), and mental health providers must not only be made aware of cyberbullying and its consequences, but must also have access to ways to deal with this growing concern.

Two years ago, cyberbullying was considered to be a "new territory" for exploration (Li, 2007, p. 1778) because there was limited information about bullying through "electronic means" (Li, p. 1780). In contrast, today studies on cyberbullying, including some descriptions of the worst cyberbullying incidences (Maag, 2007; Stelter, 2008; Zifcak, 2006), are becoming more prevalent (Beale & Hall, 2007; Carney, 2008; Kowalski & Limber, 2007; Li, 2007). At this time, there is a need to raise awareness about the effects of cyberbullying and to create educational opportunities to serve multiple audiences (i.e., teachers, teacher educators, school administrators, school counselors, mental health professionals, students, parents) in the quest to identify and hopefully prevent cyberbullying in the future. Consequently, to facilitate a multifaceted understanding of

Defin

Casey-Canon et al., 2001; Patchin & Hinduja, 2006). Cyberbullying has been defined as "bullying through the e-mail, instant messaging, in a chat room, on a website, or though digital messages or images sent to a cell phone" (Kowalski & Limber, 2007, p. 822). There are numerous methods to engage in cyberbullying, including e-mail, instant messaging, online gaming, chat rooms, and text messaging (Beale & Hall, 2007; Li, 2007). In addition,

- Flaming: sending
- Harassment: sendin
- Denigration: se
- Cyberstalking: using
- Impersonation: pret
- Outing or trickery: information
- Exclusion: excluding

Patchin, 2008; Kowalski & Limber, 2007; Li, 2007; Pellegrini & Bartini, 2000; Smith, Mahdavi, Carvalho, & Tippett, 2006; Williams & Guerra, 2007). Of the middle school grades, 6th grade students are usually the

Abstract 

This study examined cyberbullying in three distinct phases to facilitate a multifaceted understanding of cyberbullying. The phases included (a) a quantitative survey, (b) a qualitative focus group, and (c) development of educational scenarios/simulations (within the Second Life virtual environment). Phase III was based on adolescent feedback about cyberbullying from Phases I and II of this study. In all three phases, adolescent reactions to cyberbullying were examined and reported to raise awareness and to

2 Research suggests that cyberbullying has distinct gender and age differences. According to the literature, girls are more likely to be online and to cyberbully (Beale & Hall, 2007; Kowalski & Limber, 2007; Li, 2006, 2007). This finding is "opposite of what happens off-line," where boys are more likely to bully than girls (Beale & Hall, p. 8). Age also appears to be a factor in cyberbullying. Cyberbullying increases in the elementary years, peaks during the middle school years, and declines in the high school years (Beale & Hall). Based on the literature, cyberbullying is a growing concern among middle school-aged children (Beale & Hall; Hinduja & Patchin, 2008; Kowalski & Limber, 2007; Li, 2007; Pellegrini & Bartini, 2000; Smith, Mahdavi, Carvalho, & Tippett, 2006; Williams & Guerra, 2007). Of the middle school grades, 6th grade students are usually the

3 **Table 2: Percentage of Students Who Experienced Cyberbullying through Various Methods**

	E-mail	Facebook	MySpace	Cell Phone	Online Video	Chat Rooms
Victim	35.3%	11.8%	52.9%	50%	14.7%	11.8%
Bully	17.6%	0%				

4 **References**

Bainbridge, W. S. (2007, July). The scientific research potential of virtual worlds. *Science, 317*, 472–476.

07, September/October). Cyberbullying: nd parents) can do. *The Clearing House,*

ns of bullying and associated trauma dur- *chool Counseling, 11*(3), 179–187.

, C., & Gowen, K. (2001). Middle school

5

Vivian H. Wright is an associate professor of instructional technology at the University of Alabama. In addition to teaching in the graduate program, Dr. Wright works with teacher educators on innovative ways to infuse technology in the curriculum to enhance teaching and learning. She has helped initiate and develop projects such as the Master Technology Teacher and Technology on Wheels. Dr. Wright's scholarship includes publications and presentations in the research areas of K–12 technology integration, emerging technologies, and asynchronous education.

Wright, Vivian H., et al. "Cyberbullying: Using Virtual Scenarios to Educate and Raise Awareness." *Journal of Computing in Teacher Education* 26.1 (2009): 35-42.

COMMON FEATURES OF A POPULAR SOURCE

1 Often has a provocative title.
2 Author is typically a staff reporter, not an expert.
3 The bulk of the article presents anecdotes about the topic.
4 Presents a summary of research but no original research.
5 No consistent citation of sources.

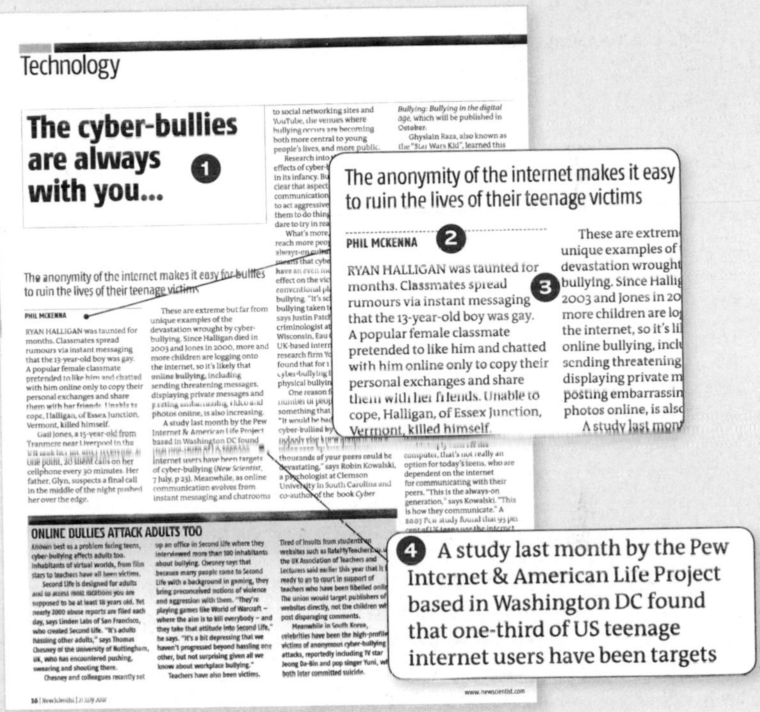

Technology

The cyber-bullies are always with you... 1

The anonymity of the internet makes it easy for bullies to ruin the lives of their teenage victims

PHIL MCKENNA 2

RYAN HALLIGAN was taunted for months. Classmates spread rumours via instant messaging that the 13-year-old boy was gay. A popular female classmate pretended to like him and chatted with him online only to copy their personal exchanges and share them with her friends. Unable to cope, Halligan, of Essex Junction, Vermont, killed himself. 3

Gail Jones, a 15-year-old from Tranmere near Liverpool in the UK ... her cellphone every 30 minutes. Her father, Glyn, suspects a final call in the middle of the night pushed her over the edge.

These are extreme but far from unique examples of the devastation wrought by cyber-bullying. Since Halligan died in 2003 and Jones in 2000, more and more children are logging onto the internet, so it's likely that online bullying, including sending threatening messages, displaying private messages and posting embarrassing video and photos online, is also increasing.

4 A study last month by the Pew Internet & American Life Project based in Washington DC found that one-third of US teenage internet users have been targets of cyber-bullying (*New Scientist*, 7 July, p 23). Meanwhile, as online communication evolves from instant messaging and chatrooms to social networking sites and YouTube, the venues where bullying occurs are becoming both more central to young people's lives, and more public.

ONLINE BULLIES ATTACK ADULTS TOO

www.newscientist.com

"The lack of face-to-face contact might tempt bullies to new levels of cruelty"

communication. "There is a distancing of the self and immediacy in response that we don't have in any other form of communication," she says. "On the computer, it's like it's not really you." 5

So what can be done? Led by Ruth Aylett of Heriot-Watt University in Edinburgh, UK,

Meanwhile, some governments have taken legislative action. In January 2006, the US Congress passed a law making it a federal crime to "annoy, abuse, threaten or harass" another person over the internet. Approximately 36 states have enacted similar legislation. And in South Korea, the "internet real-

McKenna, Phil. "The Cyber-Bullies Are Always with You. . . ." *New Scientist* July 2007: 26-27.

Determining if a source is scholarly

For many college assignments, you will be asked to use scholarly sources. These are written by experts for a knowledgeable audience and usually go into more depth than books and articles written for a general audience. (Scholarly sources are sometimes called *refereed* or *peer-reviewed* because the work is evaluated by experts in the field before publication.) To determine if a source is scholarly, look for the following:

- Formal language and presentation
- Authors with academic or scientific credentials
- Footnotes or a bibliography documenting the works cited by the author in the source
- Original research and interpretation (rather than a summary of other people's work)
- Quotations from and analysis of primary sources (in humanities disciplines such as literature, history, and philosophy)
- A description of research methods or a review of related research (in the sciences and social sciences)

See pages 350–51 for a sample scholarly source and popular source.

NOTE: In some databases, searches can be limited to refereed or peer-reviewed journals.

Selecting appropriate versions of electronic sources

An online source may appear as an abstract, an excerpt, or a full-text article or book. It is important to distinguish among these versions of sources and to use a complete version of a source for your research.

Abstracts and excerpts are shortened versions of complete works. An abstract—a summary of a work's contents—might appear in a database record for a periodical article. An excerpt is the first few sentences or paragraphs of a newspaper or magazine article; it sometimes appears in a list of hits in an online search. Abstracts and excerpts often provide enough information for you to determine whether the complete article would be useful for your paper. Both are brief (usually fewer than five hundred words) and generally do not contain enough information to function alone as sources in a research paper. Reading the complete article is the best way to understand the author's argument before referring to it in your own writing. A full-text work may appear online as a PDF (portable document format) file or as an HTML file (sometimes called a *text file*). If your source is available in both formats, choose the PDF file for your research because it will include page numbers for your citations.

R2-c Read with an open mind and a critical eye.

As you begin reading the sources you have chosen, keep an open mind. Do not let your personal beliefs prevent you from listening to new ideas and opposing viewpoints. Your research question—not a snap judgment about the question—should guide your reading.

When you read critically, you are not necessarily judging an author's work harshly; you are simply examining its assumptions, assessing its evidence, and weighing its conclusions. (For one student's careful reading of a source text, see p. 434.)

Academic English When you research on the Web, it is easy to ignore views different from your own. Web pages that appeal to you will often link to other pages that support the same viewpoint. If your sources all seem to agree with you—and with one another—seek out opposing views and evaluate them with an open mind.

Distinguishing between primary and secondary sources

As you begin assessing evidence in a source, determine whether you are reading a primary or a secondary source. Primary sources are original documents such as letters, diaries, photographs, legislative bills, laboratory studies, field research reports, and eyewitness accounts. Secondary sources are commentaries on primary sources—another writer's opinions about or interpretation of a primary source. A primary source for Ned Bishop was Nathan Bedford Forrest's official report on the battle at Fort Pillow. Bishop also consulted a number of secondary sources, some of which relied heavily on primary sources such as letters.

Although a primary source is not necessarily more reliable than a secondary source, it has the advantage of being a firsthand account. Naturally, you can better evaluate what a secondary source says if you have first read any primary sources it discusses.

Being alert for signs of bias

Some sources are more objective than others. Even publications that are considered reputable can be editorially biased. For example, *USA Today*, *National Review*, and the *Economist* are all credible sources, but they are also likely to interpret events quite differently from one another. If you are uncertain about a periodical's special interests, consult *Magazines for Libraries.* To check for bias in a book, see what book reviewers have written about it. A reference librarian can help you locate reviews and assess the credibility of both the book and the reviewers.

Evaluating all sources

Checking for signs of bias

- Does the author or publisher endorse political or religious views that could affect objectivity?
- Is the author or publisher associated with a special-interest group, such as Greenpeace or the National Rifle Association, that might present only one side of an issue?
- Are alternative views presented and addressed? How fairly does the author treat opposing views? (See A3-c.)
- Does the author's language show signs of bias?

Assessing an argument

- What is the author's central claim or thesis?
- How does the author support this claim—with relevant and sufficient evidence or with just a few anecdotes or emotional examples?
- Are statistics consistent with those you encounter in other sources? Have they been used fairly? (It is possible to "lie" with statistics by using them selectively or by omitting details.) Does the author explain where the statistics come from?
- Are any of the author's assumptions questionable?
- Does the author consider opposing arguments and refute them persuasively? (See A3-c.)
- Does the author fall prey to any logical fallacies? (See A3-a.)

Like publishers, some authors are more objective than others. If you have reason to believe that a writer is particularly biased, you will want to assess his or her arguments with special care. For questions to ask about a source's possible bias, see the chart on this page.

Assessing the author's argument

In nearly all academic writing, there is some element of argument, so don't be surprised to encounter experts who disagree. When you find areas of disagreement, you will want to read each source's arguments with special care, testing them with your own critical intelligence. The questions in the chart on this page can help you weigh the strengths and weaknesses of each author's argument.

Making the most of your handbook

Good college writers read critically.

- ▶ Judging whether a source is reasonable: **A3-a**
- ▶ Judging whether a source is fair: **A3-c**

Evaluating Web sources

Authorship

- Does the Web site or document have an author? You may need to do some clicking and scrolling to find the author's name. If you have landed directly on an internal page of a site, for example, you may need to navigate to the home page or find an "about this site" link to learn the name of the author.
- If there is an author, can you tell whether he or she is knowledgeable and credible? When the author's qualifications aren't listed on the site itself, look for links to the author's home page, which may provide evidence of his or her interests and expertise.

Sponsorship

- Who, if anyone, sponsors the site? The sponsor of a site is often named and described on the home page and is sometimes listed alongside the copyright date: © 2009 Plymouth State College.
- What does the URL tell you? The domain name extension often indicates the type of group hosting the site: commercial (.com), educational (.edu), nonprofit (.org), governmental (.gov), military (.mil), or network (.net). URLs may also indicate a country of origin: .uk (United Kingdom) or .jp (Japan), for instance.

Purpose and audience

- Why was the site created: To argue a position? To sell a product? To inform readers?
- Who is the site's intended audience?

Currency

- How current is the site? Check for the date of publication or the latest update, often located at the bottom of the home page or at the beginning or end of an internal page.
- How current are the site's links? If many of the links no longer work, the site may be too dated for your purposes.

R2-d Assess Web sources with special care.

Web sources can provide valuable information, but verifying their credibility may take time. Before using a Web source in your paper, make sure you know who created the material and for what purpose.

Many sophisticated-looking sites contain questionable information. Even a well-designed hate site may at first appear unbiased and

EVALUATING A WEB SITE: CHECKING RELIABILITY

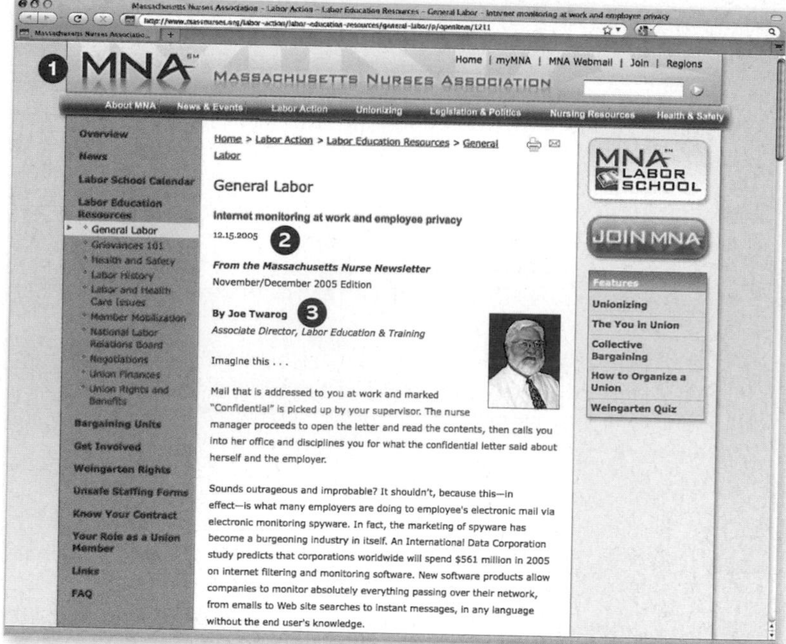

1 This article on Internet monitoring is on a site sponsored by the Massachusetts Nurses Association, a professional health care association and union whose staff and members advocate for nurses in the workplace. The URL ending .org marks this sponsor as a nonprofit organization.

2 Clear dates of publication show currency.

3 The author is a credible expert whose credentials can be verified.

informative. Sites with reliable information, however, can stand up to careful scrutiny. For a checklist on evaluating Web sources, see the chart on page 355.

In researching Internet surveillance and workplace privacy, Anna Orlov encountered sites that raised her suspicions. In particular, some sites were authored by surveillance software companies, which have an obvious interest in emphasizing the benefits of such software to company management. When you know something about the creator of a site and have a sense of the site's purpose, you can quickly determine whether a source is reliable, credible, and worth a closer look. Consider, for example, the two sites pictured on this page and on page 357. Anna Orlov decided that the first Web site would be more useful for her project than sites like the second.

EVALUATING A WEB SITE: CHECKING PURPOSE

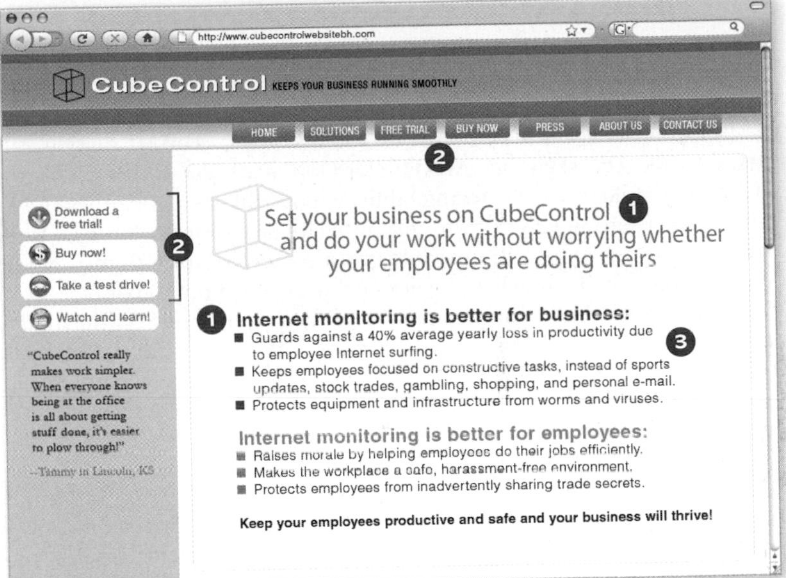

1 The site is sponsored by a company that specializes in employee monitoring software.

2 Repeated links for trial downloads and purchase suggest the site's intended audience: consumers seeking to purchase software (probably not researchers seeking detailed information about employees' use of the Internet in the workplace).

3 The site appears to provide information and even shows statistics from studies, but ultimately the purpose of the site is to sell a product.

R3 Managing information; avoiding plagiarism

An effective researcher is a good record keeper. Whether you decide to keep records on paper or on your computer—or both—your challenge as a researcher will be to find systematic ways of managing information. More specifically, you will need methods for maintaining a working bibliography, keeping track of source materials, and taking notes without plagiarizing your sources. (For more on avoiding plagiarism, see MLA-2, APA-2, or CMS-2.)

R3-a Maintain a working bibliography.

Keep a record of any sources you decide to consult. You will need this record, called a *working bibliography*, when you compile the list of sources that will appear at the end of your paper. The format of this list depends on the documentation style you are using. (For MLA style, see MLA-4b; for APA style, see APA-4b; for CMS style, see CMS-4c.) Using the proper style in your working bibliography will ensure that you have all the information you need to correctly cite any sources you use. Your working bibliography will probably contain more sources than you will actually include in your list of works cited in your final paper.

Most researchers print or save bibliographic information from the library's online catalog, its periodical databases, and the Web. The information you need to collect is given in the chart on page 360. If you download a visual, you must gather the same information as for a print source.

For Web sources, some bibliographic information may not be available, but spend time looking for it before assuming that it doesn't exist. When information isn't available on the home page, you may have to drill into the site, following links to interior pages. Look especially for the author's name, the date of publication (or latest update), and the name of any sponsoring organization. Do not omit such information unless it is genuinely unavailable.

Once you have created a working bibliography, you can annotate it. Writing several brief sentences summarizing key points of a source will help you identify how it relates to your argument and to your other sources. You should evaluate the source in your own words and use quotations sparingly. Clarifying the source's ideas at this stage will help you separate them from your own and avoid plagiarizing them later.

SAMPLE ANNOTATED BIBLIOGRAPHY ENTRY (MLA STYLE)

Gonsalves, Chris. "Wasting Away on the Web." *eWeek.com*. Ziff Davis Enterprise Holdings, 8 Aug. 2005. Web. 16 Feb. 2009.

Summarize the source.

Annotations should be three to seven sentences long.

In this editorial, Gonsalves considers the implications of several surveys, including one in which 61% of respondents said that their companies have the right to spy on them. The author agrees with this majority, claiming that it's fine if his company chooses to monitor him as long as the company discloses its monitoring practices. He argues that "the days of Internet freedom at work are

Use quotations sparingly. Put quotation marks around any words from the source.

MODELS **hackerhandbooks.com/writersref**
> Model papers > MLA annotated bibliography: Orlov
> APA annotated bibliography: Haddad

justifiably finished," adding that he would prefer not to know the extent of the surveillance. Gonsalves writes for *eWeek.com*, a publication focused on technology products. He presents himself as an employee who is comfortable with being monitored, but his job may be a source of bias. This editorial contradicts some of my other sources, which claim that employees want to know and should know all the details of their company's monitoring procedures.

Interpret the relationship between this source and others in the bibliography.

Evaluate the source for bias and relevance.

R3-b Keep track of source materials.

The best way to keep track of source materials is to save a copy of each one. Many database subscription services will allow you to e-mail, save, or print citations or full texts of articles, and you can easily download, copy, or take screen shots of information from the Web.

Working with photocopies, printouts, and electronic files—as opposed to relying on memory or hastily written notes—has several benefits. You can highlight key passages, perhaps even color-coding them to reflect topics in your outline. You can annotate the source in the margins by hand or with your word processing program's comment feature and get a head start on note taking (for an example, see the annotated article on p. 434). Finally, you reduce the chances of unintentional plagiarism, since you will be able to compare your use of a source in your paper with the actual source, not just with your notes (see R3-c).

NOTE: It's especially important to keep print or electronic copies of Web sources, which may change or even become inaccessible over time. Make sure that your copy includes the site's URL and your date of access.

TIP: Your school may provide citation software, which allows researchers to download references directly from online sources. Similarly, many databases format citations with a mouse click, and Web sites offer fill-in-the-blank forms for generating formatted citations. You must proofread such citations carefully, however, because the programs sometimes provide incorrect results.

R3-c As you take notes, avoid unintentional plagiarism.

When you take notes and jot down ideas, be very careful not to use language from your sources unless you clearly identify borrowed words and phrases as quotations. Even if you half-copy the author's

Information for a working bibliography

For an entire book

- All authors; any editors or translators
- Title and subtitle
- Edition (if not the first)
- Publication information: city, publisher, and date

For a periodical article

- All authors of the article
- Title and subtitle of the article
- Title of the magazine, journal, or newspaper
- Date; volume, issue, and page numbers

For a periodical article retrieved from a database (in addition to preceding information)

- Name of the database and an item number, if available
- Name of the subscription service
- URL of the subscription service (for an online database)
- Accession number or other number assigned by the database
- Digital object identifier (DOI), if there is one
- Date you retrieved the source

NOTE: Use particular care when printing or saving articles in PDF format. These files may not include some of the elements you need to properly cite the source. You may need to record additional information from the database or Web site where you retrieved the file.

For a Web source (including visuals)

- All authors, editors, or creators of the source
- Editor or compiler of the Web site, if there is one
- Title and subtitle of the source
- Title of the site
- Publication information for the source, if available
- Page or paragraph numbers, if any
- Date of online publication (or latest update)
- Sponsor of the site
- Date you accessed the source
- The site's URL

NOTE: For the exact bibliographic format to use in your working bibliography and in the final paper, see MLA-4b, APA-4b, or CMS-4c.

sentences—either by mixing the author's phrases with your own without using quotation marks or by plugging your synonyms into the author's sentence structure—you are committing plagiarism, a serious academic offense. (For examples of this kind of plagiarism, see MLA-2, APA-2, and CMS-2.)

To prevent unintentional borrowing, resist the temptation to look at the source as you take notes—except when you are quoting. Keep the source close by so you can check for accuracy, but don't try to put ideas in your own words with the source's sentences in front of you. When you need to quote the exact words of a source, make sure you copy the words precisely and put quotation marks around them.

TIP: Be especially careful when using copy and paste functions in electronic files. Some researchers have unintentionally plagiarized their sources because they lost track of which words came from sources and which were their own. To prevent unintentional plagiarism, put quotation marks around any exact language you save from your sources.

Academic English Even in the early stages of note taking, it is important to keep in mind that, in the United States, written texts are considered an author's property. (This "property" isn't a physical object, so it is often referred to as *intellectual property*.) The author (or publisher) owns the language as well as any original ideas contained in the writing, whether the source is published in print or electronic form. When you use another author's property in your own writing, you need to follow certain conventions for citing the material; if you don't, you risk committing *plagiarism*.

Summarizing, paraphrasing, and quoting are three ways of taking notes. Be sure to include exact page references for all three types of notes, since you will need the page numbers later if you use the information in your paper.

Summarizing without plagiarizing

A summary condenses information, perhaps reducing a chapter to a short paragraph or a paragraph to a single sentence. A summary should be written in your own words; if you use phrases from the source, put them in quotation marks.

On page 362 is a passage from a source about mountain lions. Following the passage is the student's summary. (The bibliographic information is recorded in MLA style.)

ORIGINAL SOURCE

In some respects, the increasing frequency of mountain lion encounters in California has as much to do with a growing *human* population as it does with rising mountain lion numbers. The scenic solitude of the western ranges is prime cougar habitat, and it is falling swiftly to the developer's spade. Meanwhile, with their ideal habitat already at its carrying capacity, mountain lions are forcing younger cats into less suitable terrain, including residential areas. Add that cougars have generally grown bolder under a lengthy ban on their being hunted, and an unsettling scenario begins to emerge.

— Rychnovsky, Ray. "Clawing into Controversy." *Outdoor Life* Jan. 1995: 38–42. Print. [p. 40]

SUMMARY

Source: Rychnovsky, Ray. "Clawing into Controversy." *Outdoor Life* Jan. 1995: 38–42. Print. [p. 40]

Encounters between mountain lions and humans are on the rise in California because increasing numbers of lions are competing for a shrinking habitat. As the lions' wild habitat shrinks, older lions force younger lions into residential areas. These lions have lost some of their fear of humans because of a ban on hunting (Rychnovsky 40).

Paraphrasing without plagiarizing

Like a summary, a paraphrase is written in your own words; but whereas a summary reports significant information in fewer words than the source, a paraphrase retells the information in roughly the same number of words. If you retain occasional choice phrases from the source, use quotation marks so that later you will know which phrases are not your own.

As you read the following paraphrase of the original source at the top of this page, notice that the language is significantly different from that in the original.

PARAPHRASE

Source: Rychnovsky, Ray. "Clawing into Controversy." *Outdoor Life* Jan. 1995: 38–42. Print. [p. 40]

Californians are encountering mountain lions more frequently because increasing numbers of humans and a rising population of lions are competing for the same territory. Humans have moved into mountainous regions once dominated by the lions, and the wild habitat that is left cannot sustain the current lion population.

Therefore, the older lions are forcing younger lions into residential areas. And because of a ban on hunting, these younger lions have become bolder—less fearful of encounters with humans (Rychnovsky 40).

Using quotation marks to avoid plagiarizing

A quotation consists of the exact words from a source. In your notes, put all quoted material in quotation marks; do not assume that you will remember later which words, phrases, and passages you have quoted and which are your own. When you quote, be sure to copy the words of your source exactly, including punctuation and capitalization.

QUOTATION

Source: Rychnovsky, Ray. "Clawing into Controversy." *Outdoor Life* Jan. 1995: 38–42. Print. [p. 40]

Rychnovsky explains that as humans expand residential areas into mountain ranges, the cougar's natural habitat "is falling swiftly to the developer's spade" (40).

Avoiding Internet plagiarism

UNDERSTAND WHAT PLAGIARISM IS. When you use another author's intellectual property—language, visuals, or ideas—in your own writing without giving proper credit, you commit a kind of academic theft called *plagiarism*.

TREAT WEB SOURCES IN THE SAME WAY YOU TREAT PRINT SOURCES. Any language that you find on the Internet must be carefully cited, even if the material is in the public domain or is publicly accessible on free sites. When you use material from Web sites sponsored by federal, state, or municipal governments (.gov sites) or by nonprofit organizations (.org sites), you must acknowledge that material, too, as intellectual property owned by those agencies.

KEEP TRACK OF WHICH WORDS COME FROM SOURCES AND WHICH ARE YOUR OWN. To prevent unintentional plagiarism when you copy and paste passages from Web sources to an electronic file, put quotation marks around any text that you have inserted into your own notes or paper. In addition, during note taking and drafting, you might use highlighting or a different color font to draw attention to text taken from sources—so that material from articles, Web sites, and other sources stands out unmistakably as someone else's words.

Integrating and citing sources to avoid plagiarism

Source text

> Our language is constantly changing. Like the Mississippi, it keeps forging new channels and abandoning old ones, picking up debris, depositing unwanted silt, and frequently bursting its banks. In every generation there are people who deplore changes in the language and many who wish to stop its flow. But if our language stopped changing it would mean that American society had ceased to be dynamic, innovative, pulsing with life—that the great river had frozen up.
>
> —Robert MacNeil and William Cran, *Do You Speak American?*, p. 1

NOTE: The examples in this chart follow MLA style (see MLA-4). For information on APA and CMS (*Chicago*) styles, see APA-4 and CMS-4, respectively.

If you are using an exact sentence from a source, with no changes . . .	➔	. . . put quotation marks around the sentence. Use a signal phrase and include a page number in parentheses. MacNeil and Cran write, "Our language is constantly changing" (1).
If you are using a few exact words from the source but not an entire sentence . . .	➔	. . . put quotation marks around the exact words that you have used from the source. Use a signal phrase and include a page number in parentheses. The English language, according to MacNeil and Cran, is "like the Mississippi" (1).
If you are using near-exact words from the source but changing some word forms (*I* to *she*, *walk* to *walked*) or adding words to clarify and make the quotation flow with your own text . . .	➔	. . . put quotation marks around the quoted words, and put brackets around the changes you have introduced. Include a signal phrase and follow the quotation with the page number in parentheses. MacNeil and Cran compare the English language to the Mississippi River, which "forg[es] new channels and abandon[s] old ones" (1).

		MacNeil and Cran write, "In every generation there are people who deplore changes in the [English] language and many who wish to stop its flow" (1).
If you are paraphrasing or summarizing the source, using the author's ideas but not any of the author's exact words . . .	→	. . . introduce the ideas with a signal phrase and put the page number at the end of your sentence. Do not use quotation marks. (See MLA-2, APA-2, and CMS-2.) MacNeil and Cran argue that changes in the English language are natural and that they represent cultural progress (1).
If you have used the source's sentence structure but substituted a few synonyms for the author's words . . .	→	STOP! This is a form of plagiarism even if you use a signal phrase and a page number. Change your sentence by using one of the techniques given in this chart or in MLA-3, APA-3, or CMS-3. **PLAGIARIZED** MacNeil and Cran claim that, like a river, English creates new waterways and discards old ones. **INTEGRATED AND CITED CORRECTLY** MacNeil and Cran claim, "Like the Mississippi, [English] keeps forging new channels and abandoning old ones" (1).

AVOID WEB SITES THAT BILL THEMSELVES AS "RESEARCH SERVICES" AND SELL ESSAYS. When you use Web search engines to research a topic, you will often see links to sites that appear to offer legitimate writing support but that actually sell college essays. Of course, submitting a paper that you have purchased is cheating, but even using material from such a paper is considered plagiarism.

For more on avoiding plagiarism while working with sources, see MLA-2, APA-2, or CMS-2.

R4 Choosing a documentation style

The various academic disciplines use their own style for citing sources and for listing the works that are cited in a paper. *A Writer's Reference* describes three commonly used styles: MLA (Modern Language Association), APA (American Psychological Association), and CMS (*Chicago Manual of Style*). See the appropriate tabbed section for details about each style.

NOTE: For a list of style manuals in a variety of disciplines, visit *Research and Documentation Online* at hackerhandbooks.com/resdoc.

R4-a Select a style appropriate for your discipline.

In researched writing, sources are cited for several reasons. First, it is important to acknowledge the contributions of others. If you fail to credit sources properly, you commit plagiarism, a serious academic offense. Second, by choosing appropriate sources, you will add credibility to your work; in a sense, you are calling on authorities to serve as expert witnesses. The more care you have taken in choosing reliable sources, the stronger your argument will be. Finally—and most importantly—you are engaging in a scholarly conversation: when you cite your sources, you show readers where they can pursue your topic in greater depth.

All of the academic disciplines cite sources for these same reasons. However, the different styles for citing sources are based on the values and intellectual goals of scholars in different disciplines.

MLA and APA in-text citations

MLA style and APA style both use citations in the text of a paper that refer to a list of works at the end of the paper. The systems work somewhat differently, however, because MLA style was created for scholars in English composition and literature and APA style was created for researchers in the social sciences.

MLA IN-TEXT CITATION

Brandon Conran argues that the story is written from "a bifocal point of view" (111).

APA IN-TEXT CITATION

As researchers Yanovski and Yanovski (2002) have explained, obesity was once considered "either a moral failing or evidence of underlying psychopathology" (p. 592).

While MLA and APA styles work in a similar way, some basic disciplinary differences show up in these key elements:

- author's name
- date of publication
- page numbers
- verb tense in signal phrases

MLA style gives the author's full name when it is first mentioned. This approach emphasizes authorship and interpretation. APA style, which uses only the last names of authors, gives a date after the author's name. This approach reflects the social scientist's concern with the currency of research. MLA style places the date in the works cited list but omits it in the text. While currency is important, what someone had to say a century ago may be as significant as the latest contribution to the field.

Both styles include page numbers for quotations. MLA style requires page numbers for summaries and paraphrases as well; with a page number, readers can easily find the original passage that has been summarized or paraphrased. While APA does not require page numbers for summaries and paraphrases, it recommends that writers use a page number if doing so would help readers find the passage in a longer work.

Finally, MLA style uses the present tense (such as *argues*) to introduce cited material, whereas APA style uses the past or present perfect tense (such as *argued* or *have argued*) in signal phrases. The present tense evokes the timelessness of a literary text; the past or present perfect tense emphasizes that research or experimentation occurred in the past.

CMS footnotes or endnotes

Most historians and many scholars in the humanities use the style of footnotes or endnotes recommended by *The Chicago Manual of Style* (CMS). Historians base their work on a wide variety of primary and secondary sources, all of which must be cited. The CMS note system has the virtue of being relatively unobtrusive; even when a paper or an article is thick with citations, readers will not be overwhelmed. In the text of the paper, only a raised number appears. Readers who are interested can consult the accompanying numbered note, which is given either at the foot of the page or at the end of the paper.

TEXT

Historian Albert Castel quotes several eyewitnesses on both the Union and the Confederate sides as saying that Forrest ordered his men to stop firing.[7]

NOTE

7. Albert Castel, "The Fort Pillow Massacre: A Fresh Examination of the Evidence," *Civil War History* 4, no. 1 (1958): 44-45.

The CMS system gives as much information as the MLA or APA system, but less of that information appears in the text of the paper.

MLA

MLA Papers

MLA MLA Papers

Directory to MLA in-text citation models, 371

Directory to MLA works cited models, 371

MLA-1 Supporting a thesis, 373

- a Forming a thesis, 373
- b Organizing your ideas, 374
- c Using sources to inform and support your argument, 374

MLA-2 Citing sources; avoiding plagiarism, 376

- a Citing quotations and borrowed ideas, 376
- b Enclosing borrowed language in quotation marks, 378
- c Putting summaries and paraphrases in your own words, 378

MLA-3 Integrating sources, 379

- a Using quotations appropriately, 380
- b Using signal phrases, 382
- c Synthesizing sources, 386

MLA-4 Documenting sources, 388

- a MLA in-text citations, 389
- b MLA list of works cited, 398

MLA CITATIONS AT A GLANCE
Article in a periodical, 402
Book, 406
Selection from an anthology, 410
Short work from a Web site, 414
Article from a database, 416

- c MLA information notes, 428

MLA-5 Manuscript format; sample paper, 429

- a Manuscript format, 429
- b Highlights of one student's research process, 431
- c Sample MLA paper, 435

Directory to MLA in-text citation models

BASIC RULES FOR PRINT AND ONLINE SOURCES

1. Author named in a signal phrase, 390
2. Author named in parentheses, 390
3. Author unknown, 390
4. Page number unknown, 391
5. One-page source, 391

VARIATIONS ON THE BASIC RULES

6. Two or three authors, 392
7. Four or more authors, 392
8. Organization as author, 392
9. Authors with the same last name, 393
10. Two or more works by the same author, 393
11. Two or more works in one citation, 393
12. Repeated citations from the same source, 393
13. Encyclopedia or dictionary entry, 394
14. Multivolume work, 394
15. Entire work, 394
16. Selection in an anthology, 395
17. Government document, 395
18. Historical document, 395
19. Legal source, 395
20. Visual such as a photograph, map, or chart, 396
21. E-mail, letter, or personal interview, 396
22. Web site or other electronic source, 396
23. Indirect source (source quoted in another source), 396

LITERARY WORKS AND SACRED TEXTS

24. Literary work without parts or line numbers, 397
25. Verse play or poem, 397
26. Novel with numbered divisions, 397
27. Sacred text, 398

Directory to MLA works cited models

LISTING AUTHORS (PRINT AND ONLINE)

1. Single author, 399
2. Two or three authors, 399
3. Four or more authors, 399
4. Organization as author, 400
5. Unknown author, 400
6. Two or more works by the same author, 401

ARTICLES IN PERIODICALS (PRINT)

7. Article in a journal (paginated by volume or by issue), 401
8. Article in a monthly magazine, 401
9. Article in a weekly magazine, 403
10. Article in a daily newspaper, 403
11. Abstract of a journal article, 403
12. Article with a title in its title, 404
13. Editorial or other unsigned article, 404
14. Letter to the editor, 404
15. Review, 404

BOOKS (PRINT)

16. Basic format for a book, 404
17. Book with an author and an editor, 405
18. Book with an author and a translator, 405
19. Book with an editor, 405
20. Graphic narrative or illustrated book, 405
21. Book with an author using a pseudonym, 407
22. Book in a language other than English, 407
23. Entire anthology, 407
24. One or more selections from an anthology, 407
25. Edition other than the first, 408
26. Multivolume work, 408
27. Encyclopedia or dictionary entry, 409
28. Sacred text, 409

Directory to MLA works cited models (continued)

BOOKS (PRINT) (continued)

29. Foreword, introduction, preface, or afterword, 409
30. Book with a title in its title, 411
31. Book in a series, 411
32. Republished book, 411
33. Publisher's imprint, 411

ONLINE SOURCES

34. Entire Web site, 412
35. Short work from a Web site, 413
36. Web site with an author using a pseudonym, 413
37. Article in an online journal, 413
38. Article in an online magazine, 415
39. Article in an online newspaper, 415
40. Work from a database, 415
41. Online book-length work, 417
42. Part of an online book, 417
43. Digital archives, 417
44. Entry in an online reference work, 418
45. Online poem, 418
46. Entire blog (Weblog), 418
47. Entry or comment in a blog (Weblog), 418
48. Academic course or department home page, 418
49. Online video clip, 419
50. Online abstract, 419
51. Online editorial or letter to the editor, 419
52. Online review, 419
53. E-mail message, 419
54. Posting to an online discussion list, 420
55. Entry in a wiki, 420

AUDIO AND VISUAL SOURCES (INCLUDING ONLINE VERSIONS)

56. Digital file, 420
57. Podcast, 421
58. Musical score, 421
59. Sound recording, 421
60. Film, 421
61. DVD, 422
62. Special feature on a DVD, 422
63. CD-ROM, 422
64. Computer software or video game, 422
65. Radio or television program, 422
66. Radio or television interview, 423
67. Live performance, 423
68. Lecture or public address, 423
69. Work of art, 423
70. Cartoon, 424
71. Advertisement, 424
72. Map or chart, 424

OTHER SOURCES (INCLUDING ONLINE VERSIONS)

73. Government document, 424
74. Historical document, 425
75. Legal source, 425
76. Pamphlet or brochure, 426
77. Unpublished dissertation, 426
78. Published dissertation, 426
79. Abstract of a dissertation, 426
80. Published proceedings of a conference, 427
81. Paper in conference proceedings, 427
82. Published interview, 427
83. Personal interview, 427
84. Personal letter, 427
85. Published letter, 428
86. Manuscript, 428

MLA Papers

Most English instructors and some humanities instructors will ask you to document your sources with the Modern Language Association (MLA) system of citations described in MLA-4. When writing an MLA paper that is based on sources, you face three main challenges: (1) supporting a thesis, (2) citing your sources and avoiding plagiarism, and (3) integrating quotations and other source material.

Examples in this tabbed section are drawn from a student's research about online monitoring of employees' computer use. Anna Orlov's research paper, in which she argues that electronic surveillance in the workplace threatens employees' privacy, appears on pages 436–40. (See highlights of Anna Orlov's research process on pp. 432–35.)

MLA-1 Supporting a thesis

Most research assignments ask you to form a thesis, or main idea, and to support that thesis with well-organized evidence.

MLA-1a Form a working thesis.

Once you have read a variety of sources and considered your issue from different perspectives, you are ready to form a working thesis: a one-sentence (or occasionally a two-sentence) statement of your central idea (see also C2-a). Because it is a working, or tentative, thesis, you can remain flexible and revise it as your ideas develop. In a research paper, your thesis will answer the central research question you pose (see R1-a). Here, for example, are Anna Orlov's research question and working thesis.

RESEARCH QUESTION

Should employers monitor their employees' online activities in the workplace?

WORKING THESIS

Employers should not monitor their employees' online activities because electronic surveillance can compromise workers' privacy.

After you have written a rough draft and perhaps done more reading, you may decide to revise your thesis, as Orlov did.

REVISED THESIS

Although companies often have legitimate concerns that lead them to monitor employees' Internet usage—from expensive security breaches to reduced productivity—the benefits of electronic surveillance are outweighed by its costs to employees' privacy and autonomy.

The thesis usually appears at the end of the introductory paragraph. To read Anna Orlov's thesis in the context of her introduction, see page 436.

PRACTICE **hackerhandbooks.com/writersref**
> MLA > MLA 1–1

MLA-1b Organize ideas with a rough outline.

The body of your paper will consist of evidence in support of your thesis. Instead of getting tangled up in a formal outline early in the process, sketch an informal plan that organizes your ideas in bold strokes. Anna Orlov, for example, used this simple plan to outline the structure of her argument:

- Compared with older types of surveillance, electronic surveillance allows employers to monitor workers more efficiently.
- Some experts argue that companies have important financial and legal reasons to monitor employees' Internet usage.
- But monitoring employees' Internet usage may lower worker productivity when the threat to privacy creates distrust.
- Current laws do little to protect employees' privacy rights, so employees and employers have to negotiate the potential risks and benefits of electronic surveillance.

After you have written a rough draft, a more formal outline can be a useful way to shape the complexities of your argument. See C1-d for an example.

Making the most of your handbook

It's helpful to start off with a working thesis and a rough outline—especially when writing from sources.

▶ Drafting a working thesis: C1-c
▶ Sketching a plan: C1-d

MLA-1c Use sources to inform and support your argument.

Used thoughtfully, the source materials you have gathered will make your argument more complex and convincing for readers. Sources can play several different roles as you develop your points.

Providing background information or context

You can use facts and statistics to support generalizations or to emphasize the importance of your topic, as student writer Anna Orlov does in her introduction.

> As the Internet has become an integral tool of businesses, company policies on Internet usage have become as common as policies regarding vacation days or sexual harassment. A 2005 study by the American Management Association and ePolicy Institute found that 76% of companies monitor employees' use of the Web,

and the number of companies that block employees' access to certain Web sites has increased 27% since 2001 (1).

Explaining terms or concepts

If readers are unlikely to be familiar with words or ideas important to your topic, you must explain them. Quoting or paraphrasing a source can help you define terms and concepts in accessible language.

> One popular monitoring method is keystroke logging, which is done by means of an undetectable program on employees' computers. . . . As Lane explains, these programs record every key entered into the computer in hidden directories that can later be accessed or uploaded by supervisors; the programs can even scan for keywords tailored to individual companies (128-29).

Supporting your claims

As you draft your argument, make sure to back up your assertions with facts, examples, and other evidence from your research. (See also A2-e.) Orlov, for example, uses an anecdote from one of her sources to support her claim that limiting computer access causes resentment among a company's staff.

> Monitoring online activities can have the unintended effect of making employees resentful. . . . Kesan warns that "prohibiting personal use can seem extremely arbitrary and can seriously harm morale. . . . Imagine a concerned parent who is prohibited from checking on a sick child by a draconian company policy" (315-16). As this analysis indicates, employees can become disgruntled when Internet usage policies are enforced to their full extent.

Lending authority to your argument

Expert opinion can give weight to your argument. (See also A2-e.) But don't rely on experts to make your argument for you. Construct your argument in your own words and, when appropriate, cite the judgment of an authority in the field to support your position.

> Additionally, many experts disagree with employers' assumption that online monitoring can increase productivity. Employment law attorney Joseph Schmitt argues that, particularly for employees who are paid a salary rather than an hourly wage, "a company shouldn't care whether employees spend one or 10 hours on the Internet as long as they are getting their jobs done—and provided that they are not accessing inappropriate sites" (qtd. in Verespej).

Anticipating and countering objections

Do not ignore sources that seem contrary to your position or that offer arguments different from your own. Instead, use them to give voice to opposing points of view and to state potential objections to your argument before you counter them (see A-2f). Anna Orlov, for example, cites conflicting evidence to acknowledge that some readers may feel that unlimited Internet access in the workplace hinders productivity. In doing so, she creates an opportunity to counter that objection and persuade those readers.

> On the one hand, computers and Internet access give employees powerful tools to carry out their jobs; on the other hand, the same technology offers constant temptations to avoid work. As a 2005 study by *Salary.com* and *America Online* indicates, the Internet ranked as the top choice among employees for ways of wasting time on the job; it beat talking with co-workers—the second most popular method—by a margin of nearly two to one (Frauenheim).

MLA-2 Citing sources; avoiding plagiarism

Your research paper is a collaboration between you and your sources. To be fair and ethical, you must acknowledge your debt to the writers of those sources. If you don't, you commit plagiarism, a serious academic offense.

In general, these three acts are considered plagiarism: (1) failing to cite quotations and borrowed ideas, (2) failing to enclose borrowed language in quotation marks, and (3) failing to put summaries and paraphrases in your own words. Definitions of plagiarism may vary; it's a good idea to find out how your school defines academic dishonesty.

MLA-2a Cite quotations and borrowed ideas.

Sources are cited for two reasons:

1. to tell readers where your information comes from—so that they can assess its reliability and, if interested, find and read the original source

PRACTICE **hackerhandbooks.com/writersref**
> MLA > MLA 2–1 to MLA 2–6

2. to give credit to the writers from whom you have borrowed words and ideas

You must cite anything you borrow from a source, including direct quotations; statistics and other specific facts; visuals such as cartoons, graphs, and diagrams; and any ideas you present in a summary or paraphrase.

Making the most of your handbook

When you use exact language from a source, you need to show that it is a quotation.

▶ Quotation marks for direct quotations: P5-a

The only exception is common knowledge—information your readers could easily find in any number of general sources. For example, most encyclopedias will tell readers that Alfred Hitchcock directed *Notorious* in 1946 and that Emily Dickinson published only a handful of her many poems during her lifetime.

As a rule, when you have seen information repeatedly in your reading, you don't need to cite it. However, when information has appeared in only one or two sources, when it is highly specific (as with statistics), or when it is controversial, you should cite the source. If a topic is new to you and you are not sure what is considered common knowledge or what is controversial, ask your instructor or someone else with expertise. When in doubt, cite the source.

The Modern Language Association recommends a system of in-text citations. Here, briefly, is how the MLA citation system usually works:

1. The source is introduced by a signal phrase that names its author.
2. The material being cited is followed by a page number in parentheses.
3. At the end of the paper, a list of works cited (arranged alphabetically by authors' last names) gives complete publication information about the source.

IN-TEXT CITATION

Legal scholar Jay Kesan points out that the law holds employers liable for employees' actions such as violations of copyright laws, the distribution of offensive or graphic sexual material, and illegal disclosure of confidential information (312).

ENTRY IN THE LIST OF WORKS CITED

Kesan, Jay P. "Cyber-Working or Cyber-Shirking? A First Principles Examination of Electronic Privacy in the Workplace." *Florida Law Review* 54.2 (2002): 289-332. Print.

This basic MLA format varies for different types of sources. For a detailed discussion of other models, see MLA-4.

MLA-2b Enclose borrowed language in quotation marks.

To indicate that you are using a source's exact phrases or sentences, you must enclose them in quotation marks unless they have been set off from the text by indenting (see the bottom of p. 381). To omit the quotation marks is to claim—falsely—that the language is your own. Such an omission is plagiarism even if you have cited the source.

ORIGINAL SOURCE

Without adequate discipline, the World Wide Web can be a tremendous time sink; no other medium comes close to matching the Internet's depth of materials, interactivity, and sheer distractive potential.

—Frederick Lane, *The Naked Employee*, p. 142

PLAGIARISM

Frederick Lane points out that if people do not have adequate discipline, the World Wide Web can be a tremendous time sink; no other medium comes close to matching the Internet's depth of materials, interactivity, and sheer distractive potential (142).

BORROWED LANGUAGE IN QUOTATION MARKS

Frederick Lane points out that for those not exercising self-control, "the World Wide Web can be a tremendous time sink; no other medium comes close to matching the Internet's depth of materials, interactivity, and sheer distractive potential" (142).

MLA-2c Put summaries and paraphrases in your own words.

A summary condenses information from a source; a paraphrase conveys the information using roughly the same number of words as the original source. When you summarize or paraphrase, it is not enough to name the source; you must restate the source's meaning using your own language. (See also R3-c.) You commit plagiarism if you half-copy the author's sentences—either by mixing the author's phrases with your own without using quotation marks or by plugging your synonyms into the author's sentence structure.

The first paraphrase of the following source is plagiarized—even though the source is cited—because too much of its language is borrowed from the original. The underlined strings of words have been copied exactly (without quotation marks). In addition, the writer has closely echoed the sentence structure of the source, merely substituting some synonyms (*restricted* for *limited*, *modern era* for *computer age*, *monitoring* for *surveillance*, and *inexpensive* for *cheap*).

ORIGINAL SOURCE

In earlier times, surveillance was limited to the information that a supervisor could observe and record firsthand and to primitive counting devices. In the computer age surveillance can be instantaneous, unblinking, cheap, and, maybe most importantly, easy.

—Carl Botan and Mihaela Vorvoreanu, "What Do Employees Think about Electronic Surveillance at Work?" p. 126

PLAGIARISM: UNACCEPTABLE BORROWING

Scholars Carl Botan and Mihaela Vorvoreanu argue that in earlier times monitoring of employees was restricted to the information that a supervisor could observe and record firsthand. In the modern era, monitoring can be instantaneous, inexpensive, and, most importantly, easy (126).

To avoid plagiarizing an author's language, resist the temptation to look at the source while you are summarizing or paraphrasing. After you have read the original passage, set the source aside. Ask yourself, "What is the author's meaning?" In your own words, state the author's basic point. Return to the source and check that you haven't used the author's language or sentence structure or misrepresented the author's ideas. When you fully understand another writer's meaning, you can more easily and accurately present those ideas in your own words.

ACCEPTABLE PARAPHRASE

Scholars Carl Botan and Mihaela Vorvoreanu claim that the nature of workplace surveillance has changed over time. Before the arrival of computers, managers could collect only small amounts of information about their employees based on what they saw or heard. Now, because computers are standard workplace technology, employers can monitor employees efficiently (126).

MLA-3 Integrating sources

Quotations, summaries, paraphrases, and facts will help you develop your argument, but they cannot speak for you. You can use several strategies to integrate information from research sources into your paper while maintaining your own voice.

MLA-3a Use quotations appropriately.

Limiting your use of quotations

Although it is tempting to insert many quotations in your paper and to use your own words only for connecting passages, do not quote excessively. In your academic writing, keep the emphasis on your ideas; use your own words to summarize and to paraphrase your sources and to explain your points. Sometimes, however, quotations can be the most effective way to integrate a source's ideas.

WHEN TO USE QUOTATIONS

- When language is especially vivid or expressive
- When exact wording is needed for technical accuracy
- When it is important to let the debaters of an issue explain their positions in their own words
- When the words of an authority lend weight to an argument
- When the language of a source is the topic of your discussion (as in an analysis or interpretation)

It is not always necessary to quote full sentences from a source. To reduce your reliance on the words of others, you can often integrate language from a source into your own sentence structure. (For the use of signal phrases in integrating quotations, see MLA-3b.)

> Kizza and Ssanyu observe that technology in the workplace has been accompanied by "an array of problems that needed quick answers" such as electronic monitoring to prevent security breaches (4).

Using the ellipsis mark and brackets

Two useful marks of punctuation, the ellipsis mark and brackets, allow you to keep quoted material to a minimum and to integrate it smoothly into your text.

The ellipsis mark To condense a quoted passage, you can use the ellipsis mark (three periods, with spaces between) to indicate that you have left words out. What remains must be grammatically complete.

> Lane acknowledges the legitimate reasons that many companies have for monitoring their employees' online activities, particularly management's concern about preventing "the theft of information that can be downloaded to a . . . disk, e-mailed to oneself . . . , or even posted to a Web page for the entire world to see" (12).

The writer has omitted from the source the words *floppy or Zip* before *disk* and *or a confederate* after *oneself.*

On the rare occasions when you want to leave out one or more full sentences, use a period before the three ellipsis dots.

> Charles Lewis, director of the Center for Public Integrity, points out that "by 1987, employers were administering nearly 2,000,000 polygraph tests a year to job applicants and employees. . . . Millions of workers were required to produce urine samples under observation for drug testing . . ." (22).

Ordinarily, do not use an ellipsis mark at the beginning or at the end of a quotation. Your readers will understand that the quoted material is taken from a longer passage, so such marks are not necessary. The only exception occurs when you have dropped words at the end of the final quoted sentence. In such cases, put three ellipsis dots before the closing quotation mark and parenthetical reference, as in the previous example.

Make sure omissions and ellipsis marks do not distort the meaning of your source.

Brackets Brackets allow you to insert your own words into quoted material. You can insert words in brackets to clarify a confusing reference or to keep a sentence grammatical in your context. You also use brackets to indicate that you are changing a letter from capital to lowercase (or vice versa) to fit into your sentence.

> Legal scholar Jay Kesan notes that "[a] decade ago, losses [from employees' computer crimes] were already mounting to five billion dollars annually" (311).

This quotation began *A decade ago . . .* in the source, so the writer indicated the change to lowercase with brackets and inserted words in brackets to clarify the meaning of *losses*.

To indicate an error such as a misspelling in a quotation, insert [sic], including the brackets, right after the error.

> Johnson argues that "while online monitoring is often imagined as harmles [sic], the practice may well threaten employees' rights to privacy" (14).

Setting off long quotations

When you quote more than four typed lines of prose or more than three lines of poetry, set off the quotation by indenting it one inch from the left margin.

Long quotations should be introduced by an informative sentence, usually followed by a colon. Quotation marks are unnecessary because the indented format tells readers that the passage is taken word-for-word from the source.

> Botan and Vorvoreanu examine the role of gender in company practices of electronic surveillance:
>
> > There has never been accurate documentation of the extent of gender differences in surveillance, but by the middle 1990s, estimates of the proportion of surveilled employees that were women ranged from 75% to 85%. . . . Ironically, this gender imbalance in workplace surveillance may be evening out today because advances in surveillance technology are making surveillance of traditionally male dominated fields, such as long-distance truck driving, cheap, easy, and frequently unobtrusive. (127)

Notice that at the end of an indented quotation the parenthetical citation goes outside the final mark of punctuation. (When a quotation is run into your text, the opposite is true. See the sample citations on p. 380.)

MLA-3b Use signal phrases to integrate sources.

Whenever you include a paraphrase, summary, or direct quotation of another writer in your paper, prepare your readers for it with a *signal phrase*. A signal phrase usually names the author of the source and often provides some context. It commonly appears before the source material. To vary your sentence structure, you may decide to interrupt source material with a signal phrase or place the signal phrase after your paraphrase, summary, or direct quotation.

When you write a signal phrase, choose a verb that is appropriate for the way you are using the source (see MLA-1c). Are you providing background, explaining a concept, supporting a claim, lending authority, or refuting a belief? See the chart on page 383 for a list of verbs commonly used in signal phrases. Note that MLA style calls for verbs in the present or present perfect tense (*argues* or *has argued*) to introduce source material unless you include a date that specifies the time of the original author's writing.

Marking boundaries

Readers need to move from your words to the words of a source without feeling a jolt. Avoid dropping quotations into the text without warning. Instead, provide clear signal phrases, including at least the author's name, to indicate the boundary between your words and the source's words. (The signal phrase is highlighted in the second example.)

Using signal phrases in MLA papers

To avoid monotony, try to vary both the language and the placement of your signal phrases.

Model signal phrases

In the words of researchers Greenfield and Davis, ". . ."

As legal scholar Jay Kesan has noted, ". . ."

The ePolicy Institute, an organization that advises companies about reducing risks from technology, reports that ". . ."

". . . ," writes Daniel Tynan, ". . ."

". . . ," attorney Schmitt claims.

Kizza and Ssanyu offer a persuasive counterargument: ". . ."

Verbs in signal phrases

acknowledges	comments	endorses	reasons
adds	compares	grants	refutes
admits	confirms	illustrates	rejects
agrees	contends	implies	reports
argues	declares	insists	responds
asserts	denies	notes	suggests
believes	disputes	observes	thinks
claims	emphasizes	points out	writes

DROPPED QUOTATION

Some experts have argued that a range of legitimate concerns justifies employer monitoring of employee Internet usage. "Employees could accidentally (or deliberately) spill confidential corporate information . . . or allow worms to spread throughout a corporate network" (Tynan).

QUOTATION WITH SIGNAL PHRASE

Some experts have argued that a range of legitimate concerns justifies employer monitoring of employee Internet usage. As *PC World* columnist Daniel Tynan points out, "Employees could accidentally (or deliberately) spill confidential corporate information . . . or allow worms to spread throughout a corporate network."

Establishing authority

Good research writing uses evidence from reliable sources. The first time you mention a source, include in the signal phrase the author's title, credentials, or experience—anything that would help your readers recognize the source's authority. (Signal phrases are highlighted in the next two examples.)

SOURCE WITH NO CREDENTIALS

> Jay Kesan points out that the law holds employers liable for employees' actions such as violations of copyright laws, the distribution of offensive or graphic sexual material, and illegal disclosure of confidential information (312).

SOURCE WITH CREDENTIALS

> Legal scholar Jay Kesan points out that the law holds employers liable for employees' actions such as violations of copyright laws, the distribution of offensive or graphic sexual material, and illegal disclosure of confidential information (312).

When you establish your source's authority, as with the phrase *Legal scholar* in the previous example, you also signal to readers your own credibility as a responsible researcher who has located trustworthy sources.

Introducing summaries and paraphrases

Introduce most summaries and paraphrases with a signal phrase that names the author and places the material in the context of your argument. Readers will then understand that everything between the signal phrase and the parenthetical citation summarizes or paraphrases the cited source.

Without the signal phrase (highlighted) in the following example, readers might think that only the quotation at the end is being cited, when in fact the whole paragraph is based on the source.

> Frederick Lane believes that the personal computer has posed new challenges for employers worried about workplace productivity. Whereas early desktop computers were primitive enough to prevent employees from using them to waste time, the machines have become so sophisticated that they now make non-work-related computer activities easy and inviting. Many employees spend considerable company time customizing features and playing games on their computers. But perhaps most problematic from the employer's point of view, Lane asserts, is giving employees access to the Internet, "roughly the equivalent of installing a gazillion-channel television set for each employee" (15-16).

There are times when a summary or a paraphrase does not require a signal phrase naming the author. When the context makes clear where the cited material begins, you may omit the signal phrase and include the author's last name in parentheses.

Integrating statistics and other facts

When you are citing a statistic or another specific fact, a signal phrase is often not necessary. In most cases, readers will understand that the citation refers to the statistic or fact (not the whole paragraph).

> Roughly 60% of responding companies reported disciplining employees who had used the Internet in ways the companies deemed inappropriate; 30% had fired their employees for those transgressions (Greenfield and Davis 347).

There is nothing wrong, however, with using a signal phrase to introduce a statistic or another fact.

Putting source material in context

Readers should not have to guess why source material appears in your paper. A signal phrase can help you connect your own ideas and those of another writer by clarifying how the source will contribute to your paper (see R2-a).

If you use another writer's words, you must explain how they relate to your point. In other words, you must put the source in context. It's a good idea to embed a quotation between sentences of your own. In addition to introducing it with a signal phrase, follow it with interpretive comments that link the quotation to your paper's argument (see also MLA-3c).

QUOTATION WITH EFFECTIVE CONTEXT

The difference, Lane argues, between old methods of data gathering and electronic surveillance involves quantity:

> Technology makes it possible for employers to gather enormous amounts of data about employees, often far beyond what is necessary to satisfy safety or productivity concerns. And the trends that drive technology—faster, smaller, cheaper—make it possible for larger and larger numbers of employers to gather ever-greater amounts of personal data. (3-4)

In an age when employers can collect data whenever employees use their computers—when they send e-mail, surf the Web, or even arrive at or depart from their workstations—the challenge for both employers and employees is to determine how much is too much.

MLA-3c Synthesize sources.

When you synthesize multiple sources in a research paper, you create a conversation about your research topic. You show readers that your argument is based on your active analysis and integration of ideas, not just a list of quotations and paraphrases. Your synthesis will show how your sources relate to one another; one source may support, extend, or counter the ideas of another. Readers should be able to see how each source functions in your argument (see R2-a).

Considering how sources relate to your argument

Before you integrate sources and show readers how they relate to one another, consider how each one might contribute to your own argument. As student writer Anna Orlov became more informed about Internet surveillance in the workplace, she asked herself these questions: *What do I think about monitoring employees online? Which sources might extend or illustrate the points I want to make? Which sources voice opposing points of view that I need to address?* With these questions in mind, Orlov read and annotated sources, including an argument in favor of workplace surveillance. (See the example on p. 434.)

Placing sources in conversation

When you synthesize sources, you show readers how the ideas of one source relate to those of another by connecting and analyzing the ideas in the context of your argument. Keep the emphasis on your own writing. After all, you've done the research and thought through the issues, so you should control the conversation. The thread of your argument should be easy to identify and to understand, with or without your sources.

SAMPLE SYNTHESIS (DRAFT)

Student writer Anna Orlov begins with a claim that needs support.

Signal phrases indicate how sources contribute to Orlov's paper and show that the ideas that follow are not her own.

Student writer

Productivity is not easily measured in the wired workplace. As a result, employers find it difficult to determine how much freedom to allow their employees. On the one hand, computers and Internet access give employees powerful tools to carry out their jobs; on the other hand, the same technology offers constant temptations to avoid work. As a 2005 study by *Salary.com* and *America Online* indicates, the Internet ranked as the top choice among employees for ways of wasting time on the job (Frauenheim). Chris Gonsalves, an editor for

Source 1

PRACTICE hackerhandbooks.com/writersref
> MLA > MLA 3–1 to MLA 3–4

eWeek.com, argues that technology has changed the terms between employers and employees: "While bosses can easily detect and interrupt water-cooler chatter," he writes, "the employee who is shopping at Lands' End or IMing with fellow fantasy baseball managers may actually appear to be working." The gap between observable behaviors and actual online activities has motivated some employers to invest in surveillance programs.

Source 2

Student writer

Orlov presents a counterposition to extend her argument.

Many experts, however, disagree with employers' assumption that online monitoring can increase productivity. Employment law attorney Joseph Schmitt argues that, particularly for salaried employees, "a company shouldn't care whether employees spend one or 10 hours on the Internet as long as they are getting their jobs done—and provided that they are not accessing inappropriate sites" (qtd. in Verespej). Other experts even argue that time spent on personal Internet browsing can actually be productive for companies. According to Bill Coleman, an executive at *Salary.com,* "Personal Internet use and casual office conversations often turn into new business ideas or suggestions for gaining operating efficiencies" (qtd. in Frauenheim). Employers, in other words, may benefit from showing more faith in their employees' ability to exercise their autonomy.

Source 3

Student writer

Orlov builds her case—each quoted passage offers a more detailed claim or example in support of her larger claim.

Source 4

Student writer

In this draft, Orlov uses her own analyses to shape the conversation among her sources. She does not simply string quotations together or allow her sources to overwhelm her writing. The final sentence, written in her own voice, gives her an opportunity to explain to readers how the various sources support her argument.

When synthesizing sources, ask yourself the following questions:

- Which sources inform, support, or extend your argument?
- Have you varied the function of sources—to provide background, to explain concepts, to lend authority, and to anticipate counterarguments? Do you use signal phrases to indicate these functions?
- Do you explain how your sources support your argument?
- Do you connect and analyze sources in your own voice?
- Is your own argument easy to identify and to understand, with or without your sources?

Reviewing an MLA paper: Use of sources

Use of quotations

- Is quoted material enclosed in quotation marks (unless it has been set off from the text)? (See MLA-2b.)
- Is quoted language word-for-word accurate? If not, do brackets or ellipsis marks indicate the changes or omissions? (See pp. 380–81.)
- Does a clear signal phrase (usually naming the author) prepare readers for each quotation and for the purpose the quotation serves? (See MLA-3b.)
- Does a parenthetical citation follow each quotation? (See MLA-4a.)
- Is each quotation put in context? (See MLA-3c.)

Use of summaries and paraphrases

- Are summaries and paraphrases free of plagiarized wording—not copied or half-copied from the source? (See MLA-2c.)
- Are summaries and paraphrases documented with parenthetical citations? (See MLA-4a.)
- Do readers know where the cited material begins? In other words, does a signal phrase mark the boundary between your words and the summary or paraphrase? Or does the context alone make clear exactly what you are citing? (See MLA-3b.)
- Does a signal phrase prepare readers for the purpose the summary or paraphrase has in your argument?

Use of statistics and other facts

- Are statistics and facts (other than common knowledge) documented with parenthetical citations? (See MLA-2a.)
- If there is no signal phrase, will readers understand exactly which facts are being cited? (See MLA-3b.)

MLA-4 Documenting sources

In English and other humanities classes, you may be asked to use the MLA (Modern Language Association) system for documenting sources, which is set forth in the *MLA Handbook for Writers of Research Papers,* 7th ed. (New York: MLA, 2009).

MLA recommends in-text citations that refer readers to a list of works cited. A typical in-text citation names the author of the source, often in a signal phrase, and gives a page number in parentheses. At the end of the paper, a list of works cited provides publication information about the source; the list is alphabetized by authors' last names (or by titles for works without authors). There is a direct connection between the in-text citation and the alphabetized listing. In the following example, that connection is highlighted in orange.

IN-TEXT CITATION

Jay Kesan notes that even though many companies now routinely monitor employees through electronic means, "there may exist less intrusive safeguards for employers" (293).

ENTRY IN THE LIST OF WORKS CITED

Kesan, Jay P. "Cyber-Working or Cyber-Shirking? A First Principles Examination of Electronic Privacy in the Workplace." *Florida Law Review* 54.2 (2002): 289-332. Print.

For a list of works cited that includes this entry, see page 440.

MLA-4a MLA in-text citations

MLA in-text citations are made with a combination of signal phrases and parenthetical references. A signal phrase introduces information taken from a source (a quotation, summary, paraphrase, or fact); usually the signal phrase includes the author's name. The parenthetical reference comes after the cited material, often at the end of the sentence. It includes at least a page number (except for unpaginated sources, such as those found online). In the models in MLA-4a, the elements of the in-text citation are highlighted in orange.

IN-TEXT CITATION

Kwon points out that the Fourth Amendment does not give employees any protections from employers' "unreasonable searches and seizures" (6).

Readers can look up the author's last name in the alphabetized list of works cited, where they will learn the work's title and other publication information. If readers decide to consult the source, the page number will take them straight to the passage that has been cited.

For a directory to the in-text citation models in this section, see page 371, immediately following the tabbed divider.

PRACTICE **hackerhandbooks.com/writersref**
> MLA > MLA 4–1 to MLA 4–3

Basic rules for print and online sources

The MLA system of in-text citations, which depends heavily on authors' names and page numbers, was created with print sources in mind. Although many online sources have unclear authorship and lack page numbers, the basic rules are the same for both print and online sources.

The models in this section (items 1–5) show how the MLA system usually works and explain what to do if your source has no author or page numbers.

1. Author named in a signal phrase Ordinarily, introduce the material being cited with a signal phrase that includes the author's name. In addition to preparing readers for the source, the signal phrase allows you to keep the parenthetical citation brief.

> Frederick Lane reports that employers do not necessarily have to use software to monitor how their employees use the Web: employers can "use a hidden video camera pointed at an employee's monitor" and even position a camera "so that a number of monitors [can] be viewed at the same time" (147).

The signal phrase—*Frederick Lane reports*—names the author; the parenthetical citation gives the page number of the book in which the quoted words may be found.

Notice that the period follows the parenthetical citation. When a quotation ends with a question mark or an exclamation point, leave the end punctuation inside the quotation mark and add a period at the end of your sentence. (See also the note on p. 284.)

> O'Connor asks a critical question: "When does Internet surveillance cross the line between corporate responsibility and invasion of privacy?" (16).

2. Author named in parentheses If a signal phrase does not name the author, put the author's last name in parentheses along with the page number. Use no punctuation between the name and the page number.

> Companies can monitor employees' every keystroke without legal penalty, but they may have to combat low morale as a result (Lane 129).

3. Author unknown Either use the complete title in a signal phrase or use a short form of the title in parentheses. Titles of books are italicized; titles of articles are put in quotation marks.

> A popular keystroke logging program operates invisibly on workers' computers yet provides supervisors with details of the workers' online activities ("Automatically").

TIP: Before assuming that a Web source has no author, do some detective work. Often the author's name is available but is not easy to find. For example, it may appear at the end of the page, in tiny print. Or it may appear on another page of the site, such as the home page.

NOTE: If a source has no author and is sponsored by a corporation or government agency, name the corporation or agency as the author (see items 8 and 17 on pp. 392 and 395, respectively).

4. Page number unknown Do not include the page number if a work lacks page numbers, as is the case with many Web sources. Even if a printout from a Web site shows page numbers, treat the source as unpaginated in the in-text citation because not all printouts give the same page numbers. (When the pages of a Web source are stable, as in PDF files, supply a page number in your in-text citation.)

> As a 2005 study by *Salary.com* and *America Online* indicates, the Internet ranked as the top choice among employees for ways of wasting time on the job; it beat talking with co-workers—the second most popular method—by a margin of nearly two to one (Frauenheim).

If a source has numbered paragraphs or sections, use "par." (or "pars.") or "sec." (or "secs.") in the parentheses: (Smith, par. 4). Notice that a comma follows the author's name.

5. One-page source If the source is one page long, MLA allows (but does not require) you to omit the page number. Even so, it's a good idea to supply the page number because without it readers may not know where your citation ends or, worse, may not realize that you have provided a citation at all.

NO PAGE NUMBER IN CITATION

> Anush Yegyazarian reports that in 2000 the National Labor Relations Board's Office of the General Counsel helped win restitution for two workers who had been dismissed because their employers were displeased by the employees' e-mails about work-related issues. The case points to the ongoing struggle to define what constitutes protected speech in the workplace.

PAGE NUMBER IN CITATION

> Anush Yegyazarian reports that in 2000 the National Labor Relations Board's Office of the General Counsel helped win restitution for two workers who had been dismissed because their employers were displeased by the employees' e-mails about work-related issues (62). The case points to the ongoing struggle to define what constitutes protected speech in the workplace.

Variations on the basic rules

This section describes the MLA guidelines for handling a variety of situations not covered by the basic rules in items 1–5. These rules for in-text citations are the same for both print and online sources.

6. Two or three authors Name the authors in a signal phrase, as in the following example, or include their last names in the parenthetical reference: (Kizza and Ssanyu 2).

> Kizza and Ssanyu note that "employee monitoring is a dependable, capable, and very affordable process of electronically or otherwise recording all employee activities at work" and elsewhere (2).

When three authors are named in the parentheses, separate the names with commas: (Alton, Davies, and Rice 56).

7. Four or more authors Name all of the authors or include only the first author's name followed by "et al." (Latin for "and others"). The format you use should match the format in your works cited entry (see item 3 on p. 399).

> The study was extended for two years, and only after results were reviewed by an independent panel did the researchers publish their findings (Blaine et al. 35).

8. Organization as author When the author is a corporation or an organization, name that author either in the signal phrase or in the parentheses. (For a government agency as author, see item 17 on p. 395.)

> According to a 2001 survey of human resources managers by the American Management Association, more than three-quarters of the responding companies reported disciplining employees for "misuse or personal use of office telecommunications equipment" (2).

In the list of works cited, the American Management Association is treated as the author and alphabetized under *A*. When you give the organization name in parentheses, abbreviate common words in the name: "Assn.," "Dept.," "Natl.," "Soc.," and so on.

> In a 2001 survey of human resources managers, more than three-quarters of the responding companies reported disciplining employees for "misuse or personal use of office telecommunications equipment" (Amer. Management Assn. 2).

9. Authors with the same last name If your list of works cited includes works by two or more authors with the same last name, include the author's first name in the signal phrase or first initial in the parentheses.

> Estimates of the frequency with which employers monitor employees' use of the Internet each day vary widely (A. Jones 15).

10. Two or more works by the same author Mention the title of the work in the signal phrase or include a short version of the title in the parentheses.

> The American Management Association and ePolicy Institute have tracked employers' practices in monitoring employees' e-mail use. The groups' 2003 survey found that one-third of companies had a policy of keeping and reviewing employees' e-mail messages ("2003 E-mail" 2); in 2005, more than 55% of companies engaged in e-mail monitoring ("2005 Electronic" 1).

Titles of articles and other short works are placed in quotation marks; titles of books are italicized.

In the rare case when both the author's name and a short title must be given in parentheses, separate them with a comma.

> A 2004 survey found that 20% of employers responding had employees' e-mail "subpoenaed in the course of a lawsuit or regulatory investigation," up 7% from the previous year (Amer. Management Assn. and ePolicy Inst., "2004 Workplace" 1).

11. Two or more works in one citation To cite more than one source in the parentheses, give the citations in alphabetical order and separate them with a semicolon.

> Several researchers have analyzed the reasons that companies monitor employees' use of the Internet at work (Botan and Vorvoreanu 128-29; Kesan 317-19; Kizza and Ssanyu 3-7).

Multiple citations can be distracting, so you should not overuse the technique. If you want to point to several sources that discuss a particular topic, consider using an information note instead (see MLA-4c).

12. Repeated citations from the same source When your paper is about a single work of fiction or nonfiction (such as an essay), you do not need to include the author's name each time you quote from or paraphrase the work. After you mention the author's name at the beginning of your paper, you may include just the page numbers in your parenthetical citations.

> In Susan Glaspell's short story "A Jury of Her Peers," two women accompany their husbands and a county attorney to an isolated house where a farmer named John Wright has been choked to death in his bed with a rope. The chief suspect is Wright's wife, Minnie, who is in jail awaiting trial. The sheriff's wife, Mrs. Peters, has come along to gather some personal items for Minnie, and Mrs. Hale has joined her. Early in the story, Mrs. Hale sympathizes with Minnie and objects to the way the male investigators are "snoopin' round and criticizin'" her kitchen (191). In contrast, Mrs. Peters shows respect for the law, saying that the men are doing "no more than their duty" (191).

In a paper with multiple sources, if you are citing a source more than once in a paragraph, you may omit the author's name after the first mention in the paragraph as long as it is clear that you are still referring to the same source.

13. Encyclopedia or dictionary entry Unless an entry in an encyclopedia or a dictionary has an author, the source will be alphabetized in the list of works cited under the word or entry that you consulted (see item 27 on p. 409). Either in your text or in your parenthetical citation, mention the word or entry. No page number is required, since readers can easily look up the word or entry.

> The word *crocodile* has a surprisingly complex etymology ("Crocodile").

14. Multivolume work If your paper cites more than one volume of a multivolume work, indicate in the parentheses the volume you are referring to, followed by a colon and the page number.

> In his studies of gifted children, Terman describes a pattern of accelerated language acquisition (2: 279).

If you cite only one volume of a multivolume work throughout your paper, you will include the volume number in the list of works cited and will not need to include it in the parentheses. (See the second example in item 26, at the top of p. 409.)

15. Entire work Use the author's name in a signal phrase or a parenthetical citation. There is no need to use a page number.

> Lane explores the evolution of surveillance in the workplace.

16. Selection in an anthology Put the name of the author of the selection (not the editor of the anthology) in the signal phrase or the parentheses.

In "Love Is a Fallacy," the narrator's logical teachings disintegrate when Polly declares that she should date Petey because "[h]e's got a raccoon coat" (Shulman 379).

In the list of works cited, the work is alphabetized by the author's last name, not by the name of the editor of the anthology. (See item 24 on pp. 407–08.)

Shulman, Max. "Love Is a Fallacy." *Current Issues and Enduring Questions.* Ed. Sylvan Barnet and Hugo Bedau. 8th ed. Boston: Bedford, 2008. 371-79. Print.

17. Government document When a government agency is the author, you will alphabetize it in the list of works cited under the name of the government, such as *United States* or *Great Britain* (see item 73 on p. 424). For this reason, you must name the government as well as the agency in your in-text citation.

Online monitoring by the United States Department of the Interior over a one-week period found that employees' use of "sexually explicit and gambling websites . . . accounted for over 24 hours of Internet use" and that "computer users spent over 2,004 hours accessing game and auction sites" during the same period (3).

18. Historical document For a historical document, such as the United States Constitution or the Canadian Charter of Rights and Freedoms, provide the document title, neither italicized nor in quotation marks, along with relevant article and section numbers. In parenthetical citations, use common abbreviations such as "art." and "sec." and abbreviations of well-known titles (US Const., art. 1, sec. 2).

While the United States Constitution provides for the formation of new states (art. 4, sec. 3), it does not explicitly allow or prohibit the secession of states.

For other historical documents, cite as you would any other work, by the first element in the works cited entry (see item 74 on p. 425).

19. Legal source For legislative acts (laws) and court cases, name the act or case either in a signal phrase or in parentheses. Italicize the names of cases but not the names of acts.

The Jones Act of 1917 granted US citizenship to Puerto Ricans.

In 1857, Chief Justice Roger B. Taney declared in *Dred Scott v. Sandford* that blacks, whether enslaved or free, could not be citizens of the United States.

20. Visual such as a photograph, map, or chart To cite a visual that has a figure number in the source, use the abbreviation "fig." and the number in place of a page number in your parenthetical citation: (Manning, fig. 4). Spell out the word "figure" if you refer to it in your text.

To cite a visual that does not have a figure number in a print source, use the visual's title or a general description in your text and cite the author and page number as for any other source.

For a visual that is not contained in a source such as a book or periodical, identify the visual in your text and then cite it using the first element in the works cited entry: the photographer's or artist's name or the title of the work. (See items 69 and 72 on pp. 423 and 424.)

Photographs such as *Woman Aircraft Worker* (Bransby) and *Women Welders* (Parks) demonstrate the US government's attempt to document the contributions of women on the home front during World War II.

21. E-mail, letter, or personal interview Cite e-mail messages, personal letters, and personal interviews by the name listed in the works cited entry, as you would for any other source. Identify the type of source in your text if you feel it is necessary. (See item 53 on p. 419 and items 83 and 84 on p. 427.)

22. Web site or other electronic source Your in-text citation for an electronic source should follow the same guidelines as for other sources. If the source lacks page numbers but has numbered paragraphs, sections, or divisions, use those numbers with the appropriate abbreviation in your in-text citation: "par.," "sec.," "ch.," "pt.," and so on. Do not add such numbers if the source itself does not use them; simply give the author or title in your in-text citation.

Julian Hawthorne points out profound differences between his father and Ralph Waldo Emerson but concludes that, in their lives and their writing, "together they met the needs of nearly all that is worthy in human nature" (ch. 4).

23. Indirect source (source quoted in another source) When a writer's or a speaker's quoted words appear in a source written by someone else, begin the parenthetical citation with the abbreviation "qtd. in."

According to Bill Coleman, an executive at *Salary.com,* "Personal Internet use and casual office conversations often turn into new business ideas or suggestions for gaining operating efficiencies" (qtd. in Frauenheim).

Literary works and sacred texts

Literary works and sacred texts are usually available in a variety of editions. Your list of works cited will specify which edition you are using, and your in-text citation will usually consist of a page number from the edition you consulted (see item 24). When possible, give enough information—such as book parts, play divisions, or line numbers—so that readers can locate the cited passage in any edition of the work (see items 25–27).

24. Literary work without parts or line numbers Many literary works, such as most short stories and many novels and plays, do not have parts or line numbers. In such cases, simply cite the page number.

> At the end of Kate Chopin's "The Story of an Hour," Mrs. Mallard drops dead upon learning that her husband is alive. In the final irony of the story, doctors report that she has died of a "joy that kills" (25).

25. Verse play or poem For verse plays, give act, scene, and line numbers that can be located in any edition of the work. Use arabic numerals and separate the numbers with periods.

> In Shakespeare's *King Lear,* Gloucester, blinded for suspected treason, learns a profound lesson from his tragic experience: "A man may see how this world goes / with no eyes" (4.2.148-49).

For a poem, cite the part, stanza, and line numbers, if it has them, separated by periods.

> The Green Knight claims to approach King Arthur's court "because the praise of you, prince, is puffed so high, / And your manor and your men are considered so magnificent" (1.12.258-59).

For poems that are not divided into numbered parts or stanzas, use line numbers. For a first reference, use the word "lines": (lines 5-8). Thereafter use just the numbers: (12-13).

26. Novel with numbered divisions When a novel has numbered divisions, put the page number first, followed by a semicolon and the book, part, or chapter in which the passage may be found. Use abbreviations such as "bk.," "pt.," and "ch."

> One of Kingsolver's narrators, teenager Rachel, pushes her vocabulary beyond its limits. For example, Rachel complains that being forced to live in the Congo with her missionary family is "a sheer tapestry of justice" because her chances of finding a boyfriend are "dull and void" (117; bk. 2, ch. 10).

27. Sacred text When citing a sacred text such as the Bible or the Qur'an, name the edition you are using in your works cited entry (see item 28 on p. 409). In your parenthetical citation, give the book, chapter, and verse (or their equivalent), separated with periods. Common abbreviations for books of the Bible are acceptable.

> Consider the words of Solomon: "If your enemy is hungry, give him bread to eat; and if he is thirsty, give him water to drink" (*Oxford Annotated Bible,* Prov. 25.21).

The title of a sacred work is italicized when it refers to a specific edition of the work, as in the preceding example. If you refer to the book in a general sense in your text, neither italicize it nor put it in quotation marks. (See also the note in P10-a, p. 305.)

> The Bible and the Qur'an provide allegories that help readers understand how to lead a moral life.

MLA-4b MLA list of works cited

An alphabetized list of works cited, which appears at the end of your research paper, gives publication information for each of the sources you have cited in the paper. Include only sources that you have quoted, summarized, or paraphrased. (For information about preparing the list, see p. 431; for a sample list of works cited, see p. 440.)

For a directory to the works cited models in this section, see pages 371–72, immediately following the tabbed divider.

General guidelines for works cited in MLA style

In an MLA works cited entry, invert the first author's name (last name first, followed by a comma and the first name); put all other names in normal order. In titles of works, capitalize all words except articles (*a*, *an*, *the*), prepositions (*into*, *between*, and so on), coordinating conjunctions (*and*, *but*, *or*, *nor*, *for*, *so*, *yet*), and the *to* in infinitives—unless they are the first or last word of the title or subtitle. Use quotation marks for titles of articles and other short works, such as brief documents from Web sites; italicize titles of books and other long works, such as entire Web sites.

Give the city of publication without a state name. Shorten publishers' names, usually to the first principal word ("Wiley" for "John Wiley and Sons," for instance); abbreviate "University" and "Press" in the names of university publishers: UP of Florida. For the date of publication, use the date on the title page or the most recent date on the copyright page.

For all works cited entries, include the medium in which a work was published, produced, or delivered. Usually put the medium at the end of the entry, capitalized but neither italicized nor in quotation marks. Typical designations for the medium are "Print," "Web," "Radio," "Television," "CD," "Film," "Videocassette," "DVD," "Photograph," "Performance," "Lecture," "MP3 file," and "PDF file." (See specific items throughout MLA-4b.)

Listing authors (print and online)

Alphabetize entries in the list of works cited by authors' last names (or by title if a work has no author). The author's name is important because citations in the text of the paper refer to it and readers will look for it at the beginning of an entry in the alphabetized list.

NAME CITED IN TEXT

According to Nancy Flynn, . . .

BEGINNING OF WORKS CITED ENTRY

Flynn, Nancy.

1. Single author

author: last name first | title (book) | city of publication | publisher | date | medium

Wood, James. *How Fiction Works*. New York: Farrar, 2008. Print.

2. Two or three authors

first author: last name first | second author: in normal order | title (book) | city of publication | publisher | date | medium

Gourevitch, Philip, and Errol Morris. *Standard Operating Procedure*. New York: Penguin, 2008. Print.

first author: last name first | other authors: in normal order | title (newspaper article) | newspaper title | date of publication | page(s) | medium

Farmer, John, John Azzarello, and Miles Kara. "Real Heroes, Fake Stories." *New York Times* 14 Sept. 2008: WK10. Print.

3. Four or more authors

first author: last name first | other authors: in normal order | title (book) | edition number | city of publication | publisher | date | medium

Harris, Shon, Allen Harper, Chris Eagle, and Jonathan Ness. *Gray Hat Hacking*. 2nd ed. New York: McGraw, 2007. Print.

Name all the authors or name the first author followed by "et al." (Latin for "and others"). In an in-text citation, use the same form for the authors' names as you use in the works cited entry. See item 7 on page 392.

4. Organization as author

author: organization name, not abbreviated
title (book)
National Wildlife Federation. *Rain Check: Conservation Groups Monitor Mercury Levels in Milwaukee's Rain.* Ann Arbor: Natl. Wildlife Federation, 2001. Print.
city of publication
publisher, with common abbreviations
date
medium
Women of Protest: Photographs from the Records of the National Woman's Party. Lib. of Cong., n.d. Web. 29 Sept. 2008.

For a publication by a government agency, see item 73. Your in-text citation should also treat the organization as the author (see item 8 on p. 392).

5. Unknown author

Article or other short work

title (newspaper article) | label | newspaper title | date of publication | page(s) | medium

"Poverty, by Outdated Numbers." Editorial. *Boston Globe* 20 Sept. 2008: A16. Print.

title (TV episode) | title (TV program) | producer | network | station | city of broadcast | date of broadcast | medium

"Heat." *Frontline.* Prod. Martin Smith. PBS. KTWU, Topeka. 21 Oct. 2008. Television.

For other examples of an article with no author and of a television program, see items 13 and 65, respectively.

Book, entire Web site, or other long work

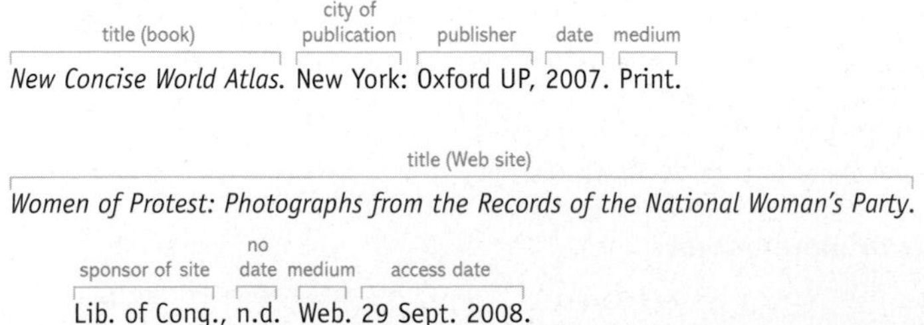

Before concluding that the author of an online source is unknown, check carefully (see the tip at the top of p. 391). Also remember

that an organization or a government may be the author (see items 4 and 73).

6. Two or more works by the same author If your list of works cited includes two or more works by the same author, first alphabetize the works by title (ignoring the article *A*, *An*, or *The* at the beginning of a title). Use the author's name for the first entry only; for subsequent entries, use three hyphens followed by a period. The three hyphens must stand for exactly the same name or names as in the first entry.

Knopp, Lisa. *Field of Vision.* Iowa City: U of Iowa P, 1996. Print.

---. *The Nature of Home: A Lexicon and Essays.* Lincoln: U of Nebraska P, 2002. Print.

Articles in periodicals (print)

This section shows how to prepare works cited entries for articles in print magazines, journals, and newspapers. See "General guidelines" and "Listing authors" on pages 398 and 399 for how to handle basic parts of the entries. See also "Online sources" beginning on page 412 for articles from Web sites and articles accessed through a library's database.

For articles appearing on consecutive pages, provide the range of pages (see items 7 and 8). When an article does not appear on consecutive pages, give the first page number followed by a plus sign: 32+. For dates requiring a month, abbreviate all but May, June, and July. For an illustrated citation of an article in a periodical, see pages 402–03.

7. Article in a journal (paginated by volume or by issue)

author: last name first | article title | journal title

Blackburn, Robin. "Economic Democracy: Meaningful, Desirable, Feasible?" *Daedalus*

volume, issue | year | page(s) | medium

136.3 (2007): 36-45. Print.

8. Article in a monthly magazine

author: last name first | article title | magazine title | date: month + year | page(s)

Lanting, Frans. "Life: A Journey through Time." *Audubon* Nov.-Dec. 2006: 48-52.

medium

Print.

Citation at a glance: Article in a periodical (MLA)

To cite an article in a print periodical in MLA style, include the following elements:

1 Author of article
2 Title and subtitle of article
3 Title of periodical
4 Volume and issue number (for journal)
5 Date or year of publication
6 Page number(s) of article
7 Medium

TITLE PAGE

FIRST PAGE OF ARTICLE

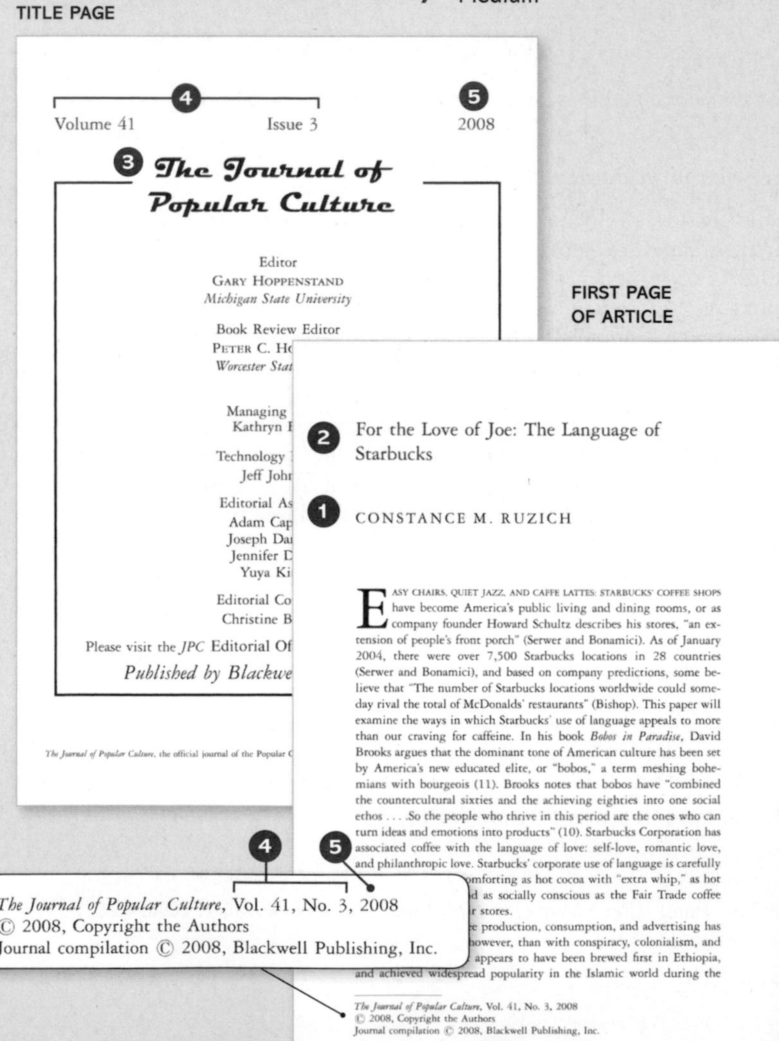

WORKS CITED ENTRY FOR AN ARTICLE IN A PRINT PERIODICAL

1 2 3

Ruzich, Constance M. "For the Love of Joe: The Language of Starbucks." *Journal of*

4 5 6 7

Popular Culture 41.3 (2008): 428-42. Print.

For more on citing print periodical articles in MLA style, see pages 401–04.

9. Article in a weekly magazine

author: last name first | article title | magazine title | date: day + month + year | page(s) | medium

von Drehle, David. "The Ghosts of Memphis." *Time* 7 Apr. 2008: 34-37. Print.

10. Article in a daily newspaper Give the page range of the article. If the article does not appear on consecutive pages, use a plus sign (+) after the first page number. If the city of publication is not obvious from the title of the newspaper, include the city in brackets after the name of the newspaper.

If sections are identified by letter, include the section letter as part of the page number. If sections are numbered, include the section number between the date and the page number, using the abbreviation "sec."

Page number with section letter

author: last name first | article title | newspaper title | date: day + month + year

McKenna, Phil. "It Takes Just One Village." *New York Times* 23 Sept. 2008, New

name of edition | page | medium

England ed.: D1. Print.

Page number with section number

author: last name first | article title | newspaper title | city of publication

Knox, David Blake. "Lord Archer, Storyteller." *Sunday Independent* [Dublin]

date: day + month + year | section | page | medium

14 Sept. 2008, sec. 2: 9. Print.

11. Abstract of a journal article Include the word "Abstract" after the title of the article.

Walker, Joyce. "Narratives in the Database: Memorializing September 11th Online." Abstract. *Computers and Composition* 24.2 (2007): 121. Print.

12. Article with a title in its title Use single quotation marks around a title of a short work or a quoted term that appears in an article title. Italicize a title or term normally italicized. (See also P5-c.)

Shen, Min. "'Quite a Moon!' The Archetypal Feminine in *Our Town*." *American Drama* 16.2 (2007): 1-14. Print.

13. Editorial or other unsigned article Begin with the article title and alphabetize the entry by the title in the list of works cited.

"Getting the Message: Communicating Electronically with Doctors Can Spur Honesty from Young Patients." Editorial. *Columbus* [OH] *Dispatch* 19 June 2008: 10A. Print.

14. Letter to the editor

Morris, David. "Fiercely Proud." Letter. *Progressive* Feb. 2008: 6. Print.

15. Review For a review of a book, a film, or another type of work, begin with the name of the reviewer and the title of the review, if it has one. Add the words "Rev. of" and the title of the work reviewed, followed by the author, director, or other significant contributor. Give the publication information for the periodical in which the review appears. If the review has no author and no title, begin with "Rev. of" and alphabetize the entry by the first principal word in the title of the work reviewed.

Dodge, Chris. Rev. of *The Radical Jack London: Writings on War and Revolution*, ed. Jonah Raskni. *Utne Reader* Sept.-Oct. 2008: 35. Print.

Lane, Anthony. "Dream On." Rev. of *The Science of Sleep* and *Renaissance*, dir. Michel Gondry. *New Yorker* 25 Sept. 2006: 155-57. Print.

Books (print)

Items 16–33 apply to print books. For online books, see items 41 and 42. For an illustrated citation of a print book, see page 406.

16. Basic format for a book

author: last name first | book title | city of publication | publisher | date

Sacks, Oliver. *Musicophilia: Tales of Music and the Brain*. New York: Knopf, 2007. Print.

medium

Take the information about the book from its title page and copyright page. Use a short form of the publisher's name; omit terms such as "Press," "Inc.," and "Co." except when naming university presses ("Howard UP," for example). If the copyright page lists more than one date, use the most recent one.

17. Book with an author and an editor

author: last name first | book title | editor: in normal order | city of publication | imprint-publisher | date | medium

Plath, Sylvia. *The Unabridged Journals of Sylvia Plath.* Ed. Karen V. Kukil. New York: Anchor-Doubleday, 2000. Print.

The abbreviation "Ed." means "Edited by," so it is the same for one or multiple editors.

18. Book with an author and a translator "Trans." means "Translated by," so it is the same for one or multiple translators.

Scirocco, Alfonso. *Garibaldi: Citizen of the World.* Trans. Allan Cameron. Princeton: Princeton UP, 2007. Print.

19. Book with an editor Begin with the editor's name. For one editor, use "ed." (for "editor") after the name; for multiple editors, use "eds." (for "editors").

Lago, Mary, Linda K. Hughes, and Elizabeth MacLeod Walls, eds. *The BBC Talks of E. M. Forster, 1929-1960.* Columbia: U of Missouri P, 2008. Print.

20. Graphic narrative or illustrated book For a book that combines text and illustrations, begin your citation with the person you wish to emphasize (writer, illustrator, artist) and list any other contributors after the title of the book. Use the abbreviation "illus." and other common labels to identify contributors. If the writer and illustrator are the same person, cite the work as you would a book, with no labels.

Weaver, Dustin, illus. *The Tenth Circle.* By Jodi Picoult. New York: Washington Square, 2006. Print.

Moore, Alan. *V for Vendetta.* Illus. David Lloyd. New York: Vertigo-DC Comics, 2008. Print.

Thompson, Craig. *Blankets.* Marietta: Top Shelf, 2005.

Citation at a glance: Book (MLA)

To cite a print book in MLA style, include the following elements:

1 Author
2 Title and subtitle
3 City of publication
4 Publisher
5 Date of publication
6 Medium

TITLE PAGE

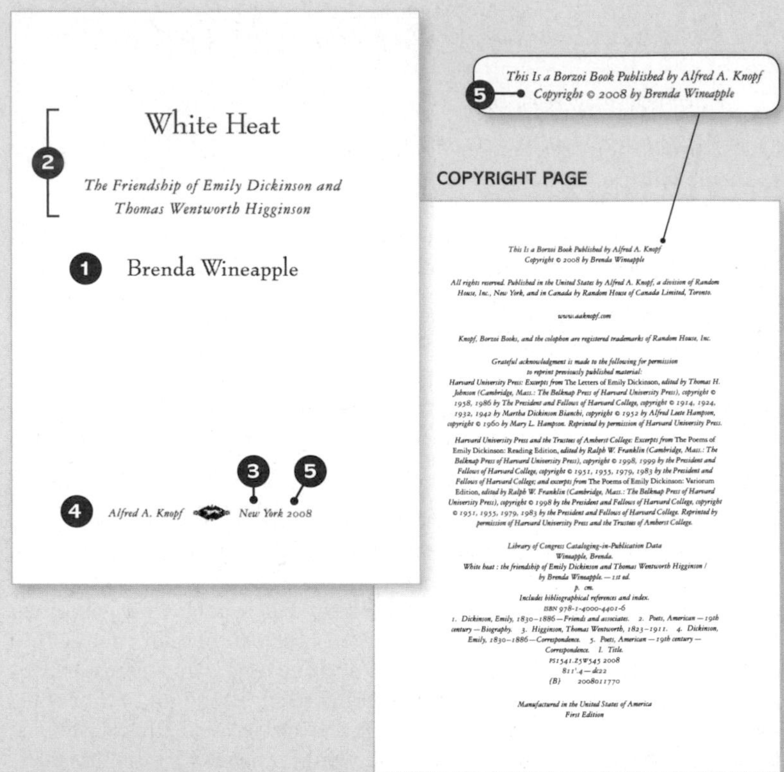

This Is a Borzoi Book Published by Alfred A. Knopf
Copyright © 2008 by Brenda Wineapple

All rights reserved. Published in the United States by Alfred A. Knopf, a division of Random House, Inc., New York, and in Canada by Random House of Canada Limited, Toronto.

www.aaknopf.com

Knopf, Borzoi Books, and the colophon are registered trademarks of Random House, Inc.

Grateful acknowledgment is made to the following for permission to reprint previously published material:
Harvard University Press: Excerpts from The Letters of Emily Dickinson, edited by Thomas H. Johnson (Cambridge, Mass.: The Belknap Press of Harvard University Press), copyright © 1958, 1986 by The President and Fellows of Harvard College, copyright © 1914, 1924, 1932, 1942 by Martha Dickinson Bianchi, copyright © 1952 by Alfred Leete Hampson, copyright © 1960 by Mary L. Hampson. Reprinted by permission of Harvard University Press.

Harvard University Press and the Trustees of Amherst College: Excerpts from The Poems of Emily Dickinson: Reading Edition, edited by Ralph W. Franklin (Cambridge, Mass.: The Belknap Press of Harvard University Press), copyright © 1998, 1999 by the President and Fellows of Harvard College, copyright © 1951, 1955, 1979, 1983 by the President and Fellows of Harvard College; and excerpts from The Poems of Emily Dickinson: Variorum Edition, edited by Ralph W. Franklin (Cambridge, Mass.: The Belknap Press of Harvard University Press), copyright © 1998 by the President and Fellows of Harvard College, copyright © 1951, 1955, 1979, 1983 by the President and Fellows of Harvard College. Reprinted by permission of Harvard University Press and the Trustees of Amherst College.

Library of Congress Cataloging-in-Publication Data
Wineapple, Brenda.
White heat : the friendship of Emily Dickinson and Thomas Wentworth Higginson / by Brenda Wineapple. — 1st ed.
p. cm.
Includes bibliographical references and index.
ISBN 978-1-4000-4401-6
1. Dickinson, Emily, 1830–1886—Friends and associates. 2. Poets, American—19th century—Biography. 3. Higginson, Thomas Wentworth, 1823–1911. 4. Dickinson, Emily, 1830–1886—Correspondence. 5. Poets, American—19th century—Correspondence. I. Title.
PS1541.Z5W545 2008
811'.4—dc22
(B) 2008011770

Manufactured in the United States of America
First Edition

WORKS CITED ENTRY FOR A PRINT BOOK

Wineapple, Brenda. (1) *White Heat: The Friendship of Emily Dickinson and Thomas Wentworth Higginson.* (2) New York: (3) Knopf, (4) 2008. (5) Print. (6)

For more on citing print books in MLA style, see pages 404–11.

21. Book with an author using a pseudonym Give the author's name as it appears on the title page (the pseudonym), and follow it with the author's real name in brackets.

Dinesen, Isak [Karen Blixen]. *Winter's Tales.* 1942. New York: Vintage, 1993. Print.

22. Book in a language other than English If your readers are not familiar with the language of the book, include a translation of the title, italicized and in brackets. Capitalize the title according to the conventions of the book's language, and give the original publication information.

Nemtsov, Boris, and Vladimir Milov. *Putin. Itogi. Nezavisimyi Ekspertnyi Doklad* [*Putin. The Results: An Independent Expert Report*]. Moscow: Novaya Gazeta, 2008. Print.

23. Entire anthology An anthology is a collection of works on a common theme, often with different authors for the selections and usually with an editor for the entire volume. (For an anthology with one editor, use the abbreviation "ed." after the editor's name. For more than one editor, use "eds.")

Dumanis, Michael, and Cate Marvin, eds. *Legitimate Dangers: American Poets of the New Century.* Louisville: Sarabande, 2006. Print.

24. One or more selections from an anthology

One selection from anthology

author of selection: last name first — Brouwer, Joel.
title of selection — "The Spots."
title of anthology — *Legitimate Dangers: American Poets of the New Century.*
editor(s) of anthology: name(s) in normal order — Ed. Michael Dumanis and Cate Marvin.
city of publication — Louisville:
publisher — Sarabande,
date — 2006.
page(s) of selection — 51-52.
medium — Print.

Brouwer, Joel. "The Spots." *Legitimate Dangers: American Poets of the New Century.* Ed. Michael Dumanis and Cate Marvin. Louisville: Sarabande, 2006. 51-52. Print.

The abbreviation "Ed." means "Edited by," so it is the same for one or multiple editors. For an illustrated citation of a selection from an anthology, see pages 410–11.

Two or more selections, with separate anthology entry

If you use two or more works from the same anthology in your paper, provide an entry for the entire anthology (see item 23) and give a shortened entry for each selection. Use the medium only in the entry for the complete anthology. For an illustrated citation of a selection from an anthology, see pages 410–11.

author of selection | title of selection | editor(s) of anthology: last name(s) only | pages(s) of selection

Brouwer, Joel. "The Spots." Dumanis and Marvin 51-52.

editor(s) of anthology | title of anthology | city of publication | publisher | date | medium

Dumanis, Michael, and Cate Marvin, eds. *Legitimate Dangers: American Poets of the New Century.* Louisville: Sarabande, 2006. Print.

author of selection | title of selection | editor(s) of anthology: last name(s) only | page(s) of selection

Keith, Sally. "Orphean Song." Dumanis and Marvin 195-96.

25. Edition other than the first Include the number of the edition (1st, 2nd, 3rd, and so on). If the book has a translator or an editor in addition to the author, give the name of the translator or editor before the edition number, using the abbreviation "Trans." for "Translated by" (see item 18) or "Ed." for "Edited by" (see item 17).

Auletta, Ken. *The Underclass.* 2nd ed. Woodstock: Overlook, 2000. Print.

26. Multivolume work Include the total number of volumes before the city and publisher, using the abbreviation "vols." If the volumes were published over several years, give the inclusive dates of publication. The abbreviation "Ed." means "Edited by," so it is the same for one or multiple editors.

author: last name first | title | editor in normal order | total volumes | city of publication | publisher | inclusive dates | medium

Stark, Freya. *Letters.* Ed. Lucy Moorehead. 8 vols. Salisbury: Compton, 1974-82. Print.

If you cite only one of the volumes in your paper, include the volume number before the city and publisher and give the date of publication for that volume. After the date, give the medium of publication followed by the total number of volumes.

author: last name first | title | editor: in normal order | volume cited | city of publication | publisher | date of volume | medium

Stark, Freya. *Letters*. Ed. Lucy Moorehead. Vol. 5. Salisbury: Compton, 1978. Print.

total volumes

8 vols.

27. Encyclopedia or dictionary entry List the author of the entry (if there is one), the title of the entry, the title of the reference work, the edition number (if any), the date of the edition, and the medium. Volume and page numbers are not necessary because the entries in the source are arranged alphabetically and are therefore easy to locate.

Posner, Rebecca. "Romance Languages." *The Encyclopaedia Britannica: Macropaedia.* 15th ed. 1987. Print.

"Sonata." *The American Heritage Dictionary of the English Language*. 4th ed. 2000. Print.

28. Sacred text Give the title of the sacred text (taken from the title page), italicized; the editor's or translator's name (if any); publication information; and the medium. Add the name of the version, if there is one.

The Oxford Annotated Bible with the Apocrypha. Ed. Herbert G. May and Bruce M. Metzger. New York: Oxford UP, 1965. Print. Rev. Standard Vers.

The Qur'an: Translation. Trans. Abdullah Yusuf Ali. Elmhurst: Tahrike, 2000. Print.

29. Foreword, introduction, preface, or afterword

author of foreword: last name first | book part | book title

Bennett, Hal Zina. Foreword. *Shimmering Images: A Handy Little Guide to Writing*

author of book: in normal order | city of publication | imprint-publisher | date | page(s) of foreword

Memoir. By Lisa Dale Norton. New York: Griffin-St. Martin's, 2008. xiii-xvi.

medium

Print.

If the book part has a title, include it in quotation marks immediately after the author's name and before the label for the book part. If the author of the book part is also the author or editor of the complete work, give only the last name of the author the second time it is used.

Ozick, Cynthia. "Portrait of the Essay as a Warm Body." Introduction. *The Best American Essays 1998*. Ed. Ozick. Boston: Houghton, 1998. xv-xxi. Print.

Citation at a glance: Selection from an anthology (MLA)

To cite a selection from a print anthology in MLA style, include the following elements:

1. Author of selection
2. Title of selection
3. Title and subtitle of anthology
4. Editor(s) of anthology
5. City of publication
6. Publisher
7. Date of publication
8. Page number(s) of selection
9. Medium

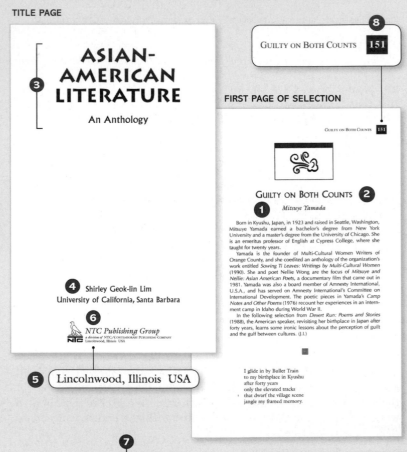

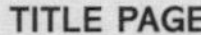
TITLE PAGE

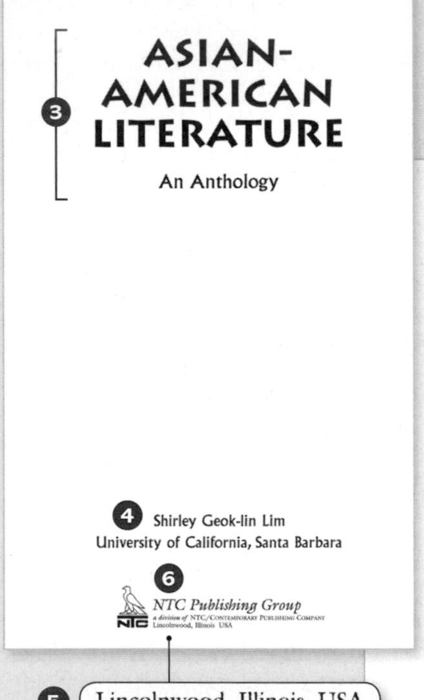
3 ASIAN-AMERICAN LITERATURE

An Anthology

4 Shirley Geok-lin Lim

University of California, Santa Barbara

6 NTC Publishing Group

a division of NTC/Contemporary Publishing Company

Lincolnwood, Illinois USA

5 Lincolnwood, Illinois USA

8 GUILTY ON BOTH COUNTS 151

FIRST PAGE OF SELECTION

GUILTY ON BOTH COUNTS 151

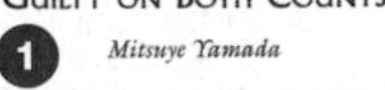
GUILTY ON BOTH COUNTS 2

1 *Mitsuye Yamada*

Born in Kyushu, Japan, in 1923 and raised in Seattle, Washington, Mitsuye Yamada earned a bachelor's degree from New York University and a master's degree from the University of Chicago. She is an emeritus professor of English at Cypress College, where she taught for twenty years.

Yamada is the founder of Multi-Cultural Women Writers of Orange County, and she coedited an anthology of the organization's work entitled *Sowing Ti Leaves: Writings by Multi-Cultural Women* (1990). She and poet Nellie Wong are the focus of *Mitsuye and Nellie: Asian American Poets*, a documentary film that came out in 1981. Yamada was also a board member of Amnesty International, U.S.A., and has served on Amnesty International's Committee on International Development. The poetic pieces in Yamada's *Camp Notes and Other Poems* (1976) recount her experiences in an internment camp in Idaho during World War II.

In the following selection from *Desert Run: Poems and Stories* (1988), the American speaker, revisiting her birthplace in Japan after forty years, learns some ironic lessons about the perception of guilt and the gulf between cultures. (J.L.)

I glide in by Bullet Train
to my birthplace in Kyushu
after forty years
only the elevated tracks
that dwarf the village scene
jangle my framed memory.

FROM COPYRIGHT PAGE

7 Published by NTC/Contemporary Publishing Group, Inc.
4255 West Touhy Avenue, Lincolnwood (Chicago), Illinois 60646-1975 U.S.A.
©2000 NTC/Contemporary Publishing Group, Inc.

WORKS CITED ENTRY FOR A SELECTION FROM AN ANTHOLOGY

1 2 3
Yamada, Mitsuye. "Guilty on Both Counts." *Asian-American Literature: An Anthology.*

4 5 6 7 8 9
Ed. Shirley Geok-lin Lim. Lincolnwood: NTC, 2000. 151-54. Print.

For more on citing selections from anthologies in MLA style, see pages 407–08.

30. Book with a title in its title If the book title contains a title normally italicized, neither italicize the internal title nor place it in quotation marks.

Woodson, Jon. *A Study of Joseph Heller's* Catch-22: *Going Around Twice*. New York: Lang, 2001. Print.

If the title within the title is normally put in quotation marks, retain the quotation marks and italicize the entire book title.

Millás, Juan José. *"Personality Disorders" and Other Stories*. Trans. Gregory B. Kaplan. New York: MLA, 2007. Print. MLA Texts and Trans.

31. Book in a series After the publication information, give the medium of publication and then the series name as it appears on the title page, followed by the series number, if any.

Douglas, Dan. *Assessing Languages for Specific Purposes*. Cambridge: Cambridge UP, 2000. Print. Cambridge Applied Linguistics Ser.

32. Republished book After the title of the book, give the original publication date, followed by the current publication information. If the republished book contains new material, such as an introduction or afterword, include information about the new material after the original date.

Trilling, Lionel. *The Liberal Imagination*. 1950. Introd. Louis Menand. New York: New York Review of Books, 2008. Print.

33. Publisher's imprint If a book was published by a division (an imprint) of a publishing company, give the name of the imprint, a hyphen, and the name of the publisher.

Ackroyd, Peter. *The Fall of Troy*. New York: Talese-Doubleday, 2007. Print.

Online sources

MLA guidelines assume that readers can locate most online sources by entering the author, title, or other identifying information in a search engine or a database. Consequently, the *MLA Handbook* does not require a Web address (URL) in citations for online sources. If your instructor requires one, see the note at the end of item 34.

MLA style calls for a sponsor or a publisher in works cited entries for most online sources. If a source has no sponsor or publisher, use the abbreviation "N.p." (for "No publisher") in the sponsor position. If there is no date of publication or update, use "n.d." (for "no date") after the sponsor. For an article in an online journal or an article from a database, give page numbers if they are available; if they are not, use the abbreviation "n. pag." (See item 37.)

34. Entire Web site

Web site with author

author: last name first | title of Web site | sponsor of site (personal page) | update | medium

Peterson, Susan Lynn. *The Life of Martin Luther*. Susan Lynn Peterson, 2005. Web.

date of access: day + month + year

24 Jan. 2009.

Web site with organization (group) as author

organization name: not abbreviated | title of Web site | sponsor: abbreviated | update | medium

American Library Association. *American Library Association*. ALA, 2008. Web.

date of access: day + month + year

14 Jan. 2009.

Web site with no author

title of Web site | sponsor of site | update | medium

Margaret Sanger Papers Project. History Dept., New York U, 18 Oct. 2000. Web.

date of access: day + month + year

6 Jan. 2009.

Web site with editor

See item 19 (p. 405) for listing the name(s) of editor(s).

Halsall, Paul, ed. *Internet Modern History Sourcebook*. Fordham U, 22 Sept. 2001. Web. 19 Jan. 2009.

Web site with no title

Use the label "Home page" or another appropriate description in place of a title.

Yoon, Mina. Home page. Oak Ridge Natl. Laboratory, 28 Dec. 2006. Web. 12 Jan. 2009.

NOTE: If your instructor requires a URL for Web sources, include the URL, enclosed in angle brackets, at the end of the entry. When a URL in a works cited entry must be divided at the end of a line, break it after a slash. Do not insert a hyphen.

Peterson, Susan Lynn. *The Life of Martin Luther.* Susan Lynn Peterson, 2005. Web. 24 Jan. 2009. <http://www.susanlynnpeterson.com/index_files/luther.htm>.

35. Short work from a Web site Short works include articles, poems, and other documents that are not book length or that appear as internal pages on a Web site. For an illustrated citation of a short work from a Web site, see pages 414–15.

Short work with author

author: last name first | title of short work | title of Web site | sponsor | no update date | medium | date of access: day + month + year

Shiva, Vandana. "Bioethics: A Third World Issue." *NativeWeb.* NativeWeb, n.d. Web. 22 Jan. 2010.

Short work with no author

title of short work | title of Web site | sponsor of site | update | medium | date of access: day + month + year

"Sister Aimee." *American Experience*. PBS Online, 2 Apr. 2007. Web. 30 Oct. 2010.

36. Web site with an author using a pseudonym Begin the entry with the pseudonym and add the author's or creator's real name, if known, in brackets. Follow with the information required for a Web site or a short work from a Web site (see item 34 or 35).

Grammar Girl [Mignon Fogarty]. "What Is the Plural of 'Mouse'?" *Grammar Girl: Quick and Dirty Tips for Better Writing*. Holtzbrinck, 16 Sept. 2008. Web. 10 Nov. 2010.

37. Article in an online journal

author: last name first | article title

Mason, John Edwin. "'Mannenberg': Notes on the Making of an Icon and Anthem."

journal title | volume, issue | year | not paginated | medium | date of access: day + month + year

African Studies Quarterly 9.4 (2007): n. pag. Web. 23 Feb. 2010.

Citation at a glance: Short work from a Web site (MLA)

To cite a short work from a Web site in MLA style, include the following elements:

1 Author of short work (if any)
2 Title of short work
3 Title of Web site
4 Sponsor of Web site ("N.p." if none)
5 Update date ("n.d." if none)
6 Medium
7 Date you accessed the source

INTERNAL PAGE OF WEB SITE

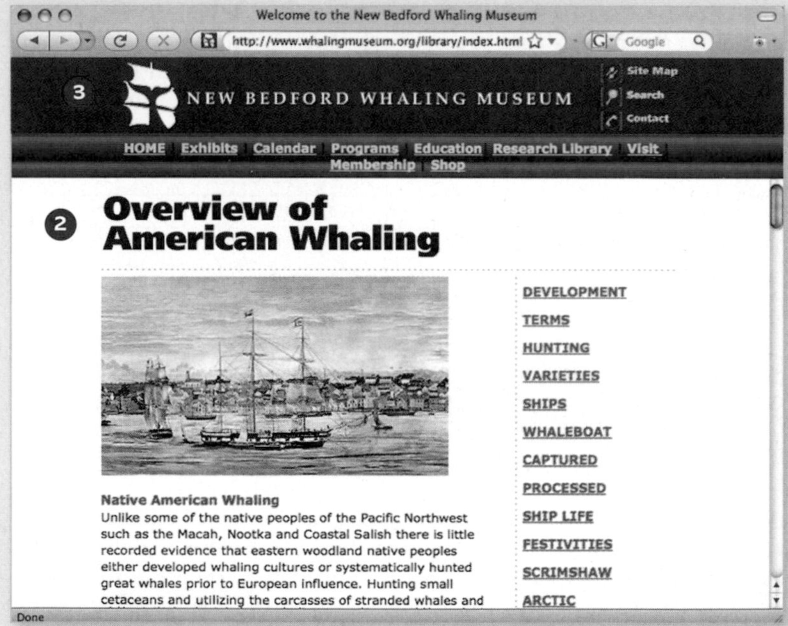

FOOTER ON HOME PAGE

the local area. It houses the most extensive collection of art, artifacts, and manuscripts pertaining to American whaling in the age of sail - late eighteenth century to the early twentieth, when sailing ships dominated merchant trade and whaling.

18 Johnny Cake Hill | New Bedford, MA | 02740-6398 | Tel. (508) 997-0046
Fax: (508) 997-0018 | Library Fax: (508) 207-1064

5

©Copyright 2009 Old Dartmouth Historical Society / New Bedford Whaling Museum 

WORKS CITED ENTRY FOR A SHORT WORK FROM A WEB SITE

2 3 4

"Overview of American Whaling." *New Bedford Whaling Museum*. Old Dartmouth Hist.

5 6 7

Soc./New Bedford Whaling Museum, 2009. Web. 27 Oct. 2009.

For more on citing sources from Web sites in MLA style, see pages 412–13.

38. Article in an online magazine Give the author; the title of the article, in quotation marks; the title of the magazine, italicized; the sponsor or publisher of the site (use "N.p." if there is none); the date of publication; the medium; and your date of access.

Burton, Robert. "The Certainty Epidemic." *Salon.com*. Salon Media Group, 29 Feb. 2008. Web. 18 Jan. 2010.

39. Article in an online newspaper Give the author; the title of the article, in quotation marks; the title of the newspaper, italicized; the sponsor or publisher of the site (use "N.p." if there is none); the date of publication; the medium; and your date of access.

Smith, Andrew D. "Poll: More than 70% of US Workers Use Internet on the Job." *Dallasnews.com*. Dallas Morning News, 25 Sept. 2008. Web. 29 Sept. 2008.

40. Work from a database For a source retrieved from a library's subscription database, first list the publication information for the source (see items 7–15) and then provide information about the database. For an illustrated citation of an article from a database, see page 416.

author of source: last name first | title of article | journal title | volume, issue | year | page(s)

Heyen, William. "Sunlight." *American Poetry Review* 36.2 (2007): 55-56. *Expanded*

database name | medium | date of access: day + month + year

Academic ASAP. Web. 24 Mar. 2010.

Barrera, Rebeca María. "A Case for Bilingual Education." *Scholastic Parent and Child* Nov.-Dec. 2004: 72-73. *Academic Search Premier*. Web. 1 Feb. 2009.

Williams, Jeffrey J. "Why Today's Publishing World Is Reprising the Past." *Chronicle of Higher Education* 13 June 2008: n. pag. *LexisNexis Academic*. Web. 29 Sept. 2009.

Citation at a glance: Article from a database (MLA)

To cite an article from a database in MLA style, include the following elements:

1 Author of article
2 Title of article
3 Title of periodical
4 Volume and issue numbers (for journal)
5 Date or year of publication
6 Page number(s) of article ("n. pag." if none)
7 Name of database
8 Medium
9 Date you accessed the source

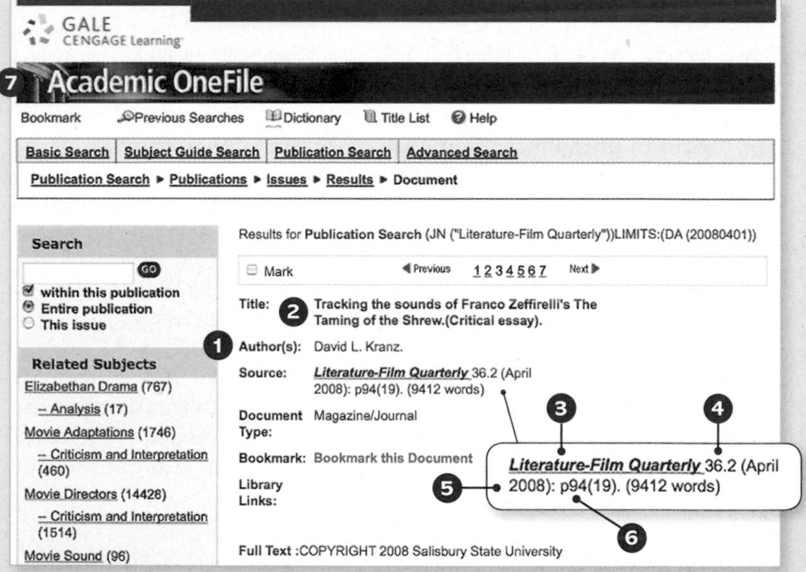

WORKS CITED ENTRY FOR AN ARTICLE FROM A DATABASE

Kranz, David L. "Tracking the Sounds of Franco Zeffirelli's *The Taming of the Shrew*." *Literature-Film Quarterly* 36.2 (2008): 94-112. *Academic OneFile*. Web. 28 Oct. 2009.

(Labels: 1 = Kranz, David L.; 2 = "Tracking the Sounds of Franco Zeffirelli's *The Taming of the Shrew*."; 3 = *Literature-Film Quarterly*; 4 = 36.2; 5 = (2008); 6 = 94-112; 7 = *Academic OneFile*; 8 = Web; 9 = 28 Oct. 2009)

For more on citing articles from a database in MLA style, see item 40.

41. Online book-length work Cite an online book or an online book-length work, such as a play or a long poem, as you would a short work from a Web site (see item 35), but italicize the title of the work.

author: last name first | title of long poem | title of Web site | sponsor of site | update | medium

Milton, John. *Paradise Lost: Book I*. *Poetryfoundation.org*. Poetry Foundation, 2008. Web.

date of access: day + month + year

14 Dec. 2009.

Give the print publication information for the work, if available (see items 16–33), followed by the title of the Web site, the medium, and your date of access.

author: last name first | book title | editor of original book

Jacobs, Harriet A. *Incidents in the Life of a Slave Girl: Written by Herself*. Ed. L. Maria Child.

city of publication | year | title of Web site | medium | date of access: day + month + year

Boston, 1861. *Documenting the American South*. Web. 3 Feb. 2010.

42. Part of an online book Begin as for a part of a print book (see item 29 on p. 409). If the online book part has no page numbers, use "N. pag." following the publication information. End with the Web site on which the work is found, the medium, and your date of access.

Adams, Henry. "Diplomacy." *The Education of Henry Adams*. Boston: Houghton, 1918. N. pag. *Bartleby.com: Great Books Online*. Web. 8 Jan. 2010.

43. Digital archives Digital archives are online collections of documents or records—books, letters, photographs, data—that have been converted to digital form. Cite publication information for the original document, if it is available, using the models throughout section MLA-4b. Then give the location of the document, if any, neither italicized nor in quotation marks; the name of the archive, italicized; the medium ("Web"); and your date of access.

Fiore, Mark. *Shockwaves*. 18 Oct. 2001. *September 11 Digital Archive*. Web. 3 Apr. 2009.

Oblinger, Maggie. Letter to Charlie Thomas. 31 Mar. 1895. Nebraska State Hist. Soc. *Prairie Settlement: Nebraska Photographs and Family Letters, 1862-1912*. Web. 3 Nov. 2009.

WPA Household Census for 1047 W. 50th Street, Los Angeles County. 1939. USC Lib. Spec. Collections. *USC Libraries Digital Archive*. Web. 12 Mar. 2010.

44. Entry in an online reference work Give the author of the entry, if there is one. Otherwise begin with the title of the entry, in quotation marks. Then give the title of the site; the sponsor and the update date (use "n.d." if there is none); the medium; and your date of access.

"Native American Church." *Britannica*. Encyclopaedia Britannica, 2008. Web. 29 Jan. 2010.

45. Online poem Cite as you would a short work from a Web site (item 35) or part of an online book (item 42).

Bell, Acton [Anne Brontë]. "Mementos." *Poems by Currer, Ellis, and Acton Bell*. London, 1846. N. pag. *A Celebration of Women Writers*. Web. 18 Sept. 2009.

46. Entire blog (Weblog) Cite a blog as you would an entire Web site (see item 34).

Gristmill. Grist Magazine, 2008. Web. 19 Jan. 2009.

47. Entry or comment in a blog (Weblog) Cite an entry or a comment (a response to an entry) in a blog as you would a short work from a Web site (see item 35). If the comment or entry has no title, use the label "Weblog entry" or "Weblog comment." Follow with the remaining information as for an entire blog in item 46.

"Social Media: Facebook and MySpace as University Curricula." *Open Education*. Open Education.net, n.d. Web. 19 Sept. 2008.

Cynthia. Weblog comment. *Open Education*. Open Education.net, 8 Jan. 2010. Web. 14 Feb. 2010.

48. Academic course or department home page Cite as a short work from a Web site (see item 35). For a course home page, begin with the name of the instructor and the title of the course or title of the page (use "Course home page" if there is no other title). For a department home page, begin with the name of the department and the label "Dept. home page."

Marrone, Carole. "355:301: College Writing and Research." *Rutgers School of Arts and Sciences*. Writing Program, Rutgers U, 2010. Web. 19 Mar. 2010.

Comparative Media Studies. Dept. home page. *Massachusetts Institute of Technology*. MIT, 2010. Web. 6 Feb. 2010.

49. Online video clip Cite as you would a short work from a Web site (see item 35).

author: last name first | video title | title of Web site | sponsor | update | medium

Murphy, Beth. "Tips for a Good Profile Piece." *YouTube*. YouTube, 7 Sept. 2008. Web.

date of access: day + month + year

19 Apr. 2010.

50. Online abstract Cite as you would an abstract of a journal article (see item 11), giving whatever print information is available, followed by the medium and your date of access. If you found the abstract in an online periodical database, include the name of the database after the print publication information (see item 40).

Turner, Fred. "Romantic Automatism: Art, Technology, and Collaborative Labor in Cold War America." Abstract. *Journal of Visual Culture* 7.1 (2008): 5. Web. 25 Oct. 2009.

51. Online editorial or letter to the editor Cite as you would an editorial or a letter to the editor in a print publication (see item 13 or 14), followed by information for a short work from a Web site (see item 35).

"Compromise Is Key with Religion at Work." Editorial. *StarTribune.com*. Star Tribune, 18 June 2008. Web. 25 June 2008.

52. Online review Begin the entry as you would for a review in a magazine or newspaper (see item 15). If the review is published in print as well as online, first give publication information as for an article in a periodical (see items 7–10). Then add the Web site on which the review appears, the medium ("Web"), and your date of access. If the review is published only on the Web, give the information required for a short work from a Web site (see item 35). If you found the review in a database, cite as in item 40.

Greer, W. R. "Who's the Fairest One of All?" Rev. of *Mirror, Mirror*, by Gregory Maguire. *Reviewsofbooks.com*. Reviewsofbooks.com, 2003. Web. 26 Oct. 2009.

53. E-mail message Begin with the writer's name and the subject line. Then write "Message to" followed by the name of the recipient. End with the date of the message and the medium ("E-mail").

Lowe, Walter. "Review Questions." Message to the author. 15 Mar. 2010. E-mail.

54. Posting to an online discussion list When possible, cite archived versions of postings. If you cannot locate an archived version, keep a copy of the posting for your records. Begin with the author's name, followed by the title or subject line, in quotation marks (use the label "Online posting" if the posting has no title). Then proceed as for a short work from a Web site (see item 35).

Fainton, Peter. "Re: Backlash against New Labour." *Media Lens Message Board*. Media Lens, 7 May 2008. Web. 2 June 2008.

55. Entry in a wiki A wiki is an online reference that is openly edited by its users. Treat an entry in a wiki as you would a short work from a Web site (see item 35). Because wiki content is, by definition, collectively edited and can be updated frequently, do not include an author. Give the title of the entry; the name of the wiki, italicized; the sponsor or publisher of the wiki (use "N.p." if there is none); the date of the last update; the medium; and your date of access.

"Hip Hop Music." *Wikipedia*. Wikimedia Foundation, 2 Mar. 2010. Web. 18 Mar. 2010.

"Negation in Languages." *UniLang Wiki*. UniLang, 12 Jan. 2009. Web. 9 Mar. 2010.

Audio and visual sources (including online versions)

56. Digital file A digital file is any document or image that exists in digital form, independent of a Web site. To cite a digital file, begin with information required for the source (such as a photograph, a report, a sound recording, or a radio program), following the guidelines throughout MLA-4b. Then for the medium, indicate the type of file: "JPEG file," "PDF file," "MP3 file," and so on.

photographer | photograph title | date of composition | location of photograph

Hine, Lewis W. *Girl in Cherryville Mill*. 1908. Prints and Photographs Div., Lib. of Cong. JPEG file.

medium: file type

"Scenes from a Recession." *This American Life*. Narr. Ira Glass. NPR, 30 Mar. 2009. MP3 file.

National Institute of Mental Health. *What Rescue Workers Can Do*. Washington: US Dept. of Health and Human Services, 2006. PDF file.

57. Podcast If you view or listen to a podcast online, cite it as you would a short work from a Web site (see item 35). If you download the podcast and view or listen to it on a computer or portable player, cite it as a digital file (see item 56).

Podcast online

"Calculating the Demand for Charter Schools." Narr. David Guenthner. *Texas PolicyCast.* Texas Public Policy Foundation, 28 Aug. 2008. Web. 10 Jan. 2009.

Podcast downloaded as digital file

"Calculating the Demand for Charter Schools." Narr. David Guenthner. *Texas PolicyCast.* Texas Public Policy Foundation, 28 Aug. 2008. MP3 file.

58. Musical score For print and online, begin with the composer's name; the title of the work, italicized (unless it is named by form, number, and key); and the date of composition. For a print source, give the place, publisher, date of publication, and medium. For an online source, give the title of the Web site; the publisher or sponsor; the date of Web publication; the medium; and your date of access.

Handel, G. F. *Messiah: An Oratorio*. N.d. *CCARH Publications: Scores and Parts*. Center for Computer Assisted Research in the Humanities, 2003. Web. 5 Jan. 2009.

59. Sound recording Begin with the name of the person you want to emphasize: the composer, conductor ("Cond."), or performer ("Perf."). For a long work, give the title, italicized (unless it is named by form, number, and key); the names of pertinent artists (such as performers, readers, or musicians); and the orchestra and conductor, if relevant. End with the manufacturer, the date, and the medium.

Bizet, Georges. *Carmen*. Perf. Jennifer Laramore, Thomas Moser, Angela Gheorghiu, and Samuel Ramey. Bavarian State Orch. and Chorus. Cond. Giuseppe Sinopoli. Warner, 1996. CD.

For a song, put the title in quotation marks. If you include the name of the album or CD, italicize it.

Blige, Mary J. "Be without You." *The Breakthrough*. Geffen, 2005. CD.

60. Film Typically, begin with the title, italicized, followed by the director and lead actors ("Perf.") or narrator ("Narr."); the distributor; the year of the film's release; and the medium ("Film," "Videocassette").

If your paper emphasizes a person involved with the film, you may begin with that person, as in the first example in item 61.

movie title / director / major performers

Frozen River. Dir. Courtney Hunt. Perf. Melissa Leo, Charlie McDermott, and Misty Upham.

distributor / release date / medium

Sony, 2008. Film.

61. DVD For a film on DVD, cite as you would a film, giving "DVD" as the medium. If you are citing the film as a whole, use the model in item 60. If your paper emphasizes a particular person, begin with that person's name and title, as shown here.

Forster, Marc, dir. *Finding Neverland*. Perf. Johnny Depp, Kate Winslet, Julie Christie, Radha Mitchell, and Dustin Hoffman. Miramax, 2004. DVD.

For any other work on DVD, such as an educational work or a game, cite as you would a film, giving whatever information is available about the author, director, distributor, and so on.

Across the Drafts: Students and Teachers Talk about Feedback. Harvard Expository Writing Program, 2005. DVD.

62. Special feature on a DVD Begin with the title of the feature, in quotation marks, and the names of any important contributors, as for films or DVDs (item 60 or 61). End with information about the DVD, as in item 61, including the disc number, if any.

"Sweeney's London." Prod. Eric Young. *Sweeney Todd: The Demon Barber of Fleet Street*. Dir. Tim Burton. DreamWorks, 2007. DVD. Disc 2.

63. CD-ROM At the end, add the medium ("CD-ROM").

"Pimpernel." *The American Heritage Dictionary of the English Language*. 4th ed. Boston: Houghton, 2000. CD-ROM.

64. Computer software or video game List the developer or author of the software (if any); the title, italicized; the distributor and date of publication; and the platform or medium.

Firaxis Games. *Sid Meier's Civilization Revolution*. Take-Two Interactive, 2008. Xbox 360.

65. Radio or television program Begin with the title of the radio segment or television episode (if there is one), in quotation marks. Then give the title of the program or series, italicized; relevant information about the program, such as the writer ("By"), director ("Dir."), performers ("Perf."), or narrator ("Narr."); the network; the local station (if any) and location; the date of broadcast; and the medium ("Television," "Radio"). For a program you accessed online, after the information about the program give the network, the original broadcast date, the title of the Web site, the medium ("Web"), and your date of access.

"Machines of the Gods." *Ancient Discoveries*. History Channel. 14 Oct. 2008. Television.

"Elif Shafak: Writing under a Watchful Eye." *Fresh Air*. Narr. Terry Gross. Natl. Public Radio, 6 Feb. 2007. *NPR.org*. Web. 22 Feb. 2009.

66. Radio or television interview Begin with the name of the person who was interviewed, followed by the word "Interview" and the interviewer's name, if relevant. End with information about the program as in item 65.

De Niro, Robert, Barry Levinson, and Art Linson. Interview by Charlie Rose. *Charlie Rose*. PBS. WGBH, Boston, 13 Oct. 2008. Television.

67. Live performance For a live performance of a concert, a play, a ballet, or an opera, begin with the title of the work performed, italicized. Then give the author or composer of the work ("By"); relevant information such as the director ("Dir."), the choreographer ("Chor."), the conductor ("Cond."), or the major performers ("Perf."); the orchestra or the theater, ballet, or opera company, if any; the theater and location; the date of the performance; and the label "Performance."

The Brothers Size. By Tarell Alvin McCraney. Dir. Bijan Sheibani. Young Vic Theatre, London. 15 Oct. 2008. Performance.

Symphony no. 4 in G. By Gustav Mahler. Cond. Mark Wigglesworth. Perf. Juliane Banse and Boston Symphony Orch. Symphony Hall, Boston. 17 Apr. 2009. Performance.

68. Lecture or public address Begin with the speaker's name, followed by the title of the lecture (if any), in quotation marks; the organization sponsoring the lecture; the location; the date; and a label such as "Lecture" or "Address."

Wellbery, David E. "On a Sentence of Franz Kafka." Franke Inst. for the Humanities. Gleacher Center, Chicago. 1 Feb. 2006. Lecture.

69. Work of art Cite the artist's name; the title of the artwork, italicized; the date of composition; the medium of composition (for instance, "Lithograph on paper," "Photograph," "Charcoal on paper"); and the institution and city in which the artwork is located. For artworks found online, omit the medium of composition and include the title of the Web site, the medium ("Web"), and your date of access.

Constable, John. *Dedham Vale*. 1802. Oil on canvas. Victoria and Albert Museum, London.

Hessing, Valjean. *Caddo Myth*. 1976. Joslyn Art Museum, Omaha. *Joslyn Art Museum*. Web. 19 Apr. 2009.

70. Cartoon Give the cartoonist's name; the title of the cartoon, if it has one, in quotation marks; the label "Cartoon" or "Comic strip"; publication information; and the medium. To cite an online cartoon, instead of publication information give the title of the Web site, the sponsor or publisher, the medium, and your date of access.

Keefe, Mike. "Veterans Affairs Overruns." Cartoon. *Denverpost.com*. Denver Post, 11 Oct. 2009. Web. 12 Dec. 2009.

71. Advertisement Name the product or company being advertised, followed by the word "Advertisement." Give publication information for the source in which the advertisement appears.

Truth by Calvin Klein. Advertisement. *Vogue* Dec. 2000: 95-98. Print.

Arbella Insurance. Advertisement. *Boston.com*. NY Times, n.d. Web. 3 Sept. 2009.

72. Map or chart Cite a map or a chart as you would a book or a short work within a longer work. Use the word "Map" or "Chart" following the title. Add the medium and, for an online source, the sponsor or publisher and the date of access.

Joseph, Lori, and Bob Laird. "Driving While Phoning Is Dangerous." Chart. *USA Today* 16 Feb. 2001: 1A. Print.

"Serbia." Map. *Syrena Maps*. Syrena, 2 Feb. 2001. Web. 17 Mar. 2009.

Other sources (including online versions)

This section includes a variety of sources not covered elsewhere. For online sources, consult the appropriate model in this section and also see items 34–55.

73. Government document Treat the government agency as the author, giving the name of the government followed by the name of the department and the agency, if any. For print sources, add the medium at the end of the entry. For online sources, follow the model for an entire Web site (item 34) or a short work from a Web site (item 35).

government | department | agency | document title | Web site title | publisher/sponsor | publication date | medium | date of access: day + month + year

United States. Dept. of the Interior. Office of Inspector General. "Excessive Indulgences: Personal Use of the Internet at the Department of the Interior." *Office of Inspector General*. Dept. of the Interior, Sept. 1999. Web. 20 May 2010.

Canada. Minister of Indian Affairs and Northern Dev. *Gathering Strength: Canada's Aboriginal Action Plan*. Ottawa: Minister of Public Works and Govt. Services Can., 2000. Print.

74. Historical document To cite a historical document, such as the US Constitution or the Canadian Charter of Rights and Freedoms, begin with the document author, if it has one, and then give the document title, neither italicized nor in quotation marks, and the document date. For a print version, continue as for a selection in an anthology (see item 24) or for a book (with the title not italicized). For an online version, cite as a short work from a Web site (see item 35).

Jefferson, Thomas. First Inaugural Address. 1801. *The American Reader*. Ed. Diane Ravitch. New York: Harper, 1990. 42-44. Print.

The Virginia Declaration of Rights. 1776. *A Chronology of US Historical Documents*. U of Oklahoma Coll. of Law, 2008. Web. 23 Feb. 2009.

75. Legal source

Legislative act (law)

Begin with the name of the act, neither italicized nor in quotation marks. Then provide the act's Public Law number; its Statutes at Large volume and page numbers; its date of enactment; and the medium of publication.

Electronic Freedom of Information Act Amendments of 1996. Pub. L. 104-231. 110 Stat. 3048. 2 Oct. 1996. Print.

Court case

Name the first plaintiff and the first defendant. Then give the volume, name, and page numbers of the law report; the court name; the year of the decision; and publication information. Do not italicize the name of the case. (In the text of the paper, the name of the case is italicized; see item 19 on p. 395.)

Utah v. Evans. 536 US 452. Supreme Court of the US. 2002. *Supreme Court Collection*. Legal Information Inst., Cornell U Law School, n.d. Web. 30 Apr. 2008.

76. Pamphlet or brochure Cite as you would a book (see items 16–33).

Commonwealth of Massachusetts. Dept. of Jury Commissioner. *A Few Facts about Jury Duty*. Boston: Commonwealth of Massachusetts, 2004. Print.

77. Unpublished dissertation Begin with the author's name, followed by the dissertation title in quotation marks; the abbreviation "Diss."; the name of the institution; the year the dissertation was accepted; and the medium of the dissertation.

Jackson, Shelley. "Writing Whiteness: Contemporary Southern Literature in Black and White." Diss. U of Maryland, 2000. Print.

78. Published dissertation For dissertations that have been published in book form, italicize the title. After the title and before the book's publication information, give the abbreviation "Diss.," the name of the institution, and the year the dissertation was accepted. Add the medium of publication at the end.

Damberg, Cheryl L. *Healthcare Reform: Distributional Consequences of an Employer Mandate for Workers in Small Firms*. Diss. Rand Graduate School, 1995. Santa Monica: Rand, 1996. Print.

79. Abstract of a dissertation Cite an abstract as you would an unpublished dissertation. After the dissertation date, give the abbreviation *DA* or *DAI* (for *Dissertation Abstracts* or *Dissertation Abstracts International*), followed by the volume and issue numbers; the year of publication; inclusive page numbers or, if the abstract is not numbered, the item number; and the medium of publication. For an abstract accessed in an online database, give the item number in place of the page number, followed by the name of the database, the medium, and your date of access.

Chen, Shu-Ling. "Mothers and Daughters in Morrison, Tan, Marshall, and Kincaid." Diss. U of Washington, 2000. *DAI* 61.6 (2000): AAT9975963. *ProQuest Dissertations and Theses*. Web. 22 Feb. 2009.

80. Published proceedings of a conference Cite as you would a book, adding the name, date, and location of the conference after the title.

Urgo, Joseph R., and Ann J. Abadie, eds. *Faulkner and Material Culture*. Proc. of Faulkner and Yoknapatawpha Conf., 25-29 July 2004, U of Mississippi. Jackson: UP of Mississippi, 2007. Print.

81. Paper in conference proceedings Cite as you would a selection in an anthology (see item 24), giving information about the conference after the title and editors of the conference proceedings (see item 80).

Henninger, Katherine R. "Faulkner, Photography, and a Regional Ethics of Form." *Faulkner and Material Culture*. Ed. Joseph R. Urgo and Ann J. Abadie. Proc. of Faulkner and Yoknapatawpha Conf., 25-29 July 2004, U of Mississippi. Jackson: UP of Mississippi, 2007. 121-38. Print.

82. Published interview Name the person interviewed, followed by the title of the interview (if there is one). If the interview does not have a title, include the word "Interview" after the interviewee's name. Give publication information for the work in which the interview was published.

Simon, David. "Beyond the Choir: An Interview with David Simon." *Film Quarterly* 62.2 (2008/2009): 44-49. Print.

If you wish to include the name of the interviewer, put it after the title of the interview (or after the name of the interviewee if there is no title).

Florida, Richard. "The Great Reset." Interview by Conor Clarke. *Atlantic*. Atlantic Monthly Group, Feb. 2009. Web. 28 Feb. 2010.

83. Personal interview To cite an interview that you conducted, begin with the name of the person interviewed. Then write "Personal interview" or "Telephone interview," followed by the date of the interview.

Akufo, Dautey. Personal interview. 11 Apr. 2010.

84. Personal letter To cite a letter that you received, begin with the writer's name and add the phrase "Letter to the author," followed by the date. Add the medium ("MS" for "manuscript," or a handwritten letter; "TS" for "typescript," or a typed letter).

Primak, Shoshana. Letter to the author. 6 May 2010. TS.

85. Published letter Begin with the writer of the letter, the words "Letter to" and the recipient, and the date of the letter (use "N.d." if the letter is undated). Then add the title of the collection and proceed as for a selection in an anthology (see item 24).

Wharton, Edith. Letter to Henry James. 28 Feb. 1915. *Henry James and Edith Wharton: Letters, 1900-1915*. Ed. Lyall H. Powers. New York: Scribner's, 1990. 323-26. Print.

86. Manuscript Give the author, a title or a description of the manuscript, and the date of composition, followed by the abbreviation "MS" for "manuscript" (handwritten) or "TS" for "typescript." Add the name and location of the institution housing the material. For a manuscript found online, give the preceding information but omit "MS" or "TS." Then list the title of the Web site, the medium ("Web"), and your date of access.

Arendt, Hannah. *Between Past and Presen*t. N.d. 1st draft. Hannah Arendt Papers. MS Div., Lib. of Cong. *Manuscript Division, Library of Congress*. Web. 24 Apr. 2009.

MLA-4c MLA information notes (optional)

Researchers who use the MLA system of parenthetical documentation may also use information notes for one of two purposes:

1. to provide additional material that is important but might interrupt the flow of the paper
2. to refer to several sources that support a single point or to provide comments on sources

Information notes may be either footnotes or endnotes. Footnotes appear at the foot of the page; endnotes appear on a separate page at the end of the paper, just before the list of works cited. For either style, the notes are numbered consecutively throughout the paper. The text of the paper contains a raised arabic numeral that corresponds to the number of the note.

TEXT

In the past several years, employees have filed a number of lawsuits against employers because of online monitoring practices.[1]

NOTE

1. For a discussion of federal law applicable to electronic surveillance in the workplace, see Kesan 293.

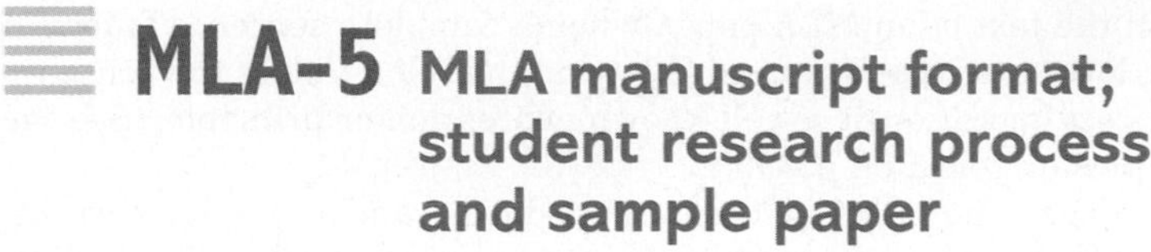

MLA-5 MLA manuscript format; student research process and sample paper

The following guidelines are consistent with advice given in the *MLA Handbook for Writers of Research Papers*, 7th ed. (New York: MLA, 2009), and with typical requirements for student papers. For a sample MLA paper, see pages 436–40.

MLA-5a MLA manuscript format

Formatting the paper

Papers written in MLA style should be formatted as follows.

Materials and font Use good-quality 8½″ × 11″ white paper. If your instructor does not require a specific font, choose one that is standard and easy to read (such as Times New Roman).

Title and identification MLA does not require a title page. On the first page of your paper, place your name, your instructor's name, the course title, and the date on separate lines against the left margin. Then center your title. (See p. 436 for a sample first page.)

If your instructor requires a title page, ask for formatting guidelines. A format similar to the one on page 532 may be acceptable.

Pagination Put the page number preceded by your last name in the upper right corner of each page, one-half inch below the top edge. Use arabic numerals (1, 2, 3, and so on).

Margins, line spacing, and paragraph indents Leave margins of one inch on all sides of the page. Left-align the text.

Double-space throughout the paper. Do not add extra space above or below the title of the paper or between paragraphs.

Indent the first line of each paragraph one-half inch from the left margin.

Capitalization and italics In titles of works, capitalize all words except articles (*a*, *an*, *the*), prepositions (*to*, *from*, *between*, and so on), coordinating conjunctions (*and*, *but*, *or*, *nor*, *for*, *so*, *yet*), and the *to* in infinitives—unless they are the first or last word of the title or subtitle. Follow these guidelines in your paper even if the title appears in all capital or all lowercase letters in the source.

In the text of an MLA paper, when a complete sentence follows a colon, lowercase the first word following the colon unless the sentence is a direct quotation or a well-known expression or principle. (See the examples in item 1 on p. 390.)

Italicize the titles of books, periodicals, and other long works, such as Web sites. Use quotation marks around the titles of periodical articles, short stories, poems, and other short works. (If your instructor prefers underlining, use it consistently in place of italics.)

Long quotations When a quotation is longer than four typed lines of prose or three lines of verse, set it off from the text by indenting the entire quotation one inch from the left margin. Double-space the indented quotation, and do not add extra space above or below it.

Quotation marks are not needed when a quotation has been set off from the text by indenting. See page 436 for an example.

URLs (Web addresses) When you need to break a URL at the end of a line in the text of your paper, break it only after a slash and do not insert a hyphen. For MLA rules on dividing URLs in your list of works cited, see page 431.

Headings MLA neither encourages nor discourages the use of headings and provides no guidelines for their use. If you would like to insert headings in a long essay or research paper, check first with your instructor.

Visuals MLA classifies visuals as tables and figures (figures include graphs, charts, maps, photographs, and drawings). Label each table with an arabic numeral ("Table 1," "Table 2," and so on) and provide a clear caption that identifies the subject. Capitalize the caption as you would a title (see P8-c); do not italicize the label and caption or place them in quotation marks. The label and caption should appear on separate lines above the table, flush with the left margin.

For a table that you have borrowed or adapted, give the source below the table in a note like the following:

> Source: David N. Greenfield and Richard A. Davis; "Lost in Cyberspace: The Web @ Work"; *CyberPsychology and Behavior* 5.4 (2002): 349; print.

For each figure, place the figure number (using the abbreviation "Fig.") and a caption below the figure, flush left. Capitalize the caption as you would a sentence; include source information following the caption. (When referring to the figure in your paper, use the abbreviation "fig." in parenthetical citations; otherwise spell out the word.) See page 439 for an example of a figure in a paper.

Place visuals in the text, as close as possible to the sentences that relate to them, unless your instructor prefers that visuals appear in an appendix.

Preparing the list of works cited

Begin the list of works cited on a new page at the end of the paper. Center the title "Works Cited" about one inch from the top of the page. Double-space throughout. See page 440 for a sample list of works cited.

Alphabetizing the list Alphabetize the list by the last names of the authors (or editors); if a work has no author or editor, alphabetize by the first word of the title other than *A*, *An*, or *The*.

If your list includes two or more works by the same author, use the author's name for the first entry only. For subsequent entries, use three hyphens followed by a period. List the titles in alphabetical order. (See item 6 on p. 401.)

Indenting Do not indent the first line of each works cited entry, but indent any additional lines one-half inch. This technique highlights the beginning of each entry, making it easy for readers to scan the alphabetized list. See page 440.

URLs (Web addresses) If you need to include a URL in a works cited entry and it must be divided across lines, break the URL only after a slash. Do not insert a hyphen at the end of the line. Insert angle brackets around the URL. (See the note following item 34 on p. 413.) If your word processing program automatically turns URLs into links (by underlining them and changing the color), turn off this feature.

MLA-5b Highlights of one student's research process

The following pages describe key steps in student writer Anna Orlov's research process, from selecting a research question to documenting sources. At each step, cross-references in the margins point to more discussion and examples elsewhere in the handbook. Samples from Orlov's process illustrate strategies and skills she used to create an accurate and effective essay. See pages 436–40 for Orlov's final paper.

Making the most of your handbook
Highlights of one student's research process (MLA style)

Anna Orlov, a student in a composition class, was assigned a research essay related to technology and the American workplace. The assignment called for her to use a variety of print and electronic sources and to follow MLA style. She developed some questions and strategies to guide her research and writing.

"How do I begin a research paper?"

Before getting started, Orlov worked with a writing tutor to break her research plan into several stages. (Section numbers in blue refer to relevant discussions throughout the book.)

- *Ask worthwhile questions about my topic.* **C1-b, R1-a**
- *Talk with a reference librarian about useful types of sources and where to find them.* **R1-b**
- *Consider how each source can contribute to my paper.* **R2-a**
- *Decide which search results are worth a closer look.* **R2-b**
- *Evaluate the sources.* **R2-c, R2-d**
- *Take notes and keep track of the sources.* **R3**
- *Write a working thesis.* **C1-c, MLA-1a**
- *Write a draft and integrate sources.* **C2, MLA-3, MLA-4a**
- *Document sources.* **MLA-4**

R1-a: Posing questions for a research paper

Orlov began by jotting down her research question: *Is Internet surveillance in the workplace fair or unfair to employees?* She thought the practice might be unfair but wanted to consider all sides of the issue. Orlov knew she would have to be open-minded and flexible and revisit her main ideas as she examined the information and arguments in her sources.

"What sources do I need, and where should I look for them?"

R2-a: Roles sources can play in a paper

Orlov worked with a reference librarian to develop a search strategy. She looked for sources that would provide that background, evidence, and counterevidence.

R1-b: Working with reference librarians

Library databases Because her topic was current, Orlov turned to her library's subscription databases for trustworthy, scholarly, up-to-date articles with concrete examples of workplace Internet surveillance.

R1-c to R1-e: Searching databases, library catalogs, and the Web

Library catalogs Orlov looked for recently published books that could offer in-depth context, including the history of online monitoring and the laws governing workplace surveillance. One book on the topic had the subject heading "electronic monitoring in the workplace." Using that heading as a search term, Orlov found a more focused list of books.

The Web Using a general search engine, Orlov found Web sites, articles, and government publications that would explain the software used by employers and various opinions held by those who use the Internet and e-mail in the workplace.

"What search terms should I use?"

Orlov asked a librarian to help her conduct a narrower search with her library's general periodical database. She could count on the database for fewer, more reliable results than an Internet search could provide.

Orlov's search terms	Date restrictions
employee	Past five years
internet use	**Number of results**
surveillance	20

R1-c and p. 338: Refining keyword searches, selecting search terms

"How do I select sources from my search results?"

Orlov used several criteria to decide which results from her general periodical database search were worth a closer look. Would a source

- be relevant to her topic?
- provide authoritative support?
- provide background information?
- offer a range of views or evidence that Orlov could address when forming her argument?

R2: Evaluating sources

DATABASE SCREEN: SEARCH RESULTS

This article's focus on surveillance cameras was not relevant.

"A New Look at Big Brother"
Business Week Online, December 20, 2007, Technology, 959 words, Peter Burrows

Orlov would want to respond to this survey if she argued that Internet surveillance is unfair.

"Wasting Away on the Web; More Employers Taking Workers' Web Use Seriously"
eWeek, August 8, 2005, 692 words, Chris Gonsalves

The *Wall Street Journal* is widely respected and might offer background for Orlov's topic.

"Snooping E-Mail by Software Is Now a Workplace Norm"
The Wall Street Journal Online, March 9, 2005, Pui-Wing Tam et al.

Orlov wondered if the *Progressive* had a political slant. She made a note to check for bias.

"Snooping Bosses; Electronic Surveillance Program"
The Progressive, February 1, 2006: 14, Barbara Ehrenreich

Reviewed by legal experts, a law review article could provide legal context and lend credibility.

"Cyber-Working or Cyber-Shirking? A First Principles Examination of Electronic Privacy in the Workplace"
Florida Law Review 54.2 (2002): 289-332, Jay P. Kesan

"How do I evaluate my sources?"

R2-b to R2-d: Assessing print and online sources

After Orlov had conducted several searches and narrowed her list of results, she downloaded her sources and began evaluating them. She wanted to see what evidence and claims she would need to address to strengthen her argument.

R3: Managing your information

She looked carefully at an article in *eWeek*, an online business computing magazine. To keep track of her thoughts about the author's text, she made notes in the margins as she read. Taking good notes would help her to begin forming her own lines of argument and avoid plagiarism.

ORLOV'S NOTES ON AN ARTICLE

Wasting Away on the Web

Opinion: More employers are taking workers' Web use seriously.

Writer is sympathetic to employers?

By Chris Gonsalves
2005-08-08

SECTION: OPINION; Pg. 26

Consider statistics. Is spending work time on personal Internet use so bad?

The issue of IT surveillance was driven home last month when Salary.com and America Online released a survey of 10,000 American workers, many of whom admitted that goofing off on the Internet was their primary method of frittering away the workday. In a sign of the times, it beat out socializing with co-workers, 45 percent to 23 percent.

Strong case for surveillance, but I'm not convinced. Counter with useful work-place Web surfing?

While bosses can easily detect and interrupt water-cooler chatter, the employee who is shopping at Lands' End or IMing with fellow fantasy baseball managers may actually appear to be working. Thwarting the activity is a technology challenge, and it's one that more and more enterprises are taking seriously, despite resistance from privacy advocates and some employees themselves.

Common examples—readers can relate.

According to the American Management Association, 78 percent of large U.S. employers are regularly checking workers' e-mail messages, Internet use, computer files and phone calls. Nearly half of such employers store employee e-mail messages for review. The AMA also found that 65 percent of enterprises had disciplined employees for misuse of e-mail or the Internet at work, and 27 percent had actually fired someone over such offenses.

Does the AMA side with employers? Survey results—good for background and counter-argument.

According to a recent poll of workers in technology-related fields published by the executive recruiting company FPC, 61 percent said they felt their bosses had the right to cyber-spy on them, but only with consent. Just 28 percent felt IT had the right to monitor their activity without consent, and only 1 percent said an employer never has the right to monitor Internet use.

Employees want employers to be up front about monitoring.

"It's not surprising that companies want to assure that their employees' time is predominantly spent on work-related computer usage," said FPC President Ron Herzog. "The majority of employees ... would like to be informed, so it is always in the company's best interest to have an Internet usage policy clearly outlining the company's expectations, which all employees sign upon hiring."

When is workplace surveillance unfair and when not?

As the stakes grow beyond a few wasted man-hours and some misappropriated bandwidth, it grows increasingly important for IT to let everyone in the company know they might be watched.

Executive Editor/News Chris Gonsalves can be contacted at chris_gonsalves@ziffdavis.com.

LOAD-DATE: August 8, 2005

LANGUAGE: English

Copyright 2005 Ziff Davis Media Inc. All Rights Reserved

"How do I integrate sources into my paper?"

C1-c and MLA-1a: Writing a working thesis

After reading and evaluating a number of sources, Orlov wrote her working thesis: *Though companies may have legitimate reasons to monitor employees' Internet usage, electronic surveillance is more unfair than beneficial to employees since it threatens their privacy.* She then sketched an informal plan to organize her ideas and began writing a rough draft. As she wrote and revised, she integrated sources from her research.

C1–C2: Planning and drafting

For example, Orlov had selected a book on electronic surveillance in the workplace, written by Frederick Lane III. She looked through the table of contents and selected a few chapters that seemed relevant to her working thesis. She read the chapters for ideas and information that she could paraphrase, summarize, or quote to provide background, support her argument, and help her counter the kind of pro-surveillance position that Chris Gonsalves takes in his *eWeek* article.

R3-c and MLA-2: Quoting, summarizing, and paraphrasing

"How do I keep track of and document my sources?"

R3-b: Keeping track of source materials

Because Orlov took careful notes about publication information and page numbers for source material throughout her research process, she didn't need to hunt down information as she cited her sources.

She followed the MLA (Modern Language Association) system to document her sources.

MLA-4: Documenting sources

ENTRY IN WORKS CITED LIST

author — title and subtitle

Lane, Frederick S., III. *The Naked Employee: How Technology Is Compromising Workplace Privacy*. New York: Amer. Management Assn., 2003. Print.

city of publication — publisher — publication date — medium

MLA-5c Sample research paper: MLA style

On the following pages is a research paper on the topic of electronic surveillance in the workplace, written by Anna Orlov, a student in a composition class. Orlov's paper is documented with in-text citations and a list of works cited in MLA style. Annotations in the margins of the paper draw your attention to Orlov's use of MLA style and her effective writing.

MODELS **hackerhandbooks.com/writersref**
> Model papers > MLA research papers: Orlov; Daly; Levi
> MLA annotated bibliography: Orlov

Orlov 1

Anna Orlov

Professor Willis

English 101

17 March 2009

Title is centered.

Online Monitoring:

A Threat to Employee Privacy in the Wired Workplace

Opening sentences provide background for the thesis.

As the Internet has become an integral tool of businesses, company policies on Internet usage have become as common as policies regarding vacation days or sexual harassment. A 2005 study by the American Management Association and ePolicy Institute found that 76% of companies monitor employees' use of the Web, and the number of companies that block employees' access to certain Web sites has increased 27% since 2001 (1). Unlike other company rules, however, Internet usage policies often include language authorizing companies to secretly monitor their employees, a practice that raises questions about rights in the workplace. Although companies often have legitimate concerns that lead them to monitor employees' Internet usage—from expensive security breaches to reduced productivity—the benefits of electronic surveillance are outweighed by its costs to employees' privacy and autonomy.

Thesis asserts Orlov's main point.

While surveillance of employees is not a new phenomenon, electronic surveillance allows employers to monitor workers with unprecedented efficiency. In his book *The Naked Employee*, Frederick Lane describes offline ways in which employers have been permitted to intrude on employees' privacy for decades, such as drug testing, background checks, psychological exams, lie detector tests, and in-store video surveillance. The difference, Lane argues, between these old methods of data gathering and electronic surveillance involves quantity:

Summary and long quotation are each introduced with a signal phrase naming the author.

> Technology makes it possible for employers to gather enormous amounts of data about employees, often far beyond what is necessary to satisfy safety or productivity concerns. And the trends that drive technology—faster, smaller, cheaper—make it possible for larger and larger numbers of employers to gather ever-greater amounts of personal data. (3-4)

Long quotation is set off from the text; quotation marks are omitted.

Page number is given in parentheses after the final period.

In an age when employers can collect data whenever employees use their

Marginal annotations indicate MLA-style formatting and effective writing.

Orlov 2

computers—when they send e-mail, surf the Web, or even arrive at or depart from their workstations—the challenge for both employers and employees is to determine how much is too much.

Another key difference between traditional surveillance and electronic surveillance is that employers can monitor workers' computer use secretly. One popular monitoring method is keystroke logging, which is done by means of an undetectable program on employees' computers. The Web site of a vendor for Spector Pro, a popular keystroke logging program, explains that the software can be installed to operate in "Stealth" mode so that it "does not show up as an icon, does not appear in the Windows system tray, . . . [and] cannot be uninstalled without the Spector Pro password which YOU specify" ("Automatically"). As Lane explains, these programs record every key entered into the computer in hidden directories that can later be accessed or uploaded by supervisors; the programs can even scan for keywords tailored to individual companies (128-29).

Clear topic sentences, like this one, are used throughout the paper.

Source with an unknown author is cited by a shortened title.

Some experts have argued that a range of legitimate concerns justifies employer monitoring of employee Internet usage. As *PC World* columnist Daniel Tynan points out, companies that don't monitor network traffic can be penalized for their ignorance: "Employees could accidentally (or deliberately) spill confidential information . . . or allow worms to spread throughout a corporate network." The ePolicy Institute, an organization that advises companies about reducing risks from technology, reported that breaches in computer security cost institutions $100 million in 1999 alone (Flynn). Companies also are held legally accountable for many of the transactions conducted on their networks and with their technology. Legal scholar Jay Kesan points out that the law holds employers liable for employees' actions such as violations of copyright laws, the distribution of offensive or graphic sexual material, and illegal disclosure of confidential information (312).

Orlov anticipates objections and provides sources for opposing views.

These kinds of concerns should give employers, in certain instances, the right to monitor employee behavior. But employers rushing to adopt surveillance programs might not be adequately weighing the effect such programs can have on employee morale. Employers must consider the possibility that employees will perceive surveillance as a breach of trust that can make them feel like disobedient children, not responsible

Transition helps readers move from one paragraph to the next.

adults who wish to perform their jobs professionally and autonomously.

Orlov treats both sides fairly; she provides a transition to her own argument.

Yet determining how much autonomy workers should be given is complicated by the ambiguous nature of productivity in the wired workplace. On the one hand, computers and Internet access give employees powerful tools to carry out their jobs; on the other hand, the same technology offers constant temptations to avoid work. As a 2005 study by *Salary.com* and *America Online* indicates, the Internet ranked as the top choice among employees for ways of wasting time on the job; it beat talking with co-workers—the second most popular method—by a margin of nearly two to one (Frauenheim). Chris Gonsalves, an editor for *eWeek.com*, argues that the technology has changed the terms between employers and employees: "While bosses can easily detect and interrupt water-cooler chatter," he writes, "the employee who is shopping at Lands' End or IMing with fellow fantasy baseball managers may actually appear to be working." The gap between behaviors that are observable to managers and the employee's actual activities when sitting behind a computer has created additional motivations for employers to invest in surveillance programs. "Dilbert," a popular cartoon that spoofs office culture, aptly captures how rampant recreational Internet use has become in the workplace (see fig. 1).

No page number is available for this Web source.

Orlov counters opposing views and provides support for her argument.

But monitoring online activities can have the unintended effect of making employees resentful. As many workers would be quick to point out, Web surfing and other personal uses of the Internet can provide needed outlets in the stressful work environment; many scholars have argued that limiting and policing these outlets can exacerbate tensions between employees and managers. Kesan warns that "prohibiting personal use can seem extremely arbitrary and can seriously harm morale. . . . Imagine a concerned parent who is prohibited from checking on a sick child by a draconian company policy" (315-16). As this analysis indicates, employees can become disgruntled when Internet usage policies are enforced to their full extent.

Orlov uses a brief signal phrase to move from her argument to the words of a source.

Additionally, many experts disagree with employers' assumption that online monitoring can increase productivity. Employment law attorney Joseph Schmitt argues that, particularly for employees who are paid a salary rather than an hourly wage, "a company shouldn't care whether employees spend one or 10 hours on the Internet as long as they are

Orlov 4

Fig. 1. This "Dilbert" comic strip suggests that personal Internet usage is widespread in the workplace (Adams 106).

Illustration has figure number, caption, and source information.

getting their jobs done—and provided that they are not accessing inappropriate sites" (qtd. in Verespej). Other experts even argue that time spent on personal Internet browsing can actually be productive for companies. According to Bill Coleman, an executive at *Salary.com*, "Personal Internet use and casual office conversations often turn into new business ideas or suggestions for gaining operating efficiencies" (qtd. in Frauenheim). Employers, in other words, may benefit from showing more faith in their employees' ability to exercise their autonomy.

Orlov cites an indirect source: words quoted in another source.

Employees' right to privacy and autonomy in the workplace, however, remains a murky area of the law. Although evaluating where to draw the line between employee rights and employer powers is often a duty that falls to the judicial system, the courts have shown little willingness to intrude on employers' exercise of control over their computer networks. Federal law provides few guidelines related to online monitoring of employees, and only Connecticut and Delaware require companies to disclose this type of surveillance to employees (Tam et al.). "It is unlikely that we will see a legally guaranteed zone of privacy in the American workplace," predicts Kesan (293). This reality leaves employees and employers to sort the potential risks and benefits of technology in contract agreements and terms of employment. With continuing advances in technology, protecting both employers and employees will require greater awareness of these programs, better disclosure to employees, and a more public discussion about what types of protections are necessary to guard individual freedoms in the wired workplace.

Orlov sums up her argument and suggests a course of action.

Orlov 5

Heading is centered.

Works Cited

List is alphabetized by authors' last names (or by title when a work has no author).

Abbreviation "n.d." indicates that the online source has no update date.

First line of each entry is at the left margin; extra lines are indented 1/2".

Double-spacing is used throughout.

A work with four authors is listed by the first author's name and the abbreviation "et al." (for "and others").

Adams, Scott. *Dilbert and the Way of the Weasel.* New York: Harper, 2002. Print.

American Management Association and ePolicy Institute. "2005 Electronic Monitoring and Surveillance Survey." *American Management Association.* Amer. Management Assn., 2005. Web. 15 Feb. 2009.

"Automatically Record Everything They Do Online! Spector Pro 5.0 FAQ's." *Netbus.org.* Netbus.Org, n.d. Web. 17 Feb. 2009.

Flynn, Nancy. "Internet Policies." *ePolicy Institute.* ePolicy Inst., n.d. Web. 15 Feb. 2009.

Frauenheim, Ed. "Stop Reading This Headline and Get Back to Work." *CNET News.com.* CNET Networks, 11 July 2005. Web. 17 Feb. 2009.

Gonsalves, Chris. "Wasting Away on the Web." *eWeek.com.* Ziff Davis Enterprise Holdings, 8 Aug. 2005. Web. 16 Feb. 2009.

Kesan, Jay P. "Cyber-Working or Cyber-Shirking? A First Principles Examination of Electronic Privacy in the Workplace." *Florida Law Review* 54.2 (2002): 289-332. Print.

Lane, Frederick S., III. *The Naked Employee: How Technology Is Compromising Workplace Privacy.* New York: Amer. Management Assn., 2003. Print.

Tam, Pui-Wing, et al. "Snooping E-Mail by Software Is Now a Workplace Norm." *Wall Street Journal* 9 Mar. 2005: B1+. Print.

Tynan, Daniel. "Your Boss Is Watching." *PC World.* PC World Communications, 6 Oct. 2004. Web. 17 Sept. 2009.

Verespej, Michael A. "Inappropriate Internet Surfing." *Industry Week.* Penton Media, 7 Feb. 2000. Web. 16 Feb. 2009.

APA
CMS

APA and CMS Papers

APA/CMS APA and CMS Papers

Directory to APA in-text citation models, 443

Directory to APA reference list models, 443

APA Papers

APA-1 Supporting a thesis, 445

- a Forming a thesis, 445
- b Organizing your ideas, 446
- c Using sources to inform and support your argument, 446

APA-2 Citing sources; avoiding plagiarism, 448

- a Citing quotations and borrowed ideas, 448
- b Enclosing borrowed language in quotation marks, 449
- c Putting summaries and paraphrases in your own words, 450

APA-3 Integrating sources, 451

- a Using quotations appropriately, 451
- b Using signal phrases, 453
- c Synthesizing sources, 456

APA-4 Documenting sources, 458

- a APA in-text citations, 459
- b APA list of references, 463

APA CITATIONS AT A GLANCE
Article in a journal or magazine, 467
Book, 470
Article from a database, 474
Section in a Web document, 478

APA-5 Manuscript format; sample paper, 483

- a Manuscript format, 484
- b Sample APA paper, 487

Directory to CMS-style note and bibliography models, 498

CMS (*Chicago*) Papers

CMS-1 Supporting a thesis, 499

- a Forming a thesis, 499
- b Organizing your ideas, 500
- c Using sources to inform and support your argument, 500

CMS-2 Citing sources; avoiding plagiarism, 502

- a Citing quotations and borrowed ideas, 502
- b Enclosing borrowed language in quotation marks, 503
- c Putting summaries and paraphrases in your own words, 503

CMS-3 Integrating sources, 505

- a Using quotations appropriately, 505
- b Using signal phrases, 507

CMS-4 Documenting sources, 510

- a First and subsequent notes, 510
- b Bibliography, 511
- c Model notes and bibliography entries, 511

CMS CITATIONS AT A GLANCE
Book, 514
Letter in a published collection, 518
Article in a scholarly journal, 520
Journal article from a database, 522
Primary source from a Web site, 526

CMS-5 Manuscript format; sample pages, 528

- a Manuscript format, 529
- b Sample CMS pages, 531

Directory to APA in-text citation models

1. Basic format for a quotation, 459
2. Basic format for a summary or a paraphrase, 459
3. Work with two authors, 460
4. Work with three to five authors, 460
5. Work with six or more authors, 460
6. Work with unknown author, 460
7. Organization as author, 461
8. Authors with the same last name, 461
9. Two or more works by the same author in the same year, 461
10. Two or more works in the same parentheses, 461
11. Personal communication, 462
12. Electronic source, 462
13. Indirect source, 463
14. Sacred or classical text, 463

Directory to APA reference list models

GENERAL GUIDELINES FOR LISTING AUTHORS (PRINT AND ONLINE)

1. Single author, 464
2. Multiple authors, 464
3. Organization as author, 465
4. Unknown author, 465
5. Two or more works by the same author, 465
6. Two or more works by the same author in the same year, 465

ARTICLES IN PERIODICALS (PRINT)

7. Article in a journal, 466
8. Article in a magazine, 466
9. Article in a newspaper, 466
10. Article with three to seven authors, 466
11. Article with eight or more authors, 466
12. Abstract of a journal article, 466
13. Letter to the editor, 468
14. Editorial or other unsigned article, 468
15. Newsletter article, 468
16. Review, 468

BOOKS (PRINT)

17. Basic format for a book, 468
18. Book with an editor, 469
19. Book with an author and an editor, 469
20. Book with an author and a translator, 469
21. Edition other than the first, 469
22. Article or chapter in an edited book or an anthology, 469
23. Multivolume work, 471
24. Introduction, preface, foreword, or afterword, 471
25. Dictionary or other reference work, 471
26. Article in a reference work, 471
27. Republished book, 471
28. Book with a title in its title, 471
29. Sacred or classical text, 471

ONLINE SOURCES

30. Article in an online journal, 472
31. Article in an online magazine, 472
32. Article in an online newspaper, 472
33. Supplemental material published only online, 473
34. Article from a database, 473
35. Abstract for an online article, 473
36. Online book, 473
37. Chapter in an online book, 473
38. Online reference work, 475

*Directory to **CMS-style note and bibliography models** is on page 498.*

Directory to APA reference list models (continued)

ONLINE SOURCES (continued)

39. Report or long document from a Web site, 475
40. Section in a Web document, 476
41. Short work from a Web site, 476
42. Document from a university or government agency Web site, 476
43. Article in an online newsletter, 476
44. Podcast, 476
45. Blog (Weblog) post, 477
46. Online audio or video file, 477
47. Entry in a wiki, 477
48. Data set or graphic representation, 477
49. Conference hearing, 480
50. E-mail, 480
51. Online posting, 480

OTHER SOURCES (INCLUDING ONLINE VERSIONS)

52. Dissertation from a database, 480
53. Unpublished dissertation, 480
54. Government document, 480
55. Report from a private organization, 481
56. Legal source, 481
57. Conference proceedings, 481
58. Paper presented at a meeting or symposium (unpublished), 481
59. Poster session at a conference, 481
60. Map or chart, 481
61. Advertisement, 481
62. Published interview, 482
63. Lecture, speech, or address, 482
64. Work of art or photograph, 482
65. Brochure, pamphlet, or fact sheet, 482
66. Presentation slides, 482
67. Film or video (motion picture), 482
68. Television program, 483
69. Sound recording, 483
70. Computer software or video game, 483

This tabbed section shows how to document sources in APA style for the social sciences and fields like nursing and business, and in CMS (*Chicago*) style for history and some humanities classes. It also includes discipline-specific advice on three important topics: supporting a thesis, citing sources and avoiding plagiarism, and integrating sources.

NOTE: For advice on finding and evaluating sources and on managing information in courses across the disciplines, see the tabbed section R, Researching.

APA Papers

Many writing assignments in the social sciences are either reports of original research or reviews of the literature (previously published research) on a particular topic. Often an original research report contains a "review of the literature" section that places the writer's project in the context of previous research.

Most social science instructors will ask you to document your sources with the American Psychological Association (APA) system of in-text citations and references described in APA-4. You face three main challenges when writing a social science paper that draws on sources: (1) supporting a thesis, (2) citing your sources and avoiding plagiarism, and (3) integrating quotations and other source material.

Examples in this section appear in APA style and are drawn from one student's research for a review of the literature on treatments for childhood obesity. Luisa Mirano's complete paper appears on pages 488–96.

APA-1 Supporting a thesis

Most assignments ask you to form a thesis, or main idea, and to support that thesis with well-organized evidence. In a paper reviewing the literature on a topic, this thesis analyzes the often competing conclusions drawn by a variety of researchers.

APA-1a Form a working thesis.

Once you have read a variety of sources and considered your issue from different perspectives, you are ready to form a working thesis: a one-sentence (or occasionally a two-sentence) statement of your central idea. (See also C1-c.) Because it is a working, or tentative, thesis, you can remain flexible and revise it as your ideas develop. Ultimately, your thesis will express not just your opinion but your informed, reasoned answer to your research question (see R1-a). Here, for example, is a research question posed by Luisa Mirano, a student in a psychology class, followed by her thesis in answer to that question.

RESEARCH QUESTION

Is medication the right treatment for the escalating problem of childhood obesity?

WORKING THESIS

Treating cases of childhood obesity with medication alone is too narrow an approach for this growing problem.

Notice that the thesis expresses a view on a debatable issue—an issue about which intelligent, well-meaning people might disagree. The writer's job is to persuade such readers that this view is worth taking seriously.

PRACTICE **hackerhandbooks.com/writersref**
> APA > APA 1–1 and APA 1–2

APA-1b Organize your ideas.

The American Psychological Association encourages the use of headings to help readers follow the organization of a paper. For an original research report, the major headings often follow a standard model: Method, Results, Discussion. The introduction is not given a heading; it consists of the material between the title of the paper and the first heading.

For a literature review, headings will vary. The student who wrote about treatments for childhood obesity used four questions to focus her research; the questions then became headings in her paper (see pp. 488–96).

Making the most of your handbook

A working thesis and rough outline can help writers get started.

▶ Drafting a working thesis: C1-c

▶ Sketching a plan: C1-d

APA-1c Use sources to inform and support your argument.

Used thoughtfully, your source materials will make your argument more complex and convincing for readers. Sources can play several different roles as you develop your points.

Providing background information or context

You can use facts and statistics to support generalizations or to establish the importance of your topic, as student writer Luisa Mirano does in her introduction.

> In March 2004, U.S. Surgeon General Richard Carmona called attention to a health problem in the United States that, until recently, has been overlooked: childhood obesity. Carmona said that the "astounding" 15% child obesity rate constitutes an "epidemic." Since the early 1980s, that rate has "doubled in children and tripled in adolescents." Now more than 9 million children are classified as obese.

Explaining terms or concepts

If readers are unlikely to be familiar with a word, a phrase, or an idea important to your topic, you must explain it for them. Quoting or paraphrasing a source can help you define terms and concepts in accessible language. Luisa Mirano uses a scholarly source to explain how one of the major obesity drugs functions.

> Sibutramine suppresses appetite by blocking the reuptake of the neurotransmitters serotonin and norepinephrine in the brain (Yanovski & Yanovski, 2002, p. 594).

Supporting your claims

As you draft your argument, make sure to back up your assertions with facts, examples, and other evidence from your research (see also A2-e). Luisa Mirano, for example, uses one source's findings to support her central idea that the medical treatment of childhood obesity has limitations.

> As journalist Greg Critser (2003) noted in his book *Fat Land*, use of weight-loss drugs is unlikely to have an effect without the proper "support system"—one that includes doctors, facilities, time, and money (p. 3).

Lending authority to your argument

Expert opinion can add credibility to your argument (see also A2-e). But don't rely on experts to make your argument for you. Construct your argument in your own words and, when appropriate, cite the judgment of an authority in the field for support.

> Both medical experts and policymakers recognize that solutions might come not only from a laboratory but also from policy, education, and advocacy. A handbook designed to educate doctors on obesity called for "major changes in some aspects of western culture" (Hoppin & Taveras, 2004, Conclusion section, para. 1).

Anticipating and countering alternative interpretations

Do not ignore sources that seem contrary to your position or that offer interpretations different from your own. Instead, use them to give voice to opposing points of view and alternative interpretations before you counter them (see A2-f). Readers often have objections in mind already, whether or not they agree with you. Mirano uses a source to acknowledge value in her opponents' position that medication alone can successfully treat childhood obesity.

> As researchers Yanovski and Yanovski (2002) have explained, obesity was once considered "either a moral failing or evidence of underlying psychopathology" (p. 592). But this view has shifted: Many medical professionals now consider obesity a biomedical rather than a moral condition, influenced by both genetic

and environmental factors. Yanovski and Yanovski have further noted that the development of weight-loss medications in the early 1990s showed that "obesity should be treated in the same manner as any other chronic disease . . . through the long-term use of medication" (p. 592).

APA-2 Citing sources; avoiding plagiarism

Your research paper is a collaboration between you and your sources. To be fair and ethical, you must acknowledge your debt to the writers of those sources. Failure to do so is a form of academic dishonesty known as *plagiarism*.

Three different acts are considered plagiarism: (1) failing to cite quotations and borrowed ideas, (2) failing to enclose borrowed language in quotation marks, and (3) failing to put summaries and paraphrases in your own words. It's a good idea to find out how your school defines and addresses academic dishonesty. (See also R3-c.)

APA-2a Cite quotations and borrowed ideas.

Sources are cited for two reasons:

- to tell readers where your information comes from—so that they can assess its reliability and, if interested, find and read the original source
- to give credit to the writers from whom you have borrowed words and ideas

You must cite anything you borrow from a source, including direct quotations; statistics and other specific facts; visuals such as tables, graphs, and diagrams; and any ideas you present in a summary or paraphrase.

The only exception is common knowledge—information that your readers may know or could easily locate in any number of reference sources. For example, most general encyclopedias will tell readers that Sigmund Freud wrote *The Interpretation of Dreams* and that chimpanzees can learn American Sign Language.

As a rule, when you have seen certain information repeatedly in your reading, you don't need to cite it. However, when information has appeared in only a few sources, when it is highly specific (as with statistics), or when it is controversial, you should cite the source.

PRACTICE **hackerhandbooks.com/writersref**
> APA > APA 2–1 to APA 2–5

The American Psychological Association recommends an author-date system of citations. The following is a brief description of how the author-date system often works.

1. The source is introduced by a signal phrase that includes the last name of the author followed by the date of publication in parentheses.
2. The material being cited is followed by a page number in parentheses.
3. At the end of the paper, an alphabetized list of references gives complete publication information for the source.

IN-TEXT CITATION

As researchers Yanovski and Yanovski (2002) have explained, obesity was once considered "either a moral failing or evidence of underlying psychopathology" (p. 592).

ENTRY IN THE LIST OF REFERENCES

Yanovski, S. Z., & Yanovski, J. A. (2002). Drug therapy: Obesity. *The New England Journal of Medicine, 346,* 591-602.

This basic APA format varies for different types of sources. For a detailed discussion and other models, see APA-4.

APA-2b Enclose borrowed language in quotation marks.

To indicate that you are using a source's exact phrases or sentences, you must enclose them in quotation marks unless they have been set off from the text by indenting (see p. 453). To omit the quotation marks is to claim—falsely—that the language is your own. Such an omission is plagiarism even if you have cited the source.

ORIGINAL SOURCE

In an effort to seek the causes of this disturbing trend, experts have pointed to a range of important potential contributors to the rise in childhood obesity that are unrelated to media: a reduction in physical education classes and after-school athletic programs, an increase in the availability of sodas and snacks in public schools, the growth in the number of fast-food outlets across the country, the trend toward "super-sizing" food portions in restaurants, and the increasing number of highly processed high-calorie and high-fat grocery products.

—Henry J. Kaiser Family Foundation, "The Role of Media in Childhood Obesity" (2004), p. 1

PLAGIARISM

According to the Henry J. Kaiser Family Foundation (2004), experts have pointed to a range of important potential contributors to the rise in childhood obesity that are unrelated to media (p. 1).

BORROWED LANGUAGE IN QUOTATION MARKS

According to the Henry J. Kaiser Family Foundation (2004), "experts have pointed to a range of important potential contributors to the rise in childhood obesity that are unrelated to media" (p. 1).

NOTE: When quoted sentences are set off from the text by indenting, quotation marks are not needed (see p. 453).

APA-2c Put summaries and paraphrases in your own words.

Summaries and paraphrases are written in your own words. A summary condenses information; a paraphrase conveys the information using roughly the same number of words as in the original source. When you summarize or paraphrase, it is not enough to name the source; you must restate the source's meaning using your own language. (See also R3-c.) You commit plagiarism if you half-copy the author's sentences—either by mixing the author's phrases with your own without using quotation marks or by plugging your own synonyms into the author's sentence structure. The following paraphrases are plagiarized—even though the source is cited—because their language and sentence structure are too close to those of the source.

ORIGINAL SOURCE

In an effort to seek the causes of this disturbing trend, experts have pointed to a range of important potential contributors to the rise in childhood obesity that are unrelated to media.

—Henry J. Kaiser Family Foundation, "The Role of Media in Childhood Obesity" (2004), p. 1

UNACCEPTABLE BORROWING OF PHRASES

According to the Henry J. Kaiser Family Foundation (2004), experts have indicated a range of significant potential contributors to the rise in childhood obesity that are not linked to media (p. 1).

UNACCEPTABLE BORROWING OF STRUCTURE

According to the Henry J. Kaiser Family Foundation (2004), experts have identified a variety of key factors causing a rise in childhood obesity, factors that are not tied to media (p. 1).

To avoid plagiarizing an author's language, resist the temptation to look at the source while you are summarizing or paraphrasing. After you have read the passage you want to paraphrase, set the source aside. Ask yourself, "What is the author's meaning?" In your own words, state your understanding of the author's basic point. Return to the source and check that you haven't used the author's language or sentence structure or misrepresented the author's ideas. When you fully understand another writer's meaning, you can more easily and accurately present those ideas in your own words.

ACCEPTABLE PARAPHRASE

A report by the Henry J. Kaiser Family Foundation (2004) described causes other than media for the childhood obesity crisis (p. 1).

APA-3 Integrating sources

Quotations, summaries, paraphrases, and facts will help you develop your argument, but they cannot speak for you. You can use several strategies to integrate information from sources into your paper while maintaining your own voice.

APA-3a Use quotations appropriately.

In your academic writing, keep the emphasis on your ideas; use your own words to summarize and to paraphrase your sources and to explain your points. Sometimes, however, quotations can be the most effective way to integrate a source.

WHEN TO USE QUOTATIONS

- When language is especially vivid or expressive
- When exact wording is needed for technical accuracy
- When it is important to let the debaters of an issue explain their positions in their own words
- When the words of an authority lend weight to an argument
- When the language of a source is the topic of your discussion

Limiting your use of quotations Although it is tempting to insert many quotations in your paper and to use your own words only for connecting passages, do not quote excessively. It is almost impossible to integrate numerous long quotations smoothly into your own text.

It is not always necessary to quote full sentences from a source. To reduce your reliance on the words of others, you can often integrate language from a source into your own sentence structure.

> Carmona (2004) advised the subcommittee that the situation constitutes an "epidemic" and that the skyrocketing statistics are "astounding."

> As researchers continue to face a number of unknowns about obesity, it may be helpful to envision treating the disorder, as Yanovski and Yanovski (2002) suggested, "in the same manner as any other chronic disease" (p. 592).

Using the ellipsis mark To condense a quoted passage, you can use the ellipsis mark (three periods, with spaces between) to indicate that you have omitted words. What remains must be grammatically complete.

> Roman (2003) reported that "social factors are nearly as significant as individual metabolism in the formation of . . . dietary habits of adolescents" (p. 345).

The writer has omitted the words *both healthy and unhealthy* from the source.

When you want to leave out one or more full sentences, use a period before the three ellipsis dots.

> According to Sothern and Gordon (2003), "Environmental factors may contribute as much as 80% to the causes of childhood obesity. . . . Research suggests that obese children demonstrate decreased levels of physical activity and increased psychosocial problems" (p. 104).

Ordinarily, do not use an ellipsis mark at the beginning or at the end of a quotation. Readers will understand that you have taken the quoted material from a longer passage, so such marks are not necessary. The only exception occurs when you have dropped words at the end of the final quoted sentence. In such cases, put three ellipsis dots before the closing quotation mark. Make sure that omissions and ellipsis marks do not distort the meaning of your source.

Using brackets Brackets allow you to insert your own words into quoted material. You can insert words in brackets to clarify a confusing reference or to keep a sentence grammatical in your context.

> The cost of treating obesity currently totals $117 billion per year—a price, according to the surgeon general, "second only to the cost of [treating] tobacco use" (Carmona, 2004).

To indicate an error such as a misspelling in a quotation, insert [*sic*], italicized and with brackets around it, right after the error. (See P6-b.)

Setting off long quotations When you quote forty or more words from a source, set off the quotation by indenting it one-half inch from the left margin. Use the normal right margin and do not single-space the quotation.

Long quotations should be introduced by an informative sentence, usually followed by a colon. Quotation marks are unnecessary because the indented format tells readers that the passage is taken word-for-word from the source.

> Yanovski and Yanovski (2002) have described earlier treatments of obesity that focused on behavior modification:
>
> > With the advent of behavioral treatments for obesity in the 1960s, hope arose that modification of maladaptive eating and exercise habits would lead to sustained weight loss, and that time-limited programs would produce permanent changes in weight. Medications for the treatment of obesity were proposed as short-term adjuncts for patients, who would presumably then acquire the skills necessary to continue to lose weight, reach "ideal body weight," and maintain a reduced weight indefinitely. (p. 592)

Notice that at the end of an indented quotation the parenthetical citation goes outside the final mark of punctuation. (When a quotation is run into your text, the opposite is true. See the sample citations on p. 452.)

APA-3b Use signal phrases to integrate sources.

Whenever you include a paraphrase, summary, or direct quotation of another writer's work in your paper, prepare your readers for it with a signal phrase. A signal phrase usually names the author of the source, gives the publication year in parentheses, and often provides some context. It commonly appears before the source material. To vary your sentence structure, you may decide to interrupt source material with a signal phrase or place the signal phrase after your paraphrase, summary, or direct quotation. It is generally acceptable in the social sciences to call authors by their last name only, even on a first mention. If your paper refers to two authors with same last name, use initials as well.

Using signal phrases in APA papers

To avoid monotony, try to vary both the language and the placement of your signal phrases.

Model signal phrases

In the words of Carmona (2004), "..."

As Yanovski and Yanovski (2002) have noted, "..."

Hoppin and Taveras (2004), medical researchers, pointed out that "..."

"...," claimed Critser (2003).

"...," wrote Duenwald (2004), "..."

Researchers McDuffie et al. (2003) have offered a compelling argument for this view: "..."

Hilts (2002) answered objections with the following analysis: "..."

Verbs in signal phrases

admitted	contended	reasoned
agreed	declared	refuted
argued	denied	rejected
asserted	emphasized	reported
believed	insisted	responded
claimed	noted	suggested
compared	observed	thought
confirmed	pointed out	wrote

When you write a signal phrase, choose a verb that is appropriate for the way you are using the source (see APA-1c). Are you providing background, explaining a concept, supporting a claim, lending authority, or refuting an argument? See the chart on this page for a list of verbs commonly used in signal phrases. Note that APA requires using verbs in the past tense or present perfect tense (*explained* or *has explained*) to introduce source material. Use the present tense only for discussing the results of an experiment (*the results show*) or knowledge that has been clearly established (*researchers agree*).

Marking boundaries

Readers need to move from your words to the words of a source without feeling a jolt. Avoid dropping direct quotations into your text without warning. Instead, provide clear signal phrases, including at least the author's name and the year of publication. Signal phrases mark the boundaries between source material and your own words; they can also tell readers why a source is worth quoting. (The signal phrase is highlighted in the second example.)

DROPPED QUOTATION

Obesity was once considered in a very different light. "For many years, obesity was approached as it if were either a moral failing or evidence of underlying psychopathology" (Yanovski & Yanovski, 2002, p. 592).

QUOTATION WITH SIGNAL PHRASE

Obesity was once considered in a very different light. As researchers Yanovski and Yanovski (2002) have explained, obesity was widely thought of as "either a moral failing or evidence of underlying psychopathology" (p. 592).

Using signal phrases with summaries and paraphrases

As with quotations, you should introduce most summaries and paraphrases with a signal phrase that mentions the author and the year and places the material in the context of your argument. Readers will then understand where the summary or paraphrase begins.

Without the signal phrase (highlighted) in the following example, readers might think that only the last sentence is being cited, when in fact the whole paragraph is based on the source.

Carmona (2004) advised a Senate subcommittee that the problem of childhood obesity is dire and that the skyrocketing statistics—which put the child obesity rate at 15%—are cause for alarm. More than 9 million children, double the number in the early 1980s, are classified as obese. Carmona warned that obesity can cause myriad physical problems that only worsen as children grow older.

There are times, however, when a summary or a paraphrase does not require a signal phrase naming the author. When the context makes clear where the cited material begins, you may omit the signal phrase and include the author's name and the year in parentheses. Unless the work is short, also include the page number in the parentheses.

Integrating statistics and other facts

When you are citing a statistic or another specific fact, a signal phrase is often not necessary. In most cases, readers will understand that the citation refers to the statistic or fact (not the whole paragraph).

In purely financial terms, the drugs cost more than $3 a day on average (Duenwald, 2004).

There is nothing wrong, however, with using a signal phrase to introduce a statistic or another fact.

> Duenwald (2004) reported that the drugs cost more than $3 a day on average.

Putting source material in context

Readers should not have to guess why source material appears in your paper. If you use another writer's words, you must explain how they relate to your point. In other words, you must put the source in context. It's a good idea to embed a quotation between sentences of your own, introducing it with a signal phrase and following it up with interpretive comments that link the quotation to your paper's argument. (See also APA-3c.)

QUOTATION WITH EFFECTIVE CONTEXT

A report by the Henry J. Kaiser Family Foundation (2004) outlined trends that may have contributed to the childhood obesity crisis, including food advertising for children as well as

> a reduction in physical education classes . . . , an increase in the availability of sodas and snacks in public schools, the growth in the number of fast-food outlets . . . , and the increasing number of highly processed high-calorie and high-fat grocery products. (p. 1)

Addressing each of these areas requires more than a doctor armed with a prescription pad; it requires a broad mobilization not just of doctors and concerned parents but of educators, food industry executives, advertisers, and media representatives.

APA-3c Synthesize sources.

When you synthesize multiple sources in a research paper, you create a conversation about your research topic. You show readers that your argument is based on your active analysis and integration of ideas, not just a list of quotations and paraphrases. Your synthesis will show how your sources relate to one another; one source may support, extend, or counter the ideas of another. Readers should be able to see how each one functions in your argument (see R2-a).

Considering how sources relate to your argument

Before you integrate sources and show readers how they relate to one another, consider how each one might contribute to your own argument. As student writer Luisa Mirano became more informed through her research about treatments for childhood obesity, she asked herself these questions: *What do I think about the various treatments for childhood obesity? Which sources might support my ideas? Which sources might help extend or illustrate the points I want to make? What common counterarguments do I need to address to strengthen my position?* Mirano kept these questions in mind as she read and annotated sources.

Placing sources in conversation

When you synthesize sources, you show readers how the ideas of one source relate to those of another by connecting and analyzing the ideas in the context of your argument. Keep the emphasis on your own writing. After all, you've done the research and thought through the issues, so you should control the conversation. The thread of your argument should be easy to identify and to understand, with or without your sources.

SAMPLE SYNTHESIS (DRAFT)

Student writer Luisa Mirano begins with a claim that needs support.

Signal phrases indicate how sources contribute to Mirano's paper and show that the ideas that follow are not her own.

Mirano interprets and connects sources. Each paragraph ends with her own thoughts.

Medical treatments have clear costs for individual patients, including unpleasant side effects, little information about long term use, and uncertainty that they will yield significant weight loss. The financial burden is heavy as well; the drugs cost more than $3 a day on average (Duenwald, 2004). In each of the clinical trials, use of medication was accompanied by expensive behavioral therapies, including counseling, nutrition education, fitness advising, and monitoring. As Critser (2003) noted in his book *Fat Land*, use of weight-loss drugs is unlikely to have an effect without the proper "support system"—one that includes doctors, facilities, time, and money (p. 3). For many families, this level of care is prohibitively expensive.

Both medical experts and policymakers recognize that solutions might come not only from a laboratory but also from policy, education, and advocacy. A handbook designed to educate doctors on obesity called for "major changes in some aspects of western culture" (Hoppin & Taveras, 2004, Conclusion section, para. 1). Solving the childhood obesity problem will require broad mobilization of doctors and concerned parents and also of educators, food industry executives, advertisers, and media representatives.

Student writer
Source 1
Student writer
Source 2
Student writer
Source 3
Student writer

In this draft, Mirano uses her own analyses to shape the conversation among her sources. She does not simply string quotations and statistics together or allow her sources to overwhelm her writing. The final sentence, written in her own voice, gives her an opportunity to explain to readers how her sources support and extend her argument.

When synthesizing sources, ask yourself these questions:

- Which sources inform, support, or extend your argument?
- Have you varied the functions of sources—to provide background, explain concepts, lend authority, and anticipate counterarguments? Do your signal phrases indicate these functions?
- Do you explain how your sources support your argument?
- Do you connect and analyze sources in your own voice?
- Is your own argument easy to identify and to understand, with or without your sources?

APA-4 Documenting sources

In most social science classes, you will be asked to use the APA system for documenting sources, which is set forth in the *Publication Manual of the American Psychological Association,* 6th ed. (Washington: APA, 2010). APA recommends in-text citations that refer readers to a list of references.

An in-text citation usually gives the author of the source (often in a signal phrase), the year of publication, and at times a page number in parentheses. At the end of the paper, a list of references provides publication information about the source (see p. 496 for a sample list). The direct link between the in-text citation and the entry in the reference list is highlighted in green in the following example.

IN-TEXT CITATION

Yanovski and Yanovski (2002) reported that "the current state of the treatment for obesity is similar to the state of the treatment of hypertension several decades ago" (p. 600).

ENTRY IN THE LIST OF REFERENCES

Yanovski, S. Z., & Yanovski, J. A. (2002). Drug therapy: Obesity. *The New England Journal of Medicine, 346,* 591-602.

For a reference list that includes this entry, see page 496.

APA-4a APA in-text citations

APA's in-text citations provide at least the author's last name and the year of publication. For direct quotations and some paraphrases, a page number is given as well.

For a directory to the in-text citation models in this section, see page 443, immediately following the tabbed divider.

NOTE: APA style requires the use of the past tense or the present perfect tense in signal phrases introducing cited material: *Smith (2005) reported . . . , Smith (2005) has argued. . . .*

1. Basic format for a quotation Ordinarily, introduce the quotation with a signal phrase that includes the author's last name followed by the year of publication in parentheses. Put the page number preceded by "p." (or "pp." for more than one page) in parentheses after the quotation.

> Critser (2003) noted that despite growing numbers of overweight Americans, many health care providers still "remain either in ignorance or outright denial about the health danger to the poor and the young" (p. 5).

If the author is not named in the signal phrase, place the author's name, the year, and the page number in parentheses after the quotation: (Critser, 2003, p. 5).

NOTE: APA style requires the year of publication in an in-text citation. Do not include a month, even if the entry in the reference list includes the month.

2. Basic format for a summary or a paraphrase Include the author's last name and the year either in a signal phrase introducing the material or in parentheses following it. Give a page number to help readers find the passage you are citing. (For the use of paragraph numbers and headings in online sources, see "No page numbers" on pp. 462–63.)

> Yanovski and Yanovski (2002) explained that sibutramine suppresses appetite by blocking the reuptake of the neurotransmitters serotonin and norepinephrine in the brain (p. 594).

> Sibutramine suppresses appetite by blocking the reuptake of the neurotransmitters serotonin and norepinephrine in the brain (Yanovski & Yanovski, 2002, p. 594).

PRACTICE **hackerhandbooks.com/writersref**
> APA > APA 4–1 to APA 4–3

3. Work with two authors Give the names of both authors in the signal phrase or the parentheses each time you cite the work. In the parentheses, use "&" between the authors' names; in the signal phrase, use "and."

> According to Sothern and Gordon (2003), "Environmental factors may contribute as much as 80% to the causes of childhood obesity" (p. 104).

> Obese children often engage in limited physical activity (Sothern & Gordon, 2003, p. 104).

4. Work with three to five authors Identify all authors in the signal phrase or the parentheses the first time you cite the source.

> In 2003, Berkowitz, Wadden, Tershakovec, and Cronquist concluded, "Sibutramine . . . must be carefully monitored in adolescents, as in adults, to control increases in [blood pressure] and pulse rate" (p. 1811).

In subsequent citations, use the first author's name followed by "et al." in either the signal phrase or the parentheses.

> As Berkowitz et al. (2003) advised, "Until more extensive safety and efficacy data are available, . . . weight-loss medications should be used only on an experimental basis for adolescents" (p. 1811).

5. Work with six or more authors Use the first author's name followed by "et al." in the signal phrase or the parentheses.

> McDuffie et al. (2002) tested 20 adolescents, aged 12-16, over a three-month period and found that orlistat, combined with behavioral therapy, produced an average weight loss of 4.4 kg, or 9.7 pounds (p. 646).

6. Work with unknown author If the author is unknown, mention the work's title in the signal phrase or give the first word or two of the title in the parenthetical citation. Titles of short works such as articles and chapters are put in quotation marks; titles of long works such as books and reports are italicized. (For online sources with no author, see item 12 on p. 462.)

> Children struggling to control their weight must also struggle with the pressures of television advertising that, on the one hand, encourages the consumption of junk food and, on the other, celebrates thin celebrities ("Television," 2002).

NOTE: In the rare case when "Anonymous" is specified as the author, treat it as if it were a real name: (Anonymous, 2001). In the list of references, also use the name Anonymous as author.

7. Organization as author If the author is a government agency or another organization, name the organization in the signal phrase or in the parenthetical citation the first time you cite the source.

> Obesity puts children at risk for a number of medical complications, including Type 2 diabetes, hypertension, sleep apnea, and orthopedic problems (Henry J. Kaiser Family Foundation, 2004, p. 1).

If the organization has a familiar abbreviation, you may include it in brackets the first time you cite the source and use the abbreviation alone in later citations.

FIRST CITATION (Centers for Disease Control and Prevention [CDC], 2009)

LATER CITATIONS (CDC, 2009)

8. Authors with the same last name To avoid confusion, use initials with the last names if your reference list includes two or more authors with the same last name.

> Research by E. Smith (1989) revealed that. . . .

9. Two or more works by the same author in the same year When your list of references includes more than one work by the same author in the same year, use lowercase letters ("a," "b," and so on) with the year to order the entries in the reference list. (See item 6 on p. 465.) Use those same letters with the year in the in-text citation.

> Research by Durgin (2003b) has yielded new findings about the role of counseling in treating childhood obesity.

10. Two or more works in the same parentheses When your parenthetical citation names two or more works, put them in the same order that they appear in the reference list, separated with semicolons.

> Researchers have indicated that studies of pharmacological treatments for childhood obesity are inconclusive (Berkowitz et al., 2003; McDuffie et al., 2002).

11. Personal communication Personal interviews, memos, letters, e-mail, and similar unpublished communications should be cited in the text only, not in the reference list. (Use the first initial with the last name in parentheses.)

> One of Atkinson's colleagues, who has studied the effect of the media on children's eating habits, has contended that advertisers for snack foods will need to design ads responsibly for their younger viewers (F. Johnson, personal communication, October 20, 2009).

12. Electronic source When possible, cite electronic sources, including online sources, as you would any other source, giving the author and the year.

> Atkinson (2001) found that children who spent at least four hours a day watching TV were less likely to engage in adequate physical activity during the week.

Electronic sources sometimes lack authors' names, dates, or page numbers.

Unknown author

If no author is named in the source, mention the title of the source in the signal phrase or give the first word or two of the title in the parentheses (see also item 6). (If an organization serves as the author, see item 7.)

> The body's basal metabolic rate, or BMR, is a measure of its at-rest energy requirement ("Exercise," 2003).

Unknown date

When the date is unknown, use the abbreviation "n.d." (for "no date").

> Attempts to establish a definitive link between television programming and children's eating habits have been problematic (Magnus, n.d.).

No page numbers

APA requires page numbers for quotations, summaries, and paraphrases. When an electronic source lacks stable numbered pages, include paragraph numbers or headings, if the source has them, to help readers locate the particular passage you are citing.

If the source has numbered paragraphs, use the paragraph number preceded by the abbreviation "para.": (Hall, 2008, para. 5). If the source contains headings, cite the appropriate heading in parentheses; you may also indicate the paragraph under the heading that you are referring to, even if the paragraphs are not numbered.

Hoppin and Taveras (2004) pointed out that several other medications were classified by the Drug Enforcement Administration as having the "potential for abuse" (Weight-Loss Drugs section, para. 6).

NOTE: Electronic files in portable document format (PDF) often have stable page numbers. For such sources, give the page number in the parenthetical citation.

13. Indirect source If you use a source that was cited in another source (a secondary source), name the original source in your signal phrase. List the secondary source in your reference list and include it in your parenthetical citation, preceded by the words "as cited in." In the following example, Satcher is the original source, and Critser is the secondary source, given in the reference list.

Former surgeon general Dr. David Satcher described "a nation of young people seriously at risk of starting out obese and dooming themselves to the difficult task of overcoming a tough illness" (as cited in Critser, 2003, p. 4).

14. Sacred or classical text Identify the text, the version or edition you used, and the relevant part (chapter, verse, line). It is not necessary to include the source in the reference list.

Peace activists have long cited the biblical prophet's vision of a world without war: "And they shall beat their swords into plowshares, and their spears into pruning hooks; nation shall not lift up sword against nation, neither shall they learn war any more" (Isaiah 2:4, Revised Standard Version).

APA-4b APA list of references

In APA style, the alphabetical list of works cited, which appears at the end of the paper, is titled "References." For advice on preparing the list, see pages 486–87. For a sample reference list, see page 496.

For a directory to the reference list models in this section, see pages 443–44, immediately following the tabbed divider.

Alphabetize entries in the list of references by authors' last names; if a work has no author, alphabetize it by its title. The first element of each entry is important because citations in the text of the paper refer to it and readers will be looking for it in the alphabetized list. The date of publication appears immediately after the first element of the citation.

In APA style, titles of books are italicized; titles of articles are neither italicized nor put in quotation marks. (For rules on capitalization of titles, see p. 485.)

PRACTICE **hackerhandbooks.com/writersref**
> APA > APA 4–4 to APA 4–8

General guidelines for listing authors (print and online)

In APA style, all authors' names are inverted (the last name comes first), and initials are used for all first and middle names.

NAME AND DATE CITED IN TEXT

Duncan (2008) has reported that. . . .

BEGINNING OF ENTRY IN THE LIST OF REFERENCES

Duncan, B. (2008).

1. Single author

author: last name + initial(s) | year | title (book)

Egeland, J. (2008). *A billion lives: An eyewitness report from the frontlines of humanity.*

place of publication | publisher

New York, NY: Simon & Schuster.

2. Multiple authors List up to seven authors by last names followed by initials. Use an ampersand (&) before the name of the last author. If there are more than seven authors, list the first six followed by three ellipsis dots and the last author's name. (See p. 460 for citing works with multiple authors in the text of your paper.)

Two to seven authors

all authors: last name + initial(s) | year | title (book) | place of publication | publisher

Musick, M. A., & Wilson, J. (2007). *Volunteers: A social profile.* Bloomington: Indiana University Press.

all authors: last name + initial(s) | year | title (article) | journal title | volume | page(s)

Diessner, R., Solom, R. C., Frost, N. K., Parsons, L., & Davidson, J. (2008). Engagement with beauty: Appreciating natural, artistic, and moral beauty. *The Journal of Psychology, 142,* 303-329.

Eight or more authors

Mulvaney, S. A., Mudasiru, E., Schlundt, D. G., Baughman, C. L., Fleming, M., VanderWoude, A., . . . Rothman, R. (2008). Self-management in Type 2 diabetes: The adolescent perspective. *The Diabetes Educator, 34,* 118-127.

3. Organization as author

author: organization name — year — title (book)

American Psychiatric Association. (1994). *Diagnostic and statistical manual of mental*

edition number — place of publication — organization as author and publisher

disorders (4th ed.). Washington, DC: Author.

If the publisher is not the same as the author, give the publisher's name at the end as you would for any other source.

4. Unknown author Begin the entry with the work's title.

title (book) — year — place of publication — publisher

New concise world atlas. (2007). New York, NY: Oxford University Press.

title (article) — year + month + day (for weekly publication) — journal title — volume, issue — page(s)

Order in the jungle. (2008, March 15). *The Economist, 386*(8571), 83-85.

5. Two or more works by the same author Use the author's name for all entries. List the entries by year, the earliest first.

Barry, P. (2007, December 8). Putting tumors on pause. *Science News, 172,* 365.

Barry, P. (2008, August 2). Finding the golden genes. *Science News, 174,* 16-21.

6. Two or more works by the same author in the same year List the works alphabetically by title. In the parentheses, following the year add "a," "b," and so on. Use these same letters when giving the year in the in-text citation. (See also p. 486.)

Elkind, D. (2008a, Spring). Can we play? *Greater Good, 4*(4), 14-17.

Elkind, D. (2008b, June 27). The price of hurrying children [Web log post]. Retrieved from http://blogs.psychologytoday.com/blog/digital-children

Articles in periodicals (print)

Periodicals include journals, magazines, and newspapers. For a journal or a magazine, give only the volume number if the publication is paginated continuously throughout each volume; give the volume and issue numbers if each issue of the volume begins on page 1. Italicize the volume number and put the issue number, not italicized, in parentheses.

For all periodicals, when an article appears on consecutive pages, provide the range of pages. When an article does not appear on consecutive pages, give all page numbers: A1, A17. (See also "Online sources" beginning on p. 472 for online articles and articles accessed through a library's database.) For an illustrated citation of an article in a print journal or magazine, see page 467.

7. Article in a journal

author: last name + initial(s) | year | article title | journal title | volume | page(s)

Zhang, L.-F. (2008). Teachers' styles of thinking: An exploratory study. *The Journal of Psychology, 142,* 37-55.

8. Article in a magazine

8. Article in a magazine Cite as you would a journal article, but give the year and the month for monthly magazines; add the day for weekly magazines.

McKibben, B. (2007, October). Carbon's new math. *National Geographic, 212*(4), 32-37.

9. Article in a newspaper

author: last name + initial(s) | year + month + day (for daily publication) | article title | newspaper title | page(s)

Svoboda, E. (2008, October 21). Deep in the rain forest, stalking the next pandemic. *The New York Times,* p. D5.

Give the year, month, and day for daily and weekly newspapers. Use "p." or "pp." before page numbers.

10. Article with three to seven authors

Ungar, M., Brown, M., Liebenberg, L., Othman, R., Kwong, W. M., Armstrong, M., & Gilgun, J. (2007). Unique pathways to resilience across cultures. *Adolescence, 42,* 287-310.

11. Article with eight or more authors List the first six authors followed by three ellipsis dots and the last author.

Krippner, G., Granovetter, M., Block, F., Biggart, N., Beamish, T., Hsing, Y., . . . O'Riain, S. (2004). Polanyi Symposium: A conversation on embeddedness. *Socio-Economic Review, 2,* 109-135.

12. Abstract of a journal article

Lahm, K. (2008). Inmate-on-inmate assault: A multilevel examination of prison violence [Abstract]. *Criminal Justice and Behavior, 35*(1), 120-137.

Citation at a glance: Article in a journal or magazine (APA)

To cite an article in a print journal or magazine in APA style, include the following elements:

1. Author
2. Year of publication for journal; complete date for magazine
3. Title of article
4. Name of journal or magazine
5. Volume number; issue number, if required (see p. 466)
6. Page number(s) of article

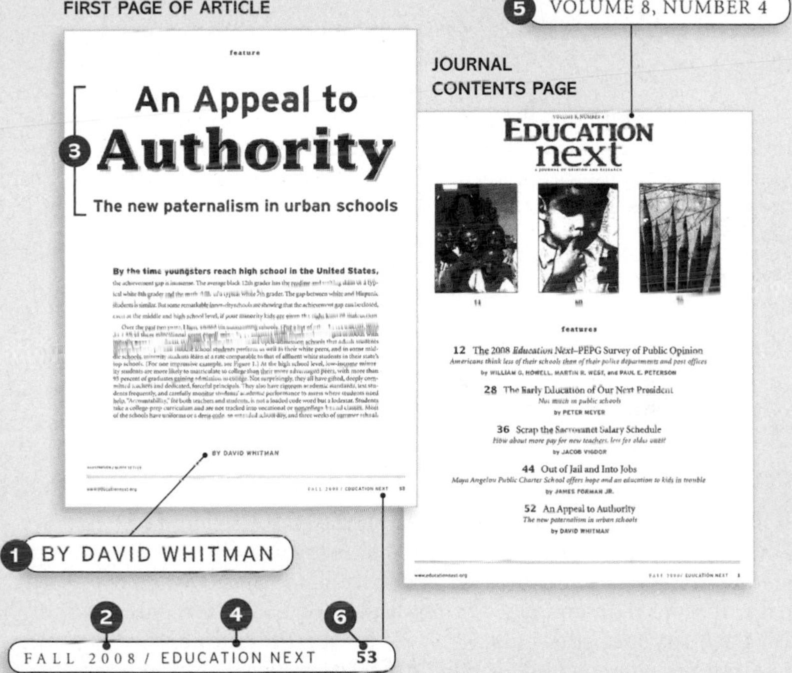

FIRST PAGE OF ARTICLE
5 VOLUME 8, NUMBER 4
feature
An Appeal to
3 Authority
The new paternalism in urban schools
By the time youngsters reach high school in the United States,
BY DAVID WHITMAN
FALL 2008 / EDUCATION NEXT 53
JOURNAL CONTENTS PAGE
EDUCATION next
features
12 The 2008 Education Next–PEPG Survey of Public Opinion
by WILLIAM G. HOWELL, MARTIN R. WEST, and PAUL E. PETERSON
28 The Early Education of Our Next President
by PETER MEYER
36 Scrap the Sacrosanct Salary Schedule
by JACOB VIGDOR
44 Out of Jail and Into Jobs
by JAMES FORMAN JR.
52 An Appeal to Authority
The new paternalism in urban schools
by DAVID WHITMAN
1 BY DAVID WHITMAN
2 4 6
FALL 2008 / EDUCATION NEXT 53

REFERENCE LIST ENTRY FOR AN ARTICLE IN A PRINT JOURNAL OR MAGAZINE

(1) Whitman, D. (2) (2008). (3) An appeal to authority: The new paternalism in urban schools. (4) *Education Next,* (5) *8*(4), (6) 53-58.

For variations on citing articles in print journals or magazines in APA style, see pages 466–68.

13. Letter to the editor Follow the appropriate model for a journal, magazine, or newspaper (see items 7–9) and insert the words "Letter to the editor" in brackets after the title of the letter. If the letter has no title, use the bracketed words as the title.

Park, T. (2008, August). Defining the line [Letter to the editor]. *Scientific American, 299*(2), 10.

14. Editorial or other unsigned article

The global justice movement [Editorial]. (2005). *Multinational Monitor, 26*(7/8), 6.

15. Newsletter article

Setting the stage for remembering. (2006, September). *Mind, Mood, and Memory, 2*(9), 4-5.

16. Review Give the author and title of the review (if any) and, in brackets, the type of work, the title, and the author for a book or the year for a motion picture. If the review has no author or title, use the material in brackets as the title.

Applebaum, A. (2008, February 14). A movie that matters [Review of the motion picture *Katyn,* 2007]. *The New York Review of Books, 55*(2), 13-15.

Agents of change. (2008, February 2). [Review of the book *The power of unreasonable people: How social entrepreneurs create markets that change the world,* by J. Elkington & P. Hartigan]. *The Economist, 386*(8565), 94.

Books (print)

Items 17–29 apply to print books. For online books, see items 36 and 37. For an illustrated citation of a print book, see page 470.

Take the information about a book from its title page and copyright page. If more than one place of publication is listed, use only the first. Give the city and state (abbreviated) for all US cities or the city and country (not abbreviated) for all non-US cities; also include the province (not abbreviated) for Canadian cities. Do not give a state if the publisher's name includes it (as in many university presses, for example).

17. Basic format for a book

author: last name + initial(s) | year of publication | book title

McKenzie, F. R. (2008). *Theory and practice with adolescents: An applied approach.*

place of publication | publisher

Chicago, IL: Lyceum Books.

18. Book with an editor

all editors: last name + initial(s) | year of publication | book title | edition

Aronson, J., & Aronson, E. (Eds.). (2008). *Readings about the social animal* (10th ed.).

place of publication | publisher

New York, NY: Worth.

The abbreviation "Eds." is for multiple editors. If the book has one editor, use "Ed."

19. Book with an author and an editor

author: last name + initial(s) | year of publication | book title | name(s) of editor(s): in normal order

McLuhan, M. (2003). *Understanding me: Lectures and interviews* (S. McLuhan & D. Staine,

place of publication (city, province, country) | publisher

Eds.). Toronto, Ontario, Canada: McClelland & Stewart.

The abbreviation "Eds." is for multiple editors. If the book has one editor, use "Ed."

20. Book with an author and a translator After the title, name the translator, followed by "Trans.," in parentheses. Add the original date of publication at the end of the entry.

Steinberg, M. D. (2003). *Voices of revolution, 1917* (M. Schwartz, Trans.). New Haven, CT: Yale University Press. (Original work published 2001)

21. Edition other than the first

O'Brien, J. A. (Ed.). (2006). *The production of reality: Essays and readings on social interaction* (4th ed.). Thousand Oaks, CA: Pine Forge Press.

If the entry also requires volume numbers (see item 23), put the volume numbers after the edition number: (3rd ed., Vols. 1-3).

22. Article or chapter in an edited book or an anthology

author of chapter: last name + initial(s) | year of publication | title of chapter

Denton, N. A. (2006). Segregation and discrimination in housing. In R. G. Bratt,

book editor(s): in normal order | book title

M. E. Stone, & C. Hartman (Eds.), *A right to housing: Foundation of a new*

page(s) for chapter | place of publication | publisher

social agenda (pp. 61-81). Philadelphia, PA: Temple University Press.

Citation at a glance: Book (APA)

To cite a print book in APA style, include the following elements:

1 Author
2 Year of publication
3 Title and subtitle
4 Place of publication
5 Publisher

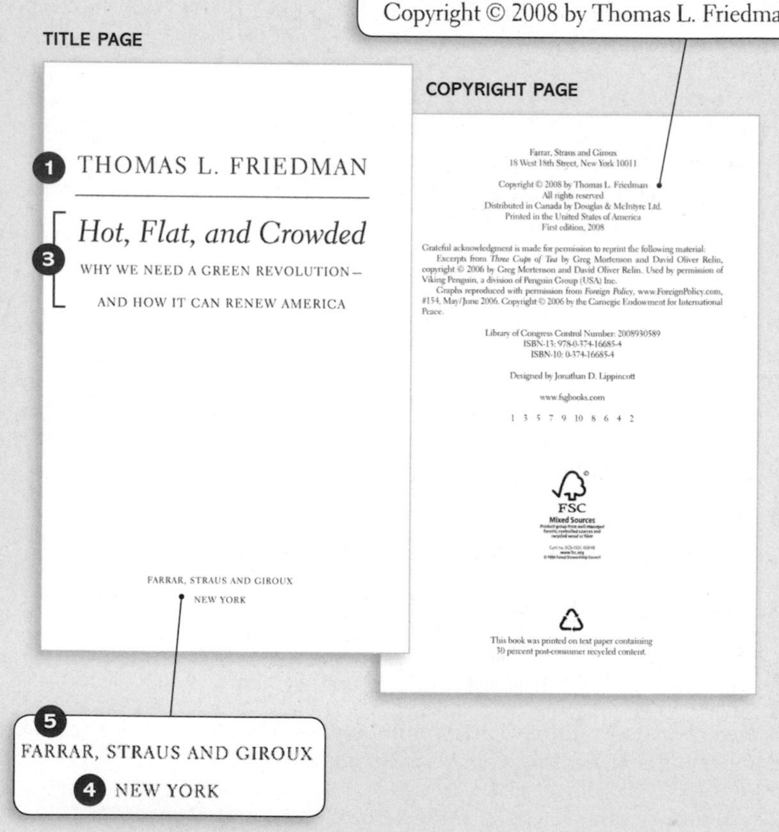

REFERENCE LIST ENTRY FOR A PRINT BOOK

Friedman, T. L.[1] (2008).[2] *Hot, flat, and crowded: Why we need a green revolution—And how it can renew America.*[3] New York, NY:[4] Farrar, Straus and Giroux.[5]

For more on citing print books in APA style, see pages 468–71.

The abbreviation "Eds." is for multiple editors. If the book has one editor, use "Ed."

23. Multivolume work Give the number of volumes after the title.

Luo, J. (Ed.). (2005). *China today: An encyclopedia of life in the People's Republic* (Vols. 1-2). Westport, CT: Greenwood Press.

If the work is published in an edition other than the first (see item 21), put the edition number before the volume numbers: (3rd ed., Vols. 1-3).

24. Introduction, preface, foreword, or afterword

Gore, A. (2000). Foreword. In B. Katz (Ed.), *Reflections on regionalism* (pp. ix-x). Washington, DC: Brookings Institution Press.

25. Dictionary or other reference work

Leong, F. T. L. (Ed.). (2008). *Encyclopedia of counseling* (Vols. 1-4). Thousand Oaks, CA: Sage.

26. Article in a reference work

Konijn, E. A. (2008). Affects and media exposure. In W. Donsbach (Ed.), *The international encyclopedia of communication* (Vol. 1, pp. 123-129). Malden, MA: Blackwell.

27. Republished book

Mailer, N. (2008). *Miami and the siege of Chicago: An informal history of the Republican and Democratic conventions of 1968.* New York, NY: New York Review Books. (Original work published 1968)

28. Book with a title in its title If the book title contains another book title or an article title, neither italicize the internal title nor place it in quotation marks.

Marcus, L. (Ed.). (1999). *Sigmund Freud's* The interpretation of dreams*: New interdisciplinary essays.* Manchester, England: Manchester University Press.

29. Sacred or classical text It is not necessary to list sacred works such as the Bible or the Qur'an or classical Greek and Roman works in your reference list. See item 14 on page 463 for how to cite these sources in the text of your paper.

Online sources

When citing an online article, include publication information as for a print periodical (see items 7–16) and add information about the online version (see items 30–35).

Online articles and books sometimes include a DOI (digital object identifier). APA uses the DOI, when available, in place of a URL in reference list entries.

Use a retrieval date for an online source only if the content is likely to change. Most of the examples in this section do not show a retrieval date because the content of the sources is stable; if you are unsure about whether to use a retrieval date, consult your instructor.

If you must break a DOI or a URL at the end of a line, break it after a double slash or before any other mark of punctuation; do not add a hyphen. Do not put a period at the end of the entry.

30. Article in an online journal

author: last name + initial(s) | year of publication | article title | journal title | volume

Whitmeyer, J. M. (2000). Power through appointment. *Social Science Research, 29,*

page(s) | DOI

535-555. doi:10.1006/ssre.2000.0680

If there is no DOI, include the URL for the journal's home page.

Ashe, D. D., & McCutcheon, L. E. (2001). Shyness, loneliness, and attitude toward celebrities. *Current Research in Social Psychology, 6,* 124-133. Retrieved from http://www.uiowa.edu/~grpproc/crisp/crisp.html

31. Article in an online magazine Give the author, date, article title, and magazine title. Follow with the volume, issue, and page numbers, if they are available. End with the URL for the magazine's home page.

Shelburne, E. C. (2008, September). The great disruption. *The Atlantic, 302*(2). Retrieved from http://www.theatlantic.com/

Rupley, S. (2010, February 26). The myth of the benign monopoly. *Salon.* Retrieved from http://www.salon.com/

32. Article in an online newspaper Give the author, date, article title, and newspaper title. Follow with the page numbers, if they are available. End with the URL for the newspaper's home page.

Watson, P. (2008, October 19). Biofuel boom endangers orangutan habitat. *Los Angeles Times.* Retrieved from http://www.latimes.com/

33. Supplemental material published only online If a journal, magazine, or newspaper contains extra material (an article or a chart, for example) only in its online version, give whatever publication information is available in the source and add the description "Supplemental material" in brackets after the title.

Samuel, T. (2009, March 27). Mind the wage gap [Supplemental material]. *The American Prospect*. Retrieved from http://www.prospect.org/

34. Article from a database Start with the publication information for the source (see items 7–16). If the database entry includes a DOI for the article, use the DOI number at the end. For an illustrated citation of a work from a database, see page 474.

all authors: last name + initial(s) | year | article title

Eskritt, M., & McLeod, K. (2008). Children's note taking as a mnemonic tool.

journal title | volume | page(s) | DOI

Journal of Experimental Child Psychology, 101, 52-74. doi:10.1016 /jecp.2008.05.007

If there is no DOI, include the URL for the home page of the journal. If the URL is not included in the database entry, you can search for it on the Web.

Howard, K. R. (2007). Childhood overweight: Parental perceptions and readiness for change. *The Journal of School Nursing, 23,* 73-79. Retrieved from http://jsn .sagepub.com/

35. Abstract for an online article

Brockerhoff, E. G., Jactel, H., Parrotta, J. A., Quine, C. P., & Sayer, J. (2008). Plantation forests and biodiversity: Oxymoron or opportunity? [Abstract]. *Biodiversity and Conservation, 17,* 925-951. doi:10.1007/s10531-008-9380-x

36. Online book

Adams, B. (2004). *The theory of social revolutions.* Retrieved from http://www .gutenberg.org/catalog/world/readfile?fk_files=44092 (Original work published 1913)

37. Chapter in an online book

Clinton, S. J. (1999). What can be done to prevent childhood obesity? In *Understanding childhood obesity* (pp. 81-98). Retrieved from http://www.questia.com/

Citation at a glance: Article from a database (APA)

To cite an article from a database in APA style, include the following elements:

1. Author(s)
2. Date of publication
3. Title of article
4. Name of periodical
5. Volume number; issue number, if required (see p. 465)
6. Page number(s)
7. DOI (digital object identifier)
8. URL for journal's home page (if there is no DOI)

ON-SCREEN VIEW OF DATABASE RECORD

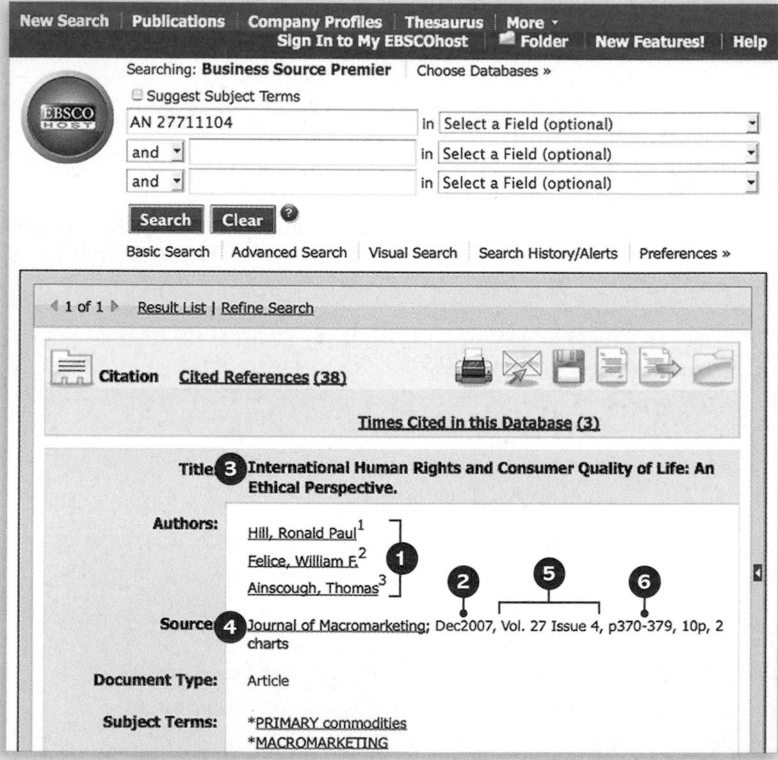

END OF DATABASE RECORD

ISSN:	0276-1467
DOI:	10.1177/027614670307128 7

REFERENCE LIST ENTRY FOR AN ARTICLE FROM A DATABASE

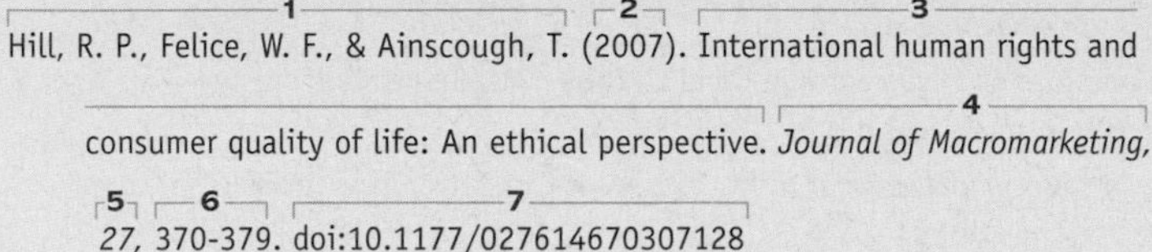

1
2
3
Hill, R. P., Felice, W. F., & Ainscough, T. (2007). International human rights and
4
consumer quality of life: An ethical perspective. *Journal of Macromarketing,*
5
6
7
27, 370-379. doi:10.1177/027614670307128

For more on citing articles from a database in APA style, see item 34.

38. Online reference work

Swain, C. M. (2004). Sociology of affirmative action. In N. J. Smelser & P. B. Baltes (Eds.), *International encyclopedia of the social and behavioral sciences.* Retrieved from http://www.sciencedirect.com/science/referenceworks/9780080430768

Include a retrieval date only if the content of the work is likely to change.

39. Report or long document from a Web site List the author's name, publication date (or "n.d." if there is no date), document title (in italics), and URL for the document. Give a retrieval date only if the content of the source is likely to change. If a source has no author, begin with the title and follow it with the date in parentheses (see item 4 on p. 465).

Source with date

all authors: last name + initial(s) | online publication date | document title

Cain, A., & Burris, M. (1999, April). *Investigation of the use of mobile phones while driving.* Retrieved from http://www.cutr.usf.edu/pdf/mobile_phone.PDF

URL

Source with no date

Archer, D. (n.d.). *Exploring nonverbal communication.* Retrieved from http://nonverbal .ucsc.edu

40. Section in a Web document

author (organization) | year | title of section | title of Web document | URL

National Institute on Media and the Family. (2009). Mobile networking. In *Guide to social networking: Risks*. Retrieved from http://www.mediafamily.org/network_pdf/MediaWise_Guide_to_Social_Networking_Risks_09.pdf

For an illustrated citation of a section in a Web document, see page 478.

41. Short work from a Web site

NATO statement endangers patients in Afghanistan. (2010, March 11). *Médecins sans frontières/Doctors without borders*. Retrieved from http://www.doctorswithoutborders.org/

42. Document from a university or government agency Web site

Cosmides, L., & Tooby, J. (1997). *Evolutionary psychology: A primer.* Retrieved from University of California, Santa Barbara, Center for Evolutionary Psychology website: http://www.psych.ucsb.edu/research/cep/primer.html

43. Article in an online newsletter Cite as an online article (see items 30–32), giving the title of the newsletter and whatever other information is available, including volume and issue numbers.

In the face of extinction. (2008, May). *NSF Current*. Retrieved from http://www.nsf.gov/news/newsletter/may_08/index.jsp

44. Podcast

organization as producer | date of posting | podcast title | descriptive label | series title | URL

National Academies (Producer). (2007, June 6). Progress in preventing childhood obesity: How do we measure up? [Audio podcast]. *The sounds of science podcast*. Retrieved from http://media.nap.edu/podcasts/

writer/presenter | date of posting | podcast title | podcast number | descriptive label | Web site hosting podcast | URL

Chesney, M. (2007, September 13). Gender differences in the use of complementary and alternative medicine (No. 12827) [Audio podcast]. Retrieved from University of California Television website: http://www.uctv.tv/ondemand

45. Blog (Weblog) post Give the writer's name, the date of the post, the subject, the label "Web log post" in brackets, and the URL. For a response to a post, use the label "Web log comment."

Kellermann, M. (2007, May 23). Disclosing clinical trials [Web log post]. Retrieved from http://www.iq.harvard.edu/blog/sss/archives/2007/05

46. Online audio or video file Give the medium or a description of the source file in brackets following the title.

writer/presenter | no date | title | descriptive label | URL

Chomsky, N. (n.d.). The new imperialism [Audio file]. Retrieved from http://www.rhapsody.com/noamchomsky

Zakaria, F. (Host), & McCullough, C. (Writer). (2007, March 6). In focus: American teens, Rwandan truths [Video file]. Retrieved from http://www.pulitzercenter.org/showproject.cfm?id=26

47. Entry in a wiki Begin with the title of the entry and the date of posting, if there is one (use "n.d." for "no date" if there is not). Then add your retrieval date and the URL for the wiki entry. Include the date of retrieval because the content of a wiki can change frequently. If an author or an editor is identified, include that name at the beginning of the entry.

Ethnomethodology. (n.d.). Retrieved June 18, 2010, from http://stswiki.org/index.php?title/Ethnomethodology

48. Data set or graphic representation Give information about the type of source in brackets following the title. If there is no title, give a brief description of the content of the source in brackets in place of the title.

U.S. Department of Agriculture, Economic Research Service. (2009). *Eating and health module (ATUS): 2007 data* [Data set]. Retrieved from http://www.ers.usda.gov/Data/ATUS/Data/2007/2007data.htm

Gallup. (2008, October 23). *No increase in proportion of first-time voters* [Graphs]. Retrieved from http://www.gallup.com/poll/111331/No-Increase-Proportion-First-Time-Voters.aspx

Citation at a glance: Section in a Web document (APA)

To cite a section from a Web document in APA style, include the following elements:

1 Author
2 Date of publication or most recent update
3 Title of section
4 Title of document
5 URL of section or of document

BROWSER PRINTOUT OF WEB SITE

2008 Minnesota Health Statistics Annual Summary – Minnesota Dept. of Health

1 *Minnesota Department of Health*
Protecting, maintaining and improving the health of all Minnesotans

4 2008 Minnesota Health Statistics Annual Summary

The Minnesota "Annual Summary" or "Minnesota Health Statistics" is a report published yearly. The most recent version of this report is ***2008 Minnesota Health Statistics***, published January 2010. This report provides statistical data on the following subjects for the state of Minnesota.

2 published January 2010.

To view the PDF files, you will need Adobe Acrobat Re[...] site).

- Introduction, Technical Notes, Definitions (PDF: 42KB/7 pages)
- Overview of 2008 Annual Summary (PDF: 66KB/11 pages)
- Live Births (PDF: 196KB/21 pages)
- Fertility (PDF: 26KB/2 pages)  3
- Infant Mortality and Fetal Deaths (PDF: 188KB/15 pages)
- General Mortality (PDF: 333KB/40 pages)
- Marriage/Dissolution of Marriage Divorce (PDF: 25KB/2 pages)
- Population (PDF: 73KB/12 pages)

Note: Induced abortion statistics previously reported in this publication are now published separately.
See Report to the Legislature: Induced Abortions in Minnesota

See also Minnesota Health Statistics Annual Summary Main Page

For further information about the Annual Summary, please contact:

Center for Health Statistics
Minnesota Department of Health
Golden Rule Building, 3rd Floor
85 East Seventh Place

http://www.health.state.mn.us/divs/chs/annsum/08annsum/index.html Page 1 of 2

ON-SCREEN VIEW OF DOCUMENT

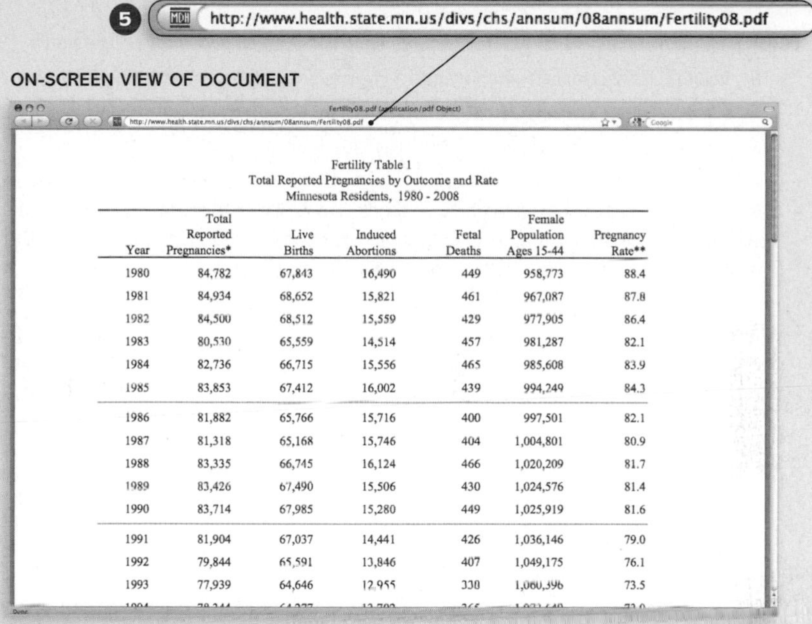

Fertility Table 1
Total Reported Pregnancies by Outcome and Rate
Minnesota Residents, 1980 - 2008

Year	Total Reported Pregnancies*	Live Births	Induced Abortions	Fetal Deaths	Female Population Ages 15-44	Pregnancy Rate**
1980	84,782	67,843	16,490	449	958,773	88.4
1981	84,934	68,652	15,821	461	967,087	87.8
1982	84,500	68,512	15,559	429	977,905	86.4
1983	80,530	65,559	14,514	457	981,287	82.1
1984	82,736	66,715	15,556	465	985,608	83.9
1985	83,853	67,412	16,002	439	994,249	84.3
1986	81,882	65,766	15,716	400	997,501	82.1
1987	81,318	65,168	15,746	404	1,004,801	80.9
1988	83,335	66,745	16,124	466	1,020,209	81.7
1989	83,426	67,490	15,506	430	1,024,576	81.4
1990	83,714	67,985	15,280	449	1,025,919	81.6
1991	81,904	67,037	14,441	426	1,036,146	79.0
1992	79,844	65,591	13,846	407	1,049,175	76.1
1993	77,939	64,646	12,955	338	1,060,396	73.5

REFERENCE LIST ENTRY FOR A SECTION IN A WEB DOCUMENT

1 2 3 4

Minnesota Department of Health. (2010, January). Fertility. In *2008 Minnesota health statistics annual summary*. Retrieved from http://www.health.state.mn.us/divs/chs/annsum/08annsum/Fertility08.pdf

5

For more on citing documents from Web sites in APA style, see pages 475–80.

49. Conference hearing

Carmona, R. H. (2004, March 2). *The growing epidemic of childhood obesity.* Testimony before the Subcommittee on Competition, Foreign Commerce, and Infrastructure of the U.S. Senate Committee on Commerce, Science, and Transportation. Retrieved from http://www.hhs.gov/asl/testify/t040302.html

50. E-mail E-mail messages, letters, and other personal communications are not included in the list of references. (See item 11 on p. 462 for citing these sources in the text of your paper.)

51. Online posting If an online posting is not archived, cite it as a personal communication in the text of your paper and do not include it in the list of references. If the posting is archived, give the URL and the name of the discussion list if it is not part of the URL.

McKinney, J. (2006, December 19). Adult education-healthcare partnerships [Electronic mailing list message]. Retrieved from http://www.nifl.gov/pipermail /healthliteracy/2006/000524.html

Other sources (including online versions)

52. Dissertation from a database

Hymel, K. M. (2009). *Essays in urban economics* (Doctoral dissertation). Available from ProQuest Dissertations and Theses database. (AAT 3355930)

53. Unpublished dissertation

Mitchell, R. D. (2007). *The Wesleyan Quadrilateral: Relocating the conversation* (Unpublished doctoral dissertation). Claremont School of Theology, Claremont, CA.

54. Government document

U.S. Census Bureau. (2006). *Statistical abstract of the United States.* Washington, DC: Government Printing Office.

U.S. Census Bureau, Bureau of Economic Analysis. (2008, August). *U.S. international trade in goods and services* (Report No. CB08-121, BEA08-37, FT-900). Retrieved from http://www.census.gov/foreign-trade/Press-Release/2008pr /06/ftdpress.pdf

55. Report from a private organization If the publisher is also the author, begin with the publisher's name in the author position. For a print source, use "Author" in the publisher position at the end of the entry (see item 3 on p. 465); for an online source, give the URL. If the report has a number, put it in parentheses following the title.

Ford Foundation. (n.d.). *Helping citizens to understand and influence state budgets.* Retrieved from http://www.fordfound.org/pdfs/impact/evaluations/state_fiscal_initiative.pdf

56. Legal source

Sweatt v. Painter, 339 U.S. 629 (1950). Retrieved from Cornell University Law School, Legal Information Institute website: http://www.law.cornell.edu/supct/html/historics/USSC_CR_0339_0629_ZS.html

57. Conference proceedings

Stahl, G. (Ed.). (2002). *Proceedings of CSCL '02: Computer support for collaborative learning.* Hillsdale, NJ: Erlbaum.

58. Paper presented at a meeting or symposium (unpublished)

Anderson, D. N. (2008, May). *Cab-hailing and the micropolitics of gesture.* Paper presented at the Arizona Linguistics and Anthropology Symposium, Tucson, AZ.

59. Poster session at a conference

Wang, Z., & Keogh, T. (2008, June). *A click away: Student response to clickers.* Poster session presented at the annual conference of the American Library Association, Anaheim, CA.

60. Map or chart

Ukraine [Map]. (2008). Retrieved from the University of Texas at Austin Perry-Castañeda Library Map Collection website: http://www.lib.utexas.edu/maps/cia08/ukraine_sm_2008.gif

61. Advertisement

Xbox 360 [Advertisement]. (2007, February). *Wired, 15*(2), 71.

62. Published interview

Murphy, C. (2007, June 22). As the Romans did [Interview by G. Hahn]. Retrieved from http://www.theatlantic.com/

63. Lecture, speech, or address

Fox, V. (2008, March 5). *Economic growth, poverty, and democracy in Latin America: A president's perspective.* Address at the Freeman Spogli Institute, Stanford University, Stanford, CA.

64. Work of art or photograph

Weber, J. (1992). *Toward freedom* [Outdoor mural]. Sherman Oaks, CA.

Newkirk, K. (2006). *Gainer (part II)*. Museum of Contemporary Art, Chicago, IL.

65. Brochure, pamphlet, or fact sheet

National Council of State Boards of Nursing. (n.d.). *Professional boundaries* [Brochure]. Retrieved from https://www.ncsbn.org/Professional_Boundaries_2007_Web.pdf

World Health Organization. (2007, October). *Health of indigenous peoples* (No. 326) [Fact sheet]. Retrieved from http://www.who.int/mediacentre/factsheets/fs326/en/index.html

66. Presentation slides

Boeninger, C. F. (2008, August). *Web 2.0 tools for reference and instructional services* [Presentation slides]. Retrieved from http://libraryvoice.com/archives/2008/08/04/opal-20-conference-presentation-slides/

67. Film or video (motion picture) Give the director, producer, and other relevant contributors, followed by the year of the film's release, the title, the description "Motion picture" in brackets, the country where the film was made, and the studio. If you viewed the film on videocassette or DVD, indicate that medium in brackets in place of "Motion picture." If the original release date and the date of the DVD or videocassette are different, add "Original release" and that date in parentheses at the end of the entry. If the motion picture would be difficult for your readers to find, include the name and address of its distributor instead of the country and studio.

Guggenheim, D. (Director), & Bender, L. (Producer). (2006). *An inconvenient truth* [DVD]. United States: Paramount Home Entertainment.

Spurlock, M. (Director). (2004). *Super size me* [Motion picture]. Available from IDP Films, 1133 Broadway, Suite 926, New York, NY 10010

68. Television program List the producer and the date of the program. Give the title, followed by "Television broadcast" in brackets, the city, and the television network or service.

Pratt, C. (Executive producer). (2008, October 5). *Face the nation* [Television broadcast]. Washington, DC: CBS News.

For a television series, use the year in which the series was produced, and follow the title with "Television series" in brackets. For an episode in a series, list the writer and director and the year. After the episode title, put "Television series episode" in brackets. Follow with information about the series.

Fanning, D. (Executive producer). (2008). *Frontline* [Television series]. Boston, MA: WGBH.

Smith, M. (Writer/producer). (2008). Heat [Television series episode]. In D. Fanning (Executive producer), *Frontline*. Boston, MA: WGBH.

69. Sound recording

Thomas, G. (1996). Breath. On *Didgeridoo: Ancient sound of the future* [CD]. Oxnard, CA: Aquarius International Music.

70. Computer software or video game Add the words "Computer software" in brackets after the title of the program.

Sims 2 [Computer software]. (2005). New York, NY: Maxis.

APA-5 Manuscript format; sample paper

The American Psychological Association makes a number of recommendations for formatting a paper and preparing a list of references. The following guidelines are consistent with advice given in the *Publication Manual of the American Psychological Association*, 6th ed. (Washington: APA, 2010).

APA-5a Manuscript format

The APA manual provides guidelines for papers prepared for publication in a scholarly journal; it does not provide separate guidelines for papers prepared for undergraduate classes. The formatting guidelines in this section and the sample paper on pages 488–96 can be used for either type of paper. (See p. 497 for alternative formatting.) If you are in doubt about the specific format preferred or required in your course, ask your instructor.

Formatting the paper

Many instructors in the social sciences require students to follow APA guidelines for formatting a paper.

Materials and font Use good-quality 8½″× 11″ white paper. If your instructor does not require a specific font, choose one that is standard and easy to read (such as Times New Roman).

Title page Begin at the top left with the words "Running head," followed by a colon and the title of your paper (shortened to no more than fifty characters) in all capital letters. Put the page number 1 flush with the right margin.

About halfway down the page, center the full title of your paper (capitalizing all words of four letters or more), your name, and your school's name. At the bottom of the page, you may add the heading "Author Note," centered, followed by a brief paragraph that lists specific information about the course or department or provides acknowledgments or contact information. See page 488 for a sample title page.

Some instructors may instead require a title page like the one on page 497. If in doubt about the requirements in your course, check with your instructor.

Page numbers and running head Number all pages with arabic numerals (1, 2, and so on) in the upper right corner about one-half inch from the top of the page. The title page should be numbered 1.

On every page, in the upper left corner on the same line as the page number, place a running head. The running head consists of the title of the paper (shortened to no more than fifty characters) in all capital letters. (On the title page only, include the words "Running head" followed by a colon before the shortened title.) See pages 488–96. (See an alternative running head on p. 497.)

Margins, line spacing, and paragraph indents Use margins of one inch on all sides of the page. Left-align the text.

Double-space throughout the paper. Indent the first line of each paragraph one-half inch.

Capitalization, italics, and quotation marks Capitalize all words of four letters or more in titles of works and in headings that appear in the text of the paper. Capitalize the first word after a colon if the word begins a complete sentence.

Italicize the titles of books, periodicals, and other long works, such as Web sites. Use quotation marks around the titles of periodical articles, short stories, poems, and other short works.

NOTE: APA has different requirements for titles in the reference list. See page 487.

Long quotations and footnotes When a quotation is longer than forty words, set it off from the text by indenting it one-half inch from the left margin. Double-space the quotation. Do not use quotation marks around it. See page 495 for an example.

If you insert a footnote number in the text of your paper, place the note at the bottom of the page on which the number appears. Insert an extra double-spaced line between the last line of text on the page and the footnote. Double-space the footnote and indent the first line one-half inch. Begin the note with the superscript arabic numeral that corresponds to the number in the text. See page 490 for an example.

Abstract If your instructor requires an abstract, include it immediately after the title page. Center the word "Abstract" one inch from the top of the page; double-space the abstract.

An abstract is a 100-to-150-word paragraph that provides readers with a quick overview of your essay. It should express your main idea and your key points; it might also briefly suggest any implications or applications of the research you discuss in the paper. See page 489 for an example.

Headings Although headings are not always necessary, their use is encouraged in the social sciences. For most undergraduate papers, one level of heading will usually be sufficient.

In APA style, major headings are centered and boldface. Capitalize the first word of the heading along with all words except articles, short prepositions, and coordinating conjunctions. See the sample paper on pages 488–96 for the use of headings.

Visuals APA classifies visuals as tables and figures (figures include graphs, charts, drawings, and photographs). Keep visuals as simple as possible.

Label each table with an arabic numeral (Table 1, Table 2, and so on) and provide a clear title. The label and title should appear on separate lines above the table, flush left and double-spaced.

Below the table, give its source in a note. If any data in the table require an explanatory footnote, use a superscript lowercase letter in the body of the table and in a footnote following the source note. Double-space source notes and footnotes and do not indent the first line of each note. See page 493 for an example of a table in a student paper.

For each figure, place a label and a caption below the figure, flush left and double-spaced. The label and caption need not appear on separate lines.

In the text of your paper, discuss significant features of each visual. Place the visual as close as possible to the sentences that relate to it unless your instructor prefers that visuals appear in an appendix.

Preparing the list of references

Begin your list of references on a new page at the end of the paper. Center the title "References" one inch from the top of the page, and double-space throughout. For a sample reference list, see page 496.

Indenting entries Use a hanging indent in the reference list: Type the first line of each entry flush left and indent any additional lines one-half inch, as shown on page 496.

Alphabetizing the list Alphabetize the reference list by the last names of the authors (or editors); when a work has no author (or editor), alphabetize by the first word of the title other than *A*, *An*, or *The*.

If your list includes two or more works by the same author, arrange the entries by year, the earliest first. If your list includes two or more works by the same author in the same year, arrange the works alphabetically by title. Add the letters "a," "b," and so on within the parentheses after the year. Use only the year and the letter for articles in journals: (2002a). Use the full date and the letter for articles in magazines and newspapers in the reference list: (2005a, July 7). Use only the year and the letter in the in-text citation.

Authors' names Invert all authors' names and use initials instead of first names. Separate the names with commas. With two to seven authors, use an ampersand (&) before the last author's name. If there are eight or more authors, give the first six authors, three ellipsis dots, and the last author (see p. 464).

Titles of books and articles Italicize the titles and subtitles of books. Do not italicize or use quotation marks around the titles of articles. Capitalize only the first word of the title and subtitle (and all proper nouns) of books and articles. Capitalize names of periodicals as you would capitalize them normally (see P8-c).

Abbreviations for page numbers Abbreviations for "page" and "pages" ("p." and "pp.") are used before page numbers of newspaper articles and articles in edited books (see item 9 on p. 466 and item 22 on p. 469) but not before page numbers of articles in magazines and scholarly journals (see items 7 and 8 on p. 466).

Breaking a URL or DOI When a URL or a DOI (digital object identifier) must be divided, break it after a double slash or before any other mark of punctuation. Do not insert a hyphen, and do not add a period at the end.

For information about the exact format of each entry in your list, consult the models on pages 464–83.

APA-5b Sample research paper: APA style

On pages 488–96 is a research paper on the effectiveness of treatments for childhood obesity, written by Luisa Mirano, a student in a psychology class. Mirano's assignment was to write a review of the literature and document it with APA-style citations and references. (See p. 497 for a sample of alternative formatting.)

MODELS hackerhandbooks.com/writersref
> Model papers > APA papers: Mirano; Charat; Gibson; Riss
> APA annotated bibliography: Haddad

A running head, which will be used in the printed journal article, consists of a title (shortened to no more than fifty characters) in all capital letters. On the title page, it is preceded by the label "Running head." Page numbers appear in the upper right corner.

Running head: CAN MEDICATION CURE OBESITY IN CHILDREN? 1

Full title, writer's name, and school name are centered halfway down the page.

Can Medication Cure Obesity in Children?

A Review of the Literature

Luisa Mirano

Northwest-Shoals Community College

An author's note lists specific information about the course or department and can provide acknowledgments and contact information.

Author Note

This paper was prepared for Psychology 108, Section B, taught by Professor Kang.

Marginal annotations indicate APA-style formatting and effective writing.

Abstract

In recent years, policymakers and medical experts have expressed alarm about the growing problem of childhood obesity in the United States. While most agree that the issue deserves attention, consensus dissolves around how to respond to the problem. This literature review examines one approach to treating childhood obesity: medication. The paper compares the effectiveness for adolescents of the only two drugs approved by the Food and Drug Administration (FDA) for long-term treatment of obesity, sibutramine and orlistat. This examination of pharmacological treatments for obesity points out the limitations of medication and suggests the need for a comprehensive solution that combines medical, social, behavioral, and political approaches to this complex problem.

Abstract appears on a separate page.

Full title, centered.

Can Medication Cure Obesity in Children?
A Review of the Literature

In March 2004, U.S. Surgeon General Richard Carmona called attention to a health problem in the United States that, until recently, has been overlooked: childhood obesity. Carmona said that the "astounding" 15% child obesity rate constitutes an "epidemic." Since the early 1980s, that rate has "doubled in children and tripled in adolescents." Now more than 9 million children are classified as obese.[1] While the traditional response to a medical epidemic is to hunt for a vaccine or a cure-all pill, childhood obesity is more elusive. The lack of success of recent initiatives suggests that medication might not be the answer for the escalating problem. This literature review considers whether the use of medication is a promising approach for solving the childhood obesity problem by responding to the following questions:

Mirano sets up her organization by posing four questions.

1. What are the implications of childhood obesity?
2. Is medication effective at treating childhood obesity?
3. Is medication safe for children?
4. Is medication the best solution?

Mirano states her thesis.

Understanding the limitations of medical treatments for children highlights the complexity of the childhood obesity problem in the United States and underscores the need for physicians, advocacy groups, and policymakers to search for other solutions.

Headings, centered, help readers follow the organization.

What Are the Implications of Childhood Obesity?

Obesity can be a devastating problem from both an individual and a societal perspective. Obesity puts children at risk for a number of medical complications, including Type 2 diabetes, hypertension, sleep apnea, and orthopedic problems (Henry J. Kaiser Family Foundation, 2004, p. 1). Researchers Hoppin and Taveras (2004) have noted that obesity is often associated with psychological issues such as depression, anxiety, and binge eating (Table 4).

In a signal phrase, the word "and" links the names of two authors; the date is given in parentheses.

Obesity also poses serious problems for a society struggling to cope with rising health care costs. The cost of treating obesity currently totals

Mirano uses a footnote to define an essential term that would be cumbersome to define within the text.

[1]Obesity is measured in terms of body-mass index (BMI): weight in kilograms divided by square of height in meters. A child or an adolescent with a BMI in the 95th percentile for his or her age and gender is considered obese.

CAN MEDICATION CURE OBESITY IN CHILDREN? 4

$117 billion per year—a price, according to the surgeon general, "second only to the cost of [treating] tobacco use" (Carmona, 2004). And as the number of children who suffer from obesity grows, long-term costs will only increase.

Because the author (Carmona) is not named in the signal phrase, his name and the date appear in parentheses.

Is Medication Effective at Treating Childhood Obesity?

The widening scope of the obesity problem has prompted medical professionals to rethink old conceptions of the disorder and its causes. As researchers Yanovski and Yanovski (2002) have explained, obesity was once considered "either a moral failing or evidence of underlying psychopathology" (p. 592). But this view has shifted: Many medical professionals now consider obesity a biomedical rather than a moral condition, influenced by both genetic and environmental factors. Yanovski and Yanovski have further noted that the development of weight-loss medications in the early 1990s showed that "obesity should be treated in the same manner as any other chronic disease . . . through the long-term use of medication" (p. 592).

Ellipsis mark indicates omitted words.

The search for the right long-term medication has been complicated. Many of the drugs authorized by the Food and Drug Administration (FDA) in the early 1990s proved to be a disappointment. Two of the medications—fenfluramine and dexfenfluramine—were withdrawn from the market because of severe side effects (Yanovski & Yanovski, 2002, p. 592), and several others were classified by the Drug Enforcement Administration as having the "potential for abuse" (Hoppin & Taveras, 2004, Weight-Loss Drugs section, para. 6). Currently only two medications have been approved by the FDA for long-term treatment of obesity: sibutramine (marketed as Meridia) and orlistat (marketed as Xenical). This section compares studies on the effectiveness of each.

In a parenthetical citation, an ampersand links the names of two authors.

Sibutramine suppresses appetite by blocking the reuptake of the neurotransmitters serotonin and norepinephrine in the brain (Yanovski & Yanovski, 2002, p. 594). Though the drug won FDA approval in 1998, experiments to test its effectiveness for younger patients came considerably later. In 2003, University of Pennsylvania researchers Berkowitz, Wadden, Tershakovec, and Cronquist released the first double-blind placebo study testing the effect of sibutramine on adolescents, aged 13-17, over a 12-month period. Their findings are summarized in Table 1.

Mirano draws attention to an important article.

After 6 months, the group receiving medication had lost 4.6 kg (about 10 pounds) more than the control group. But during the second half of the study, when both groups received sibutramine, the results were more ambiguous. In months 6-12, the group that continued to take sibutramine gained an average of 0.8 kg, or roughly 2 pounds; the control group, which switched from placebo to sibutramine, lost 1.3 kg, or roughly 3 pounds (p. 1808). Both groups received behavioral therapy covering diet, exercise, and mental health.

These results paint a murky picture of the effectiveness of the medication: While initial data seemed promising, the results after one year raised questions about whether medication-induced weight loss could be sustained over time. As Berkowitz et al. (2003) advised, "Until more extensive safety and efficacy data are available, . . . weight-loss medications should be used only on an experimental basis for adolescents" (p. 1811).

A study testing the effectiveness of orlistat in adolescents showed similarly ambiguous results. The FDA approved orlistat in 1999 but did not authorize it for adolescents until December 2003. Roche Laboratories (2003), maker of orlistat, released results of a one-year study testing the drug on 539 obese adolescents, aged 12-16. The drug, which promotes weight loss by blocking fat absorption in the large intestine, showed some effectiveness in adolescents: an average loss of 1.3 kg, or roughly 3 pounds, for subjects taking orlistat for one year, as opposed to an average gain of 0.67 kg, or 1.5 pounds, for the control group (pp. 8-9). See Table 1.

Short-term studies of orlistat have shown slightly more dramatic results. Researchers at the National Institute of Child Health and Human Development tested 20 adolescents, aged 12-16, over a three-month period and found that orlistat, combined with behavioral therapy, produced an average weight loss of 4.4 kg, or 9.7 pounds (McDuffie et al., 2002, p. 646). The study was not controlled against a placebo group; therefore, the relative effectiveness of orlistat in this case remains unclear.

For a source with six or more authors, the first author's surname followed by "et al." is used for the first and subsequent references.

Is Medication Safe for Children?

While modest weight loss has been documented for both medications, each carries risks of certain side effects. Sibutramine has been observed to increase blood pressure and pulse rate. In 2002, a

Table 1

Effectiveness of Sibutramine and Orlistat in Adolescents

Medication	Subjects	Treatment[a]	Side effects	Average weight loss/gain
Sibutramine	Control	0-6 mos.: placebo 6-12 mos.: sibutramine	Mos. 6-12: increased blood pressure; increased pulse rate	After 6 mos.: loss of 3.2 kg (7 lb) After 12 mos.: loss of 4.5 kg (9.9 lb)
	Medicated	0-12 mos.: sibutramine	Increased blood pressure; increased pulse rate	After 6 mos.: loss of 7.8 kg (17.2 lb) After 12 mos.: loss of 7.0 kg (15.4 lb)
Orlistat	Control	0-12 mos.: placebo	None	Gain of 0.67 kg (1.5 lb)
	Medicated	0-12 mos.: orlistat	Oily spotting; flatulence; abdominal discomfort	Loss of 1.3 kg (2.9 lb)

Note. The data on sibutramine are adapted from "Behavior Therapy and Sibutramine for the Treatment of Adolescent Obesity," by R. I. Berkowitz, T. A. Wadden, A. M. Tershakovec, & J. L. Cronquist, 2003, *Journal of the American Medical Association, 289*, pp. 1807-1809. The data on orlistat are adapted from *Xenical (Orlistat) Capsules: Complete Product Information*, by Roche Laboratories, December 2003, retrieved from http://www.rocheusa.com/products/xenical/pi.pdf

[a]The medication and/or placebo were combined with behavioral therapy in all groups over all time periods.

Mirano uses a table to summarize the findings presented in two sources.

A note gives the source of the data.

A content note explains data common to all subjects.

consumer group claimed that the medication was related to the deaths of 19 people and filed a petition with the Department of Health and Human Services to ban the medication (Hilts, 2002). The sibutramine study by Berkowitz et al. (2003) noted elevated blood pressure as a side effect, and dosages had to be reduced or the medication discontinued in 19 of the 43 subjects in the first six months (p. 1809).

When this article was first cited, all four authors were named. In subsequent citations of a work with three to five authors, "et al." is used after the first author's name.

The main side effects associated with orlistat were abdominal discomfort, oily spotting, fecal incontinence, and nausea (Roche Laboratories, 2003, p. 13). More serious for long-term health is the concern that orlistat, being a fat-blocker, would affect absorption of fat-soluble vitamins, such as vitamin D. However, the study found that this side effect can be minimized or eliminated if patients take vitamin supplements two hours before or after administration of orlistat (p. 10). With close monitoring of patients taking the medication, many of the risks can be reduced.

Is Medication the Best Solution?

The data on the safety and efficacy of pharmacological treatments of childhood obesity raise the question of whether medication is the best solution for the problem. The treatments have clear costs for individual patients, including unpleasant side effects, little information about long-term use, and uncertainty that they will yield significant weight loss.

In purely financial terms, the drugs cost more than $3 a day on average (Duenwald, 2004). In each of the clinical trials, use of medication was accompanied by an expensive regime of behavioral therapies, including counseling, nutritional education, fitness advising, and monitoring. As journalist Greg Critser (2003) noted in his book *Fat Land,* use of weight-loss drugs is unlikely to have an effect without the proper "support system"—one that includes doctors, facilities, time, and money (p. 3). For some, this level of care is prohibitively expensive.

A third complication is that the studies focused on adolescents aged 12-16, but obesity can begin at a much younger age. Few data exist to establish the safety or efficacy of medication for treating very young children.

Mirano develops the paper's thesis.

While the scientific data on the concrete effects of these medications in children remain somewhat unclear, medication is not the only avenue for addressing the crisis. Both medical experts and

CAN MEDICATION CURE OBESITY IN CHILDREN? 8

policymakers recognize that solutions might come not only from a laboratory but also from policy, education, and advocacy. A handbook designed to educate doctors on obesity called for "major changes in some aspects of western culture" (Hoppin & Taveras, 2004, Conclusion section, para. 1). Cultural change may not be the typical realm of medical professionals, but the handbook urged doctors to be proactive and "focus [their] energy on public policies and interventions" (Conclusion section, para. 1).

Brackets indicate a word not in the original source.

The solutions proposed by a number of advocacy groups underscore this interest in political and cultural change. A report by the Henry J. Kaiser Family Foundation (2004) outlined trends that may have contributed to the childhood obesity crisis, including food advertising for children as well as

> a reduction in physical education classes and after-school athletic programs, an increase in the availability of sodas and snacks in public schools, the growth in the number of fast-food outlets . . . , and the increasing number of highly processed high-calorie and high-fat grocery products. (p. 1)

A quotation longer than forty words is indented without quotation marks.

Addressing each of these areas requires more than a doctor armed with a prescription pad; it requires a broad mobilization not just of doctors and concerned parents but of educators, food industry executives, advertisers, and media representatives.

Mirano interprets the evidence; she doesn't just report it.

The barrage of possible approaches to combating childhood obesity—from scientific research to political lobbying—indicates both the severity and the complexity of the problem. While none of the medications currently available is a miracle drug for curing the nation's 9 million obese children, research has illuminated some of the underlying factors that affect obesity and has shown the need for a comprehensive approach to the problem that includes behavioral, medical, social, and political change.

The tone of the conclusion is objective.

List of references begins on a new page. Heading is centered.

List is alphabetized by authors' last names. All authors' names are inverted.

The first line of an entry is at the left margin; subsequent lines indent ½".

Double-spacing is used throughout.

CAN MEDICATION CURE OBESITY IN CHILDREN? 9

References

Berkowitz, R. I., Wadden, T. A., Tershakovec, A. M., & Cronquist, J. L. (2003). Behavior therapy and sibutramine for the treatment of adolescent obesity. *Journal of the American Medical Association, 289,* 1805-1812.

Carmona, R. H. (2004, March 2). *The growing epidemic of childhood obesity.* Testimony before the Subcommittee on Competition, Foreign Commerce, and Infrastructure of the U.S. Senate Committee on Commerce, Science, and Transportation. Retrieved from http://www.hhs.gov/asl/testify/t040302.html

Critser, G. (2003). *Fat land.* Boston, MA: Houghton Mifflin.

Duenwald, M. (2004, January 6). Slim pickings: Looking beyond ephedra. *The New York Times,* p. F1. Retrieved from http://nytimes.com/

Henry J. Kaiser Family Foundation. (2004, February). *The role of media in childhood obesity.* Retrieved from http://www.kff.org /entmedia/7030.cfm

Hilts, P. J. (2002, March 20). Petition asks for removal of diet drug from market. *The New York Times,* p. A26. Retrieved from http:// nytimes.com/

Hoppin, A. G., & Taveras, E. M. (2004, June 25). Assessment and management of childhood and adolescent obesity. *Clinical Update.* Retrieved from http://www.medscape.com/viewarticle/481633

McDuffie, J. R., Calis, K. A., Uwaifo, G. I., Sebring, N. G., Fallon, E. M., Hubbard, V. S., & Yanovski, J. A. (2002). Three-month tolerability of orlistat in adolescents with obesity-related comorbid conditions. *Obesity Research, 10,* 642-650.

Roche Laboratories. (2003, December). *Xenical (orlistat) capsules: Complete product information.* Retrieved from http://www.rocheusa .com/products/xenical/pi.pdf

Yanovski, S. Z., & Yanovski, J. A. (2002). Drug therapy: Obesity. *The New England Journal of Medicine, 346,* 591-602.

ALTERNATIVE APA TITLE PAGE

Obesity in Children 1

Short title and page number in the upper right corner on all pages.

Can Medication Cure Obesity in Children?

A Review of the Literature

Full title, centered.

Luisa Mirano

Psychology 108, Sector B

Professor Kang

October 31, 2004

Writer's name, course, instructor's name, and date, all centered at the bottom of the page.

ALTERNATIVE APA RUNNING HEAD

Obesity in Children 5

were classified by the Drug Enforcement Administration as having the "potential for abuse" (Hoppin & Taveras, 2004, Weight-Loss Drugs section, para. 6). Currently only two medications have been approved by the FDA for long-term treatment of obesity: sibutramine (marketed

Marginal annotations indicate APA-style formatting.

Directory to CMS-style note and bibliography models

BOOKS (PRINT AND ONLINE)

1. Basic format for a print book, 512
2. Basic format for an online book, 512
3. Basic format for an e-book (electronic book), 512
4. Two or more authors, 512
5. Organization as author, 513
6. Unknown author, 513
7. Multiple works by the same author, 513
8. Edited work without an author, 513
9. Edited work with an author, 513
10. Translated work, 513
11. Edition other than the first, 513
12. Volume in a multivolume work, 515
13. Work in an anthology, 515
14. Introduction, preface, foreword, or afterword, 515
15. Republished book, 515
16. Work with a title in its title, 516
17. Letter in a published collection, 516
18. Work in a series, 516
19. Encyclopedia or dictionary entry, 516
20. Sacred text, 516
21. Source quoted in another source, 517

ARTICLES IN PERIODICALS (PRINT AND ONLINE)

22. Article in a print journal, 517
23. Article in an online journal, 517
24. Journal article from a database, 517
25. Article in a print magazine, 521
26. Article in an online magazine, 521
27. Magazine article from a database, 521
28. Article in a print newspaper, 521
29. Article in an online newspaper, 523
30. Newspaper article from a database, 523
31. Unsigned newspaper article, 523
32. Book review, 524
33. Letter to the editor, 524

ONLINE SOURCES

34. Web site, 524
35. Short work from a Web site, 524
36. Online posting or e-mail, 524
37. Blog (Weblog) post, 525
38. Podcast, 525
39. Online audio or video, 525

OTHER SOURCES (INCLUDING ONLINE VERSIONS)

40. Government document, 525
41. Unpublished dissertation, 527
42. Personal communication, 527
43. Published or broadcast interview, 527
44. Published proceedings of a conference, 527
45. Video or DVD, 528
46. Sound recording, 528
47. Musical score or composition, 528
48. Work of art, 528
49. Performance, 528

CMS (*Chicago*) Papers

Most assignments in history and other humanities classes are based to some extent on reading. At times you will be asked to respond to one or two readings, such as essays or historical documents. At other times you may be asked to write a research paper that draws on a wide variety of sources.

Many history instructors and some humanities instructors require you to document sources with footnotes or endnotes based on *The Chicago Manual of Style*, 16th ed. (Chicago: U of Chicago P, 2010). (See CMS-4.) When you write a paper using sources, you face three main challenges: (1) supporting a thesis, (2) citing your sources and avoiding plagiarism, and (3) integrating quotations and other source material.

Examples in this section appear in CMS style and are drawn from one student's research on the Fort Pillow massacre. Sample pages from Ned Bishop's paper appear on pages 532–37.

CMS-1 Supporting a thesis

Most research assignments ask you to form a thesis, or main idea, and to support that thesis with well-organized evidence.

CMS-1a Form a working thesis.

Once you have read a variety of sources and considered your issue from different perspectives, you are ready to form a working thesis: a one-sentence (or occasionally a two-sentence) statement of your central idea. (See also C1-c.) In a research paper, your thesis will answer the central research question that you pose. Here, for example, are student writer Ned Bishop's research question and working thesis statement.

RESEARCH QUESTION

To what extent was Confederate Major General Nathan Bedford Forrest responsible for the massacre of Union troops at Fort Pillow?

WORKING THESIS

By encouraging racism among his troops, Nathan Bedford Forrest was directly responsible for the massacre of Union troops at Fort Pillow.

Notice that the thesis expresses a view on a debatable issue—an issue about which intelligent, well-meaning people might disagree. The writer's job is to persuade such readers that this view is worth taking seriously. To read Ned Bishop's thesis in the context of his introduction, see page 533.

PRACTICE **hackerhandbooks.com/writersref**
> CMS (*Chicago*) > CMS 1-1

CMS-1b Organize your ideas.

The body of your paper will consist of evidence in support of your thesis. Instead of getting tangled up in a formal outline early in the process, sketch an informal plan that organizes your ideas in bold strokes. Ned Bishop, for example, used a simple outline to structure his ideas. In the paper itself, these points became headings that help readers follow his line of argument.

What happened at Fort Pillow?

Did Forrest order the massacre?

Can Forrest be held responsible for the massacre?

CMS-1c Use sources to inform and support your argument.

Used thoughtfully, your source materials will make your argument more complex and convincing for readers. Sources can play several different roles as you develop your points.

Providing background information or context

You can use facts and statistics to support generalizations or to establish the importance of your topic, as student writer Ned Bishop does early in his paper.

> Fort Pillow, Tennessee, which sat on a bluff overlooking the Mississippi River, had been held by the Union for two years. It was garrisoned by 580 men, 292 of them from United States Colored Heavy and Light Artillery regiments, 285 from the white Thirteenth Tennessee Cavalry. Nathan Bedford Forrest commanded about 1,500 troops.[1]

Explaining terms or concepts

If readers are unlikely to be familiar with a word, a phrase, or an idea important to your topic, you must explain it for them. Quoting or paraphrasing a source can help you define terms and concepts clearly and concisely.

> The Civil War practice of giving no quarter to an enemy—in other words, "denying [an enemy] the right of survival"—defied Lincoln's mandate for humane and merciful treatment of prisoners.[9]

Supporting your claims

As you draft your argument, make sure to back up your assertions with facts, examples, and other evidence from your research (see also A2-e). Ned Bishop, for example, uses an eyewitness report of the racially motivated violence perpetrated by Nathan Bedford Forrest's troops.

> The slaughter at Fort Pillow was no doubt driven in large part by racial hatred. . . . A Southern reporter traveling with Forrest makes clear that the discrimination was deliberate: "Our troops maddened by the excitement, shot down the ret[r]eating Yankees, and not until they had attained t[h]e water's edge and turned to beg for mercy, did any prisoners fall in [t]o our hands—Thus the whites received quarter, but the negroes were shown no mercy."[19]

Lending authority to your argument

Expert opinion can give weight to your argument (see also A2-e). But don't rely on experts to make your argument for you. Construct your argument in your own words and, when appropriate, cite the judgment of an authority in the field for support.

> Fort Pillow is not the only instance of a massacre or threatened massacre of black soldiers by troops under Forrest's command. Biographer Brian Steel Wills points out that at Brice's Cross Roads in June 1864, "black soldiers suffered inordinately" as Forrest looked the other way and Confederate soldiers deliberately sought out those they termed "the damned negroes."[21]

Anticipating and countering alternative interpretations

Do not ignore sources that seem contrary to your position or that offer interpretations different from your own. Instead, use them to give voice to opposing points of view and alternative interpretations before you counter them (see A2-f). Readers often have objections in mind already, whether or not they agree with you. Ned Bishop, for example, presents conflicting evidence to acknowledge that some readers may credit Nathan Bedford Forrest with stopping the massacre. In doing so, Bishop creates an opportunity to counter that objection and persuade those readers that Forrest can be held accountable.

> Hurst suggests that the temperamental Forrest "may have ragingly ordered a massacre and even intended to carry it out—until he rode inside the fort and viewed the horrifying result" and ordered it stopped.[15] While this is an intriguing interpretation of events, even Hurst would probably admit that it is merely speculation.

CMS-2 Citing sources; avoiding plagiarism

Your research paper is a collaboration between you and your sources. To be fair and ethical, you must acknowledge your debt to the writers of those sources. Failure to do so is a form of academic dishonesty known as *plagiarism*.

Three different acts are generally considered plagiarism: (1) failing to cite quotations and borrowed ideas, (2) failing to enclose borrowed language in quotation marks, and (3) failing to put summaries and paraphrases in your own words. Definitions of plagiarism may vary; it's a good idea to find out how your school defines and addresses academic dishonesty. (See also R3-c.)

CMS-2a Cite quotations and borrowed ideas.

You must cite anything you borrow from a source, including direct quotations; statistics and other facts; visuals such as tables, maps, and photographs; and any ideas you present in a summary or paraphrase.

The only exception is common knowledge—information your readers could easily find in any number of general sources. For example, most encyclopedias will tell readers that the Korean War ended in 1953 and that President Theodore Roosevelt was the first American to receive a Nobel Prize. As a rule, when you have seen certain information repeatedly in your reading, you don't need to cite it. However, when information has appeared in only a few sources, when it is highly specific (as with statistics), or when it is controversial, you should cite the source.

CMS citations consist of superscript numbers in the text of the paper that refer readers to notes with corresponding numbers either at the foot of the page (footnotes) or at the end of the paper (endnotes).

TEXT

Governor John Andrew was not allowed to recruit black soldiers from out of state. "Ostensibly," writes Peter Burchard, "no recruiting was done outside Massachusetts but it was an open secret that Andrew's agents were working far and wide."[1]

NOTE

1. Peter Burchard, *One Gallant Rush: Robert Gould Shaw and His Brave Black Regiment* (New York: St. Martin's, 1965), 85.

PRACTICE hackerhandbooks.com/writersref
> CMS (*Chicago*) > CMS 2–1 to CMS 2–5

This basic CMS format varies for different types of sources. For a detailed discussion and other models, see CMS-4. When you use footnotes or endnotes, you will usually need to provide a bibliography as well (see CMS-4b).

CMS-2b Enclose borrowed language in quotation marks.

To indicate that you are using a source's exact phrases or sentences, you must enclose them in quotation marks unless they have been set off from the text by indenting (see the bottom of p. 506). To omit the quotation marks is to claim—falsely—that the language is your own. Such an omission is plagiarism even if you have cited the source.

ORIGINAL SOURCE

For many Southerners it was psychologically impossible to see a black man bearing arms as anything but an incipient slave uprising complete with arson, murder, pillage, and rapine.

—Dudley Taylor Cornish, *The Sable Arm*, p. 158

PLAGIARISM

According to Civil War historian Dudley Taylor Cornish, for many Southerners it was psychologically impossible to see a black man bearing arms as anything but an incipient slave uprising complete with arson, murder, pillage, and rapine.[2]

BORROWED LANGUAGE IN QUOTATION MARKS

According to Civil War historian Dudley Taylor Cornish, "For many Southerners it was psychologically impossible to see a black man bearing arms as anything but an incipient slave uprising complete with arson, murder, pillage, and rapine."[2]

NOTE: Long quotations are set off from the text by indenting and do not need quotation marks (see the example on p. 507).

CMS-2c Put summaries and paraphrases in your own words.

Summaries and paraphrases are written in your own words. A summary condenses information; a paraphrase conveys the information using roughly the same number of words as in the original source. When you summarize or paraphrase, it is not enough to name the source; you must restate the source's meaning using your own language. (See also R3-c.) You commit plagiarism if you half-copy the author's sentences—either by mixing the author's phrases with your own without using quotation marks or by plugging your own synonyms into the author's sentence structure.

The first paraphrase of the following source is plagiarized—even though the source is cited—because too much of its language is borrowed from the original. The underlined strings of words have been copied exactly (without quotation marks). In addition, the writer has closely followed the sentence structure of the original source, merely making a few substitutions (such as *Fifty percent* for *Half* and *angered and perhaps frightened* for *enraged and perhaps terrified*).

ORIGINAL SOURCE

Half of the force holding Fort Pillow were Negroes, former slaves now enrolled in the Union Army. Toward them Forrest's troops had the fierce, bitter animosity of men who had been educated to regard the colored race as inferior and who for the first time had encountered that race armed and fighting against white men. The sight enraged and perhaps terrified many of the Confederates and aroused in them the ugly spirit of a lynching mob.

—Albert Castel, "The Fort Pillow Massacre," pp. 46–47

PLAGIARISM: UNACCEPTABLE BORROWING

Albert Castel suggests that much of the brutality at Fort Pillow can be traced to racial attitudes. Fifty percent of the troops holding Fort Pillow were Negroes, former slaves who had joined the Union Army. Toward them Forrest's soldiers displayed the savage hatred of men who had been taught the inferiority of blacks and who for the first time had confronted them armed and fighting against white men. The vision angered and perhaps frightened the Confederates and aroused in them the ugly spirit of a lynching mob.[3]

To avoid plagiarizing an author's language, resist the temptation to look at the source while you are summarizing or paraphrasing. After you have read the passage you want to paraphrase, set the source aside. Ask yourself, "What is the author's meaning?" In your own words, state your understanding of the author's basic point. Return to the source and check that you haven't used the author's language or sentence structure or misrepresented the author's ideas. When you fully understand another writer's meaning, you can more easily and accurately present those ideas in your own words.

ACCEPTABLE PARAPHRASE

Albert Castel suggests that much of the brutality at Fort Pillow can be traced to racial attitudes. Nearly half of the Union troops were blacks, men whom the Confederates had been raised to consider their inferiors. The shock and perhaps fear of facing armed ex-slaves in battle for the first time may well have unleashed the fury that led to the massacre.[3]

CMS-3 Integrating sources

Quotations, summaries, paraphrases, and facts will help you develop your argument, but they cannot speak for you. You can use several strategies to integrate information from sources into your paper while maintaining your own voice.

CMS-3a Use quotations appropriately.

In your academic writing, keep the emphasis on your ideas; use your own words to summarize and to paraphrase your sources and to explain your points. Sometimes, however, quotations can be the most effective way to integrate a source.

WHEN TO USE QUOTATIONS

- When language is especially vivid or expressive
- When exact wording is needed for technical accuracy
- When it is important to let the debaters of an issue explain their positions in their own words
- When the words of an authority lend weight to an argument
- When the language of a source is the topic of your discussion

Limiting your use of quotations Although it is tempting to insert many quotations in your paper and to use your own words only for connecting passages, do not quote excessively. It is almost impossible to integrate numerous long quotations smoothly into your own text.

It is not always necessary to quote full sentences from a source. To reduce your reliance on the words of others, you can often integrate language from a source into your own sentence structure.

> As Hurst has pointed out, until "an outcry erupted in the Northern press," even the Confederates did not deny that there had been a massacre at Fort Pillow.[4]

> Union surgeon Dr. Charles Fitch testified that after he was in custody, he "saw" Confederate soldiers "kill every negro that made his appearance dressed in Federal uniform."[20]

Two useful marks of punctuation, the ellipsis mark and brackets, allow you to keep quoted material to a minimum and to integrate it smoothly into your text.

PRACTICE hackerhandbooks.com/writersref
> CMS (*Chicago*) > CMS 3–1 to CMS 3–4

Using the ellipsis mark To condense a quoted passage, you can use the ellipsis mark (three periods, with spaces between) to indicate that you have omitted words. What remains must be grammatically complete.

> Union surgeon Fitch's testimony that all women and children had been evacuated from Fort Pillow before the attack conflicts with Forrest's report: "We captured . . . about 40 negro women and children."[6]

The writer has omitted several words not relevant to the issue at hand: *164 Federals, 75 negro troops, and.*

When you want to leave out one or more full sentences, use a period before the three ellipsis dots. For an example, see the long quotation on page 507.

Ordinarily, do not use an ellipsis mark at the beginning or at the end of a quotation. Readers will understand that you have taken the quoted material from a longer passage, so such marks are not necessary. The only exception occurs when you have dropped words at the end of the final quoted sentence. In such cases, put three ellipsis dots before the closing quotation mark.

Using brackets Brackets allow you to insert your own words into quoted material, perhaps to explain a confusing reference or to keep a sentence grammatical in your context.

> According to Albert Castel, "It can be reasonably argued that he [Forrest] was justified in believing that the approaching steamships intended to aid the garrison [at Fort Pillow]."[7]

NOTE: To indicate an error such as a misspelling in a quotation, insert the word [*sic*], italicized and with brackets around it, right after the error. (See the example on p. 507 and in P6-b for more information.)

Setting off long quotations CMS style allows you some flexibility in deciding whether to set off a long quotation or run it into your text. For emphasis, you may want to set off a quotation of more than four or five typed lines of text; almost certainly you should set off quotations of ten or more lines. To set off a quotation, indent it one-half inch from the left margin and use the normal right margin. Double-space the indented quotation.

Long quotations should be introduced by an informative sentence, often followed by a colon. Quotation marks are unnecessary because the indented format tells readers that the passage is taken word-for-word from the source.

In a letter home, Confederate officer Achilles V. Clark recounted what happened at Fort Pillow:

> Words cannot describe the scene. The poor deluded negroes would run up to our men fall upon their knees and with uplifted hands scream for mercy but they were ordered to their feet and then shot down. The whitte [*sic*] men fared but little better. . . . I with several others tried to stop the butchery and at one time had partially succeeded, but Gen. Forrest ordered them shot down like dogs, and the carnage continued.[8]

CMS-3b Use signal phrases to integrate sources.

Whenever you include a paraphrase, summary, or direct quotation of another writer's work in your paper, prepare your readers for it with a *signal phrase*. A signal phrase usually names the author of the source and often provides some context. It commonly appears before the source material. To vary your sentence structure, you may decide to interrupt source material with a signal phrase or place the signal phrase after your paraphrase, summary, or direct quotation.

When the signal phrase includes a verb, choose one that is appropriate for the way you are using the source (see CMS-1c). Are you providing background, explaining a concept, supporting a claim, lending authority, or refuting an argument? See the chart on page 508 for a list of verbs commonly used in signal phrases.

Note that CMS style calls for verbs in the present tense or present perfect tense (*points out* or *has pointed out*) to introduce source material unless you include a date that specifies the time of the original author's writing.

The first time you mention an author, use the full name: *Shelby Foote argues. . . .* When you refer to the author again, you may use the last name only: *Foote raises an important question.*

Marking boundaries

Readers need to move from your words to the words of a source without feeling a jolt. Avoid dropping quotations into your text without warning. Instead, provide clear signal phrases, usually including the author's name, to indicate the boundary between your words and the source's words. (The signal phrase is highlighted in the second example on page 508.)

Using signal phrases in CMS papers

To avoid monotony, try to vary both the language and the placement of your signal phrases.

Model signal phrases

In the words of historian James M. McPherson, ". . ."[1]

As Dudley Taylor Cornish has argued, ". . ."[2]

In a letter to his wife, a Confederate soldier who witnessed the massacre wrote that ". . ."[3]

". . . ," claims Benjamin Quarles.[4]

". . . ," writes Albert Castel, ". . ."[5]

Shelby Foote offers an intriguing interpretation: ". . ."[6]

Verbs in signal phrases

admits	compares	insists	rejects
agrees	confirms	notes	reports
argues	contends	observes	responds
asserts	declares	points out	suggests
believes	denies	reasons	thinks
claims	emphasizes	refutes	writes

DROPPED QUOTATION

Not surprisingly, those testifying on the Union and Confederate sides recalled events at Fort Pillow quite differently. Unionists claimed that their troops had abandoned their arms and were in full retreat. "The Confederates, however, all agreed that the Union troops retreated to the river with arms in their hands."[9]

QUOTATION WITH SIGNAL PHRASE

Not surprisingly, those testifying on the Union and Confederate sides recalled events at Fort Pillow quite differently. Unionists claimed that their troops had abandoned their arms and were in full retreat. "The Confederates, however," writes historian Albert Castel, "all agreed that the Union troops retreated to the river with arms in their hands."[9]

Using signal phrases with summaries and paraphrases

As with quotations, you should introduce most summaries and paraphrases with a signal phrase that mentions the author and places the material in the context of your argument. Readers will then understand where the summary or paraphrase begins.

Without the signal phrase (highlighted) in the following example, readers might think that only the last sentence is being cited, when in fact the whole paragraph is based on the source.

> According to Jack Hurst, official Confederate policy was that black soldiers were to be treated as runaway slaves; in addition, the Confederate Congress decreed that white Union officers commanding black troops be killed. Confederate Lieutenant General Kirby Smith went one step further, declaring that he would kill all captured black troops. Smith's policy never met with strong opposition from the Richmond government.[10]

Integrating statistics and other facts

When you are citing a statistic or another specific fact, a signal phrase is often not necessary. In most cases, readers will understand that the citation refers to the statistic or another fact (not the whole paragraph).

> Of 295 white troops garrisoned at Fort Pillow, 168 were taken prisoner. Black troops fared worse, with only 58 of 262 captured and most of the rest presumably killed or wounded.[12]

There is nothing wrong, however, with using a signal phrase to introduce a statistic or fact.

> Shelby Foote notes that of 295 white troops garrisoned at Fort Pillow, 168 were taken prisoner but that black troops fared worse, with only 58 of 262 captured and most of the rest presumably killed or wounded.[12]

Putting source material in context

Readers should not have to guess why source material appears in your paper. If you use another writer's words, you must explain how they relate to your point. In other words, you must put the source in context. It's a good idea to embed a quotation between sentences of your own, introducing it with a signal phrase and following it up with interpretive comments that link the quotation to your paper's argument.

QUOTATION WITH EFFECTIVE CONTEXT

> In a respected biography of Nathan Bedford Forrest, Hurst suggests that the temperamental Forrest "may have ragingly ordered a massacre and even intended

to carry it out—until he rode inside the fort and viewed the horrifying result" and ordered it stopped.[11] While this is an intriguing interpretation of events, even Hurst would probably admit that it is merely speculation.

NOTE: When you bring other sources into a conversation about your research topic, you are synthesizing. For more on synthesis, see MLA-3c.

CMS-4 Documenting sources

In history and some humanities courses, you may be asked to use the documentation system set forth in *The Chicago Manual of Style*, 16th ed. (Chicago: U of Chicago P, 2010). In *Chicago* (CMS) style, superscript numbers in the text of the paper refer readers to notes with corresponding numbers either at the foot of the page (footnotes) or at the end of the paper (endnotes). A bibliography is often required as well; it appears at the end of the paper and gives publication information for all the works cited in the notes.

TEXT

A Union soldier, Jacob Thompson, claimed to have seen Forrest order the killing, but when asked to describe the six-foot-two general, he called him "a little bit of a man."[12]

FOOTNOTE OR ENDNOTE

12. Brian Steel Wills, *A Battle from the Start: The Life of Nathan Bedford Forrest* (New York: HarperCollins, 1992), 187.

BIBLIOGRAPHY ENTRY

Wills, Brian Steel. *A Battle from the Start: The Life of Nathan Bedford Forrest.* New York: HarperCollins, 1992.

CMS-4a First and subsequent notes for a source

The first time you cite a source, the note should include publication information for that work as well as the page number on which the passage being cited may be found.

PRACTICE hackerhandbooks.com/writersref
> CMS (*Chicago*) > CMS 4–1 to CMS 4–8

1. Peter Burchard, *One Gallant Rush: Robert Gould Shaw and His Brave Black Regiment* (New York: St. Martin's, 1965), 85.

For subsequent references to a source you have already cited, you may simply give the author's last name, a short form of the title, and the page or pages cited. A short form of the title of a book is italicized; a short form of the title of an article is put in quotation marks.

4. Burchard, *One Gallant Rush,* 31.

When you have two consecutive notes from the same source, you may use "Ibid." (meaning "in the same place") and the page number for the second note. Use "Ibid." alone if the page number is the same.

5. Jack Hurst, *Nathan Bedford Forrest: A Biography* (New York: Knopf, 1993), 8.

6. Ibid., 174.

CMS-4b CMS-style bibliography

A bibliography, which appears at the end of your paper, lists every work you have cited in your notes; in addition, it may include works that you consulted but did not cite. For advice on constructing the list, see page 531. A sample bibliography appears on page 537.

NOTE: If you include a bibliography, *The Chicago Manual of Style* suggests that you shorten all notes, including the first reference to a source, as described at the top of this page. Check with your instructor, however, to see whether using an abbreviated note for a first reference to a source is acceptable.

CMS-4c Model notes and bibliography entries

The following models are consistent with guidelines in *The Chicago Manual of Style*, 16th ed. For each type of source, a model note appears first, followed by a model bibliography entry. The note shows the format you should use when citing a source for the first time. For subsequent citations of a source, use shortened notes (see CMS-4a). For a directory to models in this section, see page 498.

Some online sources, typically periodical articles, use a permanent locator called a digital object identifier (DOI). Use the DOI, when it is available, in place of a URL in your citations of online sources.

When a URL (Web address) or a DOI must break across lines, do not insert a hyphen or break at a hyphen if the URL or DOI contains one. Instead, break after a colon or a double slash or before any other mark of punctuation.

Books (print and online)

1. Basic format for a print book

1. Mary N. Woods, *Beyond the Architect's Eye: Photographs and the American Built Environment* (Philadelphia: University of Pennsylvania Press, 2009).

Woods, Mary N. *Beyond the Architect's Eye: Photographs and the American Built Environment*. Philadelphia: University of Pennsylvania Press, 2009.

For an illustrated citation of a print book, see pages 514–15.

2. Basic format for an online book

2. John Dewey, *Democracy and Education* (1916; ILT Digital Classics, 1994), chap. 4, http://www.ilt.columbia.edu/publications/dewey.html.

Dewey, John. *Democracy and Education*. 1916. ILT Digital Classics, 1994. http://www.ilt.columbia.edu/publications/dewey.html.

3. Basic format for an e-book (electronic book)

3. Leo Tolstoy, *War and Peace*, trans. Richard Pevear and Larissa Volokhonsky (New York: Knopf, 2007), Kindle edition, vol. 1, pt. 1, chap. 3.

Tolstoy, Leo. *War and Peace*. Translated by Richard Pevear and Larissa Volokhonsky. New York: Knopf, 2007. Kindle edition.

4. Two or more authors For a work with two or three authors, give all authors' names in both the note and the bibliography entry. For a work with four or more authors, in the note give the first author's name followed by "et al." (for "and others"); in the bibliography entry, list all authors' names.

4. Chris Stringer and Peter Andrews, *The Complete World of Human Evolution* (London: Thames and Hudson, 2005), 45.

Stringer, Chris, and Peter Andrews. *The Complete World of Human Evolution*. London: Thames and Hudson, 2005.

4. Lynn Hunt et al., *The Making of the West: Peoples and Cultures,* 3rd ed. (Boston: Bedford/St. Martin's, 2009), 541.

Hunt, Lynn, Thomas R. Martin, Barbara H. Rosenwein, R. Po-chia Hsia, and Bonnie G. Smith. *The Making of the West: Peoples and Cultures.* 3rd ed. Boston: Bedford/St. Martin's, 2009.

5. Organization as author

5. Dormont Historical Society, *Images of America: Dormont* (Charleston, SC: Arcadia Publishing, 2008), 24.

Dormont Historical Society. *Images of America: Dormont.* Charleston, SC: Arcadia Publishing, 2008.

6. Unknown author

6. *The Men's League Handbook on Women's Suffrage* (London, 1912), 23.

The Men's League Handbook on Women's Suffrage. London, 1912.

7. Multiple works by the same author In the bibliography, use six hyphens in place of the author's name in the second and subsequent entries. Arrange the entries alphabetically by title.

Harper, Raymond L. *A History of Chesapeake, Virginia.* Charleston, SC: History Press, 2008.

------. *South Norfolk, Virginia, 1661-2005.* Charleston, SC: History Press, 2005.

8. Edited work without an author

8. Jack Beatty, ed., *Colossus: How the Corporation Changed America* (New York: Broadway Books, 2001), 127.

Beatty, Jack, ed. *Colossus: How the Corporation Changed America.* New York: Broadway Books, 2001.

9. Edited work with an author

9. Ted Poston, *A First Draft of History,* ed. Kathleen A. Hauke (Athens: University of Georgia Press, 2000), 46.

Poston, Ted. *A First Draft of History.* Edited by Kathleen A. Hauke. Athens: University of Georgia Press, 2000.

10. Translated work

10. Tonino Guerra, *Abandoned Places,* trans. Adria Bernardi (Barcelona: Guernica, 1999), 71.

Guerra, Tonino. *Abandoned Places.* Translated by Adria Bernardi. Barcelona: Guernica, 1999.

11. Edition other than the first

11. Arnoldo DeLeon, *Mexican Americans in Texas: A Brief History*, 3rd ed. (Wheeling, IL: Harlan Davidson, 2009), 34.

DeLeon, Arnoldo. *Mexican Americans in Texas: A Brief History*. 3rd ed. Wheeling, IL: Harlan Davidson, 2009.

Citation at a glance: Book (CMS)

To cite a print book in CMS (*Chicago*) style, include the following elements:

1. Author
2. Title and subtitle
3. City of publication
4. Publisher
5. Year of publication
6. Page number(s) cited (for notes)

TITLE PAGE

A MIDWIFE'S TALE

The Life of Martha Ballard, Based on Her Diary, 1785–1812

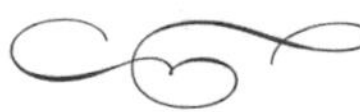

Laurel Thatcher Ulrich

Vintage Books
A Division of Random House, Inc.
New York

JUNE 1991

COPYRIGHT PAGE

FIRST VINTAGE BOOKS EDITION, JUNE 1991

Copyright © 1990 by Laurel Thatcher Ulrich
Maps copyright © 1990 by Karen Hansen

reserved under International and Pan-American Copyright
Published in the United States by Vintage Books, a division of
se, Inc., New York, and simultaneously in Canada by Random
a Limited, Toronto. Originally published in hardcover by Alfred
A. Knopf, Inc., New York, in 1990.

brary of Congress Cataloging-in-Publication Data
Ulrich, Laurel.
: the life of Martha Ballard, based on her diary, 1785-1812 / Laurel
Thatcher Ulrich.—1st Vintage Books ed.
p. cm.
cludes bibliographical references (p.) and index.
ISBN 0-679-73376-0
rtha, 1735-1812. 2. Hallowell (Me.)—Biography. 3. Augusta
(Me.)—Biography. 4. Kennebec River Valley (Me.)—Social life and customs.
5. Midwives—Maine—Hallowell—Biography. 6. Midwives—Maine—
Augusta—Biography. I. Title.
[F29.H15U47 1991]
974.1'6—dc20
[B] 90-55674
CIP

Design by Dorothy Schmiderer Baker

Manufactured in the United States of America
79D8

NOTE

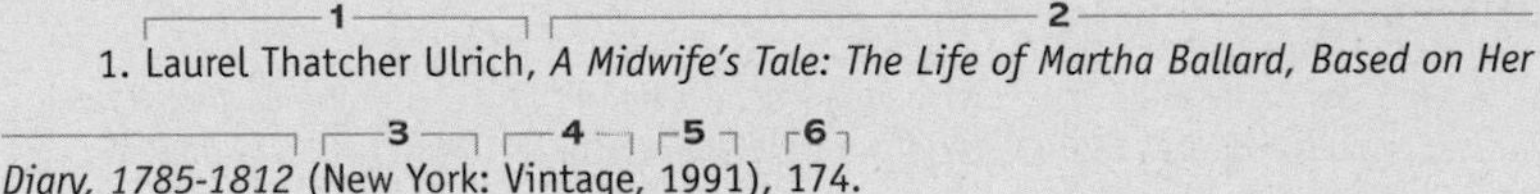

1. Laurel Thatcher Ulrich, *A Midwife's Tale: The Life of Martha Ballard, Based on Her Diary, 1785-1812* (New York: Vintage, 1991), 174.

BIBLIOGRAPHY

Ulrich, Laurel Thatcher. *A Midwife's Tale: The Life of Martha Ballard, Based on Her Diary, 1785-1812*. New York: Vintage, 1991.

For more on citing books in CMS (*Chicago*) style, see pages 512–17.

12. Volume in a multivolume work

12. Charles Reagan Wilson, ed., *Myth, Manner, and Memory,* vol. 4 of *The New Encyclopedia of Southern Culture* (Chapel Hill: University of North Carolina Press, 2006), 198.

Wilson, Charles Reagan, ed. *Myth, Manner, and Memory*. Vol. 4 of *The New Encyclopedia of Southern Culture*. Chapel Hill: University of North Carolina Press, 2006.

13. Work in an anthology

13. Zora Neale Hurston, "From *Dust Tracks on a Road,*" in *The Norton Book of American Autobiography,* ed. Jay Parini (New York: Norton, 1999), 336.

Hurston, Zora Neale. "From *Dust Tracks on a Road.*" In *The Norton Book of American Autobiography,* edited by Jay Parini, 333-43. New York: Norton, 1999.

14. Introduction, preface, foreword, or afterword

14. Nelson DeMille, foreword to *Flag: An American Biography,* by Marc Leepson (New York: Thomas Dunne, 2005), xii.

DeMille, Nelson. Foreword to *Flag: An American Biography,* by Marc Leepson, xi-xiv. New York: Thomas Dunne, 2005.

15. Republished book

15. Garry Wills, *Inventing America: Jefferson's Declaration of Independence* (1978; repr., Boston: Houghton Mifflin, 2002), 86.

Wills, Garry. *Inventing America: Jefferson's Declaration of Independence.* 1978. Reprint, Boston: Houghton Mifflin, 2002.

16. Work with a title in its title Use quotation marks around any title within an italicized title.

16. Gary Schmidgall, ed., *Conserving Walt Whitman's Fame: Selections from Horace Traubel's "Conservator," 1890-1919* (Iowa City: University of Iowa Press, 2006), 165.

Schmidgall, Gary, ed. *Conserving Walt Whitman's Fame: Selections from Horace Traubel's "Conservator," 1890-1919.* Iowa City: University of Iowa Press, 2006.

17. Letter in a published collection Use the day-month-year form for the date of the letter. If the letter writer's name is part of the book title, begin the note with only the writer's last name but begin the bibliography entry with the full name.

17. Mitford to Esmond Romilly, 29 July 1940, in *Decca: The Letters of Jessica Mitford*, ed. Peter Y. Sussman (New York: Knopf, 2006), 55-56.

Mitford, Jessica. *Decca: The Letters of Jessica Mitford.* Edited by Peter Y. Sussman. New York: Knopf, 2006.

For an illustrated citation of a letter in a published collection, see pages 518–19.

18. Work in a series

18. R. Keith Schoppa, *The Columbia Guide to Modern Chinese History,* Columbia Guides to Asian History (New York: Columbia University Press, 2000), 256-58.

Schoppa, R. Keith. *The Columbia Guide to Modern Chinese History*. Columbia Guides to Asian History. New York: Columbia University Press, 2000.

19. Encyclopedia or dictionary entry

19. *Encyclopaedia Britannica,* 15th ed., s.v. "Monroe Doctrine."

19. Bryan A. Garner, *Garner's Modern American Usage* (Oxford: Oxford University Press, 2003), s.v. "brideprice."

Garner, Bryan A. *Garner's Modern American Usage.* Oxford: Oxford University Press, 2003.

The abbreviation "s.v." is for the Latin *sub verbo* ("under the word").

Well-known reference works such as encyclopedias do not require publication information and are usually not included in the bibliography.

20. Sacred text

20. Matt. 20:4-9 (Revised Standard Version).

20. Qur'an 18:1-3.

Sacred texts are usually not included in the bibliography.

21. Source quoted in another source

21. Ron Grossman and Charles Leroux, "A Local Outpost of Democracy," *Chicago Tribune,* March 5, 1996, quoted in William Julius Wilson and Richard P. Taub, *There Goes the Neighborhood: Racial, Ethnic, and Class Tensions in Four Chicago Neighborhoods and Their Meaning for America* (New York: Knopf, 2006), 18.

Grossman, Ron, and Charles Leroux. "A Local Outpost of Democracy." *Chicago Tribune,* March 5, 1996. Quoted in William Julius Wilson and Richard P. Taub, *There Goes the Neighborhood: Racial, Ethnic, and Class Tensions in Four Chicago Neighborhoods and Their Meaning for America* (New York: Knopf, 2006), 18.

Articles in periodicals (print and online)

22. Article in a print journal Include the volume and issue numbers and the date; end the bibliography entry with the page range of the article.

For an illustrated citation of an article in a journal, see pages 520–21.

22. T. H. Breen, "Will American Consumers Buy a Second American Revolution?," *Journal of American History* 93, no. 2 (2006): 405.

Breen, T. H. "Will American Consumers Buy a Second American Revolution?" *Journal of American History* 93, no. 2 (2006): 404-8.

23. Article in an online journal Give the DOI if the article has one; if there is no DOI, give the URL for the article. For an unpaginated online article, in your note you may include locators, such as numbered paragraphs (if the article has them), or headings from the article.

23. Brian Lennon, "New Media Critical Homologies," *Postmodern Culture* 19, no. 2 (2009), http://pmc.iath.virginia.edu/text-only/issue.109/19.2lennon.txt.

Lennon, Brian. "New Media Critical Homologies." *Postmodern Culture* 19, no. 2 (2009). http://pmc.iath.virginia.edu/text-only/issue.109/19.2lennon.txt.

24. Journal article from a database Give whatever identifying information is available in the database listing: a DOI for the article; the name of the database and the number assigned by the database; or a "stable" or "persistent" URL for the article.

For an illustrated citation of an article from a database, see pages 522–23.

24. Constant Leung, "Language and Content in Bilingual Education," *Linguistics and Education* 16, no. 2 (2005): 239, doi:10.1016/j.linged.2006.01.004.

Leung, Constant. "Language and Content in Bilingual Education." *Linguistics and Education* 16, no. 2 (2005): 238-52. doi:10.1016/j.linged.2006.01.004.

Citation at a glance: Letter in a published collection (CMS)

To cite a letter in a published collection in CMS (*Chicago*) style, include the following elements:

1 Author of letter
2 Recipient of letter
3 Date of letter
4 Title of collection
5 Editor of collection
6 City of publication
7 Publisher
8 Year of publication
9 Page number(s) cited (for notes); page range of letter (for bibliography)

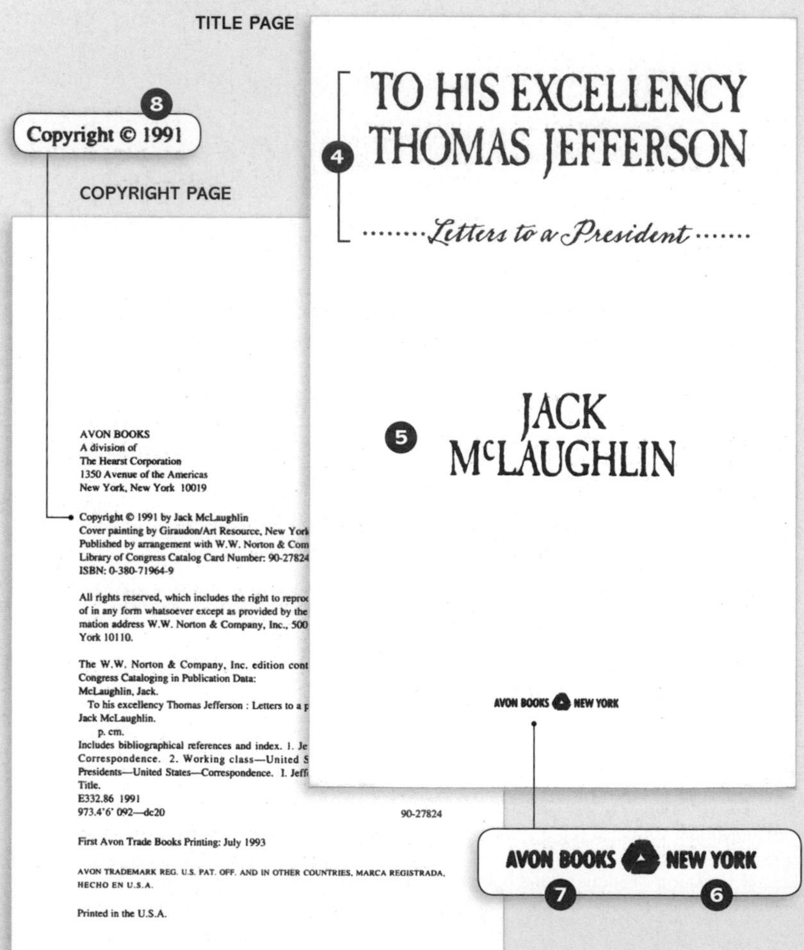

TITLE PAGE
TO HIS EXCELLENCY THOMAS JEFFERSON
Letters to a President
JACK McLAUGHLIN
AVON BOOKS NEW YORK
Copyright © 1991
COPYRIGHT PAGE
AVON BOOKS
A division of
The Hearst Corporation
1350 Avenue of the Americas
New York, New York 10019
Copyright © 1991 by Jack McLaughlin
Cover painting by Giraudon/Art Resource, New York
Published by arrangement with W.W. Norton & Com
Library of Congress Catalog Card Number: 90-27824
ISBN: 0-380-71964-9
All rights reserved, which includes the right to repro
of in any form whatsoever except as provided by the
mation address W.W. Norton & Company, Inc., 500
York 10110.
The W.W. Norton & Company, Inc. edition cont
Congress Cataloging in Publication Data:
McLaughlin, Jack.
To his excellency Thomas Jefferson : Letters to a p
Jack McLaughlin.
p. cm.
Includes bibliographical references and index. 1. Je
Correspondence. 2. Working class—United S
Presidents—United States—Correspondence. I. Jeff
Title.
E332.86 1991
973.4'6' 092—dc20
90-27824
First Avon Trade Books Printing: July 1993
AVON TRADEMARK REG. U.S. PAT. OFF. AND IN OTHER COUNTRIES, MARCA REGISTRADA, HECHO EN U.S.A.
Printed in the U.S.A.
AVON BOOKS NEW YORK

Washington 30th. Oct 1805 

His Excellency Ths. Jefferson **2**

Sir,

I have not the honor to be personally known to your Excellency therefore you will no doubt think it strange to receive this letter from a person of whom you have not the smallest knowledge. But in order to state to your Excellency in as few words as possible the purport of this address, I am a young man, a Roman Catholic who had been born and partly educated in Ireland but finding like many others who had been compelled to Migrate from that Kingdom in con-

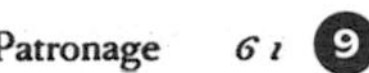

Patronage 61 **9**

your Excellency this very prolix letter which should it please your Excellency to give me some little Office or appointment in that extensive Country of Louisiana It should be my constant endeavour to merit the same by fidelity and an indefatigable attention to whatever business I should be assigned. May I have the satisfaction in whatsoever Country or situation [I] may be in to hear of your Excellencies long continuence of your Natural powers unempaired to conduct the Helm of this Extensive Country which are the sincere wishes of your Excellencies Mo. Obt. Hum. Servt.

1 John O'Neill

NOTE

1. John O'Neill to Thomas Jefferson, 30 October 1805, in *To His Excellency Thomas Jefferson: Letters to a President*, ed. Jack McLaughlin (New York: Avon Books, 1991), 61.

BIBLIOGRAPHY

O'Neill, John. John O'Neill to Thomas Jefferson, 30 October 1805. In *To His Excellency Thomas Jefferson: Letters to a President*, edited by Jack McLaughlin, 59-61. New York: Avon Books, 1991.

For another citation of a letter in CMS (*Chicago*) style, see item 17.

Citation at a glance: Article in a scholarly journal (CMS)

To cite a print article in a scholarly journal in CMS (*Chicago*) style, include the following elements:

1 Author
2 Title of article
3 Title of journal
4 Volume and issue numbers
5 Year of publication
6 Page number(s) cited (for notes); page range of article (for bibliography)

TITLE PAGE OF JOURNAL

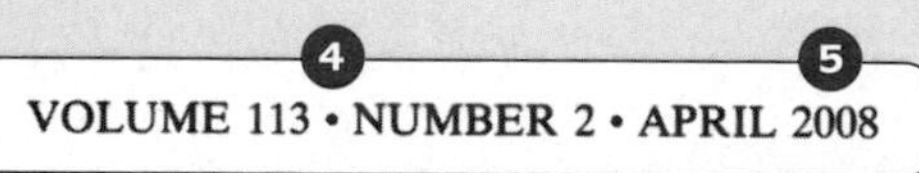

VOLUME 113 • NUMBER 2 • APRIL 2008

The American Historical Review 3

AMERICAN HISTORICAL ASSOCIATION

Editor: ROBERT A.
Associate Editor: S
Reviews Editor: MOU
Articles Editor: J
Production Manager:
Office Manager: MARY
Editorial Assistants: ELIZABE
KEVIN P. COLEMAN, ANDREW M. K
JENNIFER SOVDE, M. BENJAMIN
Advertising Manager: C
University of Chic

Board of E

TOBY L. DITZ, *Johns Hopkins University*
JANET J. EW, *Duke Unive*
GARY GERSTLE, *Vanderbilt University*
LLOYD S. KR, *University of Carolina, Cha*
BENJAMIN NATHANS, *University of Pennsylvania*
MRINALINI S, *Pennsylvania Universit*
WILLIAM B. TAYLOR, *University of California, Berkeley*
JEFFREY N. WASS, *University California, I*

FIRST PAGE OF ARTICLE

2 An Age of Imperial Revolutions

1 JEREMY ADELMAN

WHEN THE VENEZUELAN CREOLE FRANCISCO DE MIRANDA led an expeditionary force to the shores of his native land to liberate it from Spanish rule in the summer of 1806, he brought with him a new weapon for making revolutions: a printing press. He hoped that his band of white, black, and mulatto patriots would start a revolt to free a continent with an alliance of swords and ideas. After dawdling for ten days, Miranda learned that royal troops (also white, black, and mulatto) were marching from Caracas. He withdrew before the two multiracial forces could clash. Consider Miranda's reasons for retreat: The nation he sought to free from its chains was not, in his opinion, a nation at all. While Venezuelans yearned for "Civil Liberty," they did not know how to grasp and protect it. They needed a liberation that would tutor them in the ways of liberty and fraternity, to create a nation of virtuous citizens out of a colony of subjects. This was why Miranda treated the printing press, a portable factory of words about liberty and sovereignty, as part of the arsenal of change: he wanted to create public opinion where there was none. But faced with the prospect of a violent clash and a scourge of "opposition and internal divisions," of a war waged mainly with swords, he preferred to pull out and bide his time.[1]

Miranda's dilemma—whether or not to move forward knowing how revolutions worked in imperial settings when their protagonists did not presume that their cause was self-evidently bound to triumph—evokes questions about the embedded politics of what we might now call, with a wince, "regime change." As empires gave way to successor systems in their colonies, those regimes began to call themselves nations not in order to cause imperial crises, but as the result of such crises. The study of imperial crises and the study of the origins of nationalism in colonial societies should inform each other more than they do. Bringing these two separate fields of scholarship together, and questioning the tacit and not-so-tacit beliefs upon which they rest, can help us reframe the complex passages from empires to successor states, free

I want to extend my thanks to Howard Adelman, Steve Aron, Tom Bender, Graham Burnett, Jorge Cañizares-Esguerra, Josep Fradera, Roy Hora, Dina Khapaeva, and Rafe Blaufarb for their suggestions on this article, and to the *AHR*'s thoughtful reviewers and editors. Versions of this essay were presented as papers at the Universidad San Andrés in Buenos Aires, Smolny College in St. Petersburg, Russia, and the University of Texas at Austin.

[1] Archivo General de Indias (Seville) [hereafter AGI], Gobierno, Caracas, Legajo 458, September 13, 1806, Manuel de Guevara Vasconcelos to Principe de la Paz; September 5, 1806, Francisco Cavallero Sarmiento to Principe de la Plaz; Estado/Caracas, 71/9, November 8, 1808, "Informe de Secretaría á S.M. sobre el asunto de Miranda"; Francisco de Miranda, "Todo pende de nuestra voluntad," in Miranda, *América espera* (Caracas, 1982), 356; Karen Racine, *Francisco de Miranda: A Transatlantic Life in the Age of Revolution* (Wilmington, Del., 2003).

6 319

319

NOTE

1 2 3

1. Jeremy Adelman, "An Age of Imperial Revolutions," *American Historical Review*

4 5 6

113, no. 2 (2008): 321.

BIBLIOGRAPHY

1 2 3 4

Adelman, Jeremy. "An Age of Imperial Revolutions," *American Historical Review* 113,

5 6

no. 2 (2008): 319-40.

For more on citing articles from scholarly journals in CMS (*Chicago*) style, see page 517.

25. Article in a print magazine

25. Tom Bissell, "Improvised, Explosive, and Divisive," *Harper's,* January 2006, 42.

Bissell, Tom. "Improvised, Explosive, and Divisive." *Harper's,* January 2006, 41-54.

26. Article in an online magazine Include the URL for the article.

26. Katharine Mieszkowski, "A Deluge Waiting to Happen," *Salon,* July 3, 2008, http://www.salon.com/news/feature/2008/07/03/floods/index.html.

Mieszkowski, Katharine. "A Deluge Waiting to Happen." *Salon,* July 3, 2008. http://www .salon.com/news/feature/2008/07/03/floods/index.html.

27. Magazine article from a database Give whatever identifying information is available in the database listing: a DOI for the article; the name of the database and the number assigned by the database; or a "stable" or "persistent" URL for the article.

27. "Facing Facts in Afghanistan," *National Review,* November 2, 2009, 14, Expanded Academic ASAP (A209905060).

"Facing Facts in Afghanistan." *National Review,* November 2, 2009, 14. Expanded Academic ASAP (A209905060).

28. Article in a print newspaper Page numbers are not necessary; a section letter or number, if available, is sufficient.

28. Randal C. Archibold, "These Neighbors Are Good Ones without a New Fence," *New York Times,* October 22, 2008, sec. A.

Archibold, Randal C. "These Neighbors Are Good Ones without a New Fence." *New York Times,* October 22, 2008, sec. A.

Citation at a glance: Journal article from a database (CMS)

To cite a journal article from a database in CMS (*Chicago*) style, include the following elements:

1 Author
2 Title of article
3 Title of journal
4 Volume and issue numbers
5 Year of publication
6 Page number(s) cited (for notes); page range of article (for bibliography)
7 DOI; database name and article number; *or* "stable" or "persistent" URL for article

ON-SCREEN VIEW OF DATABASE RECORD

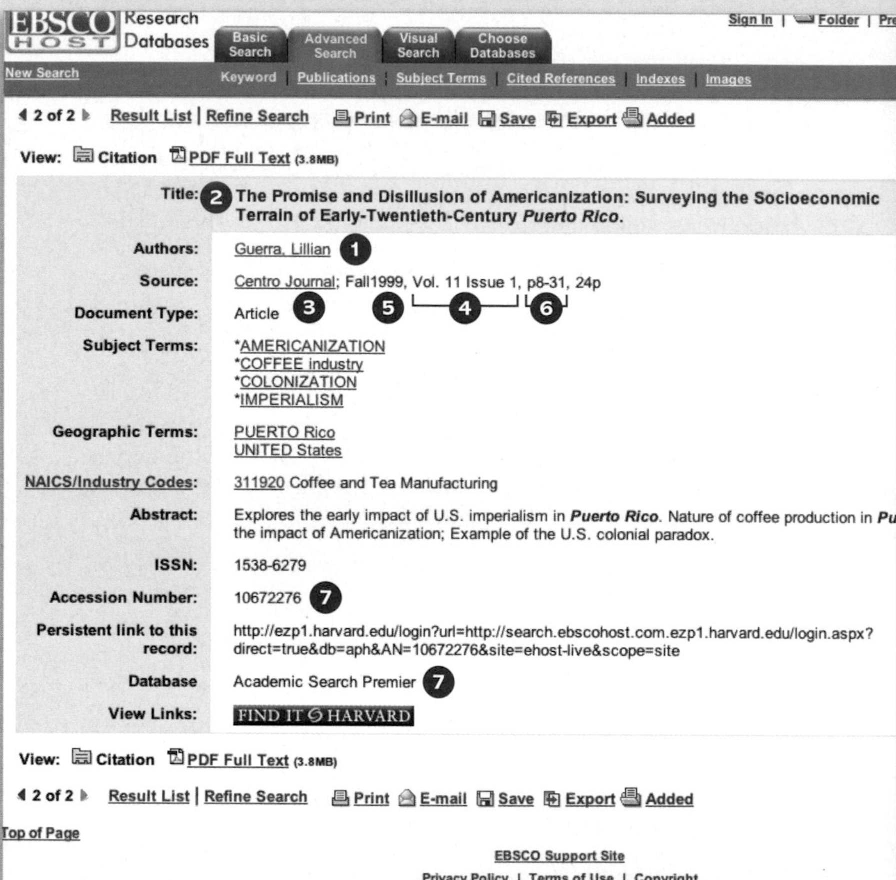

NOTE

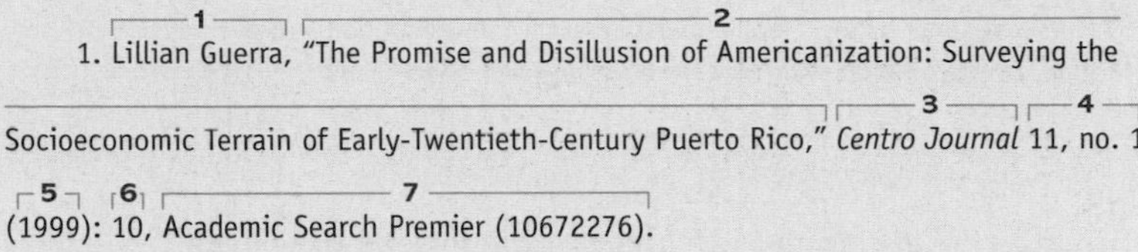

1. Lillian Guerra, "The Promise and Disillusion of Americanization: Surveying the Socioeconomic Terrain of Early-Twentieth-Century Puerto Rico," *Centro Journal* 11, no. 1 (1999): 10, Academic Search Premier (10672276).

BIBLIOGRAPHY

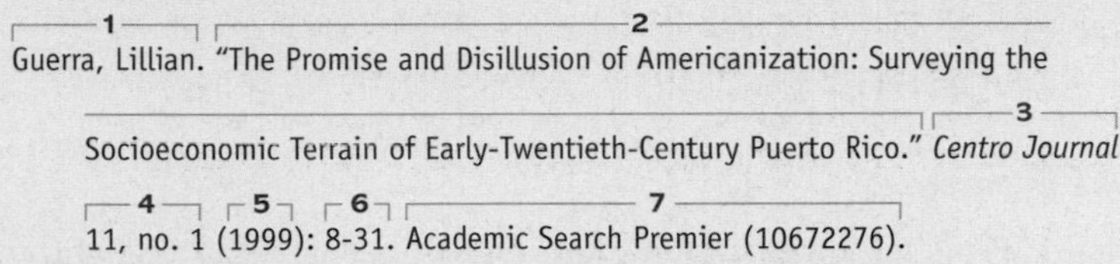

Guerra, Lillian. "The Promise and Disillusion of Americanization: Surveying the Socioeconomic Terrain of Early-Twentieth-Century Puerto Rico." *Centro Journal* 11, no. 1 (1999): 8-31. Academic Search Premier (10672276).

For more on citing journal, magazine, and newspaper articles from databases in CMS (*Chicago*) style, see pages 517, 521, and 523.

29. Article in an online newspaper Include the URL for the article; if the URL is very long, use the URL for the newspaper's home page. Omit page numbers, even if the source provides them.

29. Doyle McManus, "The Candor War," *Chicago Tribune*, July 29, 2010, http://www.chicagotribune.com/.

McManus, Doyle. "The Candor War." *Chicago Tribune*, July 29, 2010. http://www.chicagotribune.com/.

30. Newspaper article from a database Give whatever identifying information is available in the database listing: a DOI for the article; the name of the database and the number assigned by the database; or a "stable" or "persistent" URL for the article.

30. Clifford J. Levy, "In Kyrgyzstan, Failure to Act Adds to Crisis," *New York Times*, June 18, 2010, General OneFile (A229196045).

Levy, Clifford J. "In Kyrgyzstan, Failure to Act Adds to Crisis." *New York Times*, June 18, 2010. General OneFile (A229196045).

31. Unsigned newspaper article

31. "Renewable Energy Rules," *Boston Globe,* August 11, 2003, sec. A.

Boston Globe. "Renewable Energy Rules." August 11, 2003, sec. A.

32. Book review

32. Benjamin Wittes, "Remember the Titan," review of *Louis D. Brandeis: A Life*, by Melvin T. Urofsky, *Wilson Quarterly* 33, no. 4 (2009): 100.

Wittes, Benjamin. "Remember the Titan." Review of *Louis D. Brandeis: A Life*, by Melvin T. Urofsky. *Wilson Quarterly* 33, no. 4 (2009): 100-101.

33. Letter to the editor Do not use the letter's title, even if the publication gives one.

33. David Harlan, letter to the editor, *New York Review of Books*, October 9, 2008.

Harlan, David. Letter to the editor. *New York Review of Books*, October 9, 2008.

Online sources

For most Web sites, include an author if a site has one, the title of the site, the sponsor, the date of publication or modified date (date of most recent update), and the site's URL. Do not italicize a Web site title unless the site is an online book or periodical. Use quotation marks for the titles of sections or pages in a Web site. If a site does not have a date of publication or modified date, give the date you accessed the site ("accessed January 3, 2010").

34. Web site

34. Chesapeake and Ohio Canal National Historical Park, National Park Service, last modified April 9, 2010, http://www.nps.gov/choh/index.htm.

Chesapeake and Ohio Canal National Historical Park. National Park Service. Last modified April 9, 2010. http://www.nps.gov/choh/index.htm.

35. Short work from a Web site Place the title of the short work in quotation marks.

For an illustrated citation of a primary source from a Web site, see pages 526–27.

35. George P. Landow, "Victorian and Victorianism," Victorian Web, last modified August 2, 2009, http://victorianweb.org/vn/victor4.html.

Landow, George P. "Victorian and Victorianism." Victorian Web. Last modified August 2, 2009. http://victorianweb.org/vn/victor4.html.

36. Online posting or e-mail If an online posting has been archived, include a URL. E-mails that are not part of an online discussion are treated as personal communications (see item 42). Online postings and e-mails are not included in the bibliography.

36. Susanna J. Sturgis to Copyediting-L discussion list, July 17, 2010, http://listserv.indiana.edu/archives/copyediting-l.html.

37. Blog (Weblog) post Treat as a short document from a Web site (see item 35). Put the title of the posting in quotation marks, and italicize the name of the blog. Insert "blog" in parentheses after the name if the word *blog* is not part of the name.

37. Miland Brown, "The Flawed Montevideo Convention of 1933," *World History Blog*, May 31, 2008, http://www.worldhistoryblog.com/2008/05/flawed-montevideo-convention-of-1933.html.

Brown, Miland. "The Flawed Montevideo Convention of 1933." *World History Blog*. May 31, 2008. http://www.worldhistoryblog.com/2008/05/flawed-montevideo-convention-of-1933.html.

38. Podcast Treat as a short work from a Web site (see item 35), including the following, if available: the author's (or speaker's) name; the title of the podcast, in quotation marks; an identifying number, if any; the title of the site on which the podcast appears; the sponsor of the site; and the URL. Before the URL, identify the type of podcast or file format and the date of posting or your date of access.

38. Paul Tiyambe Zeleza, "Africa's Global Past," Episode 40, Africa Past and Present, African Online Digital Library, podcast audio, April 29, 2010, http://afripod.aodl.org/.

Zeleza, Paul Tiyambe. "Africa's Global Past." Episode 40. Africa Past and Present. African Online Digital Library. Podcast audio. April 29, 2010. http://afripod.aodl.org/.

39. Online audio or video Cite as a short work from a Web site (see item 35). If the source is a downloadable file, identify the file format or medium before the URL.

39. Richard B. Freeman, "Global Capitalism, Labor Markets, and Inequality," Institute of International Studies, University of California at Berkeley, October 31, 2007, http://www.youtube.com/watch?v=cgNCFsXGUa0.

Freeman, Richard B. "Global Capitalism, Labor Markets, and Inequality." Institute of International Studies, University of California at Berkeley. October 31, 2007. http://www.youtube.com/watch?v=cgNCFsXGUa0.

Other sources (including online versions)

40. Government document

40. U.S. Department of State, *Foreign Relations of the United States: Diplomatic Papers, 1943* (Washington, DC: GPO, 1965), 562.

U.S. Department of State. *Foreign Relations of the United States: Diplomatic Papers, 1943*. Washington, DC: GPO, 1965.

Citation at a glance: Primary source from a Web site (CMS)

To cite a primary source (or any other document) from a Web site in CMS (*Chicago*) style, include as many of the following elements as are available:

1. Author
2. Title of document
3. Title of site
4. Sponsor of site
5. Publication date or modified date; date of access if none
6. URL

FIRST PAGE OF DOCUMENT

WEB SITE HOME PAGE

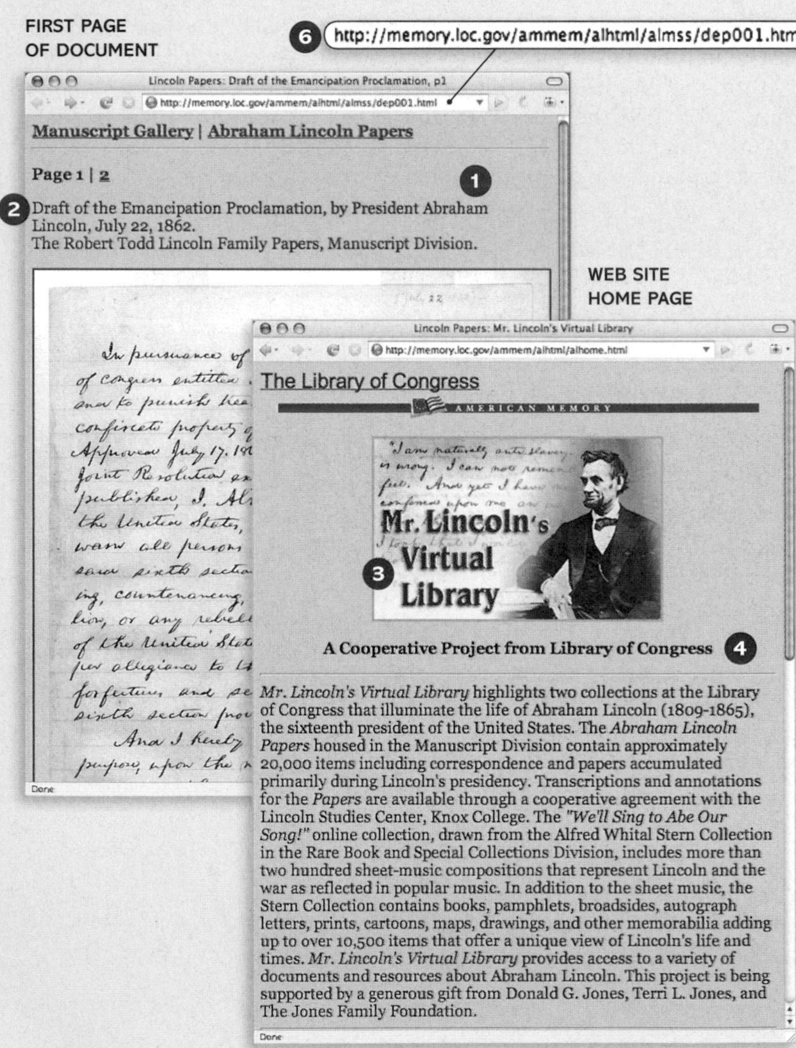

NOTE

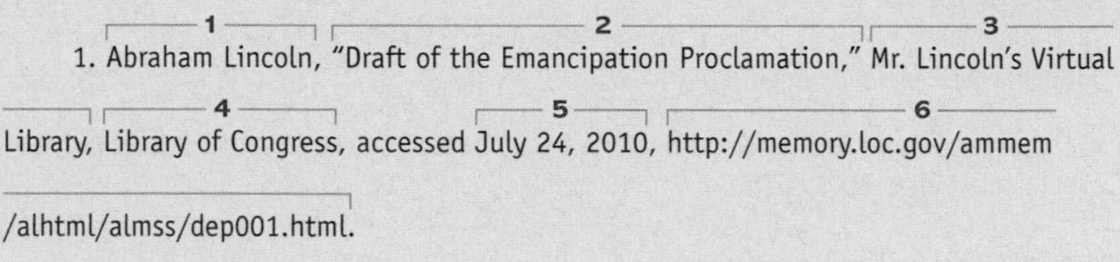
1. Abraham Lincoln, "Draft of the Emancipation Proclamation," Mr. Lincoln's Virtual Library, Library of Congress, accessed July 24, 2010, http://memory.loc.gov/ammem/alhtml/almss/dep001.html.

BIBLIOGRAPHY

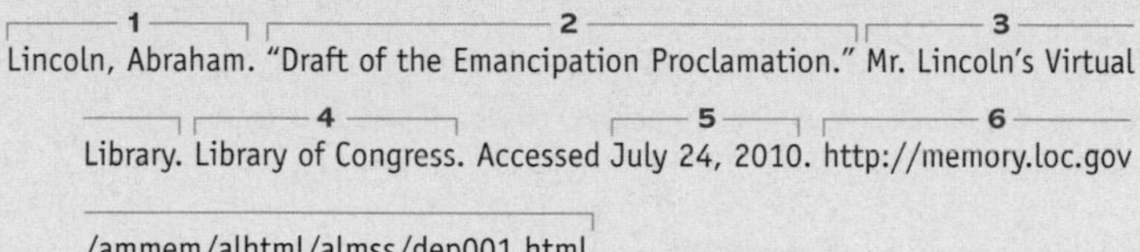
Lincoln, Abraham. "Draft of the Emancipation Proclamation." Mr. Lincoln's Virtual Library. Library of Congress. Accessed July 24, 2010. http://memory.loc.gov/ammem/alhtml/almss/dep001.html.

For more on citing documents from Web sites in CMS (*Chicago*) style, see pages 524–25.

41. Unpublished dissertation

41. Stephanie Lynn Budin, "The Origins of Aphrodite" (PhD diss., University of Pennsylvania, 2000), 301-2, ProQuest (AAT 9976404).

Budin, Stephanie Lynn. "The Origins of Aphrodite." PhD diss., University of Pennsylvania, 2000. ProQuest (AAT 9976404).

42. Personal communication

42. Sara Lehman, e-mail message to author, August 13, 2010.

Personal communications are not included in the bibliography.

43. Published or broadcast interview

43. Robert Downey Jr., interview by Graham Norton, *The Graham Norton Show*, BBC America, December 14, 2009.

Downey, Robert, Jr. Interview by Graham Norton. *The Graham Norton Show*. BBC America, December 14, 2009.

44. Published proceedings of a conference

44. Julie Kimber, Peter Love, and Phillip Deery, eds., *Labour Traditions: Proceedings of the Tenth National Labour History Conference,* University of Melbourne, Carlton, Victoria, Australia, July 4-6, 2007 (Melbourne: Australian Society for the Study of Labour History, 2007), 5.

Kimber, Julie, Peter Love, and Phillip Deery, eds. *Labour Traditions: Proceedings of the Tenth National Labour History Conference.* University of Melbourne, Carlton, Victoria, Australia, July 4-6, 2007. Melbourne: Australian Society for the Study of Labour History, 2007.

45. Video or DVD

45. *The Secret of Roan Inish,* directed by John Sayles (1993; Culver City, CA: Columbia TriStar Home Video, 2000), DVD.

The Secret of Roan Inish. Directed by John Sayles. 1993; Culver City, CA: Columbia TriStar Home Video, 2000. DVD.

46. Sound recording

46. Gustav Holst, *The Planets,* Royal Philharmonic Orchestra, conducted by André Previn, Telarc 80133, compact disc.

Holst, Gustav. *The Planets.* Royal Philharmonic Orchestra. Conducted by André Previn. Telarc 80133, compact disc.

47. Musical score or composition

47. Antonio Vivaldi, *L'Estro armonico,* op. 3, ed. Eleanor Selfridge-Field (Mineola, NY: Dover, 1999).

Vivaldi, Antonio. *L'Estro armonico,* op. 3. Edited by Eleanor Selfridge-Field. Mineola, NY: Dover, 1999.

48. Work of art

48. Aaron Siskind, *Untitled (The Most Crowded Block),* gelatin silver print, 1939, Kemper Museum of Contemporary Art, Kansas City, MO.

Siskind, Aaron. *Untitled (The Most Crowded Block)*. Gelatin silver print, 1939. Kemper Museum of Contemporary Art, Kansas City, MO.

49. Performance

49. Robert Schenkkan, *The Kentucky Cycle,* directed by Richard Elliott, Willows Theatre, Concord, CA, August 31, 2007.

Schenkkan, Robert. *The Kentucky Cycle.* Directed by Richard Elliott. Willows Theatre, Concord, CA, August 31, 2007.

CMS-5 Manuscript format; sample pages

The following guidelines for formatting a CMS-style paper and preparing its endnotes and bibliography are based on *The Chicago Manual of Style*, 16th ed. (Chicago: U of Chicago P, 2010). For pages from a sample paper, see CMS-5b.

CMS-5a Manuscript format

Formatting the paper

CMS manuscript guidelines are fairly generic because they were not created with a specific type of writing in mind.

Materials and font Use good-quality 8½″ × 11″ white paper. If your instructor does not require a specific font, choose one that is standard and easy to read (such as Times New Roman).

Title page Include the full title of your paper, your name, the course title, the instructor's name, and the date. See page 532 for a sample title page.

Pagination Using arabic numerals, number the pages in the upper right corner. Do not number the title page but count it in the numbering; that is, the first page of the text will be numbered 2. Depending on your instructor's preference, you may also use a short title or your last name before the page numbers to help identify pages.

Margins and line spacing Leave margins of at least one inch at the top, bottom, and sides of the page. Double-space the body of the paper, including long quotations that have been set off from the text. (For line spacing in notes and the bibliography, see p. 531.) Left-align the text.

Long quotations You can choose to set off a long quotation of five to ten typed lines by indenting the entire quotation one half inch from the left margin. (You should always set off quotations of ten or more lines.) Double-space the quotation; do not use quotation marks. (See p. 533 for a long quotation in the text of a paper; see also pp. 506–07.)

Capitalization and italics In titles of works, capitalize all words except articles (*a*, *an*, *the*), prepositions (*at, from, between,* and so on), coordinating conjunctions (*and*, *but*, *or*, *nor*, *for*, *so*, *yet*), and *to* and *as*—unless one of these words is first or last in the title or subtitle. Follow these guidelines in your paper even if the title is styled differently in the source.

Lowercase the first word following a colon even if the word begins a complete sentence. When the colon introduces a series of sentences or questions, capitalize all sentences in the series, including the first.

Italicize the titles of books, periodicals, and other long works. Use quotation marks around the titles of periodical articles, short stories, poems, and other short works.

Visuals CMS classifies visuals as tables and illustrations (illustrations, or figures, include drawings, photographs, maps, and charts). Keep visuals as simple as possible.

Label each table with an arabic numeral ("Table 1," "Table 2," and so on) and provide a clear title that identifies the table's subject. The label and the title should appear on separate lines above the table, flush left. Below the table, give its source in a note like this one:

> *Source:* Edna Bonacich and Richard P. Appelbaum, *Behind the Label* (Berkeley: University of California Press, 2000), 145.

For each figure, place a label and a caption below the figure, flush left. The label and caption need not appear on separate lines. The word "Figure" may be abbreviated "Fig."

In the text of your paper, discuss significant features of each visual. Place visuals as close as possible to the sentences that relate to them unless your instructor prefers that visuals appear in an appendix.

URLs (Web addresses) When a URL must break across lines, do not insert a hyphen or break at a hyphen if the URL contains one. Instead, break the URL after a colon or a double slash or before any other mark of punctuation. If your word processing program automatically turns URLs into links (by underlining them and changing the color), turn off this feature.

Headings CMS does not provide guidelines for the use of headings in student papers. If you would like to insert headings in a long essay or research paper, check first with your instructor. See the sample pages of a CMS-style paper on pages 532–37 for typical placement and formatting of headings.

Preparing the endnotes

Begin the endnotes on a new page at the end of the paper. Center the title "Notes" about one inch from the top of the page, and number the pages consecutively with the rest of the manuscript. See page 536 for an example.

Indenting and numbering Indent the first line of each note one-half inch from the left margin; do not indent additional lines in the note. Begin the note with the arabic numeral that corresponds to the number in the text. Put a period after the number.

Line spacing Single-space each note and double-space between notes (unless your instructor prefers double-spacing throughout).

Preparing the bibliography

Typically, the notes in CMS-style papers are followed by a bibliography, an alphabetically arranged list of all the works cited or consulted. Center the title "Bibliography" about one inch from the top of the page. Number bibliography pages consecutively with the rest of the paper. See page 537 for a sample bibliography.

Alphabetizing the list Alphabetize the bibliography by the last names of the authors (or editors); when a work has no author or editor, alphabetize it by the first word of the title other than *A*, *An*, or *The*.

If your list includes two or more works by the same author, use six hyphens instead of the author's name in all entries after the first. Arrange the entries alphabetically by title.

Indenting and line spacing Begin each entry at the left margin, and indent any additional lines one-half inch. Single-space each entry and double-space between entries (unless your instructor prefers double-spacing throughout).

CMS-5b Sample pages from a research paper: CMS style

Following are pages from a research paper by Ned Bishop, a student in a history class. The assignment required CMS-style endnotes and bibliography. Bishop followed CMS guidelines in preparing his manuscript as well.

Title of paper.

The Massacre at Fort Pillow:
Holding Nathan Bedford Forrest Accountable

Writer's name.

Ned Bishop

Title of course, instructor's name, and date.

History 214
Professor Citro
March 22, 2008

Marginal annotations indicate CMS-style formatting and effective writing.

Bishop 2

Although Northern newspapers of the time no doubt exaggerated some of the Confederate atrocities at Fort Pillow, most modern sources agree that a massacre of Union troops took place there on April 12, 1864. It seems clear that Union soldiers, particularly black soldiers, were killed after they had stopped fighting or had surrendered or were being held prisoner. Less clear is the role played by Major General Nathan Bedford Forrest in leading his troops. Although we will never know whether Forrest directly ordered the massacre, evidence suggests that he was responsible for it.

Thesis asserts Bishop's main point.

What happened at Fort Pillow?

Headings, centered, help readers follow the organization.

Fort Pillow, Tennessee, which sat on a bluff overlooking the Mississippi River, had been held by the Union for two years. It was garrisoned by 580 men, 292 of them from United States Colored Heavy and Light Artillery regiments, 285 from the white Thirteenth Tennessee Cavalry. Nathan Bedford Forrest commanded about 1,500 troops.[1]

Statistics are cited with an endnote.

The Confederates attacked Fort Pillow on April 12, 1864, and had virtually surrounded the fort by the time Forrest arrived on the battlefield. At 3:30 p.m., Forrest demanded the surrender of the Union forces, sending in a message of the sort he had used before: "The conduct of the officers and men garrisoning Fort Pillow has been such as to entitle them to being treated as prisoners of war. . . . Should my demand be refused, I cannot be responsible for the fate of your command."[2] Union Major William Bradford, who had replaced Major Booth, killed earlier by sharpshooters, asked for an hour to consider the demand. Forrest, worried that vessels in the river were bringing in more troops, "shortened the time to twenty minutes."[3] Bradford refused to surrender, and Forrest quickly ordered the attack.

Ellipsis mark indicates that words have been omitted.

Quotation is cited with an endnote.

The Confederates charged to the fort, scaled the parapet, and fired on the forces within. Victory came quickly, with the Union forces running toward the river or surrendering. Shelby Foote describes the scene like this:

> Some kept going, right on into the river, where a number drowned and the swimmers became targets for marksmen on the bluff. Others, dropping their guns in terror, ran back toward the Confederates with their hands up, and of these some were spared as prisoners, while others were shot down in the act of surrender.[4]

Long quotation is set off from text by indenting. Quotation marks are omitted.

In his own official report, Forrest makes no mention of the massacre. He does make much of the fact that the Union flag was not lowered by the

Bishop uses a primary source as well as secondary sources.

Union forces, saying that if his own men had not taken down the flag, "few, if any, would have survived unhurt another volley."[5] However, as Jack Hurst points out and Forrest must have known, in this twenty-minute battle, "Federals running for their lives had little time to concern themselves with a flag."[6]

Quotation is introduced with a signal phrase.

The federal congressional report on Fort Pillow, which charged the Confederates with appalling atrocities, was strongly criticized by Southerners. Respected writer Shelby Foote, while agreeing that the report was "largely" fabrication, points out that the "casualty figures . . . indicated strongly that unnecessary killing had occurred."[7] In an important article, John Cimprich and Robert C. Mainfort Jr. argue that the most trustworthy evidence is that written within about ten days of the battle, before word of the congressional hearings circulated and Southerners realized the extent of Northern outrage. The article reprints a group of letters and newspaper sources written before April 22 and thus "untainted by the political overtones the controversy later assumed."[8] Cimprich and Mainfort conclude that these sources "support the case for the occurrence of a massacre" but that Forrest's role "remains clouded" because of inconsistencies in testimony.[9]

Bishop draws attention to an article that reprints primary sources.

Did Forrest order the massacre?

We will never really know whether Forrest directly ordered the massacre, but it seems unlikely. True, Confederate soldier Achilles Clark, who had no reason to lie, wrote to his sisters that "I with several others tried to stop the butchery . . . but Gen. Forrest ordered them [Negro and white Union troops] shot down like dogs, and the carnage continued."[10] But it is not clear whether Clark heard Forrest giving the orders or was just reporting hearsay. Many Confederates had been shouting "No quarter! No quarter!" and, as Shelby Foote points out, these shouts were "thought by some to be at Forrest's command."[11] A Union soldier, Jacob Thompson, claimed to have seen Forrest order the killing, but when asked to describe the six-foot-two general, he called him "a little bit of a man."[12]

Topic sentence states the main idea for this section.

Bishop presents a balanced view of the evidence.

Perhaps the most convincing evidence that Forrest did not order the massacre is that he tried to stop it once it had begun. Historian Albert Castel quotes several eyewitnesses on both the Union and Confederate sides as saying that Forrest ordered his men to stop firing.[13] In a letter to his wife three days after the battle, Confederate soldier Samuel Caldwell wrote that "if General Forrest had not run between our men & the Yanks with his pistol and sabre drawn not a man would have been spared."[14]

In a respected biography of Nathan Bedford Forrest, Hurst suggests that the temperamental Forrest "may have ragingly ordered a massacre and even intended to carry it out—until he rode inside the fort and viewed the horrifying result" and ordered it stopped.[15] While this is an intriguing interpretation of events, even Hurst would probably admit that it is merely speculation.

Can Forrest be held responsible for the massacre?

Even assuming that Forrest did not order the massacre, he can still be held accountable for it. That is because he created an atmosphere ripe for the possibility of atrocities and did nothing to ensure that it wouldn't happen. Throughout his career Forrest repeatedly threatened "no quarter," particularly with respect to black soldiers, so Confederate troops had good reason to think that in massacring the enemy they were carrying out his orders. As Hurst writes, "About all he had to do to produce a massacre was issue no order against one."[16] Dudley Taylor Cornish agrees:

Topic sentence for this section reinforces the thesis.

> It has been asserted again and again that Forrest did not order a massacre. He did not need to. He had sought to terrify the Fort Pillow garrison by a threat of no quarter, as he had done at Union City and at Paducah in the days just before he turned on Pillow. If his men did enter the fort shouting "Give them no quarter, kill them; kill them; it is General Forrest's orders," he should not have been surprised.[17]

The slaughter at Fort Pillow was no doubt driven in large part by racial hatred. Numbers alone suggest this: of 295 white troops, 168 were taken prisoner, but of 262 black troops, only 58 were taken into custody, with the rest either dead or too badly wounded to walk.[18] A Southern reporter traveling with Forrest makes clear that the discrimination was deliberate: "Our troops maddened by the excitement, shot down the ret[r]eating Yankees, and not until they had attained t[h]e water's edge and turned to beg for mercy, did any prisoners fall in [t]o our hands—Thus the whites received quarter, but the negroes were shown no mercy."[19] Union surgeon Dr. Charles Fitch, who was taken prisoner by Forrest, testified that after he was in custody he "saw" Confederate soldiers "kill every negro that made his appearance dressed in Federal uniform."[20]

Notes begin on a new page.

First line of each note is indented ½".

Note number is not raised and is followed by a period.

Authors' names are not inverted.

Last name and title refer to an earlier note by the same author.

Notes are single-spaced, with double-spacing between notes. (Some instructors may prefer double-spacing throughout.)

Bishop 6

Notes

1. John Cimprich and Robert C. Mainfort Jr., eds., "Fort Pillow Revisited: New Evidence about an Old Controversy," *Civil War History* 28, no. 4 (1982): 293-94.

2. Quoted in Brian Steel Wills, *A Battle from the Start: The Life of Nathan Bedford Forrest* (New York: HarperCollins, 1992), 182.

3. Ibid., 183.

4. Shelby Foote, *The Civil War, a Narrative: Red River to Appomattox* (New York: Vintage, 1986), 110.

5. Nathan Bedford Forrest, "Report of Maj. Gen. Nathan B. Forrest, C. S. Army, Commanding Cavalry, of the Capture of Fort Pillow," Shotgun's Home of the American Civil War, accessed March 6, 2008, http://www.civilwarhome.com/forrest.htm.

6. Jack Hurst, *Nathan Bedford Forrest: A Biography* (New York: Knopf, 1993), 174.

7. Foote, *Civil War,* 111.

8. Cimprich and Mainfort, "Fort Pillow," 295.

9. Ibid., 305.

10. Ibid., 299.

11. Foote, *Civil War,* 110.

12. Quoted in Wills, *Battle from the Start,* 187.

13. Albert Castel, "The Fort Pillow Massacre: A Fresh Examination of the Evidence," *Civil War History* 4, no. 1 (1958): 44-45.

14. Cimprich and Mainfort, "Fort Pillow," 300.

15. Hurst, *Nathan Bedford Forrest,* 177.

16. Ibid.

17. Dudley Taylor Cornish, *The Sable Arm: Black Troops in the Union Army, 1861-1865* (Lawrence: University Press of Kansas, 1987), 175.

18. Foote, *Civil War,* 111.

19. Cimprich and Mainfort, "Fort Pillow," 304.

20. Quoted in Wills, *Battle from the Start,* 189.

21. Ibid., 215.

22. Quoted in Hurst, *Nathan Bedford Forrest,* 177.

23. Quoted in James M. McPherson, *Battle Cry of Freedom: The Civil War Era* (New York: Oxford University Press, 1988), 402.

Bishop 8

Bibliography begins on a new page.

Bibliography

Castel, Albert. "The Fort Pillow Massacre: A Fresh Examination of the Evidence." *Civil War History* 4, no. 1 (1958): 37-50.

Cimprich, John, and Robert C. Mainfort Jr., eds. "Fort Pillow Revisited: New Evidence about an Old Controversy." *Civil War History* 28, no. 4 (1982): 293-306.

Cornish, Dudley Taylor. *The Sable Arm: Black Troops in the Union Army, 1861-1865*. Lawrence: University Press of Kansas, 1987.

Foote, Shelby. *The Civil War, a Narrative: Red River to Appomattox*. New York: Vintage, 1986.

Forrest, Nathan Bedford. "Report of Maj. Gen. Nathan B. Forrest, C. S. Army, Commanding Cavalry, of the Capture of Fort Pillow." Shotgun's Home of the American Civil War. Accessed March 6, 2008. http://www .civilwarhome.com/forrest.htm.

Hurst, Jack. *Nathan Bedford Forrest: A Biography*. New York: Knopf, 1993.

McPherson, James M. *Battle Cry of Freedom: The Civil War Era*. New York: Oxford University Press, 1988.

Wills, Brian Steel. *A Battle from the Start: The Life of Nathan Bedford Forrest*. New York: HarperCollins, 1992.

Entries are alphabetized by authors' last names.

First line of entry is at left margin; additional lines are indented ½".

Entries are single-spaced, with double-spacing between entries. (Some instructors may prefer double-spacing throughout.)

Acknowledgments

Scott Adams, "Dilbert and the Way of the Weasel" comic from a student paper. DILBERT: © Scott Adams/Dist. by United Feature Syndicate, Inc. Reprinted with permission.

American Heritage Dictionary, definition for "regard" from *The American Heritage Dictionary of the English Language, Fourth Edition.* Copyright © 2009 by Houghton Mifflin Harcourt Publishing Company. Reproduced by permission of Houghton Mifflin Harcourt Publishing Company.

EBSCO Information Services, various screen shots of database search results. Copyright © 2010 by EBSCO Publishing, Inc. All rights reserved. Reprinted with permission.

Equal Exchange, annotated advertisement. Copyright © 2007 by Equal Exchange. Reprinted with permission.

Gale, screen shot from ACADEMIC ONEFILE. Copyright © Gale, a part of Cengage Learning, Inc. Reproduced by permission. www.cengage.com/permission.

Chris Gonsalves, excerpt from "Wasting Away on the Web" from *eWeek*, August 8, 2005. Copyright © 2005 Ziff Davis Media Inc. All rights reserved. Reprinted with permission of Ziff Davis Media Inc.

Massachusetts Nurses Association, screen shot of labor relations Web page from www.massnurses.org. Copyright © Massachusetts Nurses Association. Reprinted with permission.

Merriam-Webster Online, screen shot of online dictionary entry for "regard" from *Merriam-Webster's Collegiate ® Dictionary, 11th Edition*. Copyright © 2010 by Merriam-Webster, Incorporated (www.Merriam-Webster.com). Reprinted with permission.

New Bedford Whaling Museum, screen shot of "Overview of American Whaling" Web page. Courtesy of the New Bedford Whaling Museum. Reprinted by permission.

The New York Times, "Cullings: Proportion of respondents who attribute 'very great prestige' to the following professions" chart. Copyright © 2008 The New York Times. Reprinted by permission.

The New York Times, screen shot of the article page "Sales Reflect End of Car Rebate Plan" by Jack Healy. Copyright © 2009 The New York Times. Reprinted by permission.

Screen shots of various pages from *The American Historical Review*, 113.2 (April 2008). Copyright © 2008. Reprinted by permission of University of Chicago Press.

Screen shots of the Table of Contents Page and the first page of "An Appeal to Authority" by David Whitman, from *Education Next* 8 (4) 2008 issue. Copyright © Education Next. All rights reserved. Reprinted by permission.

Screen shots of the Copyright Page and Title Page from *Asian American Literature: An Anthology* by Shirley Geok-lin Lim. Copyright © 1999 by McGraw-Hill Companies. Reprinted by permission of McGraw-Hill Companies.

Screen shots of the article page "For the Love of Joe: The Language of Starbucks" by Constance M. Ruzich and the Title Page of *The Journal of Popular Culture*. Copyright © 2008 by Blackwell Publishers, Ltd. Reprinted with the permission of Blackwell Publishers, Ltd.

Screen shots of the Copyright Page and Title Page from *Hot, Flat, and Crowded* by Thomas L. Friedman. Copyright © 2008 by Farrar, Straus and Giroux, LLC. Reprinted by permission of Farrar, Straus and Giroux, LLC.

Screen shots of the Copyright Page and Title Page from *A Midwife's Tale: The Life of Martha Ballard, Based on Her Diary, 1785–1812*. Copyright © 1990 by Laurel Thatcher Ulrich. Reprinted with the permission of Alfred A. Knopf, a division of Random House, Inc. For online information about other Random House, Inc. books and authors, see the Internet Web site at http://www.randomhouse.com.

Screen shots of the Copyright Page and Title Page from *To His Excellency Thomas Jefferson: Letters to a President*. Copyright © 1990 by Jack McLaughlin. Reprinted with the permission of HarperCollins Publishers.

Screen shots of the Copyright Page and Title Page from *White Heat: The Friendship of Emily Dickinson and Thomas Wentworth Higginson* by Brenda Wineapple. Copyright © 2008 by Brenda Wineapple. Used by permission of Alfred A. Knopf, a division of Random House, Inc.

Snapshot of the article page "The Cyberbullies Are Always with You . . ." by P. McKenna, from *New Scientist* 195, 2007 issue. Copyright © 2007 New Scientist. Reprinted with permission.

Snapshot of the article page "Cyberbullying: Using Virtual Scenarios to Educate and Raise Awareness" by Vivian H. Wright, Joy J. Burnham, Christopher T. Inman, and Heather N. Ogorchock, from *Journal of Computing in Teacher Education* 26 (1) 2009 issue. Copyright © 2009 International Society of Technology in Education. Reprinted with permission.

University of Minnesota Libraries, screen shots. Copyright © 2009 Regents of the University of Minnesota. All rights reserved. Reprinted with permission.

Fred Zwicky, "Tornado Touch" photo, from *Peoria Journal Star*. Copyright © 2004 by Fred Zwicky. Reprinted by permission of the author.

Index

Index

In addition to giving you page numbers, this index shows you which tabbed section to flip to. For example, the entry "*a* vs. *an*" directs you to section **W** (Word Choice), page 139, and to section **M** (Multilingual Writers and ESL Challenges), pages 239–40. Just flip to the appropriate tabbed section and then track down the exact pages you need.

A

a, *an*. *See also the*
a vs. *an*, **W**: 139, **M**: 239–40
choosing, with common nouns, **M**: 241–42
defined, **M**: 237
multilingual/ESL challenges with, **M**: 237–40, 241–44
needed, **S**: 117
omission of, **S**: 117, **M**: 241–44
Abbreviations, **P**: 300–02
capitalizing, **P**: 299
familiar, **P**: 300
inappropriate, **P**: 302
Latin, **P**: 301
periods with, **P**: 286–87, 300–01
plurals of, **P**: 280
for titles with proper names, **P**: 300
abide by (not *with*) *a decision*, **W**: 167
Absolute concepts (such as *unique*), **G**: 212
Absolute phrases
commas with, **P**: 266–67
defined, **B**: 323
Abstract nouns, **W**: 165–66
Abstracts
in APA papers, **APA**: 485, 489
in databases, **R**: 337, 352
Academic writing, **A**: 65–108
analysis papers, **A**: 67–77
argument papers, **A**: 78–100
audience for, **C**: 3–4
highlights of the research process, **MLA**: 432–35
manuscript formats, **C**: 54–56. *See also* APA papers; CMS (*Chicago*) papers; MLA papers
process of, **A**: 101
questions asked in the disciplines, **A**: 100–02
research papers, **R**: 329–68
writing in the disciplines, **A**: 100–08. *See also* APA papers; CMS (*Chicago*) papers; MLA papers
accept, *except*, **W**: 139
according to (not *with*), **W**: 167
Active reading, **A**: 67–77. *See also* Reading
Active verbs, **W**: 156–58. *See also* Active voice
Active voice
vs. *be* verbs, **W**: 158
changing to passive, **B**: 318–19
vs. passive, **W**: 157–58
shifts between passive and, avoiding, **S**: 124–25
and wordy sentences, **W**: 155
adapt, *adopt*, **W**: 139
AD, *BC* (*CE*, *BCE*), **P**: 301
Addresses
commas with, **P**: 268
e-mail, **P**: 296
numbers in, **P**: 303
URLs (Web addresses), **P**: 296, **MLA**: 412, 430, 431, **APA**: 472, 487, **CMS**: 512, 530
ad hominem fallacy, **A**: 98
Adjective clauses
avoiding repetition in, **M**: 248
defined, **B**: 333
punctuation of, **P**: 263–64
words introducing, **B**: 325
Adjective phrases
infinitive, **B**: 322
introductory, with comma, **P**: 260
participial, **B**: 321–22
prepositional, **B**: 320
punctuation of, **P**: 264–65
restrictive (essential) vs. nonrestrictive (nonessential), **P**: 264–65
Adjectives
and absolute concepts, **G**: 212
and adverbs, **G**: 207–12, **B**: 314
comparative forms (with *more*), **G**: 210–12

Adjectives (*continued*)
  commas with coordinate, **P**: 261–62
  defined, **B**: 313
  after direct objects (object complements), **G**: 209, **B**: 319
  hyphens with, **P**: 294–95
  after linking verbs (subject complements), **G**: 208–09, **B**: 318
  no commas with cumulative, **P**: 271
  order of, **M**: 251–52
  with prepositions (idioms), **M**: 254–55
  superlative forms (with *most*), **G**: 210–12
adopt. See *adapt*, *adopt*, **W**: 139
Adverb clauses
  comma with, **P**: 260
  defined, **B**: 324
  no comma with, **P**: 272
  punctuation of, **P**: 260, 272
  words introducing, **B**: 325
Adverb phrases
  infinitive, **B**: 322
  prepositional, **B**: 320–21
Adverbs. *See also* Conjunctive adverbs
  and adjectives, **G**: 207–12
  avoiding repetition of, in clauses, **M**: 248
  comparative forms (with *-er*, *more*), **G**: 210–12
  defined, **B**: 314
  introducing clauses, **M**: 248, **B**: 325
  placement of, **M**: 249–50
  relative, **M**: 248, **B**: 325
  superlative forms (with *-est*, *most*), **G**: 210–12
adverse, *averse*, **W**: 139
Advertisements, writing about. *See* Texts, visual
advice, *advise*, **W**: 139
affect, *effect*, **W**: 139
aggravate, **W**: 139
Agreement of pronoun and antecedent, **G**: 197–99
  with antecedents joined by *and*, **G**: 199
  with antecedents joined by *or* or *nor*, **G**: 199
  with collective nouns (*audience*, *family*, *team*, etc.), **G**: 198–99
  with generic nouns, **G**: 198
  with indefinite pronouns, **G**: 197–98
  and sexist language, avoiding, **G**: 197–98
Agreement of subject and verb, **G**: 175–83
  with collective nouns (*audience*, *family*, *team*, etc.), **G**: 179–80
  with company names, **G**: 182–83
  with gerund phrases, **G**: 182–83
  with indefinite pronouns, **G**: 179
  with intervening words, **G**: 175–77
  with nouns of plural form, singular meaning (*athletics*, *economics*, etc.), **G**: 182
  standard subject-verb combinations, **G**: 175, 176–77
  with subject, not subject complement, **G**: 181
  with subject after verb, **G**: 180–81
  with subjects joined with *and*, **G**: 178
  with subjects joined with *or* or *nor*, **G**: 178
  with *the number*, *a number*, **G**: 180
  with *there is*, *there are*, **G**: 180–81
  with titles of works, **G**: 182–83
  with units of measurement, **G**: 180
  with *who*, *which*, *that*, **G**: 181–82

with words between subject and verb, **G**: 175–77
with words used as words, **G**: 182–83
agree to, *agree with*, **W**: 140, 167
ain't (nonstandard), **W**: 140
Aircraft, italics for names of, **P**: 305
Alignment of text (left, right, centered, justified), **MLA**: 429, **APA**: 485, **CMS**: 529
all (singular or plural), **G**: 179
all-, as prefix, with hyphen, **P**: 295
all ready, *already*, **W**: 140
all right (not *alright*), **W**: 140
all together, *altogether*, **W**: 140
allude, **W**: 140
allusion, *illusion*, **W**: 140
almost, placement of, **S**: 117–18
a lot (not *alot*), **W**: 140
already. See *all ready*, *already*, **W**: 140
alright (nonstandard). See *all right*, **W**: 140
although
avoiding with *but* or *however*, **M**: 249
introducing subordinate clause, **B**: 315
no comma after, **P**: 273
altogether. See *all together*, *altogether*, **W**: 140
American Psychological Association. *See* APA papers
among, *between*. See *between*, *among*, **W**: 142
amongst, **W**: 140
amoral, *immoral*, **W**: 140
amount, *number*, **W**: 140
a.m., *p.m.*, *AM*, *PM*, **P**: 301
am vs. *is* or *are*. *See* Agreement of subject and verb
an, *a*. *See a*, *an*
Analogy
as argument strategy, **A**: 93
false, **A**: 93
as pattern of organization, **C**: 37–38
Analysis
critical thinking, **A**: 67–77
synthesizing sources, **MLA**: 386–87, **APA**: 456–58
of visual texts, **A**: 67–74, 77
of written texts, **A**: 67–77
Analysis papers, **A**: 67–77
and critical thinking, **A**: 67–77
evidence for, **A**: 74, 77
interpretation in, **A**: 74, 77
sample paper, **A**: 75–76
summaries in, **C**: 26, **A**: 72–73
thesis in, **A**: 74
and
antecedents joined by, **G**: 199
comma with, **P**: 259
as coordinating conjunction, **S**: 112, **B**: 315
excessive use of, **S**: 132
no comma with, **P**: 269–70, 273
no semicolon with, **P**: 276
parallelism and, **S**: 112
subjects joined by, **G**: 178
and etc. (nonstandard), **W**: 140
and/or
avoiding, **W**: 140
slash with, **P**: 291
angry with (not *at*), **W**: 140, 167
Annotated bibliography, sample entry (MLA style), **R**: 358–59
Annotating a text, **C**: 7, **A**: 67–70
sample annotated visual text, **A**: 70
sample annotated written texts, **A**: 69, **MLA**: 434
ante-, *anti-*, **W**: 140–41
Antecedent
agreement of pronoun and, **G**: 197–99
defined, **G**: 197, 199, **B**: 309
pronoun reference, **G**: 199
singular vs. plural, **G**: 197–99
unclear or unstated, **G**: 199–200
of *who*, *which*, *that*, **G**: 181–82

Anthology, selection in, **MLA**: 395, 407–08, **APA**: 469, 471, **CMS**: 515
  citation at a glance, **MLA**: 410–11
anti-, *ante-*. See *ante-*, *anti-*, **W**: 140–41
Antonyms (opposites), **W**: 172
a number (plural), *the number* (singular), **G**: 180
anxious, **W**: 141
any, **G**: 179
anybody (singular), **W**: 141, **G**: 179, 197–98
anymore, **W**: 141
anyone (singular), **W**: 141, **G**: 179, 197–98
anyone, *any one*, **W**: 141
anyplace, **W**: 141
anything (singular), **G**: 179, 197–98
anyways, *anywheres* (nonstandard), **W**: 141
APA papers, **APA**: 443–97
  abstracts in, **APA**: 485, 489
  authority in, **APA**: 447
  citation at a glance
    article from a database, **APA**: 474–75
    article in a journal or magazine, **APA**: 467
    book, **APA**: 470
    section in a Web document, **APA**: 478–79
  citations, in-text
    directory to models for, **APA**: 443
    models for, **APA**: 459–63
  evidence for, **APA**: 446–48
  footnotes
    formatting, **APA**: 485
    sample, **APA**: 490
  manuscript format, **APA**: 484–87
  organizing, **APA**: 446
  plagiarism in, avoiding, **APA**: 448–51
  reference list
    directory to models for, **APA**: 443–44
    models for, **APA**: 463–83
    sample, **APA**: 496
  sample paper, **APA**: 488–97
  signal phrases in, **APA**: 453–54
  sources
    citing, **APA**: 458–83
    integrating, **APA**: 451–58
    synthesizing, **APA**: 456–58
    uses of, **APA**: 446–48
  supporting arguments in, **APA**: 446–48, 456–58
  tenses in, **APA**: 454, 459
  thesis in, **APA**: 445
  title page
    formatting, **APA**: 484
    samples, **APA**: 488, 497
  URLs (Web addresses) in, **APA**: 472, 487
  visuals
    formatting, **APA**: 486
    sample table, **APA**: 493
Apostrophes, **P**: 278–81
  in contractions, **P**: 279
  misuse of, **P**: 280–81
  in plurals, **P**: 279–80
  in possessives, **P**: 278–79
Apposition, faulty, **S**: 128
Appositive phrases, **B**: 323
Appositives (nouns that rename other nouns)
  case of pronouns with, **G**: 203–04
  colon with, **P**: 276
  commas with, **P**: 265
  dashes with, **P**: 288
  defined, **P**: 265
  no commas with, **P**: 271–72
  as sentence fragments, **G**: 215–16
Appropriate language (avoiding jargon, slang, etc.), **W**: 159–64
Archives, digital, **R**: 342–43
  MLA citation of, **MLA**: 417

are vs. *is*. *See* Agreement of subject and verb
Argument papers, **A**: 78–100. *See also* Arguments, evaluating
  audience for, **A**: 79–80
  common ground in, **A**: 80–81, 86
  countering opposing arguments in, **C**: 25–26, **A**: 85–86, 98–100
  credibility in, **A**: 80–81
  evidence in, **A**: 82–84
  introduction to, **A**: 80–81
  lines of argument in, **A**: 81–82
  providing context in, **A**: 79
  researching, **A**: 79
  sample paper, **A**: 87–91
  support for, **A**: 81–82
  thesis in, **A**: 80–81
Arguments, evaluating, **A**: 92–100. *See also* Argument papers
  argumentative tactics, **A**: 92–98
  assumptions, **A**: 95–96
  bias, **R**: 354
  claims, **A**: 95–96
  deductive reasoning, **A**: 96–97
  emotional appeals, **A**: 97–99
  fairness, **A**: 97–99
  generalizations, faulty, **A**: 92–93
  inductive reasoning, **A**: 92–93, 94
  logical fallacies, **A**: 92–97
Article from a database. *See also* Articles in periodicals
  citing in papers, **MLA**: 415–16, **APA**: 473–75, **CMS**: 517, 521–23
  citation at a glance, **MLA**: 416, **APA**: 474–75, **CMS**: 522–23
Articles (*a*, *an*, *the*), **M**: 237–45. *See also a*, *an*; *the*
Articles in periodicals. *See also* Article from a database
  capitalizing titles of, **P**: 298, **MLA**: 398, 429–30, **APA**: 485, 487, **CMS**: 529
  citation at a glance, **MLA**: 402–03, **APA**: 467, **CMS**: 520–21
  citing in paper, **MLA**: 401–04, 413, 415–16, **APA**: 465–68, 472–75, **CMS**: 517, 520–24
  finding, **R**: 336–40, **MLA**: 432–33
  previewing, **R**: 348
  quotation marks for titles of, **P**: 283, **MLA**: 398, 429–30, **APA**: 485, 487, **CMS**: 511, 529
Artwork, italics for title of, **P**: 304
as
  ambiguous use of, **W**: 141
  needed word, **S**: 116
  parallelism and, **S**: 113
  pronoun after, **G**: 204
as, *like*. See *like*, *as*, **W**: 147
Assignments
  understanding, **C**: 5, **A**: 104–08
  samples of, **A**: 105–08
Assumptions, in arguments, **A**: 95–96
as to, **W**: 141
at
  in idioms (common expressions), **M**: 252–53, 255
  multilingual/ESL challenges with, **M**: 252–53, 255
audience. *See* Collective nouns
Audience
  for argument paper, **A**: 79–80
  assessing, **C**: 3–4, 6
  and document design, **C**: 46–47
  and global (big-picture) revision, **C**: 21
  and level of formality, **W**: 162
Authority, establishing in research papers, **MLA**: 375, 383–84, **APA**: 447, **CMS**: 501
Autoformatting, **C**: 63
Auxiliary verbs. *See* Helping verbs
averse. See *adverse*, *averse*, **W**: 139
awful, **W**: 141
awhile, *a while*, **W**: 141
Awkward sentences, **S**: 126–28

B

back up, *backup*, **W**: 141
bad, *badly*, **W**: 141, **G**: 209
Bandwagon appeal fallacy, **A**: 98
Base form of verb, **G**: 183, **B**: 312
  modal (*can*, *might*, *should*, etc.) with, **G**: 190, **M**: 230
  in negatives with *do*, **M**: 230–31
BC, *AD* (*BCE*, *CE*), **P**: 301
be, as irregular verb, **G**: 184, **M**: 225–26
be, forms of, **G**: 176, **M**: 225–26, **B**: 312
  vs. active verbs, **W**: 158
  and agreement with subject, **G**: 175–83
  in conditional sentences, **M**: 234
  as helping verbs, **W**: 158, **M**: 227–28, 229, **B**: 312
  as linking verbs, **W**: 158, **G**: 190, **M**: 246, **B**: 318
  in passive voice, **W**: 157–58, **M**: 226, 229–30
  in progressive forms, **G**: 191–92, **M**: 227–28
  and subjunctive mood, **G**: 195–96
  in tenses, **G**: 184, 191–92
  as weak verbs, **W**: 158
because
  avoiding after *reason is*, **S**: 128, **W**: 149
  avoiding with *so* or *therefore*, **M**: 249
  introducing subordinate clause, **B**: 315
  not omitting, **S**: 113–14
Beginning of essays. *See* Introduction
Beginning of sentences
  capitalizing words at, **P**: 298–99
  numbers at, **P**: 303
  varying, **S**: 135
being as, *being that* (nonstandard), **W**: 141
beside, *besides*, **W**: 142
better, *best*, **G**: 210–11
between, *among*, **W**: 142
Bias, signs of, **R**: 353–54
Biased language, **A**: 98, **W**: 164. *See also* Sexist language
Bible
  citing in paper, **MLA**: 398, 409, **APA**: 463, 471, **CMS**: 000
  no italics for, **P**: 305
  punctuation between chapter and verse, **P**: 277
Bibliography. *See also* Reference list (APA); Works cited list (MLA)
  annotated, sample entry (MLA style), **R**: 358–59
  CMS (*Chicago*) style
    directory to models for, **CMS**: 498
    formatting, **CMS**: 511–12, 531
    models for, **CMS**: 512–28
    sample, **CMS**: 537
  working, **R**: 358–59, 360
    information for, **C**: 64, **R**: 360
Big picture, revising for (global revision), **C**: 20–21. *See also* Revising with comments
Block quotation. *See* Quotations, long
Blog (Weblog)
  citing in paper, **MLA**: 418, **APA**: 477, **CMS**: 525
  to explore ideas, **C**: 10
  as information source, **R**: 344
Body of essay, **C**: 18–19
Boldface, for emphasis, **C**: 46
Books
  capitalizing titles of, **P**: 298, **MLA**: 398, 429–30, **APA**: 485, 487, **CMS**: 529
  citation at a glance, **MLA**: 406, 410–11, **APA**: 470, **CMS**: 514–15
  citing in paper, **MLA**: 404–11, 417, **APA**: 468–71, 473, 475, **CMS**: 512–19
  italics for titles of, **P**: 304–05, **MLA**: 398, 429–30, **APA**: 485, 487, **CMS**: 511, 529

library catalog for finding, **R**: 340–41, 348–49, **MLA**: 432
previewing, **R**: 348–49, **MLA**: 435
Borrowed language and ideas. *See* Citing sources; Plagiarism, avoiding
both . . . and, **B**: 315
parallelism and, **S**: 112–13
Brackets, **P**: 289–90, **MLA**: 381, **APA**: 452–53, **CMS**: 506
Brainstorming, to generate ideas, **C**: 7–8
bring, *take*, **W**: 142
Broad reference of *this*, *that*, *which*, *it*, **G**: 200–01
burst, *bursted*; *bust*, *busted*, **W**: 142
Business writing, **C**: 57–62
audience for, **C**: 3
e-mail, **C**: 60, 62
letters, **C**: 57–58
memos, **C**: 60, 61
résumés, **C**: 58–60
sample assignment and proposal, **A**: 106
but
avoiding with *although* or *however*, **M**: 249
comma with, **P**: 259
as coordinating conjunction, **S**: 112, **B**: 315
excessive use of, **S**: 132
no comma with, **P**: 269–70, 273
no semicolon with, **P**: 276
parallelism and, **S**: 112
as preposition, **B**: 314
by, not omitting, **S**: 113–14

C

Call numbers, in library, **R**: 340
can, as modal verb, **M**: 230, 232–33, **B**: 312
can, *may*, **W**: 142
capable of (not *to*), **W**: 167
capital, *capitol*, **W**: 142
Capitalization, **P**: 296–99
of abbreviations, **P**: 299
after colon, **P**: 277, 299, **MLA**: 430, **APA**: 485, **CMS**: 529
of first word of sentence, **P**: 298–99
misuse of, **P**: 296–97
of proper nouns, **P**: 296–97
in quotations, **P**: 299
of titles of persons, **P**: 298
of titles of works, **P**: 298, **MLA**: 398, 429–30, **APA**: 485, 487, **CMS**: 529
capitol. See *capital*, *capitol*, **W**: 142
Case. *See* Pronoun case
Case study. *See* Research process, highlights of
Catalog, library, **R**: 340–41, 348–49, **MLA**: 432
Cause and effect
as pattern of organization, **C**: 38
reasoning, **A**: 94–95
censor, *censure*, **W**: 142
Central idea. *See* Focus; Thesis
cf., **P**: 301
Charts, using in documents, **C**: 50–54, **MLA**: 430–31, **APA**: 486, **CMS**: 530
Chicago Manual of Style, The, **R**: 367, **CMS**: 499, 511
Choppy sentences, **S**: 130–31
Citation at a glance
APA style
article from a database, **APA**: 474–75
article in a journal or magazine, **APA**: 467
book, **APA**: 470
section in a Web document, **APA**: 478–79
CMS (*Chicago*) style
article in a scholarly journal, **CMS**: 520–21
book, **CMS**: 514–15
journal article from a database, **CMS**: 522–23

Citation at a glance (*continued*)
CMS (*Chicago*) style (*continued*)
letter in a published collection, **CMS**: 518–19
primary source from a Web site, **CMS**: 526–27
MLA style
article from a database, **MLA**: 416
article in a periodical, **MLA**: 402–03
book, **MLA**: 406
selection from an anthology, **MLA**: 410–11
short work from a Web site, **MLA**: 414–15
Citations. *See* Citation at a glance; Citing sources; Documenting sources
cited in, for a source in another source, **APA**: 463. *See also quoted in*
cite, *site*, **W**: 142
Citing sources. *See also* Documenting sources; Plagiarism, avoiding; Quotations
APA style, **APA**: 448–51, 458–83
choosing a citation style, **A**: 103, **R**: 366–68
CMS (*Chicago*) style, **CMS**: 502–04, 510–28
common knowledge, **MLA**: 377, **APA**: 448, **CMS**: 502
general guidelines for, **R**: 364–65
MLA style, **MLA**: 376–79, 388–428
software for, **R**: 359
Claims. *See* Arguments, evaluating; Thesis
class. *See* Collective nouns
Classification, as pattern of organization, **C**: 38
Clauses. *See* Independent clauses; Subordinate clauses
Clichés, **W**: 167–68
climactic, *climatic*, **W**: 142
Clustering, of ideas, **C**: 8
CMS (*Chicago*) papers, **CMS**: 498–537
authority in, **CMS**: 501
bibliography, **CMS**: 510–28
directory to models for, **CMS**: 498
models for, **CMS**: 510–28
sample, **CMS**: 537
citation at a glance
article in a scholarly journal, **CMS**: 520–21
book, **CMS**: 514–15
journal article from a database, **CMS**: 522–23
letter in a published collection, **CMS**: 518–19
primary source from a Web site, **CMS**: 526–27
evidence for, **CMS**: 500–01
footnotes or endnotes, **CMS**: 510–11
directory to models for, **CMS**: 498
ibid. in, **CMS**: 511
models for, **CMS**: 510–28
sample, **CMS**: 536
manuscript format, **CMS**: 528–31
organizing, **CMS**: 500
plagiarism in, avoiding, **CMS**: 502–04
sample pages, **CMS**: 532–37
signal phrases in, **CMS**: 507–10
sources in
citing, **CMS**: 502–04, 510–28
integrating, **CMS**: 505–10
uses of, **CMS**: 500–01
supporting arguments in, **CMS**: 500–01
tenses in, **CMS**: 507
thesis in, **CMS**: 499
URLs (Web addresses) in, **CMS**: 512, 530
coarse, *course*, **W**: 142
Coherence, **C**: 39–44

Collaborative writing. *See* Reviewers
Collective nouns (*audience*, *family*, *team*, etc.)
  agreement of pronouns with, **G**: 198–99
  agreement of verbs with, **G**: 179–80
College writing. *See* Academic writing
Colloquial words, **W**: 172
Colon, **P**: 276–77
  with appositives (nouns that rename other nouns), **P**: 277
  capitalization after, **P**: 277, 299, **MLA**: 430, **APA**: 485, **CMS**: 529
  to fix run-on sentences, **G**: 220–21
  with greetings and salutations, **P**: 277
  between hours and minutes, **P**: 277
  introducing quotations, **P**: 276–77, 284
  with lists, **P**: 277
  misuse of, **P**: 277
  outside quotation marks, **P**: 284
  with ratios, **P**: 277
  between titles and subtitles of works, **P**: 277
Combining sentences (coordination and subordination), **S**: 129–30
Commands. *See* Imperative mood; Imperative sentences
Commas, **P**: 259–73. *See also* Commas, unnecessary
  with absolute phrases, **P**: 266–67
  in addresses, **P**: 268
  with *and*, *but*, etc., **P**: 259
  between coordinate adjectives, **P**: 261–62
  before coordinating conjunctions, **P**: 259
  in dates, **P**: 268
  with interrogative tags, **P**: 267
  with interruptions (*he said* etc.), **P**: 265–67
  after introductory elements, **P**: 260
  with items in a series, **P**: 261
  joining ideas with, **P**: 259
  with mild interjections, **P**: 267
  with modifiers, **P**: 261–62
  with nonrestrictive (nonessential) elements, **P**: 262–65
  with nouns of direct address, **P**: 267
  in numbers, **P**: 268–69
  with parenthetical expressions, **P**: 266
  to prevent confusion, **P**: 269
  with quotation marks, **P**: 267–68, 283–84
  with semicolons, **P**: 275
  to set off words or phrases, **P**: 265–67
  with titles following names, **P**: 268
  with transitional expressions, **P**: 265–66
  before *which* or *who*, **P**: 263–65
  with word groups expressing contrast, **P**: 267
  with *yes* and *no*, **P**: 267
Commas, unnecessary, **P**: 269–73
  between adjective and noun, **P**: 271
  after *although*, **P**: 273
  after *and*, *but*, etc., **P**: 273
  between compound elements, **P**: 269–70
  before concluding adverb clauses, **P**: 272
  after a coordinating conjunction, **P**: 273
  between cumulative adjectives, **P**: 271
  with indirect quotations, **P**: 273
  in an inverted sentence (verb before subject), **P**: 272–73
  with mildly parenthetical elements, **P**: 271–72

Commas, unnecessary (*continued*)
before a parenthesis, **P**: 273
with a question mark or an exclamation point, **P**: 273
with restrictive (essential) elements, **P**: 271–72
before or after a series, **P**: 270–71
after a signal phrase, **P**: 270
between subject and verb, **P**: 270
after *such as* or *like*, **P**: 273
before *than*, **P**: 273
between verb and object, **P**: 270
Comma splices. *See* Run-on sentences
Comments on a draft, understanding. *See* Revising with comments
committee. *See* Collective nouns
Common ground, establishing in an argument, **A**: 80–81, 86
Common knowledge, **MLA**: 377, **APA**: 448, **CMS**: 502
Common nouns, **M**: 238–39, 240–43, **P**: 296–97
Company names
abbreviations in, **P**: 302
agreement of verb with, **G**: 182–83
Comparative form of adjectives and adverbs (with *-er* or *more*), **G**: 210–12
compare to, *compare with*, **W**: 142–43
Comparisons
with adjectives and adverbs, **G**: 210–12
needed words in, **S**: 115–16
parallel elements in, **S**: 113
as pattern of organization, **C**: 36–37
with pronoun following *than* or *as*, **G**: 204
complement, *compliment*, **W**: 143
Complements, object, **B**: 319
Complements, subject
adjectives as, **G**: 208–09, **B**: 318
case of pronouns as, **G**: 202
defined, **B**: 318
and subject-verb agreement, **G**: 181
Complete subject, **B**: 316
Complex sentences, **B**: 327
compliment. See *complement*, *compliment*, **W**: 143
comply with (not *to*), **W**: 167
Compound antecedents, **G**: 199
Compound-complex sentences, **B**: 327
Compound elements
case of pronoun in, **G**: 203
comma with, **P**: 259
needed words in, **S**: 114–15
no comma with, **P**: 269–70
parallelism and, **S**: 112–13
Compound nouns, plural of, **P**: 279
Compound numbers, hyphens with, **P**: 295
Compound predicate
fragmented, **G**: 216
no comma in, **P**: 259, 269–70
Compound sentences
comma in, **P**: 259
defined, **B**: 326
excessive use of, **S**: 132
semicolon in, **P**: 274
Compound subjects
agreement of pronoun with, **G**: 199
agreement of verb with, **G**: 178
defined, **B**: 317
Compound verb. *See* Compound predicate
Compound words
in dictionary entry, **W**: 169
hyphens with, **P**: 294
plural of, **P**: 292
Computers, writing with, **C**: 62–64
Conciseness, **W**: 153–56
Conclusion
in deductive reasoning, **A**: 96–97
of essay, **C**: 19–20
in inductive reasoning, **A**: 92–93, 94

Concrete nouns, **W**: 165–66
Conditional sentences, **M**: 231–34. *See also* Subjunctive mood
Confused words, **W**: 166. *See also* Glossary of usage
Conjunctions, **B**: 315. *See also* Conjunctive adverbs
  in coordination and subordination, **S**: 129–30
  in fixing run-on sentences, **G**: 220
Conjunctive adverbs
  comma after, **P**: 265–66
  and coordination, **S**: 129
  defined, **B**: 315
  and run-on sentences, **G**: 219, 220
  semicolon with, **P**: 274–75
Connotation (implied meaning of word), **W**: 165
conscience, *conscious*, **W**: 143
Consistency
  in mood and voice, **S**: 124–25
  in paragraphs, **C**: 41–42
  in phrasing of headings, **C**: 48–49
  in point of view, **S**: 123–24
  in questions and quotations, **S**: 125–26
  in verb tense, **S**: 124
Context, establishing, **A**: 79
continual, *continuous*, **W**: 143
Contractions, apostrophe in, **P**: 279
Contrary-to-fact clauses, **G**: 195–96, **M**: 234
Contrast, as pattern of organization, **C**: 36–37
Contrasted elements, comma with, **P**: 267
Conversation among sources. *See* Synthesizing sources
Coordinate adjectives, comma with, **P**: 261–62
Coordinating conjunctions
  comma before, **P**: 259
  coordination and, **S**: 129
  defined, **B**: 315
  to fix run-on sentences, **G**: 220
  no comma with, **P**: 269–70, 273
  no semicolon with, **P**: 276
  parallelism and, **S**: 112
Coordination, **S**: 129, 132
Copies, of drafts, saving, **C**: 63–64
Correlative conjunctions
  defined, **B**: 315
  parallelism with, **S**: 112–13
could, as modal verb, **M**: 230, 232, **B**: 312
could care less (nonstandard), **W**: 143
could of (nonstandard), **W**: 143
council, *counsel*, **W**: 143
Countering arguments, **C**: 25–26, **A**: 85–86, 98–100, **MLA**: 376, **APA**: 447–48, **CMS**: 501
Count nouns, articles (*a*, *an*, *the*) with, **M**: 238–42
couple. *See* Collective nouns
course. See *coarse*, *course*, **W**: 142
Cover letters
  for portfolios, **C**: 29–31
  for résumés, **C**: 58
Credibility, establishing, **A**: 80–81. *See also* Authority
criteria, **W**: 143
Critical reading. *See* Reading
Critical thinking, **A**: 67–77, 92–100, **R**: 353–57
crowd. *See* Collective nouns
Cumulative adjectives
  no comma with, **P**: 271
  order of, **M**: 251–52
Cuts, in quotations. *See* Brackets; Ellipsis mark

D

-d, *-ed*, verb ending, **G**: 184, 188–89, **M**: 227
Dangling modifiers, **S**: 120–23
Dashes, **P**: 288–89
  to fix run-on sentences, **G**: 220
data, **W**: 143
Database, article from. *See* Article from a database

Databases, for finding sources, **R**: 336–39, 348. *See also* Indexes to periodical articles, print
Dates
abbreviations in, **P**: 301
commas with, **P**: 268
numbers in, **P**: 303
Days of the week
abbreviations of, **P**: 302
capitalization of, **P**: 297
Deadlines, **C**: 6, **R**: 331
Debates. *See* Argument papers; Arguments, evaluating
Declarative sentences, **B**: 327
Deductive reasoning, **A**: 96–97
Definite article. *See the*
Definition
as pattern of organization, **C**: 39
of words, **W**: 165, 172
Degree. *See* Comparative form of adjectives and adverbs; Superlative form of adjectives and adverbs
Demonstrative pronouns, **B**: 311
Denotation (dictionary definition of word), **W**: 165
Dependent clauses. *See* Subordinate clauses
Description, as pattern of organization, **C**: 36
Descriptive word groups. *See* Adjective phrases; Adverb phrases
desirous of (not *to*), **W**: 167
Detail, adequate, **C**: 24–25, 33–34. *See also* Development; Evidence
Determiners, **M**: 237–45
Development. *See also* Organization, patterns of
adequate, **C**: 21, 24–25, 33–34
Diagrams, using in documents, **C**: 50–54
Dialects, **W**: 161
Dialogue
paragraphing of, **P**: 281–82
quotation marks in, **P**: 281–82
Diction. *See* Words
Dictionaries
guide to use of, **W**: 169–72
sample online entry, **W**: 171
sample print entry, **W**: 170
different from, *different than*, **W**: 143, 167
differ from, *differ with*, **W**: 143
Digital archives, **R**: 342–43
MLA citation of, **MLA**: 417
Digital file, MLA citation of, **MLA**: 420
Digital object identifier (DOI), **APA**: 472, **CMS**: 511
Direct address, commas with, **P**: 267
Direct language, **W**: 154–55
Direct objects
case of pronouns as, **G**: 202
defined, **B**: 318
followed by adjective or noun (object complement), **B**: 319
placement of adverbs and, **M**: 249–50
transitive verbs and, **B**: 318–19
Directories, to documentation models, **MLA**: 371–72, **APA**: 443–44, **CMS**: 498
Directories, Web, **R**: 342
Direct questions. *See* Questions, direct and indirect
Direct quotations. *See* Quotations, direct and indirect
disinterested, *uninterested*, **W**: 143
Division, as pattern of organization, **C**: 38–39
Division of words
in dictionary entry, **W**: 169
hyphen and, **P**: 296
do, as irregular verb, **G**: 185
do, forms of
in forming negatives, **M**: 230–31
as helping verbs, **B**: 312
and subject-verb agreement, **G**: 176, 188
do vs. *does*. *See* Agreement of subject and verb
Document design, **C**: 45–62
academic manuscripts, **C**: 54–56

APA format, **APA**: 484–87
CMS (*Chicago*) format, **CMS**: 528–31
MLA format, **C**: 54-56, **MLA**: 429–31
business letters, **C**: 58
e-mail, **C**: 60, 62
format options, **C**: 6, 46–47, 62–63
headings, **C**: 47–49
layout, **C**: 46
lists, displayed, **C**: 49–50
memos, **C**: 60, 61
page setup, **C**: 46–47
résumés, **C**: 58–60
visuals, **C**: 50–54
and word processing programs, **C**: 62–63
Documenting sources
APA style, **APA**: 458–83
choosing a documentation style, **R**: 366–68
CMS (*Chicago*) style, **CMS**: 510–28
in the disciplines, **A**: 103
MLA style, **MLA**: 388–428, 435
reviewer comments about, **C**: 27
does vs. *do*. *See* Agreement of subject and verb
DOI (digital object identifier), **APA**: 472, **CMS**: 511, 517, 521–23
don't vs. *doesn't*, **W**: 144. *See also* Agreement of subject and verb
Dots, ellipsis. *See* Ellipsis mark
Double comparatives and superlatives, avoiding, **G**: 211
Double negatives, avoiding, **G**: 212, **M**: 231
Doublespeak, avoiding, **W**: 159–60
Double subjects, avoiding, **M**: 247–48
Draft, comments on. *See* Revising with comments
Drafting essays
body, **C**: 18–19
conclusion, **C**: 19–20
introduction, **C**: 14–18
and saving files, **C**: 63–64
thesis, **C**: 10–11, 14–18
Drawing conclusions (deductive reasoning), **A**: 96–97
Dropped quotation, avoiding, **MLA**: 382–83, **APA**: 454–55, **CMS**: 507–08
due to, **W**: 144

E

each (singular), **W**: 144, **G**: 179, 197–98
economics (singular), **G**: 182
-ed, verb ending, **G**: 184, 188–89, **M**: 227
Editing sentences, **C**: 21–22
Effect. *See* Cause and effect
effect. See *affect*, *effect*, **W**: 139
e.g. (meaning "for example"), **W**: 144, **P**: 301
either (singular), **W**: 144, **G**: 179, 197–98
either . . . or
and parallelism, **S**: 112–13
and pronoun-antecedent agreement, **G**: 199
and subject-verb agreement, **G**: 178
either . . . or fallacy, **A**: 95
-elect, hyphen with, **P**: 295
Electronic documents
annotating, **A**: 67
creating, **C**: 59–60, 63–64
e-mail messages, **C**: 60, 62
managing, **C**: 63–64
Electronic sources
abstracts, **R**: 337
archives, digital, **R**: 342–43
avoiding plagiarism with, **R**: 361, 363–65
books, **CMS**: 512
citation at a glance, **MLA**: 414–15, 416, **APA**: 474–75, 478–79, **CMS**: 522–23, 526–27
citation software for, **R**: 359
citing in paper, **MLA**: 412–28, **APA**: 472–82, **CMS**: 512, 524–27

Electronic sources (*continued*)
databases, for periodical articles, **R**: 336–39, **MLA**: 432–33
evaluating, **R**: 355–57
finding online, **R**: 341–45
in library catalog, **R**: 340–41, 348–49
previewing, **R**: 348–49
search engines for, **R**: 342
selecting appropriate versions of, **R**: 352
elicit, *illicit*, **W**: 144
Ellipsis mark
in arguments, **A**: 99–100
for deleted lines of poetry, **P**: 290
for omissions in sources, **P**: 290, **MLA**: 380–81, **APA**: 452, **CMS**: 506
for unfinished thoughts, **P**: 291
Elliptical clause, dangling, **S**: 121
E-mail
addresses, division of, **P**: 296
audience for, **C**: 27–28
effective, **C**: 60, 62
for feedback on drafts, **C**: 27–28
italics in, **P**: 304
emigrate from, *immigrate to*, **W**: 144
eminent, *imminent*, **W**: 144
Emotional appeals, in argument, **A**: 97–98
Emphasis, **S**: 129–34
active verbs for, **W**: 156–58
boldface for, **C**: 47
choppy sentences and, **S**: 130–31
colon for, **P**: 276–77
dash for, **P**: 288
document design for, **C**: 47
exclamation point for, **P**: 287–88
italics for, **C**: 47
parallel structure and, **S**: 134
sentence endings for, **S**: 133
short sentences for, **S**: 134
subordinating minor ideas for, **S**: 132–33
Encyclopedias, **R**: 345–46
Ending. *See* Conclusion
Endnotes. *See* Footnotes or endnotes
End punctuation, **P**: 286–88
English as a second language (ESL). *See* Multilingual writers
enthused, **W**: 144
-er ending (*faster*, *stronger*), **G**: 210–11
ESL (English as a second language). *See* Multilingual writers
especially, and sentence fragments, **G**: 217
-es, *-s*
spelling rules, for plurals, **P**: 292
as verb ending, **G**: 175, 176–77, 187–88
Essays. *See also* Research process, highlights of; Sample essays
drafting, **C**: 14–20
planning, **C**: 3–14
researching, **R**: 329–68
revising, **C**: 20–28. *See also* Revising with comments
saving drafts of, **C**: 63–64
-est ending (*fastest*, *strongest*), **G**: 210–11
et al., **P**: 301, **MLA**: 392, 400, **APA**: 460, **CMS**: 512
etc., **W**: 144, **P**: 301
Etymology, **W**: 172
Euphemisms, avoiding, **W**: 159–60
Evaluating arguments. *See* Arguments, evaluating
Evaluating sources, **R**: 346–57, **MLA**: 433–34
even, placement of, **S**: 117–18
eventually, *ultimately*, **W**: 144
everybody, *everyone*, *everything* (singular), **W**: 144, **G**: 179, 197–98
everyone, *every one*, **W**: 144
Evidence
adding for support, **C**: 25
in analysis papers, **A**: 74, 77

in APA papers, **APA**: 446–48
in argument papers, **A**: 82–84, 102, 103
in CMS (*Chicago*) papers, **CMS**: 500–01
in MLA papers, **MLA**: 374–76
for papers in the disciplines, **C**: 5, **A**: 102, 103
ex-, hyphen with, **P**: 295
Exact language, **W**: 165–69
Examples
as evidence, **C**: 25, **A**: 83
as pattern of organization, **C**: 34–35
as sentence fragments, **G**: 217
except. See *accept*, *except*, **W**: 139
Excerpts, of articles and books, online, **R**: 352
Exclamation points, **P**: 287–88
and MLA citation, **P**: 284, **MLA**: 390
no comma with, **P**: 273
with quotation marks, **P**: 284
Exclamations. *See* Interjections
Exclamatory sentence, **B**: 327
expect, **W**: 145
Expert opinion, using as support, **A**: 84
Explaining a point, **C**: 24–25
Expletives *there*, *it*
and subject following verb, **M**: 246–47, **B**: 317
and subject-verb agreement, **G**: 180–81
and wordy sentences, **W**: 155
explicit, *implicit*, **W**: 145
Expressions
idiomatic (common), **W**: 167
regional, **W**: 160–61
transitional, **P**: 265–66, 274–75
trite. *See* Clichés
worn-out. *See* Clichés

F

Facts
in APA papers, **APA**: 446
in argument papers, **A**: 82–83
in CMS (*Chicago*) papers, **CMS**: 500
in MLA papers, **MLA**: 374–75
scientific, and verb tense, **G**: 192–93
Fairness, in arguments, **A**: 85–86, 97–100
Fallacies, logical
either . . . or fallacy, **A**: 95
false analogy, **A**: 93
hasty generalization, **A**: 92–93
non sequitur, **A**: 96
post hoc fallacy, **A**: 95
stereotype, **A**: 92–93
False analogy, **A**: 93
family. *See* Collective nouns
farther, *further*, **W**: 145
Faulty apposition, **S**: 128
Faulty predication, **S**: 128
Feedback, using, **C**: 23. *See also* Revising with comments
fewer, *less*, **W**: 145
Field research, **R**: 346
Figures. *See* Numbers; Visuals
Figures of speech, **W**: 168–69
Files, managing, **C**: 63–64
finalize, **W**: 145
firstly, **W**: 145
First-person point of view, **C**: 21, **S**: 123
Flow. *See* Coherence
Flowcharts, using in documents, **C**: 50–54
Focus. *See also* Thesis
of essay, **C**: 10–11, 14–18, 21, **A**: 80–81
of paragraph, **C**: 32–33
Fonts (typeface), **C**: 47
Footnotes or endnotes
APA style, **APA**: 485, 490
CMS (*Chicago*) style, **R**: 367–68, **CMS**: 510–11
directory to models for, **CMS**: 498
models for, **CMS**: 510–28
sample, **CMS**: 536
MLA style, **MLA**: 428

for
  comma before, **P**: 259
  as coordinating conjunction, **S**: 112, **B**: 315
  as preposition, **B**: 314
Foreign words, italics for, **P**: 305
for example
  no colon after, **P**: 277
  and sentence fragments, **G**: 217
Formality, level of, **C**: 27–28, **W**: 162
Formal outline, **C**: 12–14, **A**: 71. *See also* Informal outline
Format, manuscript. *See* Document design
Fractions
  hyphens with, **P**: 295
  numerals for, **P**: 303
Fragments, sentence
  acceptable, **G**: 218
  clauses as, **G**: 215
  for emphasis or effect, **G**: 218
  examples as, **G**: 217
  finding and recognizing, **G**: 212–14
  fixing, **G**: 214–17
  lists as, **G**: 217
  phrases as, **G**: 215–16
  predicates as, **G**: 216
  testing for, **G**: 213
Freewriting, **C**: 9
Full stop. *See* Periods
further. See *farther*, *further*, **W**: 145
Fused sentences. *See* Run-on sentences
Future perfect tense, **G**: 191
Future progressive forms, **G**: 191–92
Future tense, **G**: 191, **M**: 227, 229

G

Gender, and pronoun agreement, **G**: 197–98
Gender-neutral language, **W**: 162–64, **G**: 197–98
Generalization, hasty, **A**: 92–93
Generic *he*, **W**: 146, 163, **G**: 197–98
Generic nouns, **G**: 198
Geographic names, *the* with, **M**: 244–45
Gerund phrases
  agreement of verb with, **G**: 182–83
  defined, **B**: 322
Gerunds
  following prepositions, **M**: 253–54
  following verbs, **M**: 235
  possessives as modifiers of, **G**: 205
get, **W**: 145
Global (big-picture) revisions, **C**: 20–21. *See also* Revising with comments
Glossary of usage, **W**: 139–52
good, *well*, **W**: 145, **G**: 209–10
Government Web sites, **R**: 343–44
graduate, **W**: 145
Grammar, mixed. *See* Mixed constructions
Grammar checkers, **C**: 62–63
Graphic narrative, MLA citation of, **MLA**: 405
Graphs, using in documents, **C**: 50–54
Greetings and salutations, colon with, **P**: 277
grow, **W**: 145

H

hanged, *hung*, **W**: 145
hardly, **W**: 146
  with negative word, avoiding, **G**: 212
  placement of, **S**: 117–18
has got, *have got*, avoiding, **W**: 146
Hasty generalization, **A**: 92–93
has vs. *have*, **G**: 176, 188. *See also* Agreement of subject and verb

have, as irregular verb, **G**: 185
have, forms of
as helping verbs, **M**: 228–29, **B**: 312
and passive voice, **M**: 226, 229–30
and perfect tenses, **M**: 228–29
and subject-verb agreement, **G**: 176, 188
have vs. *has*, **G**: 176, 188. *See also* Agreement of subject and verb
Headings
in APA papers, **APA**: 446, 485
in CMS (*Chicago*) papers, **CMS**: 500, 530
and document design, **C**: 47–49
in MLA papers, **MLA**: 430
to organize ideas, **APA**: 446, **CMS**: 500
parallel phrasing of, **C**: 48–49
placement of, **C**: 49
planning with, **APA**: 446, **CMS**: 500
style of, **C**: 49
he, *him*, *his*, sexist use of, **W**: 146, 163, **G**: 197–98
Helping verbs
contractions with, **G**: 190
defined, **G**: 190, **B**: 312
and forming passive voice, **G**: 184, **M**: 226, 229–30
and forming perfect tenses, **G**: 184, 191, 193–94, **M**: 228–29
and forming verb tenses, **G**: 184, **M**: 227–29
modals (*can*, *might*, *should*, etc.) as, **G**: 190, **M**: 230, 232–33, **B**: 312
needed, **G**: 190
and progressive forms, **M**: 227–28
here, not used as subject, **M**: 247
her vs. *she*, **G**: 201–05
he said, *she said*, comma with, **P**: 267–68, 285
he/she, *his/her*, **W**: 146, **P**: 291
he vs. *him*, **G**: 201–05
Highlights of the research process. *See* Research process, highlights of
hisself (nonstandard), **W**: 146
Homophones (words that sound alike), **P**: 293–94
Hook, in introduction, **C**: 15, 24
hopefully, **W**: 146
however
avoiding with *but* or *although*, **M**: 249
at beginning of sentence, **W**: 146
comma with, **P**: 265–66
semicolon with, **P**: 274–75
HTML documents, as sources, **R**: 352
Humanities, writing in the, **A**: 100–04. *See also* MLA papers; CMS (*Chicago*) papers
hung. See *hanged*, *hung*, **W**: 145
Hyphens, **P**: 294–96
with adjectives, **P**: 294–95
to avoid confusion, **P**: 295–96
in compound words, **P**: 294
and division of words, **P**: 296
in e-mail addresses, **P**: 296
to form dash, **P**: 288
in fractions, **P**: 295
in numbers, **P**: 295
with prefixes and suffixes, **P**: 295
in a series, **P**: 295
in URLs (Web addresses), **P**: 296, **MLA**: 430, 431, **APA**: 472, 487, **CMS**: 512, 530

I

I
vs. *me*, **G**: 201–05
point of view, **C**: 21, **S**: 123
shifts with *you*, *he*, or *she*, avoiding, **S**: 123
ibid., **CMS**: 511, 536

Ideas
borrowed. *See* Citing sources; Plagiarism, avoiding
clustering, **C**: 8
coordinating and subordinating, **S**: 129–30
exploring, for essay, **C**: 4–10
joining
with colon, **P**: 277
with comma and coordinating conjunction, **P**: 259
with semicolon, **P**: 274
listing, **C**: 7–8
names of. *See* Nouns
organizing. *See* Organization
original, **A**: 74
paired, parallelism and, **S**: 112–13
parallel, **S**: 111–14
repetition of, unnecessary, **W**: 153–54
synthesizing, **MLA**: 386–87, **APA**: 456–58
transitions between, **C**: 42–44
Idioms (common expressions)
adjective + preposition combinations, **M**: 255
with prepositions showing time and place (*at*, *on*, *in*, etc.), **M**: 252–53
standard, **W**: 167
verb + preposition combinations, **M**: 255
i.e. (meaning "that is"), **W**: 146, **P**: 301
-ie, *-ei*, spelling rule, **P**: 291
if clauses
conditional sentences, **M**: 231–34
contrary to fact (subjunctive), **G**: 195–96
if, *whether*, **W**: 146
illicit. See *elicit*, *illicit*, **W**: 144
illusion. See *allusion*, *illusion*, **W**: 140
Illustrated book, MLA citation of, **MLA**: 405
Illustrations (examples). *See also* Visuals
as evidence, **A**: 83
as pattern of organization, **C**: 34–35
Images. *See* Visuals
immigrate. See *emigrate from*, *immigrate to*, **W**: 144
imminent. See *eminent*, *imminent*, **W**: 144
immoral. See *amoral*, *immoral*, **W**: 140
Imperative mood, **G**: 195–96
Imperative sentences
defined, **B**: 317, 327
you understood in, **M**: 246, **B**: 317
implement, **W**: 146
implicit. See *explicit*, *implicit*, **W**: 145
Implied meaning of word (connotation), **W**: 165
imply, *infer*, **W**: 146
in, in idioms (common expressions)
with adjectives, **M**: 254–55
vs. *at*, *on*, to show time and place, **M**: 252–53
with verbs, **M**: 255
including, no colon after, **P**: 277
Inclusive language, **W**: 163–64, **G**: 197–98
Incomplete comparison, **S**: 115–16
Incomplete construction, **S**: 114–17
Incomplete sentences. *See* Sentence fragments
Indefinite articles. *See a*, *an*
Indefinite pronouns
agreement of verb with, **G**: 179
as antecedents, **G**: 197–98
apostrophe with, **P**: 279
defined, **B**: 311
Indenting
in APA reference list, **APA**: 486
in CMS (*Chicago*) bibliography, **CMS**: 531
in CMS (*Chicago*) notes, **CMS**: 530

of long quotations, **P**: 282
APA style, **APA**: 453, 485, 495
CMS (*Chicago*) style, **CMS**: 506–07, 529, 533
MLA style, **MLA**: 381–82, 430, 436
no quotation marks with, **P**: 282
in MLA works cited list, **MLA**: 431
in outlines, **C**: 12–14
Independent clauses
colon between, **P**: 277
combined with subordinate clauses, **B**: 327
and comma with coordinating conjunction, **P**: 259
defined, **B**: 326
and run-on sentences, **G**: 218–22
semicolon between, **P**: 274–75
Indexes to periodical articles, print, **R**: 339–40. *See also* Databases, for finding sources
Indicative mood, **G**: 195–96
Indirect objects
case of pronouns as, **G**: 202
defined, **B**: 319
Indirect questions
no question mark after, **P**: 287
shifts to direct questions, avoiding, **S**: 125–26
Indirect quotations
no comma with, **P**: 273
shifts to direct quotations, avoiding, **S**: 126
Inductive reasoning, **A**: 92–93, 94
infer. See *imply*, *infer*, **W**: 146
Infinitive phrases, **B**: 322–23
Infinitives
case of pronouns with, **G**: 204–05
dangling, **S**: 121
following verbs, **M**: 235–37
marked (with *to*), **M**: 235–36, 254
and sequence of tenses, **G**: 194–95
split, **S**: 120
subject of, objective case for, **G**: 204–05
to, infinitive marker vs. preposition, **M**: 254
unmarked (without *to*), **M**: 237
Inflated phrases, **W**: 154–55
Informal language, **W**: 162
Informal outline, **C**: 12, **A**: 71–72. *See also* Formal outline
Information, for essay
finding, **R**: 329–68, **MLA**: 432–33
managing, **R**: 357–65, **MLA**: 434
sources of, **C**: 6
working bibliography, **R**: 358–59
Information notes (MLA), **MLA**: 428
-ing verb ending. *See* Gerunds; Present participles
in, *into*, **W**: 147
in regards to, **W**: 147
Inserted material, in quotations. *See* Brackets
Institutional review board (IRB), for research subjects, **R**: 346
Instructor's comments, revising with. *See* Revising with comments
Integrating sources, **R**: 364–65
in APA papers, **APA**: 451–58
in CMS (*Chicago*) papers, **CMS**: 505–10
highlights of one student's research process, **MLA**: 435
in MLA papers, **MLA**: 379–88
intend to do (not *on doing*), **W**: 167
Intensive pronouns, **B**: 310
Interjections (exclamations)
commas with, **P**: 267
defined, **B**: 316
exclamation point with, **P**: 287–88

Internet
addresses. *See* URLs
avoiding plagiarism from, **R**: 363–65
citation at a glance, **MLA**: 414–15, **APA**: 478–79, **CMS**: 526–27
citing in paper, **MLA**: 412–28, **APA**: 472–82, **CMS**: 512, 517, 521–27
evaluating sources from, **R**: 349, 352, 355–57
finding sources on, **R**: 336, 341–45, **MLA**: 432
previewing sources on, **R**: 349, 352
searching, **R**: 336, 341–45, **MLA**: 432
scanning results, **R**: 349, 352
topic directories, **R**: 342
Interpretation
in analysis papers, **A**: 74, 77
of visual texts, **A**: 67–68, 70, 72–73
of written texts, **A**: 67–69, 71–77
Interrogative pronouns
defined, **B**: 310
who, *whom*, **G**: 205–07
Interrogative sentences, **B**: 327
Interrogative tags, commas with, **P**: 267
Interruptions, commas with, **P**: 265–67
Interviews, as information source, **R**: 346
In-text citations. *See also* CMS (*Chicago*) papers, footnotes or endnotes; Integrating sources
APA style
directory to models for, **APA**: 443
models for, **APA**: 459–63
choosing a documentation style for, **R**: 366–68
MLA style
directory to models for, **MLA**: 371
models for, **MLA**: 389–98
into. See *in*, *into*, **W**: 147
Intransitive verbs
defined, **B**: 319–20
not used in passive voice, **M**: 230
Introduction. *See also* Thesis
in argument paper, **A**: 80–81
of essay, **C**: 14–18
to portfolio, **C**: 29–31
revising, **C**: 24
Introductory word groups, comma with, **P**: 260
Invention. *See* Ideas, exploring, for essay
Inverted sentence order
for emphasis, **S**: 133
with expletives *there*, *it*, **G**: 180–81, **M**: 246–47, **B**: 317
no comma with, **P**: 272–73
and position of subject, **B**: 317
in questions, **B**: 317
and subject-verb agreement, **G**: 180–81
for variety, **S**: 135–36
IRB (institutional review board), for research subjects, **R**: 346
irregardless (nonstandard), **W**: 147
Irregular verbs, **G**: 183–86
be, *am*, *is*, *are*, *was*, *were*, **G**: 184
do, *does*, **G**: 185, 188
have, *has*, **G**: 185, 188
lie, *lay*, **G**: 186–87
list of, **G**: 184–86
is vs. *are*. *See* Agreement of subject and verb
is when, *is where*, avoiding, **S**: 128, **W**: 147
it
broad reference of, **G**: 200–01
as expletive (placeholder), **M**: 246–47

indefinite use of, **G**: 201
as subject of sentence, **M**: 246–47
Italics, **P**: 304–05
in e-mail, **P**: 304
for emphasis, **C**: 47
for foreign words, **P**: 305
for names of ships, spacecraft, and aircraft, **P**: 305
for titles of works, **P**: 304–05, **MLA**: 398, 429–30, **APA**: 485, 487, **CMS**: 511, 529
for words as words, **P**: 305
its, it's, **W**: 147, **P**: 279, 280, 293

J

Jargon, **W**: 159
Journal, keeping a, **C**: 10
Journalist's questions, **C**: 9
Journals. *See* Periodicals
jury. See Collective nouns
just, placement of, **S**: 117–18

K

Key words, repeating for coherence, **C**: 40–41
Keyword searching
in databases, **R**: 338–39
example of, **MLA**: 433
in library catalog, **R**: 340
scanning results of, **R**: 347–49
in search engines, **R**: 338, 342
kind(s), **W**: 147
kind of, sort of, **W**: 147

L

Labels for visuals, **C**: 51, **MLA**: 430–31, **APA**: 486, **CMS**: 530
Language. *See also* Tone; Words
appropriate, **W**: 159–64
biased, avoiding, **W**: 164
borrowed. *See* Citing sources; Plagiarism, avoiding
clichés, avoiding, **W**: 167–68
direct, **W**: 154–55
doublespeak, avoiding, **W**: 159–60
euphemisms, avoiding, **W**: 159–60
exact, **W**: 165–69
formality of, **W**: 162
idioms (common expressions), **W**: 167
jargon, **A**: 102, **W**: 159
nonstandard English, avoiding, **W**: 160–61
offensive, avoiding, **W**: 164
plain, **W**: 159–60
pretentious, avoiding, **W**: 159–60
regionalisms, avoiding, **W**: 160–61
sexist, avoiding, **W**: 162–64
slang, avoiding, **W**: 160–61
specialized, **C**: 5, **A**: 102
wordy, **W**: 153–56
Latin abbreviations, **P**: 301
laying vs. *lying*, **G**: 186–87
lay, lie, **W**: 147, **G**: 186–87
Layout of documents. *See* Document design
lead, led, **W**: 147
learn, teach, **W**: 147
leave, let, **W**: 147
Length
of paper, **C**: 6
of paragraph, **C**: 44–45
less. See *fewer, less*, **W**: 145
let. See *leave, let*, **W**: 147
Letter in a published collection, citation at a glance, **CMS**: 518–19
Letters, business, **C**: 57–58
Letters, of the alphabet
capitalizing, **P**: 296–99
as letters, italics for, **P**: 305
as letters, plural of, **P**: 279–80
liable, **W**: 147

Library resources. *See also* Electronic sources
articles in periodicals, **R**: 336–40
databases, **R**: 336–39, **MLA**: 432–33
print index, **R**: 339–40
bibliographies, **R**: 346
books, **R**: 340–41
catalog, **R**: 340–41, 348–49
reference librarians, **R**: 334, **MLA**: 432
reference works, **R**: 345–46
scholarly citations, **R**: 346
Web page, library, **R**: 334–35
lie, *lay*, **W**: 147, **G**: 186–87
like
no comma after, **P**: 273
and sentence fragments, **G**: 217
like, *as*, **W**: 147
Limiting modifiers (*only*, *almost*, etc.), **S**: 117–18
Line spacing, **MLA**: 429, **APA**: 485, **CMS**: 529, 530, 531
and document design, **C**: 46
Linking verbs
adjective after, **G**: 208–09, **B**: 318
defined, **B**: 318
omission of, **G**: 190, **M**: 246
pronoun after, **G**: 202
Listing ideas, **C**: 7–8
List of sources. *See* Bibliography, CMS (*Chicago*) style; Reference list (APA); Works cited list (MLA)
Lists. *See also* Series
with colon, **P**: 276
with dash, **P**: 288–89
and document design, **C**: 49–50
as fragments, **G**: 217
parallelism and, **S**: 111–12
Literary present tense, **A**: 104, **S**: 124, **G**: 192–93
Literature review, sample paper, **APA**: 488–97
Logic
analogies, **A**: 93
cause-and-effect reasoning, **A**: 94–95
deductive reasoning, **A**: 96–97
fallacies
either . . . or fallacy, **A**: 95
false analogy, **A**: 93
hasty generalization, **A**: 92–93
non sequitur, **A**: 96
post hoc fallacy, **A**: 95
stereotype, **A**: 92–93
inductive reasoning, **A**: 92–93, 94
rational appeals, **A**: 92–97
of sentences, **S**: 128
loose, *lose*, **W**: 148
lots, *lots of*, **W**: 148
-ly ending on adverbs, **G**: 207
lying vs. *laying*, **G**: 186–87

M

Magazines. *See* Periodicals
Main clauses. *See* Independent clauses
Main point. *See* Focus; Thesis; Topic sentence
Main verbs, **M**: 225, **B**: 312
with modals (*can*, *might*, *should*, etc.), **G**: 190, **M**: 230, 232–33
man, sexist use of, **W**: 163
mankind, sexist use of, **W**: 148, 163
Manuscript formats. *See also* Document design
academic formats, **C**: 54–56
APA style, **APA**: 484–87
CMS (*Chicago*) style, **CMS**: 528–31
MLA style, **MLA**: 429–31
business formats, **C**: 57–62
electronic formats, **C**: 59–60
Mapping. *See* Outlines
Maps, using in documents, **C**: 50–54

Margins, **MLA**: 429, **APA**: 485, **CMS**: 529
and document design, **C**: 46
Mass nouns. *See* Noncount nouns
mathematics (singular), **G**: 182
may. See *can*, *may*, **W**: 142
may, as modal verb, **M**: 230, 232–33, **B**: 312
maybe, *may be*, **W**: 148
may of, *might of* (nonstandard), **W**: 148
Meaning, finding in a text, **A**: 74–77
measles (singular), **G**: 182
media, *medium*, **W**: 148
Memos, **C**: 60, 61
Metaphor, **W**: 168–69
me vs. *I*, **G**: 201–05
might, as modal verb, **M**: 230, 232–33, **B**: 312
might of. See *may of*, *might of*, **W**: 148
Minor ideas. *See* Subordination
Misplaced modifiers, **S**: 117–19. *See also* Modifiers
Missing claims, in arguments, **A**: 95–96
Missing words. *See* Needed words
Misuse of words, **W**: 166, 172
Mixed constructions
illogical connections, **S**: 128
is when, *is where*, **S**: 128
mixed grammar, **S**: 126–27
reason . . . is because, **S**: 128
Mixed metaphors, **W**: 168–69
MLA Handbook for Writers of Research Papers, **MLA**: 388, 429
MLA papers, **MLA**: 369–440. *See also* Research process, highlights of
authority in, **MLA**: 375, 383–84
citation at a glance
article from a database, **MLA**: 416
article in a periodical, **MLA**: 402–03
book, **MLA**: 406
selection from an anthology, **MLA**: 410–11
short work from a Web site, **MLA**: 414–15
citations, in-text
directory to models for, **MLA**: 371
models for, **MLA**: 389–98
evidence for, **MLA**: 374–76
footnotes or endnotes (optional), **MLA**: 428
highlights of one student's research process (case study), **MLA**: 432–35
manuscript format, **C**: 54–56, **MLA**: 429–31
organizing, **MLA**: 374
plagiarism, avoiding, **MLA**: 376–79, 434–35
sample papers
analysis, **A**: 75–76
argument, **A**: 87–91
research, **MLA**: 436–40
signal phrases in, **MLA**: 382–85
sources in
citing, **MLA**: 376–79, 435
integrating, **MLA**: 379–88, 435
synthesizing, **MLA**: 386–87
uses of, **MLA**: 374–76, 432–33
supporting arguments in, **MLA**: 374–76, 386–87
tenses in, **MLA**: 382
thesis in, **MLA**: 373, 432, 435
visuals in
formatting, **MLA**: 430–31
sample figure, **MLA**: 439
works cited list, **MLA**: 398–428, 431
directory to models for, **MLA**: 371–72
medium of publication in, **MLA**: 398–99
models for, **MLA**: 398–428
sample, **MLA**: 440
URLs (Web addresses), **MLA**: 412, 431

Modal verbs (*can*, *might*, *should*, etc.), **G**: 190, **M**: 230, 232–33, **B**: 312. *See also* Helping verbs
Modern Language Association. *See* MLA papers
Modifiers
adjectives as, **G**: 207–12, **B**: 313
adverbs as, **G**: 207–12, **B**: 314
commas with, **P**: 261–62
dangling, **S**: 120–23
essential and nonessential, **P**: 262–65
of gerunds, **G**: 205
limiting, **S**: 117–18
misplaced, **S**: 117–19
redundant, **W**: 153
split infinitives: **S**: 120
squinting, **S**: 118–19
Money, abbreviations for, **P**: 301
Mood of verbs, **G**: 195–96. *See also* Conditional sentences
shifts in, avoiding, **S**: 124–25
more, *most* (comparative, superlative), **G**: 210–12
moreover
comma with, **P**: 265–66
semicolon with, **P**: 274–75
most, **W**: 148
Motive. *See* Purpose in writing; Writing situation
Multilingual writers, **M**: 223–55
adjectives, **M**: 250–52
adjectives and adverbs, placement of, **M**: 251–52
articles (*a*, *an*, *the*), **M**: 237–45
idioms (common expressions), **M**: 252–55
omitted subjects or expletives, **M**: 246–47
omitted verbs, **M**: 246
nouns, types of, **M**: 238–40
participles, present vs. past, **M**: 250–51
prepositions
with adjectives, **M**: 254–55
with nouns and *-ing* forms, **M**: 253–54
to show time and place (*at*, *in*, *on*, etc.), **M**: 252–53
with verbs, **M**: 255
repeated objects or adverbs, **S**: 131, **M**: 248
repeated subjects, **S**: 127, **M**: 247–48
sentence structure, **M**: 245–50
verbs
active voice, **M**: 227–28
conditional, **M**: 231–34
forms of, **M**: 225–30
with gerunds or infinitives, **M**: 235–37
modals (*can*, *might*, *should*, etc.), **M**: 230, 232–33
negative forms, **M**: 230–31
passive voice, **M**: 226, 229–30
tenses, **M**: 225, 227–29
must, as modal verb, **M**: 230, 232, **B**: 312
must of. See *may of*, *might of*, **W**: 148
myself, **W**: 148, **G**: 203

N

namely, and sentence fragments, **G**: 217
Narration, as pattern of organization, **C**: 35
Narrowing a subject, **C**: 6, **R**: 333–34, **MLA**: 432
N.B., **P**: 301
nearly, placement of, **S**: 117–18
Needed words, **S**: 114–17
articles (*a*, *an*, *the*), **S**: 117, **M**: 237–45
in comparisons, **S**: 115–16
in compound structures, **S**: 114–15
it, **M**: 246–47
in parallel structures, **S**: 113–14
subjects, **M**: 246–47
that, **S**: 115

there, **M**: 246–47
verbs, **G**: 190, **M**: 246
Negatives
double, avoiding, **G**: 212, **M**: 231
forming, **M**: 230–31
not and *never*, **B**: 314
neither (singular), **W**: 148, **G**: 179, 197–98
neither . . . nor
and parallel structure, **S**: 112–13
and pronoun-antecedent agreement, **G**: 199
and subject-verb agreement, **G**: 178
never
as adverb, **B**: 314
in double negatives, avoiding, **G**: 212
nevertheless
comma with, **P**: 265–66
semicolon with, **P**: 274–75
news (singular), **G**: 182
Newspapers. *See* Periodicals
News sites, **R**: 343–44
no
comma with, **P**: 267
in double negatives, avoiding, **G**: 212, **M**: 231
nobody (singular), **G**: 179, 197–98
Noncount nouns, **M**: 238–41, 243–44
none, **W**: 148, **G**: 179
Nonrestrictive (nonessential) elements, commas with, **P**: 262–65
Non sequitur, **A**: 96
Nonsexist language, **W**: 162–64, **G**: 197–98
Nonstandard English, avoiding, **W**: 160–61
no one (singular), **G**: 179, 197–98
nor
comma with, **P**: 259
as coordinating conjunction, **S**: 112, **B**: 315
parallelism and, **S**: 112
and pronoun-antecedent agreement, **G**: 199
and subject-verb agreement, **G**: 178
not
as adverb, **M**: 230–31, **B**: 314
in double negatives, avoiding, **G**: 212, **M**: 230–31
in forming negatives, **M**: 230–31
placement of, **S**: 117–18
Notes. *See* Footnotes or endnotes; Information notes (MLA)
Note taking
for analysis, **A**: 67–70
and avoiding plagiarism, **R**: 359–65, **MLA**: 434–35
on drafts, **C**: 64
to generate ideas, **C**: 7
sample notes, **A**: 69, 70
nothing (singular), **G**: 179, 197–98
not only . . . but also, **B**: 315
and parallel structure, **S**: 112–13
and pronoun-antecedent agreement, **G**: 199
and subject-verb agreement, **G**: 178
Noun/adjectives, **B**: 309, 313
Noun clauses, **B**: 324–25
words introducing, **B**: 325
Noun markers, **M**: 237–45
Nouns. *See also* Nouns, types of
adjectives with, **B**: 313
articles with, **M**: 237–45
capitalizing, **P**: 296–97
defined, **B**: 309
of direct address, comma with, **P**: 267
plural form, singular meaning (*athletics*, *economics*, etc.), **G**: 182
plural of, **P**: 292
after prepositions, **M**: 253–54
renaming other nouns. *See* Appositives
shifts between singular and plural, avoiding, **S**: 123–24

Nouns, types of. *See also* Nouns
abstract, **W**: 165–66
collective (*audience*, *family*, *team*, etc.), **G**: 179–80, 198–99
common, **M**: 238–39, 240–43, **P**: 296–97
concrete, **W**: 165–66
count, **M**: 238–42, 244
defined, **B**: 309
generic, **G**: 198
noncount, **M**: 238–40, 243–44
possessive, **P**: 278–79
proper, **M**: 238–40, 244–45, **P**: 296–97
singular and plural, **M**: 238–40
specific, concrete, **W**: 165–66
specific vs. general, **M**: 238–40
Novels, titles of
capitalization of, **P**: 298
italics for, **P**: 304
nowheres (nonstandard), **W**: 148
number. See *amount*, *number*, **W**: 140
number, agreement of verb with, **G**: 180
Number and person
shifts in, avoiding, **S**: 123–24
and subject-verb agreement, **G**: 175–77
Numbers
commas in, **P**: 268–69
consistency of, **P**: 302
hyphens with, **P**: 295
spelled out vs. numerals, **P**: 302–03
APA style, **P**: 302
CMS (*Chicago*) style, **P**: 302
MLA style, **P**: 302
Numbers mentioned as numbers
italics for, **P**: 305
plural of, **P**: 279

O

Object complements, **B**: 319
adjectives as, following direct object, **G**: 209
Objections, to arguments, **A**: 85–86
Objective case, of pronouns
for objects, **G**: 202
for subjects and objects of infinitives, **G**: 204–05
whom, **G**: 205–07
Objectivity
assessing in sources, **A**: 98–100, **R**: 353–54
in writing a summary, **A**: 73
Objects
direct, **B**: 318
indirect, **B**: 319
of infinitives, **G**: 204–05
no comma between verb and, **P**: 270
objective case for, **G**: 202, 205
of prepositions, **B**: 320
pronouns as, **G**: 202
repetition of, avoiding, **M**: 248
of, after *could*, *would*, *may*, etc. (nonstandard), **W**: 148
Offensive language, **W**: 164
off of (nonstandard), **W**: 148, 167
OK, *O.K.*, *okay*, **W**: 148
Omission of needed words. *See* Needed words
Omissions of letters and words, indicated by
apostrophe, **P**: 279
comma, **P**: 269
ellipsis mark, **P**: 290
on
in idioms (common expressions), **M**: 252–53, 255
multilingual/ESL challenges with, **M**: 252–53
one of the, agreement of verb with, **G**: 182
Online sources. *See* Electronic sources; Internet
only, placement of, **S**: 117–18
only one of the, agreement of verb with, **G**: 182
Opening. *See* Introduction
Opinion, expert, using as support, **A**: 84

Opposing arguments. *See* Countering arguments
or
comma with, **P**: 259
as coordinating conjunction, **S**: 112, **B**: 315
excessive use of, **S**: 132
parallelism and, **S**: 112
and pronoun-antecedent agreement, **G**: 199
and subject-verb agreement, **G**: 178
Organization. *See also* Outlines
of APA papers, **APA**: 446
of CMS (*Chicago*) papers, **CMS**: 500
improving, **C**: 21
patterns of
analogy, **C**: 37–38
cause and effect, **C**: 38–39
classification, **C**: 38–39
comparison and contrast, **C**: 36–37
definition, **C**: 39
description, **C**: 36
division, **C**: 38–39
examples and illustrations, **C**: 34–35
narration, **C**: 35
process, **C**: 36
of MLA papers, **MLA**: 374
Other sides or views, in arguments, **A**: 85–86, 98–100
ought to, as modal verb, **B**: 312
Outlines
for essay, **C**: 12–14
formal, **C**: 12–14, **A**: 71
informal, **C**: 12, **A**: 71–72
for MLA paper, **MLA**: 374
for summary or analysis, **A**: 71–72
Ownership. *See* Possessive case

P

Page numbers, in papers, **MLA**: 429, **APA**: 484, **CMS**: 529
Page setup. *See* Document design; Manuscript formats
Paired ideas, parallelism and, **S**: 112–13
Paragraph patterns. *See also* Paragraphs
analogy, **C**: 37–38
cause and effect, **C**: 38
classification, **C**: 38
comparison and contrast, **C**: 36–37
definition, **C**: 39
description, **C**: 36
division, **C**: 38–39
examples, **C**: 34–35
illustrations, **C**: 34–35
narration, **C**: 35
process, **C**: 36
Paragraphs, **C**: 32–45. *See also* Paragraph patterns
coherence in, **C**: 39–44
concluding, **C**: 19–20
details in, **C**: 24–25, 33–34
development of, **C**: 33–34
focus of, **C**: 32–33
introductory, **C**: 14–18
length of, **C**: 44–45
main point in, **C**: 32–34
revising, **C**: 21, 24–27
too many points in, **C**: 26–27
topic sentences in, **C**: 32
transitions in, **C**: 32, 42–44
unity of, **C**: 26–27, 33
Parallelism
for emphasis, **S**: 134
in headings, **C**: 48–49
in paragraphs, **C**: 41
in sentences, **S**: 111–14
parameters, **W**: 148
Paraphrases
in APA papers, **APA**: 448–51, 453–56, 459
in CMS (*Chicago*) papers, **CMS**: 502–04, 508–09
integrating, **R**: 364–65
in MLA papers, **MLA**: 376–79, 382–85, 388
no quotation marks for, **P**: 282
and note taking, **R**: 362–63

Parentheses, **P**: 289
  no comma before, **P**: 273
Parenthetical citations. *See* In-text citations
Parenthetical elements
  commas with, **P**: 266
  dashes with, **P**: 288
Participial phrases. *See also* Past participles; Present participles
  dangling, **S**: 120–23
  defined, **B**: 321
Participles. *See* Past participles; Present participles
Particles, with verbs, **B**: 312–13
Parts of speech, **B**: 309–16
  adjectives, **B**: 313
  adverbs, **B**: 314
  conjunctions, **B**: 315
  in dictionary entry, **W**: 171
  interjections (exclamations), **B**: 316
  nouns, **B**: 309
  prepositions, **B**: 314–15
  pronouns, **B**: 309–11
  verbs, **B**: 311–13
passed, *past*, **W**: 148–49
Passive voice
  vs. active voice, **W**: 156–58
  appropriate uses of, **W**: 156–58
  forming, **M**: 226, 229–30
  shifts between active and, avoiding, **S**: 124–25
  and wordy sentences, **W**: 155
past. See *passed*, *past*, **W**: 148–49
Past participles
  as adjectives, **M**: 250–51
  defined, **G**: 184
  of irregular verbs, **G**: 183–86
  in participial phrases, **B**: 321–22
  and passive voice, **M**: 226, 229–30
  and perfect tenses, **G**: 191, 193–94, **M**: 228–29
  vs. present participles, **M**: 250–51
  of regular verbs, **G**: 188–89
  as verbals, **B**: 321–22
Past perfect tense, **G**: 191, 193–94, **M**: 228–29
Past progressive form, **G**: 191–92, **M**: 228–29
Past tense
  in APA papers, **APA**: 454, 459
  and *-d*, *-ed* endings, **G**: 184, 188–89
  defined, **G**: 191, **M**: 227, 229
  of irregular verbs, **G**: 183–86
  vs. past perfect, **G**: 193–94
  of regular verbs, **G**: 183–84, 188–89
Patterns of organization. *See* Paragraph patterns
PDF documents, as sources, **R**: 352
Peer reviewers. *See* Reviewers; Revising with comments
Percentages, numerals for, **P**: 303. *See also* Statistics
percent, *per cent*, *percentage*, **W**: 149
Perfect progressive forms, **G**: 191–92, **M**: 228
Perfect tenses, **G**: 191, 193–94, **M**: 228–29
Periodicals. *See also* Articles in periodicals
  capitalizing titles of, **P**: 298, **APA**: 485, 487
  italics for titles of, **P**: 304, **MLA**: 398, 429, **APA**: 485, 487, **CMS**: 529
Periods, **P**: 286–87
  with abbreviations, **P**: 286–87, 300–01
  with ellipsis mark, **P**: 290
  to end a sentence, **P**: 286
  with quotation marks, **P**: 283–84
Personal pronouns
  case of, **G**: 201–05
  defined, **B**: 310
Personal titles. *See* Titles of persons
Person and number
  shifts in, avoiding, **S**: 123–24

and subject-verb agreement, **G**: 175–77
Persons, names of. *See* Nouns
Persuasive writing. *See* Argument papers
phenomena, **W**: 149
Photographs, using in documents, **C**: 50–54
Phrasal verbs. *See* Particles, with verbs
Phrases. *See also* Phrases, types of
dangling, **S**: 120–23
empty or inflated, **W**: 154–55
fragmented, **G**: 215–16
introductory, comma after, **P**: 260
misplaced, **S**: 118–19
as modifiers, **B**: 321–22
nonrestrictive (nonessential), with commas, **P**: 262–65
restrictive (essential), with no commas, **P**: 262–65, 271–72
separating subject and verb, **S**: 119
Phrases, types of. *See also* Phrases
absolute, **B**: 323
appositive, **B**: 323
gerund, **B**: 322
infinitive, **B**: 322–23
participial, **B**: 321–22
prepositional, **B**: 320–21
verbal, **B**: 321–23
physics (singular), **G**: 182
Pictures, using in documents, **C**: 50–54
Places, names of. *See* Nouns
Plagiarism, avoiding
in APA papers, **APA**: 448–51
in CMS (*Chicago*) papers, **CMS**: 502–04
and drafting, **C**: 19
and integrating sources, **R**: 364–65
and Internet sources, **C**: 54, **R**: 361, 363–65
in MLA papers, **MLA**: 376–79
and note taking, **R**: 359–65
reviewer comments about, **C**: 27
working bibliography as a strategy for, **R**: 358–59, 360
Planning an essay. *See also* Outlines
assessing the writing situation, **C**: 3–4
exploring ideas, **C**: 4–10
highlights of one student's research process, **MLA**: 432–33
working thesis, **C**: 10–11
plan to do (not *on doing*), **W**: 167
Plays, titles of
capitalizing, **P**: 298
italics for, **P**: 304
Plurals. *See also* Agreement of pronoun and antecedent; Agreement of subject and verb; Singular vs. plural
of abbreviations, **P**: 280
of compound nouns, **P**: 279
of letters used as letters, **P**: 279–80
of numbers used as numbers, **P**: 279
spelling of, **P**: 292–93
of words used as words, **P**: 280
plus, **W**: 149
PM, *AM*, *p.m.*, *a.m.*, **P**: 301
Podcast, citing in paper, **MLA**: 421, **APA**: 476, **CMS**: 525
Poems, titles of
capitalizing, **P**: 298
quotation marks with, **P**: 283
Point, main. *See* Focus; Thesis
Point of view
consistency in, **C**: 21, 41–42, **S**: 123–24
in humanities papers, **A**: 104
opposing, in arguments, **C**: 25–26, **A**: 85–86, 98–100
in science and social science papers, **A**: 104
in writing for different disciplines, **A**: 104
politics (singular), **G**: 182
Popular sources, **R**: 351

Portfolio
  organizing, **C**: 63–64
  preparing, **C**: 28–31
  reflective writing for, **C**: 28–31
  sample cover letter for, **C**: 29–31
Position, stating, **C**: 23–24
Possessive case
  apostrophe for, **P**: 278–79
  with gerund, **G**: 205
Possessive pronouns
  defined, **B**: 310
  no apostrophe in, **P**: 280
Post hoc fallacy, **A**: 95
precede, *proceed*, **W**: 149
Predicate
  compound, **G**: 216
  defined, **G**: 216
  fragmented, **G**: 216
Predicate adjective. *See* Subject complements
Predicate noun. *See* Subject complements
Predication, faulty, **S**: 128
preferable to (not *than*), **W**: 167
Prefixes, hyphen after, **P**: 295
Premises, in deductive reasoning, **A**: 96–97
Prepositional phrases
  defined, **B**: 320–21
  fragmented, **G**: 215–16
  restrictive (essential) vs. nonrestrictive (nonessential), **P**: 264–65
  between subject and verb, **G**: 176–77
Prepositions
  after adjectives, **M**: 254–55
  at, *in*, *on* to show time and place, **M**: 252–53
  defined, **B**: 314
  followed by nouns or *-ing* forms, not verbs, **M**: 253–54
  in idioms (common expressions), **W**: 167, **M**: 252–55
  list of, **B**: 314
  objects of, **B**: 320–21
  repeating, for parallel structure, **S**: 113–14
  after verbs, **M**: 255, **B**: 312–13
Present participles
  as adjectives, **M**: 250–51
  in gerund phrases, **B**: 322
  in participial phrases, **B**: 321–22
  vs. past participles, **M**: 250–51
  and progressive forms, **G**: 191–92, **M**: 228
  and sequence of tenses, **G**: 194–95
Present perfect tense, **G**: 191, 193–94, **M**: 228, **APA**: 454, 459
Present progressive form, **G**: 191–92, **M**: 227
Present tense, **G**: 191, **M**: 227
  subject-verb agreement in, **G**: 175–83
  and tense shifts, avoiding, **S**: 124
  in writing about literature, **A**: 104, **S**: 124, **G**: 192–93
  in writing about science, **G**: 192–93
Pretentious language, **W**: 159–60
Previewing sources, **R**: 347–49
Prewriting strategies
  annotating texts, **C**: 7
  asking questions, **C**: 9
  blogging, **C**: 10
  clustering, **C**: 8
  freewriting, **C**: 9
  keeping a journal, **C**: 10
  listing, **C**: 7–8
  talking and listening, **C**: 4
Primary sources, **R**: 353
  citing in a CMS (*Chicago*) paper, **CMS**: 524, 526–27
principal, *principle*, **W**: 149
Print indexes, of periodicals, **R**: 339–40. *See also* Databases, for finding sources
prior to (not *than*), **W**: 167
proceed. See *precede*, *proceed*, **W**: 149

Process
  as pattern of organization, **C**: 36
  of writing an essay
    drafting, **C**: 16–20
    planning, **C**: 3–14
    revising, **C**: 20–28
  of writing a research paper, highlights of, **MLA**: 432–35
Progressive forms, **G**: 191–92, **M**: 227–29
Pronoun/adjectives, **B**: 309–10
Pronoun-antecedent agreement, **G**: 197–99
  with collective nouns (*jury*, *class*, etc.), **G**: 198–99
  with compounds with *and*, **G**: 199
  with compounds with *either . . . or* or *neither . . . nor*, **G**: 199
  with compounds with *or*, **G**: 199
  with indefinite pronouns (*anyone*, *each*, etc.), **G**: 197–98
  sexist language with, avoiding, **G**: 197–98
Pronoun case
  I vs. *me*, etc., **G**: 201–05
  who vs. *whom*, **G**: 205–07
  you vs. *your*, etc., **G**: 205
Pronoun reference, **G**: 199–201
  ambiguous, **G**: 199–200
  broad *this*, *that*, *which*, *it*, **G**: 200–01
  implied, **G**: 200
  indefinite *they*, *it*, *you*, **G**: 201
  remote, **G**: 199–200
  unstated antecedent, **G**: 200
  who (not *that*, *which*) for persons, **W**: 152
Pronouns. *See also* Pronouns, types of
  adjectives with, **B**: 313
  agreement of verbs with, **G**: 175–83
  agreement with antecedent, **G**: 197–99
  as appositives, **G**: 203–04
  case (*I* vs. *me*, etc.), **G**: 201–05
  defined, **B**: 309
  lists of, **B**: 310–11
  as objects, **G**: 202
  pronoun/adjectives, **B**: 309–10
  reference of, **G**: 199–201
  shifts in person and number, avoiding, **S**: 123–24
  singular vs. plural, **G**: 197–99
  as subjects, **G**: 202
  who, *whom*, **G**: 205–07
Pronouns, types of, **B**: 310–11. *See also* Pronouns
  demonstrative (*those*, *that*, etc.), **B**: 311
  indefinite (*some*, *any*, etc.), **B**: 311
  intensive (*herself*, *themselves*, etc.), **B**: 310
  interrogative (*who*, *which*, etc.), **B**: 310
  personal (*you*, *they*, etc.), **B**: 310
  possessive (*your*, *his*, etc.), **G**: 205, **B**: 310
  reciprocal (*each other* etc.), **B**: 311
  reflexive (*myself*, *yourselves*, etc.), **B**: 310
  relative (*that*, *which*, etc.), **B**: 310
Pronunciation, in dictionary entry, **W**: 170
Proof. *See* Evidence
Proofreading, **C**: 28
Proper nouns, **M**: 238–40
  capitalizing, **P**: 296–97
  the with, **M**: 244–45
Publication Manual of the American Psychological Association, **APA**: 458, 483
Punctuation, **P**: 259–91
  apostrophe. *See* Apostrophes
  brackets. *See* Brackets
  colon. *See* Colon
  comma. *See* Commas; Commas, unnecessary
  dash. *See* Dashes

Punctuation (*continued*)
ellipsis mark. *See* Ellipsis mark
exclamation point. *See* Exclamation points
parentheses. *See* Parentheses
period. *See* Periods
question mark. *See* Question mark
quotation marks. *See* Quotation marks
with quotation marks, **P**: 283–85
semicolon. *See* Semicolon
Purpose in writing, **C**: 3, 5, 47
and finding sources, **R**: 334–36, **MLA**: 432–33

Q

Quantifiers with noncount nouns, **M**: 243–44
Question mark, **P**: 287
and MLA citations, **P**: 284, **MLA**: 390
no comma with, **P**: 273
with quotation marks, **P**: 284
Questions
direct and indirect, **S**: 125–26, **P**: 287
pronouns for, **B**: 310
punctuation of, **P**: 287
recognizing, in assignments, **C**: 5
subject in, **B**: 317
Questions to ask
for assignments in the disciplines, **A**: 100–02
to generate ideas, **C**: 9
about a research subject, **R**: 332–34, **MLA**: 373, 432, **APA**: 445, **CMS**: 499
Quotation marks, **P**: 281–86. *See also* Quotations
to avoid plagiarism, **C**: 27, **R**: 363
with direct quotations (exact language), **P**: 281–82, **R**: 363
misuses of, **P**: 285–86
not used with indented (long) quotations, **P**: 282
other punctuation with, **P**: 283–85
single, **P**: 282, **MLA**: 404
with titles of works, **P**: 283, **MLA**: 398, 429–30, **APA**: 485, 487, **CMS**: 511, 516, 529
with words used as words, **P**: 283
quotation, *quote*. See *quote*, *quotation*, **W**: 149
Quotations. *See also* Quotation marks
in APA papers
accuracy of, **APA**: 452–53
appropriate use of, **APA**: 451–58
avoiding plagiarism in, **APA**: 448–50
brackets with, **APA**: 452–53
citing, **APA**: 448–49, 458–83
dropped, avoiding, **APA**: 454–55
ellipsis mark with, **APA**: 452
embedding, **APA**: 456
indenting, **APA**: 453, 485, 495
integrating, **APA**: 451–58
long (indented), **APA**: 453, 485, 495
quotation marks for, **APA**: 449–50
sic for errors in, **APA**: 453
with signal phrase, **APA**: 453–56
synthesizing, **APA**: 456–58
in argument papers, **A**: 99–100
capitalization in, **P**: 299
in CMS (*Chicago*) papers
accuracy of, **CMS**: 506
appropriate use of, **CMS**: 505–07
avoiding plagiarism in, **CMS**: 502–03

brackets with, **CMS**: 506
citing, **CMS**: 502–03, 510–28
dropped, avoiding, **CMS**: 507–08
ellipsis mark with, **CMS**: 506
embedding, **CMS**: 509–10
indenting, **CMS**: 506–07, 529
integrating, **CMS**: 505–10
long (indented), **CMS**: 506–07, 529
quotation marks for, **CMS**: 503
sic for errors in, **CMS**: 506
with signal phrase, **CMS**: 507–10
direct and indirect, **S**: 126, **P**: 281–82
ellipsis marks to indicate cuts in, **P**: 290-91
integrating, **R**: 364–65
long (indented), **P**: 282
in MLA papers
accuracy of, **MLA**: 380–81
appropriate use of, **MLA**: 380–82
avoiding plagiarism in, **MLA**: 376–78
brackets with, **MLA**: 381
citing, **MLA**: 376–77, 388–428
dropped, avoiding, **MLA**: 382–83
ellipsis mark with, **MLA**: 380–81
embedding, **MLA**: 385
indenting, **MLA**: 381–82, 430, 436
integrating, **MLA**: 379–88
long (indented), **MLA**: 381–82, 430, 436
quotation marks for, **MLA**: 378
sic for errors in, **MLA**: 381
with signal phrase, **MLA**: 382–85
synthesizing, **MLA**: 386–87
punctuation of, **P**: 281–86
within quotations, **P**: 282
quote, quotation, **W**: 149
quoted in (qtd. in), for a source in another source, **MLA**: 396, 439, **CMS**: 516. *See also cited in*
quotes. *See* Quotations

R

raise, rise, **W**: 149
Ratios, colon with, **P**: 277
Readability, document design for, **C**: 46–50
Readers, engaging, **C**: 15, 24
Reading
active and critical, **A**: 67–77, **R**: 353–57
evaluating arguments, **A**: 92–100
evaluating sources, **R**: 346–57, **MLA**: 434
exploring a subject, **C**: 7
previewing sources, **R**: 347–52, **MLA**: 433–35
real, really, **W**: 149, **G**: 209–10
Reasoning. *See also* Argument papers
deductive, **A**: 96–97
inductive, **A**: 92–93, 94
logical fallacies, **A**: 92–99
reason . . . is because (nonstandard), **S**: 128, **W**: 149
reason why (nonstandard), **W**: 149
Reciprocal pronouns, **B**: 311
Red herring fallacy, **A**: 98
Redundancies, **W**: 153
Reference list (APA). *See also* Bibliography, CMS (*Chicago*) style; Works cited list (MLA)
directory to models for, **APA**: 443–44
formatting, **APA**: 486–87
models for, **APA**: 463–83
sample, **APA**: 496

Reference of pronouns. *See* Pronoun reference
Reference works, **R**: 345–46
Reflective writing, for portfolio, **C**: 28–31
Reflexive pronouns, **B**: 310
Regional expressions, **W**: 160–61
Regular verbs
- *-d*, *-ed* endings on, **G**: 184, 188–89
- defined, **G**: 184, **B**: 312
- *-s* forms of, **G**: 187–88

relation, *relationship*, **W**: 149
Relative adverbs
- defined, **B**: 325
- introducing adjective clauses, **M**: 248, **B**: 323

Relative pronouns
- agreement with verb, **G**: 181–82
- defined, **B**: 310, 325
- introducing adjective clauses, **M**: 248, **B**: 325
- in noun clauses, **B**: 325
- *who*, *whom*, **G**: 205–07

Repetition
- of function words, for parallel structure, **S**: 113–14
- of key words, **C**: 40–41
- unnecessary
  - ideas, **W**: 153–54
  - nouns and pronouns, **M**: 247–48
  - objects or adverbs, **M**: 248
  - words, **W**: 153–54

Requests, subjunctive mood for, **G**: 196
Researched writing. *See also* Researching a topic; Research process, highlights of
- APA papers, **APA**: 443–97
- CMS (*Chicago*) papers, **CMS**: 498–537
- MLA papers, **MLA**: 369–440
- sample student papers, **MLA**: 436–40, **APA**: 488–97, **CMS**: 532–37

Researching a topic, **R**: 329–68. *See also* Researched writing; Research process, highlights of
- bibliography
  - annotated, sample entry, **R**: 358–59
  - scholarly, **R**: 346
  - working, **R**: 358–59, 360
- catalog, library, **R**: 340–41, 348–49, **MLA**: 432
- databases and indexes, **R**: 336–40
- documentation styles, differences in, **R**: 366–68
- evaluating sources, **R**: 346–57, **MLA**: 433–34
- field research, **R**: 346
- getting started, **R**: 331–36, **MLA**: 432–33
- keeping records and copies of sources, **R**: 358–59, **MLA**: 435
- keyword searches, **R**: 338–40, **MLA**: 433
- library resources, **R**: 334–41, 345–46, **MLA**: 432–33
- library Web site, **R**: 334–35
- managing information, **R**: 357–65
- narrowing the focus, **R**: 333–34
- note taking, **R**: 359–65, **MLA**: 434–35
- planning, **R**: 331–32, **MLA**: 432–33
- purpose and, **R**: 334–36
- reading critically, **R**: 353–57, **MLA**: 434
- reading selectively, **R**: 347–52
- reference librarians, **R**: 334, **MLA**: 432
- reference works, **R**: 345–46
- research questions, **R**: 332–34, **MLA**: 432
- schedule for, **R**: 331
- search strategy, **R**: 334–36
- shortcuts to related sources, **R**: 346
- Web resources, **R**: 341–45

Research process, highlights of, **MLA**: 432–35
keyword searches, **MLA**: 433
note taking, **MLA**: 434–35
plagiarism, avoiding, **MLA**: 434–35
planning, **MLA**: 432–33
research questions, **MLA**: 432
sources
documenting, **MLA**: 435
evaluating, **MLA**: 434
finding, **MLA**: 432–33
integrating, **MLA**: 435
previewing, **MLA**: 433–34
selecting, **MLA**: 433
uses of, **MLA**: 432–33
respectfully, *respectively*, **W**: 149–50
Restrictive (essential) elements, no commas with, **P**: 262–65, 271–72
Résumés, **C**: 58–60
Reviewers, **C**: 6, 20, 22, 23. *See also* Revising with comments
Review of the literature, sample of, **A**: 105, **APA**: 488–97
Revising with comments, **C**: 23–28
"Be specific," **C**: 25
"Consider opposing viewpoints," **C**: 25–26
"Develop more," **C**: 24–25
"More than one point in this paragraph," **C**: 26–27
"Narrow your introduction," **C**: 24
"Summarize less, analyze more," **C**: 26
"Unclear thesis," **C**: 23–24
"Your words?" **C**: 27
Revision, **C**: 20–28
global (big-picture), **C**: 20–21
sentence-level, **C**: 21–22
software tools for, **C**: 62–64
strategies for, **C**: 23–28
rise. See *raise*, *rise*, **W**: 149
Run-on sentences
finding and recognizing, **G**: 218–19, 221
fixing, **G**: 219–22
with colon or dash, **G**: 220–21
with comma and coordinating conjunction, **G**: 220
by making two sentences, **G**: 222
by restructuring, **G**: 222
with semicolon, **G**: 220

S

-s
and apostrophe, **P**: 278–81
and spelling, **P**: 292
as verb ending, **G**: 175, 176–77, 187–88
Salutations and greetings, colon with, **P**: 277
Sample essays. *See also* Research process, highlights of
analysis, **A**: 75–76
argument, **A**: 87–91
in the disciplines, excerpts
business proposal, **A**: 106
lab report, **A**: 107
nursing practice paper, **A**: 108
psychology literature review, **A**: 105
introduction to portfolio, **C**: 29–31
research
APA style, **APA**: 488–97
CMS (*Chicago*) style (excerpt), **CMS**: 532–37
MLA style, **MLA**: 436–40
Scholarly sources
determining if a source is scholarly, **R**: 352
vs. popular sources, **R**: 350
Sciences, writing in the, **A**: 100–08

Scientific facts, and verb tense, **G**: 192–93
Scores, numerals for, **P**: 303
Search engines, **R**: 338, 342
Search strategy, **R**: 334–36
Secondary sources, **R**: 353
Second-person point of view, **C**: 21, **S**: 123
self-, hyphen with, **P**: 295
Self-assessment, in portfolio, **C**: 28–31
Semicolon, **P**: 274–76
  with commas, **P**: 275
  to fix run-on sentences, **G**: 220
  and independent clauses, **P**: 274
  misuse of, **P**: 276
  with quotation marks, **P**: 284
  with series, **P**: 275
  transitional expressions with, **P**: 274–75
sensual, *sensuous*, **W**: 150
Sentence fragments. *See* Fragments, sentence
Sentence purposes, **B**: 327
Sentences. *See also* Sentence types awkward, **S**: 126–28
  choppy, coordination and subordination for, **S**: 130–31
  conditional, **M**: 231–34
  fragments. *See* Fragments, sentence
  fused. *See* Run-on sentences
  incomplete. *See* Fragments, sentence
  inverted (verb before subject), **S**: 135–36, **G**: 180–81, **M**: 246–47, **B**: 317
  logical, **S**: 128
  parts of, **B**: 316–20
  revising and editing, **C**: 21–22
  run-on. *See* Run-on sentences
  thesis. *See* Thesis
  topic, **C**: 32
  transitional, **C**: 42–44
  variety in, **S**: 134–36
  wordy, **W**: 153–56
Sentence structure
  mixed constructions, **S**: 126–28
  multilingual/ESL challenges with, **M**: 245–50
    adjectives, placement of, **M**: 251–52
    adverbs, placement of, **M**: 249–50
    although, *because*, **M**: 249
    linking verb between subject and subject complement, **M**: 246
    present participle vs. past participle, **M**: 250–51
    repetition of object or adverb, avoiding, **M**: 248
    repetition of subject, avoiding, **M**: 247–48
    subject, needed, **M**: 246–47
    there, *it*, **M**: 246–47
  simplifying, **W**: 155
  variety in, **S**: 134–36
Sentence types, **B**: 325–27
  complex, **B**: 327
  compound, **B**: 326
  compound-complex, **B**: 327
  declarative, **B**: 327
  exclamatory, **B**: 327
  imperative, **B**: 327
  interrogative, **B**: 327
  simple, **B**: 326
Series
  comma with, **P**: 261
  parallelism and, **S**: 111–12
  parentheses with, **P**: 289
  questions in, **P**: 287
  semicolon with, **P**: 275
set, *sit*, **W**: 150
Setup, page. *See* Document design; Manuscript formats
Sexist language, avoiding, **W**: 162–64, **G**: 197–98
shall, as modal verb, **M**: 230, **B**: 312
shall, *will*, **W**: 150
she, *her*, *hers*, sexist use of, **W**: 163, **G**: 197–98
she said, *he said*, comma with, **P**: 267–68, 285
she vs. *her*, **G**: 201–05

Shifts, avoiding
from indirect to direct questions or quotations, **S**: 125–26
in mood or voice, **S**: 124–25
in point of view (person and number), **S**: 123–24
in verb tense, **S**: 124
Ships, italics for names of, **P**: 305
Short stories, titles of
capitalizing, **P**: 298, **APA**: 485
quotation marks for, **P**: 283, **MLA**: 398, 430, **APA**: 485, **CMS**: 529
should, as modal verb, **M**: 230, 232–33, **B**: 312
should of (nonstandard), **W**: 150
Showing, not telling, **C**: 26
sic, **P**: 289–90, **MLA**: 381, **APA**: 453, **CMS**: 506
Signal phrases, **MLA**: 382–85, **APA**: 453–56, **CMS**: 507–10
Simile, **W**: 168–69
Simple sentences, **B**: 326
Simple subjects, **B**: 317
Simple tenses, **G**: 191, **M**: 227, 229
since, **W**: 150
Singular vs. plural
antecedents, **G**: 197–99
nouns, **G**: 175–83, 187–88
pronouns, **G**: 197–99
subjects, **G**: 175–83, 187–88
sit. See *set*, *sit*, **W**: 150
site. See *cite*, *site*, **W**: 142
Slang, avoiding, **W**: 160–61
Slash, **P**: 291
so
comma with, **P**: 259
as coordinating conjunction, **B**: 315
Social sciences, writing in, **A**: 100–05. *See also* APA papers
Software. *See* Word processing programs
some, **G**: 179
somebody, *someone*, *something* (singular), **W**: 150, **G**: 179, 197–98
something (singular), **W**: 150
sometime, *some time*, *sometimes*, **W**: 150
Songs, titles of, quotation marks for, **P**: 283
sort of. See *kind of*, *sort of*, **W**: 147
Sound-alike words. *See* Homophones
Sources. *See also* Electronic sources; Internet
citation software for, **R**: 359
citing. *See* Citing sources
documenting, **C**: 54. *See also* APA papers; CMS (*Chicago*) papers; MLA papers
evaluating, **R**: 346–57, **MLA**: 433–34
finding, **R**: 336–46, **MLA**: 432–33
integrating, **R**: 364–65
in APA papers, **APA**: 451–58
in CMS (*Chicago*) papers, **CMS**: 505–10
in MLA papers, **MLA**: 379–88, 435
introducing. *See* Signal phrases
list of. *See* Bibliography, CMS (*Chicago*) style; Reference list (APA); Works cited list (MLA)
popular, **R**: 351
and purpose of research project, **R**: 334–36, 347, **MLA**: 432–33
quoted in another source, **MLA**: 396, **APA**: 463, **CMS**: 517
scholarly, **R**: 350, 352
selecting, **R**: 347–52, **MLA**: 433
synthesizing
in APA papers, **APA**: 456–58
in MLA papers, **MLA**: 386–87
uses of, **R**: 347
in APA papers, **APA**: 446–48
in CMS (*Chicago*) papers, **CMS**: 500–01

Sources (*continued*)
uses of (*continued*)
in MLA papers, **MLA**: 374–76
of visuals, crediting, **C**: 54
Spacecraft, italics for names of, **P**: 305
Spacing. *See* Line spacing
Specific nouns, **W**: 165–66
the with, **M**: 240–42
Spell checkers, **C**: 62–63
Spelling, **P**: 291–94
Split infinitives, **S**: 120
Squinting modifiers, **S**: 118–19. *See also* Misplaced modifiers
Standard English, **W**: 160–61
Statements contrary to fact, **G**: 195–96, **M**: 234
statistics (singular), **G**: 182
Statistics
in APA papers, **APA**: 455–56
in argument papers, **A**: 82–83
in CMS (*Chicago*) papers, **CMS**: 509
in MLA papers, **MLA**: 385
numerals for, **P**: 303
Stereotypes, avoiding, **A**: 92–93, **W**: 164
Strategies for revising. *See* Revising with comments
Straw man fallacy, **A**: 99
Student essays. *See* Sample essays
Subject, grammatical
and agreement with verb, **G**: 175–83
case of, **G**: 202
complete, **B**: 316
compound, **B**: 317
following verb, **S**: 135–36, **G**: 180–81, **M**: 246–47, **B**: 317
identifying, **G**: 181
of infinitive, **G**: 204–05
naming the actor (active voice), **W**: 156–58
naming the receiver (passive voice), **W**: 156–58
pronoun as, **G**: 202
in questions, **B**: 317
repeated, **M**: 247–48
required in sentences, **M**: 246–47
separated from verb, **S**: 119
simple, **B**: 317
singular vs. plural, **G**: 187–88
understood (*you*), **M**: 246, **B**: 317
Subject, of paper
exploring, **C**: 4–10
narrowing, **C**: 6, **R**: 333–34
of research paper, **R**: 332–34
Subject complements
adjectives as, **G**: 208–09, **B**: 318
case of pronouns as, **G**: 202
defined, **B**: 318
with linking verbs, **B**: 318
and subject-verb agreement, **G**: 181
Subjective case, of pronouns, **G**: 202
who, whom, **G**: 205–07
Subjects, of field research, **R**: 346
Subject-verb agreement. *See* Agreement of subject and verb
Subjunctive mood, **G**: 195–96. *See also* Conditional sentences
Subordinate clauses, **B**: 323–25
adjective (beginning with *who*, *that*, etc.), **B**: 323–24
adverb (beginning with *if*, *when*, *where*, etc.), **B**: 324
avoiding repeated elements in, **M**: 248
combined with independent clauses, **B**: 327
defined, **B**: 323, 326
fragmented, **G**: 215
minor ideas in, **S**: 132–33
misplaced, **S**: 118–19
noun, **B**: 324–25
and sentence types, **B**: 326–27
words introducing, **B**: 323–25
Subordinate word groups, **B**: 320–25
Subordinating conjunctions, **B**: 315, 324

Subordination
  for combining ideas of unequal importance, **S**: 129–30
  for fixing run-on sentences, **G**: 222
  for fixing sentence fragments, **G**: 214–17
  of major ideas, avoiding, **S**: 132–33
  overuse of, **S**: 133
Subtitles of works
  capitalizing, **P**: 298, **MLA**: 398, 429, **APA**: 485, 487, **CMS**: 529
  colon between title and, **P**: 277
such as
  no colon after, **P**: 277
  no comma after, **P**: 273
  and sentence fragments, **G**: 217
Suffixes
  hyphen before, **P**: 295
  spelling rules for, **P**: 292
Summary
  vs. analysis, **C**: 26
  in APA papers, **APA**: 448–51, 453–56, 459
  in CMS (*Chicago*) papers, **CMS**: 502–04, 508–09
  integrating, **R**: 364–65
  in MLA papers, **MLA**: 376–79, 382–85, 388
  no quotation marks for, **P**: 282
  and note taking, **R**: 361–62
  writing, **A**: 72–73
superior to (not *than*), **W**: 167
Superlative form of adjectives and adverbs (with *-est* or *most*), **G**: 210–12
Support. *See* Evidence
suppose to (nonstandard), **W**: 150
sure and (nonstandard), **W**: 150, 167
Surveys, as information source, **R**: 346
Syllables, division of words into
  in dictionary, **W**: 169
  hyphen for, **P**: 296
Synonyms, **W**: 165, 172
Synthesizing sources, **MLA**: 386–87, **APA**: 456–58

T

Tables, using in documents, **C**: 50–54, **MLA**: 430–31, **APA**: 486, 493, **CMS**: 530
take. See *bring*, *take*, **W**: 142
Taking notes. *See* Note taking
Talking and listening, to generate ideas, **C**: 4
teach. See *learn*, *teach*, **W**: 147
Teacher's comments, responding to. *See* Revising with comments
team. *See* Collective nouns
Technology, writing with, **C**: 62–64
Tenses, verb, **G**: 190–95
  in active voice, **M**: 227–28
  and agreement with subject, **G**: 175–83
  conditional, **M**: 231–34
  in the disciplines, **A**: 104, **MLA**: 382–83, **APA**: 454, 459, **CMS**: 507
  multilingual/ESL challenges with, **M**: 225, 227–29, 231–34
  in passive voice, **M**: 229
  present
    in writing about literature, **S**: 124, **G**: 192–93
    in writing about science, **G**: 192–93
  sequence of, **G**: 194–95
  shifts in, avoiding, **S**: 124
Texts, visual (photograph, advertisement, etc.)
  analyzing, **A**: 67–70, 77
  writing about, **A**: 72–74
Texts, written
  analyzing, **A**: 67–69, 71–72, 77
  sample paper, **A**: 75–76
  writing about, **A**: 72–76

than
in comparisons, **S**: 115–16
no comma before, **P**: 273
parallelism with, **S**: 113
pronoun after, **G**: 204
than, *then*, **W**: 150
that
agreement of verb with, **G**: 181–82
broad reference of, **G**: 200–01
needed word, **S**: 113–14, 115
vs. *which*, **W**: 151, **P**: 264
vs. *who*. See *who*, *which*, *that*, **W**: 152
the. *See also a*, *an*
multilingual/ESL challenges with, **M**: 237–42, 244–45
with geographic names, **M**: 244–45
omission of, **S**: 117, **M**: 244–45
with proper nouns, **M**: 244–45
their
misuse of, with singular antecedent, **S**: 124, **G**: 197–98
vs. *there*, *they're*, **W**: 151
vs. *they*, **W**: 151
theirselves (nonstandard), **W**: 151
them vs. *they*, **G**: 201–05
them vs. *those*, **W**: 151
then, *than*. See *than*, *then*, **W**: 150
the number, *a number*, **G**: 180
there, as expletive (placeholder)
not used as subject, **M**: 247
and sentence order (verb before subject), **M**: 246–47, **B**: 317
and subject-verb agreement, **G**: 180–81
with verb, **M**: 246–47
and wordy sentences, **W**: 155
therefore
comma with, **P**: 265–66
semicolon with, **P**: 274–75
there, *their*, *they're*, **W**: 151
Thesaurus, **W**: 172
Thesis
in analysis papers, **A**: 74
in APA papers, **APA**: 445
in argument papers, **A**: 80–81
in CMS (*Chicago*) papers, **CMS**: 499
drafting, **C**: 10–11, **MLA**: 432, 435
effective, **C**: 16–18
in essays, **C**: 10–11, 14–18, 21
in MLA papers, **MLA**: 373, 432, 435
revising, **C**: 16–18, 21, 23–24
testing, **C**: 11
working, **C**: 10–11, **MLA**: 373, 432, 435, **APA**: 445
they
indefinite reference of, **G**: 201
vs. *I* or *you*, **S**: 123
misuse of, with singular antecedent, **G**: 197–98
nonstandard for *their*, **W**: 151
vs. *them*, **G**: 201–05
they're. See *there*, *their*, *they're*, **W**: 151
Third-person point of view, **C**: 21, **S**: 123–24
this, broad reference of, **G**: 200–01
this kind. See *kind(s)*, **W**: 147
Time
abbreviations for, **P**: 301
colon with, **P**: 277
numerals for, **P**: 303
Title page
for APA paper
formatting, **APA**: 484
samples, **APA**: 488, 497
for CMS (*Chicago*) paper
formatting, **CMS**: 529
sample, **CMS**: 532
for MLA paper (optional)
formatting, **MLA**: 429
Titles of persons
abbreviations with names, **P**: 300
capitalizing, **P**: 298
comma with, **P**: 268
Titles of works
capitalizing, **P**: 298, **MLA**: 398, 429–30, **APA**: 485, 487, **CMS**: 529

italics for, **P**: 304–05, **MLA**: 398, 429–30, **APA**: 485, 487, **CMS**: 511, 529
quotation marks for, **P**: 283, **MLA**: 398, 429–30, **APA**: 485, 487, **CMS**: 511, 529
treated as singular, **G**: 182–83
to
needed word, **P**: 113–14
as preposition vs. infinitive marker, **M**: 254
Tone (voice). *See also* Language
in argument paper, **A**: 78
in e-mail, **C**: 27–28, 62
Topic
exploring, **C**: 4–10
narrowing, **C**: 6, **R**: 333–34
Topic sentence, **C**: 32
to, *too*, *two*, **W**: 151
toward, *towards*, **W**: 151
Transfer (fallacy), **A**: 98
Transitional expressions
commas with, **P**: 265–66
list of, **P**: 274–75
semicolon with, **P**: 274–75
Transitions, for coherence, **C**: 42–44
Transitive verbs, **M**: 230, **B**: 318–19
Trite expressions. *See* Clichés
troop. *See* Collective nouns
try and (nonstandard), **W**: 151, 167
Tutors, working with. *See* Reviewers; Revising with comments
two. See *to*, *too*, *two*, **W**: 151
type of (not *of a*), **W**: 167
Typing. *See* Document design

U

ultimately. See *eventually*, *ultimately*, **W**: 144
Unclear thesis, revising, **C**: 23–24
Underlining. *See* Italics
Understood subject (*you*), **M**: 246, **B**: 317
uninterested. See *disinterested*, *uninterested*, **W**: 143
unique, **W**: 151, **G**: 212
Unity. *See* Focus
URLs (Web addresses)
citing, **MLA**: 412, 413, **APA**: 472, **CMS**: 512
dividing, **P**: 296, **MLA**: 430, 431, **APA**: 472, 487, **CMS**: 512, 530
Usage
glossary of, **W**: 139–52
labels in dictionary, **W**: 172
usage, **W**: 151
use to (nonstandard), **W**: 151
Using sources
in APA papers, **APA**: 446–48
in CMS (*Chicago*) papers, **CMS**: 500–01
in MLA papers, **MLA**: 374–76
highlights of one student's research process, **MLA**: 432–33
Using the library. *See* Library resources
us vs. *we*, **G**: 201–05
utilize, **W**: 151

V

Vague thesis, revising, **C**: 23–24
Variety
in sentences, **S**: 134–36
in signal phrases, **MLA**: 382–83, **APA**: 453–54, **CMS**: 507–08
Verbal phrases, **B**: 321–23
fragmented, **G**: 215–16
gerund, **B**: 322
infinitive, **B**: 322–23
participial, **B**: 321–22
Verbs. *See also* Verbs, types of
active, **W**: 156–58, **M**: 226–28
adverbs as modifiers of, **B**: 314
agreement with subjects, **G**: 175–83
be, forms of, vs. active, **W**: 158
compound predicates, **G**: 216

Verbs (*continued*)
in conditional sentences, **M**: 231–34
-d, *-ed* ending on, **G**: 184, 188–89
defined, **B**: 311
followed by gerunds or infinitives, **M**: 235–37
forms of, **M**: 225–26, 227–31
mood of, **G**: 195–96
multilingual/ESL challenges with. *See* Multilingual writers, verbs
needed, **G**: 190
negative forms of, **M**: 230–31
without objects, **B**: 319–20
passive, **W**: 156–58, **M**: 226, 229–30
with prepositions (idioms), **M**: 255
separated from subjects, **S**: 119
-s form of, **G**: 175, 176–77, 187–88
shifts in tense, mood, voice, avoiding, **S**: 124–25
in signal phrases, **MLA**: 382–83, **APA**: 454, 459 **CMS**: 507–08
with singular vs. plural subjects, **G**: 187–88
standard forms of, **G**: 183–86
strong, vs. *be* and passive verbs, **W**: 155, 156–58
before subjects (inverted sentences), **S**: 135–36, **G**: 180–81, **M**: 246–47, **B**: 317
tenses of. *See* Tenses, verb
two-word, **B**: 312
voice of (active, passive), **W**: 156–58, **M**: 226–30
Verbs, types of. *See also* Verbs
helping. *See* Helping verbs
intransitive (no direct object), **B**: 319–20
irregular, **G**: 183–86, **M**: 225–26, **B**: 312
linking, **G**: 208–09, **M**: 246, **B**: 318
main, **G**: 190–95, **M**: 230, **B**: 312
modal (*can*, *might*, *should*, etc.). *See* Modal verbs
phrasal. *See* Particles
regular, **G**: 183–84, 188–89, **M**: 225–26, **B**: 312
transitive (with direct object), **B**: 318–19
Video clip, online, citing in paper, **MLA**: 419, **APA**: 477, **CMS**: 525
Viewpoints, differing, in arguments, **A**: 85–86, 98–100, **R**: 354
Visuals, in documents
choosing, **C**: 50, 52–53
citing sources of, **C**: 54, **MLA**: 430–31, **APA**: 486, **CMS**: 530
and document design, **C**: 50–54
as evidence, **A**: 83–84
labeling, **C**: 51, **MLA**: 430–31, **APA**: 486, **CMS**: 530
placement of, **C**: 51
purposes for, **C**: 50, 52–53, **A**: 83–84
types of
bar graph, **C**: 54
diagram, **C**: 53
flowchart, **C**: 53
line graph, **C**: 51, 52
map, **C**: 53
photograph, **C**: 53
pie chart, **C**: 52
table, **C**: 51, 52
Visual texts. *See* Texts, visual
Vocabulary, specialized, **C**: 5, **A**: 102
Voice
active vs. passive, **W**: 156–58, **M**: 227–30, **B**: 318–19
shifts between active and passive, avoiding, **S**: 124–25

W

wait for, *wait on*, **W**: 151
was vs. *were*, **G**: 176
in conditional sentences, **M**: 231–34
and subject-verb agreement, **G**: 175–83

and subjunctive mood, **G**: 195–96
ways, **W**: 151
we
vs. *us*, **G**: 201–05
vs. *you* or *they*, **S**: 123
weather, *whether*, **W**: 152
Web, World Wide. *See* Electronic sources; Internet
Weblog. *See* Blog
Web résumés, **C**: 60
well, *good*, **G**: 209–10. See also *good*, *well*, **W**: 145
were, in conditional sentences, **G**: 195–96, **M**: 231–34
were vs. *was*. *See was* vs. *were*
when clauses, **G**: 195–96, **M**: 231–34
where vs. *that*, **W**: 152
whether. See *if*, *whether*, **W**: 146; *weather*, *whether*, **W**: 152
whether . . . or, **S**: 112–13, **B**: 315
which
agreement of verb with, **G**: 181–82
broad reference of, **G**: 200–01
vs. *that*, **W**: 151, **P**: 264
vs. *who*. See *who*, *which*, *that*, **W**: 152
while, **W**: 152
who
agreement of verb with, **G**: 181–82
omission of, **S**: 114–15
vs. *which* or *that*. See *who*, *which*, *that*, **W**: 152
vs. *whom*, **W**: 152, **G**: 205–07
who, *which*, *that*, **W**: 152
who's, *whose*, **W**: 152, **P**: 281
Wiki
citing in paper, **MLA**: 420, **APA**: 477
as information source, **R**: 344–45
Wikipedia, as source, **R**: 344–45
will, as modal verb, **M**: 230, 233, **B**: 312
will, *shall*. See *shall*, *will*, **W**: 150
Wishes, subjunctive mood for, **G**: 196
Word groups. *See* Independent clauses; Phrases; Subordinate clauses
Wordiness, **W**: 153–56
Word processing programs
and automatic division of words, **P**: 296
and citing sources, **R**: 359
and document design, **C**: 46–47, 63
grammar checkers, **C**: 62–63
and keeping track of files, **C**: 63–64
spell checkers, **C**: 62–63
Words. *See also* Language; Spelling
abstract vs. concrete, **W**: 165–66
antonyms (opposites), **W**: 172
colloquial, **W**: 172
compound, **W**: 169, **P**: 294
confused, **W**: 166. *See also* Glossary of usage
connotation and denotation of, **W**: 165
division of, **W**: 169, **P**: 296
foreign, italics for, **P**: 305
general vs. specific, **W**: 165–66, **M**: 239–40
homophones (sound alike), **P**: 293–94
meaning of, **W**: 165, 172
misuse of, **W**: 166, 172
needed. *See* Needed words
origin of (etymology), **W**: 172
sound-alike. *See* Homophones
spelling of, **P**: 291–94
suffixes (endings of), **P**: 292, 295
synonyms (words with similar meanings), **W**: 165, 172
unnecessary repetition of, **W**: 153–54
using your own (paraphrase, summary), **A**: 72–73, **MLA**: 378–79, **APA**: 450–51, **CMS**: 503–04

Words used as words
italics for, **P**: 305
plural of, **P**: 280
quotation marks for, **P**: 283
treated as singular, **G**: 182–83
Work in an anthology. *See* Anthology, selection in
Working bibliography, **R**: 358–59, 360
Working thesis. *See* Thesis, drafting
Works cited list (MLA)
directory to models for, **MLA**: 371–72
formatting, **MLA**: 431
models for, **MLA**: 398–428
sample, **MLA**: 440
World Wide Web. *See* Electronic sources; Internet
Worn-out expressions. *See* Clichés
would, as modal verb, **M**: 230, 233, **B**: 312
would of (nonstandard), **W**: 152
Writing in the disciplines. *See also* Academic writing
asking questions, **A**: 100–02
assignments
business proposal, **A**: 106
lab report, **A**: 107
nursing practice paper, **A**: 108
psychology literature review, **A**: 105
understanding, **C**: 5, **A**: 104–08
choosing a citation style, **A**: 103, **R**: 366–68
general advice, **A**: 101
language conventions, **A**: 102
using evidence, **A**: 102, 103
Writing process. *See also* Research process, highlights of
for academic writing, **A**: 101
drafting, **C**: 14–20
planning, **C**: 3–14
revising, **C**: 20–28
Writing situation, **C**: 3–4, 6
Writing tutors, working with. *See* Revising with comments

Y

yes, *no*, commas with, **P**: 267
yet
comma before, **P**: 259
as coordinating conjunction, **B**: 315
you
appropriate use of, **S**: 123, **G**: 201
inappropriate use of, **W**: 152, **G**: 201
vs. *I* or *they*, **S**: 123–24
and shifts in point of view, avoiding, **S**: 123
understood, **M**: 246, **B**: 317
your, *you're*, **W**: 152
YouTube. *See* Video clip

Directory to model papers and other sample documents

ANALYSIS PAPER

A1-e "Rethinking Big-Box Stores" by Emilia Sanchez (MLA)

ARGUMENT PAPER

A2-h "From Lecture to Conversation: Redefining What's 'Fit to Print'" by Sam Jacobs (MLA)

PORTFOLIO COVER LETTER

C3-e Reflective letter by Lucy Bonilla

RESEARCH PAPERS

MLA-5 "Online Monitoring: A Threat to Employee Privacy in the Wired Workplace" by Anna Orlov

CMS-5 "The Massacre at Fort Pillow: Holding Nathan Bedford Forrest Accountable" by Ned Bishop

REVIEW OF THE LITERATURE

APA-5 "Can Medicine Cure Obesity in Children? A Review of the Literature" by Luisa Mirano

SAMPLE BUSINESS DOCUMENTS

C5-f Business letter (APA)

C5-f Business memo (APA)

C5-f Résumé (APA)

Visit **hackerhandbooks.com/writersref** for more than thirty model documents in five citation styles.

Multilingual/ESL Menu

A complete section for multilingual writers:

M Multilingual Writers and ESL Challenges

M1 Verbs **225**
- a Form and tense 225
- b Passive voice 226
- c Base form after modal 230
- d Negative forms 230
- e Conditional sentences 231
- f With gerunds or infinitives 235

M2 Articles **237**
- a Articles and other noun markers 237
- b When to use *the* 240
- c When to use *a* or *an* 241
- d When not to use *a* or *an* 243
- e With general nouns 244
- f With proper nouns 244

M3 Sentence structure **245**
- a Linking verb with subject and complement 246
- b Omitted subjects 246
- c Repeated nouns, pronouns 247
- d Repeated objects, adverbs 248
- e Mixed constructions 249
- f Adverb placement 249

M4 Using adjectives **250**
- a Present and past participles 250
- b Order of adjectives 251

M5 Prepositions and idiomatic expressions **252**
- a *at*, *on*, *in* 252
- b Noun (and *-ing* form) after preposition 253
- c Adjective + preposition 254
- d Verb + preposition 255

ESL and Academic English notes in other sections:

C Composing and Revising
- The writing situation 4
- Using a direct approach 16
- Choosing transitions 42

A Academic Writing
- Making an argument 78
- Avoiding hasty generalizations 93

S Sentence Style
- Missing words 114
- Articles 117
- Adverb placement 119
- Double subjects, repeated objects 127
- Repeated objects or adverbs 131

W Word Choice
- Passive voice 157
- Idioms 167

G Grammatical Sentences
- Problems with verbs 183
- Omitted verbs 190
- Verb tenses 192
- Pronoun-antecedent gender agreement 197
- Adjective and adverb placement 208
- No plural adjectives 208
- Adverb placement 210
- Omitted subjects, verbs 214

P Punctuation and Mechanics
- American and British English spelling 293

R Researching
- Researching with an open mind 353
- Recognizing intellectual property 361

OP

Oral Presentations in the Composition Course

A Brief Guide

Matthew Duncan
Gustav W. Friedrich

Oral Presentations in the Composition Course
A BRIEF GUIDE

Oral Presentations in the Composition Course

A BRIEF GUIDE

Matthew Duncan
Northern Illinois University

Gustav W. Friedrich
Rutgers University

Bedford/St. Martin's Boston ◆ New York

For Bedford/St. Martin's

Developmental Editor: Caroline Thompson
Production Editor: Kerri A. Cardone
Senior Production Supervisor: Joe Ford
Marketing Manager: Kevin Feyen
Editorial Assistant: Jennifer Lyford
Copyeditor: Lisa Wehrle
Text Design and Compostion: Claire Seng-Niemoeller
Cover Design: Donna Dennison, Kim Cevoli
Printing and Binding: Malloy Lithographing

President: Joan E. Feinberg
Editorial Director: Denise B. Wydra
Editor in Chief: Karen S. Henry
Director of Marketing: Karen Melton Soeltz
Director of Editing, Design, and Production: Marcia Cohen
Managing Editor: Elizabeth M. Schaaf

Library of Congress Control Number: 2005938006

Manufactured in the United States of America.

0 9 8 7 6
f e d c b a

For information, write: Bedford/St. Martin's, 75 Arlington Street, Boston, MA 02116 (617-399-4000)

ISBN: 0-312-41784-5
EAN: 978-0-312-41784-0

Contents

Introduction 1

1. Choosing a Topic 3
   - Brainstorming 3
   - Consulting with Others 4
   - Researching Ideas 4
   - Making a Choice 5

2. Determining Your Purpose 6
   - Informative Presentations 8
     - *Description* 8
     - *Demonstration* 10
     - *Definition* 11
     - *Explanation* 13
   - Persuasive Presentations 14
     - *Propositions of Fact* 14
     - *Propositions of Value* 14
     - *Concerns about a Problem* 15
     - *Propositions of Policy* 15
   - A Final Word 16

3. Analyzing Your Audience 17
   - Types of Audiences 18
     - *The Selected Audience and the Concerted Audience* 18
     - *The Passive Audience* 19
     - *The Pedestrian Audience and the Organized Audience* 19

◆ BOX: Audience Characteristics and Strategies 20
Audience Attitudes 21
Hostile Audiences 22
Sympathetic Audiences 22
Neutral Audiences 23
Communication Barriers 23
Barriers That Involve Content 24
Barriers That Involve Audience and Delivery 27

4. Adapting Your Ideas and Evidence 29

Listening and Learning 29
Choosing Forms of Support 30
Explanation 30
Examples 31
Statistics 32
Testimony 35
Visual Aids 36
Choosing Forms of Proof 36
Motivational Proof or Pathos 37
Ethical Proof or Ethos 37
Logical Proof or Logos 38

5. Organizing Your Presentation 40

Creating an Outline 40
Choosing an Organizational Pattern 43
Chronological Pattern 44
Topical Pattern 44
Spatial or Geographical Pattern 45
Cause-Effect Pattern 45
Problem-Solution Pattern 45
Compare and Contrast Pattern 46
◆ BOX: Patterns of Organization 46

6. Developing Effective Introductions, Transitions, and Conclusions 49

The Introduction 49
Language Choices 52
Transitions 54
The Conclusion 55

7. Using Visual Aids 57

Choosing Effective Visuals 57
Choosing a Mode of Delivery 59
Chalkboard or Whiteboard 59
Handouts 59
Overhead Transparencies 60
Presentation Software 61
Designing Visual Aids 64
Fonts 64
Contrast and Spacing 65
Color 65
Images 66
Avoiding Technical Problems 66

8. Practicing, Polishing, and Delivering the Presentation 68

Modes of Speaking 68
Impromptu Speaking 68
Extemporaneous Speaking 70
Scripted Speaking 71
Memorized Speaking 72
Voice and Body Language 73
Dealing with Stage Fright 74
Polishing the Presentation 76

9. **Presenting as a Group** 78
Dividing the Work 78
Transitioning between Speakers 80
Acknowledging Nonspeaking Group Members 81

10. **Evaluating Presentations** 82
Checklist for Evaluating a Presentation 83
The Speaker's Delivery 83
Content and Coherence 84
Argument and Persuasion 85
Thinking Critically about Your Own Presentation 86

Introduction

In your composition course, you are asked to write a number of different types of papers for different purposes. Your assignments probably include personal essays, descriptions, arguments, research papers, literary papers, or multimedia projects. Many of these and other modes of writing lend themselves to oral presentations such as leading a class discussion after researching a topic, talking about a paper in progress, or presenting a final writing project. You already may have taken a public speaking course, or perhaps you will take such a course later. Outside of your college courses, you are also likely to be asked to speak in front of a group. One of the most practical applications of a composition course is authoring and developing speeches and presentations. Many professions and disciplines require presentations, from sales to human resources training, from advertising to politics, from psychology to biology. Both modes of communication—writing and speaking—are critically important no matter where your plans after college take you, and neither happens in isolation.

This supplement offers guidelines and strategies for adapting your written research, analyses, and arguments for oral presentations. You will recognize some of this information since many of the strategies for creating good oral presentations are the same as those for writing good compositions. Even if you have not already written a paper about your topic, this guide will help you develop a presentation from brainstorming through organization to delivery.

This supplement prepares you to do the following:

- Identify a specific purpose and topic for an oral presentation and select an organizational pattern
- Analyze audiences in terms of their expectations, attitudes toward your position, and group cohesiveness
- Construct and adapt outlines for oral presentations
- Compose effective introductions, transitions, and conclusions
- Incorporate effective visual aids into your presentation
- Describe four modes of speaking and how they are effective for different situations
- Understand how your voice and body language affect your audience
- Cope with nervousness and stage fright
- Organize an effective group presentation
- Evaluate presentations made by your fellow students and other speakers

Choosing a Topic 1

The first step in preparing any oral presentation is to carefully read the assignment. What is it asking you to do? Inform your audience about a topic? Persuade them to change their thinking about an issue? If you are unsure about any of the assignment's requirements, ask your instructor for clarification (and do so well in advance of the due date!). Remember, too, that the requirements for your written composition assignment may differ from those for your oral presentation. Only after you understand what the assignment is asking you to do can you narrow your focus to find a good topic.

And what's a good topic? One that fulfills the requirements of your assignment, one that is manageable and specific, and one that you know something about and are interested in. You'll notice that these are the same qualities you use when choosing a topic for an essay or research paper.

In searching for a good topic, try the following strategies for generating ideas: brainstorming, consulting with others, and researching ideas.

Brainstorming

Brainstorming—listing any topic ideas that occur to you, without censoring yourself—starts by examining your own interests and expertise. What are you interested in? What would you like to find out more about? What are your experiences? What do you know? (Be sure to distinguish between what you know and what you believe: Knowledge is based on facts that you can support; belief is based on values and opinions.) In addition to listing your ideas, you could try grouping them in clusters and mapping their connections to one another. These visual types of brainstorming strategies may reveal emergent connections you hadn't originally considered.

For example, assume that the assignment requires you to give a 2- to 3-minute speech describing a place. In choosing a topic, begin to think about this assignment from your personal experiences. What places do you know around your college or university? Your local community? Your state? The United States? Other countries? Also ask yourself what places, in each of these settings, you would like to know more about.

As you brainstorm, avoid evaluation and judgment (for example, "The class won't want to know about that!" or "The teacher already knows this!"). Just write down as many ideas as you can. Evaluation comes later, when you sort through the multiple possibilities to find the one topic that will become your focus.

Consulting with Others

Conversations with friends, classmates, professors, family members, and others can be important sources of topics for oral presentations. Not only can consulting with others help you generate topics that you may not think of on your own, but also, by providing your first "audience," it can help you evaluate the potential value of topics.

Researching Ideas

Another valuable source of topics for presentations is the library's collection of books, journals, online databases, and other materials. Sometimes just browsing through current newspapers and periodicals will remind you of or spark your interest in a particular topic. The reference librarian can also advise you on library resources. The Internet, especially the World Wide Web, may also help you explore ideas for your presentation. But do not rely too heavily on the Web for inspiration. Although a huge amount of free information is available online almost immediately, much of the Web lacks the editorial standards and fact-checking requirements of traditional print media. If you find good ideas through a Web search, be sure to follow up on those ideas at the library.

Making a Choice

You have searched for potential topics by solo brainstorming, talking with others, searching online, and visiting the library. The next task is crucial and perhaps the most difficult of all. You must filter all the information you have gathered and select the topic that best meets the following three criteria:

1. Is it a topic you are interested in and know something about?
2. Is it a topic that satisfies the requirements specified in the assignment?
3. Is it a topic that your audience will find worthwhile?

Once you have chosen an appropriate topic, you will need to narrow your focus to begin developing your thesis for your paper (if the assignment calls for one) or your presentation. Writing guides and handbooks are good sources of information for advice on developing an effective thesis or presentation.

2 *Determining Your Purpose*

If your oral presentation is based on a paper you've written for your composition course, you may feel that the best course is merely to read the paper to the class. Few things, however, are more tedious and less engaging than listening to someone read a research paper aloud. Multiply that by the number of students in your class and you can understand why oral presentations take more preparation and consideration.

When you give your oral presentation, you must articulate the main idea of your paper in a statement of specific purpose—a single declarative sentence that specifies what you expect the audience to know, do, believe, and feel after you speak. Here are some examples:

- "I want the audience to know about the history and current use of inline skates."
- "I want the audience to vote against repealing Title IX."
- "I want the audience to understand the various meanings of the word *communication*."
- "I want the audience to understand what AIDS is and what we need to do to prevent it from spreading."
- "I want the audience to appreciate the contributions of Eleanor Roosevelt to our society."

Your paper should have a thesis statement—a sentence that summarizes what you want the audience to get out of your oral presentation. Whereas the specific purpose summarizes how you want your audience to respond to your oral presentation (for example, "I want the audience to vote for Joyce Jones for Congress"), your thesis statement captures what you want your audience to remember even if they later forgot much of the rest of what you said ("I want the audience to vote for Joyce Jones for Congress *because* she is honest, informed, and effective"). If you do not already have a clear, concise thesis statement in your paper, consider revising your introduction. When you are giving the presentation, stick to your thesis statement. Make it obvious to your audience that this is your purpose and goal.

Presentations usually have one of two general purposes: to inform or to persuade. Oral presentations that inform try to provide audiences with information that they will find new, relevant, and useful. Such presentations can take a variety of forms. For example, a presentation could explain a process, such as how to play various styles of music on the guitar, how to change the oil in a car, or how to mix music and scratch using two turntables. It could describe objects or places, like the Vietnam Memorial, inline skates, or the beach in Cancun. Informative presentations often define things, for example, hip hop, coordinating conjunctions, or the field of communication studies. Informative presentations also attempt to answer questions that we have about the world: What are tidal waves? What was the impact of Martin Luther King Jr.'s "I Have a Dream" speech? What are the differences between computer hacking and cracking?

While informative presentations deal with facts and procedures, persuasive writing and speaking focus on beliefs, values, and opinions. Instead of describing what exists, persuasion focuses on building a case for what should be. Although persuasive presentations most frequently ask for a change in belief, attitude, or behavior ("Boycott this corporation to protest its monopolistic practices"), they can also reaffirm existing attitudes and actions ("We should continue to use the existing grading structure at our university").

Informative Presentations

Informative presentations generally take one of four forms: description, demonstration, definition, or explanation. As you read the following discussions of these forms, keep in mind that you may need to combine them depending on the topic of your informative presentation.

Description

Description is one of the most basic categories for presenting information. Description requires you to put into words what you have experienced with your senses. You want your audience to feel, hear, and see what you felt, heard, and saw. You must have a clear idea of what you want to describe and why, and you should emphasize vital details and eliminate the trivial ones. In choosing which details to use, carefully consider your audience. Details that one audience finds clear and vivid another may find less so. (See Chapter 3 for more on analyzing your audience.)

Following is an excerpt from a descriptive speech by Major James N. Rowe; it was delivered to students of the U.S. Army General Staff and Command College at Leavenworth, Kansas. Major Rowe delivered the speech extemporaneously—that is, he prepared his ideas in advance but composed his precise wording at the moment he spoke. Notice how he calls up details of his surroundings and his feelings as he describes his experience as a U.S. prisoner of war in South Vietnam.

> Now, in the camp, the physical conditions in South Vietnam with the Viet Cong are primitive. I was in the U Minh Forest; the camps were temporary at best. You had two to three feet of standing water during the rainy season; in the dry season it sank out, and you were hunting for drinking water. We had two meals of rice a day, and generally we got salt and nuoc mam [a fish sauce used to flavor food] with them. We did get infrequent fish from the guards, but always the castoff that the guards didn't want. If we got greens, it was maybe one meal's worth every two or three months. Immediately vitamin deficiency and malnutri-

> tion were a problem. This is a thing you are going to fight the whole way through. And you are fighting on two sides. You are fighting for physical survival, and you are fighting for mental survival. The physical survival is just staying alive. We found that we had to eat a quart pan of rice each meal, two meals a day, just to stay alive. We found that [we did better] if we could put down everything we had, and I think the most difficult thing initially was the nuoc mam. It is high in protein value, but the VC don't have that much money to spend on nuoc mam. You don't get Saigon nuoc mam. Theirs is called ten-meter nuoc mam. You can smell it within ten meters, and it is either repulsive or inedible, depending on how long you have been there. But this was the type of thing you are eating for nutritional value, and not for taste. So you are fighting on that side.[1]

Note Major Rowe's choice of words at the outset, "the physical conditions . . . are primitive." The rest of this passage fleshes out this statement. Rowe describes first the environmental conditions of rising and falling water levels. He bases his definition of "primitive" on two basic human needs, shelter and food. The majority of the passage deals with food, a choice that offers his audience compelling examples to which they can relate. Rowe moves from the general (a broad overview of the climate) to the very specific (nuoc mam). He even uses wry, dark humor as a subtle example of a survival technique—the prisoners' name for the fish sauce, "ten meter nuoc mam," is a grim joke about the smell. This final sensory description will linger with a listener and draw the audience in to the rest of Rowe's presentation.

Presentations about literature or film are often descriptive. Poetry analysis is one type of descriptive process that uses a very specific format and vocabulary. By identifying the meter and rhyme scheme in a poem, a writer is describing the poem's technical features. The same is usually true when discussing the lighting, cinematography, or dialogue in a film or television show. Usually, academic writing assignments involve some degree of description along with some other mode, such as definition or explanation.

[1] Richard L. Johannesen, R. R. Allen, and Wil L. Linkugel, *Contemporary American Speeches,* 7th ed. (Dubuque, IA: Kendall/Hunt, 1992) 52.

Demonstration

Demonstration presentations narrate how to do something. Giving a demonstration presentation seems natural and easy enough. After all, if we have figured out how things happen or work, we should be able to explain them to others! If we know how to get to the mall, we should be able to tell another person how to get there. Unfortunately, as you know, this is not always the case.

To prepare a demonstration presentation, start by identifying your audience and their level of knowledge about your topic. For example, if you are giving directions to a location in Chicago, you must first assess the audience's familiarity with Chicago before referring to "The Eisenhower" rather than "I-290." Similarly, if you are working with a computer novice, you probably should use "turn the computer on" instead of "boot the machine." With a clear statement of purpose in mind, give a broad outline of the process and discuss the major steps in chronological order. Use transitional words such as "first . . . , next . . . , finally . . ." (see Chapter 6). Be sure your language is appropriate for your audience; when necessary, define terms. Do not dwell on insignificant details. Relate each major step to the whole process. Occasionally, remind the audience where you are in the process.

The following outline of the first steps in the printmaking process of producing woodcuts illustrates a demonstration speech. You can imagine the speaker showing each step.

A. To prepare the block
   1. Use a power sander to smooth rough, scratched, or dented boards.
   2. Lightly sandpaper the surface to ensure an even flatness.
   3. To enhance the grain quality in prints, run a wire brush over the surface in the direction of the grain.

B. To transfer the design, use one of three methods.
   1. Coat the block with white gouache, and draw directly on it.

   2. Place carbon paper on the block, then your drawing, then tracing paper; press firmly with a pencil to draw in the main elements.
   3. Paste the drawing onto the surface of the block and cut away the white areas.

C. To cut the block

   1. Hold the knife with your forefinger along the top of the blade to apply downward pressure, and use your other fingers as guides.
   2. Use a gouge by gently tapping it with a mallet; always direct the point of the tool away from your body.[2]

As you might guess, demonstration presentations often rely heavily on the use of visual aids and handouts. (See Chapter 7 for more about using visual aids.) Demonstration presentations also often involve specialized vocabulary. *Gouache* stands out in the example above, but some audiences may not even be familiar with tools like *power sanders, mallets,* and *gouges.* When making a demonstration presentation, define your terms first and repeat their definitions when you use them again. Another good idea when making a demonstration presentation is to move slowly and deliberately through each step of the process. If your audience is attempting to work along with you, pause or ask them whether they need more time before you continue.

Definition

Definition involves answering questions like "What is this thing?" Formal definitions—those found in dictionaries—have three parts: the name of the thing, the class or group to which it belongs, and the qualities that distinguish it from other members of its class. Thus, to define *notation,* you could say that it is "a system of figures or symbols used to represent numbers, quantities, etc."

[2] Adapted from Bruce Robertson and David Gormley, *Step-by-Step Printmaking* (London: Diagram Visual Information Ltd., 1987) 71.

Thing	*Class or group*	*Qualities*
Notation is	a system of figures or symbols	used to represent numbers, quantities, etc.

But simple definitions like these are often inadequate for describing complex ideas. Figures of speech—metaphors, similes, analogies, and the like—can help listeners understand complex concepts. You can compare and contrast a term with similar ones or use examples. Because your task is to establish a meaning the audience will understand and accept, you need to be as specific and concrete as possible. Defining an *ollie* as "a skateboard trick" is inadequate; a much better definition includes details about the placement of the skater's feet and the motion of one foot kicking downward to snap the tail of the board against the ground while the other foot slides along the board as it rises off the ground. Even comparing the trick to a short hopping jump makes the image of an ollie clearer to your audience.

Robert M. White, then president of the National Academy of Engineering, defined *invention* in the following excerpt from his speech, "Inventors, Invention, and Innovation":

> Invention is more than the development of useful and productive devices, although these are vital for material progress. Instead, it is a manifestation of the creativity in all human activities. The invention of the Gothic arch permitted the soaring cathedrals of the Middle Ages and the Renaissance. The paintings of Monet and Pissarro brought us the glories of impressionism. Our daily lives are uplifted by the songs of Irving Berlin and the symphonies of Beethoven.
>
> In short, invention is where you find it. And so it is in industry. Whatever the function, whether in research and development, design, production, or distribution of goods and services, inventions are at the root of new products and processes and also the source of the economic success of companies. Inventions are the lifeblood coursing through the heart of industrial competitiveness.[3]

[3] Johannesen, Allen, and Linkugel 66.

Note that White begins with a practical definition of invention, "the development of useful and productive devices." He qualifies that definition by adding the complex abstract idea "manifestation of creativity." By using the examples of the Gothic arch and Monet paintings, he illustrates—makes concrete—his complex idea. White goes on to summarize his definition by applying it, making it real for his audience and offering good reasons why they should care about invention.

Explanation

An explanatory presentation may seem similar to a descriptive presentation, but describing how to surf the Web, for example, is fundamentally different from explaining how Web browsers interpret HTML to display Web sites. Describing how to surf the Web creates awareness. Explaining how it works creates understanding. Explanatory speeches create understanding in an audience because they answer the questions "Why?" or "What does that mean?" They typically deal with problems and with plans and policies. Thus, they are usually more abstract than descriptive and demonstration speeches. The challenge to the speaker is to explain a problem, action, or decision without persuading the audience.

There are at least three ways in which answers to "why" questions may be difficult for uninitiated audiences to understand:

1. They may have difficulty in understanding the meaning and use of a term.
2. They may have difficulty abstracting the main points from complex information.
3. They may be hesitant to accept an implausible proposition (such as Einstein's notion that we are accelerating toward the center of the earth).

Your challenge as an explanatory speaker is to assess the main difficulty facing the audience and to shape the presentation to overcome that difficulty.

Persuasive Presentations

As we know from the discussion of informative oral presentations, the task of an informative speaker is to present information in such a fashion that an audience will focus on, understand, and remember it. The persuasive speaker has a different task: to present a message that, if accepted, requires the audience to change beliefs, attitudes, values, or behaviors. Historically, persuasive messages have been categorized according to four types: propositions of fact, propositions of value, concerns about a problem, and propositions of policy.[4]

Propositions of Fact

Propositions of fact make and support claims. That is, you pose and answer the questions "Was it true? Is it true? and Will it be true?" The supposed fact that you want the audience to accept as true can concern an individual, an event, a process, a condition, a concept, or a policy. The following are examples of propositions that claim the existence of a fact:

- "The federal government has evidence that flying saucers are real."
- "Workers in smoky bars and restaurants face a great risk of lung cancer."
- "Your dealership will lose money on its sales of compact cars because your inventory is too small."

Propositions of Value

Propositions of value make evaluative assertions. That is, they answer the questions "How important is it?" and "What is its worth?" In presentations of this type, you seek to convince an audience of something's specific degree of goodness or quality: an individual, an event, an object, a way of life, a process, a condition, or

[4] Johannesen, Allen, and Linkugel.

another value. You can urge your audience to adopt a new value or, through redefining an old value, to change their perspective. You can also motivate your audience to renew their commitment to a value they already hold. Consider the following examples:

- "Lee Jones is the best professor in our English department."
- "Nuclear weapons are immoral."
- "Organized religion has produced more harm than good."

Concerns about a Problem

Presentations that create concern about a problem usually define a situation and add more information to raise awareness. They answer the question "What is it?" Such presentations ask an audience to agree that specific conditions should be perceived as a problem requiring a solution. In addition to making a compelling presentation concerning the nature of the problem, such presentations attempt to create concern by showing the impact of the problem on the audience. The following are examples of propositions asserting problems:

- "The United States' sale of arms to other countries is a cause for concern."
- "Sexual harassment is a continuing problem on college and university campuses."
- "We should be concerned about the depiction of violence on children's television shows."

Propositions of Policy

In presentations that affirm propositions of policy, you advocate adoption of a new policy. That is, you answer the question "What course of action should be pursued?" Additionally, you can recommend continuing or discontinuing an existing policy or rejecting a proposed one. Your task as the speaker is to promote a course of action or policy as necessary and desirable (or unnecessary and undesirable). Examples of such propositions include the following:

- "Gays and lesbians should have the same rights as all U.S. citizens."
- "Colleges and universities should not limit free speech."
- "Certain illegal drugs such as marijuana should be legalized for medicinal purposes."

A Final Word

Presentations, like the papers you write in composition class, tend to fall into the two general categories–informative presentations and persuasive presentations–discussed in this chapter. But few of the presentations you make (or papers you write) will fit perfectly within one category, subcategory, or style of presentation. An informative presentation, for example, may raise questions whose answers require a more persuasive approach. Or a presentation about an e. e. cummings sonnet may require several different informative strategies: definition (of *sonnet*), description (of the elements in a sonnet), and explanation (of why cummings's use of the sonnet form is surprising). Likewise, a persuasive presentation may use several informative techniques. Or a topic in one of the four persuasive subcategories may easily fit into another.

No matter which type (or types) of presentation you prepare, make your purpose and goal obvious to your audience. Everything you say during the presentation, all the examples you offer, and all the visual aids or handouts you use should focus on your thesis and purpose. Before you give your presentation, be sure that you can clearly state in your own words the point you are trying to make. Keep this point always in mind as you write your paper, as you adapt the presentation from your paper, and as you deliver the presentation.

3 Analyzing Your Audience

Public speaking audiences base their expectations on many factors, which include internal as well as external ones. Audience members' existing beliefs and values, their knowledge (or lack of knowledge) about the speaker or topic, events happening in the outside world, and even the time of day or comfort of the speaking room all influence an audience's expectations. You need to know about these expectations in order to fulfill or deal with them. For every speaking situation, therefore, it is important to ask these questions:

- Why are members of the audience here?
- What are they expecting to hear in this kind of situation?
- What expectations do they have about me?
- What are they expecting to hear from me on this topic?
- What features of the environment (both internal to the speaking room and external to it) might affect audience expectations?
- In what ways will it benefit my presentation or argument to fulfill the audience's expectations?
- In what ways will it benefit my presentation or argument to violate these expectations? (For example, if your audience expects to be bored by a dry and lifeless presentation, how can you confront their expectations?)

How do you determine the beliefs, attitudes, values, experiences, and needs of an audience? One way to begin is to classify the audience in terms of its cohesiveness or togetherness. You can group audiences into five types: selected, concerted, passive, pedestrian, or organized.[1] Whatever its type, any audience will also have an existing attitude toward your position or topic—hostile, sympathetic, or neutral. In the following sections, we look first at the five types of audiences and then at audience attitudes.

Types of Audiences

The Selected Audience and the Concerted Audience

In a selected audience, the speaker and audience share a common and known purpose, but they do not necessarily agree on the best way to achieve their shared goals. As Democrats or Republicans gather at their convention, for example, they agree, in general, on what will help get their party's candidates elected. Nevertheless, as they work on the party platform, many disagreements arise concerning the best approach to take on issues like the economy or defense policy. Thus, your first task when addressing a selected audience is to channel any shared motives into a direction you have planned and developed.

The concerted audience is a subset of a selected audience and is therefore quite similar to it. Its members share a need to achieve some end and are usually positively disposed toward the speaker and the topic. They are inclined to do what the speaker suggests, but they still need to be convinced. When members of the Republican Party meet to put together a party platform, they are a selected audience—they have a common goal. But different wings of the party are likely to have different concerns about what should be included in the platform—each wing is a concerted audience. Your task when addressing a concerted audience is to capitalize on the audience's predisposition to accept your ideas.

Selected and concerted audiences are not common in a classroom setting, but it may be to your advantage to consider treating your classmates as one of these types of audiences. Ideally, all students at a university or college should share some goals and values.

[1] Harry L. Hollingsworth, *The Psychology of the Audience* (New York: American Book, 1935).

In particular, everyone is there to learn and grow. While this may seem idealistic, you should work from this basic assumption that your audience is invested in learning. The more you invest in your topic and your presentation, the more likely it is that your peers will be engaged and respond to your message.

The Passive Audience

In a classroom setting, you are most likely to encounter a passive audience. The passive audience is a group that is already gathered to hear the speaker, but its motivation level is low. When you speak in class, for example, an attendance requirement guarantees you the presence of an audience; it does not guarantee, however, that your audience will be interested in everything (or anything!) you have to say. Any time you address a passive audience, your first goal is to gain their attention. Then, your main task is to sustain and direct listeners' interest.

One way to sustain the interest of a passive audience is to treat them the way you might treat a selected or concerted audience. By speaking as if your audience shares your purpose, you change not only your expectations about the audience, but also their potential responses to your message or argument. Making a presentation to a class is a type of performance. You can shape an audience's response to your message by treating them as if they are already allies (as with a concerted audience). If the demeanor of your presentation positions your audience as sympathetic, but acknowledges a need to allay fears or address concerns (as with a selected audience), even the harshest critics may respond more favorably. But a skilled public speaker never assumes too much about an audience. While this tactic may work more successfully in a first-year composition class, a careful and practiced speaker will treat each presentation separately and analyze each audience carefully.

The Pedestrian Audience and the Organized Audience

The least cohesive group is the pedestrian audience—people who have no obvious connection with either the speaker or one another. For example, a fundamentalist preacher might stand on a busy

Audience Characteristics and Strategies

	Characteristics	*Examples*	*Strategies*
Selected	• Speaker and audience share a common and known purpose • Speaker and audience do not necessarily agree on best way to achieve shared goals	• Political party convention attendees • Students attending a campus meeting to discuss a specific problem	• Channel any shared motives into a planned and developed direction • Treat as sympathetic, but acknowledge need to calm fears or address concerns
Concerted	• Subset of a *selected* audience • Members share a need to achieve some end • Usually positively disposed toward the speaker and the topic • Inclined to do what the speaker suggests, but still need to be convinced	• A faction within a political party • A division within a company • Members of a campus club or organization	• Treat as if already allies • Capitalize on expected willingness to accept your ideas
Passive	• Already gathered to hear the speaker • Motivation level is low	• Your classmates • Office staff	• Capture their attention • Sustain and direct interest • Consider treating as *selected* or *concerted* (see above)
Pedestrian	• No obvious connection with either the speaker or one another • Least cohesive group	• Passersby on a street corner • People on the subway	• Work to attract the audience • Entertain them • Invite controversy
Organized	• Completely devoted to the speaker and to the speaker's purpose • Most cohesive group	• Some religious groups • Fan clubs	• Focus less on informing and persuading • Celebrate with them

street corner and attempt to attract a pedestrian audience (literally) by vividly describing people's sins and their need for salvation. Most of us are familiar with how such an audience reacts. At the other end of the spectrum is the organized audience. Organized audiences are completely devoted to the speaker and to the speaker's purpose. Some religious and political groups fall into this category, as do audiences who have committed themselves to a noncontroversial cause, such as honoring basketball star Allen Iverson on his birthday. Thus, informing and persuading organized audiences is typically less important than celebrating with them. An extreme such as the pedestrian or organized audience is unlikely in a classroom situation. Your audience is most likely to be passive, and in ideal situations, the audience may be selected or concerted.

Audience Attitudes

Identifying the type of audience you are facing is an important component of audience analysis, but it is only the first step. You also need to discover your audience's attitude toward and knowledge about your topic.

- A *hostile* audience is resistant to your message.
- A *sympathetic* audience probably already agrees with many of the points you are making, or at least is willing to listen to your position.
- A *neutral* audience does not have strong feelings one way or another.

Not every member of an audience need share the same disposition, but the prevailing attitude of the audience is important to identify and acknowledge. The degree to which your audience is hostile, sympathetic, or neutral to your message can have a dramatic effect on how you deliver it.

The audience's attitude is sometimes difficult to predict, but often depends on the level of controversy surrounding your topic. You may have to assess the audience as you make the presentation and meet their reactions with your own counterresponses. Keep in mind that the audience's attitude toward your message is independent of what type of audience they are. For example, your class may be a passive audience, but they may also be hostile to your message. They just may not care to voice those differing perspectives. A passive audience may also be sympathetic, which may greatly decrease the dynamic feedback they offer. And a pedestrian audience is not always going to be neutral. Usually, any audience is made up of a mixture of hostile, sympathetic, and neutral members. Small clusters of any faction, though, may influence your presentation.

Hostile Audiences

Although hostile audiences are not necessarily angry with the speaker or throwing rotten tomatoes, they do begin the presentation with a bias against the message of the speaker. Hostile audiences often offer feedback with their body language, for example, by looking away from the speaker, sitting with their arms crossed, or scowling and shaking their heads. Facing a hostile audience is challenging, but it also provides a potential source of energy for your presentation. The tension between the audience and your message can invigorate your delivery. A hostile audience is likely to pay more attention to your presentation, if only to scrutinize every detail and pick apart your arguments. Do not let the hostility of the audience members shake your delivery style; do not let any hostile audience members derail your train of thought or lead you off on unrelated tangents. Be prepared to answer a number of questions.

Sympathetic Audiences

Sympathetic audiences agree with at least the main idea of the presentation. Their opinions may still differ from that expressed in your presentation, but they are willing to listen to and consider your message with open minds. The fact that the audience is sympathetic may not be the most beneficial situation, though, for a dynamic or rousing presentation. If the audience is so sympathetic that they already know the details you are presenting or they feel that what you are arguing is a foregone conclusion, then you may find them becoming hostile, not to your message, but to the situation. They may feel that you are "preaching to the choir" and question your choice of subject. They may also become (or remain) passive. If you know in advance that the audience is sympathetic, do not rely on their body language or feedback to drive your delivery. Instead, keep them engaged through interesting new insights, dynamic body language and verbal delivery, and challenging explorations of the merits of the opposing arguments.

Neutral Audiences

Many audiences are neutral to your message. They may have no previous knowledge about your topic or have no firm opinions about the subject matter. The neutral audience is possibly the most interesting group to address because the substance of your presentation is likely to help sway their opinions one way or another. The next time you address this audience about the same subject matter, they may have shifted from neutral to sympathetic. Many of the challenges faced in dealing with a passive audience are also present with a neutral audience. Your main tasks are to gain the neutral audience's attention and to sustain their interest.

Communication Barriers

Communication barriers are problems that prevent you from getting your message across or that prevent your audience from responding in the way you hope. Listed on the next page are eight of the most common communication barriers that speakers encounter.[2] Most of these barriers arise from extremes and are resolved by seeking balance and compromise.

[2] R. P. Hart, *Lecturing as Communication,* unpublished manuscript, Purdue University, Purdue Research Foundation, 1975.

Barriers that involve content

- Too much or too little information
- Information is fact-heavy or opinion-heavy
- Information is too concrete or too abstract
- Information is too general or too specific

Barriers that involve audience and delivery

- Level of feedback from the audience
- Pace of presentation
- Chronology and logical organization
- Intensity of speaker's delivery

Barriers That Involve Content

Your choices of information to include in an oral presentation may elicit the following communication barriers.

- *Too much information.* "Information overload" produces frustration as an audience feels buried by an avalanche of information and stops listening. You must analyze, filter, and succinctly and precisely deliver information in order for it to become useful knowledge. Your audience is attempting to analyze and filter that same information based on what you say and how you say it.

  EXPLAIN SPECIALIZED LANGUAGE: Technical jargon and acronyms (mp3, AAC, RIAA, MPAA, 802.11b, IEEE 1394, etc.) are often confusing. Handouts or visual aids are useful for defining terms and abbreviations. (See Chapter 7 for more about using visual aids.)

  AVOID UNNECESSARY DETAILS: When giving a 5-minute presentation on copyright and media licensing, do not spend most of your time citing Senate propositions and House bills by number and date. Instead, give a broad overview with general terms and a handout with links and citations for more information to make your point more effectively.

- *Too little information.* Be aware of your audience's level of expertise and present enough information to challenge the average member. If you do not have enough information, you risk boring or insulting your audience. It is unlikely that you will complete the requirements of the assignment if you have too little information. But be careful not to confuse clarity and precision with having too little information. Seek a balance between "overload" and "skimming the surface."

  DEFINE NEW TERMS: Take time when introducing each new term in context. Again, handouts are useful, as are projected presentations (PowerPoint, overheads, etc.). If the terms are not new for your audience, move more quickly through the material.

  STAY FOCUSED: If your task is to compare and contrast the features of several blog service providers, spend only one paragraph in your paper, and one slide in your software or overhead presentation, defining a blog as a "web log" or online journal. Make the majority of the paper or presentation about the various service providers, not the uses of blogs, especially in a course about online communication.

- *Information is too factual or too inferential.* Ideal speakers are neither fact-spewing computers nor rambling philosophers. Rather, they know how to extend their listeners' knowledge by blending hard data and intelligent speculation. Most audiences want enough facts to support your inferences and enough inferences to answer the question "So what?" about the facts.

  MAKE FACTS EASY TO DIGEST: Consider placing numerical or statistical facts in a chart or graph. Audiences respond better to visualized information, especially when confronted with many numbers and figures.

  USE SOUND LOGIC: Do not fall into the trap of logical fallacies. Does your data really support what you are saying, or is it just conveniently similar to your own opinion? (For more about providing logical evidence, see Chapter 4.)

- *Information is too concrete or too abstract.* Curious, searching audiences demand that speakers satisfy their needs for both concrete and abstract information. If you carefully mix and match concrete and abstract material, you should be able to satisfy both of these audience demands.

  INTERPRET FACTS: Facts and figures are concrete. If you recite only fact after fact, your audience will grow bored or, worse, confused. You need to provide some analysis and interpretation of the facts for your audience.

  SUPPORT OPINIONS: Ideas, analyses, and interpretations tend to be abstract. If you offer only ideas and opinions, but have no concrete evidence to support your claims, an audience may find you untrustworthy or doubt your conclusions.

- *Information is too general or too specific.* By carefully and consciously moving from the general to the specific and back again, the speaker can introduce variety and improve the audience's chances of seeing both the forest and the trees.

  EXAMPLE: An article about assessing the reliability of an online encyclopedia offers a *general* statement that the task of checking facts and accuracy in an encyclopedia is too huge to do exhaustively or consistently. Not every article can be double and triple checked, so statistical and representative tests are used to verify reliability. The article then goes on to provide a *specific* example, noting that biographical information about Revolutionary War figure Alexander Hamilton offers a useful representative test due to conflicting information about his date of birth.[3]

[3] Robert McHenry, "The Faith-Based Encyclopedia," *Tech Central Station* 15 Nov. 2004, 3 May 2005 <http://www.techcentralstation.com/111504A.html>.

Barriers That Involve Audience and Delivery

Four additional barriers to communication involve the circumstances of the presentation and the speaker's style in organizing and delivering the presentation.

- *Audience provides too much or too little feedback.* Because a presentation is primarily a one-way transmission of information, the speaker must find ways to assess whether the audience understands the content of the presentation. You can use a variety of techniques to obtain feedback from your audience—for example, you can watch the reactions of one or two representative members of an audience, or you can pause periodically to invite the audience to ask questions. Of course, if you focus too much on one or two members of an audience, you may lose the focus of your message. On the other hand, too much feedback or too many questions from the audience can disrupt the flow of your presentation or take up valuable time that you need to present your message. You need to balance getting feedback from the audience while keeping your presentation on course.
- *Information is presented too rapidly or too slowly.* Research suggests that "normal conversational delivery" is the best pace for covering material clearly and efficiently. If you talk too quickly or too slowly or do not allow enough time for the audience to absorb your major points, the audience will not be able to understand and retain as much information. Keep in mind that someone reading your paper can backtrack and reread complex points; someone listening to your presentation cannot.
- *Information is presented too soon or too late.* Fortunately, with careful preparation and the knowledge of a few elementary principles of organization, the "too soon/too late" problem is easily solved. For example, by remembering that listeners find it easier to move from the simple to the complex, from the concrete to the abstract, and from the immediate to the anticipated, you can often avoid moving into material too quickly.

Similarly, by knowing that listeners have a need for pattern, chronology, and completeness, you are reminded that information must be "packaged" and organized for an audience to be able to absorb and retain it. (For more about organizing your presentation, see Chapter 5.)

- *Information is presented with too much or too little intensity.* If you get overly involved in the material you are presenting, the audience may feel you are more concerned about preaching or performing than you are about sharing information. On the other hand, if you merely go through the motions without conveying any interest in your topic, the audience will probably share your lack of enthusiasm.

By analyzing your audience and determining their attitudes and expectations, you will be better prepared to overcome potential communication barriers when you deliver your presentation. In the next chapter, you will learn more about choosing the information and evidence that will be most useful and convincing to your specific audience.

Adapting Your Ideas and Evidence 4

In your composition class, written assignments come with specific requirements, one of which may be to present your paper's information orally. Although writing and speaking are related and interdependent, your work is not finished when your paper is written. You may not have time to orally present all of the details in your paper. You need to identify the main ideas that will best help you accomplish the purpose of your presentation and the key evidence that will lead the audience members to accept what you tell them. Remember that you are *presenting* your ideas and scholarship, not *reading* the paper in its entirety.

If you have already written the paper, use the topic sentences of your paragraphs to help you identify main ideas to cover in your presentation. (If you did not create an outline before writing your paper, it's a good idea to do so now.) If you have more than three to five main points to cover in your presentation, consider ways to combine or synthesize the ones that are similar. You also need to decide which pieces of evidence from your paper will be most convincing to your audience of listeners.

Listening and Learning

Your oral presentation probably will present information to your audience that they do not know or that they have only a passing familiarity with. You want them to listen to you and internalize the information you provide. In other words, you want them to learn. You should keep in mind that your presentation is facilitating the audience as they learn new information. The following points may help you relate more effectively to your audience.

- *Individuals have different motivations for learning.* Although "What's in it for me?" and "There might be something of value that I can use" may reflect the bottom-line motivation of audience members, each person has a different motivator. Thus, it is important to build your message on audience analysis.
- *Learning is an individual activity.* The accumulation of knowledge, skills, and attitudes is an experience that occurs within and is activated by the learner. Although you can set the stage and do much to orchestrate a climate conducive to learning, learning is still an internal process.
- *Audience members have prior experiences.* The more you incorporate an audience's life experiences into the construction of a message, the more the audience will retain and use the information provided.
- *Learning results from stimulation to the senses.* An audience member learns better when you appeal to multiple senses. Learners learn best by doing. As Confucius stated it: "I hear and I forget; I see and I remember; I do and I understand."

Choosing Forms of Support

Within a learning framework, then, what specific verbal and nonverbal forms of support can you use to make it easier for the audience to retain and accept your message? Consider the following five forms of support: explanation, examples, statistics, testimony, and visual aids.

Explanation

Explanation is the act or process of making something plain or comprehensible. Providing a definition is one mode of explanation. This alternative can take a variety of forms.

- *Providing a dictionary definition.* Defining typically involves placing the item to be defined in a category and then explaining the features that distinguish the item from all other members of the category—for example, "*Primary* is a word that means 'first in time, order, or importance.'"

- *Using synonyms and/or antonyms.* Synonyms are words with approximately the same meaning—for example, "*Mawkish* as an adjective indicates that someone or something is sentimental, maudlin, or gushy." Antonyms are words that have opposite meanings.
- *Using comparisons and contrasts.* Comparisons show listeners the similarities between something unfamiliar and something familiar. Contrasts emphasize the differences between two things.
- *Defining by etymology (word origin) and history.* For example, "*Pedagogy*, a term used to describe the art and science of teaching children, is derived from the Greek words *paid* meaning 'child,' and *agogus*, meaning 'leader of.'"
- *Providing an operational definition.* An operational definition defines a process by describing the steps involved in that process—for example, "To create calligraphy, you begin with a wide-nibbed pen . . ."

To be effective, explanations must be framed within the experiences of the audience and should not be too long or abstract. You may have explanations in your paper that work well for your presentation as they are. For those that don't, adapt them for listeners—for example, turn a written operational definition into a live demonstration that shows the process to your audience.

Examples

Examples serve as illustrations, models, or instances of what is being explained. An example can be either developed in detail (an illustration) or presented in abbreviated, undeveloped fashion (a specific instance). An illustration—an extended example presented in narrative form—can be either hypothetical (a story that could but did not happen) or factual (a story that did happen). For example, a presenter might involve the listeners in a hypothetical illustration by suggesting, "Imagine yourself getting ready to give an oral presentation. You reach into your bag for the manuscript that you carefully prepared over the course of the past week. It isn't there! You madly search through everything in the bag." Whether hypothetical or factual, an illustration should be relevant and appropriate to the audience, typical rather than exceptional, and vivid and impressive in detail.

A specific instance is an undeveloped or condensed example. It requires listeners to recognize the names, events, or situations in the instance. A presenter, for example, who uses "President Dewey" as a specific instance of the dangers of poor sampling techniques when engaged in public opinion polling must know in advance that the audience will understand that Thomas Dewey was Harry Truman's Republican opponent who was mistakenly announced as the winner in the 1948 presidential election. Otherwise, this example will not make the point clear and vivid and, in fact, probably will confuse or distract the audience.

You may have specific instances in your paper that you can develop further into illustrations so that your audience can get involved and relate to what you are saying. Likewise, you may have illustrations in your paper that you want to mention but not take time to develop in full detail. You could reduce some of those illustrations to specific instances.

Statistics

Statistics describe the end result of collecting, organizing, and interpreting numerical data. They are often presented in graph or table form. Statistics are especially useful when reducing large masses of information to more specific categories, as in the following example accompanied by a bar graph.

- Adults who start smoking in their early teens are less likely to quit by age 30 than those who start later. Of those who start after the age of 16, 13.6 percent quit by age 30. But only 9.6

percent of those who start at the ages of 14–15 and 4.4 percent of those who start before age 14 quit by age 30.

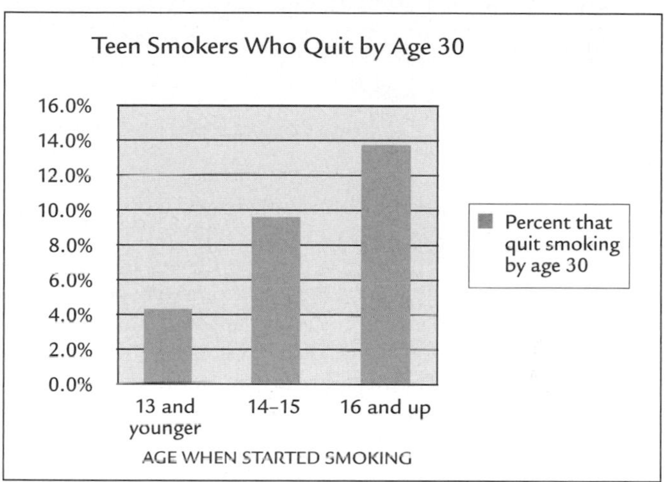

Statistics are also useful for emphasizing the largeness or smallness of something, as in the following example.

- Adults spend an average of 16 times as many hours selecting clothes—145.6 hours a year—as on planning for retirement—9.1 hours a year.

And finally, statistics can describe indications of trends—where we've been and where we're going. The following example describes a trend and summarizes the information in a table.

- According to a 1996 survey of 800 newspapers and magazines, 25 percent distributed at least part of their publications electronically. Another 31 percent intended to do so within 2 years; 19 percent intended to do so within 5 years; and 23 percent had no plans to do so.

ELECTRONIC DISTRIBUTION OF NEWSPAPERS AND MAGAZINES IN 1996	
Already doing it (at least partially)	25%
Within 2 years	31%
Within 5 years	19%
No plans	23%

When using statistics, you should be aware of two basic concerns:

1. Are the statistics accurate and unbiased?
2. Are the statistics clear and meaningful?

To address the first issue, you need to answer such questions as these: Are the statistical techniques appropriate, and are they appropriately used? Do the statistics cover enough cases and a sufficient length of time? Although you may not have the expertise to answer such questions, you can ask about the credibility of the source of the statistics. Do you have any reason to believe that the person or group from whom you got the statistics might be biased? Are these statistics consistent with other things you know about the situation?

Addressing the second issue involves more pragmatic considerations: Can you translate difficult-to-comprehend numbers into more immediately understandable terms? How in the smoking example, for instance, might you make the difference between 4.4 percent and 13.6 percent more vivid? How can you provide an adequate context for the data? Is it useful in the electronic publishing example, for instance, to put together both newspapers and magazines when exploring use of electronic publication? Is the comparison between planning for retirement and selecting clothing a fair one? Would a graph or visual aid clarify the data and statistical trends? As we will see in Chapter 7, supplementing a verbal presentation with visual aids can greatly increase the audience's comprehension and retention.

If conducted with rigor and proper scientific methodology, statistical research offers useful analysis of trends and potential outcomes. Be certain, though, that you properly cite the source of your statistics and do not rely on "they say" or "experts report." Also, be sure to give the context and scope of the study you cite. One danger of using statistics is the tendency to oversimplify the complexity of the critical question asked in the research study and to downplay the limiting factors that impact the outcomes. For example, a research study may find a statistical link between members of a specific cultural background and left-handedness, but if the study was limited to a test group of art school students, you should be sure to mention that the test group was in art school. You should not assume that the study's findings apply to members of the same cultural group who are interested in engineering or mathematics.

Testimony

Testimony involves using a credible person's statement to lend weight and authority to aspects of your presentation. For this to happen, the person being cited must be qualified; that is, the testimony must come from a person who is an expert on this topic and free of bias and self-interest. Just as important as actual credentials is the perception the audience has of the source of the testimony. Is the individual known to the audience? If not, you will need to tell the audience why the individual is a good authority. If known, is the person accepted by the audience as both knowledgeable and unbiased on the topic? In short, to lend support to a message, the testimony of a source must both be actually credible and be perceived as credible.

For example, recent articles on technology Web sites have debated the value of the online reference site Wikipedia.org. One such article, "The Faith-Based Encyclopedia," critiques not only the reliability of the data in Wikipedia entries, but also the entire notion of accountability within a free online reference written and edited completely by unpaid volunteers. Though the author of the article, Robert McHenry, is an expert on encyclopedias, his bias against the Wikipedia may perhaps be explained (or complicated) by his former position as editor-in-chief of the print edition of *Encyclopaedia Britannica*. Another related article, "Why Wikipedia Must Jettison Its Anti-Elitism," which appeared on the news Web site Kuro5hin.org, appears to be more even-handed in its critique of the Wikipedia; however, the article was written by L. Sanger, one of the founders of the Wikipedia, whose disagreements over how to run the Wikipedia "forked" the project in a new direction into another project called Nupedia. Though Sanger is a reliable source of information about Wikipedia due to his early involvement, his personal reasons for leaving may color and tarnish his objectivity about the subject. Appropriately objective information is found in a third article by technology writer Edward W. Felten, who has no ties to either Britannica or Wikipedia. Together, the three articles offer a number of informed perspectives, but Felten's piece is in many ways more compelling, even though he has no experience in reference writing or editing, either online or in print.

Visual Aids

Visual aids are primarily used to enhance the clarity and credibility of your message. They can also help you control your own nervousness by providing a safety net in an uncertain situation, reminding you of the structure of your presentation and the important points you want to make. Obtaining these advantages requires skill in selecting appropriate aids and using them well. (For more on visual aids, see Chapter 7.)

Choosing Forms of Proof

What motivates the audience to accept your claim about a fact, value, problem, or policy? Since the time of the ancient Greek philosopher Aristotle, forms of proof have been organized into three categories. Aristotle called them *pathos* (motivational proof based on the drives, values, or aspirations of the audience), *ethos* (ethical proof based on the credibility of the source of the message), and *logos* (logical proof based on evidence, such as statistics and examples).

Motivational Proof or Pathos

At the heart of persuasion is the ability to adapt a message to the feelings, needs, and values of an audience. People want and need to interact with others and belong to social groups. They need to feel worthy and to be recognized for their merits. Most, if they have their most basic needs met, develop a desire to grow and achieve their full potential. As you speak, make clear the ways in which your message answers or addresses these needs for the audience. Pathos often involves relating to the audience on a visceral, emotional level. Empathy, which means identifying with and understanding another person's feelings, motivations, or circumstances, shares the same root as *pathos*. If you recognize and anticipate the ways your words will resonate with your audience, you can tie your argument to the emotions you evoke.

In his famous speech, President John F. Kennedy urged Americans to "[a]sk not what your country can do for you. Ask what you can do for your country." By appealing to the traditional work ethic in the American tradition, President Kennedy tapped into an emotional wellspring within the hearts and minds of the public. By using the feelings of responsibility, duty, and even a hint of shame in his stern command that Americans not ask but instead give, Kennedy tied his message to deep, personal feelings in his audience.

Ethical Proof or Ethos

The persuasiveness of a message is commonly assumed to be influenced by the person who delivers it. For example, in social conversations, you may drop the names of respectable sources even as you pass along rumors and gossip. Source credibility—an audience's perception of the speaker separate from the speaker's intent or purpose—is an important factor in whether listeners accept the message. The ethos of a speaker takes into consideration both public reputation and personal standards of conduct. The external evidence of a person's ethical and consistent behavior is one part of ethos. Another is the person's actual behavior, no matter who is watching or what the perceptions of others are. Audiences are confident in a speaker who is known for her deeds, actions, accomplishments, and positions—the letter of the law and evidence of compliance. Speakers gain confidence in themselves by relying on their own morals, responsibilities, and values—the spirit of the law and thoughtful compliance no matter what the repercussions.

Logical Proof or Logos

Logos is one root of any word ending in *-logy*. In Greek, it means "word," but it has come to mean "science," "study," or "theory." *Logical* also comes from *logos*. Appeals to logos involve logical, scientific evidence. We described five verbal and nonverbal devices that you can use to help an audience understand and accept your message: explanations, examples, statistics, testimony, and visual aids. Three of these devices (examples, statistics, and testimony) are especially useful as evidence—that is, information used as logical proof by a speaker. Evidence increases the persuasiveness of a message.[1] As you might expect, highly credible evidence sources are more persuasive than less credible ones. High-quality evidence is especially effective if the audience is unfamiliar with the subject and if the evidence is from multiple sources. Outdated evidence and evidence already familiar to the audience are not as highly persuasive.

To be persuasive, you should use multiple types of evidence. Although research does not suggest that one form of evidence is superior to the others, there is some indication that examples may have greater impact than statistical evidence, perhaps because they create vivid images in the minds of receivers.

Not all sources of information are of equal value, but how can you decide which are more credible than others? In order to evaluate sources, whether you are presenting or listening to a persuasive

[1]John C. Reinard, "The Empirical Study of the Persuasive Effects of Evidence: The Status After Fifty Years of Research," *Human Communication Research* 15 (1988): 3–59.

message, consider the following criteria: Is the source reliable? Recent? Complete? Accurate?[2]

The reliability test holds that sources should be objective and competent. Be skeptical of sources who might have something to gain from promoting a particular point of view. Sources should be in a position to know about the subject at hand, and they should be competent to judge or comment on the specific issue, item, or idea. Strive for the most up-to-date information possible. To meet the completeness criterion, evidence should be based on as many sources as possible. Having multiple sources lets you test the evidence for accuracy. Accurate information is redundant and verifiable. In other words, a variety of sources should present similar information. You should be skeptical of the aberrant figure or idea.

As you choose which ideas and forms of support to include in your presentation, keep in mind that combining different forms of support and forms of proof is often effective. For example, presenting only statistics can result in a dry presentation; presenting only emotional testimony from individuals with no logical evidence can result in an unconvincing presentation. Include in your presentation the same variety of forms of support and proof as in your paper. Balance in both will produce the most persuasive argument possible.

[2] Patricia Bradley Andrews, *Basic Public Speaking* (New York: Harper & Row, 1985).

5 Organizing Your Presentation

Once you have your statement of purpose, your thesis, and your supporting details, you need to reorganize the ideas in your paper so they are most effective when you make your presentation. When an audience reads a paper, they have the advantages of written text: They can move at their own speed, reread confusing or complicated passages, and look up new vocabulary. In an oral presentation, the audience has few of these options. As a speaker, you have several advantages, however. You can accentuate certain points by altering your tone, volume, or speed, and by gesturing, making eye contact, and using body language. The key task is determining how to translate what you wrote in your paper into a clear, coherent, and effective oral presentation. An outline visually displays the main points and subpoints of your presentation (as well as the support for those points) in a way that helps you develop the presentation.

Creating an Outline

A good strategy for beginning to organize your oral presentation is to turn your paper into a complete sentence outline. Once you have developed such an outline, you may find it useful to reduce it to a topic outline or speaker's outline, which uses brief phrases and keywords in place of sentences. Often presentations do not allow enough time to cover every detail found in the paper. As you outline and organize your presentation, hit all the main points and use examples only sparingly if time is an issue. You may want to include more examples and details in a handout, but speak about only two or three during the presentation.

An outline generally includes several main points (I, II, III, etc.) and at least two subpoints (A, B, etc.) that develop each of the main points. Further subpoints are included for supporting material such as examples, testimony, statistics, and illustrations. In this way, an outline alternates numbers and letters in clearly identifiable columns and can accommodate as many levels of headings as you need. The following example shows a portion of an outline for a presentation on the merits of a popular online encyclopedia:

I. Are free online resources like Wikipedia equal to traditional purchased, print encyclopedias?
    A. What is Wikipedia?
        1. definition of *wiki*
        2. mission statement of Wikipedia.org
    B. What value does online encyclopedia offer?
        1. easy access
        2. current information
        3. multiple volunteer authors
    C. What potential problems?
        1. volunteer status of authors
        2. instability/constant changes
        3. ease of access for uneducated writers and users
            a. writing not of consistent quality
            b. readers not analytical enough
            c. might not be problem, but advantage

II. Wikipedia's reliability . . .

Although the type of labeling used in the above outline is the most common, another popular style is legal-style or decimal-number labeling. The next portion of the sample outline is shown in this style:

2. Wikipedia's reliability
    2.1. Edward W. Felten Sept. 2004 "spot check" of Wikipedia[1]
        2.1.1. checked entries on 6 topics he was well-versed in
        2.1.2. on advice of colleague, checked Britannica online entries same items
    2.2. Sanger, Wikipedia co-founder, on Kuro5hin[2]
        2.2.1. first problem is not how reliable but public's perception of reliability
        2.2.2. acknowledges Wikipedia not reliable for specialized topics, and better sources exist
            2.2.2.1. *Stanford Encyclopedia of Philosophy*
            2.2.2.2. *Internet Encyclopedia of Philosophy*
    2.3. Robert McHenry, former editor-in-chief of *Encyclopaedia Britannica*[3]
        2.3.1. explains fact checking in encyclopedias is similar to Felten's approach
        2.3.2. statistical and representative tests are used . . .

Headings at a particular level of an outline should be of equal importance and written using parallel structure. In the first example, the main points, indicated by roman numerals, are the main divisions of the presentation and are of equal importance. The subpoints

[1] Edward W. Felten, "Wikipedia vs. Britannica Smackdown," *Freedom to Tinker* 7 Sept. 2004, 3 May 2005 <http://www.freedom-to-tinker.com/archives/000675.html>.

[2] L. Sanger, "Why Wikipedia Must Jettison Its Anti-Elitism," *Kuro5hin: Technology and Culture, from the Trenches,* 31 Dec. 2004, 3 May 2005 <http://www.kuro5hin.org/story/2004/12/30/142458/25>.

[3] Robert McHenry, "The Faith-Based Encyclopedia," *Tech Central Station,* 15 Nov. 2004, 3 May 2005 <http://www.techcentralstation.com/111504A.html>.

(A, B, and C) also designate equally important divisions of the main point to which they refer. The outline has two or more elements at any level; that is, there are two or more main points, two or more subpoints under any main point, and two or more levels of support. This is normally the case because a topic is not "divided" unless it has at least two parts. If you wish to make only one subpoint, do not show it on the outline as a subpoint but include it as part of the main point.

Choosing an Organizational Pattern

When adapting a paper for an oral presentation, you may need to rearrange the organization of information. What represents a logical progression of ideas in a paper may leave your listeners confused since, unlike readers, they cannot reread passages or look back to important points that preceded. For a presentation, it is often better to provide an overview at the outset, clearly stating which points you intend to cover. Doing so gives your audience a frame of reference that helps them follow and understand your points as you speak. It is sometimes best to cover the most important points first, both because the audience is still fresh and because you have limited time. Alternatively, if you're covering only a few points, you might want to build up to the most important idea so that it remains fresh in the audience's minds after you finish speaking. During your presentation your audience will also rely on you to occasionally summarize or remind them of what you've already covered. The structure of your paper offers a good starting point for organizing your ideas and indeed may be the best structure for your presentation as well. But don't be afraid to experiment with a different pattern of organization for your presentation.

Although you can organize ideas in many ways, the following six organizational patterns are common: chronological, topical, spatial or geographical, cause-effect, problem-solution, and compare and contrast. You will likely already have used at least one of these organizational patterns in your paper.

Chronological Pattern

When using the chronological pattern, you organize your main points in a time-related sequence: that is, forward (or backward) in a systematic fashion. You might, for example, focus on the past, present, and future of digital recording technology. When describing a process step by step, you are also using a chronological pattern. The following terms make good transitions in a chronological pattern:

first . . .	next . . .	afterwards . . .
to begin . . .	before you continue . . .	eventually . . .
at the outset . . .	when that is completed . . .	finally . . .

Topical Pattern

Also known as a categorical pattern, the topical pattern organizes the main points as parallel elements of the topic itself. Perhaps the most common way of organizing a presentation, the topical pattern is useful when describing components of persons, places, things, or processes. A secondary concern when selecting this approach is the sequencing of topics. Depending on the circumstances, this is often best handled in ascending or descending order—that is, according to the relative importance, familiarity, or complexity of the topics. The example that follows begins with a specific question about a particular online resource and progresses to more complex questions about the reliability of online resources in general.

I. Are free online resources like Wikipedia equal to traditional purchased, print encyclopedias?

II. Wikipedia's reliability is a question of both real and perceived accuracy.

III. Can some solution be achieved, or are critics just complaining without offering to help?

IV. Is the question of reliability in online resources really a problem? Why?

Spatial or Geographical Pattern

The spatial or geographical pattern arranges main points in terms of their physical proximity to or direction from each other (north to south, east to west, bottom to top, left to right, near to far, outside to inside, and so on). It is most useful when explaining objects, places, or scenes in terms of their component parts.

Cause-Effect Pattern

With the cause-effect pattern, you attempt to organize the message around cause-to-effect or effect-to-cause relationships. That is, you might move from a discussion of the origins or causes of a phenomenon, say increases in the cost of fuel, to the eventual results or effects, such as increases in the cost of airplane tickets. Or, you could move from a description of present conditions (effects) to an identification and description of apparent causes. The choice of strategy is often based on which element—cause or effect—is more familiar to the intended audience. The cause-effect pattern of organization is especially useful when your purpose is to achieve understanding or agreement, rather than action, from the recipients of a message.

Problem-Solution Pattern

The problem-solution pattern involves dramatizing an obstacle and then narrowing alternative remedies to the one that you recommend. Thus, the main points of a message are organized to show that (1) there is a problem that requires a change in attitude, belief, or behavior; (2) a number of possible solutions might solve this problem; and (3) your solution is the one that will most effectively and efficiently provide a remedy. Topics that lend themselves to this organizational pattern include a wide range of business, social, economic, and political problems for which you can propose a workable solution. The problem-solution pattern of organization is especially useful when the purpose of a message is to generate audience action.

Compare and Contrast Pattern

One of the most common assignments (and most commonly misunderstood assignments) is a comparison paper or compare and contrast paper. Comparing is the act of identifying similarities, the characteristics shared by two or more distinct items or topics. Contrasting is identifying differences, the characteristics not shared by those items or topics. If your instructor assigns this type of presentation, be sure you understand whether you are supposed to compare only, contrast only, or both. Ask questions if you are unsure.

Patterns of Organization

Chronological organization

I want my audience to know that building a new student center on campus is a complex process.

- Gain approval of board of trustees
- Garner community support
- Raise additional funds
- Work with architects, engineers, consultants, and contractors
- Anticipate and solve problems caused by construction

Topical organization

I want my audience to know that there are three major issues for the college to consider before deciding whether to build a new student center.

- The cost of the project
- The short-term problems associated with the project
- The potential long-term benefits of the project

Spatial organization

I want my audience to know that the proposed student center will have four main areas.

- Café
- Game room
- Computer lab
- Club offices

Cause-effect organization

I want my audience to know that campuses with good student centers have a better sense of community among the student body.

- *Cause:* Good student center
- *Effect:* Greater sense of community

Problem-solution organization I want my audience to know that a problem associated with building a new student center is lack of funds for the project, and that the problem can be solved by using more effective fundraising techniques. • *Problem:* Lack of funds • *Solution:* Better fundraising techniques • *Advantage:* Increased income for the project
Comparison organization I want my audience to know that the new student center and the existing athletic center will be similar in three ways. • Open to all students • Appeals to incoming applicants • Provides work-study job opportunities for students
Contrast organization I want my audience to know that the new student center and the existing athletic center will be different in two ways. • *Student center:* Open to students only; no classes meet there • *Athletic center:* Open for paid public use during certain hours; some required courses meet there

Writers and speakers rarely use only one structure in the course of a paper or oral presentation. Effective speakers tend to use more complex combinations of several patterns to develop each main point of an oral presentation, as illustrated in the following partial outline.

> There are three major issues for the college to consider before deciding whether to build a new student center on campus:
>
> I. The cost-effectiveness of the project — TOPICAL
>
> A. Not enough money in the current budget to fund the project
>
> B. Enough funds can be attained through better fundraising techniques — [A–B: PROBLEM-SOLUTION]
>
> 1. Special campaign to target recent alumni
>
> 2. Joint fundraising efforts with clubs and other student organizations on campus — [1–2: TOPICAL]

II. The short-term problems associated with the project	TOPICAL
A. An unsightly construction site	CAUSE-EFFECT
B. Detours and traffic flow problems along the main campus road	
C. Potential security risks	
III. The potential long-term benefits of the project . . .	TOPICAL

Once you have determined the overall pattern of organization for your presentation, examine each main point in your outline. On the basis of each point, choose appropriate subpatterns for developing your ideas. If ideas fall naturally into a particular pattern of organization, do not force them into some other pattern; develop whatever combination of patterns works best for your ideas and achieves your purpose.

6 Developing Effective Introductions, Transitions, and Conclusions

Composing a paper (at least a good paper!), is a process, one in which you discover new ideas, and new ways to organize your ideas, as you write. After writing a first draft, for example, you may find that your thesis statement isn't as clear or as narrowly focused as you intended. Or perhaps you decide that your thesis statement needs stronger supporting points. You may find too that your conclusion needs to be summarized or restated. Writers who compose strong and persuasive papers regularly use all of these strategies.

Another part of the composing process involves choosing words and transitions. All the information in your paper needs connective words and phrases that link your points together into one cohesive and coherent argument. Rethinking their word choices during writing of second drafts is common among strong writers.

All of the composition principles true for writing papers are also true for making oral presentations. You need to write an introduction and a conclusion, and tie the sections of your presentation together with transitions.

The Introduction

When you give an oral presentation outside of class, the setting or the person introducing you may have already provided an overview of your message. Your audience may be so fired up about the topic that motivating them to listen to you is not necessary. Maybe your credibility as a speaker on the topic is so high that it does not require additional development. For most of your presentations in class, however, this is not the case. To compensate, you need to provide an overview of your message, motivate your audience to pay attention, and establish your credibility as a speaker on the topic.

Your introduction often is the most important part of the presentation. You must be clear, concise, and efficient when beginning your presentation in order to keep your audience's attention and prepare them for your message. Writing your introduction last, after you have written the rest of your paper or presentation, is often a good strategy because doing so gives you the opportunity to prepare your audience for all the main points you will cover. Keep in mind that your audience cannot refer back to your introduction in the same way they can when reading a paper. Refer back to your main points at strategic times throughout your presentation.

When you get up to speak, your audience probably has questions: What will this presentation be like? Will I like and trust this speaker? What will I get out of listening to this presentation? A good introduction answers these and other important questions. Dedicate about 5 to 10 percent of your speaking time to answering questions like these about your intent, the audience's relationship to both you and to the material, and the importance of this presentation to their lives or ways of thinking.

Although there is no guaranteed approach to making your intentions clear, consider explicitly stating the topic, thesis, title, or purpose. Previewing the structure of the message ("The three points I will develop are . . .") may be another useful plan. You may also want to explain why you narrowed the topic down from something more complex or involved.

A good way to motivate your audience to listen is to link your topic and thesis to their lives. Showing how the topic has, does, or will affect the audience's past, present, or future will help gain their interest and investment. You may also succeed in gaining the interest of your audience by demonstrating how the topic is linked to a basic need or goal, of either people in general or this audience specifically. Make the audience feel important through your introduction; show the audience how important they are in your details and supporting information.

Of course, you need to motivate your audience and build your credibility throughout your presentation, not only in your introduction. Many of the ways to build credibility are similar to those you use in writing a paper; however, when you are speaking in front of an audience, you are also communicating your credibility and trustworthiness through your body language and your ability to connect with the audience. Strategies for building credibility include the following.

- Cite highly credible individuals and reliable sources.
    - "Robert McHenry, former editor-in-chief of *Encyclopaedia Britannica,* has written . . ."
    - "In a speech from his hospital bed, Ambassador Morris B. Abram, a lawyer, educator, civil rights activist, and diplomat, has said that 'the question of treatment . . . should be based not on the length of time from birth but on the length of time from death.' "[1]
- Place your topic in historical context.
    - "Since the advent of digital music technology, especially the CD in the 1980s and the mp3 in the 1990s, . . ."
    - "Before the advent of the World Wide Web, this discussion would not have made sense. In fact, even as recently as 2000, the topic of a publicly edited free encyclopedia would have sounded more like a dream than reality to most people."
- Describe your personal acquaintance with the topic.
    - "I was an early adopter of Napster, and after legal problems changed their business model, I switched to Morpheus and KaZaa."

[1] Morris B. Abram, "Some Views on Ethics and Later Life," *Controversies in Ethics in Long-Term Care,* ed. Ellen Olson, Eileen R. Chichin, and Leslie S. Libow (New York: Springer, 1995) 146.

- "My parents both have living wills, and I, myself, am an organ donor, as you can see by this symbol on my driver's license."

- Entertain alternative points of view to show that you are speaking from a balanced perspective.
- Be sure your body language supports what you claim to think and feel about your topic.
- Be gracious and polite with your audience, even if they seem hostile to your message.
- Use relevant humor, if appropriate, to demonstrate that both you and your listeners laugh at the same things.

The introduction to your presentation need not accomplish all of these goals. However, many opening strategies can function in multiple ways, allowing you to state your topic, establish a connection with the audience, and begin to demonstrate your credibility. For example, a story or an analogy can do all three of those things—"The reason I am so impassioned about end-of-life care is readily summed up in this story about my grandmother. . . ." Humor can both emphasize your motivation for making the presentation and help develop a better relationship between you and the audience. The best advice is to make your introduction as brief as possible while fulfilling the audience's expectations concerning what you want to do, how you relate to them, and why you feel the way you do about the topic.

Language Choices

When you begin to think through how best to convey the main ideas of a message, it is imperative that you examine your word and language choices; the best choices make your message relevant, clear, and unbiased for audience members. Here are some guidelines that can help you achieve this goal for your oral presentation.

- *Public language should be personal.* Don't borrow someone else's vocabulary. Use language that you can use easily. Never use a word in an oral presentation that you haven't said out loud previously. Practice pronouncing a new word until you make it yours.

- *Public language should be fitting.* Listen carefully to the language patterns of your listeners before you speak to them. Adjust the formality of your language to fit the situation. Resist the temptation to use a pet phrase just because you like it. Don't be flip with a serious topic or melodramatic with a light one.
  - APPROPRIATE WORD CHOICE FOR A RESIDENCE HALL FLOOR MEETING: "So we have to stop leaving a mess in the bathroom, know what I'm saying? You can't be leaving surprises for the janitors, you feel me?"
  - MORE APPROPRIATE LANGUAGE FOR A CLASS PRESENTATION: "The defacement of public property on campus is the responsibility of the entire campus community, as I am sure you will agree."
- *Public language should be strategic.* If you're dealing with touchy topics or hostile listeners, try out several different ways of phrasing a volatile idea in order to achieve the right tone. Don't depend on the inspiration of the moment to guide your language choice. Think in advance about what you're going to say and how you're going to say it. Compare the tone of the following three examples.
  - "The ROTC needs to get off campus now."
  - "The college needs to expel the recruiters immediately."
  - "While the military offers a number of benefits to recruits as far as job placement and tuition support, perhaps the time has come for the administration of this university to examine its policies regarding on-campus recruiting."
- *Public language should be oral.* Except in certain rare circumstances, do not read your presentation; instead, make your presentation in an expository fashion. An oral presentation is meant for the ear, not the eye. Listen to the words and

phrases you intend to use. Put "catch phrases" in your outline rather than long, elaborate sentences. Use your voice and body to signal irony and rhetorical questions and to emphasize important points. And practice reading your presentation at least several times, ideally with a friend or family member as a test audience.

- *Public language should be precise.* If you're talking about bulldozers, don't call them *earth-moving vehicles.* As in a paper, avoid unnecessary jargon and define all technical terms for your listeners. Try to avoid vague generalities; instead, use concrete and specific language when providing descriptions.
- *Public language should be simple.* Readers have an easier time understanding complicated sentences than listeners do. When speaking, use simple sentences as often as possible, and use five-syllable words sparingly.
- *Public language should be unaffected.* Don't seek to have your listeners remember your language. Don't get carried away with metaphors; a single simple image is always superior to several complex ones. Don't invent "cute" phrases. Euphemistic language often sounds ludicrous or evasive (for example, referring to firing employees as *downsizing*).[2]

Transitions

Transitions guide an audience through your presentation. They are signs that tell the audience where you are, where you are going, and where you have been. Thus, they need to be overt, clear, and frequent. You might, for example, preview the structure of the message toward the end of the introduction ("Today, I will talk about five behaviors that characterize effective leaders. They are . . ."). Overt tactics like this ground your message for the audience and maintain the context of the information.

[2] Robert P. Hart, Gustav W. Friedrich, Barry Brummet, *Public Communication,* 2nd ed. (New York: Harper & Row, 1983) 170–171.

Informative presentations benefit from direct and overt descriptions and lists. Persuasive arguments may also benefit from such directness, but more subtle transitions are often more useful and reveal a greater degree of sophistication. Sometimes it is enough to put the elements of your presentation in the proper order and then allow your audience to arrive at the same conclusions without you telling them what comes next. Be sure, though, that you move from point to point in a logical fashion, and that you occasionally remind your audience of the thesis, topic, or main idea.

As the presentation proceeds, you can use internal previews and summaries to review a main point and anticipate the next one ("Having described why leaders need to challenge the process, let's turn now to the need to inspire a shared vision"). Sequential terms like *First . . .*, *Next . . .*, *And finally . . .* help tie points together. Too-frequent use of these types of transitions, however, can make your presentation sound clinical or sterile, like a user manual or cookbook.

Occasional use of coordinating conjunctions (such as *and, but,* and *or*), correlative conjunctions (such as *either . . . or, not only . . . but also*) and similar grammatical constructions often alleviates the "step-by-step" feel. Use *further* or *furthermore* to enhance certain points and build on previous information. *Again* can accomplish a similar goal. A semicolon (in the written outline) followed by *however* can introduce another perspective and reveal the depth of your research and the degree of your objectivity. Be certain that you use these constructions correctly, and don't overuse the same one. Starting every sentence with "*However . . .*" or "*Though . . .*" quickly grows boring. Check your writing guide or handbook for advice on making smooth transitions in your paper; many of the same techniques work well in a presentation. Remember, however, that you need to summarize and even repeat points more frequently in speaking than in writing.

The Conclusion

A conclusion typically summarizes the main points of the presentation and reinforces the importance of the message by demonstrating its potential impact. An effective way to accomplish this is by using the conclusion to elaborate on an example, illustration, or quotation that was used in the introduction. The conclusion might include a final summary that revisits your transitions ("I've talked today about five behaviors that characterize effective leaders. Effective leaders . . .").

The introduction and conclusion of your presentation act as a frame or set of bookends for your message. As you write the conclusion, consider your introduction carefully. Has your presentation covered all the material you mention in your introduction? Is your thesis statement or main idea supported by the details in the presentation? If you have a rough outline but have not written the details of the presentation, try writing your conclusion first. The conclusion then becomes a target toward which you aim as you compose the presentation. You may want to write more than one conclusion. The one you decide *not* to use as a conclusion may be a good model for your introduction.

Using Visual Aids 7

Visual aids are useful tools for presentations both because they help sustain the audience's interest and because they deliver certain types of information in a more potent or easily understood way than speaking does alone. Charts, graphs, outlines, and even props for a demonstration are all types of visuals. They can be displayed by using slides, overhead transparencies, handouts, or other methods, such as drawing on a whiteboard or chalkboard. Using visual aids requires careful planning to decide what information is best suited for visual display. You may find yourself tempted to load your presentation with lots of visuals in an attempt to entertain or impress your audience, but too many visuals—or too much information on each visual—can be confusing. A visual aid should never distract but instead help your audience follow your presentation while keeping them focused on what you are saying. Above all else, do not spend more time developing your visual aids than you spend researching and writing your presentation.

Choosing Effective Visuals

A powerful tactic for persuading an audience or demonstrating a task is to show an example. Telling your audience about your topic but never actually showing them what you are describing limits their ability to grasp and internalize the situation or problem. For example, if you are discussing Impressionist painters and paintings, imagine the difference between describing several paintings and displaying those paintings on a screen or in color handouts. Or, suppose you are discussing how a particular writer's childhood experiences influenced his or her later work. You might show the audience a photograph of the writer's hometown to help them imagine the environment. Similarly, medical or scientific presentations benefit greatly from photographs or diagrams, particularly when different items are being compared. For example, for a presentation on different methods of fruit farming, you might use photographs or even bring in several types of apples or oranges to show differences in their growth based on the farming methods used.

Certain types of visuals are more effective than others for certain purposes. Photographs and drawings are especially useful for illustrating a description of an object, a person, or a place. For showing steps in a process, flowcharts, live demonstrations using props, or demonstrations on video are useful. Video clips that show events or provide quotes in a source's own voice reinforce your message both visually and aurally. Showing a written outline of your presentation helps the audience keep track of your main points and follow your line of argument.

Charts and graphs work especially well for displaying statistics, survey results, or other kinds of numerical information. Presenting complex data in visual form through a chart or graph helps your listeners more quickly process, retain, and compare the information. Keeping track of numbers is usually difficult for the audience, but a chart or graph offers them the chance to more clearly comprehend your data and its significance. If possible, use color or distinct markings in your graphs. Label the data clearly, using a key at the side of the chart or with clearly legible units and labels. (For examples of charts and graphs, see the section on statistics in Chapter 4.)

Always use caution and judgment regarding the appropriateness and practicality of your examples. Bringing a live animal to the classroom may be more effective than showing photographs, but it may not be safe or practical! Ask your instructor if you are uncertain about the examples you have chosen. In addition, be sure to cite your source for any visuals you use. If you create a visual such as a chart or graph yourself, cite your source for the information that the chart or graph displays.

Choosing a Mode of Delivery

Whatever type of visuals you choose, you have several options for displaying them to your audience. You can write or draw them on a chalkboard or whiteboard, print them on paper to hand out to the audience, display them onscreen using a projector, or use some combination of these methods. Each method has its own advantages and disadvantages, so you need to consider carefully your purpose, your audience's needs, the equipment available, and the physical setup of the room where you will be presenting.

Chalkboard or Whiteboard

One of the simplest ways to illustrate a point or to show your audience a basic graphic is to write or draw it on a chalkboard or whiteboard at the front of the room. Nearly every classroom has a chalkboard or whiteboard, and you won't need to waste time setting up any special equipment. For illustrating just a few points for a small audience, a chalkboard or whiteboard works well. However, if you are presenting in a large room or need to show extensive or complicated visual examples, a chalkboard or whiteboard is probably not your best choice.

Handouts

Handouts are useful for oral presentations for many reasons:

- A handout provides written information, such as an outline or quotes, to reinforce the content and organization of your message.
- A handout allows the audience to see spellings of difficult terms or definitions of unfamiliar jargon.
- A handout gives the audience a place to take notes and tie their comments and questions to specific portions of your presentation.
- A handout provides a bibliography so that your audience can follow up on any sources that strike their interest.

- A handout shows detailed charts, graphs, or visuals more legibly than a projected onscreen image will.
- A handout gives the audience something to take home as a reminder of your message.

Handouts have disadvantages as well. If you distribute a handout at the beginning of your presentation, the audience may spend their time reading the handout instead of listening to you. The time the audience spends looking down at the handout means fewer opportunities for you to make eye contact and connect with your audience. Sometimes audience members think they don't need to pay attention at all because they can read the handout later. And in a large classroom or lecture hall, distributing handouts to everyone may take too much time away from your presentation. Distributing handouts at the end of the presentation avoids some of these problems but deprives the audience of the opportunity to take notes on or refer to the handout. You may want to ask a classmate to distribute the handouts for you at an appropriate time during your presentation, but this, too, is distracting. You need to decide whether the benefits of using a handout outweigh the disadvantages in your particular situation.

If you choose to create a handout, be sure to make it concise and relevant. Do not give every member of your audience a typed copy of your presentation; instead, use your outline as a starting point and include only the major points and most important details. Significant examples and support should appear on the handout, as should citations for the most relevant and useful research sources you consulted for your paper or presentation. Be sure to include the title of your presentation and your name. You may also want to include the name of the course, the semester, the date, or your e-mail address so that the audience can contact you later with any questions.

Overhead Transparencies

Overhead projectors allow you to display transparencies on a screen. Transparencies are clear sheets of plastic film on which you can print information. Opaque projectors are used in a similar way but can display information from opaque sheets of paper. By using overheads, you display information legibly to a large audience and keep the audience's attention focused on you and your message as you speak. You can point to particular images or evidence, or even write on overheads with a marker during your presentation to make visual links between ideas and examples.

Overheads should display simplified versions of your information. While a single handout could outline your entire presentation, multiple overhead transparencies can break up that information over several screens and help organize subtopics within your presentation. Transparencies also offer you flexibility because you can easily go back to a previous transparency to revisit a point, overlay transparencies to build up an idea, or change the order if you are short on time and need to skip something.

One of the disadvantages of using transparencies is that you have to load each one onto the projector by hand. For this reason, too many transparencies can easily lead to confusion or fumbling. You'll have enough to concern you during the presentation, so try to limit the number of transparencies you use. Three or four transparencies to cover your main subtopics, along with one as an overview, is plenty. If you plan to show charts or examples, it may be best to have one overview transparency and a transparency for each chart or example. You can also put more than one example or section on the same transparency and cover one or the other with a sheet of paper until time for display. Attaching sticky notes or colored tabs to your transparencies also helps with organization and quick switching.

Presentation Software

Presentation software allows you to create slides and display them onscreen with a computer projector, which avoids many of the problems of using transparencies and overhead projectors. Most computers come equipped with a basic version of at least one presentation software package; Microsoft PowerPoint, Open Office Present, and Apple Keynote are just three brands of this software.

The main advantage to presentation software packages is that they allow the mingling of a variety of delivery modes. Most presentation software allows you to include text, digital graphics, screen shots, and other elements within your slides. These types of programs allow you to quickly and easily create polished and professional slide presentations. Unlike overhead transparencies, they allow smooth and speedy transitions from one slide or image to another. Most of these programs also make it easy to create handouts for your audience because you can print out your slides, as shown in Screen 1, or print out a selected number of slides per page, as shown in screens 2 and 3. Most programs also allow you to print "notes pages," which include extra space with each slide for adding handwritten notes.

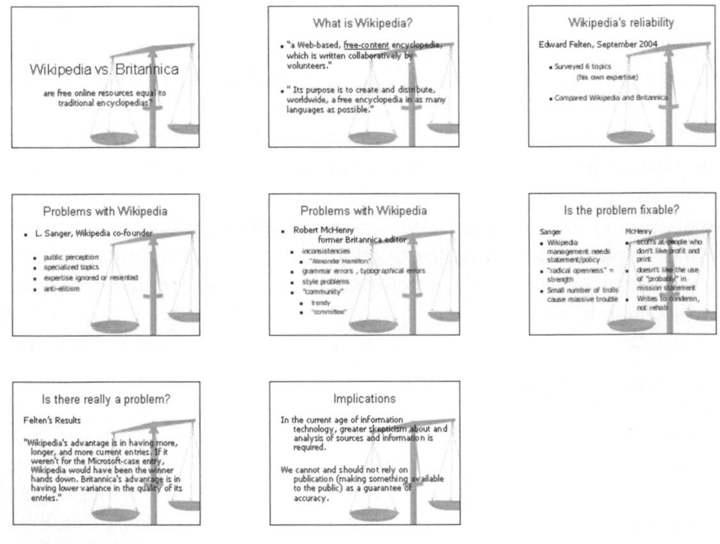

Screen 1: Presentation slides

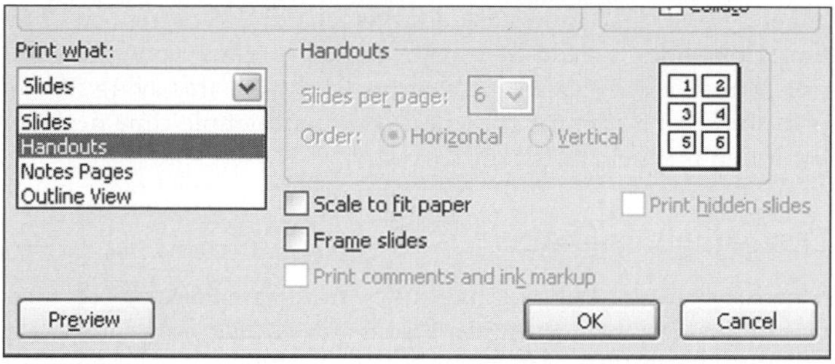

Screen 2: Printing handouts

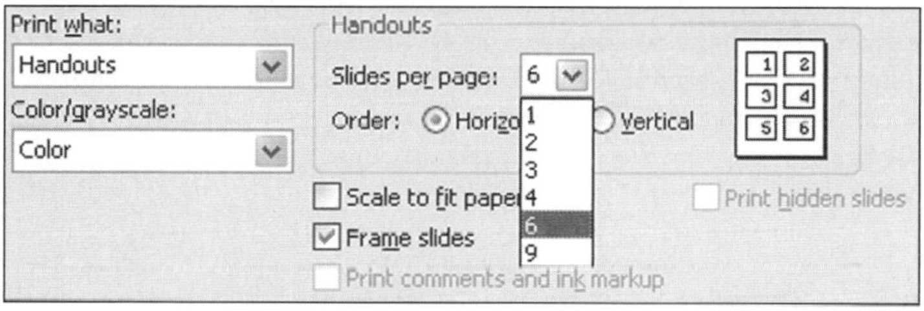

Screen 3: Selecting the number of slides per handout

A common mistake that speakers make in creating presentation slides is loading each slide with too much information. Slides work well for reminding the audience of your main points, signaling transitions, and displaying important graphics. But you, not your slides, are giving the presentation. Your audience does not need to see all of your information and examples on slides because you are there to explain the information. Your slides need only include general overviews, main points, and significant graphics or examples. Complete sentences are not necessary where a single word or a concise phrase will do. Do not read your slides directly from the screen because doing so faces you away from the audience. Feel free to approach the screen to point or gesture to a chart or graph, but remember that the slides are there for the audience's benefit, not to take your place. Any visual aid, and particularly presentation slides, should help your audience follow your presentation while keeping them focused on what you are saying. If you plan to do an electronic presentation, spend ample time developing it and practicing with the software.

Designing Visual Aids

Whether you are designing handouts, transparencies, or presentation slides, keep things simple. Visual aids should not repeat every word in your outline or your original paper; they need only present a skeleton or thumbnail sketch of the most important details or visuals. As the speaker, you will fill in the remaining details. Limit the amount of text you include, and use bulleted or numbered lists to keep the material concise. Try to limit handouts to one or two pages, double-sided if you use two pages. For slides and transparencies, "less is more." The focus of your presentation should be the words you say and how you say them, not what's happening over your shoulder.

Fonts

Stick to conventional fonts such as Times, Arial, Palatino, and Helvetica for the main body text, and use display fonts (those that look like band logos, dripping liquids, or other exotic components) only for the heading of the page or slide, if at all. Make sure the text is readable. For a transparency or slide that is projected onscreen, a 24-point font is generally the minimum size that your audience will be able to see from a distance; use even larger type if you can. Sans-serif fonts are easier for audiences to read on a screen. (Serifs are the small extensions on letters in certain fonts, as shown in the examples below. Sans-serif fonts do not have serifs.)

Recommended Serif Fonts	*Recommended Sans-Serif Fonts*	*Display or Headline Fonts*
Times	Arial	**Futura Bold**
Palatino	Verdana	*Monotype Corsiva*

Contrast and Spacing

As you consider design, pay attention to negative space and contrast. Negative space is the (usually white) unfilled portion of the page or screen. Do not cram too many items and words into the small space. Leave room for your information to "breathe." You want your audience to be able to quickly and comfortably access the information you project or hand out. Contrast is the degree of difference in thickness, darkness, or complexity of your text. The headings on this page are set in boldface because that boldness offers a contrast to the normal text on the page, making the heading stand out. The heading also stands out because of the amount of white space surrounding it. For another example, look at the contrast in the title slide of a presentation:

Wikipedia vs. Britannica

Are free online resources equal to traditional encyclopedias?

The first line of text is set in a serif font set in italics with conventional capitalization. The second line, the subtitle, uses a smaller sans-serif font set in boldface with no capitalization. Note that although this example uses several contrasting elements, it still uses fonts that are easy to read.

Color

Use very few colors in your design—two is probably enough; three is likely too many. Stick to basic colors and avoid those that are too bright or have a neon effect. If you are designing presentation slides, either light text on a very dark background or dark text on a very light background works well. Be especially cautious when using the ready-made slide templates that most presentation software packages include—not all of them are well designed.

Be judicious as well in using special features such as animation and sound effects in presentation slides. Most animation is distracting and most sound effects are unnecessary during a presentation. The first time a slide transitions to the next with an explosion or a flash of laser light is surprising and maybe interesting. The fifth time is neither.

Images

One or two meaningful and well-chosen images help reinforce your message, but avoid adding meaningless clip art or excessive decoration. In the following overview slide from a presentation on film piracy, the image of the ticket reinforces the topic by boldly claiming "ADMIT ONE," drawing a link between film piracy and the price of admission. The image suits the topic and adds to the message more so than, say, a clip art image of a movie camera or a director's chair. Note as well that plenty of white space surrounds the image and text. The bulleted list uses single words, rather than sentences, to point out main subpoints of the presentation.

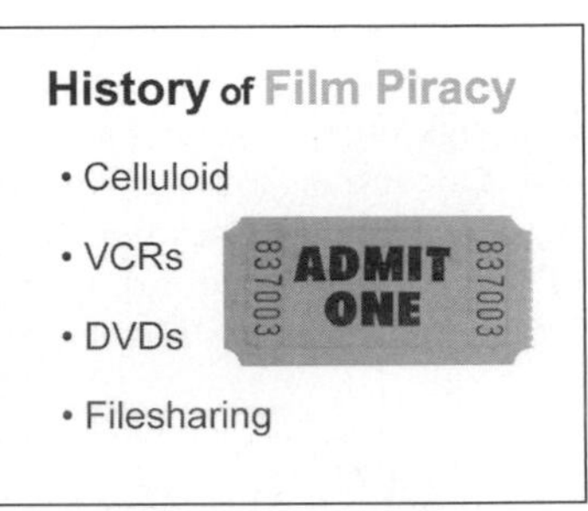

Overview slide

Avoiding Technical Problems

Before you devote time to creating visual aids, make sure that the classroom where you will be presenting has the equipment you need. You may need to request or reserve a projector in advance. If you are using presentation software or displaying other files with an LCD (liquid crystal display) projector, check to be sure that your software and all of your files will work on the computer you'll be using during the presentation. (HTML, JPG, GIF, RTF, and PDF files work best with the widest variety of computers and operating systems.)

Computer media can be unreliable, so save multiple copies of all your visual aids in different locations. Copy your handout and your software presentation on more than one disk. Burn a CD-ROM or copy the file to a flash drive. E-mail the presentation to yourself. Save the file on the hard drive of the computer you will use for the presentation (if you are permitted to do so) a day or more before the due date. If doing a group presentation, give every member of the group a copy of the files. Know the size of your audience in advance so that you can print enough handouts, and always bring extra handouts to the presentation. Finally, always have a Plan B, and if you have time and resources, have a Plan C.

8 *Practicing, Polishing, and Delivering the Presentation*

Good speakers thoroughly plan both the content of their presentations and their style of delivery. Although it is fundamental to have a clear and logical message to present, that message must be presented effectively. Otherwise, the only person who will understand and accept it is the speaker. Once you have prepared an effective message, you must develop effective strategies to deliver it. Your mode of speaking and your voice, body language, and comfort level all have a significant effect on your audience.

Modes of Speaking

Presentations involve any of four modes of speaking: impromptu, extemporaneous, scripted, or memorized.

Impromptu Speaking

Impromptu speaking is done on the spur of the moment without any formal preparation. By definition, this kind of speaking is not the kind you will be doing if you are preparing an oral presentation for class. But you are likely to be called on to do this type of speaking in other situations, for example, in a classroom setting in which the teacher asks you to summarize and give your opinion of the most recent reading assignment, or in a committee meeting in which you have special expertise on the topic at hand. You cannot prepare your exact words in advance, but you can anticipate the situation and prepare your ideas. When you are asked to answer a question or describe something on the spur of the moment, do the following.

- Quickly identify why you are speaking (for example, to supply needed information, to urge action, to clarify an issue, to provide humor).
  - "In order to defend the position that online reference works such as Wikipedia are sometimes more useful than traditional encyclopedias . . ."
  - "What are the real issues at the heart of the debate over Digital Rights Management and downloading music? I will offer a brief list of concerns . . ."
- Use an organizational strategy (for example, chronological, cause-effect, problem-solution).
  - "Before the early days of the movie industry, film piracy was usually a matter of theft and copying the actual film stock . . . The development of the VCR in the 1970s changed the way the film industry thought about piracy . . . Recent technology like TiVo and the DVD have once again changed perspectives about copyright infringement . . ."
- Grab the audience's attention and relate the core of your message in your introduction.
  - "I get angry every time I pay $10 to see a film at a movie theater and have to sit through a public service announcement warning me not to copy and trade movies because I will put all the members of the film crew out of work. Maybe you have felt this way, too. We paid for this movie! Why are they preaching at us?"
- Speak briefly. If you ramble on, the audience will miss your point.
- When in doubt, summarize. A quick review often restores your perspective and gets you back on track.
  - "I have explained Mr. Sanger's involvement in creating the Wikipedia. I have also detailed Mr. McHenry's former employment with *Encyclopaedia Britannica*. These roles are significant because . . ."

    - "So, licensing is a complicated issue. As I said originally, the owners of copyrighted material and the companies that distribute that material are often working from a different perspective than we, the customers, are. While we believe that we own a song or movie, as I have discussed, they believe that they have only licensed a copy of the performance or film for us to use in our homes. You can see why copying and playing those performances is such a complex subject . . ."

- Finish up with a brief summary stating the outcomes of accepting your message.
    - "If you want to see better quality free resources, you will have to be conscientious, both as a reader and as a writer. Rather than complaining like Robert McHenry about problems with online resources, we need to read them carefully. Analysis is the most important skill we can learn and use in the current age of information technology. When we see problems, it is up to us to make changes and take part—to give back. I hope what I have said today will make two things clear—that information is not true just because we see it in print, whether online or in a book, and that we have a responsibility to double-check and help correct the information we find online."
- Whatever you do, don't apologize—for your lack of preparation, your lack of information, or your lack of ability as a speaker.

Extemporaneous Speaking

Extemporaneous speaking is characterized by advance preparation of ideas and supporting material, with the precise wording to be composed at the moment of speaking. As a result, no matter how many times the presentation is delivered, the expression of the ideas is never exactly the same. Extemporaneous speaking has a number of important advantages.

- It allows the speaker to adapt to unforeseen situations (for example, by adding a reference to something that occurred in the setting and adding or deleting an argument based on audience response).
- It promotes a more personal relationship between the speaker and the audience.
- It leads, with experience, to a superior delivery—greater earnestness, greater sincerity, and greater power.

Because of these advantages, extemporaneous speaking is the preferred mode of speaking for most situations. Extemporaneous speakers construct a detailed outline and reduce it to a speaker's outline. (For more about outlining, see Chapter 5.) Using the speaker's outline, the speaker rehearses the presentation in front of a mirror, an audio- or video-recorder, and/or helpful friends. During the presentation, the speaker watches the audience for clues about how they are receiving the message and modifies the presentation based on that feedback.

Scripted Speaking

Although extemporaneous is the preferred mode of delivery for most situations, some occasions require you to write out a speech word for word and read the resulting document to the audience. Situations that require or encourage scripted speaking are those for which precision of expression is crucial. When the president of the United States makes a major policy statement on an important issue, he wants to be sure that the wording of the statement will not be misunderstood. Thus, he (or a speech writer) is likely to write out that statement and read it. Scripted speaking is also encouraged in situations that require precise timing (for example, a 2-minute speech written for inclusion in a political commercial).

Preparing a scripted presentation involves the same process as preparing an extemporaneous presentation. That is, you start with a detailed outline, reduce it to a speaker's outline, and rehearse from this outline. (For more about outlining, see Chapter 5.) Once you have experimented with a conversational style for presenting the message, write it down word for word and then rehearse and rewrite, rehearse and rewrite. Once in final form, the scripted presentation is prepared for easy reading—that is, put in a format and type size that are easy to read and marked appropriately to indicate any special emphases. The following example shows an excerpt from a scripted presentation.

- "If you want to see better quality free resources, you will have to be conscientious, [*pause*] both as a reader and as a writer. Rather than complaining about problems with online resources, we need to read them carefully. Analysis is the most important skill we can learn and use in the current age of information technology. When we see problems, it is up to us to make changes and take part—[*pause*] to give back. I hope what I have said today will make two things clear—[*pause*] that information is not true just because we see it in print, whether online or in a book, [*pause*] and that we have a responsibility to double-check and help correct the information we find online."

When presenting a scripted oral presentation, you attempt to establish a level of contact with the audience that approaches that of the extemporaneous mode, including steady eye contact and a conversational style of delivery.

Memorized Speaking

Memorized speaking adds one step to a scripted presentation: After writing out the manuscript, you memorize the presentation and then deliver it from memory rather than reading it. In many situations, speakers combine these two approaches: They read parts of the manuscript and deliver other parts of the message from memory in an extemporaneous fashion. In some situations, however, speakers make the extra effort of memorizing the whole document, especially for ceremonial speeches such as tributes and eulogies. When speakers make a special effort to memorize a presentation, they also make a special effort to deliver it using a style of delivery that is as close to an extemporaneous style of delivery as possible. Such a style is best developed by observing the skills of effective speakers, learning to evaluate your own delivery, and practicing to improve your skills.

Voice and Body Language

Once you have chosen a mode of delivery, you next need to consider how to use delivery to focus attention on the message and not on you. This means delivering the message in a conversational style that the audience can both hear and understand. Chapter 3 covers the following potential barriers to effective communication with your audience:

- The amount of information you include
- The type of information you include
- The level of feedback from the audience
- The pace of the presentation
- Organization and timing
- The intensity with which you present the information

As you practice your presentation, you need to consider two other factors that affect the audience—your vocal delivery and your body language.

Whether you are speaking extemporaneously or from a script, speak loudly enough, slowly enough, and clearly enough for the audience members at the back of the room to hear and understand you. If you have the opportunity to practice your presentation in the room where you will be presenting, ask a friend to sit at the back of the room to test whether you are speaking loudly enough. Nervousness may tempt you to rush through your presentation, and you may end up speaking faster than you think you do. Slow down and pause between major points so that your audience has time to absorb what you're saying. Take care to pronounce your words clearly and to speak in a natural, conversational style. Finally, avoid using distracting filler words such as *uh, um, like,* and *you know.* A brief pause is often more effective for helping you get your thoughts together without distracting the audience.

Your audience will be watching you as well as listening to you, of course, so use body language to your advantage. Natural, conversational gestures help you emphasize important ideas or direct the audience's attention to key visuals. Making eye contact with the audience is extremely important—doing so helps them feel a connection to you and your message, and it also helps you to monitor your audience's reaction. By making eye contact, you'll be able to tell whether the audience is paying close attention and whether they understand your message. Don't be afraid to move around as you speak—movement can help the audience stay focused on you—but avoid pacing back and forth or fidgeting, as these activities will distract them.

Dealing with Stage Fright

Another potential barrier to effective delivery is your level of anxiety about speaking in front of a group. Many people experience stage fright when asked to speak in front of a group, regardless of whether they are habitually nervous about communicating with others or they generally feel comfortable communicating.

Stage fright is most often a situational attack of anxiety that depends on factors such as

- the size of your audience;
- how well you know the people you are talking with;
- how well you know your subject;
- the status of the individuals you are talking with.

For example, you may feel relaxed when talking with a friend about a movie you saw the previous evening, but feel a sudden surge of panic when asked to describe your reaction to that same movie for a professor and your classmates in an English class. Or you may feel comfortable offering a lengthy response to a question from the professor during class, but feel extremely nervous about getting up in front of the class to give an oral presentation on that same topic.

To overcome nervousness before or during a presentation, try the following.

- *Develop a constructive attitude toward fear and anxiety.* Instead of wondering how you will get rid of these common emotions, ask yourself how you can use them. Individuals need tension—feelings of excitement and challenge—to increase their thinking ability and powers of concentration. Realize that everyone who speaks publicly experiences some apprehension and fear before speaking and that, in fact, some measure of anxiety is necessary for you to do your best. If you have ever participated in sports, this may sound familiar. Let the adrenaline energize your performance by using all that pent-up energy like fuel. Being nervous is similar to being excited, so channel your nervousness into a positive energy.
- *Grab every opportunity to practice and gain experience.* Whether you are snowboarding, building a Web site, or speaking in front of a group, knowledge of the requirements is likely to increase your comfort level. For example, you naturally will be more comfortable the tenth time you've gone scuba diving than the first time. Seek out opportunities to practice and gain experience. Sometimes this will be easier around people you know, but for some, it is easier to perform for an anonymous audience. Because you will be making your presentation in class, where you may know many but not all of your classmates, practice in both types of situations.
- *Prepare thoroughly for each presentation.* If you are worried about what you will say, how you will say it, *and* what the outcome will be, you certainly will be more anxious than if your *only* concern is about the outcome. Prepare. Rehearse. Be thorough. Then, when you rise to speak, you will be able to concentrate on the outcome. Control all the things you can control *before* the day of the presentation.
- *Concentrate on communicating with your audience.* Ask yourself, "How do I know that these individuals are hearing and understanding what I'm saying?" If, as you speak, you work hard to observe the reactions of your audience and to adapt to them, you will be much too busy to worry about your anxiety or fear.

- *Remember that your listeners want you to succeed.* Your listeners are just like you—friendly people. Just as they want to succeed when they get up to speak, they want you to do well when you speak. Even if you do make a slip, they will understand and forgive you! Not even the best speakers perform flawlessly every single time they speak. Do not hold yourself to an unreasonable standard, and remember that others are not holding you to that standard.
- *Keep in mind that it will be over more quickly than you expect.* You have prepared for days or weeks, but the presentation will be over in only a few minutes.

Polishing the Presentation

One of the best ways to alleviate nervousness and to be sure you are well prepared is to polish your presentation through rehearsal. It's best to have your presentation ready several days to a week in advance to allow time to practice several times in front of a mirror or your friends. Assuming that you intend to speak extemporaneously, use the first few rehearsals to test various phrasings of your ideas. As you start to feel comfortable with the flow of your presentation, begin to work on time. Most classroom assignments will give you a time limit or a range (say 3 to 5 minutes).

Develop your presentation with the middle of the range in mind. That is, if the range is 3 to 5 minutes, develop a presentation that requires 3 to 4 minutes to deliver during practice. When you make the actual presentation, you may find that because of audience reaction, impromptu remarks, and so on, the presentation takes longer than it did during rehearsal. You may also find, though, that you speak more quickly during the presentation than you did during practice. Pace yourself.

As the day of the actual presentation approaches, try to practice in the classroom where you will speak. This will add to your comfort level and allow you to anticipate the unexpected. This is especially important if you are using unfamiliar equipment, such as a microphone, presentation software, an overhead projector, or an LCD projector.

If you are extremely nervous or feel unsure about your ability to give a presentation, be proactive; address the problem early and directly. But keep in mind that you do have sources of support. Seek help from campus resources, such as the writing center or your instructor during office hours. Seek help well in advance of the due date. The night before the presentation is due is usually too late. Some of the advice in this chapter may not seem practical, but keep in mind that in most cases you will have at least a week, and often two or three, to complete an assignment. Don't forget that the instructor's goal is to help you learn and grow, and he or she understands that you may be nervous about presenting.

9 *Presenting as a Group*

Many of the oral presentations you give are culminations of group projects. Teachers often assign group work and expect an oral report as the end result. Group work is rewarding and emulates many job situations in which teams work on projects. But group work also presents challenges. Among these challenges are equally dividing the work, smoothly transitioning between multiple speakers, and adequately acknowledging nonspeaking (but contributing) group members.

Dividing the Work

Groups work best when members know and understand the roles they are expected to fill. Often instructors assign these roles, but just as often the group determines them. Even if the instructor does not assign specific tasks to various group members, the group should specify tasks for each member. This may be through nominating one member to act as a leader, who then assigns roles to each group member. Students may also volunteer to perform certain duties.

Having a leader is often useful because that person can coordinate communication among group members and with the instructor. A leader can also settle disputes or finalize decisions. The leader must strive to be objective and fair. Leading is a position not only of power but also of responsibility. The leader should gather contact information for all members of the group and set a schedule for achieving goals and deadlines. The leader need not dictate these goals, but should enforce any deadlines. Think of this person as a manager or film director.

The group should have one person serve as secretary or writer. The writer takes notes at all meetings (either as formal minutes or shorthand records). There may be a role for more than one writer in the group. One may serve as a secretary, while another compiles the group's research and composes that information in a draft. Another subset of the writer category could include production workers or designers. Designers build the visual aids and handouts the group will use during the presentation. They might also revise and proofread the final draft of the paper or check citation formats.

Both informative and persuasive group presentations require researchers. The researchers should spend time in the library, on the Web, and among peers or experts, taking notes and conducting interviews. The researchers should be responsible for gathering the raw materials used in the presentation. They should also be expected to double-check their information for reliability and credibility, and they should adequately cite their sources. If all members of the group are taking part in research, you may wish to divide the work; for example, two members of the group could conduct research at the library, while the other two members conduct an interview. The entire group could then gather to compare notes and decide on the best direction for the presentation.

When the time comes to give the presentation, one or more members of the group will need to speak. The instructor may require all members to speak during the presentation, but not always. Some group members may be more well versed in public speaking. Some may have more knowledge about specific areas of the presentation and be better suited to presenting that information orally. The speakers for the group should have the information they need well in advance of the presentation time. They should also be expected to have read the information several times and to have practiced speaking. If more than one person is speaking for the group, the speakers should also rehearse transitions between speakers.

Transitioning between Speakers

One mode of giving a group oral presentation is to have each speaking member talk in sequence. This very simple and straightforward mode of delivery often works well. In this setup, however, group members should wrap up their section of the presentation with an introduction of the next member and offer some form of transition bridging the gap between the subtopics.

- ". . . and this is why I believe that living wills and Do Not Resuscitate orders should be respected by doctors, families, and the government. To offer another perspective, I now turn the floor over to Tricia. . . ."

Another tactic is to have one group member serve as a sort of "master of ceremonies" or "emcee." The emcee introduces the topic of the discussion and then introduces each speaker in turn. One benefit of this arrangement is that the emcee can guide the pace of the presentation, urging rambling presenters to conclude or prompting terse presenters for more detail by asking questions or probing for more detail. The emcee can serve as a facilitator for a more interactive presentation as well. If the group decides to take questions during the presentation (rather than afterward), the emcee can field those questions and even direct them to the most qualified member of the group.

Groups should designate who will answer certain types of questions before they make their presentations. Some group members may be more qualified to field questions about research sources, while other group members may be better qualified to deal with on-the-spot application of the material to indirectly related material. Having a "go to" person for these types of questions helps avoid embarrassment and confusion during the presentation. Group members may freeze or come up blank due to stage fright or other pressures, so groups should devise a plan for dealing with these situations, including graceful and supportive methods for offering one another on-the-spot assistance.

These roles need not be exclusive. More than one group member can perform most of these roles. Likewise, any one group member can perform a number of roles within the group. A researcher may be a speaker, while the leader could also be a secretary.

Acknowledging Nonspeaking Group Members

Not every member of the group needs to speak during the presentation unless the instructor so requires. If certain members of the group do not speak during the presentation, the group leader or the emcee should mention the contributions of all members of the group. This can happen at the beginning or end of the presentation in a sort of summary. Alternatively, during the presentation the speakers may mention who performed what research or reference specific tasks and responsibilities. Whatever the case, it is good practice to know the names of your fellow group members. Transitions will be smoother if group members can refer to one another by name and do so occasionally throughout the presentation.

Nonspeaking members can help with other important tasks during the presentation, such as working the projector, passing out handouts, or demonstrating a process while one of the speakers explains.

10 *Evaluating Presentations*

In addition to your role as a presenter, you have another important role as an audience member for your classmates' presentations. You may be asked to evaluate their work, to offer suggestions for improvement, or even to demonstrate your understanding of the information they share. The following checklist will help you identify strengths and weaknesses in a presentation, both in the content and the speaker's delivery. As a student and a listener, you probably assess many of these strengths and weaknesses subconsciously. Being aware of the following components of a presentation (or paper) can change your mode of listening to one that is more active and critical.

At first, listening critically may seem like hard work, but as time goes on you will become comfortable and confident in this new style of listening. Paying attention to all of the items on this list is not easy or even advised. Instead, pay attention to the items that you already tend to notice and feel confident about evaluating. Pick a few other areas to concentrate on each time you hear a new speaker. Eventually, you will build better listening and analysis skills. A final recommendation: During a presentation, *make* (not *take*) notes. Writing every word the speaker says is never a good idea, but making comments in the margins of a handout or keeping a bulleted list or outline to trigger memories is very helpful, especially if you want to ask questions later.

Checklist for Evaluating a Presentation

The Speaker's Delivery

While the topic and the content are the most important parts of any presentation, the speaker has an incredible impact on the success of any presentation. The point is not to critique the speaker's every word or gesture; instead, note the places where the speaker's poise, demeanor, and performance help or hurt the presentation's message.

- ☐ **Voice**
  - ☐ Can you understand the speaker?
  - ☐ Is the speaker loud enough (but not too loud)?
- ☐ **Pace**
  - ☐ Is the speaker's pace comfortable, not too fast or too slow?
  - ☐ Does the speaker take time to allow for questions or repeat complex or confusing concepts?
- ☐ **Nervousness**
  - ☐ Does the speaker seem relaxed and comfortable?
  - ☐ Does the speaker avoid most meaningless filler words such as *uh* or *um*? (Do not nitpick, but is the number of *ums* distracting?)
- ☐ **Engagement with the audience**
  - ☐ Does the speaker avoid simply reading his or her paper?
  - ☐ Does the speaker make eye contact?
  - ☐ Is the speaker aware of the audience's responses or reactions?
  - ☐ Has the speaker adapted the material well for the audience?
- ☐ **Use of visual aids**
  - ☐ Do the visual aids help you understand the speaker's message?

- ☐ Are the visual aids well designed and free of distracting or confusing elements?
- ☐ Does the speaker direct your attention to key points or visuals? Does the speaker adequately explain their significance?

Content and Coherence

Coherence refers to the degree to which all the parts and details in a paper or presentation work together toward the statement of purpose and thesis. If a presentation lacks coherence, it will seem to ramble all over and go off on tangents, not really making one clear point. A strong thesis and attention to coherence will make for a much stronger presentation.

- ☐ **Thesis**
  - ☐ Is the thesis clearly expressed?
  - ☐ Does the thesis make sense? Can you restate it in your own words?
  - ☐ Is there only one apparent thesis or purpose?
  - ☐ Do all of the main ideas go together?
- ☐ **Language choices**
  - ☐ Does the speaker avoid using jargon?
  - ☐ Does the speaker define key terms and unfamiliar words?
  - ☐ Does the speaker address the audience using an appropriate and effective tone?
- ☐ **Transitions**
  - ☐ Does the speaker clearly and smoothly link ideas and sections of the presentation?
  - ☐ Are transitional words and phrases used correctly? For example, sometimes speakers overuse or misuse certain conjunctive adverbs in an attempt to sound more formal

or "educated." The most common of these adverbs have very specific implications, as follows:

- *therefore* = because of what I just said
- *however* = in spite of what I just said
- *furthermore* = in addition to what I just said

☐ **Support**

- ☐ Does the speaker's support for his or her thesis make sense?
- ☐ Are examples and evidence appropriate and credible? Do they mean what the speaker says they mean?
- ☐ Do the examples and evidence support the speaker's claim(s)? Do you come to a similar conclusion based on these examples? Has the speaker mentioned other possible conclusions?

Argument and Persuasion

☐ **Does the speaker avoid logical fallacies? Does the speaker**

- offer only two options or solutions, when many more really may exist? (*false dilemma*)
- assume that an event that follows another event happens *because* of the first, even though this may not be true? (*post hoc ergo propter hoc,* "after this, therefore because of this")
- suggest that one decision will lead to more bad outcomes, even though there is very little evidence supporting this suggestion? For example, "if we legalize drugs, then everyone will have access to drugs all the time, and we will become a nation of drug addicts." (*slippery slope*)
- claim that something is true simply because most people believe that it is true? "Ninety-five percent of people surveyed believe that the sun does, in fact, revolve around the earth." (*popularity*)

- use other fallacies like these? (Books and Web sites about argument list many other fallacies. Consult your instructor if you have trouble understanding the occasionally complex definitions of some fallacies.)

☐ **Does the speaker seem credible and convincing?**

☐ **Do you agree with the speaker? Did the presentation make you change your opinion? Why or why not?**

☐ **Even if you disagree with the speaker, does the speaker adequately explain and defend his or her position?**

Thinking Critically about Your Own Presentation

The checklist above is a good guide for evaluating your own presentation too. One problem many people face when evaluating their own work is being too close to the material and too invested in the paper or the argument. A good way to evaluate your work critically is to distance yourself from it for a while. If possible, record yourself practicing the presentation, either on audio or video. Then spend a day or two (or longer if you have the time) not working on the project. When you return to the paper or presentation, read, view, or listen to the entire piece. Pretend that you are an audience member and use the above checklists to evaluate your own work. Do not be afraid to play devil's advocate and take an opposing view or to adopt a hostile attitude toward the presentation's message; however, rather than attacking all your own thoughts, ideas, and statements, instead be fair and tough. Envision how you would defend your ideas and statements to an audience member making the same kinds of critical comments and asking similarly probing questions. If you can, rework your project to anticipate and address these issues before making your presentation.

Revision Symbols

Letter-number codes refer to sections of this book.

abbr	faulty abbreviation **P9**
adj	misuse of adjective **G4**
add	add needed word **S2**
adv	misuse of adverb **G4**
agr	faulty agreement **G1, G3-a**
appr	inappropriate language **W4**
art	article **M2**
awk	awkward
cap	capital letter **P8**
case	error in case **G3-c, G3-d**
cliché	cliché **W5-e**
coh	coherence **C4-d**
coord	faulty coordination **S6-c**
cs	comma splice **G6**
dev	inadequate development **C4-b**
dm	dangling modifier **S3-e**
-ed	error in *-ed* ending **G2-d**
emph	emphasis **S6**
ESL	ESL grammar **M1, M2, M3, M4, M5**
exact	inexact language **W5**
frag	sentence fragment **G5**
fs	fused sentence **G6**
gl/us	see glossary of usage **W1**
hyph	error in use of hyphen **P7**
idiom	idiom **W5-d**
inc	incomplete construction **S2**
irreg	error in irregular verb **G2-a**
ital	italics **P10**
jarg	jargon **W4-a**
lc	lowercase letter **P8**
mix	mixed construction **S5**
mm	misplaced modifier **S3-b**
mood	error in mood **G2-g**
nonst	nonstandard usage **W4-c**
num	error in use of number **P9**
om	omitted word **S2**
¶	new paragraph **C4**
p	error in punctuation
^,	comma **P1**
no ,	no comma **P2**
;	semicolon **P3**
:	colon **P3**
’	apostrophe **P4**
“ ”	quotation marks **P5**
. ?	period, question mark,
!	exclamation point,
— ( )	dash, parentheses,
[ ] . . .	brackets, ellipsis mark,
/	slash **P6**
pass	ineffective passive **W3**
pn agr	pronoun agreement **G3-a**
proof	proofreading problem **C3-d**
ref	error in pronoun reference **G3-b**
run-on	run-on sentence **G6**
-s	error in *-s* ending **G2-c**
sexist	sexist language **W4-e**
shift	distracting shift **S4**
sl	slang **W4-c**
sp	misspelled word **P7**
sub	faulty subordination **S6-d**
sv agr	subject-verb agreement **G1, G2-c**
t	error in verb tense **G2-f**
trans	transition needed **C4-d**
usage	see glossary of usage **W1**
v	voice **W3**
var	sentence variety **S6-b, S6-c, S7**
vb	verb error **G2**
w	wordy **W2**
//	faulty parallelism **S1**
^	insert
x	obvious error
#	insert space
⁀	close up space

Detailed Menu

C Composing and Revising 1

C1 Planning 3
C2 Drafting 14
C3 Revising 20
C4 Writing paragraphs 32
C5 Designing documents 45
C6 Writing with technology 62

A Academic Writing 65

A1 Writing about texts 67
a reading actively: annotating the text
b outlining
c summarizing
d analyzing
e sample analysis paper
A2 Constructing reasonable arguments 78
a examining contexts
b viewing the audience as jury
c establishing credibility
d backing up the thesis
e supporting claims
f countering arguments
g building common ground
h sample argument paper
A3 Evaluating arguments 92
a distinguishing argumentative tactics
b distinguishing emotional appeals
c judging how a writer handles opposing views
A4 Writing in the disciplines 100
a finding commonalities
b recognizing questions
c understanding evidence
d noting conventions
e citing sources
f understanding assignments

S Sentence Style 109

S1 Parallelism 111
a items in a series
b paired ideas
c repeated words
S2 Needed words 114
a compound structures
b *that*
c comparisons
d *a*, *an*, and *the*
S3 Problems with modifiers 117
a limiting modifiers
b misplaced modifiers
c awkward placement
d split infinitives
e dangling modifiers
S4 Shifts 123
a point of view
b verb tense
c verb mood and voice
d indirect to direct questions, quotations
S5 Mixed constructions 126
a mixed grammar
b illogical connections
c *is when*, *is where*, *reason . . . is because*
S6 Sentence emphasis 129
a coordination and subordination
b choppy sentences
c ineffective coordination
d ineffective subordination
e excessive subordination
f special techniques
S7 Sentence variety 134

W Word Choice 137

W1 Glossary of usage 139
W2 Wordy sentences 153
a redundancy
b repetition
c empty phrases
d simplified structure
e reducing clauses to phrases, phrases to words
W3 Active verbs 156
a replacing passive verbs
b replacing *be* verbs
W4 Appropriate language 159
a jargon
b pretentious language
c slang, regionalisms, nonstandard English
d levels of formality
e nonsexist language
f offensive language
W5 Exact language 165
a connotations
b concrete nouns
c misused words
d standard idioms
e clichés
f figures of speech
W6 The dictionary and thesaurus 169

G Grammatical Sentences 173

G1 Subject-verb agreement 175
a standard forms
b words between subject and verb
c subjects with *and*
d subjects with *or*, *nor*
e indefinite pronouns
f collective nouns
g subject after verb
h subject complement
i *who*, *which*, *that*
j plural form, singular meaning
k titles, company names, words as words, etc.
G2 Verb forms, tenses, and moods 183
a irregular verbs
b *lie* and *lay*
c *-s* endings
d *-ed* endings
e omitted verbs
f tense
g subjunctive mood
G3 Pronouns 196
a pronoun-antecedent agreement
b pronoun reference
c pronoun case (*I* vs. *me* etc.)
d *who* and *whom*
G4 Adjectives and adverbs 207
a adjectives
b adverbs
c comparatives, superlatives
d double negatives
G5 Sentence fragments 212
a subordinate clauses
b phrases
c other word groups
d acceptable fragments
G6 Run-on sentences 218
a revision with conjunction
b with semicolon
c by separating sentences
d by restructuring

M Multilingual Writers and ESL Challenges 223

M1 Verbs 225
a form and tense
b passive voice
c base form after modal
d negative forms
e conditional sentences
f with gerunds or infinitives
M2 Articles 237
a articles and other noun markers
b *the*
c *a* or *an*
d for approximate amounts
e with general nouns
f with proper nouns

CORRECTNESS

G Grammatical Sentences
- G1 Subject-verb agreement
- G2 Verb forms, tenses, and moods
- G3 Pronouns
- G4 Adjectives and adverbs
- G5 Sentence fragments
- G6 Run-on sentences

M Multilingual Writers and ESL Challenges
- M1 Verbs
- M2 Articles
- M3 Sentence structure
- M4 Using adjectives
- M5 Prepositions and idiomatic expressions

P Punctuation and Mechanics
- P1 The comma
- P2 Unnecessary commas
- P3 The semicolon and the colon
- P4 The apostrophe
- P5 Quotation marks
- P6 Other punctuation marks
- P7 Spelling and hyphenation
- P8 Capitalization
- P9 Abbreviations and numbers
- P10 Italics

B Basic Grammar
- B1 Parts of speech
- B2 Parts of sentences
- B3 Subordinate word groups
- B4 Sentence types

RESEARCH

R Researching
- R1 Conducting research
- R2 Evaluating sources
- R3 Managing information; avoiding plagiarism
- R4 Choosing a documentation style

MLA Papers
- MLA-1 Supporting a thesis
- MLA-2 Citing sources; avoiding plagiarism
- MLA-3 Integrating sources
- MLA-4 Documenting sources
- MLA-5 Manuscript format; sample paper

SAMPLE PAPER

APA and CMS Papers
(Coverage parallels MLA's)

APA	CMS
APA-1	CMS-1
APA-2	CMS-2
APA-3	CMS-3
APA-4	CMS-4
APA-5	CMS-5
SAMPLE PAPER	SAMPLE PAGES

I Index

Directory to model papers
Multilingual/ESL menu
Revision symbols
Detailed menu